REALTY B P9-BIL-291

PHONE OR FAX YOUR ORDER NOW...

CONTENTS

SALES TECHNIQUES
Listing Techniques
Selling Techniques

FINANCING
Mortgage Instruments
The Mortgage Market
Conventional Financing
FHA Financing
VA Financing
Truth in Lending Act & RESPA

CHECKLISTS
Listing Data Checklist
Disclosure Checklists

CONTRACT CLAUSES
Legal Aspects of Contract Preparation
Purchase Agreements
Exchange Agreements
Options
Leases

TAX INFORMATION
Capital Improvements vs. Repairs
Capital vs. Ordinary Gain or Loss
Depreciation – Cost Recovery
Limitation on Interest and Other Deductions
Investment Tax Credit
Tax-Free Exchanges
Exchange Analysis
Installment Sales
Imputed Interest
Personal Residences

Prices	1 Copy	5 Copies	25 Copies
Bluebook I	$16.00 ea	$13.00 ea	$11.00 ea

PROFESSIONAL PUBLISHING CORPORATION
122 PAUL DRIVE SAN RAFAEL, CA 94903
Order Dept.: (800) 288-2006
Customer Service: (415) 472-1964
Fax number: (415) 472-2069

i

CORRESPONDENCE COURSES

Bluebook Course "A": Tables and Financing
Bluebook Course "B": Contracts and Taxes

**Each Course Approved For 21 Hours
Continuing Education**

**California Department of Real Estate
Sponsor No. 0974**

**Nevada Department of Real Estate
Sponsor No. CE 0417**

**$85.00 each course – $125.00 for both courses
Shipping & Handling: $6.00 for one course
$8.00 for both courses
California residents add 6% Sales Tax**

Agency Course

**Approved for 3 Hours
Continuing Education Credit**

**California Department of Real Estate
Sponsor No. 0974**

**$25.00 plus $2.00 Shipping & Handling
California residents add 6% Sales Tax**

Ask for Information sheet and Enrollment Form

PROFESSIONAL
PUBLISHING
CORPORATION

122 Paul Drive
San Rafael, California 94903
Order Dept. (800) 288-2006
For Customer Service (415) 472-1964

REAL ESTATE SEMINARS
"Professionalism through Education"

Professional Publishing offers a series of exciting live Continuing Education Seminars on a variety of topics that are important to the Real Estate Profession at this time. All of the seminars listed on this page are available for sponsorship by Boards of REALTORS, Title and Escrow Companies and Brokerages. Call our office to find out how your Board or Company can sponsor a seminar taught by a nationally recognized speaker.

- **SALES TECHNIQUES**
- **REALTY BLUEBOOK "COVER TO COVER"**
- **REALTY BLUEBOOK "FORMS AND CONTRACTS"**
- **REALTY BLUEBOOK "CONVENTIONAL, FHA & VA FINANCING"**
- **REALTY BLUEBOOK "TAX INFORMATION"**
- **REAL ESTATE INVESTMENT AND EXCHANGE**

HEWLETT PACKARD CALCULATOR COURSES
- **HP-12C**
- **BUSINESS CONSULTANT HP-17B, HP-18C & HP-19B**

8 separate seminars available for sponsorship.

Instructed by: James F. Little – MBA & Broker

$9.00

REALTY

BLUEBOOK II®

TABLES

By
ROBERT DE HEER
President

**PROFESSIONAL
PUBLISHING
CORPORATION**

122 Paul Drive
San Rafael, California 94903
Order Dept.: (800) 288-2006
For Customer Service: (415) 472-1964
Fax number: (415) 472-2069

This publication is designed to provide accurate and au-
thoritative information in regard to the subject matter co-
vered. It is sold with the understanding that the publisher
is not engaged in rendering legal, accounting or other professional service. If legal advice or other expert assistance
is required, the services of a competent professional person
should be sought.

*From a Declaration of Principles jointly
adopted by a Committee of the American Bar
Association and a Committee of Publishers and
Associations.*

⊠ **PROFESSIONAL PUBLISHING CORPORATION**

122 PAUL DRIVE ● SAN RAFAEL CA 94903 ● (415) 472-1964

FORM SAMPLES

Sample Sets contain the following forms

SALES

FORM #:	100	Buyer-Broker Contract
	101	Residential Purchase Agreement (One Page)
	101 CAL	Same as 101/California Version
	101-R.1	Residential Purchase Agreement (Page 1 & 2)
	101-R.1 CAL	Same as 101R.1/California Version
	101-R.2	Residential Purchase Agreement (Page 3 & 4)
	101-R.2 CAL	Same as 101-R.2/California Version
	101-C	Commercial Purchase Agreement (One Page)
	101-C.1	Commercial Purchase Agreement (Page 1 & 2)
	101-C.2	Commercial Purchase Agreement (Page 3 & 4)
	101-S.1	Information for Escrow Holder (Page 1 of 2)
	101-S.2	Information for Escrow Holder (Page 2 of 2)
	101-BO.1	Business Oppor. Purchase Agree. (Page 1 of 2)
	101-BO.2	Business Oppor. Purchase Agree. (Page 2 of 2)
	421	Land Purchase Agreement
	421-A	Addendum to Land Purchase Agreement
	106	Residential Lease with Option to Purchase
	106-C	Commercial Lease with Option to Purchase
	108	Option to Purchase
	108 CAL	Same as 108/California Version
	101-A	Counter Offer
	101-AC	Counter Offer (Checklist format)
	101-AC CAL	Same as 101-AC/California Version
	101-AS	Invitation to Submit New Offer
	101-B	Addendum
	101-F/G	Contingency Release-Notice-Waiver
	101-H	Waiver of Conditions
	101-L CAL	Commission Agreement (one transaction)
	101-P	Arbitration Addendum
	101-X CAL	Liquidated Damages Addendum
	103	Agreement to Occupy Prior to Close of Escrow
	104	Guaranteed Home Trade-in Agreement
	118	Extension of Contract Terms
	141	Deposit Note
	142	Buyer's Property Inspection Report
	143	Receipt for Documents
	144	Receipt for Documents (Checklist format)

DISCLOSURES

101-BI	Inspection Addendum
101-V	Non-Foreign Seller Affidavit
101-W	FIRPTA Buyer Certification
125	Estimated Buyer's Costs
126	Estimated Seller's Proceeds
131 CAL	Seller Financing Disclosure
134 CAL	Calif. Mortgage Disclosure Statement
109.1	Seller's Property Disclosure (Page 1 of 2)
109.2	Seller's Property Disclosure (Page 2 of 2)
109.3 CAL	Real Estate Transfer Discl Stmt (Page 1 of 2)
109.4 CAL	R.E. Transfer Discl Stmt (Page 2 of 2)
109.5 CAL	R.E. Transfer Disclosure Supplement
109-AD CAL	Agency Disclosure (Calif. Version)
109-AD NAR	Agency Disclosure (NAR Version)
109-RF	Red Flags Inspection Checklist
145 CAL	Request for Condo Documents

LISTING

109	Exclusive Authorization to Sell
109-A	Farm-Ranch Listing Information Sheet

Prices and actual samples of our complete line of approved real estate forms, as well as descriptive literature and other samples, will be mailed upon receipt of $6.00.

TABLES

CONTENTS

Based on 365 days per year.

INTEREST→ YEARS	6%	6⅛%	6¼%	6⅜%	6½%	6⅝%	6¾%	6⅞%	MOS
.5	169.5955	169.6568	169.7181	169.7794	169.8407	169.9020	169.9633	170.0246	6
1.0	86.0665	86.1239	86.1814	86.2389	86.2965	86.3540	86.4116	86.4692	12
1.5	58.2318	58.2883	58.3449	58.4015	58.4582	58.5148	58.5715	58.6283	18
2.0	44.3207	44.3770	44.4334	44.4898	44.5463	44.6028	44.6594	44.7160	24
2.5	35.9790	36.0354	36.0919	36.1484	36.2050	36.2617	36.3184	36.3751	30
3.0	30.4220	30.4787	30.5354	30.5922	30.6491	30.7060	30.7630	30.8200	36
3.5	26.4563	26.5133	26.5703	26.6274	26.6847	26.7419	26.7993	26.8567	42
4.0	23.4851	23.5424	23.5999	23.6574	23.7150	23.7727	23.8305	23.8883	48
4.5	21.1769	21.2347	21.2925	21.3505	21.4085	21.4666	21.5249	21.5832	54
5.0	19.3329	19.3910	19.4493	19.5077	19.5662	19.6248	19.6835	19.7423	60
5.5	17.8263	17.8849	17.9437	18.0025	18.0615	18.1206	18.1798	18.2391	66
6.0	16.5729	16.6320	16.6912	16.7505	16.8100	16.8696	16.9293	16.9891	72
6.5	15.5143	15.5738	15.6335	15.6933	15.7532	15.8133	15.8735	15.9339	78
7.0	14.6086	14.6686	14.7287	14.7890	14.8495	14.9101	14.9708	15.0317	84
7.5	13.8253	13.8858	13.9464	14.0072	14.0682	14.1293	14.1905	14.2519	90
8.0	13.1415	13.2024	13.2635	13.3248	13.3863	13.4479	13.5097	13.5716	96
8.5	12.5395	12.6010	12.6626	12.7243	12.7863	12.8484	12.9108	12.9733	102
9.0	12.0058	12.0677	12.1298	12.1921	12.2546	12.3172	12.3801	12.4431	108
9.5	11.5295	11.5919	11.6545	11.7173	11.7803	11.8435	11.9060	11.9704	114
10.0	11.1021	11.1650	11.2281	11.2913	11.3548	11.4186	11.4825	11.5466	120
10.5	10.7165	10.7799	10.8435	10.9073	10.9713	11.0355	11.0999	11.1646	126
11.0	10.3671	10.4309	10.4950	10.5593	10.6238	10.6886	10.7535	10.8187	132
11.5	10.0491	10.1134	10.1780	10.2428	10.3078	10.3731	10.4386	10.5043	138
12.0	9.7586	9.8234	9.8884	9.9537	10.0193	10.0850	10.1511	10.2173	144
12.5	9.4922	9.5575	9.6231	9.6889	9.7549	9.8212	9.8878	9.9546	150
13.0	9.2473	9.3131	9.3791	9.4454	9.5120	9.5788	9.6459	9.7132	156
13.5	9.0214	9.0876	9.1541	9.2209	9.2880	9.3553	9.4229	9.4908	162
14.0	8.8124	8.8791	8.9462	9.0134	9.0810	9.1489	9.2170	9.2854	168
14.5	8.6187	8.6859	8.7534	8.8212	8.8892	8.9576	9.0262	9.0952	174
15.0	8.4386	8.5063	8.5743	8.6426	8.7111	8.7800	8.8491	8.9186	180
15.5	8.2709	8.3391	8.4075	8.4763	8.5454	8.6147	8.6844	8.7544	186
16.0	8.1144	8.1831	8.2520	8.3212	8.3908	8.4607	8.5309	8.6013	192
16.5	7.9681	8.0372	8.1066	8.1763	8.2464	8.3168	8.3875	8.4585	198
17.0	7.8311	7.9006	7.9705	8.0407	8.1113	8.1821	8.2533	8.3248	204
17.5	7.7025	7.7725	7.8429	7.9136	7.9846	8.0559	8.1276	8.1997	210
18.0	7.5817	7.6522	7.7230	7.7942	7.8657	7.9375	8.0097	8.0822	216
18.5	7.4680	7.5389	7.6102	7.6819	7.7539	7.8262	7.8989	7.9719	222
19.0	7.3609	7.4323	7.5040	7.5761	7.6486	7.7214	7.7946	7.8681	228
19.5	7.2598	7.3317	7.4039	7.4765	7.5494	7.6227	7.6964	7.7704	234
20.0	7.1644	7.2367	7.3093	7.3824	7.4558	7.5296	7.6037	7.6782	240
20.5	7.0741	7.1468	7.2200	7.2935	7.3673	7.4416	7.5162	7.5912	246
21.0	6.9886	7.0618	7.1354	7.2093	7.2837	7.3584	7.4335	7.5089	252
21.5	6.9076	6.9813	7.0553	7.1297	7.2045	7.2797	7.3552	7.4312	258
22.0	6.8308	6.9049	6.9793	7.0542	7.1294	7.2051	7.2811	7.3575	264
22.5	6.7578	6.8323	6.9073	6.9826	7.0583	7.1344	7.2108	7.2877	270
23.0	6.6885	6.7635	6.8388	6.9145	6.9907	7.0672	7.1442	7.2215	276
23.5	6.6226	6.6980	6.7737	6.8499	6.9265	7.0035	7.0809	7.1587	282
24.0	6.5598	6.6356	6.7118	6.7884	6.8655	6.9429	7.0208	7.0990	288
24.5	6.5000	6.5763	6.6529	6.7299	6.8074	6.8853	6.9636	7.0423	294
25.0	6.4431	6.5197	6.5967	6.6742	6.7521	6.8304	6.9092	6.9883	300
25.5	6.3887	6.4657	6.5432	6.6211	6.6994	6.7782	6.8574	6.9369	306
26.0	6.3368	6.4143	6.4922	6.5705	6.6492	6.7284	6.8080	6.8880	312
26.5	6.2873	6.3651	6.4434	6.5222	6.6013	6.6809	6.7609	6.8414	318
27.0	6.2399	6.3182	6.3969	6.4760	6.5556	6.6356	6.7161	6.7969	324
27.5	6.1946	6.2733	6.3524	6.4319	6.5119	6.5924	6.6732	6.7545	330
28.0	6.1513	6.2303	6.3099	6.3898	6.4702	6.5510	6.6323	6.7140	336
28.5	6.1098	6.1893	6.2692	6.3495	6.4303	6.5116	6.5932	6.6754	342
29.0	6.0701	6.1499	6.2302	6.3110	6.3922	6.4738	6.5559	6.6384	348
29.5	6.0320	6.1123	6.1929	6.2741	6.3557	6.4377	6.5202	6.6031	354
29.8	6.0075	6.0880	6.1690	6.2504	6.3322	6.4145	6.4972	6.5804	358
30.0	5.9956	6.0762	6.1572	6.2387	6.3207	6.4032	6.4860	6.5693	360
35.0	5.7019	5.7861	5.8708	5.9560	6.0416	6.1277	6.2142	6.3012	420
40.0	5.5022	5.5896	5.6774	5.7658	5.8546	5.9439	6.0336	6.1238	480

MONTHLY PAYMENT NECESSARY
TO AMORTIZE A $1,000 LOAN

INTEREST► YEARS	7%	7⅛%	7¼%	7⅜%	7½%	7⅝%	7¾%	7⅞%	MOS
.5	170.0860	170.1473	170.2087	170.2701	170.3315	170.3929	170.4543	170.5157	6
1.0	86.5268	86.5844	86.6421	86.6998	86.7575	86.8152	86.8729	86.930/	12
1.5	58.6850	58.7418	58.7987	58.8555	58.9124	58.9694	59.0263	59.0833	18
2.0	44.7726	44.8293	44.8860	44.9428	44.9996	45.0565	45.1134	45.1704	24
2.5	36.4320	36.4888	36.5457	36.6027	36.6597	36.7168	36.7739	36.8311	30
3.0	30.8771	30.9343	30.9916	31.0489	31.1063	31.1637	31.2212	31.2788	36
3.5	26.9143	26.9718	27.0295	27.0872	27.1450	27.2029	27.2609	27.3189	42
4.0	23.9463	24.0043	24.0625	24.1207	24.1790	24.2373	24.2958	24.3543	48
4.5	21.6416	21.7001	21.7588	21.8175	21.8763	21.9352	21.9942	22.0533	54
5.0	19.8012	19.8603	19.9194	19.9787	20.0380	20.0975	20.1570	20.2167	60
5.5	18.2985	18.3581	18.4178	18.4775	18.5374	18.5975	18.6576	18.7178	66
6.0	17.0491	17.1091	17.1694	17.2297	17.2902	17.3508	17.4115	17.4723	72
6.5	15.9944	16.0550	16.1158	16.1767	16.2377	16.2989	16.3602	16.4216	78
7.0	15.0927	15.1539	15.2152	15.2767	15.3383	15.4001	15.4620	15.5241	84
7.5	14.3135	14.3752	14.4371	14.4992	14.5614	14.6237	14.6863	14.7489	90
8.0	13.6338	13.6961	13.7585	13.8211	13.8839	13.9469	14.0100	14.0733	96
8.5	13.0359	13.0988	13.1618	13.2250	13.2884	13.3519	13.4156	13.4795	102
9.0	12.5063	12.5697	12.6333	12.6971	12.7611	12.8252	12.8895	12.9541	108
9.5	12.0342	12.0982	12.1623	12.2267	12.2912	12.3560	12.4209	12.4860	114
10.0	11.6109	11.6754	11.7402	11.8051	11.8702	11.9356	12.0011	12.0669	120
10.5	11.2295	11.2945	11.3598	11.4253	11.4911	11.5570	11.6232	11.6895	126
11.0	10.8842	10.9498	11.0157	11.0817	11.1481	11.2146	11.2813	11.3483	132
11.5	10.5703	10.6365	10.7029	10.7696	10.8364	10.9036	10.9709	11.0385	138
12.0	10.2839	10.3506	10.4176	10.4848	10.5523	10.6200	10.6880	10.7562	144
12.5	10.0216	10.0889	10.1565	10.2243	10.2923	10.3606	10.4292	10.4980	150
13.0	9.7808	9.8486	9.9168	9.9851	10.0538	10.1226	10.1918	10.2612	156
13.5	9.5589	9.6273	9.6960	9.7650	9.8341	9.9036	9.9733	10.0433	162
14.0	9.3541	9.4230	9.4922	9.5617	9.6315	9.7015	9.7718	9.8424	168
14.5	9.1644	9.2338	9.3036	9.3737	9.4440	9.5146	9.5855	9.6566	174
15.0	8.9883	9.0584	9.1287	9.1993	9.2702	9.3413	9.4128	9.4845	180
15.5	8.8246	8.8952	8.9661	9.0372	9.1087	9.1804	9.2524	9.3248	186
16.0	8.6721	8.7432	8.8146	8.8863	8.9583	9.0306	9.1032	9.1761	192
16.5	8.5298	8.6014	8.6733	8.7456	8.8181	8.8910	8.9641	9.0376	198
17.0	8.3967	8.4688	8.5413	8.6140	8.6871	8.7605	8.8343	8.9083	204
17.5	8.2720	8.3447	8.4177	8.4910	8.5646	8.6386	8.7128	8.7874	210
18.0	8.1551	8.2283	8.3018	8.3756	8.4498	8.5243	8.5991	8.6742	216
18.5	8.0453	8.1190	8.1930	8.2674	8.3421	8.4171	8.4924	8.5681	222
19.0	7.9420	8.0162	8.0907	8.1656	8.2408	8.3164	8.3923	8.4685	228
19.5	7.8447	7.9194	7.9945	8.0699	8.1456	8.2217	8.2981	8.3749	234
20.0	7.7530	7.8282	7.9038	7.9797	8.0560	8.1326	8.2095	8.2868	240
20.5	7.6665	7.7422	7.8183	7.8947	7.9715	8.0486	8.1261	8.2039	246
21.0	7.5848	7.6610	7.7375	7.8144	7.8917	7.9693	8.0473	8.1257	252
21.5	7.5075	7.5841	7.6612	7.7386	7.8164	7.8945	7.9730	8.0518	258
22.0	7.4343	7.5115	7.5890	7.6669	7.7452	7.8238	7.9028	7.9821	264
22.5	7.3650	7.4426	7.5206	7.5990	7.6778	7.7569	7.8364	7.9162	270
23.0	7.2992	7.3773	7.4558	7.5347	7.6139	7.6936	7.7735	7.8539	276
23.5	7.2369	7.3154	7.3944	7.4737	7.5535	7.6336	7.7140	7.7948	282
24.0	7.1776	7.2567	7.3361	7.4159	7.4961	7.5767	7.6576	7.7389	288
24.5	7.1214	7.2009	7.2807	7.3610	7.4417	7.5227	7.6041	7.6859	294
25.0	7.0678	7.1478	7.2281	7.3088	7.3900	7.4715	7.5533	7.6356	300
25.5	7.0169	7.0973	7.1781	7.2593	7.3408	7.4228	7.5051	7.5878	306
26.0	6.9684	7.0493	7.1305	7.2121	7.2941	7.3765	7.4593	7.5425	312
26.5	6.9222	7.0035	7.0852	7.1672	7.2497	7.3325	7.4158	7.4994	318
27.0	6.8782	6.9599	7.0420	7.1245	7.2074	7.2907	7.3744	7.4584	324
27.5	6.8362	6.9183	7.0008	7.0838	7.1671	7.2508	7.3349	7.4194	330
28.0	6.7961	6.8787	6.9616	7.0450	7.1287	7.2129	7.2974	7.3823	336
28.5	6.7579	6.8408	6.9242	7.0080	7.0921	7.1767	7.2617	7.3470	342
29.0	6.7214	6.8047	6.8885	6.9727	7.0573	7.1422	7.2276	7.3134	348
29.5	6.6864	6.7702	6.8544	6.9390	7.0240	7.1094	7.1951	7.2813	354
29.8	6.6640	6.7481	6.8325	6.9174	7.0026	7.0883	7.1743	7.2608	358
30.0	6.6531	6.7372	6.8218	6.9068	6.9922	7.0780	7.1642	7.2507	360
35.0	6.3886	6.4765	6.5647	6.6534	6.7425	6.8319	6.9218	7.0120	420
40.0	6.2144	6.3054	6.3968	6.4886	6.5808	6.6733	6.7662	6.8595	480

MONTHLY PAYMENT NECESSARY
TO AMORTIZE A $1,000 LOAN

INTEREST↓ YEARS	8%	8⅛%	8¼%	8⅜%	8½%	8⅝%	8¾%	8⅞%	MOS
.5	170.5771	170.6385	170.7000	170.7614	170.8229	170.8844	170.9459	171.0074	6
1.0	86.9884	87.0462	87.1041	87.1619	87.2198	87.2777	87.3356	87.3935	12
1.5	59.1403	59.1974	59.2544	59.3116	59.3687	59.4259	59.4831	59.5404	18
2.0	45.2273	45.2843	45.3414	45.3985	45.4557	45.5129	45.5701	45.6274	24
2.5	36.8883	36.9456	37.0030	37.0604	37.1178	37.1753	37.2329	37.2905	30
3.0	31.3364	31.3941	31.4518	31.5096	31.5675	31.6255	31.6835	31.7416	36
3.5	27.3770	27.4352	27.4934	27.5517	27.6102	27.6686	27.7272	27.7858	42
4.0	24.4129	24.4716	24.5304	24.5893	24.6483	24.7074	24.7665	24.8257	48
4.5	22.1124	22.1717	22.2311	22.2906	22.3501	22.4098	22.4696	22.5294	54
5.0	20.2764	20.3363	20.3963	20.4563	20.5165	20.5768	20.6372	20.6977	60
5.5	18.7782	18.8386	18.8992	18.9599	19.0208	19.0817	19.1428	19.2040	66
6.0	17.5332	17.5943	17.6556	17.7169	17.7784	17.8400	17.9017	17.9636	72
6.5	16.4832	16.5449	16.6068	16.6688	16.7309	16.7931	16.8555	16.9181	78
7.0	15.5862	15.6486	15.7111	15.7737	15.8365	15.8994	15.9625	16.0257	84
7.5	14.8117	14.8747	14.9378	15.0011	15.0646	15.1282	15.1919	15.2558	90
8.0	14.1367	14.2003	14.2641	14.3280	14.3921	14.4564	14.5208	14.5854	96
8.5	13.5436	13.6078	13.6722	13.7368	13.8016	13.8666	13.9317	13.9970	102
9.0	13.0187	13.0836	13.1487	13.2139	13.2794	13.3450	13.4108	13.4767	108
9.5	12.5513	12.6168	12.6826	12.7485	12.8145	12.8808	12.9473	13.0140	114
10.0	12.1328	12.1989	12.2653	12.3318	12.3986	12.4655	12.5327	12.6000	120
10.5	11.7560	11.8228	11.8898	11.9570	12.0244	12.0920	12.1599	12.2279	126
11.0	11.4154	11.4829	11.5505	11.6183	11.6864	11.7547	11.8232	11.8919	132
11.5	11.1063	11.1743	11.2426	11.3110	11.3797	11.4487	11.5178	11.5872	138
12.0	10.8245	10.8932	10.9621	11.0312	11.1006	11.1701	11.2400	11.3100	144
12.5	10.5670	10.6362	10.7057	10.7755	10.8455	10.9157	10.9862	11.0569	150
13.0	10.3307	10.4006	10.4708	10.5412	10.6118	10.6827	10.7538	10.8252	156
13.5	10.1135	10.1840	10.2548	10.3258	10.3970	10.4686	10.5403	10.6124	162
14.0	9.9132	9.9843	10.0557	10.1273	10.1992	10.2713	10.3438	10.4164	168
14.5	9.7280	9.7997	9.8717	9.9440	10.0165	10.0893	10.1623	10.2356	174
15.0	9.5565	9.6288	9.7014	9.7743	9.8474	9.9208	9.9945	10.0684	180
15.5	9.3973	9.4702	9.5434	9.6168	9.6906	9.7646	9.8389	9.9135	186
16.0	9.2493	9.3227	9.3965	9.4706	9.5449	9.6195	9.6945	9.7697	192
16.5	9.1113	9.1854	9.2597	9.3344	9.4093	9.4846	9.5601	9.6359	198
17.0	8.9826	9.0572	9.1321	9.2074	9.2829	9.3588	9.4349	9.5113	204
17.5	8.8622	8.9375	9.0130	9.0888	9.1649	9.2413	9.3181	9.3951	210
18.0	8.7496	8.8254	8.9015	8.9779	9.0546	9.1316	9.2089	9.2865	216
18.5	8.6441	8.7204	8.7970	8.8740	8.9513	9.0289	9.1068	9.1850	222
19.0	8.5450	8.6219	8.6991	8.7766	8.8545	8.9326	9.0111	9.0899	228
19.5	8.4519	8.5294	8.6071	8.6852	8.7636	8.8423	8.9214	9.0007	234
20.0	8.3644	8.4424	8.5207	8.5993	8.6782	8.7575	8.8371	8.9170	240
20.5	8.2820	8.3605	8.4393	8.5185	8.5980	8.6778	8.7579	8.8384	246
21.0	8.2043	8.2833	8.3627	8.4424	8.5224	8.6028	8.6835	8.7645	252
21.5	8.1310	8.2105	8.2904	8.3706	8.4512	8.5321	8.6133	8.6949	258
22.0	8.0618	8.1418	8.2222	8.3030	8.3841	8.4655	8.5472	8.6293	264
22.5	7.9964	8.0769	8.1578	8.2391	8.3207	8.4026	8.4849	8.5675	270
23.0	7.9345	8.0156	8.0970	8.1788	8.2609	8.3433	8.4261	8.5092	276
23.5	7.8760	7.9575	8.0394	8.1217	8.2043	8.2873	8.3706	8.4542	282
24.0	7.8205	7.9026	7.9850	8.0677	8.1508	8.2343	8.3181	8.4022	288
24.5	7.7680	7.8505	7.9334	8.0166	8.1002	8.1841	8.2684	8.3530	294
25.0	7.7182	7.8012	7.8845	7.9682	8.0523	8.1367	8.2214	8.3065	300
25.5	7.6709	7.7543	7.8381	7.9223	8.0069	8.0917	8.1770	8.2625	306
26.0	7.6260	7.7099	7.7942	7.8788	7.9638	8.0491	8.1348	8.2209	312
26.5	7.5833	7.6677	7.7524	7.8375	7.9230	8.0088	8.0949	8.1814	318
27.0	7.5428	7.6276	7.7128	7.7983	7.8842	7.9705	8.0570	8.1440	324
27.5	7.5043	7.5895	7.6751	7.7611	7.8474	7.9341	8.0211	8.1085	330
28.0	7.4676	7.5533	7.6393	7.7257	7.8125	7.8996	7.9871	8.0749	336
28.5	7.4327	7.5188	7.6053	7.6921	7.7793	7.8668	7.9547	8.0429	342
29.0	7.3995	7.4860	7.5729	7.6601	7.7477	7.8357	7.9240	8.0126	348
29.5	7.3678	7.4547	7.5420	7.6297	7.7177	7.8061	7.8948	7.9838	354
29.8	7.3475	7.4347	7.5223	7.6102	7.6985	7.7871	7.8761	7.9654	358
30.0	7.3376	7.4250	7.5127	7.6007	7.6891	7.7779	7.8670	7.9564	360
35.0	7.1026	7.1936	7.2849	7.3766	7.4686	7.5610	7.6536	7.7466	420
40.0	6.9531	7.0471	7.1414	7.2360	7.3309	7.4262	7.5217	7.6175	480

INTEREST↓ YEARS	9%	9⅛%	9¼%	9⅜%	9½%	9⅝%	9¾%	9⅞%	MOS
.5	171.0689	171.1304	171.1920	171.2535	171.3151	171.3766	171.4382	171.4998	6
1.0	87.4515	87.5095	87.5675	87.6255	87.6835	87.7416	87.7997	87.8578	12
1.5	59.5977	59.6550	59.7123	59.7697	59.8271	59.8846	59.9420	59.9995	18
2.0	45.6847	45.7421	45.7995	45.8570	45.9145	45.9720	46.0296	46.0873	24
2.5	37.3482	37.4059	37.4637	37.5215	37.5794	37.6373	37.6953	37.7533	30
3.0	31.7997	31.8579	31.9162	31.9746	32.0330	32.0914	32.1499	32.2085	36
3.5	27.8445	27.9033	27.9621	28.0211	28.0801	28.1392	28.1983	28.2575	42
4.0	24.8850	24.9444	25.0039	25.0635	25.1231	25.1829	25.2427	25.3026	48
4.5	22.5894	22.6494	22.7096	22.7698	22.8301	22.8906	22.9511	23.0117	54
5.0	20.7584	20.8191	20.8799	20.9408	21.0019	21.0630	21.1242	21.1856	60
5.5	19.2652	19.3266	19.3882	19.4498	19.5116	19.5734	19.6354	19.6975	66
6.0	18.0255	18.0876	18.1499	18.2122	18.2747	18.3373	18.4000	18.4629	72
6.5	16.9807	17.0435	17.1065	17.1696	17.2328	17.2961	17.3596	17.4232	78
7.0	16.0891	16.1526	16.2162	16.2800	16.3440	16.4081	16.4723	16.5367	84
7.5	15.3199	15.3841	15.4485	15.5130	15.5777	15.6425	15.7075	15.7726	90
8.0	14.6502	14.7151	14.7802	14.8455	14.9109	14.9765	15.0422	15.1081	96
8.5	14.0624	14.1281	14.1939	14.2599	14.3260	14.3923	14.4588	14.5255	102
9.0	13.5429	13.6093	13.6758	13.7425	13.8094	13.8764	13.9437	14.0111	108
9.5	13.0808	13.1479	13.2151	13.2825	13.3502	13.4180	13.4859	13.5541	114
10.0	12.6676	12.7353	12.8033	12.8714	12.9398	13.0083	13.0770	13.1460	120
10.5	12.2961	12.3646	12.4332	12.5021	12.5712	12.6404	12.7099	12.7796	126
11.0	11.9608	12.0299	12.0993	12.1689	12.2386	12.3086	12.3788	12.4493	132
11.5	11.6568	11.7267	11.7967	11.8670	11.9375	12.0082	12.0791	12.1503	138
12.0	11.3803	11.4508	11.5216	11.5925	11.6637	11.7352	11.8068	11.8787	144
12.5	11.1279	11.1991	11.2705	11.3422	11.4141	11.4862	11.5586	11.6312	150
13.0	10.8968	10.9687	11.0408	11.1131	11.1857	11.2586	11.3316	11.4049	156
13.5	10.6846	10.7572	10.8300	10.9030	10.9763	11.0498	11.1236	11.1976	162
14.0	10.4894	10.5626	10.6360	10.7097	10.7837	10.8579	10.9324	11.0071	168
14.5	10.3092	10.3831	10.4572	10.5316	10.6062	10.6811	10.7562	10.8316	174
15.0	10.1427	10.2172	10.2919	10.3670	10.4422	10.5178	10.5936	10.6697	180
15.5	9.9884	10.0635	10.1389	10.2146	10.2905	10.3668	10.4432	10.5200	186
16.0	9.8452	9.9209	9.9970	10.0733	10.1499	10.2268	10.3039	10.3813	192
16.5	9.7120	9.7884	9.8651	9.9420	10.0193	10.0968	10.1746	10.2527	198
17.0	9.5880	9.6651	9.7423	9.8199	9.8978	9.9760	10.0544	10.1331	204
17.5	9.4724	9.5500	9.6280	9.7062	9.7847	9.8634	9.9425	10.0219	210
18.0	9.3644	9.4427	9.5212	9.6000	9.6791	9.7585	9.8382	9.9182	216
18.5	9.2635	9.3423	9.4214	9.5008	9.5806	9.6606	9.7409	9.8215	222
19.0	9.1690	9.2484	9.3281	9.4081	9.4884	9.5690	9.6499	9.7311	228
19.5	9.0804	9.1604	9.2406	9.3212	9.4021	9.4833	9.5648	9.6466	234
20.0	8.9973	9.0778	9.1587	9.2398	9.3213	9.4031	9.4852	9.5675	240
20.5	8.9192	9.0003	9.0817	9.1635	9.2455	9.3279	9.4105	9.4935	246
21.0	8.8458	8.9275	9.0094	9.0917	9.1743	9.2573	9.3405	9.4240	252
21.5	8.7768	8.8590	8.9415	9.0243	9.1075	9.1909	9.2747	9.3588	258
22.0	8.7117	8.7945	8.8775	8.9609	9.0446	9.1286	9.2129	9.2975	264
22.5	8.6505	8.7337	8.8173	8.9012	8.9855	9.0700	9.1548	9.2400	270
23.0	8.5927	8.6765	8.7606	8.8450	8.9297	9.0148	9.1002	9.1858	276
23.5	8.5381	8.6224	8.7071	8.7920	8.8772	8.9628	9.0487	9.1349	282
24.0	8.4866	8.5714	8.6566	8.7420	8.8277	8.9138	9.0002	9.0869	288
24.5	8.4380	8.5233	8.6089	8.6948	8.7811	8.8676	8.9545	9.0417	294
25.0	8.3920	8.4777	8.5638	8.6502	8.7370	8.8240	8.9114	8.9990	300
25.5	8.3484	8.4347	8.5212	8.6081	8.6953	8.7829	8.8707	8.9588	306
26.0	8.3072	8.3939	8.4810	8.5683	8.6560	8.7440	8.8323	8.9209	312
26.5	8.2682	8.3554	8.4429	8.5307	8.6188	8.7072	8.7960	8.8850	318
27.0	8.2313	8.3189	8.4068	8.4950	8.5836	8.6725	8.7617	8.8512	324
27.5	8.1962	8.2843	8.3726	8.4613	8.5503	8.6396	8.7293	8.8192	330
28.0	8.1630	8.2515	8.3403	8.4294	8.5188	8.6086	8.6986	8.7890	336
28.5	8.1315	8.2204	8.3096	8.3991	8.4890	8.5791	8.6696	8.7604	342
29.0	8.1016	8.1909	8.2805	8.3705	8.4607	8.5513	8.6421	8.7333	348
29.5	8.0732	8.1629	8.2529	8.3433	8.4339	8.5249	8.6162	8.7077	354
29.8	8.0551	8.1450	8.2353	8.3259	8.4169	8.5081	8.5996	8.6914	358
30.0	8.0462	8.1363	8.2268	8.3175	8.4085	8.4999	8.5915	8.6835	360
35.0	7.8399	7.9335	8.0274	8.1216	8.2161	8.3109	8.4059	8.5012	420
40.0	7.7136	7.8100	7.9066	8.0035	8.1006	8.1980	8.2956	8.3934	480

A-4

MONTHLY PAYMENT NECESSARY
TO AMORTIZE A $1,000 LOAN

INTEREST→ YEARS	10%	10⅛%	10¼%	10⅜%	10½%	10⅝%	10¾%	10⅞%	MOS
.5	171.5614	171.6230	171.6846	171.7462	171.8079	171.8695	171.9312	171.9929	6
1.0	87.9159	87.9740	88.0322	88.0904	88.1486	88.2068	88.2651	88.3234	12
1.5	60.0571	60.1147	60.1723	60.2299	60.2876	60.3453	60.4030	60.4607	18
2.0	46.1449	46.2026	46.2604	46.3182	46.3760	46.4339	46.4919	46.5498	24
2.5	37.8114	37.8696	37.9278	37.9860	38.0443	38.1027	38.1611	38.2195	30
3.0	32.2672	32.3259	32.3847	32.4435	32.5024	32.5614	32.6205	32.6796	36
3.5	28.3168	28.3762	28.4356	28.4952	28.5547	28.6144	28.6742	28.7340	42
4.0	25.3626	25.4227	25.4828	25.5431	25.6034	25.6638	25.7243	25.7849	48
4.5	23.0724	23.1332	23.1941	23.2551	23.3162	23.3774	23.4387	23.5000	54
5.0	21.2470	21.3086	21.3703	21.4320	21.4939	21.5559	21.6180	21.6801	60
5.5	19.7597	19.8220	19.8845	19.9470	20.0097	20.0725	20.1354	20.1984	66
6.0	18.5258	18.5889	18.6522	18.7155	18.7790	18.8426	18.9063	18.9701	72
6.5	17.4869	17.5508	17.6148	17.6790	17.7432	17.8077	17.8722	17.9369	78
7.0	16.6012	16.6658	16.7306	16.7956	16.8607	16.9259	16.9913	17.0568	84
7.5	15.8379	15.9034	15.9690	16.0347	16.1006	16.1666	16.2328	16.2992	90
8.0	15.1742	15.2404	15.3068	15.3733	15.4400	15.5069	15.5739	15.6411	96
8.5	14.5923	14.6593	14.7265	14.7938	14.8613	14.9290	14.9969	15.0649	102
9.0	14.0787	14.1465	14.2144	14.2826	14.3509	14.4193	14.4880	14.5568	108
9.5	13.6225	13.6910	13.7598	13.8287	13.8978	13.9671	14.0366	14.1062	114
10.0	13.2151	13.2844	13.3539	13.4236	13.4935	13.5636	13.6339	13.7043	120
10.5	12.8494	12.9195	12.9898	13.0603	13.1310	13.2018	13.2729	13.3442	126
11.0	12.5199	12.5907	12.6618	12.7330	12.8045	12.8761	12.9480	13.0201	132
11.5	12.2216	12.2932	12.3650	12.4370	12.5093	12.5817	12.6543	12.7272	138
12.0	11.9508	12.0231	12.0957	12.1684	12.2414	12.3146	12.3880	12.4617	144
12.5	11.7040	11.7771	11.8503	11.9239	11.9976	12.0716	12.1458	12.2202	150
13.0	11.4785	11.5523	11.6263	11.7005	11.7750	11.8497	11.9247	11.9999	156
13.5	11.2718	11.3463	11.4211	11.4961	11.5713	11.6467	11.7224	11.7984	162
14.0	11.0820	11.1572	11.2327	11.3084	11.3843	11.4605	11.5370	11.6136	168
14.5	10.9073	10.9832	11.0593	11.1358	11.2124	11.2893	11.3665	11.4439	174
15.0	10.7461	10.8227	10.8995	10.9766	11.0540	11.1316	11.2095	11.2876	180
15.5	10.5970	10.6743	10.7518	10.8297	10.9077	10.9860	11.0646	11.1434	186
16.0	10.4590	10.5370	10.6152	10.6937	10.7724	10.8514	10.9307	11.0102	192
16.5	10.3310	10.4096	10.4885	10.5677	10.6471	10.7268	10.8067	10.8869	198
17.0	10.2121	10.2914	10.3709	10.4507	10.5308	10.6112	10.6918	10.7727	204
17.5	10.1015	10.1814	10.2616	10.3420	10.4228	10.5038	10.5851	10.6666	210
18.0	9.9984	10.0790	10.1598	10.2409	10.3223	10.4039	10.4858	10.5680	216
18.5	9.9023	9.9835	10.0649	10.1467	10.2287	10.3110	10.3935	10.4763	222
19.0	9.8126	9.8944	9.9764	10.0588	10.1414	10.2243	10.3075	10.3909	228
19.5	9.7287	9.8111	9.8937	9.9767	10.0599	10.1434	10.2272	10.3113	234
20.0	9.6502	9.7332	9.8164	9.9000	9.9838	10.0679	10.1523	10.2370	240
20.5	9.5767	9.6603	9.7441	9.8282	9.9126	9.9973	10.0823	10.1675	246
21.0	9.5078	9.5919	9.6763	9.7610	9.8460	9.9313	10.0168	10.1026	252
21.5	9.4432	9.5278	9.6128	9.6980	9.7836	9.8694	9.9555	10.0419	258
22.0	9.3825	9.4677	9.5532	9.6390	9.7251	9.8114	9.8981	9.9850	264
22.5	9.3254	9.4112	9.4972	9.5836	9.6702	9.7571	9.8443	9.9318	270
23.0	9.2718	9.3581	9.4447	9.5315	9.6187	9.7061	9.7938	9.8818	276
23.5	9.2214	9.3082	9.3952	9.4826	9.5703	9.6582	9.7465	9.8350	282
24.0	9.1739	9.2612	9.3488	9.4366	9.5248	9.6133	9.7020	9.7910	288
24.5	9.1292	9.2169	9.3050	9.3934	9.4820	9.5710	9.6602	9.7497	294
25.0	9.0870	9.1753	9.2638	9.3527	9.4418	9.5312	9.6209	9.7109	300
25.5	9.0473	9.1360	9.2250	9.3143	9.4040	9.4938	9.5840	9.6744	306
26.0	9.0098	9.0990	9.1885	9.2782	9.3683	9.4586	9.5492	9.6401	312
26.5	8.9744	9.0640	9.1540	9.2442	9.3347	9.4255	9.5165	9.6079	318
27.0	8.9410	9.0311	9.1214	9.2121	9.3030	9.3943	9.4857	9.5775	324
27.5	8.9094	8.9999	9.0907	9.1818	9.2732	9.3648	9.4567	9.5489	330
28.0	8.8796	8.9705	9.0618	9.1533	9.2450	9.3371	9.4294	9.5220	336
28.5	8.8514	8.9428	9.0344	9.1263	9.2185	9.3109	9.4036	9.4966	342
29.0	8.8248	8.9165	9.0085	9.1008	9.1934	9.2862	9.3793	9.4727	348
29.5	8.7996	8.8917	8.9841	9.0768	9.1697	9.2630	9.3564	9.4502	354
29.8	8.7835	8.8759	8.9686	9.0615	9.1547	9.2482	9.3419	9.4358	358
30.0	8.7757	8.8682	8.9610	9.0541	9.1474	9.2410	9.3348	9.4289	360
35.0	8.5967	8.6925	8.7886	8.8848	8.9813	9.0781	9.1750	9.2722	420
40.0	8.4915	8.5897	8.6882	8.7868	8.8857	8.9847	9.0840	9.1834	480

MONTHLY PAYMENT NECESSARY
TO AMORTIZE A $1,000 LOAN

INTEREST► YEARS	11%	11⅛%	11¼%	11⅜%	11½%	11⅝%	11¾%	11⅞%	MOS
.5	172.0545	172.1162	172.1779	172.2397	172.3014	172.3631	172.4248	172.4866	6
1.0	88.3817	88.4400	88.4983	88.5567	88.6151	88.6735	88.7319	88.7903	12
1.5	60.5185	60.5764	60.6342	60.6921	60.7500	60.8080	60.8660	60.9240	18
2.0	46.6078	46.6659	46.7240	46.7821	46.8403	46.8985	46.9568	47.0151	24
2.5	38.2781	38.3366	38.3953	38.4539	38.5127	38.5714	38.6303	38.6892	30
3.0	32.7387	32.7979	32.8572	32.9166	32.9760	33.0355	33.0950	33.1546	36
3.5	28.7939	28.8538	28.9139	28.9740	29.0342	29.0944	29.1547	29.2151	42
4.0	25.8455	25.9063	25.9671	26.0280	26.0890	26.1501	26.2113	26.2725	48
4.5	23.5615	23.6230	23.6847	23.7464	23.8083	23.8702	23.9322	23.9944	54
5.0	21.7424	21.8048	21.8673	21.9299	21.9926	22.0554	22.1183	22.1813	60
5.5	20.2615	20.3247	20.3881	20.4515	20.5151	20.5788	20.6426	20.7065	66
6.0	19.0341	19.0982	19.1624	19.2267	19.2912	19.3557	19.4204	19.4853	72
6.5	18.0017	18.0666	18.1317	18.1969	18.2622	18.3277	18.3933	18.4590	78
7.0	17.1224	17.1882	17.2542	17.3202	17.3865	17.4528	17.5193	17.5860	84
7.5	16.3657	16.4323	16.4991	16.5661	16.6332	16.7004	16.7678	16.8354	90
8.0	15.7084	15.7759	15.8436	15.9114	15.9794	16.0475	16.1158	16.1842	96
8.5	15.1330	15.2014	15.2699	15.3386	15.4074	15.4764	15.5456	15.6150	102
9.0	14.6259	14.6950	14.7644	14.8339	14.9037	14.9735	15.0436	15.1138	108
9.5	14.1761	14.2461	14.3163	14.3867	14.4572	14.5280	14.5989	14.6700	114
10.0	13.7750	13.8459	13.9169	13.9881	14.0595	14.1312	14.2029	14.2749	120
10.5	13.4157	13.4873	13.5592	13.6313	13.7035	13.7760	13.8486	13.9215	126
11.0	13.0923	13.1648	13.2375	13.3104	13.3835	13.4568	13.5303	13.6040	132
11.5	12.8003	12.8736	12.9471	13.0208	13.0947	13.1688	13.2431	13.3177	138
12.0	12.5356	12.6096	12.6839	12.7584	12.8332	12.9081	12.9833	13.0586	144
12.5	12.2948	12.3697	12.4448	12.5201	12.5956	12.6713	12.7473	12.8235	150
13.0	12.0753	12.1509	12.2268	12.3029	12.3792	12.4557	12.5325	12.6095	156
13.5	11.8745	11.9509	12.0276	12.1044	12.1815	12.2588	12.3364	12.4142	162
14.0	11.6905	11.7677	11.8451	11.9227	12.0006	12.0786	12.1570	12.2355	168
14.5	11.5215	11.5994	11.6776	11.7559	11.8345	11.9134	11.9925	12.0718	174
15.0	11.3660	11.4446	11.5234	11.6026	11.6819	11.7615	11.8413	11.9214	180
15.5	11.2225	11.3018	11.3814	11.4613	11.5413	11.6216	11.7022	11.7830	186
16.0	11.0900	11.1700	11.2503	11.3309	11.4117	11.4927	11.5740	11.6555	192
16.5	10.9674	11.0481	11.1291	11.2103	11.2918	11.3736	11.4556	11.5378	198
17.0	10.8538	10.9352	11.0169	11.0988	11.1810	11.2634	11.3461	11.4290	204
17.5	10.7484	10.8305	10.9128	10.9954	11.0782	11.1613	11.2447	11.3283	210
18.0	10.6505	10.7332	10.8162	10.8994	10.9830	11.0667	11.1507	11.2350	216
18.5	10.5594	10.6428	10.7264	10.8103	10.8945	10.9789	11.0635	11.1484	222
19.0	10.4746	10.5586	10.6429	10.7274	10.8122	10.8972	10.9825	11.0681	228
19.5	10.3956	10.4802	10.5651	10.6502	10.7356	10.8213	10.9072	10.9933	234
20.0	10.3219	10.4071	10.4926	10.5783	10.6643	10.7506	10.8371	10.9238	240
20.5	10.2530	10.3388	10.4249	10.5112	10.5978	10.6847	10.7718	10.8591	246
21.0	10.1887	10.2751	10.3617	10.4486	10.5358	10.6232	10.7109	10.7988	252
21.5	10.1285	10.2155	10.3027	10.3901	10.4779	10.5658	10.6541	10.7426	258
22.0	10.0722	10.1597	10.2475	10.3355	10.4237	10.5123	10.6011	10.6901	264
22.5	10.0195	10.1075	10.1958	10.2843	10.3731	10.4622	10.5515	10.6411	270
23.0	9.9701	10.0586	10.1474	10.2365	10.3258	10.4154	10.5052	10.5953	276
23.5	9.9237	10.0128	10.1021	10.1917	10.2815	10.3716	10.4619	10.5525	282
24.0	9.8803	9.9698	10.0596	10.1497	10.2400	10.3306	10.4214	10.5125	288
24.5	9.8395	9.9295	10.0198	10.1103	10.2011	10.2922	10.3835	10.4751	294
25.0	9.8011	9.8916	9.9824	10.0734	10.1647	10.2562	10.3480	10.4400	300
25.5	9.7651	9.8561	9.9473	10.0388	10.1305	10.2225	10.3147	10.4072	306
26.0	9.7313	9.8227	9.9144	10.0063	10.0984	10.1909	10.2835	10.3764	312
26.5	9.6994	9.7913	9.8834	9.9757	10.0683	10.1612	10.2543	10.3476	318
27.0	9.6695	9.7618	9.8543	9.9471	10.0401	10.1333	10.2268	10.3205	324
27.5	9.6413	9.7340	9.8269	9.9201	10.0135	10.1072	10.2011	10.2952	330
28.0	9.6148	9.7079	9.8012	9.8948	9.9886	10.0826	10.1769	10.2714	336
28.5	9.5898	9.6833	9.7770	9.8710	9.9652	10.0596	10.1542	10.2491	342
29.0	9.5663	9.6601	9.7542	9.8486	9.9431	10.0379	10.1329	10.2281	348
29.5	9.5441	9.6383	9.7328	9.8275	9.9224	10.0175	10.1129	10.2085	354
29.8	9.5301	9.6245	9.7192	9.8141	9.9093	10.0046	10.1002	10.1960	358
30.0	9.5232	9.6178	9.7126	9.8077	9.9029	9.9984	10.0941	10.1900	360
35.0	9.3696	9.4672	9.5649	9.6629	9.7611	9.8594	9.9579	10.0566	420
40.0	9.2829	9.3827	9.4826	9.5826	9.6828	9.7832	9.8836	9.9843	480

A-6

MONTHLY PAYMENT NECESSARY
TO AMORTIZE A $1,000 LOAN

INTEREST→ YEARS	12%	12⅛%	12¼%	12⅜%	12½%	12⅝%	12¾%	12⅞%	MOS
.5	172.5484	172.6101	172.6719	172.7337	172.7955	172.8573	172.9192	172.9810	6
1.0	88.8488	88.9073	88.9658	89.0243	89.0829	89.1414	89.2000	89.2586	12
1.5	60.9820	61.0401	61.0982	61.1564	61.2146	61.2728	61.3310	61.3893	18
2.0	47.0735	47.1319	47.1903	47.2488	47.3073	47.3659	47.4245	47.4831	24
2.5	38.7481	38.8071	38.8662	38.9253	38.9844	39.0436	39.1029	39.1622	30
3.0	33.2143	33.2740	33.3338	33.3937	33.4536	33.5136	33.5737	33.6338	36
3.5	29.2756	29.3362	29.3968	29.4575	29.5183	29.5791	29.6400	29.7010	42
4.0	26.3338	26.3953	26.4568	26.5183	26.5800	26.6417	26.7036	26.7655	48
4.5	24.0566	24.1189	24.1813	24.2438	24.3064	24.3691	24.4318	24.4947	54
5.0	22.2444	22.3077	22.3710	22.4344	22.4979	22.5616	22.6253	22.6891	60
5.5	20.7705	20.8347	20.8989	20.9633	21.0278	21.0923	21.1570	21.2218	66
6.0	19.5502	19.6153	19.6804	19.7458	19.8112	19.8767	19.9424	20.0082	72
6.5	18.5249	18.5909	18.6570	18.7232	18.7896	18.8561	18.9228	18.9896	78
7.0	17.6527	17.7197	17.7867	17.8539	17.9212	17.9887	18.0563	18.1241	84
7.5	16.9031	16.9709	17.0389	17.1070	17.1753	17.2437	17.3123	17.3810	90
8.0	16.2528	16.3216	16.3905	16.4596	16.5288	16.5982	16.6677	16.7374	96
8.5	15.6845	15.7541	15.8240	15.8940	15.9641	16.0344	16.1049	16.1756	102
9.0	15.1842	15.2548	15.3256	15.3965	15.4676	15.5388	15.6102	15.6810	108
9.5	14.7413	14.8128	14.8844	14.9563	15.0283	15.1004	15.1728	15.2453	114
10.0	14.3471	14.4194	14.4920	14.5647	14.6376	14.7107	14.7840	14.8574	120
10.5	13.9945	14.0678	14.1412	14.2148	14.2886	14.3626	14.4368	14.5111	126
11.0	13.6779	13.7520	13.8263	13.9007	13.9754	14.0503	14.1254	14.2006	132
11.5	13.3924	13.4674	13.5425	13.6179	13.6934	13.7692	13.8451	13.9213	138
12.0	13.1342	13.2100	13.2860	13.3622	13.4386	13.5152	13.5920	13.6690	144
12.5	12.8999	12.9765	13.0533	13.1303	13.2076	13.2851	13.3627	13.4406	150
13.0	12.6867	12.7641	12.8417	12.9196	12.9977	13.0760	13.1545	13.2332	156
13.5	12.4922	12.5704	12.6488	12.7275	12.8064	12.8855	12.9648	13.0443	162
14.0	12.3143	12.3933	12.4725	12.5520	12.6317	12.7116	12.7917	12.8721	168
14.5	12.1513	12.2311	12.3111	12.3913	12.4718	12.5525	12.6334	12.7146	174
15.0	12.0017	12.0822	12.1630	12.2440	12.3252	12.4067	12.4884	12.5703	180
15.5	11.8640	11.9453	12.0268	12.1086	12.1906	12.2728	12.3552	12.4379	186
16.0	11.7373	11.8193	11.9015	11.9840	12.0667	12.1496	12.2328	12.3162	192
16.5	11.6203	11.7030	11.7859	11.8691	11.9526	12.0362	12.1201	12.2043	198
17.0	11.5122	11.5956	11.6792	11.7631	11.8473	11.9316	12.0162	12.1011	204
17.5	11.4121	11.4962	11.5806	11.6652	11.7500	11.8350	11.9203	12.0059	210
18.0	11.3195	11.4043	11.4893	11.5745	11.6600	11.7457	11.8317	11.9179	216
18.5	11.2336	11.3190	11.4047	11.4906	11.5767	11.6631	11.7497	11.8366	222
19.0	11.1539	11.2399	11.3262	11.4127	11.4995	11.5865	11.6738	11.7613	228
19.5	11.0798	11.1664	11.2533	11.3405	11.4279	11.5155	11.6034	11.6915	234
20.0	11.0109	11.0981	11.1856	11.2734	11.3614	11.4496	11.5381	11.6268	240
20.5	10.9467	11.0346	11.1227	11.2110	11.2996	11.3885	11.4775	11.5668	246
21.0	10.8870	10.9754	11.0641	11.1530	11.2422	11.3316	11.4212	11.5111	252
21.5	10.8313	10.9203	11.0095	11.0990	11.1887	11.2787	11.3689	11.4593	258
22.0	10.7794	10.8689	10.9587	11.0487	11.1390	11.2294	11.3202	11.4111	264
22.5	10.7309	10.8210	10.9113	11.0018	11.0926	11.1836	11.2748	11.3663	270
23.0	10.6856	10.7762	10.8670	10.9581	11.0494	11.1409	11.2326	11.3246	276
23.5	10.6434	10.7344	10.8257	10.9173	11.0091	11.1011	11.1933	11.2857	282
24.0	10.6038	10.6954	10.7872	10.8792	10.9714	11.0639	11.1566	11.2495	288
24.5	10.5668	10.6589	10.7511	10.8436	10.9363	11.0293	11.1224	11.2158	294
25.0	10.5322	10.6247	10.7174	10.8104	10.9035	10.9969	11.0905	11.1843	300
25.5	10.4999	10.5928	10.6859	10.7793	10.8729	10.9667	11.0607	11.1550	306
26.0	10.4695	10.5629	10.6565	10.7503	10.8443	10.9385	11.0329	11.1276	312
26.5	10.4411	10.5349	10.6289	10.7231	10.8175	10.9121	11.0070	11.1020	318
27.0	10.4145	10.5087	10.6030	10.6977	10.7925	10.8875	10.9827	11.0781	324
27.5	10.3895	10.4841	10.5789	10.6739	10.7690	10.8644	10.9600	11.0558	330
28.0	10.3661	10.4611	10.5562	10.6516	10.7471	10.8429	10.9388	11.0350	336
28.5	10.3442	10.4395	10.5350	10.6307	10.7266	10.8227	10.9190	11.0155	342
29.0	10.3236	10.4192	10.5151	10.6112	10.7074	10.8039	10.9005	10.9973	348
29.5	10.3043	10.4003	10.4964	10.5928	10.6894	10.7862	10.8832	10.9803	354
29.8	10.2920	10.3883	10.4847	10.5813	10.6781	10.7751	10.8722	10.9696	358
30.0	10.2861	10.3824	10.4790	10.5757	10.6726	10.7697	10.8669	10.9644	360
35.0	10.1555	10.2545	10.3537	10.4531	10.5525	10.6522	10.7520	10.8519	420
40.0	10.0850	10.1859	10.2869	10.3880	10.4892	10.5905	10.6920	10.7935	480

INTEREST▸ YEARS	13%	13⅛%	13¼%	13⅜%	13½%	13⅝%	13¾%	13⅞%	MOS
.5	173.0429	173.1047	173.1666	173.2285	173.2903	173.3522	173.4142	173.4761	6
1.0	89.3173	89.3759	89.4346	89.4933	89.5520	89.6108	89.6695	89.7283	12
1.5	61.4476	61.5059	61.5643	61.6227	61.6811	61.7396	61.7981	61.8566	18
2.0	47.5418	47.6006	47.6593	47.7182	47.7770	47.8359	47.8949	47.9539	24
2.5	39.2215	39.2810	39.3404	39.4000	39.4595	39.5192	39.5788	39.6386	30
3.0	33.6940	33.7542	33.8145	33.8749	33.9353	33.9958	34.0563	34.1170	36
3.5	29.7621	29.8232	29.8844	29.9457	30.0071	30.0685	30.1300	30.1916	42
4.0	26.8275	26.8896	26.9517	27.0140	27.0763	27.1387	27.2012	27.2638	48
4.5	24.5577	24.6207	24.6839	24.7471	24.8104	24.8739	24.9374	25.0010	54
5.0	22.7531	22.8171	22.8813	22.9455	23.0098	23.0743	23.1388	23.2035	60
5.5	21.2868	21.3518	21.4170	21.4822	21.5476	21.6131	21.6787	21.7444	66
6.0	20.0741	20.1401	20.2063	20.2726	20.3390	20.4055	20.4721	20.5389	72
6.5	19.0565	19.1235	19.1907	19.2579	19.3254	19.3929	19.4606	19.5284	78
7.0	18.1920	18.2600	18.3282	18.3965	18.4649	18.5335	18.6022	18.6710	84
7.5	17.4499	17.5189	17.5881	17.6574	17.7268	17.7964	17.8662	17.9361	90
8.0	16.8073	16.8773	16.9474	17.0177	17.0882	17.1588	17.2295	17.3004	96
8.5	16.2464	16.3174	16.3885	16.4598	16.5312	16.6028	16.6746	16.7465	102
9.0	15.7536	15.8255	15.8976	15.9699	16.0423	16.1149	16.1877	16.2606	108
9.5	15.3180	15.3909	15.4640	15.5372	15.6106	15.6842	15.7579	15.8318	114
10.0	14.9311	15.0049	15.0789	15.1531	15.2274	15.3020	15.3767	15.4516	120
10.5	14.5857	14.6604	14.7354	14.8105	14.8858	14.9612	15.0369	15.1128	126
11.0	14.2761	14.3518	14.4276	14.5036	14.5799	14.6563	14.7329	14.8097	132
11.5	13.9976	14.0742	14.1509	14.2279	14.3050	14.3823	14.4598	14.5376	138
12.0	13.7463	13.8237	13.9013	13.9791	14.0572	14.1354	14.2138	14.2925	144
12.5	13.5187	13.5970	13.6755	13.7542	13.8331	13.9122	13.9915	14.0710	150
13.0	13.3121	13.3912	13.4706	13.5502	13.6299	13.7099	13.7901	13.8704	156
13.5	13.1241	13.2041	13.2843	13.3647	13.4453	13.5261	13.6071	13.6883	162
14.0	12.9526	13.0334	13.1144	13.1956	13.2771	13.3587	13.4406	13.5226	168
14.5	12.7959	12.8775	12.9593	13.0413	13.1236	13.2060	13.2887	13.3715	174
15.0	12.6524	12.7348	12.8174	12.9002	12.9832	13.0664	13.1499	13.2335	180
15.5	12.5208	12.6039	12.6873	12.7708	12.8546	12.9386	13.0228	13.1073	186
16.0	12.3999	12.4837	12.5678	12.6521	12.7367	12.8214	12.9064	12.9916	192
16.5	12.2886	12.3732	12.4580	12.5431	12.6283	12.7138	12.7995	12.8854	198
17.0	12.1861	12.2714	12.3570	12.4427	12.5287	12.6149	12.7013	12.7879	204
17.5	12.0916	12.1776	12.2638	12.3503	12.4369	12.5238	12.6109	12.6982	210
18.0	12.0043	12.0910	12.1779	12.2650	12.3523	12.4399	12.5276	12.6156	216
18.5	11.9236	12.0109	12.0985	12.1863	12.2742	12.3624	12.4509	12.5395	222
19.0	11.8490	11.9369	12.0251	12.1135	12.2021	12.2910	12.3800	12.4693	228
19.5	11.7798	11.8684	11.9572	12.0462	12.1354	12.2249	12.3146	12.4044	234
20.0	11.7158	11.8049	11.8943	11.9839	12.0737	12.1638	12.2541	12.3445	240
20.5	11.6563	11.7461	11.8360	11.9262	12.0166	12.1072	12.1981	12.2891	246
21.0	11.6011	11.6915	11.7820	11.8727	11.9637	12.0549	12.1463	12.2379	252
21.5	11.5499	11.6408	11.7318	11.8231	11.9146	12.0063	12.0983	12.1904	258
22.0	11.5023	11.5937	11.6853	11.7771	11.8691	11.9613	12.0538	12.1464	264
22.5	11.4580	11.5499	11.6420	11.7343	11.8269	11.9196	12.0125	12.1057	270
23.0	11.4168	11.5092	11.6018	11.6946	11.7876	11.8808	11.9743	12.0679	276
23.5	11.3784	11.4713	11.5644	11.6577	11.7512	11.8449	11.9388	12.0329	282
24.0	11.3427	11.4360	11.5296	11.6233	11.7173	11.8114	11.9058	12.0003	288
24.5	11.3094	11.4032	11.4972	11.5914	11.6858	11.7804	11.8751	11.9701	294
25.0	11.2784	11.3726	11.4670	11.5616	11.6564	11.7515	11.8467	11.9420	300
25.5	11.2494	11.3441	11.4389	11.5339	11.6292	11.7246	11.8202	11.9160	306
26.0	11.2224	11.3175	11.4127	11.5082	11.6038	11.6996	11.7956	11.8917	312
26.5	11.1973	11.2927	11.3883	11.4841	11.5801	11.6763	11.7727	11.8692	318
27.0	11.1738	11.2696	11.3656	11.4618	11.5581	11.6547	11.7514	11.8483	324
27.5	11.1518	11.2480	11.3444	11.4409	11.5376	11.6345	11.7316	11.8288	330
28.0	11.1313	11.2279	11.3246	11.4214	11.5185	11.6157	11.7131	11.8107	336
28.5	11.1122	11.2091	11.3061	11.4033	11.5007	11.5982	11.6959	11.7938	342
29.0	11.0943	11.1915	11.2889	11.3864	11.4841	11.5819	11.6799	11.7781	348
29.5	11.0776	11.1751	11.2728	11.3706	11.4686	11.5667	11.6650	11.7635	354
29.8	11.0671	11.1648	11.2626	11.3606	11.4588	11.5572	11.6556	11.7543	358
30.0	11.0620	11.1598	11.2577	11.3559	11.4541	11.5525	11.6511	11.7499	360
35.0	10.9519	11.0521	11.1524	11.2529	11.3534	11.4541	11.5549	11.6557	420
40.0	10.8951	10.9969	11.0987	11.2006	11.3026	11.4047	11.5069	11.6091	480

MONTHLY PAYMENT NECESSARY
TO AMORTIZE A $1,000 LOAN

INTEREST► YEARS	14%	14⅛%	14¼%	14⅜%	14½%	14⅝%	14¾%	14⅞%	MOS
.5	173.5380	173.5999	173.6619	173.7239	173.7858	173.8478	173.9098	173.9718	6
1.0	89.7871	89.8459	89.9048	89.9637	90.0225	90.0815	90.1404	90.1993	12
1.5	61.9152	61.9738	62.0324	62.0910	62.1497	62.2084	62.2672	62.3260	18
2.0	48.0129	48.0720	48.1311	48.1902	48.2494	48.3087	48.3680	48.4273	24
2.5	39.6984	39.7582	39.8181	39.8780	39.9380	39.9981	40.0582	40.1183	30
3.0	34.1776	34.2384	34.2992	34.3600	34.4210	34.4820	34.5430	34.6041	36
3.5	30.2532	30.3150	30.3768	30.4386	30.5006	30.5626	30.6247	30.6868	42
4.0	27.3265	27.3892	27.4521	27.5150	27.5780	27.6410	27.7042	27.7674	48
4.5	25.0647	25.1285	25.1924	25.2563	25.3204	25.3846	25.4488	25.5132	54
5.0	23.2683	23.3331	23.3981	23.4631	23.5283	23.5935	23.6589	23.7244	60
5.5	21.8102	21.8761	21.9421	22.0083	22.0745	22.1409	22.2074	22.2740	66
6.0	20.6057	20.6727	20.7398	20.8071	20.8744	20.9419	21.0095	21.0772	72
6.5	19.5963	19.6644	19.7326	19.8009	19.8693	19.9379	20.0066	20.0754	78
7.0	18.7400	18.8091	18.8784	18.9478	19.0173	19.0870	19.1568	19.2267	84
7.5	18.0061	18.0763	18.1466	18.2170	18.2876	18.3584	18.4293	18.5003	90
8.0	17.3715	17.4427	17.5141	17.5856	17.6573	17.7291	17.8010	17.8731	96
8.5	16.8186	16.8909	16.9633	17.0358	17.1085	17.1814	17.2544	17.3276	102
9.0	16.3337	16.4070	16.4804	16.5540	16.6277	16.7016	16.7757	16.8499	108
9.5	15.9059	15.9802	16.0546	16.1292	16.2040	16.2789	16.3540	16.4293	114
10.0	15.5266	15.6019	15.6773	15.7529	15.8287	15.9046	15.9807	16.0570	120
10.5	15.1888	15.2650	15.3414	15.4180	15.4947	15.5717	15.6488	15.7261	126
11.0	14.8867	14.9638	15.0412	15.1187	15.1964	15.2743	15.3524	15.4307	132
11.5	14.6155	14.6936	14.7719	14.8503	14.9290	15.0079	15.0869	15.1661	138
12.0	14.3713	14.4503	14.5295	14.6089	14.6885	14.7683	14.8483	14.9284	144
12.5	14.1507	14.2306	14.3107	14.3911	14.4716	14.5522	14.6331	14.7142	150
13.0	13.9510	14.0318	14.1128	14.1940	14.2754	14.3570	14.4387	14.5207	156
13.5	13.7698	13.8514	13.9333	14.0153	14.0976	14.1800	14.2627	14.3455	162
14.0	13.6049	13.6874	13.7701	13.8529	13.9360	14.0193	14.1028	14.1865	168
14.5	13.4546	13.5379	13.6214	13.7051	13.7890	13.8731	13.9575	14.0420	174
15.0	13.3174	13.4015	13.4858	13.5703	13.6550	13.7399	13.8250	13.9104	180
15.5	13.1919	13.2768	13.3619	13.4471	13.5326	13.6183	13.7042	13.7903	186
16.0	13.0770	13.1626	13.2484	13.3345	13.4207	13.5071	13.5938	13.6806	192
16.5	12.9716	13.0579	13.1445	13.2312	13.3182	13.4054	13.4928	13.5804	198
17.0	12.8748	12.9618	13.0491	13.1366	13.2242	13.3121	13.4002	13.4885	204
17.5	12.7858	12.8735	12.9615	13.0496	13.1380	13.2266	13.3153	13.4043	210
18.0	12.7038	12.7922	12.8809	12.9697	13.0587	13.1480	13.2374	13.3271	216
18.5	12.6284	12.7174	12.8067	12.8962	12.9859	13.0757	13.1658	13.2561	222
19.0	12.5588	12.6485	12.7384	12.8285	12.9188	13.0093	13.1000	13.1909	228
19.5	12.4945	12.5848	12.6753	12.7660	12.8570	12.9481	13.0394	13.1309	234
20.0	12.4352	12.5261	12.6172	12.7085	12.8000	12.8917	12.9836	13.0756	240
20.5	12.3804	12.4718	12.5635	12.6554	12.7474	12.8397	12.9321	13.0247	246
21.0	12.3297	12.4217	12.5139	12.6063	12.6989	12.7917	12.8847	12.9778	252
21.5	12.2827	12.3753	12.4680	12.5609	12.6541	12.7474	12.8409	12.9346	258
22.0	12.2393	12.3323	12.4256	12.5190	12.6126	12.7065	12.8004	12.8946	264
22.5	12.1990	12.2926	12.3863	12.4802	12.5743	12.6686	12.7631	12.8578	270
23.0	12.1617	12.2557	12.3500	12.4443	12.5389	12.6337	12.7286	12.8237	276
23.5	12.1271	12.2216	12.3163	12.4111	12.5061	12.6013	12.6967	12.7922	282
24.0	12.0950	12.1900	12.2851	12.3803	12.4758	12.5714	12.6672	12.7632	288
24.5	12.0653	12.1606	12.2561	12.3518	12.4477	12.5437	12.6399	12.7363	294
25.0	12.0376	12.1334	12.2293	12.3254	12.4216	12.5181	12.6146	12.7114	300
25.5	12.0119	12.1081	12.2044	12.3009	12.3975	12.4943	12.5913	12.6884	306
26.0	11.9881	12.0846	12.1813	12.2781	12.3751	12.4723	12.5696	12.6671	312
26.5	11.9659	12.0628	12.1598	12.2570	12.3544	12.4519	12.5496	12.6474	318
27.0	11.9453	12.0425	12.1399	12.2375	12.3351	12.4330	12.5310	12.6291	324
27.5	11.9262	12.0237	12.1214	12.2193	12.3173	12.4155	12.5138	12.6122	330
28.0	11.9084	12.0062	12.1043	12.2024	12.3007	12.3992	12.4978	12.5965	336
28.5	11.8918	11.9900	12.0883	12.1868	12.2854	12.3841	12.4830	12.5820	342
29.0	11.8764	11.9749	12.0735	12.1722	12.2711	12.3701	12.4693	12.5686	348
29.5	11.8621	11.9608	12.0597	12.1587	12.2579	12.3571	12.4566	12.5561	354
29.8	11.8531	11.9520	12.0510	12.1502	12.2496	12.3490	12.4486	12.5483	358
30.0	11.8487	11.9477	12.0469	12.1462	12.2456	12.3451	12.4448	12.5445	360
35.0	11.7567	11.8578	11.9590	12.0603	12.1617	12.2632	12.3647	12.4664	420
40.0	11.7114	11.8138	11.9162	12.0187	12.1213	12.2240	12.3267	12.4294	480

MONTHLY PAYMENT NECESSARY
TO AMORTIZE A $1,000 LOAN

INTEREST► YEARS	15%	15⅛%	15¼%	15⅜%	15½%	15⅝%	15¾%	15⅞%	MOS
.5	174.0338	174.0958	174.1579	174.2199	174.2820	174.3440	174.4061	174.4682	6
1.0	90.2583	90.3173	90.3763	90.4354	90.4944	90.5535	90.6126	90.6717	12
1.5	62.3848	62.4436	62.5025	62.5614	62.6204	62.6793	62.7383	62.7974	18
2.0	48.4866	48.5461	48.6055	48.6650	48.7245	48.7841	48.8437	48.9034	24
2.5	40.1785	40.2388	40.2991	40.3595	40.4199	40.4804	40.5409	40.6015	30
3.0	34.6653	34.7266	34.7879	34.8492	34.9107	34.9722	35.0337	35.0954	36
3.5	30.7491	30.8114	30.8737	30.9362	30.9987	31.0613	31.1240	31.1867	42
4.0	27.8307	27.8942	27.9576	28.0212	28.0849	28.1486	28.2124	28.2763	48
4.5	25.5776	25.6421	25.7068	25.7715	25.8363	25.9012	25.9661	26.0312	54
5.0	23.7899	23.8556	23.9214	23.9872	24.0532	24.1193	24.1854	24.2517	60
5.5	22.3406	22.4075	22.4744	22.5414	22.6085	22.6758	22.7431	22.8106	66
6.0	21.1450	21.2130	21.2810	21.3492	21.4175	21.4859	21.5544	21.6231	72
6.5	20.1444	20.2134	20.2826	20.3520	20.4214	20.4910	20.5607	20.6305	78
7.0	19.2968	19.3670	19.4373	19.5077	19.5783	19.6491	19.7199	19.7909	84
7.5	18.5715	18.6428	18.7142	18.7858	18.8575	18.9294	19.0014	19.0736	90
8.0	17.9454	18.0178	18.0904	18.1631	18.2359	18.3089	18.3821	18.4554	96
8.5	17.4009	17.4744	17.5481	17.6219	17.6958	17.7699	17.8442	17.9186	102
9.0	16.9243	16.9989	17.0736	17.1485	17.2235	17.2987	17.3741	17.4496	108
9.5	16.5047	16.5804	16.6561	16.7321	16.8082	16.8844	16.9609	17.0374	114
10.0	16.1335	16.2101	16.2869	16.3639	16.4411	16.5184	16.5958	16.6735	120
10.5	15.8035	15.8812	15.9590	16.0370	16.1152	16.1935	16.2720	16.3507	126
11.0	15.5092	15.5878	15.6666	15.7456	15.8247	15.9041	15.9836	16.0633	132
11.5	15.2455	15.3251	15.4049	15.4849	15.5650	15.6453	15.7259	15.8065	138
12.0	15.0088	15.0893	15.1700	15.2509	15.3320	15.4133	15.4948	15.5764	144
12.5	14.7955	14.8769	14.9586	15.0404	15.1225	15.2047	15.2871	15.3696	150
13.0	14.6029	14.6852	14.7678	14.8505	14.9335	15.0166	15.0999	15.1834	156
13.5	14.4285	14.5118	14.5952	14.6788	14.7626	14.8466	14.9308	15.0152	162
14.0	14.2704	14.3545	14.4388	14.5232	14.6079	14.6928	14.7778	14.8630	168
14.5	14.1267	14.2116	14.2967	14.3820	14.4675	14.5532	14.6391	14.7251	174
15.0	13.9959	14.0816	14.1675	14.2536	14.3399	14.4264	14.5131	14.5999	180
15.5	13.8766	13.9631	14.0498	14.1367	14.2237	14.3110	14.3985	14.4861	186
16.0	13.7677	13.8549	13.9424	14.0300	14.1179	14.2059	14.2941	14.3825	192
16.5	13.6681	13.7561	13.8443	13.9327	14.0212	14.1100	14.1989	14.2881	198
17.0	13.5770	13.6657	13.7546	13.8437	13.9329	14.0224	14.1120	14.2019	204
17.5	13.4935	13.5829	13.6724	13.7622	13.8522	13.9423	14.0326	14.1231	210
18.0	13.4169	13.5069	13.5972	13.6876	13.7782	13.8690	13.9600	14.0511	216
18.5	13.3466	13.4373	13.5281	13.6192	13.7104	13.8018	13.8935	13.9852	222
19.0	13.2820	13.3733	13.4647	13.5564	13.6483	13.7403	13.8325	13.9249	228
19.5	13.2226	13.3144	13.4065	13.4988	13.5912	13.6838	13.7766	13.8696	234
20.0	13.1679	13.2603	13.3530	13.4458	13.5388	13.6320	13.7253	13.8189	240
20.5	13.1176	13.2106	13.3037	13.3971	13.4906	13.5844	13.6783	13.7723	246
21.0	13.0712	13.1647	13.2584	13.3523	13.4464	13.5406	13.6350	13.7296	252
21.5	13.0284	13.1225	13.2167	13.3111	13.4056	13.5004	13.5952	13.6903	258
22.0	12.9890	13.0835	13.1782	13.2731	13.3681	13.4633	13.5587	13.6542	264
22.5	12.9526	13.0476	13.1427	13.2381	13.3336	13.4292	13.5251	13.6210	270
23.0	12.9190	13.0144	13.1100	13.2058	13.3018	13.3979	13.4941	13.5905	276
23.5	12.8880	12.9838	13.0799	13.1761	13.2724	13.3689	13.4656	13.5624	282
24.0	12.8593	12.9556	13.0520	13.1486	13.2454	13.3423	13.4394	13.5366	288
24.5	12.8328	12.9295	13.0263	13.1233	13.2205	13.3177	13.4152	13.5128	294
25.0	12.8083	12.9054	13.0026	13.0999	13.1975	13.2951	13.3929	13.4908	300
25.5	12.7857	12.8831	12.9807	13.0784	13.1762	13.2742	13.3724	13.4706	306
26.0	12.7647	12.8625	12.9604	13.0584	13.1566	13.2550	13.3534	13.4520	312
26.5	12.7453	12.8434	12.9417	13.0400	13.1385	13.2372	13.3360	13.4348	318
27.0	12.7274	12.8258	12.9243	13.0230	13.1218	13.2208	13.3198	13.4190	324
27.5	12.7108	12.8095	12.9083	13.0073	13.1064	13.2056	13.3050	13.4044	330
28.0	12.6954	12.7944	12.8935	12.9928	13.0922	13.1916	13.2913	13.3910	336
28.5	12.6812	12.7804	12.8798	12.9793	13.0790	13.1787	13.2786	13.3786	342
29.0	12.6680	12.7675	12.8672	12.9669	13.0668	13.1668	13.2669	13.3671	348
29.5	12.6558	12.7555	12.8554	12.9554	13.0556	13.1558	13.2561	13.3566	354
29.8	12.6481	12.7481	12.8481	12.9483	13.0485	13.1489	13.2494	13.3500	358
30.0	12.6444	12.7445	12.8446	12.9448	13.0452	13.1456	13.2462	13.3468	360
35.0	12.5681	12.6699	12.7718	12.8738	12.9758	13.0780	13.1801	13.2824	420
40.0	12.5322	12.6351	12.7380	12.8410	12.9440	13.0471	13.1502	13.2533	480

A-10

INTEREST→ YEARS	16%	16⅛%	16¼%	16⅜%	16½%	16⅝%	16¾%	16⅞%	MOS
.5	174.5303	174.5924	174.6545	174.7166	174.7788	174.8409	174.9031	174.9652	6
1.0	90.7309	90.7900	90.8492	90.9084	90.9676	91.0269	91.0862	91.1454	12
1.5	62.8564	62.9155	62.9747	63.0338	63.0930	63.1522	63.2115	63.2708	18
2.0	48.9631	49.0229	49.0826	49.1425	49.2024	49.2623	49.3222	49.3822	24
2.5	40.6621	40.7228	40.7835	40.8443	40.9051	40.9660	41.0269	41.0879	30
3.0	35.1570	35.2188	35.2806	35.3425	35.4044	35.4664	35.5284	35.5905	36
3.5	31.2495	31.3124	31.3754	31.4384	31.5015	31.5646	31.6279	31.6912	42
4.0	28.3403	28.4043	28.4685	28.5327	28.5970	28.6614	28.7259	28.7904	48
4.5	26.0964	26.1616	26.2270	26.2924	26.3580	26.4236	26.4893	26.5551	54
5.0	24.3181	24.3845	24.4511	24.5178	24.5845	24.6514	24.7184	24.7854	60
5.5	22.8781	22.9458	23.0136	23.0815	23.1495	23.2176	23.2858	23.3541	66
6.0	21.6918	21.7607	21.8297	21.8988	21.9681	22.0374	22.1069	22.1764	72
6.5	20.7005	20.7705	20.8407	20.9111	20.9815	21.0521	21.1228	21.1936	78
7.0	19.8621	19.9333	20.0047	20.0762	20.1479	20.2197	20.2916	20.3636	84
7.5	19.1459	19.2183	19.2909	19.3636	19.4364	19.5094	19.5825	19.6558	90
8.0	18.5288	18.6024	18.6761	18.7500	18.8240	18.8981	18.9724	19.0469	96
8.5	17.9932	18.0679	18.1427	18.2178	18.2929	18.3682	18.4437	18.5193	102
9.0	17.5253	17.6011	17.6771	17.7532	17.8295	17.9059	17.9825	18.0593	108
9.5	17.1142	17.1911	17.2682	17.3454	17.4228	17.5004	17.5781	17.6560	114
10.0	16.7513	16.8293	16.9074	16.9858	17.0642	17.1429	17.2217	17.3006	120
10.5	16.4296	16.5086	16.5878	16.6671	16.7467	16.8264	16.9062	16.9863	126
11.0	16.1432	16.2232	16.3034	16.3838	16.4644	16.5451	16.6260	16.7071	132
11.5	15.8874	15.9684	16.0496	16.1310	16.2126	16.2943	16.3762	16.4583	138
12.0	15.6583	15.7403	15.8224	15.9048	15.9873	16.0700	16.1529	16.2360	144
12.5	15.4524	15.5354	15.6185	15.7018	15.7853	15.8689	15.9528	16.0368	150
13.0	15.2670	15.3509	15.4349	15.5192	15.6036	15.6881	15.7729	15.8578	156
13.5	15.0997	15.1845	15.2694	15.3545	15.4398	15.5253	15.6109	15.6968	162
14.0	14.9485	15.0341	15.1199	15.2058	15.2920	15.3783	15.4648	15.5515	168
14.5	14.8114	14.8978	14.9845	15.0713	15.1582	15.2454	15.3328	15.4203	174
15.0	14.6870	14.7743	14.8617	14.9493	15.0371	15.1251	15.2132	15.3015	180
15.5	14.5740	14.6620	14.7502	14.8386	14.9272	15.0159	15.1048	15.1939	186
16.0	14.4711	14.5599	14.6488	14.7380	14.8273	14.9168	15.0065	15.0963	192
16.5	14.3774	14.4669	14.5566	14.6464	14.7365	14.8267	14.9171	15.0076	198
17.0	14.2919	14.3821	14.4725	14.5630	14.6538	14.7447	14.8358	14.9270	204
17.5	14.2138	14.3047	14.3957	14.4870	14.5784	14.6700	14.7617	14.8536	210
18.0	14.1425	14.2340	14.3257	14.4176	14.5096	14.6018	14.6942	14.7868	216
18.5	14.0772	14.1694	14.2617	14.3542	14.4468	14.5396	14.6326	14.7258	222
19.0	14.0175	14.1102	14.2031	14.2962	14.3895	14.4829	14.5764	14.6702	228
19.5	13.9627	14.0560	14.1495	14.2432	14.3370	14.4310	14.5251	14.6194	234
20.0	13.9126	14.0064	14.1005	14.1947	14.2890	14.3835	14.4782	14.5730	240
20.5	13.8665	13.9609	14.0555	14.1502	14.2451	14.3401	14.4353	14.5306	246
21.0	13.8243	13.9192	14.0143	14.1095	14.2048	14.3004	14.3960	14.4919	252
21.5	13.7855	13.8809	13.9764	14.0721	14.1680	14.2640	14.3601	14.4564	258
22.0	13.7499	13.8457	13.9417	14.0379	14.1342	14.2306	14.3272	14.4239	264
22.5	13.7172	13.8134	13.9099	14.0064	14.1032	14.2000	14.2970	14.3942	270
23.0	13.6871	13.7838	13.8806	13.9776	14.0747	14.1720	14.2694	14.3669	276
23.5	13.6594	13.7565	13.8537	13.9511	14.0486	14.1463	14.2441	14.3420	282
24.0	13.6339	13.7314	13.8290	13.9268	14.0247	14.1227	14.2208	14.3191	288
24.5	13.6105	13.7083	13.8063	13.9044	14.0027	14.1010	14.1995	14.2981	294
25.0	13.5889	13.6871	13.7854	13.8839	13.9824	14.0811	14.1800	14.2789	300
25.5	13.5690	13.6675	13.7662	13.8650	13.9639	14.0629	14.1620	14.2613	306
26.0	13.5507	13.6496	13.7485	13.8476	13.9468	14.0461	14.1456	14.2451	312
26.5	13.5339	13.6330	13.7323	13.8316	13.9311	14.0307	14.1304	14.2302	318
27.0	13.5183	13.6178	13.7173	13.8169	13.9167	14.0166	14.1165	14.2166	324
27.5	13.5040	13.6037	13.7035	13.8034	13.9034	14.0036	14.1038	14.2041	330
28.0	13.4908	13.5908	13.6908	13.7910	13.8912	13.9916	14.0921	14.1926	336
28.5	13.4787	13.5789	13.6791	13.7795	13.8800	13.9806	14.0813	14.1821	342
29.0	13.4674	13.5679	13.6684	13.7690	13.8697	13.9705	14.0714	14.1724	348
29.5	13.4571	13.5577	13.6585	13.7593	13.8602	13.9612	14.0623	14.1635	354
29.8	13.4507	13.5514	13.6523	13.7533	13.8543	13.9554	14.0567	14.1580	358
30.0	13.4476	13.5484	13.6493	13.7504	13.8515	13.9527	14.0540	14.1553	360
35.0	13.3847	13.4871	13.5895	13.6920	13.7945	13.8971	13.9998	14.1025	420
40.0	13.3565	13.4597	13.5630	13.6663	13.7696	13.8730	13.9764	14.0798	480

MONTHLY PAYMENT NECESSARY
TO AMORTIZE A $1,000 LOAN

INTEREST YEARS	17%	17⅛%	17¼%	17⅜%	17½%	17⅝%	17¾%	17⅞%	MOS
.5	175.0274	175.0896	175.1518	175.2140	175.2762	175.3385	175.4007	175.4630	6
1.0	91.2048	91.2641	91.3234	91.3828	91.4422	91.5016	91.5611	91.6205	12
1.5	63.3301	63.3894	63.4488	63.5082	63.5677	63.6272	63.6867	63.7462	18
2.0	49.4423	49.5023	49.5625	49.6226	49.6828	49.7431	49.8034	49.8637	24
2.5	41.1490	41.2101	41.2712	41.3324	41.3937	41.4550	41.5163	41.5777	30
3.0	35.6527	35.7150	35.7773	35.8396	35.9021	35.9646	36.0271	36.0897	36
3.5	31.7546	31.8180	31.8816	31.9452	32.0089	32.0726	32.1364	32.2003	42
4.0	28.8550	28.9198	28.9845	29.0494	29.1144	29.1794	29.2445	29.3097	48
4.5	26.6210	26.6870	26.7531	26.8192	26.8855	26.9518	27.0182	27.0848	54
5.0	24.8526	24.9198	24.9872	25.0547	25.1222	25.1899	25.2576	25.3255	60
5.5	23.4226	23.4911	23.5597	23.6285	23.6974	23.7663	23.8354	23.9046	66
6.0	22.2461	22.3159	22.3859	22.4559	22.5260	22.5963	22.6667	22.7372	72
6.5	21.2645	21.3356	21.4068	21.4781	21.5495	21.6211	21.6927	21.7645	78
7.0	20.4358	20.5081	20.5805	20.6531	20.7258	20.7986	20.8716	20.9446	84
7.5	19.7291	19.8027	19.8763	19.9501	20.0241	20.0981	20.1723	20.2467	90
8.0	19.1215	19.1962	19.2710	19.3461	19.4212	19.4965	19.5719	19.6475	96
8.5	18.5951	18.6710	18.7470	18.8232	18.8996	18.9760	19.0527	19.1295	102
9.0	18.1362	18.2132	18.2905	18.3678	18.4453	18.5230	18.6008	18.6788	108
9.5	17.7340	17.8122	17.8905	17.9690	18.0477	18.1265	18.2054	18.2846	114
10.0	17.3798	17.4591	17.5385	17.6181	17.6979	17.7778	17.8579	17.9381	120
10.5	17.0665	17.1468	17.2274	17.3080	17.3889	17.4699	17.5511	17.6324	126
11.0	16.7883	16.8697	16.9513	17.0330	17.1149	17.1970	17.2792	17.3616	132
11.5	16.5406	16.6230	16.7056	16.7883	16.8713	16.9543	17.0376	17.1210	138
12.0	16.3192	16.4026	16.4862	16.5700	16.6539	16.7380	16.8222	16.9066	144
12.5	16.1210	16.2053	16.2899	16.3746	16.4594	16.5445	16.6297	16.7151	150
13.0	15.9430	16.0282	16.1137	16.1993	16.2851	16.3711	16.4572	16.5435	156
13.5	15.7828	15.8690	15.9553	16.0418	16.1285	16.2154	16.3024	16.3896	162
14.0	15.6384	15.7254	15.8126	15.9000	15.9876	16.0753	16.1632	16.2513	168
14.5	15.5080	15.5959	15.6839	15.7721	15.8605	15.9491	16.0378	16.1267	174
15.0	15.3900	15.4787	15.5676	15.6566	15.7458	15.8351	15.9247	16.0144	180
15.5	15.2832	15.3727	15.4623	15.5521	15.6420	15.7322	15.8225	15.9129	186
16.0	15.1863	15.2765	15.3669	15.4574	15.5481	15.6390	15.7300	15.8212	192
16.5	15.0984	15.1893	15.2804	15.3716	15.4630	15.5546	15.6463	15.7382	198
17.0	15.0184	15.1100	15.2018	15.2937	15.3858	15.4780	15.5704	15.6630	204
17.5	14.9457	15.0380	15.1304	15.2229	15.3157	15.4086	15.5016	15.5948	210
18.0	14.8795	14.9724	15.0654	15.1586	15.2520	15.3455	15.4391	15.5329	216
18.5	14.8191	14.9126	15.0062	15.1000	15.1940	15.2881	15.3823	15.4768	222
19.0	14.7641	14.8581	14.9524	15.0467	15.1412	15.2359	15.3307	15.4257	228
19.5	14.7139	14.8085	14.9032	14.9981	15.0932	15.1884	15.2837	15.3792	234
20.0	14.6680	14.7631	14.8584	14.9538	15.0494	15.1451	15.2410	15.3370	240
20.5	14.6261	14.7217	14.8175	14.9134	15.0095	15.1057	15.2020	15.2985	246
21.0	14.5878	14.6839	14.7802	14.8766	14.9731	15.0698	15.1666	15.2635	252
21.5	14.5528	14.6494	14.7461	14.8429	14.9399	15.0370	15.1342	15.2316	258
22.0	14.5208	14.6178	14.7149	14.8122	14.9095	15.0071	15.1047	15.2025	264
22.5	14.4914	14.5889	14.6864	14.7841	14.8819	14.9798	15.0778	15.1760	270
23.0	14.4646	14.5624	14.6603	14.7584	14.8565	14.9548	15.0532	15.1518	276
23.5	14.4400	14.5382	14.6365	14.7349	14.8334	14.9321	15.0308	15.1297	282
24.0	14.4175	14.5160	14.6147	14.7134	14.8123	14.9113	15.0104	15.1096	288
24.5	14.3969	14.4957	14.5947	14.6938	14.7930	14.8923	14.9917	15.0912	294
25.0	14.3780	14.4771	14.5764	14.6758	14.7753	14.8749	14.9746	15.0744	300
25.5	14.3606	14.4601	14.5597	14.6594	14.7591	14.8590	14.9590	15.0591	306
26.0	14.3447	14.4445	14.5443	14.6443	14.7443	14.8445	14.9447	15.0451	312
26.5	14.3302	14.4302	14.5303	14.6305	14.7308	14.8312	14.9317	15.0323	318
27.0	14.3168	14.4171	14.5174	14.6179	14.7184	14.8191	14.9198	15.0206	324
27.5	14.3045	14.4050	14.5056	14.6063	14.7071	14.8080	14.9089	15.0099	330
28.0	14.2933	14.3940	14.4948	14.5957	14.6967	14.7978	14.8989	15.0002	336
28.5	14.2829	14.3839	14.4849	14.5860	14.6872	14.7885	14.8898	14.9913	342
29.0	14.2734	14.3746	14.4758	14.5771	14.6785	14.7800	14.8815	14.9831	348
29.5	14.2647	14.3661	14.4675	14.5690	14.6705	14.7722	14.8739	14.9757	354
29.8	14.2593	14.3608	14.4623	14.5639	14.6656	14.7674	14.8692	14.9711	358
30.0	14.2568	14.3583	14.4599	14.5615	14.6633	14.7651	14.8669	14.9689	360
35.0	14.2053	14.3081	14.4109	14.5138	14.6168	14.7197	14.8228	14.9258	420
40.0	14.1832	14.2867	14.3902	14.4938	14.5973	14.7009	14.8045	14.9082	480

A-12

MONTHLY PAYMENT NECESSARY
TO AMORTIZE A $1,000 LOAN

INTEREST↓ YEARS	18%	18⅛%	18¼%	18⅜%	18½%	18⅝%	18¾%	18⅞%	MOS
.5	175.5252	175.5875	175.6498	175.7121	175.7744	175.8367	175.8990	175.9613	6
1.0	91.6800	91.7395	91.7990	91.8586	91.9181	91.9777	92.0373	92.0969	12
1.5	63.8058	63.8654	63.9250	63.9847	64.0444	64.1041	64.1639	64.2237	18
2.0	49.9241	49.9845	50.0450	50.1055	50.1660	50.2266	50.2872	50.3479	24
2.5	41.6392	41.7007	41.7623	41.8239	41.8855	41.9473	42.0090	42.0709	30
3.0	36.1524	36.2151	36.2779	36.3408	36.4037	36.4667	36.5297	36.5929	36
3.5	32.2643	32.3283	32.3924	32.4566	32.5208	32.5851	32.6495	32.7140	42
4.0	29.3750	29.4404	29.5058	29.5713	29.6369	29.7026	29.7684	29.8342	48
4.5	27.1514	27.2181	27.2849	27.3518	27.4187	27.4858	27.5529	27.6202	54
5.0	25.3934	25.4615	25.5296	25.5979	25.6662	25.7346	25.8032	25.8718	60
5.5	23.9739	24.0432	24.1127	24.1823	24.2521	24.3219	24.3918	24.4618	66
6.0	22.8078	22.8785	22.9493	23.0203	23.0914	23.1625	23.2338	23.3052	72
6.5	21.8365	21.9085	21.9806	22.0529	22.1253	22.1978	22.2705	22.3432	78
7.0	21.0178	21.0912	21.1646	21.2382	21.3119	21.3858	21.4597	21.5338	84
7.5	20.3211	20.3957	20.4705	20.5453	20.6203	20.6955	20.7707	20.8461	90
8.0	19.7237	19.7991	19.8751	19.9512	20.0274	20.1038	20.1804	20.2571	96
8.5	19.2064	19.2835	19.3607	19.4380	19.5155	19.5932	19.6709	19.7489	102
9.0	18.7569	18.8351	18.9136	18.9921	19.0708	19.1497	19.2287	19.3078	108
9.5	18.3638	18.4433	18.5228	18.6026	18.6824	18.7625	18.8426	18.9230	114
10.0	18.0185	18.0991	18.1798	18.2606	18.3417	18.4228	18.5041	18.5856	120
10.5	17.7139	17.7955	17.8774	17.9593	18.0414	18.1237	18.2061	18.2887	126
11.0	17.4442	17.5269	17.6098	17.6928	17.7760	17.8593	17.9428	18.0265	132
11.5	17.2046	17.2884	17.3723	17.4563	17.5406	17.6249	17.7095	17.7942	138
12.0	16.9912	17.0759	17.1608	17.2459	17.3311	17.4165	17.5021	17.5878	144
12.5	16.8006	16.8863	16.9722	17.0582	17.1444	17.2308	17.3173	17.4040	150
13.0	16.6300	16.7166	16.8034	16.8904	16.9775	17.0648	17.1523	17.2399	156
13.5	16.4770	16.5645	16.6522	16.7401	16.8281	16.9163	17.0046	17.0931	162
14.0	16.3395	16.4279	16.5165	16.6052	16.6941	16.7831	16.8723	16.9616	168
14.5	16.2158	16.3050	16.3944	16.4839	16.5736	16.6635	16.7535	16.8437	174
15.0	16.1042	16.1942	16.2844	16.3747	16.4652	16.5559	16.6467	16.7376	180
15.5	16.0035	16.0943	16.1852	16.2763	16.3676	16.4590	16.5506	16.6423	186
16.0	15.9126	16.0041	16.0957	16.1875	16.2795	16.3716	16.4639	16.5564	192
16.5	15.8303	15.9225	16.0148	16.1073	16.2000	16.2928	16.3858	16.4789	198
17.0	15.7557	15.8486	15.9416	16.0348	16.1281	16.2216	16.3152	16.4090	204
17.5	15.6882	15.7817	15.8754	15.9692	16.0631	16.1572	16.2514	16.3458	210
18.0	15.6269	15.7210	15.8153	15.9097	16.0043	16.0989	16.1938	16.2887	216
18.5	15.5713	15.6660	15.7608	15.8558	15.9509	16.0462	16.1416	16.2371	222
19.0	15.5208	15.6160	15.7114	15.8069	15.9026	15.9984	16.0943	16.1904	228
19.5	15.4749	15.5706	15.6665	15.7626	15.8588	15.9551	16.0515	16.1480	234
20.0	15.4331	15.5294	15.6258	15.7223	15.8190	15.9158	16.0127	16.1097	240
20.5	15.3951	15.4919	15.5887	15.6857	15.7828	15.8801	15.9774	16.0749	246
21.0	15.3605	15.4577	15.5550	15.6525	15.7500	15.8477	15.9455	16.0434	252
21.5	15.3291	15.4267	15.5244	15.6223	15.7202	15.8183	15.9165	16.0148	258
22.0	15.3004	15.3984	15.4965	15.5948	15.6931	15.7916	15.8902	15.9889	264
22.5	15.2742	15.3726	15.4711	15.5697	15.6685	15.7673	15.8662	15.9653	270
23.0	15.2504	15.3492	15.4480	15.5470	15.6461	15.7452	15.8445	15.9439	276
23.5	15.2287	15.3278	15.4270	15.5263	15.6257	15.7252	15.8248	15.9245	282
24.0	15.2089	15.3083	15.4078	15.5074	15.6071	15.7069	15.8068	15.9068	288
24.5	15.1908	15.2905	15.3903	15.4902	15.5902	15.6903	15.7905	15.8908	294
25.0	15.1743	15.2743	15.3744	15.4746	15.5748	15.6752	15.7757	15.8762	300
25.5	15.1592	15.2595	15.3599	15.4603	15.5608	15.6615	15.7622	15.8629	306
26.0	15.1455	15.2460	15.3466	15.4473	15.5481	15.6489	15.7499	15.8509	312
26.5	15.1330	15.2337	15.3346	15.4355	15.5365	15.6375	15.7387	15.8399	318
27.0	15.1215	15.2225	15.3235	15.4247	15.5259	15.6272	15.7285	15.8300	324
27.5	15.1110	15.2122	15.3135	15.4148	15.5162	15.6177	15.7193	15.8209	330
28.0	15.1015	15.2029	15.3043	15.4059	15.5075	15.6091	15.7109	15.8127	336
28.5	15.0928	15.1943	15.2960	15.3977	15.4995	15.6013	15.7032	15.8052	342
29.0	15.0848	15.1865	15.2883	15.3902	15.4922	15.5942	15.6962	15.7983	348
29.5	15.0775	15.1794	15.2814	15.3834	15.4855	15.5877	15.6899	15.7921	354
29.8	15.0730	15.1750	15.2771	15.3792	15.4814	15.5836	15.6859	15.7883	358
30.0	15.0709	15.1729	15.2750	15.3772	15.4794	15.5817	15.6841	15.7865	360
35.0	15.0289	15.1321	15.2352	15.3384	15.4417	15.5449	15.6483	15.7516	420
40.0	15.0118	15.1155	15.2192	15.3229	15.4266	15.5304	15.6342	15.7379	480

A-13

MONTHLY PAYMENT NECESSARY
TO AMORTIZE A $1,000 LOAN

EREST† YEARS	19%	19⅛%	19¼%	19⅜%	19½%	19⅝%	19¾%	19⅞%	MOS
.5	176.0237	176.0860	176.1484	176.2108	176.2731	176.3355	176.3979	176.4604	6
1.0	92.1566	92.2162	92.2759	92.3356	92.3954	92.4551	92.5149	92.5747	12
1.5	64.2835	64.3433	64.4032	64.4631	64.5231	64.5831	64.6431	64.7031	18
2.0	50.4086	50.4694	50.5302	50.5910	50.6519	50.7128	50.7738	50.8348	24
2.5	42.1327	42.1947	42.2566	42.3187	42.3808	42.4429	42.5051	42.5673	30
3.0	36.6560	36.7193	36.7825	36.8459	36.9093	36.9728	37.0363	37.0999	36
3.5	32.7785	32.8431	32.9078	32.9725	33.0373	33.1022	33.1672	33.2322	42
4.0	29.9001	29.9661	30.0322	30.0984	30.1646	30.2309	30.2973	30.3638	48
4.5	27.6875	27.7549	27.8224	27.8900	27.9577	28.0255	28.0933	28.1613	54
5.0	25.9406	26.0094	26.0783	26.1473	26.2164	26.2857	26.3550	26.4244	60
5.5	24.5319	24.6022	24.6725	24.7429	24.8135	24.8841	24.9549	25.0258	66
6.0	23.3767	23.4483	23.5201	23.5919	23.6639	23.7360	23.8081	23.8804	72
6.5	22.4161	22.4891	22.5622	22.6354	22.7088	22.7822	22.8558	22.9295	78
7.0	21.6080	21.6824	21.7568	21.8314	21.9061	21.9810	22.0559	22.1310	84
7.5	20.9217	20.9973	21.0731	21.1490	21.2251	21.3012	21.3775	21.4540	90
8.0	20.3339	20.4108	20.4879	20.5651	20.6425	20.7199	20.7976	20.8753	96
8.5	19.8269	19.9051	19.9835	20.0620	20.1406	20.2193	20.2982	20.3773	102
9.0	19.3871	19.4665	19.5461	19.6258	19.7057	19.7857	19.8658	19.9461	108
9.5	19.0034	19.0840	19.1648	19.2457	19.3268	19.4080	19.4893	19.5708	114
10.0	18.6672	18.7490	18.8309	18.9130	18.9952	19.0776	19.1601	19.2428	120
10.5	18.3715	18.4544	18.5374	18.6206	18.7039	18.7874	18.8711	18.9549	126
11.0	18.1103	18.1943	18.2784	18.3627	18.4471	18.5317	18.6164	18.7013	132
11.5	17.8790	17.9641	18.0492	18.1346	18.2200	18.3057	18.3914	18.4774	138
12.0	17.6736	17.7597	17.8458	17.9322	18.0187	18.1053	18.1921	18.2790	144
12.5	17.4908	17.5778	17.6649	17.7522	17.8397	17.9273	18.0150	18.1029	150
13.0	17.3276	17.4155	17.5036	17.5918	17.6802	17.7687	17.8574	17.9462	156
13.5	17.1818	17.2706	17.3595	17.4487	17.5379	17.6273	17.7169	17.8066	162
14.0	17.0511	17.1408	17.2306	17.3206	17.4107	17.5010	17.5914	17.6819	168
14.5	16.9340	17.0245	17.1151	17.2059	17.2968	17.3879	17.4791	17.5705	174
15.0	16.8288	16.9200	17.0114	17.1030	17.1947	17.2866	17.3785	17.4707	⅟80
15.5	16.7341	16.8261	16.9183	17.0106	17.1030	17.1956	17.2884	17.3812	186
16.0	16.6489	16.7416	16.8345	16.9275	17.0207	17.1140	17.2074	17.3010	192
16.5	16.5721	16.6655	16.7591	16.8528	16.9466	17.0405	17.1346	17.2289	198
17.0	16.5029	16.5969	16.6911	16.7854	16.8799	16.9745	17.0692	17.1640	204
17.5	16.4403	16.5350	16.6298	16.7247	16.8198	16.9150	17.0103	17.1057	210
18.0	16.3838	16.4791	16.5745	16.6700	16.7656	16.8613	16.9572	17.0532	216
18.5	16.3328	16.4286	16.5245	16.6205	16.7167	16.8130	16.9094	17.0059	222
19.0	16.2866	16.3829	16.4793	16.5759	16.6725	16.7694	16.8663	16.9633	228
19.5	16.2447	16.3415	16.4385	16.5355	16.6327	16.7300	16.8274	16.9249	234
20.0	16.2068	16.3041	16.4015	16.4990	16.5966	16.6944	16.7922	16.8902	240
20.5	16.1725	16.2702	16.3681	16.4660	16.5641	16.6622	16.7605	16.8589	246
21.0	16.1414	16.2396	16.3378	16.4362	16.5346	16.6332	16.7318	16.8306	252
21.5	16.1132	16.2118	16.3104	16.4091	16.5080	16.6069	16.7059	16.8051	258
22.0	16.0876	16.1865	16.2855	16.3846	16.4838	16.5831	16.6825	16.7820	264
22.5	16.0644	16.1637	16.2630	16.3625	16.4620	16.5616	16.6613	16.7612	270
23.0	16.0434	16.1429	16.2426	16.3424	16.4422	16.5422	16.6422	16.7423	276
23.5	16.0243	16.1241	16.2241	16.3242	16.4243	16.5245	16.6249	16.7253	282
24.0	16.0069	16.1071	16.2073	16.3077	16.4081	16.5086	16.6092	16.7099	288
24.5	15.9911	16.0916	16.1921	16.2927	16.3934	16.4942	16.5950	16.6959	294
25.0	15.9768	16.0775	16.1783	16.2791	16.3801	16.4811	16.5821	16.6833	300
25.5	15.9638	16.0647	16.1657	16.2668	16.3680	16.4692	16.5705	16.6719	306
26.0	15.9520	16.0531	16.1544	16.2557	16.3570	16.4585	16.5600	16.6616	312
26.5	15.9412	16.0426	16.1440	16.2455	16.3471	16.4487	16.5504	16.6522	318
27.0	15.9315	16.0330	16.1347	16.2364	16.3381	16.4399	16.5418	16.6437	324
27.5	15.9226	16.0243	16.1261	16.2280	16.3299	16.4319	16.5340	16.6361	330
28.0	15.9145	16.0164	16.1184	16.2205	16.3225	16.4247	16.5269	16.6292	336
28.5	15.9072	16.0093	16.1114	16.2136	16.3158	16.4181	16.5205	16.6229	342
29.0	15.9005	16.0027	16.1050	16.2074	16.3097	16.4122	16.5147	16.6172	348
29.5	15.8944	15.9968	16.0992	16.2017	16.3042	16.4068	16.5094	16.6120	354
29.8	15.8907	15.9932	16.0957	16.1982	16.3008	16.4035	16.5062	16.6089	358
30.0	15.8889	15.9914	16.0940	16.1966	16.2992	16.4019	16.5046	16.6074	360
35.0	15.8549	15.9583	16.0618	16.1652	16.2687	16.3722	16.4757	16.5792	420
40.0	15.8417	15.9456	16.0494	16.1532	16.2571	16.3610	16.4648	16.5687	480

A-14

MONTHLY PAYMENT NECESSARY
TO AMORTIZE A $1,000 LOAN

INTEREST↓ YEARS	20%	20⅛%	20¼%	20⅜%	20½%	20⅝%	20¾%	20⅞%	MOS
.5	176.5228	176.5852	176.6477	176.7101	176.7726	176.8351	176.8976	176.9600	6
1.0	92.6345	92.6943	92.7542	92.8141	92.8740	92.9339	92.9938	93.0538	12
1.5	64.7632	64.8233	64.8834	64.9436	65.0038	65.0640	65.1243	65.1846	18
2.0	50.8958	50.9569	51.0180	51.0792	51.1404	51.2016	51.2629	51.3243	24
2.5	42.6296	42.6919	42.7543	42.8168	42.8793	42.9418	43.0044	43.0671	30
3.0	37.1636	37.2273	37.2911	37.3549	37.4188	37.4828	37.5468	37.6109	36
3.5	33.2973	33.3624	33.4277	33.4930	33.5584	33.6238	33.6893	33.7549	42
4.0	30.4304	30.4970	30.5637	30.6305	30.6974	30.7644	30.8314	30.8985	48
4.5	28.2293	28.2974	28.3656	28.4339	28.5023	28.5708	28.6393	28.7080	54
5.0	26.4939	26.5635	26.6332	26.7030	26.7729	26.8428	26.9129	26.9831	60
5.5	25.0967	25.1678	25.2390	25.3102	25.3816	25.4531	25.5247	25.5963	66
6.0	23.9528	24.0253	24.0980	24.1707	24.2435	24.3165	24.3895	24.4627	72
6.5	23.0033	23.0773	23.1513	23.2255	23.2998	23.3742	23.4487	23.5233	78
7.0	22.2062	22.2815	22.3570	22.4325	22.5082	22.5841	22.6600	22.7360	84
7.5	21.5305	21.6072	21.6840	21.7610	21.8381	21.9153	21.9926	22.0700	90
8.0	20.9532	21.0312	21.1094	21.1876	21.2661	21.3446	21.4233	21.5021	96
8.5	20.4565	20.5358	20.6152	20.6948	20.7745	20.8544	20.9343	21.0145	102
9.0	20.0265	20.1071	20.1878	20.2686	20.3496	20.4307	20.5120	20.5933	108
9.5	19.6524	19.7342	19.8161	19.8982	19.9804	20.0627	20.1452	20.2278	114
10.0	19.3256	19.4085	19.4916	19.5749	19.6582	19.7418	19.8254	19.9092	120
10.5	19.0388	19.1229	19.2071	19.2915	19.3760	19.4607	19.5455	19.6304	126
11.0	18.7863	18.8715	18.9568	19.0423	19.1279	19.2137	19.2996	19.3856	132
11.5	18.5634	18.6497	18.7360	18.8225	18.9092	18.9960	19.0830	19.1701	138
12.0	18.3661	18.4533	18.5407	18.6282	18.7159	18.8037	18.8917	18.9798	144
12.5	18.1910	18.2792	18.3675	18.4560	18.5446	18.6334	18.7223	18.8114	150
13.0	18.0352	18.1243	18.2136	18.3030	18.3926	18.4823	18.5721	18.6621	156
13.5	17.8965	17.9865	18.0766	18.1669	18.2574	18.3479	18.4387	18.5295	162
14.0	17.7727	17.8635	17.9545	18.0456	18.1369	18.2283	18.3199	18.4116	168
14.5	17.6620	17.7536	17.8454	17.9374	18.0295	18.1217	18.2140	18.3065	174
15.0	17.5630	17.6554	17.7479	17.8406	17.9335	18.0264	18.1195	18.2128	180
15.5	17.4742	17.5674	17.6607	17.7541	17.8476	17.9413	18.0351	18.1291	186
16.0	17.3947	17.4885	17.5825	17.6766	17.7708	17.8652	17.9596	18.0543	192
16.5	17.3232	17.4177	17.5123	17.6071	17.7020	17.7970	17.8921	17.9873	198
17.0	17.2590	17.3541	17.4494	17.5447	17.6402	17.7358	17.8316	17.9274	204
17.5	17.2013	17.2970	17.3928	17.4888	17.5848	17.6810	17.7773	17.8737	210
18.0	17.1494	17.2456	17.3420	17.4385	17.5351	17.6318	17.7286	17.8256	216
18.5	17.1026	17.1994	17.2963	17.3933	17.4904	17.5876	17.6850	17.7824	222
19.0	17.0605	17.1577	17.2551	17.3526	17.4502	17.5479	17.6457	17.7436	228
19.5	17.0225	17.1202	17.2181	17.3160	17.4141	17.5122	17.6105	17.7088	234
20.0	16.9882	17.0864	17.1847	17.2831	17.3815	17.4801	17.5788	17.6776	240
20.5	16.9574	17.0559	17.1546	17.2534	17.3523	17.4512	17.5503	17.6495	246
21.0	16.9295	17.0284	17.1275	17.2267	17.3259	17.4253	17.5247	17.6242	252
21.5	16.9043	17.0036	17.1031	17.2026	17.3022	17.4019	17.5016	17.6015	258
22.0	16.8816	16.9812	17.0810	17.1808	17.2808	17.3808	17.4809	17.5811	264
22.5	16.8611	16.9610	17.0611	17.1613	17.2615	17.3618	17.4622	17.5627	270
23.0	16.8425	16.9428	17.0432	17.1436	17.2441	17.3447	17.4454	17.5461	276
23.5	16.8257	16.9263	17.0269	17.1277	17.2284	17.3293	17.4302	17.5312	282
24.0	16.8106	16.9114	17.0123	17.1133	17.2143	17.3154	17.4166	17.5178	288
24.5	16.7969	16.8980	16.9991	17.1003	17.2016	17.3029	17.4043	17.5058	294
25.0	16.7845	16.8858	16.9872	17.0886	17.1901	17.2916	17.3932	17.4949	300
25.5	16.7733	16.8748	16.9764	17.0780	17.1797	17.2814	17.3832	17.4851	306
26.0	16.7632	16.8649	16.9666	17.0685	17.1703	17.2723	17.3743	17.4763	312
26.5	16.7540	16.8559	16.9578	17.0598	17.1619	17.2640	17.3661	17.4684	318
27.0	16.7457	16.8478	16.9499	17.0521	17.1543	17.2565	17.3588	17.4612	324
27.5	16.7382	16.8405	16.9427	17.0450	17.1474	17.2498	17.3522	17.4547	330
28.0	16.7315	16.8338	16.9362	17.0387	17.1412	17.2437	17.3463	17.4489	336
28.5	16.7253	16.8278	16.9304	17.0329	17.1356	17.2382	17.3410	17.4437	342
29.0	16.7198	16.8224	16.9251	17.0278	17.1305	17.2333	17.3361	17.4390	348
29.5	16.7147	16.8175	16.9203	17.0231	17.1259	17.2288	17.3318	17.4347	354
29.8	16.7117	16.8145	16.9173	17.0202	17.1231	17.2261	17.3291	17.4321	358
30.0	16.7102	16.8130	16.9159	17.0188	17.1218	17.2248	17.3278	17.4309	360
35.0	16.6828	16.7864	16.8900	16.9936	17.0972	17.2009	17.3046	17.4083	420
40.0	16.6726	16.7766	16.8805	16.9844	17.0884	17.1923	17.2963	17.4003	480

MONTHLY PAYMENT NECESSARY
TO AMORTIZE A $1,000 LOAN

INTEREST→ YEARS	21%	21⅛%	21¼%	21⅜%	21½%	21⅝%	21¾%	21⅞%	MOS
.5	177.0226	177.0851	177.1476	177.2101	177.2727	177.3352	177.3978	177.4604	6
1.0	93.1138	93.1738	93.2338	93.2938	93.3539	93.4140	93.4741	93.5342	12
1.5	65.2449	65.3053	65.3657	65.4261	65.4865	65.5470	65.6075	65.6681	18
2.0	51.3857	51.4471	51.5085	51.5700	51.6316	51.6932	51.7548	51.8164	24
2.5	43.1298	43.1925	43.2553	43.3182	43.3811	43.4440	43.5070	43.5701	30
3.0	37.6751	37.7393	37.8035	37.8679	37.9323	37.9967	38.0612	38.1258	36
3.5	33.8206	33.8863	33.9521	34.0180	34.0839	34.1499	34.2160	34.2821	42
4.0	30.9657	31.0330	31.1003	31.1677	31.2353	31.3028	31.3705	31.4383	48
4.5	28.7767	28.8455	28.9144	28.9834	29.0525	29.1217	29.1910	29.2603	54
5.0	27.0534	27.1237	27.1942	27.2647	27.3354	27.4061	27.4770	27.5479	60
5.5	25.6681	25.7400	25.8120	25.8841	25.9563	26.0286	26.1010	26.1735	66
6.0	24.5360	24.6094	24.6829	24.7565	24.8302	24.9040	24.9779	25.0520	72
6.5	23.5981	23.6729	23.7479	23.8230	23.8982	23.9735	24.0489	24.1245	78
7.0	22.8122	22.8885	22.9649	23.0415	23.1181	23.1949	23.2718	23.3488	84
7.5	22.1476	22.2253	22.3031	22.3811	22.4591	22.5373	22.6157	22.6941	90
8.0	21.5810	21.6601	21.7393	21.8186	21.8980	21.9776	22.0573	22.1371	96
8.5	21.0947	21.1751	21.2556	21.3362	21.4170	21.4979	21.5790	21.6601	102
9.0	20.6749	20.7565	20.8383	20.9203	21.0023	21.0845	21.1668	21.2493	108
9.5	20.3106	20.3935	20.4765	20.5597	20.6430	20.7264	20.8100	20.8937	114
10.0	19.9932	20.0773	20.1615	20.2458	20.3303	20.4150	20.4997	20.5846	120
10.5	19.7155	19.8007	19.8861	19.9716	20.0572	20.1430	20.2289	20.3150	126
11.0	19.4718	19.5581	19.6446	19.7312	19.8179	19.9048	19.9918	20.0790	132
11.5	19.2573	19.3447	19.4322	19.5199	19.6076	19.6956	19.7836	19.8719	138
12.0	19.0680	19.1564	19.2449	19.3336	19.4224	19.5113	19.6004	19.6896	144
12.5	18.9006	18.9899	19.0794	19.1690	19.2588	19.3487	19.4387	19.5289	150
13.0	18.7522	18.8425	18.9329	19.0234	19.1141	19.2049	19.2958	19.3869	156
13.5	18.6205	18.7116	18.8029	18.8943	18.9858	19.0775	19.1693	19.2612	162
14.0	18.5034	18.5953	18.6874	18.7797	18.8720	18.9645	19.0571	19.1499	168
14.5	18.3991	18.4918	18.5847	18.6777	18.7709	18.8641	18.9575	19.0510	174
15.0	18.3061	18.3996	18.4932	18.5870	18.6808	18.7748	18.8690	18.9632	180
15.5	18.2231	18.3173	18.4117	18.5061	18.6007	18.6954	18.7902	18.8851	186
16.0	18.1490	18.2439	18.3388	18.4339	18.5292	18.6245	18.7200	18.8155	192
16.5	18.0827	18.1782	18.2738	18.3695	18.4654	18.5613	18.6574	18.7536	198
17.0	18.0234	18.1195	18.2157	18.3120	18.4084	18.5049	18.6016	18.6983	204
17.5	17.9702	18.0669	18.1636	18.2605	18.3575	18.4545	18.5517	18.6490	210
18.0	17.9226	18.0198	18.1171	18.2145	18.3119	18.4095	18.5072	18.6050	216
18.5	17.8799	17.9776	18.0754	18.1732	18.2712	18.3693	18.4674	18.5657	222
19.0	17.8417	17.9398	18.0380	18.1363	18.2347	18.3332	18.4318	18.5305	228
19.5	17.8073	17.9058	18.0045	18.1032	18.2021	18.3010	18.4000	18.4991	234
20.0	17.7764	17.8754	17.9744	18.0736	18.1728	18.2721	18.3715	18.4710	240
20.5	17.7487	17.8481	17.9475	18.0470	18.1466	18.2463	18.3460	18.4459	246
21.0	17.7238	17.8235	17.9233	18.0231	18.1231	18.2231	18.3232	18.4234	252
21.5	17.7014	17.8015	17.9016	18.0017	18.1020	18.2023	18.3028	18.4032	258
22.0	17.6813	17.7816	17.8821	17.9825	18.0831	18.1837	18.2844	18.3852	264
22.5	17.6632	17.7638	17.8645	17.9653	18.0661	18.1670	18.2680	18.3691	270
23.0	17.6470	17.7478	17.8488	17.9498	18.0509	18.1521	18.2533	18.3546	276
23.5	17.6323	17.7335	17.8347	17.9359	18.0373	18.1387	18.2401	18.3416	282
24.0	17.6191	17.7205	17.8219	17.9234	18.0250	18.1266	18.2283	18.3300	288
24.5	17.6073	17.7089	17.8105	17.9122	18.0140	18.1158	18.2177	18.3196	294
25.0	17.5966	17.6984	17.8003	17.9022	18.0041	18.1061	18.2082	18.3103	300
25.5	17.5870	17.6890	17.7910	17.8931	17.9952	18.0974	18.1996	18.3019	306
26.0	17.5784	17.6805	17.7827	17.8850	17.9873	18.0896	18.1920	18.2944	312
26.5	17.5706	17.6729	17.7753	17.8777	17.9801	18.0826	18.1851	18.2877	318
27.0	17.5636	17.6661	17.7685	17.8711	17.9737	18.0763	18.1790	18.2817	324
27.5	17.5573	17.6599	17.7625	17.8652	17.9679	18.0706	18.1734	18.2762	330
28.0	17.5516	17.6543	17.7571	17.8599	17.9627	18.0656	18.1685	18.2714	336
28.5	17.5465	17.6493	17.7522	17.8551	17.9580	18.0610	18.1640	18.2671	342
29.0	17.5419	17.6448	17.7478	17.8508	17.9538	18.0569	18.1600	18.2632	348
29.5	17.5377	17.6408	17.7438	17.8469	17.9501	18.0532	18.1564	18.2597	354
29.8	17.5352	17.6383	17.7414	17.8446	17.9478	18.0510	18.1543	18.2575	358
30.0	17.5340	17.6371	17.7403	17.8435	17.9467	18.0499	18.1532	18.2565	360
35.0	17.5120	17.6157	17.7195	17.8232	17.9270	18.0308	18.1346	18.2384	420
40.0	17.5042	17.6082	17.7122	17.8162	17.9202	18.0242	18.1283	18.2323	480

MONTHLY PAYMENT NECESSARY TO AMORTIZE A $1,000 LOAN

INTEREST ▸ YEARS	22%	22⅛%	22¼%	22⅜%	22½%	22⅝%	22¾%	22⅞%	MOS
.5	177.5230	177.5856	177.6482	177.7108	177.7734	177.8361	177.8987	177.9614	6
1.0	93.5944	93.6545	93.7147	93.7750	93.8352	93.8954	93.9557	94.0160	12
1.5	65.7287	65.7893	65.8499	65.9106	65.9713	66.0320	66.0928	66.1536	18
2.0	51.8782	51.9399	52.0017	52.0635	52.1254	52.1873	52.2493	52.3113	24
2.5	43.6332	43.6964	43.7596	43.8228	43.8862	43.9495	44.0129	44.0764	30
3.0	38.1905	38.2552	38.3199	38.3847	38.4496	38.5145	38.5795	38.6446	36
3.5	34.3484	34.4147	34.4810	34.5474	34.6139	34.6805	34.7471	34.8138	42
4.0	31.5061	31.5740	31.6420	31.7100	31.7782	31.8464	31.9147	31.9830	48
4.5	29.3297	29.3992	29.4688	29.5385	29.6083	29.6782	29.7481	29.8181	54
5.0	27.6189	27.6900	27.7612	27.8325	27.9039	27.9754	28.0470	28.1187	60
5.5	26.2461	26.3188	26.3916	26.4645	26.5375	26.6106	26.6838	26.7571	66
6.0	25.1261	25.2004	25.2747	25.3492	25.4238	25.4984	25.5732	25.6481	72
6.5	24.2001	24.2759	24.3518	24.4278	24.5039	24.5801	24.6564	24.7329	78
7.0	23.4259	23.5032	23.5806	23.6580	23.7356	23.8134	23.8912	23.9691	84
7.5	22.7727	22.8513	22.9302	23.0091	23.0881	23.1673	23.2466	23.3260	90
8.0	22.2171	22.2972	22.3774	22.4577	22.5381	22.6187	22.6994	22.7802	96
8.5	21.7414	21.8229	21.9044	21.9861	22.0679	22.1498	22.2319	22.3141	102
9.0	21.3319	21.4146	21.4975	21.5805	21.6636	21.7468	21.8302	21.9137	108
9.5	20.9776	21.0615	21.1456	21.2299	21.3143	21.3988	21.4834	21.5681	114
10.0	20.6697	20.7549	20.8402	20.9256	21.0112	21.0969	21.1827	21.2687	120
10.5	20.4012	20.4875	20.5740	20.6606	20.7473	20.8341	20.9211	21.0082	126
11.0	20.1663	20.2537	20.3413	20.4290	20.5168	20.6047	20.6928	20.7810	132
11.5	19.9602	20.0487	20.1373	20.2260	20.3149	20.4039	20.4930	20.5823	138
12.0	19.7789	19.8684	19.9580	20.0478	20.1376	20.2276	20.3177	20.4080	144
12.5	19.6192	19.7096	19.8002	19.8908	19.9817	20.0726	20.1637	20.2549	150
13.0	19.4781	19.5694	19.6609	19.7525	19.8442	19.9360	20.0280	20.1201	156
13.5	19.3533	19.4455	19.5378	19.6302	19.7228	19.8155	19.9083	20.0012	162
14.0	19.2427	19.3357	19.4288	19.5221	19.6154	19.7089	19.8025	19.8962	168
14.5	19.1447	19.2384	19.3323	19.4263	19.5204	19.6146	19.7090	19.8035	174
15.0	19.0576	19.1520	19.2466	19.3414	19.4362	19.5311	19.6262	19.7214	180
15.5	18.9801	19.0753	19.1706	19.2659	19.3614	19.4571	19.5528	19.6486	186
16.0	18.9112	19.0070	19.1029	19.1990	19.2951	19.3913	19.4877	19.5841	192
16.5	18.8499	18.9463	19.0428	19.1394	19.2361	19.3329	19.4299	19.5269	198
17.0	18.7952	18.8921	18.9892	19.0864	19.1836	19.2810	19.3785	19.4761	204
17.5	18.7464	18.8439	18.9415	19.0392	19.1370	19.2349	19.3328	19.4309	210
18.0	18.7029	18.8009	18.8990	18.9971	19.0954	19.1938	19.2922	19.3908	216
18.5	18.6640	18.7625	18.8610	18.9597	19.0584	19.1572	19.2561	19.3551	222
19.0	18.6293	18.7282	18.8272	18.9262	19.0254	19.1246	19.2239	19.3233	228
19.5	18.5983	18.6976	18.7970	18.8964	18.9959	19.0956	19.1952	19.2950	234
20.0	18.5706	18.6703	18.7700	18.8698	18.9697	19.0697	19.1697	19.2698	240
20.5	18.5458	18.6458	18.7459	18.8461	18.9463	19.0466	19.1470	19.2474	246
21.0	18.5236	18.6240	18.7244	18.8248	18.9254	19.0260	19.1267	19.2274	252
21.5	18.5038	18.6044	18.7051	18.8059	18.9067	19.0076	19.1086	19.2096	258
22.0	18.4861	18.5870	18.6879	18.7890	18.8901	18.9912	19.0925	19.1938	264
22.5	18.4702	18.5713	18.6726	18.7739	18.8752	18.9766	19.0781	19.1796	270
23.0	18.4559	18.5573	18.6588	18.7603	18.8619	18.9636	19.0653	19.1670	276
23.5	18.4432	18.5448	18.6465	18.7483	18.8501	18.9519	19.0538	19.1558	282
24.0	18.4318	18.5336	18.6355	18.7375	18.8395	18.9415	19.0436	19.1457	288
24.5	18.4216	18.5236	18.6257	18.7278	18.8300	18.9322	19.0345	19.1368	294
25.0	18.4124	18.5146	18.6169	18.7192	18.8215	18.9239	19.0263	19.1288	300
25.5	18.4042	18.5066	18.6090	18.7114	18.8139	18.9165	19.0191	19.1217	306
26.0	18.3969	18.4994	18.6019	18.7045	18.8072	18.9099	19.0126	19.1153	312
26.5	18.3903	18.4929	18.5956	18.6984	18.8011	18.9039	19.0068	19.1096	318
27.0	18.3844	18.4872	18.5900	18.6928	18.7957	18.8986	19.0016	19.1046	324
27.5	18.3791	18.4820	18.5849	18.6879	18.7909	18.8939	18.9970	19.1001	330
28.0	18.3744	18.4774	18.5804	18.6835	18.7866	18.8897	18.9929	19.0960	336
28.5	18.3701	18.4732	18.5764	18.6795	18.7827	18.8859	18.9892	19.0924	342
29.0	18.3663	18.4695	18.5727	18.6760	18.7793	18.8826	18.9859	19.0892	348
29.5	18.3629	18.4662	18.5695	18.6728	18.7762	18.8795	18.9829	19.0864	354
29.8	18.3608	18.4642	18.5675	18.6709	18.7743	18.8777	18.9812	19.0846	358
30.0	18.3598	18.4632	18.5666	18.6700	18.7734	18.8768	18.9803	19.0838	360
35.0	18.3422	18.4461	18.5499	18.6538	18.7577	18.8616	18.9655	19.0694	420
40.0	18.3363	18.4404	18.5444	18.6485	18.7525	18.8566	18.9606	19.0647	480

INTEREST► YEARS	23%	23⅛%	23¼%	23⅜%	23½%	23⅝%	23¾%	23⅞%	MOS
.5	178.0241	178.0868	178.1494	178.2121	178.2749	178.3376	178.4003	178.4631	6
1.0	94.0763	94.1367	94.1970	94.2574	94.3178	94.3782	94.4387	94.4991	12
1.5	66.2144	66.2752	66.3361	66.3970	66.4580	66.5190	66.5800	66.6410	18
2.0	52.3733	52.4354	52.4975	52.5597	52.6219	52.6841	52.7464	52.8087	24
2.5	44.1399	44.2035	44.2671	44.3308	44.3945	44.4583	44.5221	44.5860	30
3.0	38.7097	38.7749	38.8401	38.9054	38.9708	39.0362	39.1017	39.1673	36
3.5	34.8806	34.9475	35.0144	35.0814	35.1484	35.2155	35.2827	35.3500	42
4.0	32.0515	32.1200	32.1886	32.2573	32.3260	32.3949	32.4638	32.5328	48
4.5	29.8883	29.9585	30.0287	30.0991	30.1696	30.2401	30.3108	30.3815	54
5.0	28.1905	28.2623	28.3343	28.4063	28.4785	28.5507	28.6230	28.6955	60
5.5	26.8305	26.9040	26.9776	27.0513	27.1251	27.1990	27.2729	27.3470	66
6.0	25.7231	25.7982	25.8734	25.9487	26.0241	26.0997	26.1753	26.2510	72
6.5	24.8094	24.8861	24.9628	25.0397	25.1167	25.1938	25.2710	25.3483	78
7.0	24.0472	24.1254	24.2037	24.2821	24.3606	24.4392	24.5180	24.5968	84
7.5	23.4055	23.4852	23.5649	23.6448	23.7248	23.8050	23.8852	23.9655	90
8.0	22.8612	22.9423	23.0235	23.1048	23.1862	23.2677	23.3494	23.4312	96
8.5	22.3964	22.4788	22.5614	22.6441	22.7269	22.8098	22.8929	22.9761	102
9.0	21.9973	22.0811	22.1650	22.2490	22.3331	22.4173	22.5017	22.5862	108
9.5	21.6530	21.7380	21.8232	21.9085	21.9939	22.0794	22.1650	22.2508	114
10.0	21.3548	21.4410	21.5274	21.6138	21.7004	21.7872	21.8740	21.9610	120
10.5	21.0955	21.1829	21.2704	21.3580	21.4458	21.5336	21.6216	21.7098	126
11.0	20.8694	20.9579	21.0465	21.1352	21.2240	21.3130	21.4021	21.4913	132
11.5	20.6717	20.7612	20.8508	20.9406	21.0305	21.1205	21.2106	21.3009	138
12.0	20.4984	20.5889	20.6795	20.7703	20.8611	20.9521	21.0433	21.1345	144
12.5	20.3462	20.4376	20.5292	20.6209	20.7127	20.8046	20.8967	20.9888	150
13.0	20.2123	20.3046	20.3970	20.4896	20.5823	20.6751	20.7680	20.8611	156
13.5	20.0942	20.1874	20.2807	20.3741	20.4676	20.5612	20.6550	20.7488	162
14.0	19.9901	20.0840	20.1781	20.2723	20.3666	20.4610	20.5555	20.6501	168
14.5	19.8980	19.9927	20.0875	20.1825	20.2775	20.3726	20.4679	20.5632	174
15.0	19.8166	19.9120	20.0075	20.1031	20.1988	20.2947	20.3906	20.4866	180
15.5	19.7445	19.8406	19.9367	20.0330	20.1293	20.2258	20.3224	20.4190	186
16.0	19.6807	19.7773	19.8741	19.9709	20.0679	20.1649	20.2621	20.3593	192
16.5	19.6240	19.7212	19.8186	19.9160	20.0135	20.1111	20.2088	20.3066	198
17.0	19.5737	19.6715	19.7693	19.8673	19.9653	20.0634	20.1617	20.2600	204
17.5	19.5291	19.6273	19.7257	19.8241	19.9226	20.0212	20.1199	20.2187	210
18.0	19.4894	19.5881	19.6869	19.7858	19.8848	19.9838	20.0830	20.1822	216
18.5	19.4541	19.5533	19.6525	19.7518	19.8512	19.9507	20.0502	20.1499	222
19.0	19.4228	19.5223	19.6219	19.7216	19.8214	19.9213	20.0212	20.1212	228
19.5	19.3949	19.4948	19.5948	19.6949	19.7950	19.8952	19.9955	20.0958	234
20.0	19.3700	19.4703	19.5706	19.6710	19.7715	19.8721	19.9727	20.0733	240
20.5	19.3479	19.4485	19.5492	19.6499	19.7507	19.8515	19.9524	20.0534	246
21.0	19.3283	19.4291	19.5301	19.6311	19.7321	19.8333	19.9345	20.0357	252
21.5	19.3107	19.4119	19.5131	19.6144	19.7157	19.8171	19.9185	20.0200	258
22.0	19.2951	19.3965	19.4980	19.5995	19.7011	19.8027	19.9044	20.0061	264
22.5	19.2812	19.3828	19.4845	19.5863	19.6881	19.7899	19.8918	19.9937	270
23.0	19.2688	19.3707	19.4726	19.5745	19.6765	19.7785	19.8806	19.9828	276
23.5	19.2578	19.3598	19.4619	19.5640	19.6662	19.7685	19.8707	19.9730	282
24.0	19.2479	19.3501	19.4524	19.5547	19.6571	19.7595	19.8619	19.9644	288
24.5	19.2391	19.3415	19.4440	19.5464	19.6490	19.7515	19.8541	19.9567	294
25.0	19.2313	19.3338	19.4364	19.5391	19.6417	19.7444	19.8472	19.9499	300
25.5	19.2243	19.3270	19.4297	19.5325	19.6353	19.7381	19.8410	19.9439	306
26.0	19.2181	19.3209	19.4238	19.5267	19.6296	19.7325	19.8355	19.9385	312
26.5	19.2125	19.3155	19.4185	19.5215	19.6245	19.7275	19.8306	19.9338	318
27.0	19.2076	19.3106	19.4137	19.5168	19.6200	19.7231	19.8263	19.9295	324
27.5	19.2032	19.3063	19.4095	19.5127	19.6159	19.7192	19.8225	19.9258	330
28.0	19.1992	19.3025	19.4057	19.5090	19.6123	19.7157	19.8190	19.9224	336
28.5	19.1957	19.2990	19.4024	19.5058	19.6091	19.7126	19.8160	19.9194	342
29.0	19.1926	19.2960	19.3994	19.5028	19.6063	19.7098	19.8133	19.9168	348
29.5	19.1898	19.2933	19.3968	19.5003	19.6038	19.7073	19.8109	19.9145	354
29.8	19.1881	19.2916	19.3951	19.4987	19.6023	19.7058	19.8094	19.9131	358
30.0	19.1873	19.2908	19.3944	19.4980	19.6015	19.7051	19.8088	19.9124	360
35.0	19.1733	19.2772	19.3811	19.4851	19.5890	19.6930	19.7969	19.9009	420
40.0	19.1688	19.2729	19.3769	19.4810	19.5851	19.6892	19.7933	19.8974	480

QUARTERLY PAYMENTS TO AMORTIZE A $1,000 LOAN

YRS	6%	6¼%	6½%	6¾%	7%	7¼%	7½%	7¾%
.5	511.28	511.75	512.23	512.70	513.17	513.64	514.11	514.58
1.0	259.45	259.85	260.24	260.64	261.04	261.43	261.83	262.23
1.5	175.53	175.90	176.28	176.65	177.03	177.40	177.78	178.15
2.0	133.59	133.95	134.32	134.68	135.05	135.41	135.78	136.15
2.5	108.44	108.80	109.16	109.52	109.88	110.24	110.60	110.97
3.0	91.68	92.04	92.40	92.76	93.12	93.48	93.84	94.20
3.5	79.73	80.09	80.44	80.80	81.16	81.52	81.88	82.24
4.0	70.77	71.13	71.49	71.84	72.20	72.57	72.93	73.29
4.5	63.81	64.17	64.53	64.89	65.25	65.61	65.98	66.34
5.0	58.25	58.61	58.97	59.33	59.70	60.06	60.43	60.79
5.5	53.71	54.07	54.43	54.80	55.16	55.53	55.90	56.27
6.0	49.93	50.29	50.66	51.02	51.39	51.76	52.13	52.50
6.5	46.74	47.10	47.47	47.84	48.21	48.58	48.95	49.33
7.0	44.01	44.37	44.74	45.11	45.49	45.86	46.24	46.62
7.5	41.64	42.01	42.39	42.76	43.13	43.51	43.89	44.27
8.0	39.58	39.95	40.33	40.70	41.08	41.46	41.85	42.23
8.5	37.77	38.14	38.52	38.90	39.28	39.66	40.05	40.43
9.0	36.16	36.53	36.91	37.30	37.68	38.07	38.45	38.85
9.5	34.72	35.10	35.48	35.87	36.25	36.64	37.04	37.43
10.0	33.43	33.81	34.20	34.59	34.98	35.37	35.76	36.16
10.5	32.27	32.65	33.04	33.43	33.83	34.22	34.62	35.02
11.0	31.22	31.60	31.99	32.39	32.78	33.18	33.58	33.99
11.5	30.26	30.65	31.04	31.44	31.84	32.24	32.64	33.05
12.0	29.38	29.77	30.17	30.57	30.97	31.38	31.78	32.19
12.5	28.58	28.97	29.37	29.77	30.18	30.59	31.00	31.41
13.0	27.84	28.24	28.64	29.04	29.45	29.86	30.28	30.69
13.5	27.16	27.56	27.96	28.37	28.78	29.20	29.61	30.03
14.0	26.53	26.93	27.34	27.75	28.16	28.58	29.00	29.42
14.5	25.94	26.35	26.76	27.17	27.59	28.01	28.43	28.86
15.0	25.40	25.81	26.22	26.64	27.06	27.48	27.91	28.34
15.5	24.89	25.30	25.72	26.14	26.56	26.99	27.42	27.85
16.0	24.42	24.84	25.25	25.68	26.10	26.53	26.97	27.40
16.5	23.98	24.40	24.82	25.24	25.67	26.11	26.54	26.98
17.0	23.57	23.99	24.41	24.84	25.27	25.71	26.15	26.59
17.5	23.18	23.60	24.03	24.46	24.89	25.33	25.78	26.22
18.0	22.81	23.24	23.67	24.10	24.54	24.98	25.43	25.88
18.5	22.47	22.90	23.33	23.77	24.21	24.65	25.10	25.56
19.0	22.15	22.58	23.01	23.45	23.90	24.34	24.80	25.25
19.5	21.84	22.28	22.71	23.16	23.60	24.05	24.51	24.97
20.0	21.55	21.99	22.43	22.88	23.33	23.78	24.24	24.70
20.5	21.28	21.72	22.16	22.61	23.06	23.52	23.98	24.45
21.0	21.02	21.46	21.91	22.36	22.82	23.28	23.74	24.21
21.5	20.78	21.22	21.67	22.13	22.58	23.05	23.51	23.98
22.0	20.55	20.99	21.45	21.90	22.36	22.83	23.30	23.77
22.5	20.33	20.78	21.23	21.69	22.15	22.62	23.09	23.57
23.0	20.12	20.57	21.03	21.49	21.95	22.42	22.90	23.38
23.5	19.92	20.37	20.83	21.30	21.77	22.24	22.72	23.20
24.0	19.73	20.19	20.65	21.11	21.59	22.06	22.54	23.03
24.5	19.55	20.01	20.47	20.94	21.42	21.89	22.38	22.87
25.0	19.38	19.84	20.30	20.78	21.25	21.74	22.22	22.71
25.5	19.21	19.68	20.15	20.62	21.10	21.58	22.07	22.57
26.0	19.05	19.52	19.99	20.47	20.95	21.44	21.93	22.43
26.5	18.90	19.37	19.85	20.33	20.81	21.30	21.80	22.30
27.0	18.76	19.23	19.71	20.19	20.68	21.17	21.67	22.17
27.5	18.63	19.10	19.58	20.06	20.55	21.05	21.55	22.05
28.0	18.49	18.97	19.45	19.94	20.43	20.93	21.43	21.94
28.5	18.37	18.85	19.33	19.82	20.32	20.82	21.32	21.83
29.0	18.25	18.73	19.22	19.71	20.20	20.71	21.21	21.72
29.5	18.13	18.62	19.11	19.60	20.10	20.60	21.11	21.63
30.0	18.02	18.51	19.00	19.50	20.00	20.50	21.02	21.53
35.0	17.14	17.64	18.16	18.67	19.20	19.72	20.26	20.80
40.0	16.53	17.06	17.59	18.13	18.67	19.21	19.77	20.32

QUARTERLY PAYMENTS TO AMORTIZE A $1,000 LOAN

YRS	8%	8¼%	8½%	8¾%	9%	9¼%	9½%	9¾%
.5	515.05	515.53	516.00	516.47	516.94	517.41	517.89	518.36
1.0	262.63	263.03	263.43	263.82	264.22	264.62	265.02	265.42
1.5	178.53	178.91	179.28	179.66	180.04	180.42	180.80	181.18
2.0	136.51	136.88	137.25	137.62	137.99	138.36	138.73	139.10
2.5	111.33	111.70	112.06	112.43	112.79	113.16	113.53	113.90
3.0	94.56	94.93	95.29	95.66	96.02	96.39	96.76	97.12
3.5	82.61	82.97	83.34	83.70	84.07	84.43	84.80	85.17
4.0	73.66	74.02	74.39	74.75	75.12	75.49	75.86	76.23
4.5	66.71	67.07	67.44	67.81	68.18	68.55	68.93	69.30
5.0	61.16	61.53	61.90	62.27	62.65	63.02	63.40	63.77
5.5	56.64	57.01	57.38	57.76	58.13	58.51	58.89	59.27
6.0	52.88	53.25	53.63	54.01	54.39	54.77	55.15	55.53
6.5	49.70	50.08	50.46	50.84	51.23	51.61	52.00	52.38
7.0	46.99	47.38	47.76	48.14	48.53	48.92	49.31	49.70
7.5	44.65	45.04	45.43	45.81	46.20	46.60	46.99	47.39
8.0	42.62	43.00	43.39	43.79	44.18	44.57	44.97	45.37
8.5	40.82	41.22	41.61	42.00	42.40	42.80	43.20	43.61
9.0	39.24	39.63	40.03	40.43	40.83	41.23	41.64	42.05
9.5	37.83	38.22	38.62	39.03	39.43	39.84	40.25	40.66
10.0	36.56	36.96	37.37	37.77	38.18	38.59	39.01	39.42
10.5	35.42	35.83	36.24	36.65	37.06	37.47	37.89	38.31
11.0	34.39	34.80	35.21	35.63	36.04	36.46	36.88	37.31
11.5	33.46	33.87	34.29	34.70	35.12	35.55	35.97	36.40
12.0	32.61	33.02	33.44	33.86	34.29	34.71	35.14	35.58
12.5	31.83	32.25	32.67	33.10	33.52	33.95	34.39	34.82
13.0	31.11	31.54	31.96	32.39	32.82	33.26	33.70	34.14
13.5	30.46	30.88	31.31	31.75	32.18	32.62	33.06	33.51
14.0	29.85	30.28	30.71	31.15	31.59	32.03	32.48	32.93
14.5	29.29	29.73	30.16	30.60	31.04	31.49	31.94	32.39
15.0	28.77	29.21	29.65	30.09	30.54	30.99	31.44	31.90
15.5	28.29	28.73	29.18	29.62	30.07	30.53	30.98	31.44
16.0	27.84	28.29	28.73	29.19	29.64	30.10	30.56	31.02
16.5	27.43	27.87	28.32	28.78	29.24	29.70	30.16	30.63
17.0	27.04	27.49	27.94	28.40	28.86	29.32	29.79	30.26
17.5	26.67	27.13	27.58	28.05	28.51	28.98	29.45	29.92
18.0	26.33	26.79	27.25	27.71	28.18	28.65	29.13	29.61
18.5	26.01	26.47	26.94	27.40	27.88	28.35	28.83	29.31
19.0	25.71	26.18	26.64	27.11	27.59	28.07	28.55	29.04
19.5	25.43	25.90	26.37	26.84	27.32	27.80	28.29	28.78
20.0	25.17	25.64	26.11	26.59	27.07	27.55	28.04	28.54
20.5	24.92	25.39	25.87	26.35	26.83	27.32	27.81	28.31
21.0	24.68	25.16	25.64	26.12	26.61	27.10	27.60	28.10
21.5	24.46	24.94	25.42	25.91	26.40	26.89	27.39	27.90
22.0	24.25	24.73	25.22	25.71	26.20	26.70	27.20	27.71
22.5	24.05	24.54	25.03	25.52	26.02	26.52	27.02	27.53
23.0	23.86	24.35	24.84	25.34	25.84	26.34	26.85	27.36
23.5	23.69	24.18	24.67	25.17	25.68	26.18	26.69	27.21
24.0	23.52	24.01	24.51	25.01	25.52	26.03	26.54	27.06
24.5	23.36	23.86	24.36	24.86	25.37	25.88	26.40	26.92
25.0	23.21	23.71	24.21	24.72	25.23	25.75	26.27	26.79
25.5	23.06	23.57	24.07	24.58	25.10	25.62	26.14	26.67
26.0	22.93	23.43	23.94	24.46	24.97	25.49	26.02	26.55
26.5	22.80	23.31	23.82	24.33	24.85	25.38	25.91	26.44
27.0	22.68	23.19	23.70	24.22	24.74	25.27	25.80	26.33
27.5	22.56	23.07	23.59	24.11	24.64	25.16	25.70	26.23
28.0	22.45	22.96	23.48	24.01	24.53	25.07	25.60	26.14
28.5	22.34	22.86	23.38	23.91	24.44	24.97	25.51	26.05
29.0	22.24	22.76	23.29	23.81	24.35	24.88	25.42	25.97
29.5	22.14	22.67	23.19	23.73	24.26	24.80	25.34	25.89
30.0	22.05	22.58	23.11	23.64	24.18	24.72	25.27	25.81
35.0	21.34	21.89	22.44	22.99	23.55	24.11	24.68	25.25
40.0	20.88	21.45	22.02	22.59	23.16	23.74	24.32	24.91

A-20

QUARTERLY PAYMENTS TO AMORTIZE A $1,000 LOAN

YRS	10%	10¼%	10½%	10¾%	11%	11¼%	11½%	11¾%
.5	518.83	519.30	519.78	520.25	520.72	521.20	521.67	522.14
1.0	265.82	266.22	266.62	267.02	267.43	267.83	268.23	268.63
1.5	181.55	181.93	182.31	182.70	183.08	183.46	183.84	184.22
2.0	139.47	139.84	140.22	140.59	140.96	141.34	141.71	142.09
2.5	114.26	114.63	115.00	115.37	115.74	116.12	116.49	116.86
3.0	97.49	97.86	98.23	98.60	98.97	99.35	99.72	100.09
3.5	85.54	85.91	86.28	86.66	87.03	87.40	87.78	88.15
4.0	76.60	76.98	77.35	77.73	78.10	78.48	78.86	79.24
4.5	69.68	70.05	70.43	70.81	71.19	71.57	71.95	72.33
5.0	64.15	64.53	64.91	65.29	65.68	66.06	66.45	66.83
5.5	59.65	60.03	60.42	60.80	61.19	61.58	61.97	62.36
6.0	55.92	56.30	56.69	57.08	57.47	57.87	58.26	58.66
6.5	52.77	53.16	53.56	53.95	54.35	54.74	55.14	55.54
7.0	50.09	50.49	50.88	51.28	51.68	52.08	52.49	52.89
7.5	47.78	48.18	48.58	48.99	49.39	49.80	50.20	50.61
8.0	45.77	46.18	46.58	46.99	47.40	47.81	48.22	48.64
8.5	44.01	44.42	44.83	45.24	45.65	46.07	46.49	46.91
9.0	42.46	42.87	43.28	43.70	44.12	44.54	44.96	45.38
9.5	41.08	41.49	41.91	42.33	42.75	43.18	43.60	44.03
10.0	39.84	40.26	40.68	41.11	41.54	41.97	42.40	42.83
10.5	38.73	39.16	39.59	40.02	40.45	40.88	41.32	41.76
11.0	37.74	38.16	38.60	39.03	39.47	39.90	40.35	40.79
11.5	36.83	37.27	37.70	38.14	38.58	39.02	39.47	39.92
12.0	36.01	36.45	36.89	37.33	37.78	38.22	38.67	39.13
12.5	35.26	35.70	36.15	36.60	37.05	37.50	37.95	38.41
13.0	34.58	35.03	35.47	35.93	36.38	36.84	37.30	37.76
13.5	33.95	34.40	34.86	35.31	35.77	36.23	36.69	37.16
14.0	33.38	33.83	34.29	34.75	35.21	35.68	36.14	36.62
14.5	32.85	33.31	33.77	34.23	34.70	35.17	35.64	36.12
15.0	32.36	32.82	33.29	33.75	34.23	34.70	35.18	35.66
15.5	31.91	32.37	32.84	33.31	33.79	34.27	34.75	35.23
16.0	31.49	31.96	32.43	32.91	33.39	33.87	34.35	34.84
16.5	31.10	31.57	32.05	32.53	33.01	33.50	33.99	34.48
17.0	30.74	31.22	31.70	32.18	32.67	33.16	33.65	34.15
17.5	30.40	30.88	31.37	31.86	32.35	32.84	33.34	33.84
18.0	30.09	30.57	31.06	31.55	32.05	32.55	33.05	33.55
18.5	29.80	30.29	30.78	31.27	31.77	32.27	32.78	33.29
19.0	29.52	30.02	30.51	31.01	31.51	32.02	32.53	33.04
19.5	29.27	29.77	30.26	30.77	31.27	31.78	32.29	32.81
20.0	29.03	29.53	30.03	30.54	31.05	31.56	32.08	32.60
20.5	28.81	29.31	29.82	30.33	30.84	31.35	31.87	32.40
21.0	28.60	29.10	29.61	30.13	30.64	31.16	31.68	32.21
21.5	28.40	28.91	29.42	29.94	30.46	30.98	31.51	32.04
22.0	28.22	28.73	29.25	29.76	30.29	30.81	31.34	31.87
22.5	28.04	28.56	29.08	29.60	30.13	30.66	31.19	31.72
23.0	27.88	28.40	28.92	29.45	29.98	30.51	31.04	31.58
23.5	27.73	28.25	28.77	29.30	29.83	30.37	30.91	31.45
24.0	27.58	28.11	28.63	29.17	29.70	30.24	30.78	31.32
24.5	27.45	27.97	28.50	29.04	29.58	30.12	30.66	31.21
25.0	27.32	27.85	28.38	28.92	29.46	30.00	30.55	31.10
25.5	27.20	27.73	28.27	28.81	29.35	29.90	30.44	31.00
26.0	27.08	27.62	28.16	28.70	29.25	29.79	30.35	30.90
26.5	26.97	27.51	28.05	28.60	29.15	29.70	30.25	30.81
27.0	26.87	27.41	27.96	28.51	29.06	29.61	30.17	30.73
27.5	26.78	27.32	27.87	28.42	28.97	29.53	30.09	30.65
28.0	26.68	27.23	27.78	28.33	28.89	29.45	30.01	30.57
28.5	26.60	27.15	27.70	28.25	28.81	29.37	29.94	30.50
29.0	26.52	27.07	27.62	28.18	28.74	29.30	29.87	30.44
29.5	26.44	26.99	27.55	28.11	28.67	29.24	29.81	30.38
30.0	26.37	26.92	27.48	28.04	28.61	29.18	29.75	30.32
35.0	25.82	26.39	26.97	27.55	28.14	28.72	29.31	29.90
40.0	25.50	26.09	26.68	27.27	27.87	28.47	29.07	29.67

QUARTERLY PAYMENTS TO AMORTIZE A $1,000 LOAN

YRS	12%	12¼%	12½%	12¾%	13%	13¼%	13½%	13¾%
.5	522.62	523.09	523.56	524.04	524.51	524.98	525.46	525.93
1.0	269.03	269.43	269.84	270.24	270.64	271.05	271.45	271.85
1.5	184.60	184.99	185.37	185.75	186.13	186.52	186.90	187.29
2.0	142.46	142.84	143.21	143.59	143.97	144.35	144.72	145.10
2.5	117.24	117.61	117.98	118.36	118.74	119.11	119.49	119.87
3.0	100.47	100.84	101.22	101.59	101.97	102.35	102.73	103.11
3.5	88.53	88.91	89.29	89.67	90.05	90.43	90.81	91.19
4.0	79.62	80.00	80.38	80.76	81.15	81.53	81.92	82.30
4.5	72.71	73.10	73.48	73.87	74.26	74.65	75.04	75.43
5.0	67.22	67.61	68.00	68.39	68.78	69.18	69.57	69.97
5.5	62.75	63.15	63.54	63.94	64.33	64.73	65.13	65.53
6.0	59.05	59.45	59.85	60.25	60.65	61.06	61.46	61.87
6.5	55.94	56.35	56.75	57.16	57.56	57.97	58.38	58.80
7.0	53.30	53.71	54.12	54.53	54.94	55.35	55.77	56.19
7.5	51.02	51.44	51.85	52.27	52.69	53.11	53.53	53.95
8.0	49.05	49.47	49.89	50.31	50.73	51.16	51.59	52.02
8.5	47.33	47.75	48.18	48.60	49.03	49.46	49.89	50.33
9.0	45.81	46.24	46.67	47.10	47.53	47.97	48.41	48.85
9.5	44.46	44.90	45.33	45.77	46.21	46.65	47.09	47.54
10.0	43.27	43.71	44.15	44.59	45.03	45.48	45.93	46.38
10.5	42.20	42.64	43.09	43.53	43.98	44.43	44.89	45.34
11.0	41.23	41.68	42.13	42.59	43.04	43.50	43.96	44.42
11.5	40.37	40.82	41.28	41.73	42.19	42.66	43.12	43.59
12.0	39.58	40.04	40.50	40.96	41.43	41.90	42.37	42.84
12.5	38.87	39.33	39.80	40.27	40.74	41.21	41.68	42.16
13.0	38.22	38.69	39.16	39.63	40.11	40.58	41.06	41.54
13.5	37.63	38.10	38.58	39.05	39.53	40.02	40.50	40.99
14.0	37.09	37.57	38.04	38.53	39.01	39.50	39.99	40.48
14.5	36.59	37.07	37.56	38.04	38.53	39.02	39.52	40.01
15.0	36.14	36.62	37.11	37.60	38.09	38.59	39.09	39.59
15.5	35.72	36.21	36.70	37.20	37.69	38.19	38.70	39.20
16.0	35.33	35.83	36.32	36.82	37.32	37.83	38.34	38.85
16.5	34.98	35.47	35.97	36.48	36.98	37.49	38.00	38.52
17.0	34.65	35.15	35.65	36.16	36.67	37.18	37.70	38.22
17.5	34.34	34.85	35.36	35.87	36.38	36.90	37.42	37.94
18.0	34.06	34.57	35.08	35.60	36.12	36.64	37.16	37.69
18.5	33.80	34.31	34.83	35.35	35.87	36.39	36.92	37.45
19.0	33.55	34.07	34.59	35.11	35.64	36.17	36.70	37.23
19.5	33.33	33.85	34.37	34.90	35.43	35.96	36.50	37.03
20.0	33.12	33.64	34.17	34.70	35.23	35.77	36.31	36.85
20.5	32.92	33.45	33.98	34.51	35.05	35.59	36.13	36.67
21.0	32.74	33.27	33.80	34.34	34.88	35.42	35.97	36.52
21.5	32.57	33.10	33.64	34.18	34.72	35.27	35.82	36.37
22.0	32.41	32.95	33.49	34.03	34.58	35.13	35.68	36.23
22.5	32.26	32.80	33.35	33.89	34.44	34.99	35.55	36.10
23.0	32.12	32.67	33.21	33.76	34.31	34.87	35.43	35.99
23.5	31.99	32.54	33.09	33.64	34.20	34.75	35.31	35.88
24.0	31.87	32.42	32.97	33.53	34.09	34.65	35.21	35.77
24.5	31.76	32.31	32.87	33.42	33.98	34.55	35.11	35.68
25.0	31.65	32.21	32.76	33.33	33.89	34.45	35.02	35.59
25.5	31.55	32.11	32.67	33.23	33.80	34.37	34.94	35.51
26.0	31.46	32.02	32.58	33.15	33.72	34.29	34.86	35.43
26.5	31.37	31.93	32.50	33.07	33.64	34.21	34.79	35.36
27.0	31.29	31.86	32.42	32.99	33.57	34.14	34.72	35.30
27.5	31.21	31.78	32.35	32.92	33.50	34.08	34.65	35.24
28.0	31.14	31.71	32.28	32.86	33.43	34.01	34.60	35.18
28.5	31.07	31.65	32.22	32.80	33.38	33.96	34.54	35.13
29.0	31.01	31.58	32.16	32.74	33.32	33.90	34.49	35.08
29.5	30.95	31.53	32.11	32.69	33.27	33.85	34.44	35.03
30.0	30.89	31.47	32.05	32.64	33.22	33.81	34.40	34.99
35.0	30.49	31.09	31.68	32.28	32.88	33.48	34.08	34.69
40.0	30.27	30.88	31.48	32.09	32.70	33.31	33.92	34.53

YRS	14%	14¼%	14½%	14¾%	15%	15¼%	15½%	15¾%
.5	526.41	526.88	527.35	527.83	528.30	528.78	529.25	529.73
1.0	272.26	272.66	273.06	273.47	273.87	274.28	274.68	275.09
1.5	187.67	188.06	188.44	188.83	189.22	189.60	189.99	190.38
2.0	145.48	145.86	146.24	146.62	147.00	147.39	147.77	148.15
2.5	120.25	120.63	121.01	121.39	121.77	122.15	122.53	122.91
3.0	103.49	103.87	104.25	104.63	105.02	105.40	105.79	106.17
3.5	91.58	91.96	92.35	92.73	93.12	93.51	93.89	94.28
4.0	82.69	83.08	83.47	83.86	84.25	84.64	85.04	85.43
4.5	75.82	76.22	76.61	77.01	77.40	77.80	78.20	78.60
5.0	70.37	70.76	71.16	71.57	71.97	72.37	72.77	73.18
5.5	65.94	66.34	66.75	67.15	67.56	67.97	68.38	68.79
6.0	62.28	62.69	63.10	63.51	63.92	64.34	64.76	65.17
6.5	59.21	59.63	60.04	60.46	60.88	61.30	61.72	62.15
7.0	56.61	57.03	57.45	57.87	58.30	58.73	59.16	59.59
7.5	54.38	54.80	55.23	55.66	56.09	56.53	56.96	57.40
8.0	52.45	52.88	53.31	53.75	54.19	54.63	55.07	55.51
8.5	50.76	51.20	51.64	52.08	52.53	52.97	53.42	53.87
9.0	49.29	49.73	50.18	50.63	51.08	51.53	51.98	52.44
9.5	47.99	48.44	48.89	49.34	49.80	50.25	50.71	51.17
10.0	46.83	47.29	47.74	48.20	48.66	49.13	49.59	50.06
10.5	45.80	46.26	46.73	47.19	47.66	48.13	48.60	49.07
11.0	44.88	45.35	45.82	46.29	46.76	47.23	47.71	48.19
11.5	44.06	44.53	45.00	45.48	45.95	46.43	46.92	47.40
12.0	43.31	43.79	44.27	44.75	45.23	45.72	46.20	46.69
12.5	42.64	43.12	43.60	44.09	44.58	45.07	45.56	46.06
13.0	42.03	42.52	43.01	43.50	43.39	44.49	44.98	45.48
13.5	41.48	41.97	42.46	42.96	43.46	43.96	44.46	44.97
14.0	40.97	41.47	41.97	42.47	42.97	43.48	43.99	44.50
14.5	40.51	41.01	41.52	42.02	42.53	43.04	43.56	44.07
15.0	40.09	40.60	41.11	41.62	42.13	42.65	43.16	43.68
15.5	39.71	40.22	40.73	41.25	41.77	42.29	42.81	43.33
16.0	39.36	39.87	40.39	40.91	41.43	41.96	42.48	43.01
16.5	39.04	39.55	40.08	40.60	41.13	41.65	42.19	42.72
17.0	38.74	39.26	39.79	40.32	40.85	41.38	41.91	42.45
17.5	38.47	38.99	39.52	40.06	40.59	41.13	41.67	42.21
18.0	38.21	38.75	39.28	39.82	40.35	40.89	41.44	41.98
18.5	37.98	38.52	39.06	39.60	40.14	40.68	41.23	41.78
19.0	37.77	38.31	38.85	39.39	39.94	40.49	41.04	41.59
19.5	37.57	38.11	38.66	39.21	39.76	40.31	40.86	41.42
20.0	37.39	37.94	38.48	39.03	39.59	40.14	40.70	41.26
20.5	37.22	37.77	38.32	38.88	39.43	39.99	40.55	41.11
21.0	37.07	37.62	38.17	38.73	39.29	39.85	40.41	40.98
21.5	36.92	37.48	38.03	38.59	39.16	39.72	40.29	40.85
22.0	36.79	37.35	37.91	38.47	39.03	39.60	40.17	40.74
22.5	36.66	37.22	37.79	38.35	38.92	39.49	40.06	40.64
23.0	36.55	37.11	37.68	38.25	38.82	39.39	39.96	40.54
23.5	36.44	37.01	37.58	38.15	38.72	39.30	39.87	40.45
24.0	36.34	36.91	37.48	38.06	38.63	39.21	39.79	40.37
24.5	36.25	36.82	37.40	37.97	38.55	39.13	39.71	40.30
25.0	36.16	36.74	37.32	37.89	38.47	39.06	39.64	40.23
25.5	36.08	36.66	37.24	37.82	38.40	38.99	39.57	40.16
26.0	36.01	36.59	37.17	37.75	38.34	38.92	39.51	40.10
26.5	35.94	36.52	37.11	37.69	38.28	38.87	39.46	40.05
27.0	35.88	36.46	37.05	37.63	38.22	38.81	39.40	40.00
27.5	35.82	36.40	36.99	37.58	38.17	38.76	39.36	39.95
28.0	35.76	36.35	36.94	37.53	38.12	38.72	39.31	39.91
28.5	35.71	36.30	36.89	37.48	38.08	38.67	39.27	39.87
29.0	35.66	36.25	36.85	37.44	38.04	38.63	39.23	39.83
29.5	35.62	36.21	36.81	37.40	38.00	38.60	39.20	39.80
30.0	35.58	36.17	36.77	37.36	37.96	38.56	39.16	39.77
35.0	35.29	35.90	36.50	37.11	37.72	38.33	38.95	39.56
40.0	35.15	35.76	36.38	36.99	37.61	38.23	38.84	39.46

QUARTERLY PAYMENTS TO AMORTIZE A $1,000 LOAN

YRS	16%	16¼%	16½%	16¾%	17%	17¼%	17½%	17¾%
.5	530.20	530.68	531.15	531.63	532.10	532.58	533.05	533.53
1.0	275.50	275.90	276.31	276.71	277.12	277.53	277.93	278.34
1.5	190.77	191.16	191.54	191.93	192.32	192.71	193.10	193.49
2.0	148.53	148.92	149.30	149.68	150.07	150.46	150.84	151.23
2.5	123.30	123.68	124.06	124.45	124.84	125.22	125.61	126.00
3.0	106.56	106.94	107.33	107.72	108.11	108.50	108.89	109.28
3.5	94.67	95.07	95.46	95.85	96.24	96.64	97.03	97.43
4.0	85.82	86.22	86.62	87.02	87.42	87.82	88.22	88.62
4.5	79.00	79.40	79.80	80.21	80.61	81.02	81.42	81.83
5.0	73.59	73.99	74.40	74.81	75.22	75.64	76.05	76.47
5.5	69.20	69.62	70.03	70.45	70.87	71.29	71.71	72.13
6.0	65.59	66.01	66.43	66.86	67.28	67.71	68.13	68.56
6.5	62.57	63.00	63.43	63.86	64.29	64.72	65.15	65.59
7.0	60.02	60.45	60.89	61.32	61.76	62.20	62.64	63.08
7.5	57.84	58.27	58.72	59.16	59.60	60.05	60.50	60.95
8.0	55.95	56.40	56.85	57.30	57.75	58.20	58.65	59.11
8.5	54.32	54.77	55.23	55.68	56.14	56.60	57.06	57.52
9.0	52.89	53.35	53.81	54.27	54.74	55.20	55.67	56.14
9.5	51.64	52.10	52.57	53.04	53.51	53.98	54.45	54.93
10.0	50.53	51.00	51.47	51.95	52.42	52.90	53.38	53.86
10.5	49.55	50.02	50.50	50.98	51.46	51.95	52.44	52.92
11.0	48.67	49.15	49.64	50.12	50.61	51.10	51.60	52.09
11.5	47.89	48.38	48.87	49.36	49.85	50.35	50.85	51.35
12.0	47.19	47.68	48.18	48.67	49.17	49.68	50.18	50.69
12.5	46.56	47.05	47.56	48.06	48.57	49.07	49.58	50.09
13.0	45.99	46.49	47.00	47.51	48.02	48.53	49.05	49.56
13.5	45.47	45.98	46.50	47.01	47.53	48.04	48.56	49.09
14.0	45.01	45.52	46.04	46.56	47.08	47.60	48.13	48.66
14.5	44.59	45.11	45.63	46.15	46.68	47.21	47.74	48.27
15.0	44.21	44.73	45.26	45.79	46.32	46.85	47.38	47.92
15.5	43.86	44.39	44.92	45.45	45.99	46.52	47.06	47.60
16.0	43.54	44.08	44.61	45.15	45.69	46.23	46.77	47.32
16.5	43.25	43.79	44.33	44.87	45.42	45.96	46.51	47.06
17.0	42.99	43.53	44.08	44.62	45.17	45.72	46.27	46.82
17.5	42.75	43.30	43.84	44.39	44.94	45.50	46.05	46.61
18.0	42.53	43.08	43.63	44.18	44.74	45.30	45.86	46.42
18.5	42.33	42.88	43.44	43.99	44.55	45.11	45.68	46.24
19.0	42.14	42.70	43.26	43.82	44.38	44.95	45.51	46.08
19.5	41.97	42.53	43.10	43.66	44.23	44.79	45.36	45.93
20.0	41.82	42.38	42.95	43.51	44.08	44.65	45.23	45.80
20.5	41.68	42.24	42.81	43.38	43.95	44.53	45.10	45.68
21.0	41.55	42.11	42.69	43.26	43.83	44.41	44.99	45.57
21.5	41.43	42.00	42.57	43.15	43.72	44.30	44.88	45.47
22.0	41.31	41.89	42.47	43.04	43.62	44.21	44.79	45.37
22.5	41.21	41.79	42.37	42.95	43.53	44.12	44.70	45.29
23.0	41.12	41.70	42.28	42.86	43.45	44.04	44.62	45.21
23.5	41.03	41.62	42.20	42.78	43.37	43.96	44.55	45.14
24.0	40.95	41.54	42.12	42.71	43.30	43.89	44.48	45.08
24.5	40.88	41.47	42.06	42.65	43.24	43.83	44.42	45.02
25.0	40.81	41.40	41.99	42.58	43.18	43.77	44.37	44.97
25.5	40.75	41.34	41.93	42.53	43.12	43.72	44.32	44.92
26.0	40.69	41.29	41.88	42.48	43.07	43.67	44.27	44.87
26.5	40.64	41.24	41.83	42.43	43.03	43.63	44.23	44.83
27.0	40.59	41.19	41.79	42.38	42.98	43.59	44.19	44.79
27.5	40.55	41.15	41.74	42.34	42.95	43.55	44.15	44.76
28.0	40.51	41.11	41.71	42.31	42.91	43.51	44.12	44.73
28.5	40.47	41.07	41.67	42.27	42.88	43.48	44.09	44.70
29.0	40.43	41.03	41.64	42.24	42.85	43.45	44.06	44.67
29.5	40.40	41.00	41.61	42.21	42.82	43.43	44.04	44.65
30.0	40.37	40.97	41.58	42.19	42.79	43.40	44.01	44.62
35.0	40.17	40.78	41.40	42.01	42.63	43.25	43.86	44.48
40.0	40.08	40.70	41.32	41.94	42.56	43.18	43.80	44.42

QUARTERLY PAYMENTS TO AMORTIZE A $1,000 LOAN

YRS	18%	18¼%	18½%	18¾%	19%	19¼%	19½%	19¾%
.5	534.00	534.48	534.95	535.43	535.91	536.38	536.86	537.33
1.0	278.75	279.16	279.56	279.97	280.38	280.79	281.20	281.61
1.5	193.88	194.27	194.67	195.06	195.45	195.84	196.24	196.63
2.0	151.61	152.00	152.39	152.78	153.17	153.56	153.95	154.34
2.5	126.38	126.77	127.16	127.55	127.94	128.33	128.72	129.12
3.0	109.67	110.06	110.46	110.85	111.25	111.64	112.04	112.43
3.5	97.83	98.22	98.62	99.02	99.42	99.82	100.22	100.63
4.0	89.02	89.42	89.83	90.23	90.64	91.05	91.46	91.86
4.5	82.24	82.65	83.06	83.48	83.89	84.30	84.72	85.13
5.0	76.88	77.30	77.72	78.14	78.56	78.98	79.40	79.82
5.5	72.55	72.97	73.40	73.83	74.25	74.68	75.11	75.54
6.0	68.99	69.42	69.86	70.29	70.72	71.16	71.60	72.04
6.5	66.03	66.46	66.90	67.34	67.79	68.23	68.68	69.12
7.0	63.53	63.97	64.42	64.87	65.32	65.77	66.22	66.67
7.5	61.40	61.85	62.30	62.76	63.21	63.67	64.13	64.59
8.0	59.57	60.03	60.49	60.95	61.41	61.88	62.35	62.82
8.5	57.99	58.45	58.92	59.39	59.86	60.33	60.81	61.28
9.0	56.61	57.00	57.56	58.03	58.51	58.99	59.47	59.96
9.5	55.41	55.89	56.37	56.85	57.33	57.82	58.31	58.80
10.0	54.35	54.83	55.32	55.81	56.30	56.79	57.29	57.79
10.5	53.41	53.91	54.40	54.90	55.39	55.89	56.39	56.90
11.0	52.59	53.08	53.58	54.09	54.59	55.09	55.60	56.11
11.5	51.85	52.35	52.86	53.37	53.88	54.39	54.90	55.42
12.0	51.19	51.70	52.22	52.73	53.24	53.76	54.28	54.80
12.5	50.61	51.12	51.64	52.16	52.68	53.20	53.73	54.25
13.0	50.08	50.60	51.13	51.65	52.18	52.70	53.23	53.77
13.5	49.61	50.14	50.66	51.19	51.73	52.26	52.79	53.33
14.0	49.19	49.72	50.25	50.78	51.32	51.86	52.40	52.94
14.5	48.80	49.34	49.88	50.42	50.96	51.50	52.05	52.59
15.0	48.46	49.00	49.54	50.09	50.63	51.18	51.73	52.28
15.5	48.15	48.69	49.24	49.79	50.34	50.89	51.44	52.00
16.0	47.87	48.42	48.97	49.52	50.07	50.63	51.19	51.75
16.5	47.61	48.16	48.72	49.28	49.83	50.40	50.96	51.52
17.0	47.38	47.94	48.50	49.06	49.62	50.18	50.75	51.32
17.5	47.17	47.73	48.29	48.86	49.42	49.99	50.56	51.13
18.0	46.98	47.54	48.11	48.68	49.25	49.82	50.39	50.97
18.5	46.81	47.37	47.94	48.52	49.09	49.66	50.24	50.82
19.0	46.65	47.22	47.79	48.37	48.94	49.52	50.10	50.68
19.5	46.51	47.08	47.66	48.23	48.81	49.39	49.97	50.56
20.0	46.38	46.95	47.53	48.11	48.69	49.28	49.86	50.45
20.5	46.26	46.84	47.42	48.00	48.59	49.17	49.76	50.35
21.0	46.15	46.73	47.32	47.90	48.49	49.08	49.67	50.26
21.5	46.05	46.64	47.22	47.81	48.40	48.99	49.58	50.18
22.0	45.96	46.55	47.14	47.73	48.32	48.91	49.51	50.10
22.5	45.88	46.47	47.06	47.65	48.25	48.84	49.44	50.03
23.0	45.80	46.40	46.99	47.58	48.18	48.78	49.37	49.97
23.5	45.73	46.33	46.92	47.52	48.12	48.72	49.32	49.92
24.0	45.67	46.27	46.87	47.46	48.06	48.66	49.27	49.87
24.5	45.62	46.21	46.81	47.41	48.01	48.62	49.22	49.82
25.0	45.56	46.16	46.76	47.37	47.97	48.57	49.18	49.78
25.5	45.52	46.12	46.72	47.32	47.93	48.53	49.14	49.74
26.0	45.47	46.07	46.68	47.28	47.89	48.50	49.10	49.71
26.5	45.43	46.04	46.64	47.25	47.85	48.46	49.07	49.68
27.0	45.40	46.00	46.61	47.22	47.82	48.43	49.04	49.65
27.5	45.36	45.97	46.58	47.19	47.79	48.41	49.02	49.63
28.0	45.33	45.94	46.55	47.16	47.77	48.38	48.99	49.60
28.5	45.30	45.91	46.52	47.13	47.75	48.36	48.97	49.58
29.0	45.28	45.89	46.50	47.11	47.72	48.34	48.95	49.56
29.5	45.26	45.87	46.48	47.09	47.70	48.32	48.93	49.55
30.0	45.23	45.85	46.46	47.07	47.69	48.30	48.92	49.53
35.0	45.10	45.72	46.34	46.96	47.58	48.20	48.82	49.44
40.0	45.04	45.67	46.29	46.91	47.53	48.16	48.78	49.40

SEMI-ANNUAL PAYMENTS TO AMORTIZE A $1,000 LOAN

YRS	6%	6¼%	6½%	6¾%	7%	7¼%	7½%	7¾%
.5	1030.01	1031.25	1032.50	1033.75	1035.00	1036.25	1037.51	1038.75
1.0	522.62	523.56	524.51	525.46	526.41	527.35	528.30	529.25
1.5	353.54	354.39	355.24	356.09	356.94	357.79	358.65	359.50
2.0	269.03	269.84	270.64	271.45	272.26	273.06	273.87	274.68
2.5	218.36	219.14	219.92	220.70	221.49	222.27	223.06	223.84
3.0	184.60	185.37	186.13	186.90	187.67	188.44	189.22	189.99
3.5	160.51	161.27	162.03	162.79	163.55	164.31	165.08	165.85
4.0	142.46	143.21	143.97	144.72	145.48	146.24	147.00	147.77
4.5	128.44	129.19	129.94	130.69	131.45	132.21	132.97	133.73
5.0	117.24	117.98	118.74	119.49	120.25	121.01	121.77	122.53
5.5	108.08	108.83	109.58	110.34	111.10	111.86	112.62	113.39
6.0	100.47	101.22	101.97	102.73	103.49	104.25	105.02	105.79
6.5	94.03	94.79	95.54	96.30	97.07	97.83	98.60	99.37
7.0	88.53	89.29	90.05	90.81	91.58	92.35	93.12	93.89
7.5	83.77	84.53	85.29	86.06	86.83	87.60	88.38	89.16
8.0	79.62	80.38	81.15	81.92	82.69	83.47	84.25	85.04
8.5	75.96	76.72	77.49	78.27	79.05	79.83	80.62	81.41
9.0	72.71	73.48	74.26	75.04	75.82	76.61	77.40	78.20
9.5	69.82	70.59	71.37	72.16	72.95	73.74	74.54	75.34
10.0	67.22	68.00	68.78	69.57	70.37	71.16	71.97	72.77
10.5	64.88	65.66	66.45	67.24	68.04	68.85	69.65	70.47
11.0	62.75	63.54	64.33	65.13	65.94	66.75	67.56	68.38
11.5	60.82	61.61	62.41	63.21	64.02	64.84	65.66	66.48
12.0	59.05	59.85	60.65	61.46	62.28	63.10	63.92	64.76
12.5	57.43	58.24	59.04	59.86	60.68	61.51	62.34	63.17
13.0	55.94	56.75	57.56	58.38	59.21	60.04	60.88	61.72
13.5	54.57	55.38	56.20	57.03	57.86	58.69	59.54	60.39
14.0	53.30	54.12	54.94	55.77	56.61	57.45	58.30	59.16
14.5	52.12	52.94	53.77	54.61	55.45	56.30	57.15	58.02
15.0	51.02	51.85	52.69	53.53	54.38	55.23	56.09	56.96
15.5	50.00	50.84	51.68	52.52	53.38	54.24	55.11	55.98
16.0	49.05	49.89	50.73	51.59	52.45	53.31	54.19	55.07
16.5	48.16	49.00	49.85	50.71	51.58	52.45	53.33	54.22
17.0	47.33	48.18	49.03	49.89	50.76	51.64	52.53	53.42
17.5	46.54	47.40	48.26	49.13	50.00	50.89	51.78	52.68
18.0	45.81	46.67	47.53	48.41	49.29	50.18	51.08	51.98
18.5	45.12	45.98	46.85	47.73	48.62	49.51	50.42	51.33
19.0	44.46	45.33	46.21	47.09	47.99	48.89	49.80	50.71
19.5	43.85	44.72	45.60	46.49	47.39	48.30	49.21	50.14
20.0	43.27	44.15	45.03	45.93	46.83	47.74	48.66	49.59
20.5	42.72	43.60	44.49	45.39	46.30	47.22	48.15	49.08
21.0	42.20	43.09	43.98	44.89	45.80	46.73	47.66	48.60
21.5	41.70	42.60	43.50	44.41	45.33	46.26	47.20	48.14
22.0	41.23	42.13	43.04	43.96	44.88	45.82	46.76	47.71
22.5	40.79	41.69	42.61	43.53	44.46	45.40	46.35	47.30
23.0	40.37	41.28	42.19	43.12	44.06	45.00	45.95	46.92
23.5	39.97	40.88	41.80	42.73	43.67	44.62	45.58	46.55
24.0	39.58	40.50	41.43	42.37	43.31	44.27	45.23	46.20
24.5	39.22	40.14	41.07	42.02	42.97	43.93	44.90	45.88
25.0	38.87	39.80	40.74	41.68	42.64	43.60	44.58	45.56
25.5	38.54	39.47	40.41	41.37	42.33	43.30	44.28	45.27
26.0	38.22	39.16	40.11	41.06	42.03	43.01	43.99	44.98
26.5	37.92	38.86	39.81	40.77	41.75	42.73	43.72	44.72
27.0	37.63	38.58	39.53	40.50	41.48	42.46	43.46	44.46
27.5	37.35	38.30	39.27	40.24	41.22	42.21	43.21	44.22
28.0	37.09	38.04	39.01	39.99	40.97	41.97	42.97	43.99
28.5	36.84	37.80	38.77	39.75	40.74	41.74	42.75	43.77
29.0	36.59	37.56	38.53	39.52	40.51	41.52	42.53	43.56
29.5	36.36	37.33	38.31	39.30	40.30	41.31	42.33	43.36
30.0	36.14	37.11	38.09	39.09	40.09	41.11	42.13	43.16
35.0	34.34	35.36	36.38	37.42	38.47	39.52	40.59	41.67
40.0	33.12	34.17	35.23	36.31	37.39	38.48	39.59	40.70

SEMI-ANNUAL PAYMENTS TO AMORTIZE A $1,000 LOAN

YRS	8%	8¼%	8½%	8¾%	9%	9¼%	9½%	9¾%
.5	1040.00	1041.25	1042.50	1043.75	1045.00	1046.26	1047.50	1048.75
1.0	530.20	531.15	532.10	533.05	534.00	534.95	535.91	536.86
1.5	360.35	361.21	362.06	362.92	363.78	364.64	365.49	366.35
2.0	275.50	276.31	277.12	277.93	278.75	279.56	280.38	281.20
2.5	224.63	225.42	226.21	227.00	227.80	228.59	229.39	230.18
3.0	190.77	191.54	192.32	193.10	193.88	194.67	195.45	196.24
3.5	166.61	167.39	168.16	168.93	169.71	170.48	171.26	172.04
4.0	148.53	149.30	150.07	150.84	151.61	152.39	153.17	153.95
4.5	134.50	135.27	136.03	136.81	137.58	138.36	139.13	139.91
5.0	123.30	124.06	124.84	125.61	126.38	127.16	127.94	128.72
5.5	114.15	114.92	115.70	116.47	117.25	118.03	118.82	119.60
6.0	106.56	107.33	108.11	108.89	109.67	110.46	111.25	112.04
6.5	100.15	100.93	101.71	102.49	103.28	104.07	104.86	105.66
7.0	94.67	95.46	96.24	97.03	97.83	98.62	99.42	100.22
7.5	89.95	90.73	91.53	92.32	93.12	93.92	94.73	95.53
8.0	85.82	86.62	87.42	88.22	89.02	89.83	90.64	91.46
8.5	82.20	83.00	83.81	84.61	85.42	86.24	87.06	87.88
9.0	79.00	79.80	80.61	81.42	82.24	83.06	83.89	84.72
9.5	76.14	76.95	77.77	78.59	79.41	80.24	81.07	81.91
10.0	73.59	74.40	75.22	76.05	76.88	77.72	78.56	79.40
10.5	71.29	72.11	72.94	73.77	74.61	75.45	76.29	77.15
11.0	69.20	70.03	70.87	71.71	72.55	73.40	74.25	75.11
11.5	67.31	68.15	68.99	69.84	70.69	71.54	72.40	73.27
12.0	65.59	66.43	67.28	68.13	68.99	69.86	70.72	71.60
12.5	64.02	64.87	65.72	66.58	67.44	68.31	69.19	70.07
13.0	62.57	63.43	64.29	65.15	66.03	66.90	67.79	68.68
13.5	61.24	62.11	62.97	63.85	64.72	65.61	66.50	67.40
14.0	60.02	60.89	61.76	62.64	63.53	64.42	65.32	66.22
14.5	58.88	59.76	60.64	61.53	62.42	63.32	64.22	65.13
15.0	57.84	58.72	59.60	60.50	61.40	62.30	63.21	64.13
15.5	56.86	57.75	58.64	59.54	60.45	61.36	62.28	63.21
16.0	55.95	56.85	57.75	58.65	59.57	60.49	61.41	62.35
16.5	55.11	56.01	56.92	57.83	58.75	59.68	60.61	61.55
17.0	54.32	55.23	56.14	57.06	57.99	58.92	59.86	60.81
17.5	53.58	54.50	55.41	56.34	57.28	58.22	59.16	60.12
18.0	52.89	53.81	54.74	55.67	56.61	57.56	58.51	59.47
18.5	52.24	53.17	54.10	55.04	55.99	56.94	57.90	58.87
19.0	51.64	52.57	53.51	54.45	55.41	56.37	57.33	58.31
19.5	51.07	52.00	52.95	53.90	54.86	55.83	56.80	57.78
20.0	50.53	51.47	52.42	53.38	54.35	55.32	56.30	57.29
20.5	50.02	50.97	51.93	52.89	53.87	54.85	55.83	56.83
21.0	49.55	50.50	51.46	52.44	53.41	54.40	55.39	56.39
21.5	49.09	50.06	51.03	52.00	52.99	53.98	54.98	55.98
22.0	48.67	49.64	50.61	51.60	52.59	53.58	54.59	55.60
22.5	48.27	49.24	50.22	51.21	52.21	53.21	54.22	55.24
23.0	47.89	48.87	49.85	50.85	51.85	52.86	53.88	54.90
23.5	47.53	48.51	49.50	50.50	51.51	52.53	53.55	54.58
24.0	47.19	48.18	49.17	50.18	51.19	52.22	53.24	54.28
24.5	46.86	47.86	48.86	49.87	50.89	51.92	52.95	54.00
25.0	46.56	47.56	48.57	49.58	50.61	51.64	52.68	53.73
25.5	46.26	47.27	48.28	49.31	50.34	51.38	52.42	53.47
26.0	45.99	47.00	48.02	49.05	50.08	51.13	52.18	53.23
26.5	45.72	46.74	47.77	48.80	49.84	50.89	51.94	53.01
27.0	45.47	46.50	47.53	48.56	49.61	50.66	51.73	52.79
27.5	45.24	46.26	47.30	48.34	49.39	50.45	51.52	52.59
28.0	45.01	46.04	47.08	48.13	49.19	50.25	51.32	52.40
28.5	44.79	45.83	46.88	47.93	48.99	50.06	51.13	52.22
29.0	44.59	45.63	46.68	47.74	48.80	49.88	50.96	52.05
29.5	44.39	45.44	46.49	47.56	48.63	49.71	50.79	51.88
30.0	44.21	45.26	46.32	47.38	48.46	49.54	50.63	51.73
35.0	42.75	43.84	44.94	46.05	47.17	48.29	49.42	50.56
40.0	41.82	42.95	44.08	45.23	46.38	47.53	48.69	49.86

SEMI-ANNUAL PAYMENTS TO AMORTIZE A $1,000 LOAN

YRS	10%	10¼%	10½%	10¾%	11%	11¼%	11½%	11¾%
.5	1050.00	1051.25	1052.51	1053.76	1055.00	1056.25	1057.50	1058.75
1.0	537.81	538.76	539.72	540.67	541.62	542.58	543.53	544.49
1.5	367.21	368.07	368.94	369.80	370.66	371.52	372.39	373.25
2.0	282.02	282.84	283.66	284.48	285.30	286.12	286.95	287.77
2.5	230.98	231.78	232.58	233.38	234.18	234.98	235.79	236.59
3.0	197.02	197.81	198.60	199.39	200.18	200.98	201.77	202.57
3.5	172.82	173.61	174.39	175.18	175.97	176.76	177.55	178.34
4.0	154.73	155.51	156.29	157.08	157.87	158.66	159.45	160.25
4.5	140.70	141.48	142.27	143.05	143.84	144.64	145.43	146.23
5.0	129.51	130.30	131.09	131.88	132.67	133.47	134.27	135.07
5.5	120.39	121.19	121.98	122.78	123.58	124.38	125.18	125.99
6.0	112.83	113.63	114.43	115.23	116.03	116.84	117.65	118.47
6.5	106.46	107.26	108.07	108.88	109.69	110.50	111.32	112.14
7.0	101.03	101.84	102.65	103.47	104.28	105.11	105.93	106.76
7.5	96.35	97.16	97.98	98.80	99.63	100.46	101.29	102.13
8.0	92.27	93.10	93.92	94.75	95.59	96.42	97.27	98.11
8.5	88.70	89.53	90.37	91.21	92.05	92.89	93.74	94.59
9.0	85.55	86.39	87.23	88.08	88.92	89.78	90.64	91.50
9.5	82.75	83.60	84.44	85.30	86.16	87.02	87.88	88.75
10.0	80.25	81.10	81.96	82.82	83.68	84.55	85.43	86.31
10.5	78.00	78.86	79.73	80.60	81.47	82.35	83.23	84.12
11.0	75.98	76.84	77.72	78.59	79.48	80.36	81.25	82.15
11.5	74.14	75.02	75.90	76.78	77.67	78.57	79.47	80.37
12.0	72.48	73.36	74.25	75.14	76.04	76.94	77.85	78.77
12.5	70.96	71.85	72.75	73.65	74.55	75.47	76.38	77.30
13.0	69.57	70.47	71.37	72.28	73.20	74.12	75.04	75.97
13.5	68.30	69.20	70.12	71.03	71.96	72.89	73.82	74.76
14.0	67.13	68.04	68.96	69.89	70.82	71.76	72.70	73.65
14.5	66.05	66.97	67.90	68.83	69.77	70.72	71.67	72.62
15.0	65.06	65.99	66.92	67.86	68.81	69.76	70.72	71.68
15.5	64.14	65.07	66.02	66.97	67.92	68.88	69.85	70.82
16.0	63.29	64.23	65.18	66.14	67.10	68.07	69.04	70.02
16.5	62.50	63.45	64.41	65.37	66.34	67.32	68.30	69.28
17.0	61.76	62.72	63.69	64.66	65.63	66.62	67.61	68.60
17.5	61.08	62.04	63.02	63.99	64.98	65.97	66.97	67.97
18.0	60.44	61.41	62.39	63.38	64.37	65.37	66.37	67.38
18.5	59.84	60.83	61.81	62.81	63.80	64.81	65.82	66.84
19.0	59.29	60.28	61.27	62.27	63.28	64.29	65.31	66.33
19.5	58.77	59.76	60.76	61.77	62.78	63.80	64.83	65.86
20.0	58.28	59.28	60.29	61.31	62.33	63.35	64.38	65.42
20.5	57.83	58.83	59.85	60.87	61.90	62.93	63.97	65.01
21.0	57.40	58.41	59.43	60.46	61.49	62.53	63.58	64.63
21.5	57.00	58.02	59.05	60.08	61.12	62.16	63.22	64.27
22.0	56.62	57.65	58.68	59.72	60.77	61.82	62.88	63.94
22.5	56.27	57.30	58.34	59.38	60.44	61.49	62.56	63.63
23.0	55.93	56.97	58.02	59.07	60.13	61.19	62.26	63.34
23.5	55.62	56.66	57.71	58.77	59.84	60.91	61.98	63.06
24.0	55.32	56.37	57.43	58.49	59.56	60.64	61.72	62.81
24.5	55.04	56.10	57.16	58.23	59.31	60.39	61.48	62.57
25.0	54.78	55.84	56.91	57.99	59.07	60.15	61.25	62.35
25.5	54.53	55.60	56.67	57.75	58.84	59.93	61.03	62.13
26.0	54.30	55.37	56.45	57.54	58.63	59.72	60.83	61.94
26.5	54.08	55.16	56.24	57.33	58.43	59.53	60.64	61.75
27.0	53.87	54.95	56.04	57.14	58.24	59.34	60.46	61.58
27.5	53.67	54.76	55.85	56.95	58.06	59.17	60.29	61.41
28.0	53.49	54.58	55.68	56.78	57.89	59.01	60.13	61.26
28.5	53.31	54.41	55.51	56.62	57.73	58.86	59.98	61.11
29.0	53.14	54.24	55.35	56.46	57.59	58.71	59.84	60.98
29.5	52.98	54.09	55.20	56.32	57.44	58.57	59.71	60.85
30.0	52.83	53.94	55.06	56.18	57.31	58.45	59.59	60.73
35.0	51.70	52.85	54.01	55.17	56.33	57.50	58.68	59.86
40.0	51.03	52.21	53.40	54.58	55.77	56.97	58.17	59.37

SEMI-ANNUAL PAYMENTS TO AMORTIZE A $1,000 LOAN

YRS	12%	12¼%	12½%	12¾%	13%	13¼%	13½%	13¾%
.5	1060.00	1061.25	1062.50	1063.75	1065.00	1066.26	1067.50	1068.75
1.0	545.44	546.40	547.35	548.31	549.27	550.22	551.18	552.14
1.5	374.11	374.98	375.85	376.71	377.58	378.45	379.32	380.19
2.0	288.60	289.42	290.25	291.08	291.91	292.74	293.57	294.40
2.5	237.40	238.21	239.02	239.83	240.64	241.45	242.27	243.08
3.0	203.37	204.17	204.97	205.77	206.57	207.38	208.18	208.99
3.5	179.14	179.94	180.73	181.53	182.34	183.14	183.94	184.75
4.0	161.04	161.84	162.64	163.44	164.24	165.05	165.85	166.66
4.5	147.03	147.83	148.63	149.44	150.24	151.05	151.86	152.68
5.0	135.87	136.68	137.49	138.30	139.11	139.92	140.74	141.56
5.5	126.80	127.61	128.42	129.24	130.06	130.88	131.71	132.53
6.0	119.28	120.10	120.92	121.75	122.57	123.40	124.23	125.07
6.5	112.97	113.79	114.62	115.45	116.29	117.13	117.97	118.81
7.0	107.59	108.42	109.26	110.10	110.95	111.79	112.64	113.49
7.5	102.97	103.81	104.66	105.51	106.36	107.21	108.07	108.93
8.0	98.96	99.81	100.66	101.52	102.38	103.25	104.12	104.99
8.5	95.45	96.31	97.17	98.04	98.91	99.79	100.66	101.55
9.0	92.36	93.23	94.10	94.98	95.86	96.74	97.63	98.52
9.5	89.63	90.50	91.39	92.27	93.16	94.05	94.95	95.85
10.0	87.19	88.08	88.97	89.86	90.76	91.66	92.57	93.48
10.5	85.01	85.91	86.81	87.71	88.62	89.53	90.45	91.37
11.0	83.05	83.96	84.86	85.78	86.70	87.62	88.55	89.48
11.5	81.28	82.20	83.12	84.04	84.97	85.90	86.83	87.77
12.0	79.68	80.61	81.53	82.47	83.40	84.34	85.29	86.24
12.5	78.23	79.16	80.10	81.04	81.99	82.94	83.89	84.85
13.0	76.91	77.85	78.79	79.74	80.70	81.66	82.62	83.59
13.5	75.70	76.65	77.61	78.56	79.53	80.50	81.47	82.45
14.0	74.60	75.56	76.52	77.49	78.46	79.44	80.42	81.41
14.5	73.58	74.55	75.52	76.50	77.48	78.47	79.46	80.45
15.0	72.65	73.63	74.61	75.59	76.58	77.58	78.58	79.58
15.5	71.80	72.78	73.77	74.76	75.76	76.76	77.77	78.78
16.0	71.01	72.00	72.99	74.00	75.00	76.01	77.03	78.05
16.5	70.28	71.28	72.28	73.29	74.30	75.32	76.35	77.38
17.0	69.60	70.61	71.62	72.64	73.66	74.69	75.72	76.76
17.5	68.98	69.99	71.01	72.04	73.07	74.10	75.14	76.19
18.0	68.40	69.42	70.45	71.48	72.52	73.56	74.61	75.66
18.5	67.86	68.89	69.93	70.97	72.01	73.06	74.12	75.18
19.0	67.36	68.40	69.44	70.49	71.54	72.60	73.66	74.73
19.5	66.90	67.94	68.99	70.04	71.10	72.17	73.24	74.31
20.0	66.47	67.52	68.57	69.63	70.70	71.77	72.85	73.93
20.5	66.06	67.12	68.18	69.25	70.32	71.40	72.48	73.57
21.0	65.69	66.75	67.82	68.89	69.97	71.06	72.15	73.24
21.5	65.34	66.41	67.48	68.56	69.65	70.74	71.83	72.94
22.0	65.01	66.09	67.17	68.25	69.35	70.44	71.54	72.65
22.5	64.71	65.79	66.87	67.97	69.06	70.17	71.28	72.39
23.0	64.42	65.51	66.60	67.70	68.80	69.91	71.02	72.14
23.5	64.15	65.25	66.34	67.45	68.56	69.67	70.79	71.91
24.0	63.90	65.00	66.11	67.22	68.33	69.45	70.57	71.70
24.5	63.67	64.77	65.88	67.00	68.12	69.24	70.37	71.51
25.0	63.45	64.56	65.67	66.79	67.92	69.05	70.18	71.32
25.5	63.24	64.36	65.48	66.60	67.73	68.87	70.01	71.15
26.0	63.05	64.17	65.30	66.43	67.56	68.70	69.84	70.99
26.5	62.87	64.00	65.12	66.26	67.40	68.54	69.69	70.84
27.0	62.70	63.83	64.96	66.10	67.25	68.40	69.55	70.71
27.5	62.54	63.68	64.81	65.96	67.11	68.26	69.42	70.58
28.0	62.39	63.53	64.67	65.82	66.97	68.13	69.29	70.46
28.5	62.25	63.39	64.54	65.69	66.85	68.01	69.18	70.34
29.0	62.12	63.27	64.42	65.57	66.73	67.90	69.07	70.24
29.5	62.00	63.15	64.30	65.46	66.63	67.79	68.97	70.14
30.0	61.88	63.04	64.19	65.36	66.53	67.70	68.87	70.05
35.0	61.04	62.22	63.42	64.61	65.81	67.01	68.21	69.42
40.0	60.58	61.79	63.00	64.21	65.43	66.65	67.87	69.09

SEMI-ANNUAL PAYMENTS TO AMORTIZE A $1,000 LOAN

YRS	14%	14¼%	14½%	14¾%	15%	15¼%	15½%	15¾%
.5	1070.00	1071.25	1072.50	1073.75	1075.01	1076.25	1077.50	1078.75
1.0	553.10	554.06	555.01	555.97	556.93	557.89	558.85	559.81
1.5	381.06	381.93	382.80	383.67	384.54	385.42	386.29	387.16
2.0	295.23	296.07	296.90	297.74	298.57	299.41	300.25	301.09
2.5	243.90	244.71	245.53	246.35	247.17	247.99	248.81	249.64
3.0	209.80	210.61	211.42	212.24	213.05	213.87	214.68	215.50
3.5	185.56	186.37	187.18	187.99	188.81	189.62	190.44	191.26
4.0	167.47	168.28	169.10	169.91	170.73	171.55	172.37	173.20
4.5	153.49	154.31	155.13	155.95	156.77	157.60	158.42	159.25
5.0	142.38	143.21	144.03	144.86	145.69	146.52	147.36	148.20
5.5	133.36	134.19	135.03	135.86	136.70	137.54	138.39	139.23
6.0	125.91	126.75	127.59	128.43	129.28	130.13	130.99	131.84
6.5	119.66	120.50	121.36	122.21	123.07	123.93	124.79	125.66
7.0	114.35	115.21	116.07	116.93	117.80	118.67	119.55	120.42
7.5	109.80	110.67	111.54	112.41	113.29	114.17	115.06	115.94
8.0	105.86	106.74	107.62	108.51	109.40	110.29	111.18	112.08
8.5	102.43	103.32	104.21	105.11	106.01	106.91	107.81	108.72
9.0	99.42	100.32	101.22	102.12	103.03	103.95	104.86	105.78
9.5	96.76	97.67	98.58	99.50	100.42	101.34	102.27	103.20
10.0	94.40	95.32	96.24	97.17	98.10	99.03	99.97	100.91
10.5	92.29	93.22	94.16	95.09	96.03	96.98	97.93	98.88
11.0	90.41	91.35	92.29	93.24	94.19	95.15	96.11	97.07
11.5	88.72	89.67	90.62	91.58	92.54	93.51	94.48	95.45
12.0	87.19	88.15	89.12	90.08	91.06	92.03	93.01	93.99
12.5	85.82	86.78	87.76	88.73	89.72	90.70	91.69	92.69
13.0	84.57	85.54	86.53	87.51	88.50	89.50	90.50	91.50
13.5	83.43	84.42	85.41	86.41	87.41	88.41	89.42	90.44
14.0	82.40	83.39	84.39	85.40	86.41	87.42	88.44	89.47
14.5	81.45	82.46	83.47	84.48	85.50	86.53	87.55	88.59
15.0	80.59	81.61	82.62	83.65	84.68	85.71	86.75	87.79
15.5	79.80	80.82	81.85	82.88	83.92	84.96	86.01	87.06
16.0	79.08	80.11	81.15	82.19	83.23	84.28	85.33	86.39
16.5	78.41	79.45	80.50	81.55	82.60	83.66	84.72	85.79
17.0	77.80	78.85	79.90	80.96	82.02	83.09	84.16	85.23
17.5	77.24	78.29	79.35	80.42	81.49	82.56	83.64	84.72
18.0	76.72	77.78	78.85	79.92	81.00	82.08	83.17	84.26
18.5	76.24	77.31	78.39	79.47	80.55	81.64	82.73	83.83
19.0	75.80	76.88	77.96	79.05	80.14	81.23	82.33	83.44
19.5	75.39	76.48	77.56	78.66	79.76	80.86	81.96	83.08
20.0	75.01	76.11	77.20	78.30	79.41	80.51	81.63	82.74
20.5	74.66	75.76	76.86	77.97	79.08	80.20	81.32	82.44
21.0	74.34	75.44	76.55	77.67	78.78	79.90	81.03	82.16
21.5	74.04	75.15	76.27	77.38	78.51	79.63	80.77	81.90
22.0	73.76	74.88	76.00	77.12	78.25	79.38	80.52	81.66
22.5	73.50	74.63	75.75	76.88	78.02	79.15	80.30	81.44
23.0	73.26	74.39	75.52	76.66	77.80	78.94	80.09	81.24
23.5	73.04	74.17	75.31	76.45	77.60	78.75	79.90	81.05
24.0	72.84	73.97	75.11	76.26	77.41	78.56	79.72	80.88
24.5	72.64	73.79	74.93	76.08	77.24	78.40	79.56	80.72
25.0	72.46	73.61	74.76	75.92	77.08	78.24	79.41	80.58
25.5	72.30	73.45	74.61	75.77	76.93	78.10	79.27	80.44
26.0	72.14	73.30	74.46	75.62	76.79	77.96	79.14	80.31
26.5	72.00	73.16	74.32	75.49	76.66	77.84	79.02	80.20
27.0	71.87	73.03	74.20	75.37	76.55	77.72	78.91	80.09
27.5	71.74	72.91	74.08	75.26	76.44	77.62	78.80	79.99
28.0	71.63	72.80	73.97	75.15	76.33	77.52	78.71	79.90
28.5	71.52	72.69	73.87	75.05	76.24	77.43	78.62	79.82
29.0	71.42	72.60	73.78	74.96	76.15	77.35	78.54	79.74
29.5	71.32	72.50	73.69	74.88	76.07	77.27	78.46	79.66
30.0	71.23	72.42	73.61	74.80	76.00	77.19	78.39	79.60
35.0	70.62	71.84	73.05	74.26	75.48	76.70	77.92	79.15
40.0	70.32	71.55	72.77	74.00	75.24	76.47	77.70	78.94

SEMI-ANNUAL PAYMENTS TO AMORTIZE A $1,000 LOAN

YRS	16%	16¼%	16½%	16¾%	17%	17¼%	17½%	17¾%
.5	1080.00	1081.25	1082.50	1083.75	1085.00	1086.25	1087.50	1088.75
1.0	560.77	561.74	562.70	563.66	564.62	565.58	566.55	567.51
1.5	388.04	388.91	389.79	390.67	391.54	392.42	393.30	394.18
2.0	301.93	302.77	303.61	304.45	305.29	306.14	306.98	307.83
2.5	250.46	251.29	252.11	252.94	253.77	254.60	255.43	256.26
3.0	216.32	217.14	217.96	218.79	219.61	220.44	221.27	222.09
3.5	192.08	192.90	193.72	194.55	195.37	196.20	197.03	197.86
4.0	174.02	174.85	175.67	176.50	177.34	178.17	179.00	179.84
4.5	160.08	160.92	161.75	162.59	163.43	164.27	165.11	165.96
5.0	149.03	149.88	150.72	151.56	152.41	153.26	154.11	154.97
5.5	140.08	140.93	141.78	142.64	143.50	144.36	145.22	146.08
6.0	132.70	133.56	134.42	135.29	136.16	137.03	137.90	138.78
6.5	126.53	127.40	128.27	129.15	130.03	130.91	131.79	132.68
7.0	121.30	122.18	123.07	123.96	124.85	125.74	126.64	127.54
7.5	116.83	117.73	118.62	119.52	120.43	121.33	122.24	123.15
8.0	112.98	113.89	114.79	115.70	116.62	117.54	118.46	119.38
8.5	109.63	110.55	111.47	112.39	113.32	114.25	115.18	116.11
9.0	106.71	107.63	108.56	109.50	110.44	111.38	112.32	113.27
9.5	104.13	105.07	106.01	106.96	107.91	108.86	109.81	110.77
10.0	101.86	102.81	103.76	104.72	105.68	106.64	107.61	108.58
10.5	99.84	100.80	101.76	102.73	103.70	104.68	105.65	106.64
11.0	98.04	99.01	99.98	100.96	101.94	102.93	103.92	104.91
11.5	96.43	97.41	98.39	99.38	100.38	101.37	102.37	103.38
12.0	94.98	95.98	96.97	97.97	98.97	99.98	100.99	102.01
12.5	93.68	94.69	95.69	96.70	97.72	98.73	99.76	100.78
13.0	92.51	93.52	94.54	95.56	96.59	97.61	98.65	99.68
13.5	91.45	92.48	93.50	94.53	95.57	96.60	97.64	98.69
14.0	90.49	91.53	92.56	93.60	94.64	95.69	96.74	97.80
14.5	89.62	90.66	91.71	92.76	93.81	94.87	95.93	96.99
15.0	88.83	89.88	90.94	91.99	93.06	94.12	95.19	96.26
15.5	88.11	89.17	90.23	91.30	92.37	93.44	94.52	95.60
16.0	87.46	88.52	89.59	90.67	91.75	92.83	93.92	95.01
16.5	86.86	87.93	89.01	90.09	91.18	92.27	93.37	94.46
17.0	86.31	87.39	88.48	89.57	90.66	91.76	92.87	93.97
17.5	85.81	86.90	87.99	89.09	90.19	91.30	92.41	93.52
18.0	85.35	86.45	87.55	88.66	89.77	90.88	92.00	93.12
18.5	84.93	86.03	87.14	88.26	89.37	90.49	91.62	92.74
19.0	84.54	85.66	86.77	87.89	89.01	90.14	91.27	92.41
19.5	84.19	85.31	86.43	87.56	88.69	89.82	90.96	92.10
20.0	83.87	84.99	86.12	87.25	88.39	89.53	90.67	91.82
20.5	83.57	84.70	85.83	86.97	88.11	89.26	90.41	91.56
21.0	83.29	84.43	85.57	86.71	87.86	89.01	90.17	91.32
21.5	83.04	84.18	85.33	86.48	87.63	88.79	89.95	91.11
22.0	82.81	83.95	85.11	86.26	87.42	88.58	89.74	90.91
22.5	82.59	83.75	84.90	86.06	87.22	88.39	89.56	90.73
23.0	82.39	83.55	84.71	85.88	87.05	88.22	89.39	90.57
23.5	82.21	83.38	84.54	85.71	86.88	88.06	89.24	90.42
24.0	82.05	83.21	84.38	85.56	86.73	87.91	89.09	90.28
24.5	81.89	83.06	84.24	85.41	86.60	87.78	88.96	90.15
25.0	81.75	82.92	84.10	85.28	86.47	87.66	88.85	90.04
25.5	81.62	82.80	83.98	85.16	86.35	87.54	88.74	89.93
26.0	81.49	82.68	83.86	85.05	86.24	87.44	88.64	89.83
26.5	81.38	82.57	83.76	84.95	86.15	87.34	88.54	89.75
27.0	81.28	82.47	83.66	84.86	86.06	87.26	88.46	89.66
27.5	81.18	82.38	83.57	84.77	85.97	87.18	88.38	89.59
28.0	81.09	82.29	83.49	84.69	85.90	87.10	88.31	89.52
28.5	81.01	82.21	83.41	84.62	85.83	87.03	88.24	89.46
29.0	80.94	82.14	83.34	84.55	85.76	86.97	88.18	89.40
29.5	80.87	82.07	83.28	84.49	85.70	86.91	88.13	89.35
30.0	80.80	82.01	83.22	84.43	85.65	86.86	88.08	89.30
35.0	80.37	81.60	82.83	84.06	85.29	86.52	87.75	88.99
40.0	80.17	81.41	82.65	83.89	85.13	86.37	87.61	88.85

SEMI-ANNUAL PAYMENTS TO AMORTIZE A $1,000 LOAN

YRS	18%	18¼%	18½%	18¾%	19%	19¼%	19½%	19¾%
.5	1090.01	1091.26	1092.50	1093.75	1095.00	1096.26	1097.50	1098.75
1.0	568.47	569.44	570.40	571.37	572.33	573.30	574.26	575.23
1.5	395.06	395.94	396.82	397.70	398.58	399.47	400.35	401.24
2.0	308.67	309.52	310.37	311.22	312.07	312.92	313.77	314.62
2.5	257.10	257.93	258.77	259.60	260.44	261.28	262.12	262.96
3.0	222.92	223.76	224.59	225.42	226.26	227.09	227.93	228.77
3.5	198.70	199.53	200.37	201.20	202.04	202.88	203.72	204.57
4.0	180.68	181.52	182.36	183.21	184.05	184.90	185.75	186.60
4.5	166.80	167.65	168.50	169.36	170.21	171.07	171.92	172.78
5.0	155.83	156.68	157.54	158.41	159.27	160.14	161.01	161.88
5.5	146.95	147.82	148.69	149.57	150.44	151.32	152.20	153.08
6.0	139.66	140.54	141.42	142.30	143.19	144.08	144.98	145.87
6.5	133.57	134.46	135.36	136.26	137.16	138.06	138.97	139.87
7.0	128.44	129.34	130.25	131.16	132.07	132.99	133.91	134.83
7.5	124.06	124.98	125.90	126.82	127.75	128.68	129.61	130.54
8.0	120.30	121.23	122.17	123.10	124.04	124.98	125.92	126.87
8.5	117.05	117.99	118.94	119.89	120.84	121.79	122.75	123.71
9.0	114.22	115.17	116.13	117.09	118.05	119.02	119.99	120.96
9.5	111.74	112.70	113.67	114.64	115.62	116.60	117.58	118.56
10.0	109.55	110.53	111.51	112.49	113.48	114.47	115.47	116.46
10.5	107.62	108.61	109.60	110.60	111.60	112.60	113.61	114.62
11.0	105.91	106.91	107.91	108.92	109.93	110.95	111.96	112.99
11.5	104.39	105.40	106.41	107.43	108.45	109.48	110.51	111.54
12.0	103.03	104.05	105.08	106.11	107.14	108.18	109.21	110.26
12.5	101.81	102.84	103.88	104.92	105.96	107.01	108.06	109.12
13.0	100.72	101.76	102.81	103.86	104.91	105.97	107.03	108.10
13.5	99.74	100.79	101.85	102.91	103.97	105.04	106.11	107.19
14.0	98.86	99.92	100.99	102.06	103.13	104.21	105.29	106.37
14.5	98.06	99.13	100.21	101.29	102.37	103.46	104.54	105.64
15.0	97.34	98.42	99.51	100.59	101.69	102.78	103.88	104.98
15.5	96.69	97.78	98.87	99.97	101.07	102.17	103.28	104.39
16.0	96.10	97.20	98.30	99.40	100.51	101.62	102.74	103.86
16.5	95.57	96.67	97.78	98.89	100.01	101.13	102.25	103.38
17.0	95.08	96.19	97.31	98.43	99.55	100.68	101.81	102.94
17.5	94.64	95.76	96.89	98.01	99.14	100.28	101.41	102.55
18.0	94.24	95.37	96.50	97.63	98.77	99.91	101.05	102.20
18.5	93.88	95.01	96.15	97.29	98.43	99.58	100.73	101.88
19.0	93.54	94.68	95.83	96.97	98.12	99.28	100.43	101.59
19.5	93.24	94.39	95.54	96.69	97.85	99.00	100.17	101.33
20.0	92.96	94.12	95.27	96.43	97.59	98.76	99.92	101.09
20.5	92.71	93.87	95.03	96.20	97.36	98.53	99.70	100.88
21.0	92.48	93.65	94.81	95.98	97.15	98.33	99.50	100.68
21.5	92.27	93.44	94.61	95.79	96.96	98.14	99.32	100.51
22.0	92.08	93.25	94.43	95.61	96.79	97.97	99.16	100.35
22.5	91.91	93.08	94.26	95.45	96.63	97.82	99.01	100.20
23.0	91.75	92.93	94.11	95.30	96.49	97.68	98.87	100.07
23.5	91.60	92.79	93.97	95.17	96.36	97.55	98.75	99.95
24.0	91.47	92.66	93.85	95.04	96.24	97.44	98.64	99.84
24.5	91.34	92.54	93.73	94.93	96.13	97.33	98.54	99.74
25.0	91.23	92.43	93.63	94.83	96.03	97.24	98.44	99.65
25.5	91.13	92.33	93.53	94.74	95.94	97.15	98.36	99.57
26.0	91.04	92.24	93.44	94.65	95.86	97.07	98.28	99.50
26.5	90.95	92.16	93.36	94.57	95.79	97.00	98.21	99.43
27.0	90.87	92.08	93.29	94.50	95.72	96.93	98.15	99.37
27.5	90.80	92.01	93.22	94.44	95.65	96.87	98.09	99.31
28.0	90.73	91.95	93.16	94.38	95.60	96.82	98.04	99.26
28.5	90.67	91.89	93.11	94.33	95.55	96.77	97.99	99.22
29.0	90.62	91.83	93.05	94.28	95.50	96.72	97.95	99.18
29.5	90.57	91.79	93.01	94.23	95.46	96.68	97.91	99.14
30.0	90.52	91.74	92.97	94.19	95.42	96.64	97.87	99.10
35.0	90.22	91.46	92.69	93.93	95.17	96.41	97.65	98.89
40.0	90.10	91.34	92.58	93.83	95.07	96.32	97.56	98.81

ANNUAL PAYMENTS TO AMORTIZE A $1,000 LOAN

YRS	6%	6¼%	6½%	6¾%	7%	7¼%	7½%	7¾%
1.0	1060.00	1062.50	1065.00	1067.50	1070.00	1072.50	1075.01	1077.50
2.0	545.44	547.35	549.27	551.18	553.10	555.01	556.93	558.85
3.0	374.11	375.85	377.58	379.32	381.06	382.80	384.54	386.29
4.0	288.60	290.25	291.91	293.57	295.23	296.90	298.57	300.25
5.0	237.40	239.02	240.64	242.27	243.90	245.53	247.17	248.81
6.0	203.37	204.97	206.57	208.18	209.80	211.42	213.05	214.68
7.0	179.14	180.73	182.34	183.94	185.56	187.18	188.81	190.44
8.0	161.04	162.64	164.24	165.85	167.47	169.10	170.73	172.37
9.0	147.03	148.63	150.24	151.86	153.49	155.13	156.77	158.42
10.0	135.87	137.49	139.11	140.74	142.38	144.03	145.69	147.36
11.0	126.80	128.42	130.06	131.71	133.36	135.03	136.70	138.39
12.0	119.28	120.92	122.57	124.23	125.91	127.59	129.28	130.99
13.0	112.97	114.62	116.29	117.97	119.66	121.36	123.07	124.79
14.0	107.59	109.26	110.95	112.64	114.35	116.07	117.80	119.55
15.0	102.97	104.66	106.36	108.07	109.80	111.54	113.29	115.06
16.0	98.96	100.66	102.38	104.12	105.86	107.62	109.40	111.18
17.0	95.45	97.17	98.91	100.66	102.43	104.21	106.01	107.81
18.0	92.36	94.10	95.86	97.63	99.42	101.22	103.03	104.86
19.0	89.63	91.39	93.16	94.95	96.76	98.58	100.42	102.27
20.0	87.19	88.97	90.76	92.57	94.40	96.24	98.10	99.97
21.0	85.01	86.81	88.62	90.45	92.29	94.16	96.03	97.93
22.0	83.05	84.86	86.70	88.55	90.41	92.29	94.19	96.11
23.0	81.28	83.12	84.97	86.83	88.72	90.62	92.54	94.48
24.0	79.68	81.53	83.40	85.29	87.19	89.12	91.06	93.01
25.0	78.23	80.10	81.99	83.89	85.82	87.76	89.72	91.69
26.0	76.91	78.79	80.70	82.62	84.57	86.53	88.50	90.50
27.0	75.70	77.61	79.53	81.47	83.43	85.41	87.41	89.42
28.0	74.60	76.52	78.46	80.42	82.40	84.39	86.41	88.44
29.0	73.58	75.52	77.48	79.46	81.45	83.47	85.50	87.55
30.0	72.65	74.61	76.58	78.58	80.59	82.62	84.68	86.75
35.0	68.98	71.01	73.07	75.14	77.24	79.35	81.49	83.64
40.0	66.47	68.57	70.70	72.85	75.01	77.20	79.41	81.63

ANNUAL PAYMENTS TO AMORTIZE A $1,000 LOAN

YRS	8%	8¼%	8½%	8¾%	9%	9¼%	9½%	9¾%
1.0	1080.00	1082.50	1085.00	1087.50	1090.01	1092.50	1095.00	1097.50
2.0	560.77	562.70	564.62	566.55	568.47	570.40	572.33	574.26
3.0	388.04	389.79	391.54	393.30	395.06	396.82	398.58	400.35
4.0	301.93	303.61	305.29	306.98	308.67	310.37	312.07	313.77
5.0	250.46	252.11	253.77	255.43	257.10	258.77	260.44	262.12
6.0	216.32	217.96	219.61	221.27	222.92	224.59	226.26	227.93
7.0	192.08	193.72	195.37	197.03	198.70	200.37	202.04	203.72
8.0	174.02	175.67	177.34	179.00	180.68	182.36	184.05	185.75
9.0	160.08	161.75	163.43	165.11	166.80	168.50	170.21	171.92
10.0	149.03	150.72	152.41	154.11	155.83	157.54	159.27	161.01
11.0	140.08	141.78	143.50	145.22	146.95	148.69	150.44	152.20
12.0	132.70	134.42	136.16	137.90	139.66	141.42	143.19	144.98
13.0	126.53	128.27	130.03	131.79	133.57	135.36	137.16	138.97
14.0	121.30	123.07	124.85	126.64	128.44	130.25	132.07	133.91
15.0	116.83	118.62	120.43	122.24	124.06	125.90	127.75	129.61
16.0	112.98	114.79	116.62	118.46	120.30	122.17	124.04	125.92
17.0	109.63	111.47	113.32	115.18	117.05	118.94	120.84	122.75
18.0	106.71	108.56	110.44	112.32	114.22	116.13	118.05	119.99
19.0	104.13	106.01	107.91	109.81	111.74	113.67	115.62	117.58
20.0	101.86	103.76	105.68	107.61	109.55	111.51	113.48	115.47
21.0	99.84	101.76	103.70	105.65	107.62	109.60	111.60	113.61
22.0	98.04	99.98	101.94	103.92	105.91	107.91	109.93	111.96
23.0	96.43	98.39	100.38	102.37	104.39	106.41	108.45	110.51
24.0	94.98	96.97	98.97	100.99	103.03	105.08	107.14	109.21
25.0	93.68	95.69	97.72	99.76	101.81	103.88	105.96	108.06
26.0	92.51	94.54	96.59	98.65	100.72	102.81	104.91	107.03
27.0	91.45	93.50	95.57	97.64	99.74	101.85	103.97	106.11
28.0	90.49	92.56	94.64	96.74	98.86	100.99	103.13	105.29
29.0	89.62	91.71	93.81	95.93	98.06	100.21	102.37	104.54
30.0	88.83	90.94	93.06	95.19	97.34	99.51	101.69	103.88
35.0	85.81	87.99	90.19	92.41	94.64	96.89	99.14	101.41
40.0	83.87	86.12	88.39	90.67	92.96	95.27	97.59	99.92

ANNUAL PAYMENTS TO AMORTIZE A $1,000 LOAN

YRS	10%	10¼%	10½%	10¾%	11%	11¼%	11½%	11¾%
1.0	1100.00	1102.50	1105.00	1107.50	1110.00	1112.50	1115.00	1117.50
2.0	576.20	578.13	580.06	582.00	583.94	585.88	587.82	589.76
3.0	402.12	403.89	405.66	407.44	409.22	411.00	412.78	414.57
4.0	315.48	317.18	318.90	320.61	322.33	324.05	325.78	327.51
5.0	263.80	265.49	267.18	268.88	270.58	272.28	273.99	275.70
6.0	229.61	231.30	232.99	234.68	236.38	238.09	239.80	241.51
7.0	205.41	207.10	208.80	210.51	212.22	213.94	215.66	217.39
8.0	187.45	189.16	190.87	192.60	194.33	196.06	197.80	199.55
9.0	173.65	175.37	177.11	178.86	180.61	182.37	184.13	185.90
10.0	162.75	164.50	166.26	168.03	169.81	171.59	173.38	175.18
11.0	153.97	155.74	157.53	159.32	161.13	162.94	164.76	166.58
12.0	146.77	148.57	150.38	152.20	154.03	155.87	157.72	159.58
13.0	140.78	142.61	144.45	146.30	148.16	150.02	151.90	153.79
14.0	135.75	137.61	139.47	141.35	143.23	145.13	147.04	148.95
15.0	131.48	133.36	135.25	137.16	139.07	140.99	142.93	144.87
16.0	127.82	129.73	131.65	133.58	135.52	137.47	139.44	141.41
17.0	124.67	126.60	128.55	130.51	132.48	134.46	136.45	138.45
18.0	121.94	123.90	125.87	127.85	129.85	131.85	133.87	135.90
19.0	119.55	121.54	123.54	125.55	127.57	129.60	131.65	133.70
20.0	117.46	119.48	121.50	123.53	125.58	127.64	129.71	131.79
21.0	115.63	117.66	119.71	121.77	123.84	125.93	128.02	130.13
22.0	114.01	116.07	118.14	120.22	122.32	124.43	126.54	128.67
23.0	112.58	114.66	116.75	118.86	120.98	123.11	125.25	127.40
24.0	111.30	113.41	115.52	117.65	119.79	121.94	124.11	126.28
25.0	110.17	112.30	114.43	116.58	118.75	120.92	123.10	125.30
26.0	109.16	111.31	113.47	115.64	117.82	120.01	122.22	124.43
27.0	108.26	110.43	112.60	114.79	116.99	119.21	121.43	123.66
28.0	107.46	109.64	111.83	114.04	116.26	118.49	120.73	122.99
29.0	106.73	108.93	111.15	113.37	115.61	117.86	120.12	122.39
30.0	106.08	108.30	110.53	112.78	115.03	117.29	119.57	121.85
35.0	103.69	105.99	108.29	110.61	112.93	115.27	117.61	119.96
40.0	102.26	104.62	106.98	109.35	111.72	114.11	116.50	118.90

ANNUAL PAYMENTS TO AMORTIZE A $1,000 LOAN

YRS	12%	12¼%	12½%	12¾%	13%	13¼%	13½%	13¾%
1.0	1120.00	1122.50	1125.00	1127.50	1130.00	1132.50	1135.00	1137.50
2.0	591.70	593.65	595.59	597.54	599.49	601.44	603.39	605.34
3.0	416.35	418.14	419.94	421.73	423.53	425.33	427.13	428.93
4.0	329.24	330.97	332.71	334.45	336.20	337.95	339.70	341.45
5.0	277.41	279.13	280.86	282.59	284.32	286.06	287.80	289.54
6.0	243.23	244.96	246.68	248.42	250.16	251.90	253.65	255.40
7.0	219.12	220.86	222.61	224.36	226.12	227.88	229.65	231.42
8.0	201.31	203.07	204.84	206.61	208.39	210.18	211.97	213.77
9.0	187.68	189.47	191.27	193.07	194.87	196.69	198.51	200.34
10.0	176.99	178.80	180.63	182.46	184.29	186.14	187.99	189.85
11.0	168.42	170.26	172.12	173.98	175.85	177.72	179.61	181.50
12.0	161.44	163.32	165.20	167.09	168.99	170.90	172.82	174.74
13.0	155.68	157.59	159.50	161.42	163.36	165.30	167.24	169.20
14.0	150.88	152.81	154.76	156.71	158.67	160.64	162.63	164.62
15.0	146.83	148.79	150.77	152.75	154.75	156.75	158.76	160.78
16.0	143.40	145.39	147.39	149.41	151.43	153.46	155.51	157.56
17.0	140.46	142.48	144.52	146.56	148.61	150.68	152.75	154.83
18.0	137.94	139.99	142.05	144.12	146.21	148.30	150.40	152.51
19.0	135.77	137.85	139.93	142.03	144.14	146.26	148.38	150.52
20.0	133.88	135.99	138.10	140.22	142.36	144.50	146.66	148.82
21.0	132.25	134.37	136.51	138.66	140.82	142.99	145.17	147.35
22.0	130.82	132.97	135.13	137.30	139.48	141.68	143.88	146.09
23.0	129.56	131.74	133.92	136.12	138.32	140.54	142.76	144.99
24.0	128.47	130.66	132.87	135.09	137.31	139.55	141.79	144.05
25.0	127.50	129.72	131.95	134.18	136.43	138.69	140.95	143.22
26.0	126.66	128.89	131.14	133.39	135.66	137.93	140.22	142.51
27.0	125.91	128.16	130.43	132.70	134.98	137.28	139.57	141.88
28.0	125.25	127.52	129.80	132.09	134.39	136.70	139.02	141.34
29.0	124.67	126.95	129.25	131.56	133.87	136.20	138.53	140.86
30.0	124.15	126.45	128.77	131.09	133.42	135.75	138.10	140.45
35.0	122.32	124.69	127.06	129.45	131.83	134.23	136.63	139.04
40.0	121.31	123.72	126.14	128.56	130.99	133.42	135.86	138.30

ANNUAL PAYMENTS TO AMORTIZE A $1,000 LOAN

YRS	14%	14¼%	14½%	14¾%	15%	15¼%	15½%	15¾%
1.0	1140.00	1142.50	1145.00	1147.50	1150.00	1152.50	1155.00	1157.50
2.0	607.29	609.25	611.21	613.16	615.12	617.08	619.04	621.00
3.0	430.74	432.54	434.35	436.17	437.98	439.80	441.62	443.44
4.0	343.21	344.97	346.73	348.50	350.27	352.04	353.82	355.60
5.0	291.29	293.04	294.80	296.56	298.32	300.09	301.86	303.64
6.0	257.16	258.93	260.69	262.47	264.24	266.02	267.81	269.60
7.0	233.20	234.98	236.77	238.57	240.37	242.17	243.98	245.80
8.0	215.58	217.39	219.20	221.03	222.86	224.69	226.53	228.38
9.0	202.17	204.01	205.86	207.72	209.58	211.45	213.32	215.20
10.0	191.72	193.59	195.47	197.36	199.26	201.16	203.07	204.98
11.0	183.40	185.31	187.22	189.14	191.07	193.01	194.96	196.91
12.0	176.67	178.62	180.56	182.52	184.49	186.46	188.44	190.43
13.0	171.17	173.14	175.13	177.12	179.12	181.12	183.14	185.16
14.0	166.61	168.62	170.64	172.66	174.69	176.73	178.78	180.84
15.0	162.81	164.85	166.90	168.96	171.02	173.10	175.18	177.27
16.0	159.62	161.69	163.77	165.86	167.95	170.06	172.17	174.29
17.0	156.92	159.02	161.13	163.25	165.37	167.51	169.65	171.80
18.0	154.63	156.75	158.89	161.04	163.19	165.35	167.52	169.70
19.0	152.67	154.82	156.99	159.16	161.34	163.53	165.73	167.93
20.0	150.99	153.17	155.36	157.56	159.77	161.98	164.20	166.43
21.0	149.55	151.76	153.97	156.19	158.42	160.66	162.91	165.16
22.0	148.31	150.54	152.77	155.02	157.27	159.53	161.80	164.08
23.0	147.24	149.49	151.74	154.01	156.28	158.56	160.85	163.15
24.0	146.31	148.58	150.86	153.14	155.43	157.74	160.04	162.36
25.0	145.50	147.79	150.09	152.39	154.70	157.02	159.35	161.68
26.0	144.81	147.11	149.43	151.75	154.07	156.41	158.75	161.10
27.0	144.20	146.52	148.85	151.19	153.53	155.88	158.24	160.60
28.0	143.67	146.01	148.35	150.70	153.06	155.43	157.80	160.17
29.0	143.21	145.56	147.92	150.29	152.66	155.03	157.42	159.80
30.0	142.81	145.17	147.54	149.92	152.31	154.69	157.09	159.49
35.0	141.45	143.86	146.28	148.71	151.14	153.57	156.01	158.45
40.0	140.75	143.20	145.65	148.11	150.57	153.03	155.49	157.96

ANNUAL PAYMENTS TO AMORTIZE A $1,000 LOAN

YRS	16%	16¼%	16½%	16¾%	17%	17¼%	17½%	17¾%
1.0	1160.00	1162.50	1165.00	1167.50	1170.00	1172.50	1175.00	1177.50
2.0	622.97	624.93	626.90	628.87	630.83	632.80	634.78	636.75
3.0	445.26	447.09	448.92	450.75	452.58	454.41	456.25	458.09
4.0	357.38	359.17	360.95	362.74	364.54	366.34	368.14	369.94
5.0	305.41	307.20	308.98	310.77	312.57	314.37	316.17	317.97
6.0	271.39	273.19	275.00	276.81	278.62	280.44	282.26	284.08
7.0	247.62	249.44	251.27	253.11	254.95	256.80	258.65	260.51
8.0	230.23	232.09	233.95	235.82	237.69	239.58	241.46	243.35
9.0	217.09	218.98	220.88	222.78	224.70	226.61	228.54	230.46
10.0	206.91	208.84	210.77	212.71	214.66	216.62	218.58	220.55
11.0	198.87	200.83	202.80	204.78	206.77	208.76	210.76	212.77
12.0	192.42	194.42	196.43	198.45	200.47	202.50	204.54	206.58
13.0	187.19	189.23	191.27	193.32	195.38	197.45	199.52	201.60
14.0	182.90	184.97	187.05	189.14	191.24	193.34	195.45	197.56
15.0	179.36	181.47	183.58	185.70	187.83	189.96	192.10	194.25
16.0	176.42	178.55	180.70	182.85	185.01	187.18	189.35	191.53
17.0	173.96	176.12	178.30	180.48	182.67	184.86	187.06	189.27
18.0	171.89	174.08	176.29	178.49	180.71	182.93	185.16	187.40
19.0	170.15	172.37	174.60	176.83	179.07	181.32	183.58	185.84
20.0	168.67	170.92	173.17	175.43	177.70	179.97	182.25	184.53
21.0	167.42	169.69	171.96	174.25	176.54	178.83	181.13	183.44
22.0	166.36	168.65	170.94	173.25	175.56	177.87	180.19	182.52
23.0	165.45	167.76	170.08	172.40	174.73	177.06	179.40	181.74
24.0	164.68	167.01	169.34	171.68	174.02	176.38	178.73	181.09
25.0	164.02	166.36	168.71	171.07	173.43	175.79	178.17	180.54
26.0	163.45	165.81	168.18	170.55	172.92	175.30	177.69	180.08
27.0	162.97	165.34	167.72	170.10	172.49	174.89	177.28	179.69
28.0	162.55	164.94	167.33	169.73	172.13	174.53	176.94	179.35
29.0	162.20	164.59	167.00	169.40	171.81	174.23	176.65	179.07
30.0	161.89	164.30	166.71	169.13	171.55	173.97	176.40	178.83
35.0	160.90	163.35	165.80	168.25	170.71	173.16	175.63	178.09
40.0	160.43	162.90	165.37	167.85	170.32	172.80	175.28	177.76

ANNUAL PAYMENTS TO AMORTIZE A $1,000 LOAN

YRS	18%	18¼%	18½%	18¾%	19%	19¼%	19½%	19¾%
1.0	1180.00	1182.50	1185.00	1187.50	1190.00	1192.50	1195.00	1197.50
2.0	638.72	640.70	642.67	644.65	646.63	648.61	650.59	652.57
3.0	459.93	461.77	463.62	465.46	467.31	469.16	471.02	472.87
4.0	371.74	373.55	375.36	377.18	379.00	380.82	382.64	384.47
5.0	319.78	321.60	323.41	325.23	327.06	328.88	330.71	332.55
6.0	285.92	287.75	289.59	291.43	293.28	295.13	296.99	298.85
7.0	262.37	264.23	266.10	267.98	269.86	271.75	273.64	275.53
8.0	245.25	247.15	249.06	250.97	252.89	254.81	256.74	258.68
9.0	232.40	234.34	236.29	238.24	240.20	242.16	244.13	246.10
10.0	222.52	224.50	226.49	228.48	230.48	232.48	234.49	236.51
11.0	214.78	216.80	218.83	220.86	222.90	224.94	226.99	229.05
12.0	208.63	210.69	212.75	214.82	216.90	218.98	221.07	223.17
13.0	203.69	205.79	207.89	209.99	212.11	214.23	216.35	218.49
14.0	199.68	201.81	203.95	206.09	208.24	210.39	212.56	214.72
15.0	196.41	198.57	200.74	202.91	205.10	207.29	209.48	211.68
16.0	193.72	195.91	198.11	200.32	202.53	204.75	206.97	209.20
17.0	191.49	193.71	195.94	198.18	200.42	202.67	204.92	207.18
18.0	189.64	191.89	194.15	196.41	198.68	200.95	203.23	205.52
19.0	188.11	190.38	192.66	194.95	197.24	199.54	201.84	204.15
20.0	186.82	189.12	191.43	193.74	196.05	198.37	200.70	203.03
21.0	185.75	188.07	190.39	192.72	195.06	197.40	199.74	202.09
22.0	184.85	187.19	189.53	191.88	194.23	196.59	198.96	201.32
23.0	184.10	186.45	188.81	191.18	193.55	195.92	198.30	200.68
24.0	183.46	185.83	188.21	190.59	192.97	195.36	197.75	200.15
25.0	182.92	185.31	187.70	190.09	192.49	194.89	197.30	199.71
26.0	182.47	184.87	187.27	189.68	192.09	194.50	196.92	199.34
27.0	182.09	184.50	186.92	189.33	191.75	194.18	196.61	199.04
28.0	181.77	184.19	186.61	189.04	191.47	193.91	196.34	198.78
29.0	181.50	183.93	186.36	188.80	191.24	193.68	196.12	198.57
30.0	181.27	183.71	186.15	188.59	191.04	193.49	195.94	198.39
35.0	180.56	183.02	185.49	187.96	190.44	192.91	195.39	197.87
40.0	180.25	182.73	185.21	187.70	190.19	192.67	195.16	197.65

TERM→ AMOUNT	3 YEARS	5 YEARS	10 YEARS	15 YEARS	20 YEARS	25 YEARS	30 YEARS	40 YEARS
$ 100	3.09	1.99	1.17	.90	.78	.71	.67	.63
200	6.18	3.97	2.33	1.80	1.56	1.42	1.34	1.25
300	9.27	5.95	3.49	2.70	2.33	2.13	2.00	1.87
400	12.36	7.93	4.65	3.60	3.11	2.83	2.67	2.49
500	15.44	9.91	5.81	4.50	3.88	3.54	3.33	3.11
600	18.53	11.89	6.97	5.40	4.66	4.25	4.00	3.73
700	21.62	13.87	8.13	6.30	5.43	4.95	4.66	4.36
800	24.71	15.85	9.29	7.20	6.21	5.66	5.33	4.98
900	27.79	17.83	10.45	8.09	6.98	6.37	5.99	5.60
1 000	30.88	19.81	11.62	8.99	7.76	7.07	6.66	6.22
1 000	30.88	19.81	11.62	8.99	7.76	7.07	6.66	6.22
2 000	61.76	39.61	23.23	17.98	15.51	14.14	13.31	12.43
3 000	92.64	59.41	34.84	26.97	23.26	21.21	19.96	18.65
4 000	123.51	79.21	46.45	35.96	31.02	28.28	26.62	24.86
5 000	154.39	99.01	58.06	44.95	38.77	35.34	33.27	31.08
6 000	185.27	118.81	69.67	53.93	46.52	42.41	39.92	37.29
7 000	216.14	138.61	81.28	62.92	54.28	49.48	46.58	43.51
8 000	247.02	158.41	92.89	71.91	62.03	56.55	53.23	49.72
9 000	277.90	178.22	104.50	80.90	69.78	63.62	59.88	55.93
10 000	308.78	198.02	116.11	89.89	77.53	70.68	66.54	62.15
11 000	339.65	217.82	127.72	98.88	85.29	77.75	73.19	68.36
12 000	370.53	237.62	139.34	107.86	93.04	84.82	79.84	74.58
13 000	401.41	257.42	150.95	116.85	100.79	91.89	86.49	80.79
14 000	432.28	277.22	162.56	125.84	108.55	98.95	93.15	87.01
15 000	463.16	297.02	174.17	134.83	116.30	106.02	99.80	93.22
16 000	494.04	316.82	185.78	143.82	124.05	113.09	106.45	99.43
17 000	524.92	336.63	197.39	152.81	131.81	120.16	113.11	105.65
18 000	555.79	356.43	209.00	161.79	139.56	127.23	119.76	111.86
19 000	586.67	376.23	220.61	170.78	147.31	134.29	126.41	118.08
20 000	617.55	396.03	232.22	179.77	155.06	141.36	133.07	124.29
21 000	648.42	415.83	243.83	188.76	162.82	148.43	139.72	130.51
22 000	679.30	435.63	255.44	197.75	170.57	155.50	146.37	136.72
23 000	710.18	455.43	267.05	206.74	178.32	162.56	153.02	142.93
24 000	741.06	475.23	278.67	215.72	186.08	169.63	159.68	149.15
25 000	771.93	495.03	290.28	224.71	193.83	176.70	166.33	155.36
26 000	802.81	514.84	301.89	233.70	201.58	183.77	172.98	161.58
27 000	833.69	534.64	313.50	242.69	209.34	190.84	179.64	167.79
28 000	864.56	554.44	325.11	251.68	217.09	197.90	186.29	174.01
29 000	895.44	574.24	336.72	260.67	224.84	204.97	192.94	180.22
30 000	926.32	594.04	348.33	269.65	232.59	212.04	199.60	186.43
31 000	957.20	613.84	359.94	278.64	240.35	219.11	206.25	192.65
32 000	988.07	633.64	371.55	287.63	248.10	226.17	212.90	198.86
33 000	1018.95	653.44	383.16	296.62	255.85	233.24	219.55	205.08
34 000	1049.83	673.25	394.77	305.61	263.61	240.31	226.21	211.29
35 000	1080.70	693.05	406.38	314.59	271.36	247.38	232.86	217.51
36 000	1111.58	712.85	418.00	323.58	279.11	254.45	239.51	223.72
37 000	1142.46	732.65	429.61	332.57	286.87	261.51	246.17	229.93
38 000	1173.33	752.45	441.22	341.56	294.62	268.58	252.82	236.15
39 000	1204.21	772.25	452.83	350.55	302.37	275.65	259.47	242.36
40 000	1235.09	792.05	464.44	359.54	310.12	282.72	266.13	248.58
41 000	1265.97	811.85	476.05	368.52	317.88	289.78	272.78	254.79
42 000	1296.84	831.66	487.66	377.51	325.63	296.85	279.43	261.01
43 000	1327.72	851.46	499.27	386.50	333.38	303.92	286.09	267.22
44 000	1358.60	871.26	510.88	395.49	341.14	310.99	292.74	273.43
45 000	1389.47	891.06	522.49	404.48	348.89	318.06	299.39	279.65

FOR OTHER RATES AND TERMS SEE PAGE A-1.

TERM▶ AMOUNT	10 YEARS	15 YEARS	20 YEARS	25 YEARS	30 YEARS	40 YEARS
$46 000	534.10	413.47	356.64	325.12	306.04	285.86
47 000	545.71	422.45	364.40	332.19	312.70	292.08
48 000	557.33	431.44	372.15	339.26	319.35	298.29
49 000	568.94	440.43	379.90	346.33	326.00	304.51
50 000	580.55	449.42	387.65	353.39	332.66	310.72
51 000	592.16	458.41	395.41	360.46	339.31	316.93
52 000	603.77	467.40	403.16	367.53	345.96	323.15
53 000	615.38	476.38	410.91	374.60	352.62	329.36
54 000	626.99	485.37	418.67	381.67	359.27	335.58
55 000	638.60	494.36	426.42	388.73	365.92	341.79
56 000	650.21	503.35	434.17	395.80	372.57	348.01
57 000	661.82	512.34	441.93	402.87	379.23	354.22
58 000	673.43	521.33	449.68	409.94	385.88	360.44
59 000	685.05	530.31	457.43	417.00	392.53	366.65
60 000	696.66	539.30	465.18	424.07	399.19	372.86
61 000	708.27	548.29	472.94	431.14	405.84	379.08
62 000	719.88	557.28	480.69	438.21	412.49	385.29
63 000	731.49	566.27	488.44	445.28	419.15	391.51
64 000	743.10	575.26	496.20	452.34	425.80	397.72
65 000	754.71	584.24	503.95	459.41	432.45	403.94
66 000	766.32	593.23	511.70	466.48	439.10	410.15
67 000	777.93	602.22	519.46	473.55	445.76	416.36
68 000	789.54	611.21	527.21	480.61	452.41	422.58
69 000	801.15	620.20	534.96	487.68	459.06	428.79
70 000	812.76	629.18	542.71	494.75	465.72	435.01
71 000	824.38	638.17	550.47	501.82	472.37	441.22
72 000	835.99	647.16	558.22	508.89	479.02	447.44
73 000	847.60	656.15	565.97	515.95	485.68	453.65
74 000	859.21	665.14	573.73	523.02	492.33	459.86
75 000	870.82	674.13	581.48	530.09	498.98	466.08
76 000	882.43	683.11	589.23	537.16	505.63	472.29
77 000	894.04	692.10	596.99	544.22	512.29	478.51
78 000	905.65	701.09	604.74	551.29	518.94	484.72
79 000	917.26	710.08	612.49	558.36	525.59	490.94
80 000	928.87	719.07	620.24	565.43	532.25	497.15
81 000	940.48	728.06	628.00	572.50	538.90	503.36
82 000	952.09	737.04	635.75	579.56	545.55	509.58
83 000	963.71	746.03	643.50	586.63	552.21	515.79
84 000	975.32	755.02	651.26	593.70	558.86	522.01
85 000	986.93	764.01	659.01	600.77	565.51	528.22
86 000	998.54	773.00	666.76	607.84	572.17	534.44
87 000	1010.15	781.99	674.52	614.90	578.82	540.65
88 000	1021.76	790.97	682.27	621.97	585.47	546.86
89 000	1033.37	799.96	690.02	629.04	592.12	553.08
90 000	1044.98	808.95	697.77	636.11	598.78	559.29
91 000	1056.59	817.94	705.53	643.17	605.43	565.51
92 000	1068.20	826.93	713.28	650.24	612.08	571.72
93 000	1079.81	835.92	721.03	657.31	618.74	577.94
94 000	1091.42	844.90	728.79	664.38	625.39	584.15
95 000	1103.04	853.89	736.54	671.45	632.04	590.36
96 000	1114.65	862.88	744.29	678.51	638.70	596.58
97 000	1126.26	871.87	752.04	685.58	645.35	602.79
98 000	1137.87	880.86	759.80	692.65	652.00	609.01
99 000	1149.48	889.84	767.55	699.72	658.65	615.22
100 000	1161.09	898.83	775.30	706.78	665.31	621.44

FOR **OTHER RATES AND TERMS** *SEE PAGE A-1.*

MONTHLY LOAN AMORTIZATION PAYMENTS

TERM➡ AMOUNT	3 YEARS	5 YEARS	10 YEARS	15 YEARS	20 YEARS	25 YEARS	30 YEARS	40 YEARS
$ 100	3.10	2.00	1.18	.92	.80	.73	.69	.64
200	6.20	3.99	2.35	1.83	1.59	1.45	1.37	1.28
300	9.30	5.98	3.53	2.74	2.38	2.17	2.05	1.92
400	12.40	7.97	4.70	3.66	3.17	2.90	2.73	2.56
500	15.50	9.96	5.88	4.57	3.96	3.62	3.42	3.20
600	18.60	11.96	7.05	5.48	4.75	4.34	4.10	3.84
700	21.70	13.95	8.22	6.40	5.54	5.06	4.78	4.48
800	24.80	15.94	9.40	7.31	6.33	5.79	5.46	5.12
900	27.90	17.93	10.57	8.22	7.12	6.51	6.14	5.76
1 000	31.00	19.92	11.75	9.13	7.91	7.23	6.83	6.40
1 000	31.00	19.92	11.75	9.13	7.91	7.23	6.83	6.40
2 000	61.99	39.84	23.49	18.26	15.81	14.46	13.65	12.80
3 000	92.98	59.76	35.23	27.39	23.72	21.69	20.47	19.20
4 000	123.97	79.68	46.97	36.52	31.62	28.92	27.29	25.59
5 000	154.96	99.60	58.71	45.65	39.52	36.15	34.11	31.99
6 000	185.95	119.52	70.45	54.78	47.43	43.37	40.94	38.39
7 000	216.95	139.44	82.19	63.91	55.33	50.60	47.76	44.78
8 000	247.94	159.36	93.93	73.03	63.24	57.83	54.58	51.18
9 000	278.93	179.28	105.67	82.16	71.14	65.06	61.40	57.58
10 000	309.92	199.20	117.41	91.29	79.04	72.29	68.22	63.97
11 000	340.91	219.12	129.15	100.42	86.95	79.51	75.04	70.37
12 000	371.90	239.04	140.89	109.55	94.85	86.74	81.87	76.77
13 000	402.89	258.96	152.63	118.68	102.75	93.97	88.69	83.16
14 000	433.89	278.88	164.37	127.81	110.66	101.20	95.51	89.56
15 000	464.88	298.80	176.11	136.93	118.56	108.43	102.33	95.96
16 000	495.87	318.71	187.85	146.06	126.47	115.65	109.15	102.35
17 000	526.86	338.63	199.59	155.19	134.37	122.88	115.97	108.75
18 000	557.85	358.55	211.33	164.32	142.27	130.11	122.80	115.15
19 000	588.84	378.47	223.07	173.45	150.18	137.34	129.62	121.54
20 000	619.84	398.39	234.81	182.58	158.08	144.57	136.44	127.94
21 000	650.83	418.31	246.55	191.71	165.98	151.79	143.26	134.34
22 000	681.82	438.23	258.29	200.83	173.89	159.02	150.08	140.73
23 000	712.81	458.15	270.03	209.96	181.79	166.25	156.91	147.13
24 000	743.80	478.07	281.77	219.09	189.70	173.48	163.73	153.53
25 000	774.79	497.99	293.51	228.22	197.60	180.71	170.55	159.92
26 000	805.78	517.91	305.25	237.35	205.50	187.93	177.37	166.32
27 000	836.78	537.83	316.99	246.48	213.41	195.16	184.19	172.72
28 000	867.77	557.75	328.73	255.61	221.31	202.39	191.01	179.11
29 000	898.76	577.67	340.47	264.74	229.21	209.62	197.84	185.51
30 000	929.75	597.59	352.21	273.86	237.12	216.85	204.66	191.91
31 000	960.74	617.51	363.95	282.99	245.02	224.08	211.48	198.30
32 000	991.73	637.42	375.69	292.12	252.93	231.30	218.30	204.70
33 000	1022.73	657.34	387.43	301.25	260.83	238.53	225.12	211.10
34 000	1053.72	677.26	399.18	310.38	268.73	245.76	231.94	217.49
35 000	1084.71	697.18	410.91	319.51	276.64	252.99	238.77	223.89
36 000	1115.70	717.10	422.65	328.64	284.54	260.22	245.59	230.29
37 000	1146.69	737.02	434.39	337.76	292.44	267.44	252.41	236.68
38 000	1177.68	756.94	446.13	346.89	300.35	274.67	259.23	243.08
39 000	1208.67	776.86	457.87	356.02	308.25	281.90	266.05	249.48
40 000	1239.67	796.78	469.61	365.15	316.16	289.13	272.88	255.87
41 000	1270.66	816.70	481.35	374.28	324.06	296.36	279.70	262.27
42 000	1301.65	836.62	493.09	383.41	331.96	303.58	286.52	268.67
43 000	1332.64	856.54	504.83	392.54	339.87	310.81	293.34	275.06
44 000	1363.63	876.46	516.57	401.66	347.77	318.04	300.16	281.46
45 000	1394.62	896.38	528.31	410.79	355.67	325.27	306.98	287.86

FOR **OTHER RATES AND TERMS** *SEE PAGE A-1.*

TERM ➧ AMOUNT	10 YEARS	15 YEARS	20 YEARS	25 YEARS	30 YEARS	40 YEARS
$46 000	540.05	419.92	363.58	332.50	313.81	294.25
47 000	551.79	429.05	371.48	339.72	320.63	300.65
48 000	563.53	438.18	379.39	346.95	327.45	307.05
49 000	575.27	447.31	387.29	354.18	334.27	313.44
50 000	587.01	456.44	395.19	361.41	341.09	319.84
51 000	598.75	465.57	403.10	368.64	347.91	326.24
52 000	610.49	474.69	411.00	375.86	354.74	332.63
53 000	622.23	483.82	418.90	383.09	361.56	339.03
54 000	633.97	492.95	426.81	390.32	368.38	345.43
55 000	645.71	502.08	434.71	397.55	375.20	351.82
56 000	657.45	511.21	442.62	404.78	382.02	358.22
57 000	669.19	520.34	450.52	412.00	388.85	364.62
58 000	680.93	529.47	458.42	419.23	395.67	371.01
59 000	692.67	538.59	466.33	426.46	402.49	377.41
60 000	704.41	547.72	474.23	433.69	409.31	383.81
61 000	716.15	556.85	482.13	440.92	416.13	390.20
62 000	727.89	565.98	490.04	448.15	422.95	396.60
63 000	739.63	575.11	497.94	455.37	429.78	403.00
64 000	751.37	584.24	505.85	462.60	436.60	409.40
65 000	763.11	593.37	513.75	469.83	443.42	415.79
66 000	774.85	602.49	521.65	477.06	450.24	422.19
67 000	786.59	611.62	529.56	484.29	457.06	428.59
68 000	798.33	620.75	537.46	491.51	463.88	434.98
69 000	810.07	629.88	545.36	498.74	470.71	441.38
70 000	821.81	639.01	553.27	505.97	477.53	447.78
71 000	833.55	648.14	561.17	513.20	484.35	454.17
72 000	845.29	657.27	569.08	520.43	491.17	460.57
73 000	857.03	666.39	576.98	527.65	497.99	466.97
74 000	868.77	675.52	584.88	534.88	504.82	473.36
75 000	880.51	684.65	592.79	542.11	511.64	479.76
76 000	892.25	693.78	600.69	549.34	518.46	486.16
77 000	903.99	702.91	608.59	556.57	525.28	492.55
78 000	915.73	712.04	616.50	563.79	532.10	498.95
79 000	927.47	721.17	624.40	571.02	538.92	505.35
80 000	939.21	730.30	632.31	578.25	545.75	511.74
81 000	950.95	739.42	640.21	585.48	552.57	518.14
82 000	962.69	748.55	648.11	592.71	559.39	524.54
83 000	974.43	757.68	656.02	599.93	566.21	530.93
84 000	986.17	766.81	663.92	607.16	573.03	537.33
85 000	997.91	775.94	671.82	614.39	579.85	543.73
86 000	1009.65	785.07	679.73	621.62	586.68	550.12
87 000	1021.39	794.20	687.63	628.85	593.50	556.52
88 000	1033.13	803.32	695.54	636.08	600.32	562.92
89 000	1044.87	812.45	703.44	643.30	607.14	569.31
90 000	1056.61	821.58	711.34	650.53	613.96	575.71
91 000	1068.35	830.71	719.25	657.76	620.79	582.11
92 000	1080.09	839.84	727.15	664.99	627.61	588.50
93 000	1091.83	848.97	735.05	672.22	634.43	594.90
94 000	1103.57	858.10	742.96	679.44	641.25	601.30
95 000	1115.31	867.22	750.86	686.67	648.07	607.69
96 000	1127.05	876.35	758.77	693.90	654.89	614.09
97 000	1138.80	885.48	766.67	701.13	661.72	620.49
98 000	1150.54	894.61	774.57	708.36	668.54	626.88
99 000	1162.28	903.74	782.48	715.58	675.36	633.28
100 000	1174.02	912.87	790.38	722.81	682.18	639.68

FOR OTHER RATES AND TERMS SEE PAGE A-1.

TERM▸ AMOUNT	3 YEARS	5 YEARS	10 YEARS	15 YEARS	20 YEARS	25 YEARS	30 YEARS	40 YEARS
$ 100	3.12	2.01	1.19	.93	.81	.74	.70	.66
200	6.23	4.01	2.38	1.86	1.62	1.48	1.40	1.32
300	9.34	6.02	3.57	2.79	2.42	2.22	2.10	1.98
400	12.45	8.02	4.75	3.71	3.23	2.96	2.80	2.64
500	15.56	10.02	5.94	4.64	4.03	3.70	3.50	3.30
600	18.67	12.03	7.13	5.57	4.84	4.44	4.20	3.95
700	21.78	14.03	8.31	6.49	5.64	5.18	4.90	4.61
800	24.89	16.04	9.50	7.42	6.45	5.92	5.60	5.27
900	28.00	18.04	10.69	8.35	7.26	6.66	6.30	5.93
1 000	31.11	20.04	11.88	9.28	8.06	7.39	7.00	6.59
1 000	31.11	20.04	11.88	9.28	8.06	7.39	7.00	6.59
2 000	62.22	40.08	23.75	18.55	16.12	14.78	13.99	13.17
3 000	93.32	60.12	35.62	27.82	24.17	22.17	20.98	19.75
4 000	124.43	80.16	47.49	37.09	32.23	29.56	27.97	26.33
5 000	155.54	100.19	59.36	46.36	40.28	36.95	34.97	32.91
6 000	186.64	120.23	71.23	55.63	48.34	44.34	41.96	39.49
7 000	217.75	140.27	83.10	64.90	56.40	51.73	48.95	46.07
8 000	248.85	160.31	94.97	74.17	64.45	59.12	55.94	52.65
9 000	279.96	180.35	106.84	83.44	72.51	66.51	62.93	59.23
10 000	311.07	200.38	118.71	92.71	80.56	73.90	69.93	65.81
11 000	342.17	220.42	130.58	101.98	88.62	81.29	76.92	72.39
12 000	373.28	240.46	142.45	111.25	96.68	88.68	83.91	78.97
13 000	404.39	260.50	154.32	120.52	104.73	96.07	90.90	85.55
14 000	435.49	280.54	166.19	129.79	112.79	103.46	97.90	92.13
15 000	466.60	300.57	178.06	139.06	120.84	110.85	104.89	98.72
16 000	497.70	320.61	189.93	148.33	128.90	118.24	111.88	105.30
17 000	528.81	340.65	201.80	157.60	136.96	125.63	118.87	111.88
18 000	559.92	360.69	213.67	166.87	145.01	133.02	125.86	118.46
19 000	591.02	380.73	225.54	176.14	153.07	140.41	132.86	125.04
20 000	622.13	400.76	237.41	185.41	161.12	147.80	139.85	131.62
21 000	653.24	420.80	249.28	194.68	169.18	155.19	146.84	138.20
22 000	684.34	440.84	261.15	203.95	177.24	162.58	153.83	144.78
23 000	715.45	460.88	273.02	213.22	185.29	169.97	160.82	151.36
24 000	746.55	480.92	284.89	222.49	193.35	177.36	167.82	157.94
25 000	777.66	500.95	296.76	231.76	201.40	184.75	174.81	164.52
26 000	808.77	520.99	308.63	241.03	209.46	192.14	181.80	171.10
27 000	839.87	541.03	320.50	250.30	217.52	199.53	188.79	177.68
28 000	870.98	561.07	332.37	259.57	225.57	206.92	195.79	184.26
29 000	902.09	581.11	344.24	268.84	233.63	214.31	202.78	190.85
30 000	933.19	601.14	356.11	278.11	241.68	221.70	209.77	197.43
31 000	964.30	621.18	367.98	287.38	249.74	229.09	216.76	204.01
32 000	995.40	641.22	379.85	296.65	257.79	236.48	223.75	210.59
33 000	1026.51	661.26	391.72	305.92	265.85	243.87	230.75	217.17
34 000	1057.62	681.30	403.59	315.19	273.91	251.26	237.74	223.75
35 000	1088.72	701.33	415.46	324.46	281.96	258.65	244.73	230.33
36 000	1119.83	721.37	427.33	333.73	290.02	266.04	251.72	236.91
37 000	1150.94	741.41	439.20	343.00	298.07	273.43	258.71	243.49
38 000	1182.04	761.45	451.07	352.27	306.13	280.82	265.71	250.07
39 000	1213.15	781.48	462.94	361.54	314.19	288.21	272.70	256.65
40 000	1244.25	801.52	474.81	370.81	322.24	295.60	279.69	263.23
41 000	1275.36	821.56	486.68	380.08	330.30	302.99	286.68	269.81
42 000	1306.47	841.60	498.55	389.35	338.35	310.38	293.68	276.39
43 000	1337.57	861.64	510.42	398.62	346.41	317.77	300.67	282.98
44 000	1368.68	881.67	522.29	407.89	354.47	325.16	307.66	289.56
45 000	1399.78	901.71	534.16	417.16	362.52	332.55	314.65	296.14

FOR **OTHER RATES AND TERMS** *SEE PAGE A-1.*

TERM→ AMOUNT	10 YEARS	15 YEARS	20 YEARS	25 YEARS	30 YEARS	40 YEARS
$46 000	546.03	426.43	370.58	339.94	321.64	302.72
47 000	557.90	435.70	378.63	347.33	328.64	309.30
48 000	569.77	444.97	386.69	354.72	335.63	315.88
49 000	581.64	454.24	394.75	362.11	342.62	322.46
50 000	593.51	463.51	402.80	369.50	349.61	329.04
51 000	605.38	472.78	410.86	376.89	356.60	335.62
52 000	617.25	482.05	418.91	384.28	363.60	342.20
53 000	629.12	491.32	426.97	391.67	370.59	348.78
54 000	640.99	500.59	435.03	399.06	377.58	355.36
55 000	652.86	509.86	443.08	406.45	384.57	361.94
56 000	664.73	519.13	451.14	413.84	391.57	368.52
57 000	676.61	528.40	459.19	421.23	398.56	375.11
58 000	688.48	537.67	467.25	428.62	405.55	381.69
59 000	700.35	546.94	475.30	436.01	412.54	388.27
60 000	712.22	556.21	483.36	443.40	419.53	394.85
61 000	724.09	565.48	491.42	450.79	426.53	401.43
62 000	735.96	574.75	499.47	458.18	433.52	408.01
63 000	747.83	584.02	507.53	465.57	440.51	414.59
64 000	759.70	593.29	515.58	472.96	447.50	421.17
65 000	771.57	602.56	523.64	480.35	454.49	427.75
66 000	783.44	611.83	531.70	487.74	461.49	434.33
67 000	795.31	621.10	539.75	495.13	468.48	440.91
68 000	807.18	630.37	547.81	502.52	475.47	447.49
69 000	819.05	639.64	555.86	509.91	482.46	454.07
70 000	830.92	648.91	563.92	517.30	489.46	460.65
71 000	842.79	658.18	571.98	524.69	496.45	467.24
72 000	854.66	667.45	580.03	532.08	503.44	473.82
73 000	866.53	676.72	588.09	539.47	510.43	480.40
74 000	878.40	685.99	596.14	546.86	517.42	486.98
75 000	890.27	695.26	604.20	554.25	524.42	493.56
76 000	902.14	704.53	612.26	561.64	531.41	500.14
77 000	914.01	713.80	620.31	569.03	538.40	506.72
78 000	925.88	723.07	628.37	576.42	545.39	513.30
79 000	937.75	732.34	636.42	583.81	552.38	519.88
80 000	949.62	741.61	644.48	591.20	559.38	526.46
81 000	961.49	750.89	652.54	598.59	566.37	533.04
82 000	973.36	760.16	660.59	605.98	573.36	539.62
83 000	985.23	769.43	668.65	613.37	580.35	546.20
84 000	997.10	778.70	676.70	620.76	587.35	552.78
85 000	1008.97	787.97	684.76	628.15	594.34	559.37
86 000	1020.84	797.24	692.82	635.54	601.33	565.95
87 000	1032.71	806.51	700.87	642.93	608.32	572.53
88 000	1044.58	815.78	708.93	650.32	615.31	579.11
89 000	1056.45	825.05	716.98	657.71	622.31	585.69
90 000	1068.32	834.32	725.04	665.10	629.30	592.27
91 000	1080.19	843.59	733.09	672.49	636.29	598.85
92 000	1092.06	852.86	741.15	679.88	643.28	605.43
93 000	1103.93	862.13	749.21	687.27	650.27	612.01
94 000	1115.80	871.40	757.26	694.66	657.27	618.59
95 000	1127.67	880.67	765.32	702.05	664.26	625.17
96 000	1139.54	889.94	773.37	709.44	671.25	631.75
97 000	1151.41	899.21	781.43	716.83	678.24	638.33
98 000	1163.28	908.48	789.49	724.22	685.24	644.91
99 000	1175.15	917.75	797.54	731.61	692.23	651.50
100 000	1187.02	927.02	805.60	739.00	699.22	658.08

FOR **OTHER RATES AND TERMS** *SEE PAGE A-1.*

TERM→ AMOUNT	3 YEARS	5 YEARS	10 YEARS	15 YEARS	20 YEARS	25 YEARS	30 YEARS	40 YEARS
$ 100	3.13	2.02	1.21	.95	.83	.76	.72	.68
200	6.25	4.04	2.41	1.89	1.65	1.52	1.44	1.36
300	9.37	6.05	3.61	2.83	2.47	2.27	2.15	2.03
400	12.49	8.07	4.81	3.77	3.29	3.03	2.87	2.71
500	15.62	10.08	6.01	4.71	4.11	3.78	3.59	3.39
600	18.74	12.10	7.21	5.65	4.93	4.54	4.30	4.06
700	21.86	14.11	8.41	6.59	5.75	5.29	5.02	4.74
800	24.98	16.13	9.61	7.54	6.57	6.05	5.74	5.42
900	28.10	18.15	10.81	8.48	7.39	6.80	6.45	6.09
1 000	31.23	20.16	12.01	9.42	8.21	7.56	7.17	6.77
1 000	31.23	20.16	12.01	9.42	8.21	7.56	7.17	6.77
2 000	62.45	40.32	24.01	18.83	16.42	15.11	14.33	13.54
3 000	93.67	60.48	36.01	28.24	24.63	22.66	21.50	20.30
4 000	124.89	80.63	48.01	37.66	32.84	30.22	28.66	27.07
5 000	156.11	100.79	60.01	47.07	41.05	37.77	35.83	33.84
6 000	187.33	120.95	72.01	56.48	49.26	45.32	42.99	40.60
7 000	218.55	141.10	84.01	65.89	57.47	52.88	50.15	47.37
8 000	249.77	161.26	96.01	75.31	65.68	60.43	57.32	54.13
9 000	281.00	181.42	108.01	84.72	73.89	67.98	64.48	60.90
10 000	312.22	201.57	120.02	94.13	82.10	75.54	71.65	67.67
11 000	343.44	221.73	132.02	103.55	90.31	83.09	78.81	74.43
12 000	374.66	241.89	144.02	112.96	98.52	90.64	85.97	81.20
13 000	405.88	262.05	156.02	122.37	106.73	98.20	93.14	87.97
14 000	437.10	282.20	168.02	131.78	114.94	105.75	100.30	94.73
15 000	468.32	302.36	180.02	141.20	123.15	113.30	107.47	101.50
16 000	499.54	322.52	192.02	150.61	131.36	120.86	114.63	108.26
17 000	530.76	342.67	204.02	160.02	139.57	128.41	121.80	115.03
18 000	561.99	362.83	216.02	169.43	147.78	135.96	128.96	121.80
19 000	593.21	382.99	228.03	178.85	155.99	143.52	136.12	128.56
20 000	624.43	403.14	240.03	188.26	164.19	151.07	143.29	135.33
21 000	655.65	423.30	252.03	197.67	172.40	158.62	150.45	142.10
22 000	686.87	443.46	264.03	207.09	180.61	166.18	157.62	148.86
23 000	718.09	463.62	276.03	216.50	188.82	173.73	164.78	155.63
24 000	749.31	483.77	288.03	225.91	197.03	181.28	171.94	162.39
25 000	780.53	503.93	300.03	235.32	205.24	188.84	179.11	169.16
26 000	811.76	524.09	312.03	244.74	213.45	196.39	186.27	175.93
27 000	842.98	544.24	324.03	254.15	221.66	203.94	193.44	182.69
28 000	874.20	564.40	336.03	263.56	229.87	211.50	200.60	189.46
29 000	905.42	584.56	348.04	272.97	238.08	219.05	207.76	196.22
30 000	936.64	604.71	360.04	282.39	246.29	226.60	214.93	202.99
31 000	967.86	624.87	372.04	291.80	254.50	234.16	222.09	209.76
32 000	999.08	645.03	384.04	301.21	262.71	241.71	229.26	216.52
33 000	1030.30	665.18	396.04	310.63	270.92	249.26	236.42	223.29
34 000	1061.52	685.34	408.04	320.04	279.13	256.82	243.59	230.06
35 000	1092.75	705.50	420.04	329.45	287.34	264.37	250.75	236.82
36 000	1123.97	725.66	432.04	338.86	295.55	271.92	257.91	243.59
37 000	1155.19	745.81	444.04	348.28	303.76	279.48	265.08	250.35
38 000	1186.41	765.97	456.05	357.69	311.97	287.03	272.24	257.12
39 000	1217.63	786.13	468.05	367.10	320.17	294.58	279.41	263.89
40 000	1248.85	806.28	480.05	376.52	328.38	302.14	286.57	270.65
41 000	1280.07	826.44	492.05	385.93	336.59	309.69	293.73	277.42
42 000	1311.29	846.60	504.05	395.34	344.80	317.24	300.90	284.19
43 000	1342.52	866.75	516.05	404.75	353.01	324.80	308.06	290.95
44 000	1373.74	886.91	528.05	414.17	361.22	332.35	315.23	297.72
45 000	1404.96	907.07	540.05	423.58	369.43	339.90	322.39	304.48

FOR **OTHER RATES AND TERMS** *SEE PAGE A-1.*

TERM➡ AMOUNT	10 YEARS	15 YEARS	20 YEARS	25 YEARS	30 YEARS	40 YEARS
$46 000	552.05	432.99	377.64	347.46	329.55	311.25
47 000	564.05	442.40	385.85	355.01	336.72	318.02
48 000	576.06	451.82	394.06	362.56	343.88	324.78
49 000	588.06	461.23	402.27	370.12	351.05	331.55
50 000	600.06	470.64	410.48	377.67	358.21	338.31
51 000	612.06	480.06	418.69	385.22	365.38	345.08
52 000	624.06	489.47	426.90	392.78	372.54	351.85
53 000	636.06	498.88	435.11	400.33	379.70	358.61
54 000	648.06	508.29	443.32	407.88	386.87	365.38
55 000	660.06	517.71	451.53	415.44	394.03	372.15
56 000	672.06	527.12	459.74	422.99	401.20	378.91
57 000	684.07	536.53	467.95	430.54	408.36	385.68
58 000	696.07	545.94	476.16	438.10	415.52	392.44
59 000	708.07	555.36	484.36	445.65	422.69	399.21
60 000	720.07	564.77	492.57	453.20	429.85	405.98
61 000	732.07	574.18	500.78	460.76	437.02	412.74
62 000	744.07	583.60	508.99	468.31	444.18	419.51
63 000	756.07	593.01	517.20	475.86	451.34	426.28
64 000	768.07	602.42	525.41	483.42	458.51	433.04
65 000	780.07	611.83	533.62	490.97	465.67	439.81
66 000	792.08	621.25	541.83	498.52	472.84	446.57
67 000	804.08	630.66	550.04	506.08	480.00	453.34
68 000	816.08	640.07	558.25	513.63	487.17	460.11
69 000	828.08	649.49	566.46	521.18	494.33	466.87
70 000	840.08	658.90	574.67	528.74	501.49	473.64
71 000	852.08	668.31	582.88	536.29	508.66	480.41
72 000	864.08	677.72	591.09	543.84	515.82	487.17
73 000	876.08	687.14	599.30	551.39	522.99	493.94
74 000	888.08	696.55	607.51	558.95	530.15	500.70
75 000	900.08	705.96	615.72	566.50	537.31	507.47
76 000	912.09	715.37	623.93	574.05	544.48	514.24
77 000	924.09	724.79	632.14	581.61	551.64	521.00
78 000	936.09	734.20	640.34	589.16	558.81	527.77
79 000	948.09	743.61	648.55	596.71	565.97	534.53
80 000	960.09	753.03	656.76	604.27	573.13	541.30
81 000	972.09	762.44	664.97	611.82	580.30	548.07
82 000	984.09	771.85	673.18	619.37	587.46	554.83
83 000	996.09	781.26	681.39	626.93	594.63	561.60
84 000	1008.09	790.68	689.60	634.48	601.79	568.37
85 000	1020.10	800.09	697.81	642.03	608.96	575.13
86 000	1032.10	809.50	706.02	649.59	616.12	581.90
87 000	1044.10	818.91	714.23	657.14	623.28	588.66
88 000	1056.10	828.33	722.44	664.69	630.45	595.43
89 000	1068.10	837.74	730.65	672.25	637.61	602.20
90 000	1080.10	847.15	738.86	679.80	644.78	608.96
91 000	1092.10	856.57	747.07	687.35	651.94	615.73
92 000	1104.10	865.98	755.28	694.91	659.10	622.50
93 000	1116.10	875.39	763.49	702.46	666.27	629.26
94 000	1128.10	884.80	771.70	710.01	673.43	636.03
95 000	1140.11	894.22	779.91	717.57	680.60	642.79
96 000	1152.11	903.63	788.12	725.12	687.76	649.56
97 000	1164.11	913.04	796.33	732.67	694.92	656.33
98 000	1176.11	922.46	804.53	740.23	702.09	663.09
99 000	1188.11	931.87	812.74	747.78	709.25	669.86
100 000	1200.11	941.28	820.95	755.33	716.42	676.62

FOR **OTHER RATES AND TERMS** *SEE PAGE A-1.*

TERM→ AMOUNT	3 YEARS	5 YEARS	10 YEARS	15 YEARS	20 YEARS	25 YEARS	30 YEARS	40 YEARS
$ 100	3.14	2.03	1.22	.96	.84	.78	.74	.70
200	6.27	4.06	2.43	1.92	1.68	1.55	1.47	1.40
300	9.41	6.09	3.64	2.87	2.51	2.32	2.21	2.09
400	12.54	8.12	4.86	3.83	3.35	3.09	2.94	2.79
500	15.67	10.14	6.07	4.78	4.19	3.86	3.67	3.48
600	18.81	12.17	7.28	5.74	5.02	4.64	4.41	4.18
700	21.94	14.20	8.50	6.69	5.86	5.41	5.14	4.87
800	25.07	16.23	9.71	7.65	6.70	6.18	5.88	5.57
900	28.21	18.25	10.92	8.61	7.53	6.95	6.61	6.26
1 000	31.34	20.28	12.14	9.56	8.37	7.72	7.34	6.96
1 000	31.34	20.28	12.14	9.56	8.37	7.72	7.34	6.96
2 000	62.68	40.56	24.27	19.12	16.73	15.44	14.68	13.91
3 000	94.01	60.83	36.40	28.67	25.10	23.16	22.02	20.86
4 000	125.35	81.11	48.54	38.23	33.46	30.88	29.36	27.82
5 000	156.69	101.39	60.67	47.79	41.83	38.60	36.69	34.77
6 000	188.02	121.66	72.80	57.34	50.19	46.31	44.03	41.72
7 000	219.36	141.94	84.93	66.90	58.56	54.03	51.37	48.68
8 000	250.70	162.22	97.07	76.46	66.92	61.75	58.71	55.63
9 000	282.03	182.49	109.20	86.01	75.28	69.47	66.04	62.58
10 000	313.37	202.77	121.33	95.57	83.65	77.19	73.38	69.54
11 000	344.71	223.05	133.47	105.13	92.01	84.90	80.72	76.49
12 000	376.04	243.32	145.60	114.68	100.38	92.62	88.06	83.44
13 000	407.38	263.60	157.73	124.24	108.74	100.34	95.39	90.40
14 000	438.71	283.87	169.86	133.80	117.11	108.06	102.73	97.35
15 000	470.05	304.15	182.00	143.35	125.47	115.78	110.07	104.30
16 000	501.39	324.43	194.13	152.91	133.84	123.50	117.41	111.25
17 000	532.72	344.70	206.26	162.47	142.20	131.21	124.74	118.21
18 000	564.06	364.98	218.39	172.02	150.56	138.93	132.08	125.16
19 000	595.40	385.26	230.53	181.58	158.93	146.65	139.42	132.11
20 000	626.73	405.53	242.66	191.14	167.29	154.37	146.76	139.07
21 000	658.07	425.81	254.79	200.69	175.66	162.09	154.10	146.02
22 000	689.41	446.09	266.93	210.25	184.02	169.80	161.43	152.97
23 000	720.74	466.36	279.06	219.80	192.39	177.52	168.77	159.93
24 000	752.08	486.64	291.19	229.36	200.75	185.24	176.11	166.88
25 000	783.41	506.91	303.32	238.92	209.12	192.96	183.45	173.83
26 000	814.75	527.19	315.46	248.47	217.48	200.68	190.78	180.79
27 000	846.09	547.47	327.59	258.03	225.84	208.40	198.12	187.74
28 000	877.42	567.74	339.72	267.59	234.21	216.11	205.46	194.69
29 000	908.76	588.02	351.86	277.14	242.57	223.83	212.80	201.65
30 000	940.10	608.30	363.99	286.70	250.94	231.55	220.13	208.60
31 000	971.43	628.57	376.12	296.26	259.30	239.27	227.47	215.55
32 000	1002.77	648.85	388.25	305.81	267.67	246.99	234.81	222.50
33 000	1034.11	669.13	400.39	315.37	276.03	254.70	242.15	229.46
34 000	1065.44	689.40	412.52	324.93	284.39	262.42	249.48	236.41
35 000	1096.78	709.68	424.65	334.48	292.76	270.14	256.82	243.36
36 000	1128.11	729.96	436.78	344.04	301.12	277.86	264.16	250.32
37 000	1159.45	750.23	448.92	353.60	309.49	285.58	271.50	257.27
38 000	1190.79	770.51	461.05	363.15	317.85	293.30	278.84	264.22
39 000	1222.12	790.78	473.18	372.71	326.22	301.01	286.17	271.18
40 000	1253.46	811.06	485.32	382.27	334.58	308.73	293.51	278.13
41 000	1284.80	831.34	497.45	391.82	342.95	316.45	300.85	285.08
42 000	1316.13	851.61	509.58	401.38	351.31	324.17	308.19	292.04
43 000	1347.47	871.89	521.71	410.94	359.67	331.89	315.52	298.99
44 000	1378.81	892.17	533.85	420.49	368.04	339.60	322.86	305.94
45 000	1410.14	912.44	545.98	430.05	376.40	347.32	330.20	312.90

FOR **OTHER RATES AND TERMS** *SEE PAGE A-1.*

TERM ♦ AMOUNT	10 YEARS	15 YEARS	20 YEARS	25 YEARS	30 YEARS	40 YEARS
$46 000	558.11	439.60	384.77	355.04	337.54	319.85
47 000	570.24	449.16	393.13	362.76	344.87	326.80
48 000	582.38	458.72	401.50	370.48	352.21	333.75
49 000	594.51	468.27	409.86	378.19	359.55	340.71
50 000	606.64	477.83	418.23	385.91	366.89	347.66
51 000	618.78	487.39	426.59	393.63	374.22	354.61
52 000	630.91	496.94	434.95	401.35	381.56	361.57
53 000	643.04	506.50	443.32	409.07	388.90	368.52
54 000	655.17	516.06	451.68	416.79	396.24	375.47
55 000	667.31	525.61	460.05	424.50	403.58	382.43
56 000	679.44	535.17	468.41	432.22	410.91	389.38
57 000	691.57	544.73	476.78	439.94	418.25	396.33
58 000	703.71	554.28	485.14	447.66	425.59	403.29
59 000	715.84	563.84	493.50	455.38	432.93	410.24
60 000	727.97	573.40	501.87	463.09	440.26	417.19
61 000	740.10	582.95	510.23	470.81	447.60	424.15
62 000	752.24	592.51	518.60	478.53	454.94	431.10
63 000	764.37	602.07	526.96	486.25	462.28	438.05
64 000	776.50	611.62	535.33	493.97	469.61	445.00
65 000	788.63	621.18	543.69	501.69	476.95	451.96
66 000	800.77	630.74	552.06	509.40	484.29	458.91
67 000	812.90	640.29	560.42	517.12	491.63	465.86
68 000	825.03	649.85	568.78	524.84	498.96	472.82
69 000	837.17	659.40	577.15	532.56	506.30	479.77
70 000	849.30	668.96	585.51	540.28	513.64	486.72
71 000	861.43	678.52	593.88	547.99	520.98	493.68
72 000	873.56	688.07	602.24	555.71	528.32	500.63
73 000	885.70	697.63	610.61	563.43	535.65	507.58
74 000	897.83	707.19	618.97	571.15	542.99	514.54
75 000	909.96	716.74	627.34	578.87	550.33	521.49
76 000	922.09	726.30	635.70	586.59	557.67	528.44
77 000	934.23	735.86	644.06	594.30	565.00	535.40
78 000	946.36	745.41	652.43	602.02	572.34	542.35
79 000	958.49	754.97	660.79	609.74	579.68	549.30
80 000	970.63	764.53	669.16	617.46	587.02	556.25
81 000	982.76	774.08	677.52	625.18	594.35	563.21
82 000	994.89	783.64	685.89	632.89	601.69	570.16
83 000	1007.02	793.20	694.25	640.61	609.03	577.11
84 000	1019.16	802.75	702.61	648.33	616.37	584.07
85 000	1031.29	812.31	710.98	656.05	623.70	591.02
86 000	1043.42	821.87	719.34	663.77	631.04	597.97
87 000	1055.56	831.42	727.71	671.49	638.38	604.93
88 000	1067.69	840.98	736.07	679.20	645.72	611.88
89 000	1079.82	850.54	744.44	686.92	653.06	618.83
90 000	1091.95	860.09	752.80	694.64	660.39	625.79
91 000	1104.09	869.65	761.17	702.36	667.73	632.74
92 000	1116.22	879.20	769.53	710.08	675.07	639.69
93 000	1128.35	888.76	777.89	717.79	682.41	646.64
94 000	1140.48	898.32	786.26	725.51	689.74	653.60
95 000	1152.62	907.87	794.62	733.23	697.08	660.55
96 000	1164.75	917.43	802.99	740.95	704.42	667.50
97 000	1176.88	926.99	811.35	748.67	711.76	674.46
98 000	1189.02	936.54	819.72	756.38	719.09	681.41
99 000	1201.15	946.10	828.08	764.10	726.43	688.36
100 000	1213.28	955.66	836.45	771.82	733.77	695.32

FOR **OTHER RATES AND TERMS** *SEE PAGE A-1.*

TERM▸ AMOUNT	3 YEARS	5 YEARS	10 YEARS	15 YEARS	20 YEARS	25 YEARS	30 YEARS	40 YEARS
$ 100	3.15	2.04	1.23	.98	.86	.79	.76	.72
200	6.30	4.08	2.46	1.95	1.71	1.58	1.51	1.43
300	9.44	6.12	3.68	2.92	2.56	2.37	2.26	2.15
400	12.59	8.16	4.91	3.89	3.41	3.16	3.01	2.86
500	15.73	10.20	6.14	4.86	4.27	3.95	3.76	3.58
600	18.88	12.24	7.36	5.83	5.12	4.74	4.51	4.29
700	22.02	14.28	8.59	6.80	5.97	5.52	5.26	5.00
800	25.17	16.32	9.82	7.77	6.82	6.31	6.02	5.72
900	28.31	18.36	11.04	8.74	7.67	7.10	6.77	6.43
1 000	31.46	20.40	12.27	9.71	8.53	7.89	7.52	7.15
1 000	31.46	20.40	12.27	9.71	8.53	7.89	7.52	7.15
2 000	62.91	40.80	24.54	19.41	17.05	15.77	15.03	14.29
3 000	94.36	61.19	36.80	29.11	25.57	23.66	22.54	21.43
4 000	125.81	81.59	49.07	38.81	34.09	31.54	30.06	28.57
5 000	157.26	101.99	61.33	48.51	42.61	39.43	37.57	35.71
6 000	188.72	122.38	73.60	58.21	51.13	47.31	45.08	42.85
7 000	220.17	142.78	85.86	67.91	59.65	55.20	52.59	49.99
8 000	251.62	163.18	98.13	77.62	68.17	63.08	60.11	57.14
9 000	283.07	183.57	110.39	87.32	76.69	70.97	67.62	64.28
10 000	314.52	203.97	122.66	97.02	85.21	78.85	75.13	71.42
11 000	345.98	224.36	134.92	106.72	93.73	86.73	82.64	78.56
12 000	377.43	244.76	147.19	116.42	102.25	94.62	90.16	85.70
13 000	408.88	265.16	159.45	126.12	110.77	102.50	97.67	92.84
14 000	440.33	285.55	171.72	135.82	119.29	110.39	105.18	99.98
15 000	471.78	305.95	183.98	145.53	127.81	118.27	112.69	107.13
16 000	503.23	326.35	196.25	155.23	136.34	126.16	120.21	114.27
17 000	534.69	346.74	208.51	164.93	144.86	134.04	127.72	121.41
18 000	566.14	367.14	220.78	174.63	153.38	141.93	135.23	128.55
19 000	597.59	387.53	233.04	184.33	161.90	149.81	142.75	135.69
20 000	629.04	407.93	245.31	194.03	170.42	157.70	150.26	142.83
21 000	660.49	428.33	257.58	203.73	178.94	165.58	157.77	149.97
22 000	691.95	448.72	269.84	213.44	187.46	173.46	165.28	157.12
23 000	723.40	469.12	282.11	223.14	195.98	181.35	172.80	164.26
24 000	754.85	489.52	294.37	232.84	204.50	189.23	180.31	171.40
25 000	786.30	509.91	306.64	242.54	213.02	197.12	187.82	178.54
26 000	817.75	530.31	318.90	252.24	221.54	205.00	195.33	185.68
27 000	849.20	550.70	331.17	261.94	230.06	212.89	202.85	192.82
28 000	880.66	571.10	343.43	271.64	238.58	220.77	210.36	199.96
29 000	912.11	591.50	355.70	281.35	247.10	228.66	217.87	207.11
30 000	943.56	611.89	367.96	291.05	255.62	236.54	225.38	214.25
31 000	975.01	632.29	380.23	300.75	264.15	244.42	232.90	221.39
32 000	1006.46	652.69	392.49	310.45	272.67	252.31	240.41	228.53
33 000	1037.92	673.08	404.76	320.15	281.19	260.19	247.92	235.67
34 000	1069.37	693.48	417.02	329.85	289.71	268.08	255.44	242.81
35 000	1100.82	713.87	429.29	339.55	298.23	275.96	262.95	249.95
36 000	1132.27	734.27	441.55	349.26	306.75	283.85	270.46	257.09
37 000	1163.72	754.67	453.82	358.96	315.27	291.73	277.97	264.24
38 000	1195.17	775.06	466.08	368.66	323.79	299.62	285.49	271.38
39 000	1226.63	795.46	478.35	378.36	332.31	307.50	293.00	278.52
40 000	1258.08	815.86	490.62	388.06	340.83	315.39	300.51	285.66
41 000	1289.53	836.25	502.88	397.76	349.35	323.27	308.02	292.80
42 000	1320.98	856.65	515.15	407.46	357.87	331.15	315.54	299.94
43 000	1352.43	877.04	527.41	417.17	366.39	339.04	323.05	307.08
44 000	1383.89	897.44	539.68	426.87	374.91	346.92	330.56	314.23
45 000	1415.34	917.84	551.94	436.57	383.43	354.81	338.07	321.37

FOR **OTHER RATES AND TERMS** *SEE PAGE A-1.*

TERM → AMOUNT	10 YEARS	15 YEARS	20 YEARS	25 YEARS	30 YEARS	40 YEARS
$46 000	564.21	446.27	391.96	362.69	345.59	328.51
47 000	576.47	455.97	400.48	370.58	353.10	335.65
48 000	588.74	465.67	409.00	378.46	360.61	342.79
49 000	601.00	475.37	417.52	386.35	368.13	349.93
50 000	613.27	485.08	426.04	394.23	375.64	357.07
51 000	625.53	494.78	434.56	402.11	383.15	364.22
52 000	637.80	504.48	443.08	410.00	390.66	371.36
53 000	650.06	514.18	451.60	417.88	398.18	378.50
54 000	662.33	523.88	460.12	425.77	405.69	385.64
55 000	674.59	533.58	468.64	433.65	413.20	392.78
56 000	686.86	543.28	477.16	441.54	420.71	399.92
57 000	699.12	552.99	485.68	449.42	428.23	407.06
58 000	711.39	562.69	494.20	457.31	435.74	414.21
59 000	723.66	572.39	502.72	465.19	443.25	421.35
60 000	735.92	582.09	511.24	473.08	450.76	428.49
61 000	748.19	591.79	519.77	480.96	458.28	435.63
62 000	760.45	601.49	528.29	488.84	465.79	442.77
63 000	772.72	611.19	536.81	496.73	473.30	449.91
64 000	784.98	620.89	545.33	504.61	480.82	457.05
65 000	797.25	630.60	553.85	512.50	488.33	464.20
66 000	809.51	640.30	562.37	520.38	495.84	471.34
67 000	821.78	650.00	570.89	528.27	503.35	478.48
68 000	834.04	659.70	579.41	536.15	510.87	485.62
69 000	846.31	669.40	587.93	544.04	518.38	492.76
70 000	858.57	679.10	596.45	551.92	525.89	499.90
71 000	870.84	688.80	604.97	559.80	533.40	507.04
72 000	883.10	698.51	613.49	567.69	540.92	514.18
73 000	895.37	708.21	622.01	575.57	548.43	521.33
74 000	907.63	717.91	630.53	583.46	555.94	528.47
75 000	919.90	727.61	639.05	591.34	563.45	535.61
76 000	932.16	737.31	647.57	599.23	570.97	542.75
77 000	944.43	747.01	656.10	607.11	578.48	549.89
78 000	956.70	756.71	664.62	615.00	585.99	557.03
79 000	968.96	766.42	673.14	622.88	593.51	564.17
80 000	981.23	776.12	681.66	630.77	601.02	571.32
81 000	993.49	785.82	690.18	638.65	608.53	578.46
82 000	1005.76	795.52	698.70	646.53	616.04	585.60
83 000	1018.02	805.22	707.22	654.42	623.56	592.74
84 000	1030.29	814.92	715.74	662.30	631.07	599.88
85 000	1042.55	824.62	724.26	670.19	638.58	607.02
86 000	1054.82	834.33	732.78	678.07	646.09	614.16
87 000	1067.08	844.03	741.30	685.96	653.61	621.31
88 000	1079.35	853.73	749.82	693.84	661.12	628.45
89 000	1091.61	863.43	758.34	701.73	668.63	635.59
90 000	1103.88	873.13	766.86	709.61	676.14	642.73
91 000	1116.14	882.83	775.38	717.49	683.66	649.87
92 000	1128.41	892.53	783.91	725.38	691.17	657.01
93 000	1140.67	902.24	792.43	733.26	698.68	664.15
94 000	1152.94	911.94	800.95	741.15	706.20	671.30
95 000	1165.20	921.64	809.47	749.03	713.71	678.44
96 000	1177.47	931.34	817.99	756.92	721.22	685.58
97 000	1189.74	941.04	826.51	764.80	728.73	692.72
98 000	1202.00	950.74	835.03	772.69	736.25	699.86
99 000	1214.27	960.44	843.55	780.57	743.76	707.00
100 000	1226.53	970.15	852.07	788.46	751.27	714.14

FOR **OTHER RATES AND TERMS** *SEE PAGE A-1.*

TERM◆ AMOUNT	3 YEARS	5 YEARS	10 YEARS	15 YEARS	20 YEARS	25 YEARS	30 YEARS	40 YEARS
$ 100	3.16	2.06	1.24	.99	.87	.81	.77	.74
200	6.32	4.11	2.48	1.97	1.74	1.62	1.54	1.47
300	9.48	6.16	3.72	2.96	2.61	2.42	2.31	2.20
400	12.63	8.21	4.96	3.94	3.48	3.23	3.08	2.94
500	15.79	10.26	6.20	4.93	4.34	4.03	3.85	3.67
600	18.95	12.31	7.44	5.91	5.21	4.84	4.62	4.40
700	22.10	14.37	8.68	6.90	6.08	5.64	5.39	5.14
800	25.26	16.42	9.92	7.88	6.95	6.45	6.16	5.87
900	28.42	18.47	11.16	8.87	7.82	7.25	6.93	6.60
1 000	31.57	20.52	12.40	9.85	8.68	8.06	7.69	7.34
1 000	31.57	20.52	12.40	9.85	8.68	8.06	7.69	7.34
2 000	63.14	41.04	24.80	19.70	17.36	16.11	15.38	14.67
3 000	94.71	61.55	37.20	29.55	26.04	24.16	23.07	22.00
4 000	126.28	82.07	49.60	39.39	34.72	32.21	30.76	29.33
5 000	157.84	102.59	62.00	49.24	43.40	40.27	38.45	36.66
6 000	189.41	123.10	74.40	59.09	52.07	48.32	46.14	43.99
7 000	220.98	143.62	86.79	68.94	60.75	56.37	53.83	51.32
8 000	252.55	164.14	99.19	78.78	69.43	64.42	61.52	58.65
9 000	284.11	184.65	111.59	88.63	78.11	72.48	69.21	65.98
10 000	315.68	205.17	123.99	98.48	86.79	80.53	76.90	73.31
11 000	347.25	225.69	136.39	108.33	95.47	88.58	84.59	80.65
12 000	378.82	246.20	148.79	118.17	104.14	96.63	92.27	87.98
13 000	410.38	266.72	161.19	128.02	112.82	104.68	99.96	95.31
14 000	441.95	287.24	173.58	137.87	121.50	112.74	107.65	102.64
15 000	473.52	307.75	185.98	147.72	130.18	120.79	115.34	109.97
16 000	505.09	328.27	198.38	157.56	138.86	128.84	123.03	117.30
17 000	536.65	348.79	210.78	167.41	147.53	136.89	130.72	124.63
18 000	568.22	369.30	223.18	177.26	156.21	144.95	138.41	131.96
19 000	599.79	389.82	235.58	187.11	164.89	153.00	146.10	139.29
20 000	631.36	410.34	247.98	196.95	173.57	161.05	153.79	146.62
21 000	662.92	430.85	260.37	206.80	182.25	169.10	161.48	153.95
22 000	694.49	451.37	272.77	216.65	190.93	177.15	169.17	161.29
23 000	726.06	471.89	285.17	226.50	199.60	185.21	176.86	168.62
24 000	757.63	492.40	297.57	236.34	208.28	193.26	184.54	175.95
25 000	789.19	512.92	309.97	246.19	216.96	201.31	192.23	183.28
26 000	820.76	533.43	322.37	256.04	225.64	209.36	199.92	190.61
27 000	852.33	553.95	334.77	265.88	234.32	217.42	207.61	197.94
28 000	883.90	574.47	347.16	275.73	243.00	225.47	215.30	205.27
29 000	915.46	594.98	359.56	285.58	251.67	233.52	222.99	212.60
30 000	947.03	615.50	371.96	295.43	260.35	241.57	230.68	219.93
31 000	978.60	636.02	384.36	305.27	269.03	249.63	238.37	227.26
32 000	1010.17	656.53	396.76	315.12	277.71	257.68	246.06	234.60
33 000	1041.73	677.05	409.16	324.97	286.39	265.73	253.75	241.93
34 000	1073.30	697.57	421.56	334.82	295.06	273.78	261.44	249.26
35 000	1104.87	718.08	433.95	344.66	303.74	281.83	269.12	256.59
36 000	1136.44	738.60	446.35	354.51	312.42	289.89	276.81	263.92
37 000	1168.00	759.12	458.75	364.36	321.10	297.94	284.50	271.25
38 000	1199.57	779.63	471.15	374.21	329.78	305.99	292.19	278.58
39 000	1231.14	800.15	483.55	384.05	338.46	314.04	299.88	285.91
40 000	1262.71	820.67	495.95	393.90	347.13	322.10	307.57	293.24
41 000	1294.27	841.18	508.35	403.75	355.81	330.15	315.26	300.57
42 000	1325.84	861.70	520.74	413.60	364.49	338.20	322.95	307.90
43 000	1357.41	882.22	533.14	423.44	373.17	346.25	330.64	315.24
44 000	1388.98	902.73	545.54	433.29	381.85	354.30	338.33	322.57
45 000	1420.54	923.25	557.94	443.14	390.53	362.36	346.02	329.90

FOR **OTHER RATES AND TERMS** *SEE PAGE A-1.*

TERM➧ AMOUNT	10 YEARS	15 YEARS	20 YEARS	25 YEARS	30 YEARS	40 YEARS
$46 000	570.34	452.99	399.20	370.41	353.71	337.23
47 000	582.74	462.83	407.88	378.46	361.39	344.56
48 000	595.14	472.68	416.56	386.51	369.08	351.89
49 000	607.53	482.53	425.24	394.57	376.77	359.22
50 000	619.93	492.37	433.92	402.62	384.46	366.55
51 000	632.33	502.22	442.59	410.67	392.15	373.88
52 000	644.73	512.07	451.27	418.72	399.84	381.21
53 000	657.13	521.92	459.95	426.78	407.53	388.54
54 000	669.53	531.76	468.63	434.83	415.22	395.88
55 000	681.93	541.61	477.31	442.88	422.91	403.21
56 000	694.32	551.46	485.99	450.93	430.60	410.54
57 000	706.72	561.31	494.66	458.98	438.29	417.87
58 000	719.12	571.15	503.34	467.04	445.97	425.20
59 000	731.52	581.00	512.02	475.09	453.66	432.53
60 000	743.92	590.85	520.70	483.14	461.35	439.86
61 000	756.32	600.70	529.38	491.19	469.04	447.19
62 000	768.72	610.54	538.06	499.25	476.73	454.52
63 000	781.11	620.39	546.73	507.30	484.42	461.85
64 000	793.51	630.24	555.41	515.35	492.11	469.19
65 000	805.91	640.09	564.09	523.40	499.80	476.52
66 000	818.31	649.93	572.77	531.45	507.49	483.85
67 000	830.71	659.78	581.45	539.51	515.18	491.18
68 000	843.11	669.63	590.12	547.56	522.87	498.51
69 000	855.51	679.48	598.80	555.61	530.56	505.84
70 000	867.90	689.32	607.48	563.66	538.24	513.17
71 000	880.30	699.17	616.16	571.72	545.93	520.50
72 000	892.70	709.02	624.84	579.77	553.62	527.83
73 000	905.10	718.86	633.52	587.82	561.31	535.16
74 000	917.50	728.71	642.19	595.87	569.00	542.49
75 000	929.90	738.56	650.87	603.93	576.69	549.83
76 000	942.30	748.41	659.55	611.98	584.38	557.16
77 000	954.69	758.25	668.23	620.03	592.07	564.49
78 000	967.09	768.10	676.91	628.08	599.76	571.82
79 000	979.49	777.95	685.59	636.13	607.45	579.15
80 000	991.89	787.80	694.26	644.19	615.14	586.48
81 000	1004.29	797.64	702.94	652.24	622.82	593.81
82 000	1016.69	807.49	711.62	660.29	630.51	601.14
83 000	1029.09	817.34	720.30	668.34	638.20	608.47
84 000	1041.48	827.19	728.98	676.40	645.09	615.80
85 000	1053.88	837.03	737.65	684.45	653.58	623.13
86 000	1066.28	846.88	746.33	692.50	661.27	630.47
87 000	1078.68	856.73	755.01	700.55	668.96	637.80
88 000	1091.08	866.58	763.69	708.60	676.65	645.13
89 000	1103.48	876.42	772.37	716.66	684.34	652.46
90 000	1115.88	886.27	781.05	724.71	692.03	659.79
91 000	1128.27	896.12	789.72	732.76	699.72	667.12
92 000	1140.67	905.97	798.40	740.81	707.41	674.45
93 000	1153.07	915.81	807.08	748.87	715.09	681.78
94 000	1165.47	925.66	815.76	756.92	722.78	689.11
95 000	1177.87	935.51	824.44	764.97	730.47	696.44
96 000	1190.27	945.35	833.12	773.02	738.16	703.78
97 000	1202.67	955.20	841.79	781.08	745.85	711.11
98 000	1215.06	965.05	850.47	789.13	753.54	718.44
99 000	1227.46	974.90	859.15	797.18	761.23	725.77
100 000	1239.86	984.74	867.83	805.23	768.92	733.10

FOR **OTHER RATES AND TERMS** *SEE PAGE A-1.*

TERM► AMOUNT	3 YEARS	5 YEARS	10 YEARS	15 YEARS	20 YEARS	25 YEARS	30 YEARS	40 YEARS
$ 100	3.17	2.07	1.26	1.00	.89	.83	.79	.76
200	6.34	4.13	2.51	2.00	1.77	1.65	1.58	1.51
300	9.51	6.20	3.76	3.00	2.66	2.47	2.37	2.26
400	12.68	8.26	5.02	4.00	3.54	3.29	3.15	3.01
500	15.85	10.32	6.27	5.00	4.42	4.12	3.94	3.77
600	19.02	12.39	7.52	6.00	5.31	4.94	4.73	4.52
700	22.18	14.45	8.78	7.00	6.19	5.76	5.51	5.27
800	25.35	16.51	10.03	8.00	7.07	6.58	6.30	6.02
900	28.52	18.58	11.28	9.00	7.96	7.40	7.09	6.77
1 000	31.69	20.64	12.54	10.00	8.84	8.23	7.87	7.53
1 000	31.69	20.64	12.54	10.00	8.84	8.23	7.87	7.53
2 000	63.37	41.28	25.07	19.99	17.68	16.45	15.74	15.05
3 000	95.06	61.92	37.60	29.99	26.52	24.67	23.61	22.57
4 000	126.74	82.55	50.14	39.98	35.35	32.89	31.47	30.09
5 000	158.42	103.19	62.67	49.98	44.19	41.11	39.34	37.61
6 000	190.11	123.83	75.20	59.97	53.03	49.33	47.21	45.14
7 000	221.79	144.47	87.73	69.97	61.86	57.56	55.07	52.66
8 000	253.47	165.10	100.27	79.96	70.70	65.78	62.94	60.18
9 000	285.16	185.74	112.80	89.96	79.54	74.00	70.81	67.70
10 000	316.84	206.38	125.33	99.95	88.38	82.22	78.68	75.22
11 000	348.52	227.01	137.86	109.94	97.21	90.44	86.54	82.74
12 000	380.21	247.65	150.40	119.94	106.05	98.66	94.41	90.27
13 000	411.89	268.29	162.93	129.93	114.89	106.88	102.28	97.79
14 000	443.57	288.93	175.46	139.93	123.72	115.11	110.14	105.31
15 000	475.26	309.56	188.00	149.92	132.56	123.33	118.01	112.83
16 000	506.94	330.20	200.53	159.92	141.40	131.55	125.88	120.35
17 000	538.62	350.84	213.06	169.91	150.24	139.77	133.74	127.87
18 000	570.31	371.48	225.59	179.91	159.07	147.99	141.61	135.40
19 000	601.99	392.11	238.13	189.90	167.91	156.21	149.48	142.92
20 000	633.68	412.75	250.66	199.89	176.75	164.43	157.35	150.44
21 000	665.36	433.39	263.19	209.89	185.58	172.66	165.21	157.96
22 000	697.04	454.02	275.72	219.88	194.42	180.88	173.08	165.48
23 000	728.73	474.66	288.26	229.88	203.26	189.10	180.95	173.00
24 000	760.41	495.30	300.79	239.87	212.10	197.32	188.81	180.53
25 000	792.09	515.94	313.32	249.87	220.93	205.54	196.68	188.05
26 000	823.78	536.57	325.85	259.86	229.77	213.76	204.55	195.57
27 000	855.46	557.21	338.39	269.86	238.61	221.98	212.41	203.09
28 000	887.14	577.85	350.92	279.85	247.44	230.21	220.28	210.61
29 000	918.83	598.48	363.45	289.85	256.28	238.43	228.15	218.13
30 000	950.51	619.12	375.99	299.84	265.12	246.65	236.02	225.66
31 000	982.19	639.76	388.52	309.83	273.96	254.87	243.88	233.18
32 000	1013.88	660.40	401.05	319.83	282.79	263.09	251.75	240.70
33 000	1045.56	681.03	413.58	329.82	291.63	271.31	259.62	248.22
34 000	1077.24	701.67	426.12	339.82	300.47	279.53	267.48	255.74
35 000	1108.93	722.31	438.65	349.81	309.30	287.76	275.35	263.26
36 000	1140.61	742.95	451.18	359.81	318.14	295.98	283.22	270.79
37 000	1172.29	763.58	463.71	369.80	326.98	304.20	291.08	278.31
38 000	1203.98	784.22	476.25	379.80	335.82	312.42	298.95	285.83
39 000	1235.66	804.86	488.78	389.79	344.65	320.64	306.82	293.35
40 000	1267.35	825.49	501.31	399.78	353.49	328.86	314.69	300.87
41 000	1299.03	846.13	513.84	409.78	362.33	337.08	322.55	308.39
42 000	1330.71	866.77	526.38	419.77	371.16	345.31	330.42	315.92
43 000	1362.40	887.41	538.91	429.77	380.00	353.53	338.29	323.44
44 000	1394.08	908.04	551.44	439.76	388.84	361.75	346.15	330.96
45 000	1425.76	928.68	563.98	449.76	397.67	369.97	354.02	338.48

FOR **OTHER RATES AND TERMS** *SEE PAGE A-1.*

TERM→ AMOUNT	10 YEARS	15 YEARS	20 YEARS	25 YEARS	30 YEARS	40 YEARS
$46 000	576.51	459.75	406.51	378.19	361.89	346.00
47 000	589.04	469.75	415.35	386.41	369.75	353.53
48 000	601.57	479.74	424.19	394.63	377.62	361.05
49 000	614.11	489.73	433.02	402.86	385.49	368.57
50 000	626.64	499.73	441.86	411.08	393.36	376.09
51 000	639.17	509.72	450.70	419.30	401.22	383.61
52 000	651.70	519.72	459.53	427.52	409.09	391.13
53 000	664.24	529.71	468.37	435.74	416.96	398.66
54 000	676.77	539.71	477.21	443.96	424.82	406.18
55 000	689.30	549.70	486.05	452.18	432.69	413.70
56 000	701.83	559.70	494.88	460.41	440.56	421.22
57 000	714.37	569.69	503.72	468.63	448.42	428.74
58 000	726.90	579.69	512.56	476.85	456.29	436.26
59 000	739.43	589.68	521.39	485.07	464.16	443.79
60 000	751.97	599.67	530.23	493.29	472.03	451.31
61 000	764.50	609.67	539.07	501.51	479.89	458.83
62 000	777.03	619.66	547.91	509.73	487.76	466.35
63 000	789.56	629.66	556.74	517.96	495.63	473.87
64 000	802.10	639.65	565.58	526.18	503.49	481.39
65 000	814.63	649.65	574.42	534.40	511.36	488.92
66 000	827.16	659.64	583.25	542.62	519.23	496.44
67 000	839.69	669.64	592.09	550.84	527.09	503.96
68 000	852.23	679.63	600.93	559.06	534.96	511.48
69 000	864.76	689.62	609.77	567.28	542.83	519.00
70 000	877.29	699.62	618.60	575.51	550.70	526.52
71 000	889.82	709.61	627.44	583.73	558.56	534.05
72 000	902.36	719.61	636.28	591.95	566.43	541.57
73 000	914.89	729.60	645.11	600.17	574.30	549.09
74 000	927.42	739.60	653.95	608.39	582.16	556.61
75 000	939.96	749.59	662.79	616.61	590.03	564.13
76 000	952.49	759.59	671.63	624.83	597.90	571.65
77 000	965.02	769.58	680.46	633.06	605.76	579.18
78 000	977.55	779.57	689.30	641.28	613.63	586.70
79 000	990.09	789.57	698.14	649.50	621.50	594.22
80 000	1002.62	799.56	706.97	657.72	629.37	601.74
81 000	1015.15	809.56	715.81	665.94	637.23	609.26
82 000	1027.68	819.55	724.65	674.16	645.10	616.78
83 000	1040.22	829.55	733.48	682.38	652.97	624.31
84 000	1052.75	839.54	742.32	690.61	660.83	631.83
85 000	1065.28	849.54	751.16	698.83	668.70	639.35
86 000	1077.82	859.53	760.00	707.05	676.57	646.87
87 000	1090.35	869.53	768.83	715.27	684.43	654.39
88 000	1102.88	879.52	777.67	723.49	692.30	661.92
89 000	1115.41	889.51	786.51	731.71	700.17	669.44
90 000	1127.95	899.51	795.34	739.93	708.04	676.96
91 000	1140.48	909.50	804.18	748.16	715.90	684.48
92 000	1153.01	919.50	813.02	756.38	723.77	692.00
93 000	1165.54	929.49	821.86	764.60	731.64	699.52
94 000	1178.08	939.49	830.69	772.82	739.50	707.05
95 000	1190.61	949.48	839.53	781.04	747.37	714.57
96 000	1203.14	959.48	848.37	789.26	755.24	722.09
97 000	1215.67	969.47	857.20	797.48	763.10	729.61
98 000	1228.21	979.46	866.04	805.71	770.97	737.13
99 000	1240.74	989.46	874.88	813.93	778.84	744.65
100 000	1253.27	999.45	883.72	822.15	786.71	752.18

FOR **OTHER RATES AND TERMS** *SEE PAGE A-1.*

TERM➡ AMOUNT	3 YEARS	5 YEARS	10 YEARS	15 YEARS	20 YEARS	25 YEARS	30 YEARS	40 YEARS
$ 100	3.18	2.08	1.27	1.02	.90	.84	.81	.78
200	6.36	4.16	2.54	2.03	1.80	1.68	1.61	1.55
300	9.54	6.23	3.81	3.05	2.70	2.52	2.42	2.32
400	12.72	8.31	5.07	4.06	3.60	3.36	3.22	3.09
500	15.90	10.38	6.34	5.08	4.50	4.20	4.03	3.86
600	19.08	12.46	7.61	6.09	5.40	5.04	4.83	4.63
700	22.26	14.54	8.87	7.10	6.30	5.88	5.64	5.40
800	25.44	16.61	10.14	8.12	7.20	6.72	6.44	6.18
900	28.62	18.69	11.41	9.13	8.10	7.56	7.25	6.95
1 000	31.80	20.76	12.67	10.15	9.00	8.40	8.05	7.72
1 000	31.80	20.76	12.67	10.15	9.00	8.40	8.05	7.72
2 000	63.60	41.52	25.34	20.29	18.00	16.79	16.10	15.43
3 000	95.40	62.28	38.01	30.43	27.00	25.18	24.14	23.15
4 000	127.20	83.04	50.68	40.58	35.99	33.57	32.19	30.86
5 000	159.00	103.80	63.34	50.72	44.99	41.96	40.24	38.57
6 000	190.80	124.56	76.01	60.86	53.99	50.36	48.28	46.29
7 000	222.60	145.31	88.68	71.00	62.99	58.75	56.33	54.00
8 000	254.40	166.07	101.35	81.15	71.98	67.14	64.37	61.71
9 000	286.20	186.83	114.01	91.29	80.98	75.53	72.42	69.43
10 000	318.00	207.59	126.68	101.43	89.98	83.92	80.47	77.14
11 000	349.80	228.35	139.35	111.57	98.97	92.32	88.51	84.85
12 000	381.60	249.11	152.02	121.72	107.97	100.71	96.56	92.57
13 000	413.40	269.86	164.68	131.86	116.97	109.10	104.61	100.28
14 000	445.20	290.62	177.35	142.00	125.97	117.49	112.65	108.00
15 000	477.00	311.38	190.02	152.14	134.96	125.88	120.70	115.71
16 000	508.80	332.14	202.69	162.29	143.96	134.28	128.74	123.42
17 000	540.60	352.90	215.35	172.43	152.96	142.67	136.79	131.14
18 000	572.40	373.66	228.02	182.57	161.96	151.06	144.84	138.85
19 000	604.20	394.41	240.69	192.72	170.95	159.45	152.88	146.56
20 000	636.00	415.17	253.36	202.86	179.95	167.84	160.93	154.28
21 000	667.80	435.93	266.02	213.00	188.95	176.24	168.98	161.99
22 000	699.60	456.69	278.69	223.14	197.94	184.63	177.02	169.70
23 000	731.40	477.45	291.36	233.29	206.94	193.02	185.07	177.42
24 000	763.20	498.21	304.03	243.43	215.94	201.41	193.11	185.13
25 000	795.00	518.96	316.69	253.57	224.94	209.80	201.16	192.85
26 000	826.80	539.72	329.36	263.71	233.93	218.20	209.21	200.56
27 000	858.60	560.48	342.03	273.86	242.93	226.59	217.25	208.27
28 000	890.40	581.24	354.70	284.00	251.93	234.98	225.30	215.99
29 000	922.20	602.00	367.36	294.14	260.93	243.37	233.35	223.70
30 000	954.00	622.76	380.03	304.28	269.92	251.76	241.39	231.41
31 000	985.80	643.51	392.70	314.43	278.92	260.16	249.44	239.13
32 000	1017.60	664.27	405.37	324.57	287.92	268.55	257.48	246.84
33 000	1049.40	685.03	418.04	334.71	296.91	276.94	265.53	254.55
34 000	1081.20	705.79	430.70	344.86	305.91	285.33	273.58	262.27
35 000	1113.00	726.55	443.37	355.00	314.91	293.72	281.62	269.98
36 000	1144.80	747.31	456.04	365.14	323.91	302.12	289.67	277.70
37 000	1176.60	768.06	468.71	375.28	332.90	310.51	297.72	285.41
38 000	1208.39	788.82	481.37	385.43	341.90	318.90	305.76	293.12
39 000	1240.19	809.58	494.04	395.57	350.90	327.29	313.81	300.84
40 000	1271.99	830.34	506.71	405.71	359.90	335.68	321.85	308.55
41 000	1303.79	851.10	519.38	415.85	368.89	344.08	329.90	316.26
42 000	1335.59	871.86	532.04	426.00	377.89	352.47	337.95	323.98
43 000	1367.39	892.61	544.71	436.14	386.89	360.86	345.99	331.69
44 000	1399.19	913.37	557.38	446.28	395.88	369.25	354.04	339.40
45 000	1430.99	934.13	570.05	456.42	404.88	377.64	362.09	347.12

FOR **OTHER RATES AND TERMS** *SEE PAGE A-1.*

TERM➡ AMOUNT	10 YEARS	15 YEARS	20 YEARS	25 YEARS	30 YEARS	40 YEARS
$46 000	582.71	466.57	413.88	386.04	370.13	354.83
47 000	595.38	476.71	422.88	394.43	378.18	362.54
48 000	608.05	486.85	431.87	402.82	386.22	370.26
49 000	620.72	497.00	440.87	411.21	394.27	377.97
50 000	633.38	507.14	449.87	419.60	402.32	385.69
51 000	646.05	517.28	458.87	428.00	410.36	393.40
52 000	658.72	527.42	467.86	436.39	418.41	401.11
53 000	671.39	537.57	476.86	444.78	426.45	408.83
54 000	684.05	547.71	485.86	453.17	434.50	416.54
55 000	696.72	557.85	494.85	461.56	442.55	424.25
56 000	709.39	567.99	503.85	469.95	450.59	431.97
57 000	722.06	578.14	512.85	478.35	458.64	439.68
58 000	734.72	588.28	521.85	486.74	466.69	447.39
59 000	747.39	598.42	530.84	495.13	474.73	455.11
60 000	760.06	608.56	539.84	503.52	482.78	462.82
61 000	772.73	618.71	548.84	511.91	490.82	470.54
62 000	785.39	628.85	557.84	520.31	498.87	478.25
63 000	798.06	638.99	566.83	528.70	506.92	485.96
64 000	810.73	649.14	575.83	537.09	514.96	493.68
65 000	823.40	659.28	584.83	545.48	523.01	501.39
66 000	836.07	669.42	593.82	553.87	531.06	509.10
67 000	848.73	679.56	602.82	562.27	539.10	516.82
68 000	861.40	689.71	611.82	570.66	547.15	524.53
69 000	874.07	699.85	620.82	579.05	555.19	532.24
70 000	886.74	709.99	629.81	587.44	563.24	539.96
71 000	899.40	720.13	638.81	595.83	571.29	547.67
72 000	912.07	730.28	647.81	604.23	579.33	555.39
73 000	924.74	740.42	656.80	612.62	587.38	563.10
74 000	937.41	750.56	665.80	621.01	595.43	570.81
75 000	950.07	760.70	674.80	629.40	603.47	578.53
76 000	962.74	770.85	683.80	637.79	611.52	586.24
77 000	975.41	780.99	692.79	646.19	619.56	593.95
78 000	988.08	791.13	701.79	654.58	627.61	601.67
79 000	1000.74	801.28	710.79	662.97	635.66	609.38
80 000	1013.41	811.42	719.79	671.36	643.70	617.09
81 000	1026.08	821.56	728.78	679.75	651.75	624.81
82 000	1038.75	831.70	737.78	688.15	659.80	632.52
83 000	1051.41	841.85	746.78	696.54	667.84	640.24
84 000	1064.08	851.99	755.77	704.93	675.89	647.95
85 000	1076.75	862.13	764.77	713.32	683.93	655.66
86 000	1089.42	872.27	773.77	721.71	691.98	663.38
87 000	1102.08	882.42	782.77	730.11	700.03	671.09
88 000	1114.75	892.56	791.76	738.50	708.07	678.80
89 000	1127.42	902.70	800.76	746.89	716.12	686.52
90 000	1140.09	912.84	809.76	755.28	724.17	694.23
91 000	1152.75	922.99	818.76	763.67	732.21	701.94
92 000	1165.42	933.13	827.75	772.07	740.26	709.66
93 000	1178.09	943.27	836.75	780.46	748.30	717.37
94 000	1190.76	953.42	845.75	788.85	756.35	725.08
95 000	1203.42	963.56	854.74	797.24	764.40	732.80
96 000	1216.09	973.70	863.74	805.63	772.44	740.51
97 000	1228.76	983.84	872.74	814.03	780.49	748.23
98 000	1241.43	993.99	881.74	822.42	788.54	755.94
99 000	1254.10	1004.13	890.73	830.81	796.58	763.65
100 000	1266.76	1014.27	899.73	839.20	804.63	771.37

FOR **OTHER RATES AND TERMS** *SEE PAGE A-1.*

TERM➧ AMOUNT	3 YEARS	5 YEARS	10 YEARS	15 YEARS	20 YEARS	25 YEARS	30 YEARS	40 YEARS
$ 100	3.20	2.09	1.29	1.03	.92	.86	.83	.80
200	6.39	4.18	2.57	2.06	1.84	1.72	1.65	1.59
300	9.58	6.27	3.85	3.09	2.75	2.57	2.47	2.38
400	12.77	8.36	5.13	4.12	3.67	3.43	3.30	3.17
500	15.96	10.44	6.41	5.15	4.58	4.29	4.12	3.96
600	19.15	12.53	7.69	6.18	5.50	5.14	4.94	4.75
700	22.35	14.62	8.97	7.21	6.42	6.00	5.76	5.54
800	25.54	16.71	10.25	8.24	7.33	6.86	6.59	6.33
900	28.73	18.80	11.53	9.27	8.25	7.71	7.41	7.12
1 000	31.92	20.88	12.81	10.30	9.16	8.57	8.23	7.91
1 000	31.92	20.88	12.81	10.30	9.16	8.57	8.23	7.91
2 000	63.84	41.76	25.61	20.59	18.32	17.13	16.46	15.82
3 000	95.75	62.64	38.41	30.88	27.48	25.70	24.69	23.72
4 000	127.67	83.52	51.22	41.17	36.64	34.26	32.91	31.63
5 000	159.59	104.40	64.02	51.46	45.80	42.82	41.14	39.54
6 000	191.50	125.28	76.82	61.76	54.96	51.39	49.37	47.44
7 000	223.42	146.16	89.63	72.05	64.12	59.95	57.59	55.35
8 000	255.33	167.04	102.43	82.34	73.27	68.52	65.82	63.26
9 000	287.25	187.92	115.23	92.63	82.43	77.08	74.05	71.16
10 000	319.17	208.80	128.04	102.92	91.59	85.64	82.27	79.07
11 000	351.08	229.68	140.84	113.22	100.75	94.21	90.50	86.98
12 000	383.00	250.56	153.64	123.51	109.91	102.77	98.73	94.88
13 000	414.92	271.44	166.45	133.80	119.07	111.33	106.95	102.79
14 000	446.83	292.32	179.25	144.09	128.23	119.90	115.18	110.70
15 000	478.75	313.20	192.05	154.38	137.39	128.46	123.41	118.60
16 000	510.66	334.08	204.86	164.68	146.54	137.03	131.63	126.51
17 000	542.58	354.96	217.66	174.97	155.70	145.59	139.86	134.42
18 000	574.50	375.84	230.46	185.26	164.86	154.15	148.09	142.32
19 000	606.41	396.72	243.27	195.55	174.02	162.72	156.31	150.23
20 000	638.33	417.60	256.07	205.84	183.18	171.28	164.54	158.14
21 000	670.25	438.48	268.87	216.14	192.34	179.85	172.77	166.04
22 000	702.16	459.50	281.68	226.43	201.50	188.41	180.99	173.95
23 000	734.08	480.24	294.48	236.72	210.65	196.97	189.22	181.86
24 000	765.99	501.12	307.28	247.01	219.81	205.54	197.45	189.76
25 000	797.91	522.00	320.09	257.30	228.97	214.10	205.67	197.67
26 000	829.83	542.88	332.89	267.59	238.13	222.66	213.90	205.58
27 000	861.74	563.76	345.69	277.89	247.29	231.23	222.13	213.48
28 000	893.66	584.64	358.50	288.18	256.45	239.79	230.35	221.39
29 000	925.58	605.52	371.30	298.47	265.61	248.36	238.58	229.30
30 000	957.49	626.40	384.10	308.76	274.77	256.92	246.81	237.20
31 000	989.41	647.28	396.91	319.05	283.92	265.48	255.03	245.11
32 000	1021.32	668.16	409.71	329.35	293.08	274.05	263.26	253.02
33 000	1053.24	689.04	422.51	339.64	302.24	282.61	271.49	260.92
34 000	1085.16	709.92	435.32	349.93	311.40	291.17	279.71	268.83
35 000	1117.07	730.80	448.12	360.22	320.56	299.74	287.94	276.74
36 000	1148.99	751.68	460.92	370.51	329.72	308.30	296.17	284.64
37 000	1180.90	772.56	473.73	380.81	338.88	316.87	304.39	292.55
38 000	1212.82	793.44	486.53	391.10	348.03	325.43	312.62	300.46
39 000	1244.74	814.32	499.33	401.39	357.19	333.99	320.85	308.36
40 000	1276.65	835.20	512.14	411.68	366.35	342.56	329.08	316.27
41 000	1308.57	856.08	524.94	421.97	375.51	351.12	337.30	324.18
42 000	1340.49	876.96	537.74	432.27	384.67	359.69	345.53	332.08
43 000	1372.40	897.84	550.55	442.56	393.83	368.25	353.76	339.99
44 000	1404.32	918.72	563.35	452.85	402.99	376.81	361.98	347.90
45 000	1436.23	939.60	576.15	463.14	412.15	385.38	370.21	355.80

FOR **OTHER RATES AND TERMS** *SEE PAGE A-1.*

TERM→ AMOUNT	10 YEARS	15 YEARS	20 YEARS	25 YEARS	30 YEARS	40 YEARS
$46 000	588.96	473.43	421.30	393.94	378.44	363.71
47 000	601.76	483.73	430.46	402.50	386.66	371.62
48 000	614.56	494.02	439.62	411.07	394.89	379.52
49 000	627.37	504.31	448.78	419.63	403.12	387.43
50 000	640.17	514.60	457.94	428.20	411.34	395.34
51 000	652.97	524.89	467.10	436.76	419.57	403.24
52 000	665.78	535.18	476.26	445.32	427.80	411.15
53 000	678.58	545.48	485.41	453.89	436.02	419.06
54 000	691.38	555.77	494.57	462.45	444.25	426.96
55 000	704.18	566.06	503.73	471.02	452.48	434.87
56 000	716.99	576.35	512.89	479.58	460.70	442.77
57 000	729.79	586.64	522.05	488.14	468.93	450.68
58 000	742.59	596.94	531.21	496.71	477.16	458.59
59 000	755.40	607.23	540.37	505.27	485.38	466.49
60 000	768.20	617.52	549.53	513.83	493.61	474.40
61 000	781.00	627.81	558.68	522.40	501.84	482.31
62 000	793.81	638.10	567.84	530.96	510.06	490.21
63 000	806.61	648.40	577.00	539.53	518.29	498.12
64 000	819.41	658.69	586.16	548.09	526.52	506.03
65 000	832.22	668.98	595.32	556.65	534.74	513.93
66 000	845.02	679.27	604.48	565.22	542.97	521.84
67 000	857.82	689.56	613.64	573.78	551.20	529.75
68 000	870.63	699.86	622.79	582.34	559.42	537.65
69 000	883.43	710.15	631.95	590.91	567.65	545.56
70 000	896.23	720.44	641.11	599.47	575.88	553.47
71 000	909.04	730.73	650.27	608.04	584.10	561.37
72 000	921.84	741.02	659.43	616.60	592.33	569.28
73 000	934.64	751.32	668.59	625.16	600.56	577.19
74 000	947.45	761.61	677.75	633.73	608.78	585.09
75 000	960.25	771.90	686.91	642.29	617.01	593.00
76 000	973.05	782.19	696.06	650.86	625.24	600.91
77 000	985.86	792.48	705.22	659.42	633.47	608.81
78 000	998.66	802.77	714.38	667.98	641.69	616.72
79 000	1011.46	813.07	723.54	676.55	649.92	624.63
80 000	1024.27	823.36	732.70	685.11	658.15	632.53
81 000	1037.07	833.65	741.86	693.67	666.37	640.44
82 000	1049.87	843.94	751.02	702.24	674.60	648.35
83 000	1062.68	854.23	760.17	710.80	682.83	656.25
84 000	1075.48	864.53	769.33	719.37	691.05	664.16
85 000	1088.28	874.82	778.49	727.93	699.28	672.07
86 000	1101.09	885.11	787.65	736.49	707.51	679.97
87 000	1113.89	895.40	796.81	745.06	715.73	687.88
88 000	1126.69	905.69	805.97	753.62	723.96	695.79
89 000	1139.50	915.99	815.13	762.18	732.19	703.69
90 000	1152.30	926.28	824.29	770.75	740.41	711.60
91 000	1165.10	936.57	833.44	779.31	748.64	719.51
92 000	1177.91	946.86	842.60	787.88	756.87	727.41
93 000	1190.71	957.15	851.76	796.44	765.09	735.32
94 000	1203.51	967.45	860.92	805.00	773.32	743.23
95 000	1216.32	977.74	870.08	813.57	781.55	751.13
96 000	1229.12	988.03	879.24	822.13	789.77	759.04
97 000	1241.92	998.32	888.40	830.70	798.00	766.95
98 000	1254.73	1008.61	897.55	839.26	806.23	774.85
99 000	1267.53	1018.91	906.71	847.82	814.45	782.76
100 000	1280.33	1029.20	915.87	856.39	822.68	790.67

FOR **OTHER RATES AND TERMS** *SEE PAGE A-1.*

TERM ► AMOUNT	3 YEARS	5 YEARS	10 YEARS	15 YEARS	20 YEARS	25 YEARS	30 YEARS	40 YEARS
$ 100	3.21	2.11	1.30	1.05	.94	.88	.85	.82
200	6.41	4.21	2.59	2.09	1.87	1.75	1.69	1.63
300	9.61	6.31	3.89	3.14	2.80	2.63	2.53	2.44
400	12.82	8.41	5.18	4.18	3.73	3.50	3.37	3.25
500	16.02	10.51	6.47	5.23	4.67	4.37	4.21	4.06
600	19.22	12.61	7.77	6.27	5.60	5.25	5.05	4.87
700	22.43	14.71	9.06	7.31	6.53	6.12	5.89	5.68
800	25.63	16.81	10.36	8.36	7.46	6.99	6.73	6.49
900	28.83	18.91	11.65	9.40	8.39	7.87	7.57	7.30
1 000	32.04	21.01	12.94	10.45	9.33	8.74	8.41	8.11
1 000	32.04	21.01	12.94	10.45	9.33	8.74	8.41	8.11
2 000	64.07	42.01	25.88	20.89	18.65	17.48	16.82	16.21
3 000	96.10	63.01	38.82	31.33	27.97	26.22	25.23	24.31
4 000	128.14	84.01	51.76	41.77	37.29	34.95	33.64	32.41
5 000	160.17	105.01	64.70	52.22	46.61	43.69	42.05	40.51
6 000	192.20	126.02	77.64	62.66	55.93	52.43	50.46	48.61
7 000	224.24	147.02	90.58	73.10	65.25	61.16	58.86	56.71
8 000	256.27	168.02	103.52	83.54	74.58	69.90	67.27	64.81
9 000	288.30	189.02	116.46	93.99	83.90	78.64	75.68	72.91
10 000	320.33	210.02	129.40	104.43	93.22	87.37	84.09	81.01
11 000	352.37	231.03	142.34	114.87	102.54	96.11	92.50	89.11
12 000	384.40	252.03	155.28	125.31	111.86	104.85	100.91	97.21
13 000	416.43	273.03	168.22	135.75	121.18	113.59	109.32	105.31
14 000	448.47	294.03	181.16	146.20	130.50	122.32	117.72	113.41
15 000	480.50	315.03	194.10	156.64	139.82	131.06	126.13	121.51
16 000	512.53	336.03	207.04	167.08	149.15	139.80	134.54	129.61
17 000	544.57	357.04	219.98	177.52	158.47	148.53	142.95	137.72
18 000	576.60	378.04	232.92	187.97	167.79	157.27	151.36	145.82
19 000	608.63	399.04	245.86	198.41	177.11	166.01	159.77	153.92
20 000	640.66	420.04	258.80	208.85	186.43	174.74	168.18	162.02
21 000	672.70	441.04	271.74	219.29	195.75	183.48	176.58	170.12
22 000	704.73	462.05	284.68	229.73	205.07	192.22	184.99	178.22
23 000	736.76	483.05	297.62	240.18	214.40	200.96	193.40	186.32
24 000	768.80	504.05	310.56	250.62	223.72	209.69	201.81	194.42
25 000	800.83	525.05	323.50	261.06	233.04	218.43	210.22	202.52
26 000	832.86	546.05	336.44	271.50	242.36	227.17	218.63	210.62
27 000	864.89	567.06	349.38	281.95	251.68	235.90	227.04	218.72
28 000	896.93	588.06	362.32	292.39	261.00	244.64	235.44	226.82
29 000	928.96	609.06	375.26	302.83	270.32	253.38	243.85	234.92
30 000	960.99	630.06	388.20	313.27	279.64	262.11	252.26	243.02
31 000	993.03	651.06	401.14	323.71	288.97	270.85	260.67	251.12
32 000	1025.06	672.06	414.08	334.16	298.29	279.59	269.08	259.22
33 000	1057.09	693.07	427.02	344.60	307.61	288.32	277.49	267.33
34 000	1089.13	714.07	439.96	355.04	316.93	297.06	285.90	275.43
35 000	1121.16	735.07	452.90	365.48	326.25	305.80	294.30	283.53
36 000	1153.19	756.07	465.84	375.93	335.57	314.54	302.71	291.63
37 000	1185.22	777.07	478.78	386.37	344.89	323.27	311.12	299.73
38 000	1217.26	798.08	491.72	396.81	354.21	332.01	319.53	307.83
39 000	1249.29	819.08	504.66	407.25	363.54	340.75	327.94	315.93
40 000	1281.32	840.08	517.60	417.69	372.86	349.48	336.35	324.03
41 000	1313.36	861.08	530.53	428.14	382.18	358.22	344.76	332.13
42 000	1345.39	882.08	543.47	438.58	391.50	366.96	353.16	340.23
43 000	1377.42	903.09	556.41	449.02	400.82	375.69	361.57	348.33
44 000	1409.45	924.09	569.35	459.46	410.14	384.43	369.98	356.43
45 000	1441.49	945.09	582.29	469.91	419.46	393.17	378.39	364.53

FOR **OTHER RATES AND TERMS** *SEE PAGE A-1.*

TERM➟ AMOUNT	10 YEARS	15 YEARS	20 YEARS	25 YEARS	30 YEARS	40 YEARS
$46 000	595.23	480.35	428.79	401.91	386.80	372.63
47 000	608.17	490.79	438.11	410.64	395.21	380.73
48 000	621.11	501.23	447.43	419.38	403.62	388.83
49 000	634.05	511.68	456.75	428.12	412.02	396.94
50 000	646.99	522.12	466.07	436.85	420.43	405.04
51 000	659.93	532.56	475.39	445.59	428.84	413.14
52 000	672.87	543.00	484.71	454.33	437.25	421.24
53 000	685.81	553.44	494.03	463.06	445.66	429.34
54 000	698.75	563.89	503.36	471.80	454.07	437.44
55 000	711.69	574.33	512.68	480.54	462.47	445.54
56 000	724.63	584.77	522.00	489.28	470.88	453.64
57 000	737.57	595.21	531.32	498.01	479.29	461.74
58 000	750.51	605.66	540.64	506.75	487.70	469.84
59 000	763.45	616.10	549.96	515.49	496.11	477.94
60 000	776.39	626.54	559.28	524.22	504.52	486.04
61 000	789.33	636.98	568.61	532.96	512.93	494.14
62 000	802.27	647.42	577.93	541.70	521.33	502.24
63 000	815.21	657.87	587.25	550.43	529.74	510.34
64 000	828.15	668.31	596.57	559.17	538.15	518.44
65 000	841.09	678.75	605.89	567.91	546.56	526.55
66 000	854.03	689.19	615.21	576.64	554.97	534.65
67 000	866.97	699.64	624.53	585.38	563.38	542.75
68 000	879.91	710.08	633.85	594.12	571.79	550.85
69 000	892.85	720.52	643.18	602.86	580.19	558.95
70 000	905.79	730.96	652.50	611.59	588.60	567.05
71 000	918.73	741.40	661.82	620.33	597.01	575.15
72 000	931.67	751.85	671.14	629.07	605.42	583.25
73 000	944.61	762.29	680.46	637.80	613.83	591.35
74 000	957.55	772.73	689.78	646.54	622.24	599.45
75 000	970.49	783.17	699.10	655.28	630.65	607.55
76 000	983.43	793.62	708.42	664.01	639.05	615.65
77 000	996.37	804.06	717.75	672.75	647.46	623.75
78 000	1009.31	814.50	727.07	681.49	655.87	631.85
79 000	1022.25	824.94	736.39	690.23	664.28	639.95
80 000	1035.19	835.38	745.71	698.96	672.69	648.05
81 000	1048.13	845.83	755.03	707.70	681.10	656.15
82 000	1061.06	856.27	764.35	716.44	689.51	664.26
83 000	1074.00	866.71	773.67	725.17	697.91	672.36
84 000	1086.94	877.15	783.00	733.91	706.32	680.46
85 000	1099.88	887.60	792.32	742.65	714.73	688.56
86 000	1112.82	898.04	801.64	751.38	723.14	696.66
87 000	1125.76	908.48	810.96	760.12	731.55	704.76
88 000	1138.70	918.92	820.28	768.86	739.96	712.86
89 000	1151.64	929.36	829.60	777.60	748.37	720.96
90 000	1164.58	939.81	838.92	786.33	756.77	729.06
91 000	1177.52	950.25	848.24	795.07	765.18	737.16
92 000	1190.46	960.69	857.57	803.81	773.59	745.26
93 000	1203.40	971.13	866.89	812.54	782.00	753.36
94 000	1216.34	981.58	876.21	821.28	790.41	761.46
95 000	1229.28	992.02	885.53	830.02	798.82	769.56
96 000	1242.22	1002.46	894.85	838.75	807.23	777.66
97 000	1255.16	1012.90	904.17	847.49	815.63	785.76
98 000	1268.10	1023.35	913.49	856.23	824.04	793.87
99 000	1281.04	1033.79	922.81	864.96	832.45	801.97
100 000	1293.98	1044.23	932.14	873.70	840.86	810.07

FOR **OTHER RATES AND TERMS** *SEE PAGE A-1.*

TERM ♦ AMOUNT	3 YEARS	5 YEARS	10 YEARS	15 YEARS	20 YEARS	25 YEARS	30 YEARS	40 YEARS
$ 100	3.22	2.12	1.31	1.06	.95	.90	.86	.83
200	6.43	4.23	2.62	2.12	1.90	1.79	1.72	1.66
300	9.65	6.34	3.93	3.18	2.85	2.68	2.58	2.49
400	12.86	8.45	5.24	4.24	3.80	3.57	3.44	3.32
500	16.08	10.57	6.54	5.30	4.75	4.46	4.30	4.15
600	19.29	12.68	7.85	6.36	5.70	5.35	5.16	4.98
700	22.51	14.79	9.16	7.42	6.64	6.24	6.02	5.81
800	25.72	16.90	10.47	8.48	7.59	7.13	6.88	6.64
900	28.94	19.02	11.77	9.54	8.54	8.03	7.74	7.47
1 000	32.15	21.13	13.08	10.60	9.49	8.92	8.60	8.30
1 000	32.15	21.13	13.08	10.60	9.49	8.92	8.60	8.30
2 000	64.30	42.25	26.16	21.19	18.98	17.83	17.19	16.60
3 000	96.45	63.38	39.24	31.79	28.46	26.74	25.78	24.89
4 000	128.60	84.50	52.31	42.38	37.95	35.65	34.37	33.19
5 000	160.75	105.63	65.39	52.97	47.43	44.56	42.96	41.48
6 000	192.90	126.75	78.47	63.57	56.92	53.47	51.55	49.78
7 000	225.05	147.87	91.54	74.16	66.40	62.38	60.15	58.07
8 000	257.20	169.00	104.62	84.75	75.89	71.30	68.74	66.37
9 000	289.35	190.12	117.70	95.35	85.37	80.21	77.33	74.67
10 000	321.50	211.25	130.78	105.94	94.86	89.12	85.92	82.96
11 000	353.65	232.37	143.85	116.53	104.34	98.03	94.51	91.26
12 000	385.80	253.50	156.93	127.13	113.83	106.94	103.10	99.55
13 000	417.95	274.62	170.01	137.72	123.31	115.85	111.70	107.85
14 000	450.10	295.74	183.08	148.32	132.80	124.76	120.29	116.14
15 000	482.25	316.87	196.16	158.91	142.28	133.68	128.88	124.44
16 000	514.40	337.99	209.24	169.50	151.77	142.59	137.47	132.73
17 000	546.55	359.12	222.31	180.10	161.25	151.50	146.06	141.03
18 000	578.70	380.24	235.39	190.69	170.74	160.41	154.65	149.33
19 000	610.85	401.37	248.47	201.28	180.22	169.32	163.24	157.62
20 000	643.00	422.49	261.55	211.88	189.71	178.23	171.84	165.92
21 000	675.15	443.61	274.62	222.47	199.19	187.14	180.43	174.21
22 000	707.30	464.74	287.70	233.06	208.68	196.06	189.02	182.51
23 000	739.45	485.86	300.78	243.66	218.16	204.97	197.61	190.80
24 000	771.60	506.99	313.85	254.25	227.65	213.88	206.20	199.10
25 000	803.75	528.11	326.93	264.85	237.13	222.79	214.79	207.39
26 000	835.90	549.24	340.01	275.44	246.62	231.70	223.39	215.69
27 000	868.05	570.36	353.08	286.03	256.10	240.61	231.98	223.99
28 000	900.20	591.48	366.16	296.63	265.59	249.52	240.57	232.28
29 000	932.35	612.61	379.24	307.22	275.07	258.43	249.16	240.58
30 000	964.50	633.73	392.32	317.81	284.56	267.35	257.75	248.87
31 000	996.65	654.86	405.39	328.41	294.05	276.26	266.34	257.17
32 000	1028.80	675.98	418.47	339.00	303.53	285.17	274.93	265.46
33 000	1060.95	697.11	431.55	349.59	313.02	294.08	283.53	273.76
34 000	1093.10	718.23	444.62	360.19	322.50	302.99	292.12	282.05
35 000	1125.25	739.35	457.70	370.78	331.99	311.90	300.71	290.35
36 000	1157.40	760.48	470.78	381.38	341.47	320.81	309.30	298.65
37 000	1189.55	781.60	483.85	391.97	350.96	329.73	317.89	306.94
38 000	1221.70	802.73	496.93	402.56	360.44	338.64	326.48	315.24
39 000	1253.85	823.85	510.01	413.16	369.93	347.55	335.08	323.53
40 000	1286.00	844.97	523.09	423.75	379.41	356.46	343.67	331.83
41 000	1318.15	866.10	536.16	434.34	388.90	365.37	352.26	340.12
42 000	1350.30	887.22	549.24	444.94	398.38	374.28	360.85	348.42
43 000	1382.45	908.35	562.32	455.53	407.87	383.19	369.44	356.72
44 000	1414.60	929.47	575.39	466.12	417.35	392.11	378.03	365.01
45 000	1446.75	950.60	588.47	476.72	426.84	401.02	386.62	373.31

FOR **OTHER RATES AND TERMS** *SEE PAGE A-1.*

TERM ◆ AMOUNT	10 YEARS	15 YEARS	20 YEARS	25 YEARS	30 YEARS	40 YEARS
$46 000	601.55	487.31	436.32	409.93	395.22	381.60
47 000	614.63	497.91	445.81	418.84	403.81	389.90
48 000	627.70	508.50	455.29	427.75	412.40	398.19
49 000	640.78	519.09	464.78	436.66	420.99	406.49
50 000	653.86	529.69	474.26	445.57	429.58	414.78
51 000	666.93	540.28	483.75	454.49	438.17	423.08
52 000	680.01	550.87	493.23	463.40	446.77	431.38
53 000	693.09	561.47	502.72	472.31	455.36	439.67
54 000	706.16	572.06	512.20	481.22	463.95	447.97
55 000	719.24	582.65	521.69	490.13	472.54	456.26
56 000	732.32	593.25	531.17	499.04	481.13	464.56
57 000	745.40	603.84	540.66	507.95	489.72	472.85
58 000	758.47	614.44	550.14	516.86	498.31	481.15
59 000	771.55	625.03	559.63	525.78	506.91	489.44
60 000	784.63	635.62	569.12	534.69	515.50	497.74
61 000	797.70	646.22	578.60	543.60	524.09	506.04
62 000	810.78	656.81	588.09	552.51	532.68	514.33
63 000	823.86	667.40	597.57	561.42	541.27	522.63
64 000	836.93	678.00	607.06	570.33	549.86	530.92
65 000	850.01	688.59	616.54	579.24	558.46	539.22
66 000	863.09	699.18	626.03	588.16	567.05	547.51
67 000	876.17	709.78	635.51	597.07	575.64	555.81
68 000	889.24	720.37	645.00	605.98	584.23	564.10
69 000	902.32	730.97	654.48	614.89	592.82	572.40
70 000	915.40	741.56	663.97	623.80	601.41	580.70
71 000	928.47	752.15	673.45	632.71	610.00	588.99
72 000	941.55	762.75	682.94	641.62	618.60	597.29
73 000	954.63	773.34	692.42	650.54	627.19	605.58
74 000	967.70	783.93	701.91	659.45	635.78	613.88
75 000	980.78	794.53	711.39	668.36	644.37	622.17
76 000	993.86	805.12	720.88	677.27	652.96	630.47
77 000	1006.94	815.71	730.36	686.18	661.55	638.77
78 000	1020.01	826.31	739.85	695.09	670.15	647.06
79 000	1033.09	836.90	749.33	704.00	678.74	655.36
80 000	1046.17	847.50	758.82	712.91	687.33	663.65
81 000	1059.24	858.09	768.30	721.83	695.92	671.95
82 000	1072.32	868.68	777.79	730.74	704.51	680.24
83 000	1085.40	879.28	787.27	739.65	713.10	688.54
84 000	1098.48	889.87	796.76	748.56	721.69	696.83
85 000	1111.55	900.46	806.24	757.47	730.29	705.13
86 000	1124.63	911.06	815.73	766.38	738.88	713.43
87 000	1137.71	921.65	825.21	775.29	747.47	721.72
88 000	1150.78	932.24	834.70	784.21	756.06	730.02
89 000	1163.86	942.84	844.18	793.12	764.65	738.31
90 000	1176.94	953.43	853.67	802.03	773.24	746.61
91 000	1190.01	964.03	863.16	810.94	781.84	754.90
92 000	1203.09	974.62	872.64	819.85	790.43	763.20
93 000	1216.17	985.21	882.13	828.76	799.02	771.49
94 000	1229.25	995.81	891.61	837.67	807.61	779.79
95 000	1242.32	1006.40	901.10	846.59	816.20	788.09
96 000	1255.40	1016.99	910.58	855.50	824.79	796.38
97 000	1268.48	1027.59	920.07	864.41	833.38	804.68
98 000	1281.55	1038.18	929.55	873.32	841.98	812.97
99 000	1294.63	1048.77	939.04	882.23	850.57	821.27
100 000	1307.71	1059.37	948.52	891.14	859.16	829.56

FOR **OTHER RATES AND TERMS** *SEE PAGE A-1.*

TERM➡ AMOUNT	3 YEARS	5 YEARS	10 YEARS	15 YEARS	20 YEARS	25 YEARS	30 YEARS	40 YEARS
$ 100	3.23	2.13	1.33	1.08	.97	.91	.88	.85
200	6.46	4.25	2.65	2.15	1.94	1.82	1.76	1.70
300	9.69	6.38	3.97	3.23	2.90	2.73	2.64	2.55
400	12.91	8.50	5.29	4.30	3.87	3.64	3.52	3.40
500	16.14	10.63	6.61	5.38	4.83	4.55	4.39	4.25
600	19.37	12.75	7.93	6.45	5.80	5.46	5.27	5.10
700	22.59	14.88	9.26	7.53	6.76	6.37	6.15	5.95
800	25.82	17.00	10.58	8.60	7.73	7.27	7.03	6.80
900	29.05	19.13	11.90	9.68	8.69	8.18	7.90	7.65
1 000	32.27	21.25	13.22	10.75	9.66	9.09	8.78	8.50
1 000	32.27	21.25	13.22	10.75	9.66	9.09	8.78	8.50
2 000	64.54	42.50	26.44	21.50	19.31	18.18	17.56	16.99
3 000	96.81	63.75	39.65	32.24	28.96	27.27	26.33	25.48
4 000	129.07	84.99	52.87	42.99	38.61	36.35	35.11	33.97
5 000	161.34	106.24	66.08	53.74	48.26	45.44	43.88	42.46
6 000	193.61	127.49	79.30	64.48	57.91	54.53	52.66	50.95
7 000	225.88	148.73	92.51	75.23	67.56	63.61	61.44	59.45
8 000	258.14	169.98	105.73	85.97	77.21	72.70	70.21	67.94
9 000	290.41	191.23	118.94	96.72	86.86	81.79	78.99	76.43
10 000	322.68	212.48	132.16	107.47	96.51	90.88	87.76	84.92
11 000	354.94	233.72	145.37	118.21	106.16	99.96	96.54	93.41
12 000	387.21	254.97	158.59	128.96	115.81	109.05	105.31	101.90
13 000	419.48	276.22	171.80	139.70	125.46	118.14	114.09	110.39
14 000	451.75	297.46	185.02	150.45	135.11	127.22	122.87	118.89
15 000	484.01	318.71	198.23	161.20	144.76	136.31	131.64	127.38
16 000	516.28	339.96	211.45	171.94	154.41	145.40	140.42	135.87
17 000	548.55	361.20	224.66	182.69	164.06	154.48	149.19	144.36
18 000	580.81	382.45	237.88	193.43	173.71	163.57	157.97	152.85
19 000	613.08	403.70	251.09	204.18	183.36	172.66	166.74	161.34
20 000	645.35	424.95	264.31	214.93	193.01	181.75	175.52	169.83
21 000	677.62	446.19	277.52	225.67	202.66	190.83	184.30	178.33
22 000	709.88	467.44	290.74	236.42	212.31	199.92	193.07	186.82
23 000	742.15	488.69	303.95	247.16	221.96	209.01	201.85	195.31
24 000	774.42	509.93	317.17	257.91	231.61	218.09	210.62	203.80
25 000	806.68	531.18	330.38	268.66	241.26	227.18	219.40	212.29
26 000	838.95	552.43	343.60	279.40	250.91	236.27	228.17	220.78
27 000	871.22	573.68	356.81	290.15	260.56	245.35	236.95	229.27
28 000	903.49	594.92	370.03	300.89	270.21	254.44	245.73	237.77
29 000	935.75	616.17	383.24	311.64	279.86	263.53	254.50	246.26
30 000	968.02	637.42	396.46	322.39	289.51	272.62	263.28	254.75
31 000	1000.29	658.66	409.67	333.13	299.16	281.70	272.05	263.24
32 000	1032.55	679.91	422.89	343.88	308.81	290.79	280.83	271.73
33 000	1064.82	701.16	436.10	354.62	318.46	299.88	289.60	280.22
34 000	1097.09	722.40	449.32	365.37	328.11	308.96	298.38	288.71
35 000	1129.36	743.65	462.53	376.12	337.76	318.05	307.16	297.21
36 000	1161.62	764.90	475.75	386.86	347.41	327.14	315.93	305.70
37 000	1193.89	786.15	488.96	397.61	357.06	336.22	324.71	314.19
38 000	1226.16	807.39	502.18	408.35	366.71	345.31	333.48	322.68
39 000	1258.43	828.64	515.39	419.10	376.36	354.40	342.26	331.17
40 000	1290.69	849.89	528.61	429.85	386.01	363.49	351.03	339.66
41 000	1322.96	871.13	541.82	440.59	395.66	372.57	359.81	348.15
42 000	1355.23	892.38	555.04	451.34	405.31	381.66	368.59	356.65
43 000	1387.49	913.63	568.25	462.09	414.96	390.75	377.36	365.14
44 000	1419.76	934.87	581.47	472.83	424.61	399.83	386.14	373.63
45 000	1452.03	956.12	594.68	483.58	434.26	408.92	394.91	382.12

FOR **OTHER RATES AND TERMS** *SEE PAGE A-1.*

TERM◆ AMOUNT	10 YEARS	15 YEARS	20 YEARS	25 YEARS	30 YEARS	40 YEARS
$46 000	607.90	494.32	443.91	418.01	403.69	390.61
47 000	621.11	505.07	453.57	427.09	412.46	399.10
48 000	634.33	515.82	463.22	436.18	421.24	407.60
49 000	647.54	526.56	472.87	445.27	430.02	416.09
50 000	660.76	537.31	482.52	454.36	438.79	424.58
51 000	673.97	548.05	492.17	463.44	447.57	433.07
52 000	687.19	558.80	501.82	472.53	456.34	441.56
53 000	700.40	569.55	511.47	481.62	465.12	450.05
54 000	713.62	580.29	521.12	490.70	473.89	458.54
55 000	726.83	591.04	530.77	499.79	482.67	467.04
56 000	740.05	601.78	540.42	508.88	491.45	475.53
57 000	753.26	612.53	550.07	517.96	500.22	484.02
58 000	766.48	623.28	559.72	527.05	509.00	492.51
59 000	779.69	634.02	569.37	536.14	517.77	501.00
60 000	792.91	644.77	579.02	545.23	526.55	509.49
61 000	806.12	655.51	588.67	554.31	535.32	517.98
62 000	819.34	666.26	598.32	563.40	544.10	526.48
63 000	832.55	677.01	607.97	572.49	552.88	534.97
64 000	845.77	687.75	617.62	581.57	561.65	543.46
65 000	858.98	698.50	627.27	590.66	570.43	551.95
66 000	872.20	709.24	636.92	599.75	579.20	560.44
67 000	885.41	719.99	646.57	608.83	587.98	568.93
68 000	898.63	730.74	656.22	617.92	596.75	577.42
69 000	911.85	741.48	665.87	627.01	605.53	585.92
70 000	925.06	752.23	675.52	636.10	614.31	594.41
71 000	938.28	762.97	685.17	645.18	623.08	602.90
72 000	951.49	773.72	694.82	654.27	631.86	611.39
73 000	964.71	784.47	704.47	663.36	640.63	619.88
74 000	977.92	795.21	714.12	672.44	649.41	628.37
75 000	991.14	805.96	723.77	681.53	658.18	636.86
76 000	1004.35	816.70	733.42	690.62	666.96	645.36
77 000	1017.57	827.45	743.07	699.70	675.74	653.85
78 000	1030.78	838.20	752.72	708.79	684.51	662.34
79 000	1044.00	848.94	762.37	717.88	693.29	670.83
80 000	1057.21	859.69	772.02	726.97	702.06	679.32
81 000	1070.43	870.44	781.67	736.05	710.84	687.81
82 000	1083.64	881.18	791.32	745.14	719.61	696.30
83 000	1096.86	891.93	800.97	754.23	728.39	704.80
84 000	1110.07	902.67	810.62	763.31	737.17	713.29
85 000	1123.29	913.42	820.27	772.40	745.94	721.78
86 000	1136.50	924.17	829.92	781.49	754.72	730.27
87 000	1149.72	934.91	839.57	790.57	763.49	738.76
88 000	1162.93	945.66	849.22	799.66	772.27	747.25
89 000	1176.15	956.40	858.87	808.75	781.04	755.74
90 000	1189.36	967.15	868.52	817.84	789.82	764.24
91 000	1202.58	977.90	878.17	826.92	798.60	772.73
92 000	1215.79	988.64	887.82	836.01	807.37	781.22
93 000	1229.01	999.39	897.48	845.10	816.15	789.71
94 000	1242.22	1010.13	907.13	854.18	824.92	798.20
95 000	1255.44	1020.88	916.78	863.27	833.70	806.69
96 000	1268.65	1031.63	926.43	872.36	842.47	815.19
97 000	1281.87	1042.37	936.08	881.44	851.25	823.68
98 000	1295.08	1053.12	945.73	890.53	860.03	832.17
99 000	1308.30	1063.86	955.38	899.62	868.80	840.66
100 000	1321.51	1074.61	965.03	908.71	877.58	849.15

FOR **OTHER RATES AND TERMS** *SEE PAGE A-1.*

TERM➔ AMOUNT	3 YEARS	5 YEARS	10 YEARS	15 YEARS	20 YEARS	25 YEARS	30 YEARS	40 YEARS
$ 100	3.24	2.14	1.34	1.09	.99	.93	.90	.87
200	6.48	4.28	2.68	2.18	1.97	1.86	1.80	1.74
300	9.72	6.42	4.01	3.27	2.95	2.78	2.69	2.61
400	12.96	8.55	5.35	4.36	3.93	3.71	3.59	3.48
500	16.20	10.69	6.68	5.45	4.91	4.64	4.49	4.35
600	19.44	12.83	8.02	6.54	5.89	5.56	5.38	5.22
700	22.67	14.96	9.35	7.63	6.88	6.49	6.28	6.09
800	25.91	17.10	10.69	8.72	7.86	7.42	7.17	6.96
900	29.15	19.24	12.02	9.81	8.84	8.34	8.07	7.82
1 000	32.39	21.38	13.36	10.90	9.82	9.27	8.97	8.69
1 000	32.39	21.38	13.36	10.90	9.82	9.27	8.97	8.69
2 000	64.77	42.75	26.71	21.80	19.64	18.53	17.93	17.38
3 000	97.16	64.12	40.07	32.70	29.45	27.80	26.89	26.07
4 000	129.54	85.49	53.42	43.60	39.27	37.06	35.85	34.76
5 000	161.93	106.86	66.77	54.50	49.09	46.32	44.81	43.45
6 000	194.31	128.23	80.13	65.40	58.90	55.59	53.77	52.13
7 000	226.70	149.60	93.48	76.30	68.72	64.85	62.73	60.82
8 000	259.08	170.97	106.84	87.20	78.54	74.12	71.69	69.51
9 000	291.47	192.34	120.19	98.10	88.35	83.38	80.65	78.20
10 000	323.85	213.71	133.54	109.00	98.17	92.64	89.62	86.89
11 000	356.24	235.08	146.90	119.90	107.99	101.91	98.58	95.58
12 000	388.62	256.45	160.25	130.80	117.80	111.17	107.54	104.26
13 000	421.01	277.82	173.61	141.70	127.62	120.43	116.50	112.95
14 000	453.39	299.19	186.96	152.60	137.44	129.70	125.46	121.64
15 000	485.78	320.56	200.31	163.50	147.25	138.96	134.42	130.33
16 000	518.16	341.93	213.67	174.40	157.07	148.23	143.38	139.02
17 000	550.54	363.30	227.02	185.30	166.88	157.49	152.34	147.70
18 000	582.93	384.67	240.38	196.20	176.70	166.75	161.30	156.39
19 000	615.31	406.04	253.73	207.10	186.52	176.02	170.26	165.08
20 000	647.70	427.41	267.08	218.00	196.33	185.28	179.23	173.77
21 000	680.08	448.78	280.44	228.89	206.15	194.55	188.19	182.46
22 000	712.47	470.15	293.79	239.79	215.97	203.81	197.15	191.15
23 000	744.85	491.52	307.14	250.69	225.78	213.07	206.11	199.83
24 000	777.24	512.89	320.50	261.59	235.60	222.34	215.07	208.52
25 000	809.62	534.26	333.85	272.49	245.42	231.60	224.03	217.21
26 000	842.01	555.63	347.21	283.39	255.23	240.86	232.99	225.90
27 000	874.39	577.00	360.56	294.29	265.05	250.13	241.95	234.59
28 000	906.78	598.37	373.91	305.19	274.87	259.39	250.91	243.27
29 000	939.16	619.74	387.27	316.09	284.68	268.66	259.87	251.96
30 000	971.55	641.11	400.62	326.99	294.50	277.92	268.84	260.65
31 000	1003.93	662.48	413.98	337.89	304.31	287.18	277.80	269.34
32 000	1036.32	683.85	427.33	348.79	314.13	296.45	286.76	278.03
33 000	1068.70	705.22	440.68	359.69	323.95	305.71	295.72	286.72
34 000	1101.08	726.59	454.04	370.59	333.76	314.98	304.68	295.40
35 000	1133.47	747.96	467.39	381.49	343.58	324.24	313.64	304.09
36 000	1165.85	769.33	480.75	392.39	353.40	333.50	322.60	312.78
37 000	1198.24	790.70	494.10	403.29	363.21	342.77	331.56	321.47
38 000	1230.62	812.08	507.45	414.19	373.03	352.03	340.52	330.16
39 000	1263.01	833.45	520.81	425.09	382.85	361.29	349.48	338.84
40 000	1295.39	854.82	534.16	435.99	392.66	370.56	358.45	347.53
41 000	1327.78	876.19	547.51	446.88	402.48	379.82	367.41	356.22
42 000	1360.16	897.56	560.87	457.78	412.30	389.09	376.37	364.91
43 000	1392.55	918.93	574.22	468.68	422.11	398.35	385.33	373.60
44 000	1424.93	940.30	587.58	479.58	431.93	407.61	394.29	382.29
45 000	1457.32	961.67	600.93	490.48	441.74	416.88	403.25	390.97

FOR **OTHER RATES AND TERMS** *SEE PAGE A-1.*

TERM→ AMOUNT	10 YEARS	15 YEARS	20 YEARS	25 YEARS	30 YEARS	40 YEARS
$46 000	614.28	501.38	451.56	426.14	412.21	399.66
47 000	627.64	512.28	461.38	435.41	421.17	408.35
48 000	640.99	523.18	471.19	444.67	430.13	417.04
49 000	654.35	534.08	481.01	453.93	439.09	425.73
50 000	667.70	544.98	490.83	463.20	448.06	434.41
51 000	681.05	555.88	500.64	472.46	457.02	443.10
52 000	694.41	566.78	510.46	481.72	465.98	451.79
53 000	707.76	577.68	520.28	490.99	474.94	460.48
54 000	721.12	588.58	530.09	500.25	483.90	469.17
55 000	734.47	599.48	539.91	509.52	492.86	477.86
56 000	747.82	610.38	549.73	518.78	501.82	486.54
57 000	761.18	621.28	559.54	528.04	510.78	495.23
58 000	774.53	632.18	569.36	537.31	519.74	503.92
59 000	787.89	643.08	579.17	546.57	528.70	512.61
60 000	801.24	653.98	588.99	555.83	537.67	521.30
61 000	814.59	664.88	598.81	565.10	546.63	529.98
62 000	827.95	675.77	608.62	574.36	555.59	538.67
63 000	841.30	686.67	618.44	583.63	564.55	547.36
64 000	854.65	697.57	628.26	592.89	573.51	556.05
65 000	868.01	708.47	638.07	602.15	582.47	564.74
66 000	881.36	719.37	647.89	611.42	591.43	573.43
67 000	894.72	730.27	657.71	620.68	600.39	582.11
68 000	908.07	741.17	667.52	629.95	609.35	590.80
69 000	921.42	752.07	677.34	639.21	618.31	599.49
70 000	934.78	762.97	687.16	648.47	627.28	608.18
71 000	948.13	773.87	696.97	657.74	636.24	616.87
72 000	961.49	784.77	706.79	667.00	645.20	625.55
73 000	974.84	795.67	716.60	676.26	654.16	634.24
74 000	988.19	806.57	726.42	685.53	663.12	642.93
75 000	1001.55	817.47	736.24	694.79	672.08	651.62
76 000	1014.90	828.37	746.05	704.06	681.04	660.31
77 000	1028.26	839.27	755.87	713.32	690.00	669.00
78 000	1041.61	850.17	765.69	722.58	698.96	677.68
79 000	1054.96	861.07	775.50	731.85	707.93	686.37
80 000	1068.32	871.97	785.32	741.11	716.89	695.06
81 000	1081.67	882.87	795.14	750.38	725.85	703.75
82 000	1095.02	893.76	804.95	759.64	734.81	712.44
83 000	1108.38	904.66	814.77	768.90	743.77	721.12
84 000	1121.73	915.56	824.59	778.17	752.73	729.81
85 000	1135.09	926.46	834.40	787.43	761.69	738.50
86 000	1148.44	937.36	844.22	796.69	770.65	747.19
87 000	1161.79	948.26	854.03	805.96	779.61	755.88
88 000	1175.15	959.16	863.85	815.22	788.57	764.57
89 000	1188.50	970.06	873.67	824.49	797.54	773.25
90 000	1201.86	980.96	883.48	833.75	806.50	781.94
91 000	1215.21	991.86	893.30	843.01	815.46	790.63
92 000	1228.56	1002.76	903.12	852.28	824.42	799.32
93 000	1241.92	1013.66	912.93	861.54	833.38	808.01
94 000	1255.27	1024.56	922.75	870.81	842.34	816.69
95 000	1268.63	1035.46	932.57	880.07	851.30	825.38
96 000	1281.98	1046.36	942.38	889.33	860.26	834.07
97 000	1295.33	1057.26	952.20	898.60	869.22	842.76
98 000	1308.69	1068.16	962.02	907.86	878.18	851.45
99 000	1322.04	1079.06	971.83	917.12	887.15	860.14
100 000	1335.40	1089.96	981.65	926.39	896.11	868.82

FOR **OTHER RATES AND TERMS** *SEE PAGE A-1.*

TERM→ AMOUNT	3 YEARS	5 YEARS	10 YEARS	15 YEARS	20 YEARS	25 YEARS	30 YEARS	40 YEARS
$ 100	3.26	2.15	1.35	1.11	1.00	.95	.92	.89
200	6.51	4.30	2.70	2.22	2.00	1.89	1.83	1.78
300	9.76	6.45	4.05	3.32	3.00	2.84	2.75	2.67
400	13.01	8.60	5.40	4.43	4.00	3.78	3.66	3.56
500	16.26	10.75	6.75	5.53	5.00	4.73	4.58	4.45
600	19.51	12.90	8.10	6.64	6.00	5.67	5.49	5.34
700	22.76	15.05	9.45	7.74	6.99	6.61	6.41	6.22
800	26.01	17.20	10.80	8.85	7.99	7.56	7.32	7.11
900	29.26	19.35	12.15	9.95	8.99	8.50	8.24	8.00
1 000	32.51	21.50	13.50	11.06	9.99	9.45	9.15	8.89
1 000	32.51	21.50	13.50	11.06	9.99	9.45	9.15	8.89
2 000	65.01	42.99	26.99	22.11	19.97	18.89	18.30	17.78
3 000	97.51	64.49	40.49	33.17	29.96	28.33	27.45	26.66
4 000	130.01	85.98	53.98	44.22	39.94	37.77	36.59	35.55
5 000	162.52	107.47	67.47	55.27	49.92	47.21	45.74	44.43
6 000	195.02	128.97	80.97	66.33	59.91	56.66	54.89	53.32
7 000	227.52	150.46	94.46	77.38	69.89	66.10	64.04	62.20
8 000	260.02	171.96	107.95	88.44	79.88	75.54	73.18	71.09
9 000	292.53	193.45	121.45	99.49	89.86	84.98	82.33	79.98
10 000	325.03	214.94	134.94	110.54	99.84	94.42	91.48	88.86
11 000	357.53	236.44	148.43	121.60	109.83	103.86	100.63	97.75
12 000	390.03	257.93	161.93	132.65	119.81	113.31	109.77	106.63
13 000	422.54	279.43	175.42	143.71	129.79	122.75	118.92	115.52
14 000	455.04	300.92	188.91	154.76	139.78	132.19	128.07	124.40
15 000	487.54	322.41	202.41	165.81	149.76	141.63	137.22	133.29
16 000	520.04	343.91	215.90	176.87	159.75	151.07	146.36	142.18
17 000	552.55	365.40	229.39	187.92	169.73	160.52	155.51	151.06
18 000	585.05	386.90	242.89	198.98	179.71	169.96	164.66	159.95
19 000	617.55	408.39	256.38	210.03	189.70	179.40	173.81	168.83
20 000	650.05	429.88	269.87	221.08	199.68	188.84	182.95	177.72
21 000	682.56	451.38	283.37	232.14	209.66	198.28	192.10	186.60
22 000	715.06	472.87	296.86	243.19	219.65	207.72	201.25	195.49
23 000	747.56	494.36	310.36	254.25	229.63	217.17	210.40	204.38
24 000	780.06	515.86	323.85	265.30	239.62	226.61	219.54	213.26
25 000	812.57	537.35	337.34	276.35	249.60	236.05	228.69	222.15
26 000	845.07	558.85	350.84	287.41	259.58	245.49	237.84	231.03
27 000	877.57	580.34	364.33	298.46	269.57	254.93	246.98	239.92
28 000	910.07	601.83	377.82	309.52	279.55	264.38	256.13	248.80
29 000	942.58	623.33	391.32	320.57	289.54	273.82	265.28	257.69
30 000	975.08	644.82	404.81	331.62	299.52	283.26	274.43	266.58
31 000	1007.58	666.32	418.30	342.68	309.50	292.70	283.57	275.46
32 000	1040.08	687.81	431.80	353.73	319.49	302.14	292.72	284.35
33 000	1072.59	709.30	445.29	364.79	329.47	311.58	301.87	293.23
34 000	1105.09	730.80	458.78	375.84	339.45	321.03	311.02	302.12
35 000	1137.59	752.29	472.28	386.89	349.44	330.47	320.16	311.00
36 000	1170.09	773.79	485.77	397.95	359.42	339.91	329.31	319.89
37 000	1202.60	795.28	499.26	409.00	369.41	349.35	338.46	328.78
38 000	1235.10	816.77	512.76	420.06	379.39	358.79	347.61	337.66
39 000	1267.60	838.27	526.25	431.11	389.37	368.24	356.75	346.55
40 000	1300.10	859.76	539.74	442.16	399.36	377.68	365.90	355.43
41 000	1332.61	881.25	553.24	453.22	409.34	387.12	375.05	364.32
42 000	1365.11	902.75	566.73	464.27	419.32	396.56	384.20	373.20
43 000	1397.61	924.24	580.23	475.33	429.31	406.00	393.34	382.09
44 000	1430.11	945.74	593.72	486.38	439.29	415.44	402.49	390.98
45 000	1462.61	967.23	607.21	497.43	449.28	424.89	411.64	399.86

FOR **OTHER RATES AND TERMS** *SEE PAGE A-1.*

TERM➤ AMOUNT	10 YEARS	15 YEARS	20 YEARS	25 YEARS	30 YEARS	40 YEARS
$46 000	620.71	508.49	459.26	434.33	420.79	408.75
47 000	634.20	519.54	469.24	443.77	429.93	417.63
48 000	647.69	530.60	479.23	453.21	439.08	426.52
49 000	661.19	541.65	489.21	462.65	448.23	435.40
50 000	674.68	552.70	499.19	472.10	457.37	444.29
51 000	688.17	563.76	509.18	481.54	466.52	453.18
52 000	701.67	574.81	519.16	490.98	475.67	462.06
53 000	715.16	585.87	529.15	500.42	484.82	470.95
54 000	728.65	596.92	539.13	509.86	493.96	479.83
55 000	742.15	607.97	549.11	519.30	503.11	488.72
56 000	755.64	619.03	559.10	528.75	512.26	497.60
57 000	769.13	630.08	569.08	538.19	521.41	506.49
58 000	782.63	641.14	579.07	547.63	530.55	515.38
59 000	796.12	652.19	589.05	557.07	539.70	524.26
60 000	809.61	663.24	599.03	566.51	548.85	533.15
61 000	823.11	674.30	609.02	575.96	558.00	542.03
62 000	836.60	685.35	619.00	585.40	567.14	550.92
63 000	850.10	696.41	628.98	594.84	576.29	559.80
64 000	863.59	707.46	638.97	604.28	585.44	568.69
65 000	877.08	718.51	648.95	613.72	594.59	577.58
66 000	890.58	729.57	658.94	623.16	603.73	586.46
67 000	904.07	740.62	668.92	632.61	612.88	595.35
68 000	917.56	751.68	678.90	642.05	622.03	604.23
69 000	931.06	762.73	688.89	651.49	631.18	613.12
70 000	944.55	773.78	698.87	660.93	640.32	622.00
71 000	958.04	784.84	708.85	670.37	649.47	630.89
72 000	971.54	795.89	718.84	679.82	658.62	639.78
73 000	985.03	806.95	728.82	689.26	667.76	648.66
74 000	998.52	818.00	738.81	698.70	676.91	657.55
75 000	1012.02	829.05	748.79	708.14	686.06	666.43
76 000	1025.51	840.11	758.77	717.58	695.21	675.32
77 000	1039.00	851.16	768.76	727.02	704.35	684.20
78 000	1052.50	862.22	778.74	736.47	713.50	693.09
79 000	1065.99	873.27	788.73	745.91	722.65	701.98
80 000	1079.48	884.32	798.71	755.35	731.80	710.86
81 000	1092.98	895.38	808.69	764.79	740.94	719.75
82 000	1106.47	906.43	818.68	774.23	750.09	728.63
83 000	1119.97	917.49	828.66	783.68	759.24	737.52
84 000	1133.46	928.54	838.64	793.12	768.39	746.40
85 000	1146.95	939.59	848.63	802.56	777.53	755.29
86 000	1160.45	950.65	858.61	812.00	786.68	764.18
87 000	1173.94	961.70	868.60	821.44	795.83	773.06
88 000	1187.43	972.76	878.58	830.88	804.98	781.95
89 000	1200.93	983.81	888.56	840.33	814.12	790.83
90 000	1214.42	994.86	898.55	849.77	823.27	799.72
91 000	1227.91	1005.92	908.53	859.21	832.42	808.60
92 000	1241.41	1016.97	918.51	868.65	841.57	817.49
93 000	1254.90	1028.03	928.50	878.09	850.71	826.38
94 000	1268.39	1039.08	938.48	887.54	859.86	835.26
95 000	1281.89	1050.13	948.47	896.98	869.01	844.15
96 000	1295.38	1061.19	958.45	906.42	878.15	853.03
97 000	1308.87	1072.24	968.43	915.86	887.30	861.92
98 000	1322.37	1083.30	978.42	925.30	896.45	870.80
99 000	1335.86	1094.35	988.40	934.74	905.60	879.69
100 000	1349.35	1105.40	998.38	944.19	914.74	888.58

FOR **OTHER RATES AND TERMS** *SEE PAGE A-1.*

TERM► AMOUNT	3 YEARS	5 YEARS	10 YEARS	15 YEARS	20 YEARS	25 YEARS	30 YEARS	40 YEARS
$ 100	3.27	2.17	1.37	1.13	1.02	.97	.94	.91
200	6.53	4.33	2.73	2.25	2.04	1.93	1.87	1.82
300	9.79	6.49	4.10	3.37	3.05	2.89	2.81	2.73
400	13.05	8.65	5.46	4.49	4.07	3.85	3.74	3.64
500	16.32	10.81	6.82	5.61	5.08	4.82	4.67	4.55
600	19.58	12.98	8.19	6.73	6.10	5.78	5.61	5.46
700	22.84	15.14	9.55	7.85	7.11	6.74	6.54	6.36
800	26.10	17.30	10.91	8.97	8.13	7.70	7.47	7.27
900	29.36	19.46	12.28	10.09	9.14	8.66	8.41	8.18
1 000	32.63	21.62	13.64	11.21	10.16	9.63	9.34	9.09
1 000	32.63	21.62	13.64	11.21	10.16	9.63	9.34	9.09
2 000	65.25	43.24	27.27	22.42	20.31	19.25	18.67	18.17
3 000	97.87	64.86	40.91	33.63	30.46	28.87	28.01	27.26
4 000	130.49	86.48	54.54	44.84	40.61	38.49	37.34	36.34
5 000	163.11	108.09	68.17	56.05	50.77	48.11	46.68	45.42
6 000	195.73	129.71	81.81	67.26	60.92	57.73	56.01	54.51
7 000	228.35	151.33	95.44	78.47	71.07	67.35	65.35	63.59
8 000	260.97	172.95	109.08	89.68	81.22	76.97	74.68	72.68
9 000	293.59	194.57	122.71	100.89	91.38	86.59	84.02	81.76
10 000	326.21	216.18	136.34	112.10	101.53	96.21	93.35	90.84
11 000	358.83	237.80	149.98	123.31	111.68	105.84	102.69	99.93
12 000	391.45	259.42	163.61	134.52	121.83	115.46	112.02	109.01
13 000	424.07	281.04	177.25	145.73	131.98	125.08	121.36	118.10
14 000	456.69	302.66	190.88	156.94	142.14	134.70	130.69	127.18
15 000	489.31	324.27	204.51	168.15	152.29	144.32	140.03	136.26
16 000	521.93	345.89	218.15	179.36	162.44	153.94	149.36	145.35
17 000	554.55	367.51	231.78	190.57	172.59	163.56	158.70	154.43
18 000	587.17	389.13	245.41	201.78	182.75	173.18	168.03	163.52
19 000	619.79	410.75	259.05	212.99	192.90	182.80	177.37	172.60
20 000	652.41	432.36	272.68	224.19	203.05	192.42	186.70	181.68
21 000	685.03	453.98	286.32	235.40	213.20	202.04	196.04	190.77
22 000	717.65	475.60	299.95	246.61	223.36	211.67	205.37	199.85
23 000	750.28	497.22	313.58	257.82	233.51	221.29	214.71	208.94
24 000	782.90	518.84	327.22	269.03	243.66	230.91	224.04	218.02
25 000	815.52	540.45	340.85	280.24	253.81	240.53	233.38	227.10
26 000	848.14	562.07	354.49	291.45	263.96	250.15	242.71	236.19
27 000	880.76	583.69	368.12	302.66	274.12	259.77	252.04	245.27
28 000	913.38	605.31	381.75	313.87	284.27	269.39	261.38	254.36
29 000	946.00	626.93	395.39	325.08	294.42	279.01	270.71	263.44
30 000	978.62	648.54	409.02	336.29	304.57	288.63	280.05	272.52
31 000	1011.24	670.16	422.65	347.50	314.73	298.25	289.38	281.61
32 000	1043.86	691.78	436.29	358.71	324.88	307.87	298.72	290.69
33 000	1076.48	713.40	449.92	369.92	335.03	317.50	308.05	299.78
34 000	1109.10	735.02	463.56	381.13	345.18	327.12	317.39	308.86
35 000	1141.72	756.63	477.19	392.34	355.34	336.74	326.72	317.94
36 000	1174.34	778.25	490.82	403.55	365.49	346.36	336.06	327.03
37 000	1206.96	799.87	504.46	414.76	375.64	355.98	345.39	336.11
38 000	1239.58	821.49	518.09	425.97	385.79	365.60	354.73	345.20
39 000	1272.20	843.11	531.73	437.17	395.94	375.22	364.06	354.28
40 000	1304.82	864.72	545.36	448.38	406.10	384.84	373.40	363.36
41 000	1337.44	886.34	558.99	459.59	416.25	394.46	382.73	372.45
42 000	1370.06	907.96	572.63	470.80	426.40	404.08	392.07	381.53
43 000	1402.68	929.58	586.26	482.01	436.55	413.70	401.40	390.62
44 000	1435.30	951.19	599.90	493.22	446.71	423.33	410.74	399.70
45 000	1467.93	972.81	613.53	504.43	456.86	432.95	420.07	408.78

FOR OTHER RATES AND TERMS SEE PAGE A-1.

TERM ▶ AMOUNT	10 YEARS	15 YEARS	20 YEARS	25 YEARS	30 YEARS	40 YEARS
$46 000	627.16	515.64	467.01	442.57	429.41	417.87
47 000	640.80	526.85	477.16	452.19	438.74	426.95
48 000	654.43	538.06	487.31	461.81	448.08	436.04
49 000	668.06	549.27	497.47	471.43	457.41	445.12
50 000	681.70	560.48	507.62	481.05	466.75	454.20
51 000	695.33	571.69	517.77	490.67	476.08	463.29
52 000	708.97	582.90	527.92	500.29	485.42	472.37
53 000	722.60	594.11	538.08	509.91	494.75	481.46
54 000	736.23	605.32	548.23	519.54	504.08	490.54
55 000	749.87	616.53	558.38	529.16	513.42	499.62
56 000	763.50	627.74	568.53	538.78	522.75	508.71
57 000	777.14	638.95	578.69	548.40	532.09	517.79
58 000	790.77	650.15	588.84	558.02	541.42	526.88
59 000	804.40	661.36	598.99	567.64	550.76	535.96
60 000	818.04	672.57	609.14	577.26	560.09	545.04
61 000	831.67	683.78	619.29	586.88	569.43	554.13
62 000	845.30	694.99	629.45	596.50	578.76	563.21
63 000	858.94	706.20	639.60	606.12	588.10	572.30
64 000	872.57	717.41	649.75	615.74	597.43	581.38
65 000	886.21	728.62	659.90	625.37	606.77	590.46
66 000	899.84	739.83	670.06	634.99	616.10	599.55
67 000	913.47	751.04	680.21	644.61	625.44	608.63
68 000	927.11	762.25	690.36	654.23	634.77	617.72
69 000	940.74	773.46	700.51	663.85	644.11	626.80
70 000	954.38	784.67	710.67	673.47	653.44	635.88
71 000	968.01	795.88	720.82	683.09	662.78	644.97
72 000	981.64	807.09	730.97	692.71	672.11	654.05
73 000	995.28	818.30	741.12	702.33	681.45	663.13
74 000	1008.91	829.51	751.27	711.95	690.78	672.22
75 000	1022.55	840.72	761.43	721.57	700.12	681.30
76 000	1036.18	851.93	771.58	731.20	709.45	690.39
77 000	1049.81	863.13	781.73	740.82	718.79	699.47
78 000	1063.45	874.34	791.88	750.44	728.12	708.55
79 000	1077.08	885.55	802.04	760.06	737.46	717.64
80 000	1090.71	896.76	812.19	769.68	746.79	726.72
81 000	1104.35	907.97	822.34	779.30	756.12	735.81
82 000	1117.98	919.18	832.49	788.92	765.46	744.89
83 000	1131.62	930.39	842.65	798.54	774.79	753.97
84 000	1145.25	941.60	852.80	808.16	784.13	763.06
85 000	1158.88	952.81	862.95	817.78	793.46	772.14
86 000	1172.52	964.02	873.10	827.40	802.80	781.23
87 000	1186.15	975.23	883.25	837.03	812.13	790.31
88 000	1199.79	986.44	893.41	846.65	821.47	799.39
89 000	1213.42	997.65	903.56	856.27	830.80	808.48
90 000	1227.05	1008.86	913.71	865.89	840.14	817.56
91 000	1240.69	1020.07	923.86	875.51	849.47	826.65
92 000	1254.32	1031.28	934.02	885.13	858.81	835.73
93 000	1267.95	1042.49	944.17	894.75	868.14	844.81
94 000	1281.59	1053.70	954.32	904.37	877.48	853.90
95 000	1295.22	1064.91	964.47	913.99	886.81	862.98
96 000	1308.86	1076.12	974.62	923.61	896.15	872.07
97 000	1322.49	1087.32	984.78	933.23	905.48	881.15
98 000	1336.12	1098.53	994.93	942.86	914.82	890.23
99 000	1349.76	1109.74	1005.08	952.48	924.15	899.32
100 000	1363.39	1120.95	1015.23	962.10	933.49	908.40

FOR **OTHER RATES AND TERMS** *SEE PAGE A-1.*

TERM→ AMOUNT	3 YEARS	5 YEARS	10 YEARS	15 YEARS	20 YEARS	25 YEARS	30 YEARS	40 YEARS
$ 100	3.28	2.18	1.38	1.14	1.04	.99	.96	.93
200	6.55	4.35	2.76	2.28	2.07	1.97	1.91	1.86
300	9.83	6.53	4.14	3.41	3.10	2.95	2.86	2.79
400	13.10	8.70	5.52	4.55	4.13	3.93	3.81	3.72
500	16.37	10.88	6.89	5.69	5.17	4.91	4.77	4.65
600	19.65	13.05	8.27	6.82	6.20	5.89	5.72	5.57
700	22.92	15.22	9.65	7.96	7.23	6.87	6.67	6.50
800	26.20	17.40	11.03	9.10	8.26	7.85	7.62	7.43
900	29.47	19.57	12.40	10.23	9.29	8.83	8.58	8.36
1 000	32.74	21.75	13.78	11.37	10.33	9.81	9.53	9.29
1 000	32.74	21.75	13.78	11.37	10.33	9.81	9.53	9.29
2 000	65.48	43.49	27.56	22.74	20.65	19.61	19.05	18.57
3 000	98.22	65.23	41.33	34.10	30.97	29.41	28.57	27.85
4 000	130.96	86.97	55.11	45.47	41.29	39.21	38.10	37.14
5 000	163.70	108.72	68.88	56.83	51.61	49.01	47.62	46.42
6 000	196.44	130.46	82.66	68.20	61.94	58.81	57.14	55.70
7 000	229.18	152.20	96.43	79.57	72.26	68.61	66.67	64.99
8 000	261.91	173.94	110.21	90.93	82.58	78.41	76.19	74.27
9 000	294.65	195.69	123.98	102.30	92.90	88.22	85.71	83.55
10 000	327.39	217.43	137.76	113.66	103.22	98.02	95.24	92.83
11 000	360.13	239.17	151.53	125.03	113.55	107.82	104.76	102.12
12 000	392.87	260.91	165.31	136.40	123.87	117.62	114.28	111.40
13 000	425.61	282.66	179.08	147.76	134.19	127.42	123.81	120.68
14 000	458.35	304.40	192.86	159.13	144.51	137.22	133.33	129.97
15 000	491.09	326.14	206.63	170.49	154.83	147.02	142.85	139.25
16 000	523.82	347.88	220.41	181.86	165.16	156.82	152.38	148.53
17 000	556.56	369.63	234.18	193.23	175.48	166.62	161.90	157.82
18 000	589.30	391.37	247.96	204.59	185.80	176.43	171.42	167.10
19 000	622.04	413.11	261.73	215.96	196.12	186.23	180.95	176.38
20 000	654.78	434.85	275.51	227.32	206.44	196.03	190.47	185.66
21 000	687.52	456.60	289.28	238.69	216.76	205.83	199.99	194.95
22 000	720.26	478.34	303.06	250.06	227.09	215.63	209.52	204.23
23 000	753.00	500.08	316.83	261.42	237.41	225.43	219.04	213.51
24 000	785.73	521.82	330.61	272.79	247.73	235.23	228.56	222.80
25 000	818.47	543.57	344.38	284.15	258.05	245.03	238.09	232.08
26 000	851.21	565.31	358.16	295.52	268.37	254.83	247.61	241.36
27 000	883.95	587.05	371.93	306.89	278.70	264.64	257.13	250.64
28 000	916.69	608.79	385.71	318.25	289.02	274.44	266.66	259.93
29 000	949.43	630.54	399.48	329.62	299.34	284.24	276.18	269.21
30 000	982.17	652.28	413.26	340.98	309.66	294.04	285.70	278.49
31 000	1014.91	674.02	427.03	352.35	319.98	303.84	295.23	287.78
32 000	1047.64	695.76	440.81	363.72	330.31	313.64	304.75	297.06
33 000	1080.38	717.50	454.58	375.08	340.63	323.44	314.27	306.34
34 000	1113.12	739.25	468.36	386.45	350.95	333.24	323.79	315.63
35 000	1145.86	760.99	482.13	397.81	361.27	343.04	333.32	324.91
36 000	1178.60	782.73	495.91	409.18	371.59	352.85	342.84	334.19
37 000	1211.34	804.47	509.68	420.55	381.91	362.65	352.36	343.47
38 000	1244.08	826.22	523.46	431.91	392.24	372.45	361.89	352.76
39 000	1276.81	847.96	537.23	443.28	402.56	382.25	371.41	362.04
40 000	1309.55	869.70	551.01	454.64	412.88	392.05	380.93	371.32
41 000	1342.29	891.44	564.78	466.01	423.20	401.85	390.46	380.61
42 000	1375.03	913.19	578.56	477.38	433.52	411.65	399.98	389.89
43 000	1407.77	934.93	592.33	488.74	443.85	421.45	409.50	399.17
44 000	1440.51	956.67	606.11	500.11	454.17	431.25	419.03	408.45
45 000	1473.25	978.41	619.88	511.47	464.49	441.06	428.55	417.74

FOR **OTHER RATES AND TERMS** *SEE PAGE A-1.*

TERM ⬥ AMOUNT	10 YEARS	15 YEARS	20 YEARS	25 YEARS	30 YEARS	40 YEARS
$46 000	633.66	522.84	474.81	450.86	438.07	427.02
47 000	647.43	534.21	485.13	460.66	447.60	436.30
48 000	661.21	545.57	495.46	470.46	457.12	445.59
49 000	674.98	556.94	505.78	480.26	466.64	454.87
50 000	688.76	568.30	516.10	490.06	476.17	464.15
51 000	702.53	579.67	526.42	499.86	485.69	473.44
52 000	716.31	591.04	536.74	509.66	495.21	482.72
53 000	730.08	602.40	547.06	519.46	504.74	492.00
54 000	743.86	613.77	557.39	529.27	514.26	501.28
55 000	757.63	625.13	567.71	539.07	523.78	510.57
56 000	771.41	636.50	578.03	548.87	533.31	519.85
57 000	785.18	647.87	588.35	558.67	542.83	529.13
58 000	798.96	659.23	598.67	568.47	552.35	538.42
59 000	812.73	670.60	609.00	578.27	561.88	547.70
60 000	826.51	681.96	619.32	588.07	571.40	556.98
61 000	840.28	693.33	629.64	597.87	580.92	566.26
62 000	854.06	704.70	639.96	607.68	590.45	575.55
63 000	867.83	716.06	650.28	617.48	599.97	584.83
64 000	881.61	727.43	660.61	627.28	609.49	594.11
65 000	895.38	738.79	670.93	637.08	619.02	603.40
66 000	909.16	750.16	681.25	646.88	628.54	612.68
67 000	922.93	761.52	691.57	656.68	638.06	621.96
68 000	936.71	772.89	701.89	666.48	647.58	631.25
69 000	950.48	784.26	712.21	676.28	657.11	640.53
70 000	964.26	795.62	722.54	686.08	666.63	649.81
71 000	978.03	806.99	732.86	695.89	676.15	659.09
72 000	991.81	818.35	743.18	705.69	685.68	668.38
73 000	1005.58	829.72	753.50	715.49	695.20	677.66
74 000	1019.36	841.09	763.82	725.29	704.72	686.94
75 000	1033.13	852.45	774.15	735.09	714.25	696.23
76 000	1046.91	863.82	784.47	744.89	723.77	705.51
77 000	1060.68	875.18	794.79	754.69	733.29	714.79
78 000	1074.46	886.55	805.11	764.49	742.82	724.07
79 000	1088.23	897.92	815.43	774.29	752.34	733.36
80 000	1102.01	909.28	825.76	784.10	761.86	742.64
81 000	1115.78	920.65	836.08	793.90	771.39	751.92
02 000	1129.56	932.01	846.40	803.70	780.91	761.21
83 000	1143.33	943.38	856.72	813.50	790.43	770.49
84 000	1157.11	954.75	867.04	823.30	799.96	779.77
85 000	1170.88	966.11	877.37	833.10	809.48	789.06
86 000	1184.66	977.48	887.69	842.90	819.00	798.34
87 000	1198.43	988.84	898.01	852.70	828.53	807.62
88 000	1212.21	1000.21	908.33	862.50	838.05	816.90
89 000	1225.98	1011.58	918.65	872.31	847.57	826.19
90 000	1239.76	1022.94	928.97	882.11	857.10	835.47
91 000	1253.53	1034.31	939.30	891.91	866.62	844.75
92 000	1267.31	1045.67	949.62	901.71	876.14	854.04
93 000	1281.08	1057.04	959.94	911.51	885.67	863.32
94 000	1294.86	1068.41	970.26	921.31	895.19	872.60
95 000	1308.63	1079.77	980.58	931.11	904.71	881.88
96 000	1322.41	1091.14	990.91	940.91	914.24	891.17
97 000	1336.18	1102.50	1001.23	950.71	923.76	900.45
98 000	1349.96	1113.87	1011.55	960.52	933.28	909.73
99 000	1363.73	1125.24	1021.87	970.32	942.81	919.02
100 000	1377.51	1136.60	1032.19	980.12	952.33	928.30

FOR **OTHER RATES AND TERMS** *SEE PAGE A-1.*

11¼%

11¼%

TERM ➡ AMOUNT	3 YEARS	5 YEARS	10 YEARS	15 YEARS	20 YEARS	25 YEARS	30 YEARS	40 YEARS
$ 100	3.29	2.19	1.40	1.16	1.05	1.00	.98	.95
200	6.58	4.38	2.79	2.31	2.10	2.00	1.95	1.90
300	9.86	6.57	4.18	3.46	3.15	3.00	2.92	2.85
400	13.15	8.75	5.57	4.61	4.20	4.00	3.89	3.80
500	16.43	10.94	6.96	5.77	5.25	5.00	4.86	4.75
600	19.72	13.13	8.36	6.92	6.30	5.99	5.83	5.69
700	23.01	15.31	9.75	8.07	7.35	6.99	6.80	6.64
800	26.29	17.50	11.14	9.22	8.40	7.99	7.78	7.59
900	29.58	19.69	12.53	10.38	9.45	8.99	8.75	8.54
1 000	32.86	21.87	13.92	11.53	10.50	9.99	9.72	9.49
1 000	32.86	21.87	13.92	11.53	10.50	9.99	9.72	9.49
2 000	65.72	43.74	27.84	23.05	20.99	19.97	19.43	18.97
3 000	98.58	65.61	41.76	34.58	31.48	29.95	29.14	28.45
4 000	131.43	87.47	55.67	46.10	41.98	39.93	38.86	37.94
5 000	164.29	109.34	69.59	57.62	52.47	49.92	48.57	47.42
6 000	197.15	131.21	83.51	69.15	62.96	59.90	58.28	56.90
7 000	230.01	153.08	97.42	80.67	73.45	69.88	67.99	66.38
8 000	262.86	174.94	111.34	92.19	83.95	79.86	77.71	75.87
9 000	295.72	196.81	125.26	103.72	94.44	89.85	87.42	85.35
10 000	328.58	218.68	139.17	115.24	104.93	99.83	97.13	94.83
11 000	361.43	240.55	153.09	126.76	115.42	109.81	106.84	104.31
12 000	394.29	262.41	167.01	138.29	125.92	119.79	116.56	113.80
13 000	427.15	284.28	180.92	149.81	136.41	129.78	126.27	123.28
14 000	460.01	306.15	194.84	161.33	146.90	139.76	135.98	132.76
15 000	492.86	328.01	208.76	172.86	157.39	149.74	145.69	142.24
16 000	525.72	349.88	222.68	184.38	167.89	159.72	155.41	151.73
17 000	558.58	371.75	236.59	195.90	178.38	169.71	165.12	161.21
18 000	591.44	393.62	250.51	207.43	188.87	179.69	174.83	170.69
19 000	624.29	415.48	264.43	218.95	199.36	189.67	184.54	180.17
20 000	657.15	437.35	278.34	230.47	209.86	199.65	194.26	189.66
21 000	690.01	459.22	292.26	242.00	220.35	209.64	203.97	199.14
22 000	722.86	481.09	306.18	253.52	230.84	219.62	213.68	208.62
23 000	755.72	502.95	320.09	265.04	241.33	229.60	223.40	218.10
24 000	788.58	524.82	334.01	276.57	251.83	239.58	233.11	227.59
25 000	821.44	546.69	347.93	288.09	262.32	249.56	242.82	237.07
26 000	854.29	568.56	361.84	299.61	272.81	259.55	252.53	246.55
27 000	887.15	590.42	375.76	311.14	283.30	269.53	262.25	256.03
28 000	920.01	612.29	389.68	322.66	293.80	279.51	271.96	265.52
29 000	952.86	634.16	403.59	334.18	304.29	289.49	281.67	275.00
30 000	985.72	656.02	417.51	345.71	314.78	299.48	291.38	284.48
31 000	1018.58	677.89	431.43	357.23	325.27	309.46	301.10	293.96
32 000	1051.44	699.76	445.35	368.76	335.77	319.44	310.81	303.45
33 000	1084.29	721.63	459.26	380.28	346.26	329.42	320.52	312.93
34 000	1117.15	743.49	473.18	391.80	356.75	339.41	330.23	322.41
35 000	1150.01	765.36	487.10	403.33	367.24	349.39	339.95	331.90
36 000	1182.87	787.23	501.01	414.85	377.74	359.37	349.66	341.38
37 000	1215.72	809.10	514.93	426.37	388.23	369.35	359.37	350.86
38 000	1248.58	830.96	528.85	437.90	398.72	379.34	369.08	360.34
39 000	1281.44	852.83	542.76	449.42	409.21	389.32	378.80	369.83
40 000	1314.29	874.70	556.68	460.94	419.71	399.30	388.51	379.31
41 000	1347.15	896.56	570.60	472.47	430.20	409.28	398.22	388.79
42 000	1380.01	918.43	584.51	483.99	440.69	419.27	407.93	398.27
43 000	1412.87	940.30	598.43	495.51	451.19	429.25	417.65	407.76
44 000	1445.72	962.17	612.35	507.04	461.68	439.23	427.36	417.24
45 000	1478.58	984.03	626.27	518.56	472.17	449.21	437.07	426.72

FOR **OTHER RATES AND TERMS** *SEE PAGE A-1.*

TERM ➡ AMOUNT	10 YEARS	15 YEARS	20 YEARS	25 YEARS	30 YEARS	40 YEARS
$46 000	640.18	530.08	482.66	459.20	446.79	436.20
47 000	654.10	541.61	493.16	469.18	456.50	445.69
48 000	668.02	553.13	503.65	479.16	466.21	455.17
49 000	681.93	564.65	514.14	489.14	475.92	464.65
50 000	695.85	576.18	524.63	499.12	485.64	474.13
51 000	709.77	587.70	535.13	509.11	495.35	483.62
52 000	723.68	599.22	545.62	519.09	505.06	493.10
53 000	737.60	610.75	556.11	529.07	514.77	502.58
54 000	751.52	622.27	566.60	539.05	524.49	512.06
55 000	765.43	633.79	577.10	549.04	534.20	521.55
56 000	779.35	645.32	587.59	559.02	543.91	531.03
57 000	793.27	656.84	598.08	569.00	553.62	540.51
58 000	807.18	668.36	608.57	578.98	563.34	549.99
59 000	821.10	679.89	619.07	588.97	573.05	559.48
60 000	835.02	691.41	629.56	598.95	582.76	568.96
61 000	848.94	702.94	640.05	608.93	592.47	578.44
62 000	862.85	714.46	650.54	618.91	602.19	587.92
63 000	876.77	725.98	661.04	628.90	611.90	597.41
64 000	890.69	737.51	671.53	638.88	621.61	606.89
65 000	904.60	749.03	682.02	648.86	631.32	616.37
66 000	918.52	760.55	692.51	658.84	641.04	625.85
67 000	932.44	772.08	703.01	668.83	650.75	635.34
68 000	946.35	783.60	713.50	678.81	660.46	644.82
69 000	960.27	795.12	723.99	688.79	670.18	654.30
70 000	974.19	806.65	734.48	698.77	679.89	663.79
71 000	988.10	818.17	744.98	708.76	689.60	673.27
72 000	1002.02	829.69	755.47	718.74	699.31	682.75
73 000	1015.94	841.22	765.96	728.72	709.03	692.23
74 000	1029.86	852.74	776.45	738.70	718.74	701.72
75 000	1043.77	864.26	786.95	748.68	728.45	711.20
76 000	1057.69	875.79	797.44	758.67	738.16	720.68
77 000	1071.61	887.31	807.93	768.65	747.88	730.16
78 000	1085.52	898.83	818.42	778.63	757.59	739.65
79 000	1099.44	910.36	828.92	788.61	767.30	749.13
80 000	1113.36	921.88	839.41	798.60	777.01	758.61
81 000	1127.27	933.40	849.90	808.58	786.73	768.09
82 000	1141.19	944.93	860.39	818.56	796.44	777.58
83 000	1155.11	956.45	870.89	828.54	806.15	787.06
84 000	1169.02	967.97	881.38	838.53	815.86	796.54
85 000	1182.94	979.50	891.87	848.51	825.58	806.02
86 000	1196.86	991.02	902.37	858.49	835.29	815.51
87 000	1210.77	1002.54	912.86	868.47	845.00	824.99
88 000	1224.69	1014.07	923.35	878.46	854.72	834.47
89 000	1238.61	1025.59	933.84	888.44	864.43	843.95
90 000	1252.53	1037.12	944.34	898.42	874.14	853.44
91 000	1266.44	1048.64	954.83	908.40	883.85	862.92
92 000	1280.36	1060.16	965.32	918.39	893.57	872.40
93 000	1294.28	1071.69	975.81	928.37	903.28	881.88
94 000	1308.19	1083.21	986.31	938.35	912.99	891.37
95 000	1322.11	1094.73	996.80	948.33	922.70	900.85
96 000	1336.03	1106.26	1007.29	958.31	932.42	910.33
97 000	1349.94	1117.78	1017.78	968.30	942.13	919.81
98 000	1363.86	1129.30	1028.28	978.28	951.84	929.30
99 000	1377.78	1140.83	1038.77	988.26	961.55	938.78
100 000	1391.69	1152.35	1049.26	998.24	971.27	948.26

FOR **OTHER RATES AND TERMS** *SEE PAGE A-1.*

TERM→ AMOUNT	3 YEARS	5 YEARS	10 YEARS	15 YEARS	20 YEARS	25 YEARS	30 YEARS	40 YEARS
$ 100	3.30	2.20	1.41	1.17	1.07	1.02	1.00	.97
200	6.60	4.40	2.82	2.34	2.14	2.04	1.99	1.94
300	9.90	6.60	4.22	3.51	3.20	3.05	2.98	2.91
400	13.20	8.80	5.63	4.68	4.27	4.07	3.97	3.88
500	16.49	11.00	7.03	5.85	5.34	5.09	4.96	4.85
600	19.79	13.20	8.44	7.01	6.40	6.10	5.95	5.81
700	23.09	15.40	9.85	8.18	7.47	7.12	6.94	6.78
800	26.39	17.60	11.25	9.35	8.54	8.14	7.93	7.75
900	29.68	19.80	12.66	10.52	9.60	9.15	8.92	8.72
1 000	32.98	22.00	14.06	11.69	10.67	10.17	9.91	9.69
1 000	32.98	22.00	14.06	11.69	10.67	10.17	9.91	9.69
2 000	65.96	43.99	28.12	23.37	21.33	20.33	19.81	19.37
3 000	98.93	65.98	42.18	35.05	32.00	30.50	29.71	29.05
4 000	131.91	87.98	56.24	46.73	42.66	40.66	39.62	38.74
5 000	164.89	109.97	70.30	58.41	53.33	50.83	49.52	48.42
6 000	197.86	131.96	84.36	70.10	63.99	60.99	59.42	58.10
7 000	230.84	153.95	98.42	81.78	74.66	71.16	69.33	67.78
8 000	263.81	175.95	112.48	93.46	85.32	81.32	79.23	77.47
9 000	296.79	197.94	126.54	105.14	95.98	91.49	89.13	87.15
10 000	329.77	219.93	140.60	116.82	106.65	101.65	99.03	96.83
11 000	362.74	241.92	154.66	128.51	117.31	111.82	108.94	106.52
12 000	395.72	263.92	168.72	140.19	127.98	121.98	118.84	116.20
13 000	428.69	285.91	182.78	151.87	138.64	132.15	128.74	125.88
14 000	461.67	307.90	196.84	163.55	149.31	142.31	138.65	135.56
15 000	494.65	329.89	210.90	175.23	159.97	152.48	148.55	145.25
16 000	527.62	351.89	224.96	186.92	170.63	162.64	158.45	154.93
17 000	560.60	373.88	239.02	198.60	181.30	172.80	168.35	164.61
18 000	593.57	395.87	253.08	210.28	191.96	182.97	178.26	174.30
19 000	626.55	417.86	267.14	221.96	202.63	193.13	188.16	183.98
20 000	659.53	439.86	281.20	233.64	213.29	203.30	198.06	193.66
21 000	692.50	461.85	295.26	245.32	223.96	213.46	207.97	203.34
22 000	725.48	483.84	309.31	257.01	234.62	223.63	217.87	213.03
23 000	758.45	505.83	323.37	268.69	245.28	233.79	227.77	222.71
24 000	791.43	527.83	337.43	280.37	255.95	243.96	237.67	232.39
25 000	824.41	549.82	351.49	292.05	266.61	254.12	247.58	242.08
26 000	857.38	571.81	365.55	303.73	277.28	264.29	257.48	251.76
27 000	890.36	593.81	379.61	315.42	287.94	274.45	267.38	261.44
28 000	923.33	615.80	393.67	327.10	298.61	284.62	277.29	271.12
29 000	956.31	637.79	407.73	338.78	309.27	294.78	287.19	280.81
30 000	989.29	659.78	421.79	350.46	319.93	304.95	297.09	290.49
31 000	1022.26	681.78	435.85	362.14	330.60	315.11	307.00	300.17
32 000	1055.24	703.77	449.91	373.83	341.26	325.28	316.90	309.86
33 000	1088.21	725.76	463.97	385.51	351.93	335.44	326.80	319.54
34 000	1121.19	747.75	478.03	397.19	362.59	345.60	336.70	329.22
35 000	1154.17	769.75	492.09	408.87	373.26	355.77	346.61	338.90
36 000	1187.14	791.74	506.15	420.55	383.92	365.93	356.51	348.59
37 000	1220.12	813.73	520.21	432.24	394.58	376.10	366.41	358.27
38 000	1253.09	835.72	534.27	443.92	405.25	386.26	376.32	367.95
39 000	1286.07	857.72	548.33	455.60	415.91	396.43	386.22	377.63
40 000	1319.05	879.71	562.39	467.28	426.58	406.59	396.12	387.32
41 000	1352.02	901.70	576.45	478.96	437.24	416.76	406.02	397.00
42 000	1385.00	923.69	590.51	490.64	447.91	426.92	415.93	406.68
43 000	1417.97	945.69	604.57	502.33	458.57	437.09	425.83	416.37
44 000	1450.95	967.68	618.62	514.01	469.23	447.25	435.73	426.05
45 000	1483.93	989.67	632.68	525.69	479.90	457.42	445.64	435.73

FOR **OTHER RATES AND TERMS** *SEE PAGE A-1.*

TERM ➧ AMOUNT	10 YEARS	15 YEARS	20 YEARS	25 YEARS	30 YEARS	40 YEARS
$46 000	646.74	537.37	490.56	467.58	455.54	445.41
47 000	660.80	549.05	501.23	477.75	465.44	455.10
48 000	674.86	560.74	511.89	487.91	475.34	464.78
49 000	688.92	572.42	522.56	498.07	485.25	474.46
50 000	702.98	584.10	533.22	508.24	495.15	484.15
51 000	717.04	595.78	543.88	518.40	505.05	493.83
52 000	731.10	607.46	554.55	528.57	514.96	503.51
53 000	745.16	619.15	565.21	538.73	524.86	513.19
54 000	759.22	630.83	575.88	548.90	534.76	522.88
55 000	773.28	642.51	586.54	559.06	544.67	532.56
56 000	787.34	654.19	597.21	569.23	554.57	542.24
57 000	801.40	665.87	607.87	579.39	564.47	551.93
58 000	815.46	677.56	618.53	589.56	574.37	561.61
59 000	829.52	689.24	629.20	599.72	584.28	571.29
60 000	843.58	700.92	639.86	609.89	594.18	580.97
61 000	857.64	712.60	650.53	620.05	604.08	590.66
62 000	871.70	724.28	661.19	630.22	613.99	600.34
63 000	885.76	735.96	671.86	640.38	623.89	610.02
64 000	899.82	747.65	682.52	650.55	633.79	619.71
65 000	913.88	759.33	693.18	660.71	643.69	629.39
66 000	927.93	771.01	703.85	670.87	653.60	639.07
67 000	941.99	782.69	714.51	681.04	663.50	648.75
68 000	956.05	794.37	725.18	691.20	673.40	658.44
69 000	970.11	806.06	735.84	701.37	683.31	668.12
70 000	984.17	817.74	746.51	711.53	693.21	677.80
71 000	998.23	829.42	757.17	721.70	703.11	687.49
72 000	1012.29	841.10	767.83	731.86	713.01	697.17
73 000	1026.35	852.78	778.50	742.03	722.92	706.85
74 000	1040.41	864.47	789.16	752.19	732.82	716.53
75 000	1054.47	876.15	799.83	762.36	742.72	726.22
76 000	1068.53	887.83	810.49	772.52	752.63	735.90
77 000	1082.59	899.51	821.16	782.69	762.53	745.58
78 000	1096.65	911.19	831.82	792.85	772.43	755.26
79 000	1110.71	922.87	842.48	803.02	782.34	764.95
80 000	1124.77	934.56	853.15	813.18	792.24	774.63
81 000	1138.83	946.24	863.81	823.34	802.14	784.31
82 000	1152.89	957.92	874.48	833.51	812.04	794.00
83 000	1166.95	969.60	885.14	843.67	821.95	803.68
84 000	1181.01	981.28	895.81	853.84	831.85	813.36
85 000	1195.07	992.97	906.47	864.00	841.75	823.04
86 000	1209.13	1004.65	917.13	874.17	851.66	832.73
87 000	1223.19	1016.33	927.80	884.33	861.56	842.41
88 000	1237.24	1028.01	938.46	894.50	871.46	852.09
89 000	1251.30	1039.69	949.13	904.66	881.36	861.78
90 000	1265.36	1051.38	959.79	914.83	891.27	871.46
91 000	1279.42	1063.06	970.46	924.99	901.17	881.14
92 000	1293.48	1074.74	981.12	935.16	911.07	890.82
93 000	1307.54	1086.42	991.78	945.32	920.98	900.51
94 000	1321.60	1098.10	1002.45	955.49	930.88	910.19
95 000	1335.66	1109.79	1013.11	965.65	940.78	919.87
96 000	1349.72	1121.47	1023.78	975.82	950.68	929.56
97 000	1363.78	1133.15	1034.44	985.98	960.59	939.24
98 000	1377.84	1144.83	1045.11	996.14	970.49	948.92
99 000	1391.90	1156.51	1055.77	1006.31	980.39	958.60
100 000	1405.96	1168.19	1066.43	1016.47	990.30	968.29

FOR **OTHER RATES AND TERMS** *SEE PAGE A-1.*

TERM ▶ AMOUNT	3 YEARS	5 YEARS	10 YEARS	15 YEARS	20 YEARS	25 YEARS	30 YEARS	40 YEARS
$ 100	3.31	2.22	1.43	1.19	1.09	1.04	1.01	.99
200	6.62	4.43	2.85	2.37	2.17	2.07	2.02	1.98
300	9.93	6.64	4.27	3.56	3.26	3.11	3.03	2.97
400	13.24	8.85	5.69	4.74	4.34	4.14	4.04	3.96
500	16.55	11.06	7.11	5.93	5.42	5.18	5.05	4.95
600	19.86	13.28	8.53	7.11	6.51	6.21	6.06	5.94
700	23.17	15.49	9.95	8.29	7.59	7.25	7.07	6.92
800	26.48	17.70	11.37	9.48	8.67	8.28	8.08	7.91
900	29.79	19.91	12.79	10.66	9.76	9.32	9.09	8.90
1 000	33.10	22.12	14.21	11.85	10.84	10.35	10.10	9.89
1 000	33.10	22.12	14.21	11.85	10.84	10.35	10.10	9.89
2 000	66.20	44.24	28.41	23.69	21.68	20.70	20.19	19.77
3 000	99.29	66.36	42.61	35.53	32.52	31.05	30.29	29.66
4 000	132.39	88.48	56.82	47.37	43.35	41.40	40.38	39.54
5 000	165.48	110.60	71.02	59.21	54.19	51.74	50.48	49.42
6 000	198.58	132.71	85.22	71.05	65.03	62.09	60.57	59.31
7 000	231.67	154.83	99.43	82.89	75.86	72.44	70.66	69.19
8 000	264.77	176.95	113.63	94.74	86.70	82.79	80.76	79.07
9 000	297.86	199.07	127.83	106.58	97.54	93.14	90.85	88.96
10 000	330.96	221.19	142.03	118.42	108.38	103.48	100.95	98.84
11 000	364.05	243.31	156.24	130.26	119.21	113.83	111.04	108.73
12 000	397.15	265.42	170.44	142.10	130.05	124.18	121.13	118.61
13 000	430.24	287.54	184.64	153.94	140.89	134.53	131.23	128.49
14 000	463.34	309.66	198.85	165.78	151.72	144.88	141.32	138.38
15 000	496.43	331.78	213.05	177.62	162.56	155.22	151.42	148.26
16 000	529.53	353.90	227.25	189.47	173.40	165.57	161.51	158.14
17 000	562.62	376.02	241.46	201.31	184.24	175.92	171.60	168.03
18 000	595.72	398.13	255.66	213.15	195.07	186.27	181.70	177.91
19 000	628.81	420.25	269.86	224.99	205.91	196.62	191.79	187.79
20 000	661.91	442.37	284.06	236.83	216.75	206.96	201.89	197.68
21 000	695.00	464.49	298.27	248.67	227.58	217.31	211.98	207.56
22 000	728.10	486.61	312.47	260.51	238.42	227.66	222.08	217.45
23 000	761.19	508.73	326.67	272.36	249.26	238.01	232.17	227.33
24 000	794.29	530.84	340.88	284.20	260.09	248.36	242.26	237.21
25 000	827.38	552.96	355.08	296.04	270.93	258.70	252.36	247.10
26 000	860.48	575.08	369.28	307.88	281.77	269.05	262.45	256.98
27 000	893.57	597.20	383.48	319.72	292.61	279.40	272.55	266.86
28 000	926.67	619.32	397.69	331.56	303.44	289.75	282.64	276.75
29 000	959.76	641.44	411.89	343.40	314.28	300.10	292.73	286.63
30 000	992.86	663.55	426.09	355.24	325.12	310.44	302.83	296.51
31 000	1025.95	685.67	440.30	367.09	335.95	320.79	312.92	306.40
32 000	1059.05	707.79	454.50	378.93	346.79	331.14	323.02	316.28
33 000	1092.14	729.91	468.70	390.77	357.63	341.49	333.11	326.17
34 000	1125.24	752.03	482.91	402.61	368.47	351.84	343.20	336.05
35 000	1158.33	774.15	497.11	414.45	379.30	362.18	353.30	345.93
36 000	1191.43	796.26	511.31	426.29	390.14	372.53	363.39	355.82
37 000	1224.52	818.38	525.51	438.13	400.98	382.88	373.49	365.70
38 000	1257.62	840.50	539.72	449.97	411.81	393.23	383.58	375.58
39 000	1290.71	862.62	553.92	461.82	422.65	403.58	393.67	385.47
40 000	1323.81	884.74	568.12	473.66	433.49	413.92	403.77	395.35
41 000	1356.90	906.86	582.33	485.50	444.32	424.27	413.86	405.23
42 000	1390.00	928.97	596.53	497.34	455.16	434.62	423.96	415.12
43 000	1423.09	951.09	610.73	509.18	466.00	444.97	434.05	425.00
44 000	1456.19	973.21	624.93	521.02	476.84	455.32	444.15	434.89
45 000	1489.28	995.33	639.14	532.86	487.67	465.66	454.24	444.77

FOR **OTHER RATES AND TERMS** *SEE PAGE A-1.*

TERM▸ AMOUNT	10 YEARS	15 YEARS	20 YEARS	25 YEARS	30 YEARS	40 YEARS
$46 000	653.34	544.71	498.51	476.01	464.33	454.65
47 000	667.54	556.55	509.35	486.36	474.43	464.54
48 000	681.75	568.39	520.18	496.71	484.52	474.42
49 000	695.95	580.23	531.02	507.06	494.62	484.30
50 000	710.15	592.07	541.86	517.40	504.71	494.19
51 000	724.36	603.91	552.70	527.75	514.80	504.07
52 000	738.56	615.75	563.53	538.10	524.90	513.95
53 000	752.76	627.59	574.37	548.45	534.99	523.84
54 000	766.96	639.44	585.21	558.80	545.09	533.72
55 000	781.17	651.28	596.04	569.14	555.18	543.61
56 000	795.37	663.12	606.88	579.49	565.27	553.49
57 000	809.57	674.96	617.72	589.84	575.37	563.37
58 000	823.78	686.80	628.56	600.19	585.46	573.26
59 000	837.98	698.64	639.39	610.54	595.56	583.14
60 000	852.18	710.48	650.23	620.88	605.65	593.02
61 000	866.38	722.33	661.07	631.23	615.74	602.91
62 000	880.59	734.17	671.90	641.58	625.84	612.79
63 000	894.79	746.01	682.74	651.93	635.93	622.67
64 000	908.99	757.85	693.58	662.28	646.03	632.56
65 000	923.20	769.69	704.41	672.62	656.12	642.44
66 000	937.40	781.53	715.25	682.97	666.22	652.33
67 000	951.60	793.37	726.09	693.32	676.31	662.21
68 000	965.81	805.21	736.93	703.67	686.40	672.09
69 000	980.01	817.06	747.76	714.02	696.50	681.98
70 000	994.21	828.90	758.60	724.36	706.59	691.86
71 000	1008.41	840.74	769.44	734.71	716.69	701.74
72 000	1022.62	852.58	780.27	745.06	726.78	711.63
73 000	1036.82	864.42	791.11	755.41	736.87	721.51
74 000	1051.02	876.26	801.95	765.76	746.97	731.39
75 000	1065.23	888.10	812.79	776.10	757.06	741.28
76 000	1079.43	899.94	823.62	786.45	767.16	751.16
77 000	1093.63	911.79	834.46	796.80	777.25	761.05
78 000	1107.83	923.63	845.30	807.15	787.34	770.93
79 000	1122.04	935.47	856.13	817.50	797.44	780.81
80 000	1136.24	947.31	866.97	827.84	807.53	790.70
81 000	1150.44	959.15	877.81	838.19	817.63	800.58
82 000	1164.65	970.99	888.64	848.54	827.72	810.46
83 000	1178.85	982.83	899.48	858.89	837.82	820.35
84 000	1193.05	994.68	910.32	869.24	847.91	830.23
85 000	1207.26	1006.52	921.16	879.58	858.00	840.11
86 000	1221.46	1018.36	931.99	889.93	868.10	850.00
87 000	1235.66	1030.20	942.83	900.28	878.19	859.88
88 000	1249.86	1042.04	953.67	910.63	888.29	869.77
89 000	1264.07	1053.88	964.50	920.98	898.38	879.65
90 000	1278.27	1065.72	975.34	931.32	908.47	889.53
91 000	1292.47	1077.56	986.18	941.67	918.57	899.42
92 000	1306.68	1089.41	997.02	952.02	928.66	909.30
93 000	1320.88	1101.25	1007.85	962.37	938.76	919.18
94 000	1335.08	1113.09	1018.69	972.72	948.85	929.07
95 000	1349.28	1124.93	1029.53	983.06	958.94	938.95
96 000	1363.49	1136.77	1040.36	993.41	969.04	948.83
97 000	1377.69	1148.61	1051.20	1003.76	979.13	958.72
98 000	1391.89	1160.45	1062.04	1014.11	989.23	968.60
99 000	1406.10	1172.30	1072.87	1024.46	999.32	978.49
100 000	1420.30	1184.14	1083.71	1034.80	1009.41	988.37

FOR OTHER RATES AND TERMS SEE PAGE A-1.

TERM◆ AMOUNT	3 YEARS	5 YEARS	10 YEARS	15 YEARS	20 YEARS	25 YEARS	30 YEARS	40 YEARS
$ 100	3.33	2.23	1.44	1.21	1.11	1.06	1.03	1.01
200	6.65	4.45	2.87	2.41	2.21	2.11	2.06	2.02
300	9.97	6.68	4.31	3.61	3.31	3.16	3.09	3.03
400	13.29	8.90	5.74	4.81	4.41	4.22	4.12	4.04
500	16.61	11.13	7.18	6.01	5.51	5.27	5.15	5.05
600	19.93	13.35	8.61	7.21	6.61	6.32	6.18	6.06
700	23.26	15.58	10.05	8.41	7.71	7.38	7.21	7.06
800	26.58	17.80	11.48	9.61	8.81	8.43	8.23	8.07
900	29.90	20.03	12.92	10.81	9.91	9.48	9.26	9.08
1 000	33.22	22.25	14.35	12.01	11.02	10.54	10.29	10.09
1 000	33.22	22.25	14.35	12.01	11.02	10.54	10.29	10.09
2 000	66.43	44.49	28.70	24.01	22.03	21.07	20.58	20.17
3 000	99.65	66.74	43.05	36.01	33.04	31.60	30.86	30.26
4 000	132.86	88.98	57.39	48.01	44.05	42.13	41.15	40.34
5 000	166.08	111.23	71.74	60.01	55.06	52.67	51.44	50.43
6 000	199.29	133.47	86.09	72.02	66.07	63.20	61.72	60.51
7 000	232.51	155.72	100.43	84.02	77.08	73.73	72.01	70.60
8 000	265.72	177.96	114.78	96.02	88.09	84.26	82.29	80.68
9 000	298.93	200.21	129.13	108.02	99.10	94.80	92.58	90.77
10 000	332.15	222.45	143.48	120.02	110.11	105.33	102.87	100.85
11 000	365.36	244.69	157.82	132.02	121.12	115.86	113.15	110.94
12 000	398.58	266.94	172.17	144.03	132.14	126.39	123.44	121.02
13 000	431.79	289.18	186.52	156.03	143.15	136.92	133.72	131.11
14 000	465.01	311.43	200.86	168.03	154.16	147.46	144.01	141.19
15 000	498.22	333.67	215.21	180.03	165.17	157.99	154.30	151.28
16 000	531.43	355.92	229.56	192.03	176.18	168.52	164.58	161.36
17 000	564.65	378.16	243.91	204.03	187.19	179.05	174.87	171.45
18 000	597.86	400.41	258.25	216.04	198.20	189.59	185.16	181.53
19 000	631.08	422.65	272.60	228.04	209.21	200.12	195.44	191.62
20 000	664.29	444.89	286.95	240.04	220.22	210.65	205.73	201.70
21 000	697.51	467.14	301.29	252.04	231.23	221.18	216.01	211.79
22 000	730.72	489.38	315.64	264.04	242.24	231.71	226.30	221.87
23 000	763.93	511.63	329.99	276.04	253.25	242.25	236.59	231.96
24 000	797.15	533.87	344.34	288.05	264.27	252.78	246.87	242.04
25 000	830.36	556.12	358.68	300.05	275.28	263.31	257.16	252.13
26 000	863.58	578.36	373.03	312.05	286.29	273.84	267.44	262.21
27 000	896.79	600.61	387.38	324.05	297.30	284.38	277.73	272.30
28 000	930.01	622.85	401.72	336.05	308.31	294.91	288.02	282.38
29 000	963.22	645.09	416.07	348.05	319.32	305.44	298.30	292.47
30 000	996.43	667.34	430.42	360.06	330.33	315.97	308.59	302.55
31 000	1029.65	689.58	444.76	372.06	341.34	326.50	318.87	312.64
32 000	1062.86	711.83	459.11	384.06	352.35	337.04	329.16	322.72
33 000	1096.08	734.07	473.46	396.06	363.36	347.57	339.45	332.81
34 000	1129.29	756.32	487.81	408.06	374.37	358.10	349.73	342.89
35 000	1162.51	778.56	502.15	420.06	385.39	368.63	360.02	352.98
36 000	1195.72	800.81	516.50	432.07	396.40	379.17	370.31	363.06
37 000	1228.93	823.05	530.85	444.07	407.41	389.70	380.59	373.15
38 000	1262.15	845.29	545.19	456.07	418.42	400.23	390.88	383.23
39 000	1295.36	867.54	559.54	468.07	429.43	410.76	401.16	393.32
40 000	1328.58	889.78	573.89	480.07	440.44	421.29	411.45	403.40
41 000	1361.79	912.03	588.24	492.07	451.45	431.83	421.74	413.49
42 000	1395.01	934.27	602.58	504.08	462.46	442.36	432.02	423.57
43 000	1428.22	956.52	616.93	516.08	473.47	452.89	442.31	433.66
44 000	1461.43	978.76	631.28	528.08	484.48	463.42	452.59	443.74
45 000	1494.65	1001.01	645.62	540.08	495.49	473.96	462.88	453.83

FOR **OTHER RATES AND TERMS** *SEE PAGE A-1.*

TERM▶ AMOUNT	10 YEARS	15 YEARS	20 YEARS	25 YEARS	30 YEARS	40 YEARS
$46 000	659.97	552.08	506.50	484.49	473.17	463.91
47 000	674.32	564.08	517.52	495.02	483.45	474.00
48 000	688.67	576.09	528.53	505.55	493.74	484.08
49 000	703.01	588.09	539.54	516.08	504.03	494.17
50 000	717.36	600.09	550.55	526.62	514.31	504.25
51 000	731.71	612.09	561.56	537.15	524.60	514.34
52 000	746.05	624.09	572.57	547.68	534.88	524.42
53 000	760.40	636.09	583.58	558.21	545.17	534.51
54 000	774.75	648.10	594.59	568.75	555.46	544.59
55 000	789.10	660.10	605.60	579.28	565.74	554.68
56 000	803.44	672.10	616.61	589.81	576.03	564.76
57 000	817.79	684.10	627.62	600.34	586.31	574.85
58 000	832.14	696.10	638.63	610.88	596.60	584.93
59 000	846.48	708.10	649.65	621.41	606.89	595.02
60 000	860.83	720.11	660.66	631.94	617.17	605.10
61 000	875.18	732.11	671.67	642.47	627.46	615.19
62 000	889.52	744.11	682.68	653.00	637.74	625.27
63 000	903.87	756.11	693.69	663.54	648.03	635.36
64 000	918.22	768.11	704.70	674.07	658.32	645.44
65 000	932.57	780.11	715.71	684.60	668.60	655.53
66 000	946.91	792.12	726.72	695.13	678.89	665.61
67 000	961.26	804.12	737.73	705.67	689.18	675.70
68 000	975.61	816.12	748.74	716.20	699.46	685.78
69 000	989.95	828.12	759.75	726.73	709.75	695.87
70 000	1004.30	840.12	770.77	737.26	720.03	705.95
71 000	1018.65	852.12	781.78	747.79	730.32	716.04
72 000	1033.00	864.13	792.79	758.33	740.61	726.12
73 000	1047.34	876.13	803.80	768.86	750.89	736.21
74 000	1061.69	888.13	814.81	779.39	761.18	746.29
75 000	1076.04	900.13	825.82	789.92	771.46	756.38
76 000	1090.38	912.13	836.83	800.46	781.75	766.46
77 000	1104.73	924.13	847.84	810.99	792.04	776.55
78 000	1119.08	936.14	858.85	821.52	802.32	786.63
79 000	1133.43	948.14	869.86	832.05	812.61	796.72
80 000	1147.77	960.14	880.87	842.58	822.90	806.80
81 000	1162.12	972.14	891.88	853.12	833.18	816.89
82 000	1176.47	984.14	902.90	863.65	843.47	826.97
83 000	1190.81	996.14	913.91	874.18	853.75	837.06
84 000	1205.16	1008.15	924.92	884.71	864.04	847.14
85 000	1219.51	1020.15	935.93	895.25	874.33	857.23
86 000	1233.86	1032.15	946.94	905.78	884.61	867.31
87 000	1248.20	1044.15	957.95	916.31	894.90	877.40
88 000	1262.55	1056.15	968.96	926.84	905.18	887.48
89 000	1276.90	1068.15	979.97	937.37	915.47	897.57
90 000	1291.24	1080.16	990.98	947.91	925.76	907.65
91 000	1305.59	1092.16	1001.99	958.44	936.04	917.74
92 000	1319.94	1104.16	1013.00	968.97	946.33	927.82
93 000	1334.28	1116.16	1024.02	979.50	956.61	937.91
94 000	1348.63	1128.16	1035.03	990.04	966.90	947.99
95 000	1362.98	1140.16	1046.04	1000.57	977.19	958.08
96 000	1377.33	1152.17	1057.05	1011.10	987.47	968.16
97 000	1391.67	1164.17	1068.06	1021.63	997.76	978.25
98 000	1406.02	1176.17	1079.07	1032.16	1008.05	988.33
99 000	1420.37	1188.17	1090.08	1042.70	1018.33	998.42
100 000	1434.71	1200.17	1101.09	1053.23	1028.62	1008.50

FOR **OTHER RATES AND TERMS** *SEE PAGE A-1.*

TERM♦ AMOUNT	3 YEARS	5 YEARS	10 YEARS	15 YEARS	20 YEARS	25 YEARS	30 YEARS	40 YEARS
$ 100	3.34	2.24	1.45	1.22	1.12	1.08	1.05	1.03
200	6.67	4.48	2.90	2.44	2.24	2.15	2.10	2.06
300	10.01	6.72	4.35	3.65	3.36	3.22	3.15	3.09
400	13.34	8.95	5.80	4.87	4.48	4.29	4.20	4.12
500	16.67	11.19	7.25	6.09	5.60	5.36	5.24	5.15
600	20.01	13.43	8.70	7.30	6.72	6.44	6.29	6.18
700	23.34	15.66	10.15	8.52	7.83	7.51	7.34	7.21
800	26.67	17.90	11.60	9.74	8.95	8.58	8.39	8.23
900	30.01	20.14	13.05	10.95	10.07	9.65	9.44	9.26
1 000	33.34	22.38	14.50	12.17	11.19	10.72	10.48	10.29
1 000	33.34	22.38	14.50	12.17	11.19	10.72	10.48	10.29
2 000	66.67	44.75	28.99	24.33	22.38	21.44	20.96	20.58
3 000	100.01	67.12	43.48	36.49	33.56	32.16	31.44	30.87
4 000	133.34	89.49	57.97	48.66	44.75	42.87	41.92	41.15
5 000	166.67	111.86	72.46	60.82	55.93	53.59	52.40	51.44
6 000	200.01	134.23	86.96	72.98	67.12	64.31	62.88	61.73
7 000	233.34	156.60	101.45	85.15	78.30	75.03	73.36	72.01
8 000	266.68	178.97	115.94	97.31	89.49	85.74	83.84	82.30
9 000	300.01	201.34	130.43	109.47	100.68	96.46	94.32	92.59
10 000	333.34	223.71	144.92	121.63	111.86	107.18	104.79	102.87
11 000	366.68	246.09	159.42	133.80	123.05	117.90	115.27	113.16
12 000	400.01	268.46	173.91	145.96	134.23	128.61	125.75	123.45
13 000	433.34	290.83	188.40	158.12	145.42	139.33	136.23	133.73
14 000	466.68	313.20	202.89	170.29	156.60	150.05	146.71	144.02
15 000	500.01	335.57	217.38	182.45	167.79	160.77	157.19	154.31
16 000	533.35	357.94	231.88	194.61	178.98	171.48	167.67	164.59
17 000	566.68	380.31	246.37	206.78	190.16	182.20	178.15	174.88
18 000	600.01	402.68	260.86	218.94	201.35	192.92	188.63	185.17
19 000	633.35	425.05	275.35	231.10	212.53	203.64	199.11	195.46
20 000	666.68	447.42	289.84	243.26	223.72	214.35	209.58	205.74
21 000	700.02	469.80	304.34	255.43	234.90	225.07	220.06	216.03
22 000	733.35	492.17	318.83	267.59	246.09	235.79	230.54	226.32
23 000	766.68	514.54	333.32	279.75	257.27	246.51	241.02	236.60
24 000	800.02	536.91	347.81	291.92	268.46	257.22	251.50	246.89
25 000	833.35	559.28	362.30	304.08	279.65	267.94	261.98	257.18
26 000	866.68	581.65	376.80	316.24	290.83	278.66	272.46	267.46
27 000	900.02	604.02	391.29	328.41	302.02	289.38	282.94	277.75
28 000	933.35	626.39	405.78	340.57	313.20	300.09	293.42	288.04
29 000	966.69	648.76	420.27	352.73	324.39	310.81	303.89	298.32
30 000	1000.02	671.13	434.76	364.89	335.57	321.53	314.37	308.61
31 000	1033.35	693.51	449.26	377.06	346.76	332.25	324.85	318.90
32 000	1066.69	715.88	463.75	389.22	357.95	342.96	335.33	329.18
33 000	1100.02	738.25	478.24	401.38	369.13	353.68	345.81	339.47
34 000	1133.36	760.62	492.73	413.55	380.32	364.40	356.29	349.76
35 000	1166.69	782.99	507.22	425.71	391.50	375.12	366.77	360.05
36 000	1200.02	805.36	521.72	437.87	402.69	385.83	377.25	370.33
37 000	1233.36	827.73	536.21	450.04	413.87	396.55	387.73	380.62
38 000	1266.69	850.10	550.70	462.20	425.06	407.27	398.21	390.91
39 000	1300.02	872.47	565.19	474.36	436.25	417.99	408.68	401.19
40 000	1333.36	894.84	579.68	486.52	447.43	428.70	419.16	411.48
41 000	1366.69	917.22	594.18	498.69	458.62	439.42	429.64	421.77
42 000	1400.03	939.59	608.67	510.85	469.80	450.14	440.12	432.05
43 000	1433.36	961.96	623.16	523.01	480.99	460.85	450.60	442.34
44 000	1466.69	984.33	637.65	535.18	492.17	471.57	461.08	452.63
45 000	1500.03	1006.70	652.14	547.34	503.36	482.29	471.56	462.91

FOR **OTHER RATES AND TERMS** SEE PAGE A-1.

TERM➡ AMOUNT	10 YEARS	15 YEARS	20 YEARS	25 YEARS	30 YEARS	40 YEARS
$46 000	666.64	559.50	514.54	493.01	482.04	473.20
47 000	681.13	571.67	525.73	503.72	492.52	483.49
48 000	695.62	583.83	536.92	514.44	503.00	493.77
49 000	710.11	595.99	548.10	525.16	513.47	504.06
50 000	724.60	608.15	559.29	535.88	523.95	514.35
51 000	739.10	620.32	570.47	546.59	534.43	524.63
52 000	753.59	632.48	581.66	557.31	544.91	534.92
53 000	768.08	644.64	592.84	568.03	555.39	545.21
54 000	782.57	656.81	604.03	578.75	565.87	555.50
55 000	797.06	668.97	615.22	589.46	576.35	565.78
56 000	811.56	681.13	626.40	600.18	586.83	576.07
57 000	826.05	693.30	637.59	610.90	597.31	586.36
58 000	840.54	705.46	648.77	621.62	607.78	596.64
59 000	855.03	717.62	659.96	632.33	618.26	606.93
60 000	869.52	729.78	671.14	643.05	628.74	617.22
61 000	884.02	741.95	682.33	653.77	639.22	627.50
62 000	898.51	754.11	693.52	664.49	649.70	637.79
63 000	913.00	766.27	704.70	675.20	660.18	648.08
64 000	927.49	778.44	715.89	685.92	670.66	658.36
65 000	941.98	790.60	727.07	696.64	681.14	668.65
66 000	956.48	802.76	738.26	707.36	691.62	678.94
67 000	970.97	814.93	749.44	718.07	702.10	689.22
68 000	985.46	827.09	760.63	728.79	712.57	699.51
69 000	999.95	839.25	771.81	739.51	723.05	709.80
70 000	1014.44	851.41	783.00	750.23	733.53	720.09
71 000	1028.94	863.58	794.19	760.94	744.01	730.37
72 000	1043.43	875.74	805.37	771.66	754.49	740.66
73 000	1057.92	887.90	816.56	782.38	764.97	750.95
74 000	1072.41	900.07	827.74	793.10	775.45	761.23
75 000	1086.90	912.23	838.93	803.81	785.93	771.52
76 000	1101.40	924.39	850.11	814.53	796.41	781.81
77 000	1115.89	936.56	861.30	825.25	806.89	792.09
78 000	1130.38	948.72	872.49	835.97	817.36	802.38
79 000	1144.87	960.88	883.67	846.68	827.84	812.67
80 000	1159.36	973.04	894.86	857.40	838.32	822.95
81 000	1173.86	985.21	906.04	868.12	848.80	833.24
82 000	1188.35	997.37	917.23	878.83	859.28	843.53
83 000	1202.84	1009.53	928.41	889.55	869.76	853.81
84 000	1217.33	1021.70	939.60	900.27	880.24	864.10
85 000	1231.82	1033.86	950.78	910.99	890.72	874.39
86 000	1246.32	1046.02	961.97	921.70	901.20	884.68
87 000	1260.81	1058.18	973.16	932.42	911.67	894.96
88 000	1275.30	1070.35	984.34	943.14	922.15	905.25
89 000	1289.79	1082.51	995.53	953.86	932.63	915.54
90 000	1304.28	1094.67	1006.71	964.57	943.11	925.82
91 000	1318.78	1106.84	1017.90	975.29	953.59	936.11
92 000	1333.27	1119.00	1029.08	986.01	964.07	946.40
93 000	1347.76	1131.16	1040.27	996.73	974.55	956.68
94 000	1362.25	1143.33	1051.46	1007.44	985.03	966.97
95 000	1376.74	1155.49	1062.64	1018.16	995.51	977.26
96 000	1391.24	1167.65	1073.83	1028.88	1005.99	987.54
97 000	1405.73	1179.81	1085.01	1039.60	1016.46	997.83
98 000	1420.22	1191.98	1096.20	1050.31	1026.94	1008.12
99 000	1434.71	1204.14	1107.38	1061.03	1037.42	1018.40
100 000	1449.20	1216.30	1118.57	1071.75	1047.90	1028.69

FOR **OTHER RATES AND TERMS** *SEE PAGE A-1.*

TERM ➤ AMOUNT	3 YEARS	5 YEARS	10 YEARS	15 YEARS	20 YEARS	25 YEARS	30 YEARS	40 YEARS
$ 100	3.35	2.25	1.47	1.24	1.14	1.10	1.07	1.05
200	6.70	4.50	2.93	2.47	2.28	2.19	2.14	2.10
300	10.04	6.75	4.40	3.70	3.41	3.28	3.21	3.15
400	13.39	9.00	5.86	4.94	4.55	4.37	4.27	4.20
500	16.73	11.25	7.32	6.17	5.69	5.46	5.34	5.25
600	20.08	13.50	8.79	7.40	6.82	6.55	6.41	6.30
700	23.42	15.75	10.25	8.63	7.96	7.64	7.48	7.35
800	26.77	18.00	11.72	9.87	9.09	8.73	8.54	8.40
900	30.11	20.25	13.18	11.10	10.23	9.82	9.61	9.45
1 000	33.46	22.50	14.64	12.33	11.37	10.91	10.68	10.49
1 000	33.46	22.50	14.64	12.33	11.37	10.91	10.68	10.49
2 000	66.91	45.00	29.28	24.66	22.73	21.81	21.35	20.98
3 000	100.37	67.50	43.92	36.98	34.09	32.72	32.02	31.47
4 000	133.82	90.00	58.56	49.31	45.45	43.62	42.70	41.96
5 000	167.27	112.49	73.19	61.63	56.81	54.52	53.37	52.45
6 000	200.73	134.99	87.83	73.96	68.17	65.43	64.04	62.94
7 000	234.18	157.49	102.47	86.28	79.53	76.33	74.71	73.43
8 000	267.63	179.99	117.11	98.61	90.90	87.23	85.39	83.92
9 000	301.09	202.49	131.74	110.93	102.26	98.14	96.06	94.41
10 000	334.54	224.98	146.38	123.26	113.62	109.04	106.73	104.90
11 000	367.99	247.48	161.02	135.58	124.98	119.94	117.40	115.39
12 000	401.45	269.98	175.66	147.91	136.34	130.85	128.08	125.88
13 000	434.90	292.48	190.29	160.23	147.70	141.75	138.75	136.36
14 000	468.36	314.98	204.93	172.56	159.06	152.65	149.42	146.85
15 000	501.81	337.47	219.57	184.88	170.43	163.56	160.09	157.34
16 000	535.26	359.97	234.21	197.21	181.79	174.46	170.77	167.83
17 000	568.72	382.47	248.84	209.53	193.15	185.37	181.44	178.32
18 000	602.17	404.97	263.48	221.86	204.51	196.27	192.11	188.81
19 000	635.62	427.47	278.12	234.18	215.87	207.17	202.78	199.30
20 000	669.08	449.96	292.76	246.51	227.23	218.08	213.46	209.79
21 000	702.53	472.46	307.39	258.83	238.59	228.98	224.13	220.28
22 000	735.98	494.96	322.03	271.16	249.96	239.88	234.80	230.77
23 000	769.44	517.46	336.67	283.49	261.32	250.79	245.47	241.26
24 000	802.89	539.96	351.31	295.81	272.68	261.69	256.15	251.75
25 000	836.35	562.45	365.95	308.14	284.04	272.59	266.82	262.23
26 000	869.80	584.95	380.58	320.46	295.40	283.50	277.49	272.72
27 000	903.25	607.45	395.22	332.79	306.76	294.40	288.16	283.21
28 000	936.71	629.95	409.86	345.11	318.12	305.30	298.84	293.70
29 000	970.16	652.45	424.50	357.44	329.49	316.21	309.51	304.19
30 000	1003.61	674.94	439.13	369.76	340.85	327.11	320.18	314.68
31 000	1037.07	697.44	453.77	382.09	352.21	338.01	330.85	325.17
32 000	1070.52	719.94	468.41	394.41	363.57	348.92	341.53	335.66
33 000	1103.97	742.44	483.05	406.74	374.93	359.82	352.20	346.15
34 000	1137.43	764.93	497.68	419.06	386.29	370.73	362.87	356.64
35 000	1170.88	787.43	512.32	431.39	397.65	381.63	373.55	367.13
36 000	1204.34	809.93	526.96	443.71	409.02	392.53	384.22	377.62
37 000	1237.79	832.43	541.60	456.04	420.38	403.44	394.89	388.11
38 000	1271.24	854.93	556.23	468.36	431.74	414.34	405.56	398.59
39 000	1304.70	877.42	570.87	480.69	443.10	425.24	416.24	409.08
40 000	1338.15	899.92	585.51	493.01	454.46	436.15	426.91	419.57
41 000	1371.60	922.42	600.15	505.34	465.82	447.05	437.58	430.06
42 000	1405.06	944.92	614.78	517.66	477.18	457.95	448.25	440.55
43 000	1438.51	967.42	629.42	529.99	488.55	468.86	458.93	451.04
44 000	1471.96	989.91	644.06	542.31	499.91	479.76	469.60	461.53
45 000	1505.42	1012.41	658.70	554.64	511.27	490.66	480.27	472.02

FOR **OTHER RATES AND TERMS** *SEE PAGE A-1.*

TERM◆ AMOUNT	10 YEARS	15 YEARS	20 YEARS	25 YEARS	30 YEARS	40 YEARS
$46 000	673.34	566.97	522.63	501.57	490.94	482.51
47 000	687.97	579.29	533.99	512.47	501.62	493.00
48 000	702.61	591.62	545.35	523.37	512.29	503.49
49 000	717.25	603.94	556.71	534.28	522.96	513.98
50 000	731.89	616.27	568.08	545.18	533.63	524.46
51 000	746.52	628.59	579.44	556.09	544.31	534.95
52 000	761.16	640.92	590.80	566.99	554.98	545.44
53 000	775.80	653.24	602.16	577.89	565.65	555.93
54 000	790.44	665.57	613.52	588.80	576.32	566.42
55 000	805.07	677.89	624.88	599.70	587.00	576.91
56 000	819.71	690.22	636.24	610.60	597.67	587.40
57 000	834.35	702.54	647.61	621.51	608.34	597.89
58 000	848.99	714.87	658.97	632.41	619.01	608.38
59 000	863.62	727.19	670.33	643.31	629.69	618.87
60 000	878.26	739.52	681.69	654.22	640.36	629.36
61 000	892.90	751.84	693.05	665.12	651.03	639.85
62 000	907.54	764.17	704.41	676.02	661.70	650.34
63 000	922.17	776.49	715.77	686.93	672.38	660.82
64 000	936.81	788.82	727.13	697.83	683.05	671.31
65 000	951.45	801.14	738.50	708.74	693.72	681.80
66 000	966.09	813.47	749.86	719.64	704.40	692.29
67 000	980.73	825.79	761.22	730.54	715.07	702.78
68 000	995.36	838.12	772.58	741.45	725.74	713.27
69 000	1010.00	850.45	783.94	752.35	736.41	723.76
70 000	1024.64	862.77	795.30	763.25	747.09	734.25
71 000	1039.28	875.10	806.66	774.16	757.76	744.74
72 000	1053.91	887.42	818.03	785.06	768.43	755.23
73 000	1068.55	899.75	829.39	795.96	779.10	765.72
74 000	1083.19	912.07	840.75	806.87	789.78	776.21
75 000	1097.83	924.40	852.11	817.77	800.45	786.69
76 000	1112.46	936.72	863.47	828.67	811.12	797.18
77 000	1127.10	949.05	874.83	839.58	821.79	807.67
78 000	1141.74	961.37	886.19	850.48	832.47	818.16
79 000	1156.38	973.70	897.56	861.38	843.14	828.65
80 000	1171.01	986.02	908.92	872.29	853.81	839.14
81 000	1185.65	998.35	920.28	883.19	864.48	849.63
82 000	1200.29	1010.67	931.64	894.10	875.16	860.12
83 000	1214.93	1023.00	943.00	905.00	885.83	870.61
84 000	1229.56	1035.32	954.36	915.90	896.50	881.10
85 000	1244.20	1047.65	965.72	926.81	907.17	891.59
86 000	1258.84	1059.97	977.09	937.71	917.85	902.08
87 000	1273.48	1072.30	988.45	948.61	928.52	912.56
88 000	1288.12	1084.62	999.81	959.52	939.19	923.05
89 000	1302.75	1096.95	1011.17	970.42	949.86	933.54
90 000	1317.39	1109.27	1022.53	981.32	960.54	944.03
91 000	1332.03	1121.60	1033.89	992.23	971.21	954.52
92 000	1346.67	1133.93	1045.25	1003.13	981.88	965.01
93 000	1361.30	1146.25	1056.62	1014.03	992.55	975.50
94 000	1375.94	1158.58	1067.98	1024.94	1003.23	985.99
95 000	1390.58	1170.90	1079.34	1035.84	1013.90	996.48
96 000	1405.22	1183.23	1090.70	1046.74	1024.57	1006.97
97 000	1419.85	1195.55	1102.06	1057.65	1035.25	1017.46
98 000	1434.49	1207.88	1113.42	1068.55	1045.92	1027.95
99 000	1449.13	1220.20	1124.78	1079.46	1056.59	1038.44
100 000	1463.77	1232.53	1136.15	1090.36	1067.26	1048.92

FOR OTHER RATES AND TERMS SEE PAGE A-1.

TERM→ AMOUNT	3 YEARS	5 YEARS	10 YEARS	15 YEARS	20 YEARS	25 YEARS	30 YEARS	40 YEARS
$ 100	3.36	2.27	1.48	1.25	1.16	1.11	1.09	1.07
200	6.72	4.53	2.96	2.50	2.31	2.22	2.18	2.14
300	10.08	6.79	4.44	3.75	3.47	3.33	3.27	3.21
400	13.43	9.06	5.92	5.00	4.62	4.44	4.35	4.28
500	16.79	11.32	7.40	6.25	5.77	5.55	5.44	5.35
600	20.15	13.58	8.88	7.50	6.93	6.66	6.53	6.42
700	23.51	15.84	10.35	8.75	8.08	7.77	7.61	7.49
800	26.86	18.11	11.83	10.00	9.24	8.88	8.70	8.56
900	30.22	20.37	13.31	11.24	10.39	9.99	9.79	9.63
1 000	33.58	22.63	14.79	12.49	11.54	11.10	10.87	10.70
1 000	33.58	22.63	14.79	12.49	11.54	11.10	10.87	10.70
2 000	67.15	45.26	29.57	24.98	23.08	22.19	21.74	21.39
3 000	100.73	67.88	44.36	37.47	34.62	33.28	32.61	32.08
4 000	134.30	90.51	59.14	49.96	46.16	44.37	43.47	42.77
5 000	167.87	113.13	73.92	62.45	57.70	55.46	54.34	53.46
6 000	201.45	135.76	88.71	74.94	69.23	66.55	65.21	64.16
7 000	235.02	158.38	103.49	87.42	80.77	77.64	76.07	74.85
8 000	268.59	181.01	118.28	99.91	92.31	88.73	86.94	85.54
9 000	302.17	203.63	133.06	112.40	103.85	99.82	97.81	96.23
10 000	335.74	226.26	147.84	124.89	115.39	110.91	108.67	106.92
11 000	369.32	248.88	162.63	137.38	126.92	122.00	119.54	117.62
12 000	402.89	271.51	177.41	149.87	138.46	133.09	130.41	128.31
13 000	436.46	294.13	192.20	162.35	150.00	144.18	141.28	139.00
14 000	470.04	316.76	206.98	174.84	161.54	155.27	152.14	149.69
15 000	503.61	339.38	221.76	187.33	173.08	166.36	163.01	160.38
16 000	537.18	362.01	236.55	199.82	184.61	177.45	173.88	171.08
17 000	570.76	384.64	251.33	212.31	196.15	188.54	184.74	181.77
18 000	604.33	407.26	266.12	224.80	207.69	199.63	195.61	192.46
19 000	637.90	429.89	280.90	237.28	219.23	210.72	206.48	203.15
20 000	671.48	452.51	295.68	249.77	230.77	221.82	217.34	213.84
21 000	705.05	475.14	310.47	262.26	242.31	232.91	228.21	224.54
22 000	738.63	497.76	325.25	274.75	253.84	244.00	239.08	235.23
23 000	772.20	520.39	340.04	287.24	265.38	255.09	249.94	245.92
24 000	805.77	543.01	354.82	299.73	276.92	266.18	260.81	256.61
25 000	839.35	565.64	369.60	312.21	288.46	277.27	271.68	267.30
26 000	872.92	588.26	384.39	324.70	300.00	288.36	282.55	278.00
27 000	906.49	610.89	399.17	337.19	311.53	299.45	293.41	288.69
28 000	940.07	633.51	413.96	349.68	323.07	310.54	304.28	299.38
29 000	973.64	656.14	428.74	362.17	334.61	321.63	315.15	310.07
30 000	1007.21	678.76	443.52	374.66	346.15	332.72	326.01	320.76
31 000	1040.79	701.39	458.31	387.14	357.69	343.81	336.88	331.46
32 000	1074.36	724.01	473.09	399.63	369.22	354.90	347.75	342.15
33 000	1107.94	746.64	487.88	412.12	380.76	365.99	358.61	352.84
34 000	1141.51	769.27	502.66	424.61	392.30	377.08	369.48	363.53
35 000	1175.08	791.89	517.44	437.10	403.84	388.17	380.35	374.22
36 000	1208.66	814.52	532.23	449.59	415.38	399.26	391.21	384.92
37 000	1242.23	837.14	547.01	462.07	426.92	410.35	402.08	395.61
38 000	1275.80	859.77	561.80	474.56	438.45	421.44	412.95	406.30
39 000	1309.38	882.39	576.58	487.05	449.99	432.54	423.82	416.99
40 000	1342.95	905.02	591.36	499.54	461.53	443.63	434.68	427.68
41 000	1376.53	927.64	606.15	512.03	473.07	454.72	445.55	438.38
42 000	1410.10	950.27	620.93	524.52	484.61	465.81	456.42	449.07
43 000	1443.67	972.89	635.72	537.00	496.14	476.90	467.28	459.76
44 000	1477.25	995.52	650.50	549.49	507.68	487.99	478.15	470.45
45 000	1510.82	1018.14	665.28	561.98	519.22	499.08	489.02	481.14

*FOR **OTHER RATES AND TERMS** SEE PAGE A-1.*

TERM ➡ AMOUNT	10 YEARS	15 YEARS	20 YEARS	25 YEARS	30 YEARS	40 YEARS
$46 000	680.07	574.47	530.76	510.17	499.88	491.84
47 000	694.85	586.96	542.30	521.26	510.75	502.53
48 000	709.64	599.45	553.83	532.35	521.62	513.22
49 000	724.42	611.94	565.37	543.44	532.48	523.91
50 000	739.20	624.42	576.91	554.53	543.35	534.60
51 000	753.99	636.91	588.45	565.62	554.22	545.30
52 000	768.77	649.40	599.99	576.71	565.09	555.99
53 000	783.56	661.89	611.53	587.80	575.95	566.68
54 000	798.34	674.38	623.06	598.89	586.82	577.37
55 000	813.12	686.87	634.60	609.98	597.69	588.06
56 000	827.91	699.35	646.14	621.07	608.55	598.75
57 000	842.69	711.84	657.68	632.16	619.42	609.45
58 000	857.48	724.33	669.22	643.26	630.29	620.14
59 000	872.26	736.82	680.75	654.35	641.15	630.83
60 000	887.04	749.31	692.29	665.44	652.02	641.52
61 000	901.83	761.80	703.83	676.53	662.89	652.21
62 000	916.61	774.28	715.37	687.62	673.75	662.91
63 000	931.40	786.77	726.91	698.71	684.62	673.60
64 000	946.18	799.26	738.44	709.80	695.49	684.29
65 000	960.96	811.75	749.98	720.89	706.36	694.98
66 000	975.75	824.24	761.52	731.98	717.22	705.67
67 000	990.53	836.73	773.06	743.07	728.09	716.37
68 000	1005.32	849.21	784.60	754.16	738.96	727.06
69 000	1020.10	861.70	796.14	765.25	749.82	737.75
70 000	1034.88	874.19	807.67	776.34	760.69	748.44
71 000	1049.67	886.68	819.21	787.43	771.56	759.13
72 000	1064.45	899.17	830.75	798.52	782.42	769.83
73 000	1079.24	911.66	842.29	809.61	793.29	780.52
74 000	1094.02	924.14	853.83	820.70	804.16	791.21
75 000	1108.80	936.63	865.36	831.79	815.02	801.90
76 000	1123.59	949.12	876.90	842.88	825.89	812.59
77 000	1138.37	961.61	888.44	853.98	836.76	823.29
78 000	1153.16	974.10	899.98	865.07	847.63	833.98
79 000	1167.94	986.59	911.52	876.16	858.49	844.67
80 000	1182.72	999.07	923.05	887.25	869.36	855.36
81 000	1197.51	1011.56	934.59	898.34	880.23	866.05
82 000	1212.29	1024.05	946.13	909.43	891.09	876.75
83 000	1227.08	1036.54	957.67	920.52	901.96	887.44
84 000	1241.86	1049.03	969.21	931.61	912.83	898.13
85 000	1256.64	1061.52	980.74	942.70	923.69	908.82
86 000	1271.43	1074.00	992.28	953.79	934.56	919.51
87 000	1286.21	1086.49	1003.82	964.88	945.43	930.21
88 000	1301.00	1098.98	1015.36	975.97	956.30	940.90
89 000	1315.78	1111.47	1026.90	987.06	967.16	951.59
90 000	1330.56	1123.96	1038.44	998.15	978.03	962.28
91 000	1345.35	1136.45	1049.97	1009.24	988.90	972.97
92 000	1360.13	1148.94	1061.51	1020.33	999.77	983.67
93 000	1374.92	1161.42	1073.05	1031.42	1010.63	994.36
94 000	1389.70	1173.91	1084.59	1042.51	1021.50	1005.05
95 000	1404.48	1186.40	1096.13	1053.60	1032.36	1015.74
96 000	1419.27	1198.89	1107.66	1064.70	1043.23	1026.43
97 000	1434.05	1211.38	1119.20	1075.79	1054.10	1037.13
98 000	1448.84	1223.87	1130.74	1086.88	1064.96	1047.82
99 000	1463.62	1236.35	1142.28	1097.97	1075.83	1058.51
100 000	1478.40	1248.84	1153.82	1109.06	1086.70	1069.20

FOR **OTHER RATES AND TERMS** *SEE PAGE A-1.*

TERM➡ AMOUNT	3 YEARS	5 YEARS	10 YEARS	15 YEARS	20 YEARS	25 YEARS	30 YEARS	40 YEARS
$ 100	3.37	2.28	1.50	1.27	1.18	1.13	1.11	1.09
200	6.74	4.56	2.99	2.54	2.35	2.26	2.22	2.18
300	10.11	6.83	4.48	3.80	3.52	3.39	3.32	3.27
400	13.48	9.11	5.98	5.07	4.69	4.52	4.43	4.36
500	16.85	11.38	7.47	6.33	5.86	5.64	5.54	5.45
600	20.22	13.66	8.96	7.60	7.03	6.77	6.64	6.54
700	23.59	15.93	10.46	8.86	8.21	7.90	7.75	7.63
800	26.96	18.21	11.95	10.13	9.38	9.03	8.85	8.72
900	30.33	20.48	13.44	11.39	10.55	10.16	9.96	9.81
1 000	33.70	22.76	14.94	12.66	11.72	11.28	11.07	10.90
1 000	33.70	22.76	14.94	12.66	11.72	11.28	11.07	10.90
2 000	67.39	45.51	29.87	25.31	23.44	22.56	22.13	21.80
3 000	101.09	68.26	44.80	37.96	35.15	33.84	33.19	32.69
4 000	134.78	91.02	59.73	50.61	46.87	45.12	44.25	43.59
5 000	168.47	113.77	74.66	63.27	58.58	56.40	55.31	54.48
6 000	202.17	136.52	89.59	75.92	70.30	67.68	66.38	65.38
7 000	235.86	159.28	104.52	88.57	82.02	78.95	77.44	76.27
8 000	269.56	182.03	119.45	101.22	93.73	90.23	88.50	87.17
9 000	303.25	204.78	134.38	113.88	105.45	101.51	99.56	98.06
10 000	336.94	227.54	149.32	126.53	117.16	112.79	110.62	108.96
11 000	370.64	250.29	164.25	139.18	128.88	124.07	121.69	119.85
12 000	404.33	273.04	179.18	151.83	140.59	135.35	132.75	130.75
13 000	438.03	295.79	194.11	164.49	152.31	146.62	143.81	141.64
14 000	471.72	318.55	209.04	177.14	164.03	157.90	154.87	152.54
15 000	505.41	341.30	223.97	189.79	175.74	169.18	165.93	163.43
16 000	539.11	364.05	238.90	202.44	187.46	180.46	177.00	174.33
17 000	572.80	386.81	253.83	215.10	199.17	191.74	188.06	185.22
18 000	606.50	409.56	268.76	227.75	210.89	203.02	199.12	196.12
19 000	640.19	432.31	283.70	240.40	222.60	214.29	210.18	207.01
20 000	673.88	455.07	298.63	253.05	234.32	225.57	221.24	217.91
21 000	707.58	477.82	313.56	265.71	246.04	236.85	232.31	228.80
22 000	741.27	500.57	328.49	278.36	257.75	248.13	243.37	239.70
23 000	774.97	523.33	343.42	291.01	269.47	259.41	254.43	250.59
24 000	808.66	546.08	358.35	303.66	281.18	270.69	265.49	261.49
25 000	842.35	568.83	373.28	316.32	292.90	281.96	276.55	272.38
26 000	876.05	591.58	388.21	328.97	304.61	293.24	287.62	283.28
27 000	909.74	614.34	403.14	341.62	316.33	304.52	298.68	294.17
28 000	943.44	637.09	418.08	354.27	328.05	315.80	309.74	305.07
29 000	977.13	659.84	433.01	366.93	339.76	327.08	320.80	315.96
30 000	1010.82	682.60	447.94	379.58	351.48	338.36	331.86	326.86
31 000	1044.52	705.35	462.87	392.23	363.19	349.63	342.92	337.75
32 000	1078.21	728.10	477.80	404.88	374.91	360.91	353.99	348.65
33 000	1111.91	750.86	492.73	417.53	386.62	372.19	365.05	359.54
34 000	1145.60	773.61	507.66	430.19	398.34	383.47	376.11	370.44
35 000	1179.29	796.36	522.59	442.84	410.06	394.75	387.17	381.33
36 000	1212.99	819.12	537.52	455.49	421.77	406.03	398.24	392.23
37 000	1246.68	841.87	552.45	468.14	433.49	417.30	409.30	403.13
38 000	1280.38	864.62	567.39	480.80	445.20	428.58	420.36	414.02
39 000	1314.07	887.37	582.32	493.45	456.92	439.86	431.42	424.92
40 000	1347.76	910.13	597.25	506.10	468.64	451.14	442.48	435.81
41 000	1381.46	932.88	612.18	518.75	480.35	462.42	453.55	446.71
42 000	1415.15	955.63	627.11	531.41	492.07	473.70	464.61	457.60
43 000	1448.84	978.39	642.04	544.06	503.78	484.97	475.67	468.50
44 000	1482.54	1001.14	656.97	556.71	515.50	496.25	486.73	479.39
45 000	1516.23	1023.89	671.90	569.36	527.21	507.53	497.79	490.29

FOR **OTHER RATES AND TERMS** *SEE PAGE A-1.*

TERM➨ AMOUNT	10 YEARS	15 YEARS	20 YEARS	25 YEARS	30 YEARS	40 YEARS
$46 000	686.83	582.02	538.93	518.81	508.86	501.18
47 000	701.77	594.67	550.65	530.09	519.92	512.08
48 000	716.70	607.32	562.36	541.37	530.98	522.97
49 000	731.63	619.97	574.08	552.64	542.04	533.87
50 000	746.56	632.63	585.79	563.92	553.10	544.76
51 000	761.49	645.28	597.51	575.20	564.17	555.66
52 000	776.42	657.93	609.22	586.48	575.23	566.55
53 000	791.35	670.58	620.94	597.76	586.29	577.45
54 000	806.28	683.24	632.66	609.04	597.35	588.34
55 000	821.21	695.89	644.37	620.31	608.41	599.24
56 000	836.15	708.54	656.09	631.59	619.48	610.13
57 000	851.08	721.19	667.80	642.87	630.54	621.03
58 000	866.01	733.85	679.52	654.15	641.60	631.92
59 000	880.94	746.50	691.23	665.43	652.66	642.82
60 000	895.87	759.15	702.95	676.71	663.72	653.71
61 000	910.80	771.80	714.67	687.98	674.79	664.61
62 000	925.73	784.46	726.38	699.26	685.85	675.50
63 000	940.66	797.11	738.10	710.54	696.91	686.40
64 000	955.59	809.76	749.81	721.82	707.97	697.29
65 000	970.52	822.41	761.53	733.10	719.03	708.19
66 000	985.46	835.06	773.24	744.38	730.10	719.08
67 000	1000.39	847.72	784.96	755.65	741.16	729.98
68 000	1015.32	860.37	796.68	766.93	752.22	740.87
69 000	1030.25	873.02	808.39	778.21	763.28	751.77
70 000	1045.18	885.67	820.11	789.49	774.34	762.66
71 000	1060.11	898.33	831.82	800.77	785.41	773.56
72 000	1075.04	910.98	843.54	812.05	796.47	784.46
73 000	1089.97	923.63	855.26	823.32	807.53	795.35
74 000	1104.90	936.28	866.97	834.60	818.59	806.25
75 000	1119.84	948.94	878.69	845.88	829.65	817.14
76 000	1134.77	961.59	890.40	857.16	840.72	828.04
77 000	1149.70	974.24	902.12	868.44	851.78	838.93
78 000	1164.63	986.89	913.83	879.72	862.84	849.83
79 000	1179.56	999.55	925.55	890.99	873.90	860.72
80 000	1194.49	1012.20	937.27	902.27	884.96	871.62
81 000	1209.42	1024.85	948.98	913.55	896.03	882.51
82 000	1224.35	1037.50	960.70	924.83	907.09	893.41
83 000	1239.28	1050.16	972.41	936.11	918.15	904.30
84 000	1254.22	1062.81	984.13	947.39	929.21	915.20
85 000	1269.15	1075.46	995.84	958.67	940.27	926.09
86 000	1284.08	1088.11	1007.56	969.94	951.34	936.99
87 000	1299.01	1100.77	1019.28	981.22	962.40	947.88
88 000	1313.94	1113.42	1030.99	992.50	973.46	958.78
89 000	1328.87	1126.07	1042.71	1003.78	984.52	969.67
90 000	1343.80	1138.72	1054.42	1015.06	995.58	980.57
91 000	1358.73	1151.38	1066.14	1026.34	1006.65	991.46
92 000	1373.66	1164.03	1077.85	1037.61	1017.71	1002.36
93 000	1388.59	1176.68	1089.57	1048.89	1028.77	1013.25
94 000	1403.53	1189.33	1101.29	1060.17	1039.83	1024.15
95 000	1418.46	1201.99	1113.00	1071.45	1050.89	1035.04
96 000	1433.39	1214.64	1124.72	1082.73	1061.96	1045.94
97 000	1448.32	1227.29	1136.43	1094.01	1073.02	1056.83
98 000	1463.25	1239.94	1148.15	1105.28	1084.08	1067.73
99 000	1478.18	1252.59	1159.86	1116.56	1095.14	1078.62
100 000	1493.11	1265.25	1171.58	1127.84	1106.20	1089.52

FOR **OTHER RATES AND TERMS** *SEE PAGE A-1.*

TERM▶ AMOUNT	3 YEARS	5 YEARS	10 YEARS	15 YEARS	20 YEARS	25 YEARS	30 YEARS	40 YEARS
$ 100	3.39	2.29	1.51	1.29	1.19	1.15	1.13	1.11
200	6.77	4.58	3.02	2.57	2.38	2.30	2.26	2.22
300	10.15	6.87	4.53	3.85	3.57	3.45	3.38	3.33
400	13.53	9.16	6.04	5.13	4.76	4.59	4.51	4.44
500	16.91	11.45	7.54	6.41	5.95	5.74	5.63	5.55
600	20.29	13.73	9.05	7.70	7.14	6.89	6.76	6.66
700	23.68	16.02	10.56	8.98	8.33	8.03	7.89	7.77
800	27.06	18.31	12.07	10.26	9.52	9.18	9.01	8.88
900	30.44	20.60	13.58	11.54	10.71	10.33	10.14	9.99
1 000	33.82	22.89	15.08	12.82	11.90	11.47	11.26	11.10
1 000	33.82	22.89	15.08	12.82	11.90	11.47	11.26	11.10
2 000	67.63	45.77	30.16	25.64	23.79	22.94	22.52	22.20
3 000	101.45	68.65	45.24	38.46	35.69	34.41	33.78	33.30
4 000	135.26	91.53	60.32	51.27	47.58	45.87	45.04	44.40
5 000	169.08	114.41	75.40	64.09	59.48	57.34	56.29	55.50
6 000	202.89	137.29	90.48	76.91	71.37	68.81	67.55	66.60
7 000	236.71	160.17	105.56	89.73	83.27	80.27	78.81	77.70
8 000	270.52	183.06	120.64	102.54	95.16	91.74	90.07	88.79
9 000	304.34	205.94	135.72	115.36	107.05	103.21	101.32	99.89
10 000	338.15	228.82	150.79	128.18	118.95	114.68	112.58	110.99
11 000	371.96	251.70	165.87	141.00	130.84	126.14	123.84	122.09
12 000	405.78	274.58	180.95	153.81	142.74	137.61	135.10	133.19
13 000	439.59	297.46	196.03	166.63	154.63	149.08	146.36	144.29
14 000	473.41	320.34	211.11	179.45	166.53	160.54	157.61	155.39
15 000	507.22	343.22	226.19	192.27	178.42	172.01	168.87	166.49
16 000	541.04	366.11	241.27	205.08	190.31	183.48	180.13	177.58
17 000	574.85	388.99	256.35	217.90	202.21	194.94	191.39	188.68
18 000	608.67	411.87	271.43	230.72	214.10	206.41	202.64	199.78
19 000	642.48	434.75	286.50	243.53	226.00	217.88	213.90	210.88
20 000	676.29	457.63	301.58	256.35	237.89	229.35	225.16	221.98
21 000	710.11	480.51	316.66	269.17	249.79	240.81	236.42	233.08
22 000	743.92	503.39	331.74	281.99	261.68	252.28	247.68	244.18
23 000	777.74	526.27	346.82	294.80	273.57	263.75	258.93	255.28
24 000	811.55	549.16	361.90	307.62	285.47	275.21	270.19	266.37
25 000	845.37	572.04	376.98	320.44	297.36	286.68	281.45	277.47
26 000	879.18	594.92	392.06	333.26	309.26	298.15	292.71	288.57
27 000	913.00	617.80	407.14	346.07	321.15	309.61	303.96	299.67
28 000	946.81	640.68	422.21	358.89	333.05	321.08	315.22	310.77
29 000	980.63	663.56	437.29	371.71	344.94	332.55	326.48	321.87
30 000	1014.44	686.44	452.37	384.53	356.83	344.02	337.74	332.97
31 000	1048.25	709.32	467.45	397.34	368.73	355.48	348.99	344.06
32 000	1082.07	732.21	482.53	410.16	380.62	366.95	360.25	355.16
33 000	1115.88	755.09	497.61	422.98	392.52	378.42	371.51	366.26
34 000	1149.70	777.97	512.69	435.80	404.41	389.88	382.77	377.36
35 000	1183.51	800.85	527.77	448.61	416.31	401.35	394.03	388.46
36 000	1217.33	823.73	542.85	461.43	428.20	412.82	405.28	399.56
37 000	1251.14	846.61	557.92	474.25	440.09	424.28	416.54	410.66
38 000	1284.96	869.49	573.00	487.06	451.99	435.75	427.80	421.76
39 000	1318.77	892.37	588.08	499.88	463.88	447.22	439.06	432.85
40 000	1352.58	915.26	603.16	512.70	475.78	458.69	450.31	443.95
41 000	1386.40	938.14	618.24	525.52	487.67	470.15	461.57	455.05
42 000	1420.21	961.02	633.32	538.33	499.57	481.62	472.83	466.15
43 000	1454.03	983.90	648.40	551.15	511.46	493.09	484.09	477.25
44 000	1487.84	1006.78	663.48	563.97	523.35	504.55	495.35	488.35
45 000	1521.66	1029.66	678.56	576.79	535.25	516.02	506.60	499.45

FOR **OTHER RATES AND TERMS** *SEE PAGE A-1.*

TERM➡ AMOUNT	10 YEARS	15 YEARS	20 YEARS	25 YEARS	30 YEARS	40 YEARS
$46 000	693.63	589.60	547.14	527.49	517.86	510.55
47 000	708.71	602.42	559.04	538.95	529.12	521.64
48 000	723.79	615.24	570.93	550.42	540.38	532.74
49 000	738.87	628.06	582.83	561.89	551.63	543.84
50 000	753.95	640.87	594.72	573.36	562.89	554.94
51 000	769.03	653.69	606.61	584.82	574.15	566.04
52 000	784.11	666.51	618.51	596.29	585.41	577.14
53 000	799.19	679.33	630.40	607.76	596.66	588.24
54 000	814.27	692.14	642.30	619.22	607.92	599.33
55 000	829.34	704.96	654.19	630.69	619.18	610.43
56 000	844.42	717.78	666.09	642.16	630.44	621.53
57 000	859.50	730.59	677.98	653.62	641.70	632.63
58 000	874.58	743.41	689.87	665.09	652.95	643.73
59 000	889.66	756.23	701.77	676.56	664.21	654.83
60 000	904.74	769.05	713.66	688.03	675.47	665.93
61 000	919.82	781.86	725.56	699.49	686.73	677.03
62 000	934.90	794.68	737.45	710.96	697.98	688.12
63 000	949.98	807.50	749.35	722.43	709.24	699.22
64 000	965.05	820.32	761.24	733.89	720.50	710.32
65 000	980.13	833.13	773.13	745.36	731.76	721.42
66 000	995.21	845.95	785.03	756.83	743.02	732.52
67 000	1010.29	858.77	796.92	768.29	754.27	743.62
68 000	1025.37	871.59	808.82	779.76	765.53	754.72
69 000	1040.45	884.40	820.71	791.23	776.79	765.82
70 000	1055.53	897.22	832.61	802.70	788.05	776.91
71 000	1070.61	910.04	844.50	814.16	799.30	788.01
72 000	1085.69	922.86	856.40	825.63	810.56	799.11
73 000	1100.76	935.67	868.29	837.10	821.82	810.21
74 000	1115.84	948.49	880.18	848.56	833.08	821.31
75 000	1130.92	961.31	892.08	860.03	844.34	832.41
76 000	1146.00	974.12	903.97	871.50	855.59	843.51
77 000	1161.08	986.94	915.87	882.96	866.85	854.60
78 000	1176.16	999.76	927.76	894.43	878.11	865.70
79 000	1191.24	1012.58	939.66	905.90	889.37	876.80
80 000	1206.32	1025.39	951.55	917.37	900.62	887.90
81 000	1221.40	1038.21	963.44	928.83	911.88	899.00
82 000	1236.47	1051.03	975.34	940.30	923.14	910.10
83 000	1251.55	1063.85	987.23	951.77	934.40	921.20
84 000	1266.63	1076.66	999.13	963.23	945.65	932.30
85 000	1281.71	1089.48	1011.02	974.70	956.91	943.39
86 000	1296.79	1102.30	1022.92	986.17	968.17	954.49
87 000	1311.87	1115.12	1034.81	997.63	979.43	965.59
88 000	1326.95	1127.93	1046.70	1009.10	990.69	976.69
89 000	1342.03	1140.75	1058.60	1020.57	1001.94	987.79
90 000	1357.11	1153.57	1070.49	1032.04	1013.20	998.89
91 000	1372.18	1166.39	1082.39	1043.50	1024.46	1009.99
92 000	1387.26	1179.20	1094.28	1054.97	1035.72	1021.09
93 000	1402.34	1192.02	1106.18	1066.44	1046.97	1032.18
94 000	1417.42	1204.84	1118.07	1077.90	1058.23	1043.28
95 000	1432.50	1217.65	1129.96	1089.37	1069.49	1054.38
96 000	1447.58	1230.47	1141.86	1100.84	1080.75	1065.48
97 000	1462.66	1243.29	1153.75	1112.30	1092.01	1076.58
98 000	1477.74	1256.11	1165.65	1123.77	1103.26	1087.68
99 000	1492.82	1268.92	1177.54	1135.24	1114.52	1098.78
100 000	1507.89	1281.74	1189.44	1146.71	1125.78	1109.87

FOR **OTHER RATES AND TERMS** *SEE PAGE A-1.*

TERM♦ AMOUNT	3 YEARS	5 YEARS	10 YEARS	15 YEARS	20 YEARS	25 YEARS	30 YEARS	40 YEARS
$ 100	3.40	2.31	1.53	1.30	1.21	1.17	1.15	1.14
200	6.79	4.61	3.05	2.60	2.42	2.34	2.30	2.27
300	10.19	6.91	4.57	3.90	3.63	3.50	3.44	3.40
400	13.58	9.21	6.10	5.20	4.83	4.67	4.59	4.53
500	16.97	11.51	7.62	6.50	6.04	5.83	5.73	5.66
600	20.37	13.81	9.14	7.79	7.25	7.00	6.88	6.79
700	23.76	16.11	10.66	9.09	8.46	8.16	8.02	7.92
800	27.15	18.41	12.19	10.39	9.66	9.33	9.17	9.05
900	30.55	20.71	13.71	11.69	10.87	10.50	10.31	10.18
1 000	33.94	23.01	15.23	12.99	12.08	11.66	11.46	11.31
1 000	33.94	23.01	15.23	12.99	12.08	11.66	11.46	11.31
2 000	67.88	46.02	30.46	25.97	24.15	23.32	22.91	22.61
3 000	101.81	69.03	45.69	38.95	36.23	34.97	34.37	33.91
4 000	135.75	92.04	60.91	51.94	48.30	46.63	45.82	45.22
5 000	169.68	115.05	76.14	64.92	60.37	58.29	57.28	56.52
6 000	203.62	138.06	91.37	77.90	72.45	69.94	68.73	67.82
7 000	237.55	161.07	106.60	90.89	84.52	81.60	80.18	79.12
8 000	271.49	184.08	121.82	103.87	96.59	93.26	91.64	90.43
9 000	305.42	207.09	137.05	116.85	108.67	104.91	103.09	101.73
10 000	339.36	230.10	152.28	129.84	120.74	116.57	114.55	113.03
11 000	373.29	253.11	167.51	142.82	132.82	128.23	126.00	124.33
12 000	407.23	276.12	182.73	155.80	144.89	139.88	137.45	135.64
13 000	441.16	299.13	197.96	168.79	156.96	151.54	148.91	146.94
14 000	475.10	322.14	213.19	181.77	169.04	163.20	160.36	158.24
15 000	509.03	345.15	228.42	194.75	181.11	174.85	171.82	169.54
16 000	542.97	368.16	243.64	207.74	193.18	186.51	183.27	180.85
17 000	576.90	391.17	258.87	220.72	205.26	198.16	194.73	192.15
18 000	610.84	414.18	274.10	233.70	217.33	209.82	206.18	203.45
19 000	644.78	437.19	289.33	246.69	229.41	221.48	217.63	214.75
20 000	678.71	460.20	304.55	259.67	241.48	233.13	229.09	226.06
21 000	712.65	483.21	319.78	272.65	253.55	244.79	240.54	237.36
22 000	746.58	506.22	335.01	285.64	265.63	256.45	252.00	248.66
23 000	780.52	529.23	350.24	298.62	277.70	268.10	263.45	259.97
24 000	814.45	552.24	365.46	311.60	289.77	279.76	274.90	271.27
25 000	848.39	575.25	380.69	324.58	301.85	291.42	286.36	282.57
26 000	882.32	598.26	395.92	337.57	313.92	303.07	297.81	293.87
27 000	916.26	621.27	411.15	350.55	326.00	314.73	309.27	305.18
28 000	950.19	644.28	426.37	363.53	338.07	326.39	320.72	316.48
29 000	984.13	667.29	441.60	376.52	350.14	338.04	332.17	327.78
30 000	1018.06	690.30	456.83	389.50	362.22	349.70	343.63	339.08
31 000	1052.00	713.31	472.06	402.48	374.29	361.35	355.08	350.39
32 000	1085.93	736.32	487.28	415.47	386.36	373.01	366.54	361.69
33 000	1119.87	759.33	502.51	428.45	398.44	384.67	377.99	372.99
34 000	1153.80	782.34	517.74	441.43	410.51	396.32	389.45	384.29
35 000	1187.74	805.35	532.97	454.42	422.59	407.98	400.90	395.60
36 000	1221.68	828.36	548.19	467.40	434.66	419.64	412.35	406.90
37 000	1255.61	851.37	563.42	480.38	446.73	431.29	423.81	418.20
38 000	1289.55	874.38	578.65	493.37	458.81	442.95	435.26	429.50
39 000	1323.48	897.39	593.87	506.35	470.88	454.61	446.72	440.81
40 000	1357.42	920.40	609.10	519.33	482.95	466.26	458.17	452.11
41 000	1391.35	943.41	624.33	532.32	495.03	477.92	469.62	463.41
42 000	1425.29	966.42	639.56	545.30	507.10	489.58	481.08	474.71
43 000	1459.22	989.43	654.78	558.28	519.18	501.23	492.53	486.02
44 000	1493.16	1012.44	670.01	571.27	531.25	512.89	503.99	497.32
45 000	1527.09	1035.45	685.24	584.25	543.32	524.55	515.44	508.62

FOR **OTHER RATES AND TERMS** *SEE PAGE A-1.*

TERM➧ AMOUNT	10 YEARS	15 YEARS	20 YEARS	25 YEARS	30 YEARS	40 YEARS
$46 000	700.47	597.23	555.40	536.20	526.89	519.93
47 000	715.69	610.21	567.47	547.86	538.35	531.23
48 000	730.92	623.20	579.54	559.51	549.80	542.53
49 000	746.15	636.18	591.62	571.17	561.26	553.83
50 000	761.38	649.16	603.69	582.83	572.71	565.14
51 000	776.60	662.15	615.77	594.48	584.17	576.44
52 000	791.83	675.13	627.84	606.14	595.62	587.74
53 000	807.06	688.11	639.91	617.80	607.07	599.04
54 000	822.29	701.10	651.99	629.45	618.53	610.35
55 000	837.51	714.08	664.06	641.11	629.98	621.65
56 000	852.74	727.06	676.13	652.77	641.44	632.95
57 000	867.97	740.05	688.21	664.42	652.89	644.25
58 000	883.20	753.03	700.28	676.08	664.34	655.56
59 000	898.42	766.01	712.36	687.74	675.80	666.86
60 000	913.65	779.00	724.43	699.39	687.25	678.16
61 000	928.88	791.98	736.50	711.05	698.71	689.46
62 000	944.11	804.96	748.58	722.70	710.16	700.77
63 000	959.33	817.95	760.65	734.36	721.61	712.07
64 000	974.56	830.93	772.72	746.02	733.07	723.37
65 000	989.79	843.91	784.80	757.67	744.52	734.67
66 000	1005.02	856.90	796.87	769.33	755.98	745.98
67 000	1020.24	869.88	808.95	780.99	767.43	757.28
68 000	1035.47	882.86	821.02	792.64	778.89	768.58
69 000	1050.70	895.84	833.09	804.30	790.34	779.89
70 000	1065.93	908.83	845.17	815.96	801.79	791.19
71 000	1081.15	921.81	857.24	827.61	813.25	802.49
72 000	1096.38	934.79	869.31	839.27	824.70	813.79
73 000	1111.61	947.78	881.39	850.93	836.16	825.10
74 000	1126.83	960.76	893.46	862.58	847.61	836.40
75 000	1142.06	973.74	905.54	874.24	859.06	847.70
76 000	1157.29	986.73	917.61	885.90	870.52	859.00
77 000	1172.52	999.71	929.68	897.55	881.97	870.31
78 000	1187.74	1012.69	941.76	909.21	893.43	881.61
79 000	1202.97	1025.68	953.83	920.86	904.88	892.91
80 000	1218.20	1038.66	965.90	932.52	916.33	904.21
81 000	1233.43	1051.64	977.98	944.18	927.79	915.52
82 000	1248.65	1064.63	990.05	955.83	939.24	926.82
83 000	1263.88	1077.61	1002.13	967.49	950.70	938.12
84 000	1279.11	1090.59	1014.20	979.15	962.15	949.42
85 000	1294.34	1103.58	1026.27	990.80	973.61	960.73
86 000	1309.56	1116.56	1038.35	1002.46	985.06	972.03
87 000	1324.79	1129.54	1050.42	1014.12	996.51	983.33
88 000	1340.02	1142.53	1062.49	1025.77	1007.97	994.63
89 000	1355.25	1155.51	1074.57	1037.43	1019.42	1005.94
90 000	1370.47	1168.49	1086.64	1049.09	1030.88	1017.24
91 000	1385.70	1181.47	1098.72	1060.74	1042.33	1028.54
92 000	1400.93	1194.46	1110.79	1072.40	1053.78	1039.85
93 000	1416.16	1207.44	1122.86	1084.05	1065.24	1051.15
94 000	1431.38	1220.42	1134.94	1095.71	1076.69	1062.45
95 000	1446.61	1233.41	1147.01	1107.37	1088.15	1073.75
96 000	1461.84	1246.39	1159.08	1119.02	1099.60	1085.06
97 000	1477.07	1259.37	1171.16	1130.68	1111.05	1096.36
98 000	1492.29	1272.36	1183.23	1142.34	1122.51	1107.66
99 000	1507.52	1285.34	1195.31	1153.99	1133.96	1118.96
100 000	1522.75	1298.32	1207.38	1165.65	1145.42	1130.27

FOR OTHER RATES AND TERMS SEE PAGE A-1.

TERM➤ AMOUNT	3 YEARS	5 YEARS	10 YEARS	15 YEARS	20 YEARS	25 YEARS	30 YEARS	40 YEARS
$ 100	3.41	2.32	1.54	1.32	1.23	1.19	1.17	1.16
200	6.82	4.63	3.08	2.63	2.46	2.37	2.34	2.31
300	10.22	6.95	4.62	3.95	3.68	3.56	3.50	3.46
400	13.63	9.26	6.16	5.26	4.91	4.74	4.67	4.61
500	17.03	11.57	7.69	6.58	6.13	5.93	5.83	5.76
600	20.44	13.89	9.23	7.89	7.36	7.11	7.00	6.91
700	23.84	16.20	10.77	9.21	8.58	8.30	8.16	8.06
800	27.25	18.52	12.31	10.52	9.81	9.48	9.33	9.21
900	30.66	20.83	13.84	11.84	11.03	10.67	10.49	10.36
1 000	34.06	23.14	15.38	13.15	12.26	11.85	11.66	11.51
1 000	34.06	23.14	15.38	13.15	12.26	11.85	11.66	11.51
2 000	68.12	46.28	30.76	26.30	24.51	23.70	23.31	23.02
3 000	102.17	69.42	46.14	39.45	36.77	35.54	34.96	34.53
4 000	136.23	92.56	61.51	52.60	49.02	47.39	46.61	46.03
5 000	170.29	115.70	76.89	65.75	61.28	59.24	58.26	57.54
6 000	204.34	138.84	92.27	78.90	73.53	71.08	69.91	69.05
7 000	238.40	161.98	107.64	92.05	85.78	82.93	81.56	80.55
8 000	272.46	185.12	123.02	105.20	98.04	94.78	93.21	92.06
9 000	306.51	208.25	138.40	118.35	110.29	106.62	104.87	103.57
10 000	340.57	231.39	153.77	131.50	122.55	118.47	116.52	115.07
11 000	374.62	254.53	169.15	144.65	134.80	130.32	128.17	126.58
12 000	408.68	277.67	184.53	157.80	147.05	142.16	139.82	138.09
13 000	442.74	300.81	199.90	170.95	159.31	154.01	151.47	149.59
14 000	476.79	323.95	215.28	184.10	171.56	165.86	163.12	161.10
15 000	510.85	347.09	230.66	197.25	183.82	177.70	174.77	172.61
16 000	544.91	370.23	246.03	210.40	196.07	189.55	186.42	184.11
17 000	578.96	393.37	261.41	223.55	208.32	201.40	198.07	195.62
18 000	613.02	416.50	276.79	236.70	220.58	213.24	209.73	207.13
19 000	647.08	439.64	292.16	249.85	232.83	225.09	221.38	218.64
20 000	681.13	462.78	307.54	263.00	245.09	236.94	233.03	230.14
21 000	715.19	485.92	322.92	276.15	257.34	248.78	244.68	241.65
22 000	749.24	509.06	338.29	289.30	269.59	260.63	256.33	253.16
23 000	783.30	532.20	353.67	302.45	281.85	272.48	267.98	264.66
24 000	817.36	555.34	369.05	315.60	294.10	284.32	279.63	276.17
25 000	851.41	578.48	384.42	328.75	306.36	296.17	291.28	287.68
26 000	885.47	601.61	399.80	341.90	318.61	308.02	302.93	299.18
27 000	919.53	624.75	415.18	355.05	330.86	319.86	314.59	310.69
28 000	953.58	647.89	430.55	368.20	343.12	331.71	326.24	322.20
29 000	987.64	671.03	445.93	381.35	355.37	343.56	337.89	333.70
30 000	1021.69	694.17	461.31	394.50	367.63	355.40	349.54	345.21
31 000	1055.75	717.31	476.68	407.65	379.88	367.25	361.19	356.72
32 000	1089.81	740.45	492.06	420.80	392.13	379.10	372.84	368.22
33 000	1123.86	763.59	507.44	433.95	404.39	390.94	384.49	379.73
34 000	1157.92	786.73	522.81	447.10	416.64	402.79	396.14	391.24
35 000	1191.98	809.86	538.19	460.25	428.90	414.64	407.79	402.74
36 000	1226.03	833.00	553.57	473.40	441.15	426.48	419.45	414.25
37 000	1260.09	856.14	568.94	486.55	453.40	438.33	431.10	425.76
38 000	1294.15	879.28	584.32	499.70	465.66	450.18	442.75	437.27
39 000	1328.20	902.42	599.70	512.85	477.91	462.02	454.40	448.77
40 000	1362.26	925.56	615.07	526.00	490.17	473.87	466.05	460.28
41 000	1396.31	948.70	630.45	539.15	502.42	485.72	477.70	471.79
42 000	1430.37	971.84	645.83	552.30	514.68	497.56	489.35	483.29
43 000	1464.43	994.98	661.20	565.45	526.93	509.41	501.00	494.80
44 000	1498.48	1018.11	676.58	578.60	539.18	521.26	512.65	506.31
45 000	1532.54	1041.25	691.96	591.75	551.44	533.10	524.31	517.81

FOR **OTHER RATES AND TERMS** *SEE PAGE A-1.*

TERM → AMOUNT	10 YEARS	15 YEARS	20 YEARS	25 YEARS	30 YEARS	40 YEARS
$46 000	707.33	604.90	563.69	544.95	535.96	529.32
47 000	722.71	618.05	575.95	556.80	547.61	540.83
48 000	738.09	631.20	588.20	568.64	559.26	552.33
49 000	753.46	644.35	600.45	580.49	570.91	563.84
50 000	768.84	657.50	612.71	592.34	582.56	575.35
51 000	784.22	670.65	624.96	604.18	594.21	586.85
52 000	799.59	683.80	637.22	616.03	605.86	598.36
53 000	814.97	696.95	649.47	627.88	617.51	609.87
54 000	830.35	710.10	661.72	639.72	629.17	621.38
55 000	845.72	723.25	673.98	651.57	640.82	632.88
56 000	861.10	736.40	686.23	663.42	652.47	644.39
57 000	876.48	749.55	698.49	675.26	664.12	655.90
58 000	891.85	762.70	710.74	687.11	675.77	667.40
59 000	907.23	775.85	722.99	698.96	687.42	678.91
60 000	922.61	789.00	735.25	710.80	699.07	690.42
61 000	937.98	802.15	747.50	722.65	710.72	701.92
62 000	953.36	815.30	759.76	734.50	722.37	713.43
63 000	968.74	828.45	772.01	746.34	734.03	724.94
64 000	984.11	841.60	784.26	758.19	745.68	736.44
65 000	999.49	854.75	796.52	770.04	757.33	747.95
66 000	1014.87	867.90	808.77	781.88	768.98	759.46
67 000	1030.24	881.05	821.03	793.73	780.63	770.96
68 000	1045.62	894.20	833.28	805.58	792.28	782.47
69 000	1061.00	907.35	845.53	817.42	803.93	793.98
70 000	1076.37	920.50	857.79	829.27	815.58	805.48
71 000	1091.75	933.65	870.04	841.12	827.23	816.99
72 000	1107.13	946.80	882.30	852.96	838.89	828.50
73 000	1122.50	959.95	894.55	864.81	850.54	840.01
74 000	1137.88	973.10	906.80	876.66	862.19	851.51
75 000	1153.26	986.25	919.06	888.50	873.84	863.02
76 000	1168.63	999.40	931.31	900.35	885.49	874.53
77 000	1184.01	1012.55	943.57	912.20	897.14	886.03
78 000	1199.39	1025.70	955.82	924.04	908.79	897.54
79 000	1214.76	1038.84	968.08	935.89	920.44	909.05
80 000	1230.14	1051.99	980.33	947.74	932.10	920.55
81 000	1245.52	1065.14	992.58	959.58	943.75	932.06
82 000	1260.89	1078.29	1004.84	971.43	955.40	943.57
83 000	1276.27	1091.44	1017.09	983.28	967.05	955.07
84 000	1291.65	1104.59	1029.35	995.12	978.70	966.58
85 000	1307.02	1117.74	1041.60	1006.97	990.35	978.09
88 000	1322.40	1130.89	1053.85	1018.82	1002.00	989.59
87 000	1337.78	1144.04	1066.11	1030.66	1013.65	1001.10
88 000	1353.15	1157.19	1078.36	1042.51	1025.30	1012.61
89 000	1368.53	1170.34	1090.62	1054.36	1036.96	1024.11
90 000	1383.91	1183.49	1102.87	1066.20	1048.61	1035.62
91 000	1399.28	1196.64	1115.12	1078.05	1060.26	1047.13
92 000	1414.66	1209.79	1127.38	1089.90	1071.91	1058.64
93 000	1430.04	1222.94	1139.63	1101.74	1083.56	1070.14
94 000	1445.41	1236.09	1151.89	1113.59	1095.21	1081.65
95 000	1460.79	1249.24	1164.14	1125.44	1106.86	1093.16
96 000	1476.17	1262.39	1176.39	1137.28	1118.51	1104.66
97 000	1491.54	1275.54	1188.65	1149.13	1130.16	1116.17
98 000	1506.92	1288.69	1200.90	1160.98	1141.82	1127.68
99 000	1522.30	1301.84	1213.16	1172.82	1153.47	1139.18
100 000	1537.67	1314.99	1225.41	1184.67	1165.12	1150.69

FOR **OTHER RATES AND TERMS** SEE PAGE A-1.

TERM▶ AMOUNT	3 YEARS	5 YEARS	10 YEARS	15 YEARS	20 YEARS	25 YEARS	30 YEARS	40 YEARS
$ 100	3.42	2.33	1.56	1.34	1.25	1.21	1.19	1.18
200	6.84	4.66	3.11	2.67	2.49	2.41	2.37	2.35
300	10.26	6.99	4.66	4.00	3.74	3.62	3.56	3.52
400	13.68	9.31	6.22	5.33	4.98	4.82	4.74	4.69
500	17.09	11.64	7.77	6.66	6.22	6.02	5.93	5.86
600	20.51	13.97	9.32	8.00	7.47	7.23	7.11	7.03
700	23.93	16.29	10.87	9.33	8.71	8.43	8.30	8.20
800	27.35	18.62	12.43	10.66	9.95	9.64	9.48	9.37
900	30.76	20.95	13.98	11.99	11.20	10.84	10.67	10.55
1 000	34.18	23.27	15.53	13.32	12.44	12.04	11.85	11.72
1 000	34.18	23.27	15.53	13.32	12.44	12.04	11.85	11.72
2 000	68.36	46.54	31.06	26.64	24.88	24.08	23.70	23.43
3 000	102.54	69.81	46.58	39.96	37.31	36.12	35.55	35.14
4 000	136.72	93.08	62.11	53.27	49.75	48.16	47.40	46.85
5 000	170.89	116.35	77.64	66.59	62.18	60.19	59.25	58.56
6 000	205.07	139.61	93.16	79.91	74.62	72.23	71.10	70.27
7 000	239.25	162.88	108.69	93.23	87.05	84.27	82.95	81.98
8 000	273.43	186.15	124.22	106.54	99.49	96.31	94.79	93.70
9 000	307.60	209.42	139.74	119.86	111.92	108.34	106.64	105.41
10 000	341.78	232.69	155.27	133.18	124.36	120.38	118.49	117.12
11 000	375.96	255.96	170.80	146.50	136.79	132.42	130.34	128.83
12 000	410.14	279.22	186.32	159.81	149.23	144.46	142.19	140.54
13 000	444.31	302.49	201.85	173.13	161.66	156.49	154.04	152.25
14 000	478.49	325.76	217.38	186.45	174.10	168.53	165.89	163.96
15 000	512.67	349.03	232.90	199.77	186.53	180.57	177.74	175.68
16 000	546.85	372.30	248.43	213.08	198.97	192.61	189.58	187.39
17 000	581.02	395.57	263.96	226.40	211.40	204.64	201.43	199.10
18 000	615.20	418.83	279.48	239.72	223.84	216.68	213.28	210.81
19 000	649.38	442.10	295.01	253.04	236.27	228.72	225.13	222.52
20 000	683.56	465.37	310.54	266.35	248.71	240.76	236.98	234.23
21 000	717.74	488.64	326.06	279.67	261.14	252.79	248.83	245.94
22 000	751.91	511.91	341.59	292.99	273.58	264.83	260.68	257.66
23 000	786.09	535.17	357.12	306.31	286.01	276.87	272.53	269.37
24 000	820.27	558.44	372.64	319.62	298.45	288.91	284.37	281.08
25 000	854.45	581.71	388.17	332.94	310.89	300.95	296.22	292.79
26 000	888.62	604.98	403.70	346.26	323.32	312.98	308.07	304.50
27 000	922.80	628.25	419.22	359.58	335.76	325.02	319.92	316.21
28 000	956.98	651.52	434.75	372.89	348.19	337.06	331.77	327.92
29 000	991.16	674.78	450.28	386.21	360.63	349.10	343.62	339.64
30 000	1025.33	698.05	465.80	399.53	373.06	361.13	355.47	351.35
31 000	1059.51	721.32	481.33	412.84	385.50	373.17	367.32	363.06
32 000	1093.69	744.59	496.86	426.16	397.93	385.21	379.16	374.77
33 000	1127.87	767.86	512.38	439.48	410.37	397.25	391.01	386.48
34 000	1162.04	791.13	527.91	452.80	422.80	409.28	402.86	398.19
35 000	1196.22	814.39	543.44	466.11	435.24	421.32	414.71	409.90
36 000	1230.40	837.66	558.96	479.43	447.67	433.36	426.56	421.62
37 000	1264.58	860.93	574.49	492.75	460.11	445.40	438.41	433.33
38 000	1298.75	884.20	590.02	506.07	472.54	457.43	450.26	445.04
39 000	1332.93	907.47	605.54	519.38	484.98	469.47	462.10	456.75
40 000	1367.11	930.74	621.07	532.70	497.41	481.51	473.95	468.46
41 000	1401.29	954.00	636.60	546.02	509.85	493.55	485.80	480.17
42 000	1435.47	977.27	652.12	559.34	522.28	505.58	497.65	491.88
43 000	1469.64	1000.54	667.65	572.65	534.72	517.62	509.50	503.60
44 000	1503.82	1023.81	683.18	585.97	547.15	529.66	521.35	515.31
45 000	1538.00	1047.08	698.70	599.29	559.59	541.70	533.20	527.02

FOR **OTHER RATES AND TERMS** *SEE PAGE A-1.*

TERM➡ AMOUNT	10 YEARS	15 YEARS	20 YEARS	25 YEARS	30 YEARS	40 YEARS
$46 000	714.23	612.61	572.02	553.74	545.05	538.73
47 000	729.76	625.92	584.46	565.77	556.89	550.44
48 000	745.28	639.24	596.89	577.81	568.74	562.15
49 000	760.81	652.56	609.33	589.85	580.59	573.86
50 000	776.34	665.88	621.77	601.89	592.44	585.58
51 000	791.86	679.19	634.20	613.92	604.29	597.29
52 000	807.39	692.51	646.64	625.96	616.14	609.00
53 000	822.92	705.83	659.07	638.00	627.99	620.71
54 000	838.44	719.15	671.51	650.04	639.84	632.42
55 000	853.97	732.46	683.94	662.07	651.68	644.13
56 000	869.50	745.78	696.38	674.11	663.53	655.84
57 000	885.02	759.10	708.81	686.15	675.38	667.55
58 000	900.55	772.42	721.25	698.19	687.23	679.27
59 000	916.08	785.73	733.68	710.22	699.08	690.98
60 000	931.60	799.05	746.12	722.26	710.93	702.69
61 000	947.13	812.37	758.55	734.30	722.78	714.40
62 000	962.66	825.68	770.99	746.34	734.63	726.11
63 000	978.18	839.00	783.42	758.37	746.47	737.82
64 000	993.71	852.32	795.86	770.41	758.32	749.53
65 000	1009.24	865.64	808.29	782.45	770.17	761.25
66 000	1024.76	878.95	820.73	794.49	782.02	772.96
67 000	1040.29	892.27	833.16	806.52	793.87	784.67
68 000	1055.82	905.59	845.60	818.56	805.72	796.38
69 000	1071.34	918.91	858.03	830.60	817.57	808.09
70 000	1086.87	932.22	870.47	842.64	829.42	819.80
71 000	1102.40	945.54	882.90	854.68	841.26	831.51
72 000	1117.92	958.86	895.34	866.71	853.11	843.23
73 000	1133.45	972.18	907.78	878.75	864.96	854.94
74 000	1148.98	985.49	920.21	890.79	876.81	866.65
75 000	1164.50	998.81	932.65	902.83	888.66	878.36
76 000	1180.03	1012.13	945.08	914.86	900.51	890.07
77 000	1195.56	1025.45	957.52	926.90	912.36	901.78
78 000	1211.08	1038.76	969.95	938.94	924.20	913.49
79 000	1226.61	1052.08	982.39	950.98	936.05	925.21
80 000	1242.14	1065.40	994.82	963.01	947.90	936.92
81 000	1257.66	1078.72	1007.26	975.05	959.75	948.63
82 000	1273.19	1092.03	1019.69	987.09	971.60	960.34
83 000	1288.72	1105.35	1032.13	999.13	983.45	972.05
84 000	1304.24	1118.67	1044.56	1011.16	995.30	983.76
85 000	1319.77	1131.99	1057.00	1023.20	1007.15	995.47
86 000	1335.30	1145.30	1069.43	1035.24	1018.99	1007.19
87 000	1350.82	1158.62	1081.87	1047.28	1030.84	1018.90
88 000	1366.35	1171.94	1094.30	1059.31	1042.69	1030.61
89 000	1381.88	1185.25	1106.74	1071.35	1054.54	1042.32
90 000	1397.40	1198.57	1119.17	1083.39	1066.39	1054.03
91 000	1412.93	1211.89	1131.61	1095.43	1078.24	1065.74
92 000	1428.46	1225.21	1144.04	1107.47	1090.09	1077.45
93 000	1443.98	1238.52	1156.48	1119.50	1101.94	1089.17
94 000	1459.51	1251.84	1168.91	1131.54	1113.78	1100.88
95 000	1475.04	1265.16	1181.35	1143.58	1125.63	1112.59
96 000	1490.56	1278.48	1193.78	1155.62	1137.48	1124.30
97 000	1506.09	1291.79	1206.22	1167.65	1149.33	1136.01
98 000	1521.62	1305.11	1218.66	1179.69	1161.18	1147.72
99 000	1537.14	1318.43	1231.09	1191.73	1173.03	1159.43
100 000	1552.67	1331.75	1243.53	1203.77	1184.88	1171.15

FOR **OTHER RATES AND TERMS** *SEE PAGE A-1.*

TERM▶ AMOUNT	3 YEARS	5 YEARS	10 YEARS	15 YEARS	20 YEARS	25 YEARS	30 YEARS	40 YEARS
$ 100	3.43	2.34	1.57	1.35	1.27	1.23	1.21	1.20
200	6.86	4.68	3.14	2.70	2.53	2.45	2.41	2.39
300	10.29	7.02	4.71	4.05	3.79	3.67	3.62	3.58
400	13.72	9.36	6.28	5.40	5.05	4.90	4.82	4.77
500	17.15	11.70	7.84	6.75	6.31	6.12	6.03	5.96
600	20.58	14.04	9.41	8.10	7.58	7.34	7.23	7.15
700	24.01	16.38	10.98	9.45	8.84	8.57	8.44	8.35
800	27.44	18.72	12.55	10.79	10.10	9.79	9.64	9.54
900	30.87	21.06	14.11	12.14	11.36	11.01	10.85	10.73
1 000	34.30	23.40	15.68	13.49	12.62	12.23	12.05	11.92
1 000	34.30	23.40	15.68	13.49	12.62	12.23	12.05	11.92
2 000	68.60	46.80	31.36	26.98	25.24	24.46	24.10	23.84
3 000	102.90	70.20	47.04	40.46	37.86	36.69	36.15	35.75
4 000	137.20	93.60	62.71	53.95	50.47	48.92	48.19	47.67
5 000	171.50	117.00	78.39	67.43	63.09	61.15	60.24	59.59
6 000	205.80	140.39	94.07	80.92	75.71	73.38	72.29	71.50
7 000	240.10	163.79	109.75	94.41	88.33	85.61	84.33	83.42
8 000	274.40	187.19	125.42	107.89	100.94	97.84	96.38	95.33
9 000	308.70	210.59	141.10	121.38	113.56	110.07	108.43	107.25
10 000	343.00	233.99	156.78	134.86	126.18	122.30	120.47	119.17
11 000	377.30	257.38	172.46	148.35	138.79	134.53	132.52	131.08
12 000	411.60	280.78	188.13	161.83	151.41	146.76	144.57	143.00
13 000	445.89	304.18	203.81	175.32	164.03	158.99	156.61	154.92
14 000	480.19	327.58	219.49	188.81	176.65	171.22	168.66	166.83
15 000	514.49	350.98	235.16	202.29	189.26	183.44	180.71	178.75
16 000	548.79	374.37	250.84	215.78	201.88	195.67	192.75	190.66
17 000	583.09	397.77	266.52	229.26	214.50	207.90	204.80	202.58
18 000	617.39	421.17	282.20	242.75	227.11	220.13	216.85	214.50
19 000	651.69	444.57	297.87	256.24	239.73	232.36	228.90	226.41
20 000	685.99	467.97	313.55	269.72	252.35	244.59	240.94	238.33
21 000	720.29	491.36	329.23	283.21	264.97	256.82	252.99	250.25
22 000	754.59	514.76	344.91	296.69	277.58	269.05	265.04	262.16
23 000	788.89	538.16	360.58	310.18	290.20	281.28	277.08	274.08
24 000	823.19	561.56	376.26	323.66	302.82	293.51	289.13	285.99
25 000	857.48	584.96	391.94	337.15	315.43	305.74	301.18	297.91
26 000	891.78	608.35	407.62	350.64	328.05	317.97	313.22	309.83
27 000	926.08	631.75	423.29	364.12	340.67	330.20	325.27	321.74
28 000	960.38	655.15	438.97	377.61	353.29	342.42	337.32	333.66
29 000	994.68	678.55	454.65	391.09	365.90	354.65	349.36	345.58
30 000	1028.98	701.95	470.32	404.58	378.52	366.88	361.41	357.49
31 000	1063.28	725.34	486.00	418.06	391.14	379.11	373.46	369.41
32 000	1097.58	748.74	501.68	431.55	403.76	391.34	385.50	381.32
33 000	1131.88	772.14	517.36	445.04	416.37	403.57	397.55	393.24
34 000	1166.18	795.54	533.03	458.52	428.99	415.80	409.60	405.16
35 000	1200.48	818.94	548.71	472.01	441.61	428.03	421.65	417.07
36 000	1234.78	842.34	564.39	485.49	454.22	440.26	433.69	428.99
37 000	1269.07	865.73	580.07	498.98	466.84	452.49	445.74	440.91
38 000	1303.37	889.13	595.74	512.47	479.46	464.72	457.79	452.82
39 000	1337.67	912.53	611.42	525.95	492.08	476.95	469.83	464.74
40 000	1371.97	935.93	627.10	539.44	504.69	489.18	481.88	476.65
41 000	1406.27	959.33	642.77	552.92	517.31	501.41	493.93	488.57
42 000	1440.57	982.72	658.45	566.41	529.93	513.63	505.97	500.49
43 000	1474.87	1006.12	674.13	579.89	542.54	525.86	518.02	512.40
44 000	1509.17	1029.52	689.81	593.38	555.16	538.09	530.07	524.32
45 000	1543.47	1052.92	705.48	606.87	567.78	550.32	542.11	536.24

*FOR **OTHER RATES AND TERMS** SEE PAGE A-1.*

TERM♦ AMOUNT	10 YEARS	15 YEARS	20 YEARS	25 YEARS	30 YEARS	40 YEARS
$46 000	721.16	620.35	580.40	562.55	554.16	548.15
47 000	736.84	633.84	593.01	574.78	566.21	560.07
48 000	752.52	647.32	605.63	587.01	578.25	571.98
49 000	768.19	660.81	618.25	599.24	590.30	583.90
50 000	783.87	674.29	630.86	611.47	602.35	595.82
51 000	799.55	687.78	643.48	623.70	614.40	607.73
52 000	815.23	701.27	656.10	635.93	626.44	619.65
53 000	830.90	714.75	668.72	648.16	638.49	631.57
54 000	846.58	728.24	681.33	660.39	650.54	643.48
55 000	862.26	741.72	693.95	672.62	662.58	655.40
56 000	877.93	755.21	706.57	684.84	674.63	667.31
57 000	893.61	768.70	719.18	697.07	686.68	679.23
58 000	909.29	782.18	731.80	709.30	698.72	691.15
59 000	924.97	795.67	744.42	721.53	710.77	703.06
60 000	940.64	809.15	757.04	733.76	722.82	714.98
61 000	956.32	822.64	769.65	745.99	734.86	726.90
62 000	972.00	836.12	782.27	758.22	746.91	738.81
63 000	987.68	849.61	794.89	770.45	758.96	750.73
64 000	1003.35	863.10	807.51	782.68	771.00	762.64
65 000	1019.03	876.58	820.12	794.91	783.05	774.56
66 000	1034.71	890.07	832.74	807.14	795.10	786.48
67 000	1050.38	903.55	845.36	819.37	807.15	798.39
68 000	1066.06	917.04	857.97	831.60	819.19	810.31
69 000	1081.74	930.52	870.59	843.82	831.24	822.23
70 000	1097.42	944.01	883.21	856.05	843.29	834.14
71 000	1113.09	957.50	895.83	868.28	855.33	846.06
72 000	1128.77	970.98	908.44	880.51	867.38	857.97
73 000	1144.45	984.47	921.06	892.74	879.43	869.89
74 000	1160.13	997.95	933.68	904.97	891.47	881.81
75 000	1175.80	1011.44	946.29	917.20	903.52	893.72
76 000	1191.48	1024.93	958.91	929.43	915.57	905.64
77 000	1207.16	1038.41	971.53	941.66	927.61	917.55
78 000	1222.84	1051.90	984.15	953.89	939.66	929.47
79 000	1238.51	1065.38	996.76	966.12	951.71	941.39
80 000	1254.19	1078.87	1009.38	978.35	963.75	953.30
81 000	1269.87	1092.35	1022.00	990.58	975.80	965.22
82 000	1285.54	1105.84	1034.61	1002.81	987.85	977.14
83 000	1301.22	1119.33	1047.23	1015.03	999.90	989.05
84 000	1316.90	1132.81	1059.85	1027.26	1011.94	1000.97
85 000	1332.58	1146.30	1072.47	1039.49	1023.99	1012.88
86 000	1348.25	1159.78	1085.08	1051.72	1036.04	1024.80
87 000	1363.93	1173.27	1097.70	1063.95	1048.08	1036.72
88 000	1379.61	1186.76	1110.32	1076.18	1060.13	1048.63
89 000	1395.29	1200.24	1122.93	1088.41	1072.18	1060.55
90 000	1410.96	1213.73	1135.55	1100.64	1084.22	1072.47
91 000	1426.64	1227.21	1148.17	1112.87	1096.27	1084.38
92 000	1442.32	1240.70	1160.79	1125.10	1108.32	1096.30
93 000	1457.99	1254.18	1173.40	1137.33	1120.36	1108.21
94 000	1473.67	1267.67	1186.02	1149.56	1132.41	1120.13
95 000	1489.35	1281.16	1198.64	1161.79	1144.46	1132.05
96 000	1505.03	1294.64	1211.26	1174.02	1156.50	1143.96
97 000	1520.70	1308.13	1223.87	1186.24	1168.55	1155.88
98 000	1536.38	1321.61	1236.49	1198.47	1180.60	1167.80
99 000	1552.06	1335.10	1249.11	1210.70	1192.65	1179.71
100 000	1567.74	1348.58	1261.72	1222.93	1204.69	1191.63

FOR **OTHER RATES AND TERMS** *SEE PAGE A-1.*

TERM➧ AMOUNT	3 YEARS	5 YEARS	10 YEARS	15 YEARS	20 YEARS	25 YEARS	30 YEARS	40 YEARS
$ 100	3.45	2.36	1.59	1.37	1.28	1.25	1.23	1.22
200	6.89	4.71	3.17	2.74	2.56	2.49	2.45	2.43
300	10.33	7.06	4.75	4.10	3.84	3.73	3.68	3.64
400	13.77	9.42	6.34	5.47	5.12	4.97	4.90	4.85
500	17.22	11.77	7.92	6.83	6.40	6.22	6.13	6.07
600	20.66	14.12	9.50	8.20	7.68	7.46	7.35	7.28
700	24.10	16.47	11.09	9.56	8.96	8.70	8.58	8.49
800	27.54	18.83	12.67	10.93	10.24	9.94	9.80	9.70
900	30.98	21.18	14.25	12.29	11.52	11.18	11.03	10.91
1 000	34.43	23.53	15.83	13.66	12.80	12.43	12.25	12.13
1 000	34.43	23.53	15.83	13.66	12.80	12.43	12.25	12.13
2 000	68.85	47.06	31.66	27.32	25.60	24.85	24.50	24.25
3 000	103.27	70.59	47.49	40.97	38.40	37.27	36.74	36.37
4 000	137.69	94.12	63.32	54.63	51.20	49.69	48.99	48.49
5 000	172.11	117.65	79.15	68.28	64.00	62.11	61.23	60.61
6 000	206.53	141.17	94.98	81.94	76.80	74.53	73.48	72.73
7 000	240.95	164.70	110.81	95.59	89.60	86.96	85.72	84.85
8 000	275.37	188.23	126.63	109.25	102.40	99.38	97.97	96.98
9 000	309.79	211.76	142.46	122.90	115.20	111.80	110.22	109.10
10 000	344.21	235.29	158.29	136.56	128.00	124.22	122.46	121.22
11 000	378.64	258.82	174.12	150.21	140.80	136.64	134.71	133.34
12 000	413.06	282.34	189.95	163.87	153.60	149.06	146.95	145.46
13 000	447.48	305.87	205.78	177.52	166.40	161.49	159.20	157.58
14 000	481.90	329.40	221.61	191.18	179.20	173.91	171.44	169.70
15 000	516.32	352.93	237.44	204.83	192.00	186.33	183.69	181.82
16 000	550.74	376.46	253.26	218.49	204.80	198.75	195.93	193.95
17 000	585.16	399.99	269.09	232.14	217.60	211.17	208.18	206.07
18 000	619.58	423.51	284.92	245.80	230.40	223.59	220.43	218.19
19 000	654.00	447.04	300.75	259.45	243.20	236.02	232.67	230.31
20 000	688.42	470.57	316.58	273.11	256.00	248.44	244.92	242.43
21 000	722.85	494.10	332.41	286.76	268.80	260.86	257.16	254.55
22 000	757.27	517.63	348.24	300.42	281.60	273.28	269.41	266.67
23 000	791.69	541.16	364.06	314.07	294.40	285.70	281.65	278.80
24 000	826.11	564.68	379.89	327.73	307.20	298.12	293.90	290.92
25 000	860.53	588.21	395.72	341.38	320.00	310.55	306.14	303.04
26 000	894.95	611.74	411.55	355.04	332.80	322.97	318.39	315.16
27 000	929.37	635.27	427.38	368.69	345.60	335.39	330.64	327.28
28 000	963.79	658.80	443.21	382.35	358.40	347.81	342.88	339.40
29 000	998.21	682.33	459.04	396.00	371.20	360.23	355.13	351.52
30 000	1032.63	705.85	474.87	409.66	384.00	372.65	367.37	363.64
31 000	1067.06	729.38	490.69	423.31	396.80	385.08	379.62	375.77
32 000	1101.48	752.91	506.52	436.97	409.60	397.50	391.86	387.89
33 000	1135.90	776.44	522.35	450.62	422.40	409.92	404.11	400.01
34 000	1170.32	799.97	538.18	464.28	435.20	422.34	416.35	412.13
35 000	1204.74	823.49	554.01	477.93	448.00	434.76	428.60	424.25
36 000	1239.16	847.02	569.84	491.59	460.80	447.18	440.85	436.37
37 000	1273.58	870.55	585.67	505.24	473.60	459.61	453.09	448.49
38 000	1308.00	894.08	601.49	518.90	486.40	472.03	465.34	460.62
39 000	1342.42	917.61	617.32	532.55	499.20	484.45	477.58	472.74
40 000	1376.84	941.14	633.15	546.21	512.00	496.87	489.83	484.86
41 000	1411.27	964.66	648.98	559.86	524.80	509.29	502.07	496.98
42 000	1445.69	988.19	664.81	573.52	537.60	521.71	514.32	509.10
43 000	1480.11	1011.72	680.64	587.17	550.40	534.14	526.56	521.22
44 000	1514.53	1035.25	696.47	600.83	563.20	546.56	538.81	533.34
45 000	1548.95	1058.78	712.30	614.48	576.00	558.98	551.06	545.46

FOR **OTHER RATES AND TERMS** *SEE PAGE A-1.*

TERM→ AMOUNT	10 YEARS	15 YEARS	20 YEARS	25 YEARS	30 YEARS	40 YEARS
$46 000	728.12	628.14	588.80	571.40	563.30	557.59
47 000	743.95	641.79	601.60	583.82	575.55	569.71
48 000	759.78	655.45	614.40	596.24	587.79	581.83
49 000	775.61	669.10	627.20	608.66	600.04	593.95
50 000	791.44	682.76	640.00	621.09	612.28	606.07
51 000	807.27	696.41	652.80	633.51	624.53	618.19
52 000	823.10	710.07	665.60	645.93	636.77	630.31
53 000	838.92	723.72	678.40	658.35	649.02	642.44
54 000	854.75	737.38	691.20	670.77	661.27	654.56
55 000	870.58	751.03	704.00	683.19	673.51	666.68
56 000	886.41	764.69	716.80	695.62	685.76	678.80
57 000	902.24	778.34	729.60	708.04	698.00	690.92
58 000	918.07	792.00	742.40	720.46	710.25	703.04
59 000	933.90	805.65	755.20	732.88	722.49	715.16
60 000	949.73	819.31	768.00	745.30	734.74	727.28
61 000	965.55	832.96	780.80	757.72	746.98	739.41
62 000	981.38	846.62	793.60	770.15	759.23	751.53
63 000	997.21	860.27	806.40	782.57	771.48	763.65
64 000	1013.04	873.93	819.20	794.99	783.72	775.77
65 000	1028.87	887.58	832.00	807.41	795.97	787.89
66 000	1044.70	901.24	844.80	819.83	808.21	800.01
67 000	1060.53	914.89	857.60	832.25	820.46	812.13
68 000	1076.36	928.55	870.40	844.68	832.70	824.26
69 000	1092.18	942.20	883.20	857.10	844.95	836.38
70 000	1108.01	955.86	896.00	869.52	857.19	848.50
71 000	1123.84	969.51	908.80	881.94	869.44	860.62
72 000	1139.67	983.17	921.60	894.36	881.69	872.74
73 000	1155.50	996.82	934.40	906.78	893.93	884.86
74 000	1171.33	1010.48	947.20	919.21	906.18	896.98
75 000	1187.16	1024.13	960.00	931.63	918.42	909.10
76 000	1202.98	1037.79	972.80	944.05	930.67	921.23
77 000	1218.81	1051.44	985.60	956.47	942.91	933.35
78 000	1234.64	1065.10	998.40	968.89	955.16	945.47
79 000	1250.47	1078.75	1011.20	981.31	967.40	957.59
80 000	1266.30	1092.41	1024.00	993.74	979.65	969.71
81 000	1282.13	1106.06	1036.80	1006.16	991.90	981.83
82 000	1297.96	1119.72	1049.60	1018.58	1004.14	993.95
83 000	1313.79	1133.37	1062.40	1031.00	1016.39	1006.08
84 000	1329.61	1147.03	1075.20	1043.42	1028.63	1018.20
85 000	1345.44	1160.68	1088.00	1055.84	1040.88	1030.32
86 000	1361.27	1174.34	1100.80	1068.27	1053.12	1042.44
87 000	1377.10	1187.99	1113.60	1080.69	1065.37	1054.56
88 000	1392.93	1201.65	1126.40	1093.11	1077.61	1066.68
89 000	1408.76	1215.30	1139.20	1105.53	1089.86	1078.80
90 000	1424.59	1228.96	1152.00	1117.95	1102.11	1090.92
91 000	1440.41	1242.61	1164.80	1130.37	1114.35	1103.05
92 000	1456.24	1256.27	1177.60	1142.79	1126.60	1115.17
93 000	1472.07	1269.92	1190.40	1155.22	1138.84	1127.29
94 000	1487.90	1283.58	1203.20	1167.64	1151.09	1139.41
95 000	1503.73	1297.23	1216.00	1180.06	1163.33	1151.53
96 000	1519.56	1310.89	1228.80	1192.48	1175.58	1163.65
97 000	1535.39	1324.54	1241.60	1204.90	1187.82	1175.77
98 000	1551.22	1338.20	1254.40	1217.32	1200.07	1187.90
99 000	1567.04	1351.85	1267.20	1229.75	1212.32	1200.02
100 000	1582.87	1365.51	1280.00	1242.17	1224.56	1212.14

FOR **OTHER RATES AND TERMS** *SEE PAGE A-1.*

TERM➤ AMOUNT	3 YEARS	5 YEARS	10 YEARS	15 YEARS	20 YEARS	25 YEARS	30 YEARS	40 YEARS
$ 100	3.46	2.37	1.60	1.39	1.30	1.27	1.25	1.24
200	6.91	4.74	3.20	2.77	2.60	2.53	2.49	2.47
300	10.37	7.10	4.80	4.15	3.90	3.79	3.74	3.70
400	13.82	9.47	6.40	5.54	5.20	5.05	4.98	4.94
500	17.28	11.83	8.00	6.92	6.50	6.31	6.23	6.17
600	20.73	14.20	9.59	8.30	7.80	7.57	7.47	7.40
700	24.19	16.57	11.19	9.68	9.09	8.84	8.72	8.63
800	27.64	18.93	12.79	11.07	10.39	10.10	9.96	9.87
900	31.09	21.30	14.39	12.45	11.69	11.36	11.21	11.10
1 000	34.55	23.66	15.99	13.83	12.99	12.62	12.45	12.33
1 000	34.55	23.66	15.99	13.83	12.99	12.62	12.45	12.33
2 000	69.09	47.32	31.97	27.66	25.97	25.23	24.89	24.66
3 000	103.63	70.98	47.95	41.48	38.96	37.85	37.34	36.99
4 000	138.18	94.64	63.93	55.31	51.94	50.46	49.78	49.31
5 000	172.72	118.30	79.91	69.13	64.92	63.08	62.23	61.64
6 000	207.26	141.96	95.89	82.96	77.91	75.69	74.67	73.97
7 000	241.81	165.62	111.87	96.78	90.89	88.31	87.12	86.29
8 000	276.35	189.28	127.85	110.61	103.87	100.92	99.56	98.62
9 000	310.89	212.94	143.83	124.43	116.86	113.54	112.01	110.95
10 000	345.44	236.59	159.81	138.26	129.84	126.15	124.45	123.27
11 000	379.98	260.25	175.79	152.08	142.82	138.77	136.90	135.60
12 000	414.52	283.91	191.77	165.91	155.81	151.38	149.34	147.93
13 000	449.06	307.57	207.75	179.73	168.79	164.00	161.79	160.25
14 000	483.61	331.23	223.74	193.56	181.77	176.61	174.23	172.58
15 000	518.15	354.89	239.72	207.38	194.76	189.22	186.68	184.91
16 000	552.69	378.55	255.70	221.21	207.74	201.84	199.12	197.23
17 000	587.24	402.21	271.68	235.03	220.73	214.45	211.57	209.56
18 000	621.78	425.87	287.66	248.86	233.71	227.07	224.01	221.89
19 000	656.32	449.52	303.64	262.68	246.69	239.68	236.46	234.21
20 000	690.87	473.18	319.62	276.51	259.68	252.30	248.90	246.54
21 000	725.41	496.84	335.60	290.33	272.66	264.91	261.34	258.87
22 000	759.95	520.50	351.58	304.16	285.64	277.53	273.79	271.19
23 000	794.49	544.16	367.56	317.98	298.63	290.14	286.23	283.52
24 000	829.04	567.82	383.54	331.81	311.61	302.76	298.68	295.85
25 000	863.58	591.48	399.52	345.63	324.59	315.37	311.12	308.17
26 000	898.12	615.14	415.50	359.46	337.58	327.99	323.57	320.50
27 000	932.67	638.80	431.49	373.28	350.56	340.60	336.01	332.83
28 000	967.21	662.45	447.47	387.11	363.54	353.22	348.46	345.15
29 000	1001.75	686.11	463.45	400.93	376.53	365.83	360.90	357.48
30 000	1036.30	709.77	479.43	414.76	389.51	378.44	373.35	369.81
31 000	1070.84	733.43	495.41	428.58	402.50	391.06	385.79	382.13
32 000	1105.38	757.09	511.39	442.41	415.48	403.67	398.24	394.46
33 000	1139.92	780.75	527.37	456.23	428.46	416.29	410.68	406.79
34 000	1174.47	804.41	543.35	470.06	441.45	428.90	423.13	419.11
35 000	1209.01	828.07	559.33	483.88	454.43	441.52	435.57	431.44
36 000	1243.55	851.73	575.31	497.71	467.41	454.13	448.02	443.77
37 000	1278.10	875.38	591.29	511.53	480.40	466.75	460.46	456.09
38 000	1312.64	899.04	607.27	525.36	493.38	479.36	472.91	468.42
39 000	1347.18	922.70	623.25	539.18	506.36	491.98	485.35	480.75
40 000	1381.73	946.36	639.23	553.01	519.35	504.59	497.80	493.07
41 000	1416.27	970.02	655.22	566.83	532.33	517.21	510.24	505.40
42 000	1450.81	993.68	671.20	580.66	545.31	529.82	522.68	517.73
43 000	1485.36	1017.34	687.18	594.48	558.30	542.43	535.13	530.05
44 000	1519.90	1041.00	703.16	608.31	571.28	555.05	547.57	542.38
45 000	1554.44	1064.66	719.14	622.13	584.26	567.66	560.02	554.71

FOR **OTHER RATES AND TERMS** *SEE PAGE A-1.*

TERM→ AMOUNT	10 YEARS	15 YEARS	20 YEARS	25 YEARS	30 YEARS	40 YEARS
$46 000	735.12	635.96	597.25	580.28	572.46	567.03
47 000	751.10	649.78	610.23	592.89	584.91	579.36
48 000	767.08	663.61	623.22	605.51	597.35	591.69
49 000	783.06	677.43	636.20	618.12	609.80	604.01
50 000	799.04	691.26	649.18	630.74	622.24	616.34
51 000	815.02	705.08	662.17	643.35	634.69	628.67
52 000	831.00	718.91	675.15	655.97	647.13	640.99
53 000	846.98	732.73	688.13	668.58	659.58	653.32
54 000	862.97	746.56	701.12	681.20	672.02	665.65
55 000	878.95	760.38	714.10	693.81	684.47	677.97
56 000	894.93	774.21	727.08	706.43	696.91	690.30
57 000	910.91	788.03	740.07	719.04	709.36	702.63
58 000	926.89	801.86	753.05	731.65	721.80	714.95
59 000	942.87	815.68	766.03	744.27	734.25	727.28
60 000	958.85	829.51	779.02	756.88	746.69	739.61
61 000	974.83	843.33	792.00	769.50	759.14	751.93
62 000	990.81	857.16	804.99	782.11	771.58	764.26
63 000	1006.79	870.98	817.97	794.73	784.02	776.59
64 000	1022.77	884.81	830.95	807.34	796.47	788.91
65 000	1038.75	898.63	843.94	819.96	808.91	801.24
66 000	1054.73	912.46	856.92	832.57	821.36	813.57
67 000	1070.71	926.28	869.90	845.19	833.80	825.89
68 000	1086.70	940.11	882.89	857.80	846.25	838.22
69 000	1102.68	953.93	895.87	870.42	858.69	850.55
70 000	1118.66	967.76	908.85	883.03	871.14	862.87
71 000	1134.64	981.58	921.84	895.64	883.58	875.20
72 000	1150.62	995.41	934.82	908.26	896.03	887.53
73 000	1166.60	1009.23	947.80	920.87	908.47	899.85
74 000	1182.58	1023.06	960.79	933.49	920.92	912.18
75 000	1198.56	1036.88	973.77	946.10	933.36	924.51
76 000	1214.54	1050.71	986.76	958.72	945.81	936.83
77 000	1230.52	1064.53	999.74	971.33	958.25	949.16
78 000	1246.50	1078.36	1012.72	983.95	970.70	961.49
79 000	1262.48	1092.18	1025.71	996.56	983.14	973.81
80 000	1278.46	1106.01	1038.69	1009.18	995.59	986.14
81 000	1294.45	1119.83	1051.67	1021.79	1008.03	998.47
82 000	1310.43	1133.66	1064.66	1034.41	1020.48	1010.79
83 000	1326.41	1147.48	1077.64	1047.02	1032.92	1023.12
84 000	1342.39	1161.31	1090.62	1059.64	1045.36	1035.45
85 000	1358.37	1175.13	1103.61	1072.25	1057.81	1047.77
86 000	1374.35	1188.96	1116.59	1084.86	1070.25	1060.10
87 000	1390.33	1202.78	1129.57	1097.48	1082.70	1072.43
88 000	1406.31	1216.61	1142.56	1110.09	1095.14	1084.75
89 000	1422.29	1230.43	1155.54	1122.71	1107.59	1097.08
90 000	1438.27	1244.26	1168.52	1135.32	1120.03	1109.41
91 000	1454.25	1258.08	1181.51	1147.94	1132.48	1121.73
92 000	1470.23	1271.91	1194.49	1160.55	1144.92	1134.06
93 000	1486.21	1285.73	1207.48	1173.17	1157.37	1146.39
94 000	1502.19	1299.56	1220.46	1185.78	1169.81	1158.71
95 000	1518.18	1313.38	1233.44	1198.40	1182.26	1171.04
96 000	1534.16	1327.21	1246.43	1211.01	1194.70	1183.37
97 000	1550.14	1341.03	1259.41	1223.63	1207.15	1195.69
98 000	1566.12	1354.86	1272.39	1236.24	1219.59	1208.02
99 000	1582.10	1368.68	1285.38	1248.86	1232.04	1220.35
100 000	1598.08	1382.51	1298.36	1261.47	1244.48	1232.67

FOR **OTHER RATES AND TERMS** *SEE PAGE A-1.*

TERM ♦ AMOUNT	3 YEARS	5 YEARS	10 YEARS	15 YEARS	20 YEARS	25 YEARS	30 YEARS	40 YEARS
$ 100	3.47	2.38	1.62	1.40	1.32	1.29	1.27	1.26
200	6.94	4.76	3.23	2.80	2.64	2.57	2.53	2.51
300	10.40	7.14	4.85	4.20	3.96	3.85	3.80	3.76
400	13.87	9.52	6.46	5.60	5.27	5.13	5.06	5.02
500	17.34	11.90	8.07	7.00	6.59	6.41	6.33	6.27
600	20.80	14.28	9.69	8.40	7.91	7.69	7.59	7.52
700	24.27	16.66	11.30	9.80	9.22	8.97	8.86	8.78
800	27.74	19.04	12.91	11.20	10.54	10.25	10.12	10.03
900	31.20	21.42	14.53	12.60	11.86	11.53	11.38	11.28
1 000	34.67	23.79	16.14	14.00	13.17	12.81	12.65	12.54
1 000	34.67	23.79	16.14	14.00	13.17	12.81	12.65	12.54
2 000	69.34	47.58	32.27	28.00	26.34	25.62	25.29	25.07
3 000	104.00	71.37	48.41	41.99	39.51	38.43	37.94	37.60
4 000	138.67	95.16	64.54	55.99	52.68	51.24	50.58	50.13
5 000	173.33	118.95	80.67	69.98	65.84	64.05	63.23	62.67
6 000	208.00	142.74	96.81	83.98	79.01	76.85	75.87	75.20
7 000	242.66	166.53	112.94	97.98	92.18	89.66	88.52	87.73
8 000	277.33	190.32	129.07	111.97	105.35	102.47	101.16	100.26
9 000	311.99	214.11	145.21	125.97	118.52	115.28	113.80	112.80
10 000	346.66	237.90	161.34	139.96	131.68	128.09	126.45	125.33
11 000	381.32	261.69	177.47	153.96	144.85	140.90	139.09	137.86
12 000	415.99	285.48	193.61	167.96	158.02	153.70	151.74	150.39
13 000	450.65	309.27	209.74	181.95	171.19	166.51	164.38	162.92
14 000	485.32	333.06	225.87	195.95	184.36	179.32	177.03	175.46
15 000	519.98	356.85	242.01	209.94	197.52	192.13	189.67	187.99
16 000	554.65	380.64	258.14	223.94	210.69	204.94	202.32	200.52
17 000	589.32	404.43	274.27	237.93	223.86	217.75	214.96	213.05
18 000	623.98	428.22	290.41	251.93	237.03	230.55	227.60	225.59
19 000	658.65	452.01	306.54	265.93	250.20	243.36	240.25	238.12
20 000	693.31	475.80	322.67	279.92	263.36	256.17	252.89	250.65
21 000	727.98	499.59	338.81	293.92	276.53	268.98	265.54	263.18
22 000	762.64	523.38	354.94	307.91	289.70	281.79	278.18	275.71
23 000	797.31	547.17	371.08	321.91	302.87	294.60	290.83	288.25
24 000	831.97	570.96	387.21	335.91	316.03	307.40	303.47	300.78
25 000	866.64	594.75	403.34	349.90	329.20	320.21	316.12	313.31
26 000	901.30	618.54	419.48	363.90	342.37	333.02	328.76	325.84
27 000	935.97	642.33	435.61	377.89	355.54	345.83	341.40	338.38
28 000	970.63	666.12	451.74	391.89	368.71	358.64	354.05	350.91
29 000	1005.30	689.91	467.88	405.89	381.87	371.45	366.69	363.44
30 000	1039.96	713.70	484.01	419.88	395.04	384.25	379.34	375.97
31 000	1074.63	737.49	500.14	433.88	408.21	397.06	391.98	388.50
32 000	1109.30	761.28	516.28	447.87	421.38	409.87	404.63	401.04
33 000	1143.96	785.07	532.41	461.87	434.55	422.68	417.27	413.57
34 000	1178.63	808.86	548.54	475.86	447.71	435.49	429.92	426.10
35 000	1213.29	832.65	564.68	489.86	460.88	448.30	442.56	438.63
36 000	1247.96	856.44	580.81	503.86	474.05	461.10	455.20	451.17
37 000	1282.62	880.23	596.94	517.85	487.22	473.91	467.85	463.70
38 000	1317.29	904.02	613.08	531.85	500.39	486.72	480.49	476.23
39 000	1351.95	927.81	629.21	545.84	513.55	499.53	493.14	488.76
40 000	1386.62	951.60	645.34	559.84	526.72	512.34	505.78	501.29
41 000	1421.28	975.39	661.48	573.84	539.89	525.15	518.43	513.83
42 000	1455.95	999.18	677.61	587.83	553.06	537.95	531.07	526.36
43 000	1490.61	1022.97	693.75	601.83	566.22	550.76	543.72	538.89
44 000	1525.28	1046.76	709.88	615.82	579.39	563.57	556.36	551.42
45 000	1559.94	1070.55	726.01	629.82	592.56	576.38	569.00	563.96

FOR **OTHER RATES AND TERMS** *SEE PAGE A-1.*

TERM➧ AMOUNT	10 YEARS	15 YEARS	20 YEARS	25 YEARS	30 YEARS	40 YEARS
$46 000	742.15	643.82	605.73	589.19	581.65	576.49
47 000	758.28	657.81	618.90	602.00	594.29	589.02
48 000	774.41	671.81	632.06	614.80	606.94	601.55
49 000	790.55	685.80	645.23	627.61	619.58	614.08
50 000	806.68	699.80	658.40	640.42	632.23	626.62
51 000	822.81	713.79	671.57	653.23	644.87	639.15
52 000	838.95	727.79	684.74	666.04	657.52	651.68
53 000	855.08	741.79	697.90	678.85	670.16	664.21
54 000	871.21	755.78	711.07	691.65	682.80	676.75
55 000	887.35	769.78	724.24	704.46	695.45	689.28
56 000	903.48	783.77	737.41	717.27	708.09	701.81
57 000	919.61	797.77	750.58	730.08	720.74	714.34
58 000	935.75	811.77	763.74	742.89	733.38	726.87
59 000	951.88	825.76	776.91	755.70	746.03	739.41
60 000	968.01	839.76	790.08	768.50	758.67	751.94
61 000	984.15	853.75	803.25	781.31	771.32	764.47
62 000	1000.28	867.75	816.41	794.12	783.96	777.00
63 000	1016.42	881.74	829.58	806.93	796.60	789.54
64 000	1032.55	895.74	842.75	819.74	809.25	802.07
65 000	1048.68	909.74	855.92	832.54	821.89	814.60
66 000	1064.82	923.73	869.09	845.35	834.54	827.13
67 000	1080.95	937.73	882.25	858.16	847.18	839.67
68 000	1097.08	951.72	895.42	870.97	859.83	852.20
69 000	1113.22	965.72	908.59	883.78	872.47	864.73
70 000	1129.35	979.72	921.76	896.59	885.12	877.26
71 000	1145.48	993.71	934.93	909.39	897.76	889.79
72 000	1161.62	1007.71	948.09	922.20	910.40	902.33
73 000	1177.75	1021.70	961.26	935.01	923.05	914.86
74 000	1193.88	1035.70	974.43	947.82	935.69	927.39
75 000	1210.02	1049.70	987.60	960.63	948.34	939.92
76 000	1226.15	1063.69	1000.77	973.44	960.98	952.46
77 000	1242.28	1077.69	1013.93	986.24	973.63	964.99
78 000	1258.42	1091.68	1027.10	999.05	986.27	977.52
79 000	1274.55	1105.68	1040.27	1011.86	998.92	990.05
80 000	1290.68	1119.67	1053.44	1024.67	1011.56	1002.58
81 000	1306.82	1133.67	1066.60	1037.48	1024.20	1015.12
82 000	1322.95	1147.67	1079.77	1050.29	1036.85	1027.65
83 000	1339.09	1161.66	1092.94	1063.09	1049.49	1040.18
84 000	1355.22	1175.66	1106.11	1075.90	1062.14	1052.71
85 000	1371.35	1189.65	1119.28	1088.71	1074.78	1065.25
86 000	1387.49	1203.65	1132.44	1101.52	1087.43	1077.78
87 000	1403.62	1217.65	1145.61	1114.33	1100.07	1090.31
88 000	1419.75	1231.64	1158.78	1127.14	1112.72	1102.84
89 000	1435.89	1245.64	1171.95	1139.94	1125.36	1115.37
90 000	1452.02	1259.63	1185.12	1152.75	1138.00	1127.91
91 000	1468.15	1273.63	1198.28	1165.56	1150.65	1140.44
92 000	1484.29	1287.63	1211.45	1178.37	1163.29	1152.97
93 000	1500.42	1301.62	1224.62	1191.18	1175.94	1165.50
94 000	1516.55	1315.62	1237.79	1203.99	1188.58	1178.04
95 000	1532.69	1329.61	1250.96	1216.79	1201.23	1190.57
96 000	1548.82	1343.61	1264.12	1229.60	1213.87	1203.10
97 000	1564.95	1357.60	1277.29	1242.41	1226.52	1215.63
98 000	1581.09	1371.60	1290.46	1255.22	1239.16	1228.16
99 000	1597.22	1385.60	1303.63	1268.03	1251.80	1240.70
100 000	1613.35	1399.59	1316.79	1280.84	1264.45	1253.23

FOR **OTHER RATES AND TERMS** *SEE PAGE A-1.*

TERM➡ AMOUNT	3 YEARS	5 YEARS	10 YEARS	15 YEARS	20 YEARS	25 YEARS	30 YEARS	40 YEARS
$ 100	3.48	2.40	1.63	1.42	1.34	1.31	1.29	1.28
200	6.96	4.79	3.26	2.84	2.68	2.61	2.57	2.55
300	10.44	7.18	4.89	4.26	4.01	3.91	3.86	3.83
400	13.92	9.57	6.52	5.67	5.35	5.21	5.14	5.10
500	17.40	11.97	8.15	7.09	6.68	6.51	6.43	6.37
600	20.88	14.36	9.78	8.51	8.02	7.81	7.71	7.65
700	24.36	16.75	11.41	9.92	9.35	9.11	9.00	8.92
800	27.84	19.14	13.03	11.34	10.69	10.41	10.28	10.20
900	31.31	21.53	14.66	12.76	12.02	11.71	11.57	11.47
1 000	34.79	23.93	16.29	14.17	13.36	13.01	12.85	12.74
1 000	34.79	23.93	16.29	14.17	13.36	13.01	12.85	12.74
2 000	69.58	47.85	32.58	28.34	26.71	26.01	25.69	25.48
3 000	104.37	71.77	48.87	42.51	40.06	39.01	38.54	38.22
4 000	139.16	95.69	65.15	56.67	53.42	52.02	51.38	50.96
5 000	173.94	119.61	81.44	70.84	66.77	65.02	64.23	63.70
6 000	208.73	143.53	97.73	85.01	80.12	78.02	77.07	76.43
7 000	243.52	167.45	114.01	99.18	93.48	91.02	89.92	89.17
8 000	278.31	191.38	130.30	113.34	106.83	104.03	102.76	101.91
9 000	313.10	215.30	146.59	127.51	120.18	117.03	115.61	114.65
10 000	347.88	239.22	162.87	141.68	133.53	130.03	128.45	127.39
11 000	382.67	263.14	179.16	155.85	146.89	143.03	141.30	140.12
12 000	417.46	287.06	195.45	170.01	160.24	156.04	154.14	152.86
13 000	452.25	310.98	211.74	184.18	173.59	169.04	166.98	165.60
14 000	487.04	334.90	228.02	198.35	186.95	182.04	179.83	178.34
15 000	521.82	358.83	244.31	212.52	200.30	195.04	192.67	191.08
16 000	556.61	382.75	260.60	226.68	213.65	208.05	205.52	203.81
17 000	591.40	406.67	276.88	240.85	227.01	221.05	218.36	216.55
18 000	626.19	430.59	293.17	255.02	240.36	234.05	231.21	229.29
19 000	660.97	454.51	309.46	269.19	253.71	247.05	244.05	242.03
20 000	695.76	478.43	325.74	283.35	267.06	260.06	256.90	254.77
21 000	730.55	502.35	342.03	297.52	280.42	273.06	269.74	267.50
22 000	765.34	526.27	358.32	311.69	293.77	286.06	282.59	280.24
23 000	800.13	550.20	374.60	325.86	307.12	299.06	295.43	292.98
24 000	834.91	574.12	390.89	340.02	320.48	312.07	308.28	305.72
25 000	869.70	598.04	407.18	354.19	333.83	325.07	321.12	318.46
26 000	904.49	621.96	423.47	368.36	347.18	338.07	333.96	331.19
27 000	939.28	645.88	439.75	382.53	360.54	351.07	346.81	343.93
28 000	974.07	669.80	456.04	396.69	373.89	364.08	359.65	356.67
29 000	1008.85	693.72	472.33	410.86	387.24	377.08	372.50	369.41
30 000	1043.64	717.65	488.61	425.03	400.59	390.08	385.34	382.15
31 000	1078.43	741.57	504.90	439.20	413.95	403.09	398.19	394.88
32 000	1113.22	765.49	521.19	453.36	427.30	416.09	411.03	407.62
33 000	1148.01	789.41	537.47	467.53	440.65	429.09	423.88	420.36
34 000	1182.79	813.33	553.76	481.70	454.01	442.09	436.72	433.10
35 000	1217.58	837.25	570.05	495.87	467.36	455.10	449.57	445.84
36 000	1252.37	861.17	586.33	510.03	480.71	468.10	462.41	458.57
37 000	1287.16	885.10	602.62	524.20	494.07	481.10	475.25	471.31
38 000	1321.94	909.02	618.91	538.37	507.42	494.10	488.10	484.05
39 000	1356.73	932.94	635.20	552.54	520.77	507.11	500.94	496.79
40 000	1391.52	956.86	651.48	566.70	534.12	520.11	513.79	509.53
41 000	1426.31	980.78	667.77	580.87	547.48	533.11	526.63	522.26
42 000	1461.10	1004.70	684.06	595.04	560.83	546.11	539.48	535.00
43 000	1495.88	1028.62	700.34	609.21	574.18	559.12	552.32	547.74
44 000	1530.67	1052.54	716.63	623.37	587.54	572.12	565.17	560.48
45 000	1565.46	1076.47	732.92	637.54	600.89	585.12	578.01	573.22

FOR **OTHER RATES AND TERMS** *SEE PAGE A-1.*

TERM◆ AMOUNT	10 YEARS	15 YEARS	20 YEARS	25 YEARS	30 YEARS	40 YEARS
$46 000	749.20	651.71	614.24	598.12	590.86	585.95
47 000	765.49	665.88	627.60	611.13	603.70	598.69
48 000	781.78	680.04	640.95	624.13	616.55	611.43
49 000	798.06	694.21	654.30	637.13	629.39	624.17
50 000	814.35	708.38	667.65	650.13	642.23	636.91
51 000	830.64	722.55	681.01	663.14	655.08	649.64
52 000	846.93	736.71	694.36	676.14	667.92	662.38
53 000	863.21	750.88	707.71	689.14	680.77	675.12
54 000	879.50	765.05	721.07	702.14	693.61	687.86
55 000	895.79	779.22	734.42	715.15	706.46	700.60
56 000	912.07	793.38	747.77	728.15	719.30	713.33
57 000	928.36	807.55	761.13	741.15	732.15	726.07
58 000	944.65	821.72	774.48	754.15	744.99	738.81
59 000	960.93	835.89	787.83	767.16	757.84	751.55
60 000	977.22	850.05	801.18	780.16	770.68	764.29
61 000	993.51	864.22	814.54	793.16	783.52	777.02
62 000	1009.79	878.39	827.89	806.17	796.37	789.76
63 000	1026.08	892.56	841.24	819.17	809.21	802.50
64 000	1042.37	906.72	854.60	832.17	822.06	815.24
65 000	1058.66	920.89	867.95	845.17	834.90	827.98
66 000	1074.94	935.06	881.30	858.18	847.75	840.71
67 000	1091.23	949.23	894.66	871.18	860.59	853.45
68 000	1107.52	963.39	908.01	884.18	873.44	866.19
69 000	1123.80	977.56	921.36	897.18	886.28	878.93
70 000	1140.09	991.73	934.71	910.19	899.13	891.67
71 000	1156.38	1005.90	948.07	923.19	911.97	904.40
72 000	1172.66	1020.06	961.42	936.19	924.82	917.14
73 000	1188.95	1034.23	974.77	949.19	937.66	929.88
74 000	1205.24	1048.40	988.13	962.20	950.50	942.62
75 000	1221.53	1062.57	1001.48	975.20	963.35	955.36
76 000	1237.81	1076.73	1014.83	988.20	976.19	968.09
77 000	1254.10	1090.90	1028.18	1001.20	989.04	980.83
78 000	1270.39	1105.07	1041.54	1014.21	1001.88	993.57
79 000	1286.67	1119.24	1054.89	1027.21	1014.73	1006.31
80 000	1302.96	1133.40	1068.24	1040.21	1027.57	1019.05
81 000	1319.25	1147.57	1081.60	1053.21	1040.42	1031.78
82 000	1335.53	1161.74	1094.95	1066.22	1053.26	1044.52
83 000	1351.82	1175.91	1108.30	1079.22	1066.11	1057.26
84 000	1368.11	1190.07	1121.66	1092.22	1078.95	1070.00
85 000	1384.39	1204.24	1135.01	1105.22	1091.79	1082.74
86 000	1400.68	1218.41	1148.36	1118.23	1104.64	1095.47
87 000	1416.97	1232.58	1161.71	1131.23	1117.48	1108.21
88 000	1433.26	1246.74	1175.07	1144.23	1130.33	1120.95
89 000	1449.54	1260.91	1188.42	1157.23	1143.17	1133.69
90 000	1465.83	1275.08	1201.77	1170.24	1156.02	1146.43
91 000	1482.12	1289.25	1215.13	1183.24	1168.86	1159.17
92 000	1498.40	1303.41	1228.48	1196.24	1181.71	1171.90
93 000	1514.69	1317.58	1241.83	1209.25	1194.55	1184.64
94 000	1530.98	1331.75	1255.19	1222.25	1207.40	1197.38
95 000	1547.26	1345.92	1268.54	1235.25	1220.24	1210.12
96 000	1563.55	1360.08	1281.89	1248.25	1233.09	1222.86
97 000	1579.84	1374.25	1295.24	1261.26	1245.93	1235.59
98 000	1596.12	1388.42	1308.60	1274.26	1258.77	1248.33
99 000	1612.41	1402.59	1321.95	1287.26	1271.62	1261.07
100 000	1628.70	1416.75	1335.30	1300.26	1284.46	1273.81

FOR **OTHER RATES AND TERMS** *SEE PAGE A-1.*

TERM♦ AMOUNT	3 YEARS	5 YEARS	10 YEARS	15 YEARS	20 YEARS	25 YEARS	30 YEARS	40 YEARS
$ 100	3.50	2.41	1.65	1.44	1.36	1.32	1.31	1.30
200	6.99	4.82	3.29	2.87	2.71	2.64	2.61	2.59
300	10.48	7.22	4.94	4.31	4.07	3.96	3.92	3.89
400	13.97	9.63	6.58	5.74	5.42	5.28	5.22	5.18
500	17.46	12.03	8.23	7.17	6.77	6.60	6.53	6.48
600	20.95	14.44	9.87	8.61	8.13	7.92	7.83	7.77
700	24.44	16.84	11.51	10.04	9.48	9.24	9.14	9.07
800	27.93	19.25	13.16	11.48	10.84	10.56	10.44	10.36
900	31.42	21.65	14.80	12.91	12.19	11.88	11.75	11.65
1 000	34.92	24.06	16.45	14.34	13.54	13.20	13.05	12.95
1 000	34.92	24.06	16.45	14.34	13.54	13.20	13.05	12.95
2 000	69.83	48.11	32.89	28.68	27.08	26.40	26.10	25.89
3 000	104.74	72.16	49.33	43.02	40.62	39.60	39.14	38.84
4 000	139.65	96.22	65.77	57.36	54.16	52.79	52.19	51.78
5 000	174.56	120.27	82.21	71.70	67.70	65.99	65.23	64.72
6 000	209.47	144.32	98.65	86.04	81.24	79.19	78.28	77.67
7 000	244.38	168.38	115.09	100.38	94.78	92.39	91.32	90.61
8 000	279.29	192.43	131.53	114.72	108.32	105.58	104.37	103.56
9 000	314.20	216.48	147.97	129.06	121.85	118.78	117.41	116.50
10 000	349.11	240.54	164.42	143.40	135.39	131.98	130.46	129.44
11 000	384.02	264.59	180.86	157.74	148.93	145.18	143.50	142.39
12 000	418.93	288.64	197.30	172.08	162.47	158.37	156.55	155.33
13 000	453.84	312.70	213.74	186.42	176.01	171.57	169.59	168.28
14 000	488.75	336.75	230.18	200.76	189.55	184.77	182.64	181.22
15 000	523.67	360.80	246.62	215.10	203.09	197.97	195.68	194.16
16 000	558.58	384.86	263.06	229.44	216.63	211.16	208.73	207.11
17 000	593.49	408.91	279.50	243.78	230.16	224.36	221.77	220.05
18 000	628.40	432.96	295.94	258.12	243.70	237.56	234.82	233.00
19 000	663.31	457.02	312.39	272.46	257.24	250.76	247.86	245.94
20 000	698.22	481.07	328.83	286.80	270.78	263.95	260.91	258.88
21 000	733.13	505.12	345.27	301.14	284.32	277.15	273.95	271.83
22 000	768.04	529.18	361.71	315.48	297.86	290.35	287.00	284.77
23 000	802.95	553.23	378.15	329.82	311.40	303.55	300.04	297.72
24 000	837.86	577.28	394.59	344.16	324.94	316.74	313.09	310.66
25 000	872.77	601.33	411.03	358.50	338.48	329.94	326.13	323.60
26 000	907.68	625.39	427.47	372.84	352.01	343.14	339.18	336.55
27 000	942.59	649.44	443.91	387.18	365.55	356.34	352.22	349.49
28 000	977.50	673.49	460.35	401.52	379.09	369.53	365.27	362.44
29 000	1012.41	697.55	476.80	415.86	392.63	382.73	378.31	375.38
30 000	1047.33	721.60	493.24	430.20	406.17	395.93	391.36	388.32
31 000	1082.24	745.65	509.68	444.54	419.71	409.13	404.41	401.27
32 000	1117.15	769.71	526.12	458.88	433.25	422.32	417.45	414.21
33 000	1152.06	793.76	542.56	473.22	446.79	435.52	430.50	427.16
34 000	1186.97	817.81	559.00	487.56	460.32	448.72	443.54	440.10
35 000	1221.88	841.87	575.44	501.90	473.86	461.92	456.59	453.04
36 000	1256.79	865.92	591.88	516.24	487.40	475.11	469.63	465.99
37 000	1291.70	889.97	608.32	530.58	500.94	488.31	482.68	478.93
38 000	1326.61	914.03	624.77	544.92	514.48	501.51	495.72	491.88
39 000	1361.52	938.08	641.21	559.26	528.02	514.71	508.77	504.82
40 000	1396.43	962.13	657.65	573.60	541.56	527.90	521.81	517.76
41 000	1431.34	986.19	674.09	587.94	555.10	541.10	534.86	530.71
42 000	1466.25	1010.24	690.53	602.28	568.63	554.30	547.90	543.65
43 000	1501.16	1034.29	706.97	616.62	582.17	567.50	560.95	556.60
44 000	1536.07	1058.35	723.41	630.96	595.71	580.69	573.99	569.54
45 000	1570.99	1082.40	739.85	645.30	609.25	593.89	587.04	582.48

FOR **OTHER RATES AND TERMS** *SEE PAGE A-1.*

A-108

TERM➧ AMOUNT	10 YEARS	15 YEARS	20 YEARS	25 YEARS	30 YEARS	40 YEARS
$46 000	756.29	659.64	622.79	607.09	600.08	595.43
47 000	772.73	673.98	636.33	620.29	613.13	608.37
48 000	789.18	688.32	649.87	633.48	626.17	621.32
49 000	805.62	702.66	663.41	646.68	639.22	634.26
50 000	822.06	717.00	676.95	659.88	652.26	647.20
51 000	838.50	731.34	690.48	673.08	665.31	660.15
52 000	854.94	745.68	704.02	686.27	678.35	673.09
53 000	871.38	760.02	717.56	699.47	691.40	686.04
54 000	887.82	774.36	731.10	712.67	704.44	698.98
55 000	904.26	788.70	744.64	725.86	717.49	711.92
56 000	920.70	803.04	758.18	739.06	730.53	724.87
57 000	937.15	817.38	771.72	752.26	743.58	737.81
58 000	953.59	831.72	785.26	765.46	756.62	750.76
59 000	970.03	846.06	798.79	778.65	769.67	763.70
60 000	986.47	860.40	812.33	791.85	782.72	776.64
61 000	1002.91	874.74	825.87	805.05	795.76	789.59
62 000	1019.35	889.08	839.41	818.25	808.81	802.53
63 000	1035.79	903.42	852.95	831.44	821.85	815.48
64 000	1052.23	917.76	866.49	844.64	834.90	828.42
65 000	1068.67	932.10	880.03	857.84	847.94	841.36
66 000	1085.11	946.44	893.57	871.04	860.99	854.31
67 000	1101.56	960.78	907.11	884.23	874.03	867.25
68 000	1118.00	975.12	920.64	897.43	887.08	880.20
69 000	1134.44	989.46	934.18	910.63	900.12	893.14
70 000	1150.88	1003.80	947.72	923.83	913.17	906.08
71 000	1167.32	1018.14	961.26	937.02	926.21	919.03
72 000	1183.76	1032.48	974.80	950.22	939.26	931.97
73 000	1200.20	1046.82	988.34	963.42	952.30	944.92
74 000	1216.64	1061.16	1001.88	976.62	965.35	957.86
75 000	1233.08	1075.50	1015.42	989.81	978.39	970.80
76 000	1249.53	1089.84	1028.95	1003.01	991.44	983.75
77 000	1265.97	1104.18	1042.49	1016.21	1004.48	996.69
78 000	1282.41	1118.52	1056.03	1029.41	1017.53	1009.64
79 000	1298.85	1132.86	1069.57	1042.60	1030.57	1022.58
80 000	1315.29	1147.20	1083.11	1055.80	1043.62	1035.52
81 000	1331.73	1161.54	1096.65	1069.00	1056.66	1048.47
82 000	1348.17	1175.88	1110.19	1082.20	1069.71	1061.41
83 000	1364.61	1190.22	1123.73	1095.39	1082.75	1074.36
84 000	1381.05	1204.56	1137.26	1108.59	1095.80	1087.30
85 000	1397.49	1218.90	1150.80	1121.79	1108.84	1100.24
86 000	1413.94	1233.24	1164.34	1134.99	1121.89	1113.19
87 000	1430.38	1247.58	1177.88	1148.18	1134.93	1126.13
88 000	1446.82	1261.92	1191.42	1161.38	1147.98	1139.08
89 000	1463.26	1276.26	1204.96	1174.58	1161.03	1152.02
90 000	1479.70	1290.60	1218.50	1187.78	1174.07	1164.96
91 000	1496.14	1304.94	1232.04	1200.97	1187.12	1177.91
92 000	1512.58	1319.28	1245.58	1214.17	1200.16	1190.85
93 000	1529.02	1333.62	1259.11	1227.37	1213.21	1203.80
94 000	1545.46	1347.96	1272.65	1240.57	1226.25	1216.74
95 000	1561.91	1362.30	1286.19	1253.76	1239.30	1229.68
96 000	1578.35	1376.64	1299.73	1266.96	1252.34	1242.63
97 000	1594.79	1390.98	1313.27	1280.16	1265.39	1255.57
98 000	1611.23	1405.32	1326.81	1293.36	1278.43	1268.52
99 000	1627.67	1419.66	1340.35	1306.55	1291.48	1281.46
100 000	1644.11	1434.00	1353.89	1319.75	1304.52	1294.40

FOR **OTHER RATES AND TERMS** *SEE PAGE A-1.*

TERM➡ AMOUNT	3 YEARS	5 YEARS	10 YEARS	15 YEARS	20 YEARS	25 YEARS	30 YEARS	40 YEARS
$ 100	3.51	2.42	1.66	1.46	1.38	1.34	1.33	1.32
200	7.01	4.84	3.32	2.91	2.75	2.68	2.65	2.64
300	10.52	7.26	4.98	4.36	4.12	4.02	3.98	3.95
400	14.02	9.68	6.64	5.81	5.50	5.36	5.30	5.27
500	17.52	12.10	8.30	7.26	6.87	6.70	6.63	6.58
600	21.03	14.52	9.96	8.71	8.24	8.04	7.95	7.90
700	24.53	16.93	11.62	10.16	9.61	9.38	9.28	9.21
800	28.03	19.35	13.28	11.62	10.99	10.72	10.60	10.53
900	31.54	21.77	14.94	13.07	12.36	12.06	11.93	11.84
1 000	35.04	24.19	16.60	14.52	13.73	13.40	13.25	13.16
1 000	35.04	24.19	16.60	14.52	13.73	13.40	13.25	13.16
2 000	70.07	48.38	33.20	29.03	27.46	26.79	26.50	26.31
3 000	105.11	72.56	49.79	43.54	41.18	40.18	39.74	39.46
4 000	140.14	96.75	66.39	58.06	54.91	53.58	52.99	52.61
5 000	175.17	120.93	82.98	72.57	68.63	66.97	66.24	65.76
6 000	210.21	145.12	99.58	87.08	82.36	80.36	79.48	78.91
7 000	245.24	169.30	116.18	101.60	96.08	93.76	92.73	92.06
8 000	280.27	193.49	132.77	116.11	109.81	107.15	105.97	105.21
9 000	315.31	217.67	149.37	130.62	123.53	120.54	119.22	118.36
10 000	350.34	241.86	165.96	145.14	137.26	133.93	132.47	131.51
11 000	385.38	266.04	182.56	159.65	150.98	147.33	145.71	144.66
12 000	420.41	290.23	199.16	174.16	164.71	160.72	158.96	157.81
13 000	455.44	314.42	215.75	188.68	178.43	174.11	172.21	170.96
14 000	490.48	338.60	232.35	203.19	192.16	187.51	185.45	184.11
15 000	525.51	362.79	248.94	217.70	205.89	200.90	198.70	197.26
16 000	560.54	386.97	265.54	232.21	219.61	214.29	211.94	210.41
17 000	595.58	411.16	282.13	246.73	233.34	227.68	225.19	223.56
18 000	630.61	435.34	298.73	261.24	247.06	241.08	238.44	236.71
19 000	665.65	459.53	315.33	275.75	260.79	254.47	251.68	249.86
20 000	700.68	483.71	331.92	290.27	274.51	267.86	264.93	263.01
21 000	735.71	507.90	348.52	304.78	288.24	281.26	278.17	276.16
22 000	770.75	532.08	365.11	319.29	301.96	294.65	291.42	289.31
23 000	805.78	556.27	381.71	333.81	315.69	308.04	304.67	302.46
24 000	840.81	580.46	398.31	348.32	329.41	321.43	317.91	315.61
25 000	875.85	604.64	414.90	362.83	343.14	334.83	331.16	328.76
26 000	910.88	628.83	431.50	377.35	356.86	348.22	344.41	341.91
27 000	945.92	653.01	448.09	391.86	370.59	361.61	357.65	355.06
28 000	980.95	677.20	464.69	406.37	384.31	375.01	370.90	368.21
29 000	1015.98	701.38	481.28	420.88	398.04	388.40	384.14	381.36
30 000	1051.02	725.57	497.88	435.40	411.77	401.79	397.39	394.51
31 000	1086.05	749.75	514.48	449.91	425.49	415.18	410.64	407.66
32 000	1121.08	773.94	531.07	464.42	439.22	428.58	423.88	420.81
33 000	1156.12	798.12	547.67	478.94	452.94	441.97	437.13	433.96
34 000	1191.15	822.31	564.26	493.45	466.67	455.36	450.37	447.11
35 000	1226.19	846.49	580.86	507.96	480.39	468.76	463.62	460.26
36 000	1261.22	870.68	597.46	522.48	494.12	482.15	476.87	473.41
37 000	1296.25	894.87	614.05	536.99	507.84	495.54	490.11	486.56
38 000	1331.29	919.05	630.65	551.50	521.57	508.94	503.36	499.71
39 000	1366.32	943.24	647.24	566.02	535.29	522.33	516.61	512.86
40 000	1401.35	967.42	663.84	580.53	549.02	535.72	529.85	526.01
41 000	1436.39	991.61	680.43	595.04	562.74	549.11	543.10	539.16
42 000	1471.42	1015.79	697.03	609.55	576.47	562.51	556.34	552.31
43 000	1506.46	1039.98	713.63	624.07	590.19	575.90	569.59	565.46
44 000	1541.49	1064.16	730.22	638.58	603.92	589.29	582.84	578.61
45 000	1576.52	1088.35	746.82	653.09	617.65	602.69	596.08	591.76

FOR **OTHER RATES AND TERMS** *SEE PAGE A-1.*

TERM➔ AMOUNT	10 YEARS	15 YEARS	20 YEARS	25 YEARS	30 YEARS	40 YEARS
$46 000	763.41	667.61	631.37	616.08	609.33	604.91
47 000	780.01	682.12	645.10	629.47	622.58	618.06
48 000	796.61	696.63	658.82	642.86	635.82	631.21
49 000	813.20	711.15	672.55	656.26	649.07	644.36
50 000	829.80	725.66	686.27	669.65	662.31	657.51
51 000	846.39	740.17	700.00	683.04	675.56	670.66
52 000	862.99	754.69	713.72	696.44	688.81	683.81
53 000	879.58	769.20	727.45	709.83	702.05	696.96
54 000	896.18	783.71	741.17	723.22	715.30	710.11
55 000	912.78	798.22	754.90	736.61	728.54	723.26
56 000	929.37	812.74	768.62	750.01	741.79	736.41
57 000	945.97	827.25	782.35	763.40	755.04	749.56
58 000	962.56	841.76	796.07	776.79	768.28	762.71
59 000	979.16	856.28	809.80	790.19	781.53	775.86
60 000	995.76	870.79	823.53	803.58	794.78	789.01
61 000	1012.35	885.30	837.25	816.97	808.02	802.16
62 000	1028.95	899.82	850.98	830.36	821.27	815.31
63 000	1045.54	914.33	864.70	843.76	834.51	828.46
64 000	1062.14	928.84	878.43	857.15	847.76	841.62
65 000	1078.74	943.36	892.15	870.54	861.01	854.77
66 000	1095.33	957.87	905.88	883.94	874.25	867.92
67 000	1111.93	972.38	919.60	897.33	887.50	881.07
68 000	1128.52	986.89	933.33	910.72	900.74	894.22
69 000	1145.12	1001.41	947.05	924.11	913.99	907.37
70 000	1161.71	1015.92	960.78	937.51	927.24	920.52
71 000	1178.31	1030.43	974.50	950.90	940.48	933.67
72 000	1194.91	1044.95	988.23	964.29	953.73	946.82
73 000	1211.50	1059.46	1001.95	977.69	966.98	959.97
74 000	1228.10	1073.97	1015.68	991.08	980.22	973.12
75 000	1244.69	1088.49	1029.41	1004.47	993.47	986.27
76 000	1261.29	1103.00	1043.13	1017.87	1006.71	999.42
77 000	1277.89	1117.51	1056.86	1031.26	1019.96	1012.57
78 000	1294.48	1132.03	1070.58	1044.65	1033.21	1025.72
79 000	1311.08	1146.54	1084.31	1058.04	1046.45	1038.87
80 000	1327.67	1161.05	1098.03	1071.44	1059.70	1052.02
81 000	1344.27	1175.56	1111.76	1084.83	1072.94	1065.17
82 000	1360.86	1190.08	1125.48	1098.22	1086.19	1078.32
83 000	1377.46	1204.59	1139.21	1111.62	1099.44	1091.47
84 000	1394.06	1219.10	1152.93	1125.01	1112.68	1104.62
85 000	1410.65	1233.62	1166.66	1138.40	1125.93	1117.77
86 000	1427.25	1248.13	1180.38	1151.79	1139.18	1130.92
87 000	1443.84	1262.64	1194.11	1165.19	1152.42	1144.07
88 000	1460.44	1277.16	1207.83	1178.58	1165.67	1157.22
89 000	1477.04	1291.67	1221.56	1191.97	1178.91	1170.37
90 000	1493.63	1306.18	1235.29	1205.37	1192.16	1183.52
91 000	1510.23	1320.70	1249.01	1218.76	1205.41	1196.67
92 000	1526.82	1335.21	1262.74	1232.15	1218.65	1209.82
93 000	1543.42	1349.72	1276.46	1245.54	1231.90	1222.97
94 000	1560.01	1364.23	1290.19	1258.94	1245.15	1236.12
95 000	1576.61	1378.75	1303.91	1272.33	1258.39	1249.27
96 000	1593.21	1393.26	1317.64	1285.72	1271.64	1262.42
97 000	1609.80	1407.77	1331.36	1299.12	1284.88	1275.57
98 000	1626.40	1422.29	1345.09	1312.51	1298.13	1288.72
99 000	1642.99	1436.80	1358.81	1325.90	1311.38	1301.87
100 000	1659.59	1451.31	1372.54	1339.29	1324.62	1315.02

FOR **OTHER RATES AND TERMS** *SEE PAGE A-1.*

TERM➡ AMOUNT	3 YEARS	5 YEARS	10 YEARS	15 YEARS	20 YEARS	25 YEARS	30 YEARS	40 YEARS
$ 100	3.52	2.44	1.68	1.47	1.40	1.36	1.35	1.34
200	7.04	4.87	3.36	2.94	2.79	2.72	2.69	2.68
300	10.55	7.30	5.03	4.41	4.18	4.08	4.04	4.01
400	14.07	9.73	6.71	5.88	5.57	5.44	5.38	5.35
500	17.58	12.16	8.38	7.35	6.96	6.80	6.73	6.68
600	21.10	14.60	10.06	8.82	8.35	8.16	8.07	8.02
700	24.61	17.03	11.73	10.29	9.74	9.52	9.42	9.35
800	28.13	19.46	13.41	11.75	11.14	10.88	10.76	10.69
900	31.65	21.89	15.08	13.22	12.53	12.23	12.11	12.03
1 000	35.16	24.32	16.76	14.69	13.92	13.59	13.45	13.36
1 000	35.16	24.32	16.76	14.69	13.92	13.59	13.45	13.36
2 000	70.32	48.64	33.51	29.38	27.83	27.18	26.90	26.72
3 000	105.48	72.96	50.26	44.07	41.74	40.77	40.35	40.07
4 000	140.63	97.28	67.01	58.75	55.66	54.36	53.80	53.43
5 000	175.79	121.60	83.76	73.44	69.57	67.95	67.24	66.79
6 000	210.95	145.91	100.51	88.13	83.48	81.54	80.69	80.14
7 000	246.10	170.23	117.26	102.81	97.39	95.13	94.14	93.50
8 000	281.26	194.55	134.02	117.50	111.31	108.72	107.59	106.86
9 000	316.42	218.87	150.77	132.19	125.22	122.30	121.03	120.21
10 000	351.58	243.19	167.52	146.88	139.13	135.89	134.48	133.57
11 000	386.73	267.50	184.27	161.56	153.04	149.48	147.93	146.93
12 000	421.89	291.82	201.02	176.25	166.96	163.07	161.38	160.28
13 000	457.05	316.14	217.77	190.94	180.87	176.66	174.82	173.64
14 000	492.20	340.46	234.52	205.62	194.78	190.25	188.27	187.00
15 000	527.36	364.78	251.27	220.31	208.69	203.84	201.72	200.35
16 000	562.52	389.09	268.03	235.00	222.61	217.43	215.17	213.71
17 000	597.67	413.41	284.78	249.68	236.52	231.02	228.61	227.07
18 000	632.83	437.73	301.53	264.37	250.43	244.60	242.06	240.42
19 000	667.99	462.05	318.28	279.06	264.34	258.19	255.51	253.78
20 000	703.15	486.37	335.03	293.75	278.26	271.78	268.96	267.13
21 000	738.30	510.68	351.78	308.43	292.17	285.37	282.40	280.49
22 000	773.46	535.00	368.53	323.12	306.08	298.96	295.85	293.85
23 000	808.62	559.32	385.29	337.81	319.99	312.55	309.30	307.20
24 000	843.77	583.64	402.04	352.49	333.91	326.14	322.75	320.56
25 000	878.93	607.96	418.79	367.18	347.82	339.73	336.19	333.92
26 000	914.09	632.27	435.54	381.87	361.73	353.32	349.64	347.27
27 000	949.24	656.59	452.29	396.55	375.64	366.90	363.09	360.63
28 000	984.40	680.91	469.04	411.24	389.56	380.49	376.54	373.99
29 000	1019.56	705.23	485.79	425.93	403.47	394.08	389.98	387.34
30 000	1054.72	729.55	502.54	440.62	417.38	407.67	403.43	400.70
31 000	1089.87	753.86	519.30	455.30	431.29	421.26	416.88	414.06
32 000	1125.03	778.18	536.05	469.99	445.21	434.85	430.33	427.41
33 000	1160.19	802.50	552.80	484.68	459.12	448.44	443.77	440.77
34 000	1195.34	826.82	569.55	499.36	473.03	462.03	457.22	454.13
35 000	1230.50	851.14	586.30	514.05	486.94	475.62	470.67	467.48
36 000	1265.66	875.46	603.05	528.74	500.86	489.20	484.12	480.84
37 000	1300.82	899.77	619.80	543.42	514.77	502.79	497.57	494.19
38 000	1335.97	924.09	636.55	558.11	528.68	516.38	511.01	507.55
39 000	1371.13	948.41	653.31	572.80	542.59	529.97	524.46	520.91
40 000	1406.29	972.73	670.06	587.49	556.51	543.56	537.91	534.26
41 000	1441.44	997.05	686.81	602.17	570.42	557.15	551.36	547.62
42 000	1476.60	1021.36	703.56	616.86	584.33	570.74	564.80	560.98
43 000	1511.76	1045.68	720.31	631.55	598.25	584.33	578.25	574.33
44 000	1546.91	1070.00	737.06	646.23	612.16	597.92	591.70	587.69
45 000	1582.07	1094.32	753.81	660.92	626.07	611.50	605.15	601.05

FOR **OTHER RATES AND TERMS** *SEE PAGE A-1.*

TERM➡ AMOUNT	10 YEARS	15 YEARS	20 YEARS	25 YEARS	30 YEARS	40 YEARS
$46 000	770.57	675.61	639.98	625.09	618.59	614.40
47 000	787.32	690.29	653.90	638.68	632.04	627.76
48 000	804.07	704.98	667.81	652.27	645.49	641.12
49 000	820.82	719.67	681.72	665.86	658.94	654.47
50 000	837.57	734.36	695.63	679.45	672.38	667.83
51 000	854.32	749.04	709.55	693.04	685.83	681.19
52 000	871.07	763.73	723.46	706.63	699.28	694.54
53 000	887.82	778.42	737.37	720.22	712.73	707.90
54 000	904.58	793.10	751.28	733.80	726.17	721.26
55 000	921.33	807.79	765.20	747.39	739.62	734.61
56 000	938.08	822.48	779.11	760.98	753.07	747.97
57 000	954.83	837.16	793.02	774.57	766.52	761.32
58 000	971.58	851.85	806.93	788.16	779.96	774.68
59 000	988.33	866.54	820.85	801.75	793.41	788.04
60 000	1005.08	881.23	834.76	815.34	806.86	801.39
61 000	1021.84	895.91	848.67	828.93	820.31	814.75
62 000	1038.59	910.60	862.58	842.52	833.75	828.11
63 000	1055.34	925.29	876.50	856.10	847.20	841.46
64 000	1072.09	939.97	890.41	869.69	860.65	854.82
65 000	1088.84	954.66	904.32	883.28	874.10	868.18
66 000	1105.59	969.35	918.23	896.87	887.54	881.53
67 000	1122.34	984.03	932.15	910.46	900.99	894.89
68 000	1139.09	998.72	946.06	924.05	914.44	908.25
69 000	1155.85	1013.41	959.97	937.64	927.89	921.60
70 000	1172.60	1028.10	973.88	951.23	941.33	934.96
71 000	1189.35	1042.78	987.80	964.82	954.78	948.32
72 000	1206.10	1057.47	1001.71	978.40	968.23	961.67
73 000	1222.85	1072.16	1015.62	991.99	981.68	975.03
74 000	1239.60	1086.84	1029.53	1005.58	995.13	988.38
75 000	1256.35	1101.53	1043.45	1019.17	1008.57	1001.74
76 000	1273.10	1116.22	1057.36	1032.76	1022.02	1015.10
77 000	1289.86	1130.90	1071.27	1046.35	1035.47	1028.45
78 000	1306.61	1145.59	1085.18	1059.94	1048.92	1041.81
79 000	1323.36	1160.28	1099.10	1073.53	1062.36	1055.17
80 000	1340.11	1174.97	1113.01	1087.12	1075.81	1068.52
81 000	1356.86	1189.65	1126.92	1100.70	1089.26	1081.88
82 000	1373.61	1204.34	1140.83	1114.29	1102.71	1095.24
83 000	1390.36	1219.03	1154.75	1127.88	1116.15	1108.59
84 000	1407.12	1233.71	1168.66	1141.47	1129.60	1121.95
85 000	1423.87	1248.40	1182.57	1155.06	1143.05	1135.31
86 000	1440.62	1263.09	1196.49	1168.65	1156.50	1148.66
87 000	1457.37	1277.77	1210.40	1182.24	1169.94	1162.02
88 000	1474.12	1292.46	1224.31	1195.83	1183.39	1175.38
89 000	1490.87	1307.15	1238.22	1209.42	1196.84	1188.73
90 000	1507.62	1321.84	1252.14	1223.00	1210.29	1202.09
91 000	1524.37	1336.52	1266.05	1236.59	1223.73	1215.45
92 000	1541.13	1351.21	1279.96	1250.18	1237.18	1228.80
93 000	1557.88	1365.90	1293.87	1263.77	1250.63	1242.16
94 000	1574.63	1380.58	1307.79	1277.36	1264.08	1255.51
95 000	1591.38	1395.27	1321.70	1290.95	1277.52	1268.87
96 000	1608.13	1409.96	1335.61	1304.54	1290.97	1282.23
97 000	1624.88	1424.64	1349.52	1318.13	1304.42	1295.58
98 000	1641.63	1439.33	1363.44	1331.72	1317.87	1308.94
99 000	1658.38	1454.02	1377.35	1345.30	1331.31	1322.30
100 000	1675.14	1468.71	1391.26	1358.89	1344.76	1335.65

FOR **OTHER RATES AND TERMS** *SEE PAGE A-1.*

TERM♦ AMOUNT	3 YEARS	5 YEARS	10 YEARS	15 YEARS	20 YEARS	25 YEARS	30 YEARS	40 YEARS
$ 100	3.53	2.45	1.70	1.49	1.42	1.38	1.37	1.36
200	7.06	4.90	3.39	2.98	2.83	2.76	2.73	2.72
300	10.59	7.34	5.08	4.46	4.24	4.14	4.10	4.07
400	14.12	9.79	6.77	5.95	5.65	5.52	5.46	5.43
500	17.65	12.23	8.46	7.44	7.06	6.90	6.83	6.79
600	21.17	14.68	10.15	8.92	8.47	8.28	8.19	8.14
700	24.70	17.12	11.84	10.41	9.88	9.65	9.56	9.50
800	28.23	19.57	13.53	11.89	11.29	11.03	10.92	10.86
900	31.76	22.01	15.22	13.38	12.70	12.41	12.29	12.21
1 000	35.29	24.46	16.91	14.87	14.11	13.79	13.65	13.57
1 000	35.29	24.46	16.91	14.87	14.11	13.79	13.65	13.57
2 000	70.57	48.91	33.82	29.73	28.21	27.58	27.30	27.13
3 000	105.85	73.36	50.73	44.59	42.31	41.36	40.95	40.69
4 000	141.13	97.81	67.63	59.45	56.41	55.15	54.60	54.26
5 000	176.41	122.26	84.54	74.31	70.51	68.93	68.25	67.82
6 000	211.69	146.71	101.45	89.18	84.61	82.72	81.90	81.38
7 000	246.97	171.16	118.36	104.04	98.71	96.50	95.55	94.95
8 000	282.25	195.61	135.26	118.90	112.81	110.29	109.20	108.51
9 000	317.53	220.06	152.17	133.76	126.91	124.07	122.85	122.07
10 000	352.81	244.52	169.08	148.62	141.01	137.86	136.50	135.63
11 000	388.09	268.97	185.99	163.48	155.11	151.64	150.15	149.20
12 000	423.37	293.42	202.89	178.35	169.21	165.43	163.80	162.76
13 000	458.65	317.87	219.80	193.21	183.31	179.22	177.45	176.32
14 000	493.93	342.32	236.71	208.07	197.41	193.00	191.10	189.89
15 000	529.21	366.77	253.62	222.93	211.51	206.79	204.75	203.45
16 000	564.49	391.22	270.52	237.79	225.61	220.57	218.39	217.01
17 000	599.77	415.67	287.43	252.65	239.71	234.36	232.04	230.58
18 000	635.06	440.12	304.34	267.52	253.81	248.14	245.69	244.14
19 000	670.34	464.58	321.25	282.38	267.91	261.93	259.34	257.70
20 000	705.62	489.03	338.15	297.24	282.01	275.71	272.99	271.26
21 000	740.90	513.48	355.06	312.10	296.11	289.50	286.64	284.83
22 000	776.18	537.93	371.97	326.96	310.22	303.28	300.29	298.39
23 000	811.46	562.38	388.88	341.82	324.32	317.07	313.94	311.95
24 000	846.74	586.83	405.78	356.69	338.42	330.85	327.59	325.52
25 000	882.02	611.28	422.69	371.55	352.52	344.64	341.24	339.08
26 000	917.30	635.73	439.60	386.41	366.62	358.43	354.89	352.64
27 000	952.58	660.18	456.51	401.27	380.72	372.21	368.54	366.21
28 000	987.86	684.64	473.41	416.13	394.82	386.00	382.19	379.77
29 000	1023.14	709.09	490.32	430.99	408.92	399.78	395.84	393.33
30 000	1058.42	733.54	507.23	445.86	423.02	413.57	409.49	406.89
31 000	1093.70	757.99	524.14	460.72	437.12	427.35	423.13	420.46
32 000	1128.98	782.44	541.04	475.58	451.22	441.14	436.78	434.02
33 000	1164.26	806.89	557.95	490.44	465.32	454.92	450.43	447.58
34 000	1199.54	831.34	574.86	505.30	479.42	468.71	464.08	461.15
35 000	1234.83	855.79	591.77	520.16	493.52	482.49	477.73	474.71
36 000	1270.11	880.24	608.67	535.03	507.62	496.28	491.38	488.27
37 000	1305.39	904.70	625.58	549.89	521.72	510.07	505.03	501.83
38 000	1340.67	929.15	642.49	564.75	535.82	523.85	518.68	515.40
39 000	1375.95	953.60	659.40	579.61	549.92	537.64	532.33	528.96
40 000	1411.23	978.05	676.30	594.47	564.02	551.42	545.98	542.52
41 000	1446.51	1002.50	693.21	609.33	578.12	565.21	559.63	556.09
42 000	1481.79	1026.95	710.12	624.20	592.22	578.99	573.28	569.65
43 000	1517.07	1051.40	727.02	639.06	606.32	592.78	586.93	583.21
44 000	1552.35	1075.85	743.93	653.92	620.43	606.56	600.58	596.78
45 000	1587.63	1100.30	760.84	668.78	634.53	620.35	614.23	610.34

FOR **OTHER RATES AND TERMS** *SEE PAGE A-1.*

TERM➡ AMOUNT	10 YEARS	15 YEARS	20 YEARS	25 YEARS	30 YEARS	40 YEARS
$46 000	777.75	683.64	648.63	634.13	627.87	623.90
47 000	794.65	698.50	662.73	647.92	641.52	637.46
48 000	811.56	713.37	676.83	661.70	655.17	651.03
49 000	828.47	728.23	690.93	675.49	668.82	664.59
50 000	845.38	743.09	705.03	689.28	682.47	678.15
51 000	862.28	757.95	719.13	703.06	696.12	691.72
52 000	879.19	772.81	733.23	716.85	709.77	705.28
53 000	896.10	787.67	747.33	730.63	723.42	718.84
54 000	913.01	802.54	761.43	744.42	737.07	732.41
55 000	929.91	817.40	775.53	758.20	750.72	745.97
56 000	946.82	832.26	789.63	771.99	764.37	759.53
57 000	963.73	847.12	803.73	785.77	778.02	773.09
58 000	980.64	861.98	817.83	799.56	791.67	786.66
59 000	997.54	876.84	831.93	813.34	805.32	800.22
60 000	1014.45	891.71	846.03	827.13	818.97	813.78
61 000	1031.36	906.57	860.13	840.92	832.62	827.35
62 000	1048.27	921.43	874.23	854.70	846.26	840.91
63 000	1065.17	936.29	888.33	868.49	859.91	854.47
64 000	1082.08	951.15	902.43	882.27	873.56	868.03
65 000	1098.99	966.01	916.53	896.06	887.21	881.60
66 000	1115.90	980.88	930.64	909.84	900.86	895.16
67 000	1132.80	995.74	944.74	923.63	914.51	908.72
68 000	1149.71	1010.60	958.84	937.41	928.16	922.29
69 000	1166.62	1025.46	972.94	951.20	941.81	935.85
70 000	1183.53	1040.32	987.04	964.98	955.46	949.41
71 000	1200.43	1055.18	1001.14	978.77	969.11	962.98
72 000	1217.34	1070.05	1015.24	992.55	982.76	976.54
73 000	1234.25	1084.91	1029.34	1006.34	996.41	990.10
74 000	1251.16	1099.77	1043.44	1020.13	1010.06	1003.66
75 000	1268.06	1114.63	1057.54	1033.91	1023.71	1017.23
76 000	1284.97	1129.49	1071.64	1047.70	1037.36	1030.79
77 000	1301.88	1144.35	1085.74	1061.48	1051.00	1044.35
78 000	1318.79	1159.22	1099.84	1075.27	1064.65	1057.92
79 000	1335.69	1174.08	1113.94	1089.05	1078.30	1071.48
80 000	1352.60	1188.94	1128.04	1102.84	1091.95	1085.04
81 000	1369.51	1203.80	1142.14	1116.62	1105.60	1098.61
82 000	1386.42	1218.66	1156.24	1130.41	1119.25	1112.17
83 000	1403.32	1233.52	1170.34	1144.19	1132.90	1125.73
84 000	1420.23	1248.39	1184.44	1157.98	1146.55	1139.29
85 000	1437.14	1263.25	1198.54	1171.77	1160.20	1152.86
86 000	1454.04	1278.11	1212.64	1185.55	1173.85	1166.42
87 000	1470.95	1292.97	1226.74	1199.34	1187.50	1179.98
88 000	1487.86	1307.83	1240.85	1213.12	1201.15	1193.55
89 000	1504.77	1322.69	1254.95	1226.91	1214.80	1207.11
90 000	1521.67	1337.56	1269.05	1240.69	1228.45	1220.67
91 000	1538.58	1352.42	1283.15	1254.48	1242.10	1234.23
92 000	1555.49	1367.28	1297.25	1268.26	1255.74	1247.80
93 000	1572.40	1382.14	1311.35	1282.05	1269.39	1261.36
94 000	1589.30	1397.00	1325.45	1295.83	1283.04	1274.92
95 000	1606.21	1411.86	1339.55	1309.62	1296.69	1288.49
96 000	1623.12	1426.73	1353.65	1323.40	1310.34	1302.05
97 000	1640.03	1441.59	1367.75	1337.19	1323.99	1315.61
98 000	1656.93	1456.45	1381.85	1350.98	1337.64	1329.18
99 000	1673.84	1471.31	1395.95	1364.76	1351.29	1342.74
100 000	1690.75	1486.17	1410.05	1378.55	1364.94	1356.30

FOR **OTHER RATES AND TERMS** *SEE PAGE A-1.*

TERM▶ AMOUNT	3 YEARS	5 YEARS	10 YEARS	15 YEARS	20 YEARS	25 YEARS	30 YEARS	40 YEARS
$ 100	3.55	2.46	1.71	1.51	1.43	1.40	1.39	1.38
200	7.09	4.92	3.42	3.01	2.86	2.80	2.78	2.76
300	10.63	7.38	5.12	4.52	4.29	4.20	4.16	4.14
400	14.17	9.84	6.83	6.02	5.72	5.60	5.55	5.51
500	17.71	12.30	8.54	7.52	7.15	7.00	6.93	6.89
600	21.25	14.76	10.24	9.03	8.58	8.39	8.32	8.27
700	24.79	17.21	11.95	10.53	10.01	9.79	9.70	9.64
800	28.33	19.67	13.66	12.03	11.44	11.19	11.09	11.02
900	31.87	22.13	15.36	13.54	12.87	12.59	12.47	12.40
1 000	35.41	24.59	17.07	15.04	14.29	13.99	13.86	13.77
1 000	35.41	24.59	17.07	15.04	14.29	13.99	13.86	13.77
2 000	70.81	49.17	34.13	30.08	28.58	27.97	27.71	27.54
3 000	106.22	73.76	51.20	45.12	42.87	41.95	41.56	41.31
4 000	141.62	98.34	68.26	60.15	57.16	55.93	55.41	55.08
5 000	177.03	122.93	85.33	75.19	71.45	69.92	69.26	68.85
6 000	212.43	147.51	102.39	90.23	85.74	83.90	83.11	82.62
7 000	247.84	172.10	119.45	105.26	100.03	97.88	96.97	96.39
8 000	283.24	196.68	136.52	120.30	114.32	111.86	110.82	110.16
9 000	318.64	221.27	153.58	135.34	128.61	125.85	124.67	123.93
10 000	354.05	245.85	170.65	150.38	142.90	139.83	138.52	137.70
11 000	389.45	270.43	187.71	165.41	157.18	153.81	152.37	151.47
12 000	424.86	295.02	204.78	180.45	171.47	167.79	166.22	165.24
13 000	460.26	319.60	221.84	195.49	185.76	181.78	180.07	179.01
14 000	495.67	344.19	238.90	210.52	200.05	195.76	193.93	192.78
15 000	531.07	368.77	255.97	225.56	214.34	209.74	207.78	206.55
16 000	566.48	393.36	273.03	240.60	228.63	223.72	221.63	220.32
17 000	601.88	417.94	290.10	255.64	242.92	237.71	235.48	234.09
18 000	637.28	442.53	307.16	270.67	257.21	251.69	249.33	247.86
19 000	672.69	467.11	324.23	285.71	271.50	265.67	263.18	261.63
20 000	708.09	491.70	341.29	300.75	285.79	279.65	277.03	275.40
21 000	743.50	516.28	358.35	315.78	300.07	293.64	290.89	289.17
22 000	778.90	540.86	375.42	330.82	314.36	307.62	304.74	302.94
23 000	814.31	565.45	392.48	345.86	328.65	321.60	318.59	316.71
24 000	849.71	590.03	409.55	360.90	342.94	335.58	332.44	330.48
25 000	885.11	614.62	426.61	375.93	357.23	349.57	346.29	344.24
26 000	920.52	639.20	443.67	390.97	371.52	363.55	360.14	358.01
27 000	955.92	663.79	460.74	406.01	385.81	377.53	373.99	371.78
28 000	991.33	688.37	477.80	421.04	400.10	391.51	387.85	385.55
29 000	1026.73	712.96	494.87	436.08	414.39	405.50	401.70	399.32
30 000	1062.14	737.54	511.93	451.12	428.68	419.48	415.55	413.09
31 000	1097.54	762.13	529.00	466.15	442.96	433.46	429.40	426.86
32 000	1132.95	786.71	546.06	481.19	457.25	447.44	443.25	440.63
33 000	1168.35	811.29	563.12	496.23	471.54	461.43	457.10	454.40
34 000	1203.75	835.88	580.19	511.27	485.83	475.41	470.96	468.17
35 000	1239.16	860.46	597.25	526.30	500.12	489.39	484.81	481.94
36 000	1274.56	885.05	614.32	541.34	514.41	503.37	498.66	495.71
37 000	1309.97	909.63	631.38	556.38	528.70	517.36	512.51	509.48
38 000	1345.37	934.22	648.45	571.41	542.99	531.34	526.36	523.25
39 000	1380.78	958.80	665.51	586.45	557.28	545.32	540.21	537.02
40 000	1416.18	983.39	682.57	601.49	571.57	559.30	554.06	550.79
41 000	1451.58	1007.97	699.64	616.53	585.85	573.29	567.92	564.56
42 000	1486.99	1032.55	716.70	631.56	600.14	587.27	581.77	578.33
43 000	1522.39	1057.14	733.77	646.60	614.43	601.25	595.62	592.10
44 000	1557.80	1081.72	750.83	661.64	628.72	615.23	609.47	605.87
45 000	1593.20	1106.31	767.90	676.67	643.01	629.22	623.32	619.64

FOR **OTHER RATES AND TERMS** *SEE PAGE A-1.*

TERM➡ AMOUNT	10 YEARS	15 YEARS	20 YEARS	25 YEARS	30 YEARS	40 YEARS
$46 000	784.96	691.71	657.30	643.20	637.17	633.41
47 000	802.02	706.75	671.59	657.18	651.02	647.18
48 000	819.09	721.79	685.88	671.16	664.88	660.95
49 000	836.15	736.82	700.17	685.14	678.73	674.72
50 000	853.22	751.86	714.46	699.13	692.58	688.48
51 000	870.28	766.90	728.74	713.11	706.43	702.25
52 000	887.34	781.93	743.03	727.09	720.28	716.02
53 000	904.41	796.97	757.32	741.07	734.13	729.79
54 000	921.47	812.01	771.61	755.06	747.98	743.56
55 000	938.54	827.04	785.90	769.04	761.84	757.33
56 000	955.60	842.08	800.19	783.02	775.69	771.10
57 000	972.67	857.12	814.48	797.00	789.54	784.87
58 000	989.73	872.16	828.77	810.99	803.39	798.64
59 000	1006.79	887.19	843.06	824.97	817.24	812.41
60 000	1023.86	902.23	857.35	838.95	831.09	826.18
61 000	1040.92	917.27	871.63	852.93	844.95	839.95
62 000	1057.99	932.30	885.92	866.92	858.80	853.72
63 000	1075.05	947.34	900.21	880.90	872.65	867.49
64 000	1092.12	962.38	914.50	894.88	886.50	881.26
65 000	1109.18	977.42	928.79	908.86	900.35	895.03
66 000	1126.24	992.45	943.08	922.85	914.20	908.80
67 000	1143.31	1007.49	957.37	936.83	928.05	922.57
68 000	1160.37	1022.53	971.66	950.81	941.91	936.34
69 000	1177.44	1037.56	985.95	964.79	955.76	950.11
70 000	1194.50	1052.60	1000.24	978.78	969.61	963.88
71 000	1211.57	1067.64	1014.52	992.76	983.46	977.65
72 000	1228.63	1082.68	1028.81	1006.74	997.31	991.42
73 000	1245.69	1097.71	1043.10	1020.72	1011.16	1005.19
74 000	1262.76	1112.75	1057.39	1034.71	1025.01	1018.95
75 000	1279.82	1127.79	1071.68	1048.69	1038.87	1032.72
76 000	1296.89	1142.82	1085.97	1062.67	1052.72	1046.49
77 000	1313.95	1157.86	1100.26	1076.65	1066.57	1060.26
78 000	1331.01	1172.90	1114.55	1090.64	1080.42	1074.03
79 000	1348.08	1187.93	1128.84	1104.62	1094.27	1087.80
80 000	1365.14	1202.97	1143.13	1118.60	1108.12	1101.57
81 000	1382.21	1218.01	1157.41	1132.58	1121.97	1115.34
82 000	1399.27	1233.05	1171.70	1146.57	1135.83	1129.11
83 000	1416.34	1248.08	1185.99	1160.55	1149.68	1142.88
84 000	1433.40	1263.12	1200.28	1174.53	1163.53	1156.65
85 000	1450.46	1278.16	1214.57	1188.51	1177.38	1170.42
86 000	1467.53	1293.19	1228.86	1202.50	1191.23	1184.19
87 000	1484.59	1308.23	1243.15	1216.48	1205.08	1197.96
88 000	1501.66	1323.27	1257.44	1230.46	1218.94	1211.73
89 000	1518.72	1338.31	1271.73	1244.44	1232.79	1225.50
90 000	1535.79	1353.34	1286.02	1258.43	1246.64	1239.27
91 000	1552.85	1368.38	1300.30	1272.41	1260.49	1253.04
92 000	1569.91	1383.42	1314.59	1286.39	1274.34	1266.81
93 000	1586.98	1398.45	1328.88	1300.37	1288.19	1280.58
94 000	1604.04	1413.49	1343.17	1314.35	1302.04	1294.35
95 000	1621.11	1428.53	1357.46	1328.34	1315.90	1308.12
96 000	1638.17	1443.57	1371.75	1342.32	1329.75	1321.89
97 000	1655.24	1458.60	1386.04	1356.30	1343.60	1335.66
98 000	1672.30	1473.64	1400.33	1370.28	1357.45	1349.43
99 000	1689.36	1488.68	1414.62	1384.27	1371.30	1363.19
100 000	1706.43	1503.71	1428.91	1398.25	1385.15	1376.96

FOR **OTHER RATES AND TERMS** *SEE PAGE A-1.*

TERM➡ AMOUNT	3 YEARS	5 YEARS	10 YEARS	15 YEARS	20 YEARS	25 YEARS	30 YEARS	40 YEARS
$ 100	3.56	2.48	1.73	1.53	1.45	1.42	1.41	1.40
200	7.11	4.95	3.45	3.05	2.90	2.84	2.82	2.80
300	10.66	7.42	5.17	4.57	4.35	4.26	4.22	4.20
400	14.22	9.89	6.89	6.09	5.80	5.68	5.63	5.60
500	17.77	12.36	8.62	7.61	7.24	7.09	7.03	6.99
600	21.32	14.84	10.34	9.13	8.69	8.51	8.44	8.39
700	24.87	17.31	12.06	10.65	10.14	9.93	9.84	9.79
800	28.43	19.78	13.78	12.18	11.59	11.35	11.25	11.19
900	31.98	22.25	15.50	13.70	13.04	12.77	12.65	12.58
1 000	35.53	24.72	17.23	15.22	14.48	14.18	14.06	13.98
1 000	35.53	24.72	17.23	15.22	14.48	14.18	14.06	13.98
2 000	71.06	49.44	34.45	30.43	28.96	28.36	28.11	27.96
3 000	106.59	74.16	51.67	45.64	43.44	42.54	42.17	41.93
4 000	142.12	98.88	68.89	60.86	57.92	56.72	56.22	55.91
5 000	177.65	123.60	86.11	76.07	72.40	70.90	70.27	69.89
6 000	213.18	148.32	103.34	91.28	86.87	85.08	84.33	83.86
7 000	248.70	173.03	120.56	106.50	101.35	99.26	98.38	97.84
8 000	284.23	197.75	137.78	121.71	115.83	113.44	112.44	111.82
9 000	319.76	222.47	155.00	136.92	130.31	127.62	126.49	125.79
10 000	355.29	247.19	172.22	152.14	144.79	141.80	140.54	139.77
11 000	390.82	271.91	189.44	167.35	159.27	155.98	154.60	153.74
12 000	426.35	296.63	206.67	182.56	173.74	170.16	168.65	167.72
13 000	461.87	321.34	223.89	197.78	188.22	184.34	182.71	181.70
14 000	497.40	346.06	241.11	212.99	202.70	198.52	196.76	195.67
15 000	532.93	370.78	258.33	228.20	217.18	212.70	210.81	209.65
16 000	568.46	395.50	275.55	243.42	231.66	226.88	224.87	223.63
17 000	603.99	420.22	292.77	258.63	246.13	241.06	238.92	237.60
18 000	639.52	444.94	310.00	273.84	260.61	255.24	252.98	251.58
19 000	675.05	469.65	327.22	289.06	275.09	269.42	267.03	265.56
20 000	710.57	494.37	344.44	304.27	289.57	283.60	281.08	279.53
21 000	746.10	519.09	361.66	319.48	304.05	297.78	295.14	293.51
22 000	781.63	543.81	378.88	334.70	318.53	311.96	309.19	307.48
23 000	817.16	568.53	396.10	349.91	333.00	326.14	323.25	321.46
24 000	852.69	593.25	413.33	365.12	347.48	340.32	337.30	335.44
25 000	888.22	617.96	430.55	380.34	361.96	354.50	351.35	349.41
26 000	923.74	642.68	447.77	395.55	376.44	368.68	365.41	363.39
27 000	959.27	667.40	464.99	410.76	390.92	382.86	379.46	377.37
28 000	994.80	692.12	482.21	425.97	405.39	397.04	393.52	391.34
29 000	1030.33	716.84	499.43	441.19	419.87	411.22	407.57	405.32
30 000	1065.86	741.56	516.66	456.40	434.35	425.40	421.62	419.30
31 000	1101.39	766.27	533.88	471.61	448.83	439.58	435.68	433.27
32 000	1136.91	790.99	551.10	486.83	463.31	453.76	449.73	447.25
33 000	1172.44	815.71	568.32	502.04	477.79	467.94	463.79	461.22
34 000	1207.97	840.43	585.54	517.25	492.26	482.12	477.84	475.20
35 000	1243.50	865.15	602.76	532.47	506.74	496.30	491.89	489.18
36 000	1279.03	889.87	619.99	547.68	521.22	510.48	505.95	503.15
37 000	1314.56	914.58	637.21	562.89	535.70	524.66	520.00	517.13
38 000	1350.09	939.30	654.43	578.11	550.18	538.84	534.06	531.11
39 000	1385.61	964.02	671.65	593.32	564.65	553.02	548.11	545.08
40 000	1421.14	988.74	688.87	608.53	579.13	567.20	562.16	559.06
41 000	1456.67	1013.46	706.09	623.75	593.61	581.38	576.22	573.04
42 000	1492.20	1038.18	723.32	638.96	608.09	595.56	590.27	587.01
43 000	1527.73	1062.89	740.54	654.17	622.57	609.74	604.33	600.99
44 000	1563.26	1087.61	757.76	669.39	637.05	623.92	618.38	614.96
45 000	1598.78	1112.33	774.98	684.60	651.52	638.10	632.43	628.94

FOR **OTHER RATES AND TERMS** *SEE PAGE A-1.*

TERM▶ AMOUNT	10 YEARS	15 YEARS	20 YEARS	25 YEARS	30 YEARS	40 YEARS
$46 000	792.20	699.81	666.00	652.28	646.49	642.92
47 000	809.42	715.03	680.48	666.46	660.54	656.89
48 000	826.65	730.24	694.96	680.64	674.59	670.87
49 000	843.87	745.45	709.44	694.82	688.65	684.85
50 000	861.09	760.67	723.91	709.00	702.70	698.82
51 000	878.31	775.88	738.39	723.18	716.76	712.80
52 000	895.53	791.09	752.87	737.36	730.81	726.78
53 000	912.75	806.31	767.35	751.54	744.86	740.75
54 000	929.98	821.52	781.83	765.72	758.92	754.73
55 000	947.20	836.73	796.31	779.90	772.97	768.70
56 000	964.42	851.94	810.78	794.08	787.03	782.68
57 000	981.64	867.16	825.26	808.26	801.08	796.66
58 000	998.86	882.37	839.74	822.44	815.13	810.63
59 000	1016.08	897.58	854.22	836.62	829.19	824.61
60 000	1033.31	912.80	868.70	850.80	843.24	838.59
61 000	1050.53	928.01	883.17	864.98	857.30	852.56
62 000	1067.75	943.22	897.65	879.16	871.35	866.54
63 000	1084.97	958.44	912.13	893.34	885.40	880.52
64 000	1102.19	973.65	926.61	907.52	899.46	894.49
65 000	1119.41	988.86	941.09	921.70	913.51	908.47
66 000	1136.64	1004.08	955.57	935.88	927.57	922.44
67 000	1153.86	1019.29	970.04	950.06	941.62	936.42
68 000	1171.08	1034.50	984.52	964.24	955.67	950.40
69 000	1188.30	1049.72	999.00	978.42	969.73	964.37
70 000	1205.52	1064.93	1013.48	992.60	983.78	978.35
71 000	1222.74	1080.14	1027.96	1006.78	997.84	992.33
72 000	1239.97	1095.36	1042.44	1020.96	1011.89	1006.30
73 000	1257.19	1110.57	1056.91	1035.14	1025.94	1020.28
74 000	1274.41	1125.78	1071.39	1049.32	1040.00	1034.26
75 000	1291.63	1141.00	1085.87	1063.50	1054.05	1048.23
76 000	1308.85	1156.21	1100.35	1077.68	1068.11	1062.21
77 000	1326.07	1171.42	1114.83	1091.86	1082.16	1076.18
78 000	1343.30	1186.64	1129.30	1106.04	1096.21	1090.16
79 000	1360.52	1201.85	1143.78	1120.22	1110.27	1104.14
80 000	1377.74	1217.06	1158.26	1134.40	1124.32	1118.11
81 000	1394.96	1232.28	1172.74	1148.58	1138.38	1132.09
82 000	1412.18	1247.49	1187.22	1162.76	1152.43	1146.07
83 000	1429.40	1262.70	1201.70	1176.94	1166.48	1160.04
84 000	1446.63	1277.91	1216.17	1191.12	1180.54	1174.02
85 000	1463.85	1293.13	1230.65	1205.30	1194.59	1187.99
86 000	1481.07	1308.34	1245.13	1219.48	1208.65	1201.97
87 000	1498.29	1323.55	1259.61	1233.66	1222.70	1215.95
88 000	1515.51	1338.77	1274.09	1247.84	1236.75	1229.92
89 000	1532.73	1353.98	1288.56	1262.02	1250.81	1243.90
90 000	1549.96	1369.19	1303.04	1276.20	1264.86	1257.88
91 000	1567.18	1384.41	1317.52	1290.38	1278.91	1271.85
92 000	1584.40	1399.62	1332.00	1304.56	1292.97	1285.83
93 000	1601.62	1414.83	1346.48	1318.74	1307.02	1299.81
94 000	1618.84	1430.05	1360.96	1332.92	1321.08	1313.78
95 000	1636.06	1445.26	1375.43	1347.10	1335.13	1327.76
96 000	1653.29	1460.47	1389.91	1361.28	1349.18	1341.73
97 000	1670.51	1475.69	1404.39	1375.46	1363.24	1355.71
98 000	1687.73	1490.90	1418.87	1389.64	1377.29	1369.69
99 000	1704.95	1506.11	1433.35	1403.82	1391.35	1383.66
100 000	1722.17	1521.33	1447.82	1418.00	1405.40	1397.64

FOR **OTHER RATES AND TERMS** *SEE PAGE A-1.*

TERM◆ AMOUNT	3 YEARS	5 YEARS	10 YEARS	15 YEARS	20 YEARS	25 YEARS	30 YEARS	40 YEARS
$ 100	3.57	2.49	1.74	1.54	1.47	1.44	1.43	1.42
200	7.14	4.98	3.48	3.08	2.94	2.88	2.86	2.84
300	10.70	7.46	5.22	4.62	4.41	4.32	4.28	4.26
400	14.27	9.95	6.96	6.16	5.87	5.76	5.71	5.68
500	17.83	12.43	8.69	7.70	7.34	7.19	7.13	7.10
600	21.40	14.92	10.43	9.24	8.81	8.63	8.56	8.51
700	24.96	17.40	12.17	10.78	10.27	10.07	9.98	9.93
800	28.53	19.89	13.91	12.32	11.74	11.51	11.41	11.35
900	32.09	22.37	15.65	13.86	13.21	12.95	12.84	12.77
1 000	35.66	24.86	17.38	15.40	14.67	14.38	14.26	14.19
1 000	35.66	24.86	17.38	15.40	14.67	14.38	14.26	14.19
2 000	71.31	49.71	34.76	30.79	29.34	28.76	28.52	28.37
3 000	106.96	74.56	52.14	46.18	44.01	43.14	42.78	42.55
4 000	142.62	99.42	69.52	61.57	58.68	57.52	57.03	56.74
5 000	178.27	124.27	86.90	76.96	73.35	71.89	71.29	70.92
6 000	213.92	149.12	104.28	92.35	88.01	86.27	85.55	85.10
7 000	249.57	173.97	121.66	107.74	102.68	100.65	99.80	99.29
8 000	285.23	198.83	139.04	123.13	117.35	115.03	114.06	113.47
9 000	320.88	223.68	156.42	138.52	132.02	129.41	128.32	127.65
10 000	356.53	248.53	173.80	153.91	146.69	143.78	142.57	141.84
11 000	392.19	273.38	191.18	169.30	161.35	158.16	156.83	156.02
12 000	427.84	298.24	208.56	184.69	176.02	172.54	171.09	170.20
13 000	463.49	323.09	225.94	200.08	190.69	186.92	185.34	184.39
14 000	499.14	347.94	243.32	215.47	205.36	201.30	199.60	198.57
15 000	534.80	372.79	260.70	230.86	220.03	215.67	213.86	212.75
16 000	570.45	397.65	278.08	246.25	234.69	230.05	228.11	226.94
17 000	606.10	422.50	295.46	261.64	249.36	244.43	242.37	241.12
18 000	641.75	447.35	312.84	277.03	264.03	258.81	256.63	255.30
19 000	677.41	472.20	330.22	292.42	278.70	273.19	270.88	269.49
20 000	713.06	497.06	347.60	307.81	293.37	287.56	285.14	283.67
21 000	748.71	521.91	364.98	323.20	308.03	301.94	299.40	297.85
22 000	784.37	546.76	382.36	338.59	322.70	316.32	313.65	312.04
23 000	820.02	571.61	399.74	353.98	337.37	330.70	327.91	326.22
24 000	855.67	596.47	417.12	369.37	352.04	345.08	342.17	340.40
25 000	891.32	621.32	434.50	384.76	366.71	359.45	356.42	354.59
26 000	926.98	646.17	451.88	400.15	381.37	373.83	370.68	368.77
27 000	962.63	671.02	469.26	415.54	396.04	388.21	384.94	382.95
28 000	998.28	695.88	486.64	430.93	410.71	402.59	399.19	397.14
29 000	1033.93	720.73	504.02	446.32	425.38	416.97	413.45	411.32
30 000	1069.59	745.58	521.40	461.71	440.05	431.34	427.71	425.50
31 000	1105.24	770.43	538.78	477.10	454.71	445.72	441.96	439.69
32 000	1140.89	795.29	556.16	492.49	469.38	460.10	456.22	453.87
33 000	1176.55	820.14	573.54	507.88	484.05	474.48	470.48	468.05
34 000	1212.20	844.99	590.92	523.27	498.72	488.86	484.73	482.24
35 000	1247.85	869.85	608.30	538.66	513.39	503.23	498.99	496.42
36 000	1283.50	894.70	625.68	554.05	528.05	517.61	513.25	510.60
37 000	1319.16	919.55	643.06	569.44	542.72	531.99	527.50	524.78
38 000	1354.81	944.40	660.44	584.83	557.39	546.37	541.76	538.97
39 000	1390.46	969.26	677.82	600.22	572.06	560.75	556.02	553.15
40 000	1426.11	994.11	695.20	615.61	586.73	575.12	570.28	567.33
41 000	1461.77	1018.96	712.58	631.00	601.39	589.50	584.53	581.52
42 000	1497.42	1043.81	729.96	646.39	616.06	603.88	598.79	595.70
43 000	1533.07	1068.67	747.33	661.78	630.73	618.26	613.05	609.88
44 000	1568.73	1093.52	764.71	677.17	645.40	632.64	627.30	624.07
45 000	1604.38	1118.37	782.09	692.56	660.07	647.01	641.56	638.25

FOR **OTHER RATES AND TERMS** *SEE PAGE A-1.*

TERM→ AMOUNT	10 YEARS	15 YEARS	20 YEARS	25 YEARS	30 YEARS	40 YEARS
$46 000	799.47	707.95	674.73	661.39	655.82	652.43
47 000	816.85	723.34	689.40	675.77	670.07	666.62
48 000	834.23	738.73	704.07	690.15	684.33	680.80
49 000	851.61	754.12	718.74	704.53	698.59	694.98
50 000	868.99	769.51	733.41	718.90	712.84	709.17
51 000	886.37	784.90	748.07	733.28	727.10	723.35
52 000	903.75	800.29	762.74	747.66	741.36	737.53
53 000	921.13	815.68	777.41	762.04	755.61	751.72
54 000	938.51	831.07	792.08	776.42	769.87	765.90
55 000	955.89	846.46	806.75	790.79	784.13	780.08
56 000	973.27	861.85	821.41	805.17	798.38	794.27
57 000	990.65	877.24	836.08	819.55	812.64	808.45
58 000	1008.03	892.63	850.75	833.93	826.90	822.63
59 000	1025.41	908.02	865.42	848.30	841.15	836.82
60 000	1042.79	923.41	880.09	862.68	855.41	851.00
61 000	1060.17	938.80	894.75	877.06	869.67	865.18
62 000	1077.55	954.19	909.42	891.44	883.92	879.37
63 000	1094.93	969.58	924.09	905.82	898.18	893.55
64 000	1112.31	984.97	938.76	920.19	912.44	907.73
65 000	1129.69	1000.36	953.43	934.57	926.69	921.92
66 000	1147.07	1015.75	968.09	948.95	940.95	936.10
67 000	1164.45	1031.14	982.76	963.33	955.21	950.28
68 000	1181.83	1046.53	997.43	977.71	969.46	964.47
69 000	1199.21	1061.92	1012.10	992.08	983.72	978.65
70 000	1216.59	1077.31	1026.77	1006.46	997.98	992.83
71 000	1233.97	1092.70	1041.43	1020.84	1012.23	1007.01
72 000	1251.35	1108.09	1056.10	1035.22	1026.49	1021.20
73 000	1268.73	1123.48	1070.77	1049.60	1040.75	1035.38
74 000	1286.11	1138.87	1085.44	1063.97	1055.00	1049.56
75 000	1303.49	1154.26	1100.11	1078.35	1069.26	1063.75
76 000	1320.87	1169.65	1114.77	1092.73	1083.52	1077.93
77 000	1338.25	1185.04	1129.44	1107.11	1097.78	1092.11
78 000	1355.63	1200.43	1144.11	1121.49	1112.03	1106.30
79 000	1373.01	1215.82	1158.78	1135.86	1126.29	1120.48
80 000	1390.39	1231.21	1173.45	1150.24	1140.55	1134.66
81 000	1407.77	1246.60	1188.11	1164.62	1154.80	1148.85
82 000	1425.15	1261.99	1202.78	1179.00	1169.06	1163.03
83 000	1442.53	1277.38	1217.45	1193.38	1183.32	1177.21
84 000	1459.91	1292.77	1232.12	1207.75	1197.57	1191.40
85 000	1477.29	1308.16	1246.79	1222.13	1211.83	1205.58
86 000	1494.66	1323.55	1261.45	1236.51	1226.09	1219.76
87 000	1512.04	1338.94	1276.12	1250.89	1240.34	1233.95
88 000	1529.42	1354.33	1290.79	1265.27	1254.60	1248.13
89 000	1546.80	1369.72	1305.46	1279.64	1268.86	1262.31
90 000	1564.18	1385.11	1320.13	1294.02	1283.11	1276.50
91 000	1581.56	1400.50	1334.79	1308.40	1297.37	1290.68
92 000	1598.94	1415.89	1349.46	1322.78	1311.63	1304.86
93 000	1616.32	1431.28	1364.13	1337.16	1325.88	1319.05
94 000	1633.70	1446.67	1378.80	1351.53	1340.14	1333.23
95 000	1651.08	1462.06	1393.47	1365.91	1354.40	1347.41
96 000	1668.46	1477.45	1408.13	1380.29	1368.65	1361.60
97 000	1685.84	1492.84	1422.80	1394.67	1382.91	1375.78
98 000	1703.22	1508.23	1437.47	1409.05	1397.17	1389.96
99 000	1720.60	1523.62	1452.14	1423.42	1411.42	1404.15
100 000	1737.98	1539.01	1466.81	1437.80	1425.68	1418.33

FOR **OTHER RATES AND TERMS** *SEE PAGE A-1.*

TERM► AMOUNT	3 YEARS	5 YEARS	10 YEARS	15 YEARS	20 YEARS	25 YEARS	30 YEARS	40 YEARS
$ 100	3.58	2.50	1.76	1.56	1.49	1.46	1.45	1.44
200	7.16	5.00	3.51	3.12	2.98	2.92	2.90	2.88
300	10.74	7.50	5.27	4.68	4.46	4.38	4.34	4.32
400	14.32	10.00	7.02	6.23	5.95	5.84	5.79	5.76
500	17.89	12.50	8.77	7.79	7.43	7.29	7.23	7.20
600	21.47	15.00	10.53	9.35	8.92	8.75	8.68	8.64
700	25.05	17.50	12.28	10.90	10.41	10.21	10.13	10.08
800	28.63	19.99	14.04	12.46	11.89	11.67	11.57	11.52
900	32.20	22.49	15.79	14.02	13.38	13.12	13.02	12.96
1 000	35.78	24.99	17.54	15.57	14.86	14.58	14.46	14.40
1 000	35.78	24.99	17.54	15.57	14.86	14.58	14.46	14.40
2 000	71.56	49.98	35.08	31.14	29.72	29.16	28.92	28.79
3 000	107.34	74.97	52.62	46.71	44.58	43.73	43.38	43.18
4 000	143.11	99.95	70.16	62.28	59.44	58.31	57.84	57.57
5 000	178.89	124.94	87.70	77.84	74.30	72.89	72.30	71.96
6 000	214.67	149.93	105.24	93.41	89.16	87.46	86.76	86.35
7 000	250.45	174.92	122.77	108.98	104.01	102.04	101.22	100.74
8 000	286.22	199.90	140.31	124.55	118.87	116.62	115.68	115.13
9 000	322.00	224.89	157.85	140.11	133.73	131.19	130.14	129.52
10 000	357.78	249.88	175.39	155.68	148.59	145.77	144.60	143.91
11 000	393.55	274.86	192.93	171.25	163.45	160.35	159.06	158.30
12 000	429.33	299.85	210.47	186.82	178.31	174.92	173.52	172.69
13 000	465.11	324.84	228.01	202.38	193.16	189.50	187.98	187.08
14 000	500.89	349.83	245.54	217.95	208.02	204.07	202.44	201.47
15 000	536.66	374.81	263.08	233.52	222.88	218.65	216.90	215.86
16 000	572.44	399.80	280.62	249.09	237.74	233.23	231.36	230.25
17 000	608.22	424.79	298.16	264.65	252.60	247.80	245.82	244.64
18 000	644.00	449.77	315.70	280.22	267.46	262.38	260.28	259.03
19 000	679.77	474.76	333.24	295.79	282.31	276.96	274.74	273.42
20 000	715.55	499.75	350.78	311.36	297.17	291.53	289.20	287.81
21 000	751.33	524.74	368.31	326.92	312.03	306.11	303.66	302.20
22 000	787.10	549.72	385.85	342.49	326.89	320.69	318.12	316.59
23 000	822.88	574.71	403.39	358.06	341.75	335.26	332.58	330.98
24 000	858.66	599.70	420.93	373.63	356.61	349.84	347.04	345.37
25 000	894.44	624.68	438.47	389.19	371.47	364.42	361.50	359.76
26 000	930.21	649.67	456.01	404.76	386.32	378.99	375.96	374.15
27 000	965.99	674.66	473.54	420.33	401.18	393.57	390.42	388.54
28 000	1001.77	699.65	491.08	435.90	416.04	408.14	404.88	402.93
29 000	1037.55	724.63	508.62	451.46	430.90	422.72	419.34	417.32
30 000	1073.32	749.62	526.16	467.03	445.76	437.30	433.80	431.71
31 000	1109.10	774.61	543.70	482.60	460.62	451.87	448.26	446.10
32 000	1144.88	799.60	561.24	498.17	475.47	466.45	462.72	460.49
33 000	1180.65	824.58	578.78	513.73	490.33	481.03	477.18	474.88
34 000	1216.43	849.57	596.31	529.30	505.19	495.60	491.64	489.27
35 000	1252.21	874.56	613.85	544.87	520.05	510.18	506.10	503.66
36 000	1287.99	899.54	631.39	560.44	534.91	524.76	520.56	518.05
37 000	1323.76	924.53	648.93	576.01	549.77	539.33	535.02	532.44
38 000	1359.54	949.52	666.47	591.57	564.62	553.91	549.48	546.83
39 000	1395.32	974.51	684.01	607.14	579.48	568.49	563.94	561.22
40 000	1431.10	999.49	701.55	622.71	594.34	583.06	578.40	575.61
41 000	1466.87	1024.48	719.08	638.28	609.20	597.64	592.86	590.00
42 000	1502.65	1049.47	736.62	653.84	624.06	612.21	607.32	604.39
43 000	1538.43	1074.45	754.16	669.41	638.92	626.79	621.78	618.78
44 000	1574.20	1099.44	771.70	684.98	653.78	641.37	636.24	633.18
45 000	1609.98	1124.43	789.24	700.55	668.63	655.94	650.70	647.57

FOR **OTHER RATES AND TERMS** *SEE PAGE A-1.*

TERM → AMOUNT	10 YEARS	15 YEARS	20 YEARS	25 YEARS	30 YEARS	40 YEARS
$46 000	806.78	716.11	683.49	670.52	665.16	661.96
47 000	824.31	731.68	698.35	685.10	679.62	676.35
48 000	841.85	747.25	713.21	699.67	694.08	690.74
49 000	859.39	762.82	728.07	714.25	708.54	705.13
50 000	876.93	778.38	742.93	728.83	723.00	719.52
51 000	894.47	793.95	757.78	743.40	737.46	733.91
52 000	912.01	809.52	772.64	757.98	751.92	748.30
53 000	929.55	825.09	787.50	772.55	766.38	762.69
54 000	947.08	840.65	802.36	787.13	780.84	777.08
55 000	964.62	856.22	817.22	801.71	795.30	791.47
56 000	982.16	871.79	832.08	816.28	809.76	805.86
57 000	999.70	887.36	846.93	830.86	824.22	820.25
58 000	1017.24	902.92	861.79	845.44	838.68	834.64
59 000	1034.78	918.49	876.65	860.01	853.14	849.03
60 000	1052.32	934.06	891.51	874.59	867.60	863.42
61 000	1069.85	949.63	906.37	889.17	882.06	877.81
62 000	1087.39	965.19	921.23	903.74	896.52	892.20
63 000	1104.93	980.76	936.09	918.32	910.98	906.59
64 000	1122.47	996.33	950.94	932.90	925.44	920.98
65 000	1140.01	1011.90	965.80	947.47	939.90	935.37
66 000	1157.55	1027.46	980.66	962.05	954.36	949.76
67 000	1175.08	1043.03	995.52	976.62	968.82	964.15
68 000	1192.62	1058.60	1010.38	991.20	983.28	978.54
69 000	1210.16	1074.17	1025.24	1005.78	997.74	992.93
70 000	1227.70	1089.73	1040.09	1020.35	1012.20	1007.32
71 000	1245.24	1105.30	1054.95	1034.93	1026.65	1021.71
72 000	1262.78	1120.87	1069.81	1049.51	1041.11	1036.10
73 000	1280.32	1136.44	1084.67	1064.08	1055.57	1050.49
74 000	1297.85	1152.01	1099.53	1078.66	1070.03	1064.88
75 000	1315.39	1167.57	1114.39	1093.24	1084.49	1079.27
76 000	1332.93	1183.14	1129.24	1107.81	1098.95	1093.66
77 000	1350.47	1198.71	1144.10	1122.39	1113.41	1108.05
78 000	1368.01	1214.28	1158.96	1136.97	1127.87	1122.44
79 000	1385.55	1229.84	1173.82	1151.54	1142.33	1136.83
80 000	1403.09	1245.41	1188.68	1166.12	1156.79	1151.22
81 000	1420.62	1260.98	1203.54	1180.69	1171.25	1165.61
82 000	1438.16	1276.55	1218.40	1195.27	1185.71	1180.00
83 000	1455.70	1292.11	1233.25	1209.85	1200.17	1194.39
84 000	1473.24	1307.68	1248.11	1224.42	1214.63	1208.78
85 000	1490.78	1323.25	1262.97	1239.00	1229.09	1223.17
86 000	1508.32	1338.82	1277.83	1253.58	1243.55	1237.56
87 000	1525.85	1354.38	1292.69	1268.15	1258.01	1251.96
88 000	1543.39	1369.95	1307.55	1282.73	1272.47	1266.35
89 000	1560.93	1385.52	1322.40	1297.31	1286.93	1280.74
90 000	1578.47	1401.09	1337.26	1311.88	1301.39	1295.13
91 000	1596.01	1416.65	1352.12	1326.46	1315.85	1309.52
92 000	1613.55	1432.22	1366.98	1341.04	1330.31	1323.91
93 000	1631.09	1447.79	1381.84	1355.61	1344.77	1338.30
94 000	1648.62	1463.36	1396.70	1370.19	1359.23	1352.69
95 000	1666.16	1478.92	1411.55	1384.76	1373.69	1367.08
96 000	1683.70	1494.49	1426.41	1399.34	1388.15	1381.47
97 000	1701.24	1510.06	1441.27	1413.92	1402.61	1395.86
98 000	1718.78	1525.63	1456.13	1428.49	1417.07	1410.25
99 000	1736.32	1541.19	1470.99	1443.07	1431.53	1424.64
100 000	1753.86	1556.76	1485.85	1457.65	1445.99	1439.03

FOR **OTHER RATES AND TERMS** *SEE PAGE A-1.*

TERM➤ AMOUNT	3 YEARS	5 YEARS	10 YEARS	15 YEARS	20 YEARS	25 YEARS	30 YEARS	40 YEARS
$ 100	3.60	2.52	1.77	1.58	1.51	1.48	1.47	1.46
200	7.19	5.03	3.54	3.15	3.01	2.96	2.94	2.92
300	10.78	7.54	5.31	4.73	4.52	4.44	4.40	4.38
400	14.37	10.05	7.08	6.30	6.02	5.92	5.87	5.84
500	17.96	12.57	8.85	7.88	7.53	7.39	7.34	7.30
600	21.55	15.08	10.62	9.45	9.03	8.87	8.80	8.76
700	25.14	17.59	12.39	11.03	10.54	10.35	10.27	10.22
800	28.73	20.10	14.16	12.60	12.04	11.83	11.74	11.68
900	32.32	22.61	15.93	14.18	13.55	13.30	13.20	13.14
1 000	35.91	25.13	17.70	15.75	15.05	14.78	14.67	14.60
1 000	35.91	25.13	17.70	15.75	15.05	14.78	14.67	14.60
2 000	71.81	50.25	35.40	31.50	30.10	29.56	29.33	29.20
3 000	107.71	75.37	53.10	47.24	45.15	44.33	43.99	43.80
4 000	143.61	100.49	70.80	62.99	60.20	59.11	58.66	58.39
5 000	179.52	125.62	88.49	78.73	75.25	73.88	73.32	72.99
6 000	215.42	150.74	106.19	94.48	90.30	88.66	87.98	87.59
7 000	251.32	175.86	123.89	110.23	105.35	103.43	102.65	102.19
8 000	287.22	200.98	141.59	125.97	120.40	118.21	117.31	116.78
9 000	323.12	226.10	159.29	141.72	135.45	132.98	131.97	131.38
10 000	359.03	251.23	176.98	157.46	150.50	147.76	146.64	145.98
11 000	394.93	276.35	194.68	173.21	165.55	162.53	161.30	160.58
12 000	430.83	301.47	212.38	188.95	180.60	177.31	175.96	175.17
13 000	466.73	326.59	230.08	204.70	195.65	192.08	190.63	189.77
14 000	502.63	351.72	247.78	220.45	210.70	206.86	205.29	204.37
15 000	538.54	376.84	265.47	236.19	225.75	221.63	219.95	218.97
16 000	574.44	401.96	283.17	251.94	240.80	236.41	234.62	233.56
17 000	610.34	427.08	300.87	267.68	255.85	251.19	249.28	248.16
18 000	646.24	452.20	318.57	283.43	270.89	265.96	263.94	262.76
19 000	682.14	477.33	336.26	299.17	285.94	280.74	278.61	277.35
20 000	718.05	502.45	353.96	314.92	300.99	295.51	293.27	291.95
21 000	753.95	527.57	371.66	330.67	316.04	310.29	307.93	306.55
22 000	789.85	552.69	389.36	346.41	331.09	325.06	322.60	321.15
23 000	825.75	577.82	407.06	362.16	346.14	339.84	337.26	335.74
24 000	861.65	602.94	424.75	377.90	361.19	354.61	351.92	350.34
25 000	897.56	628.06	442.45	393.65	376.24	369.39	366.59	364.94
26 000	933.46	653.18	460.15	409.40	391.29	384.16	381.25	379.54
27 000	969.36	678.30	477.85	425.14	406.34	398.94	395.91	394.13
28 000	1005.26	703.43	495.55	440.89	421.39	413.71	410.58	408.73
29 000	1041.16	728.55	513.24	456.63	436.44	428.49	425.24	423.33
30 000	1077.07	753.67	530.94	472.38	451.49	443.26	439.90	437.93
31 000	1112.97	778.79	548.64	488.12	466.54	458.04	454.57	452.52
32 000	1148.87	803.92	566.34	503.87	481.59	472.81	469.23	467.12
33 000	1184.77	829.04	584.03	519.62	496.64	487.59	483.89	481.72
34 000	1220.68	854.16	601.73	535.36	511.69	502.37	498.56	496.31
35 000	1256.58	879.28	619.43	551.11	526.73	517.14	513.22	510.91
36 000	1292.48	904.40	637.13	566.85	541.78	531.92	527.88	525.51
37 000	1328.38	929.53	654.83	582.60	556.83	546.69	542.55	540.11
38 000	1364.28	954.65	672.52	598.34	571.88	561.47	557.21	554.70
39 000	1400.19	979.77	690.22	614.09	586.93	576.24	571.87	569.30
40 000	1436.09	1004.89	707.92	629.84	601.98	591.02	586.54	583.90
41 000	1471.99	1030.02	725.62	645.58	617.03	605.79	601.20	598.50
42 000	1507.89	1055.14	743.32	661.33	632.08	620.57	615.86	613.09
43 000	1543.79	1080.26	761.01	677.07	647.13	635.34	630.52	627.69
44 000	1579.70	1105.38	778.71	692.82	662.18	650.12	645.19	642.29
45 000	1615.60	1130.50	796.41	708.57	677.23	664.89	659.85	656.89

FOR **OTHER RATES AND TERMS** *SEE PAGE A-1.*

TERM➧ AMOUNT	10 YEARS	15 YEARS	20 YEARS	25 YEARS	30 YEARS	40 YEARS
$46 000	814.11	724.31	692.28	679.67	674.51	671.48
47 000	831.81	740.06	707.33	694.44	689.18	686.08
48 000	849.50	755.80	722.38	709.22	703.84	700.68
49 000	867.20	771.55	737.43	723.99	718.50	715.27
50 000	884.90	787.29	752.48	738.77	733.17	729.87
51 000	902.60	803.04	767.53	753.55	747.83	744.47
52 000	920.29	818.79	782.57	768.32	762.49	759.07
53 000	937.99	834.53	797.62	783.10	777.16	773.66
54 000	955.69	850.28	812.67	797.87	791.82	788.26
55 000	973.39	866.02	827.72	812.65	806.48	802.86
56 000	991.09	881.77	842.77	827.42	821.15	817.46
57 000	1008.78	897.51	857.82	842.20	835.81	832.05
58 000	1026.48	913.26	872.87	856.97	850.47	846.65
59 000	1044.18	929.01	887.92	871.75	865.14	861.25
60 000	1061.88	944.75	902.97	886.52	879.80	875.85
61 000	1079.58	960.50	918.02	901.30	894.46	890.44
62 000	1097.27	976.24	933.07	916.07	909.13	905.04
63 000	1114.97	991.99	948.12	930.85	923.79	919.64
64 000	1132.67	1007.74	963.17	945.62	938.45	934.23
65 000	1150.37	1023.48	978.22	960.40	953.12	948.83
66 000	1168.06	1039.23	993.27	975.17	967.78	963.43
67 000	1185.76	1054.97	1008.32	989.95	982.44	978.03
68 000	1203.46	1070.72	1023.37	1004.73	997.11	992.62
69 000	1221.16	1086.46	1038.41	1019.50	1011.77	1007.22
70 000	1238.86	1102.21	1053.46	1034.28	1026.43	1021.82
71 000	1256.55	1117.96	1068.51	1049.05	1041.10	1036.42
72 000	1274.25	1133.70	1083.56	1063.83	1055.76	1051.01
73 000	1291.95	1149.45	1098.61	1078.60	1070.42	1065.61
74 000	1309.65	1165.19	1113.66	1093.38	1085.09	1080.21
75 000	1327.35	1180.94	1128.71	1108.15	1099.75	1094.81
76 000	1345.04	1196.68	1143.76	1122.93	1114.41	1109.40
77 000	1362.74	1212.43	1158.81	1137.70	1129.08	1124.00
78 000	1380.44	1228.18	1173.86	1152.48	1143.74	1138.60
79 000	1398.14	1243.92	1188.91	1167.25	1158.40	1153.19
80 000	1415.84	1259.67	1203.96	1182.03	1173.07	1167.79
81 000	1433.53	1275.41	1219.01	1196.80	1187.73	1182.39
82 000	1451.23	1291.16	1234.06	1211.58	1202.39	1196.99
83 000	1468.93	1306.90	1249.11	1226.35	1217.05	1211.58
84 000	1486.63	1322.65	1264.16	1241.13	1231.72	1226.18
85 000	1504.32	1338.40	1279.21	1255.91	1246.38	1240.78
86 000	1522.02	1354.14	1294.26	1270.68	1261.04	1255.38
87 000	1539.72	1369.89	1309.30	1285.46	1275.71	1269.97
88 000	1557.42	1385.63	1324.35	1300.23	1290.37	1284.57
89 000	1575.12	1401.38	1339.40	1315.01	1305.03	1299.17
90 000	1592.81	1417.13	1354.45	1329.78	1319.70	1313.77
91 000	1610.51	1432.87	1369.50	1344.56	1334.36	1328.36
92 000	1628.21	1448.62	1384.55	1359.33	1349.02	1342.96
93 000	1645.91	1464.36	1399.60	1374.11	1363.69	1357.56
94 000	1663.61	1480.11	1414.65	1388.88	1378.35	1372.15
95 000	1681.30	1495.85	1429.70	1403.66	1393.01	1386.75
96 000	1699.00	1511.60	1444.75	1418.43	1407.68	1401.35
97 000	1716.70	1527.35	1459.80	1433.21	1422.34	1415.95
98 000	1734.40	1543.09	1474.85	1447.98	1437.00	1430.54
99 000	1752.09	1558.84	1489.90	1462.76	1451.67	1445.14
100 000	1769.79	1574.58	1504.95	1477.53	1466.33	1459.74

FOR **OTHER RATES AND TERMS** *SEE PAGE A-1.*

TERM→ AMOUNT	3 YEARS	5 YEARS	10 YEARS	15 YEARS	20 YEARS	25 YEARS	30 YEARS	40 YEARS
$ 100	3.61	2.53	1.79	1.60	1.53	1.50	1.49	1.49
200	7.21	5.06	3.58	3.19	3.05	3.00	2.98	2.97
300	10.81	7.58	5.36	4.78	4.58	4.50	4.47	4.45
400	14.42	10.11	7.15	6.37	6.10	5.99	5.95	5.93
500	18.02	12.63	8.93	7.97	7.63	7.49	7.44	7.41
600	21.62	15.16	10.72	9.56	9.15	8.99	8.93	8.89
700	25.22	17.69	12.51	11.15	10.67	10.49	10.41	10.37
800	28.83	20.21	14.29	12.74	12.20	11.98	11.90	11.85
900	32.43	22.74	16.08	14.34	13.72	13.48	13.39	13.33
1 000	36.03	25.26	17.86	15.93	15.25	14.98	14.87	14.81
1 000	36.03	25.26	17.86	15.93	15.25	14.98	14.87	14.81
2 000	72.06	50.52	35.72	31.85	30.49	29.95	29.74	29.61
3 000	108.09	75.78	53.58	47.78	45.73	44.93	44.61	44.42
4 000	144.11	101.04	71.44	63.70	60.97	59.90	59.47	59.22
5 000	180.14	126.29	89.29	79.63	76.21	74.88	74.34	74.03
6 000	216.17	151.55	107.15	95.55	91.45	89.85	89.21	88.83
7 000	252.19	176.81	125.01	111.48	106.69	104.83	104.07	103.64
8 000	288.22	202.07	142.87	127.40	121.93	119.80	118.94	118.44
9 000	324.25	227.32	160.73	143.33	137.17	134.78	133.81	133.25
10 000	360.28	252.58	178.58	159.25	152.41	149.75	148.67	148.05
11 000	396.30	277.84	196.44	175.18	167.66	164.73	163.54	162.85
12 000	432.33	303.10	214.30	191.10	182.90	179.70	178.41	177.66
13 000	468.36	328.35	232.16	207.03	198.14	194.67	193.27	192.46
14 000	504.38	353.61	250.02	222.95	213.38	209.65	208.14	207.27
15 000	540.41	378.87	267.87	238.87	228.62	224.62	223.01	222.07
16 000	576.44	404.13	285.73	254.80	243.86	239.60	237.88	236.88
17 000	612.47	429.38	303.59	270.72	259.10	254.57	252.74	251.68
18 000	648.49	454.64	321.45	286.65	274.34	269.55	267.61	266.49
19 000	684.52	479.90	339.30	302.57	289.58	284.52	282.48	281.29
20 000	720.55	505.16	357.16	318.50	304.82	299.50	297.34	296.10
21 000	756.57	530.42	375.02	334.42	320.07	314.47	312.21	310.90
22 000	792.60	555.67	392.88	350.35	335.31	329.45	327.08	325.70
23 000	828.63	580.93	410.74	366.27	350.55	344.42	341.94	340.51
24 000	864.66	606.19	428.59	382.20	365.79	359.40	356.81	355.31
25 000	900.68	631.45	446.45	398.12	381.03	374.37	371.68	370.12
26 000	936.71	656.70	464.31	414.05	396.27	389.34	386.54	384.92
27 000	972.74	681.96	482.17	429.97	411.51	404.32	401.41	399.73
28 000	1008.76	707.22	500.03	445.90	426.75	419.29	416.28	414.53
29 000	1044.79	732.48	517.88	461.82	441.99	434.27	431.15	429.34
30 000	1080.82	757.73	535.74	477.74	457.23	449.24	446.01	444.14
31 000	1116.85	782.99	553.60	493.67	472.48	464.22	460.88	458.95
32 000	1152.87	808.25	571.46	509.59	487.72	479.19	475.75	473.75
33 000	1188.90	833.51	589.32	525.52	502.96	494.17	490.61	488.55
34 000	1224.93	858.76	607.17	541.44	518.20	509.14	505.48	503.36
35 000	1260.95	884.02	625.03	557.37	533.44	524.12	520.35	518.16
36 000	1296.98	909.28	642.89	573.29	548.68	539.09	535.21	532.97
37 000	1333.01	934.54	660.75	589.22	563.92	554.07	550.08	547.77
38 000	1369.04	959.79	678.60	605.14	579.16	569.04	564.95	562.58
39 000	1405.06	985.05	696.46	621.07	594.40	584.01	579.81	577.38
40 000	1441.09	1010.31	714.32	636.99	609.64	598.99	594.68	592.19
41 000	1477.12	1035.57	732.18	652.92	624.89	613.96	609.55	606.99
42 000	1513.14	1060.83	750.04	668.84	640.13	628.94	624.42	621.80
43 000	1549.17	1086.08	767.89	684.77	655.37	643.91	639.28	636.60
44 000	1585.20	1111.34	785.75	700.69	670.61	658.89	654.15	651.40
45 000	1621.22	1136.60	803.61	716.61	685.85	673.86	669.02	666.21

FOR **OTHER RATES AND TERMS** *SEE PAGE A-1.*

MONTHLY LOAN AMORTIZATION PAYMENTS

TERM♦ AMOUNT	10 YEARS	15 YEARS	20 YEARS	25 YEARS	30 YEARS	40 YEARS
$46 000	821.47	732.54	701.09	688.84	683.88	681.01
47 000	839.33	748.46	716.33	703.81	698.75	695.82
48 000	857.18	764.39	731.57	718.79	713.62	710.62
49 000	875.04	780.31	746.81	733.76	728.48	725.43
50 000	892.90	796.24	762.05	748.73	743.35	740.23
51 000	910.76	812.16	777.30	763.71	758.22	755.04
52 000	928.61	828.09	792.54	778.68	773.08	769.84
53 000	946.47	844.01	807.78	793.66	787.95	784.65
54 000	964.33	859.94	823.02	808.63	802.82	799.45
55 000	982.19	875.86	838.26	823.61	817.69	814.25
56 000	1000.05	891.79	853.50	838.58	832.55	829.06
57 000	1017.90	907.71	868.74	853.56	847.42	843.86
58 000	1035.76	923.64	883.98	868.53	862.29	858.67
59 000	1053.62	939.56	899.22	883.51	877.15	873.47
60 000	1071.48	955.48	914.46	898.48	892.02	888.28
61 000	1089.34	971.41	929.71	913.46	906.89	903.08
62 000	1107.19	987.33	944.95	928.43	921.75	917.89
63 000	1125.05	1003.26	960.19	943.40	936.62	932.69
64 000	1142.91	1019.18	975.43	958.38	951.49	947.50
65 000	1160.77	1035.11	990.67	973.35	966.35	962.30
66 000	1178.63	1051.03	1005.91	988.33	981.22	977.10
67 000	1196.48	1066.96	1021.15	1003.30	996.09	991.91
68 000	1214.34	1082.88	1036.39	1018.28	1010.96	1006.71
69 000	1232.20	1098.81	1051.63	1033.25	1025.82	1021.52
70 000	1250.06	1114.73	1066.87	1048.23	1040.69	1036.32
71 000	1267.91	1130.66	1082.12	1063.20	1055.56	1051.13
72 000	1285.77	1146.58	1097.36	1078.18	1070.42	1065.93
73 000	1303.63	1162.51	1112.60	1093.15	1085.29	1080.74
74 000	1321.49	1178.43	1127.84	1108.13	1100.16	1095.54
75 000	1339.35	1194.35	1143.08	1123.10	1115.02	1110.35
76 000	1357.20	1210.28	1158.32	1138.07	1129.89	1125.15
77 000	1375.06	1226.20	1173.56	1153.05	1144.76	1139.95
78 000	1392.92	1242.13	1188.80	1168.02	1159.62	1154.76
79 000	1410.78	1258.05	1204.04	1183.00	1174.49	1169.56
80 000	1428.64	1273.98	1219.28	1197.97	1189.36	1184.37
81 000	1446.49	1289.90	1234.53	1212.95	1204.23	1199.17
82 000	1464.35	1305.83	1249.77	1227.92	1219.09	1213.98
83 000	1482.21	1321.75	1265.01	1242.90	1233.96	1228.78
84 000	1500.07	1337.68	1280.25	1257.87	1248.83	1243.59
85 000	1517.93	1353.60	1295.49	1272.85	1263.69	1258.39
86 000	1535.78	1369.53	1310.73	1287.82	1278.56	1273.19
87 000	1553.64	1385.45	1325.97	1302.80	1293.43	1288.00
88 000	1571.50	1401.38	1341.21	1317.77	1308.29	1302.80
89 000	1589.36	1417.30	1356.45	1332.74	1323.16	1317.61
90 000	1607.21	1433.22	1371.69	1347.72	1338.03	1332.41
91 000	1625.07	1449.15	1386.94	1362.69	1352.89	1347.22
92 000	1642.93	1465.07	1402.18	1377.67	1367.76	1362.02
93 000	1660.79	1481.00	1417.42	1392.64	1382.63	1376.83
94 000	1678.65	1496.92	1432.66	1407.62	1397.50	1391.63
95 000	1696.50	1512.85	1447.90	1422.59	1412.36	1406.44
96 000	1714.36	1528.77	1463.14	1437.57	1427.23	1421.24
97 000	1732.22	1544.70	1478.38	1452.54	1442.10	1436.04
98 000	1750.08	1560.62	1493.62	1467.52	1456.96	1450.85
99 000	1767.94	1576.55	1508.86	1482.49	1471.83	1465.65
100 000	1785.79	1592.47	1524.10	1497.46	1486.70	1480.46

FOR **OTHER RATES AND TERMS** *SEE PAGE A-1.*

TERM▶ AMOUNT	3 YEARS	5 YEARS	10 YEARS	15 YEARS	20 YEARS	25 YEARS	30 YEARS	40 YEARS
$ 100	3.62	2.54	1.81	1.62	1.55	1.52	1.51	1.51
200	7.24	5.08	3.61	3.23	3.09	3.04	3.02	3.01
300	10.85	7.62	5.41	4.84	4.63	4.56	4.53	4.51
400	14.47	10.16	7.21	6.45	6.18	6.07	6.03	6.01
500	18.08	12.70	9.01	8.06	7.72	7.59	7.54	7.51
600	21.70	15.24	10.82	9.67	9.26	9.11	9.05	9.01
700	25.31	17.78	12.62	11.28	10.81	10.63	10.55	10.51
800	28.93	20.32	14.42	12.89	12.35	12.14	12.06	12.01
900	32.54	22.86	16.22	14.50	13.89	13.66	13.57	13.52
1 000	36.16	25.40	18.02	16.11	15.44	15.18	15.08	15.02
1 000	36.16	25.40	18.02	16.11	15.44	15.18	15.08	15.02
2 000	72.31	50.79	36.04	32.21	30.87	30.35	30.15	30.03
3 000	108.46	76.19	54.06	48.32	46.30	45.53	45.22	45.04
4 000	144.61	101.58	72.08	64.42	61.74	60.70	60.29	60.05
5 000	180.77	126.97	90.10	80.53	77.17	75.88	75.36	75.06
6 000	216.92	152.37	108.12	96.63	92.60	91.05	90.43	90.08
7 000	253.07	177.76	126.13	112.73	108.04	106.23	105.50	105.09
8 000	289.22	203.15	144.15	128.84	123.47	121.40	120.57	120.10
9 000	325.38	228.55	162.17	144.94	138.90	136.57	135.64	135.11
10 000	361.53	253.94	180.19	161.05	154.34	151.75	150.71	150.12
11 000	397.68	279.33	198.21	177.15	169.77	166.92	165.78	165.14
12 000	433.83	304.73	216.23	193.26	185.20	182.10	180.86	180.15
13 000	469.99	330.12	234.25	209.36	200.64	197.27	195.93	195.16
14 000	506.14	355.51	252.26	225.46	216.07	212.45	211.00	210.17
15 000	542.29	380.91	270.28	241.57	231.50	227.62	226.07	225.18
16 000	578.44	406.30	288.30	257.67	246.93	242.79	241.14	240.19
17 000	614.60	431.69	306.32	273.78	262.37	257.97	256.21	255.21
18 000	650.75	457.09	324.34	289.88	277.80	273.14	271.28	270.22
19 000	686.90	482.48	342.36	305.98	293.23	288.32	286.35	285.23
20 000	723.05	507.87	360.38	322.09	308.67	303.49	301.42	300.24
21 000	759.21	533.27	378.39	338.19	324.10	318.67	316.49	315.25
22 000	795.36	558.66	396.41	354.30	339.53	333.84	331.56	330.27
23 000	831.51	584.05	414.43	370.40	354.97	349.01	346.63	345.28
24 000	867.66	609.45	432.45	386.51	370.40	364.19	361.71	360.29
25 000	903.81	634.84	450.47	402.61	385.83	379.36	376.78	375.30
26 000	939.97	660.23	468.49	418.71	401.27	394.54	391.85	390.31
27 000	976.12	685.63	486.51	434.82	416.70	409.71	406.92	405.32
28 000	1012.27	711.02	504.52	450.92	432.13	424.89	421.99	420.34
29 000	1048.42	736.41	522.54	467.03	447.57	440.06	437.06	435.35
30 000	1084.58	761.81	540.56	483.13	463.00	455.23	452.13	450.36
31 000	1120.73	787.20	558.58	499.24	478.43	470.41	467.20	465.37
32 000	1156.88	812.59	576.60	515.34	493.86	485.58	482.27	480.38
33 000	1193.03	837.99	594.62	531.44	509.30	500.76	497.34	495.40
34 000	1229.19	863.38	612.63	547.55	524.73	515.93	512.41	510.41
35 000	1265.34	888.77	630.65	563.65	540.16	531.11	527.48	525.42
36 000	1301.49	914.17	648.67	579.76	555.60	546.28	542.56	540.43
37 000	1337.64	939.56	666.69	595.86	571.03	561.45	557.63	555.44
38 000	1373.80	964.96	684.71	611.96	586.46	576.63	572.70	570.45
39 000	1409.95	990.35	702.73	628.07	601.90	591.80	587.77	585.47
40 000	1446.10	1015.74	720.75	644.17	617.33	606.98	602.84	600.48
41 000	1482.25	1041.14	738.76	660.28	632.76	622.15	617.91	615.49
42 000	1518.41	1066.53	756.78	676.38	648.20	637.33	632.98	630.50
43 000	1554.56	1091.92	774.80	692.49	663.63	652.50	648.05	645.51
44 000	1590.71	1117.32	792.82	708.59	679.06	667.67	663.12	660.53
45 000	1626.86	1142.71	810.84	724.69	694.50	682.85	678.19	675.54

FOR **OTHER RATES AND TERMS** *SEE PAGE A-1.*

TERM♦ AMOUNT	10 YEARS	15 YEARS	20 YEARS	25 YEARS	30 YEARS	40 YEARS
$46 000	828.86	740.80	709.93	698.02	693.26	690.55
47 000	846.88	756.90	725.36	713.20	708.34	705.56
48 000	864.89	773.01	740.79	728.37	723.41	720.57
49 000	882.91	789.11	756.23	743.55	738.48	735.58
50 000	900.93	805.22	771.66	758.72	753.55	750.60
51 000	918.95	821.32	787.09	773.89	768.62	765.61
52 000	936.97	837.42	802.53	789.07	783.69	780.62
53 000	954.99	853.53	817.96	804.24	798.76	795.63
54 000	973.01	869.63	833.39	819.42	813.83	810.64
55 000	991.02	885.74	848.83	834.59	828.90	825.66
56 000	1009.04	901.84	864.26	849.77	843.97	840.67
57 000	1027.06	917.94	879.69	864.94	859.04	855.68
58 000	1045.08	934.05	895.13	880.11	874.11	870.69
59 000	1063.10	950.15	910.56	895.29	889.19	885.70
60 000	1081.12	966.26	925.99	910.46	904.26	900.71
61 000	1099.13	982.36	941.43	925.64	919.33	915.73
62 000	1117.15	998.47	956.86	940.81	934.40	930.74
63 000	1135.17	1014.57	972.29	955.99	949.47	945.75
64 000	1153.19	1030.67	987.72	971.16	964.54	960.76
65 000	1171.21	1046.78	1003.16	986.33	979.61	975.77
66 000	1189.23	1062.88	1018.59	1001.51	994.68	990.79
67 000	1207.25	1078.99	1034.02	1016.68	1009.75	1005.80
68 000	1225.26	1095.09	1049.46	1031.86	1024.82	1020.81
69 000	1243.28	1111.20	1064.89	1047.03	1039.89	1035.82
70 000	1261.30	1127.30	1080.32	1062.21	1054.96	1050.83
71 000	1279.32	1143.40	1095.76	1077.38	1070.04	1065.84
72 000	1297.34	1159.51	1111.19	1092.55	1085.11	1080.86
73 000	1315.36	1175.61	1126.62	1107.73	1100.18	1095.87
74 000	1333.38	1191.72	1142.06	1122.90	1115.25	1110.88
75 000	1351.39	1207.82	1157.49	1138.08	1130.32	1125.89
76 000	1369.41	1223.92	1172.92	1153.25	1145.39	1140.90
77 000	1387.43	1240.03	1188.35	1168.43	1160.46	1155.92
78 000	1405.45	1256.13	1203.79	1183.60	1175.53	1170.93
79 000	1423.47	1272.24	1219.22	1198.77	1190.60	1185.94
80 000	1441.49	1288.34	1234.65	1213.95	1205.67	1200.95
81 000	1459.51	1304.45	1250.09	1229.12	1220.74	1215.96
82 000	1477.52	1320.55	1265.52	1244.30	1235.82	1230.97
83 000	1495.54	1336.65	1280.95	1259.47	1250.89	1245.99
84 000	1513.56	1352.76	1296.39	1274.65	1265.96	1261.00
85 000	1531.58	1368.86	1311.82	1289.82	1281.03	1276.01
86 000	1549.60	1384.97	1327.25	1304.99	1296.10	1291.02
87 000	1567.62	1401.07	1342.69	1320.17	1311.17	1306.03
88 000	1585.63	1417.18	1358.12	1335.34	1326.24	1321.05
89 000	1603.65	1433.28	1373.55	1350.52	1341.31	1336.06
90 000	1621.67	1449.38	1388.99	1365.69	1356.38	1351.07
91 000	1639.69	1465.49	1404.42	1380.87	1371.45	1366.08
92 000	1657.71	1481.59	1419.85	1396.04	1386.52	1381.09
93 000	1675.73	1497.70	1435.28	1411.21	1401.59	1396.10
94 000	1693.75	1513.80	1450.72	1426.39	1416.67	1411.12
95 000	1711.76	1529.90	1466.15	1441.56	1431.74	1426.13
96 000	1729.78	1546.01	1481.58	1456.74	1446.81	1441.14
97 000	1747.80	1562.11	1497.02	1471.91	1461.88	1456.15
98 000	1765.82	1578.22	1512.45	1487.09	1476.95	1471.16
99 000	1783.84	1594.32	1527.88	1502.26	1492.02	1486.18
100 000	1801.86	1610.43	1543.32	1517.43	1507.09	1501.19

FOR **OTHER RATES AND TERMS** *SEE PAGE A-1.*

APR TABLE
(Effective Interest Rate including Discount Points)

The table shows the effective interest rate of a mortgage loan taking into account the actual interest rate and the points (loan fee) required to obtain the loan. It is useful for comparing the actual cost of several mortgages over a given number of years, expressed as an Annual Percentage Rate.

PROBLEM:

Mr. and Mrs. Buyer are faced with a choice between two mortgage loans offered by different lenders. Both loans are for $150,000, to be amortized over a 30 year period.

Mortgage "A": 11¾% Interest, with a loan fee of 3 points.

Mortgage "B": 12½% Interest, with a loan fee of 1 point.

QUESTION:

If the Buyers expect to keep the property for 10 years, which loan offers the lowest APR?

ANSWER:

MORTGAGE "A" – Find the block of 11¾% in the INTEREST RATE column at the far left of the table. In the DISCOUNT POINTS column select the line of 3 Points. At the intersection of that line and the 10-YEAR column you find the APR of 12.51%.

MORTGAGE "B" – Find the block of 12½% in the INTEREST RATE column at the far left of the table. In the DISCOUNT POINTS column select the line of 1 Point. At the intersection of that line and the 10-YEAR column you find the APR of 12.25%.

Mortgage "B" has the lower APR.

ANNUAL PERCENTAGE RATES

INTEREST RATE	DISCOUNT POINTS	5 YEARS	10 YEARS	15 YEARS	20 YEARS	25 YEARS	30 YEARS
6%	1	6.42	6.22	6.16	6.13	6.11	6.09
	2	6.84	6.45	6.32	6.25	6.21	6.19
	3	7.27	6.68	6.48	6.38	6.32	6.29
	4	7.71	6.91	6.64	6.51	6.44	6.39
	5	8.15	7.15	6.81	6.65	6.55	6.49
6¼%	1	6.67	6.47	6.41	6.38	6.36	6.35
	2	7.10	6.70	6.57	6.50	6.47	6.44
	3	7.53	6.93	6.73	6.63	6.58	6.54
	4	7.97	7.16	6.90	6.77	6.69	6.64
	5	8.41	7.40	7.07	6.90	6.81	6.74
6½%	1	6.92	6.72	6.66	6.63	6.61	6.60
	2	7.35	6.95	6.82	6.76	6.72	6.70
	3	7.78	7.18	6.99	6.89	6.83	6.80
	4	8.22	7.42	7.15	7.02	6.95	6.90
	5	8.66	7.66	7.32	7.16	7.06	7.00
6¾%	1	7.17	6.98	6.91	6.88	6.86	6.85
	2	7.60	7.21	7.07	7.01	6.97	6.95
	3	8.03	7.44	7.24	7.14	7.09	7.05
	4	8.47	7.67	7.41	7.28	7.20	7.15
	5	8.92	7.91	7.58	7.41	7.32	7.26
7%	1	7.42	7.23	7.16	7.13	7.11	7.10
	2	7.85	7.46	7.33	7.26	7.23	7.20
	3	8.29	7.69	7.49	7.40	7.34	7.30
	4	8.73	7.93	7.66	7.53	7.46	7.41
	5	9.17	8.17	7.83	7.67	7.58	7.52
7¼%	1	7.67	7.48	7.41	7.38	7.36	7.35
	2	8.10	7.71	7.58	7.51	7.48	7.45
	3	8.54	7.94	7.75	7.65	7.59	7.56
	4	8.98	8.18	7.92	7.79	7.71	7.67
	5	9.43	8.42	8.09	7.93	7.83	7.77
7½%	1	7.92	7.73	7.66	7.63	7.61	7.60
	2	8.36	7.96	7.83	7.77	7.73	7.71
	3	8.79	8.20	8.00	7.90	7.85	7.81
	4	9.24	8.44	8.17	8.04	7.97	7.92
	5	9.69	8.68	8.35	8.19	8.09	8.03
7¾%	1	8.18	7.98	7.92	7.88	7.87	7.85
	2	8.61	8.21	8.08	8.02	7.98	7.96
	3	9.05	8.45	8.25	8.16	8.10	8.07
	4	9.49	8.69	8.43	8.30	8.23	8.18
	5	9.94	8.94	8.60	8.44	8.35	8.29
8%	1	8.43	8.23	8.17	8.14	8.12	8.11
	2	8.86	8.47	8.34	8.27	8.24	8.21
	3	9.30	8.70	8.51	8.41	8.36	8.32
	4	9.74	8.95	8.68	8.55	8.48	8.44
	5	10.20	9.19	8.86	8.70	8.61	8.55
8¼%	1	8.68	8.48	8.42	8.39	8.37	8.36
	2	9.11	8.72	8.59	8.53	8.49	8.47
	3	9.55	8.96	8.76	8.67	8.61	8.58
	4	10.00	9.20	8.94	8.81	8.74	8.69
	5	10.45	9.45	9.12	8.96	8.86	8.81

ANNUAL PERCENTAGE RATES

INTEREST RATE	DISCOUNT POINTS	5 YEARS	10 YEARS	15 YEARS	20 YEARS	25 YEARS	30 YEARS
8½%	1	8.93	8.73	8.67	8.64	8.62	8.61
	2	9.36	8.97	8.84	8.78	8.74	8.72
	3	9.80	9.21	9.02	8.92	8.87	8.83
	4	10.25	9.46	9.19	9.07	8.99	8.95
	5	10.71	9.70	9.37	9.21	9.12	9.07
8¾%	1	9.18	8.98	8.92	8.89	8.87	8.86
	2	9.62	9.22	9.09	9.03	9.00	8.97
	3	10.06	9.46	9.27	9.18	9.12	9.09
	4	10.51	9.71	9.45	9.32	9.25	9.21
	5	10.96	9.96	9.63	9.47	9.38	9.32
9%	1	9.43	9.24	9.17	9.14	9.12	9.11
	2	9.87	9.48	9.35	9.28	9.25	9.23
	3	10.31	9.72	9.52	9.43	9.38	9.34
	4	10.76	9.96	9.70	9.58	9.51	9.46
	5	11.22	10.21	9.89	9.73	9.64	9.58
9¼%	1	9.68	9.49	9.42	9.39	9.38	9.36
	2	10.12	9.73	9.60	9.54	9.50	9.48
	3	10.56	9.97	9.78	9.68	9.63	9.60
	4	11.01	10.22	9.96	9.83	9.76	9.72
	5	11.47	10.47	10.14	9.99	9.90	9.84
9½%	1	9.93	9.74	9.67	9.64	9.63	9.62
	2	10.37	9.98	9.85	9.79	9.76	9.73
	3	10.82	10.23	10.03	9.94	9.89	9.85
	4	11.27	10.47	10.21	10.09	10.02	9.98
	5	11.73	10.73	10.40	10.24	10.16	10.10
9¾%	1	10.18	9.99	9.93	9.90	9.88	9.87
	2	10.62	10.23	10.10	10.04	10.01	9.99
	3	11.07	10.48	10.29	10.19	10.14	10.11
	4	11.52	10.73	10.47	10.35	10.28	10.23
	5	11.98	10.98	10.66	10.50	10.41	10.36
10%	1	10.44	10.24	10.18	10.15	10.13	10.12
	2	10.88	10.48	10.36	10.30	10.26	10.24
	3	11.32	10.73	10.54	10.45	10.40	10.37
	4	11.78	10.98	10.72	10.60	10.53	10.49
	5	12.24	11.24	10.91	10.76	10.67	10.62
10¼%	1	10.69	10.49	10.43	10.40	10.38	10.37
	2	11.13	10.74	10.61	10.55	10.52	10.50
	3	11.58	10.99	10.79	10.70	10.65	10.62
	4	12.03	11.24	10.98	10.86	10.79	10.75
	5	12.49	11.50	11.17	11.02	10.93	10.88
10½%	1	10.94	10.74	10.68	10.65	10.63	10.62
	2	11.38	10.99	10.86	10.80	10.77	10.75
	3	11.83	11.24	11.05	10.96	10.91	10.88
	4	12.29	11.49	11.24	11.11	11.05	11.01
	5	12.75	11.75	11.43	11.27	11.19	11.14
10¾%	1	11.19	10.99	10.93	10.90	10.89	10.88
	2	11.63	11.24	11.11	11.06	11.02	11.00
	3	12.08	11.49	11.30	11.21	11.16	11.13
	4	12.54	11.75	11.49	11.37	11.30	11.26
	5	13.01	12.01	11.68	11.53	11.45	11.40

A-128.2

ANNUAL PERCENTAGE RATES

INTEREST RATE	DISCOUNT POINTS	5 YEARS	10 YEARS	15 YEARS	20 YEARS	25 YEARS	30 YEARS
11%	1	11.44	11.25	11.18	11.15	11.14	11.13
	2	11.88	11.49	11.37	11.31	11.28	11.26
	3	12.34	11.75	11.56	11.47	11.42	11.39
	4	12.80	12.00	11.75	11.63	11.56	11.52
	5	13.26	12.26	11.94	11.79	11.71	11.66
11¼%	1	11.69	11.50	11.43	11.40	11.39	11.38
	2	12.14	11.75	11.62	11.56	11.53	11.51
	3	12.59	12.00	11.81	11.72	11.67	11.64
	4	13.05	12.26	12.00	11.88	11.82	11.78
	5	13.52	12.52	12.20	12.05	11.97	11.92
11½%	1	11.94	11.75	11.69	11.66	11.64	11.63
	2	12.39	12.00	11.87	11.81	11.78	11.76
	3	12.84	12.25	12.06	11.98	11.93	11.90
	4	13.30	12.51	12.26	12.14	12.08	12.04
	5	13.77	12.78	12.46	12.31	12.23	12.18
11¾%	1	12.19	12.00	11.94	11.91	11.89	11.88
	2	12.64	12.25	12.13	12.07	12.04	12.02
	3	13.10	12.51	12.32	12.23	12.18	12.16
	4	13.56	12.77	12.51	12.40	12.33	12.30
	5	14.03	13.03	12.71	12.57	12.49	12.44
12%	1	12.44	12.25	12.19	12.16	12.14	12.13
	2	12.89	12.50	12.38	12.32	12.29	12.27
	3	13.35	12.76	12.57	12.49	12.44	12.41
	4	13.81	13.02	12.77	12.65	12.59	12.55
	5	14.28	13.29	12.97	12.82	12.74	12.70
12¼%	1	12.69	12.50	12.44	12.41	12.40	12.39
	2	13.15	12.76	12.63	12.57	12.54	12.53
	3	13.60	13.02	12.83	12.74	12.69	12.67
	4	14.07	13.28	13.03	12.91	12.85	12.81
	5	14.54	13.55	13.23	13.08	13.00	12.96
12½%	1	12.95	12.75	12.69	12.66	12.65	12.64
	2	13.40	13.01	12.88	12.83	12.80	12.78
	3	13.86	13.27	13.08	13.00	12.95	12.92
	4	14.32	13.53	13.28	13.17	13.11	13.07
	5	14.79	13.80	13.49	13.34	13.26	13.22
12¾%	1	13.20	13.00	12.94	12.91	12.90	12.89
	2	13.65	13.26	13.14	13.08	13.05	13.03
	3	14.11	13.52	13.34	13.25	13.21	13.18
	4	14.58	13.79	13.54	13.42	13.36	13.33
	5	15.05	14.06	13.74	13.60	13.52	13.48
13%	1	13.45	13.26	13.19	13.17	13.15	13.14
	2	13.90	13.51	13.39	13.33	13.30	13.29
	3	14.36	13.78	13.59	13.51	13.46	13.44
	4	14.83	14.04	13.79	13.68	13.62	13.59
	5	15.31	14.32	14.00	13.86	13.78	13.74
13¼%	1	13.70	13.51	13.45	13.42	13.40	13.39
	2	14.15	13.77	13.64	13.59	13.56	13.54
	3	14.62	14.03	13.85	13.76	13.72	13.69
	4	15.09	14.30	14.05	13.94	13.88	13.85
	5	15.56	14.57	14.26	14.12	14.04	14.00

ANNUAL PERCENTAGE RATES

INTEREST RATE	DISCOUNT POINTS	5 YEARS	10 YEARS	15 YEARS	20 YEARS	25 YEARS	30 YEARS
13½%	1	13.95	13.76	13.70	13.67	13.65	13.65
	2	14.41	14.02	13.90	13.84	13.81	13.80
	3	14.87	14.28	14.10	14.02	13.97	13.95
	4	15.34	14.55	14.31	14.19	14.14	14.10
	5	15.82	14.83	14.52	14.38	14.30	14.26
13¾%	1	14.20	14.01	13.95	13.92	13.91	13.90
	2	14.66	14.27	14.15	14.09	14.07	14.05
	3	15.12	14.54	14.35	14.27	14.23	14.21
	4	15.59	14.81	14.56	14.45	14.39	14.36
	5	16.07	15.09	14.77	14.64	14.56	14.52
14%	1	14.45	14.26	14.20	14.17	14.16	14.15
	2	14.91	14.52	14.40	14.35	14.32	14.31
	3	15.38	14.79	14.61	14.53	14.48	14.46
	4	15.85	15.07	14.82	14.71	14.65	14.62
	5	16.33	15.34	15.03	14.89	14.82	14.78
14¼%	1	14.70	14.51	14.45	14.42	14.41	14.40
	2	15.16	14.78	14.66	14.60	14.57	14.56
	3	15.63	15.05	14.86	14.78	14.74	14.72
	4	16.10	15.32	15.08	14.97	14.91	14.88
	5	16.58	15.60	15.29	15.15	15.08	15.05
14½%	1	14.95	14.76	14.70	14.68	14.66	14.66
	2	15.42	15.03	14.91	14.86	14.83	14.81
	3	15.88	15.30	15.12	15.04	15.00	14.97
	4	16.36	15.58	15.33	15.22	15.17	15.14
	5	16.84	15.86	15.55	15.41	15.34	15.31
14¾%	1	15.21	15.01	14.95	14.93	14.91	14.91
	2	15.67	15.28	15.16	15.11	15.08	15.07
	3	16.14	15.56	15.37	15.29	15.25	15.23
	4	16.61	15.83	15.59	15.48	15.43	15.40
	5	17.10	16.11	15.81	15.67	15.60	15.57
15%	1	15.46	15.27	15.21	15.18	15.17	15.16
	2	15.92	15.54	15.42	15.36	15.34	15.32
	3	16.39	15.81	15.63	15.55	15.51	15.49
	4	16.87	16.09	15.84	15.74	15.69	15.66
	5	17.35	16.37	16.07	15.93	15.86	15.83
15¼%	1	15.71	15.52	15.46	15.43	15.42	15.41
	2	16.17	15.79	15.67	15.62	15.59	15.58
	3	16.64	16.06	15.88	15.80	15.77	15.74
	4	17.12	16.34	16.10	16.00	15.94	15.92
	5	17.61	16.63	16.32	16.19	16.12	16.09
15½%	1	15.96	15.77	15.71	15.68	15.67	15.66
	2	16.42	16.04	15.92	15.87	15.84	15.83
	3	16.90	16.32	16.14	16.06	16.02	16.00
	4	17.38	16.60	16.36	16.25	16.20	16.17
	5	17.86	16.88	16.58	16.45	16.39	16.35
15¾%	1	16.21	16.02	15.96	15.94	15.92	15.92
	2	16.68	16.29	16.18	16.12	16.10	16.09
	3	17.15	16.57	16.39	16.32	16.28	16.26
	4	17.63	16.85	16.61	16.51	16.46	16.43
	5	18.12	17.14	16.84	16.71	16.65	16.61

ANNUAL PERCENTAGE RATES

INTEREST RATE	DISCOUNT POINTS	5 YEARS	10 YEARS	15 YEARS	20 YEARS	25 YEARS	30 YEARS
16%	1	16.46	16.27	16.21	16.19	16.17	16.17
	2	16.93	16.55	16.43	16.38	16.35	16.34
	3	17.40	16.83	16.65	16.57	16.53	16.51
	4	17.89	17.11	16.87	16.77	16.72	16.69
	5	18.38	17.40	17.10	16.97	16.91	16.88
16¼%	1	16.71	16.52	16.46	16.44	16.43	16.42
	2	17.18	16.80	16.68	16.63	16.61	16.59
	3	17.66	17.08	16.90	16.83	16.79	16.77
	4	18.14	17.37	17.13	17.03	16.98	16.95
	5	18.63	17.66	17.36	17.23	17.17	17.14
16½%	1	16.96	16.77	16.72	16.69	16.68	16.67
	2	17.43	17.05	16.93	16.89	16.86	16.85
	3	17.91	17.33	17.16	17.08	17.05	17.03
	4	18.40	17.62	17.38	17.28	17.24	17.21
	5	18.89	17.91	17.62	17.49	17.43	17.40
16¾%	1	17.21	17.03	16.97	16.94	16.93	16.93
	2	17.69	17.30	17.19	17.14	17.12	17.10
	3	18.16	17.59	17.41	17.34	17.30	17.29
	4	18.65	17.88	17.64	17.54	17.49	17.47
	5	19.14	18.17	17.87	17.75	17.69	17.66
17%	1	17.47	17.28	17.22	17.19	17.18	17.18
	2	17.94	17.56	17.44	17.39	17.37	17.36
	3	18.42	17.84	17.67	17.59	17.56	17.54
	4	18.90	18.13	17.90	17.80	17.75	17.73
	5	19.40	18.43	18.13	18.01	17.95	17.92
17¼%	1	17.72	17.53	17.47	17.45	17.44	17.43
	2	18.19	17.81	17.70	17.65	17.62	17.61
	3	18.67	18.10	17.92	17.85	17.82	17.80
	4	19.16	18.39	18.16	18.06	18.01	17.99
	5	19.66	18.68	18.39	18.27	18.21	18.18
17½%	1	17.97	17.78	17.72	17.70	17.69	17.68
	2	18.44	18.06	17.95	17.90	17.88	17.87
	3	18.92	18.35	18.18	18.11	18.07	18.06
	4	19.41	18.64	18.41	18.32	18.27	18.25
	5	19.91	18.94	18.65	18.53	18.47	18.45
17¾%	1	18.22	18.03	17.97	17.95	17.94	17.93
	2	18.70	18.32	18.20	18.15	18.13	18.12
	3	19.18	18.61	18.43	18.36	18.33	18.31
	4	19.67	18.90	18.67	18.57	18.53	18.51
	5	20.17	19.20	18.91	18.79	18.73	18.71
18%	1	18.47	18.28	18.23	18.20	18.19	18.19
	2	18.95	18.57	18.46	18.41	18.39	18.38
	3	19.43	18.86	18.69	18.62	18.59	18.57
	4	19.92	19.16	18.93	18.83	18.79	18.77
	5	20.42	19.46	19.17	19.05	19.00	18.97
18¼%	1	18.72	18.53	18.48	18.45	18.44	18.44
	2	19.20	18.82	18.71	18.66	18.64	18.63
	3	19.69	19.11	18.94	18.87	18.84	18.83
	4	20.18	19.41	19.18	19.09	19.05	19.03
	5	20.68	19.71	19.43	19.31	19.26	19.23

A-128.5

ANNUAL PERCENTAGE RATES

INTEREST RATE	DISCOUNT POINTS	5 YEARS	10 YEARS	15 YEARS	20 YEARS	25 YEARS	30 YEARS
18½%	1	18.97	18.79	18.73	18.71	18.70	18.69
	2	19.45	19.07	18.96	18.92	18.90	18.89
	3	19.94	19.37	19.20	19.13	19.10	19.08
	4	20.43	19.67	19.44	19.35	19.31	19.29
	5	20.94	19.97	19.69	19.57	19.52	19.49
18¾%	1	19.22	19.04	18.98	18.96	18.95	18.94
	2	19.70	19.33	19.22	19.17	19.15	19.14
	3	20.19	19.62	19.45	19.39	19.36	19.34
	4	20.69	19.92	19.70	19.61	19.57	19.55
	5	21.19	20.23	19.95	19.83	19.78	19.76
19%	1	19.48	19.29	19.23	19.21	19.20	19.20
	2	19.96	19.58	19.47	19.42	19.40	19.40
	3	20.45	19.88	19.71	19.64	19.61	19.60
	4	20.94	20.18	19.96	19.86	19.82	19.81
	5	21.45	20.49	20.20	20.09	20.04	20.02
19¼%	1	19.73	19.54	19.48	19.46	19.45	19.45
	2	20.21	19.83	19.72	19.68	19.66	19.65
	3	20.70	20.13	19.97	19.90	19.87	19.86
	4	21.20	20.44	20.21	20.12	20.08	20.07
	5	21.70	20.75	20.46	20.35	20.30	20.28
19½%	1	19.98	19.79	19.74	19.71	19.70	19.70
	2	20.46	20.09	19.98	19.93	19.91	19.90
	3	20.95	20.39	20.22	20.16	20.13	20.11
	4	21.45	20.69	20.47	20.38	20.34	20.33
	5	21.96	21.00	20.72	20.61	20.56	20.54
19¾%	1	20.23	20.04	19.99	19.97	19.96	19.95
	2	20.71	20.34	20.23	20.19	20.17	20.16
	3	21.21	20.64	20.48	20.41	20.38	20.37
	4	21.71	20.95	20.73	20.64	20.60	20.59
	5	22.22	21.26	20.98	20.87	20.83	20.81
20%	1	20.48	20.29	20.24	20.22	20.21	20.21
	2	20.97	20.59	20.48	20.44	20.42	20.41
	3	21.46	20.90	20.73	20.67	20.64	20.63
	4	21.96	21.20	20.98	20.90	20.86	20.85
	5	22.47	21.52	21.24	21.13	21.09	21.07
20¼%	1	20.73	20.55	20.49	20.47	20.46	20.46
	2	21.22	20.85	20.74	20.70	20.68	20.67
	3	21.71	21.15	20.99	20.92	20.90	20.89
	4	22.22	21.46	21.24	21.16	21.12	21.11
	5	22.73	21.78	21.50	21.39	21.35	21.33
20½%	1	20.98	20.80	20.74	20.72	20.71	20.71
	2	21.47	21.10	20.99	20.95	20.93	20.92
	3	21.97	21.41	21.24	21.18	21.15	21.14
	4	22.47	21.72	21.50	21.42	21.38	21.37
	5	22.99	22.03	21.76	21.66	21.61	21.59
20¾%	1	21.23	21.05	21.00	20.97	20.97	20.96
	2	21.72	21.35	21.24	21.20	21.19	21.18
	3	22.22	21.66	21.50	21.44	21.41	21.40
	4	22.73	21.97	21.76	21.67	21.64	21.62
	5	23.24	22.29	22.02	21.92	21.87	21.85

FNMA WEEKLY, BIWEEKLY PAYMENT PROGRAM
TO AMORTIZE A $1,000 LOAN

INTEREST RATE	WEEKLY PAYMENT	TERM IN YR	BIWEEKLY PAYMENT	TERM IN YR
6.00%	1.498877	24.50	2.997753	24.54
6.25%	1.539293	24.31	3.078587	24.35
6.50%	1.580170	24.12	3.160341	24.15
6.75%	1.621495	23.90	3.242991	23.92
7.00%	1.663256	23.69	3.326513	23.73
7.25%	1.705441	23.48	3.410882	23.50
7.50%	1.748037	23.27	3.496073	23.31
7.75%	1.791031	23.06	3.582062	23.08
8.00%	1.834412	22.83	3.668823	22.85
8.25%	1.878167	22.60	3.756334	22.62
8.50%	1.922284	22.37	3.844568	22.38
8.75%	1.966751	22.13	3.933503	22.15
9.00%	2.011557	21.90	4.023114	21.92
9.25%	2.056689	21.67	4.113378	21.69
9.50%	2.102136	21.42	4.204272	21.46
9.75%	2.147886	21.19	4.295773	21.23
10.00%	2.193929	20.94	4.387858	20.96
10.25%	2.240253	20.71	4.480507	20.73
10.50%	2.286848	20.46	4.573697	20.50
10.75%	2.333704	20.21	4.667407	20.23
11.00%	2.380809	19.98	4.761617	20.00
11.25%	2.428154	19.73	4.856307	19.77
11.50%	2.475729	19.48	4.951458	19.54
11.75%	2.523525	19.25	5.047049	19.27
12.00%	2.571532	19.00	5.143063	19.04
12.25%	2.619741	18.77	5.239483	18.81
12.50%	2.668145	18.52	5.336289	18.58
12.75%	2.716733	18.29	5.433467	18.31
13.00%	2.765499	18.06	5.530998	18.08
13.25%	2.814434	17.83	5.628868	17.85
13.50%	2.863531	17.60	5.727061	17.62
13.75%	2.912782	17.37	5.825563	17.38
14.00%	2.962180	17.15	5.924359	17.19
14.25%	3.011718	16.92	6.023436	16.96
14.50%	3.061390	16.71	6.122780	16.73
14.75%	3.111190	16.48	6.222379	16.54
15.00%	3.161110	16.27	6.322221	16.31
15.25%	3.211147	16.06	6.422293	16.12
15.50%	3.261293	15.87	6.522585	15.88
15.75%	3.311543	15.65	6.623086	15.69
16.00%	3.361893	15.46	6.723785	15.50
16.25%	3.412337	15.27	6.824674	15.31
16.50%	3.462870	15.08	6.925741	15.12
16.75%	3.513489	14.88	7.026978	14.92

FOR **OTHER RATES AND TERMS** *SEE PAGE A-1.*

CONSTANT ANNUAL PERCENT
EXPRESSING THE SUM OF 12 EQUAL MONTHLY PAYMENTS
NEEDED TO AMORTIZE A PRINCIPAL AMOUNT

INTEREST →	8%	8¼%	8½%	8¾%	9%	9¼%	9½%	9¾%
YEARS								
0.5	204.71	204.87	205.00	205.16	205.29	205.45	205.58	205.74
1.0	104.39	104.54	104.67	104.81	104.95	105.09	105.22	105.37
1.5	70.97	71.11	71.25	71.39	71.52	71.66	71.79	71.94
2.0	54.28	54.42	54.55	54.69	54.82	54.96	55.10	55.24
2.5	44.27	44.41	44.54	44.68	44.82	44.96	45.10	45.24
3.0	37.61	37.75	37.88	38.02	38.16	38.30	38.44	38.58
3.5	32.85	33.00	33.13	33.28	33.41	33.56	33.70	33.84
4.0	29.30	29.44	29.58	29.72	29.86	30.01	30.15	30.29
4.5	26.54	26.68	26.82	26.97	27.11	27.25	27.40	27.54
5.0	24.33	24.48	24.62	24.77	24.91	25.06	25.20	25.35
5.5	22.54	22.68	22.83	22.97	23.12	23.27	23.41	23.56
6.0	21.04	21.19	21.33	21.48	21.63	21.78	21.93	22.08
6.5	19.78	19.93	20.08	20.23	20.38	20.53	20.68	20.83
7.0	18.70	18.86	19.00	19.16	19.31	19.46	19.61	19.77
7.5	17.77	17.93	18.08	18.23	18.38	18.54	18.69	18.85
8.0	16.96	17.12	17.27	17.43	17.58	17.74	17.89	18.05
8.5	16.25	16.41	16.56	16.72	16.88	17.03	17.19	17.35
9.0	15.62	15.78	15.94	16.09	16.25	16.41	16.57	16.73
9.5	15.06	15.22	15.38	15.54	15.70	15.86	16.02	16.18
10.0	14.56	14.72	14.88	15.04	15.20	15.36	15.53	15.69
10.5	14.11	14.27	14.43	14.59	14.76	14.92	15.09	15.25
11.0	13.70	13.86	14.02	14.19	14.35	14.52	14.69	14.86
11.5	13.33	13.49	13.66	13.82	13.99	14.16	14.33	14.50
12.0	12.99	13.16	13.32	13.49	13.66	13.83	14.00	14.17
12.5	12.68	12.85	13.02	13.18	13.35	13.53	13.70	13.87
13.0	12.40	12.57	12.73	12.91	13.08	13.25	13.42	13.60
13.5	12.14	12.31	12.48	12.65	12.82	13.00	13.17	13.35
14.0	11.90	12.07	12.24	12.41	12.59	12.76	12.94	13.12
14.5	11.67	11.85	12.02	12.20	12.37	12.55	12.73	12.91
15.0	11.47	11.64	11.82	11.99	12.17	12.35	12.53	12.71
15.5	11.28	11.45	11.63	11.81	11.99	12.17	12.35	12.53
16.0	11.10	11.28	11.45	11.63	11.81	12.00	12.18	12.37
16.5	10.93	11.11	11.29	11.47	11.65	11.84	12.02	12.21
17.0	10.78	10.96	11.14	11.32	11.51	11.69	11.88	12.07
17.5	10.64	10.82	11.00	11.18	11.37	11.55	11.74	11.93
18.0	10.50	10.68	10.87	11.05	11.24	11.43	11.62	11.81
18.5	10.37	10.56	10.74	10.93	11.12	11.31	11.50	11.69
19.0	10.25	10.44	10.63	10.81	11.00	11.19	11.39	11.58
19.5	10.14	10.33	10.52	10.71	10.90	11.09	11.28	11.48
20.0	10.04	10.23	10.41	10.60	10.80	10.99	11.19	11.38
20.5	9.94	10.13	10.32	10.51	10.70	10.90	11.09	11.29
21.0	9.85	10.04	10.23	10.42	10.62	10.81	11.01	11.21
21.5	9.76	9.95	10.14	10.34	10.53	10.73	10.93	11.13
22.0	9.67	9.87	10.06	10.26	10.45	10.65	10.85	11.06
22.5	9.60	9.79	9.99	10.18	10.38	10.58	10.78	10.99
23.0	9.52	9.72	9.91	10.11	10.31	10.51	10.72	10.92
23.5	9.45	9.65	9.85	10.05	10.25	10.45	10.65	10.86
24.0	9.38	9.58	9.78	9.98	10.18	10.39	10.59	10.80
24.5	9.32	9.52	9.72	9.92	10.13	10.33	10.54	10.75
25.0	9.26	9.46	9.66	9.87	10.07	10.28	10.48	10.69
25.5	9.21	9.41	9.61	9.81	10.02	10.23	10.43	10.65
26.0	9.15	9.35	9.56	9.76	9.97	10.18	10.39	10.60
26.5	9.10	9.30	9.51	9.71	9.92	10.13	10.34	10.56
27.0	9.05	9.26	9.46	9.67	9.88	10.09	10.30	10.51
27.5	9.01	9.21	9.42	9.63	9.84	10.05	10.26	10.48
28.0	8.96	9.17	9.38	9.58	9.80	10.01	10.22	10.44
28.5	8.92	9.13	9.34	9.55	9.76	9.97	10.19	10.40
29.0	8.88	9.09	9.30	9.51	9.72	9.94	10.15	10.37
29.5	8.84	9.05	9.26	9.47	9.69	9.90	10.12	10.34
30.0	8.81	9.02	9.23	9.44	9.66	9.87	10.09	10.31
35.0	8.52	8.74	8.96	9.18	9.41	9.63	9.86	10.09
40.0	8.34	8.57	8.80	9.03	9.26	9.49	9.72	9.95

EXAMPLES *ON PAGES A-382 TO A-397*

CONSTANT ANNUAL PERCENT
EXPRESSING THE SUM OF 12 EQUAL MONTHLY PAYMENTS
NEEDED TO AMORTIZE A PRINCIPAL AMOUNT

INTEREST →	10%	10¼%	10½%	10¾%	11%	11¼%	11½%	11¾%
YEARS								
0.5	205.88	206.03	206.17	206.33	206.49	206.62	206.78	206.92
1.0	105.50	105.65	105.78	105.92	106.07	106.20	106.35	106.48
1.5	72.07	72.21	72.35	72.49	72.63	72.76	72.91	73.04
2.0	55.37	55.52	55.65	55.79	55.93	56.07	56.21	56.35
2.5	45.37	45.52	45.65	45.80	45.94	46.08	46.22	46.36
3.0	38.72	38.86	39.00	39.15	39.29	39.43	39.57	39.72
3.5	33.98	34.12	34.27	34.41	34.56	34.70	34.84	34.99
4.0	30.44	30.58	30.72	30.87	31.02	31.16	31.31	31.45
4.5	27.69	27.83	27.98	28.13	28.28	28.42	28.57	28.72
5.0	25.50	25.65	25.79	25.94	26.09	26.24	26.39	26.54
5.5	23.71	23.86	24.01	24.16	24.32	24.47	24.62	24.77
6.0	22.23	22.38	22.53	22.69	22.84	23.00	23.15	23.30
6.5	20.98	21.14	21.29	21.45	21.60	21.76	21.92	22.07
7.0	19.92	20.08	20.23	20.39	20.55	20.71	20.86	21.02
7.5	19.01	19.16	19.32	19.48	19.64	19.80	19.96	20.12
8.0	18.21	18.37	18.53	18.69	18.85	19.01	19.18	19.34
8.5	17.51	17.67	17.83	18.00	18.16	18.32	18.49	18.66
9.0	16.89	17.06	17.22	17.39	17.55	17.72	17.89	18.05
9.5	16.35	16.51	16.68	16.84	17.01	17.18	17.35	17.52
10.0	15.86	16.03	16.19	16.36	16.53	16.70	16.87	17.04
10.5	15.42	15.59	15.76	15.93	16.10	16.27	16.44	16.62
11.0	15.02	15.19	15.37	15.54	15.71	15.89	16.06	16.24
11.5	14.67	14.84	15.01	15.19	15.36	15.54	15.71	15.89
12.0	14.34	14.52	14.69	14.87	15.04	15.22	15.40	15.58
12.5	14.04	14.22	14.40	14.58	14.75	14.93	15.12	15.30
13.0	13.77	13.95	14.13	14.31	14.49	14.67	14.86	15.04
13.5	13.53	13.71	13.89	14.07	14.25	14.43	14.62	14.80
14.0	13.30	13.48	13.66	13.84	14.03	14.21	14.40	14.59
14.5	13.09	13.27	13.45	13.64	13.83	14.01	14.20	14.39
15.0	12.90	13.08	13.26	13.45	13.64	13.83	14.02	14.21
15.5	12.72	12.90	13.09	13.28	13.47	13.66	13.85	14.04
16.0	12.55	12.74	12.93	13.12	13.31	13.50	13.69	13.89
16.5	12.40	12.59	12.78	12.97	13.16	13.36	13.55	13.75
17.0	12.25	12.45	12.64	12.83	13.03	13.22	13.42	13.62
17.5	12.12	12.31	12.51	12.70	12.90	13.10	13.29	13.49
18.0	12.00	12.19	12.39	12.58	12.78	12.98	13.18	13.38
18.5	11.88	12.08	12.27	12.47	12.67	12.87	13.07	13.28
19.0	11.78	11.97	12.17	12.37	12.57	12.77	12.97	13.18
19.5	11.67	11.87	12.07	12.27	12.48	12.68	12.88	13.09
20.0	11.58	11.78	11.98	12.18	12.39	12.59	12.80	13.00
20.5	11.49	11.69	11.90	12.10	12.30	12.51	12.72	12.93
21.0	11.41	11.61	11.82	12.02	12.23	12.43	12.64	12.85
21.5	11.33	11.54	11.74	11.95	12.15	12.36	12.57	12.78
22.0	11.26	11.46	11.67	11.88	12.09	12.30	12.51	12.72
22.5	11.19	11.40	11.60	11.81	12.02	12.24	12.45	12.66
23.0	11.13	11.33	11.54	11.75	11.96	12.18	12.39	12.61
23.5	11.07	11.27	11.48	11.70	11.91	12.12	12.34	12.55
24.0	11.01	11.22	11.43	11.64	11.86	12.07	12.29	12.51
24.5	10.96	11.17	11.38	11.59	11.81	12.02	12.24	12.46
25.0	10.90	11.12	11.33	11.55	11.76	11.98	12.20	12.42
25.5	10.86	11.07	11.28	11.50	11.72	11.94	12.16	12.38
26.0	10.81	11.03	11.24	11.46	11.68	11.90	12.12	12.34
26.5	10.77	10.98	11.20	11.42	11.64	11.86	12.08	12.31
27.0	10.73	10.95	11.16	11.38	11.60	11.83	12.05	12.27
27.5	10.69	10.91	11.13	11.35	11.57	11.79	12.02	12.24
28.0	10.66	10.87	11.09	11.32	11.54	11.76	11.99	12.21
28.5	10.62	10.84	11.06	11.28	11.51	11.73	11.96	12.19
29.0	10.59	10.81	11.03	11.26	11.48	11.71	11.93	12.16
29.5	10.56	10.78	11.00	11.23	11.45	11.68	11.91	12.14
30.0	10.53	10.75	10.98	11.20	11.43	11.66	11.88	12.11
35.0	10.32	10.55	10.78	11.01	11.24	11.48	11.71	11.95
40.0	10.19	10.43	10.66	10.90	11.14	11.38	11.62	11.86

EXAMPLES *ON PAGES A-382 TO A-397*

CONSTANT ANNUAL PERCENT

EXPRESSING THE SUM OF 12 EQUAL MONTHLY PAYMENTS
NEEDED TO AMORTIZE A PRINCIPAL AMOUNT

INTEREST →	12%	12¼%	12½%	12¾%	13%	13¼%	13½%	13¾%
YEARS								
0.5	207.07	207.21	207.37	207.51	207.66	207.80	207.96	208.11
1.0	106.63	106.76	106.91	107.04	107.19	107.32	107.47	107.61
1.5	73.18	73.32	73.46	73.60	73.74	73.88	74.02	74.16
2.0	56.49	56.63	56.77	56.91	57.05	57.19	57.33	57.48
2.5	46.50	46.64	46.78	46.92	47.07	47.21	47.35	47.50
3.0	39.86	40.00	40.15	40.29	40.43	40.58	40.72	40.87
3.5	35.13	35.28	35.42	35.57	35.72	35.86	36.01	36.16
4.0	31.60	31.75	31.90	32.04	32.19	32.34	32.49	32.64
4.5	28.87	29.02	29.17	29.32	29.47	29.62	29.77	29.93
5.0	26.68	26.85	27.00	27.15	27.30	27.46	27.61	27.77
5.5	24.93	25.08	25.23	25.39	25.54	25.70	25.86	26.02
6.0	23.46	23.62	23.77	23.93	24.09	24.25	24.41	24.57
6.5	22.23	22.39	22.55	22.71	22.87	23.03	23.19	23.35
7.0	21.18	21.34	21.51	21.67	21.83	21.99	22.16	22.32
7.5	20.28	20.45	20.61	20.77	20.94	21.11	21.27	21.44
8.0	19.50	19.67	19.84	20.00	20.17	20.34	20.51	20.68
8.5	18.82	18.99	19.16	19.33	19.50	19.67	19.84	20.01
9.0	18.22	18.39	18.56	18.73	18.90	19.08	19.25	19.43
9.5	17.69	17.86	18.03	18.21	18.38	18.56	18.73	18.91
10.0	17.22	17.39	17.57	17.74	17.92	18.09	18.27	18.45
10.5	16.79	16.97	17.15	17.32	17.50	17.68	17.86	18.04
11.0	16.41	16.59	16.77	16.95	17.13	17.31	17.50	17.68
11.5	16.07	16.25	16.43	16.61	16.80	16.98	17.17	17.35
12.0	15.76	15.94	16.13	16.31	16.50	16.68	16.87	17.06
12.5	15.48	15.66	15.85	16.04	16.22	16.41	16.60	16.79
13.0	15.22	15.41	15.60	15.79	15.97	16.16	16.36	16.55
13.5	14.99	15.18	15.37	15.56	15.75	15.94	16.13	16.33
14.0	14.78	14.97	15.16	15.35	15.54	15.74	15.93	16.13
14.5	14.58	14.77	14.97	15.16	15.36	15.55	15.75	15.95
15.0	14.40	14.60	14.79	14.99	15.18	15.38	15.58	15.78
15.5	14.24	14.43	14.63	14.83	15.03	15.22	15.43	15.63
16.0	14.09	14.28	14.48	14.68	14.88	15.08	15.28	15.49
16.5	13.94	14.14	14.34	14.54	14.75	14.95	15.15	15.36
17.0	13.81	14.02	14.22	14.42	14.62	14.83	15.03	15.24
17.5	13.69	13.90	14.10	14.30	14.51	14.72	14.92	15.13
18.0	13.58	13.79	13.99	14.20	14.41	14.61	14.82	15.03
18.5	13.48	13.69	13.89	14.10	14.31	14.52	14.73	14.94
19.0	13.38	13.59	13.80	14.01	14.22	14.43	14.64	14.86
19.5	13.30	13.50	13.71	13.92	14.14	14.35	14.56	14.78
20.0	13.21	13.42	13.63	13.85	14.06	14.27	14.49	14.71
20.5	13.14	13.35	13.56	13.77	13.99	14.20	14.42	14.64
21.0	13.06	13.28	13.49	13.71	13.92	14.14	14.36	14.58
21.5	13.00	13.21	13.43	13.64	13.86	14.08	14.30	14.52
22.0	12.94	13.15	13.37	13.58	13.80	14.02	14.24	14.46
22.5	12.88	13.09	13.31	13.53	13.75	13.97	14.19	14.42
23.0	12.82	13.04	13.26	13.48	13.70	13.92	14.15	14.37
23.5	12.77	12.99	13.21	13.43	13.65	13.88	14.10	14.33
24.0	12.72	12.94	13.17	13.39	13.61	13.84	14.06	14.29
24.5	12.68	12.90	13.12	13.35	13.57	13.80	14.02	14.25
25.0	12.64	12.86	13.08	13.31	13.53	13.76	13.99	14.22
25.5	12.60	12.82	13.05	13.27	13.50	13.73	13.96	14.18
26.0	12.56	12.79	13.01	13.24	13.47	13.70	13.92	14.15
26.5	12.53	12.75	12.98	13.21	13.44	13.67	13.90	14.13
27.0	12.50	12.72	12.95	13.18	13.41	13.64	13.87	14.10
27.5	12.47	12.69	12.92	13.15	13.38	13.61	13.85	14.08
28.0	12.44	12.67	12.90	13.13	13.36	13.59	13.82	14.06
28.5	12.41	12.64	12.87	13.10	13.33	13.57	13.80	14.04
29.0	12.39	12.62	12.85	13.08	13.31	13.55	13.78	14.02
29.5	12.37	12.60	12.83	13.06	13.29	13.53	13.76	14.00
30.0	12.34	12.57	12.81	13.04	13.27	13.51	13.74	13.98
35.0	12.19	12.42	12.66	12.90	13.14	13.38	13.62	13.87
40.0	12.10	12.34	12.59	12.83	13.07	13.32	13.56	13.81

EXAMPLES *ON PAGES A-382 TO A-397*

INTEREST →	14%	14¼%	14½%	14¾%	15%	15¼%	15½%	15¾%
YEARS								
0.5	208.25	208.41	208.55	208.70	208.84	209.00	209.14	209.30
1.0	107.75	107.89	108.03	108.17	108.31	108.46	108.59	108.74
1.5	74.30	74.44	74.58	74.72	74.86	75.01	75.14	75.29
2.0	57.62	57.76	57.90	58.04	58.18	58.33	58.47	58.61
2.5	47.64	47.78	47.93	48.07	48.21	48.36	48.50	48.65
3.0	41.01	41.16	41.31	41.45	41.60	41.75	41.89	42.04
3.5	36.30	36.45	36.60	36.75	36.90	37.05	37.20	37.35
4.0	32.79	32.94	33.09	33.25	33.40	33.55	33.70	33.86
4.5	30.08	30.23	30.38	30.54	30.69	30.85	31.00	31.16
5.0	27.92	28.08	28.23	28.39	28.55	28.71	28.86	29.02
5.5	26.17	26.33	26.49	26.65	26.81	26.97	27.13	27.29
6.0	24.73	24.89	25.05	25.21	25.37	25.54	25.70	25.87
6.5	23.52	23.68	23.84	24.01	24.17	24.34	24.51	24.67
7.0	22.49	22.65	22.82	22.99	23.16	23.33	23.49	23.66
7.5	21.61	21.78	21.95	22.12	22.29	22.46	22.63	22.80
8.0	20.85	21.02	21.19	21.36	21.53	21.71	21.88	22.06
8.5	20.18	20.36	20.53	20.71	20.88	21.06	21.24	21.41
9.0	19.60	19.78	19.95	20.13	20.31	20.49	20.67	20.85
9.5	19.09	19.27	19.45	19.63	19.81	19.99	20.17	20.35
10.0	18.63	18.81	18.99	19.18	19.36	19.54	19.73	19.92
10.5	18.23	18.41	18.59	18.78	18.96	19.15	19.34	19.53
11.0	17.86	18.05	18.24	18.42	18.61	18.80	18.99	19.18
11.5	17.54	17.73	17.91	18.10	18.29	18.49	18.68	18.87
12.0	17.25	17.44	17.63	17.82	18.01	18.20	18.40	18.59
12.5	16.98	17.17	17.37	17.56	17.75	17.95	18.15	18.34
13.0	16.74	16.94	17.13	17.33	17.52	17.72	17.92	18.12
13.5	16.52	16.72	16.92	17.12	17.31	17.51	17.72	17.92
14.0	16.33	16.52	16.72	16.92	17.12	17.33	17.53	17.73
14.5	16.15	16.35	16.55	16.75	16.95	17.16	17.36	17.57
15.0	15.98	16.18	16.39	16.59	16.80	17.00	17.21	17.42
15.5	15.83	16.03	16.24	16.45	16.65	16.86	17.07	17.28
16.0	15.69	15.90	16.10	16.31	16.52	16.73	16.94	17.15
16.5	15.57	15.77	15.98	16.19	16.40	16.61	16.83	17.04
17.0	15.45	15.66	15.87	16.08	16.29	16.51	16.72	16.93
17.5	15.34	15.55	15.77	15.98	16.19	16.41	16.62	16.84
18.0	15.24	15.46	15.67	15.89	16.10	16.32	16.53	16.75
18.5	15.15	15.37	15.58	15.80	16.02	16.23	16.45	16.67
19.0	15.07	15.29	15.50	15.72	15.94	16.16	16.38	16.60
19.5	14.99	15.21	15.43	15.65	15.87	16.09	16.31	16.53
20.0	14.92	15.14	15.36	15.58	15.80	16.02	16.25	16.47
20.5	14.86	15.08	15.30	15.52	15.74	15.96	16.19	16.41
21.0	14.80	15.02	15.24	15.46	15.69	15.91	16.14	16.36
21.5	14.74	14.96	15.18	15.41	15.63	15.86	16.09	16.31
22.0	14.69	14.91	15.14	15.36	15.59	15.81	16.04	16.27
22.5	14.64	14.86	15.09	15.32	15.54	15.77	16.00	16.23
23.0	14.59	14.82	15.05	15.27	15.50	15.73	15.96	16.19
23.5	14.55	14.78	15.01	15.24	15.47	15.70	15.93	16.16
24.0	14.51	14.74	14.97	15.20	15.43	15.66	15.89	16.13
24.5	14.48	14.71	14.94	15.17	15.40	15.63	15.86	16.10
25.0	14.45	14.68	14.91	15.14	15.37	15.60	15.84	16.07
25.5	14.41	14.65	14.88	15.11	15.34	15.58	15.81	16.05
26.0	14.39	14.62	14.85	15.08	15.32	15.55	15.79	16.02
26.5	14.36	14.59	14.83	15.06	15.29	15.53	15.77	16.00
27.0	14.33	14.57	14.80	15.04	15.27	15.51	15.75	15.98
27.5	14.31	14.55	14.78	15.02	15.25	15.49	15.73	15.97
28.0	14.29	14.53	14.76	15.00	15.23	15.47	15.71	15.95
28.5	14.27	14.51	14.74	14.98	15.22	15.46	15.69	15.93
29.0	14.25	14.49	14.73	14.96	15.20	15.44	15.68	15.92
29.5	14.23	14.47	14.71	14.95	15.19	15.43	15.67	15.91
30.0	14.22	14.46	14.69	14.93	15.17	15.41	15.65	15.90
35.0	14.11	14.35	14.59	14.84	15.08	15.33	15.57	15.82
40.0	14.05	14.30	14.55	14.79	15.04	15.29	15.53	15.78

EXAMPLES *ON PAGES A-382 TO A-397*

CONSTANT ANNUAL PERCENT
EXPRESSING THE SUM OF 12 EQUAL MONTHLY PAYMENTS
NEEDED TO AMORTIZE A PRINCIPAL AMOUNT

INTEREST →	16%	17%	18%	19%	20%	21%	22%	23%
YEARS								
0.5	209.44	210.04	210.64	211.23	211.83	212.43	213.04	213.64
1.0	108.88	109.45	110.02	110.59	111.16	111.74	112.32	112.90
1.5	75.43	76.00	76.57	77.14	77.72	78.29	78.88	79.46
2.0	58.76	59.33	59.91	60.49	61.08	61.66	62.26	62.85
2.5	48.79	49.38	49.97	50.56	51.16	51.76	52.36	52.97
3.0	42.19	42.79	43.38	43.99	44.60	45.21	45.83	46.45
3.5	37.50	38.11	38.72	39.33	39.96	40.58	41.22	41.86
4.0	34.01	34.63	35.25	35.88	36.52	37.16	37.81	38.46
4.5	31.32	31.95	32.58	33.23	33.88	34.53	35.20	35.87
5.0	29.18	29.82	30.47	31.13	31.79	32.46	33.14	33.83
5.5	27.45	28.11	28.77	29.44	30.12	30.80	31.50	32.20
6.0	26.03	26.70	27.37	28.05	28.74	29.44	30.15	30.87
6.5	24.84	25.52	26.20	26.90	27.60	28.32	29.04	29.77
7.0	23.83	24.52	25.22	25.93	26.65	27.37	28.11	28.86
7.5	22.98	23.68	24.39	25.11	25.84	26.58	27.33	28.09
8.0	22.23	22.95	23.67	24.40	25.14	25.90	26.66	27.43
8.5	21.59	22.31	23.05	23.79	24.55	25.31	26.09	26.88
9.0	21.03	21.76	22.51	23.26	24.03	24.81	25.60	26.40
9.5	20.54	21.28	22.04	22.80	23.58	24.37	25.17	25.98
10.0	20.10	20.86	21.62	22.40	23.19	23.99	24.80	25.63
10.5	19.72	20.48	21.26	22.05	22.85	23.66	24.48	25.31
11.0	19.37	20.15	20.93	21.73	22.54	23.37	24.20	25.04
11.5	19.06	19.85	20.65	21.46	22.28	23.11	23.95	24.81
12.0	18.79	19.58	20.39	21.21	22.04	22.88	23.73	24.60
12.5	18.54	19.35	20.16	20.99	21.83	22.68	23.54	24.42
13.0	18.32	19.13	19.96	20.79	21.64	22.50	23.37	24.25
13.5	18.12	18.94	19.77	20.62	21.48	22.34	23.22	24.11
14.0	17.94	18.77	19.61	20.46	21.33	22.20	23.09	23.99
14.5	17.77	18.61	19.46	20.32	21.19	22.08	22.97	23.88
15.0	17.62	18.47	19.33	20.19	21.08	21.97	22.87	23.78
15.5	17.49	18.34	19.20	20.08	20.97	21.87	22.78	23.69
16.0	17.37	18.22	19.10	19.98	20.87	21.78	22.69	23.62
16.5	17.25	18.12	19.00	19.89	20.79	21.70	22.62	23.55
17.0	17.15	18.02	18.91	19.80	20.71	21.63	22.55	23.49
17.5	17.06	17.93	18.83	19.73	20.64	21.56	22.50	23.43
18.0	16.97	17.86	18.75	19.66	20.58	21.51	22.44	23.39
18.5	16.89	17.78	18.69	19.60	20.52	21.46	22.40	23.34
19.0	16.82	17.72	18.63	19.54	20.47	21.41	22.36	23.31
19.5	16.76	17.66	18.57	19.49	20.43	21.37	22.32	23.27
20.0	16.70	17.60	18.52	19.45	20.39	21.33	22.28	23.24
20.5	16.64	17.55	18.47	19.41	20.35	21.30	22.26	23.22
21.0	16.59	17.51	18.43	19.37	20.32	21.27	22.23	23.19
21.5	16.54	17.46	18.39	19.34	20.29	21.24	22.20	23.17
22.0	16.50	17.43	18.36	19.31	20.26	21.22	22.18	23.15
22.5	16.46	17.39	18.33	19.28	20.23	21.20	22.16	23.14
23.0	16.42	17.36	18.30	19.25	20.21	21.18	22.15	23.12
23.5	16.39	17.33	18.27	19.23	20.19	21.16	22.13	23.11
24.0	16.36	17.30	18.25	19.21	20.17	21.14	22.12	23.10
24.5	16.33	17.28	18.23	19.19	20.16	21.13	22.11	23.09
25.0	16.31	17.25	18.21	19.17	20.14	21.12	22.09	23.08
25.5	16.28	17.23	18.19	19.16	20.13	21.10	22.09	23.07
26.0	16.26	17.21	18.17	19.14	20.12	21.09	22.08	23.06
26.5	16.24	17.20	18.16	19.13	20.10	21.08	22.07	23.06
27.0	16.22	17.18	18.15	19.12	20.09	21.08	22.06	23.05
27.5	16.20	17.17	18.13	19.11	20.09	21.07	22.05	23.04
28.0	16.19	17.15	18.12	19.10	20.08	21.06	22.05	23.04
28.5	16.17	17.14	18.11	19.09	20.07	21.06	22.04	23.03
29.0	16.16	17.13	18.10	19.08	20.06	21.05	22.04	23.03
29.5	16.15	17.12	18.09	19.07	20.06	21.05	22.04	23.03
30.0	16.14	17.11	18.09	19.07	20.05	21.04	22.03	23.02
35.0	16.06	17.05	18.03	19.03	20.02	21.01	22.01	23.01
40.0	16.03	17.02	18.01	19.01	20.01	21.01	22.00	23.00

EXAMPLES *ON PAGES A-382 TO A-397*

INTEREST →	24%	25%	26%	27%	28%	29%	30%	35%
YEARS								
0.5	214.24	214.84	215.44	216.05	216.65	217.26	217.86	220.91
1.0	113.47	114.05	114.64	115.22	115.81	116.40	116.99	119.96
1.5	80.04	80.63	81.22	81.82	82.41	83.01	83.61	86.64
2.0	63.45	64.05	64.65	65.26	65.87	66.48	67.10	70.22
2.5	53.58	54.20	54.82	55.44	56.07	56.70	57.33	60.57
3.0	47.08	47.71	48.35	48.99	49.64	50.29	50.94	54.28
3.5	42.50	43.15	43.80	44.47	45.13	45.80	46.47	49.93
4.0	39.12	39.79	40.46	41.14	41.82	42.51	43.21	46.77
4.5	36.54	37.23	37.92	38.61	39.31	40.02	40.74	44.40
5.0	34.52	35.22	35.93	36.64	37.36	38.09	38.82	42.59
5.5	32.91	33.62	34.35	35.08	35.82	36.56	37.31	41.17
6.0	31.59	32.32	33.06	33.81	34.57	35.33	36.10	40.05
6.5	30.51	31.26	32.02	32.78	33.55	34.33	35.12	39.16
7.0	29.61	30.37	31.15	31.93	32.71	33.51	34.31	38.44
7.5	28.86	29.63	30.42	31.21	32.02	32.83	33.65	37.85
8.0	28.22	29.01	29.81	30.62	31.43	32.26	33.09	37.37
8.5	27.67	28.48	29.29	30.11	30.94	31.78	32.63	36.97
9.0	27.21	28.02	28.85	29.68	30.53	31.38	32.24	36.64
9.5	26.80	27.63	28.47	29.32	30.18	31.04	31.91	36.37
10.0	26.46	27.30	28.15	29.01	29.88	30.75	31.63	36.15
10.5	26.16	27.01	27.87	28.74	29.62	30.51	31.40	35.96
11.0	25.90	26.76	27.63	28.51	29.40	30.30	31.20	35.81
11.5	25.67	26.54	27.42	28.31	29.21	30.12	31.03	35.68
12.0	25.47	26.35	27.24	28.14	29.05	29.96	30.88	35.57
12.5	25.30	26.19	27.09	27.99	28.91	29.83	30.76	35.48
13.0	25.15	26.04	26.95	27.87	28.79	29.72	30.65	35.40
13.5	25.01	25.92	26.83	27.75	28.68	29.62	30.56	35.34
14.0	24.89	25.81	26.73	27.66	28.59	29.53	30.48	35.28
14.5	24.79	25.71	26.64	27.57	28.52	29.46	30.41	35.24
15.0	24.70	25.63	26.56	27.50	28.45	29.40	30.36	35.20
15.5	24.62	25.55	26.49	27.44	28.39	29.35	30.31	35.17
16.0	24.55	25.49	26.43	27.38	28.34	29.30	30.26	35.14
16.5	24.49	25.43	26.38	27.33	28.29	29.26	30.23	35.12
17.0	24.43	25.38	26.33	27.29	28.26	29.22	30.20	35.10
17.5	24.38	25.33	26.29	27.25	28.22	29.19	30.17	35.08
18.0	24.34	25.29	26.26	27.22	28.19	29.17	30.15	35.07
18.5	24.30	25.26	26.22	27.19	28.17	29.15	30.13	35.06
19.0	24.27	25.23	26.20	27.17	28.15	29.13	30.11	35.05
19.5	24.24	25.20	26.17	27.15	28.13	29.11	30.09	35.04
20.0	24.21	25.18	26.15	27.13	28.11	29.09	30.08	35.04
20.5	24.19	25.16	26.13	27.11	28.10	29.08	30.07	35.03
21.0	24.16	25.14	26.12	27.10	28.08	29.07	30.06	35.02
21.5	24.15	25.12	26.10	27.09	28.07	29.06	30.05	35.02
22.0	24.13	25.11	26.09	27.08	28.06	29.05	30.04	35.02
22.5	24.11	25.10	26.08	27.07	28.06	29.05	30.04	35.01
23.0	24.10	25.08	26.07	27.06	28.05	29.04	30.03	35.01
23.5	24.09	25.07	26.06	27.05	28.04	29.03	30.03	35.01
24.0	24.08	25.07	26.05	27.04	28.04	29.03	30.02	35.01
24.5	24.07	25.06	26.05	27.04	28.03	29.03	30.02	35.01
25.0	24.06	25.05	26.04	27.03	28.03	29.02	30.02	35.01
25.5	24.06	25.05	26.04	27.03	28.02	29.02	30.02	35.01
26.0	24.05	25.04	26.03	27.03	28.02	29.02	30.01	35.00
26.5	24.04	25.04	26.03	27.02	28.02	29.01	30.01	35.00
27.0	24.04	25.03	26.03	27.02	28.02	29.01	30.01	35.00
27.5	24.03	25.03	26.02	27.02	28.01	29.01	30.01	35.00
28.0	24.03	25.02	26.02	27.02	28.01	29.01	30.01	35.00
28.5	24.03	25.02	26.02	27.01	28.01	29.01	30.01	35.00
29.0	24.02	25.02	26.01	27.01	28.01	29.01	30.01	35.00
29.5	24.02	25.02	26.01	27.01	28.01	29.01	30.00	35.00
30.0	24.02	25.01	26.01	27.01	28.01	29.01	30.00	35.00
35.0	24.01	25.00	26.00	27.00	28.00	29.00	30.00	35.00
40.0	24.00	25.00	26.00	27.00	28.00	29.00	30.00	35.00

EXAMPLES *ON PAGES A-382 TO A-397*

LOAN TO APPRAISED VALUE RATIOS
Conventional Loans

APPRAISED VALUE	70%	75%	80%	85%	90%	95%
50,000	35000	37500	40000	42500	45000	47500
51,000	35700	38250	40800	43350	45900	48450
52,000	36400	39000	41600	44200	46800	49400
53,000	37100	39750	42400	45050	47700	50350
54,000	37800	40500	43200	45900	48600	51300
55,000	38500	41250	44000	46750	49500	52250
56,000	39200	42000	44800	47600	50400	53200
57,000	39900	42750	45600	48450	51300	54150
58,000	40600	43500	46400	49300	52200	55100
59,000	41300	44250	47200	50150	53100	56050
60,000	42000	45000	48000	51000	54000	57000
61,000	42700	45750	48800	51850	54900	57950
62,000	43400	46500	49600	52700	55800	58900
63,000	44100	47250	50400	53550	56700	59850
64,000	44800	48000	51200	54400	57600	60800
65,000	45500	48750	52000	55250	58500	61750
66,000	46200	49500	52800	56100	59400	62700
67,000	46900	50250	53600	56950	60300	63650
68,000	47600	51000	54400	57800	61200	64600
69,000	48300	51750	55200	58650	62100	65550
70,000	49000	52500	56000	59500	63000	66500
71,000	49700	53250	56800	60350	63900	67450
72,000	50400	54000	57600	61200	64800	68400
73,000	51100	54750	58400	62050	65700	69350
74,000	51800	55500	59200	62900	66600	70300
75,000	52500	56250	60000	63750	67500	71250
76,000	53200	57000	60800	64600	68400	72200
77,000	53900	57750	61600	65450	69300	73150
78,000	54600	58500	62400	66300	70200	74100
79,000	55300	59250	63200	67150	71100	75050
80,000	56000	60000	64000	68000	72000	76000
81,000	56700	60750	64800	68850	72900	76950
82,000	57400	61500	65600	69700	73800	77900
83,000	58100	62250	66400	70550	74700	78850
84,000	58800	63000	67200	71400	75600	79800
85,000	59500	63750	68000	72250	76500	80750
86,000	60200	64500	68800	73100	77400	81700
87,000	60900	65250	69600	73950	78300	82650
88,000	61600	66000	70400	74800	79200	83600
89,000	62300	66750	71200	75650	80100	84550
90,000	63000	67500	72000	76500	81000	85500
91,000	63700	68250	72800	77350	81900	86450
92,000	64400	69000	73600	78200	82800	87400
93,000	65100	69750	74400	79050	83700	88350
94,000	65800	70500	75200	79900	84600	89300
95,000	66500	71250	76000	80750	85500	90250
96,000	67200	72000	76800	81600	86400	91200
97,000	67900	72750	77600	82450	87300	92150
98,000	68600	73500	78400	83300	88200	93100
99,000	69300	74250	79200	84150	89100	94050

LOAN TO APPRAISED VALUE RATIOS
Conventional Loans

APPRAISED VALUE	70%	75%	80%	85%	90%	95%
100,000	70000	75000	80000	85000	90000	95000
101,000	70700	75750	80800	85850	90900	95950
102,000	71400	76500	81600	86700	91800	96900
103,000	72100	77250	82400	87550	92700	97850
104,000	72800	78000	83200	88400	93600	98800
105,000	73500	78750	84000	89250	94500	99750
106,000	74200	79500	84800	90100	95400	100700
107,000	74900	80250	85600	90950	96300	101650
108,000	75600	81000	86400	91800	97200	102600
109,000	76300	81750	87200	92650	98100	103550
110,000	77000	82500	88000	93500	99000	104500
111,000	77700	83250	88800	94350	99900	105450
112,000	78400	84000	89600	95200	100800	106400
113,000	79100	84750	90400	96050	101700	107350
114,000	79800	85500	91200	96900	102600	108300
115,000	80500	86250	92000	97750	103500	109250
116,000	81200	87000	92800	98600	104400	110200
117,000	81900	87750	93600	99450	105300	111150
118,000	82600	88500	94400	100300	106200	112100
119,000	83300	89250	95200	101150	107100	113050
120,000	84000	90000	96000	102000	108000	114000
121,000	84700	90750	96800	102850	108900	114950
122,000	85400	91500	97600	103700	109800	115900
123,000	86100	92250	98400	104550	110700	116850
124,000	86800	93000	99200	105400	111600	117800
125,000	87500	93750	100000	106250	112500	118750
126,000	88200	94500	100800	107100	113400	119700
127,000	88900	95250	101600	107950	114300	120650
128,000	89600	96000	102400	108800	115200	121600
129,000	90300	96750	103200	109650	116100	122550
130,000	91000	97500	104000	110500	117000	123500
131,000	91700	98250	104800	111350	117900	124450
132,000	92400	99000	105600	112200	118800	125400
133,000	93100	99750	106400	113050	119700	126350
134,000	93800	100500	107200	113900	120600	127300
135,000	94500	101250	108000	114750	121500	128250
136,000	95200	102000	108800	115600	122400	129200
137,000	95900	102750	109600	116450	123300	130150
138,000	96600	103500	110400	117300	124200	131100
139,000	97300	104250	111200	118150	125100	132050
140,000	98000	105000	112000	119000	126000	133000
141,000	98700	105750	112800	115850	126900	133950
142,000	99400	106500	113600	120700	127800	134900
143,000	100100	107250	114400	121550	128700	135850
144,000	100800	108000	115200	122400	129600	136800
145,000	101500	108750	116000	123250	130500	137750
146,000	102200	109500	116800	124100	131400	138700
147,000	102900	110250	117600	124950	132300	139650
148,000	103600	111000	118400	125800	133200	140600
149,000	104300	111750	119200	126650	134100	141550

LOAN TO APPRAISED VALUE RATIOS
Conventional Loans

APPRAISED VALUE	70%	75%	80%	85%	90%	95%
150,000	105000	112500	120000	127500	135000	142500
151,000	105700	113250	120800	128350	135900	143450
152,000	106400	114000	121600	129200	136800	144400
153,000	107100	114750	122400	130050	137700	145350
154,000	107800	115500	123200	130900	138600	146300
155,000	108500	116250	124000	131750	139500	147250
156,000	109200	117000	124800	132600	140400	148200
157,000	109900	117750	125600	133450	141300	149150
158,000	110600	118500	126400	134300	142200	150100
159,000	111300	119250	127200	135150	143100	151050
160,000	112000	120000	128000	136000	144000	152000
161,000	112700	120750	128800	136850	144900	152950
162,000	113400	121500	129600	137700	145800	153900
163,000	114100	122250	130400	138550	146700	154850
164,000	114800	123000	131200	139400	147600	155800
165,000	115500	123750	132000	140250	148500	156750
166,000	116200	124500	132800	141100	149400	157700
167,000	116900	125250	133600	141950	150300	158650
168,000	117600	126000	134400	142800	151200	159600
169,000	118300	126750	135200	143650	152100	160550
170,000	119000	127500	136000	144500	153000	161500
171,000	119700	128250	136800	145350	153900	162450
172,000	120400	129000	137600	146200	154800	163400
173,000	121100	129750	138400	147050	155700	164350
174,000	121800	130500	139200	147900	156600	165300
175,000	122500	131250	140000	148750	157500	166250
176,000	123200	132000	140800	149600	158400	167200
177,000	123900	132750	141600	150450	159300	168150
178,000	124600	133500	142400	151300	160200	169100
179,000	125300	134250	143200	152150	161100	170050
180,000	126000	135000	144000	153000	162000	171000
181,000	126700	135750	144800	153850	162900	171950
182,000	127400	136500	145600	154700	163800	172900
183,000	128100	137250	146400	155550	164700	173850
184,000	128800	138000	147200	156400	165600	174800
185,000	129500	138750	148000	157250	166500	175750
186,000	130200	139500	148800	158100	167400	176700
187,000	130900	140250	149600	158950	168300	177650
188,000	131600	141000	150400	159800	169200	178600
189,000	132300	141750	151200	160650	170100	179550
190,000	133000	142500	152000	161500	171000	180500
191,000	133700	143250	152800	162350	171900	181450
192,000	134400	144000	153600	163200	172800	182400
193,000	135100	144750	154400	164050	173700	183350
194,000	135800	145500	155200	164900	174600	184300
195,000	136500	146250	156000	165750	175500	185250
196,000	137200	147000	156800	166600	176400	186200
197,000	137900	147750	157600	167450	177300	187150
198,000	138600	148500	158400	168300	178200	188100
199,000	139300	149250	159200	169150	179100	189050

LOAN TO APPRAISED VALUE RATIOS
Conventional Loans

APPRAISED VALUE	70%	75%	80%	85%	90%	95%
200,000	140000	150000	160000	170000	180000	190000
201,000	140700	150750	160800	170850	180900	190950
202,000	141400	151500	161600	171700	181800	191900
203,000	142100	152250	162400	172550	182700	192850
204,000	142800	153000	163200	173400	183600	193800
205,000	143500	153750	164000	174250	184500	194750
206,000	144200	154500	164800	175100	185400	195700
207,000	144900	155250	165600	175950	186300	196650
208,000	145600	156000	166400	176800	187200	197600
209,000	146300	156750	167200	177650	188100	198550
210,000	147000	157500	168000	178500	189000	199500
211,000	147700	158250	168800	179350	189900	200450
212,000	148400	159000	169600	180200	190800	201400
213,000	149100	159750	170400	181050	191700	202350
214,000	149800	160500	171200	181900	192600	203300
215,000	150500	161250	172000	182750	193500	204250
216,000	151200	162000	172800	183600	194400	205200
217,000	151900	162750	173600	184450	195300	206150
218,000	152600	163500	174400	185300	196200	207100
219,000	153300	164250	175200	186150	197100	208050
220,000	154000	165000	176000	187000	198000	209000
221,000	154700	165750	176800	187850	198900	209950
222,000	155400	166500	177600	188700	199800	210900
223,000	156100	167250	178400	189550	200700	211850
224,000	156800	168000	179200	190400	201600	212800
225,000	157500	168750	180000	191250	202500	213750
226,000	158200	169500	180800	192100	203400	214700
227,000	158900	170250	181600	192950	204300	215650
228,000	159600	171000	182400	193800	205200	216600
229,000	160300	171750	183200	194650	206100	217550
230,000	161000	172500	184000	195500	207000	218500
231,000	161700	173250	184800	196350	207900	219450
232,000	162400	174000	185600	197200	208800	220400
233,000	163100	174750	186400	198050	209700	221350
234,000	163800	175500	187200	198900	210600	222300
235,000	164500	176250	188000	199750	211500	223250
236,000	165200	177000	188800	200600	212400	224200
237,000	165900	177750	189600	201450	213300	225150
238,000	166600	178500	190400	202300	214200	226100
239,000	167300	179250	191200	203150	215100	227050
240,000	168000	180000	192000	204000	216000	228000
241,000	168700	180750	192800	204850	216900	228950
242,000	169400	181500	193600	205700	217800	229900
243,000	170100	182250	194400	206550	218700	230850
244,000	170800	183000	195200	207400	219600	231800
245,000	171500	183750	196000	208250	220500	232750
246,000	172200	184500	196800	209100	221400	233700
247,000	172900	185250	197600	209950	222300	234650
248,000	173600	186000	198400	210800	223200	235600
249,000	174300	186750	199200	211650	224100	236550

LOAN TO APPRAISED VALUE RATIOS
Conventional Loans

APPRAISED VALUE	70%	75%	80%	85%	90%	95%
250,000	175000	187500	200000	212500	225000	237500
251,000	175700	188250	200800	213350	225900	238450
252,000	176400	189000	201600	214200	226800	239400
253,000	177100	189750	202400	215050	227700	240350
254,000	177800	190500	203200	215900	228600	241300
255,000	178500	191250	204000	216750	229500	242250
256,000	179200	192000	204800	217600	230400	243200
257,000	179900	192750	205600	218450	231300	244150
258,000	180600	193500	206400	219300	232200	245100
259,000	181300	194250	207200	220150	233100	246050
260,000	182000	195000	208000	221000	234000	247000
261,000	182700	195750	208800	221850	234900	247950
262,000	183400	196500	209600	222700	235800	248900
263,000	184100	197250	210400	223550	236700	249850
264,000	184800	198000	211200	224400	237600	250800
265,000	185500	198750	212000	225250	238500	251750
266,000	186200	199500	212800	226100	239400	252700
267,000	186900	200250	213600	226950	240300	253650
268,000	187600	201000	214400	227800	241200	254600
269,000	188300	201750	215200	228650	242100	255550
270,000	189000	202500	216000	229500	243000	256500
271,000	189700	203250	216800	230350	243900	257450
272,000	190400	204000	217600	231200	244800	258400
273,000	191100	204750	218400	232050	245700	259350
274,000	191800	205500	219200	232900	246600	260300
275,000	192500	206250	220000	233750	247500	261250
276,000	193200	207000	220800	234600	248400	262200
277,000	193900	207750	221600	235450	249300	263150
278,000	194600	208500	222400	236300	250200	264100
279,000	195300	209250	223200	237150	251100	265050
280,000	196000	210000	224000	238000	252000	266000
281,000	196700	210750	224800	238850	252900	266950
282,000	197400	211500	225600	239700	253800	267900
283,000	198100	212250	226400	240550	254700	268850
284,000	198800	213000	227200	241400	255600	269800
285,000	199500	213750	228000	242250	256500	270750
286,000	200200	214500	228800	243100	257400	271700
287,000	200900	215250	229600	243950	258300	272650
288,000	201600	216000	230400	244800	259200	273600
289,000	202300	216750	231200	245650	260100	274550
290,000	203000	217500	232000	246500	261000	275500
291,000	203700	218250	232800	247350	261900	276450
292,000	204400	219000	233600	248200	262800	277400
293,000	205100	219750	234400	249050	263700	278350
294,000	205800	220500	235200	249900	264600	279300
295,000	206500	221250	236000	250750	265500	280250
296,000	207200	222000	236800	251600	266400	281200
297,000	207900	222750	237600	252450	267300	282150
298,000	208600	223500	238400	253300	268200	283100
299,000	209300	224250	239200	254150	269100	284050

A-138

LOAN TO APPRAISED VALUE RATIOS
Conventional Loans

APPRAISED VALUE	70%	75%	80%	85%	90%	95%
300,000	210000	225000	240000	255000	270000	285000
301,000	210700	225750	240800	255850	270900	285950
302,000	211400	226500	241600	256700	271800	286900
303,000	212100	227250	242400	257550	272700	287850
304,000	212800	228000	243200	258400	273600	288800
305,000	213500	228750	244000	259250	274500	289750
306,000	214200	229500	244800	260100	275400	290700
307,000	214900	230250	245600	260950	276300	291650
308,000	215600	231000	246400	261800	277200	292600
309,000	216300	231750	247200	262650	278100	293550
310,000	217000	232500	248000	263500	279000	294500
311,000	217700	233250	248800	264350	279900	295450
312,000	218400	234000	249600	265200	280800	296400
313,000	219100	234750	250400	266050	281700	297350
314,000	219800	235500	251200	266900	282600	298300
315,000	220500	236250	252000	267750	283500	299250
316,000	221200	237000	252800	268600	284400	300200
317,000	221900	237750	253600	269450	285300	301150
318,000	222600	238500	254400	270300	286200	302100
319,000	223300	239250	255200	271150	287100	303050
320,000	224000	240000	256000	272000	288000	304000
321,000	224700	240750	256800	272850	288900	304950
322,000	225400	241500	257600	273700	289800	305900
323,000	226100	242250	258400	274550	290700	306850
324,000	226800	243000	259200	275400	291600	307800
325,000	227500	243750	260000	276250	292500	308750
326,000	228200	244500	260800	277100	293400	309700
327,000	228900	245250	261600	277950	294300	310650
328,000	229600	246000	262400	278800	295200	311600
329,000	230300	246750	263200	279650	296100	312550
330,000	231000	247500	264000	280500	297000	313500
331,000	231700	248250	264800	281350	297900	314450
332,000	232400	249000	265600	282200	298800	315400
333,000	233100	249750	266400	283050	299700	316350
334,000	233800	250500	267200	283900	300600	317300
335,000	234500	251250	268000	284750	301500	318250
336,000	235200	252000	268800	285600	302400	319200
337,000	235900	252750	269600	286450	303300	320150
338,000	236600	253500	270400	287300	304200	321100
339,000	237300	254250	271200	288150	305100	322050
340,000	238000	255000	272000	289000	306000	323000
341,000	238700	255750	272800	289850	306900	323950
342,000	239400	256500	273600	290700	307800	324900
343,000	240100	257250	274400	291550	308700	325850
344,000	240800	258000	275200	292400	309600	326800
345,000	241500	258750	276000	293250	310500	327750
346,000	242200	259500	276800	294100	311400	328700
347,000	242900	260250	277600	294950	312300	329650
348,000	243600	261000	278400	295800	313200	330600
349,000	244300	261750	279200	296650	314100	331550

LOAN TO APPRAISED VALUE RATIOS
Conventional Loans

APPRAISED VALUE	70%	75%	80%	85%	90%	95%
350,000	245000	262500	280000	297500	315000	332500
351,000	245700	263250	280800	298350	315900	333450
352,000	246400	264000	281600	299200	316800	334400
353,000	247100	264750	282400	300050	317700	335350
354,000	247800	265500	283200	300900	318600	336300
355,000	248500	266250	284000	301750	319500	337250
356,000	249200	267000	284800	302600	320400	338200
357,000	249900	267750	285600	303450	321300	339150
358,000	250600	268500	286400	304300	322200	340100
359,000	251300	269250	287200	305150	323100	341050
360,000	252000	270000	288000	306000	324000	342000
361,000	252700	270750	288800	306850	324900	342950
362,000	253400	271500	289600	307700	325800	343900
363,000	254100	272250	290400	308550	326700	344850
364,000	254800	273000	291200	309400	327600	345800
365,000	255500	273750	292000	310250	328500	346750
366,000	256200	274500	292800	311100	329400	347700
367,000	256900	275250	293600	311950	330300	348650
368,000	257600	276000	294400	312800	331200	349600
369,000	258300	276750	295200	313650	332100	350550
370,000	259000	277500	296000	314500	333000	351500
371,000	259700	278250	296800	315350	333900	352450
372,000	260400	279000	297600	316200	334800	353400
373,000	261100	279750	298400	317050	335700	354350
374,000	261800	280500	299200	317900	336600	355300
375,000	262500	281250	300000	318750	337500	356250
376,000	263200	282000	300800	319600	338400	357200
377,000	263900	282750	301600	320450	339300	358150
378,000	264600	283500	302400	321300	340200	359100
379,000	265300	284250	303200	322150	341100	360050
380,000	266000	285000	304000	323000	342000	361000
381,000	266700	285750	304800	323850	342900	361950
382,000	267400	286500	305600	324700	343800	362900
383,000	268100	287250	306400	325550	344700	363850
384,000	268800	288000	307200	326400	345600	364800
385,000	269500	288750	308000	327250	346500	365750
386,000	270200	289500	308800	328100	347400	366700
387,000	270900	290250	309600	328950	348300	367650
388,000	271600	291000	310400	329800	349200	368600
389,000	272300	291750	311200	330650	350100	369550
390,000	273000	292500	312000	331500	351000	370500
391,000	273700	293250	312800	332350	351900	371450
392,000	274400	294000	313600	333200	352800	372400
393,000	275100	294750	314400	334050	353700	373350
394,000	275800	295500	315200	334900	354600	374300
395,000	276500	296250	316000	335750	355500	375250
396,000	277200	297000	316800	336600	356400	376200
397,000	277900	297750	317600	337450	357300	377150
398,000	278600	298500	318400	338300	358200	378100
399,000	279300	299250	319200	339150	359100	379050

LOAN TO APPRAISED VALUE RATIOS
Conventional Loans

APPRAISED VALUE	70%	75%	80%	85%	90%	95%
400,000	280000	300000	320000	340000	360000	380000
401,000	280700	300750	320800	340850	360900	380950
402,000	281400	301500	321600	341700	361800	381900
403,000	282100	302250	322400	342550	362700	382850
404,000	282800	303000	323200	343400	363600	383800
405,000	283500	303750	324000	344250	364500	384750
406,000	284200	304500	324800	345100	365400	385700
407,000	284900	305250	325600	345950	366300	386650
408,000	285600	306000	326400	346800	367200	387600
409,000	286300	306750	327200	347650	368100	388550
410,000	287000	307500	328000	348500	369000	389500
411,000	287700	308250	328800	349350	369900	390450
412,000	288400	309000	329600	350200	370800	391400
413,000	289100	309750	330400	351050	371700	392350
414,000	289800	310500	331200	351900	372600	393300
415,000	290500	311250	332000	352750	373500	394250
416,000	291200	312000	332800	353600	374400	395200
417,000	291900	312750	333600	354450	375300	396150
418,000	292600	313500	334400	355300	376200	397100
419,000	293300	314250	335200	356150	377100	398050
420,000	294000	315000	336000	357000	378000	399000
421,000	294700	315750	336800	357850	378900	399950
422,000	295400	316500	337600	358700	379800	400900
423,000	296100	317250	338400	359550	380700	401850
424,000	296800	318000	339200	360400	381600	402800
425,000	297500	318750	340000	361250	382500	403750
426,000	298200	319500	340800	362100	383400	404700
427,000	298900	320250	341600	362950	384300	405650
428,000	299600	321000	342400	363800	385200	406600
429,000	300300	321750	343200	364650	386100	407550
430,000	301000	322500	344000	365500	387000	408500
431,000	301700	323250	344800	366350	387900	409450
432,000	302400	324000	345600	367200	388800	410400
433,000	303100	324750	346400	368050	389700	411350
434,000	303800	325500	347200	368900	390600	412300
435,000	304500	326250	348000	369750	391500	413250
436,000	305200	327000	348800	370600	392400	414200
437,000	305900	327750	349600	371450	393300	415150
438,000	306600	328500	350400	372300	394200	416100
439,000	307300	329250	351200	373150	395100	417050
440,000	308000	330000	352000	374000	396000	418000
441,000	308700	330750	352800	374850	396900	418950
442,000	309400	331500	353600	375700	397800	419900
443,000	310100	332250	354400	376550	398700	420850
444,000	310800	333000	355200	377400	399600	421800
445,000	311500	333750	356000	378250	400500	422750
446,000	312200	334500	356800	379100	401400	423700
447,000	312900	335250	357600	379950	402300	424650
448,000	313600	336000	358400	380800	403200	425600
449,000	314300	336750	359200	381650	404100	426550

LOAN TO APPRAISED VALUE RATIOS
Conventional Loans

APPRAISED VALUE	70%	75%	80%	85%	90%	95%
450,000	315000	337500	360000	382500	405000	427500
451,000	315700	338250	360800	383350	405900	428450
452,000	316400	339000	361600	384200	406800	429400
453,000	317100	339750	362400	385050	407700	430350
454,000	317800	340500	363200	385900	408600	431300
455,000	318500	341250	364000	386750	409500	432250
456,000	319200	342000	364800	387600	410400	433200
457,000	319900	342750	365600	388450	411300	434150
458,000	320600	343500	366400	389300	412200	435100
459,000	321300	344250	367200	390150	413100	436050
460,000	322000	345000	368000	391000	414000	437000
461,000	322700	345750	368800	391850	414900	437950
462,000	323400	346500	369600	392700	415800	438900
463,000	324100	347250	370400	393550	416700	439850
464,000	324800	348000	371200	394400	417600	440800
465,000	325500	348750	372000	395250	418500	441750
466,000	326200	349500	372800	396100	419400	442700
467,000	326900	350250	373600	396950	420300	443650
468,000	327600	351000	374400	397800	421200	444600
469,000	328300	351750	375200	398650	422100	445550
470,000	329000	352500	376000	399500	423000	446500
471,000	329700	353250	376800	400350	423900	447450
472,000	330400	354000	377600	401200	424800	448400
473,000	331100	354750	378400	402050	425700	449350
474,000	331800	355500	379200	402900	426600	450300
475,000	332500	356250	380000	403750	427500	451250
476,000	333200	357000	380800	404600	428400	452200
477,000	333900	357750	381600	405450	429300	453150
478,000	334600	358500	382400	406300	430200	454100
479,000	335300	359250	383200	407150	431100	455050
480,000	336000	360000	384000	408000	432000	456000
481,000	336700	360750	384800	408850	432900	456950
482,000	337400	361500	385600	409700	433800	457900
483,000	338100	362250	386400	410550	434700	458850
484,000	338800	363000	387200	411400	435600	459800
485,000	339500	363750	388000	412250	436500	460750
486,000	340200	364500	388800	413100	437400	461700
487,000	340900	365250	389600	413950	438300	462650
488,000	341600	366000	390400	414800	439200	463600
489,000	342300	366750	391200	415650	440100	464550
490,000	343000	367500	392000	416500	441000	465500
491,000	343700	368250	392800	417350	441900	466450
492,000	344400	369000	393600	418200	442800	467400
493,000	345100	369750	394400	419050	443700	468350
494,000	345800	370500	395200	419900	444600	469300
495,000	346500	371250	396000	420750	445500	470250
496,000	347200	372000	396800	421600	446400	471200
497,000	347900	372750	397600	422450	447300	472150
498,000	348600	373500	398400	423300	448200	473100
499,000	349300	374250	399200	424150	449100	474050

LOAN TO APPRAISED VALUE RATIOS
Conventional Loans

APPRAISED VALUE	70%	75%	80%	85%	90%	95%
500,000	350000	375000	400000	425000	450000	475000
501,000	350700	375750	400800	425850	450900	475950
502,000	351400	376500	401600	426700	451800	476900
503,000	352100	377250	402400	427550	452700	477850
504,000	352800	378000	403200	428400	453600	478800
505,000	353500	378750	404000	429250	454500	479750
506,000	354200	379500	404800	430100	455400	480700
507,000	354900	380250	405600	430950	456300	481650
508,000	355600	381000	406400	431800	457200	482600
509,000	356300	381750	407200	432650	458100	483550
510,000	357000	382500	408000	433500	459000	484500
511,000	357700	383250	408800	434350	459900	485450
512,000	358400	384000	409600	435200	460800	486400
513,000	359100	384750	410400	436050	461700	487350
514,000	359800	385500	411200	436900	462600	488300
515,000	360500	386250	412000	437750	463500	489250
516,000	361200	387000	412800	438600	464400	490200
517,000	361900	387750	413600	439450	465300	491150
518,000	362600	388500	414400	440300	466200	492100
519,000	363300	389250	415200	441150	467100	493050
520,000	364000	390000	416000	442000	468000	494000
521,000	364700	390750	416800	442850	468900	494950
522,000	365400	391500	417600	443700	469800	495900
523,000	366100	392250	418400	444550	470700	496850
524,000	366800	393000	419200	445400	471600	497800
525,000	367500	393750	420000	446250	472500	498750
526,000	368200	394500	420800	447100	473400	499700
527,000	368900	395250	421600	447950	474300	500650
528,000	369600	396000	422400	448800	475200	501600
529,000	370300	396750	423200	449650	476100	502550
530,000	371000	397500	424000	450500	477000	503500
531,000	371700	398250	424800	451350	477900	504450
532,000	372400	399000	425600	452200	478800	505400
533,000	373100	399750	426400	453050	479700	506350
534,000	373800	400500	427200	453900	480600	507300
535,000	374500	401250	428000	454750	481500	508250
536,000	375200	402000	428800	455600	482400	509200
537,000	375900	402750	429600	456450	483300	510150
538,000	376600	403500	430400	457300	484200	511100
539,000	377300	404250	431200	458150	485100	512050
540,000	378000	405000	432000	459000	486000	513000
541,000	378700	405750	432800	459850	486900	513950
542,000	379400	406500	433600	460700	487800	514900
543,000	380100	407250	434400	461550	488700	515850
544,000	380800	408000	435200	462400	489600	516800
545,000	381500	408750	436000	463250	490500	517750
546,000	382200	409500	436800	464100	491400	518700
547,000	382900	410250	437600	464950	492300	519650
548,000	383600	411000	438400	465800	493200	520600
549,000	384300	411750	439200	466650	494100	521550

NET AND GROSS SELLING PRICE

Net	Gross at 3% Commission	Gross at 3½% Commission	Gross at 4% Commission	Gross at 4½% Commission	Gross at 5% Commission	Gross at 5½% Commission	Gross at 6% Commission	Gross at 6½% Commission
25000	25773	25907	26042	26178	26316	26455	26596	26738
26000	26804	26943	27083	27225	27368	27513	27660	27807
27000	27835	27979	28125	28272	28421	28571	28723	28877
28000	28866	29016	29167	29319	29474	29630	29787	29947
29000	29897	30052	30208	30366	30526	30688	30851	31016
30000	30928	31088	31250	31414	31579	31746	31915	32086
31000	31959	32124	32292	32461	32632	32804	32979	33155
32000	32990	33161	33333	33508	33684	33862	34043	34225
33000	34021	34197	34375	34555	34737	34921	35106	35294
34000	35052	35233	35417	35602	35789	35979	36170	36364
35000	36082	36269	36458	36649	36842	37037	37234	37433
36000	37113	37306	37500	37696	37895	38095	38298	38503
37000	38144	38342	38542	38743	38947	39153	39362	39572
38000	39175	39378	39583	39791	40000	40212	40426	40642
39000	40206	40415	40625	40833	41053	41270	41489	41711
40000	41237	41451	41667	41885	42105	42328	42553	42781
41000	42268	42487	42708	42932	43158	43386	43617	43850
42000	43299	43523	43750	43979	44211	44444	44681	44920
43000	44330	44560	44792	45026	45263	45503	45745	45989
44000	45361	45596	45833	46073	46316	46561	46809	47059
45000	46392	46632	46875	47120	47368	47619	47872	48128
46000	47423	47668	47917	48168	48421	48677	48936	49198
47000	48454	48705	48958	49215	49474	49735	50000	50267
48000	49485	49741	50000	50262	50526	50794	51064	51337
49000	50515	50777	51042	51309	51579	51852	52128	52406
50000	51546	51813	52083	52356	52632	52910	53191	53476
51000	52577	52850	53125	53403	53684	53968	54255	54545
52000	53608	53886	54167	54450	54737	55026	55319	55615
53000	54639	54922	55208	55497	55789	56085	56383	56684
54000	55670	55959	56250	56545	56842	57143	57447	57754
55000	56701	56995	57292	57592	57895	58201	58511	58824
56000	57732	58031	58333	58639	58947	59259	59574	59893
57000	58763	59067	59375	59686	60000	60317	60638	60963
58000	59794	60104	60417	60733	61053	61376	61702	62032
59000	60825	61140	61458	61780	62105	62434	62766	63102
60000	61856	62176	62500	62827	63158	63492	63830	64171
61000	62887	63212	63542	63874	64211	64550	64894	65241
62000	63918	64249	64583	64921	65263	65608	65957	66310
63000	64948	65285	65625	65969	66316	66667	67021	67380
64000	65979	66321	66667	67016	67368	67725	68085	68449
65000	67010	67358	67708	68063	68421	68783	69149	69519
66000	68041	68394	68750	69110	69474	69841	70213	70588
67000	69072	69430	69792	70157	70526	70899	71277	71658
68000	70103	70466	70833	71204	71579	71958	72340	72727
69000	71134	71503	71875	72251	72632	73016	73404	73797
70000	72165	72539	72917	73298	73684	74074	74468	74866
71000	73196	73575	73958	74345	74737	75132	75532	75936
72000	74227	74611	75000	75393	75789	76190	76596	77005
73000	75258	75648	76042	76440	76842	77249	77660	78075
74000	76289	76684	77083	77487	77895	78307	78723	79144
75000	77320	77720	78125	78534	78947	79365	79787	80214
76000	78351	78756	79167	79581	80000	80423	80851	81283
77000	79381	79793	80208	80628	81053	81481	81915	82353
78000	80412	80829	81250	81675	82105	82540	82979	83422
79000	81443	81865	82292	82723	83158	83598	84043	84492
80000	82474	82902	83333	83770	84211	84656	85106	85561
81000	83505	83938	84375	84817	85263	85714	86170	86631
82000	84536	84974	85417	85864	86316	86772	87234	87701
83000	85567	86010	86458	86911	87368	87831	88298	88770
84000	86598	87047	87500	87958	88421	88889	89362	89840
85000	87629	88083	88542	89005	89474	89947	90426	90909
86000	88660	89119	89583	90052	90526	91005	91489	91979
87000	89691	90155	90625	91099	91579	92063	92553	93048
88000	90722	91192	91667	92147	92632	93122	93617	94118
89000	91753	92228	92708	93194	93684	94180	94681	95187
90000	92784	93264	93750	94241	94737	95238	95745	96257
91000	93814	94301	94792	95288	95789	96296	96809	97326
92000	94845	95337	95833	96335	96842	97354	97872	98396
93000	95876	96373	96875	97382	97895	98413	98936	99465
94000	96907	97409	97917	98429	98947	99471	100000	100535
95000	97938	98446	98958	99476	100000	100529	101064	101604
96000	98969	99482	100000	100524	101053	101587	102128	102674
97000	100000	100518	101042	101571	102105	102645	103191	103743
98000	101031	101554	102083	102618	103158	103704	104255	104813
99000	102062	102591	103125	103665	104211	104762	105319	105882
100000	103093	103627	104167	104712	105263	105820	106383	106952

NET AND GROSS SELLING PRICE

Net	Gross at 3% Commission	Gross at 3½% Commission	Gross at 4% Commission	Gross at 4½% Commission	Gross at 5% Commission	Gross at 5½% Commission	Gross at 6% Commission	Gross at 6½% Commission
101000	104124	104663	105208	105759	106316	106878	107447	108021
102000	105155	105699	106250	106806	107368	107937	108511	109091
103000	106186	106736	107292	107853	108421	108995	109574	110160
104000	107216	107772	108333	108901	109474	110053	110638	111230
105000	108247	108808	109375	109948	110526	111111	111702	112299
106000	109278	109845	110417	110995	111579	112169	112766	113369
107000	110309	110881	111458	112042	112632	113228	113830	114439
108000	111340	111917	112500	113089	113684	114286	114894	115508
109000	112371	112953	113542	114136	114737	115344	115957	116578
110000	113402	113990	114583	115183	115789	116402	117021	117647
111000	114433	115026	115625	116230	116842	117460	118085	118717
112000	115464	116062	116667	117277	117895	118519	119149	119786
113000	116495	117098	117708	118325	118947	119577	120213	120856
114000	117526	118135	118750	119372	120000	120635	121277	121925
115000	118557	119171	119792	120415	121053	121693	122340	122995
116000	119588	120207	120833	121466	122105	122751	123404	124064
117000	120619	121244	121875	122513	123158	123810	124468	125134
118000	121649	122280	122917	123560	124211	124868	125532	126203
119000	122680	123316	123958	124607	125263	125926	126596	127273
120000	123711	124352	125000	125654	126316	126984	127660	128342
121000	124742	125389	126042	126702	127368	128042	128723	129412
122000	125773	126425	127083	127749	128421	129101	129787	130481
123000	126804	127461	128125	128796	129474	130159	130851	131551
124000	127835	128497	129167	129843	130526	131217	131915	132620
125000	128866	129534	130208	130890	131579	132275	132979	133690
126000	129897	130570	131250	131937	132632	133333	134043	134759
127000	130928	131606	132292	132984	133684	134392	135106	135829
128000	131959	132642	133333	134031	134737	135450	136170	136898
129000	132990	133679	134375	135079	135789	136508	137234	137968
130000	134021	134715	135417	136126	136842	137566	138298	139037
131000	135052	135751	136458	137173	137895	138624	139362	140107
132000	136082	136788	137500	138220	138947	139683	140426	141176
133000	137113	137824	138542	139267	140000	140741	141489	142246
134000	138144	138860	139583	140314	141053	141799	142553	143316
135000	139175	139896	140625	141361	142105	142857	143617	144385
136000	140206	140933	141667	142408	143158	143915	144681	145455
137000	141237	141969	142708	143455	144211	144974	145745	146524
138000	142268	143005	143750	144503	145263	146032	146809	147594
139000	143299	144041	144792	145550	146316	147090	147872	148663
140000	144330	145078	145833	146597	147368	148148	148936	149733
141000	145361	146114	146875	147644	148421	149206	150000	150802
142000	146392	147150	147917	148691	149474	150265	151064	151872
143000	147423	148187	148958	149738	150526	151323	152128	152941
144000	148454	149223	150000	150785	151579	152381	153191	154011
145000	149485	150259	151042	151832	152632	153439	154255	155080
146000	150515	151295	152083	152880	153684	154497	155319	156150
147000	151546	152332	153125	153927	154737	155556	156383	157219
148000	152577	153368	154167	154974	155789	156614	157447	158289
149000	153608	154404	155208	156021	156842	157672	158511	159358
150000	154639	155440	156250	157068	157895	158730	159574	160428
151000	155670	156477	157292	158115	158947	159788	160638	161497
152000	156701	157513	158333	159162	160000	160847	161702	162567
153000	157732	158549	159375	160209	161053	161905	162766	163636
154000	158763	159585	160417	161257	162105	162963	163830	164706
155000	159794	160622	161458	162304	163158	164021	164894	165775
156000	160825	161658	162500	163351	164211	165079	165957	166845
157000	161856	162694	163542	164398	165263	166138	167021	167914
158000	162887	163731	164583	165445	166316	167196	168085	168984
159000	163918	164767	165625	166492	167368	168254	169149	170053
160000	164948	165803	166667	167539	168421	169312	170213	171123
161000	165979	166839	167708	168586	169474	170370	171277	172193
162000	167010	167876	168750	169634	170526	171429	172340	173262
163000	168041	168912	169792	170681	171579	172487	173404	174332
164000	169072	169948	170833	171728	172632	173545	174468	175401
165000	170103	170984	171875	172775	173684	174603	175532	176471
166000	171134	172021	172917	173822	174737	175661	176596	177540
167000	172165	173057	173958	174869	175789	176720	177660	178610
168000	173196	174093	175000	175916	176842	177778	178723	179679
169000	174227	175130	176042	176963	177895	178836	179787	180749
170000	175258	176166	177083	178011	178947	179894	180851	181818
171000	176289	177202	178125	179058	180000	180952	181915	182888
172000	177320	178238	179167	180105	181053	182011	182979	183957
173000	178351	179275	180208	181152	182105	183069	184043	185027
174000	179381	180311	181250	182199	183158	184127	185106	186096
175000	180412	181347	182292	183246	184211	185185	186170	187166
176000	181443	182383	183333	184293	185263	186243	187234	188235

Net	Gross at 3% Commission	Gross at 3½% Commission	Gross at 4% Commission	Gross at 4½% Commission	Gross at 5% Commission	Gross at 5½% Commission	Gross at 6% Commission	Gross at 6½% Commission
177000	182474	183420	184375	185340	186316	187302	188298	189305
178000	183505	184456	185417	186387	187368	188360	189362	190374
179000	184536	185492	186458	187435	188421	189418	190426	191444
180000	185567	186528	187500	188482	189474	190476	191489	192513
181000	186598	187565	188542	189529	190526	191534	192553	193583
182000	187629	.88601	189583	190576	191579	192593	193617	194652
183000	188660	189637	190625	191623	192632	193651	194681	195722
184000	189691	190674	191667	192670	193684	194709	195745	196791
185000	190722	191710	192708	193717	194737	195767	196808	197861
186000	191753	192746	193750	194764	195789	196825	197872	198930
187000	192783	193782	194792	195812	196842	197884	198936	200000
188000	193814	194819	195833	196859	197895	198942	200000	201070
189000	194845	195855	196875	197906	198947	200000	201064	202139
190000	195876	196891	197917	198953	200000	201058	202128	203209
191000	196907	197927	198958	200000	201053	202116	203191	204278
192000	197938	198964	200000	201047	202105	203175	204255	205348
193000	198969	200000	201042	202094	203158	204233	205319	206417
194000	200000	201036	202083	203141	204211	205291	206383	207487
195000	201031	202073	203125	204188	205263	206349	207447	208556
196000	202062	203109	204167	205236	206316	207407	208511	209626
197000	203093	204145	205208	206283	207368	208466	209574	210695
198000	204124	205181	206250	207330	208421	209524	210638	211765
199000	205155	206218	207292	208377	209474	210582	211702	212834
200000	206186	207254	208333	209424	210526	211640	212766	213904
201000	207216	208290	209375	210471	211579	212698	213830	214973
202000	208247	209326	210417	211518	212632	213757	214894	216043
203000	209278	210363	211458	212565	213684	214815	215957	217112
204000	210309	211399	212500	213613	214737	215873	217021	218182
205000	211340	212435	213542	214660	215789	216931	218085	219251
206000	212371	213471	214583	215707	216842	217989	219149	220321
207000	213402	214508	215625	216754	217895	219048	220213	221390
208000	214433	215544	216667	217801	218947	220106	221277	222460
209000	215464	216580	217708	218848	220000	221164	222340	223529
210000	216495	217617	218750	219895	221053	222222	223404	224599
211000	217526	218653	219792	220942	222105	223280	224468	225668
212000	218557	219689	220833	221990	223158	224339	225532	226738
213000	219588	220725	221875	223037	224211	225397	226596	227807
214000	220619	221762	222917	224084	225263	226455	227660	228877
215000	221649	222798	223958	225131	226316	227513	228723	229947
216000	222680	223834	225000	226178	227368	228571	229787	231016
217000	223711	224870	226042	227225	228421	229630	230851	232086
218000	224742	225907	227083	228272	229474	230688	231915	233155
219000	225773	226943	228125	229319	230526	231746	232979	234225
220000	226804	227979	229167	230366	231579	232804	234043	235294
221000	227835	229016	230208	231414	232632	233862	235106	236364
222000	228866	230052	231250	232461	233684	234921	236170	237433
223000	229897	231088	232292	233508	234737	235979	237234	238503
224000	230928	232124	233333	234555	235789	237037	238298	239572
225000	231959	233161	234375	235602	236842	238095	239362	240642
226000	232990	234197	235417	236649	237895	239153	240426	241711
227000	234021	235233	236458	237696	238947	240212	241489	242781
228000	235052	236269	237500	238743	240000	241270	242553	243850
229000	236082	237306	238542	239791	241053	242328	243617	244920
230000	237113	238342	239583	240838	242105	243386	244681	245989
231000	238144	239378	240625	241885	243158	244444	245745	247059
232000	239175	240414	241667	242932	244211	245503	246808	248128
233000	240206	241451	242708	243979	245263	246561	247872	249198
234000	241237	242487	243750	245026	246316	247619	248936	250267
235000	242268	243523	244792	246073	247368	248677	250000	251337
236000	243299	244560	245833	247120	248421	249735	251064	252406
237000	244330	245596	246875	248168	249474	250794	252128	253476
238000	245361	246632	247917	249215	250526	251852	253191	254545
239000	246392	247668	248958	250262	251579	252910	254255	255615
240000	247423	248705	250000	251309	252632	253968	255319	256684
241000	248454	249741	251042	252356	253684	255026	256383	257754
242000	249485	250777	252083	253403	254737	256085	257447	258824
243000	250515	251813	253125	254450	255789	257143	258511	259893
244000	251546	252850	254167	255497	256842	258201	259574	260963
245000	252577	253886	255208	256544	257895	259259	260638	262032
246000	253608	254922	256250	257592	258947	260317	261702	263102
247000	254639	255959	257292	258639	260000	261376	262766	264171
248000	255670	256995	258333	259686	261053	262434	263830	265241
249000	256701	258031	259375	260733	262105	263492	264894	266310
250000	257732	259067	260417	261780	263158	264550	265957	267380
251000	258763	260104	261458	262827	264211	265608	267021	268449
252000	259794	261140	262500	263874	265263	266667	268085	269519

Net	Gross at 3% Commission	Gross at 3½% Commission	Gross at 4% Commission	Gross at 4½% Commission	Gross at 5% Commission	Gross at 5½% Commission	Gross at 6% Commission	Gross at 6½% Commission
253000	260825	262176	263542	264921	266316	267725	269149	270588
254000	261856	263212	264583	265969	267368	268783	270213	271658
255000	262887	264249	265625	267016	268421	269841	271277	272727
256000	263918	265285	266667	268063	269474	270899	272340	273797
257000	264948	266321	267708	269110	270526	271958	273404	274866
258000	265979	267358	268750	270157	271579	273016	274468	275936
259000	267010	268394	269792	271204	272632	274074	275532	277005
260000	268041	269430	270833	272251	273684	275132	276596	278075
261000	269072	270466	271875	273298	274737	276190	277660	279144
262000	270103	271503	272917	274346	275789	277249	278723	280214
263000	271134	272539	273958	275393	276842	278307	279787	281283
264000	272165	273575	275000	276440	277895	279365	280851	282353
265000	273196	274611	276042	277487	278947	280423	281915	283422
266000	274227	275648	277083	278534	280000	281481	282979	284492
267000	275258	276684	278125	279581	281053	282540	284043	285561
268000	276289	277720	279167	280628	282105	283598	285106	286631
269000	277320	278756	280208	281675	283158	284656	286170	287701
270000	278351	279793	281250	282723	284211	285714	287234	288770
271000	279381	280829	282292	283770	285263	286772	288298	289840
272000	280412	281865	283333	284817	286316	287831	289362	290909
273000	281443	282902	284375	285864	287368	288889	290426	291979
274000	282474	283938	285417	286911	288421	289947	291489	293048
275000	283505	284974	286458	287958	289474	291005	292553	294118
276000	284536	286010	287500	289005	290526	292063	293617	295187
277000	285567	287047	288542	290052	291579	293122	294681	296257
278000	286598	288083	289583	291099	292632	294180	295745	297326
279000	287629	289119	290625	292147	293684	295238	296808	298396
280000	288660	290155	291667	293194	294737	296296	297872	299465
281000	289691	291192	292708	294241	295789	297354	298936	300535
282000	290722	292228	293750	295288	296842	298413	300000	301604
283000	291753	293264	294792	296335	297895	299471	301064	302674
284000	292783	294301	295833	297382	298947	300529	302128	303743
285000	293814	295337	296875	298429	300000	301587	303191	304813
286000	294845	296373	297917	299476	301053	302645	304255	305882
287000	295876	297409	298958	300524	302105	303704	305319	306952
288000	296907	298446	300000	301571	303158	304762	306383	308021
289000	297938	299482	301042	302618	304211	305820	307447	309091
290000	298969	300518	302083	303665	305263	306878	308511	310160
291000	300000	301554	303125	304712	306316	307936	309574	311230
292000	301031	302591	304167	305759	307368	308995	310638	312299
293000	302062	303627	305208	306806	308421	310053	311702	313369
294000	303093	304663	306250	307853	309474	311111	312766	314439
295000	304124	305699	307292	308901	310526	312169	313830	315508
296000	305155	306736	308333	309948	311579	313227	314894	316578
297000	306186	307772	309375	310995	312632	314286	315957	317647
298000	307216	308808	310417	312042	313684	315344	317021	318717
299000	308247	309845	311458	313089	314737	316402	318085	319786
300000	309278	310881	312500	314136	315789	317460	319149	320856
301000	310309	311917	313542	315183	316842	318519	320213	321925
302000	311340	312953	314583	316230	317895	319577	321277	322995
303000	312371	313990	315625	317277	318947	320635	322340	324064
304000	313402	315026	316667	318325	320000	321693	323404	325134
305000	314433	316062	317708	319372	321053	322751	324468	326203
306000	315464	317098	318750	320419	322105	323810	325532	327273
307000	316495	318135	319792	321466	323158	324868	326596	328342
308000	317526	319171	320833	322513	324211	325926	327660	329412
309000	318557	320207	321875	323560	325263	326984	328723	330481
310000	319588	321244	322917	324607	326316	328042	329787	331551
311000	320619	322280	323958	325654	327368	329101	330851	332620
312000	321649	323316	325000	326702	328421	330159	331915	333690
313000	322680	324352	326042	327749	329474	331217	332979	334759
314000	323711	325389	327083	328796	330526	332275	334043	335829
315000	324742	326425	328125	329843	331579	333333	335106	336898
316000	325773	327461	329167	330890	332632	334392	336170	337968
317000	326804	328497	330208	331937	333684	335450	337234	339037
318000	327835	329534	331250	332984	334737	336508	338298	340107
319000	328866	330570	332292	334031	335789	337566	339362	341176
320000	329897	331606	333333	335079	336842	338625	340426	342246
321000	330928	332642	334375	336126	337895	339683	341489	343316
322000	331959	333679	335417	337173	338947	340741	342553	344385
323000	332990	334715	336458	338220	340000	341799	343617	345455
324000	334021	335751	337500	339267	341053	342857	344681	346524
325000	335052	336788	338542	340314	342105	343915	345745	347594
326000	336082	337824	339583	341361	343158	344974	346808	348663
327000	337113	338860	340625	342408	344211	346032	347872	349733
328000	338144	339896	341667	343455	345263	347090	348936	350802

Net	Gross at 3% Commission	Gross at 3½% Commission	Gross at 4% Commission	Gross at 4½% Commission	Gross at 5% Commission	Gross at 5½% Commission	Gross at 6% Commission	Gross at 6½% Commission
329000	339175	340933	342708	344503	346316	348148	350000	351872
330000	340206	341969	343750	345550	347368	349206	351064	352941
331000	341237	343005	344792	346597	348421	350265	352128	354011
332000	342268	344041	345833	347644	349474	351323	353191	355080
333000	343299	345078	346875	348691	350526	352381	354255	356150
334000	344330	346114	347917	349738	351579	353439	355319	357219
335000	345361	347150	348958	350785	352632	354497	356383	358289
336000	346392	348187	350000	351832	353684	355556	357447	359358
337000	347423	349223	351042	352880	354737	356614	358511	360428
338000	348454	350259	352083	353927	355789	357672	359574	361497
339000	349485	351295	353125	354974	356842	358730	360638	362567
340000	350515	352332	354167	356021	357895	359788	361702	363636
341000	351546	353368	355208	357068	358947	360847	362766	364706
342000	352577	354404	356250	358115	360000	361905	363830	365775
343000	353608	355440	357292	359162	361053	362963	364894	366845
344000	354639	356477	358333	360209	362105	364021	365957	367914
345000	355670	357513	359375	361257	363158	365079	367021	368984
346000	356701	358549	360417	362304	364211	366138	368085	370053
347000	357732	359585	361458	363351	365263	367196	369149	371123
348000	358763	360622	362500	364398	366316	368254	370213	372193
349000	359794	361658	363542	365445	367368	369312	371277	373262
350000	360825	362694	364583	366492	368421	370370	372340	374332
351000	361856	363731	365625	367539	369474	371429	373404	375401
352000	362887	364767	366667	368586	370526	372487	374468	376471
353000	363918	365803	367708	369633	371579	373545	375532	377540
354000	364948	366839	368750	370681	372632	374603	376596	378610
355000	365979	367876	369792	371728	373684	375661	377660	379679
356000	367010	368912	370833	372775	374737	376720	378723	380749
357000	368041	369948	371875	373822	375789	377778	379787	381818
358000	369072	370984	372917	374865	376842	378836	380851	382888
359000	370103	372021	373958	375916	377895	379894	381915	383957
360000	371134	373057	375000	376963	378947	380952	382979	385027
361000	372165	374093	376042	378010	380000	382011	384043	386096
362000	373196	375130	377083	379058	381053	383069	385106	387166
363000	374227	376166	378125	380105	382105	384127	386170	388235
364000	375258	377202	379167	381152	383158	385185	387234	389305
365000	376289	378238	380208	382199	384211	386243	388298	390374
366000	377320	379275	381250	383246	385263	387302	389362	391444
367000	378351	380311	382292	384293	386316	388360	390426	392513
368000	379381	381347	383333	385340	387368	389418	391489	393583
369000	380412	382383	384375	386387	388421	390476	392553	394652
370000	381443	383420	385417	387435	389474	391534	393617	395722
371000	382474	384456	386458	388482	390526	392593	394681	396791
372000	383505	385492	387500	389529	391579	393651	395745	397861
373000	384536	386528	388542	390576	392632	394709	396808	398930
374000	385567	387565	389583	391623	393684	395767	397872	400000
375000	386598	388601	390625	392670	394737	396825	398936	401070
376000	387629	389637	391667	393717	395789	397884	400000	402139
377000	388660	390674	392708	394764	396842	398942	401064	403209
378000	389691	391710	393750	395812	397895	400000	402128	404278
379000	390722	392746	394792	396859	398947	401058	403191	405348
380000	391753	393782	395833	397906	400000	402116	404255	406417
381000	392783	394819	396875	398953	401053	403175	405319	407487
382000	393814	395855	397917	400000	402105	404233	406383	408556
383000	394845	396891	398958	401047	403158	405291	407447	409626
384000	395876	397927	400000	402094	404211	406349	408511	410695
385000	396907	398964	401042	403141	405263	407407	409574	411765
386000	397938	400000	402083	404188	406316	408466	410638	412834
387000	398969	401036	403125	405236	407368	409524	411702	413904
388000	400000	402073	404167	406283	408421	410582	412766	414973
389000	401031	403109	405208	407330	409474	411640	413830	416043
390000	402062	404145	406250	408377	410526	412698	414894	417112
391000	403093	405181	407292	409424	411579	413757	415957	418182
392000	404124	406218	408333	410471	412632	414815	417021	419251
393000	405155	407254	409375	411518	413684	415873	418085	420321
394000	406186	408290	410417	412565	414737	416931	419149	421390
395000	407216	409326	411458	413613	415789	417989	420213	422460
396000	408247	410363	412500	414660	416842	419048	421277	423529
397000	409278	411399	413542	415707	417895	420106	422340	424599
398000	410309	412435	414583	416754	418947	421164	423404	425668
399000	411340	413471	415625	417801	420000	422222	424468	426738
400000	412371	414508	416667	418848	421053	423280	425532	427807
401000	413402	415544	417708	419895	422105	424339	426596	428877
402000	414433	416580	418750	420942	423158	425397	427660	429947
403000	415464	417617	419792	421990	424211	426455	428723	431016
404000	416495	418653	420833	423037	425263	427513	429787	432086

FACTORS TO COMPUTE INTEREST PORTION OF MONTHLY LOAN PAYMENTS

Annual Interest %	Monthly Interest %	Annual Interest %	Monthly Interest %	Annual Interest %	Monthly Interest %
6	0.5000	11	0.9167	16	1.333
6¼	0.5208	11¼	0.9375	16¼	1.354
6½	0.5417	11½	0.9583	16½	1.375
6¾	0.5625	11¾	0.9792	16¾	1.396
7	0.5833	12	1.0000	17	1.417
7¼	0.6042	12¼	1.0208	17¼	1.438
7½	0.6250	12½	1.0417	17½	1.458
7¾	0.6458	12¾	1.0625	17¾	1.479
8	0.6667	13	1.0833	18	1.500
8¼	0.6875	13¼	1.1042	18¼	1.521
8½	0.7083	13½	1.1250	18½	1.542
8¾	0.7292	13¾	1.1458	18¾	1.563
9	0.7500	14	1.1667	19	1.583
9¼	0.7708	14¼	1.1875	19¼	1.604
9½	0.7917	14½	1.2083	19½	1.625
9¾	0.8125	14¾	1.2292	19¾	1.646
10	0.8333	15	1.2500	20	1.667
10¼	0.8542	15¼	1.2708	20¼	1.688
10½	0.8750	15½	1.2917	20½	1.708
10¾	0.8958	15¾	1.3125	20¾	1.729

EXAMPLE:

Loan Balance $19,866.66

Interest 10% p/yr. or 0.8333 p/mo.

Monthly Payment $300.00

Interest: 0.8333% X 19,866.66 .... (165.55)

Payment toward principal 134.45

New Loan Balance $19,732.21

Monthly Payment $300.00

Interest: 0.8333% X 19,732.21 .... (164.43)

Payment toward principal 135.57

New Loan Balance $19,596.64

AGE OF LOAN	2.0	3.0	5.0	8.0	10.0	12.0	15.0	16.0	17.0	18.0	19.0	20.0	AGE OF LOAN
						ORIGINAL TERM IN YEARS							
1	51.7	69.0	82.7	90.3	92.8	94.5	96.1	96.5	96.8	97.1	97.4	97.6	1
2	0.0	35.7	64.1	80.0	85.2	88.6	91.9	92.7	93.4	94.0	94.6	95.1	2
3	0.0	0.0	44.2	68.8	76.9	82.2	87.4	88.7	89.8	90.7	91.6	92.3	3
4	0.0	0.0	22.9	56.9	68.1	75.4	82.6	84.3	85.8	87.2	88.4	89.4	4
5	0.0	0.0	0.0	44.1	58.6	68.1	77.4	79.7	81.6	83.4	84.9	86.3	5
6	0.0	0.0	0.0	30.4	48.5	60.3	71.9	74.7	77.1	79.3	81.2	82.9	6
7	0.0	0.0	0.0	15.7	37.6	51.9	65.9	69.3	72.3	74.9	77.2	79.3	7
8	0.0	0.0	0.0	0.0	25.9	42.5	59.5	63.6	67.1	70.2	73.0	75.4	8
9	0.0	0.0	0.0	0.0	13.4	33.3	52.7	57.5	61.6	65.2	68.4	71.2	9
10	0.0	0.0	0.0	0.0	0.0	23.0	45.4	50.9	55.6	59.8	63.5	66.8	10
11	0.0	0.0	0.0	0.0	0.0	11.9	37.5	43.8	49.2	54.0	58.2	62.0	11
12	0.0	0.0	0.0	0.0	0.0	0.0	29.1	36.2	42.4	47.8	52.6	56.9	12
13	0.0	0.0	0.0	0.0	0.0	0.0	20.1	28.1	35.1	41.2	46.6	51.4	13
14	0.0	0.0	0.0	0.0	0.0	0.0	10.4	19.4	27.2	34.0	40.1	45.5	14
15	0.0	0.0	0.0	0.0	0.0	0.0	0.0	10.0	18.7	26.4	33.2	39.1	15
16	0.0	0.0	0.0	0.0	0.0	0.0	0.0	0.0	9.7	18.2	25.7	32.4	16
17	0.0	0.0	0.0	0.0	0.0	0.0	0.0	0.0	0.0	9.4	17.7	25.1	17
18	0.0	0.0	0.0	0.0	0.0	0.0	0.0	0.0	0.0	0.0	9.2	17.3	18
19	0.0	0.0	0.0	0.0	0.0	0.0	0.0	0.0	0.0	0.0	0.0	8.9	19

AGE OF LOAN	21.0	22.0	23.0	24.0	25.0	26.0	27.0	28.0	29.0	30.0	35.0	40.0	AGE OF LOAN
						ORIGINAL TERM IN YEARS							
1	97.8	98.0	98.2	98.3	98.5	98.6	98.7	98.8	98.9	99.0	99.3	99.5	1
2	95.5	95.9	96.2	96.5	96.8	97.1	97.3	97.5	97.7	97.9	98.6	99.0	2
3	93.0	93.6	94.1	94.6	95.1	95.5	95.8	96.2	96.5	96.7	97.8	98.5	3
4	90.3	91.2	91.9	92.6	93.2	93.7	94.2	94.7	95.1	95.5	96.9	97.9	4
5	87.5	88.5	89.5	90.4	91.2	91.9	92.5	93.1	93.6	94.1	96.0	97.3	5
6	84.4	85.7	86.9	88.0	89.0	89.9	90.7	91.4	92.1	92.7	95.0	96.6	6
7	81.1	82.7	84.2	85.5	86.7	87.7	88.7	89.6	90.4	91.1	94.0	95.9	7
8	77.5	79.5	81.2	82.8	84.2	85.4	86.6	87.7	88.6	89.5	92.9	95.1	8
9	73.7	76.0	78.0	79.9	81.5	83.0	84.3	85.6	86.7	87.7	91.7	94.3	9
10	69.7	72.3	74.6	76.7	78.6	80.3	81.9	83.3	84.6	85.8	90.4	93.4	10
11	65.3	68.3	71.0	73.4	75.6	77.5	79.3	80.9	82.4	83.8	89.0	92.5	11
12	60.6	64.0	67.1	69.8	72.3	74.5	76.5	78.4	80.0	81.6	87.5	91.4	12
13	55.6	59.4	62.9	65.9	68.7	71.2	73.5	75.6	77.5	79.2	85.9	90.3	13
14	50.2	54.5	58.4	61.8	64.9	67.8	70.3	72.6	74.8	76.7	84.2	89.2	14
15	44.5	49.2	53.5	57.4	60.9	64.0	66.9	69.5	71.8	74.0	82.4	87.9	15
16	38.3	43.6	48.4	52.6	56.5	60.0	63.2	66.1	68.7	71.1	80.4	86.6	16
17	31.7	37.5	42.8	47.5	51.8	55.7	59.2	62.4	65.3	68.0	78.3	85.1	17
18	24.5	31.0	36.8	42.1	46.8	51.1	55.0	58.5	61.7	64.7	76.1	83.6	18
19	16.9	24.1	30.5	36.2	41.4	46.2	50.4	54.3	57.9	61.1	73.7	81.9	19
20	8.7	16.6	23.6	30.0	35.7	40.9	45.6	49.8	53.7	57.3	71.1	80.1	20
21	0.0	8.6	16.3	23.2	29.5	35.2	40.3	45.0	49.3	53.2	68.3	78.2	21
22	0.0	0.0	8.4	16.0	22.9	29.1	34.7	39.8	44.5	48.8	65.3	76.2	22
23	0.0	0.0	0.0	8.3	15.8	22.5	28.7	34.3	39.4	44.1	62.1	74.0	23
24	0.0	0.0	0.0	0.0	8.1	15.5	22.3	28.4	33.9	39.0	58.7	71.6	24
25	0.0	0.0	0.0	0.0	0.0	8.0	15.3	22.0	28.0	33.6	55.0	69.1	25
26	0.0	0.0	0.0	0.0	0.0	0.0	7.9	15.2	21.7	27.8	51.1	66.4	26
27	0.0	0.0	0.0	0.0	0.0	0.0	0.0	7.8	15.0	21.5	46.8	63.5	27
28	0.0	0.0	0.0	0.0	0.0	0.0	0.0	0.0	7.7	14.8	42.3	60.4	28
29	0.0	0.0	0.0	0.0	0.0	0.0	0.0	0.0	0.0	7.7	37.5	57.1	29
30	0.0	0.0	0.0	0.0	0.0	0.0	0.0	0.0	0.0	0.0	32.2	53.5	30
31	0.0	0.0	0.0	0.0	0.0	0.0	0.0	0.0	0.0	0.0	26.7	49.7	31
32	0.0	0.0	0.0	0.0	0.0	0.0	0.0	0.0	0.0	0.0	20.7	45.7	32
33	0.0	0.0	0.0	0.0	0.0	0.0	0.0	0.0	0.0	0.0	14.2	41.2	33
34	0.0	0.0	0.0	0.0	0.0	0.0	0.0	0.0	0.0	0.0	7.4	36.4	34
35	0.0	0.0	0.0	0.0	0.0	0.0	0.0	0.0	0.0	0.0	0.0	31.4	35
36	0.0	0.0	0.0	0.0	0.0	0.0	0.0	0.0	0.0	0.0	0.0	25.9	36
37	0.0	0.0	0.0	0.0	0.0	0.0	0.0	0.0	0.0	0.0	0.0	20.1	37
38	0.0	0.0	0.0	0.0	0.0	0.0	0.0	0.0	0.0	0.0	0.0	13.9	38
39	0.0	0.0	0.0	0.0	0.0	0.0	0.0	0.0	0.0	0.0	0.0	7.2	39

EXAMPLES *ON PAGES A-382 TO A-397*

AGE OF LOAN	2.0	3.0	5.0	8.0	10.0	12.0	15.0	16.0	17.0	18.0	19.0	20.0	AGE OF LOAN
						ORIGINAL TERM IN YEARS							
1	51.8	69.0	82.8	90.4	92.9	94.6	96.2	96.6	96.9	97.2	97.5	97.7	1
2	0.0	35.8	64.3	80.1	85.3	88.7	92.1	92.9	93.6	94.2	94.7	95.2	2
3	0.0	0.0	44.4	69.1	77.2	82.5	87.6	88.9	90.0	90.9	91.8	92.5	3
4	0.0	0.0	23.0	57.2	68.4	75.7	82.9	84.6	86.1	87.5	88.6	89.7	4
5	0.0	0.0	0.0	44.4	58.9	68.5	77.8	80.0	82.0	83.7	85.2	86.6	5
6	0.0	0.0	0.0	30.6	48.8	60.7	72.3	75.1	77.5	79.7	81.6	83.3	6
7	0.0	0.0	0.0	15.9	37.9	52.3	66.3	69.8	72.8	75.4	77.7	79.7	7
8	0.0	0.0	0.0	0.0	26.2	43.3	60.0	64.1	67.6	70.7	73.4	75.9	8
9	0.0	0.0	0.0	0.0	13.5	33.6	53.2	57.9	62.1	65.7	68.9	71.7	9
10	0.0	0.0	0.0	0.0	0.0	23.2	45.8	51.3	56.1	60.3	64.0	67.3	10
11	0.0	0.0	0.0	0.0	0.0	12.0	37.9	44.2	49.7	54.6	58.8	62.6	11
12	0.0	0.0	0.0	0.0	0.0	0.0	29.5	36.6	42.9	48.4	53.2	57.4	12
13	0.0	0.0	0.0	0.0	0.0	0.0	20.3	28.4	35.5	41.7	47.1	51.9	13
14	0.0	0.0	0.0	0.0	0.0	0.0	10.5	19.6	27.6	34.5	40.6	46.0	14
15	0.0	0.0	0.0	0.0	0.0	0.0	0.0	10.2	19.0	26.8	33.6	39.7	15
16	0.0	0.0	0.0	0.0	0.0	0.0	0.0	0.0	9.9	18.5	26.1	32.8	16
17	0.0	0.0	0.0	0.0	0.0	0.0	0.0	0.0	0.0	9.6	18.0	25.5	17
18	0.0	0.0	0.0	0.0	0.0	0.0	0.0	0.0	0.0	0.0	9.3	17.6	18
19	0.0	0.0	0.0	0.0	0.0	0.0	0.0	0.0	0.0	0.0	0.0	9.1	19

AGE OF LOAN	21.0	22.0	23.0	24.0	25.0	26.0	27.0	28.0	29.0	30.0	35.0	40.0	AGE OF LOAN
						ORIGINAL TERM IN YEARS							
1	97.9	98.1	98.2	98.4	98.5	98.6	98.8	98.9	98.9	99.0	99.4	99.6	1
2	95.6	96.0	96.4	96.7	96.9	97.2	97.4	97.6	97.8	98.0	98.7	99.1	2
3	93.2	93.8	94.3	94.8	95.2	95.6	96.0	96.3	96.6	96.9	97.9	98.6	3
4	90.6	91.4	92.2	92.8	93.4	94.0	94.4	94.9	95.3	95.7	97.1	98.0	4
5	87.8	88.9	89.8	90.7	91.5	92.2	92.8	93.4	93.9	94.4	96.2	97.4	5
6	84.8	86.1	87.3	88.4	89.3	90.2	91.0	91.7	92.4	93.0	95.3	96.8	6
7	81.5	83.1	84.6	85.9	87.1	88.1	89.1	90.0	90.8	91.5	94.3	96.1	7
8	78.0	79.9	81.7	83.2	84.6	85.9	87.0	88.1	89.0	89.9	93.2	95.4	8
9	74.3	76.5	78.5	80.4	82.0	83.5	84.8	86.0	87.2	88.2	92.1	94.6	9
10	70.2	72.8	75.2	77.3	79.2	80.9	82.4	83.9	85.1	86.3	90.8	93.8	10
11	65.9	68.9	71.6	74.0	76.1	78.1	79.9	81.5	83.0	84.3	89.5	92.9	11
12	61.2	64.6	67.7	70.4	72.9	75.1	77.1	79.0	80.6	82.2	88.0	91.9	12
13	56.2	60.1	63.5	66.6	69.4	71.9	74.2	76.3	78.1	79.9	86.5	90.8	13
14	50.9	55.2	59.0	62.5	65.6	68.4	71.0	73.3	75.5	77.4	84.8	89.7	14
15	45.1	49.9	54.2	58.1	61.6	64.7	67.6	70.2	72.6	74.7	83.1	88.5	15
16	38.8	44.2	49.0	53.3	57.2	60.7	63.9	66.8	69.5	71.9	81.1	87.2	16
17	32.2	38.1	43.4	48.2	52.5	56.4	60.0	63.2	66.1	68.8	79.1	85.8	17
18	25.0	31.5	37.4	42.7	47.5	51.8	55.7	59.3	62.5	65.5	76.9	84.3	18
19	17.2	24.5	31.0	36.8	42.1	46.9	51.2	55.1	58.7	61.9	74.5	82.7	19
20	8.9	16.9	24.1	30.5	36.3	41.5	46.3	50.6	54.5	58.1	71.9	80.9	20
21	0.0	8.8	16.6	23.7	30.0	35.8	41.0	45.8	50.1	54.0	69.2	79.1	21
22	0.0	0.0	8.6	16.3	23.3	29.6	35.3	40.5	45.3	49.6	66.2	77.1	22
23	0.0	0.0	0.0	8.5	16.1	23.0	29.3	34.9	40.1	44.8	63.0	74.9	23
24	0.0	0.0	0.0	0.0	8.3	15.9	22.7	28.9	34.6	39.7	59.6	72.6	24
25	0.0	0.0	0.0	0.0	0.0	8.2	15.7	22.5	28.6	34.2	55.9	70.1	25
26	0.0	0.0	0.0	0.0	0.0	0.0	8.1	15.5	22.2	28.3	52.0	67.4	26
27	0.0	0.0	0.0	0.0	0.0	0.0	0.0	8.0	15.3	22.0	47.7	64.5	27
28	0.0	0.0	0.0	0.0	0.0	0.0	0.0	0.0	7.9	15.2	43.1	61.4	28
29	0.0	0.0	0.0	0.0	0.0	0.0	0.0	0.0	0.0	7.9	38.2	58.1	29
30	0.0	0.0	0.0	0.0	0.0	0.0	0.0	0.0	0.0	0.0	33.0	54.5	30
31	0.0	0.0	0.0	0.0	0.0	0.0	0.0	0.0	0.0	0.0	27.3	50.6	31
32	0.0	0.0	0.0	0.0	0.0	0.0	0.0	0.0	0.0	0.0	21.2	46.5	32
33	0.0	0.0	0.0	0.0	0.0	0.0	0.0	0.0	0.0	0.0	14.6	42.0	33
34	0.0	0.0	0.0	0.0	0.0	0.0	0.0	0.0	0.0	0.0	7.6	37.3	34
35	0.0	0.0	0.0	0.0	0.0	0.0	0.0	0.0	0.0	0.0	0.0	32.1	35
36	0.0	0.0	0.0	0.0	0.0	0.0	0.0	0.0	0.0	0.0	0.0	26.6	36
37	0.0	0.0	0.0	0.0	0.0	0.0	0.0	0.0	0.0	0.0	0.0	20.6	37
38	0.0	0.0	0.0	0.0	0.0	0.0	0.0	0.0	0.0	0.0	0.0	14.2	38
39	0.0	0.0	0.0	0.0	0.0	0.0	0.0	0.0	0.0	0.0	0.0	7.4	39

EXAMPLES *ON PAGES A-382 TO A-397*

AGE OF LOAN	ORIGINAL TERM IN YEARS												AGE OF LOAN
	2.0	3.0	5.0	8.0	10.0	12.0	15.0	16.0	17.0	18.0	19.0	20.0	
1	51.9	69.1	82.9	90.5	93.0	94.7	96.2	96.6	97.0	97.3	97.5	97.8	1
2	0.0	35.8	64.4	80.3	85.5	88.9	92.2	93.0	93.7	94.3	94.9	95.3	2
3	0.0	0.0	44.5	69.3	77.4	82.7	87.8	89.1	90.2	91.1	92.0	92.7	3
4	0.0	0.0	23.1	57.4	68.6	76.0	83.2	84.9	86.4	87.7	88.9	89.9	4
5	0.0	0.0	0.0	44.6	59.2	68.8	78.1	80.4	82.3	84.0	85.6	86.9	5
6	0.0	0.0	0.0	30.8	45.1	61.0	72.6	75.5	77.9	80.1	82.0	83.6	6
7	0.0	0.0	0.0	16.0	38.2	52.7	66.8	70.2	73.2	75.8	78.1	80.1	7
8	0.0	0.0	0.0	0.0	26.4	43.6	60.4	64.5	68.1	71.2	73.9	76.3	8
9	0.0	0.0	0.0	0.0	13.7	33.9	53.6	58.4	62.6	66.2	69.4	72.3	9
10	0.0	0.0	0.0	0.0	0.0	23.4	46.3	51.8	56.6	60.9	64.6	67.9	10
11	0.0	0.0	0.0	0.0	0.0	12.2	38.3	44.7	50.2	55.1	59.3	63.1	11
12	0.0	0.0	0.0	0.0	0.0	0.0	29.8	37.0	43.3	48.9	53.7	58.0	12
13	0.0	0.0	0.0	0.0	0.0	0.0	20.6	28.8	35.9	42.2	47.7	52.5	13
14	0.0	0.0	0.0	0.0	0.0	0.0	10.7	19.9	27.9	34.9	41.1	46.6	14
15	0.0	0.0	0.0	0.0	0.0	0.0	0.0	10.3	19.3	27.2	34.1	40.2	15
16	0.0	0.0	0.0	0.0	0.0	0.0	0.0	0.0	10.0	18.8	26.5	33.3	16
17	0.0	0.0	0.0	0.0	0.0	0.0	0.0	0.0	0.0	9.7	18.3	25.9	17
18	0.0	0.0	0.0	0.0	0.0	0.0	0.0	0.0	0.0	0.0	9.5	17.9	18
19	0.0	0.0	0.0	0.0	0.0	0.0	0.0	0.0	0.0	0.0	0.0	9.3	19

AGE OF LOAN	ORIGINAL TERM IN YEARS												AGE OF LOAN
	21.0	22.0	23.0	24.0	25.0	26.0	27.0	28.0	29.0	30.0	35.0	40.0	
1	98.0	98.1	98.3	98.5	98.6	98.7	98.8	98.9	99.0	99.1	99.4	99.6	1
2	95.8	96.1	96.5	96.8	97.1	97.3	97.5	97.7	97.9	98.1	98.7	99.1	2
3	93.4	94.0	94.5	95.0	95.4	95.8	96.1	96.5	96.8	97.0	98.0	98.7	3
4	90.8	91.7	92.4	93.0	93.6	94.2	94.7	95.1	95.5	95.9	97.3	98.2	4
5	88.1	89.2	90.1	91.0	91.7	92.4	93.1	93.6	94.1	94.6	96.4	97.6	5
6	85.1	86.5	87.6	88.7	89.7	90.5	91.3	92.0	92.7	93.3	95.5	97.0	6
7	81.9	83.5	85.0	86.3	87.5	88.5	89.5	90.3	91.1	91.8	94.6	96.4	7
8	78.5	80.4	82.1	83.7	85.1	86.3	87.5	88.5	89.4	90.3	93.5	95.7	8
9	74.8	77.0	79.0	80.9	82.5	84.0	85.3	86.5	87.6	88.6	92.4	94.9	9
10	70.8	73.4	75.7	77.8	79.7	81.4	83.0	84.4	85.6	86.8	91.2	94.1	10
11	66.5	69.5	72.1	74.6	76.7	78.7	80.5	82.1	83.5	84.8	89.9	93.2	11
12	61.8	65.2	68.3	71.0	73.5	75.7	77.7	79.6	81.2	82.7	88.6	92.3	12
13	56.8	60.7	64.1	67.2	70.0	72.5	74.8	76.9	78.8	80.5	87.1	91.3	13
14	51.4	55.8	59.7	63.1	66.3	69.1	71.7	74.0	76.1	78.0	85.4	90.2	14
15	45.6	50.5	54.8	58.7	62.2	65.4	68.3	70.9	73.3	75.4	83.7	89.0	15
16	39.4	44.8	49.6	54.0	57.9	61.4	64.6	67.5	70.2	72.6	81.8	87.8	16
17	32.6	38.6	44.0	48.9	53.2	57.2	60.7	63.9	66.9	69.5	79.8	86.4	17
18	25.4	32.0	38.0	43.3	48.2	52.5	56.5	60.0	63.3	66.3	77.6	85.0	18
19	17.5	24.9	31.5	37.4	42.7	47.5	51.9	55.5	59.4	62.7	75.3	83.4	19
20	9.1	17.2	24.5	31.0	36.9	42.2	47.0	51.3	55.3	58.9	72.7	81.7	20
21	0.0	8.9	16.9	24.1	30.5	36.4	41.7	46.5	50.8	54.8	70.0	79.8	21
22	0.0	0.0	8.8	16.6	23.7	30.2	36.0	41.2	46.0	50.4	67.1	77.9	22
23	0.0	0.0	0.0	8.6	16.4	23.4	29.8	35.6	40.8	45.6	63.9	75.7	23
24	0.0	0.0	0.0	0.0	8.5	16.2	23.2	29.5	35.2	40.4	60.5	73.5	24
25	0.0	0.0	0.0	0.0	0.0	8.4	16.0	22.9	29.2	34.9	56.8	71.0	25
26	0.0	0.0	0.0	0.0	0.0	0.0	8.3	15.8	22.7	28.9	52.8	68.3	26
27	0.0	0.0	0.0	0.0	0.0	0.0	0.0	8.2	15.7	22.5	48.6	65.4	27
28	0.0	0.0	0.0	0.0	0.0	0.0	0.0	0.0	8.1	15.5	43.9	62.4	28
29	0.0	0.0	0.0	0.0	0.0	0.0	0.0	0.0	0.0	8.0	39.0	59.0	29
30	0.0	0.0	0.0	0.0	0.0	0.0	0.0	0.0	0.0	0.0	33.6	55.4	30
31	0.0	0.0	0.0	0.0	0.0	0.0	0.0	0.0	0.0	0.0	27.9	51.6	31
32	0.0	0.0	0.0	0.0	0.0	0.0	0.0	0.0	0.0	0.0	21.7	47.4	32
33	0.0	0.0	0.0	0.0	0.0	0.0	0.0	0.0	0.0	0.0	15.0	42.9	33
34	0.0	0.0	0.0	0.0	0.0	0.0	0.0	0.0	0.0	0.0	7.7	38.0	34
35	0.0	0.0	0.0	0.0	0.0	0.0	0.0	0.0	0.0	0.0	0.0	32.8	35
36	0.0	0.0	0.0	0.0	0.0	0.0	0.0	0.0	0.0	0.0	0.0	27.2	36
37	0.0	0.0	0.0	0.0	0.0	0.0	0.0	0.0	0.0	0.0	0.0	21.1	37
38	0.0	0.0	0.0	0.0	0.0	0.0	0.0	0.0	0.0	0.0	0.0	14.6	38
39	0.0	0.0	0.0	0.0	0.0	0.0	0.0	0.0	0.0	0.0	0.0	7.6	39

EXAMPLES *ON PAGES A-382 TO A-397*

AGE OF LOAN	2.0	3.0	5.0	8.0	10.0	12.0	15.0	16.0	17.0	18.0	19.0	20.0	AGE OF LOAN
1	51.9	69.2	83.0	90.6	93.1	94.7	96.3	96.7	97.0	97.3	97.6	97.8	1
2	0.0	35.9	64.6	80.5	85.7	89.1	92.4	93.2	93.9	94.5	95.0	95.5	2
3	0.0	0.0	44.7	69.5	77.6	82.9	88.1	89.3	90.4	91.4	92.2	92.9	3
4	0.0	0.0	23.2	57.7	68.9	76.3	83.4	85.2	86.7	88.0	89.2	90.2	4
5	0.0	0.0	0.0	44.9	59.5	69.1	78.4	80.7	82.7	84.4	85.9	87.2	5
6	0.0	0.0	0.0	31.1	45.4	61.4	73.0	75.9	78.3	80.5	82.3	84.0	6
7	0.0	0.0	0.0	16.1	38.4	53.0	67.2	70.6	73.6	76.2	78.5	80.6	7
8	0.0	0.0	0.0	0.0	26.6	44.0	60.9	65.0	68.5	71.7	74.4	76.8	8
9	0.0	0.0	0.0	0.0	13.8	34.2	54.1	58.9	63.1	66.7	69.9	72.8	9
10	0.0	0.0	0.0	0.0	0.0	23.7	46.7	52.3	57.1	61.4	65.1	68.4	10
11	0.0	0.0	0.0	0.0	0.0	12.3	38.7	45.2	50.7	55.6	59.9	63.7	11
12	0.0	0.0	0.0	0.0	0.0	0.0	30.1	37.5	43.8	49.4	54.3	58.6	12
13	0.0	0.0	0.0	0.0	0.0	0.0	20.9	29.2	36.4	42.7	48.2	53.1	13
14	0.0	0.0	0.0	0.0	0.0	0.0	10.8	20.2	28.3	35.4	41.6	47.1	14
15	0.0	0.0	0.0	0.0	0.0	0.0	0.0	10.5	19.6	27.5	34.5	40.7	15
16	0.0	0.0	0.0	0.0	0.0	0.0	0.0	0.0	10.2	19.1	26.9	33.8	16
17	0.0	0.0	0.0	0.0	0.0	0.0	0.0	0.0	0.0	9.9	18.6	26.3	17
18	0.0	0.0	0.0	0.0	0.0	0.0	0.0	0.0	0.0	0.0	9.7	18.2	18
19	0.0	0.0	0.0	0.0	0.0	0.0	0.0	0.0	0.0	0.0	0.0	9.4	19

AGE OF LOAN	21.0	22.0	23.0	24.0	25.0	26.0	27.0	28.0	29.0	30.0	35.0	40.0	AGE OF LOAN
1	98.0	98.2	98.4	98.5	98.6	98.8	98.9	99.0	99.0	99.1	99.4	99.6	1
2	95.9	96.3	96.6	96.9	97.2	97.4	97.6	97.8	98.0	98.2	98.8	99.2	2
3	93.6	94.2	94.7	95.2	95.6	96.0	96.3	96.6	96.9	97.1	98.1	98.8	3
4	91.1	91.9	92.6	93.3	93.9	94.4	94.9	95.3	95.7	96.0	97.4	98.3	4
5	88.4	89.5	90.4	91.2	92.0	92.7	93.3	93.9	94.4	94.8	96.6	97.8	5
6	85.5	86.8	88.0	89.1	90.0	90.9	91.6	92.3	93.0	93.6	95.8	97.2	6
7	82.4	84.0	85.4	86.7	87.8	88.5	89.8	90.7	91.5	92.2	94.9	96.6	7
8	79.0	80.9	82.6	84.1	85.5	86.7	87.9	88.5	89.8	90.7	93.9	95.9	8
9	75.3	77.5	79.6	81.4	83.0	84.4	85.8	87.0	88.0	89.0	92.8	95.2	9
10	71.3	73.9	76.3	78.4	80.2	81.9	83.5	84.9	86.1	87.3	91.6	94.4	10
11	67.1	70.1	72.7	75.1	77.3	79.2	81.0	82.6	84.1	85.4	90.4	93.6	11
12	62.4	65.8	68.9	71.6	74.1	76.3	78.3	80.2	81.8	83.3	89.0	92.7	12
13	57.4	61.3	64.8	67.5	70.7	73.2	75.5	77.5	79.4	81.1	87.6	91.8	13
14	52.0	56.4	60.3	63.8	67.0	69.8	72.4	74.7	76.8	78.7	86.0	90.7	14
15	46.2	51.1	55.5	59.4	62.9	66.1	69.0	71.6	74.0	76.1	84.3	89.6	15
16	39.9	45.4	50.3	54.7	58.6	62.2	65.4	68.3	70.9	73.3	82.5	88.4	16
17	33.1	39.2	44.6	49.5	53.9	57.9	61.4	64.7	67.6	70.3	80.5	87.0	17
18	25.8	32.5	38.6	44.0	48.9	53.2	57.2	60.8	64.1	67.0	78.4	85.6	18
19	17.8	25.3	32.0	38.0	43.4	48.2	52.6	56.6	60.2	63.5	76.0	84.1	19
20	9.3	17.5	24.9	31.5	37.5	42.8	47.7	52.1	56.1	59.7	73.5	82.4	20
21	0.0	9.1	17.2	24.5	31.1	37.0	42.4	47.2	51.6	55.6	70.8	80.6	21
22	0.0	0.0	8.9	17.0	24.2	30.7	36.6	41.9	46.7	51.1	67.9	78.7	22
23	0.0	0.0	0.0	8.8	16.7	23.9	30.4	36.2	41.5	46.3	64.8	76.6	23
24	0.0	0.0	0.0	0.0	8.7	16.5	23.6	30.0	35.9	41.1	61.4	74.3	24
25	0.0	0.0	0.0	0.0	0.0	8.6	16.3	23.4	29.7	35.5	57.7	71.9	25
26	0.0	0.0	0.0	0.0	0.0	0.0	8.5	16.2	23.1	29.5	53.7	69.2	26
27	0.0	0.0	0.0	0.0	0.0	0.0	0.0	8.4	16.0	22.9	49.4	66.4	27
28	0.0	0.0	0.0	0.0	0.0	0.0	0.0	0.0	8.3	15.9	44.8	63.3	28
29	0.0	0.0	0.0	0.0	0.0	0.0	0.0	0.0	0.0	8.2	39.8	60.0	29
30	0.0	0.0	0.0	0.0	0.0	0.0	0.0	0.0	0.0	0.0	34.3	56.4	30
31	0.0	0.0	0.0	0.0	0.0	0.0	0.0	0.0	0.0	0.0	28.5	52.5	31
32	0.0	0.0	0.0	0.0	0.0	0.0	0.0	0.0	0.0	0.0	22.2	48.3	32
33	0.0	0.0	0.0	0.0	0.0	0.0	0.0	0.0	0.0	0.0	15.3	43.8	33
34	0.0	0.0	0.0	0.0	0.0	0.0	0.0	0.0	0.0	0.0	8.0	38.9	34
35	0.0	0.0	0.0	0.0	0.0	0.0	0.0	0.0	0.0	0.0	0.0	33.6	35
36	0.0	0.0	0.0	0.0	0.0	0.0	0.0	0.0	0.0	0.0	0.0	27.8	36
37	0.0	0.0	0.0	0.0	0.0	0.0	0.0	0.0	0.0	0.0	0.0	21.7	37
38	0.0	0.0	0.0	0.0	0.0	0.0	0.0	0.0	0.0	0.0	0.0	15.0	38
39	0.0	0.0	0.0	0.0	0.0	0.0	0.0	0.0	0.0	0.0	0.0	7.8	39

EXAMPLES *ON PAGES A-382 TO A-397*

AGE OF LOAN	ORIGINAL TERM IN YEARS												AGE OF LOAN
	2.0	3.0	5.0	8.0	10.0	12.0	15.0	16.0	17.0	18.0	19.0	20.0	
1	52.0	69.3	83.1	90.7	93.2	94.8	96.4	96.8	97.1	97.4	97.7	97.9	1
2	0.0	36.0	64.7	80.6	85.8	89.2	92.5	93.3	94.0	94.6	95.1	95.6	2
3	0.0	0.0	44.8	69.7	77.8	83.1	88.3	89.5	90.6	91.6	92.4	93.1	3
4	0.0	0.0	23.3	57.9	69.2	76.6	83.7	85.4	86.9	88.3	89.4	90.4	4
5	0.0	0.0	0.0	45.1	59.8	69.4	78.8	81.0	83.0	84.7	86.2	87.5	5
6	0.0	0.0	0.0	31.3	49.7	61.7	73.4	76.2	78.7	80.8	82.7	84.4	6
7	0.0	0.0	0.0	16.2	38.7	53.4	67.6	71.0	74.0	76.6	78.9	81.0	7
8	0.0	0.0	0.0	0.0	26.8	44.3	61.3	65.4	69.0	72.1	74.9	77.3	8
9	0.0	0.0	0.0	0.0	13.9	34.5	54.5	59.3	63.5	67.2	70.4	73.3	9
10	0.0	0.0	0.0	0.0	0.0	23.9	47.1	52.7	57.6	61.9	65.6	68.9	10
11	0.0	0.0	0.0	0.0	0.0	12.4	39.1	45.6	51.2	56.1	60.4	64.2	11
12	0.0	0.0	0.0	0.0	0.0	0.0	30.5	37.9	44.3	49.9	54.8	59.2	12
13	0.0	0.0	0.0	0.0	0.0	0.0	21.1	29.5	36.8	43.1	48.7	53.7	13
14	0.0	0.0	0.0	0.0	0.0	0.0	11.0	20.4	28.7	35.8	42.1	47.7	14
15	0.0	0.0	0.0	0.0	0.0	0.0	0.0	10.6	19.9	27.9	35.0	41.2	15
16	0.0	0.0	0.0	0.0	0.0	0.0	0.0	0.0	10.3	19.3	27.3	34.3	16
17	0.0	0.0	0.0	0.0	0.0	0.0	0.0	0.0	0.0	10.0	18.9	26.7	17
18	0.0	0.0	0.0	0.0	0.0	0.0	0.0	0.0	0.0	0.0	9.8	18.5	18
19	0.0	0.0	0.0	0.0	0.0	0.0	0.0	0.0	0.0	0.0	0.0	9.6	19

AGE OF LOAN	ORIGINAL TERM IN YEARS												AGE OF LOAN
	21.0	22.0	23.0	24.0	25.0	26.0	27.0	28.0	29.0	30.0	35.0	40.0	
1	98.1	98.3	98.4	98.6	98.7	98.8	98.9	99.0	99.1	99.2	99.5	99.6	1
2	96.0	96.4	96.7	97.0	97.3	97.5	97.7	97.9	98.1	98.3	98.9	99.3	2
3	93.8	94.3	94.9	95.3	95.7	96.1	96.4	96.8	97.0	97.3	98.2	98.8	3
4	91.3	92.1	92.9	93.5	94.1	94.6	95.1	95.5	95.9	96.2	97.5	98.4	4
5	88.7	89.7	90.7	91.5	92.3	93.0	93.6	94.1	94.6	95.1	96.8	97.9	5
6	85.8	87.2	88.3	89.4	90.3	91.2	91.9	92.6	93.3	93.8	96.0	97.4	6
7	82.8	84.4	85.8	87.1	88.2	89.2	90.2	91.0	91.8	92.5	95.1	96.8	7
8	79.4	81.3	83.0	84.6	85.9	87.2	88.3	89.3	90.2	91.0	94.2	96.2	8
9	75.8	78.0	80.0	81.8	83.4	84.9	86.2	87.4	88.5	89.4	93.1	95.5	9
10	71.9	74.5	76.8	78.9	80.8	82.4	84.0	85.3	86.6	87.7	92.0	94.8	10
11	67.6	70.6	73.3	75.7	77.9	79.8	81.5	83.1	84.6	85.9	90.8	94.0	11
12	63.0	66.4	69.5	72.2	74.7	76.9	78.9	80.7	82.4	83.9	89.5	93.1	12
13	58.0	61.9	65.4	68.5	71.3	73.8	76.1	78.1	80.0	81.7	88.1	92.2	13
14	52.6	57.0	60.9	64.5	67.6	70.4	73.0	75.3	77.4	79.3	86.6	91.2	14
15	46.8	51.7	56.1	60.1	63.6	66.8	69.7	72.3	74.6	76.8	84.9	90.1	15
16	40.5	46.0	50.9	55.3	59.3	62.8	66.1	69.0	71.6	74.0	83.1	88.9	16
17	33.6	39.8	45.2	50.2	54.6	58.6	62.2	65.4	68.4	71.0	81.2	87.6	17
18	26.2	33.0	39.1	44.6	49.5	53.9	57.9	61.5	64.8	67.8	79.1	86.2	18
19	18.1	25.7	32.5	38.6	44.0	48.9	53.3	57.4	61.0	64.3	76.8	84.7	19
20	9.4	17.8	25.3	32.0	38.1	43.5	48.4	52.8	56.8	60.5	74.3	83.1	20
21	0.0	9.3	17.5	24.9	31.6	37.6	43.0	47.9	52.3	56.4	71.6	81.4	21
22	0.0	0.0	9.1	17.3	24.6	31.2	37.2	42.6	47.5	51.9	68.7	79.5	22
23	0.0	0.0	0.0	9.0	17.1	24.3	30.9	36.8	42.2	47.1	65.6	77.4	23
24	0.0	0.0	0.0	0.0	8.9	16.8	24.1	30.6	36.5	41.8	62.2	75.2	24
25	0.0	0.0	0.0	0.0	0.0	8.8	16.7	23.8	30.3	36.2	58.5	72.8	25
26	0.0	0.0	0.0	0.0	0.0	0.0	8.7	16.5	23.6	30.0	54.5	70.1	26
27	0.0	0.0	0.0	0.0	0.0	0.0	0.0	8.6	16.3	23.4	50.2	67.3	27
28	0.0	0.0	0.0	0.0	0.0	0.0	0.0	0.0	8.5	16.2	45.6	64.2	28
29	0.0	0.0	0.0	0.0	0.0	0.0	0.0	0.0	0.0	8.4	40.5	60.9	29
30	0.0	0.0	0.0	0.0	0.0	0.0	0.0	0.0	0.0	0.0	35.0	57.3	30
31	0.0	0.0	0.0	0.0	0.0	0.0	0.0	0.0	0.0	0.0	29.1	53.4	31
32	0.0	0.0	0.0	0.0	0.0	0.0	0.0	0.0	0.0	0.0	22.6	49.2	32
33	0.0	0.0	0.0	0.0	0.0	0.0	0.0	0.0	0.0	0.0	15.7	44.6	33
34	0.0	0.0	0.0	0.0	0.0	0.0	0.0	0.0	0.0	0.0	8.1	39.6	34
35	0.0	0.0	0.0	0.0	0.0	0.0	0.0	0.0	0.0	0.0	0.0	34.3	35
36	0.0	0.0	0.0	0.0	0.0	0.0	0.0	0.0	0.0	0.0	0.0	28.5	36
37	0.0	0.0	0.0	0.0	0.0	0.0	0.0	0.0	0.0	0.0	0.0	22.2	37
38	0.0	0.0	0.0	0.0	0.0	0.0	0.0	0.0	0.0	0.0	0.0	15.4	38
39	0.0	0.0	0.0	0.0	0.0	0.0	0.0	0.0	0.0	0.0	0.0	8.0	39

EXAMPLES *ON PAGES A-382 TO A-397*

AGE OF LOAN	ORIGINAL TERM IN YEARS												AGE OF LOAN
	2.0	3.0	5.0	8.0	10.0	12.0	15.0	16.0	17.0	18.0	19.0	20.0	
1	52.0	69.4	83.1	90.8	93.3	94.9	96.5	96.9	97.2	97.5	97.7	97.9	1
2	0.0	36.1	64.8	80.8	86.0	89.4	92.7	93.4	94.1	94.7	95.3	95.7	2
3	0.0	0.0	45.0	69.9	78.1	83.4	88.5	89.7	90.8	91.8	92.6	93.3	3
4	0.0	0.0	23.4	58.1	69.5	76.8	84.0	85.7	87.2	88.5	89.7	90.7	4
5	0.0	0.0	0.0	45.3	60.1	69.8	79.1	81.3	83.3	85.0	86.5	87.8	5
6	0.0	0.0	0.0	31.4	50.0	62.1	73.8	76.6	79.1	81.2	83.1	84.7	6
7	0.0	0.0	0.0	16.4	39.0	53.7	68.0	71.5	74.4	77.1	79.4	81.4	7
8	0.0	0.0	0.0	0.0	27.0	44.7	61.7	65.5	69.4	72.6	75.3	77.7	8
9	0.0	0.0	0.0	0.0	14.1	34.8	54.9	59.8	64.0	67.7	70.9	73.8	9
10	0.0	0.0	0.0	0.0	0.0	24.2	47.6	53.2	58.1	62.4	66.2	69.5	10
11	0.0	0.0	0.0	0.0	0.0	12.6	39.5	46.1	51.7	56.6	61.0	64.8	11
12	0.0	0.0	0.0	0.0	0.0	0.0	30.8	38.3	44.8	50.4	55.4	59.7	12
13	0.0	0.0	0.0	0.0	0.0	0.0	21.4	29.9	37.2	43.6	49.3	54.2	13
14	0.0	0.0	0.0	0.0	0.0	0.0	11.1	20.7	29.0	36.3	42.6	48.2	14
15	0.0	0.0	0.0	0.0	0.0	0.0	0.0	10.8	20.1	28.3	35.4	41.8	15
16	0.0	0.0	0.0	0.0	0.0	0.0	0.0	0.0	10.5	19.6	27.6	34.7	16
17	0.0	0.0	0.0	0.0	0.0	0.0	0.0	0.0	0.0	10.2	19.2	27.1	17
18	0.0	0.0	0.0	0.0	0.0	0.0	0.0	0.0	0.0	0.0	10.0	18.8	18
19	0.0	0.0	0.0	0.0	0.0	0.0	0.0	0.0	0.0	0.0	0.0	9.8	19

AGE OF LOAN	ORIGINAL TERM IN YEARS												AGE OF LOAN
	21.0	22.0	23.0	24.0	25.0	26.0	27.0	28.0	29.0	30.0	35.0	40.0	
1	98.1	98.3	98.5	98.6	98.7	98.9	99.0	99.0	99.1	99.2	99.5	99.3	1
2	96.1	96.5	96.8	97.1	97.4	97.6	97.8	98.0	98.2	98.3	98.9	99.3	2
3	93.9	94.5	95.0	95.5	95.9	96.3	96.6	96.9	97.2	97.4	98.3	98.9	3
4	91.6	92.4	93.1	93.7	94.3	94.8	95.3	95.7	96.0	96.4	97.7	98.5	4
5	89.0	90.0	91.0	91.8	92.5	93.2	93.8	94.3	94.8	95.3	97.0	98.0	5
6	86.2	87.5	88.7	89.7	90.6	91.5	92.2	92.9	93.5	94.1	96.2	97.5	6
7	83.2	84.7	86.2	87.4	88.6	89.6	90.5	91.3	92.1	92.8	95.4	97.0	7
8	79.9	81.8	83.5	85.0	86.3	87.6	88.7	89.7	90.6	91.4	94.5	96.4	8
9	76.3	78.5	80.5	82.3	83.9	85.3	86.6	87.8	88.9	89.8	93.5	95.8	9
10	72.4	75.0	77.3	79.4	81.3	82.9	84.5	85.8	87.0	88.2	92.4	95.1	10
11	68.2	71.2	73.9	76.3	78.4	80.3	82.1	83.6	85.1	86.4	91.2	94.3	11
12	63.6	67.0	70.1	72.8	75.3	77.5	79.5	81.3	82.9	84.4	90.0	93.5	12
13	58.6	62.5	66.0	69.1	71.9	74.4	76.7	78.7	80.6	82.3	88.6	92.6	13
14	53.2	57.6	61.6	65.1	68.3	71.1	73.7	76.0	78.1	79.9	87.1	91.6	14
15	47.4	52.3	56.8	60.7	64.3	67.5	70.3	72.9	75.3	77.4	85.5	90.6	15
16	41.0	46.6	51.5	56.0	60.0	63.5	66.8	69.7	72.3	74.7	83.7	89.4	16
17	34.1	40.3	45.8	50.8	55.3	59.3	62.9	66.1	69.1	71.7	81.8	88.2	17
18	26.6	33.5	39.7	45.2	50.2	54.6	58.6	62.3	65.6	68.5	79.8	86.8	18
19	18.4	26.1	33.0	39.1	44.6	49.6	54.1	58.1	61.7	65.0	77.5	85.4	19
20	9.6	18.1	25.7	32.5	38.6	44.1	49.1	53.5	57.6	61.2	75.1	83.8	20
21	0.0	9.4	17.8	25.4	32.1	38.2	43.7	48.6	53.1	57.1	72.4	82.1	21
22	0.0	0.0	9.3	17.6	25.0	31.8	37.8	43.2	48.2	52.7	69.6	80.2	22
23	0.0	0.0	0.0	9.1	17.4	24.8	31.4	37.4	42.9	47.8	66.4	78.2	23
24	0.0	0.0	0.0	0.0	9.0	17.2	24.5	31.1	37.1	42.5	63.1	76.0	24
25	0.0	0.0	0.0	0.0	0.0	8.9	17.0	24.3	30.8	36.8	59.4	73.6	25
26	0.0	0.0	0.0	0.0	0.0	0.0	8.8	16.8	24.1	30.6	55.4	71.0	26
27	0.0	0.0	0.0	0.0	0.0	0.0	0.0	8.7	16.7	23.9	51.1	68.2	27
28	0.0	0.0	0.0	0.0	0.0	0.0	0.0	0.0	8.7	16.5	46.3	65.1	28
29	0.0	0.0	0.0	0.0	0.0	0.0	0.0	0.0	0.0	8.6	41.2	61.8	29
30	0.0	0.0	0.0	0.0	0.0	0.0	0.0	0.0	0.0	0.0	35.7	58.2	30
31	0.0	0.0	0.0	0.0	0.0	0.0	0.0	0.0	0.0	0.0	29.7	54.3	31
32	0.0	0.0	0.0	0.0	0.0	0.0	0.0	0.0	0.0	0.0	23.1	50.0	32
33	0.0	0.0	0.0	0.0	0.0	0.0	0.0	0.0	0.0	0.0	16.0	45.4	33
34	0.0	0.0	0.0	0.0	0.0	0.0	0.0	0.0	0.0	0.0	8.3	40.4	34
35	0.0	0.0	0.0	0.0	0.0	0.0	0.0	0.0	0.0	0.0	0.0	35.0	35
36	0.0	0.0	0.0	0.0	0.0	0.0	0.0	0.0	0.0	0.0	0.0	29.1	36
37	0.0	0.0	0.0	0.0	0.0	0.0	0.0	0.0	0.0	0.0	0.0	22.7	37
38	0.0	0.0	0.0	0.0	0.0	0.0	0.0	0.0	0.0	0.0	0.0	15.7	38
39	0.0	0.0	0.0	0.0	0.0	0.0	0.0	0.0	0.0	0.0	0.0	8.2	39

EXAMPLES ON PAGES A-382 TO A-397

AGE OF LOAN	2.0	3.0	5.0	8.0	10.0	12.0	15.0	16.0	17.0	18.0	19.0	20.0	AGE OF LOAN
1	52.1	69.4	83.2	90.9	93.4	95.0	96.6	96.9	97.3	97.5	97.8	98.0	1
2	0.0	36.2	65.0	81.0	86.1	89.5	92.8	93.6	94.3	94.9	95.4	95.8	2
3	0.0	0.0	45.1	70.1	78.3	83.6	88.7	89.9	91.0	91.9	92.8	93.5	3
4	0.0	0.0	23.5	58.4	69.7	77.1	84.3	86.0	87.5	88.8	89.9	90.9	4
5	0.0	0.0	0.0	45.6	60.4	70.1	79.4	81.7	83.6	85.3	86.8	88.1	5
6	0.0	0.0	0.0	31.7	50.3	62.4	74.2	77.0	79.4	81.6	83.4	85.1	6
7	0.0	0.0	0.0	16.5	39.3	54.1	68.4	71.9	74.9	77.5	79.8	81.8	7
8	0.0	0.0	0.0	0.0	27.3	45.0	62.2	66.3	69.9	73.0	75.8	78.2	8
9	0.0	0.0	0.0	0.0	14.2	35.2	55.4	60.3	64.5	68.2	71.4	74.3	9
10	0.0	0.0	0.0	0.0	0.0	24.4	48.0	53.7	58.6	62.9	66.7	70.0	10
11	0.0	0.0	0.0	0.0	0.0	12.7	39.9	46.5	52.2	57.2	61.5	65.3	11
12	0.0	0.0	0.0	0.0	0.0	0.0	31.2	38.7	45.2	50.9	55.9	60.3	12
13	0.0	0.0	0.0	0.0	0.0	0.0	21.7	30.2	37.7	44.1	49.8	54.8	13
14	0.0	0.0	0.0	0.0	0.0	0.0	11.3	21.0	29.4	36.7	43.2	48.8	14
15	0.0	0.0	0.0	0.0	0.0	0.0	0.0	10.9	20.4	28.7	35.9	42.3	15
16	0.0	0.0	0.0	0.0	0.0	0.0	0.0	0.0	10.6	19.9	28.0	35.2	16
17	0.0	0.0	0.0	0.0	0.0	0.0	0.0	0.0	0.0	10.4	19.5	27.5	17
18	0.0	0.0	0.0	0.0	0.0	0.0	0.0	0.0	0.0	0.0	10.1	19.1	18
19	0.0	0.0	0.0	0.0	0.0	0.0	0.0	0.0	0.0	0.0	0.0	9.9	19

AGE OF LOAN	21.0	22.0	23.0	24.0	25.0	26.0	27.0	28.0	29.0	30.0	35.0	40.0	AGE OF LOAN
1	98.2	98.4	98.5	98.7	98.8	98.5	99.0	99.1	99.2	99.2	99.5	99.7	1
2	96.2	96.6	96.9	97.2	97.5	97.7	97.9	98.1	98.3	98.4	99.0	99.4	2
3	94.1	94.7	95.2	95.6	96.0	96.4	96.7	97.0	97.3	97.5	98.4	99.0	3
4	91.8	92.6	93.3	93.9	94.5	95.0	95.4	95.8	96.2	96.6	97.8	98.6	4
5	89.3	90.3	91.2	92.1	92.8	93.4	94.0	94.6	95.1	95.5	97.1	98.2	5
6	86.5	87.8	89.0	90.0	90.9	91.8	92.5	93.2	93.8	94.3	96.4	97.7	6
7	83.6	85.1	86.5	87.8	88.9	89.9	90.8	91.7	92.4	93.1	95.6	97.2	7
8	80.3	82.2	83.9	85.4	86.7	88.0	89.0	90.0	90.9	91.7	94.7	96.6	8
9	76.8	79.0	81.0	82.8	84.4	85.8	87.1	88.2	89.3	90.2	93.8	96.0	9
10	72.9	75.5	77.8	79.9	81.8	83.4	84.9	86.3	87.5	88.6	92.8	95.3	10
11	68.7	71.7	74.4	76.8	78.9	80.9	82.6	84.2	85.6	86.8	91.6	94.6	11
12	64.2	67.6	70.7	73.4	75.9	78.1	80.1	81.8	83.5	84.9	90.4	93.8	12
13	59.2	63.1	66.6	69.7	72.5	75.0	77.3	79.3	81.2	82.8	89.1	93.0	13
14	53.8	58.2	62.2	65.7	68.9	71.7	74.3	76.6	78.7	80.6	87.6	92.1	14
15	47.9	52.9	57.4	61.4	64.9	68.1	71.0	73.6	76.0	78.1	86.1	91.0	15
16	41.5	47.2	52.2	56.6	60.6	64.2	67.5	70.4	73.0	75.4	84.3	89.9	16
17	34.6	40.9	46.5	51.5	55.9	60.0	63.6	66.8	69.8	72.5	82.5	88.7	17
18	27.0	34.0	40.3	45.8	50.8	55.3	59.4	63.0	66.3	69.3	80.5	87.4	18
19	18.7	26.6	33.5	39.7	45.3	50.3	54.8	58.8	62.5	65.8	78.2	86.0	19
20	9.8	18.4	26.2	33.1	39.2	44.8	49.8	54.3	58.3	62.0	75.8	84.5	20
21	0.0	9.6	18.2	25.8	32.7	38.8	44.3	49.3	53.8	57.9	73.2	82.8	21
22	0.0	0.0	9.5	17.9	25.5	32.3	38.4	43.9	48.9	53.4	70.4	81.0	22
23	0.0	0.0	0.0	9.3	17.7	25.2	32.0	38.1	43.6	48.5	67.3	79.0	23
24	0.0	0.0	0.0	0.0	9.2	17.5	25.0	31.7	37.8	43.2	63.9	76.8	24
25	0.0	0.0	0.0	0.0	0.0	9.1	17.3	24.7	31.4	37.5	60.2	74.4	25
26	0.0	0.0	0.0	0.0	0.0	0.0	9.0	17.2	24.5	31.2	56.2	71.9	26
27	0.0	0.0	0.0	0.0	0.0	0.0	0.0	8.9	17.0	24.3	51.9	69.1	27
28	0.0	0.0	0.0	0.0	0.0	0.0	0.0	0.0	8.9	16.9	47.2	66.0	28
29	0.0	0.0	0.0	0.0	0.0	0.0	0.0	0.0	0.0	8.8	42.0	62.7	29
30	0.0	0.0	0.0	0.0	0.0	0.0	0.0	0.0	0.0	0.0	36.4	59.1	30
31	0.0	0.0	0.0	0.0	0.0	0.0	0.0	0.0	0.0	0.0	30.3	55.2	31
32	0.0	0.0	0.0	0.0	0.0	0.0	0.0	0.0	0.0	0.0	23.6	50.9	32
33	0.0	0.0	0.0	0.0	0.0	0.0	0.0	0.0	0.0	0.0	16.4	46.3	33
34	0.0	0.0	0.0	0.0	0.0	0.0	0.0	0.0	0.0	0.0	8.5	41.2	34
35	0.0	0.0	0.0	0.0	0.0	0.0	0.0	0.0	0.0	0.0	0.0	35.7	35
36	0.0	0.0	0.0	0.0	0.0	0.0	0.0	0.0	0.0	0.0	0.0	29.7	36
37	0.0	0.0	0.0	0.0	0.0	0.0	0.0	0.0	0.0	0.0	0.0	23.2	37
38	0.0	0.0	0.0	0.0	0.0	0.0	0.0	0.0	0.0	0.0	0.0	16.1	38
39	0.0	0.0	0.0	0.0	0.0	0.0	0.0	0.0	0.0	0.0	0.0	8.4	39

EXAMPLES *ON PAGES A-382 TO A-397*

AGE OF LOAN	ORIGINAL TERM IN YEARS												AGE OF LOAN
	2.0	3.0	5.0	8.0	10.0	12.0	15.0	16.0	17.0	18.0	19.0	20.0	
1	52.2	69.5	83.5	91.0	93.5	95.1	96.0	97.0	97.3	97.6	97.9	98.1	1
2	0.0	36.3	65.1	81.1	86.3	89.7	92.9	93.7	94.4	95.0	95.5	96.0	2
3	0.0	0.0	45.3	70.4	78.5	83.8	88.9	90.1	91.2	92.1	92.9	93.7	3
4	0.0	0.0	23.6	58.6	70.0	77.4	84.5	86.2	87.7	89.0	90.2	91.2	4
5	0.0	0.0	0.0	45.8	60.7	70.4	79.7	82.0	83.9	85.6	87.1	88.4	5
6	0.0	0.0	0.0	31.9	50.6	62.8	74.5	77.3	79.8	81.9	83.9	85.4	6
7	0.0	0.0	0.0	16.6	39.5	54.5	68.8	72.3	75.3	77.9	80.2	82.2	7
8	0.0	0.0	0.0	0.0	27.5	45.4	62.6	66.8	70.3	73.5	76.2	78.6	8
9	0.0	0.0	0.0	0.0	14.3	35.5	55.8	60.7	65.0	68.7	71.9	74.7	9
10	0.0	0.0	0.0	0.0	0.0	24.7	48.4	54.1	59.1	63.4	67.2	70.5	10
11	0.0	0.0	0.0	0.0	0.0	12.9	40.3	47.0	52.7	57.7	62.0	65.9	11
12	0.0	0.0	0.0	0.0	0.0	0.0	31.5	39.1	45.7	51.4	56.4	60.8	12
13	0.0	0.0	0.0	0.0	0.0	0.0	21.9	30.6	38.1	44.6	50.3	55.4	13
14	0.0	0.0	0.0	0.0	0.0	0.0	11.4	21.3	29.8	37.2	43.7	49.4	14
15	0.0	0.0	0.0	0.0	0.0	0.0	0.0	11.1	20.7	29.0	36.4	42.8	15
16	0.0	0.0	0.0	0.0	0.0	0.0	0.0	0.0	10.8	20.2	28.4	35.7	16
17	0.0	0.0	0.0	0.0	0.0	0.0	0.0	0.0	0.0	10.5	19.8	27.9	17
18	0.0	0.0	0.0	0.0	0.0	0.0	0.0	0.0	0.0	0.0	10.3	19.4	18
19	0.0	0.0	0.0	0.0	0.0	0.0	0.0	0.0	0.0	0.0	0.0	10.1	19

AGE OF LOAN	ORIGINAL TERM IN YEARS												AGE OF LOAN
	21.0	22.0	23.0	24.0	25.0	26.0	27.0	28.0	29.0	30.0	35.0	40.0	
1	98.3	98.4	98.6	98.7	98.8	98.9	99.0	99.1	99.2	99.3	99.5	99.7	1
2	96.4	96.7	97.0	97.3	97.6	97.8	98.0	98.2	98.3	98.5	99.1	99.4	2
3	94.3	94.9	95.3	95.8	96.2	96.5	96.9	97.1	97.4	97.6	98.5	99.1	3
4	92.0	92.8	93.5	94.1	94.7	95.2	95.6	96.0	96.4	96.7	97.9	98.7	4
5	89.6	90.6	91.5	92.3	93.0	93.7	94.3	94.8	95.3	95.7	97.3	98.3	5
6	86.9	88.2	89.3	90.3	91.2	92.1	92.8	93.4	94.0	94.6	96.6	97.8	6
7	83.9	85.5	86.9	88.2	89.3	90.3	91.2	92.0	92.7	93.4	95.8	97.3	7
8	80.7	82.8	84.3	85.8	87.1	88.3	89.4	90.4	91.3	92.0	95.0	96.8	8
9	77.2	79.5	81.5	83.2	84.8	86.2	87.5	88.6	89.7	90.6	94.1	96.2	9
10	73.4	76.0	78.3	80.4	82.3	83.9	85.4	86.7	87.9	89.0	93.1	95.6	10
11	69.3	72.3	75.0	77.3	79.5	81.4	83.1	84.6	86.0	87.3	92.0	94.9	11
12	64.7	68.2	71.3	74.0	76.4	78.6	80.6	82.4	84.0	85.4	90.8	94.2	12
13	59.8	63.7	67.2	70.3	73.1	75.6	77.9	79.9	81.7	83.4	89.5	93.4	13
14	54.4	58.9	62.8	66.4	69.5	72.4	74.9	77.2	79.3	81.1	88.1	92.5	14
15	48.5	53.5	58.0	62.0	65.6	68.8	71.7	74.3	76.6	78.7	86.6	91.5	15
16	42.1	47.7	52.8	57.3	61.3	64.9	68.1	71.1	73.7	76.0	84.9	90.4	16
17	35.0	41.4	47.1	52.1	56.6	60.6	64.3	67.5	70.5	73.1	83.1	89.3	17
18	27.4	34.5	40.8	46.5	51.5	56.0	60.1	63.7	67.0	70.0	81.1	88.0	18
19	19.0	27.0	34.0	40.3	45.9	50.9	55.5	59.5	63.2	66.5	78.9	86.6	19
20	9.9	18.7	26.6	33.6	39.8	45.4	50.5	55.0	59.1	62.8	76.6	85.1	20
21	0.0	9.8	18.5	26.2	33.2	39.4	45.0	50.0	54.6	58.6	74.0	83.5	21
22	0.0	0.0	9.6	18.2	25.9	32.8	39.0	44.6	49.6	54.2	71.2	81.7	22
23	0.0	0.0	0.0	9.5	18.0	25.7	32.5	38.7	44.2	49.3	68.1	79.7	23
24	0.0	0.0	0.0	0.0	9.4	17.8	25.4	32.2	38.4	43.9	64.7	77.6	24
25	0.0	0.0	0.0	0.0	0.0	9.3	17.7	25.2	32.0	38.1	61.1	75.2	25
26	0.0	0.0	0.0	0.0	0.0	0.0	9.2	17.5	25.0	31.7	57.1	72.7	26
27	0.0	0.0	0.0	0.0	0.0	0.0	0.0	9.1	17.4	24.8	52.7	69.9	27
28	0.0	0.0	0.0	0.0	0.0	0.0	0.0	0.0	9.0	17.2	47.9	66.9	28
29	0.0	0.0	0.0	0.0	0.0	0.0	0.0	0.0	0.0	9.0	42.7	63.6	29
30	0.0	0.0	0.0	0.0	0.0	0.0	0.0	0.0	0.0	0.0	37.1	60.0	30
31	0.0	0.0	0.0	0.0	0.0	0.0	0.0	0.0	0.0	0.0	30.9	56.1	31
32	0.0	0.0	0.0	0.0	0.0	0.0	0.0	0.0	0.0	0.0	24.1	51.8	32
33	0.0	0.0	0.0	0.0	0.0	0.0	0.0	0.0	0.0	0.0	16.8	47.1	33
34	0.0	0.0	0.0	0.0	0.0	0.0	0.0	0.0	0.0	0.0	8.7	42.0	34
35	0.0	0.0	0.0	0.0	0.0	0.0	0.0	0.0	0.0	0.0	0.0	36.5	35
36	0.0	0.0	0.0	0.0	0.0	0.0	0.0	0.0	0.0	0.0	0.0	30.3	36
37	0.0	0.0	0.0	0.0	0.0	0.0	0.0	0.0	0.0	0.0	0.0	23.7	37
38	0.0	0.0	0.0	0.0	0.0	0.0	0.0	0.0	0.0	0.0	0.0	16.5	38
39	0.0	0.0	0.0	0.0	0.0	0.0	0.0	0.0	0.0	0.0	0.0	8.6	39

EXAMPLES *ON PAGES A-382 TO A-397*

AGE OF LOAN	2.0	3.0	5.0	8.0	10.0	12.0	15.0	16.0	17.0	18.0	19.0	20.0	AGE OF LOAN
					ORIGINAL TERM IN YEARS								
1	52.2	69.6	83.4	91.1	93.5	95.1	96.7	97.1	97.4	97.7	97.9	98.1	1
2	0.0	36.4	65.3	81.3	86.5	89.8	93.1	93.9	94.5	95.1	95.6	96.1	2
3	0.0	0.0	45.4	70.6	78.7	84.0	89.1	90.3	91.4	92.3	93.1	93.8	3
4	0.0	0.0	23.7	58.9	70.3	77.7	84.8	86.5	88.0	89.3	90.4	91.4	4
5	0.0	0.0	0.0	46.1	61.0	70.7	80.1	82.3	84.2	85.9	87.4	88.7	5
6	0.0	0.0	0.0	32.1	50.9	63.1	74.9	77.7	80.2	82.3	84.1	85.8	6
7	0.0	0.0	0.0	16.7	35.8	54.8	69.2	72.7	75.7	78.3	80.6	82.6	7
8	0.0	0.0	0.0	0.0	27.7	45.7	63.0	67.2	70.8	73.9	76.7	79.1	8
9	0.0	0.0	0.0	0.0	14.5	35.8	56.3	61.2	65.4	69.1	72.4	75.2	9
10	0.0	0.0	0.0	0.0	0.0	24.9	48.9	54.6	59.6	63.9	67.7	71.0	10
11	0.0	0.0	0.0	0.0	0.0	13.0	40.8	47.4	53.2	58.2	62.6	66.4	11
12	0.0	0.0	0.0	0.0	0.0	0.0	31.9	39.6	46.2	51.9	57.0	61.4	12
13	0.0	0.0	0.0	0.0	0.0	0.0	22.2	31.0	38.5	45.1	50.9	55.9	13
14	0.0	0.0	0.0	0.0	0.0	0.0	11.6	21.5	30.1	37.6	44.2	49.9	14
15	0.0	0.0	0.0	0.0	0.0	0.0	0.0	11.3	21.0	29.4	36.8	43.3	15
16	0.0	0.0	0.0	0.0	0.0	0.0	0.0	0.0	11.0	20.5	28.8	36.1	16
17	0.0	0.0	0.0	0.0	0.0	0.0	0.0	0.0	0.0	10.7	20.1	28.3	17
18	0.0	0.0	0.0	0.0	0.0	0.0	0.0	0.0	0.0	0.0	10.5	19.7	18
19	0.0	0.0	0.0	0.0	0.0	0.0	0.0	0.0	0.0	0.0	0.0	10.3	19

AGE OF LOAN	21.0	22.0	23.0	24.0	25.0	26.0	27.0	28.0	29.0	30.0	35.0	40.0	AGE OF LOAN
					ORIGINAL TERM IN YEARS								
1	98.3	98.5	98.6	98.8	98.9	99.0	99.1	99.2	99.2	99.3	99.6	99.7	1
2	96.5	96.8	97.1	97.4	97.7	97.9	98.1	98.3	98.4	98.6	99.1	99.4	2
3	94.5	95.0	95.5	95.9	96.3	96.7	97.0	97.3	97.5	97.8	98.6	99.1	3
4	92.3	93.0	93.7	94.3	94.9	95.4	95.8	96.2	96.5	96.9	98.0	98.8	4
5	89.8	90.9	91.8	92.6	93.3	93.9	94.5	95.0	95.5	95.9	97.4	98.4	5
6	87.2	88.5	89.6	90.6	91.5	92.3	93.1	93.7	94.3	94.8	96.8	98.0	6
7	84.3	85.9	87.3	88.5	89.6	90.6	91.5	92.3	93.0	93.6	96.0	97.5	7
8	81.2	83.1	84.7	86.2	87.5	88.7	89.8	90.7	91.6	92.4	95.2	97.0	8
9	77.7	79.9	81.9	83.7	85.2	86.6	87.9	89.0	90.0	91.0	94.4	96.5	9
10	74.0	76.5	78.9	80.9	82.7	84.4	85.8	87.2	88.4	89.4	93.4	95.9	10
11	69.8	72.8	75.5	77.9	80.0	81.9	83.6	85.1	86.5	87.8	92.4	95.2	11
12	65.3	68.8	71.8	74.6	77.0	79.2	81.2	82.9	84.5	85.9	91.2	94.5	12
13	60.4	64.3	67.8	71.0	73.7	76.2	78.5	80.5	82.3	83.5	90.0	93.7	13
14	55.0	59.5	63.4	67.0	70.2	73.0	75.5	77.8	79.9	81.7	88.6	92.9	14
15	49.1	54.1	58.6	62.7	66.2	69.5	72.3	74.9	77.2	79.3	87.1	91.9	15
16	42.6	48.3	53.4	57.9	62.0	65.6	68.8	71.7	74.3	76.7	85.5	90.9	16
17	35.5	42.0	47.7	52.7	57.3	61.3	65.0	68.2	71.2	73.8	83.7	89.8	17
18	27.8	35.0	41.4	47.1	52.2	56.7	60.8	64.4	67.7	70.7	81.8	88.5	18
19	19.4	27.4	34.5	40.9	46.6	51.6	56.2	60.3	64.0	67.3	79.6	87.2	19
20	10.1	19.1	27.0	34.1	40.4	46.1	51.2	55.7	59.8	63.5	77.3	85.7	20
21	0.0	10.0	18.8	26.7	33.7	40.0	45.7	50.7	55.3	59.4	74.7	84.1	21
22	0.0	0.0	9.8	18.6	26.4	33.4	39.6	45.3	50.3	54.9	71.9	82.4	22
23	0.0	0.0	0.0	9.7	18.4	26.1	33.1	39.3	44.9	50.0	68.9	80.4	23
24	0.0	0.0	0.0	0.0	9.6	18.2	25.9	32.8	39.0	44.6	65.5	78.3	24
25	0.0	0.0	0.0	0.0	0.0	9.5	18.0	25.7	32.5	38.8	61.9	76.0	25
26	0.0	0.0	0.0	0.0	0.0	0.0	9.4	17.9	25.5	32.3	57.9	73.5	26
27	0.0	0.0	0.0	0.0	0.0	0.0	0.0	9.3	17.7	25.3	53.5	70.8	27
28	0.0	0.0	0.0	0.0	0.0	0.0	0.0	0.0	9.3	17.6	48.7	67.8	28
29	0.0	0.0	0.0	0.0	0.0	0.0	0.0	0.0	0.0	9.2	43.5	64.5	29
30	0.0	0.0	0.0	0.0	0.0	0.0	0.0	0.0	0.0	0.0	37.8	60.9	30
31	0.0	0.0	0.0	0.0	0.0	0.0	0.0	0.0	0.0	0.0	31.5	57.0	31
32	0.0	0.0	0.0	0.0	0.0	0.0	0.0	0.0	0.0	0.0	24.6	52.6	32
33	0.0	0.0	0.0	0.0	0.0	0.0	0.0	0.0	0.0	0.0	17.2	47.9	33
34	0.0	0.0	0.0	0.0	0.0	0.0	0.0	0.0	0.0	0.0	9.0	42.8	34
35	0.0	0.0	0.0	0.0	0.0	0.0	0.0	0.0	0.0	0.0	0.0	37.2	35
36	0.0	0.0	0.0	0.0	0.0	0.0	0.0	0.0	0.0	0.0	0.0	31.0	36
37	0.0	0.0	0.0	0.0	0.0	0.0	0.0	0.0	0.0	0.0	0.0	24.2	37
	0.0	0.0	0.0	0.0	0.0	0.0	0.0	0.0	0.0	0.0	0.0	16.9	38
	0.0	0.0	0.0	0.0	0.0	0.0	0.0	0.0	0.0	0.0	0.0	8.8	39

EXAMPLES *ON PAGES A-382 TO A-397*

AGE OF LOAN	2.0	3.0	5.0	8.0	10.0	12.0	15.0	16.0	17.0	18.0	19.0	20.0	AGE OF LOAN
1	52.3	69.7	83.5	91.1	93.6	95.2	96.8	97.1	97.5	97.7	98.0	98.2	1
2	0.0	36.4	65.4	81.4	86.6	90.0	93.2	94.0	94.7	95.2	95.7	96.2	2
3	0.0	0.0	45.6	70.8	79.0	84.2	89.3	90.5	91.6	92.5	93.3	94.0	3
4	0.0	0.0	23.8	59.1	70.5	77.9	85.1	86.8	88.2	89.5	90.6	91.6	4
5	0.0	0.0	0.0	46.3	61.3	71.0	80.4	82.6	84.6	86.2	87.7	89.0	5
6	0.0	0.0	0.0	32.3	51.2	63.5	75.3	78.1	80.5	82.6	84.5	86.1	6
7	0.0	0.0	0.0	16.9	40.1	55.2	69.6	73.1	76.1	78.7	81.0	82.9	7
8	0.0	0.0	0.0	0.0	27.9	46.1	63.5	67.6	71.2	74.4	77.1	79.5	8
9	0.0	0.0	0.0	0.0	14.6	36.1	56.7	61.6	65.9	69.6	72.9	75.7	9
10	0.0	0.0	0.0	0.0	0.0	25.1	49.3	55.1	60.1	64.4	68.2	71.5	10
11	0.0	0.0	0.0	0.0	0.0	13.1	41.2	47.9	53.7	58.7	63.1	67.0	11
12	0.0	0.0	0.0	0.0	0.0	0.0	32.2	40.0	46.6	52.4	57.5	62.0	12
13	0.0	0.0	0.0	0.0	0.0	0.0	22.5	31.3	39.0	45.6	51.4	56.5	13
14	0.0	0.0	0.0	0.0	0.0	0.0	11.7	21.8	30.5	38.1	44.7	50.5	14
15	0.0	0.0	0.0	0.0	0.0	0.0	0.0	11.4	21.3	29.8	37.3	43.9	15
16	0.0	0.0	0.0	0.0	0.0	0.0	0.0	0.0	11.1	20.8	29.2	36.6	16
17	0.0	0.0	0.0	0.0	0.0	0.0	0.0	0.0	0.0	10.9	20.4	28.7	17
18	0.0	0.0	0.0	0.0	0.0	0.0	0.0	0.0	0.0	0.0	10.6	20.0	18
19	0.0	0.0	0.0	0.0	0.0	0.0	0.0	0.0	0.0	0.0	0.0	10.4	19

AGE OF LOAN	21.0	22.0	23.0	24.0	25.0	26.0	27.0	28.0	29.0	30.0	35.0	40.0	AGE OF LOAN
1	98.4	98.5	98.7	98.8	98.9	99.0	99.1	99.2	99.3	99.4	99.6	99.8	1
2	96.6	96.9	97.2	97.5	97.8	98.0	98.2	98.3	98.5	98.6	99.2	99.5	2
3	94.6	95.2	95.7	96.1	96.5	96.8	97.1	97.4	97.6	97.9	98.7	99.2	3
4	92.5	93.2	93.9	94.5	95.1	95.5	96.0	96.3	96.7	97.0	98.2	98.9	4
5	90.1	91.1	92.0	92.8	93.5	94.1	94.7	95.2	95.7	96.1	97.6	98.5	5
6	87.5	88.8	89.9	90.9	91.8	92.6	93.3	93.9	94.5	95.0	96.9	98.1	6
7	84.7	86.3	87.6	88.9	89.9	90.9	91.8	92.6	93.3	93.9	96.2	97.7	7
8	81.6	83.5	85.1	86.6	87.9	89.1	90.1	91.1	91.9	92.7	95.5	97.2	8
9	78.2	80.4	82.4	84.1	85.7	87.0	88.3	89.4	90.4	91.3	94.7	96.7	9
10	74.5	77.0	79.3	81.4	83.2	84.8	86.3	87.6	88.8	89.8	93.7	96.1	10
11	70.4	73.4	76.0	78.4	80.5	82.4	84.1	85.6	87.0	88.2	92.7	95.5	11
12	65.9	69.3	72.4	75.1	77.6	79.7	81.7	83.4	85.0	86.4	91.6	94.8	12
13	61.0	64.9	68.4	71.5	74.3	76.8	79.0	81.0	82.8	84.4	90.4	94.0	13
14	55.5	60.1	64.1	67.6	70.8	73.6	76.1	78.4	80.5	82.3	89.1	93.2	14
15	49.6	54.7	59.3	63.3	66.9	70.1	73.0	75.5	77.8	79.9	87.6	92.3	15
16	43.1	48.7	54.0	58.6	62.6	66.2	69.5	72.4	75.0	77.3	86.1	91.3	16
17	36.0	42.5	48.3	53.4	57.9	62.0	65.7	68.9	71.9	74.5	84.3	90.2	17
18	28.2	35.5	41.9	47.7	52.8	57.4	61.5	65.1	68.4	71.4	82.4	89.1	18
19	19.7	27.8	35.0	41.4	47.2	52.3	56.9	61.0	64.7	68.0	80.3	87.8	19
20	10.3	19.4	27.4	34.6	41.0	46.7	51.8	56.4	60.5	64.2	78.0	86.3	20
21	0.0	10.1	19.1	27.1	34.2	40.6	46.3	51.4	56.0	60.1	75.5	84.8	21
22	0.0	0.0	10.0	18.9	26.8	33.9	40.2	45.9	51.1	55.6	72.7	83.0	22
23	0.0	0.0	0.0	9.9	18.7	26.6	33.6	39.9	45.6	50.7	69.7	81.2	23
24	0.0	0.0	0.0	0.0	9.8	18.5	26.3	33.3	39.6	45.3	66.3	79.1	24
25	0.0	0.0	0.0	0.0	0.0	9.7	18.3	26.1	33.1	39.4	62.7	76.8	25
26	0.0	0.0	0.0	0.0	0.0	0.0	9.6	18.2	25.9	32.9	58.7	74.3	26
27	0.0	0.0	0.0	0.0	0.0	0.0	0.0	9.5	18.1	25.8	54.3	71.6	27
28	0.0	0.0	0.0	0.0	0.0	0.0	0.0	0.0	9.4	17.9	49.5	68.6	28
29	0.0	0.0	0.0	0.0	0.0	0.0	0.0	0.0	0.0	9.4	44.2	65.3	29
30	0.0	0.0	0.0	0.0	0.0	0.0	0.0	0.0	0.0	0.0	38.4	61.7	30
31	0.0	0.0	0.0	0.0	0.0	0.0	0.0	0.0	0.0	0.0	32.1	57.8	31
32	0.0	0.0	0.0	0.0	0.0	0.0	0.0	0.0	0.0	0.0	25.1	53.5	32
33	0.0	0.0	0.0	0.0	0.0	0.0	0.0	0.0	0.0	0.0	17.5	48.7	33
34	0.0	0.0	0.0	0.0	0.0	0.0	0.0	0.0	0.0	0.0	9.1	43.5	34
35	0.0	0.0	0.0	0.0	0.0	0.0	0.0	0.0	0.0	0.0	0.0	37.8	35
36	0.0	0.0	0.0	0.0	0.0	0.0	0.0	0.0	0.0	0.0	0.0	31.6	36
37	0.0	0.0	0.0	0.0	0.0	0.0	0.0	0.0	0.0	0.0	0.0	24.7	37
38	0.0	0.0	0.0	0.0	0.0	0.0	0.0	0.0	0.0	0.0	0.0	17.2	38
39	0.0	0.0	0.0	0.0	0.0	0.0	0.0	0.0	0.0	0.0	0.0	9.0	39

EXAMPLES *ON PAGES A-382 TO A-397*

AGE OF LOAN	2.0	3.0	5.0	8.0	10.0	12.0	15.0	16.0	17.0	18.0	19.0	20.0	AGE OF LOAN
					ORIGINAL TERM IN YEARS								
1	52.4	69.8	83.6	91.2	93.7	95.3	96.8	97.2	97.5	97.8	98.0	98.2	1
2	0.0	36.5	65.6	81.6	86.8	90.1	93.4	94.1	94.8	95.4	95.9	96.3	2
3	0.0	0.0	45.7	71.0	79.2	84.5	89.5	90.7	91.8	92.7	93.5	94.2	3
4	0.0	0.0	23.5	59.3	7C.8	78.2	85.3	87.0	88.5	89.8	90.9	91.8	4
5	0.0	0.0	0.0	46.5	61.6	71.4	8C.7	82.9	84.9	86.5	88.0	89.3	5
6	0.0	0.0	0.0	32.5	51.5	63.8	75.6	78.4	80.9	83.0	84.8	86.4	6
7	0.0	0.0	0.0	17.0	40.4	55.5	70.0	73.5	76.5	79.1	81.3	83.3	7
8	0.0	0.0	0.0	0.0	28.2	46.4	63.9	68.1	71.7	74.8	77.5	79.9	8
9	0.0	0.0	0.0	0.C	14.8	36.4	57.1	62.1	66.4	70.1	73.3	76.2	9
10	0.0	0.0	0.0	0.0	0.0	25.4	49.7	55.5	60.6	64.9	68.7	72.0	10
11	0.0	0.0	0.C	0.C	0.0	13.3	41.6	48.3	54.2	59.2	63.6	67.5	11
12	0.0	0.0	0.0	0.0	0.0	0.0	32.6	40.4	47.1	53.C	58.1	62.5	12
13	0.0	0.0	0.0	0.0	C.0	0.0	22.7	31.7	39.4	46.1	51.9	57.0	13
14	0.0	0.0	0.0	0.0	0.0	0.0	11.9	22.1	30.9	38.5	45.2	51.0	14
15	0.0	0.0	0.0	C.C	C.0	C.C	0.0	11.6	21.6	30.2	37.8	44.4	15
16	0.0	0.0	0.0	0.0	0.0	0.0	0.0	0.0	11.3	21.1	29.6	37.1	16
17	0.0	0.0	0.0	0.0	0.0	0.C	0.0	0.0	0.0	11.0	20.7	29.1	17
18	0.0	0.0	0.C	0.C	0.C	0.C	0.0	0.0	0.0	0.0	10.8	20.3	18
19	0.0	0.0	0.0	0.0	C.0	0.0	0.0	0.0	0.0	0.C	0.0	10.6	19

AGE OF LOAN	21.0	22.0	23.0	24.0	25.0	26.0	27.0	28.0	29.0	30.0	35.0	40.0	AGE OF LOAN
					ORIGINAL TERM IN YEARS								
1	98.4	98.6	98.7	98.5	99.0	99.1	99.2	99.2	99.3	99.4	99.6	99.8	1
2	96.7	97.0	97.3	97.6	97.8	98.1	98.2	98.4	98.6	98.7	99.2	99.5	2
3	94.8	95.3	95.8	96.2	96.6	96.9	97.2	97.5	97.7	98.0	98.8	99.2	3
4	92.7	93.4	94.1	94.7	95.2	95.7	96.1	96.5	96.8	97.1	98.3	98.9	4
5	90.4	91.4	92.3	93.0	93.7	94.3	94.9	95.4	95.8	96.2	97.7	98.6	5
6	87.9	89.1	90.2	91.2	92.1	92.9	93.6	94.2	94.7	95.3	97.1	98.2	6
7	85.1	86.6	88.0	89.2	90.3	91.2	92.1	92.9	93.5	94.2	96.4	97.8	7
8	82.0	83.9	85.5	87.0	88.3	89.4	90.5	91.4	92.2	93.0	95.7	97.4	8
9	78.7	80.9	82.8	84.5	86.1	87.5	88.7	89.8	90.8	91.7	94.9	96.9	9
10	75.0	77.5	79.8	81.9	83.7	85.3	86.7	88.0	89.2	90.2	94.0	96.3	10
11	70.9	73.9	76.6	78.9	81.0	82.5	84.6	86.1	87.4	88.6	93.1	95.7	11
12	66.4	69.9	73.0	75.7	78.1	80.3	82.2	83.9	85.5	86.9	92.0	95.1	12
13	61.5	65.5	69.0	72.1	74.9	77.4	79.6	81.6	83.4	85.0	90.8	94.4	13
14	56.1	60.7	64.7	68.2	71.4	74.2	76.7	79.0	81.0	82.8	89.6	93.6	14
15	50.2	55.3	59.9	63.9	67.5	7C.7	73.6	76.2	78.5	80.5	88.1	92.7	15
16	43.7	49.5	54.6	59.2	63.3	66.9	70.1	73.0	75.6	78.0	86.6	91.8	16
17	36.5	43.1	48.9	54.C	58.6	62.7	66.3	69.6	72.5	75.2	84.9	90.7	17
18	28.6	36.0	42.5	48.3	53.5	58.0	62.2	65.8	69.1	72.1	83.0	89.6	18
19	20.0	28.2	35.5	42.0	47.8	53.C	57.6	61.7	65.4	68.7	80.9	88.3	19
20	10.5	19.7	27.9	35.1	41.6	47.4	52.5	57.1	61.3	65.0	78.7	86.9	20
21	0.0	10.3	19.4	27.6	34.8	41.2	47.0	52.1	56.7	60.9	76.2	85.4	21
22	0.0	0.0	10.2	19.2	27.3	34.4	40.9	46.6	51.8	56.4	73.4	83.7	22
23	0.0	0.0	0.0	10.1	19.0	27.0	34.2	40.6	46.3	51.4	70.4	81.8	23
24	0.0	0.0	0.0	0.0	10.0	18.8	26.8	33.9	40.3	46.0	67.1	79.8	24
25	0.0	0.0	0.0	0.C	C.0	9.9	18.7	26.6	33.7	40.0	63.5	77.6	25
26	0.0	0.0	0.C	0.0	0.0	0.0	9.8	18.5	26.4	33.5	59.5	75.1	26
27	0.0	0.0	0.0	0.0	C.0	0.0	0.0	9.7	18.4	26.2	55.1	72.4	27
28	0.0	0.0	0.0	0.0	0.0	0.C	0.0	0.0	9.6	18.3	50.3	69.4	28
29	0.0	0.C	0.0	0.0	C.0	0.0	0.0	0.C	0.0	9.6	45.0	66.2	29
30	0.0	0.0	0.0	0.0	0.0	0.0	0.0	0.0	0.0	0.0	39.1	62.6	30
31	0.0	0.C	0.0	0.0	C.0	0.0	0.0	0.0	0.0	0.0	32.7	58.7	31
32	0.0	0.0	0.0	0.0	0.0	0.C	0.0	0.C	0.0	0.0	25.6	54.3	32
33	0.0	0.0	0.0	0.0	0.0	0.0	0.0	0.C	0.0	0.0	17.9	49.6	33
34	0.0	0.0	0.0	0.0	0.0	0.0	0.0	0.0	0.0	0.0	9.4	44.3	34
35	0.0	0.0	0.0	0.0	C.0	0.C	0.0	0.C	0.0	0.0	0.0	38.6	35
36	0.0	0.0	0.0	0.0	0.0	0.0	0.0	0.0	0.0	0.0	0.0	32.2	36
37	0.0	0.0	0.0	0.C	0.0	0.0	0.0	0.0	0.0	0.0	0.0	25.3	37
38	0.0	0.0	0.C	0.0	0.0	0.0	0.0	0.0	0.0	0.C	0.0	17.6	38
39	0.0	0.0	0.0	0.0	0.0	0.0	0.0	0.0	0.0	0.0	0.0	9.2	39

EXAMPLES *ON PAGES A-382 TO A-397*

AGE OF LOAN	2.0	3.0	5.0	8.0	10.0	12.0	15.0	16.0	17.0	18.0	19.0	20.0	AGE OF LOAN
					ORIGINAL TERM IN YEARS								
1	52.4	65.8	83.7	91.3	93.8	95.4	96.9	97.3	97.6	97.8	98.1	98.3	1
2	0.0	36.6	65.7	81.7	86.9	90.3	93.5	94.3	94.9	95.5	96.0	96.4	2
3	0.0	0.0	45.9	71.2	79.4	84.7	89.7	90.9	92.0	92.9	93.7	94.3	3
4	0.0	0.0	24.1	59.6	71.1	78.5	85.6	87.3	88.7	90.0	91.1	92.1	4
5	0.0	0.0	0.0	46.8	61.9	71.7	81.0	83.2	85.2	86.8	88.3	89.5	5
6	0.0	0.0	0.0	32.7	51.8	64.2	76.0	78.8	81.2	83.3	85.2	86.8	6
7	0.0	0.0	0.0	17.1	40.7	55.9	70.4	73.9	76.9	79.5	81.7	83.7	7
8	0.0	0.0	0.0	0.0	28.4	46.8	64.3	68.5	72.1	75.2	78.0	80.3	8
9	0.0	0.0	0.0	0.0	14.9	36.7	57.6	62.5	66.8	70.6	73.8	76.6	9
10	0.0	0.0	0.0	0.0	0.0	25.6	50.1	56.0	61.0	65.4	69.2	72.5	10
11	0.0	0.0	0.0	0.0	0.0	13.4	42.0	48.8	54.6	59.7	64.1	68.0	11
12	0.0	0.0	0.0	0.0	0.0	0.0	32.9	40.8	47.6	53.5	58.6	63.1	12
13	0.0	0.0	0.0	0.0	0.0	0.0	23.0	32.0	39.8	46.6	52.4	57.6	13
14	0.0	0.0	0.0	0.0	0.0	0.0	12.1	22.4	31.3	39.0	45.7	51.5	14
15	0.0	0.0	0.0	0.0	0.0	0.0	0.0	11.7	21.8	30.6	38.2	44.9	15
16	0.0	0.0	0.0	0.0	0.0	0.0	0.0	0.0	11.4	21.4	30.0	37.6	16
17	0.0	0.0	0.0	0.0	0.0	0.0	0.0	0.0	0.0	11.2	21.0	29.5	17
18	0.0	0.0	0.0	0.0	0.0	0.0	0.0	0.0	0.0	0.0	11.0	20.6	18
19	0.0	0.0	0.0	0.0	0.0	0.0	0.0	0.0	0.0	0.0	0.0	10.8	19

AGE OF LOAN	21.0	22.0	23.0	24.0	25.0	26.0	27.0	28.0	29.0	30.0	35.0	40.0	AGE OF LOAN
					ORIGINAL TERM IN YEARS								
1	98.5	98.6	98.8	98.9	99.0	99.1	99.2	99.3	99.4	99.4	99.6	99.8	1
2	96.8	97.1	97.4	97.7	97.9	98.1	98.3	98.5	98.6	98.8	99.3	99.5	2
3	94.9	95.5	95.9	96.4	96.7	97.1	97.3	97.6	97.8	98.1	98.8	99.3	3
4	92.9	93.6	94.3	94.9	95.4	95.9	96.3	96.6	97.0	97.3	98.4	99.0	4
5	90.6	91.6	92.5	93.3	93.9	94.6	95.1	95.6	96.0	96.4	97.8	98.7	5
6	88.2	89.4	90.5	91.5	92.3	93.1	93.8	94.4	95.0	95.5	97.3	98.3	6
7	85.4	87.0	88.3	89.5	90.6	91.5	92.4	93.1	93.8	94.4	96.6	98.0	7
8	82.4	84.3	85.9	87.3	88.6	89.8	90.8	91.7	92.5	93.3	95.9	97.5	8
9	79.1	81.3	83.2	85.0	86.5	87.8	89.1	90.1	91.1	91.1	92.0	95.2	97.1	9
10	75.5	78.0	80.3	82.3	84.1	85.7	87.1	88.4	89.6	90.6	94.3	96.6	10
11	71.4	74.4	77.1	79.4	81.5	83.4	85.0	86.5	87.8	89.0	93.4	96.0	11
12	67.0	70.4	73.5	76.2	78.6	80.8	82.7	84.4	86.0	87.3	92.4	95.4	12
13	62.1	66.1	69.6	72.7	75.5	77.9	80.1	82.1	83.9	85.4	91.2	94.7	13
14	56.7	61.2	65.3	68.8	72.0	74.8	77.3	79.6	81.6	83.4	90.0	93.9	14
15	50.8	55.9	60.5	64.5	68.1	71.3	74.2	76.8	79.0	81.1	88.6	93.1	15
16	44.2	50.1	55.2	59.8	63.9	67.5	70.8	73.7	76.3	78.6	87.1	92.2	16
17	37.0	43.6	49.4	54.6	59.2	63.3	67.0	70.3	73.2	75.8	85.4	91.2	17
18	29.0	36.5	43.1	48.9	54.1	50.7	62.8	66.5	69.8	72.8	83.6	90.0	18
19	20.3	28.6	36.0	42.6	48.4	53.6	58.2	62.4	66.1	69.4	81.6	88.8	19
20	10.6	20.0	28.3	35.6	42.2	48.0	53.2	57.8	62.0	65.7	79.3	87.5	20
21	0.0	10.5	19.8	28.0	35.3	41.8	47.6	52.8	57.4	61.6	76.9	86.0	21
22	0.0	0.0	10.3	19.5	27.7	35.0	41.5	47.3	52.5	57.1	74.2	84.3	22
23	0.0	0.0	0.0	10.2	19.3	27.5	34.7	41.2	47.0	52.1	71.2	82.5	23
24	0.0	0.0	0.0	0.0	10.1	19.2	27.2	34.4	40.9	46.7	67.9	80.5	24
25	0.0	0.0	0.0	0.0	0.0	10.0	19.0	27.0	34.2	40.7	64.3	78.3	25
26	0.0	0.0	0.0	0.0	0.0	0.0	10.0	18.9	26.9	34.0	60.3	75.9	26
27	0.0	0.0	0.0	0.0	0.0	0.0	0.0	9.9	18.8	26.7	55.9	73.2	27
28	0.0	0.0	0.0	0.0	0.0	0.0	0.0	0.0	9.8	18.6	51.0	70.3	28
29	0.0	0.0	0.0	0.0	0.0	0.0	0.0	0.0	0.0	9.8	45.7	67.0	29
30	0.0	0.0	0.0	0.0	0.0	0.0	0.0	0.0	0.0	0.0	39.8	63.4	30
31	0.0	0.0	0.0	0.0	0.0	0.0	0.0	0.0	0.0	0.0	33.3	59.5	31
32	0.0	0.0	0.0	0.0	0.0	0.0	0.0	0.0	0.0	0.0	26.1	55.1	32
33	0.0	0.0	0.0	0.0	0.0	0.0	0.0	0.0	0.0	0.0	18.2	50.3	33
34	0.0	0.0	0.0	0.0	0.0	0.0	0.0	0.0	0.0	0.0	9.5	45.1	34
35	0.0	0.0	0.0	0.0	0.0	0.0	0.0	0.0	0.0	0.0	0.0	39.3	35
36	0.0	0.0	0.0	0.0	0.0	0.0	0.0	0.0	0.0	0.0	0.0	32.8	36
37	0.0	0.0	0.0	0.0	0.0	0.0	0.0	0.0	0.0	0.0	0.0	25.8	37
38	0.0	0.0	0.0	0.0	0.0	0.0	0.0	0.0	0.0	0.0	0.0	18.0	38
39	0.0	0.0	0.0	0.0	0.0	0.0	0.0	0.0	0.0	0.0	0.0	9.4	39

EXAMPLES *ON PAGES A-382 TO A-397*

AGE OF LOAN	2.0	3.0	5.0	8.0	10.0	12.0	15.0	16.0	17.0	18.0	19.0	20.0	AGE OF LOAN
					ORIGINAL TERM IN YEARS								
1	52.5	69.9	83.8	91.4	93.9	95.5	97.0	97.3	97.6	97.9	98.1	98.3	1
2	0.0	36.7	65.8	81.5	87.1	90.4	93.6	94.4	95.0	95.6	96.1	96.5	2
3	0.0	0.0	46.0	71.4	75.6	84.9	89.9	91.1	92.1	93.0	93.8	94.5	3
4	0.0	0.0	24.2	59.8	71.3	78.8	85.8	87.5	89.0	90.2	91.3	92.3	4
5	0.0	0.0	0.0	47.0	62.2	72.0	81.3	83.5	85.5	87.1	88.5	89.8	5
6	0.0	0.0	0.0	32.9	52.1	64.5	76.3	79.1	81.6	83.7	85.5	87.1	6
7	0.0	0.0	0.0	17.3	41.0	56.2	70.8	74.3	77.3	79.9	82.1	84.1	7
8	0.0	0.0	0.0	0.0	28.6	47.1	64.7	68.9	72.5	75.7	78.4	80.7	8
9	0.0	0.0	0.0	0.0	15.0	37.0	58.0	63.0	67.3	71.0	74.3	77.1	9
10	0.0	0.0	0.0	0.0	0.0	25.9	50.6	56.5	61.5	65.5	69.7	73.0	10
11	0.0	0.0	0.0	0.0	0.0	13.6	42.4	49.2	55.1	60.2	64.7	68.5	11
12	0.0	0.0	0.0	0.0	0.0	0.0	33.3	41.2	48.1	54.0	59.1	63.6	12
13	0.0	0.0	0.0	0.0	0.0	0.0	23.3	32.4	40.3	47.1	53.0	58.1	13
14	0.0	0.0	0.0	0.0	0.0	0.0	12.2	22.7	31.6	39.4	46.2	52.1	14
15	0.0	0.0	0.0	0.0	0.0	0.0	0.0	11.9	22.1	31.0	38.7	45.4	15
16	0.0	0.0	0.0	0.0	0.0	0.0	0.0	0.0	11.6	21.7	30.4	38.0	16
17	0.0	0.0	0.0	0.0	0.0	0.0	0.0	0.0	0.0	11.4	21.3	29.9	17
18	0.0	0.0	0.0	0.0	0.0	0.0	0.0	0.0	0.0	0.0	11.2	20.9	18
19	0.0	0.0	0.0	0.0	0.0	0.0	0.0	0.0	0.0	0.0	0.0	11.0	19

AGE OF LOAN	21.0	22.0	23.0	24.0	25.0	26.0	27.0	28.0	29.0	30.0	35.0	40.0	AGE OF LOAN
					ORIGINAL TERM IN YEARS								
1	98.5	98.7	98.8	98.9	99.1	99.1	99.2	99.3	99.4	99.4	99.7	99.8	1
2	96.9	97.2	97.5	97.8	98.0	98.2	98.4	98.6	98.7	98.8	99.3	99.6	2
3	95.1	95.6	96.1	96.5	96.9	97.2	97.5	97.7	97.9	98.2	98.9	99.3	3
4	93.1	93.8	94.5	95.1	95.6	96.0	96.4	96.8	97.1	97.4	98.5	99.1	4
5	90.9	91.9	92.7	93.5	94.2	94.8	95.3	95.8	96.2	96.6	98.0	98.8	5
6	88.5	89.7	90.8	91.8	92.6	93.4	94.0	94.6	95.2	95.7	97.4	98.4	6
7	85.8	87.3	88.6	89.8	90.9	91.8	92.7	93.4	94.1	94.6	96.8	98.1	7
8	82.8	84.7	86.3	87.7	89.0	90.1	91.1	92.0	92.8	93.5	96.1	97.7	8
9	79.6	81.7	83.7	85.4	86.9	88.2	89.4	90.5	91.4	92.3	95.4	97.2	9
10	75.9	78.5	80.8	82.8	84.6	86.1	87.6	88.8	89.9	90.9	94.6	96.8	10
11	71.9	74.9	77.6	79.9	82.0	83.8	85.5	87.0	88.3	89.4	93.7	96.2	11
12	67.5	71.0	74.1	76.8	79.2	81.3	83.2	84.9	86.4	87.8	92.7	95.6	12
13	62.7	66.6	70.2	73.3	76.0	78.5	80.7	82.6	84.4	85.9	91.6	95.0	13
14	57.3	61.8	65.9	69.4	72.6	75.4	77.9	80.1	82.1	83.9	90.4	94.2	14
15	51.3	56.5	61.1	65.2	68.8	72.0	74.8	77.4	79.6	81.7	89.1	93.4	15
16	44.7	50.6	55.8	60.5	64.5	68.2	71.4	74.3	76.9	79.2	87.6	92.6	16
17	37.5	44.2	50.0	55.3	59.9	64.0	67.7	70.9	73.8	76.5	86.0	91.6	17
18	29.5	37.0	43.6	49.5	54.7	59.4	63.5	67.2	70.5	73.4	84.2	90.5	18
19	20.6	29.1	36.6	43.2	49.0	54.3	58.9	63.1	66.8	70.1	82.2	89.3	19
20	10.8	20.3	28.7	36.2	42.8	48.6	53.9	58.5	62.7	66.4	80.0	88.0	20
21	0.0	10.7	20.1	28.4	35.8	42.4	48.3	53.5	58.2	62.3	77.6	86.5	21
22	0.0	0.0	10.5	19.9	28.2	35.5	42.1	47.9	53.2	57.8	74.9	84.9	22
23	0.0	0.0	0.0	10.4	19.7	27.9	35.2	41.8	47.6	52.9	71.9	83.2	23
24	0.0	0.0	0.0	0.0	10.3	19.5	27.7	35.0	41.5	47.4	68.7	81.2	24
25	0.0	0.0	0.0	0.0	0.0	10.2	19.4	27.5	34.8	41.3	65.1	79.0	25
26	0.0	0.0	0.0	0.0	0.0	0.0	10.2	19.2	27.3	34.6	61.1	76.6	26
27	0.0	0.0	0.0	0.0	0.0	0.0	0.0	10.1	19.1	27.2	56.7	74.0	27
28	0.0	0.0	0.0	0.0	0.0	0.0	0.0	0.0	10.0	19.0	51.8	71.1	28
29	0.0	0.0	0.0	0.0	0.0	0.0	0.0	0.0	0.0	10.0	46.4	67.8	29
30	0.0	0.0	0.0	0.0	0.0	0.0	0.0	0.0	0.0	0.0	40.5	64.3	30
31	0.0	0.0	0.0	0.0	0.0	0.0	0.0	0.0	0.0	0.0	33.9	60.3	31
32	0.0	0.0	0.0	0.0	0.0	0.0	0.0	0.0	0.0	0.0	26.6	56.0	32
33	0.0	0.0	0.0	0.0	0.0	0.0	0.0	0.0	0.0	0.0	18.6	51.1	33
34	0.0	0.0	0.0	0.0	0.0	0.0	0.0	0.0	0.0	0.0	9.8	45.8	34
35	0.0	0.0	0.0	0.0	0.0	0.0	0.0	0.0	0.0	0.0	0.0	40.0	35
36	0.0	0.0	0.0	0.0	0.0	0.0	0.0	0.0	0.0	0.0	0.0	33.5	36
37	0.0	0.0	0.0	0.0	0.0	0.0	0.0	0.0	0.0	0.0	0.0	26.3	37
38	0.0	0.0	0.0	0.0	0.0	0.0	0.0	0.0	0.0	0.0	0.0	18.4	38
39	0.0	0.0	0.0	0.0	0.0	0.0	0.0	0.0	0.0	0.0	0.0	9.7	39

EXAMPLES *ON PAGES A-382 TO A-397*

AGE OF LOAN	ORIGINAL TERM IN YEARS												AGE OF LOAN
	2.0	3.0	5.0	8.0	10.0	12.0	15.0	16.0	17.0	18.0	19.0	20.0	
1	52.5	70.0	83.9	91.5	93.9	95.5	97.0	97.4	97.7	98.0	98.2	98.4	1
2	0.0	36.8	66.0	82.1	87.2	90.6	93.7	94.5	95.1	95.7	96.2	96.6	2
3	0.0	0.0	46.2	71.6	79.8	85.1	90.1	91.3	92.3	93.2	94.0	94.7	3
4	0.0	0.0	24.3	60.1	71.6	79.0	86.1	87.8	89.2	90.4	91.5	92.5	4
5	0.0	0.0	0.0	47.3	62.5	72.3	81.6	83.8	85.7	87.4	88.8	90.1	5
6	0.0	0.0	0.0	33.1	52.4	64.8	76.7	79.5	81.9	84.0	85.8	87.4	6
7	0.0	0.0	0.0	17.4	41.2	56.6	71.2	74.7	77.7	80.2	82.5	84.4	7
8	0.0	0.0	0.0	0.0	28.9	47.5	65.1	69.3	73.0	76.1	78.8	81.2	8
9	0.0	0.0	0.0	0.0	15.2	37.3	58.4	63.4	67.7	71.5	74.7	77.5	9
10	0.0	0.0	0.0	0.0	0.0	26.1	51.0	56.9	62.0	66.4	70.2	73.5	10
11	0.0	0.0	0.0	0.0	0.0	13.7	42.8	49.7	55.6	60.7	65.2	69.1	11
12	0.0	0.0	0.0	0.0	0.0	0.0	33.6	41.6	48.5	54.5	59.6	64.1	12
13	0.0	0.0	0.0	0.0	0.0	0.0	23.6	32.8	40.7	47.5	53.5	58.7	13
14	0.0	0.0	0.0	0.0	0.0	0.0	12.4	22.9	32.0	39.9	46.7	52.6	14
15	0.0	0.0	0.0	0.0	0.0	0.0	0.0	12.0	22.4	31.4	39.1	45.9	15
16	0.0	0.0	0.0	0.0	0.0	0.0	0.0	0.0	11.8	22.0	30.8	38.5	16
17	0.0	0.0	0.0	0.0	0.0	0.0	0.0	0.0	0.0	11.5	21.6	30.3	17
18	0.0	0.0	0.0	0.0	0.0	0.0	0.0	0.0	0.0	0.0	11.3	21.2	18
19	0.0	0.0	0.0	0.0	0.0	0.0	0.0	0.0	0.0	0.0	0.0	11.1	19

AGE OF LOAN	ORIGINAL TERM IN YEARS												AGE OF LOAN
	21.0	22.0	23.0	24.0	25.0	26.0	27.0	28.0	29.0	30.0	35.0	40.0	
1	98.6	98.7	98.9	99.0	99.1	99.2	99.3	99.3	99.4	99.5	99.7	99.8	1
2	97.0	97.3	97.6	97.9	98.1	98.3	98.5	98.6	98.8	98.9	99.3	99.6	2
3	95.2	95.8	96.2	96.6	97.0	97.3	97.6	97.8	98.0	98.2	99.0	99.4	3
4	93.3	94.0	94.7	95.2	95.7	96.2	96.6	96.9	97.2	97.5	98.5	99.1	4
5	91.2	92.1	93.0	93.7	94.4	95.0	95.5	95.9	96.4	96.7	98.1	98.9	5
6	88.8	90.0	91.1	92.0	92.9	93.6	94.3	94.9	95.4	95.9	97.6	98.6	6
7	86.1	87.6	89.0	90.1	91.2	92.1	92.9	93.6	94.3	94.9	97.0	98.2	7
8	83.2	85.0	86.6	88.1	89.3	90.4	91.4	92.3	93.1	93.8	96.3	97.8	8
9	80.0	82.2	84.1	85.8	87.3	88.6	89.8	90.8	91.8	92.6	95.6	97.4	9
10	76.4	79.0	81.2	83.2	85.0	86.6	87.9	89.2	90.3	91.3	94.9	97.0	10
11	72.5	75.4	78.1	80.4	82.5	84.3	85.9	87.4	88.7	89.8	94.0	96.4	11
12	68.1	71.5	74.6	77.3	79.7	81.8	83.7	85.4	86.9	88.2	93.1	95.9	12
13	63.2	67.2	70.7	73.8	76.6	79.0	81.2	83.1	84.9	86.4	92.0	95.2	13
14	57.8	62.4	66.4	70.0	73.2	76.0	78.5	80.7	82.6	84.4	90.8	94.6	14
15	51.9	57.1	61.7	65.8	69.4	72.6	75.4	77.9	80.2	82.2	89.5	93.8	15
16	45.3	51.2	56.4	61.1	65.2	68.8	72.0	74.9	77.5	79.8	88.1	92.9	16
17	38.0	44.7	50.6	55.9	60.5	64.6	68.3	71.6	74.5	77.1	86.5	92.0	17
18	29.9	37.5	44.2	50.1	55.4	60.0	64.2	67.9	71.1	74.1	84.7	90.9	18
19	20.9	29.5	37.1	43.7	49.7	54.9	59.6	63.7	67.5	70.8	82.8	89.8	19
20	11.0	20.6	29.2	36.7	43.3	49.3	54.5	59.2	63.4	67.1	80.6	88.5	20
21	0.0	10.8	20.4	28.9	36.3	43.0	48.9	54.2	58.8	63.0	78.2	87.1	21
22	0.0	0.0	10.7	20.2	28.6	36.0	42.7	48.6	53.8	58.5	75.6	85.5	22
23	0.0	0.0	0.0	10.6	20.0	28.4	35.8	42.4	48.3	53.6	72.7	83.8	23
24	0.0	0.0	0.0	0.0	10.5	19.8	28.2	35.5	42.1	48.0	69.4	81.8	24
25	0.0	0.0	0.0	0.0	0.0	10.4	19.7	28.0	35.3	41.9	65.8	79.7	25
26	0.0	0.0	0.0	0.0	0.0	0.0	10.3	19.6	27.8	35.2	61.8	77.3	26
27	0.0	0.0	0.0	0.0	0.0	0.0	0.0	10.3	19.5	27.7	57.4	74.7	27
28	0.0	0.0	0.0	0.0	0.0	0.0	0.0	0.0	10.2	19.4	52.5	71.8	28
29	0.0	0.0	0.0	0.0	0.0	0.0	0.0	0.0	0.0	10.2	47.1	68.6	29
30	0.0	0.0	0.0	0.0	0.0	0.0	0.0	0.0	0.0	0.0	41.1	65.1	30
31	0.0	0.0	0.0	0.0	0.0	0.0	0.0	0.0	0.0	0.0	34.5	61.1	31
32	0.0	0.0	0.0	0.0	0.0	0.0	0.0	0.0	0.0	0.0	27.1	56.7	32
33	0.0	0.0	0.0	0.0	0.0	0.0	0.0	0.0	0.0	0.0	19.0	51.9	33
34	0.0	0.0	0.0	0.0	0.0	0.0	0.0	0.0	0.0	0.0	10.0	46.6	34
35	0.0	0.0	0.0	0.0	0.0	0.0	0.0	0.0	0.0	0.0	0.0	40.6	35
36	0.0	0.0	0.0	0.0	0.0	0.0	0.0	0.0	0.0	0.0	0.0	34.1	36
37	0.0	0.0	0.0	0.0	0.0	0.0	0.0	0.0	0.0	0.0	0.0	26.8	37
38	0.0	0.0	0.0	0.0	0.0	0.0	0.0	0.0	0.0	0.0	0.0	18.8	38
39	0.0	0.0	0.0	0.0	0.0	0.0	0.0	0.0	0.0	0.0	0.0	9.8	39

EXAMPLES ON PAGES A-382 TO A-397

AGE OF LOAN	2.0	3.0	5.0	8.0	10.0	12.0	15.0	16.0	17.0	18.0	19.0	20.0	AGE OF LOAN
					ORIGINAL TERM IN YEARS								
1	52.6	70.1	83.9	91.6	94.0	95.6	97.1	97.5	97.8	98.0	98.2	98.4	1
2	0.0	36.9	66.1	82.2	87.4	90.7	93.9	94.6	95.3	95.8	96.3	96.7	2
3	0.0	0.0	46.3	71.8	80.0	85.3	90.3	91.5	92.5	93.4	94.1	94.8	3
4	0.0	0.0	24.4	60.3	71.9	79.3	86.3	88.0	89.4	90.7	91.7	92.7	4
5	0.0	0.0	0.0	47.5	62.8	72.6	81.9	84.1	86.0	87.7	89.1	90.3	5
6	0.0	0.0	0.0	33.3	52.7	65.2	77.0	79.8	82.2	84.3	86.1	87.7	6
7	0.0	0.0	0.0	17.5	41.5	57.0	71.6	75.1	78.0	80.6	82.8	84.8	7
8	0.0	0.0	0.0	0.0	29.1	47.8	65.6	69.8	73.4	76.5	79.2	81.6	8
9	0.0	0.0	0.0	0.0	15.3	37.7	58.9	63.9	68.2	71.9	75.2	78.0	9
10	0.0	0.0	0.0	0.0	0.0	26.4	51.4	57.4	62.5	66.9	70.7	74.0	10
11	0.0	0.0	0.0	0.0	0.0	13.9	43.2	50.1	56.1	61.2	65.7	69.6	11
12	0.0	0.0	0.0	0.0	0.0	0.0	34.0	42.1	49.0	55.0	60.1	64.7	12
13	0.0	0.0	0.0	0.0	0.0	0.0	23.8	33.1	41.1	48.0	54.0	59.2	13
14	0.0	0.0	0.0	0.0	0.0	0.0	12.5	23.2	32.4	40.3	47.2	53.2	14
15	0.0	0.0	0.0	0.0	0.0	0.0	0.0	12.2	22.7	31.8	39.6	46.4	15
16	0.0	0.0	0.0	0.0	0.0	0.0	0.0	0.0	11.9	22.3	31.2	39.0	16
17	0.0	0.0	0.0	0.0	0.0	0.0	0.0	0.0	0.0	11.7	21.9	30.7	17
18	0.0	0.0	0.0	0.0	0.0	0.0	0.0	0.0	0.0	0.0	11.5	21.5	18
19	0.0	0.0	0.0	0.0	0.0	0.0	0.0	0.0	0.0	0.0	0.0	11.3	19

AGE OF LOAN	21.0	22.0	23.0	24.0	25.0	26.0	27.0	28.0	29.0	30.0	35.0	40.0	AGE OF LOAN
					ORIGINAL TERM IN YEARS								
1	98.6	98.8	98.5	99.0	99.1	99.2	99.3	99.4	99.4	99.5	99.7	99.8	1
2	97.1	97.4	97.7	97.9	98.2	98.4	98.5	98.7	98.8	98.9	99.4	99.6	2
3	95.4	95.9	96.3	96.7	97.1	97.4	97.7	97.9	98.1	98.3	99.0	99.4	3
4	93.5	94.2	94.8	95.4	95.9	96.3	96.7	97.1	97.4	97.6	98.6	99.2	4
5	91.4	92.3	93.2	93.9	94.6	95.1	95.7	96.1	96.5	96.9	98.2	98.9	5
6	89.1	90.3	91.3	92.3	93.1	93.8	94.5	95.1	95.6	96.0	97.7	98.6	6
7	86.5	88.0	89.3	90.4	91.5	92.4	93.2	93.9	94.5	95.1	97.1	98.3	7
8	83.6	85.4	87.0	88.4	89.7	90.8	91.7	92.6	93.4	94.1	96.5	98.0	8
9	80.4	82.6	84.5	86.2	87.6	89.0	90.1	91.2	92.1	92.9	95.9	97.6	9
10	76.9	79.4	81.7	83.7	85.4	87.0	88.3	89.6	90.7	91.6	95.1	97.1	10
11	73.0	76.0	78.6	80.9	82.9	84.8	86.4	87.8	89.1	90.2	94.3	96.7	11
12	68.6	72.1	75.1	77.8	80.2	82.3	84.2	85.8	87.3	88.6	93.4	96.1	12
13	63.8	67.8	71.3	74.4	77.1	79.6	81.7	83.6	85.3	86.9	92.4	95.5	13
14	58.4	63.0	67.0	70.6	73.7	76.5	79.0	81.2	83.2	84.9	91.2	94.8	14
15	52.4	57.7	62.3	66.4	70.0	73.2	76.0	78.5	80.8	82.8	90.0	94.1	15
16	45.8	51.8	57.0	61.7	65.8	69.4	72.7	75.5	78.1	80.4	88.6	93.3	16
17	38.5	45.2	51.2	56.5	61.2	65.3	68.9	72.2	75.1	77.7	87.0	92.4	17
18	30.3	38.0	44.8	50.7	56.0	60.7	64.8	68.5	71.8	74.7	85.3	91.4	18
19	21.2	29.9	37.6	44.3	50.3	55.6	60.3	64.4	68.1	71.4	83.4	90.2	19
20	11.2	21.0	29.6	37.2	43.9	49.9	55.2	59.9	64.1	67.8	81.2	89.0	20
21	0.0	11.0	20.7	29.3	36.9	43.6	49.5	54.8	59.5	63.7	78.9	87.6	21
22	0.0	0.0	10.9	20.5	29.0	36.6	43.3	49.2	54.5	59.2	76.3	86.1	22
23	0.0	0.0	0.0	10.8	20.4	28.8	36.3	43.0	49.0	54.3	73.4	84.4	23
24	0.0	0.0	0.0	0.0	10.7	20.2	28.6	36.1	42.8	48.7	70.1	82.5	24
25	0.0	0.0	0.0	0.0	0.0	10.6	20.1	28.4	35.9	42.6	66.6	80.4	25
26	0.0	0.0	0.0	0.0	0.0	0.0	10.6	19.9	28.3	35.7	62.6	78.1	26
27	0.0	0.0	0.0	0.0	0.0	0.0	0.0	10.5	19.8	28.1	58.2	75.5	27
28	0.0	0.0	0.0	0.0	0.0	0.0	0.0	0.0	10.4	19.7	53.3	72.6	28
29	0.0	0.0	0.0	0.0	0.0	0.0	0.0	0.0	0.0	10.4	47.8	69.4	29
30	0.0	0.0	0.0	0.0	0.0	0.0	0.0	0.0	0.0	0.0	41.8	65.9	30
31	0.0	0.0	0.0	0.0	0.0	0.0	0.0	0.0	0.0	0.0	35.1	61.9	31
32	0.0	0.0	0.0	0.0	0.0	0.0	0.0	0.0	0.0	0.0	27.6	57.5	32
33	0.0	0.0	0.0	0.0	0.0	0.0	0.0	0.0	0.0	0.0	19.4	52.7	33
34	0.0	0.0	0.0	0.0	0.0	0.0	0.0	0.0	0.0	0.0	10.2	47.3	34
35	0.0	0.0	0.0	0.0	0.0	0.0	0.0	0.0	0.0	0.0	0.0	41.3	35
36	0.0	0.0	0.0	0.0	0.0	0.0	0.0	0.0	0.0	0.0	0.0	34.7	36
37	0.0	0.0	0.0	0.0	0.0	0.0	0.0	0.0	0.0	0.0	0.0	27.3	37
38	0.0	0.0	0.0	0.0	0.0	0.0	0.0	0.0	0.0	0.0	0.0	19.2	38
39	0.0	0.0	0.0	0.0	0.0	0.0	0.0	0.0	0.0	0.0	0.0	10.1	39

EXAMPLES ON PAGES A-382 TO A-397

AGE OF LOAN	2.0	3.0	5.0	8.0	10.0	12.0	15.0	16.0	17.0	18.0	19.0	20.0	AGE OF LOAN
1	52.7	70.2	84.0	91.7	94.1	95.7	97.2	97.5	97.8	98.1	98.3	98.5	1
2	0.0	37.0	66.3	82.4	87.5	90.9	94.0	94.0	94.7	95.4	95.9	96.4	96.8	2
3	0.0	0.0	46.5	72.0	80.2	85.5	90.5	91.7	92.7	93.5	94.3	95.0	3
4	0.0	0.0	24.5	60.5	72.1	79.5	86.6	88.2	89.7	90.9	92.0	92.9	4
5	0.0	0.0	0.0	47.7	63.1	72.9	82.2	84.4	86.3	87.9	89.3	90.6	5
6	0.0	0.0	0.0	33.5	53.0	65.5	77.4	80.2	82.6	84.6	86.4	88.0	6
7	0.0	0.0	0.0	17.6	41.8	57.3	72.0	75.4	78.4	81.0	83.2	85.1	7
8	0.0	0.0	0.0	0.0	29.3	48.2	66.0	70.2	73.8	76.9	79.6	82.0	8
9	0.0	0.0	0.0	0.0	15.4	38.0	59.3	64.3	68.6	72.4	75.6	78.4	9
10	0.0	0.0	0.0	0.0	0.0	26.6	51.8	57.8	62.9	67.3	71.1	74.5	10
11	0.0	0.0	0.0	0.0	0.0	14.0	43.6	50.6	56.5	61.7	66.2	70.1	11
12	0.0	0.0	0.0	0.0	0.0	0.0	34.4	42.5	49.5	55.5	60.7	65.2	12
13	0.0	0.0	0.0	0.0	0.0	0.0	24.1	33.5	41.6	48.5	54.5	59.7	13
14	0.0	0.0	0.0	0.0	0.0	0.0	12.7	23.5	32.8	40.8	47.7	53.7	14
15	0.0	0.0	0.0	0.0	0.0	0.0	0.0	12.4	23.0	32.1	40.1	47.0	15
16	0.0	0.0	0.0	0.0	0.0	0.0	0.0	0.0	12.1	22.5	31.6	39.5	16
17	0.0	0.0	0.0	0.0	0.0	0.0	0.0	0.0	0.0	11.9	22.2	31.1	17
18	0.0	0.0	0.0	0.0	0.0	0.0	0.0	0.0	0.0	0.0	11.7	21.8	18
19	0.0	0.0	0.0	0.0	0.0	0.0	0.0	0.0	0.0	0.0	0.0	11.5	19

AGE OF LOAN	21.0	22.0	23.0	24.0	25.0	26.0	27.0	28.0	29.0	30.0	35.0	40.0	AGE OF LOAN
1	98.7	98.8	98.5	99.1	99.2	99.3	99.3	99.4	99.5	99.5	99.7	99.8	1
2	97.2	97.5	97.8	98.0	98.2	98.4	98.6	98.7	98.9	99.0	99.4	99.7	2
3	95.5	96.0	96.5	96.9	97.2	97.5	97.8	98.0	98.2	98.4	99.1	99.5	3
4	93.7	94.4	95.0	95.6	96.0	96.5	96.9	97.2	97.5	97.8	98.7	99.3	4
5	91.6	92.6	93.4	94.1	94.8	95.3	95.8	96.3	96.7	97.0	98.3	99.0	5
6	89.4	90.6	91.6	92.5	93.3	94.1	94.7	95.3	95.8	96.2	97.8	98.7	6
7	86.8	88.3	89.6	90.7	91.8	92.6	93.4	94.1	94.8	95.3	97.3	98.4	7
8	84.0	85.8	87.4	88.8	90.0	91.1	92.0	92.9	93.6	94.3	96.7	98.1	8
9	80.9	83.0	84.9	86.5	88.0	89.3	90.5	91.5	92.4	93.2	96.1	97.7	9
10	77.4	79.9	82.1	84.1	85.8	87.4	88.7	89.9	91.0	91.9	95.4	97.3	10
11	73.5	76.4	79.1	81.4	83.4	85.2	86.8	88.2	89.4	90.6	94.6	96.9	11
12	69.1	72.6	75.6	78.3	80.7	82.8	84.6	86.3	87.7	89.0	93.7	96.3	12
13	64.3	68.3	71.8	74.9	77.7	80.1	82.2	84.1	85.8	87.3	92.7	95.8	13
14	58.9	63.6	67.6	71.2	74.3	77.1	79.5	81.7	83.7	85.4	91.6	95.1	14
15	53.0	58.2	62.9	67.0	70.6	73.7	76.6	79.1	81.3	83.3	90.4	94.4	15
16	46.3	52.3	57.6	62.3	66.4	70.0	73.3	76.1	78.7	80.9	89.0	93.6	16
17	38.9	45.8	51.8	57.1	61.8	65.9	69.6	72.8	75.7	78.3	87.5	92.8	17
18	30.7	38.5	45.3	51.3	56.6	61.3	65.5	69.2	72.4	75.3	85.8	91.8	18
19	21.5	30.3	38.1	44.9	50.9	56.2	60.9	65.1	68.8	72.1	83.9	90.7	19
20	11.3	21.3	30.0	37.7	44.5	50.5	55.8	60.5	64.7	68.5	81.8	89.5	20
21	0.0	11.2	21.1	29.7	37.4	44.2	50.2	55.5	60.2	64.4	79.5	88.1	21
22	0.0	0.0	11.1	20.9	29.5	37.1	43.9	49.9	55.2	59.9	76.9	86.6	22
23	0.0	0.0	0.0	11.0	20.7	29.3	36.9	43.6	49.6	54.9	74.1	85.0	23
24	0.0	0.0	0.0	0.0	10.9	20.5	29.1	36.6	43.4	49.4	70.9	83.1	24
25	0.0	0.0	0.0	0.0	0.0	10.8	20.4	28.9	36.5	43.2	67.3	81.0	25
26	0.0	0.0	0.0	0.0	0.0	0.0	10.7	20.3	28.7	36.3	63.3	78.7	26
27	0.0	0.0	0.0	0.0	0.0	0.0	0.0	10.7	20.2	28.6	58.9	76.2	27
28	0.0	0.0	0.0	0.0	0.0	0.0	0.0	0.0	10.6	20.1	54.0	73.3	28
29	0.0	0.0	0.0	0.0	0.0	0.0	0.0	0.0	0.0	10.6	48.5	70.2	29
30	0.0	0.0	0.0	0.0	0.0	0.0	0.0	0.0	0.0	0.0	42.4	66.6	30
31	0.0	0.0	0.0	0.0	0.0	0.0	0.0	0.0	0.0	0.0	35.7	62.7	31
32	0.0	0.0	0.0	0.0	0.0	0.0	0.0	0.0	0.0	0.0	28.1	58.3	32
33	0.0	0.0	0.0	0.0	0.0	0.0	0.0	0.0	0.0	0.0	19.7	53.5	33
34	0.0	0.0	0.0	0.0	0.0	0.0	0.0	0.0	0.0	0.0	10.4	48.0	34
35	0.0	0.0	0.0	0.0	0.0	0.0	0.0	0.0	0.0	0.0	0.0	42.0	35
36	0.0	0.0	0.0	0.0	0.0	0.0	0.0	0.0	0.0	0.0	0.0	35.3	36
37	0.0	0.0	0.0	0.0	0.0	0.0	0.0	0.0	0.0	0.0	0.0	27.8	37
38	0.0	0.0	0.0	0.0	0.0	0.0	0.0	0.0	0.0	0.0	0.0	19.5	38
39	0.0	0.0	0.0	0.0	0.0	0.0	0.0	0.0	0.0	0.0	0.0	10.3	39

EXAMPLES *ON PAGES A-382 TO A-397*

AGE OF LOAN	ORIGINAL TERM IN YEARS												AGE OF LOAN
	2.0	3.0	5.0	8.0	10.0	12.0	15.0	16.0	17.0	18.0	19.0	20.0	
1	52.7	70.2	84.1	91.7	94.2	95.7	97.2	97.6	97.9	98.1	98.3	98.5	1
2	0.0	37.0	66.4	82.5	87.7	91.0	94.1	94.9	95.5	96.0	96.5	96.9	2
3	0.0	0.0	46.6	72.2	80.4	85.7	90.7	91.8	92.8	93.7	94.4	95.1	3
4	0.0	0.0	24.6	60.8	72.4	79.8	86.8	88.5	89.9	91.1	92.2	93.1	4
5	0.0	0.0	0.0	48.0	63.3	73.2	82.5	84.7	36.6	88.2	89.6	90.8	5
6	0.0	0.C	0.0	33.7	53.3	65.9	77.7	80.5	82.9	85.C	86.7	88.3	6
7	0.0	0.0	0.0	17.8	42.1	57.6	72.4	75.8	78.8	81.3	83.6	85.5	7
8	0.0	0.0	0.0	0.0	29.5	48.5	66.4	70.6	74.2	77.3	80.0	82.3	8
9	0.0	0.0	0.0	0.0	15.6	38.3	59.7	64.8	69.1	72.8	76.0	78.8	9
10	0.0	0.0	0.0	0.0	C.0	26.9	52.3	58.3	63.4	67.8	71.6	74.9	10
11	0.0	0.0	0.C	0.0	0.0	14.2	44.0	51.0	57.0	62.2	66.7	70.6	11
12	0.0	0.0	0.0	0.C	C.0	0.0	34.7	42.9	49.9	55.9	61.2	65.7	12
13	0.0	0.0	0.0	0.0	0.0	C.0	24.4	33.9	42.0	49.0	55.0	60.3	13
14	0.0	0.C	0.C	0.0	0.0	0.0	12.8	23.8	33.1	41.2	48.2	54.2	14
15	0.0	0.0	0.C	0.C	0.0	0.C	0.0	12.5	23.3	32.5	40.5	47.5	15
16	0.0	0.0	0.C	0.0	0.0	0.0	0.0	0.0	12.3	22.8	32.0	39.9	16
17	0.0	0.0	0.C	0.0	0.C	0.0	0.0	0.0	0.0	12.0	22.5	31.5	17
18	0.0	0.0	0.0	0.0	C.0	0.0	0.0	0.0	0.0	0.C	11.8	22.1	18
19	0.0	0.0	0.0	0.0	0.0	0.C	0.0	0.0	0.0	0.0	0.0	11.7	19

AGE OF LOAN	ORIGINAL TERM IN YEARS												AGE OF LOAN
	21.0	22.0	23.0	24.0	25.0	26.0	27.0	28.0	29.0	30.0	35.0	40.0	
1	98.7	98.9	99.0	99.1	99.2	99.3	99.4	99.4	99.5	99.5	99.7	99.9	1
2	97.3	97.6	97.9	98.1	98.3	98.5	98.7	98.8	98.9	99.0	99.5	99.7	2
3	95.7	96.2	96.6	97.0	97.3	97.6	97.9	98.1	98.3	98.5	99.1	99.5	3
4	93.9	94.6	95.2	95.7	96.2	96.6	97.0	97.3	97.6	97.9	98.8	99.3	4
5	91.9	92.8	93.6	94.3	95.0	95.5	96.0	96.4	96.8	97.2	98.4	99.1	5
6	89.6	90.8	91.9	92.8	93.6	94.3	94.9	95.5	95.9	96.4	97.9	98.8	6
7	87.2	88.6	89.9	91.0	92.0	92.9	93.7	94.4	95.0	95.5	97.4	98.5	7
8	84.4	86.2	87.7	89.1	90.3	91.4	92.3	93.1	93.9	94.5	96.9	98.2	8
9	81.3	83.4	85.3	86.9	88.4	89.7	90.8	91.8	92.7	93.5	96.3	97.9	9
10	77.8	80.3	82.6	84.5	86.2	87.7	89.1	90.3	91.3	92.3	95.6	97.5	10
11	74.0	76.9	79.5	81.8	83.8	85.6	87.2	88.8	89.8	90.9	94.8	97.0	11
12	69.7	73.1	76.1	78.8	81.2	83.2	85.1	86.7	88.1	89.4	94.0	96.5	12
13	64.9	68.9	72.4	75.5	78.2	80.6	82.7	84.6	86.3	87.7	93.0	96.0	13
14	59.5	64.1	68.2	71.7	74.9	77.6	80.1	82.2	84.2	85.9	92.0	95.4	14
15	53.5	58.8	63.5	67.5	71.1	74.3	77.1	79.6	81.8	83.8	90.8	94.7	15
16	46.8	52.9	58.2	62.9	67.C	70.6	73.8	76.7	79.2	81.5	89.4	94.0	16
17	39.4	46.3	52.4	57.7	62.4	66.5	70.2	73.4	76.3	78.9	88.0	93.1	17
18	31.1	39.0	45.8	51.9	57.2	61.9	66.1	69.8	73.1	76.0	86.3	92.2	18
19	21.8	30.7	38.6	45.4	51.5	56.8	61.5	65.7	69.4	72.7	84.5	91.1	19
20	11.5	21.6	30.4	38.2	45.1	51.1	56.5	61.2	65.4	69.1	82.4	89.9	20
21	0.0	11.4	21.4	30.2	37.9	44.7	50.8	56.1	60.9	65.1	80.1	88.6	21
22	0.0	0.0	11.3	21.2	29.9	37.6	44.5	50.5	55.9	60.6	77.6	87.2	22
23	0.0	0.0	0.0	11.2	21.0	29.7	37.4	44.2	50.2	55.6	74.7	85.5	23
24	0.0	0.0	0.0	0.0	11.1	20.5	29.5	37.2	44.0	50.0	71.6	83.7	24
25	0.0	0.0	0.0	0.0	0.0	11.C	20.7	29.3	37.0	43.8	68.0	81.7	25
26	0.0	0.0	0.0	0.0	0.0	0.0	10.9	20.6	29.2	36.8	64.0	79.4	26
27	0.0	0.0	0.0	0.0	C.0	0.C	0.0	10.9	20.5	29.1	59.6	76.9	27
28	0.0	0.0	0.C	0.0	0.0	0.C	0.0	0.0	10.8	20.4	54.7	74.0	28
29	0.0	0.C	0.C	0.0	C.0	0.0	0.C	0.0	0.0	10.7	49.2	70.9	29
30	0.0	0.C	0.C	0.0	0.0	0.0	0.0	0.0	0.0	0.0	43.1	67.4	30
31	0.0	0.0	0.0	0.0	C.0	0.0	0.0	0.0	0.0	0.0	36.2	63.5	31
32	0.0	0.0	0.C	0.0	0.0	0.0	0.0	0.0	0.0	0.0	28.6	59.1	32
33	0.0	0.0	0.0	0.0	0.0	0.C	0.0	0.0	0.0	0.C	20.1	54.2	33
34	0.0	0.0	0.C	0.0	0.0	0.0	0.0	0.0	0.0	0.C	10.6	48.7	34
35	0.0	0.0	0.0	0.0	0.0	C.C	0.0	0.0	0.0	0.0	0.0	42.7	35
36	0.0	0.0	0.0	0.0	0.0	0.0	0.0	0.C	0.0	0.0	0.0	35.9	36
37	0.0	0.0	0.C	0.0	0.0	0.0	0.0	0.0	0.0	0.C	0.0	28.3	37
38	0.0	0.0	0.C	0.0	0.0	0.0	0.0	0.0	0.0	0.0	0.0	19.9	38
39	0.0	0.0	0.0	0.0	0.0	C.C	0.0	0.0	0.0	0.0	0.0	10.5	39

EXAMPLES *ON PAGES A-382 TO A-397*

AGE OF LOAN	ORIGINAL TERM IN YEARS												AGE OF LOAN
	2.0	3.0	5.0	8.0	10.0	12.0	15.0	16.0	17.0	18.0	19.0	20.0	
1	52.8	70.3	84.2	91.8	94.3	95.8	97.3	97.6	97.9	98.2	98.4	98.6	1
2	0.0	37.1	66.6	82.7	87.8	91.1	94.2	95.0	95.6	96.1	96.6	97.0	2
3	0.0	0.0	46.8	72.5	80.7	85.9	90.8	92.0	93.0	93.9	94.6	95.2	3
4	0.0	0.0	24.7	61.0	72.6	80.1	87.1	88.7	90.1	91.3	92.4	93.3	4
5	0.0	0.0	0.0	48.2	63.6	73.5	82.8	85.0	86.9	88.5	89.8	91.1	5
6	0.0	0.0	0.0	33.9	53.6	66.2	78.0	80.8	83.2	85.3	87.0	88.6	6
7	0.0	0.0	0.0	17.9	42.4	58.0	72.7	76.2	79.2	81.7	83.9	85.8	7
8	0.0	0.0	0.0	0.0	29.8	48.8	66.8	71.0	74.6	77.7	80.4	82.7	8
9	0.0	0.0	0.0	0.0	15.7	38.6	60.1	65.2	69.5	73.3	76.5	79.3	9
10	0.0	0.0	0.0	0.0	0.0	27.1	52.7	58.7	63.8	68.3	72.1	75.4	10
11	0.0	0.0	0.0	0.0	0.0	14.3	44.4	51.4	57.5	62.7	67.2	71.1	11
12	0.0	0.0	0.0	0.0	0.0	0.0	35.1	43.3	50.4	56.4	61.7	66.2	12
13	0.0	0.0	0.0	0.0	0.0	0.0	24.7	34.2	42.4	49.5	55.5	60.8	13
14	0.0	0.0	0.0	0.0	0.0	0.0	13.0	24.1	33.5	41.6	48.7	54.8	14
15	0.0	0.0	0.0	0.0	0.0	0.0	0.0	12.7	23.6	32.9	41.0	48.0	15
16	0.0	0.0	0.0	0.0	0.0	0.0	0.0	0.0	12.4	23.1	32.4	40.4	16
17	0.0	0.0	0.0	0.0	0.0	0.0	0.0	0.0	0.0	12.2	22.8	31.9	17
18	0.0	0.0	0.0	0.0	0.0	0.0	0.0	0.0	0.0	0.0	12.0	22.4	18
19	0.0	0.0	0.0	0.0	0.0	0.0	0.0	0.0	0.0	0.0	0.0	11.8	19

AGE OF LOAN	ORIGINAL TERM IN YEARS												AGE OF LOAN
	21.0	22.0	23.0	24.0	25.0	26.0	27.0	28.0	29.0	30.0	35.0	40.0	
1	98.8	98.5	99.0	99.1	99.2	99.3	99.4	99.5	99.5	99.6	99.8	99.9	1
2	97.4	97.7	97.9	98.2	98.4	98.6	98.7	98.5	99.0	99.1	99.5	99.7	2
3	95.8	96.3	96.7	97.1	97.4	97.7	98.0	98.2	98.4	98.6	99.2	99.5	3
4	94.1	94.7	95.3	95.9	96.3	96.7	97.1	97.4	97.7	98.0	98.9	99.4	4
5	92.1	93.0	93.8	94.5	95.1	95.7	96.2	96.6	97.0	97.3	98.5	99.1	5
6	89.9	91.1	92.1	93.0	93.8	94.5	95.1	95.6	96.1	96.6	98.1	98.9	6
7	87.5	88.9	90.2	91.3	92.3	93.2	93.9	94.6	95.2	95.7	97.6	98.6	7
8	84.7	86.5	88.1	89.4	90.6	91.7	92.6	93.4	94.1	94.8	97.1	98.3	8
9	81.7	83.8	85.7	87.3	88.7	90.0	91.1	92.1	93.0	93.7	96.5	98.0	9
10	78.3	80.8	83.0	84.9	86.6	88.1	89.4	90.6	91.6	92.6	95.8	97.6	10
11	74.5	77.4	80.0	82.3	84.3	86.0	87.6	89.0	90.2	91.3	95.1	97.2	11
12	70.2	73.6	76.7	79.3	81.6	83.7	85.5	87.1	88.5	89.8	94.3	96.7	12
13	65.4	69.4	72.9	76.0	78.7	81.1	83.2	85.1	86.7	88.2	93.3	96.2	13
14	60.0	64.7	68.7	72.3	75.4	78.2	80.6	82.7	84.6	86.3	92.3	95.6	14
15	54.1	59.4	64.0	68.1	71.7	74.9	77.7	80.2	82.3	84.3	91.2	95.0	15
16	47.4	53.5	58.8	63.5	67.6	71.2	74.4	77.3	79.8	82.0	89.9	94.3	16
17	39.9	46.9	52.9	58.3	63.0	67.1	70.8	74.0	76.9	79.4	88.4	93.4	17
18	31.5	39.5	46.4	52.5	57.8	62.6	66.7	70.4	73.7	76.6	86.8	92.5	18
19	22.2	31.2	39.1	46.0	52.1	57.5	62.2	66.4	70.1	73.4	85.0	91.5	19
20	11.7	21.9	30.9	38.7	45.6	51.7	57.1	61.9	66.1	69.8	83.0	90.4	20
21	0.0	11.6	21.7	30.6	38.4	45.3	51.4	56.8	61.6	65.8	80.7	89.1	21
22	0.0	0.0	11.5	21.5	30.4	38.2	45.1	51.1	56.5	61.3	78.2	87.7	22
23	0.0	0.0	0.0	11.4	21.4	30.2	37.9	44.8	50.9	56.3	75.4	86.1	23
24	0.0	0.0	0.0	0.0	11.3	21.2	30.0	37.7	44.6	50.7	72.3	84.3	24
25	0.0	0.0	0.0	0.0	0.0	11.2	21.1	29.8	37.6	44.4	68.7	82.3	25
26	0.0	0.0	0.0	0.0	0.0	0.0	11.1	21.0	29.7	37.4	64.8	80.1	26
27	0.0	0.0	0.0	0.0	0.0	0.0	0.0	11.1	20.9	29.6	60.4	77.6	27
28	0.0	0.0	0.0	0.0	0.0	0.0	0.0	0.0	11.0	20.8	55.4	74.8	28
29	0.0	0.0	0.0	0.0	0.0	0.0	0.0	0.0	0.0	11.0	49.9	71.6	29
30	0.0	0.0	0.0	0.0	0.0	0.0	0.0	0.0	0.0	0.0	43.7	68.1	30
31	0.0	0.0	0.0	0.0	0.0	0.0	0.0	0.0	0.0	0.0	36.8	64.2	31
32	0.0	0.0	0.0	0.0	0.0	0.0	0.0	0.0	0.0	0.0	29.1	59.8	32
33	0.0	0.0	0.0	0.0	0.0	0.0	0.0	0.0	0.0	0.0	20.5	55.0	33
34	0.0	0.0	0.0	0.0	0.0	0.0	0.0	0.0	0.0	0.0	10.8	49.5	34
35	0.0	0.0	0.0	0.0	0.0	0.0	0.0	0.0	0.0	0.0	0.0	43.4	35
36	0.0	0.0	0.0	0.0	0.0	0.0	0.0	0.0	0.0	0.0	0.0	36.5	36
37	0.0	0.0	0.0	0.0	0.0	0.0	0.0	0.0	0.0	0.0	0.0	28.8	37
38	0.0	0.0	0.0	0.0	0.0	0.0	0.0	0.0	0.0	0.0	0.0	20.3	38
39	0.0	0.0	0.0	0.0	0.0	0.0	0.0	0.0	0.0	0.0	0.0	10.7	39

EXAMPLES *ON PAGES A-382 TO A-397*

AGE OF LOAN	2.0	3.0	5.0	8.0	10.0	12.0	15.0	16.0	17.0	18.0	19.0	20.0	AGE OF LOAN
1	52.9	70.4	84.3	91.9	94.3	95.9	97.3	97.7	98.0	98.2	98.4	98.6	1
2	0.0	37.2	66.7	82.8	88.0	91.3	94.4	95.1	95.7	96.2	96.7	97.1	2
3	0.0	0.0	46.9	72.7	8C.9	86.1	91.0	92.2	93.2	94.0	94.7	95.4	3
4	0.0	0.0	24.8	61.2	72.9	80.3	87.3	88.9	90.3	91.5	92.6	93.4	4
5	0.0	0.0	0.0	48.5	63.9	73.8	83.1	85.3	87.1	88.7	90.1	91.3	5
6	0.0	0.0	0.0	34.1	53.9	66.5	78.4	81.2	83.5	85.6	87.3	88.9	6
7	0.0	0.0	0.0	18.0	42.6	58.3	73.1	76.6	79.5	82.1	84.2	86.1	7
8	0.0	0.0	0.0	0.0	30.0	49.2	67.2	71.4	75.0	78.1	80.8	83.1	8
9	0.0	0.0	0.0	0.0	15.9	38.9	60.5	65.6	70.0	73.7	76.9	79.7	9
10	0.0	0.0	0.0	0.0	0.0	27.4	53.1	59.1	64.3	68.7	72.5	75.8	10
11	0.0	0.0	0.0	0.0	0.0	14.5	44.8	51.9	58.0	63.2	67.7	71.5	11
12	0.0	0.0	0.0	0.0	0.0	0.0	35.4	43.7	50.8	56.9	62.2	66.7	12
13	0.0	0.0	0.0	0.0	0.0	0.0	24.9	34.6	42.8	49.9	56.0	61.3	13
14	0.0	0.0	0.0	0.0	0.0	0.0	13.2	24.3	33.9	42.1	49.2	55.3	14
15	0.0	0.0	0.0	0.0	0.0	0.0	0.0	12.9	23.9	33.3	41.4	48.5	15
16	0.0	0.0	0.0	0.0	0.0	0.0	0.0	0.0	12.6	23.4	32.8	40.9	16
17	0.0	0.0	0.0	0.0	0.0	0.0	0.0	0.0	0.0	12.4	23.1	32.3	17
18	0.0	0.0	0.0	0.0	0.0	0.0	0.0	0.0	0.0	0.0	12.2	22.8	18
19	0.0	0.0	0.0	0.0	0.0	0.0	0.0	0.0	0.0	0.0	0.0	12.0	19

AGE OF LOAN	21.0	22.0	23.0	24.0	25.0	26.0	27.0	28.0	29.0	30.0	35.0	40.0	AGE OF LOAN
1	98.8	98.5	99.1	99.3	99.3	99.3	99.4	99.5	99.5	99.6	99.8	99.9	1
2	97.4	97.7	98.0	98.2	98.4	98.6	98.8	98.9	99.0	99.1	99.5	99.7	2
3	95.9	96.4	96.8	97.2	97.5	97.8	98.0	98.3	98.5	98.6	99.2	99.6	3
4	94.2	94.9	95.5	96.0	96.5	96.9	97.2	97.5	97.8	98.1	98.9	99.4	4
5	92.3	93.2	94.0	94.7	95.3	95.8	96.3	96.7	97.1	97.4	98.6	99.2	5
6	90.2	91.3	92.3	93.2	94.0	94.7	95.3	95.8	96.3	96.7	98.2	99.0	6
7	87.8	89.2	90.5	91.6	92.5	93.4	94.1	94.8	95.4	95.9	97.7	98.7	7
8	85.1	86.9	88.4	89.7	90.9	91.9	92.9	93.7	94.4	95.0	97.2	98.4	8
9	82.1	84.2	86.0	87.7	89.1	90.3	91.4	92.4	93.2	94.0	96.7	98.1	9
10	78.7	81.2	83.4	85.3	87.0	88.5	89.8	90.9	92.0	92.9	96.0	97.8	10
11	74.9	77.9	80.5	82.7	84.7	86.4	88.0	89.3	90.5	91.6	95.3	97.4	11
12	70.7	74.1	77.1	79.8	82.1	84.1	85.9	87.5	88.9	90.2	94.5	96.9	12
13	65.9	69.9	73.4	76.5	79.2	81.6	83.7	85.5	87.1	88.6	93.6	96.4	13
14	60.6	65.2	69.3	72.8	75.9	78.7	81.1	83.2	85.1	86.8	92.6	95.9	14
15	54.6	59.9	64.6	68.7	72.3	75.4	78.2	80.7	82.9	84.8	91.5	95.3	15
16	47.9	54.0	59.4	64.1	68.2	71.8	75.0	77.8	80.3	82.5	90.3	94.6	16
17	40.4	47.4	53.5	58.9	63.6	67.7	71.4	74.6	77.5	80.0	88.9	93.8	17
18	31.9	39.9	46.9	53.1	58.5	63.2	67.4	71.0	74.3	77.2	87.3	92.9	18
19	22.5	31.6	39.6	46.5	52.7	58.1	62.8	67.0	70.7	74.0	85.5	91.9	19
20	11.9	22.2	31.3	39.2	46.2	52.3	57.7	62.5	66.7	70.4	83.6	90.8	20
21	0.0	11.7	22.0	31.0	38.9	45.9	52.0	57.4	62.2	66.4	81.3	89.6	21
22	0.0	0.0	11.6	21.8	30.8	38.7	45.6	51.8	57.2	62.0	78.8	88.2	22
23	0.0	0.0	0.0	11.5	21.7	30.6	38.5	45.4	51.5	56.9	76.1	86.6	23
24	0.0	0.0	0.0	0.0	11.4	21.5	30.4	38.3	45.2	51.3	72.9	84.8	24
25	0.0	0.0	0.0	0.0	0.0	11.4	21.4	30.3	38.1	45.0	69.4	82.9	25
26	0.0	0.0	0.0	0.0	0.0	0.0	11.3	21.3	30.1	37.9	65.5	80.7	26
27	0.0	0.0	0.0	0.0	0.0	0.0	0.0	11.2	21.2	30.0	61.1	78.2	27
28	0.0	0.0	0.0	0.0	0.0	0.0	0.0	0.0	11.2	21.1	56.1	75.4	28
29	0.0	0.0	0.0	0.0	0.0	0.0	0.0	0.0	0.0	11.1	50.6	72.3	29
30	0.0	0.0	0.0	0.0	0.0	0.0	0.0	0.0	0.0	0.0	44.4	68.9	30
31	0.0	0.0	0.0	0.0	0.0	0.0	0.0	0.0	0.0	0.0	37.4	65.0	31
32	0.0	0.0	0.0	0.0	0.0	0.0	0.0	0.0	0.0	0.0	29.6	60.6	32
33	0.0	0.0	0.0	0.0	0.0	0.0	0.0	0.0	0.0	0.0	20.8	55.7	33
34	0.0	0.0	0.0	0.0	0.0	0.0	0.0	0.0	0.0	0.0	11.0	50.2	34
35	0.0	0.0	0.0	0.0	0.0	0.0	0.0	0.0	0.0	0.0	0.0	44.0	35
36	0.0	0.0	0.0	0.0	0.0	0.0	0.0	0.0	0.0	0.0	0.0	37.1	36
37	0.0	0.0	0.0	0.0	0.0	0.0	0.0	0.0	0.0	0.0	0.0	29.3	37
38	0.0	0.0	0.0	0.0	0.0	0.0	0.0	0.0	0.0	0.0	0.0	20.6	38
39	0.0	0.0	0.0	0.0	0.0	0.0	0.0	0.0	0.0	0.0	0.0	10.9	39

EXAMPLES *ON PAGES A-382 TO A-397*

AGE OF LOAN	ORIGINAL TERM IN YEARS												AGE OF LOAN
	2.0	3.0	5.0	8.0	10.0	12.0	15.0	16.0	17.0	18.0	19.0	20.0	
1	52.9	70.5	84.4	92.0	94.4	96.0	97.4	97.7	98.0	98.3	98.5	98.7	1
2	0.0	37.3	66.8	83.0	88.1	91.4	94.5	95.2	95.8	96.3	96.8	97.2	2
3	0.0	0.0	47.1	72.9	81.1	86.3	91.2	92.4	93.3	94.2	94.9	95.5	3
4	0.0	0.0	24.9	61.5	73.1	80.6	87.5	89.1	90.5	91.7	92.7	93.6	4
5	0.0	0.0	0.0	48.7	64.2	74.1	83.4	85.5	87.4	89.0	90.3	91.5	5
6	0.0	0.0	0.0	34.3	54.2	66.9	78.7	81.5	83.9	85.9	87.6	89.1	6
7	0.0	0.0	0.0	18.2	42.9	58.7	73.5	76.9	79.9	82.4	84.6	86.5	7
8	0.0	0.0	0.0	0.0	30.2	49.5	67.6	71.8	75.4	78.5	81.2	83.5	8
9	0.0	0.0	0.0	0.0	16.0	39.2	61.0	66.1	70.4	74.1	77.3	80.1	9
10	0.0	0.0	0.0	0.0	0.0	27.6	53.5	59.6	64.8	69.2	73.0	76.3	10
11	0.0	0.0	0.0	0.0	0.0	14.6	45.2	52.3	58.4	63.6	68.1	72.0	11
12	0.0	0.0	0.0	0.0	0.0	0.0	35.8	44.2	51.3	57.4	62.7	67.2	12
13	0.0	0.0	0.0	0.0	0.0	0.0	25.2	35.0	43.3	50.4	56.5	61.9	13
14	0.0	0.0	0.0	0.0	0.0	0.0	13.3	24.6	34.3	42.5	49.6	55.8	14
15	0.0	0.0	0.0	0.0	0.0	0.0	0.0	13.0	24.2	33.7	41.9	49.0	15
16	0.0	0.0	0.0	0.0	0.0	0.0	0.0	0.0	12.8	23.7	33.2	41.3	16
17	0.0	0.0	0.0	0.0	0.0	0.0	0.0	0.0	0.0	12.6	23.4	32.7	17
18	0.0	0.0	0.0	0.0	0.0	0.0	0.0	0.0	0.0	0.0	12.4	23.1	18
19	0.0	0.0	0.0	0.0	0.0	0.0	0.0	0.0	0.0	0.0	0.0	12.2	19

AGE OF LOAN	ORIGINAL TERM IN YEARS												AGE OF LOAN
	21.0	22.0	23.0	24.0	25.0	26.0	27.0	28.0	29.0	30.0	35.0	40.0	
1	98.8	99.0	99.1	99.2	99.3	99.4	99.4	99.5	99.6	99.6	99.8	99.9	1
2	97.5	97.8	98.1	98.3	98.5	98.7	98.8	99.0	99.1	99.2	99.6	99.8	2
3	96.1	96.6	96.9	97.3	97.6	97.9	98.1	98.3	98.5	98.7	99.3	99.6	3
4	94.4	95.1	95.7	96.2	96.6	97.0	97.3	97.7	97.9	98.2	99.0	99.4	4
5	92.5	93.4	94.2	94.9	95.5	96.0	96.5	96.9	97.2	97.5	98.7	99.3	5
6	90.5	91.6	92.6	93.5	94.2	94.9	95.5	96.0	96.5	96.9	98.3	99.0	6
7	88.1	89.5	90.8	91.8	92.8	93.6	94.4	95.0	95.6	96.1	97.8	98.8	7
8	85.5	87.2	88.7	90.0	91.2	92.2	93.1	93.9	94.6	95.2	97.4	98.5	8
9	82.5	84.6	86.4	88.0	89.4	90.6	91.7	92.7	93.5	94.2	96.8	98.2	9
10	79.2	81.7	83.8	85.7	87.4	88.8	90.1	91.3	92.3	93.1	96.2	97.9	10
11	75.4	78.3	80.9	83.2	85.1	86.8	88.4	89.7	90.9	91.9	95.6	97.5	11
12	71.2	74.6	77.6	80.3	82.6	84.6	86.4	87.9	89.3	90.5	94.8	97.1	12
13	66.5	70.5	74.0	77.0	79.7	82.1	84.1	85.9	87.5	89.0	93.9	96.6	13
14	61.1	65.8	69.8	73.4	76.5	79.2	81.6	83.7	85.6	87.2	93.0	96.1	14
15	55.1	60.5	65.2	69.3	72.9	76.0	78.8	81.2	83.3	85.2	91.9	95.5	15
16	48.4	54.6	60.0	64.7	68.8	72.4	75.6	78.4	80.9	83.0	90.7	94.8	16
17	40.9	47.9	54.1	59.5	64.2	68.4	72.0	75.2	78.0	80.5	89.3	94.1	17
18	32.4	40.4	47.5	53.7	59.1	63.8	68.0	71.7	74.9	77.7	87.8	93.2	18
19	22.8	32.0	40.1	47.1	53.3	58.7	63.5	67.6	71.3	74.6	86.0	92.3	19
20	12.1	22.6	31.7	39.8	46.8	52.9	58.4	63.1	67.4	71.1	84.1	91.2	20
21	0.0	11.9	22.4	31.5	39.5	46.5	52.7	58.1	62.9	67.1	81.9	90.0	21
22	0.0	0.0	11.8	22.2	31.3	39.2	46.2	52.4	57.8	62.6	79.5	88.6	22
23	0.0	0.0	0.0	11.7	22.0	31.1	39.0	46.0	52.2	57.6	76.7	87.1	23
24	0.0	0.0	0.0	0.0	11.7	21.9	30.9	38.8	45.8	52.0	73.6	85.4	24
25	0.0	0.0	0.0	0.0	0.0	11.6	21.8	30.7	38.7	45.6	70.1	83.5	25
26	0.0	0.0	0.0	0.0	0.0	0.0	11.5	21.7	30.6	38.5	66.2	81.3	26
27	0.0	0.0	0.0	0.0	0.0	0.0	0.0	11.5	21.6	30.5	61.8	78.9	27
28	0.0	0.0	0.0	0.0	0.0	0.0	0.0	0.0	11.4	21.5	56.8	76.1	28
29	0.0	0.0	0.0	0.0	0.0	0.0	0.0	0.0	0.0	11.4	51.3	73.0	29
30	0.0	0.0	0.0	0.0	0.0	0.0	0.0	0.0	0.0	0.0	45.0	69.6	30
31	0.0	0.0	0.0	0.0	0.0	0.0	0.0	0.0	0.0	0.0	38.0	65.7	31
32	0.0	0.0	0.0	0.0	0.0	0.0	0.0	0.0	0.0	0.0	30.1	61.3	32
33	0.0	0.0	0.0	0.0	0.0	0.0	0.0	0.0	0.0	0.0	21.2	56.4	33
34	0.0	0.0	0.0	0.0	0.0	0.0	0.0	0.0	0.0	0.0	11.2	50.9	34
35	0.0	0.0	0.0	0.0	0.0	0.0	0.0	0.0	0.0	0.0	0.0	44.7	35
36	0.0	0.0	0.0	0.0	0.0	0.0	0.0	0.0	0.0	0.0	0.0	37.7	36
37	0.0	0.0	0.0	0.0	0.0	0.0	0.0	0.0	0.0	0.0	0.0	29.9	37
38	0.0	0.0	0.0	0.0	0.0	0.0	0.0	0.0	0.0	0.0	0.0	21.0	38
39	0.0	0.0	0.0	0.0	0.0	0.0	0.0	0.0	0.0	0.0	0.0	11.1	39

EXAMPLES ON PAGES A-382 TO A-397

AGE OF LOAN	ORIGINAL TERM IN YEARS												AGE OF LOAN
	2.0	3.0	5.0	8.0	10.0	12.0	15.0	16.0	17.0	18.0	19.0	20.0	
1	53.0	70.6	84.5	92.1	94.5	96.0	97.5	97.8	98.1	98.3	98.5	98.7	1
2	0.0	37.4	67.0	83.1	88.3	91.5	94.6	95.3	95.9	96.4	96.9	97.3	2
3	0.0	0.0	47.2	73.1	81.3	86.5	91.4	92.5	93.5	94.3	95.0	95.6	3
4	0.0	0.0	25.0	61.7	73.4	80.8	87.7	89.4	90.7	91.9	92.9	93.8	4
5	0.0	0.0	0.0	48.9	64.5	74.4	83.6	85.8	87.6	89.2	90.6	91.7	5
6	0.0	0.0	0.0	34.5	54.5	67.2	79.0	81.8	84.2	86.2	87.9	89.4	6
7	0.0	0.0	0.0	18.3	43.2	59.0	73.8	77.3	80.2	82.8	84.9	86.8	7
8	0.0	0.0	0.0	0.0	30.5	49.9	68.0	72.2	75.8	78.9	81.5	83.8	8
9	0.0	0.0	0.0	0.0	16.1	39.5	61.4	66.5	70.8	74.5	77.7	80.5	9
10	0.0	0.0	0.0	0.0	0.0	27.9	53.9	60.0	65.2	69.6	73.5	76.7	10
11	0.0	0.0	0.0	0.0	0.0	14.8	45.6	52.8	58.9	64.1	68.6	72.5	11
12	0.0	0.0	0.0	0.0	0.0	0.0	36.1	44.6	51.7	57.9	63.2	67.7	12
13	0.0	0.0	0.0	0.0	0.0	0.0	25.5	35.3	43.7	50.9	57.0	62.4	13
14	0.0	0.0	0.0	0.0	0.0	0.0	13.5	24.9	34.6	43.0	50.1	56.3	14
15	0.0	0.0	0.0	0.0	0.0	0.0	0.0	13.2	24.4	34.1	42.3	49.5	15
16	0.0	0.0	0.0	0.0	0.0	0.0	0.0	0.0	12.9	24.0	33.6	41.8	16
17	0.0	0.0	0.0	0.0	0.0	0.0	0.0	0.0	0.0	12.7	23.7	33.1	17
18	0.0	0.0	0.0	0.0	0.0	0.0	0.0	0.0	0.0	0.0	12.5	23.4	18
19	0.0	0.0	0.0	0.0	0.0	0.0	0.0	0.0	0.0	0.0	0.0	12.4	19

AGE OF LOAN	ORIGINAL TERM IN YEARS												AGE OF LOAN
	21.0	22.0	23.0	24.0	25.0	26.0	27.0	28.0	29.0	30.0	35.0	40.0	
1	98.9	99.0	99.1	99.2	99.3	99.4	99.5	99.5	99.6	99.6	99.8	99.9	1
2	97.6	97.9	98.2	98.4	98.6	98.7	98.9	99.0	99.1	99.2	99.6	99.8	2
3	96.2	96.6	97.0	97.4	97.7	98.0	98.2	98.4	98.6	98.8	99.3	99.6	3
4	94.6	95.2	55.8	96.3	96.7	97.1	97.5	97.8	98.0	98.2	99.0	99.5	4
5	92.8	93.6	94.4	95.1	95.7	96.2	96.6	97.0	97.4	97.7	98.7	99.3	5
6	90.7	91.8	92.8	93.7	94.4	95.1	95.7	96.2	96.6	97.0	98.4	99.1	6
7	88.4	89.8	91.0	92.1	93.0	93.9	94.6	95.2	95.8	96.3	98.0	98.9	7
8	85.8	87.5	89.0	90.3	91.5	92.5	93.4	94.1	94.8	95.4	97.5	98.6	8
9	82.9	85.0	86.8	88.4	89.7	90.9	92.0	92.9	93.8	94.5	97.0	98.4	9
10	79.6	82.1	84.2	86.1	87.8	89.2	90.5	91.6	92.6	93.4	96.4	98.0	10
11	75.9	78.8	81.4	83.6	85.5	87.2	88.7	90.0	91.2	92.2	95.8	97.7	11
12	71.7	75.1	78.1	80.7	83.0	85.0	86.8	88.3	89.7	90.9	95.0	97.3	12
13	67.0	71.0	74.5	77.5	80.2	82.5	84.6	86.4	88.0	89.3	94.2	96.8	13
14	61.7	66.3	70.4	73.9	77.0	79.7	82.1	84.2	86.0	87.6	93.3	96.3	14
15	55.7	61.1	65.7	69.8	73.4	76.5	79.3	81.7	83.8	85.7	92.2	95.8	15
16	48.9	55.1	60.5	65.4	69.4	73.0	76.1	78.9	81.4	83.5	91.0	95.1	16
17	41.3	48.4	54.6	60.1	64.8	68.9	72.6	75.8	78.6	81.1	89.7	94.4	17
18	32.8	40.9	48.0	54.2	59.7	64.4	68.6	72.2	75.5	78.3	88.2	93.6	18
19	23.1	32.4	40.6	47.7	53.9	59.3	64.1	68.3	71.9	75.2	86.5	92.6	19
20	12.2	22.9	32.2	40.3	47.3	53.5	59.0	63.8	68.0	71.7	84.6	91.6	20
21	0.0	12.1	22.7	31.9	40.0	47.1	53.3	58.7	63.5	67.7	82.5	90.4	21
22	0.0	0.0	12.0	22.5	31.7	39.7	46.8	53.0	58.5	63.3	80.0	89.1	22
23	0.0	0.0	0.0	11.9	22.4	31.5	39.5	46.6	52.8	58.3	77.3	87.6	23
24	0.0	0.0	0.0	0.0	11.8	22.2	31.3	39.3	46.4	52.6	74.2	85.9	24
25	0.0	0.0	0.0	0.0	0.0	11.8	22.1	31.2	39.2	46.2	70.8	84.0	25
26	0.0	0.0	0.0	0.0	0.0	0.0	11.7	22.0	31.1	39.0	66.9	81.9	26
27	0.0	0.0	0.0	0.0	0.0	0.0	0.0	11.6	21.9	31.0	62.5	79.5	27
28	0.0	0.0	0.0	0.0	0.0	0.0	0.0	0.0	11.6	21.8	57.5	76.8	28
29	0.0	0.0	0.0	0.0	0.0	0.0	0.0	0.0	0.0	11.6	51.9	73.7	29
30	0.0	0.0	0.0	0.0	0.0	0.0	0.0	0.0	0.0	0.0	45.6	70.3	30
31	0.0	0.0	0.0	0.0	0.0	0.0	0.0	0.0	0.0	0.0	38.5	66.4	31
32	0.0	0.0	0.0	0.0	0.0	0.0	0.0	0.0	0.0	0.0	30.6	62.0	32
33	0.0	0.0	0.0	0.0	0.0	0.0	0.0	0.0	0.0	0.0	21.6	57.1	33
34	0.0	0.0	0.0	0.0	0.0	0.0	0.0	0.0	0.0	0.0	11.4	51.6	34
35	0.0	0.0	0.0	0.0	0.0	0.0	0.0	0.0	0.0	0.0	0.0	45.3	35
36	0.0	0.0	0.0	0.0	0.0	0.0	0.0	0.0	0.0	0.0	0.0	38.3	36
37	0.0	0.0	0.0	0.0	0.0	0.0	0.0	0.0	0.0	0.0	0.0	30.3	37
38	0.0	0.0	0.0	0.0	0.0	0.0	0.0	0.0	0.0	0.0	0.0	21.4	38
39	0.0	0.0	0.0	0.0	0.0	0.0	0.0	0.0	0.0	0.0	0.0	11.3	39

EXAMPLES *ON PAGES A-382 TO A-397*

AGE OF LOAN	ORIGINAL TERM IN YEARS												AGE OF LOAN
	2.0	3.0	5.0	8.0	10.0	12.0	15.0	16.0	17.0	18.0	19.0	20.0	
1	53.0	70.6	84.6	92.2	94.6	96.1	97.5	97.9	98.1	98.4	98.6	98.8	1
2	0.0	37.5	67.1	83.3	88.4	91.7	94.7	95.4	96.0	96.5	97.0	97.4	2
3	0.0	0.0	47.4	73.3	81.5	86.7	91.5	92.7	93.6	94.5	95.2	95.8	3
4	0.0	0.0	25.1	62.0	73.6	81.1	88.0	89.6	90.9	92.1	93.1	94.0	4
5	0.0	0.0	0.0	49.2	64.8	74.7	83.9	86.1	87.9	89.5	90.8	92.0	5
6	0.0	0.0	0.0	34.7	54.8	67.5	79.4	82.1	84.5	86.5	88.2	89.7	6
7	0.0	0.0	0.0	18.4	43.5	59.4	74.2	77.7	80.6	83.1	85.2	87.1	7
8	0.0	0.0	0.0	0.0	30.7	50.2	68.4	72.6	76.2	79.3	81.9	84.2	8
9	0.0	0.0	0.0	0.0	16.3	39.9	61.8	66.9	71.3	75.0	78.2	80.9	9
10	0.0	0.0	0.0	0.0	0.0	28.2	54.4	60.5	65.7	70.1	73.9	77.2	10
11	0.0	0.0	0.0	0.0	0.0	14.9	46.0	53.2	59.3	64.6	69.1	73.0	11
12	0.0	0.0	0.0	0.0	0.0	0.0	36.5	45.0	52.2	58.4	63.7	68.2	12
13	0.0	0.0	0.0	0.0	0.0	0.0	25.8	35.7	44.1	51.4	57.5	62.9	13
14	0.0	0.0	0.0	0.0	0.0	0.0	13.7	25.2	35.0	43.4	50.6	56.8	14
15	0.0	0.0	0.0	0.0	0.0	0.0	0.0	13.4	24.7	34.5	42.8	50.0	15
16	0.0	0.0	0.0	0.0	0.0	0.0	0.0	0.0	13.1	24.3	34.0	42.3	16
17	0.0	0.0	0.0	0.0	0.0	0.0	0.0	0.0	0.0	12.9	24.0	33.6	17
18	0.0	0.0	0.0	0.0	0.0	0.0	0.0	0.0	0.0	0.0	12.7	23.7	18
19	0.0	0.0	0.0	0.0	0.0	0.0	0.0	0.0	0.0	0.0	0.0	12.6	19

12.25

AGE OF LOAN	ORIGINAL TERM IN YEARS												AGE OF LOAN
	21.0	22.0	23.0	24.0	25.0	26.0	27.0	28.0	29.0	30.0	35.0	40.0	
1	98.9	99.0	99.2	99.3	99.4	99.4	99.5	99.6	99.6	99.7	99.8	99.9	1
2	97.7	98.0	98.2	98.4	98.6	98.8	98.9	99.1	99.2	99.3	99.6	99.8	2
3	96.3	96.8	97.2	97.5	97.8	98.1	98.3	98.5	98.7	98.8	99.4	99.7	3
4	94.7	95.4	95.9	96.4	96.9	97.2	97.6	97.9	98.1	98.3	99.1	99.5	4
5	93.0	93.8	94.6	95.2	95.8	96.3	96.8	97.1	97.5	97.8	98.8	99.4	5
6	91.0	92.1	93.0	93.9	94.6	95.3	95.8	96.3	96.8	97.1	98.5	99.2	6
7	88.7	90.1	91.3	92.4	93.3	94.1	94.8	95.4	96.0	96.4	98.1	99.0	7
8	86.2	87.9	89.3	90.6	91.8	92.8	93.6	94.4	95.0	95.6	97.6	98.7	8
9	83.3	85.3	87.1	88.7	90.1	91.2	92.3	93.2	94.0	94.7	97.2	98.5	9
10	80.0	82.5	84.6	86.5	88.1	89.5	90.8	91.9	92.8	93.7	96.6	98.2	10
11	76.3	79.3	81.8	84.0	85.9	87.6	89.1	90.4	91.5	92.5	96.0	97.8	11
12	72.2	75.8	78.6	81.2	83.5	85.4	87.2	88.7	90.0	91.2	95.3	97.4	12
13	67.5	71.5	75.0	78.0	80.7	83.0	85.0	86.8	88.4	89.7	94.5	97.0	13
14	62.2	66.9	70.9	74.4	77.5	80.2	82.6	84.6	86.5	88.0	93.6	96.5	14
15	56.2	61.6	66.3	70.4	74.0	77.1	79.8	82.2	84.3	86.2	92.6	96.0	15
16	49.5	55.7	61.1	65.8	69.9	73.5	76.7	79.5	81.9	84.0	91.4	95.4	16
17	41.8	49.0	55.2	60.6	65.4	69.5	73.2	76.3	79.1	81.6	90.1	94.7	17
18	33.2	41.4	48.6	54.8	60.3	65.0	69.2	72.8	76.1	78.9	88.7	93.9	18
19	23.4	32.9	41.1	48.2	54.5	59.9	64.7	68.9	72.6	75.8	87.0	93.0	19
20	12.4	23.2	32.6	40.8	47.9	54.1	59.6	64.4	68.6	72.3	85.1	92.0	20
21	0.0	12.3	23.0	32.4	40.5	47.6	53.9	59.3	64.2	68.4	83.0	90.8	21
22	0.0	0.0	12.2	22.9	32.1	40.3	47.4	53.6	59.1	63.9	80.6	89.5	22
23	0.0	0.0	0.0	12.1	22.7	32.0	40.1	47.2	53.4	58.9	77.9	88.1	23
24	0.0	0.0	0.0	0.0	12.0	22.6	31.8	39.9	47.0	53.2	74.9	86.4	24
25	0.0	0.0	0.0	0.0	0.0	12.0	22.5	31.7	39.7	46.8	71.4	84.6	25
26	0.0	0.0	0.0	0.0	0.0	0.0	11.9	22.4	31.5	39.6	67.6	82.5	26
27	0.0	0.0	0.0	0.0	0.0	0.0	0.0	11.9	22.3	31.4	63.2	80.1	27
28	0.0	0.0	0.0	0.0	0.0	0.0	0.0	0.0	11.8	22.2	58.2	77.4	28
29	0.0	0.0	0.0	0.0	0.0	0.0	0.0	0.0	0.0	11.8	52.6	74.4	29
30	0.0	0.0	0.0	0.0	0.0	0.0	0.0	0.0	0.0	0.0	46.3	71.0	30
31	0.0	0.0	0.0	0.0	0.0	0.0	0.0	0.0	0.0	0.0	39.1	67.1	31
32	0.0	0.0	0.0	0.0	0.0	0.0	0.0	0.0	0.0	0.0	31.1	62.8	32
33	0.0	0.0	0.0	0.0	0.0	0.0	0.0	0.0	0.0	0.0	21.9	57.8	33
34	0.0	0.0	0.0	0.0	0.0	0.0	0.0	0.0	0.0	0.0	11.6	52.3	34
35	0.0	0.0	0.0	0.0	0.0	0.0	0.0	0.0	0.0	0.0	0.0	46.0	35
36	0.0	0.0	0.0	0.0	0.0	0.0	0.0	0.0	0.0	0.0	0.0	38.9	36
37	0.0	0.0	0.0	0.0	0.0	0.0	0.0	0.0	0.0	0.0	0.0	30.9	37
38	0.0	0.0	0.0	0.0	0.0	0.0	0.0	0.0	0.0	0.0	0.0	21.8	38
39	0.0	0.0	0.0	0.0	0.0	0.0	0.0	0.0	0.0	0.0	0.0	11.6	39

EXAMPLES ON PAGES A-382 TO A-397

AGE OF LOAN	2.0	3.0	5.0	8.0	10.0	12.0	15.0	16.0	17.0	18.0	19.0	20.0	AGE OF LOAN
						ORIGINAL TERM IN YEARS							
1	53.1	70.7	84.6	92.2	94.6	96.2	97.6	97.9	98.2	98.4	98.6	98.8	1
2	0.0	37.5	67.2	83.4	88.6	91.8	94.8	95.5	96.1	96.6	97.1	97.4	2
3	0.0	0.0	47.6	73.5	81.7	86.9	91.7	92.8	93.8	94.6	95.3	95.9	3
4	0.0	0.0	25.2	62.2	73.9	81.3	88.2	89.8	91.1	92.3	93.3	94.2	4
5	0.0	0.0	0.0	49.4	65.1	75.0	84.2	86.3	88.2	89.7	91.0	92.2	5
6	0.0	0.0	0.0	34.9	55.1	67.8	79.7	82.4	84.8	86.8	88.5	89.9	6
7	0.0	0.0	0.0	18.5	43.7	59.7	74.6	78.0	80.9	83.4	85.6	87.4	7
8	0.0	0.0	0.0	0.0	30.9	50.6	68.8	73.0	76.6	79.7	82.3	84.5	8
9	0.0	0.0	0.0	0.0	16.4	40.2	62.2	67.3	71.7	75.4	78.6	81.3	9
10	0.0	0.0	0.0	0.0	0.0	28.4	54.8	60.9	66.1	70.5	74.3	77.6	10
11	0.0	0.0	0.0	0.0	0.0	15.1	46.4	53.6	59.8	65.1	69.6	73.4	11
12	0.0	0.0	0.0	0.0	0.0	0.0	36.8	45.4	52.7	58.8	64.2	68.7	12
13	0.0	0.0	0.0	0.0	0.0	0.0	26.0	36.1	44.6	51.8	58.0	63.4	13
14	0.0	0.0	0.0	0.0	0.0	0.0	13.8	25.5	35.4	43.9	51.1	57.3	14
15	0.0	0.0	0.0	0.0	0.0	0.0	0.0	13.5	25.0	34.8	43.3	50.5	15
16	0.0	0.0	0.0	0.0	0.0	0.0	0.0	0.0	13.3	24.6	34.4	42.7	16
17	0.0	0.0	0.0	0.0	0.0	0.0	0.0	0.0	0.0	13.1	24.3	34.0	17
18	0.0	0.0	0.0	0.0	0.0	0.0	0.0	0.0	0.0	0.0	12.9	24.0	18
19	0.0	0.0	0.0	0.0	0.0	0.0	0.0	0.0	0.0	0.0	0.0	12.7	19

12.50

AGE OF LOAN	21.0	22.0	23.0	24.0	25.0	26.0	27.0	28.0	29.0	30.0	35.0	40.0	AGE OF LOAN
						ORIGINAL TERM IN YEARS							
1	99.0	99.1	99.2	99.3	99.4	99.5	99.5	99.6	99.6	99.7	99.8	99.9	1
2	97.8	98.0	98.3	98.5	98.7	98.8	99.0	99.1	99.2	99.3	99.6	99.8	2
3	96.4	96.9	97.3	97.6	97.9	98.1	98.4	98.6	98.7	98.9	99.4	99.7	3
4	94.9	95.5	96.1	96.6	97.0	97.4	97.7	98.0	98.2	98.4	99.2	99.6	4
5	93.2	94.0	94.8	95.4	96.0	96.5	96.9	97.3	97.6	97.9	98.9	99.4	5
6	91.2	92.3	93.3	94.1	94.8	95.4	96.0	96.5	96.9	97.3	98.6	99.2	6
7	89.0	90.4	91.6	92.6	93.5	94.3	95.0	95.6	96.1	96.6	98.3	98.9	7
8	86.5	88.2	89.6	90.9	92.0	93.0	93.9	94.6	95.2	95.8	97.8	98.8	8
9	83.7	85.7	87.5	89.0	90.4	91.5	92.6	93.5	94.2	94.9	97.3	98.6	9
10	80.4	82.9	85.0	86.9	88.5	89.9	91.1	92.2	93.1	93.9	96.8	98.3	10
11	76.8	79.7	82.2	84.4	86.3	88.0	89.4	90.7	91.8	92.8	96.2	98.0	11
12	72.7	76.1	79.1	81.6	83.9	85.8	87.6	89.1	90.4	91.5	95.5	97.6	12
13	68.0	72.0	75.5	78.5	81.1	83.4	85.4	87.2	88.7	90.1	94.7	97.2	13
14	62.7	67.4	71.4	74.9	78.0	80.7	83.0	85.1	86.9	88.4	93.9	96.7	14
15	56.7	62.1	66.8	70.9	74.5	77.6	80.3	82.7	84.8	86.6	92.9	96.2	15
16	50.0	56.2	61.6	66.4	70.5	74.1	77.2	80.0	82.4	84.5	91.8	95.6	16
17	42.3	49.5	55.8	61.2	66.0	70.1	73.7	76.9	79.7	82.1	90.5	94.9	17
18	33.6	41.9	49.1	55.4	60.8	65.6	69.8	73.4	76.6	79.4	89.1	94.2	18
19	23.8	33.3	41.6	48.8	55.0	60.5	65.3	69.5	73.1	76.4	87.4	93.3	19
20	12.6	23.5	33.0	41.3	48.5	54.7	60.2	65.0	69.2	72.9	85.6	92.3	20
21	0.0	12.5	23.3	32.8	41.0	48.2	54.5	60.0	64.8	69.0	83.5	91.2	21
22	0.0	0.0	12.4	23.2	32.6	40.8	48.0	54.2	59.7	64.6	81.2	90.0	22
23	0.0	0.0	0.0	12.3	23.0	32.4	40.6	47.8	54.0	59.5	78.5	88.5	23
24	0.0	0.0	0.0	0.0	12.2	22.9	32.2	40.4	47.6	53.9	75.5	86.9	24
25	0.0	0.0	0.0	0.0	0.0	12.2	22.8	32.1	40.3	47.4	72.1	85.1	25
26	0.0	0.0	0.0	0.0	0.0	0.0	12.1	22.7	32.0	40.1	68.2	83.0	26
27	0.0	0.0	0.0	0.0	0.0	0.0	0.0	12.0	22.6	31.9	63.8	80.7	27
28	0.0	0.0	0.0	0.0	0.0	0.0	0.0	0.0	12.0	22.5	58.9	78.0	28
29	0.0	0.0	0.0	0.0	0.0	0.0	0.0	0.0	0.0	12.0	53.3	75.0	29
30	0.0	0.0	0.0	0.0	0.0	0.0	0.0	0.0	0.0	0.0	46.9	71.7	30
31	0.0	0.0	0.0	0.0	0.0	0.0	0.0	0.0	0.0	0.0	39.7	67.8	31
32	0.0	0.0	0.0	0.0	0.0	0.0	0.0	0.0	0.0	0.0	31.5	63.5	32
33	0.0	0.0	0.0	0.0	0.0	0.0	0.0	0.0	0.0	0.0	22.3	58.5	33
34	0.0	0.0	0.0	0.0	0.0	0.0	0.0	0.0	0.0	0.0	11.8	52.9	34
35	0.0	0.0	0.0	0.0	0.0	0.0	0.0	0.0	0.0	0.0	0.0	46.6	35
36	0.0	0.0	0.0	0.0	0.0	0.0	0.0	0.0	0.0	0.0	0.0	39.4	36
37	0.0	0.0	0.0	0.0	0.0	0.0	0.0	0.0	0.0	0.0	0.0	31.3	37
38	0.0	0.0	0.0	0.0	0.0	0.0	0.0	0.0	0.0	0.0	0.0	22.2	38
39	0.0	0.0	0.0	0.0	0.0	0.0	0.0	0.0	0.0	0.0	0.0	11.8	39

EXAMPLES *ON PAGES A-382 TO A-397*

AGE OF LOAN	ORIGINAL TERM IN YEARS												AGE OF LOAN
	2.0	3.0	5.0	8.0	10.0	12.0	15.0	16.0	17.0	18.0	19.0	20.0	
1	53.2	70.8	84.7	92.3	94.7	96.2	97.6	98.0	98.2	98.5	98.7	98.8	1
2	0.0	37.6	67.4	83.6	88.7	91.9	94.9	95.6	96.2	96.7	97.1	97.5	2
3	0.0	0.0	47.7	73.7	81.9	87.1	91.9	93.0	93.9	94.7	95.4	96.0	3
4	0.0	0.0	25.4	62.4	74.1	81.5	88.4	90.0	91.3	92.5	93.5	94.3	4
5	0.0	0.0	0.0	49.6	65.3	75.3	84.5	86.6	88.1	89.9	91.3	92.4	5
6	0.0	0.0	0.0	35.1	55.4	68.2	80.0	82.7	85.1	87.0	88.7	90.2	6
7	0.0	0.0	0.0	18.7	44.0	60.1	74.9	78.4	81.3	83.8	85.9	87.7	7
8	0.0	0.0	0.0	C.0	31.2	50.5	69.2	73.4	77.0	80.0	82.6	84.9	8
9	0.0	0.0	0.0	0.0	16.6	40.5	62.6	67.7	72.1	75.8	79.0	81.7	9
10	0.0	0.0	0.0	0.0	0.0	28.7	55.2	61.3	66.5	71.0	74.8	78.0	10
11	0.0	0.0	0.0	0.0	0.0	15.2	46.8	54.1	60.3	65.5	70.0	73.9	11
12	0.0	0.0	0.0	0.0	0.0	0.0	37.2	45.8	53.1	59.3	64.7	69.2	12
13	0.0	0.0	0.0	0.0	0.0	0.0	26.3	36.4	45.0	52.3	58.5	63.9	13
14	0.0	0.0	0.0	0.0	0.0	0.0	14.0	25.8	35.8	44.3	51.6	57.9	14
15	0.0	0.0	0.0	C.0	0.0	0.0	0.0	13.7	25.3	35.2	43.7	51.0	15
16	0.0	0.0	0.0	0.0	0.0	0.0	0.0	0.0	13.5	24.9	34.8	43.2	16
17	0.0	0.0	0.0	0.0	0.0	0.0	0.0	0.0	0.0	13.3	24.6	34.4	17
18	0.0	0.0	0.0	0.0	0.0	0.C	0.0	0.0	0.0	0.0	13.1	24.3	18
19	0.0	0.0	0.0	0.0	0.0	0.0	0.0	0.0	0.0	0.0	0.0	12.9	19

12.75

AGE OF LOAN	ORIGINAL TERM IN YEARS												AGE OF LOAN
	21.0	22.0	23.0	24.0	25.0	26.0	27.0	28.0	29.0	30.0	35.0	40.0	
1	99.0	99.1	99.2	99.3	99.4	99.5	99.5	99.6	99.6	99.7	99.8	99.9	1
2	97.8	98.1	98.3	98.6	98.7	98.9	99.0	99.1	99.3	99.3	99.7	99.8	2
3	96.5	97.0	97.4	97.7	98.0	98.2	98.4	98.6	98.8	98.9	99.4	99.7	3
4	95.0	95.7	96.2	96.7	97.1	97.5	97.8	98.0	98.3	98.5	99.2	99.6	4
5	93.4	94.2	94.9	95.6	96.1	96.6	97.0	97.4	97.7	98.0	98.9	99.4	5
6	91.5	92.5	93.5	94.3	95.0	95.6	96.2	96.6	97.0	97.4	98.6	99.3	6
7	89.3	90.6	91.8	92.8	93.7	94.5	95.2	95.8	96.3	96.7	98.3	99.1	7
8	86.8	88.5	89.9	91.2	92.3	93.2	94.1	94.8	95.4	96.0	97.9	98.9	8
9	84.0	86.1	87.8	89.3	90.7	91.8	92.8	93.7	94.5	95.1	97.5	98.7	9
10	80.9	83.3	85.4	87.2	88.8	90.2	91.4	92.5	93.4	94.2	96.9	98.4	10
11	77.3	80.1	82.6	84.8	86.7	88.3	89.8	91.0	92.1	93.1	96.4	98.1	11
12	73.2	76.6	79.5	82.1	84.3	86.3	87.9	89.4	90.7	91.8	95.7	97.7	12
13	68.5	72.5	76.0	79.0	81.6	83.9	85.9	87.6	89.1	90.4	95.0	97.4	13
14	63.3	67.9	72.0	75.5	78.5	81.2	83.5	85.5	87.3	88.8	94.1	96.9	14
15	57.3	62.7	67.4	71.5	75.0	78.1	80.8	83.2	85.2	87.0	93.2	96.4	15
16	50.5	56.8	62.2	66.9	71.0	74.6	77.8	80.5	82.9	85.0	92.1	95.8	16
17	42.8	50.0	56.3	61.8	66.5	70.7	74.3	77.4	80.2	82.6	90.9	95.2	17
18	34.0	42.4	49.6	55.9	61.4	66.2	70.4	74.0	77.2	80.0	89.5	94.5	18
19	24.1	33.7	42.1	49.3	55.6	61.1	65.9	70.1	73.7	76.9	87.9	93.6	19
20	12.8	23.9	33.5	41.8	49.0	55.3	60.8	65.6	69.8	73.5	86.1	92.7	20
21	0.0	12.7	23.7	33.2	41.5	48.8	55.1	60.6	65.4	69.6	84.1	91.6	21
22	0.0	0.0	12.6	23.5	33.0	41.3	48.5	54.9	60.4	65.2	81.7	90.4	22
23	0.0	0.0	0.0	12.5	23.4	32.9	41.1	48.3	54.7	60.2	79.1	89.2	23
24	0.0	0.0	0.0	0.0	12.4	23.3	32.7	41.0	48.2	54.5	76.1	87.4	24
25	0.0	0.0	0.0	0.0	0.0	12.4	23.2	32.6	40.8	48.0	72.7	85.6	25
26	0.0	0.0	0.0	0.0	0.0	0.0	12.3	23.1	32.5	40.7	68.9	83.6	26
27	0.0	0.0	0.0	0.0	0.0	0.0	0.0	12.3	23.0	32.4	64.5	81.3	27
28	0.0	0.0	0.0	0.0	0.0	0.0	0.0	0.0	12.2	22.9	59.5	78.7	28
29	0.0	0.0	0.0	0.0	0.0	0.0	0.0	0.0	0.0	12.2	53.9	75.7	29
30	0.0	0.0	0.0	0.0	0.0	0.0	0.0	0.0	0.0	0.0	47.5	72.3	30
31	0.0	0.0	0.0	0.0	0.0	0.0	0.0	0.0	0.0	0.0	40.3	68.5	31
32	0.0	0.0	0.0	0.0	0.0	0.0	0.0	0.0	0.0	0.0	32.0	64.1	32
33	0.0	0.0	0.0	0.0	0.0	0.0	0.0	0.0	0.0	0.0	22.7	59.2	33
34	0.0	0.0	0.0	0.0	0.0	0.0	0.0	0.0	0.0	0.0	12.1	53.6	34
35	0.0	0.0	0.0	0.0	0.0	0.0	0.0	0.0	0.0	0.0	0.0	47.3	35
36	0.0	0.0	0.0	0.0	0.0	0.0	0.0	0.0	0.0	0.0	0.0	40.0	36
37	0.0	0.0	0.0	0.0	0.0	0.0	0.0	0.0	0.0	0.0	0.0	31.8	37
38	0.0	0.0	0.0	0.C	0.0	0.0	0.0	0.0	0.0	0.0	0.0	22.5	38
39	0.0	0.0	0.0	C.0	0.0	0.0	0.0	0.0	0.0	0.0	0.0	12.0	39

EXAMPLES *ON PAGES A-382 TO A-397*

AGE OF LOAN	ORIGINAL TERM IN YEARS												AGE OF LOAN
	2.0	3.0	5.0	8.0	10.0	12.0	15.0	16.0	17.0	18.0	19.0	20.0	
1	53.2	70.9	84.8	92.4	94.8	96.3	97.7	98.0	98.3	98.5	98.7	98.9	1
2	0.0	37.7	67.5	83.7	88.8	92.1	95.0	95.7	96.3	96.8	97.2	97.6	2
3	0.0	0.0	47.9	73.9	82.2	87.3	92.0	93.1	94.1	94.9	95.6	96.1	3
4	0.0	0.0	25.5	62.6	74.4	81.8	88.6	90.2	91.5	92.7	93.6	94.5	4
5	0.0	0.0	0.0	49.9	65.6	75.6	84.7	86.9	88.6	90.2	91.5	92.6	5
6	0.0	0.0	0.0	35.3	55.7	68.5	80.3	83.0	85.4	87.3	89.0	90.4	6
7	0.0	0.0	0.0	18.8	44.3	60.4	75.3	78.7	81.6	84.1	86.2	88.0	7
8	0.0	0.0	0.0	0.0	31.4	51.2	69.5	73.8	77.4	80.4	83.0	85.2	8
9	0.0	0.0	0.0	0.0	16.7	40.8	63.0	68.2	72.5	76.2	79.4	82.1	9
10	0.0	0.0	0.0	0.0	0.0	28.9	55.6	61.8	67.0	71.4	75.2	78.5	10
11	0.0	0.0	0.0	0.0	0.0	15.4	47.2	54.5	60.7	66.0	70.5	74.4	11
12	0.0	0.0	0.0	0.0	0.0	0.0	37.5	46.2	53.6	59.8	65.1	69.7	12
13	0.0	0.0	0.0	0.0	0.0	0.0	26.6	36.8	45.4	52.8	59.0	64.4	13
14	0.0	0.0	0.0	0.0	0.0	0.0	14.2	26.1	36.2	44.7	52.1	58.4	14
15	0.0	0.0	0.0	0.0	0.0	0.0	0.0	13.9	25.6	35.6	44.2	51.5	15
16	0.0	0.0	0.0	0.0	0.0	0.0	0.0	0.0	13.6	25.2	35.2	43.7	16
17	0.0	0.0	0.0	0.0	0.0	0.0	0.0	0.0	0.0	13.4	24.9	34.8	17
18	0.0	0.0	0.0	0.0	0.0	0.0	0.0	0.0	0.0	0.0	13.3	24.6	18
19	0.0	0.0	0.0	0.0	0.0	0.0	0.0	0.0	0.0	0.0	0.0	13.1	19

13.00

AGE OF LOAN	ORIGINAL TERM IN YEARS												AGE OF LOAN
	21.0	22.0	23.0	24.0	25.0	26.0	27.0	28.0	29.0	30.0	35.0	40.0	
1	99.0	99.1	99.3	99.4	99.4	99.5	99.6	99.6	99.7	99.7	99.8	99.9	1
2	97.9	98.2	98.4	98.6	98.8	98.9	99.1	99.2	99.3	99.4	99.7	99.8	2
3	96.6	97.1	97.4	97.8	98.1	98.3	98.5	98.7	98.9	99.0	99.5	99.7	3
4	95.2	95.8	96.4	96.8	97.2	97.6	97.9	98.1	98.4	98.6	99.3	99.6	4
5	93.6	94.4	95.1	95.7	96.3	96.7	97.1	97.5	97.8	98.1	99.0	99.5	5
6	91.7	92.8	93.7	94.5	95.2	95.8	96.3	96.8	97.2	97.5	98.7	99.3	6
7	89.6	90.9	92.1	93.1	94.0	94.7	95.4	95.9	96.5	96.9	98.4	99.2	7
8	87.1	88.8	90.2	91.5	92.5	93.5	94.3	95.0	95.6	96.2	98.0	99.0	8
9	84.4	86.4	88.1	89.6	91.0	92.1	93.1	93.9	94.7	95.4	97.6	98.7	9
10	81.3	83.7	85.8	87.6	89.1	90.5	91.7	92.7	93.6	94.4	97.1	98.5	10
11	77.7	80.6	83.1	85.2	87.1	88.7	90.1	91.3	92.4	93.4	96.6	98.2	11
12	73.6	77.0	80.0	82.5	84.7	86.6	88.3	89.8	91.0	92.1	95.9	97.9	12
13	69.0	73.0	76.5	79.4	82.0	84.3	86.3	88.0	89.5	90.8	95.2	97.5	13
14	63.8	68.4	72.5	76.0	79.0	81.6	83.9	85.9	87.7	89.2	94.4	97.1	14
15	57.8	63.2	67.9	72.0	75.5	78.6	81.3	83.6	85.7	87.4	93.5	96.6	15
16	51.0	57.3	62.8	67.5	71.6	75.2	78.3	81.0	83.3	85.4	92.4	96.1	16
17	43.2	50.5	56.9	62.3	67.1	71.2	74.8	78.0	80.7	83.1	91.2	95.4	17
18	34.4	42.9	50.2	56.5	62.0	66.8	70.9	74.5	77.7	80.5	89.9	94.7	18
19	24.4	34.1	42.5	49.8	56.2	61.7	66.5	70.7	74.3	77.5	88.3	93.9	19
20	13.0	24.2	33.9	42.3	49.6	55.9	61.4	66.2	70.4	74.1	86.6	93.0	20
21	0.0	12.9	24.0	33.7	42.0	49.3	55.7	61.2	66.0	70.2	84.6	91.9	21
22	0.0	0.0	12.8	23.8	33.5	41.8	49.1	55.4	61.0	65.8	82.3	90.8	22
23	0.0	0.0	0.0	12.7	23.7	33.3	41.6	48.9	55.3	60.8	79.7	89.4	23
24	0.0	0.0	0.0	0.0	12.6	23.6	33.2	41.5	48.8	55.1	76.7	87.9	24
25	0.0	0.0	0.0	0.0	0.0	12.6	23.5	33.0	41.3	48.6	73.3	86.1	25
26	0.0	0.0	0.0	0.0	0.0	0.0	12.5	23.4	32.9	41.2	69.5	84.1	26
27	0.0	0.0	0.0	0.0	0.0	0.0	0.0	12.4	23.3	32.8	65.2	81.8	27
28	0.0	0.0	0.0	0.0	0.0	0.0	0.0	0.0	12.4	23.3	60.2	79.3	28
29	0.0	0.0	0.0	0.0	0.0	0.0	0.0	0.0	0.0	12.4	54.5	76.3	29
30	0.0	0.0	0.0	0.0	0.0	0.0	0.0	0.0	0.0	0.0	48.1	73.0	30
31	0.0	0.0	0.0	0.0	0.0	0.0	0.0	0.0	0.0	0.0	40.8	69.2	31
32	0.0	0.0	0.0	0.0	0.0	0.0	0.0	0.0	0.0	0.0	32.5	64.8	32
33	0.0	0.0	0.0	0.0	0.0	0.0	0.0	0.0	0.0	0.0	23.0	59.9	33
34	0.0	0.0	0.0	0.0	0.0	0.0	0.0	0.0	0.0	0.0	12.2	54.3	34
35	0.0	0.0	0.0	0.0	0.0	0.0	0.0	0.0	0.0	0.0	0.0	47.9	35
36	0.0	0.0	0.0	0.0	0.0	0.0	0.0	0.0	0.0	0.0	0.0	40.6	36
37	0.0	0.0	0.0	0.0	0.0	0.0	0.0	0.0	0.0	0.0	0.0	32.3	37
38	0.0	0.0	0.0	0.0	0.0	0.0	0.0	0.0	0.0	0.0	0.0	22.9	38
39	0.0	0.0	0.0	0.0	0.0	0.0	0.0	0.0	0.0	0.0	0.0	12.2	39

EXAMPLES *ON PAGES A-382 TO A-397*

AGE OF LOAN	2.0	3.0	5.0	8.0	10.0	12.0	15.0	16.0	17.0	18.0	19.0	20.0	AGE OF LOAN
					ORIGINAL TERM IN YEARS								
1	53.3	71.0	84.9	92.5	94.8	96.4	97.7	98.1	98.3	98.6	98.7	98.9	1
2	0.0	37.8	67.7	83.9	89.0	92.2	95.2	95.8	96.4	96.9	97.3	97.7	2
3	0.0	0.0	48.0	74.1	82.3	87.4	92.2	93.3	94.2	95.0	95.7	96.3	3
4	0.0	0.0	25.6	62.9	74.6	82.0	88.8	90.4	91.7	92.9	93.8	94.6	4
5	0.0	0.0	0.0	50.1	65.9	75.8	85.0	87.1	88.9	90.4	91.7	92.8	5
6	0.0	0.0	0.0	35.6	55.9	68.8	80.6	83.3	85.6	87.6	89.3	90.7	6
7	0.0	0.0	0.0	18.9	44.6	60.8	75.6	79.1	81.9	84.4	86.5	88.3	7
8	0.0	0.0	0.0	0.0	31.6	51.6	69.9	74.2	77.7	80.8	83.3	85.6	8
9	0.0	0.0	0.0	0.0	16.9	41.1	63.4	68.6	72.9	76.6	79.7	82.4	9
10	0.0	0.0	0.0	0.0	0.0	29.2	56.0	62.2	67.4	71.9	75.6	78.9	10
11	0.0	0.0	0.0	0.0	0.0	15.5	47.6	54.9	61.2	66.4	71.0	74.8	11
12	0.0	0.0	0.0	0.0	0.0	0.0	37.9	46.6	54.0	60.3	65.6	70.2	12
13	0.0	0.0	0.0	0.0	0.0	0.0	26.9	37.2	45.8	53.2	59.5	64.9	13
14	0.0	0.0	0.0	0.0	0.0	0.0	14.3	26.4	36.5	45.2	52.6	58.9	14
15	0.0	0.0	0.0	0.0	0.0	0.0	0.0	14.1	25.9	36.0	44.6	52.0	15
16	0.0	0.0	0.0	0.0	0.0	0.0	0.0	0.0	13.8	25.6	35.6	44.1	16
17	0.0	0.0	0.0	0.0	0.0	0.0	0.0	0.0	0.0	13.6	25.2	35.2	17
18	0.0	0.0	0.0	0.0	0.0	0.0	0.0	0.0	0.0	0.0	13.4	25.0	18
19	0.0	0.0	0.0	0.0	0.0	0.0	0.0	0.0	0.0	0.0	0.0	13.3	19

13.25

AGE OF LOAN	21.0	22.0	23.0	24.0	25.0	26.0	27.0	28.0	29.0	30.0	35.0	40.0	AGE OF LOAN
					ORIGINAL TERM IN YEARS								
1	99.1	99.2	99.3	99.4	99.5	99.5	99.6	99.6	99.7	99.7	99.9	99.9	1
2	98.0	98.2	98.5	98.7	98.8	99.0	99.1	99.2	99.3	99.4	99.7	99.8	2
3	96.7	97.2	97.5	97.9	98.1	98.4	98.6	98.8	98.9	99.1	99.5	99.7	3
4	95.3	96.0	96.5	96.9	97.3	97.7	98.0	98.2	98.4	98.6	99.3	99.6	4
5	93.7	94.6	95.3	95.9	96.4	96.9	97.3	97.6	97.9	98.2	99.1	99.5	5
6	91.9	93.0	93.9	94.7	95.4	96.0	96.5	96.9	97.3	97.6	98.8	99.4	6
7	89.8	91.2	92.3	93.3	94.2	94.9	95.6	96.1	96.6	97.0	98.5	99.2	7
8	87.5	89.1	90.5	91.7	92.8	93.7	94.5	95.2	95.8	96.3	98.1	99.0	8
9	84.8	86.7	88.5	90.0	91.2	92.4	93.3	94.2	94.9	95.6	97.7	98.8	9
10	81.7	84.1	86.1	87.9	89.5	90.8	92.0	93.0	93.9	94.6	97.3	98.6	10
11	78.1	81.0	83.5	85.6	87.4	89.0	90.4	91.6	92.7	93.6	96.7	98.3	11
12	74.1	77.5	80.4	82.9	85.1	87.0	88.7	90.1	91.4	92.4	96.1	98.0	12
13	69.5	73.5	76.9	79.9	82.5	84.7	86.7	88.4	89.8	91.1	95.4	97.7	13
14	64.3	69.0	73.0	76.5	79.5	82.1	84.4	86.4	88.1	89.6	94.7	97.2	14
15	58.3	63.8	68.5	72.5	76.0	79.1	81.8	84.1	86.1	87.8	93.8	96.8	15
16	51.5	57.8	63.3	68.0	72.1	75.7	78.8	81.5	83.8	85.8	92.7	96.3	16
17	43.7	51.1	57.4	62.9	67.7	71.8	75.4	78.5	81.2	83.6	91.6	95.7	17
18	34.8	43.4	50.7	57.1	62.6	67.3	71.5	75.1	78.2	81.0	90.3	95.0	18
19	24.7	34.6	43.0	50.4	56.7	62.3	67.1	71.2	74.9	78.0	89.6	94.2	19
20	13.2	24.5	34.3	42.8	50.1	56.5	62.0	66.8	71.0	74.7	87.0	93.3	20
21	0.0	13.1	24.3	34.1	42.5	49.9	56.2	61.8	66.6	70.8	85.0	92.3	21
22	0.0	0.0	13.0	24.2	33.9	42.3	49.7	56.0	61.6	66.4	82.8	91.1	22
23	0.0	0.0	0.0	12.9	24.1	33.8	42.2	49.5	55.9	61.4	80.2	89.8	23
24	0.0	0.0	0.0	0.0	12.8	23.9	33.6	42.0	49.3	55.7	77.3	88.3	24
25	0.0	0.0	0.0	0.0	0.0	12.8	23.8	33.5	41.9	49.2	74.0	86.6	25
26	0.0	0.0	0.0	0.0	0.0	0.0	12.7	23.8	33.4	41.8	70.2	84.6	26
27	0.0	0.0	0.0	0.0	0.0	0.0	0.0	12.7	23.7	33.3	65.8	82.4	27
28	0.0	0.0	0.0	0.0	0.0	0.0	0.0	0.0	12.6	23.6	60.8	79.8	28
29	0.0	0.0	0.0	0.0	0.0	0.0	0.0	0.0	0.0	12.6	55.2	76.9	29
30	0.0	0.0	0.0	0.0	0.0	0.0	0.0	0.0	0.0	0.0	48.7	73.6	30
31	0.0	0.0	0.0	0.0	0.0	0.0	0.0	0.0	0.0	0.0	41.4	69.8	31
32	0.0	0.0	0.0	0.0	0.0	0.0	0.0	0.0	0.0	0.0	33.0	65.5	32
33	0.0	0.0	0.0	0.0	0.0	0.0	0.0	0.0	0.0	0.0	23.4	60.6	33
34	0.0	0.0	0.0	0.0	0.0	0.0	0.0	0.0	0.0	0.0	12.5	54.9	34
35	0.0	0.0	0.0	0.0	0.0	0.0	0.0	0.0	0.0	0.0	0.0	48.5	35
36	0.0	0.0	0.0	0.0	0.0	0.0	0.0	0.0	0.0	0.0	0.0	41.2	36
37	0.0	0.0	0.0	0.0	0.0	0.0	0.0	0.0	0.0	0.0	0.0	32.8	37
38	0.0	0.0	0.0	0.0	0.0	0.0	0.0	0.0	0.0	0.0	0.0	23.3	38
39	0.0	0.0	0.0	0.0	0.0	0.0	0.0	0.0	0.0	0.0	0.0	12.4	39

EXAMPLES ON PAGES A-382 TO A-397

AGE OF LOAN	ORIGINAL TERM IN YEARS												AGE OF LOAN
	2.0	3.0	5.0	8.0	10.0	12.0	15.0	16.0	17.0	18.0	19.0	20.0	
1	53.3	71.0	85.0	92.5	94.9	96.4	97.8	98.1	98.4	98.6	98.8	98.9	1
2	0.0	37.9	67.8	84.0	89.1	92.3	95.3	95.9	96.5	97.0	97.4	97.7	2
3	0.0	0.0	48.2	74.3	82.5	87.6	92.4	93.4	94.4	95.1	95.8	96.4	3
4	0.0	0.0	25.7	63.1	74.9	82.3	89.0	90.6	91.9	93.0	94.0	94.8	4
5	0.0	0.0	0.0	50.4	66.2	76.1	85.3	87.4	89.1	90.6	91.9	93.0	5
6	0.0	0.0	0.0	35.8	56.2	69.1	80.9	83.6	85.9	87.9	89.5	90.9	6
7	0.0	0.0	0.0	19.1	44.9	61.1	76.0	79.4	82.3	84.7	86.8	88.6	7
8	0.0	0.0	0.0	0.0	31.9	51.9	70.3	74.5	78.1	81.1	83.7	85.9	8
9	0.0	0.0	0.0	0.0	17.0	41.4	63.8	69.0	73.3	77.0	80.1	82.8	9
10	0.0	0.0	0.0	0.0	0.0	29.4	56.4	62.6	67.8	72.3	76.1	79.3	10
11	0.0	0.0	0.0	0.0	0.0	15.7	47.9	55.3	61.6	66.9	71.4	75.3	11
12	0.0	0.0	0.0	0.0	0.0	0.0	38.3	47.0	54.4	60.7	66.1	70.7	12
13	0.0	0.0	0.0	0.0	0.0	0.0	27.2	37.5	46.3	53.7	60.0	65.4	13
14	0.0	0.0	0.0	0.0	0.0	0.0	14.5	26.7	36.9	45.6	53.0	59.4	14
15	0.0	0.0	0.0	0.0	0.0	0.0	0.0	14.2	26.2	36.4	45.1	52.5	15
16	0.0	0.0	0.0	0.0	0.0	0.0	0.0	0.0	14.0	25.8	36.0	44.6	16
17	0.0	0.0	0.0	0.0	0.0	0.0	0.0	0.0	0.0	13.8	25.5	35.6	17
18	0.0	0.0	0.0	0.0	0.0	0.0	0.0	0.0	0.0	0.0	13.6	25.3	18
19	0.0	0.0	0.0	0.0	0.0	0.0	0.0	0.0	0.0	0.0	0.0	13.5	19

13.50

AGE OF LOAN	ORIGINAL TERM IN YEARS												AGE OF LOAN
	21.0	22.0	23.0	24.0	25.0	26.0	27.0	28.0	29.0	30.0	35.0	40.0	
1	99.1	99.2	99.3	99.4	99.5	99.5	99.6	99.7	99.7	99.7	99.9	99.9	1
2	98.0	98.3	98.5	98.7	98.9	99.0	99.2	99.3	99.4	99.4	99.7	99.9	2
3	96.9	97.3	97.6	97.9	98.2	98.4	98.6	98.8	99.0	99.1	99.5	99.8	3
4	95.5	96.1	96.6	97.0	97.4	97.8	98.1	98.3	98.5	98.7	99.3	99.7	4
5	93.9	94.7	95.4	96.0	96.5	97.0	97.4	97.7	98.0	98.3	99.1	99.6	5
6	92.1	93.2	94.1	94.9	95.5	96.1	96.6	97.0	97.4	97.8	98.9	99.4	6
7	90.1	91.4	92.5	93.5	94.4	95.1	95.7	96.3	96.8	97.2	98.6	99.2	7
8	87.8	89.4	90.8	92.0	93.0	93.9	94.7	95.4	96.0	96.5	98.2	99.1	8
9	85.1	87.1	88.8	90.2	91.5	92.6	93.6	94.4	95.1	95.7	97.8	98.9	9
10	82.1	84.4	86.5	88.3	89.8	91.1	92.3	93.2	94.1	94.9	97.4	98.7	10
11	78.6	81.4	83.9	86.0	87.8	89.4	90.7	91.9	93.0	93.9	96.9	98.4	11
12	74.7	77.9	80.8	83.4	85.5	87.4	89.0	90.4	91.7	92.7	96.3	98.1	12
13	70.0	74.0	77.4	80.4	82.9	85.1	87.1	88.7	90.2	91.4	95.7	97.8	13
14	64.8	69.5	73.5	76.9	79.9	82.5	84.8	86.8	88.5	89.9	94.9	97.4	14
15	58.8	64.3	69.0	73.0	76.5	79.6	82.2	84.5	86.5	88.2	94.0	97.0	15
16	52.0	58.4	63.8	68.6	72.7	76.2	79.3	81.9	84.3	86.3	93.0	96.5	16
17	44.2	51.6	58.0	63.5	68.2	72.3	75.9	79.0	81.7	84.0	91.9	95.9	17
18	35.2	43.8	51.2	57.6	63.1	67.5	72.0	75.6	78.8	81.5	90.6	95.2	18
19	25.3	35.0	43.5	50.9	57.3	62.8	67.6	71.8	75.4	78.6	89.1	94.5	19
20	13.3	24.8	34.7	43.3	50.7	57.0	62.6	67.4	71.6	75.2	87.4	93.6	20
21	0.0	13.2	24.7	34.5	43.0	50.4	56.8	62.4	67.2	71.4	85.5	92.6	21
22	0.0	0.0	13.2	24.5	34.3	42.8	50.2	56.6	62.2	67.0	83.3	91.5	22
23	0.0	0.0	0.0	13.1	24.4	34.2	42.7	50.1	56.5	62.0	80.8	90.2	23
24	0.0	0.0	0.0	0.0	13.0	24.3	34.1	42.5	49.9	56.3	77.9	88.7	24
25	0.0	0.0	0.0	0.0	0.0	12.9	24.2	33.9	42.4	49.8	74.6	87.1	25
26	0.0	0.0	0.0	0.0	0.0	0.0	12.9	24.1	33.8	42.3	70.8	85.1	26
27	0.0	0.0	0.0	0.0	0.0	0.0	0.0	12.8	24.0	33.7	66.4	82.9	27
28	0.0	0.0	0.0	0.0	0.0	0.0	0.0	0.0	12.8	24.0	61.5	80.4	28
29	0.0	0.0	0.0	0.0	0.0	0.0	0.0	0.0	0.0	12.8	55.8	77.5	29
30	0.0	0.0	0.0	0.0	0.0	0.0	0.0	0.0	0.0	0.0	49.8	74.2	30
31	0.0	0.0	0.0	0.0	0.0	0.0	0.0	0.0	0.0	0.0	41.9	70.5	31
32	0.0	0.0	0.0	0.0	0.0	0.0	0.0	0.0	0.0	0.0	33.4	66.1	32
33	0.0	0.0	0.0	0.0	0.0	0.0	0.0	0.0	0.0	0.0	23.8	61.2	33
34	0.0	0.0	0.0	0.0	0.0	0.0	0.0	0.0	0.0	0.0	12.7	55.6	34
35	0.0	0.0	0.0	0.0	0.0	0.0	0.0	0.0	0.0	0.0	0.0	49.1	35
36	0.0	0.0	0.0	0.0	0.0	0.0	0.0	0.0	0.0	0.0	0.0	41.7	36
37	0.0	0.0	0.0	0.0	0.0	0.0	0.0	0.0	0.0	0.0	0.0	33.3	37
38	0.0	0.0	0.0	0.0	0.0	0.0	0.0	0.0	0.0	0.0	0.0	23.6	38
39	0.0	0.0	0.0	0.0	0.0	0.0	0.0	0.0	0.0	0.0	0.0	12.6	39

EXAMPLES *ON PAGES A-382 TO A-397*

AGE OF LOAN	2.0	3.0	5.0	8.0	10.0	12.0	15.0	16.0	17.0	18.0	19.0	20.0	AGE OF LOAN
						ORIGINAL TERM IN YEARS							
1	53.4	71.1	85.1	92.6	95.0	96.5	97.8	98.1	98.4	98.6	98.8	99.0	1
2	0.0	38.0	67.9	84.2	89.2	92.4	95.4	96.0	96.6	97.1	97.5	97.8	2
3	0.0	0.0	48.3	74.5	82.7	87.8	92.5	93.6	94.5	95.3	95.9	96.5	3
4	0.0	0.0	25.8	63.3	75.1	82.5	89.3	90.8	92.1	93.2	94.1	94.9	4
5	0.0	0.0	0.0	50.6	66.4	76.4	85.5	87.6	89.4	90.8	92.1	93.2	5
6	0.0	0.0	0.0	36.0	56.5	69.4	81.2	83.9	86.2	88.1	89.8	91.2	6
7	0.0	0.0	0.0	19.2	45.1	61.4	76.3	79.7	82.6	85.0	87.1	88.9	7
8	0.0	0.0	0.0	0.0	32.1	52.2	70.7	74.9	78.5	81.5	84.0	86.2	8
9	0.0	0.0	0.0	0.0	17.1	41.7	64.2	69.4	73.7	77.4	80.5	83.2	9
10	0.0	0.0	0.0	0.0	0.0	29.7	56.8	63.0	68.3	72.7	76.5	79.7	10
11	0.0	0.0	0.0	0.0	0.0	15.8	48.3	55.8	62.0	67.3	71.8	75.7	11
12	0.0	0.0	0.0	0.0	0.0	0.0	38.6	47.4	54.9	61.2	66.5	71.1	12
13	0.0	0.0	0.0	0.0	0.0	0.0	27.4	37.9	46.7	54.1	60.5	65.9	13
14	0.0	0.0	0.0	0.0	0.0	0.0	14.6	26.9	37.3	46.0	53.5	59.8	14
15	0.0	0.0	0.0	0.0	0.0	0.0	0.0	14.4	26.5	36.8	45.5	52.9	15
16	0.0	0.0	0.0	0.0	0.0	0.0	0.0	0.0	14.1	26.1	36.3	45.0	16
17	0.0	0.0	0.0	0.0	0.0	0.0	0.0	0.0	0.0	14.0	25.8	36.0	17
18	0.0	0.0	0.0	0.0	0.0	0.0	0.0	0.0	0.0	0.0	13.8	25.6	18
19	0.0	0.0	0.0	0.0	0.0	0.0	0.0	0.0	0.0	0.0	0.0	13.6	19

13.75

AGE OF LOAN	21.0	22.0	23.0	24.0	25.0	26.0	27.0	28.0	29.0	30.0	35.0	40.0	AGE OF LOAN
						ORIGINAL TERM IN YEARS							
1	99.1	99.2	99.3	99.4	99.5	99.6	99.6	99.7	99.7	99.8	99.9	99.9	1
2	98.1	98.4	98.6	98.8	98.9	99.1	99.2	99.3	99.4	99.5	99.7	99.9	2
3	97.0	97.4	97.7	98.0	98.3	98.5	98.7	98.9	99.0	99.1	99.6	99.8	3
4	95.6	96.2	96.7	97.2	97.5	97.9	98.1	98.4	98.6	98.8	99.4	99.7	4
5	94.1	94.9	95.6	96.2	96.7	97.1	97.5	97.8	98.1	98.3	99.2	99.6	5
6	92.4	93.4	94.3	95.0	95.7	96.3	96.7	97.2	97.5	97.9	98.9	99.5	6
7	90.4	91.7	92.8	93.7	94.6	95.3	95.9	96.4	96.9	97.3	98.6	99.3	7
8	88.1	89.7	91.1	92.2	93.3	94.2	94.9	95.6	96.2	96.7	98.3	99.2	8
9	85.5	87.4	89.1	90.5	91.8	92.9	93.8	94.6	95.3	95.9	98.0	99.0	9
10	82.4	84.8	86.8	88.6	90.1	91.4	92.5	93.5	94.3	95.1	97.5	98.8	10
11	79.0	81.8	84.2	86.3	88.1	89.7	91.0	92.2	93.2	94.1	97.1	98.5	11
12	75.0	78.4	81.3	83.8	85.9	87.8	89.4	90.8	92.0	93.0	96.5	98.2	12
13	70.5	74.5	77.9	80.8	83.3	85.5	87.4	89.1	90.5	91.7	95.9	97.9	13
14	65.3	70.0	74.0	77.4	80.4	83.0	85.2	87.1	88.8	90.3	95.1	97.6	14
15	59.3	64.8	69.5	73.5	77.0	80.1	82.7	84.9	86.9	88.6	94.3	97.1	15
16	52.5	58.9	64.4	69.1	73.2	76.7	79.8	82.4	84.7	86.7	93.3	96.6	16
17	44.6	52.1	58.5	64.0	68.7	72.9	76.4	79.5	82.2	84.5	92.2	96.1	17
18	35.7	44.3	51.7	58.1	63.7	68.5	72.6	76.2	79.3	82.0	91.0	95.5	18
19	25.3	35.4	44.0	51.4	57.9	63.4	68.2	72.4	76.0	79.1	89.5	94.7	19
20	13.5	25.1	35.1	43.8	51.2	57.6	63.2	68.0	72.1	75.8	87.9	93.9	20
21	0.0	13.4	25.0	34.9	43.5	51.0	57.4	63.0	67.8	72.0	86.0	92.9	21
22	0.0	0.0	13.3	24.8	34.8	43.3	50.8	57.2	62.8	67.6	83.8	91.8	22
23	0.0	0.0	0.0	13.3	24.7	34.6	43.2	50.6	57.0	62.6	81.3	90.6	23
24	0.0	0.0	0.0	0.0	13.2	24.6	34.5	43.0	50.5	56.9	78.4	89.2	24
25	0.0	0.0	0.0	0.0	0.0	13.1	24.5	34.4	42.9	50.3	75.1	87.5	25
26	0.0	0.0	0.0	0.0	0.0	0.0	13.1	24.4	34.3	42.8	71.4	85.6	26
27	0.0	0.0	0.0	0.0	0.0	0.0	0.0	13.0	24.4	34.2	67.1	83.4	27
28	0.0	0.0	0.0	0.0	0.0	0.0	0.0	0.0	13.0	24.3	62.1	80.9	28
29	0.0	0.0	0.0	0.0	0.0	0.0	0.0	0.0	0.0	13.0	56.4	78.1	29
30	0.0	0.0	0.0	0.0	0.0	0.0	0.0	0.0	0.0	0.0	49.9	74.8	30
31	0.0	0.0	0.0	0.0	0.0	0.0	0.0	0.0	0.0	0.0	42.5	71.1	31
32	0.0	0.0	0.0	0.0	0.0	0.0	0.0	0.0	0.0	0.0	33.9	66.8	32
33	0.0	0.0	0.0	0.0	0.0	0.0	0.0	0.0	0.0	0.0	24.1	61.8	33
34	0.0	0.0	0.0	0.0	0.0	0.0	0.0	0.0	0.0	0.0	12.9	56.2	34
35	0.0	0.0	0.0	0.0	0.0	0.0	0.0	0.0	0.0	0.0	0.0	49.7	35
36	0.0	0.0	0.0	0.0	0.0	0.0	0.0	0.0	0.0	0.0	0.0	42.3	36
37	0.0	0.0	0.0	0.0	0.0	0.0	0.0	0.0	0.0	0.0	0.0	33.8	37
38	0.0	0.0	0.0	0.0	0.0	0.0	0.0	0.0	0.0	0.0	0.0	24.0	38
39	0.0	0.0	0.0	0.0	0.0	0.0	0.0	0.0	0.0	0.0	0.0	12.8	39

EXAMPLES *ON PAGES A-382 TO A-397*

AGE OF LOAN	ORIGINAL TERM IN YEARS												AGE OF LOAN
	2.0	3.0	5.0	8.0	10.0	12.0	15.0	16.0	17.0	18.0	19.0	20.0	
1	53.5	71.2	85.1	92.7	95.1	96.5	97.9	98.2	98.5	98.7	98.9	99.0	1
2	0.0	38.1	68.1	84.3	89.4	92.6	95.5	96.1	96.7	97.1	97.5	97.9	2
3	0.0	0.0	48.5	74.7	82.9	88.0	92.7	93.7	94.6	95.4	96.0	96.6	3
4	0.0	0.0	25.9	63.6	75.3	82.7	89.5	91.0	92.3	93.4	94.3	95.1	4
5	0.0	0.0	0.0	50.8	66.7	76.7	85.8	87.8	89.6	91.1	92.3	93.4	5
6	0.0	0.0	0.0	36.2	56.8	69.7	81.5	84.2	86.5	88.4	90.0	91.4	6
7	0.0	0.0	0.0	19.3	45.4	61.8	76.7	80.1	82.9	85.3	87.4	89.1	7
8	0.0	0.0	0.0	0.0	32.3	52.6	71.1	75.3	78.8	81.8	84.4	86.5	8
9	0.0	0.0	0.0	0.0	17.3	42.0	64.6	69.8	74.1	77.8	80.9	83.5	9
10	0.0	0.0	0.0	0.0	0.0	29.9	57.2	63.5	68.7	73.1	76.9	80.1	10
11	0.0	0.0	0.0	0.0	0.0	16.0	48.7	56.2	62.5	67.8	72.3	76.1	11
12	0.0	0.0	0.0	0.0	0.0	0.0	39.0	47.9	55.3	61.6	67.0	71.6	12
13	0.0	0.0	0.0	0.0	0.0	0.0	27.7	38.3	47.1	54.6	60.9	66.4	13
14	0.0	0.0	0.0	0.0	0.0	0.0	14.8	27.2	37.7	46.5	54.0	60.3	14
15	0.0	0.0	0.0	0.0	0.0	0.0	0.0	14.6	26.8	37.2	46.0	53.4	15
16	0.0	0.0	0.0	0.0	0.0	0.0	0.0	0.0	14.3	26.5	36.7	45.5	16
17	0.0	0.0	0.0	0.0	0.0	0.0	0.0	0.0	0.0	14.1	26.2	36.4	17
18	0.0	0.0	0.0	0.0	0.0	0.0	0.0	0.0	0.0	0.0	14.0	25.9	18
19	0.0	0.0	0.0	0.0	0.0	0.0	0.0	0.0	0.0	0.0	0.0	13.8	19

14.00

AGE OF LOAN	ORIGINAL TERM IN YEARS												AGE OF LOAN
	21.0	22.0	23.0	24.0	25.0	26.0	27.0	28.0	29.0	30.0	35.0	40.0	
1	99.2	99.3	99.4	99.5	99.5	99.6	99.6	99.7	99.7	99.8	99.9	99.9	1
2	98.2	98.4	98.6	98.8	99.0	99.1	99.2	99.3	99.4	99.5	99.8	99.9	2
3	97.1	97.5	97.8	98.1	98.4	98.6	98.8	98.9	99.1	99.2	99.6	99.8	3
4	95.8	96.3	96.8	97.3	97.6	97.9	98.2	98.5	98.7	98.8	99.4	99.7	4
5	94.3	95.1	95.7	96.3	96.8	97.2	97.6	97.9	98.2	98.4	99.2	99.6	5
6	92.6	93.6	94.5	95.2	95.8	96.4	96.9	97.3	97.7	98.0	99.0	99.5	6
7	90.6	91.9	93.0	93.9	94.8	95.5	96.1	96.6	97.0	97.4	98.7	99.4	7
8	88.4	90.0	91.3	92.5	93.5	94.4	95.1	95.8	96.3	96.8	98.4	99.2	8
9	85.8	87.7	89.4	90.8	92.1	93.1	94.0	94.8	95.5	96.1	98.1	99.0	9
10	82.8	85.2	87.2	88.9	90.4	91.7	92.8	93.7	94.6	95.3	97.7	98.8	10
11	79.4	82.2	84.6	86.7	88.5	90.0	91.3	92.5	93.5	94.3	97.2	98.6	11
12	75.5	78.8	81.7	84.2	86.3	88.1	89.7	91.1	92.2	93.3	96.7	98.3	12
13	71.0	74.9	78.3	81.2	83.8	85.9	87.8	89.4	90.8	92.0	96.1	98.0	13
14	65.8	70.5	74.5	77.9	80.9	83.4	85.6	87.5	89.2	90.6	95.4	97.7	14
15	59.8	65.3	70.0	74.0	77.5	80.5	83.1	85.4	87.3	89.0	94.5	97.3	15
16	53.0	59.4	64.9	69.6	73.7	77.2	80.2	82.9	85.1	87.1	93.6	96.8	16
17	45.1	52.6	59.0	64.5	69.3	73.4	76.9	80.0	82.6	84.9	92.5	96.3	17
18	36.1	44.8	52.3	58.7	64.2	69.0	73.1	76.7	79.8	82.4	91.3	95.7	18
19	25.7	35.8	44.5	52.0	58.4	64.0	68.8	72.9	76.5	79.6	89.9	95.0	19
20	13.7	25.5	35.6	44.3	51.7	58.2	63.7	68.5	72.7	76.3	88.3	94.2	20
21	0.0	13.6	25.3	35.4	44.0	51.5	58.0	63.5	68.4	72.5	86.4	93.3	21
22	0.0	0.0	13.5	25.2	35.2	43.9	51.3	57.8	63.4	68.2	84.3	92.2	22
23	0.0	0.0	0.0	13.5	25.1	35.1	43.7	51.2	57.6	63.2	81.8	91.0	23
24	0.0	0.0	0.0	0.0	13.4	25.0	34.9	43.6	51.0	57.5	79.0	89.6	24
25	0.0	0.0	0.0	0.0	0.0	13.3	24.9	34.8	43.5	50.9	75.7	87.9	25
26	0.0	0.0	0.0	0.0	0.0	0.0	13.3	24.8	34.7	43.4	72.0	86.1	26
27	0.0	0.0	0.0	0.0	0.0	0.0	0.0	13.3	24.7	34.7	67.7	83.9	27
28	0.0	0.0	0.0	0.0	0.0	0.0	0.0	0.0	13.2	24.7	62.7	81.5	28
29	0.0	0.0	0.0	0.0	0.0	0.0	0.0	0.0	0.0	13.2	57.1	78.7	29
30	0.0	0.0	0.0	0.0	0.0	0.0	0.0	0.0	0.0	0.0	50.5	75.4	30
31	0.0	0.0	0.0	0.0	0.0	0.0	0.0	0.0	0.0	0.0	43.0	71.7	31
32	0.0	0.0	0.0	0.0	0.0	0.0	0.0	0.0	0.0	0.0	34.4	67.4	32
33	0.0	0.0	0.0	0.0	0.0	0.0	0.0	0.0	0.0	0.0	24.5	62.5	33
34	0.0	0.0	0.0	0.0	0.0	0.0	0.0	0.0	0.0	0.0	13.1	56.8	34
35	0.0	0.0	0.0	0.0	0.0	0.0	0.0	0.0	0.0	0.0	0.0	50.3	35
36	0.0	0.0	0.0	0.0	0.0	0.0	0.0	0.0	0.0	0.0	0.0	42.9	36
37	0.0	0.0	0.0	0.0	0.0	0.0	0.0	0.0	0.0	0.0	0.0	34.3	37
38	0.0	0.0	0.0	0.0	0.0	0.0	0.0	0.0	0.0	0.0	0.0	24.4	38
39	0.0	0.0	0.0	0.0	0.0	0.0	0.0	0.0	0.0	0.0	0.0	13.0	39

EXAMPLES *ON PAGES A-382 TO A-397*

AGE OF LOAN	ORIGINAL TERM IN YEARS												AGE OF LOAN
	2.0	3.0	5.0	8.0	10.0	12.0	15.0	16.0	17.0	18.0	19.0	20.0	
1	53.5	71.3	85.2	92.8	95.1	96.6	97.9	98.2	98.5	98.7	98.9	99.0	1
2	0.0	38.1	68.2	84.4	89.5	92.7	95.6	96.2	96.8	97.2	97.6	98.0	2
3	0.0	0.0	48.6	74.8	83.0	88.2	92.8	93.9	94.8	95.5	96.1	96.7	3
4	0.0	0.0	26.0	63.8	75.6	83.0	89.7	91.2	92.5	93.5	94.5	95.2	4
5	0.0	0.0	0.0	51.1	67.0	77.0	86.0	88.1	89.8	91.3	92.5	93.6	5
6	0.0	0.0	0.0	36.4	57.1	70.1	81.8	84.5	86.8	88.7	90.3	91.6	6
7	0.0	0.0	0.0	19.5	45.7	62.1	77.0	80.4	83.2	85.6	87.7	89.4	7
8	0.0	0.0	0.0	0.0	32.6	52.9	71.4	75.6	79.2	82.2	84.7	86.8	8
9	0.0	0.0	0.0	0.0	17.4	42.4	65.0	70.2	74.5	78.2	81.2	83.9	9
10	0.0	0.0	0.0	0.0	0.0	30.2	57.5	63.9	69.1	73.5	77.3	80.5	10
11	0.0	0.0	0.0	0.0	0.0	16.1	49.1	56.6	62.9	68.2	72.7	76.6	11
12	0.0	0.0	0.0	0.0	0.0	0.0	39.3	48.3	55.8	62.1	67.5	72.0	12
13	0.0	0.0	0.0	0.0	0.0	0.0	28.0	38.6	47.5	55.0	61.4	66.8	13
14	0.0	0.0	0.0	0.0	0.0	0.0	15.0	27.5	38.0	46.9	54.4	60.8	14
15	0.0	0.0	0.0	0.0	0.0	0.0	0.0	14.7	27.1	37.5	46.4	53.9	15
16	0.0	0.0	0.0	0.0	0.0	0.0	0.0	0.0	14.5	26.7	37.1	45.9	16
17	0.0	0.0	0.0	0.0	0.0	0.0	0.0	0.0	0.0	14.3	26.5	36.8	17
18	0.0	0.0	0.0	0.0	0.0	0.0	0.0	0.0	0.0	0.0	14.2	26.2	18
19	0.0	0.0	0.0	0.0	0.0	0.0	0.0	0.0	0.0	0.0	0.0	14.0	19

14.25

AGE OF LOAN	ORIGINAL TERM IN YEARS												AGE OF LOAN
	21.0	22.0	23.0	24.0	25.0	26.0	27.0	28.0	29.0	30.0	35.0	40.0	
1	99.2	99.3	99.4	99.5	99.5	99.6	99.7	99.7	99.7	99.8	99.9	99.9	1
2	98.2	98.5	98.7	98.9	99.0	99.2	99.3	99.4	99.5	99.5	99.8	99.9	2
3	97.2	97.5	97.9	98.2	98.4	98.6	98.8	99.0	99.1	99.2	99.6	99.8	3
4	95.9	96.5	97.0	97.4	97.7	98.0	98.3	98.5	98.7	98.9	99.5	99.7	4
5	94.5	95.2	95.9	96.4	96.9	97.3	97.7	98.0	98.3	98.5	99.3	99.6	5
6	92.8	93.8	94.6	95.4	96.0	96.5	97.0	97.4	97.8	98.1	99.1	99.5	6
7	90.9	92.1	93.2	94.1	94.9	95.6	96.2	96.7	97.2	97.5	98.8	99.4	7
8	88.7	90.2	91.6	92.7	93.7	94.6	95.3	95.9	96.5	97.0	98.5	99.3	8
9	86.1	88.0	89.7	91.1	92.3	93.3	94.2	95.0	95.7	96.3	98.2	99.1	9
10	83.2	85.5	87.5	89.2	90.7	91.9	93.0	94.0	94.8	95.5	97.8	98.9	10
11	79.8	82.6	85.0	87.0	88.8	90.3	91.6	92.8	93.7	94.6	97.3	98.7	11
12	75.9	79.3	82.1	84.5	86.7	88.5	90.0	91.4	92.5	93.5	96.8	98.4	12
13	71.4	75.4	78.8	81.7	84.2	86.3	88.2	89.8	91.1	92.3	96.2	98.2	13
14	66.3	70.9	74.9	78.4	81.3	83.8	86.0	87.9	89.5	90.9	95.6	97.8	14
15	60.3	65.8	70.5	74.5	78.0	81.0	83.5	85.8	87.7	89.3	94.8	97.4	15
16	53.5	59.9	65.4	70.1	74.2	77.7	80.7	83.3	85.5	87.5	93.9	97.0	16
17	45.6	53.1	59.5	65.1	69.8	73.9	77.4	80.5	83.1	85.4	92.8	96.5	17
18	36.5	45.3	52.8	59.2	64.8	69.5	73.7	77.2	80.3	82.9	91.6	95.9	18
19	26.0	36.2	45.0	52.5	59.0	64.5	69.3	73.4	77.0	80.1	90.3	95.2	19
20	13.9	25.8	36.0	44.7	52.3	58.7	64.3	69.1	73.3	76.8	88.7	94.4	20
21	0.0	13.8	25.6	35.8	44.5	52.0	58.5	64.1	68.9	73.1	86.8	93.5	21
22	0.0	0.0	13.7	25.5	35.6	44.4	51.9	58.4	63.9	68.8	84.7	92.5	22
23	0.0	0.0	0.0	13.6	25.4	35.5	44.2	51.7	58.2	63.8	82.3	91.3	23
24	0.0	0.0	0.0	0.0	13.6	25.3	35.4	44.1	51.6	58.1	79.5	89.9	24
25	0.0	0.0	0.0	0.0	0.0	13.5	25.2	35.3	44.0	51.5	76.3	88.4	25
26	0.0	0.0	0.0	0.0	0.0	0.0	13.5	25.1	35.2	43.9	72.6	86.5	26
27	0.0	0.0	0.0	0.0	0.0	0.0	0.0	13.4	25.1	35.1	68.3	84.4	27
28	0.0	0.0	0.0	0.0	0.0	0.0	0.0	0.0	13.4	25.0	63.3	82.0	28
29	0.0	0.0	0.0	0.0	0.0	0.0	0.0	0.0	0.0	13.4	57.6	79.2	29
30	0.0	0.0	0.0	0.0	0.0	0.0	0.0	0.0	0.0	0.0	51.1	76.0	30
31	0.0	0.0	0.0	0.0	0.0	0.0	0.0	0.0	0.0	0.0	43.5	72.3	31
32	0.0	0.0	0.0	0.0	0.0	0.0	0.0	0.0	0.0	0.0	34.8	68.0	32
33	0.0	0.0	0.0	0.0	0.0	0.0	0.0	0.0	0.0	0.0	24.8	63.1	33
34	0.0	0.0	0.0	0.0	0.0	0.0	0.0	0.0	0.0	0.0	13.3	57.4	34
35	0.0	0.0	0.0	0.0	0.0	0.0	0.0	0.0	0.0	0.0	0.0	50.9	35
36	0.0	0.0	0.0	0.0	0.0	0.0	0.0	0.0	0.0	0.0	0.0	43.4	36
37	0.0	0.0	0.0	0.0	0.0	0.0	0.0	0.0	0.0	0.0	0.0	34.7	37
38	0.0	0.0	0.0	0.0	0.0	0.0	0.0	0.0	0.0	0.0	0.0	24.7	38
39	0.0	0.0	0.0	0.0	0.0	0.0	0.0	0.0	0.0	0.0	0.0	13.2	39

EXAMPLES ON PAGES A-382 TO A-397

AGE OF LOAN	2.0	3.0	5.0	8.0	10.0	12.0	15.0	16.0	17.0	18.0	19.0	20.0	AGE OF LOAN
					ORIGINAL TERM IN YEARS								
1	53.6	71.3	85.3	92.8	95.2	96.7	98.0	98.3	98.5	98.7	98.9	99.1	1
2	0.0	38.2	68.4	84.6	89.6	92.8	95.7	96.3	96.8	97.3	97.7	98.0	2
3	0.0	0.0	48.8	75.C	83.2	88.3	93.0	94.0	94.9	95.6	96.3	96.8	3
4	0.0	0.0	26.1	64.0	75.8	83.2	89.9	91.4	92.6	93.7	94.6	95.4	4
5	0.0	0.0	0.0	51.3	67.3	77.2	86.3	88.3	90.0	91.5	92.7	93.7	5
6	0.0	0.0	0.0	36.6	57.4	70.4	82.1	84.8	87.0	88.9	90.5	91.8	6
7	0.0	0.0	0.0	19.6	46.0	62.4	77.3	80.7	83.5	85.9	88.0	89.7	7
8	0.0	0.0	0.0	0.0	32.8	53.3	71.8	76.0	79.5	82.5	85.0	87.1	8
9	0.0	0.0	0.0	0.0	17.6	42.7	65.4	70.6	74.9	78.5	81.6	84.2	9
10	0.0	0.0	0.0	0.0	0.0	30.4	58.0	64.3	69.5	74.0	77.7	80.9	10
11	0.0	0.0	0.0	0.0	0.0	16.3	49.5	57.0	63.3	68.7	73.2	77.0	11
12	0.0	0.0	0.0	0.0	0.0	0.0	39.7	48.7	56.2	62.6	67.9	72.5	12
13	0.0	0.0	0.0	0.0	0.0	0.0	28.3	39.0	47.9	55.5	61.9	67.3	13
14	0.0	0.0	0.0	0.0	0.0	0.0	15.2	27.8	38.4	47.3	54.9	61.3	14
15	0.0	0.0	0.0	0.0	0.0	0.0	0.0	14.9	27.9	37.9	46.8	54.4	15
16	0.0	0.0	0.0	0.0	0.0	0.0	0.0	0.0	14.7	27.1	37.5	46.4	16
17	0.0	0.0	0.0	0.0	0.0	0.0	0.0	0.0	0.0	14.5	26.8	37.2	17
18	0.0	0.0	0.0	0.0	0.0	0.0	0.0	0.0	0.0	0.0	14.3	26.5	18
19	0.0	0.0	0.0	0.0	0.0	0.0	0.0	0.0	0.0	0.0	0.0	14.2	19

14.50

AGE OF LOAN	21.0	22.0	23.0	24.0	25.0	26.0	27.0	28.0	29.0	30.0	35.0	40.0	AGE OF LOAN
					ORIGINAL TERM IN YEARS								
1	99.2	99.3	99.4	99.5	99.6	99.6	99.7	99.7	99.8	99.8	99.9	100.0	1
2	98.3	98.5	98.7	98.9	99.1	99.2	99.3	99.4	99.5	99.6	99.8	99.9	2
3	97.2	97.6	98.0	98.2	98.5	98.7	98.9	99.0	99.2	99.3	99.6	99.8	3
4	96.0	96.6	97.1	97.5	97.8	98.1	98.4	98.6	98.8	99.0	99.5	99.8	4
5	94.6	95.4	96.6	96.6	97.0	97.5	97.8	98.1	98.4	98.6	99.3	99.7	5
6	93.0	94.0	94.8	95.5	96.2	96.7	97.1	97.5	97.9	98.2	99.1	99.6	6
7	91.1	92.4	93.4	94.3	95.1	95.8	96.4	96.9	97.3	97.7	98.9	99.5	7
8	89.0	90.5	91.8	93.0	93.9	94.8	95.5	96.1	96.6	97.1	98.6	99.3	8
9	86.5	88.4	90.0	91.4	92.6	93.6	94.5	95.2	95.9	96.4	98.3	99.2	9
10	83.6	85.9	87.8	89.5	91.0	92.2	93.3	94.2	95.0	95.7	97.9	99.0	10
11	80.2	83.0	85.4	87.4	89.1	90.6	91.9	93.0	94.0	94.8	97.5	98.8	11
12	76.4	79.7	82.5	84.9	87.0	88.8	90.3	91.7	92.8	93.8	97.0	98.5	12
13	71.9	75.9	79.2	82.1	84.6	86.7	88.5	90.1	91.4	92.6	96.4	98.3	13
14	66.8	71.4	75.4	78.8	81.7	84.2	86.4	88.3	89.9	91.2	95.8	97.9	14
15	60.8	66.3	71.0	75.0	78.5	81.4	84.0	86.2	88.1	89.7	95.0	97.6	15
16	54.0	60.4	65.9	70.7	74.7	78.2	81.2	83.7	86.0	87.9	94.1	97.2	16
17	46.0	53.6	60.1	65.6	70.3	74.4	77.9	80.9	83.5	85.8	93.1	96.7	17
18	36.9	45.7	53.3	59.8	65.3	70.1	74.2	77.7	80.7	83.4	92.0	96.1	18
19	26.3	36.6	45.5	53.0	59.5	65.1	69.9	74.0	77.5	80.6	90.6	95.5	19
20	14.1	26.1	36.4	45.2	52.8	59.3	64.9	69.7	73.8	77.4	89.1	94.7	20
21	0.0	14.0	26.0	36.2	45.0	52.6	59.1	64.7	69.5	73.6	87.3	93.8	21
22	0.0	0.0	13.9	25.9	36.1	44.9	52.4	58.9	64.5	69.3	85.2	92.8	22
23	0.0	0.0	0.0	13.9	25.7	35.9	44.7	52.3	58.8	64.4	82.8	91.7	23
24	0.0	0.0	0.0	0.0	13.8	25.6	35.8	44.6	52.2	58.7	80.0	90.3	24
25	0.0	0.0	0.0	0.0	0.0	13.7	25.6	35.7	44.5	52.0	76.8	88.8	25
26	0.0	0.0	0.0	0.0	0.0	0.0	13.7	25.5	35.6	44.4	73.1	87.0	26
27	0.0	0.0	0.0	0.0	0.0	0.0	0.0	13.7	25.4	35.6	68.9	84.9	27
28	0.0	0.0	0.0	0.0	0.0	0.0	0.0	0.0	13.6	25.4	63.9	82.5	28
29	0.0	0.0	0.0	0.0	0.0	0.0	0.0	0.0	0.0	13.6	58.3	79.8	29
30	0.0	0.0	0.0	0.0	0.0	0.0	0.0	0.0	0.0	0.0	51.7	76.6	30
31	0.0	0.0	0.0	0.0	0.0	0.0	0.0	0.0	0.0	0.0	44.1	72.9	31
32	0.0	0.0	0.0	0.0	0.0	0.0	0.0	0.0	0.0	0.0	35.3	68.6	32
33	0.0	0.0	0.0	0.0	0.0	0.0	0.0	0.0	0.0	0.0	25.2	63.7	33
34	0.0	0.0	0.0	0.0	0.0	0.0	0.0	0.0	0.0	0.0	13.5	58.1	34
35	0.0	0.0	0.0	0.0	0.0	0.0	0.0	0.0	0.0	0.0	0.0	51.5	35
36	0.0	0.0	0.0	0.0	0.0	0.0	0.0	0.0	0.0	0.0	0.0	43.9	36
37	0.0	0.0	0.0	0.0	0.0	0.0	0.0	0.0	0.0	0.0	0.0	35.3	37
38	0.0	0.0	0.0	0.0	0.0	0.0	0.0	0.0	0.0	0.0	0.0	25.1	38
39	0.0	0.0	0.0	0.0	0.0	0.0	0.0	0.0	0.0	0.0	0.0	13.5	39

EXAMPLES *ON PAGES A-382 TO A-397*

AGE OF LOAN	ORIGINAL TERM IN YEARS												AGE OF LOAN
	2.0	3.0	5.0	8.0	10.0	12.0	15.0	16.0	17.0	18.0	19.0	20.0	
1	53.7	71.4	85.4	92.9	95.3	96.7	98.0	98.3	98.6	98.8	99.0	99.1	1
2	0.0	38.3	68.5	84.7	89.8	92.9	95.7	96.4	96.9	97.4	97.8	98.1	2
3	0.0	0.0	48.9	75.2	83.4	88.5	93.1	94.1	95.0	95.7	96.4	96.9	3
4	0.0	0.0	26.2	64.3	76.1	83.4	90.0	91.6	92.8	93.9	94.8	95.5	4
5	0.0	0.0	0.0	51.5	67.5	77.5	86.5	88.5	90.2	91.7	92.9	93.9	5
6	0.0	0.0	0.0	36.8	57.7	70.7	82.4	85.1	87.3	89.1	90.7	92.1	6
7	0.0	0.0	0.0	19.7	46.3	62.8	77.7	81.0	83.8	86.2	88.2	89.9	7
8	0.0	0.0	0.0	0.0	33.0	53.6	72.2	76.4	79.9	82.8	85.3	87.4	8
9	0.0	0.0	0.0	0.0	17.7	43.0	65.8	71.0	75.3	78.9	82.0	84.6	9
10	0.0	0.0	0.0	0.0	0.0	30.7	58.4	64.7	69.9	74.4	78.1	81.2	10
11	0.0	0.0	0.0	0.0	0.0	16.5	49.9	57.5	63.8	69.1	73.6	77.4	11
12	0.0	0.0	0.0	0.0	0.0	0.0	40.0	49.1	56.6	63.0	68.4	72.9	12
13	0.0	0.0	0.0	0.0	0.0	0.0	28.6	39.3	48.4	55.9	62.3	67.8	13
14	0.0	0.0	0.0	0.0	0.0	0.0	15.3	28.1	38.8	47.8	55.4	61.8	14
15	0.0	0.0	0.0	0.0	0.0	0.0	0.0	15.1	27.7	38.3	47.3	54.9	15
16	0.0	0.0	0.0	0.0	0.0	0.0	0.0	0.0	14.9	27.4	37.9	46.9	16
17	0.0	0.0	0.0	0.0	0.0	0.0	0.0	0.0	0.0	14.7	27.1	37.6	17
18	0.0	0.0	0.0	0.0	0.0	0.0	0.0	0.0	0.0	0.0	14.5	26.8	18
19	0.0	0.0	0.0	0.0	0.0	0.0	0.0	0.0	0.0	0.0	0.0	14.4	19

14.75

AGE OF LOAN	ORIGINAL TERM IN YEARS												AGE OF LOAN
	21.0	22.0	23.0	24.0	25.0	26.0	27.0	28.0	29.0	30.0	35.0	40.0	
1	99.2	99.3	99.4	99.5	99.6	99.6	99.7	99.7	99.8	99.8	99.9	100.0	1
2	98.4	98.6	98.8	99.0	99.1	99.2	99.3	99.4	99.5	99.6	99.8	99.9	2
3	97.3	97.7	98.0	98.3	98.5	98.8	98.9	99.1	99.2	99.3	99.7	99.8	3
4	96.2	96.7	97.2	97.6	97.9	98.2	98.4	98.7	98.8	99.0	99.7	99.8	4
5	94.8	95.5	96.2	96.7	97.2	97.6	97.9	98.2	98.4	98.7	99.4	99.7	5
6	93.2	94.2	95.0	95.7	96.3	96.8	97.3	97.6	98.0	98.2	99.2	99.6	6
7	91.4	92.6	93.6	94.5	95.3	96.0	96.5	97.0	97.4	97.8	98.9	99.5	7
8	89.2	90.8	92.1	93.2	94.1	95.0	95.7	96.3	96.8	97.2	98.7	99.4	8
9	86.8	88.7	90.3	91.6	92.8	93.8	94.7	95.4	96.0	96.6	98.4	99.2	9
10	83.9	86.2	88.2	89.8	91.2	92.5	93.5	94.4	95.2	95.8	98.0	99.1	10
11	80.6	83.4	85.7	87.7	89.4	90.9	92.2	93.3	94.2	95.0	97.6	98.9	11
12	76.8	80.1	82.9	85.3	87.4	89.1	90.6	91.9	93.1	94.0	97.1	98.6	12
13	72.4	76.3	79.6	82.5	85.0	87.1	88.9	90.4	91.7	92.9	96.6	98.4	13
14	67.3	71.9	75.9	79.3	82.2	84.7	86.8	88.6	90.2	91.5	96.0	98.1	14
15	61.3	66.8	71.5	75.5	78.9	81.9	84.4	86.6	88.4	90.0	95.2	97.7	15
16	54.5	60.9	66.4	71.2	75.2	78.6	81.6	84.2	86.4	88.2	94.4	97.3	16
17	46.5	54.1	60.6	66.1	70.9	74.9	78.4	81.4	84.0	86.2	93.4	96.8	17
18	37.3	46.2	53.8	60.3	65.8	70.6	74.7	78.2	81.2	83.8	92.3	96.3	18
19	26.6	37.0	45.9	53.5	60.0	65.6	70.4	74.5	78.0	81.1	91.0	95.7	19
20	14.3	26.5	36.8	45.7	53.3	59.8	65.4	70.2	74.3	77.9	89.4	94.9	20
21	0.0	14.2	26.3	36.7	45.5	53.1	59.6	65.2	70.0	74.2	87.7	94.1	21
22	0.0	0.0	14.1	26.2	36.5	45.4	53.0	59.5	65.1	69.9	85.6	93.1	22
23	0.0	0.0	0.0	14.0	26.1	36.4	45.2	52.8	59.3	65.0	83.3	92.0	23
24	0.0	0.0	0.0	0.0	14.0	26.0	36.3	45.1	52.7	59.2	80.5	90.7	24
25	0.0	0.0	0.0	0.0	0.0	13.9	25.9	36.2	45.0	52.6	77.4	89.2	25
26	0.0	0.0	0.0	0.0	0.0	0.0	13.9	25.8	36.1	44.9	73.7	87.4	26
27	0.0	0.0	0.0	0.0	0.0	0.0	0.0	13.8	25.8	36.0	69.5	85.4	27
28	0.0	0.0	0.0	0.0	0.0	0.0	0.0	0.0	13.8	25.7	64.5	83.0	28
29	0.0	0.0	0.0	0.0	0.0	0.0	0.0	0.0	0.0	13.8	58.8	80.3	29
30	0.0	0.0	0.0	0.0	0.0	0.0	0.0	0.0	0.0	0.0	52.2	77.1	30
31	0.0	0.0	0.0	0.0	0.0	0.0	0.0	0.0	0.0	0.0	44.6	73.5	31
32	0.0	0.0	0.0	0.0	0.0	0.0	0.0	0.0	0.0	0.0	35.8	69.2	32
33	0.0	0.0	0.0	0.0	0.0	0.0	0.0	0.0	0.0	0.0	25.5	64.3	33
34	0.0	0.0	0.0	0.0	0.0	0.0	0.0	0.0	0.0	0.0	13.7	58.7	34
35	0.0	0.0	0.0	0.0	0.0	0.0	0.0	0.0	0.0	0.0	0.0	52.3	35
36	0.0	0.0	0.0	0.0	0.0	0.0	0.0	0.0	0.0	0.0	0.0	44.5	36
37	0.0	0.0	0.0	0.0	0.0	0.0	0.0	0.0	0.0	0.0	0.0	35.7	37
38	0.0	0.0	0.0	0.0	0.0	0.0	0.0	0.0	0.0	0.0	0.0	25.5	38
39	0.0	0.0	0.0	0.0	0.0	0.0	0.0	0.0	0.0	0.0	0.0	13.6	39

EXAMPLES *ON PAGES A-382 TO A-397*

AGE OF LOAN	ORIGINAL TERM IN YEARS												AGE OF LOAN
	2.0	3.0	5.0	8.0	10.0	12.0	15.0	16.0	17.0	18.0	19.0	20.0	
1	53.7	71.5	85.5	93.0	95.3	96.8	98.1	98.4	98.6	98.8	99.0	99.1	1
2	0.0	38.4	68.6	84.9	89.9	93.0	95.8	96.5	97.0	97.5	97.8	98.1	2
3	0.0	0.0	49.1	75.4	83.6	88.7	93.3	94.3	95.1	95.9	96.5	97.0	3
4	0.0	0.0	26.4	64.5	76.3	83.6	90.2	91.7	93.0	94.0	94.9	95.6	4
5	0.0	0.0	0.0	51.8	67.8	77.8	86.7	88.8	90.5	91.9	93.1	94.1	5
6	0.0	0.0	0.0	37.0	58.0	71.0	82.7	85.3	87.5	89.4	91.0	92.3	6
7	0.0	0.0	0.0	19.9	46.5	63.1	78.0	81.3	84.2	86.5	88.5	90.2	7
8	0.0	0.0	0.0	0.0	33.3	53.9	72.5	76.7	80.2	83.2	85.6	87.7	8
9	0.0	0.0	0.0	0.0	17.9	43.3	66.2	71.3	75.7	79.3	82.3	84.9	9
10	0.0	0.0	0.0	0.0	0.0	31.0	58.8	65.1	70.4	74.8	78.5	81.6	10
11	0.0	0.0	0.0	0.0	0.0	16.6	50.3	57.9	64.2	69.5	74.0	77.8	11
12	0.0	0.0	0.0	0.0	0.0	0.0	40.4	49.5	57.1	63.5	68.8	73.4	12
13	0.0	0.0	0.0	0.0	0.0	0.0	28.9	39.7	48.8	56.4	62.8	68.2	13
14	0.0	0.0	0.0	0.0	0.0	0.0	15.5	28.4	39.2	48.2	55.8	62.3	14
15	0.0	0.0	0.0	0.0	0.0	0.0	0.0	15.3	28.0	38.7	47.7	55.3	15
16	0.0	0.0	0.0	0.0	0.0	0.0	0.0	0.0	15.0	27.7	38.3	47.3	16
17	0.0	0.0	0.0	0.0	0.0	0.0	0.0	0.0	0.0	14.9	27.4	38.0	17
18	0.0	0.0	0.0	0.0	0.0	0.0	0.0	0.0	0.0	0.0	14.7	27.2	18
19	0.0	0.0	0.0	0.0	0.0	0.0	0.0	0.0	0.0	0.0	0.0	14.6	19

15.00

AGE OF LOAN	ORIGINAL TERM IN YEARS												AGE OF LOAN
	21.0	22.0	23.0	24.0	25.0	26.0	27.0	28.0	29.0	30.0	35.0	40.0	
1	99.3	99.4	99.5	99.5	99.6	99.7	99.7	99.7	99.8	99.8	99.9	100.0	1
2	98.4	98.6	98.8	99.0	99.1	99.3	99.4	99.5	99.5	99.6	99.8	99.9	2
3	97.4	97.8	98.1	98.4	98.6	98.8	99.0	99.1	99.2	99.3	99.7	99.9	3
4	96.3	96.8	97.3	97.7	98.0	98.3	98.5	98.7	98.9	99.1	99.6	99.8	4
5	94.9	95.7	96.3	96.8	97.3	97.7	98.0	98.3	98.5	98.7	99.4	99.7	5
6	93.4	94.3	95.2	95.8	96.4	96.9	97.4	97.7	98.1	98.3	99.2	99.6	6
7	91.6	92.8	93.8	94.7	95.5	96.1	96.7	97.1	97.5	97.9	99.0	99.5	7
8	89.5	91.0	92.3	93.4	94.3	95.1	95.8	96.4	96.9	97.3	98.7	99.4	8
9	87.1	88.9	90.5	91.9	93.0	94.0	94.9	95.6	96.2	96.7	98.5	99.3	9
10	84.3	86.5	88.5	90.1	91.5	92.7	93.7	94.6	95.4	96.0	98.1	99.1	10
11	81.0	83.7	86.1	88.1	89.8	91.2	92.4	93.5	94.4	95.2	97.7	98.9	11
12	77.2	80.5	83.3	85.7	87.7	89.4	90.9	92.2	93.3	94.2	97.3	98.7	12
13	72.8	76.7	80.1	82.9	85.3	87.4	89.2	90.7	92.0	93.1	96.8	98.5	13
14	67.7	72.4	76.3	79.7	82.6	85.0	87.2	89.0	90.5	91.8	96.2	98.2	14
15	61.8	67.3	72.0	76.0	79.4	82.3	84.8	86.9	88.8	90.3	95.4	97.8	15
16	54.9	61.4	66.9	71.7	75.7	79.1	82.1	84.6	86.7	88.6	94.6	97.5	16
17	47.0	54.6	61.1	66.6	71.4	75.4	78.9	81.9	84.4	86.6	93.7	97.0	17
18	37.7	46.7	54.3	60.8	66.4	71.1	75.2	78.7	81.7	84.2	92.6	96.5	18
19	27.0	37.5	46.4	54.1	60.6	66.1	70.9	75.0	78.5	81.5	91.3	95.9	19
20	14.5	26.8	37.3	46.2	53.8	60.4	66.0	70.7	74.8	78.4	89.8	95.2	20
21	0.0	14.4	26.6	37.1	46.0	53.7	60.2	65.8	70.6	74.7	88.1	94.4	21
22	0.0	0.0	14.3	26.5	36.9	45.9	53.5	60.0	65.6	70.5	86.1	93.4	22
23	0.0	0.0	0.0	14.2	26.4	36.8	45.7	53.4	59.9	65.5	83.7	92.3	23
24	0.0	0.0	0.0	0.0	14.2	26.3	36.7	45.6	53.2	59.8	81.0	91.0	24
25	0.0	0.0	0.0	0.0	0.0	14.1	26.2	36.6	45.5	53.1	77.9	89.5	25
26	0.0	0.0	0.0	0.0	0.0	0.0	14.1	26.2	36.5	45.4	74.3	87.8	26
27	0.0	0.0	0.0	0.0	0.0	0.0	0.0	14.1	26.1	36.5	70.0	85.8	27
28	0.0	0.0	0.0	0.0	0.0	0.0	0.0	0.0	14.0	26.1	65.1	83.5	28
29	0.0	0.0	0.0	0.0	0.0	0.0	0.0	0.0	0.0	14.0	59.4	80.8	29
30	0.0	0.0	0.0	0.0	0.0	0.0	0.0	0.0	0.0	0.0	52.8	77.7	30
31	0.0	0.0	0.0	0.0	0.0	0.0	0.0	0.0	0.0	0.0	45.2	74.0	31
32	0.0	0.0	0.0	0.0	0.0	0.0	0.0	0.0	0.0	0.0	36.3	69.8	32
33	0.0	0.0	0.0	0.0	0.0	0.0	0.0	0.0	0.0	0.0	25.9	64.9	33
34	0.0	0.0	0.0	0.0	0.0	0.0	0.0	0.0	0.0	0.0	13.9	59.3	34
35	0.0	0.0	0.0	0.0	0.0	0.0	0.0	0.0	0.0	0.0	0.0	52.7	35
36	0.0	0.0	0.0	0.0	0.0	0.0	0.0	0.0	0.0	0.0	0.0	45.0	36
37	0.0	0.0	0.0	0.0	0.0	0.0	0.0	0.0	0.0	0.0	0.0	36.1	37
38	0.0	0.0	0.0	0.0	0.0	0.0	0.0	0.0	0.0	0.0	0.0	25.8	38
39	0.0	0.0	0.0	0.0	0.0	0.0	0.0	0.0	0.0	0.0	0.0	13.9	39

EXAMPLES ON PAGES A-382 TO A-397

AGE OF LOAN	ORIGINAL TERM IN YEARS												AGE OF LOAN
	2.0	3.0	5.0	8.0	10.0	12.0	15.0	16.0	17.0	18.0	19.0	20.0	
1	53.8	71.6	95.6	93.1	95.4	96.8	98.1	98.4	98.7	98.9	99.0	99.2	1
2	0.0	38.5	68.8	85.0	90.0	93.1	95.9	96.6	97.1	97.5	97.9	98.2	2
3	0.0	0.0	49.2	75.6	83.8	88.3	93.4	94.4	95.3	96.0	96.6	97.1	3
4	0.0	0.0	26.5	64.7	76.5	83.9	90.4	91.9	93.1	94.2	95.0	95.8	4
5	0.0	0.0	0.0	52.0	68.1	78.0	87.0	89.0	90.7	92.1	93.3	94.2	5
6	0.0	0.0	0.0	37.2	58.3	71.3	83.0	85.6	87.8	89.6	91.2	92.5	6
7	0.0	0.0	0.0	20.0	46.8	63.4	78.3	81.7	84.4	86.8	88.8	90.4	7
8	0.0	0.0	0.0	0.0	33.5	54.3	72.9	77.1	80.6	83.5	85.9	88.0	8
9	0.0	0.0	0.0	0.0	18.0	43.6	66.6	71.7	76.0	79.6	82.7	85.2	9
10	0.0	0.0	0.0	0.0	0.0	31.2	59.2	65.5	70.8	75.2	78.9	82.0	10
11	0.0	0.0	0.0	0.0	0.0	16.8	50.7	58.3	64.6	69.9	74.4	78.2	11
12	0.0	0.0	0.0	0.0	0.0	0.0	40.7	49.9	57.5	63.9	69.3	73.8	12
13	0.0	0.0	0.0	0.0	0.0	0.0	29.1	40.1	49.2	56.8	63.3	68.7	13
14	0.0	0.0	0.0	0.0	0.0	0.0	15.7	28.7	39.5	48.6	56.3	62.7	14
15	0.0	0.0	0.0	0.0	0.0	0.0	0.0	15.4	28.3	39.1	48.2	55.8	15
16	0.0	0.0	0.0	0.0	0.0	0.0	0.0	0.0	15.2	28.0	38.7	47.8	16
17	0.0	0.0	0.0	0.0	0.0	0.0	0.0	0.0	0.0	15.0	27.7	38.4	17
18	0.0	0.0	0.0	0.0	0.0	0.0	0.0	0.0	0.0	0.0	14.9	27.5	18
19	0.0	0.0	0.0	0.0	0.0	0.0	0.0	0.0	0.0	0.0	0.0	14.8	19

15.25

AGE OF LOAN	ORIGINAL TERM IN YEARS												AGE OF LOAN
	21.0	22.0	23.0	24.0	25.0	26.0	27.0	28.0	29.0	30.0	35.0	40.0	
1	99.3	99.4	99.5	99.6	99.6	99.7	99.7	99.8	99.8	99.8	99.9	100.0	1
2	98.5	98.7	98.9	99.0	99.2	99.3	99.4	99.5	99.6	99.6	99.8	99.9	2
3	97.5	97.9	98.2	98.4	98.7	98.9	99.0	99.2	99.3	99.4	99.7	99.9	3
4	96.4	96.9	97.4	97.7	98.1	98.3	98.6	98.8	99.0	99.1	99.6	99.8	4
5	95.1	95.8	96.4	96.9	97.4	97.8	98.1	98.3	98.6	98.8	99.4	99.7	5
6	93.6	94.5	95.3	96.0	96.6	97.1	97.5	97.8	98.1	98.4	99.3	99.7	6
7	91.8	93.0	94.0	94.9	95.6	96.3	96.8	97.2	97.6	98.0	99.1	99.6	7
8	89.8	91.3	92.5	93.6	94.5	95.3	96.0	96.6	97.0	97.5	98.8	99.4	8
9	87.4	39.2	90.8	92.1	93.3	94.2	95.1	95.8	96.4	96.9	98.5	99.3	9
10	84.6	86.9	88.8	90.4	91.8	93.0	94.0	94.8	95.6	96.2	98.2	99.2	10
11	81.4	84.1	86.4	88.4	90.1	91.5	92.7	93.7	94.6	95.4	97.9	99.0	11
12	77.7	80.9	83.7	86.0	88.0	89.8	91.2	92.5	93.5	94.5	97.4	98.8	12
13	73.3	77.2	80.5	83.3	85.7	87.8	89.5	91.0	92.3	93.4	96.9	98.6	13
14	68.2	72.8	76.8	80.1	83.0	85.4	87.5	89.3	90.8	92.1	96.3	98.3	14
15	62.3	67.8	72.5	76.4	79.8	82.7	85.2	87.3	89.1	90.7	95.6	98.0	15
16	55.4	61.9	67.4	72.1	76.2	79.6	82.5	85.0	87.1	89.0	94.9	97.6	16
17	47.4	55.1	61.6	67.1	71.9	75.9	79.4	82.3	84.8	87.0	93.9	97.2	17
18	38.1	47.1	54.8	61.3	66.9	71.6	75.7	79.2	82.1	84.7	92.9	96.7	18
19	27.3	37.9	46.9	54.6	61.1	66.7	71.4	75.5	79.0	82.0	91.6	96.1	19
20	14.7	27.1	37.7	46.7	54.3	60.9	66.5	71.3	75.4	78.9	90.1	95.4	20
21	0.0	14.6	27.0	37.5	46.5	54.2	60.7	66.3	71.1	75.2	88.5	94.6	21
22	0.0	0.0	14.5	26.8	37.4	46.3	54.0	60.6	66.2	71.0	86.5	93.7	22
23	0.0	0.0	0.0	14.4	26.7	37.2	46.2	53.9	60.5	66.1	84.2	92.6	23
24	0.0	0.0	0.0	0.0	14.4	26.7	37.1	46.1	53.8	60.3	81.5	91.4	24
25	0.0	0.0	0.0	0.0	0.0	14.3	26.6	37.1	46.0	53.7	78.4	89.9	25
26	0.0	0.0	0.0	0.0	0.0	0.0	14.3	26.5	37.0	45.9	74.8	88.2	26
27	0.0	0.0	0.0	0.0	0.0	0.0	0.0	14.2	26.5	36.9	70.6	86.3	27
28	0.0	0.0	0.0	0.0	0.0	0.0	0.0	0.0	14.2	26.4	65.7	84.0	28
29	0.0	0.0	0.0	0.0	0.0	0.0	0.0	0.0	0.0	14.2	60.0	81.3	29
30	0.0	0.0	0.0	0.0	0.0	0.0	0.0	0.0	0.0	0.0	53.4	78.2	30
31	0.0	0.0	0.0	0.0	0.0	0.0	0.0	0.0	0.0	0.0	45.7	74.6	31
32	0.0	0.0	0.0	0.0	0.0	0.0	0.0	0.0	0.0	0.0	36.7	70.4	32
33	0.0	0.0	0.0	0.0	0.0	0.0	0.0	0.0	0.0	0.0	26.3	65.5	33
34	0.0	0.0	0.0	0.0	0.0	0.0	0.0	0.0	0.0	0.0	14.1	59.8	34
35	0.0	0.0	0.0	0.0	0.0	0.0	0.0	0.0	0.0	0.0	0.0	53.2	35
36	0.0	0.0	0.0	0.0	0.0	0.0	0.0	0.0	0.0	0.0	0.0	45.5	36
37	0.0	0.0	0.0	0.0	0.0	0.0	0.0	0.0	0.0	0.0	0.0	36.6	37
38	0.0	0.0	0.0	0.0	0.0	0.0	0.0	0.0	0.0	0.0	0.0	26.2	38
39	0.0	0.0	0.0	0.0	0.0	0.0	0.0	0.0	0.0	0.0	0.0	14.1	39

EXAMPLES *ON PAGES A-382 TO A-397*

AGE OF LOAN	2.0	3.0	5.0	8.0	10.0	12.0	15.0	16.0	17.0	18.0	19.0	20.0	AGE OF LOAN
						ORIGINAL TERM IN YEARS							
1	53.8	71.6	85.6	93.1	95.5	96.9	98.2	98.5	98.7	98.9	99.1	99.2	1
2	0.0	38.6	68.9	85.1	90.2	93.3	96.0	96.6	97.2	97.6	98.0	98.3	2
3	0.0	0.0	49.4	75.8	84.0	89.0	93.5	94.5	95.4	96.1	96.7	97.2	3
4	0.0	0.0	26.6	64.9	76.8	84.1	90.6	92.1	93.3	94.3	95.2	95.9	4
5	0.0	0.0	0.0	52.2	68.4	78.3	87.2	89.2	90.9	92.3	93.4	94.4	5
6	0.0	0.0	0.0	37.4	58.5	71.6	83.3	85.9	88.0	89.9	91.4	92.7	6
7	0.0	0.0	0.0	20.2	47.1	63.7	78.6	82.0	84.7	87.1	89.0	90.7	7
8	0.0	0.0	0.0	0.0	33.7	54.6	73.2	77.4	80.9	83.8	86.2	88.3	8
9	0.0	0.0	0.0	0.0	18.2	43.9	67.0	72.1	76.4	80.0	83.0	85.6	9
10	0.0	0.0	0.0	0.0	0.0	31.5	59.6	65.9	71.2	75.6	79.2	82.3	10
11	0.0	0.0	0.0	0.0	0.0	16.9	51.1	58.7	65.1	70.4	74.8	78.6	11
12	0.0	0.0	0.0	0.0	0.0	0.0	41.1	50.3	57.9	64.3	69.7	74.2	12
13	0.0	0.0	0.0	0.0	0.0	0.0	29.4	40.4	49.6	57.3	63.7	69.2	13
14	0.0	0.0	0.0	0.0	0.0	0.0	15.8	29.0	39.9	49.1	56.7	63.2	14
15	0.0	0.0	0.0	0.0	0.0	0.0	0.0	15.6	28.6	39.5	48.6	56.3	15
16	0.0	0.0	0.0	0.0	0.0	0.0	0.0	0.0	15.4	28.3	39.1	48.2	16
17	0.0	0.0	0.0	0.0	0.0	0.0	0.0	0.0	0.0	15.2	28.0	38.8	17
18	0.0	0.0	0.0	0.0	0.0	0.0	0.0	0.0	0.0	0.0	15.1	27.8	18
19	0.0	0.0	0.0	0.0	0.0	0.0	0.0	0.0	0.0	0.0	0.0	15.0	19

15.50

AGE OF LOAN	21.0	22.0	23.0	24.0	25.0	26.0	27.0	28.0	29.0	30.0	35.0	40.0	AGE OF LOAN
						ORIGINAL TERM IN YEARS							
1	99.3	99.4	99.5	99.6	99.6	99.7	99.7	99.8	99.8	99.8	99.9	100.0	1
2	98.5	98.7	98.9	99.1	99.2	99.3	99.4	99.5	99.6	99.6	99.8	99.9	2
3	97.6	97.9	98.2	98.5	98.7	98.9	99.1	99.2	99.3	99.4	99.7	99.9	3
4	96.5	97.0	97.5	97.8	98.1	98.4	98.6	98.8	99.0	99.2	99.6	99.8	4
5	95.2	95.9	96.5	97.0	97.5	97.8	98.2	98.4	98.7	98.8	99.5	99.8	5
6	93.8	94.7	95.5	96.1	96.7	97.2	97.6	97.9	98.2	98.5	99.3	99.7	6
7	92.0	93.2	94.2	95.1	95.8	96.4	96.9	97.4	97.7	98.1	99.1	99.6	7
8	90.0	91.5	92.8	93.8	94.7	95.5	96.1	96.7	97.2	97.6	98.9	99.5	8
9	87.7	89.5	91.1	92.4	93.5	94.4	95.2	95.9	96.5	97.0	98.6	99.4	9
10	85.0	87.2	89.1	90.7	92.0	93.2	94.2	95.0	95.7	96.4	98.3	99.2	10
11	81.8	84.5	86.8	88.7	90.3	91.7	92.9	94.0	94.8	95.6	98.0	99.1	11
12	78.1	81.3	84.1	86.4	88.4	90.1	91.5	92.7	93.8	94.7	97.5	98.9	12
13	73.7	77.6	80.9	83.7	86.1	88.1	89.8	91.3	92.6	93.6	97.1	98.6	13
14	68.7	73.3	77.2	80.6	83.4	85.8	87.9	89.6	91.1	92.4	96.5	98.4	14
15	62.8	68.3	72.9	76.9	80.3	83.1	85.6	87.7	89.5	91.0	95.8	98.1	15
16	55.9	62.4	67.9	72.6	76.6	80.0	82.9	85.4	87.5	89.3	95.1	97.7	16
17	47.9	55.6	62.1	67.7	72.4	76.4	79.8	82.7	85.2	87.4	94.2	97.3	17
18	38.5	47.6	55.3	61.8	67.4	72.1	76.2	79.6	82.6	85.1	93.1	96.8	18
19	27.6	38.3	47.4	55.1	61.6	67.2	72.0	76.0	79.5	82.4	91.9	96.3	19
20	14.9	27.4	38.1	47.2	54.9	61.4	67.0	71.8	75.9	79.3	90.5	95.6	20
21	0.0	14.8	27.3	37.9	47.0	54.7	61.3	66.9	71.7	75.7	88.8	94.8	21
22	0.0	0.0	14.7	27.2	37.8	46.8	54.6	61.1	66.7	71.5	86.9	93.9	22
23	0.0	0.0	0.0	14.6	27.1	37.7	46.7	54.4	61.0	66.6	84.6	92.9	23
24	0.0	0.0	0.0	0.0	14.6	27.0	37.6	46.6	54.3	60.9	82.0	91.7	24
25	0.0	0.0	0.0	0.0	0.0	14.5	26.9	37.5	46.5	54.2	78.9	90.3	25
26	0.0	0.0	0.0	0.0	0.0	0.0	14.5	26.9	37.4	46.4	75.3	88.6	26
27	0.0	0.0	0.0	0.0	0.0	0.0	0.0	14.5	26.8	37.4	71.2	86.7	27
28	0.0	0.0	0.0	0.0	0.0	0.0	0.0	0.0	14.4	26.8	66.3	84.4	28
29	0.0	0.0	0.0	0.0	0.0	0.0	0.0	0.0	0.0	14.4	60.6	81.8	29
30	0.0	0.0	0.0	0.0	0.0	0.0	0.0	0.0	0.0	0.0	53.9	78.7	30
31	0.0	0.0	0.0	0.0	0.0	0.0	0.0	0.0	0.0	0.0	46.2	75.2	31
32	0.0	0.0	0.0	0.0	0.0	0.0	0.0	0.0	0.0	0.0	37.2	71.0	32
33	0.0	0.0	0.0	0.0	0.0	0.0	0.0	0.0	0.0	0.0	26.6	66.1	33
34	0.0	0.0	0.0	0.0	0.0	0.0	0.0	0.0	0.0	0.0	14.3	60.4	34
35	0.0	0.0	0.0	0.0	0.0	0.0	0.0	0.0	0.0	0.0	0.0	53.8	35
36	0.0	0.0	0.0	0.0	0.0	0.0	0.0	0.0	0.0	0.0	0.0	46.1	36
37	0.0	0.0	0.0	0.0	0.0	0.0	0.0	0.0	0.0	0.0	0.0	37.1	37
38	0.0	0.0	0.0	0.0	0.0	0.0	0.0	0.0	0.0	0.0	0.0	26.6	38
39	0.0	0.0	0.0	0.0	0.0	0.0	0.0	0.0	0.0	0.0	0.0	14.3	39

EXAMPLES *ON PAGES A-382 TO A-397*

REMAINING BALANCE
IN PERCENT OF ORIGINAL LOAN AMOUNT

AGE OF LOAN	ORIGINAL TERM IN YEARS												AGE OF LOAN
	2.0	3.0	5.0	8.0	10.0	12.0	15.0	16.0	17.0	18.0	19.0	20.0	
1	53.9	71.7	85.7	93.2	95.5	96.9	98.2	98.5	98.7	98.9	99.1	99.2	1
2	0.0	38.7	69.0	85.3	90.3	93.4	96.1	96.7	97.2	97.7	98.0	98.3	2
3	0.0	0.0	49.5	76.0	84.2	89.2	93.7	94.7	95.5	96.2	96.8	97.3	3
4	0.0	0.0	26.7	65.2	77.0	84.3	90.8	92.3	93.5	94.5	95.3	96.0	4
5	0.0	0.0	0.0	52.5	68.6	78.6	87.4	89.4	91.1	92.4	93.6	94.6	5
6	0.0	0.0	0.0	37.6	58.8	71.9	83.5	86.1	88.3	90.1	91.6	92.9	6
7	0.0	0.0	0.0	20.3	47.4	64.1	79.0	82.3	85.0	87.3	89.3	90.9	7
8	0.0	0.0	0.0	0.0	34.0	54.9	73.6	77.8	81.2	84.1	86.5	88.6	8
9	0.0	0.0	0.0	0.0	18.3	44.2	67.3	72.5	76.8	80.3	83.3	85.9	9
10	0.0	0.0	0.0	0.0	0.0	31.7	60.0	66.3	71.6	75.9	79.6	82.7	10
11	0.0	0.0	0.0	0.0	0.0	17.1	51.4	59.1	65.5	70.8	75.2	79.0	11
12	0.0	0.0	0.0	0.0	0.0	0.0	41.4	50.7	58.3	64.8	70.1	74.7	12
13	0.0	0.0	0.0	0.0	0.0	0.0	29.7	40.8	50.0	57.7	64.2	69.6	13
14	0.0	0.0	0.0	0.0	0.0	0.0	16.0	29.3	40.3	49.5	57.2	63.7	14
15	0.0	0.0	0.0	0.0	0.0	0.0	0.0	15.8	28.9	39.8	49.0	56.7	15
16	0.0	0.0	0.0	0.0	0.0	0.0	0.0	0.0	15.6	28.6	39.5	48.6	16
17	0.0	0.0	0.0	0.0	0.0	0.0	0.0	0.0	0.0	15.4	28.3	39.2	17
18	0.0	0.0	0.0	0.0	0.0	0.0	0.0	0.0	0.0	0.0	15.3	28.1	18
19	0.0	0.0	0.0	0.0	0.0	0.0	0.0	0.0	0.0	0.0	0.0	15.1	19

15.75

AGE OF LOAN	ORIGINAL TERM IN YEARS												AGE OF LOAN
	21.0	22.0	23.0	24.0	25.0	26.0	27.0	28.0	29.0	30.0	35.0	40.0	
1	99.3	99.4	99.5	99.6	99.7	99.7	99.7	99.8	99.8	99.8	99.9	100.0	1
2	98.6	98.8	99.0	99.1	99.2	99.4	99.5	99.6	99.6	99.7	99.8	99.9	2
3	97.7	98.0	98.3	98.6	98.8	99.0	99.1	99.2	99.4	99.4	99.9	99.9	3
4	96.6	97.1	97.6	97.9	98.2	98.5	98.7	98.9	99.1	99.2	99.6	99.8	4
5	95.4	96.1	96.7	97.2	97.6	97.9	98.2	98.5	98.7	98.9	99.5	99.8	5
6	93.9	94.9	95.6	96.3	96.8	97.3	97.7	98.0	98.3	98.6	99.3	99.7	6
7	92.3	93.4	94.4	95.2	95.9	96.5	97.0	97.5	97.8	98.2	99.0	99.6	7
8	90.3	91.7	93.0	94.0	94.9	95.7	96.3	96.8	97.3	97.7	99.0	99.5	8
9	88.0	89.8	91.3	92.6	93.7	94.6	95.4	96.1	96.7	97.1	98.7	99.4	9
10	85.3	87.5	89.4	90.9	92.3	93.4	94.4	95.2	95.9	96.5	98.4	99.3	10
11	82.2	84.8	87.1	89.0	90.6	92.0	93.2	94.2	95.0	95.8	98.1	99.1	11
12	78.5	81.7	84.4	86.7	88.7	90.4	91.8	93.0	94.0	94.9	97.7	98.9	12
13	74.2	78.0	81.3	84.1	86.4	88.4	90.1	91.6	92.8	93.9	97.2	98.7	13
14	69.1	73.8	77.7	81.0	83.8	86.2	88.2	89.9	91.4	92.7	96.7	98.5	14
15	63.3	68.8	73.4	77.3	80.7	83.5	86.0	88.0	89.8	91.3	96.0	98.2	15
16	56.4	62.9	68.4	73.1	77.1	80.5	83.3	85.8	87.9	89.6	95.3	97.8	16
17	48.3	56.1	62.6	68.1	72.9	76.9	80.3	83.2	85.6	87.7	94.4	97.5	17
18	38.9	48.1	55.8	62.2	67.9	72.6	76.7	80.1	83.0	85.5	93.4	97.0	18
19	27.9	38.7	47.8	55.6	62.1	67.7	72.5	76.5	79.9	82.9	92.2	96.4	19
20	15.0	27.7	38.5	47.6	55.4	61.9	67.5	72.3	76.4	79.8	90.8	95.8	20
21	0.0	15.0	27.6	38.4	47.5	55.2	61.8	67.4	72.2	76.2	89.2	95.1	21
22	0.0	0.0	14.9	27.5	38.2	47.3	55.1	61.7	67.3	72.1	87.3	94.2	22
23	0.0	0.0	0.0	14.8	27.4	38.1	47.2	54.9	61.5	67.2	85.1	93.2	23
24	0.0	0.0	0.0	0.0	14.8	27.3	38.0	47.1	54.8	61.4	82.5	92.0	24
25	0.0	0.0	0.0	0.0	0.0	14.7	27.3	37.9	47.0	54.8	79.4	90.6	25
26	0.0	0.0	0.0	0.0	0.0	0.0	14.7	27.2	37.9	46.9	75.9	89.0	26
27	0.0	0.0	0.0	0.0	0.0	0.0	0.0	14.7	27.1	37.8	71.7	87.1	27
28	0.0	0.0	0.0	0.0	0.0	0.0	0.0	0.0	14.6	27.1	66.8	84.9	28
29	0.0	0.0	0.0	0.0	0.0	0.0	0.0	0.0	0.0	14.6	61.1	82.3	29
30	0.0	0.0	0.0	0.0	0.0	0.0	0.0	0.0	0.0	0.0	54.5	79.2	30
31	0.0	0.0	0.0	0.0	0.0	0.0	0.0	0.0	0.0	0.0	46.7	75.7	31
32	0.0	0.0	0.0	0.0	0.0	0.0	0.0	0.0	0.0	0.0	37.6	71.5	32
33	0.0	0.0	0.0	0.0	0.0	0.0	0.0	0.0	0.0	0.0	27.0	66.7	33
34	0.0	0.0	0.0	0.0	0.0	0.0	0.0	0.0	0.0	0.0	14.5	61.0	34
35	0.0	0.0	0.0	0.0	0.0	0.0	0.0	0.0	0.0	0.0	0.0	54.4	35
36	0.0	0.0	0.0	0.0	0.0	0.0	0.0	0.0	0.0	0.0	0.0	46.6	36
37	0.0	0.0	0.0	0.0	0.0	0.0	0.0	0.0	0.0	0.0	0.0	37.5	37
38	0.0	0.0	0.0	0.0	0.0	0.0	0.0	0.0	0.0	0.0	0.0	26.9	38
39	0.0	0.0	0.0	0.0	0.0	0.0	0.0	0.0	0.0	0.0	0.0	14.5	39

EXAMPLES *ON PAGES A-382 TO A-397*

AGE OF LOAN	ORIGINAL TERM IN YEARS												AGE OF LOAN
	2.0	3.0	5.0	8.0	10.0	12.0	15.0	16.0	17.0	18.0	19.0	20.0	
1	54.0	71.8	85.8	93.3	95.6	97.0	98.3	98.5	98.8	99.0	99.1	99.3	1
2	0.0	38.7	69.2	85.4	90.4	93.5	96.2	96.8	97.3	97.7	98.1	98.4	2
3	0.0	0.0	49.7	76.2	84.3	89.3	93.8	94.8	95.6	96.3	96.9	97.3	3
4	0.0	0.0	26.8	65.4	77.2	84.5	91.0	92.4	93.6	94.6	95.4	96.1	4
5	0.0	0.0	0.0	52.7	68.9	78.8	87.7	89.6	91.3	92.6	93.8	94.7	5
6	0.0	0.0	0.0	37.8	59.1	72.2	83.8	86.4	88.5	90.3	91.8	93.1	6
7	0.0	0.0	0.0	20.4	47.6	64.4	79.3	82.6	85.3	87.6	89.5	91.1	7
8	0.0	0.0	0.0	0.0	34.2	55.3	73.9	78.1	81.6	84.4	86.8	88.9	8
9	0.0	0.0	0.0	0.0	18.5	44.5	67.7	72.9	77.1	80.7	83.7	86.2	9
10	0.0	0.0	0.0	0.0	0.0	32.0	60.4	66.7	72.0	76.3	80.0	83.1	10
11	0.0	0.0	0.0	0.0	0.0	17.3	51.8	59.5	65.9	71.2	75.7	79.4	11
12	0.0	0.0	0.0	0.0	0.0	0.0	41.8	51.1	58.8	65.2	70.6	75.1	12
13	0.0	0.0	0.0	0.0	0.0	0.0	30.0	41.2	50.4	58.2	64.6	70.0	13
14	0.0	0.0	0.0	0.0	0.0	0.0	16.2	29.6	40.7	49.9	57.6	64.1	14
15	0.0	0.0	0.0	0.0	0.0	0.0	0.0	15.9	29.2	40.2	49.5	57.2	15
16	0.0	0.0	0.0	0.0	0.0	0.0	0.0	0.0	15.8	28.9	39.9	49.1	16
17	0.0	0.0	0.0	0.0	0.0	0.0	0.0	0.0	0.0	15.6	28.6	39.6	17
18	0.0	0.0	0.0	0.0	0.0	0.0	0.0	0.0	0.0	0.0	15.4	28.4	18
19	0.0	0.0	0.0	0.0	0.0	0.0	0.0	0.0	0.0	0.0	0.0	15.3	19

16.00

AGE OF LOAN	ORIGINAL TERM IN YEARS												AGE OF LOAN
	21.0	22.0	23.0	24.0	25.0	26.0	27.0	28.0	29.0	30.0	35.0	40.0	
1	99.4	99.5	99.5	99.6	99.7	99.7	99.8	99.8	99.8	99.9	99.9	100.0	1
2	98.6	98.8	99.0	99.2	99.3	99.4	99.5	99.6	99.6	99.7	99.9	99.9	2
3	97.8	98.1	98.4	98.6	98.8	99.0	99.2	99.3	99.4	99.5	99.8	99.9	3
4	96.7	97.2	97.6	98.0	98.3	98.6	98.8	99.0	99.1	99.2	99.7	99.8	4
5	95.5	96.2	96.8	97.3	97.7	98.0	98.3	98.6	98.8	99.0	99.5	99.8	5
6	94.1	95.0	95.8	96.4	96.9	97.4	97.8	98.1	98.4	98.6	99.4	99.7	6
7	92.5	93.6	94.6	95.4	96.1	96.7	97.2	97.6	97.9	98.3	99.2	99.6	7
8	90.5	92.0	93.2	94.2	95.1	95.8	96.4	97.0	97.4	97.8	99.0	99.6	8
9	88.3	90.1	91.6	92.8	93.9	94.8	95.6	96.2	96.8	97.3	98.8	99.4	9
10	85.6	87.8	89.7	91.2	92.5	93.6	94.6	95.4	96.1	96.7	98.5	99.3	10
11	82.5	85.2	87.4	89.3	90.9	92.3	93.4	94.4	95.2	95.9	98.2	99.2	11
12	78.9	82.1	84.8	87.1	89.0	90.6	92.0	93.2	94.2	95.1	97.8	99.0	12
13	74.6	78.5	81.7	84.5	86.8	88.8	90.4	91.9	93.1	94.1	97.3	98.8	13
14	69.6	74.2	78.1	81.4	84.2	86.5	88.5	90.2	91.7	92.9	96.8	98.6	14
15	63.7	69.2	73.9	77.8	81.1	83.9	86.3	88.4	90.1	91.6	96.2	98.3	15
16	56.8	63.4	68.9	73.6	77.5	80.9	83.7	86.2	88.2	90.0	95.5	98.0	16
17	48.8	56.5	63.1	68.6	73.3	77.3	80.7	83.6	86.0	88.1	94.6	97.6	17
18	39.3	48.5	56.3	62.9	68.4	73.1	77.1	80.5	83.4	85.9	93.7	97.1	18
19	28.2	39.1	48.3	56.1	62.6	68.2	73.0	77.0	80.4	83.3	92.5	96.6	19
20	15.2	28.1	38.9	48.1	55.9	62.5	68.1	72.8	76.8	80.3	91.1	96.0	20
21	0.0	15.2	28.0	38.8	47.9	55.7	62.3	67.9	72.7	76.7	89.5	95.3	21
22	0.0	0.0	15.1	27.8	38.7	47.8	55.6	62.2	67.8	72.6	87.7	94.4	22
23	0.0	0.0	0.0	15.0	27.8	38.5	47.7	55.5	62.1	67.7	85.5	93.5	23
24	0.0	0.0	0.0	0.0	15.0	27.7	38.5	47.6	55.4	62.0	82.9	92.3	24
25	0.0	0.0	0.0	0.0	0.0	14.9	27.6	38.4	47.5	55.3	79.9	90.9	25
26	0.0	0.0	0.0	0.0	0.0	0.0	14.9	27.6	38.3	47.5	76.4	89.4	26
27	0.0	0.0	0.0	0.0	0.0	0.0	0.0	14.9	27.5	38.3	72.2	87.5	27
28	0.0	0.0	0.0	0.0	0.0	0.0	0.0	0.0	14.8	27.5	67.4	85.3	28
29	0.0	0.0	0.0	0.0	0.0	0.0	0.0	0.0	0.0	14.8	61.7	82.7	29
30	0.0	0.0	0.0	0.0	0.0	0.0	0.0	0.0	0.0	0.0	55.0	79.7	30
31	0.0	0.0	0.0	0.0	0.0	0.0	0.0	0.0	0.0	0.0	47.2	76.2	31
32	0.0	0.0	0.0	0.0	0.0	0.0	0.0	0.0	0.0	0.0	38.1	72.1	32
33	0.0	0.0	0.0	0.0	0.0	0.0	0.0	0.0	0.0	0.0	27.3	67.3	33
34	0.0	0.0	0.0	0.0	0.0	0.0	0.0	0.0	0.0	0.0	14.8	61.6	34
35	0.0	0.0	0.0	0.0	0.0	0.0	0.0	0.0	0.0	0.0	0.0	54.9	35
36	0.0	0.0	0.0	0.0	0.0	0.0	0.0	0.0	0.0	0.0	0.0	47.1	36
37	0.0	0.0	0.0	0.0	0.0	0.0	0.0	0.0	0.0	0.0	0.0	38.0	37
38	0.0	0.0	0.0	0.0	0.0	0.0	0.0	0.0	0.0	0.0	0.0	27.3	38
39	0.0	0.0	0.0	0.0	0.0	0.0	0.0	0.0	0.0	0.0	0.0	14.7	39

EXAMPLES *ON PAGES A-382 TO A-397*

AGE OF LOAN	2.0	3.0	5.0	8.0	10.0	12.0	15.0	16.0	17.0	18.0	19.0	20.0	AGE OF LOAN
1	54.0	71.9	85.9	93.4	95.6	97.0	98.3	98.6	98.8	99.0	99.1	99.3	1
2	0.0	38.8	69.3	85.6	90.5	93.6	96.3	96.9	97.4	97.8	98.1	98.4	2
3	0.0	0.0	49.8	76.4	84.5	89.5	93.9	94.9	95.7	96.4	97.0	97.4	3
4	0.0	0.0	26.9	65.6	77.5	84.7	91.2	92.6	93.8	94.7	95.6	96.3	4
5	0.0	0.0	0.0	52.9	69.1	79.1	87.9	89.9	91.5	92.8	93.9	94.9	5
6	0.0	0.0	0.0	38.0	59.4	72.5	84.1	86.6	88.8	90.5	92.0	93.3	6
7	0.0	0.0	0.0	20.6	47.9	64.7	79.6	82.9	85.6	87.9	89.8	91.4	7
8	0.0	0.0	0.0	0.0	34.4	55.6	74.3	78.4	81.9	84.7	87.1	89.1	8
9	0.0	0.0	0.0	0.0	18.6	44.8	68.1	73.2	77.5	81.0	84.0	86.5	9
10	0.0	0.0	0.0	0.0	0.0	32.2	60.8	67.1	72.3	76.7	80.3	83.4	10
11	0.0	0.0	0.0	0.0	0.0	17.4	52.2	59.9	66.3	71.6	76.0	79.8	11
12	0.0	0.0	0.0	0.0	0.0	0.0	42.1	51.5	59.2	65.6	71.0	75.5	12
13	0.0	0.0	0.0	0.0	0.0	0.0	30.3	41.5	50.8	58.6	65.1	70.5	13
14	0.0	0.0	0.0	0.0	0.0	0.0	16.4	29.8	41.0	50.3	58.1	64.6	14
15	0.0	0.0	0.0	0.0	0.0	0.0	0.0	16.1	29.5	40.6	49.9	57.7	15
16	0.0	0.0	0.0	0.0	0.0	0.0	0.0	0.0	15.9	29.2	40.3	49.5	16
17	0.0	0.0	0.0	0.0	0.0	0.0	0.0	0.0	0.0	15.8	28.9	40.0	17
18	0.0	0.0	0.0	0.0	0.0	0.0	0.0	0.0	0.0	0.0	15.6	28.7	18
19	0.0	0.0	0.0	0.0	0.0	0.0	0.0	0.0	0.0	0.0	0.0	15.5	19

16.25

AGE OF LOAN	21.0	22.0	23.0	24.0	25.0	26.0	27.0	28.0	29.0	30.0	35.0	40.0	AGE OF LOAN
1	99.4	99.5	99.6	99.6	99.7	99.7	99.8	99.8	99.8	99.9	99.9	100.0	1
2	98.7	98.9	99.0	99.2	99.3	99.4	99.5	99.6	99.6	99.7	99.9	99.9	2
3	97.8	98.2	98.4	98.7	98.9	99.0	99.2	99.3	99.4	99.5	99.8	99.9	3
4	96.8	97.3	97.7	98.1	98.4	98.6	98.8	99.0	99.2	99.3	99.7	99.9	4
5	95.7	96.3	96.9	97.4	97.8	98.1	98.4	98.6	98.8	99.0	99.6	99.8	5
6	94.3	95.2	95.9	96.5	97.1	97.5	97.9	98.2	98.5	98.7	99.4	99.7	6
7	92.7	93.8	94.8	95.6	96.2	96.8	97.3	97.7	98.0	98.3	99.3	99.7	7
8	90.8	92.2	93.4	94.4	95.3	96.0	96.6	97.1	97.5	97.9	99.1	99.6	8
9	88.6	90.3	91.8	93.1	94.1	95.0	95.8	96.4	96.9	97.4	98.8	99.5	9
10	86.0	88.1	89.9	91.5	92.8	93.9	94.8	95.6	96.2	96.8	98.6	99.4	10
11	82.9	85.5	87.7	89.6	91.2	92.5	93.6	94.6	95.4	96.1	98.3	99.2	11
12	79.3	82.5	85.1	87.4	89.3	90.9	92.3	93.5	94.4	95.3	97.9	99.1	12
13	75.0	78.9	82.1	84.8	87.1	89.1	90.7	92.1	93.3	94.3	97.5	98.9	13
14	70.1	74.6	78.5	81.8	84.6	86.9	88.9	90.5	92.0	93.2	97.0	98.7	14
15	64.2	69.7	74.3	78.2	81.5	84.3	86.7	88.7	90.4	91.8	96.4	98.4	15
16	57.3	63.9	69.4	74.0	78.0	81.3	84.1	86.5	88.6	90.3	95.7	98.1	16
17	49.2	57.0	63.6	69.1	73.8	77.8	81.1	84.0	86.4	88.4	94.9	97.7	17
18	39.7	49.0	56.8	63.3	68.9	73.6	77.6	81.0	83.8	86.3	93.9	97.3	18
19	28.5	39.5	48.8	56.6	62.1	68.7	73.4	77.4	80.8	83.7	92.8	96.8	19
20	15.4	28.4	39.3	48.6	56.4	63.0	68.6	73.3	77.3	80.7	91.4	96.2	20
21	0.0	15.3	28.3	39.2	48.4	56.2	62.8	68.4	73.2	77.2	89.9	95.5	21
22	0.0	0.0	15.3	28.2	39.1	48.3	56.1	62.7	68.3	73.1	88.0	94.7	22
23	0.0	0.0	0.0	15.2	28.1	39.0	48.2	56.0	62.6	68.2	85.9	93.7	23
24	0.0	0.0	0.0	0.0	15.2	28.0	38.9	48.1	55.9	62.5	83.4	92.6	24
25	0.0	0.0	0.0	0.0	0.0	15.1	27.9	38.8	48.0	55.8	80.4	91.3	25
26	0.0	0.0	0.0	0.0	0.0	0.0	15.1	27.9	38.7	47.9	76.9	89.7	26
27	0.0	0.0	0.0	0.0	0.0	0.0	0.0	15.1	27.8	38.7	72.8	87.9	27
28	0.0	0.0	0.0	0.0	0.0	0.0	0.0	0.0	15.0	27.8	67.9	85.7	28
29	0.0	0.0	0.0	0.0	0.0	0.0	0.0	0.0	0.0	15.0	62.2	83.2	29
30	0.0	0.0	0.0	0.0	0.0	0.0	0.0	0.0	0.0	0.0	55.6	80.2	30
31	0.0	0.0	0.0	0.0	0.0	0.0	0.0	0.0	0.0	0.0	47.7	76.7	31
32	0.0	0.0	0.0	0.0	0.0	0.0	0.0	0.0	0.0	0.0	38.5	72.6	32
33	0.0	0.0	0.0	0.0	0.0	0.0	0.0	0.0	0.0	0.0	27.7	67.8	33
34	0.0	0.0	0.0	0.0	0.0	0.0	0.0	0.0	0.0	0.0	14.9	62.1	34
35	0.0	0.0	0.0	0.0	0.0	0.0	0.0	0.0	0.0	0.0	0.0	55.5	35
36	0.0	0.0	0.0	0.0	0.0	0.0	0.0	0.0	0.0	0.0	0.0	47.6	36
37	0.0	0.0	0.0	0.0	0.0	0.0	0.0	0.0	0.0	0.0	0.0	38.4	37
38	0.0	0.0	0.0	0.0	0.0	0.0	0.0	0.0	0.0	0.0	0.0	27.6	38
39	0.0	0.0	0.0	0.0	0.0	0.0	0.0	0.0	0.0	0.0	0.0	14.9	39

EXAMPLES *ON PAGES A-382 TO A-397*

AGE OF LOAN	2.0	3.0	5.0	8.0	10.0	12.0	15.0	16.0	17.0	18.0	19.0	20.0	AGE OF LOAN
1	54.1	72.0	86.0	93.4	95.7	97.1	98.3	98.6	98.8	99.0	99.2	99.3	1
2	0.0	38.9	69.4	85.7	90.7	93.7	96.4	97.0	97.5	97.9	98.2	98.5	2
3	0.0	0.0	50.0	76.6	84.7	89.7	94.1	95.0	95.8	96.5	97.0	97.5	3
4	0.0	0.0	27.0	65.8	77.7	84.9	91.3	92.7	93.9	94.9	95.7	96.4	4
5	0.0	0.0	0.0	53.2	69.4	79.3	88.1	90.1	91.7	93.0	94.1	95.0	5
6	0.0	0.0	0.0	38.3	59.7	72.8	84.3	86.9	89.0	90.8	92.2	93.4	6
7	0.0	0.0	0.0	20.7	48.2	65.0	79.9	83.2	85.9	88.1	90.0	91.6	7
8	0.0	0.0	0.0	0.0	34.7	55.9	74.6	78.8	82.2	85.0	87.4	89.4	8
9	0.0	0.0	0.0	0.0	18.7	45.1	68.4	73.6	77.8	81.4	84.3	86.8	9
10	0.0	0.0	0.0	0.0	0.0	32.5	61.2	67.5	72.7	77.1	80.7	83.7	10
11	0.0	0.0	0.0	0.0	0.0	17.6	52.6	60.3	66.7	72.0	76.4	80.1	11
12	0.0	0.0	0.0	0.0	0.0	0.0	42.5	51.8	59.6	66.0	71.4	75.9	12
13	0.0	0.0	0.0	0.0	0.0	0.0	30.5	41.9	51.2	59.0	65.5	70.9	13
14	0.0	0.0	0.0	0.0	0.0	0.0	16.5	30.1	41.4	50.7	58.5	65.0	14
15	0.0	0.0	0.0	0.0	0.0	0.0	0.0	16.3	29.8	41.0	50.3	58.1	15
16	0.0	0.0	0.0	0.0	0.0	0.0	0.0	0.0	16.1	29.5	40.6	50.0	16
17	0.0	0.0	0.0	0.0	0.0	0.0	0.0	0.0	0.0	15.9	29.2	40.3	17
18	0.0	0.0	0.0	0.0	0.0	0.0	0.0	0.0	0.0	0.0	15.8	29.0	18
19	0.0	0.0	0.0	0.0	0.0	0.0	0.0	0.0	0.0	0.0	0.0	15.7	19

16.50

AGE OF LOAN	21.0	22.0	23.0	24.0	25.0	26.0	27.0	28.0	29.0	30.0	35.0	40.0	AGE OF LOAN
1	99.4	99.5	99.6	99.6	99.7	99.7	99.8	99.8	99.8	99.9	99.9	100.0	1
2	98.7	98.9	99.1	99.2	99.3	99.4	99.5	99.6	99.7	99.7	99.9	99.9	2
3	97.9	98.2	98.5	98.7	98.9	99.1	99.2	99.3	99.4	99.5	99.8	99.9	3
4	96.9	97.4	97.8	98.1	98.4	98.7	98.9	99.0	99.2	99.3	99.7	99.9	4
5	95.8	96.5	97.0	97.5	97.9	98.2	98.5	98.7	98.9	99.1	99.6	99.8	5
6	94.5	95.3	96.0	96.7	97.2	97.6	98.0	98.3	98.5	98.8	99.5	99.8	6
7	92.9	94.0	94.9	95.7	96.4	96.9	97.4	97.8	98.1	98.4	99.3	99.7	7
8	91.0	92.4	93.6	94.6	95.4	96.1	96.7	97.2	97.6	98.0	99.1	99.6	8
9	88.8	90.6	92.0	93.3	94.3	95.2	95.9	96.5	97.1	97.5	98.9	99.5	9
10	86.3	88.4	90.2	91.7	93.0	94.1	95.0	95.7	96.4	96.9	98.7	99.4	10
11	83.2	85.8	88.0	89.9	91.4	92.7	93.9	94.8	95.6	96.3	98.4	99.3	11
12	79.7	82.8	85.5	87.7	89.6	91.2	92.5	93.7	94.6	95.5	98.0	99.1	12
13	75.5	79.3	82.5	85.2	87.5	89.4	91.0	92.4	93.5	94.5	97.6	98.9	13
14	70.5	75.1	78.9	82.2	84.9	87.2	89.2	90.8	92.2	93.4	97.1	98.7	14
15	64.7	70.1	74.8	78.7	81.9	84.7	87.0	89.0	90.7	92.1	96.5	98.5	15
16	57.8	64.3	69.8	74.5	78.4	81.7	84.5	86.9	88.9	90.6	95.9	98.2	16
17	49.7	57.5	64.1	69.6	74.3	78.2	81.5	84.4	86.8	88.8	95.1	97.8	17
18	40.1	49.4	57.2	63.8	69.4	74.1	78.0	81.4	84.2	86.6	94.1	97.4	18
19	28.9	39.9	49.2	57.0	63.6	69.2	73.9	77.9	81.3	84.1	93.0	96.9	19
20	15.6	28.7	39.7	49.0	56.9	63.5	69.1	73.8	77.8	81.2	91.7	96.4	20
21	0.0	15.5	28.6	39.6	48.9	56.7	63.3	68.9	73.7	77.7	90.2	95.7	21
22	0.0	0.0	15.5	28.5	39.5	48.8	56.6	63.2	68.8	73.6	88.4	94.9	22
23	0.0	0.0	0.0	15.4	28.4	39.4	48.7	56.5	63.1	68.7	86.3	94.0	23
24	0.0	0.0	0.0	0.0	15.3	28.3	39.3	48.6	56.4	63.0	83.9	92.9	24
25	0.0	0.0	0.0	0.0	0.0	15.3	28.3	39.2	48.5	56.3	80.8	91.6	25
26	0.0	0.0	0.0	0.0	0.0	0.0	15.3	28.2	39.2	48.4	77.4	90.0	26
27	0.0	0.0	0.0	0.0	0.0	0.0	0.0	15.2	28.2	39.1	73.3	88.2	27
28	0.0	0.0	0.0	0.0	0.0	0.0	0.0	0.0	15.2	28.1	68.5	86.1	28
29	0.0	0.0	0.0	0.0	0.0	0.0	0.0	0.0	0.0	15.2	62.8	83.6	29
30	0.0	0.0	0.0	0.0	0.0	0.0	0.0	0.0	0.0	0.0	56.1	80.7	30
31	0.0	0.0	0.0	0.0	0.0	0.0	0.0	0.0	0.0	0.0	48.2	77.2	31
32	0.0	0.0	0.0	0.0	0.0	0.0	0.0	0.0	0.0	0.0	38.9	73.1	32
33	0.0	0.0	0.0	0.0	0.0	0.0	0.0	0.0	0.0	0.0	28.0	68.3	33
34	0.0	0.0	0.0	0.0	0.0	0.0	0.0	0.0	0.0	0.0	15.1	62.7	34
35	0.0	0.0	0.0	0.0	0.0	0.0	0.0	0.0	0.0	0.0	0.0	56.0	35
36	0.0	0.0	0.0	0.0	0.0	0.0	0.0	0.0	0.0	0.0	0.0	48.1	36
37	0.0	0.0	0.0	0.0	0.0	0.0	0.0	0.0	0.0	0.0	0.0	38.9	37
38	0.0	0.0	0.0	0.0	0.0	0.0	0.0	0.0	0.0	0.0	0.0	28.0	38
39	0.0	0.0	0.0	0.0	0.0	0.0	0.0	0.0	0.0	0.0	0.0	15.1	39

EXAMPLES *ON PAGES A-382 TO A-397*

REMAINING BALANCE
IN PERCENT OF ORIGINAL LOAN AMOUNT

AGE OF LOAN	ORIGINAL TERM IN YEARS												AGE OF LOAN
	2.0	3.0	5.0	8.0	10.0	12.0	15.0	16.0	17.0	18.0	19.0	20.0	
1	54.1	72.0	86.0	93.5	95.8	97.2	98.4	98.6	98.9	99.0	99.2	99.3	1
2	0.0	39.0	69.6	85.8	90.8	93.8	96.5	97.0	97.5	97.9	98.3	98.5	2
3	0.0	0.0	50.1	76.8	84.9	89.8	94.2	95.1	95.9	96.6	97.1	97.6	3
4	0.0	0.0	27.1	66.0	77.9	85.1	91.5	92.9	94.1	95.0	95.8	96.5	4
5	0.0	0.0	0.0	53.4	69.7	79.6	88.3	90.3	91.8	93.2	94.3	95.2	5
6	0.0	0.0	0.0	38.5	59.9	73.1	84.6	87.1	89.2	91.0	92.4	93.6	6
7	0.0	0.0	0.0	20.8	48.5	65.3	80.2	83.4	86.1	88.4	90.2	91.8	7
8	0.0	0.0	0.0	0.0	34.9	56.2	75.0	79.1	82.5	85.3	87.7	89.6	8
9	0.0	0.0	0.0	0.0	18.9	45.5	68.8	74.0	78.2	81.7	84.6	87.1	9
10	0.0	0.0	0.0	0.0	0.0	32.7	61.5	67.9	73.1	77.4	81.1	84.1	10
11	0.0	0.0	0.0	0.0	0.0	17.7	53.0	60.7	67.1	72.4	76.8	80.5	11
12	0.0	0.0	0.0	0.0	0.0	0.0	42.8	52.2	60.0	66.5	71.8	76.3	12
13	0.0	0.0	0.0	0.0	0.0	0.0	30.8	42.2	51.6	59.4	65.9	71.3	13
14	0.0	0.0	0.0	0.0	0.0	0.0	16.7	30.4	41.8	51.1	59.0	65.5	14
15	0.0	0.0	0.0	0.0	0.0	0.0	0.0	16.5	30.1	41.4	50.7	58.6	15
16	0.0	0.0	0.0	0.0	0.0	0.0	0.0	0.0	16.3	29.8	41.0	50.4	16
17	0.0	0.0	0.0	0.0	0.0	0.0	0.0	0.0	0.0	16.1	29.5	40.7	17
18	0.0	0.0	0.0	0.0	0.0	0.0	0.0	0.0	0.0	0.0	16.0	29.3	18
19	0.0	0.0	0.0	0.0	0.0	0.0	0.0	0.0	0.0	0.0	0.0	15.9	19

16.75

AGE OF LOAN	ORIGINAL TERM IN YEARS												AGE OF LOAN
	21.0	22.0	23.0	24.0	25.0	26.0	27.0	28.0	29.0	30.0	35.0	40.0	
1	99.4	99.5	99.6	99.7	99.7	99.8	99.8	99.8	99.9	99.9	99.9	100.0	1
2	98.8	99.0	99.1	99.3	99.4	99.5	99.6	99.6	99.7	99.7	99.9	99.9	2
3	98.0	98.3	98.6	98.8	99.0	99.1	99.3	99.4	99.5	99.6	99.8	99.9	3
4	97.0	97.5	97.9	98.2	98.5	98.7	98.9	99.1	99.2	99.4	99.7	99.9	4
5	95.9	96.6	97.1	97.6	97.9	98.3	98.5	98.8	98.9	99.1	99.6	99.8	5
6	94.6	95.5	96.2	96.8	97.3	97.7	98.1	98.4	98.6	98.8	99.5	99.8	6
7	93.1	94.2	95.1	95.9	96.5	97.0	97.5	97.9	98.2	98.5	99.3	99.7	7
8	91.3	92.6	93.8	94.8	95.6	96.3	96.8	97.3	97.7	98.1	99.2	99.6	8
9	89.1	90.8	92.3	93.5	94.5	95.3	96.1	96.7	97.2	97.6	99.0	99.6	9
10	86.6	88.7	90.5	92.0	93.2	94.3	95.2	95.9	96.5	97.1	98.7	99.4	10
11	83.6	86.2	88.3	90.2	91.7	93.0	94.1	95.0	95.8	96.4	98.4	99.3	11
12	80.1	83.2	85.8	88.0	89.9	91.5	92.8	93.9	94.8	95.6	98.1	99.2	12
13	75.9	79.7	82.9	85.5	87.8	89.7	91.3	92.6	93.8	94.7	97.7	99.0	13
14	70.9	75.5	79.3	82.6	85.3	87.6	89.5	91.1	92.5	93.7	97.2	98.8	14
15	65.1	70.6	75.2	79.1	82.3	85.1	87.4	89.3	91.0	92.4	96.7	98.6	15
16	58.2	64.8	70.3	75.0	78.9	82.1	84.9	87.2	89.2	90.9	96.0	98.3	16
17	50.1	58.0	64.5	70.1	74.7	78.7	82.0	84.8	87.1	89.1	95.3	97.9	17
18	40.5	49.9	57.7	64.3	69.9	74.6	78.5	81.8	84.6	87.0	94.4	97.6	18
19	29.2	40.3	49.7	57.5	64.1	69.7	74.4	78.4	81.7	84.5	93.3	97.1	19
20	15.8	29.0	40.2	49.5	57.4	64.0	69.6	74.3	78.2	81.6	92.0	96.5	20
21	0.0	15.7	28.9	40.0	49.4	57.2	63.9	69.4	74.2	78.2	90.5	95.9	21
22	0.0	0.0	15.7	28.8	39.9	49.2	57.1	63.7	69.3	74.1	88.8	95.1	22
23	0.0	0.0	0.0	15.6	28.7	39.8	49.1	57.0	63.6	69.3	86.7	94.2	23
24	0.0	0.0	0.0	0.0	15.6	28.7	39.7	49.1	56.9	63.6	84.2	93.1	24
25	0.0	0.0	0.0	0.0	0.0	15.5	28.6	39.7	49.0	56.9	81.3	91.9	25
26	0.0	0.0	0.0	0.0	0.0	0.0	15.5	28.6	39.6	48.9	77.9	90.4	26
27	0.0	0.0	0.0	0.0	0.0	0.0	0.0	15.5	28.5	39.6	73.8	88.6	27
28	0.0	0.0	0.0	0.0	0.0	0.0	0.0	0.0	15.4	28.5	69.0	86.5	28
29	0.0	0.0	0.0	0.0	0.0	0.0	0.0	0.0	0.0	15.4	63.3	84.1	29
30	0.0	0.0	0.0	0.0	0.0	0.0	0.0	0.0	0.0	0.0	56.6	81.2	30
31	0.0	0.0	0.0	0.0	0.0	0.0	0.0	0.0	0.0	0.0	48.7	77.7	31
32	0.0	0.0	0.0	0.0	0.0	0.0	0.0	0.0	0.0	0.0	39.4	73.7	32
33	0.0	0.0	0.0	0.0	0.0	0.0	0.0	0.0	0.0	0.0	28.4	68.9	33
34	0.0	0.0	0.0	0.0	0.0	0.0	0.0	0.0	0.0	0.0	15.4	63.2	34
35	0.0	0.0	0.0	0.0	0.0	0.0	0.0	0.0	0.0	0.0	0.0	56.5	35
36	0.0	0.0	0.0	0.0	0.0	0.0	0.0	0.0	0.0	0.0	0.0	48.7	36
37	0.0	0.0	0.0	0.0	0.0	0.0	0.0	0.0	0.0	0.0	0.0	39.3	37
38	0.0	0.0	0.0	0.0	0.0	0.0	0.0	0.0	0.0	0.0	0.0	28.3	38
39	0.0	0.0	0.0	0.0	0.0	0.0	0.0	0.0	0.0	0.0	0.0	15.3	39

EXAMPLES *ON PAGES A-382 TO A-397*

AGE OF LOAN	ORIGINAL TERM IN YEARS												AGE OF LOAN
	2.0	3.0	5.0	8.0	10.0	12.0	15.0	16.0	17.0	18.0	19.0	20.0	
1	54.2	72.1	86.1	93.6	95.8	97.2	98.4	98.7	98.9	99.1	99.2	99.3	1
2	0.0	39.1	69.7	86.0	90.9	93.9	96.5	97.1	97.6	98.0	98.3	98.6	2
3	0.0	0.0	50.3	76.9	85.0	90.0	94.3	95.3	96.0	96.7	97.2	97.7	3
4	0.0	0.0	27.2	66.3	78.1	85.3	91.7	93.1	94.2	95.1	95.9	96.6	4
5	0.0	0.0	0.0	53.6	69.9	79.9	88.5	90.5	92.0	93.3	94.4	95.3	5
6	0.0	0.0	0.0	38.7	60.2	73.4	84.9	87.4	89.5	91.2	92.6	93.8	6
7	0.0	0.0	0.0	21.0	48.7	65.7	80.5	83.7	86.4	88.6	90.5	92.0	7
8	0.0	0.0	0.0	0.0	35.1	56.6	75.3	79.4	82.8	85.6	87.9	89.9	8
9	0.0	0.0	0.0	0.0	19.0	45.8	69.2	74.3	78.5	82.0	84.9	87.4	9
10	0.0	0.0	0.0	0.0	0.0	33.0	61.9	68.3	73.5	77.8	81.4	84.4	10
11	0.0	0.0	0.0	0.0	0.0	17.9	53.3	61.1	67.5	72.8	77.2	80.9	11
12	0.0	0.0	0.0	0.0	0.0	0.0	43.2	52.6	60.4	66.9	72.2	76.7	12
13	0.0	0.0	0.0	0.0	0.0	0.0	31.1	42.6	52.0	59.9	66.4	71.8	13
14	0.0	0.0	0.0	0.0	0.0	0.0	16.9	30.7	42.1	51.6	59.4	65.9	14
15	0.0	0.0	0.0	0.0	0.0	0.0	0.0	16.6	30.4	41.7	51.2	59.0	15
16	0.0	0.0	0.0	0.0	0.0	0.0	0.0	0.0	16.5	30.1	41.4	50.8	16
17	0.0	0.0	0.0	0.0	0.0	0.0	0.0	0.0	0.0	16.3	29.8	41.1	17
18	0.0	0.0	0.0	0.0	0.0	0.0	0.0	0.0	0.0	0.0	16.2	29.7	18
19	0.0	0.0	0.0	0.0	0.0	0.0	0.0	0.0	0.0	0.0	0.0	16.1	19

17.00

AGE OF LOAN	ORIGINAL TERM IN YEARS												AGE OF LOAN
	21.0	22.0	23.0	24.0	25.0	26.0	27.0	28.0	29.0	30.0	35.0	40.0	
1	99.5	99.5	99.6	99.7	99.7	99.8	99.8	99.8	99.9	99.9	99.9	100.0	1
2	98.8	99.0	99.2	99.3	99.4	99.5	99.6	99.6	99.7	99.7	99.9	100.0	2
3	98.0	98.4	98.6	98.8	99.0	99.2	99.3	99.4	99.5	99.6	99.8	99.9	3
4	97.1	97.6	98.0	98.3	98.6	98.8	99.0	99.1	99.3	99.4	99.7	99.9	4
5	96.1	96.7	97.2	97.7	98.0	98.3	98.6	98.8	99.0	99.2	99.6	99.8	5
6	94.8	95.6	96.3	96.9	97.4	97.8	98.1	98.4	98.7	98.9	99.5	99.8	6
7	93.3	94.4	95.2	96.0	96.6	97.2	97.6	98.0	98.3	98.6	99.4	99.7	7
8	91.5	92.9	94.0	94.9	95.7	96.4	97.0	97.4	97.8	98.2	99.2	99.7	8
9	89.4	91.1	92.5	93.7	94.7	95.5	96.2	96.8	97.3	97.7	99.0	99.6	9
10	86.9	89.0	90.7	92.2	93.4	94.5	95.3	96.1	96.7	97.2	98.8	99.5	10
11	83.9	86.5	88.6	90.4	91.9	93.2	94.3	95.2	95.9	96.6	98.5	99.4	11
12	80.4	83.5	86.2	88.3	90.2	91.7	93.0	94.1	95.0	95.8	98.2	99.2	12
13	76.3	80.1	83.2	85.9	88.1	90.0	91.5	92.9	94.0	94.9	97.8	99.1	13
14	71.4	75.9	79.8	83.0	85.6	87.9	89.8	91.4	92.7	93.9	97.4	98.9	14
15	65.6	71.0	75.6	79.5	82.7	85.4	87.7	89.6	91.3	92.6	96.8	98.6	15
16	58.7	65.3	70.8	75.4	79.3	82.5	85.3	87.6	89.5	91.2	96.2	98.4	16
17	50.5	58.4	65.0	70.5	75.2	79.1	82.4	85.1	87.5	89.4	95.5	98.1	17
18	40.9	50.3	58.2	64.8	70.4	75.0	78.9	82.2	85.0	87.4	94.6	97.7	18
19	29.5	40.7	50.1	58.0	64.6	70.2	74.9	78.8	82.1	84.9	93.5	97.2	19
20	16.0	29.4	40.6	50.0	57.8	64.5	70.1	74.7	78.7	82.0	92.3	96.7	20
21	0.0	15.9	29.2	40.4	49.8	57.7	64.3	69.9	74.6	78.6	90.8	96.1	21
22	0.0	0.0	15.8	29.1	40.3	49.7	57.6	64.2	69.8	74.6	89.1	95.3	22
23	0.0	0.0	0.0	15.8	29.1	40.2	49.6	57.5	64.2	69.8	87.0	94.4	23
24	0.0	0.0	0.0	0.0	15.7	29.0	40.1	49.5	57.4	64.1	84.6	93.4	24
25	0.0	0.0	0.0	0.0	0.0	15.7	28.9	40.1	49.5	57.4	81.7	92.2	25
26	0.0	0.0	0.0	0.0	0.0	0.0	15.7	28.9	40.0	49.4	78.3	90.7	26
27	0.0	0.0	0.0	0.0	0.0	0.0	0.0	15.7	28.9	40.0	74.3	89.0	27
28	0.0	0.0	0.0	0.0	0.0	0.0	0.0	0.0	15.6	28.8	69.5	86.9	28
29	0.0	0.0	0.0	0.0	0.0	0.0	0.0	0.0	0.0	15.6	63.8	84.5	29
30	0.0	0.0	0.0	0.0	0.0	0.0	0.0	0.0	0.0	0.0	57.1	81.6	30
31	0.0	0.0	0.0	0.0	0.0	0.0	0.0	0.0	0.0	0.0	49.2	78.2	31
32	0.0	0.0	0.0	0.0	0.0	0.0	0.0	0.0	0.0	0.0	39.8	74.2	32
33	0.0	0.0	0.0	0.0	0.0	0.0	0.0	0.0	0.0	0.0	28.7	69.4	33
34	0.0	0.0	0.0	0.0	0.0	0.0	0.0	0.0	0.0	0.0	15.6	63.8	34
35	0.0	0.0	0.0	0.0	0.0	0.0	0.0	0.0	0.0	0.0	0.0	57.1	35
36	0.0	0.0	0.0	0.0	0.0	0.0	0.0	0.0	0.0	0.0	0.0	49.1	36
37	0.0	0.0	0.0	0.0	0.0	0.0	0.0	0.0	0.0	0.0	0.0	39.8	37
38	0.0	0.0	0.0	0.0	0.0	0.0	0.0	0.0	0.0	0.0	0.0	28.7	38
39	0.0	0.0	0.0	0.0	0.0	0.0	0.0	0.0	0.0	0.0	0.0	15.5	39

EXAMPLES *ON PAGES A-382 TO A-397*

AGE OF LOAN	ORIGINAL TERM IN YEARS												AGE OF LOAN
	2.0	3.0	5.0	8.0	10.0	12.0	15.0	16.0	17.0	18.0	19.0	20.0	
1	54.3	72.2	86.2	93.6	95.9	97.3	98.5	98.7	98.9	99.1	99.2	99.4	1
2	0.0	39.2	69.8	86.1	91.0	94.0	96.6	97.2	97.7	98.0	98.4	98.6	2
3	0.0	0.0	50.4	77.1	85.2	90.1	94.4	95.4	96.1	96.8	97.3	97.7	3
4	0.0	0.0	27.4	66.5	78.3	85.5	91.8	93.2	94.3	95.3	96.0	96.7	4
5	0.0	0.0	0.0	53.9	70.2	80.1	88.8	90.7	92.2	93.5	94.6	95.4	5
6	0.0	0.0	0.0	38.9	60.5	73.6	85.1	87.6	89.7	91.4	92.8	94.0	6
7	0.0	0.0	0.0	21.1	49.0	66.0	80.8	84.0	86.7	88.9	90.7	92.2	7
8	0.0	0.0	0.0	0.0	35.4	56.9	75.6	79.7	83.1	85.9	88.2	90.1	8
9	0.0	0.0	0.0	0.0	19.2	46.1	69.5	74.7	78.9	82.4	85.3	87.7	9
10	0.0	0.0	0.0	0.0	0.0	33.3	62.3	68.6	73.9	78.2	81.7	84.7	10
11	0.0	0.0	0.0	0.0	0.0	18.0	53.7	61.5	67.9	73.2	77.6	81.2	11
12	0.0	0.0	0.0	0.0	0.0	0.0	43.5	53.0	60.8	67.3	72.7	77.1	12
13	0.0	0.0	0.0	0.0	0.0	0.0	31.4	42.9	52.4	60.3	66.8	72.2	13
14	0.0	0.0	0.0	0.0	0.0	0.0	17.0	31.0	42.5	52.0	59.8	66.4	14
15	0.0	0.0	0.0	0.0	0.0	0.0	0.0	16.8	30.7	42.1	51.6	59.5	15
16	0.0	0.0	0.0	0.0	0.0	0.0	0.0	0.0	16.6	30.4	41.8	51.3	16
17	0.0	0.0	0.0	0.0	0.0	0.0	0.0	0.0	0.0	16.5	30.2	41.5	17
18	0.0	0.0	0.0	0.0	0.0	0.0	0.0	0.0	0.0	0.0	16.4	30.0	18
19	0.0	0.0	0.0	0.0	0.0	0.0	0.0	0.0	0.0	0.0	0.0	16.3	19

17.25

AGE OF LOAN	ORIGINAL TERM IN YEARS												AGE OF LOAN
	21.0	22.0	23.0	24.0	25.0	26.0	27.0	28.0	29.0	30.0	35.0	40.0	
1	99.5	99.6	99.6	99.7	99.7	99.8	99.8	99.8	99.9	99.9	100.0	100.0	1
2	98.8	99.0	99.2	99.3	99.4	99.5	99.6	99.7	99.7	99.8	99.9	100.0	2
3	98.1	98.4	98.7	98.9	99.1	99.2	99.3	99.4	99.5	99.6	99.8	99.9	3
4	97.2	97.7	98.0	98.4	98.6	98.8	99.0	99.2	99.3	99.4	99.8	99.9	4
5	96.2	96.8	97.3	97.7	98.1	98.4	98.7	98.9	99.0	99.2	99.7	99.9	5
6	94.9	95.8	96.4	97.0	97.5	97.9	98.2	98.5	98.7	98.9	99.6	99.8	6
7	93.5	94.5	95.4	96.1	96.8	97.3	97.7	98.1	98.4	98.6	99.4	99.8	7
8	91.7	93.1	94.2	95.1	95.9	96.5	97.1	97.6	97.9	98.3	99.3	99.7	8
9	89.7	91.3	92.7	93.9	94.9	95.7	96.4	96.9	97.4	97.8	99.1	99.6	9
10	87.2	89.3	91.0	92.4	93.6	94.6	95.5	96.2	96.8	97.3	98.9	99.5	10
11	84.3	86.8	88.9	90.7	92.2	93.4	94.5	95.3	96.1	96.7	98.6	99.4	11
12	80.8	83.9	86.5	88.6	90.5	92.0	93.3	94.3	95.2	96.0	98.3	99.3	12
13	76.7	80.5	83.6	86.2	88.4	90.3	91.8	93.1	94.2	95.1	97.9	99.1	13
14	71.8	76.4	80.2	83.3	86.0	88.2	90.1	91.7	93.0	94.1	97.5	98.9	14
15	66.0	71.5	76.1	79.9	83.1	85.8	88.1	90.0	91.5	92.9	97.0	98.7	15
16	59.1	65.7	71.2	75.8	79.7	82.9	85.6	87.9	89.8	91.4	96.4	98.5	16
17	51.0	58.9	65.5	71.0	75.6	79.5	82.8	85.5	87.8	89.7	95.7	98.2	17
18	41.3	50.8	58.7	65.3	70.8	75.5	79.4	82.6	85.4	87.7	94.8	97.8	18
19	29.8	41.1	50.6	58.5	65.1	70.7	75.3	79.2	82.5	85.3	93.8	97.4	19
20	16.2	29.7	41.0	50.4	58.3	65.0	70.5	75.2	79.1	82.4	92.6	96.8	20
21	0.0	16.1	29.6	40.8	50.3	58.2	64.8	70.4	75.1	79.1	91.1	96.2	21
22	0.0	0.0	16.0	29.5	40.7	50.2	58.1	64.7	70.3	75.0	89.4	95.5	22
23	0.0	0.0	0.0	16.0	29.4	40.6	50.1	58.0	64.7	70.3	87.4	94.7	23
24	0.0	0.0	0.0	0.0	16.0	29.3	40.6	50.0	57.9	64.6	85.0	93.6	24
25	0.0	0.0	0.0	0.0	0.0	15.9	29.3	40.5	49.9	57.9	82.2	92.4	25
26	0.0	0.0	0.0	0.0	0.0	0.0	15.9	29.2	40.5	49.9	78.8	91.0	26
27	0.0	0.0	0.0	0.0	0.0	0.0	0.0	15.9	29.2	40.4	74.8	89.3	27
28	0.0	0.0	0.0	0.0	0.0	0.0	0.0	0.0	15.8	29.2	70.0	87.3	28
29	0.0	0.0	0.0	0.0	0.0	0.0	0.0	0.0	0.0	15.8	64.4	84.9	29
30	0.0	0.0	0.0	0.0	0.0	0.0	0.0	0.0	0.0	0.0	57.7	82.1	30
31	0.0	0.0	0.0	0.0	0.0	0.0	0.0	0.0	0.0	0.0	49.7	78.7	31
32	0.0	0.0	0.0	0.0	0.0	0.0	0.0	0.0	0.0	0.0	40.3	74.7	32
33	0.0	0.0	0.0	0.0	0.0	0.0	0.0	0.0	0.0	0.0	29.1	69.9	33
34	0.0	0.0	0.0	0.0	0.0	0.0	0.0	0.0	0.0	0.0	15.8	64.3	34
35	0.0	0.0	0.0	0.0	0.0	0.0	0.0	0.0	0.0	0.0	0.0	57.6	35
36	0.0	0.0	0.0	0.0	0.0	0.0	0.0	0.0	0.0	0.0	0.0	49.7	36
37	0.0	0.0	0.0	0.0	0.0	0.0	0.0	0.0	0.0	0.0	0.0	40.2	37
38	0.0	0.0	0.0	0.0	0.0	0.0	0.0	0.0	0.0	0.0	0.0	29.0	38
39	0.0	0.0	0.0	0.0	0.0	0.0	0.0	0.0	0.0	0.0	0.0	15.8	39

EXAMPLES *ON PAGES A-382 TO A-397*

AGE OF LOAN	2.0	3.0	5.0	8.0	10.0	12.0	15.0	16.0	17.0	18.0	19.0	20.0	AGE OF LOAN
1	54.3	72.3	86.3	93.7	95.9	97.3	98.5	98.7	99.0	99.1	99.3	99.4	1
2	0.0	39.3	70.0	86.2	91.1	94.1	96.7	97.3	97.7	98.1	98.4	98.7	2
3	0.0	0.0	50.6	77.3	85.4	90.3	94.5	95.5	96.2	96.9	97.4	97.8	3
4	0.0	0.0	27.5	66.7	78.6	85.7	92.0	93.4	94.5	95.4	96.2	96.8	4
5	0.0	0.0	0.0	54.1	70.4	80.4	89.0	90.8	92.4	93.7	94.7	95.6	5
6	0.0	0.0	0.0	39.1	60.8	73.9	85.4	87.9	89.9	91.6	93.0	94.1	6
7	0.0	0.0	0.0	21.2	49.3	66.3	81.1	84.3	86.9	89.1	90.9	92.4	7
8	0.0	0.0	0.0	0.0	35.6	57.2	76.0	80.1	83.4	86.2	88.5	90.4	8
9	0.0	0.0	0.0	0.0	19.3	46.4	69.9	75.0	79.2	82.7	85.6	87.9	9
10	0.0	0.0	0.0	0.0	0.0	33.5	62.7	69.0	74.2	78.5	82.1	85.0	10
11	0.0	0.0	0.0	0.0	0.0	18.2	54.1	61.9	68.3	73.6	78.0	81.6	11
12	0.0	0.0	0.0	0.0	0.0	0.0	43.9	53.4	61.2	67.7	73.1	77.5	12
13	0.0	0.0	0.0	0.0	0.0	0.0	31.7	43.3	52.8	60.7	67.2	72.6	13
14	0.0	0.0	0.0	0.0	0.0	0.0	17.2	31.3	42.8	52.4	60.3	66.8	14
15	0.0	0.0	0.0	0.0	0.0	0.0	0.0	17.0	31.0	42.5	52.0	59.9	15
16	0.0	0.0	0.0	0.0	0.0	0.0	0.0	0.0	16.8	30.7	42.2	51.7	16
17	0.0	0.0	0.0	0.0	0.0	0.0	0.0	0.0	0.0	16.7	30.5	41.9	17
18	0.0	0.0	0.0	0.0	0.0	0.0	0.0	0.0	0.0	0.0	16.5	30.3	18
19	0.0	0.0	0.0	0.0	0.0	0.0	0.0	0.0	0.0	0.0	0.0	16.4	19

17.50

AGE OF LOAN	21.0	22.0	23.0	24.0	25.0	26.0	27.0	28.0	29.0	30.0	35.0	40.0	AGE OF LOAN
1	99.5	99.6	99.6	99.7	99.8	99.8	99.8	99.9	99.9	99.9	100.0	100.0	1
2	98.9	99.1	99.2	99.3	99.5	99.5	99.6	99.7	99.7	99.8	99.9	100.0	2
3	98.2	98.5	98.7	98.9	99.1	99.2	99.4	99.5	99.6	99.6	99.8	99.9	3
4	97.3	97.8	98.1	98.4	98.7	98.9	99.1	99.2	99.3	99.4	99.8	99.9	4
5	96.3	96.9	97.4	97.8	98.2	98.5	98.7	98.9	99.1	99.2	99.7	99.9	5
6	95.1	95.9	96.6	97.1	97.6	98.0	98.3	98.6	98.8	99.0	99.6	99.8	6
7	93.7	94.7	95.6	96.3	96.9	97.4	97.8	98.2	98.5	98.7	99.5	99.8	7
8	91.9	93.3	94.4	95.3	96.0	96.7	97.2	97.7	98.0	98.3	99.3	99.7	8
9	89.9	91.6	92.9	94.1	95.0	95.8	96.5	97.1	97.5	97.9	99.1	99.6	9
10	87.5	89.5	91.2	92.6	93.8	94.8	95.7	96.4	96.9	97.4	98.9	99.6	10
11	84.6	87.1	89.2	91.0	92.4	93.6	94.7	95.5	96.2	96.8	98.7	99.4	11
12	81.2	84.2	86.8	88.9	90.7	92.2	93.5	94.5	95.4	96.1	98.4	99.3	12
13	77.1	80.8	83.9	86.5	88.7	90.5	92.1	93.3	94.4	95.3	98.0	99.2	13
14	72.2	76.8	80.5	83.7	86.3	88.5	90.4	91.9	93.2	94.3	97.6	99.0	14
15	66.5	71.9	76.5	80.3	83.5	86.1	88.4	90.2	91.8	93.1	97.1	98.8	15
16	59.6	66.2	71.7	76.3	80.1	83.3	86.0	88.2	90.1	91.7	96.5	98.5	16
17	51.4	59.3	65.9	71.5	76.1	79.9	83.2	85.9	88.1	90.0	95.8	98.3	17
18	41.7	51.2	59.1	65.7	71.3	75.9	79.8	83.0	85.8	88.0	95.0	97.9	18
19	30.1	41.5	51.0	59.0	65.6	71.1	75.8	79.7	82.9	85.7	94.0	97.5	19
20	16.4	30.0	41.4	50.9	58.8	65.4	71.0	75.7	79.6	82.8	92.8	97.0	20
21	0.0	16.3	29.9	41.2	50.7	58.7	65.3	70.9	75.6	79.5	91.4	96.4	21
22	0.0	0.0	16.2	29.8	41.1	50.6	58.6	65.2	70.8	75.5	89.8	95.7	22
23	0.0	0.0	0.0	16.2	29.7	41.1	50.5	58.5	65.2	70.7	87.8	94.9	23
24	0.0	0.0	0.0	0.0	16.1	29.7	41.0	50.5	58.4	65.1	85.4	93.9	24
25	0.0	0.0	0.0	0.0	0.0	16.1	29.6	40.9	50.4	58.4	82.6	92.7	25
26	0.0	0.0	0.0	0.0	0.0	0.0	16.1	29.6	40.9	50.4	79.2	91.3	26
27	0.0	0.0	0.0	0.0	0.0	0.0	0.0	16.1	29.5	40.8	75.3	89.6	27
28	0.0	0.0	0.0	0.0	0.0	0.0	0.0	0.0	16.0	29.5	70.5	87.7	28
29	0.0	0.0	0.0	0.0	0.0	0.0	0.0	0.0	0.0	16.0	64.9	85.3	29
30	0.0	0.0	0.0	0.0	0.0	0.0	0.0	0.0	0.0	0.0	58.2	82.5	30
31	0.0	0.0	0.0	0.0	0.0	0.0	0.0	0.0	0.0	0.0	50.2	79.1	31
32	0.0	0.0	0.0	0.0	0.0	0.0	0.0	0.0	0.0	0.0	40.7	75.2	32
33	0.0	0.0	0.0	0.0	0.0	0.0	0.0	0.0	0.0	0.0	29.4	70.4	33
34	0.0	0.0	0.0	0.0	0.0	0.0	0.0	0.0	0.0	0.0	16.0	64.8	34
35	0.0	0.0	0.0	0.0	0.0	0.0	0.0	0.0	0.0	0.0	0.0	58.1	35
36	0.0	0.0	0.0	0.0	0.0	0.0	0.0	0.0	0.0	0.0	0.0	50.1	36
37	0.0	0.0	0.0	0.0	0.0	0.0	0.0	0.0	0.0	0.0	0.0	40.7	37
38	0.0	0.0	0.0	0.0	0.0	0.0	0.0	0.0	0.0	0.0	0.0	29.4	38
39	0.0	0.0	0.0	0.0	0.0	0.0	0.0	0.0	0.0	0.0	0.0	16.0	39

EXAMPLES *ON PAGES A-382 TO A-397*

AGE OF LOAN	ORIGINAL TERM IN YEARS												AGE OF LOAN
	2.0	3.0	5.0	8.0	10.0	12.0	15.0	16.0	17.0	18.0	19.0	20.0	
1	54.4	72.3	86.4	93.8	96.0	97.4	98.5	98.8	99.0	99.2	99.3	99.4	1
2	0.0	39.3	70.1	86.3	91.2	94.2	96.8	97.3	97.8	98.2	98.5	98.7	2
3	0.0	0.0	50.7	77.5	85.6	90.4	94.7	95.6	96.3	97.0	97.5	97.9	3
4	0.0	0.0	27.6	66.9	78.8	86.0	92.2	93.5	94.6	95.5	96.3	96.9	4
5	0.0	0.0	0.0	54.3	70.7	80.6	89.2	91.0	92.6	93.8	94.8	95.7	5
6	0.0	0.0	0.0	39.3	61.1	74.2	85.6	88.1	90.1	91.8	93.2	94.3	6
7	0.0	0.0	0.0	21.4	49.6	66.6	81.4	84.6	87.2	89.4	91.1	92.6	7
8	0.0	0.0	0.0	0.0	35.9	57.5	76.3	80.4	83.7	86.5	88.7	90.6	8
9	0.0	0.0	0.0	0.0	19.5	46.7	70.3	75.4	79.6	83.0	85.8	88.2	9
10	0.0	0.0	0.0	0.0	0.0	33.8	63.0	69.4	74.6	78.9	82.4	85.3	10
11	0.0	0.0	0.0	0.0	0.0	18.4	54.5	62.3	68.7	74.0	78.3	81.9	11
12	0.0	0.0	0.0	0.0	0.0	0.0	44.2	53.8	61.6	68.1	73.5	77.9	12
13	0.0	0.0	0.0	0.0	0.0	0.0	32.0	43.7	53.2	61.1	67.6	73.0	13
14	0.0	0.0	0.0	0.0	0.0	0.0	17.4	31.6	43.2	52.8	60.7	67.2	14
15	0.0	0.0	0.0	0.0	0.0	0.0	0.0	17.2	31.3	42.9	52.4	60.3	15
16	0.0	0.0	0.0	0.0	0.0	0.0	0.0	0.0	17.0	31.0	42.6	52.1	16
17	0.0	0.0	0.0	0.0	0.0	0.0	0.0	0.0	0.0	16.9	30.8	42.3	17
18	0.0	0.0	0.0	0.0	0.0	0.0	0.0	0.0	0.0	0.0	16.7	30.6	18
19	0.0	0.0	0.0	0.0	0.0	0.0	0.0	0.0	0.0	0.0	0.0	16.6	19

17.75

AGE OF LOAN	ORIGINAL TERM IN YEARS												AGE OF LOAN
	21.0	22.0	23.0	24.0	25.0	26.0	27.0	28.0	29.0	30.0	35.0	40.0	
1	99.5	99.6	99.7	99.7	99.8	99.8	99.8	99.9	99.9	99.9	100.0	100.0	1
2	98.9	99.1	99.3	99.4	99.5	99.6	99.6	99.7	99.7	99.8	99.9	100.0	2
3	98.2	98.5	98.8	99.0	99.1	99.3	99.4	99.5	99.6	99.6	99.9	99.9	3
4	97.4	97.8	98.2	98.5	98.7	98.9	99.1	99.3	99.4	99.5	99.8	99.9	4
5	96.4	97.0	97.5	97.9	98.3	98.5	98.8	99.0	99.1	99.3	99.7	99.9	5
6	95.2	96.0	96.7	97.2	97.7	98.1	98.4	98.6	98.9	99.0	99.6	99.8	6
7	93.8	94.9	95.7	96.4	97.0	97.5	97.9	98.2	98.5	98.8	99.5	99.8	7
8	92.2	93.5	94.5	95.4	96.2	96.8	97.3	97.8	98.1	98.4	99.3	99.7	8
9	90.2	91.8	93.1	94.3	95.2	96.0	96.6	97.2	97.6	98.0	99.2	99.7	9
10	87.8	89.8	91.5	92.9	94.0	95.0	95.8	96.5	97.1	97.5	99.0	99.6	10
11	84.9	87.4	89.5	91.2	92.6	93.8	94.8	95.7	96.4	97.0	98.8	99.5	11
12	81.5	84.6	87.1	89.2	91.0	92.5	93.7	94.7	95.6	96.3	98.5	99.4	12
13	77.5	81.2	84.3	86.9	89.0	90.8	92.3	93.6	94.6	95.5	98.1	99.2	13
14	72.7	77.2	80.9	84.1	86.7	88.8	90.7	92.2	93.4	94.5	97.7	99.1	14
15	66.9	72.4	76.9	80.7	83.9	86.5	88.7	90.5	92.1	93.4	97.3	98.9	15
16	60.0	66.6	72.1	76.7	80.5	83.7	86.3	88.6	90.4	92.0	96.7	98.6	16
17	51.9	59.8	66.4	71.9	76.5	80.3	83.5	86.2	88.5	90.3	96.0	98.3	17
18	42.1	51.6	59.6	66.2	71.7	76.4	80.2	83.4	86.1	88.4	95.2	98.0	18
19	30.5	41.9	51.5	59.4	66.1	71.6	76.2	80.1	83.3	86.0	94.2	97.6	19
20	16.6	30.3	41.8	51.3	59.3	65.9	71.5	76.1	80.0	83.3	93.1	97.1	20
21	0.0	16.5	30.2	41.7	51.2	59.2	65.8	71.4	76.0	79.9	91.7	96.6	21
22	0.0	0.0	16.4	30.1	41.6	51.1	59.1	65.7	71.3	76.0	90.1	95.9	22
23	0.0	0.0	0.0	16.4	30.1	41.5	51.0	59.0	65.7	71.2	88.1	95.1	23
24	0.0	0.0	0.0	0.0	16.4	30.0	41.4	50.9	58.9	65.6	85.8	94.1	24
25	0.0	0.0	0.0	0.0	0.0	16.3	30.0	41.4	50.9	58.9	83.0	93.0	25
26	0.0	0.0	0.0	0.0	0.0	0.0	16.3	29.9	41.3	50.8	79.7	91.6	26
27	0.0	0.0	0.0	0.0	0.0	0.0	0.0	16.3	29.9	41.3	75.7	90.0	27
28	0.0	0.0	0.0	0.0	0.0	0.0	0.0	0.0	16.3	29.9	71.0	88.0	28
29	0.0	0.0	0.0	0.0	0.0	0.0	0.0	0.0	0.0	16.2	65.4	85.7	29
30	0.0	0.0	0.0	0.0	0.0	0.0	0.0	0.0	0.0	0.0	58.7	82.9	30
31	0.0	0.0	0.0	0.0	0.0	0.0	0.0	0.0	0.0	0.0	50.7	79.6	31
32	0.0	0.0	0.0	0.0	0.0	0.0	0.0	0.0	0.0	0.0	41.1	75.6	32
33	0.0	0.0	0.0	0.0	0.0	0.0	0.0	0.0	0.0	0.0	29.8	70.9	33
34	0.0	0.0	0.0	0.0	0.0	0.0	0.0	0.0	0.0	0.0	16.2	65.3	34
35	0.0	0.0	0.0	0.0	0.0	0.0	0.0	0.0	0.0	0.0	0.0	58.6	35
36	0.0	0.0	0.0	0.0	0.0	0.0	0.0	0.0	0.0	0.0	0.0	50.6	36
37	0.0	0.0	0.0	0.0	0.0	0.0	0.0	0.0	0.0	0.0	0.0	41.1	37
38	0.0	0.0	0.0	0.0	0.0	0.0	0.0	0.0	0.0	0.0	0.0	29.7	38
39	0.0	0.0	0.0	0.0	0.0	0.0	0.0	0.0	0.0	0.0	0.0	16.2	39

EXAMPLES ON PAGES A-382 TO A-397

AGE OF LOAN	ORIGINAL TERM IN YEARS												AGE OF LOAN
	2.0	3.0	5.0	8.0	10.0	12.0	15.0	16.0	17.0	18.0	19.0	20.0	
1	54.5	72.4	86.4	93.8	96.1	97.4	98.6	98.8	99.0	99.2	99.3	99.4	1
2	0.0	39.4	70.2	86.5	91.4	94.3	96.8	97.4	97.8	98.2	98.5	98.8	2
3	0.0	0.0	50.9	77.7	85.7	90.6	94.8	95.7	96.4	97.0	97.5	98.0	3
4	0.0	0.0	27.7	67.1	79.0	86.1	92.3	93.7	94.7	95.6	96.4	97.0	4
5	0.0	0.0	0.0	54.6	71.0	80.8	89.4	91.2	92.7	94.0	95.0	95.8	5
6	0.0	0.0	0.0	39.5	61.3	74.5	85.9	88.3	90.3	92.0	93.3	94.5	6
7	0.0	0.0	0.0	21.5	49.8	66.9	81.6	84.8	87.4	89.6	91.3	92.8	7
8	0.0	0.0	0.0	0.0	36.1	57.8	76.6	80.7	84.0	86.7	89.0	90.8	8
9	0.0	0.0	0.0	0.0	19.6	47.0	70.6	75.7	79.9	83.3	86.1	88.5	9
10	0.0	0.0	0.0	0.0	0.0	34.0	63.4	69.8	75.0	79.2	82.7	85.6	10
11	0.0	0.0	0.0	0.0	0.0	18.5	54.8	62.7	69.1	74.3	78.7	82.3	11
12	0.0	0.0	0.0	0.0	0.0	0.0	44.5	54.2	62.0	68.5	73.8	78.2	12
13	0.0	0.0	0.0	0.0	0.0	0.0	32.3	44.0	53.6	61.5	68.0	73.4	13
14	0.0	0.0	0.0	0.0	0.0	0.0	17.6	31.9	43.6	53.2	61.1	67.7	14
15	0.0	0.0	0.0	0.0	0.0	0.0	0.0	17.3	31.6	43.2	52.8	60.8	15
16	0.0	0.0	0.0	0.0	0.0	0.0	0.0	0.0	17.2	31.3	42.9	52.5	16
17	0.0	0.0	0.0	0.0	0.0	0.0	0.0	0.0	0.0	17.0	31.1	42.7	17
18	0.0	0.0	0.0	0.0	0.0	0.0	0.0	0.0	0.0	0.0	16.9	30.9	18
19	0.0	0.0	0.0	0.0	0.0	0.0	0.0	0.0	0.0	0.0	0.0	16.8	19

18.00

AGE OF LOAN	ORIGINAL TERM IN YEARS												AGE OF LOAN
	21.0	22.0	23.0	24.0	25.0	26.0	27.0	28.0	29.0	30.0	35.0	40.0	
1	99.5	99.6	99.7	99.7	99.8	99.8	99.8	99.9	99.9	99.9	100.0	100.0	1
2	99.0	99.1	99.3	99.4	99.5	99.6	99.7	99.7	99.8	99.8	99.9	100.0	2
3	98.3	98.6	98.8	99.0	99.2	99.3	99.4	99.5	99.6	99.7	99.9	99.9	3
4	97.5	97.9	98.3	98.5	98.8	99.0	99.2	99.3	99.4	99.5	99.8	99.9	4
5	96.5	97.1	97.6	98.0	98.3	98.6	98.8	99.0	99.2	99.3	99.7	99.9	5
6	95.4	96.2	96.8	97.3	97.8	98.1	98.4	98.7	98.9	99.1	99.6	99.8	6
7	94.0	95.0	95.8	96.5	97.1	97.6	98.0	98.3	98.6	98.8	99.5	99.8	7
8	92.4	93.6	94.7	95.6	96.3	96.9	97.4	97.9	98.2	98.5	99.4	99.7	8
9	90.4	92.0	93.3	94.4	95.4	96.1	96.8	97.3	97.7	98.1	99.2	99.7	9
10	88.1	90.0	91.7	93.1	94.2	95.2	96.0	96.6	97.2	97.7	99.0	99.6	10
11	85.2	87.7	89.8	91.5	92.9	94.0	95.0	95.8	96.5	97.1	98.8	99.5	11
12	81.9	84.9	87.4	89.5	91.2	92.7	93.9	94.9	95.7	96.4	98.5	99.4	12
13	77.9	81.6	84.6	87.2	89.3	91.1	92.5	93.8	94.8	95.7	98.2	99.3	13
14	73.1	77.6	81.3	84.4	87.0	89.1	90.9	92.4	93.7	94.7	97.8	99.1	14
15	67.3	72.8	77.3	81.1	84.2	86.8	89.0	90.8	92.3	93.6	97.4	98.9	15
16	60.5	67.1	72.6	77.1	80.9	84.1	86.7	88.9	90.7	92.2	96.8	98.7	16
17	52.3	60.2	66.9	72.4	76.9	80.7	83.9	86.6	88.8	90.6	96.2	98.4	17
18	42.5	52.1	60.1	66.7	72.2	76.8	80.6	83.8	86.5	88.7	95.4	98.1	18
19	30.8	42.3	51.9	59.9	66.5	72.1	76.7	80.5	83.7	86.4	94.4	97.7	19
20	16.7	30.6	42.2	51.8	59.8	66.4	71.9	76.6	80.4	83.6	93.3	97.3	20
21	0.0	16.7	30.5	42.1	51.6	59.6	66.3	71.8	76.5	80.3	92.0	96.7	21
22	0.0	0.0	16.6	30.5	42.0	51.6	59.5	66.2	71.8	76.4	90.4	96.1	22
23	0.0	0.0	0.0	16.6	30.4	41.9	51.5	59.5	66.1	71.7	88.5	95.3	23
24	0.0	0.0	0.0	0.0	16.5	30.3	41.8	51.4	59.4	66.1	86.2	94.3	24
25	0.0	0.0	0.0	0.0	0.0	16.5	30.3	41.8	51.3	59.3	83.4	93.2	25
26	0.0	0.0	0.0	0.0	0.0	0.0	16.5	30.2	41.7	51.3	80.1	91.9	26
27	0.0	0.0	0.0	0.0	0.0	0.0	0.0	16.5	30.2	41.7	76.2	90.3	27
28	0.0	0.0	0.0	0.0	0.0	0.0	0.0	0.0	16.4	30.2	71.5	88.4	28
29	0.0	0.0	0.0	0.0	0.0	0.0	0.0	0.0	0.0	16.4	65.9	86.1	29
30	0.0	0.0	0.0	0.0	0.0	0.0	0.0	0.0	0.0	0.0	59.2	83.3	30
31	0.0	0.0	0.0	0.0	0.0	0.0	0.0	0.0	0.0	0.0	51.2	80.0	31
32	0.0	0.0	0.0	0.0	0.0	0.0	0.0	0.0	0.0	0.0	41.6	76.1	32
33	0.0	0.0	0.0	0.0	0.0	0.0	0.0	0.0	0.0	0.0	30.1	71.4	33
34	0.0	0.0	0.0	0.0	0.0	0.0	0.0	0.0	0.0	0.0	16.4	65.8	34
35	0.0	0.0	0.0	0.0	0.0	0.0	0.0	0.0	0.0	0.0	0.0	59.1	35
36	0.0	0.0	0.0	0.0	0.0	0.0	0.0	0.0	0.0	0.0	0.0	51.1	36
37	0.0	0.0	0.0	0.0	0.0	0.0	0.0	0.0	0.0	0.0	0.0	41.5	37
38	0.0	0.0	0.0	0.0	0.0	0.0	0.0	0.0	0.0	0.0	0.0	30.1	38
39	0.0	0.0	0.0	0.0	0.0	0.0	0.0	0.0	0.0	0.0	0.0	16.4	39

EXAMPLES *ON PAGES A-382 TO A-397*

AGE OF LOAN	2.0	3.0	5.0	8.0	10.0	12.0	15.0	16.0	17.0	18.0	19.0	20.0	AGE OF LOAN
						ORIGINAL TERM IN YEARS							
1	54.5	72.5	86.5	93.9	96.1	97.5	98.6	98.8	99.0	99.2	99.3	99.5	1
2	0.0	39.5	70.4	86.6	91.5	94.4	96.9	97.5	97.9	98.3	98.6	98.8	2
3	0.0	0.0	51.0	77.9	85.9	90.7	94.9	95.8	96.5	97.1	97.6	98.0	3
4	0.0	0.0	27.8	67.4	79.2	86.3	92.5	93.8	94.9	95.8	96.5	97.1	4
5	0.0	0.0	0.0	54.8	71.2	81.1	89.6	91.4	92.9	94.1	95.1	96.0	5
6	0.0	0.0	0.0	39.7	61.6	74.8	86.1	88.5	90.5	92.2	93.5	94.6	6
7	0.0	0.0	0.0	21.6	50.1	67.2	81.9	85.1	87.7	89.8	91.6	93.0	7
8	0.0	0.0	0.0	0.0	36.3	58.2	76.9	81.0	84.3	87.0	89.2	91.1	8
9	0.0	0.0	0.0	0.0	19.8	47.3	71.0	76.1	80.2	83.6	86.4	88.7	9
10	0.0	0.0	0.0	0.0	0.0	34.3	63.8	70.1	75.3	79.6	83.1	86.0	10
11	0.0	0.0	0.0	0.0	0.0	18.7	55.2	63.0	69.5	74.7	79.1	82.6	11
12	0.0	0.0	0.0	0.0	0.0	0.0	44.9	54.6	62.4	68.9	74.2	78.6	12
13	0.0	0.0	0.0	0.0	0.0	0.0	32.5	44.4	54.0	61.9	68.5	73.8	13
14	0.0	0.0	0.0	0.0	0.0	0.0	17.7	32.2	43.9	53.6	61.5	68.1	14
15	0.0	0.0	0.0	0.0	0.0	0.0	0.0	17.5	31.9	43.6	53.2	61.2	15
16	0.0	0.0	0.0	0.0	0.0	0.0	0.0	0.0	17.4	31.6	43.3	53.0	16
17	0.0	0.0	0.0	0.0	0.0	0.0	0.0	0.0	0.0	17.2	31.4	43.1	17
18	0.0	0.0	0.0	0.0	0.0	0.0	0.0	0.0	0.0	0.0	0.0	17.1	31.2	18
19	0.0	0.0	0.0	0.0	0.0	0.0	0.0	0.0	0.0	0.0	0.0	17.0	19

18.25

AGE OF LOAN	21.0	22.0	23.0	24.0	25.0	26.0	27.0	28.0	29.0	30.0	35.0	40.0	AGE OF LOAN
						ORIGINAL TERM IN YEARS							
1	99.5	99.6	99.7	99.7	99.8	99.8	99.8	99.9	99.9	99.9	100.0	100.0	1
2	99.0	99.2	99.3	99.4	99.5	99.6	99.7	99.7	99.8	99.8	99.9	100.0	2
3	98.4	98.6	98.9	99.1	99.2	99.3	99.5	99.6	99.6	99.7	99.9	99.9	3
4	97.6	98.0	98.3	98.6	98.8	99.0	99.2	99.3	99.4	99.5	99.8	99.9	4
5	96.6	97.2	97.7	98.1	98.4	98.7	98.9	99.1	99.2	99.4	99.7	99.9	5
6	95.5	96.3	96.9	97.4	97.9	98.2	98.5	98.8	99.0	99.1	99.7	99.9	6
7	94.2	95.2	96.0	96.7	97.2	97.7	98.1	98.4	98.7	98.9	99.5	99.8	7
8	92.6	93.8	94.9	95.7	96.4	97.0	97.5	97.9	98.3	98.6	99.4	99.8	8
9	90.6	92.2	93.5	94.6	95.5	96.3	96.9	97.4	97.8	98.2	99.3	99.7	9
10	88.3	90.3	91.9	93.3	94.4	95.3	96.1	96.8	97.3	97.8	99.1	99.6	10
11	85.6	88.0	90.0	91.7	93.1	94.2	95.2	96.0	96.7	97.2	98.9	99.5	11
12	82.2	85.2	87.7	89.8	91.5	92.9	94.1	95.1	95.9	96.6	98.6	99.4	12
13	78.3	81.9	85.0	87.5	89.6	91.3	92.8	94.0	95.0	95.8	98.3	99.3	13
14	73.5	78.0	81.7	84.8	87.3	89.4	91.2	92.7	93.9	94.9	97.9	99.2	14
15	67.8	73.2	77.7	81.5	84.6	87.1	89.3	91.1	92.6	93.8	97.5	99.0	15
16	60.9	67.5	73.0	77.5	81.3	84.4	87.0	89.2	91.0	92.5	97.0	98.8	16
17	52.7	60.7	67.3	72.8	77.4	81.1	84.3	86.9	89.1	90.9	96.3	98.5	17
18	42.9	52.5	60.5	67.1	72.6	77.2	81.0	84.2	86.8	89.0	95.6	98.2	18
19	31.1	42.7	52.4	60.4	67.0	72.5	77.1	80.9	84.1	86.7	94.7	97.8	19
20	16.9	31.0	42.6	52.2	60.2	66.9	72.4	77.0	80.8	84.0	93.6	97.4	20
21	0.0	16.9	30.9	42.5	52.1	60.1	66.8	72.3	76.9	80.8	92.2	96.9	21
22	0.0	0.0	16.8	30.8	42.4	52.0	60.0	66.7	72.2	76.9	90.7	96.2	22
23	0.0	0.0	0.0	16.8	30.7	42.3	51.9	59.9	66.6	72.2	88.8	95.5	23
24	0.0	0.0	0.0	0.0	16.7	30.7	42.2	51.9	59.9	66.6	86.5	94.6	24
25	0.0	0.0	0.0	0.0	0.0	16.7	30.6	42.2	51.8	59.8	83.8	93.5	25
26	0.0	0.0	0.0	0.0	0.0	0.0	16.7	30.6	42.1	51.8	80.6	92.1	26
27	0.0	0.0	0.0	0.0	0.0	0.0	0.0	16.7	30.6	42.1	76.7	90.6	27
28	0.0	0.0	0.0	0.0	0.0	0.0	0.0	0.0	16.7	30.5	72.0	88.7	28
29	0.0	0.0	0.0	0.0	0.0	0.0	0.0	0.0	0.0	16.6	66.4	86.4	29
30	0.0	0.0	0.0	0.0	0.0	0.0	0.0	0.0	0.0	0.0	59.7	83.7	30
31	0.0	0.0	0.0	0.0	0.0	0.0	0.0	0.0	0.0	0.0	51.6	80.5	31
32	0.0	0.0	0.0	0.0	0.0	0.0	0.0	0.0	0.0	0.0	42.0	76.6	32
33	0.0	0.0	0.0	0.0	0.0	0.0	0.0	0.0	0.0	0.0	30.5	71.9	33
34	0.0	0.0	0.0	0.0	0.0	0.0	0.0	0.0	0.0	0.0	16.6	66.3	34
35	0.0	0.0	0.0	0.0	0.0	0.0	0.0	0.0	0.0	0.0	0.0	59.6	35
36	0.0	0.0	0.0	0.0	0.0	0.0	0.0	0.0	0.0	0.0	51.6	36
37	0.0	0.0	0.0	0.0	0.0	0.0	0.0	0.0	0.0	0.0	0.0	42.0	37
38	0.0	0.0	0.0	0.0	0.0	0.0	0.0	0.0	0.0	0.0	0.0	30.4	38
39	0.0	0.0	0.0	0.0	0.0	0.0	0.0	0.0	0.0	0.0	0.0	16.6	39

EXAMPLES ON PAGES A-382 TO A-397

AGE OF LOAN	2.0	3.0	5.0	8.0	10.0	12.0	15.0	16.0	17.0	18.0	19.0	20.0	AGE OF LOAN
1	54.6	72.6	86.6	94.0	96.2	97.5	98.6	98.9	99.1	99.2	99.4	99.5	1
2	0.0	39.6	70.5	86.7	91.6	94.5	97.0	97.5	98.0	98.3	98.6	98.8	2
3	0.0	0.0	51.2	78.0	86.1	90.9	95.0	95.9	96.6	97.2	97.7	98.1	3
4	0.0	0.0	27.9	67.6	79.4	86.5	92.6	93.9	95.0	95.9	96.6	97.2	4
5	0.0	0.0	0.0	55.0	71.5	81.3	89.8	91.6	93.1	94.3	95.3	96.1	5
6	0.0	0.0	0.0	39.9	61.9	75.1	86.3	88.8	90.7	92.3	93.7	94.8	6
7	0.0	0.0	0.0	21.8	50.4	67.5	82.2	85.4	87.9	90.0	91.8	93.2	7
8	0.0	0.0	0.0	0.0	36.6	58.5	77.3	81.3	84.6	87.3	89.5	91.3	8
9	0.0	0.0	0.0	0.0	19.9	47.6	71.3	76.4	80.5	83.9	86.7	89.0	9
10	0.0	0.0	0.0	0.0	0.0	34.5	64.1	70.5	75.7	79.9	83.4	86.2	10
11	0.0	0.0	0.0	0.0	0.0	18.8	55.6	63.4	69.8	75.1	79.4	82.9	11
12	0.0	0.0	0.0	0.0	0.0	0.0	45.2	54.9	62.8	69.3	74.6	79.0	12
13	0.0	0.0	0.0	0.0	0.0	0.0	32.8	44.7	54.4	62.4	68.9	74.2	13
14	0.0	0.0	0.0	0.0	0.0	0.0	17.9	32.4	44.3	54.0	62.0	68.5	14
15	0.0	0.0	0.0	0.0	0.0	0.0	0.0	17.7	32.1	44.0	53.7	61.6	15
16	0.0	0.0	0.0	0.0	0.0	0.0	0.0	17.5	31.9	43.7	53.4	16	
17	0.0	0.0	0.0	0.0	0.0	0.0	0.0	0.0	17.4	31.7	43.4	17	
18	0.0	0.0	0.0	0.0	0.0	0.0	0.0	0.0	0.0	17.3	31.5	18	
19	0.0	0.0	0.0	0.0	0.0	0.0	0.0	0.0	0.0	0.0	17.2	19	

18.50

AGE OF LOAN	21.0	22.0	23.0	24.0	25.0	26.0	27.0	28.0	29.0	30.0	35.0	40.0	AGE OF LOAN
1	99.6	99.6	99.7	99.8	99.8	99.8	99.9	99.9	99.9	99.9	100.0	100.0	1
2	99.0	99.2	99.3	99.5	99.5	99.6	99.7	99.7	99.8	99.8	99.9	100.0	2
3	98.4	98.7	98.9	99.1	99.2	99.4	99.5	99.6	99.6	99.7	99.9	100.0	3
4	97.7	98.1	98.4	98.7	98.9	99.1	99.2	99.4	99.5	99.6	99.8	99.9	4
5	96.7	97.3	97.8	98.1	98.5	98.7	98.9	99.1	99.3	99.4	99.8	99.9	5
6	95.7	96.4	97.0	97.5	97.9	98.3	98.6	98.8	99.0	99.2	99.7	99.9	6
7	94.3	95.3	96.1	96.8	97.3	97.8	98.1	98.5	98.7	98.9	99.6	99.8	7
8	92.8	94.0	95.0	95.9	96.6	97.1	97.6	98.0	98.4	98.6	99.5	99.8	8
9	90.9	92.4	93.7	94.8	95.7	96.4	97.0	97.5	97.9	98.3	99.3	99.7	9
10	88.6	90.5	92.2	93.5	94.6	95.5	96.3	96.9	97.4	97.9	99.1	99.7	10
11	85.9	88.3	90.3	91.9	93.3	94.4	95.4	96.2	96.8	97.3	98.9	99.6	11
12	82.6	85.6	88.0	90.1	91.7	93.1	94.3	95.3	96.1	96.7	98.7	99.5	12
13	78.6	82.3	85.3	87.8	89.9	91.6	93.0	94.2	95.2	96.0	98.4	99.4	13
14	73.9	78.4	82.0	85.1	87.6	89.7	91.4	92.9	94.1	95.1	98.0	99.2	14
15	68.2	73.6	78.1	81.8	84.9	87.5	89.6	91.3	92.8	94.0	97.6	99.0	15
16	61.4	68.0	73.4	77.9	81.7	84.8	87.3	89.5	91.3	92.7	97.1	98.8	16
17	53.1	61.1	67.8	73.2	77.8	81.5	84.6	87.2	89.4	91.2	96.5	98.6	17
18	43.3	52.9	61.0	67.6	73.1	77.6	81.4	84.5	87.2	89.3	95.7	98.3	18
19	31.4	43.1	52.8	60.8	67.4	73.0	77.5	81.3	84.5	87.1	94.9	97.9	19
20	17.1	31.3	43.0	52.7	60.7	67.3	72.8	77.4	81.2	84.4	93.8	97.5	20
21	0.0	17.1	31.2	42.9	52.5	60.6	67.2	72.8	77.4	81.2	92.5	97.0	21
22	0.0	0.0	17.0	31.1	42.8	52.5	60.5	67.2	72.7	77.3	91.0	96.4	22
23	0.0	0.0	0.0	17.0	31.0	42.7	52.4	60.4	67.1	72.6	89.1	95.7	23
24	0.0	0.0	0.0	0.0	16.9	31.0	42.6	52.3	60.4	67.0	86.9	94.8	24
25	0.0	0.0	0.0	0.0	0.0	16.9	30.9	42.6	52.3	60.3	84.2	93.7	25
26	0.0	0.0	0.0	0.0	0.0	0.0	16.9	30.9	42.6	52.2	81.0	92.4	26
27	0.0	0.0	0.0	0.0	0.0	0.0	0.0	16.9	30.9	42.5	77.1	90.9	27
28	0.0	0.0	0.0	0.0	0.0	0.0	0.0	0.0	16.8	30.8	72.5	89.0	28
29	0.0	0.0	0.0	0.0	0.0	0.0	0.0	0.0	0.0	16.8	66.9	86.8	29
30	0.0	0.0	0.0	0.0	0.0	0.0	0.0	0.0	0.0	0.0	60.2	84.1	30
31	0.0	0.0	0.0	0.0	0.0	0.0	0.0	0.0	0.0	0.0	52.1	80.9	31
32	0.0	0.0	0.0	0.0	0.0	0.0	0.0	0.0	0.0	0.0	42.4	77.0	32
33	0.0	0.0	0.0	0.0	0.0	0.0	0.0	0.0	0.0	0.0	30.8	72.4	33
34	0.0	0.0	0.0	0.0	0.0	0.0	0.0	0.0	0.0	0.0	16.8	66.8	34
35	0.0	0.0	0.0	0.0	0.0	0.0	0.0	0.0	0.0	0.0	0.0	60.1	35
36	0.0	0.0	0.0	0.0	0.0	0.0	0.0	0.0	0.0	0.0	0.0	52.1	36
37	0.0	0.0	0.0	0.0	0.0	0.0	0.0	0.0	0.0	0.0	0.0	42.4	37
38	0.0	0.0	0.0	0.0	0.0	0.0	0.0	0.0	0.0	0.0	0.0	30.8	38
39	0.0	0.0	0.0	0.0	0.0	0.0	0.0	0.0	0.0	0.0	0.0	16.8	39

EXAMPLES *ON PAGES A-382 TO A-397*

AGE OF LOAN	ORIGINAL TERM IN YEARS												AGE OF LOAN
	2.0	3.0	5.0	8.0	10.0	12.0	15.0	16.0	17.0	18.0	19.0	20.0	
1	54.6	72.6	86.7	94.0	96.2	97.5	98.7	98.9	99.1	99.3	99.4	99.5	1
2	0.0	39.7	70.6	86.9	91.7	94.6	97.1	97.6	98.0	98.4	98.6	98.9	2
3	0.0	0.0	51.3	78.2	86.2	91.0	95.1	96.0	96.7	97.3	97.8	98.1	3
4	0.0	0.0	28.0	67.8	79.6	86.7	92.8	94.1	95.1	96.0	96.7	97.3	4
5	0.0	0.0	0.0	55.2	71.7	81.6	90.0	91.8	93.2	94.4	95.4	96.2	5
6	0.0	0.0	0.0	40.1	62.2	75.3	86.6	89.0	90.9	92.5	93.8	94.9	6
7	0.0	0.0	0.0	21.9	50.7	67.8	82.5	85.6	88.2	90.3	92.0	93.4	7
8	0.0	0.0	0.0	0.0	36.8	58.8	77.6	81.6	84.8	87.5	89.7	91.5	8
9	0.0	0.0	0.0	0.0	20.1	47.9	71.6	76.7	80.8	84.2	87.0	89.2	9
10	0.0	0.0	0.0	0.0	0.0	34.8	64.5	70.9	76.0	80.2	83.7	86.5	10
11	0.0	0.0	0.0	0.0	0.0	19.0	55.9	63.8	70.2	75.5	79.8	83.3	11
12	0.0	0.0	0.0	0.0	0.0	0.0	45.6	55.3	63.2	69.7	75.0	79.3	12
13	0.0	0.0	0.0	0.0	0.0	0.0	33.1	45.1	54.8	62.8	69.3	74.6	13
14	0.0	0.0	0.0	0.0	0.0	0.0	18.1	32.7	44.7	54.4	62.4	68.9	14
15	0.0	0.0	0.0	0.0	0.0	0.0	0.0	17.9	32.4	44.3	54.1	62.1	15
16	0.0	0.0	0.0	0.0	0.0	0.0	0.0	0.0	17.7	32.2	44.1	53.8	16
17	0.0	0.0	0.0	0.0	0.0	0.0	0.0	0.0	0.0	17.6	32.0	43.8	17
18	0.0	0.0	0.0	0.0	0.0	0.0	0.0	0.0	0.0	0.0	17.5	31.8	18
19	0.0	0.0	0.0	0.0	0.0	0.0	0.0	0.0	0.0	0.0	0.0	17.4	19

18.75

AGE OF LOAN	ORIGINAL TERM IN YEARS												AGE OF LOAN
	21.0	22.0	23.0	24.0	25.0	26.0	27.0	28.0	29.0	30.0	35.0	40.0	
1	99.6	99.7	99.7	99.8	99.8	99.8	99.9	99.9	99.9	99.9	100.0	100.0	1
2	99.1	99.2	99.4	99.5	99.6	99.6	99.7	99.8	99.8	99.8	99.9	100.0	2
3	98.5	98.7	98.9	99.1	99.3	99.4	99.5	99.6	99.7	99.7	99.9	100.0	3
4	97.7	98.1	98.4	98.7	98.9	99.1	99.3	99.4	99.5	99.6	99.8	99.9	4
5	96.9	97.4	97.8	98.2	98.5	98.8	99.0	99.2	99.3	99.4	99.8	99.9	5
6	95.8	96.5	97.1	97.6	98.0	98.4	98.6	98.9	99.1	99.2	99.7	99.9	6
7	94.5	95.5	96.2	96.9	97.4	97.9	98.2	98.5	98.8	99.0	99.6	99.8	7
8	93.0	94.2	95.2	96.0	96.7	97.3	97.7	98.1	98.4	98.7	99.5	99.8	8
9	91.1	92.6	93.9	95.0	95.8	96.5	97.1	97.6	98.0	98.4	99.4	99.7	9
10	88.9	90.8	92.4	93.7	94.8	95.7	96.4	97.0	97.5	97.9	99.2	99.7	10
11	86.2	88.6	90.5	92.2	93.5	94.6	95.5	96.3	96.9	97.5	99.0	99.6	11
12	82.9	85.9	88.3	90.3	92.0	93.3	94.5	95.4	96.2	96.9	98.8	99.5	12
13	79.0	82.6	85.6	88.1	90.1	91.8	93.2	94.4	95.3	96.1	98.5	99.4	13
14	74.3	78.7	82.4	85.4	87.9	90.0	91.7	93.1	94.3	95.3	98.1	99.3	14
15	68.6	74.0	78.5	82.2	85.3	87.8	89.9	91.6	93.0	94.2	97.7	99.1	15
16	61.8	68.4	73.8	78.3	82.0	85.1	87.7	89.8	91.5	93.0	97.2	98.9	16
17	53.6	61.6	68.2	73.7	78.2	81.9	85.0	87.6	89.7	91.4	96.6	98.7	17
18	43.7	53.4	61.4	68.0	73.5	78.0	81.8	84.9	87.5	89.6	95.9	98.4	18
19	31.7	43.5	53.2	61.3	67.9	73.4	77.9	81.7	84.8	87.4	95.0	98.0	19
20	17.3	30.1	43.4	53.1	61.1	67.8	73.3	77.9	81.6	84.8	94.0	97.6	20
21	0.0	17.3	31.6	43.3	53.0	61.0	67.7	73.2	77.8	81.6	92.7	97.1	21
22	0.0	0.0	17.2	31.4	43.2	52.9	61.0	67.6	73.1	77.7	91.2	96.5	22
23	0.0	0.0	0.0	17.2	31.4	43.1	52.8	60.9	67.6	73.1	89.4	95.8	23
24	0.0	0.0	0.0	0.0	17.1	31.3	43.1	52.8	60.8	67.5	87.2	95.0	24
25	0.0	0.0	0.0	0.0	0.0	17.1	31.3	43.0	52.7	60.8	84.5	93.9	25
26	0.0	0.0	0.0	0.0	0.0	0.0	17.1	31.2	43.0	52.7	81.4	92.7	26
27	0.0	0.0	0.0	0.0	0.0	0.0	0.0	17.1	31.2	42.9	77.5	91.3	27
28	0.0	0.0	0.0	0.0	0.0	0.0	0.0	0.0	17.1	31.2	72.9	89.3	28
29	0.0	0.0	0.0	0.0	0.0	0.0	0.0	0.0	0.0	17.0	67.4	87.1	29
30	0.0	0.0	0.0	0.0	0.0	0.0	0.0	0.0	0.0	0.0	60.6	84.5	30
31	0.0	0.0	0.0	0.0	0.0	0.0	0.0	0.0	0.0	0.0	52.6	81.3	31
32	0.0	0.0	0.0	0.0	0.0	0.0	0.0	0.0	0.0	0.0	42.8	77.5	32
33	0.0	0.0	0.0	0.0	0.0	0.0	0.0	0.0	0.0	0.0	31.1	72.9	33
34	0.0	0.0	0.0	0.0	0.0	0.0	0.0	0.0	0.0	0.0	17.0	67.3	34
35	0.0	0.0	0.0	0.0	0.0	0.0	0.0	0.0	0.0	0.0	0.0	60.6	35
36	0.0	0.0	0.0	0.0	0.0	0.0	0.0	0.0	0.0	0.0	0.0	52.5	36
37	0.0	0.0	0.0	0.0	0.0	0.0	0.0	0.0	0.0	0.0	0.0	42.8	37
38	0.0	0.0	0.0	0.0	0.0	0.0	0.0	0.0	0.0	0.0	0.0	31.1	38
39	0.0	0.0	0.0	0.0	0.0	0.0	0.0	0.0	0.0	0.0	0.0	17.0	39

EXAMPLES *ON PAGES A-382 TO A-397*

AGE OF LOAN	ORIGINAL TERM IN YEARS												AGE OF LOAN
	2.0	3.0	5.0	8.0	10.0	12.0	15.0	16.0	17.0	18.0	19.0	20.0	
1	54.7	72.7	86.8	94.1	96.3	97.6	98.7	98.9	99.1	99.3	99.4	99.5	1
2	0.0	39.8	70.8	87.0	91.8	94.7	97.1	97.6	98.1	98.4	98.7	98.9	2
3	0.0	0.0	51.5	78.4	86.4	91.2	95.2	96.1	96.8	97.4	97.8	98.2	3
4	0.0	0.0	28.1	68.0	79.9	86.9	92.9	94.2	95.2	96.1	96.8	97.3	4
5	0.0	0.0	0.0	55.5	72.0	81.8	90.2	91.9	93.4	94.6	95.5	96.3	5
6	0.0	0.0	0.0	40.3	62.4	75.6	86.8	89.2	91.1	92.7	94.0	95.0	6
7	0.0	0.0	0.0	22.1	50.9	68.1	82.8	85.9	88.4	90.5	92.2	93.5	7
8	0.0	0.0	0.0	0.0	37.0	59.1	77.9	81.9	85.1	87.8	89.9	91.7	8
9	0.0	0.0	0.0	0.0	20.3	48.2	72.0	77.0	81.2	84.5	87.2	89.5	9
10	0.0	0.0	0.0	0.0	0.0	35.1	64.9	71.2	76.4	80.6	84.0	86.8	10
11	0.0	0.0	0.0	0.0	0.0	19.2	56.3	64.2	70.6	75.8	80.1	83.6	11
12	0.0	0.0	0.0	0.0	0.0	0.0	45.9	55.7	63.6	70.1	75.4	79.7	12
13	0.0	0.0	0.0	0.0	0.0	0.0	33.4	45.4	55.2	63.2	69.7	75.0	13
14	0.0	0.0	0.0	0.0	0.0	0.0	18.3	33.0	45.0	54.8	62.8	69.3	14
15	0.0	0.0	0.0	0.0	0.0	0.0	0.0	18.1	32.7	44.7	54.5	62.5	15
16	0.0	0.0	0.0	0.0	0.0	0.0	0.0	0.0	17.9	32.5	44.4	54.2	16
17	0.0	0.0	0.0	0.0	0.0	0.0	0.0	0.0	0.0	17.8	32.3	44.2	17
18	0.0	0.0	0.0	0.0	0.0	0.0	0.0	0.0	0.0	0.0	17.7	32.1	18
19	0.0	0.0	0.0	0.0	0.0	0.0	0.0	0.0	0.0	0.0	0.0	17.6	19

19.00

AGE OF LOAN	ORIGINAL TERM IN YEARS												AGE OF LOAN
	21.0	22.0	23.0	24.0	25.0	26.0	27.0	28.0	29.0	30.0	35.0	40.0	
1	99.6	99.7	99.7	99.8	99.8	99.8	99.9	99.9	99.9	99.9	100.0	100.0	1
2	99.1	99.3	99.4	99.5	99.6	99.7	99.7	99.8	99.8	99.8	99.9	100.0	2
3	98.5	98.8	99.0	99.2	99.3	99.4	99.5	99.6	99.7	99.7	99.9	100.0	3
4	97.8	98.2	98.5	98.8	99.0	99.2	99.3	99.4	99.5	99.6	99.8	99.9	4
5	97.0	97.5	97.9	98.3	98.6	98.8	99.0	99.2	99.3	99.4	99.8	99.9	5
6	95.9	96.6	97.2	97.7	98.1	98.4	98.7	98.9	99.1	99.3	99.7	99.9	6
7	94.7	95.6	96.4	97.0	97.5	97.9	98.3	98.6	98.8	99.0	99.6	99.9	7
8	93.2	94.3	95.3	96.1	96.8	97.4	97.8	98.2	98.5	98.8	99.5	99.8	8
9	91.3	92.8	94.1	95.1	96.0	96.7	97.2	97.7	98.1	98.4	99.4	99.8	9
10	89.1	91.0	92.6	93.9	94.9	95.8	96.5	97.1	97.6	98.0	99.2	99.7	10
11	86.5	88.8	90.8	92.4	93.7	94.8	95.7	96.4	97.0	97.6	99.1	99.6	11
12	83.3	86.2	88.6	90.6	92.2	93.6	94.7	95.6	96.3	97.0	98.8	99.6	12
13	79.4	83.0	85.9	88.4	90.4	92.1	93.4	94.6	95.5	96.3	98.6	99.4	13
14	74.7	79.1	82.8	85.7	88.2	90.3	91.9	93.3	94.5	95.4	98.2	99.3	14
15	69.0	74.5	78.9	82.6	85.6	88.1	90.1	91.8	93.3	94.4	97.8	99.2	15
16	62.2	68.7	74.2	78.7	82.4	85.5	88.0	90.0	91.8	93.2	97.3	99.0	16
17	54.0	62.0	68.6	74.1	78.6	82.3	85.3	87.9	90.0	91.7	96.8	98.7	17
18	44.0	53.8	61.8	68.5	73.9	78.4	82.2	85.3	87.8	89.9	96.1	98.5	18
19	32.0	43.9	53.7	61.7	68.3	73.8	78.3	82.1	85.2	87.7	95.2	98.1	19
20	17.5	31.9	43.8	53.5	61.6	68.2	73.7	78.3	82.0	85.1	94.2	97.7	20
21	0.0	17.5	31.8	43.7	53.4	61.5	68.1	73.6	78.2	82.0	93.0	97.3	21
22	0.0	0.0	17.4	31.8	43.6	53.3	61.4	68.1	73.6	78.1	91.5	96.7	22
23	0.0	0.0	0.0	17.4	31.7	43.5	53.3	61.3	68.0	73.5	89.7	96.0	23
24	0.0	0.0	0.0	0.0	17.3	31.6	43.5	53.2	61.3	68.0	87.5	95.2	24
25	0.0	0.0	0.0	0.0	0.0	17.3	31.6	43.4	53.2	61.2	84.9	94.1	25
26	0.0	0.0	0.0	0.0	0.0	0.0	17.3	31.6	43.4	53.1	81.8	92.9	26
27	0.0	0.0	0.0	0.0	0.0	0.0	0.0	17.3	31.5	43.3	78.0	91.4	27
28	0.0	0.0	0.0	0.0	0.0	0.0	0.0	0.0	17.2	31.5	73.4	89.6	28
29	0.0	0.0	0.0	0.0	0.0	0.0	0.0	0.0	0.0	17.2	67.8	87.5	29
30	0.0	0.0	0.0	0.0	0.0	0.0	0.0	0.0	0.0	0.0	61.1	84.9	30
31	0.0	0.0	0.0	0.0	0.0	0.0	0.0	0.0	0.0	0.0	53.0	81.7	31
32	0.0	0.0	0.0	0.0	0.0	0.0	0.0	0.0	0.0	0.0	43.2	77.9	32
33	0.0	0.0	0.0	0.0	0.0	0.0	0.0	0.0	0.0	0.0	31.4	73.3	33
34	0.0	0.0	0.0	0.0	0.0	0.0	0.0	0.0	0.0	0.0	17.2	67.8	34
35	0.0	0.0	0.0	0.0	0.0	0.0	0.0	0.0	0.0	0.0	0.0	61.1	35
36	0.0	0.0	0.0	0.0	0.0	0.0	0.0	0.0	0.0	0.0	0.0	53.0	36
37	0.0	0.0	0.0	0.0	0.0	0.0	0.0	0.0	0.0	0.0	0.0	43.2	37
38	0.0	0.0	0.0	0.0	0.0	0.0	0.0	0.0	0.0	0.0	0.0	31.4	38
39	0.0	0.0	0.0	0.0	0.0	0.0	0.0	0.0	0.0	0.0	0.0	17.2	39

EXAMPLES *ON PAGES A-382 TO A-397*

AGE OF LOAN	ORIGINAL TERM IN YEARS												AGE OF LOAN
	2.0	3.0	5.0	8.0	10.0	12.0	15.0	16.0	17.0	18.0	19.0	20.0	
1	54.9	73.0	87.1	94.4	96.5	97.8	98.8	99.0	99.2	99.4	99.5	99.6	1
2	0.0	40.1	71.3	87.5	92.2	95.0	97.4	97.9	98.3	98.6	98.8	99.1	2
3	0.0	0.0	52.1	79.1	87.0	91.7	95.6	96.4	97.1	97.6	98.1	98.4	3
4	0.0	0.0	28.6	68.9	80.7	87.7	93.5	94.7	95.7	96.5	97.1	97.7	4
5	0.0	0.0	0.0	56.4	72.9	82.7	90.9	92.6	94.0	95.1	96.0	96.7	5
6	0.0	0.0	0.0	41.2	63.5	76.7	87.7	90.0	91.9	93.4	94.6	95.6	6
7	0.0	0.0	0.0	22.6	52.0	69.3	83.8	86.9	89.3	91.3	92.9	94.2	7
8	0.0	0.0	0.0	0.0	38.0	60.4	79.1	83.0	86.2	88.7	90.8	92.5	8
9	0.0	0.0	0.0	0.0	20.9	49.4	73.3	78.3	82.4	85.6	88.3	90.4	9
10	0.0	0.0	0.0	0.0	0.0	36.1	66.3	72.6	77.7	81.8	85.2	87.9	10
11	0.0	0.0	0.0	0.0	0.0	19.8	57.7	65.7	72.1	77.2	81.4	84.8	11
12	0.0	0.0	0.0	0.0	0.0	0.0	47.3	57.2	65.1	71.6	76.8	81.1	12
13	0.0	0.0	0.0	0.0	0.0	0.0	34.5	46.8	56.7	64.7	71.2	76.5	13
14	0.0	0.0	0.0	0.0	0.0	0.0	19.0	34.2	46.4	56.4	64.4	70.9	14
15	0.0	0.0	0.0	0.0	0.0	0.0	0.0	18.8	33.9	46.1	56.1	64.1	15
16	0.0	0.0	0.0	0.0	0.0	0.0	0.0	0.0	18.6	33.7	45.9	55.8	16
17	0.0	0.0	0.0	0.0	0.0	0.0	0.0	0.0	0.0	18.5	33.5	45.7	17
18	0.0	0.0	0.0	0.0	0.0	0.0	0.0	0.0	0.0	0.0	18.4	33.4	18
19	0.0	0.0	0.0	0.0	0.0	0.0	0.0	0.0	0.0	0.0	0.0	18.3	19

20.00

AGE OF LOAN	ORIGINAL TERM IN YEARS												AGE OF LOAN
	21.0	22.0	23.0	24.0	25.0	26.0	27.0	28.0	29.0	30.0	35.0	40.0	
1	99.7	99.7	99.8	99.8	99.8	99.9	99.9	99.9	99.9	99.9	100.0	100.0	1
2	99.2	99.4	99.5	99.6	99.7	99.7	99.8	99.8	99.8	99.9	100.0	100.0	2
3	98.7	99.0	99.1	99.3	99.4	99.5	99.6	99.7	99.7	99.8	99.9	100.0	3
4	98.1	98.4	98.7	99.0	99.1	99.3	99.4	99.5	99.6	99.7	99.9	100.0	4
5	97.3	97.8	98.2	98.5	98.8	99.0	99.2	99.3	99.5	99.6	99.8	99.9	5
6	96.4	97.1	97.6	98.0	98.4	98.7	98.9	99.1	99.3	99.4	99.8	99.9	6
7	95.3	96.1	96.8	97.4	97.9	98.3	98.6	98.8	99.0	99.2	99.7	99.9	7
8	93.9	95.0	95.9	96.6	97.3	97.7	98.2	98.5	98.8	99.0	99.6	99.9	8
9	92.2	93.6	94.8	95.7	96.5	97.1	97.6	98.1	98.4	98.7	99.5	99.8	9
10	90.1	91.9	93.4	94.6	95.6	96.4	97.0	97.6	98.0	98.4	99.4	99.8	10
11	87.6	89.9	91.7	93.2	94.4	95.4	96.3	96.9	97.5	97.9	99.2	99.7	11
12	84.5	87.4	89.7	91.5	93.1	94.3	95.3	96.2	96.9	97.4	99.1	99.6	12
13	80.8	84.3	87.2	89.5	91.4	92.9	94.2	95.3	96.1	96.8	98.8	99.6	13
14	76.2	80.6	84.1	87.0	89.3	91.3	92.9	94.1	95.2	96.1	98.5	99.5	14
15	70.7	76.0	80.4	83.9	86.9	89.2	91.2	92.8	94.1	95.1	98.2	99.3	15
16	63.9	70.5	75.8	80.2	83.8	86.7	89.1	91.1	92.7	94.0	97.8	99.2	16
17	55.6	63.7	70.3	75.7	80.1	83.7	86.7	89.1	91.0	92.7	97.3	99.0	17
18	45.6	55.5	63.6	70.2	75.6	80.0	83.6	86.6	89.0	91.0	96.7	98.8	18
19	33.3	45.4	55.3	63.5	70.1	75.5	79.9	83.6	86.5	89.0	95.9	98.5	19
20	18.3	33.2	45.3	55.2	63.4	70.0	75.4	79.9	83.5	86.5	95.0	98.1	20
21	0.0	18.2	33.1	45.2	55.2	63.3	69.9	75.4	79.8	83.4	93.9	97.7	21
22	0.0	0.0	18.2	33.0	45.2	55.1	63.2	69.9	75.3	79.8	92.5	97.2	22
23	0.0	0.0	0.0	18.1	33.0	45.1	55.0	63.2	69.8	75.3	90.8	96.6	23
24	0.0	0.0	0.0	0.0	18.1	32.9	45.1	55.0	63.1	69.8	88.8	95.9	24
25	0.0	0.0	0.0	0.0	0.0	18.1	32.9	45.0	55.0	63.1	86.3	94.9	25
26	0.0	0.0	0.0	0.0	0.0	0.0	18.1	32.9	45.0	55.0	83.3	93.8	26
27	0.0	0.0	0.0	0.0	0.0	0.0	0.0	18.1	32.9	45.0	79.6	92.5	27
28	0.0	0.0	0.0	0.0	0.0	0.0	0.0	0.0	18.1	32.9	75.1	90.8	28
29	0.0	0.0	0.0	0.0	0.0	0.0	0.0	0.0	0.0	18.1	69.7	88.8	29
30	0.0	0.0	0.0	0.0	0.0	0.0	0.0	0.0	0.0	0.0	63.0	86.3	30
31	0.0	0.0	0.0	0.0	0.0	0.0	0.0	0.0	0.0	0.0	54.9	83.3	31
32	0.0	0.0	0.0	0.0	0.0	0.0	0.0	0.0	0.0	0.0	44.9	79.6	32
33	0.0	0.0	0.0	0.0	0.0	0.0	0.0	0.0	0.0	0.0	32.8	75.2	33
34	0.0	0.0	0.0	0.0	0.0	0.0	0.0	0.0	0.0	0.0	18.1	69.7	34
35	0.0	0.0	0.0	0.0	0.0	0.0	0.0	0.0	0.0	0.0	0.1	63.0	35
36	0.0	0.0	0.0	0.0	0.0	0.0	0.0	0.0	0.0	0.0	0.0	54.9	36
37	0.0	0.0	0.0	0.0	0.0	0.0	0.0	0.0	0.0	0.0	0.0	45.0	37
38	0.0	0.0	0.0	0.0	0.0	0.0	0.0	0.0	0.0	0.0	0.0	33.0	38
39	0.0	0.0	0.0	0.0	0.0	0.0	0.0	0.0	0.0	0.0	0.0	18.2	39

EXAMPLES ON PAGES A-382 TO A-397

BALLOON PAYMENT TABLE

Due Dates in Years →	2	3	4	5	6	7	8	9	10
Monthly Payment % ↓									

8% Interest

Payment %	2	3	4	5	6	7	8	9	10
0.70	99.13	98.65	98.12	97.55	96.93	96.26	95.54	94.75	93.90
0.75	97.84	96.62	95.30	93.88	92.33	90.66	88.84	86.88	84.75
0.90	93.95	90.54	86.85	82.86	78.53	73.84	68.76	63.27	57.31
1.00	91.36	86.49	81.22	75.51	69.32	62.63	55.38	47.52	39.02
1.10	88.76	82.43	75.58	68.16	60.12	51.42	41.99	31.78	20.72
1.20	86.17	78.38	69.95	60.81	50.92	40.21	28.60	16.04	2.43
1.25	84.87	76.35	67.13	57.14	46.32	34.60	21.91	8.16	0.0
1.30	83.58	74.33	64.31	53.46	41.72	28.99	15.22	0.29	0.0
1.40	80.98	70.27	58.68	46.12	32.51	17.78	1.83	0.0	0.0
1.50	78.39	66.22	53.04	38.77	23.31	6.57	0.0	0.0	0.0
1.60	75.80	62.17	47.41	31.42	14.11	0.0	0.0	0.0	0.0
1.70	73.20	58.11	41.77	24.07	4.91	0.0	0.0	0.0	0.0
1.75	71.91	56.09	38.95	20.40	0.31	0.0	0.0	0.0	0.0
1.80	70.61	54.06	36.14	16.73	0.0	0.0	0.0	0.0	0.0
1.90	68.02	50.01	30.50	9.38	0.0	0.0	0.0	0.0	0.0
2.00	65.42	45.95	24.87	2.03	0.0	0.0	0.0	0.0	0.0
2.10	62.83	41.90	19.23	0.0	0.0	0.0	0.0	0.0	0.0

8¼% Interest

Payment %	2	3	4	5	6	7	8	9	10
0.70	99.67	99.49	99.29	99.07	98.84	98.58	98.30	98.00	97.68
0.75	98.37	97.46	96.46	95.38	94.20	92.93	91.54	90.04	88.40
0.90	94.48	91.35	87.96	84.28	80.29	75.95	71.24	66.13	60.58
1.00	91.88	87.28	82.30	76.89	71.01	64.63	57.71	50.19	42.02
1.10	89.28	83.22	76.64	69.49	61.74	53.32	44.17	34.25	23.47
1.20	86.68	79.15	70.97	62.10	52.46	42.00	30.64	18.31	4.92
1.25	85.38	77.11	68.14	58.40	47.82	36.34	23.87	10.34	0.0
1.30	84.08	75.08	65.31	54.70	43.18	30.68	17.11	2.37	0.0
1.40	81.48	71.01	59.64	47.30	33.91	19.36	3.57	0.0	0.0
1.50	78.88	66.94	53.98	39.91	24.63	8.05	0.0	0.0	0.0
1.60	76.28	62.87	48.32	32.51	15.36	0.0	0.0	0.0	0.0
1.70	73.68	58.80	42.65	25.12	6.08	0.0	0.0	0.0	0.0
1.75	72.38	56.77	39.82	21.42	1.44	0.0	0.0	0.0	0.0
1.80	71.08	54.73	36.99	17.72	0.0	0.0	0.0	0.0	0.0
1.90	68.48	50.66	31.32	10.33	0.0	0.0	0.0	0.0	0.0
2.00	65.88	46.60	25.66	2.93	0.0	0.0	0.0	0.0	0.0
2.10	63.28	42.53	20.00	0.0	0.0	0.0	0.0	0.0	0.0

8½% Interest

Payment %	2	3	4	5	6	7	8	9	10
0.70	100.22	100.34	100.47	100.62	100.78	100.95	101.13	101.34	101.56
0.75	98.91	98.30	97.63	96.90	96.10	95.24	94.30	93.27	92.16
0.90	95.00	92.17	89.09	85.73	82.08	78.10	73.78	69.07	63.94
1.00	92.40	88.09	83.39	78.29	72.73	66.68	60.09	52.93	45.12
1.10	89.79	84.00	77.70	70.84	63.38	55.25	46.41	36.79	26.31
1.20	87.19	79.92	72.01	63.40	54.03	43.83	32.73	20.65	7.50
1.25	85.88	77.88	69.16	59.68	49.35	38.12	25.89	12.58	0.0
1.30	84.58	75.83	66.32	55.95	44.68	32.40	19.05	4.51	0.0
1.40	81.97	71.75	60.62	48.51	35.33	20.98	5.36	0.0	0.0
1.50	79.37	67.67	54.93	41.07	25.98	9.56	0.0	0.0	0.0
1.60	76.76	63.58	49.24	33.62	16.63	0.0	0.0	0.0	0.0
1.70	74.16	59.50	43.54	26.18	7.28	0.0	0.0	0.0	0.0
1.75	72.85	57.46	40.70	22.46	2.60	0.0	0.0	0.0	0.0
1.80	71.55	55.41	37.85	18.73	0.0	0.0	0.0	0.0	0.0
1.90	68.94	51.33	32.16	11.29	0.0	0.0	0.0	0.0	0.0
2.00	66.34	47.24	26.46	3.84	0.0	0.0	0.0	0.0	0.0
2.10	63.73	43.16	20.77	0.0	0.0	0.0	0.0	0.0	0.0

8¾% Interest

Payment %	2	3	4	5	6	7	8	9	10
0.70	100.76	101.19	101.67	102.18	102.74	103.36	104.03	104.76	105.56
0.75	99.45	99.14	98.81	98.44	98.03	97.59	97.11	96.59	96.02
0.90	95.54	93.00	90.22	87.20	83.90	80.30	76.37	72.08	67.40
1.00	92.92	88.90	84.50	79.71	74.47	68.76	62.53	55.74	48.32
1.10	90.31	84.80	78.78	72.21	65.05	57.23	48.70	39.40	29.24
1.20	87.70	80.70	73.06	64.72	55.62	45.70	34.87	23.05	10.16
1.25	86.39	78.65	70.19	60.97	50.91	39.93	27.95	14.88	0.62
1.30	85.09	76.60	67.33	57.23	46.20	34.17	21.04	6.71	0.0
1.40	82.47	72.50	61.61	49.73	36.77	22.63	7.20	0.0	0.0
1.50	79.86	68.40	55.89	42.24	27.35	11.10	0.0	0.0	0.0
1.60	77.25	64.30	50.17	34.75	17.92	0.0	0.0	0.0	0.0
1.70	74.64	60.20	44.44	27.25	8.50	0.0	0.0	0.0	0.0
1.75	73.33	58.15	41.58	23.51	3.79	0.0	0.0	0.0	0.0
1.80	72.02	56.10	38.72	19.76	0.0	0.0	0.0	0.0	0.0
1.90	69.41	52.00	33.00	12.27	0.0	0.0	0.0	0.0	0.0
2.00	66.80	47.90	27.28	4.77	0.0	0.0	0.0	0.0	0.0
2.10	64.19	43.80	21.55	0.0	0.0	0.0	0.0	0.0	0.0

EXAMPLES *ON PAGES A-382 TO A-397*

BALLOON PAYMENT TABLE

Due Dates in Years →	2	3	4	5	6	7	8	9	10

Monthly Payment % ↓

9% Interest

	2	3	4	5	6	7	8	9	10
0.75	100.00	100.00	100.00	100.00	100.00	100.00	100.00	100.00	100.00
0.90	96.07	93.83	91.37	88.69	85.75	82.54	79.02	75.18	70.97
1.00	93.45	89.71	85.62	81.14	76.25	70.89	65.03	58.63	51.62
1.10	90.83	85.60	79.87	73.60	66.75	59.25	51.05	42.08	32.27
1.20	88.22	81.48	74.12	66.06	57.25	47.61	37.06	25.53	12.92
1.25	86.91	79.42	71.24	62.29	52.50	41.79	30.07	17.26	3.24
1.30	85.60	77.37	68.36	58.52	47.75	35.96	23.08	8.98	0.0
1.40	82.98	73.25	62.61	50.97	38.25	24.32	9.09	0.0	0.0
1.50	80.36	65.14	56.86	43.43	28.74	12.68	0.0	0.0	0.0
1.60	77.74	65.02	51.11	35.89	19.24	1.04	0.0	0.0	0.0
1.70	75.12	60.90	45.35	28.35	9.74	0.0	0.0	0.0	0.0
1.75	73.81	58.85	42.48	24.58	4.99	0.0	0.0	0.0	0.0
1.80	72.50	56.79	39.60	20.80	0.24	0.0	0.0	0.0	0.0
1.90	69.88	52.67	33.85	13.26	0.0	0.0	0.0	0.0	0.0
2.00	67.26	48.56	28.10	5.72	0.0	0.0	0.0	0.0	0.0
2.10	64.65	44.44	22.35	0.0	0.0	0.0	0.0	0.0	0.0
2.20	62.03	40.33	16.59	0.0	0.0	0.0	0.0	0.0	0.0

9¼% Interest

	2	3	4	5	6	7	8	9	10
0.75	100.54	100.86	101.20	101.57	101.98	102.44	102.93	103.47	104.07
0.90	96.61	94.66	92.53	90.19	87.63	84.82	81.73	78.35	74.65
1.00	93.98	90.53	86.75	82.60	78.05	73.06	67.59	61.60	55.02
1.10	91.36	86.40	80.97	75.01	68.47	61.31	53.45	44.84	35.39
1.20	88.73	82.27	75.19	67.42	58.90	49.56	39.31	28.08	15.76
1.25	87.42	80.21	72.29	63.62	54.11	43.68	32.24	19.70	5.95
1.30	86.11	78.14	69.40	59.82	49.32	37.80	25.17	11.32	0.0
1.40	83.48	74.01	63.62	52.23	39.74	26.05	11.03	0.0	0.0
1.50	80.86	69.88	57.84	44.64	30.17	14.29	0.0	0.0	0.0
1.60	78.23	65.75	52.06	37.05	20.59	2.54	0.0	0.0	0.0
1.70	75.61	61.62	46.28	29.46	11.01	0.0	0.0	0.0	0.0
1.75	74.29	59.55	43.39	25.66	6.22	0.0	0.0	0.0	0.0
1.80	72.98	57.49	40.50	21.86	1.43	0.0	0.0	0.0	0.0
1.90	70.36	53.36	34.71	14.27	0.0	0.0	0.0	0.0	0.0
2.00	67.73	49.22	28.93	6.68	0.0	0.0	0.0	0.0	0.0
2.10	65.11	45.09	23.15	0.0	0.0	0.0	0.0	0.0	0.0
2.20	62.48	40.96	17.37	0.0	0.0	0.0	0.0	0.0	0.0

9½% Interest

	2	3	4	5	6	7	8	9	10
0.75	101.09	101.72	102.41	103.18	104.01	104.93	105.94	107.05	108.27
0.90	97.15	95.51	93.70	91.72	89.54	87.14	84.51	81.61	78.43
1.00	94.52	91.36	87.89	84.08	79.89	75.28	70.21	64.64	58.52
1.10	91.89	87.21	82.08	76.44	70.23	63.41	55.91	47.67	38.62
1.20	89.25	83.07	76.27	68.79	60.58	51.55	41.62	30.70	18.71
1.25	87.94	80.99	73.36	64.97	55.75	45.61	34.47	22.22	8.75
1.30	86.62	78.92	70.46	61.15	50.92	39.68	27.32	13.73	0.0
1.40	83.99	74.77	64.64	53.51	41.27	27.81	13.02	0.0	0.0
1.50	81.36	70.63	58.83	45.87	31.61	15.95	0.0	0.0	0.0
1.60	78.73	66.48	53.02	38.22	21.96	4.08	0.0	0.0	0.0
1.70	76.09	62.34	47.21	30.58	12.31	0.0	0.0	0.0	0.0
1.75	74.78	60.26	44.30	26.76	7.48	0.0	0.0	0.0	0.0
1.80	73.46	58.19	41.40	22.94	2.65	0.0	0.0	0.0	0.0
1.90	70.83	54.04	35.59	15.30	0.0	0.0	0.0	0.0	0.0
2.00	68.20	49.90	29.77	7.66	0.0	0.0	0.0	0.0	0.0
2.10	65.57	45.75	23.96	0.01	0.0	0.0	0.0	0.0	0.0
2.20	62.94	41.60	18.15	0.0	0.0	0.0	0.0	0.0	0.0

9¾% Interest

	2	3	4	5	6	7	8	9	10
0.75	101.65	102.60	103.64	104.80	106.07	107.47	109.02	110.72	112.60
0.90	97.69	96.36	94.89	93.27	91.48	89.52	87.35	84.96	82.33
1.00	95.05	92.19	89.05	85.58	81.75	77.54	72.89	67.77	62.13
1.10	92.41	88.03	83.20	77.88	72.02	65.56	58.44	50.59	41.94
1.20	89.78	83.87	77.36	70.19	62.29	53.58	43.98	33.40	21.75
1.25	88.46	81.79	74.44	66.34	57.42	47.59	36.75	24.81	11.65
1.30	87.14	79.71	71.52	62.50	52.55	41.60	29.52	16.22	1.55
1.40	84.50	75.55	65.68	54.80	42.82	29.62	15.07	0.0	0.0
1.50	81.86	71.38	59.84	47.11	33.09	17.64	0.61	0.0	0.0
1.60	79.22	67.22	53.99	39.42	23.36	5.66	0.0	0.0	0.0
1.70	76.59	63.06	48.15	31.73	13.62	0.0	0.0	0.0	0.0
1.75	75.27	60.98	45.23	27.88	8.76	0.0	0.0	0.0	0.0
1.80	73.95	58.90	42.31	24.03	3.89	0.0	0.0	0.0	0.0
1.90	71.31	54.73	36.47	16.34	0.0	0.0	0.0	0.0	0.0
2.00	68.67	50.57	30.63	8.65	0.0	0.0	0.0	0.0	0.0
2.10	66.03	46.41	24.78	0.96	0.0	0.0	0.0	0.0	0.0
2.20	63.39	42.25	18.94	0.0	0.0	0.0	0.0	0.0	0.0

EXAMPLES ON PAGES A-382 TO A-397

BALLOON PAYMENT TABLE

Due Dates in Years →	2	3	4	5	6	7	8	9	10
Monthly Payment %				10% Interest					
0.80	100.88	101.39	101.95	102.57	103.26	104.02	104.86	105.79	106.81
0.90	98.24	97.21	96.08	94.84	93.46	91.94	90.25	88.40	86.34
1.00	95.59	93.04	90.21	87.09	83.65	79.84	75.64	70.99	65.86
1.10	92.95	88.86	84.34	79.35	73.84	67.75	61.02	53.58	45.37
1.20	90.30	84.68	78.47	71.61	64.03	55.65	46.40	36.18	24.89
1.25	88.98	82.59	75.53	67.73	59.12	49.60	39.09	27.48	14.65
1.30	87.66	80.50	72.60	63.86	54.21	43.56	31.78	18.77	4.40
1.40	85.01	76.32	66.72	56.12	44.40	31.46	17.16	1.37	0.0
1.50	82.37	72.15	60.85	48.37	34.59	19.37	2.54	0.0	0.0
1.60	79.72	67.97	54.98	40.63	24.78	7.27	C.0	0.0	0.0
1.70	77.08	63.79	49.11	32.89	14.97	0.0	0.0	0.0	0.0
1.75	75.76	61.70	46.17	29.02	10.06	0.0	0.0	0.0	0.0
1.80	74.43	59.61	43.23	25.14	5.16	0.0	0.0	0.0	0.0
1.90	71.79	55.43	37.36	17.40	0.C	0.0	0.0	0.0	0.0
2.00	69.15	51.25	31.49	9.66	0.0	0.0	0.0	0.0	0.0
2.10	66.50	47.08	25.62	1.91	0.0	0.0	0.0	0.0	0.0
2.20	63.86	42.90	19.75	0.0	0.0	0.0	0.0	0.0	0.0
				10¼% Interest					
0.80	101.43	102.27	103.19	104.22	105.35	106.60	107.99	109.53	111.24
0.90	98.78	98.08	97.29	96.43	95.47	94.40	93.22	91.92	90.47
1.00	96.13	93.88	91.39	88.63	85.57	82.19	78.44	74.29	69.69
1.10	93.48	89.69	85.49	80.84	75.68	69.98	63.66	56.66	48.91
1.20	90.83	85.49	79.59	73.04	65.79	57.77	48.88	39.03	28.13
1.25	89.51	83.40	76.63	69.14	60.85	51.66	41.49	30.22	17.74
1.30	88.18	81.30	73.68	65.25	55.90	45.56	34.10	21.41	7.35
1.40	85.53	77.11	67.78	57.45	46.01	33.34	19.32	3.78	0.0
1.50	82.88	72.91	61.88	49.66	36.12	21.13	4.53	0.0	0.0
1.60	80.23	68.72	55.97	41.86	26.23	8.92	0.0	0.0	0.0
1.70	77.58	64.52	50.07	34.07	16.34	0.0	0.0	0.0	0.0
1.75	76.25	62.43	47.12	30.17	11.39	0.0	0.0	0.0	0.0
1.80	74.92	60.33	44.17	26.27	6.45	0.0	0.0	0.0	0.0
1.90	72.27	56.14	38.27	18.48	0.0	0.0	0.0	0.0	0.0
2.00	69.62	51.94	32.36	10.68	0.0	0.0	0.0	0.0	0.0
2.10	66.97	47.75	26.46	2.89	0.0	0.0	0.0	0.0	0.0
2.20	64.32	43.55	20.56	0.0	0.0	0.0	0.0	0.0	0.0
				10½% Interest					
0.80	101.99	103.15	104.45	105.88	107.47	109.24	111.20	113.38	115.79
0.90	99.33	98.95	98.51	98.04	97.50	96.91	96.26	95.53	94.73
1.00	96.68	94.74	92.58	90.19	87.53	84.59	81.31	77.68	73.65
1.10	94.02	90.53	86.65	82.34	77.56	72.26	66.37	59.83	52.57
1.20	91.36	86.32	80.72	74.50	67.59	59.93	51.42	41.97	31.48
1.25	90.03	84.21	77.75	70.57	62.61	53.76	43.94	33.04	20.94
1.30	88.70	82.11	74.78	66.65	57.62	47.60	36.47	24.12	10.40
1.40	86.05	77.90	68.85	58.80	47.65	35.27	21.52	6.26	0.0
1.50	83.39	73.69	62.92	50.96	37.68	22.94	6.58	0.0	0.0
1.60	80.73	69.48	56.98	43.11	27.71	10.61	0.0	0.0	0.0
1.70	78.07	65.27	51.05	35.26	17.74	0.0	0.0	0.0	0.0
1.75	76.74	63.16	48.08	31.34	12.75	0.0	0.0	0.0	0.0
1.80	75.42	61.06	45.11	27.42	7.77	0.0	0.0	0.0	0.0
1.90	72.76	56.85	39.18	19.57	0.0	0.0	0.0	0.0	0.0
2.00	70.10	52.64	33.25	11.72	0.C	0.0	0.0	0.0	C.0
2.10	67.44	48.43	27.31	3.88	0.0	0.0	C.0	0.0	0.0
2.20	64.78	44.22	21.38	0.0	0.0	0.0	0.0	0.0	0.0
				10¾% Interest					
0.80	102.55	104.05	105.71	107.56	109.62	111.92	114.47	117.32	120.48
0.90	99.89	99.82	99.75	99.67	99.58	99.48	99.36	99.24	99.10
1.00	97.22	95.60	93.79	91.77	89.53	87.03	84.25	81.16	77.72
1.10	94.56	91.37	87.82	83.87	79.48	74.58	69.14	63.08	56.33
1.20	91.90	87.15	81.86	75.97	69.42	62.13	54.02	44.99	34.94
1.25	90.56	85.03	78.88	72.02	64.40	55.91	46.46	35.95	24.25
1.30	89.23	82.92	75.89	68.07	59.37	49.69	38.91	26.91	13.56
1.40	86.57	78.69	69.93	60.17	49.32	37.24	23.79	8.82	0.0
1.50	83.90	74.47	63.96	52.28	39.27	24.79	8.67	0.0	0.0
1.60	81.24	70.24	58.00	44.38	29.21	12.34	C.0	0.0	0.0
1.70	78.57	66.01	52.04	36.48	19.16	0.0	0.0	0.0	0.0
1.75	77.24	63.90	49.05	32.53	14.14	0.0	0.0	0.0	0.0
1.80	75.91	61.79	46.07	28.58	9.11	0.0	0.0	0.0	0.0
1.90	73.25	57.56	40.11	20.68	0.0	0.0	0.0	0.0	0.0
2.00	70.58	53.34	34.14	12.78	0.0	0.0	0.0	0.0	0.0
2.10	67.92	49.11	28.18	4.88	0.0	0.0	0.0	0.0	0.0
2.20	65.25	44.88	22.21	0.0	0.0	0.0	0.0	0.0	0.0

EXAMPLES *ON PAGES A-382 TO A-397*

BALLOON PAYMENT TABLE

Due Dates in Years →	2	3	4	5	6	7	8	9	10
Monthly Payment % ↓									

11% Interest

	2	3	4	5	6	7	8	9	10
0.90	100.44	100.70	100.99	101.32	101.68	102.08	102.53	103.03	103.59
1.00	97.77	96.46	95.00	93.37	91.55	89.52	87.26	84.73	81.91
1.10	95.10	92.22	89.01	85.42	81.42	76.95	71.97	66.42	60.22
1.20	92.43	87.98	83.01	77.47	71.28	64.39	56.69	48.10	38.52
1.25	91.10	85.86	80.01	73.49	66.22	58.10	49.04	38.94	27.67
1.30	89.76	83.74	77.02	69.52	61.15	51.82	41.40	29.78	16.82
1.40	87.09	79.50	71.02	61.57	51.02	39.25	26.11	11.46	0.0
1.50	84.42	75.25	65.02	53.61	40.88	26.68	10.83	0.0	0.0
1.60	81.75	71.01	59.03	45.66	30.75	14.11	0.0	0.0	0.0
1.70	79.08	66.77	53.03	37.71	20.61	1.54	0.0	0.0	0.0
1.75	77.74	64.65	50.04	33.73	15.55	0.0	0.0	0.0	0.0
1.80	76.41	62.53	47.04	29.76	10.48	0.0	0.0	0.0	0.0
1.90	73.74	58.28	41.04	21.81	0.34	0.0	0.0	0.0	0.0
2.00	71.07	54.04	35.05	13.85	0.0	0.0	0.0	0.0	0.0
2.10	68.39	49.80	29.05	5.90	0.0	0.0	0.0	0.0	0.0
2.20	65.72	45.56	23.06	0.0	0.0	0.0	0.0	0.0	0.0
2.25	64.39	43.44	20.06	0.0	0.0	0.0	0.0	0.0	0.0

11¼% Interest

	2	3	4	5	6	7	8	9	10
0.90	101.00	101.59	102.25	102.99	103.82	104.74	105.78	106.93	108.23
1.00	98.33	97.34	96.23	95.00	93.61	92.07	90.34	88.40	86.24
1.10	95.65	93.08	90.21	86.99	83.40	79.37	74.88	69.85	64.22
1.20	92.97	88.82	84.18	78.99	73.18	66.68	59.42	51.29	42.20
1.25	91.63	86.69	81.17	74.98	68.07	60.34	51.69	42.01	31.19
1.30	90.29	84.56	78.15	70.98	62.96	53.99	43.96	32.74	20.19
1.40	87.62	80.30	72.12	62.98	52.74	41.30	28.50	14.18	0.0
1.50	84.94	76.05	66.10	54.97	42.53	28.61	13.04	0.0	0.0
1.60	82.26	71.79	60.07	46.97	32.31	15.92	0.0	0.0	0.0
1.70	79.58	67.53	54.04	38.96	22.09	3.23	0.0	0.0	0.0
1.75	78.25	65.40	51.03	34.96	16.98	0.0	0.0	0.0	0.0
1.80	76.91	63.27	48.02	30.96	11.88	0.0	0.0	0.0	0.0
1.90	74.23	59.01	41.99	22.95	1.66	0.0	0.0	0.0	0.0
2.00	71.55	54.75	35.96	14.95	0.0	0.0	0.0	0.0	0.0
2.10	68.87	50.49	29.94	6.94	0.0	0.0	0.0	0.0	0.0
2.20	66.20	46.24	23.91	0.0	0.0	0.0	0.0	0.0	0.0
2.25	64.86	44.11	20.90	0.0	0.0	0.0	0.0	0.0	0.0

11½% Interest

	2	3	4	5	6	7	8	9	10
0.90	101.56	102.49	103.53	104.69	106.00	107.46	109.10	110.94	113.00
1.00	98.88	98.22	97.47	96.64	95.71	94.66	93.48	92.16	90.69
1.10	96.20	93.94	91.42	88.58	85.41	81.84	77.85	73.37	68.35
1.20	93.51	89.67	85.36	80.52	75.11	69.03	62.21	54.58	46.01
1.25	92.17	87.53	82.33	76.50	69.95	62.62	54.40	45.18	34.84
1.30	90.83	85.39	79.30	72.47	64.80	56.21	46.58	35.78	23.67
1.40	88.15	81.12	73.24	64.41	54.50	43.40	30.95	16.98	1.33
1.50	85.46	76.84	67.18	56.35	44.20	30.58	15.31	0.0	0.0
1.60	82.78	72.57	61.12	48.29	33.90	17.77	0.0	0.0	0.0
1.70	80.09	68.29	55.07	40.23	23.60	4.95	0.0	0.0	0.0
1.75	78.75	66.16	52.04	36.20	18.45	0.0	0.0	0.0	0.0
1.80	77.41	64.02	49.01	32.17	13.30	0.0	0.0	0.0	0.0
1.90	74.72	59.74	42.95	24.12	3.00	0.0	0.0	0.0	0.0
2.00	72.04	55.47	36.89	16.06	0.0	0.0	0.0	0.0	0.0
2.10	69.36	51.20	30.83	8.00	0.0	0.0	0.0	0.0	0.0
2.20	66.67	46.92	24.77	0.0	0.0	0.0	0.0	0.0	0.0
2.25	65.33	44.78	21.74	0.0	0.0	0.0	0.0	0.0	0.0

11¾% Interest

	2	3	4	5	6	7	8	9	10
0.90	102.13	103.39	104.81	106.41	108.21	110.23	112.50	115.05	117.92
1.00	99.44	99.10	98.73	98.31	97.83	97.30	96.70	96.03	95.27
1.10	96.75	94.81	92.64	90.20	87.45	84.36	80.89	76.99	72.61
1.20	94.06	90.52	86.55	82.08	77.06	71.42	65.08	57.95	49.94
1.25	92.71	88.38	83.50	78.03	71.87	64.95	57.17	48.43	38.60
1.30	91.37	86.23	80.46	73.97	66.68	58.48	49.27	38.91	27.27
1.40	88.68	81.94	74.37	65.86	56.29	45.54	33.46	19.87	4.60
1.50	85.99	77.65	68.28	57.75	45.91	32.60	17.64	0.83	0.0
1.60	83.30	73.36	62.19	49.63	35.52	19.66	1.83	0.0	0.0
1.70	80.60	69.07	56.10	41.52	25.14	6.72	0.0	0.0	0.0
1.75	79.26	66.92	53.05	37.47	19.94	0.25	0.0	0.0	0.0
1.80	77.91	64.78	50.01	33.41	14.75	0.0	0.0	0.0	0.0
1.90	75.22	60.48	43.92	25.30	4.37	0.0	0.0	0.0	0.0
2.00	72.53	56.19	37.83	17.18	0.0	0.0	0.0	0.0	0.0
2.10	69.84	51.90	31.74	9.07	0.0	0.0	0.0	0.0	0.0
2.20	67.15	47.61	25.65	0.96	0.0	0.0	0.0	0.0	0.0
2.25	65.81	45.47	22.60	0.0	0.0	0.0	0.0	0.0	0.0

EXAMPLES *ON PAGES A-382 TO A-397*

BALLOON PAYMENT TABLE

Due Dates in Years →	2	3	4	5	6	7	8	9	10

Monthly Payment % ↓

12% Interest

	2	3	4	5	6	7	8	9	10
1.00	100.00	100.00	100.00	100.00	100.00	100.00	100.00	100.00	100.00
1.10	97.30	95.69	93.88	91.83	89.53	86.93	84.00	80.71	76.99
1.20	94.60	91.38	87.75	83.67	79.06	73.86	68.01	61.42	53.99
1.25	93.26	89.23	84.69	79.58	73.82	67.33	60.02	51.77	42.49
1.30	91.91	87.08	81.63	75.50	68.59	60.80	52.02	42.13	30.99
1.40	89.21	82.77	75.51	67.33	58.12	47.73	36.03	22.84	7.98
1.50	86.51	78.46	69.39	59.16	47.64	34.66	20.03	3.55	0.0
1.60	83.82	74.15	63.27	51.00	37.17	21.60	4.04	0.0	0.0
1.70	81.12	69.85	57.14	42.83	26.70	8.53	0.0	0.0	0.0
1.75	79.77	67.69	54.08	38.75	21.47	1.99	0.0	0.0	0.0
1.80	78.42	65.54	51.02	34.66	16.23	0.0	0.0	0.0	0.0
1.90	75.72	61.23	44.90	26.50	5.76	0.0	0.0	0.0	0.0
2.00	73.03	56.92	38.78	18.33	0.0	0.0	0.0	0.0	0.0
2.10	70.33	52.62	32.65	10.16	0.0	0.0	0.0	0.0	0.0
2.20	67.63	48.31	26.53	2.00	0.0	0.0	0.0	0.0	0.0
2.25	66.28	46.15	23.47	0.0	0.0	0.0	0.0	0.0	0.0
2.30	64.93	44.00	20.41	0.0	0.0	0.0	0.0	0.0	0.0

12¼% Interest

	2	3	4	5	6	7	8	9	10
1.00	100.56	100.90	101.28	101.71	102.19	102.74	103.36	104.06	104.85
1.10	97.86	96.58	95.13	93.49	91.64	89.55	87.19	84.53	81.52
1.20	95.15	92.25	88.97	85.27	81.08	76.36	71.02	64.99	58.17
1.25	93.80	90.09	85.90	81.16	75.80	69.76	62.93	55.21	46.50
1.30	92.45	87.93	82.82	77.05	70.53	63.16	54.84	45.44	34.83
1.40	89.75	83.60	76.66	68.82	59.97	49.97	38.67	25.90	11.48
1.50	87.04	79.28	70.51	60.60	49.41	36.77	22.49	6.36	0.0
1.60	84.34	74.96	64.36	52.38	38.85	23.58	6.32	0.0	0.0
1.70	81.63	70.63	58.20	44.16	28.30	10.38	0.0	0.0	0.0
1.75	80.28	68.47	55.12	40.05	23.02	3.78	0.0	0.0	0.0
1.80	78.93	66.31	52.05	35.94	17.74	0.0	0.0	0.0	0.0
1.90	76.23	61.98	45.89	27.72	7.18	0.0	0.0	0.0	0.0
2.00	73.52	57.66	39.74	19.49	0.0	0.0	0.0	0.0	0.0
2.10	70.82	53.33	33.58	11.27	0.0	0.0	0.0	0.0	0.0
2.20	68.11	49.01	27.43	3.05	0.0	0.0	0.0	0.0	0.0
2.25	66.76	46.85	24.35	0.0	0.0	0.0	0.0	0.0	0.0
2.30	65.41	44.69	21.27	0.0	0.0	0.0	0.0	0.0	0.0

12½% Interest

	2	3	4	5	6	7	8	9	10
1.00	101.13	101.81	102.57	103.44	104.43	105.54	106.81	108.23	109.85
1.10	98.42	97.47	96.39	95.17	93.79	92.22	90.45	88.45	86.18
1.20	95.71	93.13	90.20	86.89	83.15	78.90	74.09	68.65	62.49
1.25	94.35	90.96	87.11	82.75	77.82	72.24	65.91	58.75	50.64
1.30	93.00	88.79	84.02	78.62	72.50	65.58	57.73	48.85	38.80
1.40	90.29	84.44	77.83	70.34	61.86	52.25	41.37	29.05	15.10
1.50	87.58	80.10	71.64	62.06	51.21	38.92	25.01	9.25	0.0
1.60	84.86	75.76	65.46	53.78	40.57	25.60	8.65	0.0	0.0
1.70	82.15	71.42	59.27	45.51	29.92	12.27	0.0	0.0	0.0
1.75	80.80	69.25	56.18	41.37	24.60	5.61	0.0	0.0	0.0
1.80	79.44	67.08	53.08	37.23	19.28	0.0	0.0	0.0	0.0
1.90	76.73	62.74	46.90	28.95	8.63	0.0	0.0	0.0	0.0
2.00	74.02	58.40	40.71	20.68	0.0	0.0	0.0	0.0	0.0
2.10	71.31	54.06	34.52	12.40	0.0	0.0	0.0	0.0	0.0
2.20	68.60	49.72	28.34	4.12	0.0	0.0	0.0	0.0	0.0
2.25	67.25	47.55	25.24	0.0	0.0	0.0	0.0	0.0	0.0
2.30	65.89	45.38	22.15	0.0	0.0	0.0	0.0	0.0	0.0

12¾% Interest

	2	3	4	5	6	7	8	9	10
1.00	101.70	102.72	103.88	105.20	106.70	108.40	110.33	112.52	115.01
1.10	98.98	98.36	97.67	96.87	95.97	94.95	93.79	92.47	90.98
1.20	96.26	94.01	91.45	88.54	85.24	81.50	77.24	72.42	66.94
1.25	94.90	91.83	88.34	84.37	79.88	74.77	68.97	62.39	54.91
1.30	93.55	89.65	85.23	80.21	74.51	68.04	60.70	52.36	42.89
1.40	90.83	85.29	79.01	71.88	63.78	54.58	44.15	32.30	18.85
1.50	88.11	80.94	72.79	63.54	53.04	41.13	27.60	12.24	0.0
1.60	85.39	76.58	66.57	55.21	42.31	27.67	11.05	0.0	0.0
1.70	82.68	72.22	60.35	46.88	31.58	14.21	0.0	0.0	0.0
1.75	81.32	70.04	57.24	42.71	26.21	7.49	0.0	0.0	0.0
1.80	79.96	67.86	54.13	38.54	20.85	0.76	0.0	0.0	0.0
1.90	77.24	63.51	47.91	30.21	10.11	0.0	0.0	0.0	0.0
2.00	74.52	59.15	41.69	21.88	0.0	0.0	0.0	0.0	0.0
2.10	71.81	54.79	35.47	13.54	0.0	0.0	0.0	0.0	0.0
2.20	69.09	50.43	29.25	5.21	0.0	0.0	0.0	0.0	0.0
2.25	67.73	48.25	26.14	1.04	0.0	0.0	0.0	0.0	0.0
2.30	66.37	46.08	23.03	0.0	0.0	0.0	0.0	0.0	0.0

EXAMPLES ON PAGES A-382 TO A-397

BALLOON PAYMENT TABLE

Due Dates in Years →	2	3	4	5	6	7	8	9	10
Monthly Payment %				13% Interest					
1.10	99.54	99.27	98.95	98.60	98.19	97.73	97.20	96.61	95.93
1.20	96.82	94.90	92.70	90.21	87.37	84.14	80.47	76.29	71.53
1.25	95.46	92.71	89.58	86.02	81.96	77.35	72.10	66.12	59.32
1.30	94.10	90.52	86.45	81.82	76.55	70.56	63.73	55.96	47.12
1.40	91.37	86.15	80.20	73.43	65.73	56.97	48.99	35.64	22.72
1.50	88.65	81.77	73.95	65.04	54.91	43.38	30.25	15.31	0.0
1.60	85.92	77.40	67.70	56.65	44.09	29.79	13.51	0.0	0.0
1.70	83.20	73.02	61.44	48.26	33.27	16.20	0.0	0.0	0.0
1.75	81.84	70.84	58.32	44.07	27.85	9.40	0.0	0.0	0.0
1.80	80.48	68.65	55.19	39.88	22.44	2.61	0.0	0.0	0.0
1.90	77.75	64.28	48.94	31.49	11.62	0.0	0.0	0.0	0.0
2.00	75.03	59.90	42.69	23.10	0.80	0.0	0.0	0.0	0.0
2.10	72.30	55.53	36.43	14.71	0.0	0.0	0.0	0.0	0.0
2.20	69.58	51.15	30.18	6.32	0.0	0.0	0.0	0.0	0.0
2.25	68.22	48.97	27.06	2.12	0.0	0.0	0.0	0.0	0.0
2.30	66.86	46.78	23.93	0.0	0.0	0.0	0.0	0.0	0.0
2.40	64.13	42.40	17.68	0.0	0.0	0.0	0.0	0.0	0.0
				13¼% Interest					
1.10	100.11	100.18	100.25	100.34	100.44	100.56	100.69	100.84	101.00
1.20	97.38	95.79	93.98	91.90	89.54	86.85	83.77	80.26	76.26
1.25	96.02	93.60	90.83	87.68	84.09	79.98	75.30	69.97	63.87
1.30	94.65	91.40	87.69	83.46	78.63	73.12	66.84	59.67	51.49
1.40	91.92	87.01	81.41	75.01	67.72	59.40	49.91	39.08	26.72
1.50	89.19	82.62	75.12	66.57	56.81	45.67	32.97	18.48	1.95
1.60	86.46	78.23	68.83	58.12	45.50	31.95	16.04	0.0	0.0
1.70	83.73	73.84	62.55	49.67	34.98	18.23	0.0	0.0	0.0
1.75	82.36	71.64	59.41	45.45	29.53	11.36	0.0	0.0	0.0
1.80	81.00	69.44	56.26	41.23	24.07	4.50	0.0	0.0	0.0
1.90	78.27	65.05	49.98	32.78	13.16	0.0	0.0	0.0	0.0
2.00	75.54	60.66	43.69	24.34	2.25	0.0	0.0	0.0	0.0
2.10	72.80	56.27	37.41	15.89	0.0	0.0	0.0	0.0	0.0
2.20	70.07	51.88	31.12	7.44	0.0	0.0	0.0	0.0	0.0
2.25	68.71	49.68	27.98	3.22	0.0	0.0	0.0	0.0	0.0
2.30	67.34	47.49	24.84	0.0	0.0	0.0	0.0	0.0	0.0
2.40	64.61	43.10	18.55	0.0	0.0	0.0	0.0	0.0	0.0
				13½% Interest					
1.10	100.68	101.10	101.57	102.12	102.74	103.45	104.26	105.19	106.26
1.20	97.95	96.69	95.26	93.62	91.75	89.60	87.15	84.35	81.14
1.25	96.58	94.49	92.10	89.37	86.25	82.67	78.59	73.91	68.57
1.30	95.21	92.29	88.94	85.12	80.74	75.74	70.02	63.48	56.00
1.40	92.47	87.88	82.62	76.62	69.74	61.88	52.90	42.62	30.86
1.50	89.73	83.47	76.30	68.11	58.74	48.02	35.77	21.75	5.72
1.60	87.00	79.06	69.99	59.61	47.74	34.16	18.64	0.88	0.0
1.70	84.26	74.65	63.67	51.10	36.74	20.30	1.51	0.0	0.0
1.75	82.89	72.45	60.51	46.85	31.23	13.37	0.0	0.0	0.0
1.80	81.52	70.24	57.35	42.60	25.73	6.44	0.0	0.0	0.0
1.90	78.78	65.84	51.03	34.10	14.73	0.0	0.0	0.0	0.0
2.00	76.04	61.43	44.71	25.59	3.73	0.0	0.0	0.0	0.0
2.10	73.31	57.02	38.39	17.09	0.0	0.0	0.0	0.0	0.0
2.20	70.57	52.61	32.07	8.59	0.0	0.0	0.0	0.0	0.0
2.25	69.20	50.41	28.92	4.33	0.0	0.0	0.0	0.0	0.0
2.30	67.83	48.20	25.76	0.08	0.0	0.0	0.0	0.0	0.0
2.40	65.09	43.80	19.44	0.0	0.0	0.0	0.0	0.0	0.0
				13¾% Interest					
1.10	101.25	102.02	102.90	103.91	105.07	106.40	107.92	109.67	111.67
1.20	98.51	97.60	96.56	95.36	93.99	92.41	90.61	88.54	86.17
1.25	97.14	95.39	93.38	91.08	88.44	85.42	81.95	77.97	73.41
1.30	95.77	93.18	90.21	86.80	82.90	78.42	73.29	67.40	60.65
1.40	93.02	88.75	83.85	78.24	71.80	64.42	55.96	46.26	35.13
1.50	90.28	84.33	77.50	69.68	60.71	50.42	38.63	25.11	9.61
1.60	87.54	79.90	71.15	61.12	49.61	36.42	21.30	3.97	0.0
1.70	84.79	75.48	64.80	52.56	38.52	22.43	3.98	0.0	0.0
1.75	83.42	73.26	61.62	48.27	32.97	15.43	0.0	0.0	0.0
1.80	82.05	71.05	58.45	43.99	27.43	8.43	0.0	0.0	0.0
1.90	79.30	66.63	52.09	35.43	16.33	0.0	0.0	0.0	0.0
2.00	76.56	62.20	45.74	26.87	5.24	0.0	0.0	0.0	0.0
2.10	73.81	57.78	39.39	18.31	0.0	0.0	0.0	0.0	0.0
2.20	71.07	53.35	33.04	9.75	0.0	0.0	0.0	0.0	0.0
2.25	69.70	51.14	29.86	5.47	0.0	0.0	0.0	0.0	0.0
2.30	68.32	48.93	26.69	1.19	0.0	0.0	0.0	0.0	0.0
2.40	65.58	44.50	20.33	0.0	0.0	0.0	0.0	0.0	0.0

EXAMPLES *ON PAGES A-382 TO A-397*

BALLOON PAYMENT TABLE

Due Dates in Years → Monthly Payment % ↓	2	3	4	5	6	7	8	9	10
					14% Interest				
1.20	59.08	98.52	97.87	97.12	96.27	95.28	94.15	92.85	91.36
1.25	97.71	96.30	94.68	92.82	90.68	88.22	85.39	82.14	78.41
1.30	96.33	94.08	91.48	88.51	85.08	81.15	76.63	71.43	65.46
1.40	93.58	89.63	85.10	79.89	73.90	67.01	59.10	50.00	39.55
1.50	90.83	85.19	78.71	71.27	62.71	52.87	41.57	28.57	13.64
1.60	88.08	80.75	72.33	62.65	51.52	38.74	24.04	7.15	0.0
1.70	85.33	76.31	65.94	54.03	40.34	24.60	6.51	0.0	0.0
1.75	83.95	74.09	62.75	49.72	34.74	17.53	0.0	0.0	0.0
1.80	82.57	71.87	59.56	45.41	29.15	10.46	0.0	0.0	0.0
1.90	79.82	67.42	53.17	36.79	17.96	0.0	0.0	0.0	0.0
2.00	77.07	62.98	46.78	28.17	6.78	0.0	0.0	0.0	0.0
2.10	74.32	58.54	40.40	19.55	0.0	0.0	0.0	0.0	0.0
2.20	71.57	54.10	34.01	10.93	0.0	0.0	0.0	0.0	0.0
2.25	70.19	51.87	30.82	6.62	0.0	0.0	0.0	0.0	0.0
2.30	68.82	49.65	27.63	2.31	0.0	0.0	0.0	0.0	0.0
2.40	66.07	45.21	21.24	0.0	0.0	0.0	0.0	0.0	0.0
2.50	63.32	40.77	14.86	0.0	0.0	0.0	0.0	0.0	0.0
					14¼% Interest				
1.20	99.65	99.44	99.19	98.91	98.58	98.21	97.78	97.28	96.70
1.25	98.27	97.21	95.99	94.57	92.95	91.07	88.91	86.42	83.56
1.30	96.90	94.98	92.78	90.24	87.31	83.93	80.05	75.57	70.41
1.40	94.14	90.52	86.36	81.56	76.03	69.66	62.32	53.86	44.11
1.50	91.38	86.06	79.94	72.88	64.75	55.38	44.58	32.14	17.81
1.60	88.62	81.60	73.52	64.20	53.47	41.10	26.85	10.43	0.0
1.70	85.86	77.14	67.10	55.52	42.19	26.82	9.12	0.0	0.0
1.75	84.48	74.91	63.89	51.18	36.55	19.68	0.25	0.0	0.0
1.80	83.11	72.69	60.68	46.85	30.91	12.54	0.0	0.0	0.0
1.90	80.35	68.23	54.26	38.17	19.63	0.0	0.0	0.0	0.0
2.00	77.59	63.77	47.84	29.49	8.34	0.0	0.0	0.0	0.0
2.10	74.83	59.31	41.42	20.81	0.0	0.0	0.0	0.0	0.0
2.20	72.07	54.85	35.00	12.13	0.0	0.0	0.0	0.0	0.0
2.25	70.69	52.62	31.79	7.79	0.0	0.0	0.0	0.0	0.0
2.30	69.32	50.39	28.58	3.45	0.0	0.0	0.0	0.0	0.0
2.40	66.56	45.93	22.16	0.0	0.0	0.0	0.0	0.0	0.0
2.50	63.80	41.47	15.74	0.0	0.0	0.0	0.0	0.0	0.0
					14½% Interest				
1.20	100.23	100.37	100.53	100.72	100.94	101.19	101.48	101.82	102.21
1.25	98.85	98.13	97.31	96.36	95.26	93.99	92.52	90.83	88.87
1.30	97.46	95.90	94.08	91.99	89.57	86.78	83.55	79.83	75.52
1.40	94.70	91.42	87.63	83.25	78.20	72.36	65.61	57.82	48.82
1.50	91.93	86.94	81.18	74.51	66.82	57.94	47.67	35.82	22.12
1.60	89.17	82.47	74.72	65.78	55.45	43.51	29.73	13.81	0.0
1.70	86.41	77.99	68.27	57.04	44.07	29.09	11.79	0.0	0.0
1.75	85.02	75.75	65.04	52.67	38.38	21.88	2.82	0.0	0.0
1.80	83.64	73.51	61.81	48.30	32.70	14.67	0.0	0.0	0.0
1.90	80.88	69.04	55.36	39.57	21.32	0.25	0.0	0.0	0.0
2.00	78.11	64.56	48.91	30.83	9.95	0.0	0.0	0.0	0.0
2.10	75.35	60.08	42.45	22.09	0.0	0.0	0.0	0.0	0.0
2.20	72.58	55.61	36.00	13.35	0.0	0.0	0.0	0.0	0.0
2.25	71.20	53.37	32.77	8.98	0.0	0.0	0.0	0.0	0.0
2.30	69.81	51.13	29.55	4.62	0.0	0.0	0.0	0.0	0.0
2.40	67.05	46.65	23.09	0.0	0.0	0.0	0.0	0.0	0.0
2.50	64.28	42.18	16.64	0.0	0.0	0.0	0.0	0.0	0.0
					14¾% Interest				
1.20	100.81	101.31	101.89	102.56	103.34	104.24	105.28	106.49	107.89
1.25	99.42	99.06	98.65	98.16	97.61	96.96	96.21	95.35	94.34
1.30	98.04	96.82	95.40	93.77	91.87	89.68	87.14	84.20	80.79
1.40	95.26	92.32	88.92	84.97	80.40	75.11	68.99	61.90	53.69
1.50	92.49	87.83	82.43	76.17	68.93	60.55	50.84	39.60	26.58
1.60	89.72	83.33	75.94	67.38	57.46	45.98	32.69	17.30	0.0
1.70	86.95	78.84	69.45	58.58	45.99	31.42	14.54	0.0	0.0
1.75	85.56	76.59	66.21	54.18	40.26	24.13	5.46	0.0	0.0
1.80	84.18	74.35	62.96	49.78	34.52	16.85	0.0	0.0	0.0
1.90	81.40	69.85	56.47	40.98	23.05	2.28	0.0	0.0	0.0
2.00	78.63	65.36	49.99	32.19	11.58	0.0	0.0	0.0	0.0
2.10	75.86	60.86	43.50	23.39	0.11	0.0	0.0	0.0	0.0
2.20	73.09	56.37	37.01	14.59	0.0	0.0	0.0	0.0	0.0
2.25	71.70	54.12	33.77	10.19	0.0	0.0	0.0	0.0	0.0
2.30	70.32	51.88	30.52	5.80	0.0	0.0	0.0	0.0	0.0
2.40	67.55	47.38	24.03	0.0	0.0	0.0	0.0	0.0	0.0
2.50	64.77	42.89	17.54	0.0	0.0	0.0	0.0	0.0	0.0

EXAMPLES *ON PAGES A-382 TO A-397*

BALLOON PAYMENT TABLE

Due Dates in Years →	2	3	4	5	6	7	8	9	10
Monthly Payment % ↓									

15% Interest

	2	3	4	5	6	7	8	9	10
1.25	100.00	100.00	100.00	100.00	100.00	100.00	100.00	100.00	100.00
1.30	98.61	97.74	96.74	95.57	94.21	92.64	90.82	88.70	86.24
1.40	95.83	93.23	90.22	86.71	82.65	77.93	72.45	66.10	58.72
1.50	93.05	88.72	83.69	77.86	71.08	63.22	54.09	43.49	31.19
1.60	90.27	84.21	77.17	69.00	59.51	48.50	35.72	20.89	3.67
1.70	87.50	79.70	70.65	60.14	47.95	33.79	17.36	0.0	0.0
1.75	86.11	77.44	67.39	55.71	42.16	26.43	8.18	0.0	0.0
1.80	84.72	75.19	64.12	51.28	36.38	19.08	0.0	0.0	0.0
1.90	81.94	70.67	57.60	42.43	24.81	4.37	0.0	0.0	0.0
2.00	79.16	66.16	51.08	33.57	13.24	0.0	0.0	0.0	0.0
2.10	76.38	61.65	44.56	24.71	1.68	0.0	0.0	0.0	0.0
2.20	73.60	57.14	38.03	15.85	0.0	0.0	0.0	0.0	0.0
2.25	72.21	54.88	34.77	11.42	0.0	0.0	0.0	0.0	0.0
2.30	70.82	52.63	31.51	7.00	0.0	0.0	0.0	0.0	0.0
2.40	68.04	48.12	24.99	0.0	0.0	0.0	0.0	0.0	0.0
2.50	65.26	43.61	18.46	0.0	0.0	0.0	0.0	0.0	0.0
2.60	62.49	39.09	11.94	0.0	0.0	0.0	0.0	0.0	0.0

15¼% Interest

	2	3	4	5	6	7	8	9	10
1.25	100.58	100.94	101.36	101.85	102.41	103.08	103.85	104.74	105.79
1.30	99.19	98.68	98.09	97.40	96.59	95.66	94.58	93.31	91.84
1.40	96.40	94.15	91.53	88.48	84.93	80.80	76.00	70.41	63.90
1.50	93.62	89.62	84.97	79.56	73.27	65.94	57.42	47.50	35.96
1.60	90.83	85.09	78.41	70.64	61.60	51.08	38.84	24.59	8.02
1.70	88.04	80.56	71.86	61.73	49.94	36.22	20.26	1.68	0.0
1.75	86.65	78.30	68.58	57.27	44.10	28.79	10.97	0.0	0.0
1.80	85.26	76.03	65.30	52.81	38.27	21.36	1.68	0.0	0.0
1.90	82.47	71.50	58.74	43.89	26.61	6.50	0.0	0.0	0.0
2.00	79.69	66.97	52.18	34.97	14.94	0.0	0.0	0.0	0.0
2.10	76.90	62.45	45.63	26.05	3.28	0.0	0.0	0.0	0.0
2.20	74.12	57.92	39.07	17.13	0.0	0.0	0.0	0.0	0.0
2.25	72.72	55.65	35.79	12.68	0.0	0.0	0.0	0.0	0.0
2.30	71.33	53.39	32.51	8.22	0.0	0.0	0.0	0.0	0.0
2.40	68.54	48.86	25.95	0.0	0.0	0.0	0.0	0.0	0.0
2.50	65.76	44.33	19.39	0.0	0.0	0.0	0.0	0.0	0.0
2.60	62.97	39.80	12.84	0.0	0.0	0.0	0.0	0.0	0.0

15½% Interest

	2	3	4	5	6	7	8	9	10
1.25	101.16	101.89	102.74	103.73	104.89	106.24	107.81	109.65	111.79
1.30	99.77	99.62	99.45	99.25	99.01	98.74	98.43	98.06	97.63
1.40	96.97	95.07	92.86	90.27	87.25	83.74	79.63	74.84	69.26
1.50	94.18	90.53	86.26	81.29	75.49	68.72	60.83	51.62	40.88
1.60	91.39	85.98	79.67	72.31	63.73	53.71	42.03	28.41	12.51
1.70	88.60	81.43	73.08	63.33	51.96	38.70	23.23	5.19	0.0
1.75	87.20	79.16	69.78	58.84	46.08	31.20	13.83	0.0	0.0
1.80	85.80	76.89	66.49	54.35	40.20	23.69	4.43	0.0	0.0
1.90	83.01	72.34	59.89	45.37	28.44	8.68	0.0	0.0	0.0
2.00	80.22	67.79	53.30	36.39	16.67	0.0	0.0	0.0	0.0
2.10	77.43	63.25	46.71	27.42	4.91	0.0	0.0	0.0	0.0
2.20	74.63	58.70	40.12	18.44	0.0	0.0	0.0	0.0	0.0
2.25	73.24	56.43	36.82	13.95	0.0	0.0	0.0	0.0	0.0
2.30	71.84	54.15	33.52	9.46	0.0	0.0	0.0	0.0	0.0
2.40	69.05	49.61	26.93	0.48	0.0	0.0	0.0	0.0	0.0
2.50	66.25	45.06	20.34	0.0	0.0	0.0	0.0	0.0	0.0
2.60	63.46	40.51	13.74	0.0	0.0	0.0	0.0	0.0	0.0

15¾% Interest

	2	3	4	5	6	7	8	9	10
1.25	101.75	102.85	104.13	105.64	107.40	109.46	111.86	114.68	117.97
1.30	100.35	100.57	100.82	101.12	101.47	101.88	102.36	102.92	103.57
1.40	97.55	96.01	94.20	92.09	89.62	86.73	83.35	79.40	74.79
1.50	94.75	91.44	87.57	83.05	77.75	71.57	64.33	55.87	45.97
1.60	91.95	86.88	80.94	74.01	65.89	56.40	45.31	32.34	17.16
1.70	89.15	82.31	74.32	64.96	54.03	41.24	26.29	8.80	0.0
1.75	87.75	80.03	71.00	60.44	48.10	33.66	16.78	0.0	0.0
1.80	86.35	77.75	67.69	55.92	42.17	26.08	7.27	0.0	0.0
1.90	83.55	73.18	61.06	46.88	30.30	10.92	0.0	0.0	0.0
2.00	80.75	68.62	54.43	37.84	18.44	0.0	0.0	0.0	0.0
2.10	77.95	64.06	47.80	28.80	6.58	0.0	0.0	0.0	0.0
2.20	75.15	59.49	41.18	19.76	0.0	0.0	0.0	0.0	0.0
2.25	73.75	57.21	37.86	15.24	0.0	0.0	0.0	0.0	0.0
2.30	72.35	54.93	34.55	10.72	0.0	0.0	0.0	0.0	0.0
2.40	69.55	50.36	27.92	1.68	0.0	0.0	0.0	0.0	0.0
2.50	66.75	45.80	21.29	0.0	0.0	0.0	0.0	0.0	0.0
2.60	63.95	41.23	14.66	0.0	0.0	0.0	0.0	0.0	0.0

EXAMPLES *ON PAGES A-382 TO A-397*

BALLOON PAYMENT TABLE

Due Dates in Years →	2	3	4	5	6	7	8	9	10

16% Interest

Monthly Payment %	2	3	4	5	6	7	8	9	10
1.30	100.93	101.52	102.21	103.03	103.98	105.09	106.40	107.93	109.72
1.40	98.13	96.94	95.56	93.93	92.02	89.79	87.17	84.09	80.49
1.50	95.32	92.36	88.89	84.83	80.06	74.47	67.92	60.24	51.23
1.60	92.52	87.78	82.23	75.72	68.10	59.15	48.67	36.38	21.98
1.70	89.71	83.20	75.57	66.62	56.13	43.84	29.42	12.53	0.0
1.75	88.31	80.91	72.23	62.07	50.15	36.18	19.80	0.60	0.0
1.80	86.90	78.62	68.90	57.52	44.17	28.52	10.18	0.0	0.0
1.90	84.10	74.03	62.24	48.41	32.20	13.20	0.0	0.0	0.0
2.00	81.29	69.45	55.58	39.31	20.24	0.0	0.0	0.0	0.0
2.10	78.48	64.87	48.91	30.21	8.28	0.0	0.0	0.0	0.0
2.20	75.68	60.29	42.25	21.10	0.0	0.0	0.0	0.0	0.0
2.25	74.27	58.00	38.92	16.55	0.0	0.0	0.0	0.0	0.0
2.30	72.87	55.71	35.59	12.00	0.0	0.0	0.0	0.0	0.0
2.40	70.06	51.12	28.92	2.89	0.0	0.0	0.0	0.0	0.0
2.50	67.26	46.54	22.26	0.0	0.0	0.0	0.0	0.0	0.0
2.60	64.45	41.96	15.59	0.0	0.0	0.0	0.0	0.0	0.0
2.70	61.64	37.38	8.93	0.0	0.0	0.0	0.0	0.0	0.0

16¼% Interest

Monthly Payment %	2	3	4	5	6	7	8	9	10
1.30	101.52	102.49	103.62	104.96	106.52	108.37	110.53	113.07	116.06
1.40	98.71	97.89	96.93	95.80	94.47	92.90	91.07	88.91	86.38
1.50	95.90	93.29	90.23	86.63	82.40	77.43	71.59	64.73	56.67
1.60	93.08	88.69	83.53	77.46	70.34	61.96	52.12	42.55	26.96
1.70	90.27	84.09	76.83	68.30	58.27	46.49	32.64	16.37	0.0
1.75	88.86	81.79	73.48	63.72	52.24	38.75	22.90	4.28	0.0
1.80	87.46	79.49	70.13	59.13	46.21	31.02	13.17	0.0	0.0
1.90	84.64	74.89	63.43	49.97	34.14	15.54	0.0	0.0	0.0
2.00	81.83	70.29	56.73	40.80	22.08	0.07	0.0	0.0	0.0
2.10	79.01	65.69	50.03	31.63	10.01	0.0	0.0	0.0	0.0
2.20	76.20	61.09	43.33	22.47	0.0	0.0	0.0	0.0	0.0
2.25	74.79	58.79	39.98	17.88	0.0	0.0	0.0	0.0	0.0
2.30	73.39	56.49	36.63	13.30	0.0	0.0	0.0	0.0	0.0
2.40	70.57	51.89	29.94	4.13	0.0	0.0	0.0	0.0	0.0
2.50	67.76	47.29	23.24	0.0	0.0	0.0	0.0	0.0	0.0
2.60	64.95	42.69	16.54	0.0	0.0	0.0	0.0	0.0	0.0
2.70	62.13	38.09	9.84	0.0	0.0	0.0	0.0	0.0	0.0

16½% Interest

Monthly Payment %	2	3	4	5	6	7	8	9	10
1.30	102.11	103.46	105.04	106.91	109.11	111.71	114.76	118.36	122.60
1.40	99.29	98.84	98.31	97.69	96.95	96.09	95.07	93.87	92.45
1.50	96.47	94.23	91.58	88.46	84.79	80.46	75.36	69.35	62.28
1.60	93.65	89.61	84.84	79.23	72.62	64.83	55.65	44.84	32.11
1.70	90.83	84.99	78.11	70.00	60.45	49.20	35.95	20.33	1.94
1.75	89.42	82.68	74.74	65.39	54.37	41.38	26.09	8.07	0.0
1.80	88.01	80.37	71.37	60.77	48.28	33.57	16.24	0.0	0.0
1.90	85.19	75.76	64.64	51.54	36.12	17.94	0.0	0.0	0.0
2.00	82.37	71.14	57.90	42.31	23.55	2.31	0.0	0.0	0.0
2.10	79.55	66.52	51.17	33.08	11.78	0.0	0.0	0.0	0.0
2.20	76.73	61.90	44.43	23.85	0.0	0.0	0.0	0.0	0.0
2.25	75.32	59.59	41.06	19.24	0.0	0.0	0.0	0.0	0.0
2.30	73.91	57.28	37.70	14.62	0.0	0.0	0.0	0.0	0.0
2.40	71.09	52.66	30.96	5.39	0.0	0.0	0.0	0.0	0.0
2.50	68.27	48.05	24.23	0.0	0.0	0.0	0.0	0.0	0.0
2.60	65.45	43.43	17.49	0.0	0.0	0.0	0.0	0.0	0.0
2.70	62.63	38.81	10.76	0.0	0.0	0.0	0.0	0.0	0.0

16¾% Interest

Monthly Payment %	2	3	4	5	6	7	8	9	10
1.30	102.71	104.44	106.48	108.90	111.75	115.12	119.09	123.79	129.34
1.40	99.88	99.80	99.71	99.61	99.48	99.33	99.16	98.95	98.71
1.50	97.05	95.17	92.94	90.32	87.21	83.55	79.22	74.11	68.07
1.60	94.23	90.53	86.17	81.02	74.94	67.76	59.28	49.26	37.43
1.70	91.40	85.90	79.40	71.73	62.67	51.97	39.34	24.41	6.79
1.75	89.98	83.58	76.02	67.08	56.53	44.08	29.36	11.99	0.0
1.80	88.57	81.26	72.63	62.44	50.40	36.18	19.39	0.0	0.0
1.90	85.74	76.63	65.86	53.14	38.13	20.39	0.0	0.0	0.0
2.00	82.92	71.99	59.09	43.85	25.85	4.60	0.0	0.0	0.0
2.10	80.09	67.35	52.32	34.56	13.58	0.0	0.0	0.0	0.0
2.20	77.26	62.72	45.54	25.26	1.31	0.0	0.0	0.0	0.0
2.25	75.85	60.40	42.16	20.62	0.0	0.0	0.0	0.0	0.0
2.30	74.43	58.08	38.77	15.97	0.0	0.0	0.0	0.0	0.0
2.40	71.60	53.45	32.00	6.68	0.0	0.0	0.0	0.0	0.0
2.50	68.78	48.81	25.23	0.0	0.0	0.0	0.0	0.0	0.0
2.60	65.95	44.17	18.46	0.0	0.0	0.0	0.0	0.0	0.0
2.70	63.12	39.54	11.69	0.0	0.0	0.0	0.0	0.0	0.0

EXAMPLES *ON PAGES A-382 TO A-397*

BALLOON PAYMENT TABLE

Due Dates in Years →	2	3	4	5	6	7	8	9	10
Monthly Payment %									

17% Interest

	2	3	4	5	6	7	8	9	10
1.40	100.47	100.77	101.13	101.56	102.06	102.65	103.35	104.19	105.17
1.50	97.64	96.12	94.32	92.20	89.68	86.70	83.18	79.00	74.06
1.60	94.80	91.47	87.52	82.84	77.31	70.75	63.00	53.81	42.94
1.70	91.97	86.81	80.71	73.48	64.93	54.80	42.81	28.62	11.82
1.75	90.55	84.49	77.31	68.81	58.74	46.83	32.72	16.02	0.0
1.80	89.13	82.16	73.90	64.13	52.55	38.85	22.63	3.43	0.0
1.90	86.30	77.50	67.29	54.77	40.18	22.90	2.45	0.0	0.0
2.00	83.46	72.85	60.29	45.41	27.80	6.95	0.0	0.0	0.0
2.10	80.63	68.20	53.48	36.05	15.42	0.0	0.0	0.0	0.0
2.20	77.79	63.54	46.67	26.69	3.05	0.0	0.0	0.0	0.0
2.25	76.38	61.21	43.27	22.01	0.0	0.0	0.0	0.0	0.0
2.30	74.96	58.89	39.86	17.34	0.0	0.0	0.0	0.0	0.0
2.40	72.12	54.23	33.05	7.98	0.0	0.0	0.0	0.0	0.0
2.50	69.29	49.58	26.24	0.0	0.0	0.0	0.0	0.0	0.0
2.60	66.45	44.93	19.44	0.0	0.0	0.0	0.0	0.0	0.0
2.70	63.62	40.27	12.63	0.0	0.0	0.0	0.0	0.0	0.0
2.75	62.20	37.94	9.22	0.0	0.0	0.0	0.0	0.0	0.0

17¼% Interest

	2	3	4	5	6	7	8	9	10
1.40	101.06	101.75	102.56	103.53	104.68	106.04	107.65	109.57	111.84
1.50	98.22	97.08	95.72	94.11	92.20	89.93	87.23	84.03	80.24
1.60	95.38	92.41	88.88	84.69	79.71	73.81	66.81	58.49	48.63
1.70	92.54	87.73	82.03	75.26	67.23	57.70	46.38	32.96	17.02
1.75	91.12	85.40	78.61	70.55	60.99	49.64	36.17	20.19	1.21
1.80	89.70	83.06	75.19	65.84	54.75	41.58	25.96	7.42	0.0
1.90	86.86	78.39	68.34	56.42	42.27	25.47	5.53	0.0	0.0
2.00	84.01	73.72	61.50	46.99	29.78	9.35	0.0	0.0	0.0
2.10	81.17	69.04	54.65	37.57	17.30	0.0	0.0	0.0	0.0
2.20	78.33	64.37	47.81	28.15	4.82	0.0	0.0	0.0	0.0
2.25	76.91	62.04	44.39	23.44	0.0	0.0	0.0	0.0	0.0
2.30	75.49	59.70	40.96	18.73	0.0	0.0	0.0	0.0	0.0
2.40	72.65	55.03	34.12	9.30	0.0	0.0	0.0	0.0	0.0
2.50	69.80	50.36	27.27	0.0	0.0	0.0	0.0	0.0	0.0
2.60	66.96	45.68	20.43	0.0	0.0	0.0	0.0	0.0	0.0
2.70	64.12	41.01	13.58	0.0	0.0	0.0	0.0	0.0	0.0
2.75	62.70	38.67	10.16	0.0	0.0	0.0	0.0	0.0	0.0

17½% Interest

	2	3	4	5	6	7	8	9	10
1.40	101.66	102.73	104.01	105.53	107.34	109.49	112.05	115.09	118.72
1.50	98.81	98.04	97.13	96.04	94.75	93.21	91.38	89.21	86.61
1.60	95.96	93.35	90.25	86.56	82.16	76.93	70.71	63.31	54.51
1.70	93.11	88.66	83.37	77.07	69.57	60.65	50.04	37.42	22.40
1.75	91.69	86.32	79.93	72.32	63.28	52.51	39.71	24.47	6.35
1.80	90.27	83.97	76.49	67.58	56.98	44.38	29.38	11.53	0.0
1.90	87.42	79.28	69.60	58.09	44.39	28.10	8.71	0.0	0.0
2.00	84.57	74.59	62.72	48.60	31.80	11.81	0.0	0.0	0.0
2.10	81.72	69.90	55.84	39.11	19.21	0.0	0.0	0.0	0.0
2.20	78.87	65.21	48.96	29.62	6.62	0.0	0.0	0.0	0.0
2.25	77.44	62.86	45.52	24.88	0.33	0.0	0.0	0.0	0.0
2.30	76.02	60.52	42.08	20.14	0.0	0.0	0.0	0.0	0.0
2.40	73.17	55.83	35.20	10.65	0.0	0.0	0.0	0.0	0.0
2.50	70.32	51.14	28.31	1.16	0.0	0.0	0.0	0.0	0.0
2.60	67.47	46.45	21.43	0.0	0.0	0.0	0.0	0.0	0.0
2.70	64.62	41.76	14.55	0.0	0.0	0.0	0.0	0.0	0.0
2.75	63.20	39.41	11.11	0.0	0.0	0.0	0.0	0.0	0.0

17¾% Interest

	2	3	4	5	6	7	8	9	10
1.40	102.26	103.73	105.47	107.56	110.05	113.01	116.55	120.77	125.80
1.50	99.40	99.02	98.56	98.01	97.35	96.57	95.64	94.52	93.20
1.60	96.55	94.31	91.64	88.45	84.65	80.12	74.72	68.27	60.59
1.70	93.69	89.60	84.72	78.90	71.96	63.68	53.80	42.02	27.98
1.75	92.26	87.25	81.26	74.12	65.61	55.45	43.34	28.90	11.67
1.80	90.84	84.89	77.80	69.34	59.26	47.23	32.88	15.77	0.0
1.90	87.98	80.18	70.88	59.79	46.56	30.78	11.96	0.0	0.0
2.00	85.12	75.47	63.96	50.23	33.86	14.33	0.0	0.0	0.0
2.10	82.27	70.76	57.04	40.68	21.16	0.0	0.0	0.0	0.0
2.20	79.41	66.05	50.12	31.13	8.47	0.0	0.0	0.0	0.0
2.25	77.98	63.70	46.67	26.35	2.12	0.0	0.0	0.0	0.0
2.30	76.56	61.35	43.21	21.57	0.0	0.0	0.0	0.0	0.0
2.40	73.70	56.64	36.29	12.02	0.0	0.0	0.0	0.0	0.0
2.50	70.84	51.93	29.37	2.46	0.0	0.0	0.0	0.0	0.0
2.60	67.99	47.22	22.45	0.0	0.0	0.0	0.0	0.0	0.0
2.70	65.13	42.51	15.53	0.0	0.0	0.0	0.0	0.0	0.0
2.75	63.70	40.15	12.07	0.0	0.0	0.0	0.0	0.0	0.0

EXAMPLES *ON PAGES A-382 TO A-397*

BALLOON PAYMENT TABLE

Due Dates in Years →	2	3	4	5	6	7	8	9	10
Monthly Payment % ↓									

18% Interest

	2	3	4	5	6	7	8	9	10
1.50	100.00	100.00	100.00	100.00	100.00	100.00	100.00	100.00	100.00
1.60	97.14	95.27	93.04	90.38	87.19	83.38	78.82	73.38	66.87
1.70	94.27	90.54	86.09	80.76	74.38	66.76	57.65	46.76	33.74
1.75	92.84	88.18	82.61	75.94	67.98	58.45	47.07	33.45	17.17
1.80	91.41	85.82	79.13	71.13	61.58	50.15	36.48	20.14	0.61
1.90	88.55	81.09	72.17	61.51	48.77	33.53	15.31	0.0	0.0
2.00	85.68	76.36	65.22	51.89	35.96	16.91	0.0	0.0	0.0
2.10	82.82	71.63	58.26	42.27	23.15	0.30	0.0	0.0	0.0
2.20	79.96	66.91	51.30	32.65	10.35	0.0	0.0	0.0	0.0
2.25	78.52	64.54	47.83	27.84	3.94	0.0	0.0	0.0	0.0
2.30	77.09	62.18	44.35	23.03	0.0	0.0	0.0	0.0	0.0
2.40	74.23	57.45	37.39	13.41	0.0	0.0	0.0	0.0	0.0
2.50	71.37	52.72	30.43	3.78	0.0	0.0	0.0	0.0	0.0
2.60	68.50	48.00	23.48	0.0	0.0	0.0	0.0	0.0	0.0
2.70	65.64	43.27	16.52	0.0	0.0	0.0	0.0	0.0	0.0
2.75	64.21	40.90	13.04	0.0	0.0	0.0	0.0	0.0	0.0
3.00	57.05	29.09	0.0	0.0	0.0	0.0	0.0	0.0	0.0

18¼% Interest

	2	3	4	5	6	7	8	9	10
1.50	100.60	100.99	101.45	102.01	102.88	103.48	104.45	105.60	106.98
1.60	97.73	96.24	94.46	92.33	89.77	86.71	83.03	78.63	73.35
1.70	94.86	91.50	87.47	82.64	76.85	69.92	61.61	51.64	39.70
1.75	93.42	89.12	83.97	77.80	70.39	61.52	50.89	38.15	22.87
1.80	91.99	86.75	80.47	72.95	63.54	53.13	40.18	24.65	6.05
1.90	89.12	82.00	73.48	63.26	51.02	36.34	18.75	0.0	0.0
2.00	86.24	77.26	66.49	53.57	38.10	19.55	0.0	0.0	0.0
2.10	83.37	72.51	59.49	43.89	25.18	2.76	0.0	0.0	0.0
2.20	80.50	67.77	52.50	34.20	12.26	0.0	0.0	0.0	0.0
2.25	79.07	65.39	49.00	29.35	5.80	0.0	0.0	0.0	0.0
2.30	77.63	63.02	45.50	24.51	0.0	0.0	0.0	0.0	0.0
2.40	74.76	58.27	38.51	14.82	0.0	0.0	0.0	0.0	0.0
2.50	71.89	53.53	31.51	5.13	0.0	0.0	0.0	0.0	0.0
2.60	69.02	48.78	24.52	0.0	0.0	0.0	0.0	0.0	0.0
2.70	66.15	44.03	17.53	0.0	0.0	0.0	0.0	0.0	0.0
2.75	64.72	41.66	14.03	0.0	0.0	0.0	0.0	0.0	0.0
3.00	57.54	29.80	0.0	0.0	0.0	0.0	0.0	0.0	0.0

18½% Interest

	2	3	4	5	6	7	8	9	10
1.50	101.20	101.98	102.92	104.06	105.42	107.05	109.02	111.38	114.22
1.60	98.32	97.22	95.90	94.31	92.40	90.10	87.34	84.03	80.05
1.70	95.44	92.45	88.86	84.55	79.37	73.14	65.66	56.67	45.86
1.75	94.00	90.07	85.35	79.67	72.85	64.66	54.81	42.98	28.77
1.80	92.57	87.69	81.83	74.79	66.34	56.18	43.97	29.30	11.68
1.90	89.69	82.93	74.80	65.04	53.31	39.22	22.28	1.94	0.0
2.00	86.81	78.16	67.77	55.28	40.28	22.25	0.59	0.0	0.0
2.10	83.93	73.40	60.74	45.53	27.25	5.29	0.0	0.0	0.0
2.20	81.05	68.63	53.70	35.77	14.22	0.0	0.0	0.0	0.0
2.25	79.62	66.25	50.19	30.89	7.70	0.0	0.0	0.0	0.0
2.30	78.18	63.87	46.67	26.01	1.19	0.0	0.0	0.0	0.0
2.40	75.30	59.10	39.64	16.26	0.0	0.0	0.0	0.0	0.0
2.50	72.42	54.34	32.61	6.50	0.0	0.0	0.0	0.0	0.0
2.60	69.54	49.57	25.58	0.0	0.0	0.0	0.0	0.0	0.0
2.70	66.67	44.81	18.54	0.0	0.0	0.0	0.0	0.0	0.0
2.75	65.23	42.42	15.03	0.0	0.0	0.0	0.0	0.0	0.0
3.00	58.03	30.51	0.0	0.0	0.0	0.0	0.0	0.0	0.0

18¾% Interest

	2	3	4	5	6	7	8	9	10
1.50	101.80	102.99	104.41	106.13	108.20	110.70	113.70	117.32	121.68
1.60	98.92	98.20	97.35	96.31	95.07	93.57	91.76	89.59	86.97
1.70	96.03	93.42	90.28	86.49	81.93	76.43	69.81	61.84	52.24
1.75	94.59	91.03	86.74	81.58	75.36	67.86	58.84	47.97	34.87
1.80	93.15	88.64	83.21	76.66	68.78	59.29	47.86	34.09	17.51
1.90	90.26	83.85	76.14	66.84	55.64	42.16	25.91	6.34	0.0
2.00	87.38	79.07	69.07	57.02	42.50	25.02	3.96	0.0	0.0
2.10	84.49	74.29	62.00	47.19	29.36	7.88	0.0	0.0	0.0
2.20	81.61	69.50	54.93	37.37	16.21	0.0	0.0	0.0	0.0
2.25	80.17	67.11	51.39	32.45	9.64	0.0	0.0	0.0	0.0
2.30	78.72	64.72	47.85	27.54	3.07	0.0	0.0	0.0	0.0
2.40	75.84	59.94	40.78	17.72	0.0	0.0	0.0	0.0	0.0
2.50	72.95	55.15	33.71	7.89	0.0	0.0	0.0	0.0	0.0
2.60	70.07	50.37	26.64	0.0	0.0	0.0	0.0	0.0	0.0
2.70	67.18	45.59	19.57	0.0	0.0	0.0	0.0	0.0	0.0
2.75	65.74	43.19	16.04	0.0	0.0	0.0	0.0	0.0	0.0
3.00	58.53	31.24	0.0	0.0	0.0	0.0	0.0	0.0	0.0

EXAMPLES *ON PAGES A-382 TO A-397*

BALLOON PAYMENT TABLE

Due Dates in Years →	2	3	4	5	6	7	8	9	10
Monthly Payment % ↓									

19% Interest

Monthly Payment %	2	3	4	5	6	7	8	9	10
1.60	99.52	99.20	98.81	98.35	97.78	97.11	96.29	95.30	94.11
1.70	96.62	94.40	91.70	88.46	84.53	79.79	74.07	67.17	58.83
1.75	95.18	92.00	88.15	83.51	77.90	71.14	62.96	53.10	41.18
1.80	53.73	89.59	84.60	78.56	71.28	62.48	51.86	39.03	23.54
1.90	50.84	84.79	77.49	68.67	58.02	45.16	29.64	10.89	0.0
2.00	87.95	79.99	70.38	58.77	44.76	27.84	7.42	0.0	0.0
2.10	85.06	75.19	63.27	48.88	31.51	10.53	0.0	0.0	0.0
2.20	82.16	70.38	56.16	38.99	18.25	0.0	0.0	0.0	0.0
2.25	80.72	67.98	52.61	34.04	11.62	0.0	0.0	0.0	0.0
2.30	79.27	65.58	49.05	29.09	4.99	0.0	0.0	0.0	0.0
2.40	76.38	60.78	41.94	19.20	0.0	0.0	0.0	0.0	0.0
2.50	73.49	55.98	34.83	9.30	0.0	0.0	0.0	0.0	0.0
2.60	70.60	51.17	27.73	0.0	0.0	0.0	0.0	0.0	0.0
2.70	67.70	46.37	20.62	0.0	0.0	0.0	0.0	0.0	0.0
2.75	66.26	43.97	17.06	0.0	0.0	0.0	0.0	0.0	0.0
2.90	61.92	36.77	6.40	0.0	0.0	0.0	0.0	0.0	0.0
3.00	59.03	31.96	0.0	0.0	0.0	0.0	0.0	0.0	0.0

19¼% Interest

Monthly Payment %	2	3	4	5	6	7	8	9	10
1.60	100.12	100.19	100.29	100.40	100.54	100.71	100.91	101.15	101.45
1.70	97.22	95.38	93.15	90.45	87.18	83.23	78.44	72.65	65.64
1.75	95.77	92.97	89.58	85.47	80.50	74.48	67.20	58.38	47.71
1.80	94.32	90.56	86.00	80.49	73.81	65.73	55.95	44.12	29.79
1.90	91.42	85.74	78.85	70.52	60.44	48.24	33.46	15.58	0.0
2.00	88.52	80.91	71.71	60.56	47.07	30.74	10.97	0.0	0.0
2.10	85.62	76.09	64.56	50.60	33.70	13.24	0.0	0.0	0.0
2.20	82.72	71.27	57.41	40.63	20.33	0.0	0.0	0.0	0.0
2.25	81.27	68.86	53.84	35.65	13.64	0.0	0.0	0.0	0.0
2.30	79.82	66.45	50.26	30.67	6.95	0.0	0.0	0.0	0.0
2.40	76.92	61.63	43.12	20.71	0.0	0.0	0.0	0.0	0.0
2.50	74.02	56.81	35.97	10.74	0.0	0.0	0.0	0.0	0.0
2.60	71.13	51.99	28.82	0.78	0.0	0.0	0.0	0.0	0.0
2.70	68.23	47.17	21.67	0.0	0.0	0.0	0.0	0.0	0.0
2.75	66.78	44.75	18.10	0.0	0.0	0.0	0.0	0.0	0.0
2.90	62.43	37.52	7.38	0.0	0.0	0.0	0.0	0.0	0.0
3.00	59.53	32.70	0.23	0.0	0.0	0.0	0.0	0.0	0.0

19½% Interest

Monthly Payment %	2	3	4	5	6	7	8	9	10
1.60	100.72	101.20	101.79	102.50	103.36	104.40	105.66	107.20	109.06
1.70	97.82	96.37	94.61	92.47	89.88	86.74	82.92	78.29	72.67
1.75	96.37	93.95	91.01	87.46	83.14	77.90	71.54	63.82	54.46
1.80	94.91	91.53	87.42	82.44	76.39	69.06	60.16	49.35	36.25
1.90	92.01	86.69	80.24	72.41	62.91	51.38	37.39	20.42	0.0
2.00	89.10	81.85	73.05	62.37	49.42	33.70	14.62	0.0	0.0
2.10	86.19	77.01	65.86	52.34	35.93	16.02	0.0	0.0	0.0
2.20	83.29	72.17	58.68	42.31	22.44	0.0	0.0	0.0	0.0
2.25	81.83	69.75	55.08	37.29	15.70	0.0	0.0	0.0	0.0
2.30	80.38	67.33	51.49	32.27	8.95	0.0	0.0	0.0	0.0
2.40	77.47	62.49	44.30	22.24	0.0	0.0	0.0	0.0	0.0
2.50	74.57	57.65	37.12	12.20	0.0	0.0	0.0	0.0	0.0
2.60	71.66	52.81	29.93	2.17	0.0	0.0	0.0	0.0	0.0
2.70	68.75	47.96	22.74	0.0	0.0	0.0	0.0	0.0	0.0
2.75	67.30	45.54	19.15	0.0	0.0	0.0	0.0	0.0	0.0
2.90	62.94	38.28	8.37	0.0	0.0	0.0	0.0	0.0	0.0
3.00	60.03	33.44	1.18	0.0	0.0	0.0	0.0	0.0	0.0

19¾% Interest

Monthly Payment %	2	3	4	5	6	7	8	9	10
1.60	101.33	102.22	103.30	104.62	106.22	108.17	110.53	113.41	116.92
1.70	98.42	97.37	96.08	94.52	92.63	90.32	87.51	84.10	79.94
1.75	96.96	94.94	92.47	89.47	85.82	81.39	75.99	69.42	61.44
1.80	95.51	92.51	88.86	84.42	79.02	72.46	64.47	54.75	42.93
1.90	92.59	87.65	81.63	74.32	65.42	54.59	41.42	25.41	5.92
2.00	89.68	82.79	74.41	64.21	51.81	36.73	18.38	0.0	0.0
2.10	86.76	77.93	67.18	54.11	38.21	18.86	0.0	0.0	0.0
2.20	83.85	73.07	59.96	44.00	24.60	1.00	0.0	0.0	0.0
2.25	82.39	70.64	56.34	38.95	17.80	0.0	0.0	0.0	0.0
2.30	80.94	68.21	52.73	33.90	10.99	0.0	0.0	0.0	0.0
2.40	78.02	63.35	45.50	23.79	0.0	0.0	0.0	0.0	0.0
2.50	75.11	58.49	38.28	13.69	0.0	0.0	0.0	0.0	0.0
2.60	72.19	53.63	31.05	3.59	0.0	0.0	0.0	0.0	0.0
2.70	69.28	48.77	23.83	0.0	0.0	0.0	0.0	0.0	0.0
2.75	67.82	46.34	20.21	0.0	0.0	0.0	0.0	0.0	0.0
2.90	63.45	39.05	9.37	0.0	0.0	0.0	0.0	0.0	0.0
3.00	60.54	34.19	2.15	0.0	0.0	0.0	0.0	0.0	0.0

EXAMPLES *ON PAGES A-382 TO A-397*

MORTGAGE YIELD TABLE

SHOWING DISCOUNT PERCENTAGES AT VARIOUS YIELDS, MONTHLY PAYMENT RATES AND DUE DATES

DUE DATE	PAY'T RATE %	BAL REMAIN %	YIELD PERCENTAGES								
			10%	11%	12%	13%	14%	15%	16%	17%	18%
1 YR.	0.75	100.00	0.95	1.89	2.81	3.73	4.64	5.54	6.43	7.31	8.18
	1.00	96.87	0.93	1.86	2.77	3.68	4.58	5.46	6.34	7.21	8.07
	1.25	93.75	0.92	1.83	2.74	3.63	4.51	5.39	6.25	7.11	7.96
	1.50	90.62	0.91	1.81	2.70	3.58	4.45	5.31	6.17	7.01	7.85
	1.75	87.49	0.90	1.78	2.66	3.53	4.39	5.24	6.08	6.91	7.73
	2.00	84.37	0.88	1.76	2.62	3.48	4.32	5.16	5.99	6.81	7.62
	8.75	0.0	0.53	1.05	1.57	2.09	2.60	3.11	3.61	4.12	4.61
2 YRS.	0.75	100.00	1.81	3.58	5.31	7.01	8.68	10.31	11.91	13.48	15.02
	1.00	93.45	1.75	3.47	5.16	6.81	8.43	10.02	11.57	13.10	14.60
	1.25	86.91	1.70	3.37	5.00	6.60	8.18	9.72	11.23	12.71	14.17
	1.50	80.36	1.65	3.26	4.85	6.40	7.93	9.42	10.89	12.33	13.74
	1.75	73.81	1.59	3.16	4.69	6.20	7.68	9.12	10.55	11.94	13.31
	2.00	67.26	1.54	3.05	4.54	5.99	7.42	8.83	10.21	11.56	12.88
	4.57	0.0	1.00	1.98	2.95	3.91	4.85	5.78	6.70	7.60	8.49
3 YRS.	0.75	100.00	2.58	5.09	7.53	9.89	12.19	14.42	16.59	18.70	20.75
	1.00	89.71	2.47	4.86	7.19	9.45	11.65	13.79	15.87	17.89	19.85
	1.25	79.42	2.35	4.63	6.85	9.01	11.11	13.16	15.14	17.08	18.95
	1.50	69.14	2.23	4.40	6.52	8.57	10.58	12.52	14.42	16.26	18.06
	1.75	58.85	2.12	4.18	6.18	8.14	10.04	11.89	13.69	15.45	17.16
	2.00	48.56	2.00	3.95	5.85	7.70	9.50	11.26	12.97	14.64	16.27
	3.18	0.0	1.45	2.87	4.26	5.62	6.96	8.27	9.55	10.81	12.04
4 YRS.	0.75	100.00	3.29	6.45	9.49	12.43	15.25	17.97	20.58	23.10	25.53
	1.00	85.62	3.08	6.06	8.92	11.68	14.34	16.90	19.38	21.76	24.06
	1.25	71.24	2.88	5.66	8.35	10.93	13.43	15.84	18.17	20.42	22.58
	1.50	56.86	2.68	5.27	7.77	10.19	12.52	14.78	16.96	19.07	21.11
	1.75	42.48	2.48	4.88	7.20	9.44	11.62	13.72	15.76	17.73	19.64
	2.00	28.10	2.28	4.48	6.62	8.70	10.71	12.66	14.55	16.38	18.16
	2.49	0.0	1.88	3.72	5.50	7.24	8.93	10.58	12.19	13.76	15.28
5 YRS.	0.75	100.00	3.92	7.67	11.24	14.65	17.91	21.02	23.99	26.82	29.54
	1.00	81.14	3.62	7.07	10.38	13.54	16.56	19.46	22.22	24.87	27.41
	1.25	62.29	3.31	6.48	9.52	12.43	15.22	17.90	20.46	22.92	25.28
	1.50	43.43	3.00	5.89	8.66	11.32	13.88	16.34	18.70	20.97	23.15
	1.75	24.58	2.70	5.30	7.80	10.21	12.54	14.78	16.94	19.02	21.03
	2.00	5.72	2.39	4.71	6.94	9.10	11.19	13.22	15.17	17.07	18.90
	2.08	0.0	2.30	4.53	6.68	8.77	10.79	12.74	14.64	16.47	18.25
6 YRS.	0.75	100.00	4.50	8.76	12.79	16.61	20.22	23.65	26.89	29.97	32.88
	1.00	76.25	4.07	7.93	11.60	15.08	18.39	21.53	24.52	27.36	30.05
	1.25	52.50	3.64	7.11	10.42	13.56	16.56	19.42	22.15	24.74	27.22
	1.50	28.74	3.22	6.29	9.23	12.04	14.73	17.31	19.77	22.13	24.39
	1.80	0.0	2.70	5.30	7.80	10.21	12.52	14.75	16.90	18.97	20.97
7 YRS.	0.75	100.00	5.02	9.73	14.16	18.32	22.23	25.91	29.37	32.62	35.68
	1.00	70.89	4.46	8.66	12.62	16.35	19.88	23.21	26.35	29.32	32.12
	1.25	41.79	3.89	7.58	11.07	14.39	17.53	20.50	23.33	26.01	28.56
	1.50	12.68	3.33	6.50	9.53	12.42	15.17	17.80	20.31	22.71	25.00
	1.61	0.0	3.08	6.04	8.86	11.56	14.15	16.62	19.00	21.27	23.45
8 YRS.	0.75	100.00	5.49	10.61	15.38	19.83	23.99	27.86	31.48	34.86	38.03
	1.00	65.04	4.78	9.26	13.45	17.39	21.08	24.54	27.79	30.85	33.72
	1.25	30.07	4.07	7.90	11.52	14.94	18.17	21.22	24.11	26.84	29.42
	1.47	0.0	3.45	6.74	9.86	12.83	15.67	18.36	20.93	23.38	25.72
9 YRS.	0.75	100.00	5.92	11.40	16.46	21.16	25.51	29.54	33.29	36.76	39.99
	1.00	58.63	5.04	9.74	14.12	18.21	22.02	25.59	28.92	32.03	34.94
	1.25	17.26	4.17	8.09	11.79	15.26	18.54	21.63	24.55	27.30	29.90
	1.35	0.0	3.81	7.40	10.81	14.03	17.09	19.98	22.72	25.33	27.80
10 YRS.	0.75	100.00	6.31	12.10	17.43	22.32	26.84	30.99	34.82	38.36	41.62
	1.00	51.62	5.26	10.14	14.66	18.86	22.76	26.39	29.77	32.92	35.85
	1.25	3.24	4.21	8.17	11.89	15.39	18.69	21.79	24.72	27.48	30.08
	1.27	0.0	4.14	8.04	11.71	15.16	18.41	21.48	24.38	27.11	29.70

		MONTHS									
UNTIL PAID	1.00	185.53	5.73	10.98	15.79	20.20	24.25	27.98	31.42	34.60	37.54
	1.25	122.63	4.21	8.17	11.90	15.40	18.69	21.80	24.72	27.48	30.09
	1.50	92.77	3.36	6.55	9.60	12.50	15.27	17.91	20.43	22.83	25.13
	1.75	74.89	2.79	5.48	8.06	10.54	12.92	15.22	17.42	19.54	21.59
	2.00	62.90	2.40	4.72	6.96	9.12	11.22	13.24	15.20	17.10	18.93
	2.50	47.73	1.87	3.70	5.47	7.21	8.89	10.53	12.14	13.70	15.22
	3.00	38.50	1.54	3.05	4.52	5.97	7.38	8.76	10.12	11.44	12.74
	4.00	27.79	1.14	2.27	3.37	4.46	5.53	6.58	7.62	8.64	9.65

EXAMPLES *ON PAGES A-382 TO A-397*

DUE DATE	19%	20%	21%	22%	23%	24%	25%	26%	27%	28%	29%
1 YR.	9.04	9.90	10.74	11.57	12.40	13.22	14.03	14.83	15.62	16.41	17.18
	8.92	9.76	10.59	11.42	12.23	13.04	13.84	14.63	15.41	16.19	16.95
	8.80	9.63	10.45	11.26	12.07	12.86	13.65	14.43	15.20	15.97	16.72
	8.67	9.49	10.30	11.10	11.90	12.68	13.46	14.23	14.99	15.75	16.49
	8.55	9.36	10.16	10.95	11.73	12.51	13.27	14.03	14.78	15.53	16.26
	8.43	9.22	10.01	10.79	11.56	12.33	13.08	13.83	14.57	15.31	16.03
	5.11	5.60	6.08	6.56	7.04	7.52	7.99	8.46	8.92	9.38	9.84
2 YRS.	16.53	18.01	19.46	20.88	22.28	23.64	24.98	26.30	27.58	28.85	30.08
	16.06	17.50	18.91	20.30	21.65	22.98	24.29	25.57	26.82	28.06	29.26
	15.59	16.99	18.37	19.71	21.03	22.33	23.60	24.84	26.07	27.26	28.44
	15.13	16.48	17.82	19.13	20.41	21.67	22.90	24.12	25.31	26.47	27.62
	14.66	15.98	17.27	18.54	19.79	21.01	22.21	23.39	24.55	25.68	26.80
	14.19	15.47	16.72	17.95	19.16	20.35	21.52	22.66	23.79	24.89	25.98
	9.37	10.24	11.09	11.94	12.77	13.59	14.40	15.20	15.99	16.77	17.54
3 YRS.	22.73	24.67	26.54	28.37	30.14	31.86	33.53	35.16	36.74	38.28	39.77
	21.76	23.61	25.42	27.17	28.87	30.53	32.14	33.71	35.24	36.72	38.16
	20.78	22.56	24.29	25.97	27.61	29.20	30.75	32.26	33.73	35.16	36.55
	19.81	21.51	23.16	24.78	26.35	27.87	29.36	30.81	32.23	33.60	34.94
	18.83	20.45	22.04	23.58	25.08	26.55	27.97	29.36	30.72	32.04	33.33
	17.85	19.40	20.91	22.38	23.82	25.22	26.58	27.91	29.21	30.48	31.72
	13.25	14.43	15.59	16.73	17.85	18.95	20.02	21.07	22.11	23.12	24.12
4 YRS.	27.87	30.12	32.29	34.38	36.40	38.34	40.21	42.02	43.75	45.43	47.05
	26.27	28.41	30.47	32.46	34.38	36.23	38.02	39.74	41.40	43.01	44.56
	24.68	26.70	28.65	30.54	32.36	34.12	35.82	37.47	39.05	40.59	42.07
	23.08	24.99	26.83	28.62	30.34	32.01	33.63	35.19	36.70	38.17	39.59
	21.49	23.28	25.01	26.69	28.32	29.90	31.43	32.92	34.35	35.75	37.10
	19.89	21.57	23.19	24.77	26.30	27.79	29.24	30.64	32.00	33.33	34.61
	16.77	18.22	19.64	21.02	22.36	23.67	24.95	26.20	27.41	28.60	29.76
5 YRS.	32.12	34.60	36.96	39.22	41.39	43.45	45.43	47.32	49.12	50.85	52.51
	29.83	32.16	34.38	36.51	38.55	40.51	42.38	44.18	45.90	47.55	49.13
	27.54	29.72	31.80	33.80	35.72	37.56	39.34	41.04	42.67	44.24	45.75
	25.25	27.27	29.22	31.09	32.89	34.62	36.29	37.90	39.45	40.94	42.38
	22.96	24.83	26.63	28.38	30.06	31.68	33.25	34.76	36.22	37.64	39.00
	20.67	22.39	24.05	25.66	27.22	28.73	30.20	31.62	33.00	34.33	35.63
	19.98	21.65	23.27	24.84	26.36	27.84	29.28	30.67	32.02	33.33	34.60
6 YRS.	35.65	38.27	40.76	43.12	45.35	47.48	49.50	51.41	53.23	54.96	56.61
	32.62	35.06	37.38	39.59	41.69	43.69	45.60	47.42	49.15	50.80	52.37
	29.59	31.85	34.00	36.06	38.02	39.90	41.70	43.42	45.06	46.63	48.14
	26.56	28.63	30.62	32.53	34.36	36.12	37.80	39.42	40.97	42.47	43.90
	22.89	24.75	26.53	28.26	29.92	31.53	33.08	34.58	36.03	37.43	38.78
7 YRS.	38.57	41.28	43.84	46.25	48.52	50.66	52.68	54.58	56.38	58.08	59.69
	34.77	37.28	39.66	41.90	44.03	46.04	47.95	49.76	51.48	53.10	54.65
	30.98	33.29	35.47	37.56	39.54	41.42	43.22	44.94	46.57	48.13	49.61
	27.19	29.29	31.29	33.21	35.05	36.81	38.50	40.11	41.66	43.15	44.58
	25.54	27.55	29.47	31.32	33.09	34.80	36.44	38.01	39.52	40.98	42.38
8 YRS.	40.98	43.75	46.34	48.76	51.03	53.16	55.16	57.03	58.79	60.44	62.00
	36.43	38.97	41.36	43.62	45.75	47.75	49.65	51.43	53.12	54.72	56.23
	31.87	34.19	36.39	38.48	40.46	42.35	44.13	45.84	47.45	49.00	50.46
	27.95	30.08	32.12	34.06	35.92	37.69	39.39	41.02	42.58	44.07	45.50
9 YRS.	42.98	45.77	48.37	50.78	53.04	55.14	57.10	58.93	60.64	62.24	63.73
	37.67	40.23	42.63	44.88	47.00	48.98	50.85	52.61	54.27	55.84	57.31
	32.36	34.69	36.89	38.98	40.95	42.83	44.61	46.30	47.91	49.44	50.89
	30.14	32.38	34.50	36.51	38.43	40.26	42.01	43.67	45.25	46.77	48.21
10 YRS.	44.64	47.43	50.02	52.41	54.63	56.69	58.61	60.39	62.05	63.60	65.04
	38.59	41.15	43.55	45.79	47.88	49.85	51.69	53.43	55.06	56.59	58.04
	32.55	34.97	37.07	39.16	41.13	43.00	44.78	46.47	48.07	49.59	51.04
	32.14	34.45	36.64	38.71	40.68	42.55	44.32	46.00	47.60	49.12	50.57
UNTIL PAID	40.27	42.79	45.14	47.33	49.37	51.27	53.05	54.71	56.27	57.74	59.11
	32.55	34.88	37.08	39.17	41.14	43.01	44.79	46.47	48.07	49.59	51.04
	27.32	29.42	31.43	33.35	35.19	36.95	38.63	40.25	41.80	43.28	44.70
	23.55	25.45	27.27	29.03	30.72	32.36	33.93	35.45	36.92	38.33	39.70
	20.71	22.43	24.09	25.70	27.26	28.78	30.24	31.66	33.04	34.37	35.67
	16.70	18.14	19.55	20.93	22.27	23.57	24.85	26.09	27.30	28.49	29.64
	14.01	15.26	16.47	17.67	18.84	19.98	21.10	22.20	23.28	24.33	25.36
	10.64	11.61	12.57	13.51	14.44	15.36	16.26	17.14	18.02	18.88	19.72

EXAMPLES *ON PAGES A-382 TO A-397*

MORTGAGE YIELD TABLE
SHOWING DISCOUNT PERCENTAGES AT VARIOUS
YIELDS, MONTHLY PAYMENT RATES AND DUE DATES

DUE DATE	PAY'T RATE %	BAL REMAIN %	YIELD PERCENTAGES								
			10%	11%	12%	13%	14%	15%	16%	17%	18%
1 YR.	0.77	100.00	0.71	1.65	2.58	3.50	4.41	5.31	6.20	7.08	7.95
	1.00	97.13	0.70	1.63	2.55	3.45	4.35	5.24	6.12	6.99	7.85
	1.25	94.00	0.69	1.61	2.51	3.41	4.29	5.17	6.04	6.90	7.75
	1.50	90.87	0.68	1.58	2.48	3.36	4.23	5.10	5.95	6.80	7.64
	1.75	87.74	0.67	1.56	2.44	3.31	4.17	5.02	5.87	6.70	7.53
	2.00	84.61	0.66	1.54	2.40	3.26	4.11	4.95	5.78	6.61	7.42
	8.76	0.0	0.40	0.92	1.44	1.96	2.47	2.98	3.49	3.99	4.49
2 YRS.	0.77	100.00	1.35	3.13	4.87	6.57	8.24	9.88	11.49	13.06	14.61
	1.00	93.98	1.32	3.05	4.74	6.40	8.03	9.62	11.19	12.72	14.22
	1.25	87.42	1.28	2.95	4.60	6.21	7.79	9.34	10.86	12.35	13.81
	1.50	80.86	1.24	2.86	4.45	6.02	7.55	9.05	10.53	11.97	13.39
	1.75	74.29	1.20	2.77	4.31	5.83	7.31	8.77	10.20	11.60	12.97
	2.00	67.73	1.16	2.68	4.17	5.63	7.07	8.48	9.87	11.22	12.56
	4.58	0.0	0.75	1.73	2.71	3.66	4.61	5.54	6.46	7.37	8.26
3 YRS.	0.77	100.00	1.94	4.45	6.90	9.27	11.58	13.82	16.00	18.11	20.17
	1.00	90.53	1.86	4.27	6.62	8.90	11.11	13.26	15.36	17.39	19.37
	1.25	80.21	1.77	4.07	6.31	8.48	10.60	12.66	14.66	16.60	18.50
	1.50	69.88	1.68	3.87	6.00	8.07	10.09	12.05	13.96	15.82	17.62
	1.75	59.55	1.59	3.67	5.69	7.66	9.57	11.44	13.26	15.03	16.75
	2.00	49.22	1.51	3.47	5.38	7.24	9.06	10.83	12.56	14.24	15.88
	3.19	0.0	1.09	2.51	3.91	5.28	6.62	7.93	9.22	10.48	11.72
4 YRS.	0.77	100.00	2.46	5.64	8.70	11.65	14.49	17.22	19.85	22.38	24.82
	1.00	86.75	2.33	5.33	8.22	11.01	13.69	16.28	18.78	21.18	23.51
	1.25	72.30	2.17	4.98	7.69	10.30	12.83	15.26	17.61	19.88	22.07
	1.50	57.84	2.02	4.64	7.16	9.60	11.96	14.24	16.44	18.57	20.63
	1.75	43.39	1.87	4.29	6.63	8.90	11.10	13.22	15.28	17.27	19.19
	2.00	28.93	1.72	3.95	6.11	8.20	10.23	12.20	14.11	15.96	17.76
	2.53	0.0	1.41	3.26	5.05	6.80	8.50	10.16	11.77	13.35	14.88
5 YRS.	0.77	100.00	2.94	6.71	10.30	13.73	17.01	20.14	23.13	25.99	28.71
	1.00	82.60	2.73	6.23	9.58	12.78	15.84	18.77	21.57	24.25	26.81
	1.25	63.62	2.50	5.71	8.79	11.73	14.56	17.26	19.86	22.35	24.73
	1.50	44.64	2.27	5.19	7.99	10.69	13.28	15.76	18.15	20.45	22.66
	1.75	25.66	2.04	4.67	7.20	9.64	12.00	14.26	16.45	18.55	20.58
	2.00	6.68	1.81	4.15	6.41	8.60	10.72	12.76	14.74	16.65	18.51
	2.09	0.0	1.73	3.97	6.13	8.23	10.26	12.23	14.14	15.98	17.77
6 YRS.	0.77	100.00	3.37	7.66	11.72	15.57	19.21	22.66	25.93	29.03	31.97
	1.00	78.05	3.08	7.00	10.72	14.25	17.61	20.80	23.82	26.70	29.44
	1.25	54.11	2.76	6.28	9.63	12.82	15.86	18.76	21.52	24.16	26.67
	1.50	30.17	2.43	5.56	8.54	11.39	14.12	16.73	19.23	21.62	23.91
	1.81	0.0	2.03	4.65	7.16	9.59	11.92	14.16	16.33	18.41	20.42
7 YRS.	0.77	100.00	3.76	8.52	12.98	17.18	21.12	24.83	28.32	31.60	34.69
	1.00	73.06	3.38	7.65	11.68	15.48	19.06	22.44	25.64	28.65	31.50
	1.25	43.68	2.95	6.70	10.25	13.62	16.81	19.84	22.71	25.43	28.02
	1.50	14.30	2.53	5.75	8.83	11.76	14.56	17.23	19.78	22.21	24.54
	1.62	0.0	2.32	5.29	8.14	10.86	13.47	15.96	18.36	20.65	22.85
8 YRS.	0.77	100.00	4.12	9.28	14.10	18.59	22.79	26.70	30.36	33.78	36.97
	1.00	67.59	3.63	8.19	12.47	16.48	20.24	23.76	27.08	30.19	33.11
	1.25	32.24	3.09	7.00	10.69	14.17	17.45	20.56	23.50	26.27	28.90
	1.48	0.0	2.60	5.91	9.06	12.06	14.52	17.64	20.23	22.70	25.06
9 YRS.	0.77	100.00	4.44	9.97	15.09	19.84	24.23	28.31	32.10	35.61	38.87
	1.00	61.60	3.83	8.64	13.11	17.28	21.18	24.81	28.21	31.38	34.35
	1.25	19.70	3.17	7.18	10.95	14.50	17.84	20.99	23.96	26.76	29.41
	1.37	0.0	2.86	6.50	9.93	13.19	16.27	19.19	21.97	24.59	27.09
10 YRS.	0.77	100.00	4.73	10.59	15.97	20.93	25.49	29.70	33.58	37.16	40.47
	1.00	55.03	4.00	9.00	13.63	17.93	21.92	25.63	29.08	32.29	35.28
	1.25	5.95	3.21	7.26	11.07	14.65	18.01	21.18	24.16	26.98	29.63
	1.28	0.0	3.12	7.05	10.76	14.25	17.54	20.64	23.57	26.33	28.94
		MONTHS									
UNTIL PAID	1.00	191.87	4.42	9.85	14.82	19.37	23.54	27.38	30.91	34.16	37.16
	1.25	124.87	3.22	7.27	11.08	14.66	18.03	21.20	24.18	27.00	29.65
	1.50	93.94	2.55	5.81	8.91	11.86	14.67	17.36	19.92	22.36	24.69
	1.75	75.62	2.12	4.84	7.46	9.98	12.40	14.72	16.96	19.11	21.18
	2.00	63.40	1.81	4.16	6.43	8.62	10.74	12.79	14.78	16.69	18.55
	2.50	48.01	1.41	3.26	5.05	6.80	8.50	10.16	11.77	13.35	14.88
	3.00	38.68	1.16	2.68	4.17	5.62	7.05	8.44	9.80	11.14	12.45
	4.00	27.88	0.86	1.99	3.10	4.20	5.27	6.33	7.38	8.40	9.41

EXAMPLES ON PAGES A-382 TO A-397

DUE DATE	19%	20%	21%	22%	23%	24%	25%	26%	27%	28%	29%
	YIELD PERCENTAGES										
1 YR.	8.82	9.67	10.52	11.35	12.18	13.00	13.81	14.61	15.41	16.19	16.97
	8.71	9.55	10.38	11.21	12.03	12.84	13.64	14.43	15.22	15.99	16.76
	8.59	9.42	10.24	11.06	11.86	12.66	13.45	14.23	15.01	15.77	16.53
	8.47	9.29	10.10	10.90	11.70	12.49	13.27	14.04	14.80	15.56	16.31
	8.35	9.16	9.96	10.75	11.53	12.31	13.08	13.84	14.60	15.34	16.08
	8.23	9.02	9.81	10.60	11.37	12.14	12.89	13.65	14.39	15.12	15.85
	4.98	5.47	5.96	6.44	6.92	7.39	7.87	8.34	8.80	9.26	9.72
2 YRS.	16.12	17.60	19.06	20.48	21.88	23.25	24.59	25.91	27.20	28.47	29.71
	15.70	17.14	18.56	19.95	21.32	22.65	23.97	25.25	26.51	27.75	28.96
	15.24	16.65	18.03	19.38	20.70	22.01	23.28	24.54	25.76	26.97	28.15
	14.78	16.15	17.49	18.80	20.09	21.36	22.60	23.82	25.01	26.19	27.34
	14.33	15.65	16.95	18.23	19.48	20.71	21.92	23.10	24.26	25.41	26.53
	13.87	15.15	16.41	17.65	18.87	20.06	21.23	22.39	23.51	24.62	25.71
	9.14	10.01	10.87	11.72	12.55	13.38	14.19	14.99	15.78	16.56	17.33
3 YRS.	22.17	24.11	25.99	27.82	29.60	31.33	33.01	34.64	36.23	37.77	39.27
	21.29	23.16	24.98	26.74	28.46	30.13	31.75	33.33	34.87	36.36	37.81
	20.34	22.13	23.87	25.57	27.22	28.82	30.38	31.90	33.38	34.82	36.22
	19.38	21.10	22.77	24.39	25.97	27.51	29.01	30.47	31.89	33.28	34.62
	18.43	20.07	21.66	23.21	24.73	26.20	27.64	29.04	30.40	31.73	33.03
	17.48	19.03	20.55	22.04	23.48	24.89	26.27	27.61	28.92	30.19	31.44
	12.93	14.12	15.29	16.43	17.55	18.65	19.73	20.79	21.82	22.84	23.84
4 YRS.	27.17	29.44	31.62	33.72	35.75	37.70	39.58	41.40	43.15	44.83	46.46
	25.74	27.90	29.98	31.99	33.93	35.79	37.60	39.34	41.02	42.64	44.20
	24.18	26.22	28.19	30.10	31.94	33.71	35.43	37.08	38.69	40.24	41.74
	22.62	24.55	26.41	28.21	29.95	31.63	33.26	34.84	36.37	37.84	39.27
	21.06	22.87	24.62	26.32	27.96	29.55	31.10	32.59	34.04	35.45	36.81
	19.50	21.19	22.83	24.42	25.97	27.47	28.93	30.34	31.72	33.05	34.35
	16.38	17.83	19.25	20.64	21.99	23.31	24.59	25.84	27.06	28.26	29.42
5 YRS.	31.32	33.81	36.19	38.47	40.65	42.73	44.72	46.62	48.44	50.18	51.85
	29.27	31.62	33.87	36.02	38.09	40.06	41.96	43.77	45.51	47.18	48.78
	27.02	29.22	31.33	33.35	35.29	37.16	38.95	40.67	42.32	43.91	45.44
	24.78	26.82	28.79	30.68	32.50	34.25	35.94	37.56	39.13	40.64	42.09
	22.54	24.43	26.25	28.01	29.71	31.35	32.93	34.46	35.94	37.36	38.74
	20.30	22.03	23.71	25.34	26.92	28.44	29.92	31.35	32.74	34.09	35.40
	19.51	21.19	22.82	24.40	25.93	27.42	28.86	30.26	31.62	32.94	34.22
6 YRS.	34.76	37.40	39.91	42.29	44.54	46.69	48.72	50.66	52.50	54.24	55.90
	32.04	34.51	36.86	39.10	41.23	43.25	45.19	47.03	48.78	50.46	52.05
	29.07	31.35	33.54	35.62	37.61	39.52	41.33	43.07	44.74	46.33	47.85
	26.10	28.20	30.21	32.15	34.00	35.77	37.48	39.12	40.69	42.20	43.65
	22.36	24.23	26.03	27.76	29.44	31.06	32.62	34.13	35.59	36.99	38.35
7 YRS.	37.60	40.34	42.92	45.36	47.65	49.81	51.85	53.78	55.60	57.32	58.94
	34.19	36.74	39.15	41.43	43.59	45.63	47.57	49.40	51.14	52.79	54.36
	30.48	32.81	35.03	37.14	39.15	41.07	42.89	44.62	46.28	47.85	49.36
	26.76	28.89	30.92	32.86	34.72	36.50	38.21	39.84	41.41	42.92	44.36
	24.95	26.97	28.91	30.78	32.56	34.28	35.93	37.52	39.05	40.51	41.93
8 YRS.	39.96	42.75	45.37	47.82	50.12	52.28	54.30	56.19	57.98	59.65	61.22
	35.86	38.45	40.88	43.17	45.33	47.37	49.29	51.11	52.82	54.44	55.97
	31.39	33.75	35.98	38.10	40.11	42.02	43.83	45.56	47.20	48.76	50.24
	27.31	29.46	31.51	33.47	35.35	37.14	38.86	40.50	42.07	43.58	45.02
9 YRS.	41.91	44.73	47.36	49.81	52.09	54.22	56.20	58.06	59.80	61.42	62.94
	37.13	39.73	42.17	44.46	46.61	48.63	50.53	52.32	54.00	55.59	57.09
	31.91	34.28	36.51	38.63	40.64	42.54	44.35	46.06	47.69	49.23	50.70
	29.46	31.71	33.85	35.89	37.83	39.68	41.44	43.11	44.72	46.24	47.70
10 YRS.	43.53	46.35	48.98	51.40	53.66	55.75	57.69	59.50	61.19	62.76	64.22
	38.08	40.69	43.12	45.40	47.53	49.53	51.41	53.17	54.82	56.38	57.84
	32.13	34.50	36.74	38.85	40.86	42.75	44.55	46.26	47.88	49.42	50.88
	31.41	33.75	35.96	38.06	40.04	41.93	43.72	45.42	47.04	48.57	50.04
UNTIL PAID	39.94	42.52	44.91	47.13	49.19	51.12	52.92	54.60	56.18	57.66	59.04
	32.16	34.52	36.76	38.87	40.87	42.77	44.57	46.28	47.90	49.44	50.90
	26.92	29.05	31.09	33.03	34.89	36.67	38.38	40.01	41.58	43.08	44.52
	23.17	25.08	26.93	28.71	30.42	32.07	33.67	35.20	36.68	38.11	39.49
	20.34	22.08	23.76	25.39	26.97	28.50	29.98	31.41	32.80	34.15	35.45
	16.38	17.84	19.26	20.64	21.99	23.31	24.59	25.85	27.07	28.26	29.42
	13.73	14.98	16.21	17.41	18.59	19.74	20.87	21.97	23.06	24.12	25.16
	10.41	11.39	12.35	13.30	14.23	15.15	16.06	16.95	17.83	18.69	19.54

EXAMPLES *ON PAGES A-382 TO A-397*

MORTGAGE YIELD TABLE
SHOWING DISCOUNT PERCENTAGES AT VARIOUS YIELDS, MONTHLY PAYMENT RATES AND DUE DATES

DUE DATE	PAY'T RATE %	BAL REMAIN %	10%	11%	12%	13%	14%	15%	16%	17%	18%
						YIELD PERCENTAGES					
1 YR.	0.79	100.00	0.47	1.41	2.34	3.27	4.18	5.08	5.97	6.85	7.73
	1.00	97.39	0.47	1.40	2.32	3.23	4.13	5.02	5.90	6.77	7.64
	1.25	94.25	0.46	1.38	2.29	3.18	4.07	4.95	5.82	6.68	7.53
	1.50	91.12	0.46	1.36	2.25	3.14	4.01	4.88	5.74	6.59	7.43
	1.75	87.99	0.45	1.34	2.22	3.09	3.96	4.81	5.66	6.49	7.32
	2.00	84.85	0.44	1.32	2.19	3.05	3.90	4.74	5.57	6.40	7.22
	8.77	0.0	0.26	0.79	1.31	1.83	2.34	2.85	3.36	3.86	4.36
2 YRS.	0.79	100.00	0.90	2.68	4.43	6.13	7.81	9.45	11.06	12.64	14.19
	1.00	94.52	0.88	2.62	4.32	5.99	7.62	9.23	10.80	12.34	13.85
	1.25	87.94	0.85	2.54	4.19	5.81	7.40	8.95	10.48	11.98	13.45
	1.50	81.36	0.83	2.46	4.06	5.63	7.17	8.68	10.16	11.61	13.04
	1.75	74.78	0.80	2.38	3.93	5.45	6.94	8.41	9.84	11.25	12.64
	2.00	68.20	0.77	2.30	3.80	5.27	6.72	8.13	9.52	10.89	12.23
	4.59	0.0	0.50	1.49	2.46	3.42	4.37	5.30	6.23	7.14	8.03
3 YRS.	0.79	100.00	1.29	3.82	6.27	8.66	10.97	13.22	15.41	17.53	19.59
	1.00	91.36	1.24	3.67	6.04	8.33	10.57	12.74	14.84	16.89	18.88
	1.25	80.99	1.18	3.50	5.76	7.95	10.08	12.15	14.17	16.13	18.03
	1.50	70.63	1.13	3.33	5.47	7.56	9.59	11.57	13.49	15.36	17.19
	1.75	60.26	1.07	3.16	5.19	7.18	9.11	10.99	12.82	14.60	16.34
	2.00	49.90	1.01	2.99	4.91	6.79	8.62	10.40	12.14	13.83	15.49
	3.20	0.0	0.73	2.16	3.56	4.93	6.28	7.59	8.89	10.15	11.39
4 YRS.	0.79	100.00	1.64	4.84	7.91	10.87	13.72	16.47	19.11	21.66	24.11
	1.00	87.89	1.56	4.59	7.51	10.32	13.04	15.65	18.17	20.60	22.95
	1.25	73.36	1.46	4.29	7.03	9.67	12.22	14.67	17.05	19.34	21.55
	1.50	58.83	1.36	4.00	6.55	9.01	11.39	13.69	15.92	18.07	20.15
	1.75	44.30	1.25	3.70	6.07	8.36	10.57	12.71	14.79	16.80	18.74
	2.00	29.77	1.15	3.40	5.58	7.70	9.75	11.74	13.66	15.53	17.34
	2.51	0.0	0.94	2.80	4.60	6.35	8.06	9.73	11.35	12.93	14.47
5 YRS.	0.79	100.00	1.96	5.75	9.37	12.82	16.12	19.27	22.27	25.15	27.89
	1.00	84.08	1.83	5.38	8.76	12.00	15.10	18.06	20.90	23.61	26.21
	1.25	64.47	1.68	4.93	8.04	11.02	13.88	16.62	19.25	21.77	24.18
	1.50	45.87	1.52	4.48	7.32	10.05	12.66	15.18	17.60	19.92	22.16
	1.75	26.76	1.37	4.03	6.60	9.07	11.45	13.74	15.95	18.08	20.13
	2.00	7.66	1.22	3.59	5.88	8.09	10.23	12.30	14.30	16.23	18.11
	2.10	0.0	1.15	3.41	5.59	7.70	9.74	11.72	13.64	15.49	17.29
6 YRS.	0.79	100.00	2.25	6.57	10.66	14.53	18.20	21.68	24.97	28.09	31.06
	1.00	79.89	2.07	6.05	9.83	13.41	16.81	20.05	23.12	26.03	28.81
	1.25	55.75	1.85	5.43	8.83	12.07	15.15	18.09	20.89	23.56	26.11
	1.50	31.62	1.64	4.80	7.83	10.72	13.49	16.14	18.67	21.09	23.41
	1.83	0.0	1.36	3.99	6.52	8.96	11.31	13.57	15.75	17.85	19.88
7 YRS.	0.79	100.00	2.51	7.30	11.80	16.03	20.01	23.75	27.27	30.58	33.70
	1.00	75.28	2.27	6.62	10.72	14.58	18.22	21.66	24.91	27.97	30.87
	1.25	45.61	1.99	5.80	9.42	12.84	16.08	19.16	22.07	24.84	27.47
	1.50	15.95	1.70	4.99	8.11	11.10	13.94	16.65	19.24	21.71	24.07
	1.63	0.0	1.55	4.55	7.41	10.16	12.79	15.30	17.71	20.02	22.24
8 YRS.	0.79	100.00	2.75	7.96	12.82	17.35	21.59	25.54	29.23	32.69	35.91
	1.00	70.21	2.44	7.10	11.46	15.55	19.38	22.97	26.34	29.51	32.48
	1.25	34.47	2.08	6.07	9.83	13.38	16.72	19.88	22.87	25.70	28.37
	1.49	0.0	1.74	5.08	8.26	11.28	14.16	16.91	19.53	22.02	24.40
9 YRS.	0.79	100.00	2.96	8.55	13.72	18.51	22.96	27.08	30.91	34.46	37.76
	1.00	64.65	2.59	7.50	12.07	16.33	20.31	24.01	27.48	30.71	33.74
	1.25	22.22	2.15	6.24	10.09	13.71	17.12	20.33	23.36	26.21	28.91
	1.38	0.0	1.91	5.58	9.05	12.34	15.45	18.41	21.20	23.86	26.38
10 YRS.	0.79	100.00	3.15	9.07	14.52	19.53	24.15	28.41	32.34	35.96	39.31
	1.00	58.52	2.71	7.83	12.57	16.96	21.05	24.84	28.36	31.64	34.70
	1.25	8.75	2.18	6.33	10.22	13.88	17.32	20.55	23.59	26.46	29.16
	1.29	0.0	2.08	6.06	9.81	13.34	16.66	19.80	22.75	25.55	28.19
		MONTHS									
UNTIL PAID	1.00	198.92	3.03	8.67	13.82	18.52	22.82	26.76	30.38	33.71	36.78
	1.25	127.23	2.18	6.34	10.24	13.91	17.35	20.59	23.63	26.50	29.20
	1.50	95.15	1.72	5.04	8.20	11.21	14.07	16.80	19.40	21.88	24.25
	1.75	76.36	1.43	4.20	6.85	9.41	11.86	14.22	16.48	18.66	20.76
	2.00	63.90	1.22	3.60	5.90	8.12	10.26	12.34	14.34	16.28	18.16
	2.50	48.29	0.95	2.81	4.62	6.39	8.10	9.78	11.41	13.00	14.54
	3.00	38.85	0.78	2.31	3.81	5.28	6.71	8.11	9.49	10.83	12.15
	4.00	27.97	0.58	1.71	2.83	3.93	5.01	6.08	7.13	8.16	9.18

EXAMPLES *ON PAGES A-382 TO A-397*

MORTGAGE YIELD TABLE
SHOWING DISCOUNT PERCENTAGES AT VARIOUS YIELDS, MONTHLY PAYMENT RATES AND DUE DATES

DUE DATE	YIELD PERCENTAGES										
	19%	20%	21%	22%	23%	24%	25%	26%	27%	28%	29%
1 YR.	8.59	9.45	10.29	11.13	11.96	12.78	13.59	14.39	15.19	15.97	16.75
	8.49	9.34	10.18	11.00	11.82	12.63	13.44	14.23	15.02	15.80	16.57
	8.38	9.21	10.04	10.85	11.66	12.46	13.25	14.04	14.81	15.58	16.34
	8.26	9.08	9.90	10.70	11.50	12.29	13.07	13.85	14.61	15.37	16.12
	8.14	8.95	9.76	10.55	11.34	12.12	12.89	13.65	14.41	15.15	15.89
	8.02	8.82	9.62	10.40	11.18	11.94	12.70	13.46	14.20	14.94	15.67
	4.85	5.34	5.83	6.32	6.80	7.27	7.74	8.21	8.68	9.14	9.60
2 YRS.	15.70	17.19	18.65	20.08	21.48	22.85	24.20	25.52	26.82	28.09	29.33
	15.33	16.79	18.21	19.61	20.98	22.32	23.64	24.93	26.20	27.44	28.66
	14.89	16.30	17.68	19.04	20.38	21.68	22.97	24.23	25.46	26.67	27.86
	14.44	15.81	17.16	18.48	19.78	21.05	22.29	23.52	24.72	25.90	27.06
	13.99	15.32	16.63	17.91	19.17	20.41	21.62	22.81	23.98	25.13	26.25
	13.55	14.84	16.10	17.35	18.57	19.77	20.95	22.10	23.24	24.35	25.45
	8.92	9.79	10.65	11.50	12.33	13.16	13.97	14.78	15.57	16.35	17.12
3 YRS.	21.60	23.54	25.44	27.28	29.06	30.80	32.49	34.13	35.72	37.27	38.78
	20.82	22.70	24.53	26.31	28.04	29.72	31.36	32.95	34.50	36.00	37.46
	19.89	21.69	23.45	25.16	26.82	28.43	30.01	31.54	33.03	34.47	35.89
	18.96	20.68	22.36	24.00	25.59	27.14	28.65	30.12	31.56	32.95	34.31
	18.03	19.67	21.28	22.84	24.37	25.85	27.30	28.71	30.08	31.42	32.73
	17.10	18.66	20.20	21.69	23.14	24.56	25.95	27.30	28.61	29.90	31.15
	12.61	13.81	14.98	16.12	17.25	18.35	19.43	20.50	21.54	22.56	23.56
4 YRS.	26.48	28.75	30.95	33.06	35.10	37.06	38.96	40.78	42.54	44.23	45.87
	25.21	27.38	29.49	31.51	33.47	35.35	37.17	38.93	40.62	42.26	43.84
	23.68	25.74	27.73	29.65	31.51	33.30	35.03	36.71	38.32	39.89	41.40
	22.15	24.10	25.98	27.79	29.55	31.25	32.89	34.49	36.03	37.52	38.96
	20.63	22.45	24.22	25.93	27.59	29.20	30.75	32.26	33.73	35.15	36.52
	19.10	20.81	22.46	24.07	25.63	27.14	28.61	30.04	31.43	32.77	34.08
	15.98	17.44	18.87	20.26	21.62	22.94	24.23	25.49	26.72	27.92	29.08
5 YRS.	30.52	33.03	35.42	37.72	39.91	42.00	44.01	45.92	47.76	49.51	51.19
	28.69	31.07	33.35	35.53	37.61	39.61	41.53	43.37	45.13	46.81	48.43
	26.50	28.72	30.85	32.90	34.86	36.75	38.56	40.30	41.97	43.57	45.11
	24.30	26.37	28.36	30.27	32.11	33.88	35.58	37.23	38.81	40.33	41.80
	22.11	24.02	25.86	27.64	29.36	31.01	32.61	34.16	35.65	37.09	38.48
	19.92	21.67	23.37	25.01	26.60	28.14	29.64	31.08	32.49	33.85	35.16
	19.04	20.73	22.37	23.96	25.50	27.00	28.45	29.85	31.22	32.55	33.84
6 YRS.	33.87	36.53	39.06	41.46	43.73	45.90	47.95	49.90	51.76	53.52	55.19
	31.44	33.95	36.34	38.60	40.76	42.82	44.77	46.64	48.41	50.11	51.72
	28.54	30.86	33.07	35.18	37.20	39.12	40.96	42.72	44.41	46.01	47.55
	25.63	27.76	29.80	31.75	33.63	35.43	37.15	38.81	40.40	41.92	43.39
	21.83	23.71	25.52	27.27	28.96	30.59	32.16	33.68	35.14	36.56	37.93
7 YRS.	36.64	39.40	42.01	44.47	46.78	48.97	51.03	52.98	54.82	56.55	58.19
	33.60	36.19	38.63	40.95	43.14	45.21	47.17	49.03	50.80	52.47	54.06
	29.96	32.33	34.58	36.72	38.76	40.70	42.55	44.30	45.98	47.58	49.10
	26.32	28.47	30.53	32.50	34.39	36.19	37.92	39.57	41.16	42.68	44.14
	24.36	26.40	28.35	30.23	32.03	33.77	35.43	37.03	38.57	40.05	41.47
8 YRS.	38.93	41.76	44.41	46.89	49.21	51.39	53.44	55.36	57.16	58.85	60.45
	35.28	37.91	40.39	42.72	44.91	46.98	48.93	50.77	52.51	54.15	55.71
	30.90	33.29	35.56	37.71	39.75	41.69	43.53	45.27	46.94	48.52	50.02
	26.67	28.84	30.91	32.89	34.78	36.58	38.32	39.97	41.56	43.08	44.53
9 YRS.	40.83	43.69	46.35	48.83	51.14	53.30	55.31	57.19	58.95	60.60	62.14
	36.57	39.22	41.71	44.03	46.22	48.27	50.20	52.02	53.73	55.34	56.86
	31.45	33.05	36.13	38.28	40.32	42.25	44.08	45.81	47.46	49.03	50.51
	28.77	31.00	33.21	35.26	37.22	39.09	40.86	42.56	44.18	45.72	47.19
10 YRS.	42.41	45.28	47.93	50.40	52.68	54.00	56.78	58.62	60.33	61.92	63.41
	37.55	40.20	42.68	45.00	47.18	49.21	51.11	52.90	54.58	56.16	57.64
	31.71	34.11	36.39	38.54	40.57	42.49	44.32	46.04	47.69	49.24	50.72
	30.68	33.04	35.28	37.40	39.41	41.31	43.12	44.84	46.47	48.03	49.51
UNTIL PAID	39.62	42.24	44.67	46.92	49.02	50.97	52.79	54.50	56.09	57.58	58.98
	31.75	34.16	36.43	38.58	40.61	42.53	44.35	46.08	47.72	49.28	50.75
	26.51	28.67	30.74	32.71	34.59	36.40	38.12	39.78	41.36	42.88	44.33
	22.78	24.72	26.58	28.38	30.12	31.79	33.40	34.95	36.44	37.89	39.28
	19.97	21.73	23.43	25.08	26.67	28.21	29.71	31.15	32.56	33.92	35.23
	16.05	17.52	18.96	20.35	21.71	23.04	24.34	25.60	26.83	28.03	29.21
	13.44	14.70	15.94	17.15	18.33	19.49	20.63	21.74	22.83	23.90	24.95
	10.18	11.16	12.13	13.08	14.02	14.95	15.86	16.75	17.64	18.51	19.36

EXAMPLES *ON PAGES A-382 TO A-397*

MORTGAGE YIELD TABLE
SHOWING DISCOUNT PERCENTAGES AT VARIOUS YIELDS, MONTHLY PAYMENT RATES AND DUE DATES

9¾% INTEREST

DUE DATE	PAY'T RATE %	BAL REMAIN %	YIELD PERCENTAGES								
			10%	11%	12%	13%	14%	15%	16%	17%	18%
1 YR.	0.81	100.00	0.24	1.18	2.11	3.03	3.94	4.85	5.74	6.62	7.50
	1.00	97.65	0.23	1.17	2.09	3.00	3.90	4.80	5.68	6.56	7.42
	1.25	94.51	0.23	1.15	2.06	2.96	3.85	4.73	5.60	6.47	7.32
	1.50	91.37	0.23	1.13	2.03	2.92	3.80	4.66	5.52	6.37	7.22
	1.75	88.23	0.22	1.12	2.00	2.88	3.74	4.60	5.45	6.28	7.11
	2.00	85.10	0.22	1.10	1.97	2.83	3.69	4.53	5.37	6.19	7.01
	8.78	0.0	0.13	0.66	1.18	1.70	2.21	2.72	3.23	3.73	4.23
2 YRS.	0.81	100.00	0.45	2.23	3.98	5.70	7.38	9.02	10.64	12.22	13.77
	1.00	95.05	0.44	2.19	3.90	5.57	7.22	8.83	10.41	11.96	13.48
	1.25	88.46	0.43	2.12	3.78	5.41	7.00	8.57	10.10	11.61	13.08
	1.50	81.86	0.41	2.05	3.66	5.24	6.79	8.31	9.79	11.26	12.69
	1.75	75.27	0.40	1.99	3.55	5.07	6.57	8.04	9.49	10.90	12.29
	2.00	68.67	0.39	1.92	3.43	4.91	6.36	7.78	9.18	10.55	11.90
	4.60	0.0	0.25	1.24	2.22	3.18	4.13	5.07	5.99	6.90	7.80
3 YRS.	0.81	100.00	0.65	3.18	5.65	8.04	10.36	12.62	14.81	16.95	19.02
	1.00	92.20	0.62	3.07	5.45	7.77	10.02	12.20	14.33	16.39	18.40
	1.25	81.79	0.59	2.93	5.20	7.41	9.56	11.64	13.67	15.65	17.57
	1.50	71.38	0.56	2.79	4.95	7.05	9.09	11.09	13.02	14.91	16.74
	1.75	60.98	0.54	2.64	4.69	6.69	8.63	10.53	12.37	14.17	15.92
	2.00	50.57	0.51	2.50	4.44	6.33	8.17	9.97	11.72	13.43	15.09
	3.21	0.0	0.36	1.80	3.20	4.58	5.93	7.26	8.55	9.82	11.07
4 YRS.	0.81	100.00	0.82	4.03	7.12	10.10	12.96	15.72	18.38	20.94	23.40
	1.00	89.05	0.78	3.84	6.79	9.64	12.38	15.02	17.56	20.02	22.38
	1.25	74.44	0.73	3.60	6.36	9.02	11.60	14.08	16.47	18.79	21.02
	1.50	59.84	0.68	3.35	5.92	8.41	10.82	13.14	15.39	17.56	19.65
	1.75	45.23	0.63	3.10	5.49	7.80	10.04	12.20	14.30	16.33	18.29
	2.00	30.63	0.58	2.85	5.06	7.19	9.26	11.27	13.21	15.10	16.93
	2.52	0.0	0.47	2.33	4.14	5.91	7.63	9.30	10.93	12.52	14.07
5 YRS.	0.81	100.00	0.98	4.79	8.43	11.90	15.22	18.39	21.42	24.31	27.07
	1.00	85.58	0.92	4.51	7.94	11.22	14.35	17.35	20.22	22.97	25.59
	1.25	66.34	0.85	4.14	7.29	10.31	13.20	15.97	18.63	21.18	23.62
	1.50	47.11	0.77	3.76	6.63	9.39	12.04	14.59	17.04	19.39	21.65
	1.75	27.88	0.69	3.39	5.98	8.48	10.89	13.21	15.44	17.60	19.67
	2.11	0.0	0.58	2.84	5.04	7.16	9.21	11.21	13.13	15.00	16.81
6 YRS.	0.81	100.00	1.12	5.47	9.59	13.49	17.19	20.69	24.01	27.16	30.14
	1.00	81.75	1.04	5.08	8.91	12.55	16.00	19.28	22.40	25.36	28.17
	1.25	57.42	0.93	4.56	8.01	11.30	14.43	17.41	20.25	22.96	25.54
	1.50	33.09	0.83	4.04	7.11	10.04	12.85	15.53	18.10	20.55	22.91
	1.84	0.0	0.68	3.33	5.88	8.34	10.70	12.98	15.18	17.29	19.33
7 YRS.	0.81	100.00	1.25	6.08	10.62	14.89	18.90	22.67	26.22	29.56	32.71
	1.00	77.54	1.15	5.57	9.74	13.67	17.37	20.87	24.17	27.28	30.22
	1.25	47.59	1.00	4.89	8.56	12.04	15.34	18.46	21.42	24.23	26.90
	1.50	17.64	0.86	4.20	7.38	10.41	13.30	16.05	18.68	21.19	23.58
	1.65	0.0	0.78	3.80	6.69	9.45	12.10	14.64	17.07	19.39	21.63
8 YRS.	0.81	100.00	1.37	6.63	11.54	16.11	20.39	24.38	28.11	31.60	34.86
	1.00	72.89	1.24	5.98	10.43	14.59	18.50	22.16	25.59	28.81	31.84
	1.25	36.75	1.05	5.12	8.95	12.56	15.97	19.19	22.23	25.11	27.82
	1.50	0.0	0.87	4.24	7.45	10.50	13.41	16.18	18.82	21.33	23.73
9 YRS.	0.81	100.00	1.48	7.12	12.35	17.19	21.68	25.85	29.72	33.31	36.65
	1.00	67.78	1.31	6.33	11.00	15.35	19.41	23.20	26.73	30.03	33.11
	1.25	24.81	1.09	5.27	9.21	12.90	16.38	19.66	22.74	25.65	28.39
	1.39	0.0	0.96	4.66	8.17	11.49	14.63	17.61	20.44	23.12	25.66
10 YRS.	0.81	100.00	1.58	7.56	13.07	18.14	22.81	27.12	31.09	34.76	38.16
	1.00	62.14	1.38	6.62	11.47	15.97	20.15	24.02	27.62	30.97	34.09
	1.25	11.65	1.11	5.36	9.34	13.08	16.60	19.90	23.00	25.92	28.67
	1.31	0.0	1.04	5.07	8.85	12.42	15.78	18.94	21.93	24.76	27.42
		MONTHS									
UNTIL PAID	1.00	206.86	1.56	7.43	12.77	17.63	22.07	26.12	29.84	33.26	36.40
	1.25	129.73	1.11	5.38	9.38	13.13	16.65	19.96	23.07	25.99	28.74
	1.50	96.41	0.87	4.26	7.47	10.54	13.45	16.23	18.87	21.40	23.80
	1.75	77.13	0.72	3.53	6.23	8.82	11.31	13.70	16.00	18.21	20.33
	2.00	64.42	0.62	3.03	5.35	7.60	9.77	11.87	13.90	15.87	17.76
	2.50	48.57	0.48	2.36	4.19	5.97	7.70	9.39	11.04	12.64	14.20
	3.00	39.03	0.39	1.94	3.45	4.92	6.37	7.79	9.17	10.53	11.85
	4.00	28.06	0.29	1.43	2.56	3.66	4.75	5.82	6.88	7.92	8.94

EXAMPLES *ON PAGES A-382 TO A-397*

MORTGAGE YIELD TABLE

SHOWING DISCOUNT PERCENTAGES AT VARIOUS
YIELDS, MONTHLY PAYMENT RATES AND DUE DATES

DUE DATE	19%	20%	21%	22%	23%	24%	25%	26%	27%	28%	29%
					YIELD PERCENTAGES						
1 YR.	8.36	9.22	10.07	10.91	11.74	12.56	13.37	14.18	14.97	15.76	16.54
	8.28	9.13	9.97	10.80	11.62	12.43	13.24	14.03	14.82	15.60	16.37
	8.16	9.00	9.83	10.65	11.46	12.26	13.06	13.84	14.62	15.39	16.15
	8.05	8.88	9.69	10.50	11.30	12.09	12.87	13.65	14.42	15.18	15.93
	7.94	8.75	9.56	10.35	11.14	11.92	12.69	13.46	14.22	14.97	15.71
	7.82	8.62	9.42	10.20	10.98	11.75	12.51	13.27	14.02	14.75	15.49
	4.73	5.22		6.19	6.67	7.15	7.62	8.09	8.56	9.02	9.48
2 YRS.	15.29	16.78	18.24	19.68	21.08	22.46	23.81	25.14	26.43	27.71	28.96
	14.96	16.43	17.86	19.26	20.64	21.99	23.31	24.61	25.89	27.14	28.36
	14.53	15.95	17.34	18.71	20.05	21.36	22.65	23.92	25.16	26.37	27.57
	14.09	15.47	16.83	18.15	19.46	20.73	21.99	23.22	24.42	25.61	26.77
	13.66	15.00	16.31	17.60	18.86	20.11	21.32	22.52	23.69	24.85	25.98
	13.22	14.52	15.79	17.04	18.27	19.48	20.66	21.82	22.96	24.08	25.18
	8.69	9.56	10.42	11.27	12.11	12.94	13.76	14.56	15.36	16.14	16.91
3 YRS.	21.03	22.98	24.88	26.73	28.52	30.27	31.96	33.61	35.21	36.77	38.28
	20.35	22.24	24.09	25.88	27.62	29.31	30.96	32.56	34.12	35.64	37.11
	19.44	21.26	23.02	24.74	26.42	28.04	29.63	31.17	32.67	34.13	35.55
	18.53	20.27	21.96	23.61	25.21	26.77	28.29	29.77	31.22	32.62	33.99
	17.62	19.28	20.90	22.47	24.01	25.50	26.96	28.38	29.76	31.11	32.43
	16.71	18.29	19.83	21.34	22.80	24.23	25.62	26.98	28.31	29.60	30.87
	12.29	13.49	14.67	15.82	16.95	18.05	19.14	20.20	21.25	22.27	23.28
4 YRS.	25.78	28.07	30.28	32.40	34.45	36.42	38.33	40.16	41.93	43.64	45.28
	24.66	26.86	28.98	31.03	33.00	34.91	36.74	38.52	40.23	41.88	43.47
	23.17	25.25	27.26	29.20	31.07	32.88	34.63	36.32	37.95	39.53	41.06
	21.68	23.64	25.54	27.37	29.15	30.86	32.52	34.13	35.68	37.18	38.64
	20.19	22.03	23.82	25.54	27.22	28.84	30.41	31.93	33.41	34.84	36.23
	18.70	20.42	22.09	23.71	25.29	26.82	28.30	29.74	31.13	32.49	33.81
	15.58	17.05	18.48	19.88	21.24	22.57	23.87	25.13	26.37	27.57	28.75
5 YRS.	29.72	32.24	34.65	36.96	39.17	41.28	43.30	45.23	47.08	48.85	50.54
	28.11	30.51	32.82	35.02	37.13	39.16	41.10	42.95	44.73	46.44	48.07
	25.96	28.21	30.37	32.44	34.42	36.33	38.16	39.92	41.61	43.23	44.79
	23.82	25.91	27.92	29.85	31.71	33.50	35.22	36.88	38.48	40.02	41.50
	21.68	23.61	25.47	27.28	29.00	30.67	32.29	33.85	35.35	36.81	38.21
	19.53	21.30	23.02	24.68	26.29	27.84	29.35	30.81	32.23	33.60	34.93
	18.57	20.27	21.92	23.52	25.07	26.57	28.03	29.45	30.82	32.15	33.45
6 YRS.	32.97	35.66	38.21	40.63	42.93	45.11	47.18	49.15	51.02	52.79	54.48
	30.84	33.38	35.80	38.10	40.29	42.37	44.35	46.24	48.04	49.75	51.39
	28.00	30.35	32.59	34.73	36.77	38.72	40.58	42.37	44.07	45.70	47.26
	25.16	27.31	29.38	31.36	33.25	35.07	36.82	38.49	40.10	41.64	43.12
	21.29	23.18	25.01	26.77	28.47	30.11	31.69	33.22	34.70	36.13	37.51
7 YRS.	35.67	38.47	41.10	43.58	45.92	48.12	50.21	52.17	54.03	55.79	57.45
	33.00	35.63	38.11	40.46	42.68	44.78	46.77	48.66	50.45	52.15	53.76
	29.43	31.84	34.12	36.30	38.36	40.33	42.20	43.98	45.67	47.29	48.83
	25.87	28.05	30.14	32.13	34.04	35.87	37.62	39.29	40.90	42.43	43.91
	23.77	25.82	27.79	29.68	31.50	33.25	34.92	36.53	38.08	39.57	41.01
8 YRS.	37.91	40.77	43.44	45.95	48.30	50.50	52.57	54.52	56.34	58.06	59.67
	34.69	37.36	39.88	42.25	44.48	46.58	48.56	50.43	52.20	53.86	55.44
	30.39	32.82	35.13	37.31	39.38	41.35	43.21	44.98	46.67	48.27	49.79
	26.02	28.21	30.34	32.29	34.20	36.03	37.77	39.44	41.04	42.58	44.04
9 YRS.	39.76	42.65	45.34	47.85	50.20	52.38	54.42	56.33	58.11	59.78	61.34
	36.00	38.70	41.22	43.59	45.82	47.91	49.87	51.71	53.45	55.08	56.62
	30.98	33.42	35.73	37.91	39.98	41.94	43.80	45.56	47.22	48.81	50.32
	28.08	30.37	32.56	34.63	36.61	38.50	40.29	42.00	43.63	45.19	46.68
10 YRS.	41.29	44.20	46.89	49.39	51.71	53.86	55.86	57.73	59.46	61.09	62.60
	37.00	39.71	42.23	44.60	46.81	48.87	50.81	52.63	54.33	55.93	57.44
	31.27	33.72	36.03	38.21	40.27	42.22	44.07	45.82	47.48	49.06	50.56
	29.95	32.33	34.59	36.73	38.76	40.69	42.52	44.25	45.90	47.48	48.97
UNTIL PAID	39.29	41.96	44.44	46.73	48.85	50.83	52.67	54.39	56.00	57.51	58.92
	31.34	33.79	36.09	38.28	40.34	42.29	44.13	45.88	47.54	49.12	50.61
	26.10	28.29	30.38	32.38	34.29	36.12	37.86	39.54	41.14	42.67	44.14
	22.38	24.34	26.23	28.05	29.81	31.50	33.12	34.69	36.20	37.66	39.07
	19.60	21.37	23.09	24.76	26.37	27.92	29.43	30.89	32.31	33.68	35.01
	15.73	17.21	18.65	20.06	21.44	22.77	24.08	25.35	26.59	27.81	28.99
	13.15	14.42	15.67	16.89	18.08	19.25	20.39	21.51	22.61	23.69	24.74
	9.94	10.93	11.91	12.87	13.81	14.74	15.66	16.56	17.44	18.32	19.18

EXAMPLES *ON PAGES A-382 TO A-397*

MORTGAGE YIELD TABLE
SHOWING DISCOUNT PERCENTAGES AT VARIOUS
YIELDS, MONTHLY PAYMENT RATES AND DUE DATES

DUE DATE	PAY'T RATE %	BAL REMAIN %	YIELD PERCENTAGES								
			11%	12%	13%	14%	15%	16%	17%	18%	19%
1 YR.	0.83	100.00	0.94	1.88	2.80	3.71	4.62	5.51	6.40	7.27	8.14
	1.00	97.91	0.93	1.86	2.77	3.68	4.57	5.46	6.34	7.21	8.06
	1.25	94.76	0.92	1.83	2.73	3.63	4.51	5.38	6.25	7.11	7.95
	1.50	91.62	0.91	1.81	2.70	3.58	4.45	5.31	6.16	7.01	7.84
	1.75	88.48	0.89	1.78	2.66	3.52	4.38	5.23	6.07	6.91	7.73
	2.00	85.34	0.88	1.75	2.62	3.47	4.32	5.16	5.99	6.81	7.62
	8.79	0.0	0.53	1.05	1.57	2.08	2.60	3.10	3.61	4.11	4.60
2 YRS.	0.83	100.00	1.79	3.54	5.26	6.94	8.59	10.21	11.80	13.35	14.88
	1.00	95.59	1.75	3.47	5.16	6.81	8.43	10.02	11.57	13.10	14.60
	1.25	88.98	1.70	3.37	5.00	6.61	8.18	9.72	11.23	12.72	14.17
	1.50	82.37	1.65	3.26	4.85	6.40	7.93	9.43	10.89	12.33	13.75
	1.75	75.76	1.60	3.16	4.70	6.20	7.68	9.13	10.55	11.95	13.32
	2.00	69.15	1.54	3.06	4.54	6.00	7.43	8.84	10.22	11.57	12.90
	4.61	0.0	0.99	1.97	2.94	3.89	4.83	5.76	6.67	7.57	8.46
3 YRS.	0.83	100.00	2.55	5.02	7.42	9.75	12.02	14.22	16.36	18.44	20.46
	1.00	93.04	2.47	4.87	7.20	9.46	11.66	13.80	15.88	17.90	19.87
	1.25	82.59	2.35	4.64	6.87	9.03	11.13	13.18	15.17	17.10	18.98
	1.50	72.15	2.24	4.41	6.53	8.59	10.60	12.55	14.45	16.30	18.10
	1.75	61.70	2.12	4.19	6.20	8.16	10.07	11.92	13.73	15.49	17.21
	2.00	51.25	2.01	3.96	5.87	7.72	9.53	11.30	13.01	14.69	16.32
	3.23	0.0	1.44	2.85	4.23	5.59	6.92	8.22	9.50	10.75	11.97
4 YRS.	0.83	100.00	3.22	6.33	9.32	12.20	14.97	17.64	20.22	22.70	25.08
	1.00	96.21	3.09	6.07	8.94	11.71	14.37	16.94	19.42	21.81	24.11
	1.25	79.53	2.89	5.68	8.37	10.97	13.48	15.90	18.23	20.48	22.66
	1.50	60.85	2.69	5.30	7.81	10.24	12.58	14.85	17.04	19.16	21.20
	1.75	46.17	2.49	4.91	7.24	9.50	11.69	13.80	15.85	17.83	19.75
	2.00	31.49	2.30	4.52	6.68	8.76	10.79	12.75	14.66	16.50	18.30
	2.54	0.0	1.87	3.69	5.46	7.19	8.87	10.51	12.10	13.66	15.18
5 YRS.	0.83	100.00	3.83	7.49	10.99	14.33	17.51	20.56	23.47	26.25	28.91
	1.00	87.09	3.63	7.10	10.42	13.60	16.63	19.54	22.31	24.97	27.52
	1.25	67.73	3.33	6.52	9.58	12.51	15.31	18.00	20.58	23.05	25.42
	1.50	48.38	3.03	5.94	8.73	11.41	13.99	16.47	18.84	21.13	23.33
	1.75	29.02	2.73	5.36	7.89	10.32	12.67	14.93	17.11	19.21	21.23
	2.00	9.66	2.43	4.77	7.04	9.23	11.35	13.39	15.37	17.29	19.14
	2.12	0.0	2.28	4.48	6.62	8.69	10.69	12.63	14.51	16.33	18.09
6 YRS.	0.83	100.00	4.38	8.53	12.45	16.18	19.71	23.05	26.22	29.23	32.08
	1.00	83.65	4.10	7.99	11.68	15.18	18.51	21.67	24.67	27.52	30.23
	1.25	55.12	3.68	7.18	10.52	13.69	16.71	19.59	22.34	24.96	27.45
	1.50	34.59	3.26	6.38	9.35	12.20	14.92	17.52	20.01	22.39	24.67
	1.85	0.0	2.67	5.24	7.71	10.09	12.39	14.60	16.72	18.77	20.75
7 YRS.	0.83	100.00	4.87	9.44	13.74	17.79	21.59	25.17	28.54	31.72	34.71
	1.00	79.84	4.50	8.74	12.73	16.50	20.06	23.41	26.57	29.56	32.38
	1.25	49.60	3.95	7.69	11.22	14.57	17.75	20.76	23.62	26.32	28.89
	1.50	19.37	3.40	6.63	9.71	12.65	15.45	18.11	20.66	23.09	25.41
	1.66	0.0	3.04	5.56	8.74	11.41	13.97	16.42	18.76	21.01	23.17
8 YRS.	0.83	100.00	5.31	10.25	14.87	19.19	23.22	26.99	30.51	33.80	36.88
	1.00	75.64	4.84	9.37	13.62	17.60	21.32	24.82	28.10	31.19	34.08
	1.25	39.09	4.15	8.05	11.73	15.21	18.48	21.58	24.50	27.26	29.87
	1.52	0.0	3.40	6.64	9.72	12.65	15.44	18.10	20.64	23.06	25.37
9 YRS.	0.83	100.00	5.70	10.98	15.87	20.41	24.62	28.53	32.16	35.54	38.69
	1.00	70.90	5.13	9.90	14.35	18.49	22.36	25.96	29.32	32.47	35.41
	1.25	27.48	4.28	8.20	12.07	15.62	18.96	22.10	25.06	27.85	30.49
	1.41	0.0	3.74	7.28	10.63	13.81	16.81	19.67	22.37	24.94	27.38
10 YRS.	0.83	100.00	6.05	11.62	16.74	21.47	25.83	29.85	33.56	37.00	40.18
	1.00	65.86	5.37	10.34	14.95	19.22	23.18	26.87	30.29	33.47	36.43
	1.25	14.65	4.36	8.44	12.26	15.85	19.22	22.39	25.37	28.17	30.81
	1.32	0.0	4.06	7.89	11.49	14.89	18.09	21.11	23.96	26.66	29.21
		MONTHS									
UNTIL PAID	1.00	215.91	6.12	11.67	16.71	21.29	25.47	29.30	32.80	36.01	38.97
	1.25	132.38	4.38	8.48	12.33	15.93	19.31	22.49	25.47	28.28	30.92
	1.50	97.72	3.45	6.73	9.85	12.82	15.64	18.34	20.90	23.34	25.67
	1.75	77.92	2.86	5.60	8.23	10.76	13.18	15.51	17.75	19.90	21.97
	2.00	64.95	2.44	4.80	7.08	9.28	11.40	13.46	15.44	17.36	19.22
	2.50	48.86	1.00	3.75	5.55	7.30	9.00	10.66	12.28	13.86	15.39
	3.00	39.21	1.56	3.08	4.57	6.03	7.45	8.85	10.21	11.55	12.86
	4.00	28.15	1.15	2.28	3.39	4.49	5.57	6.63	7.67	8.70	9.71

EXAMPLES ON PAGES A-382 TO A-397

MORTGAGE YIELD TABLE

SHOWING DISCOUNT PERCENTAGES AT VARIOUS
YIELDS, MONTHLY PAYMENT RATES AND DUE DATES

DUE DATE	20%	21%	22%	23%	24%	25%	26%	27%	28%	29%	30%
1 YR.	9.00	9.84	10.68	11.52	12.34	13.15	13.96	14.75	15.54	16.32	17.10
	8.91	9.76	10.59	11.41	12.23	13.03	13.83	14.62	15.40	16.18	16.94
	8.79	9.62	10.44	11.26	12.06	12.86	13.64	14.42	15.20	15.96	16.72
	8.67	9.49	10.30	11.10	11.89	12.68	13.46	14.23	14.99	15.74	16.49
	8.55	9.35	10.15	10.94	11.73	12.50	13.27	14.03	14.78	15.52	16.26
	8.42	9.22	10.01	10.79	11.56	12.32	13.08	13.83	14.57	15.30	16.03
	5.09	5.58	6.07	6.55	7.03	7.50	7.97	8.44	8.90	9.36	9.82
2 YRS.	16.37	17.84	19.28	20.68	22.07	23.42	24.75	26.05	27.33	28.58	29.81
	16.06	17.50	18.91	20.30	21.65	22.99	24.29	25.57	26.83	28.06	29.26
	15.60	17.00	18.37	19.72	21.04	22.33	23.60	24.85	26.07	27.27	28.45
	15.13	16.49	17.83	19.13	20.42	21.68	22.91	24.13	25.32	26.49	27.63
	14.67	15.99	17.28	18.55	19.80	21.03	22.23	23.41	24.56	25.70	26.82
	14.20	15.48	16.74	17.97	19.18	20.37	21.54	22.69	23.81	24.92	26.00
	9.33	10.20	11.05	11.89	12.72	13.54	14.35	15.14	15.93	16.70	17.47
3 YRS.	22.42	24.33	26.18	27.99	29.74	31.44	33.09	34.70	36.26	37.78	39.26
	21.78	23.64	25.44	27.20	28.90	30.56	32.18	33.74	35.27	36.75	38.20
	20.81	22.59	24.33	26.01	27.65	29.25	30.80	32.31	33.78	35.21	36.60
	19.85	21.55	23.21	24.83	26.40	27.93	29.42	30.87	32.29	33.67	35.01
	18.88	20.51	22.10	23.64	25.15	26.62	28.05	29.44	30.80	32.12	33.41
	17.92	19.47	20.98	22.46	23.90	25.30	26.67	28.00	29.31	30.58	31.82
	13.18	14.35	15.51	16.64	17.75	18.84	19.91	20.96	21.99	23.00	23.99
4 YRS.	27.38	29.60	31.74	33.80	35.79	37.70	39.54	41.32	43.04	44.69	46.29
	26.33	28.48	30.54	32.53	34.46	36.31	38.10	39.83	41.49	43.10	44.65
	24.76	26.79	28.74	30.64	32.46	34.23	35.93	37.58	39.17	40.71	42.20
	23.18	25.10	26.95	28.74	30.47	32.14	33.76	35.33	36.85	38.32	39.74
	21.61	23.41	25.15	26.84	28.48	30.06	31.60	33.08	34.53	35.93	37.28
	20.03	21.72	23.35	24.94	26.48	27.98	29.43	30.84	32.21	33.54	34.83
	16.65	18.09	19.50	20.87	22.21	23.51	24.78	26.02	27.23	28.41	29.56
5 YRS.	31.45	33.88	36.21	38.43	40.55	42.59	44.53	46.39	48.18	49.88	51.51
	29.95	32.28	34.51	36.65	38.69	40.65	42.53	44.33	46.06	47.71	49.30
	27.69	29.88	31.97	33.98	35.90	37.76	39.53	41.24	42.88	44.45	45.97
	25.44	27.47	29.43	31.31	33.11	34.86	36.53	38.15	39.70	41.20	42.64
	23.18	25.07	26.88	28.63	30.32	31.96	33.55	35.05	36.52	37.94	39.31
	20.93	22.66	24.34	25.96	27.54	29.06	30.53	31.96	33.35	34.69	35.99
	19.80	21.46	23.07	24.63	26.14	27.61	29.04	30.42	31.76	33.06	34.33
6 YRS.	34.79	37.36	39.80	42.12	44.31	46.40	48.39	50.28	52.07	53.78	55.40
	32.81	35.26	37.59	39.80	41.91	43.92	45.83	47.66	49.39	51.05	52.62
	29.83	32.10	34.27	36.34	38.31	40.20	42.00	43.73	45.37	46.95	48.46
	26.85	28.95	30.95	32.87	34.71	36.48	38.17	39.80	41.36	42.85	44.29
	22.66	24.50	26.27	27.98	29.63	31.23	32.77	34.25	35.69	37.08	38.42
7 YRS.	37.53	40.18	42.69	45.05	47.28	49.38	51.37	53.25	55.02	56.70	58.29
	35.05	37.57	39.96	42.21	44.35	46.37	48.28	50.09	51.81	53.45	54.99
	31.34	33.65	35.86	37.95	39.94	41.84	43.64	45.36	47.00	48.56	50.05
	27.62	29.74	31.76	33.69	35.54	37.31	39.01	40.63	42.19	43.68	45.11
	25.24	27.23	29.13	30.96	32.72	34.41	36.04	37.60	39.10	40.55	41.94
8 YRS.	39.77	42.48	45.01	47.39	49.62	51.71	53.68	55.53	57.26	58.90	60.44
	36.80	39.36	41.77	44.03	46.17	48.18	50.08	51.87	53.56	55.16	56.67
	32.35	34.69	36.90	39.00	41.00	42.89	44.68	46.39	48.01	49.55	51.02
	27.58	29.69	31.70	33.62	35.47	37.23	38.91	40.53	42.07	43.55	44.97
9 YRS.	41.61	44.34	46.88	49.25	51.46	53.53	55.46	57.27	58.96	60.55	62.04
	38.16	40.73	43.14	45.40	47.53	49.52	51.39	53.15	54.81	56.37	57.85
	32.97	35.32	37.54	39.64	41.63	43.51	45.29	46.98	48.59	50.12	51.56
	29.70	31.90	34.00	36.00	37.90	39.71	41.44	43.09	44.66	46.16	47.60
10 YRS.	43.12	45.85	48.38	50.73	52.91	54.95	56.84	58.60	60.25	61.79	63.22
	39.19	41.77	44.18	46.42	48.53	50.50	52.34	54.07	55.70	57.23	58.66
	33.30	35.65	37.87	39.96	41.95	43.82	45.59	47.28	48.87	50.39	51.83
	31.62	33.90	36.07	38.12	40.06	41.91	43.67	45.33	46.92	48.43	49.87
UNTIL PAID	41.69	44.21	46.53	48.69	50.70	52.56	54.30	55.92	57.44	58.86	60.19
	33.41	35.76	37.97	40.07	42.04	43.91	45.69	47.37	48.96	50.47	51.90
	27.90	30.02	32.05	33.98	35.83	37.60	39.29	40.91	42.46	43.95	45.37
	23.96	25.88	27.72	29.49	31.20	32.85	34.43	35.96	37.43	38.85	40.22
	21.01	22.75	24.43	26.06	27.63	29.16	30.63	32.06	33.45	34.79	36.09
	16.89	18.35	19.77	21.15	22.50	23.82	25.10	26.35	27.57	28.76	29.93
	14.14	15.39	16.62	17.82	19.00	20.15	21.28	22.39	23.47	24.53	25.57
	10.71	11.69	12.65	13.60	14.53	15.45	16.36	17.25	18.13	18.99	19.84

EXAMPLES *ON PAGES A-382 TO A-397*

DUE DATE	PAY'T RATE %	BAL REMAIN %	11%	12%	13%	14%	15%	16%	17%	18%	19%
1 YR.	0.85	100.00	0.71	1.64	2.57	3.48	4.39	5.28	6.17	7.04	7.91
	1.00	98.17	0.70	1.63	2.55	3.45	4.35	5.24	6.12	6.99	7.85
	1.25	95.02	0.69	1.61	2.51	3.40	4.29	5.17	6.03	6.89	7.74
	1.50	91.88	0.68	1.58	2.47	3.36	4.23	5.09	5.95	6.80	7.63
	1.75	88.73	0.67	1.56	2.44	3.31	4.17	5.02	5.86	6.70	7.52
	2.00	85.59	0.66	1.54	2.40	3.26	4.11	4.95	5.78	6.60	7.42
	8.80		0.40	0.92	1.44	1.95	2.47	2.97	3.48	3.98	4.48
2 YRS.	0.85	100.00	1.34	3.10	4.82	6.51	8.16	9.79	11.38	12.94	14.47
	1.00	96.13	1.32	3.04	4.74	6.40	8.03	9.62	11.19	12.72	14.22
	1.25	89.51	1.28	2.95	4.60	6.21	7.79	9.34	10.86	12.35	13.81
	1.50	82.88	1.24	2.86	4.46	6.02	7.55	9.06	10.53	11.98	13.40
	1.75	76.25	1.20	2.77	4.32	5.83	7.32	8.77	10.20	11.61	12.98
	2.00	69.62	1.16	2.68	4.17	5.64	7.08	8.49	9.88	11.24	12.57
	4.63	0.0	0.75	1.73	2.70	3.65	4.59	5.52	6.44	7.34	8.23
3 YRS.	0.85	100.00	1.91	4.39	6.80	9.14	11.42	13.63	15.78	17.86	19.89
	1.00	93.88	1.86	4.27	6.62	8.91	11.12	13.28	15.37	17.41	19.39
	1.25	83.40	1.77	4.08	6.32	8.50	10.62	12.68	14.68	16.63	18.52
	1.50	72.91	1.68	3.88	6.01	8.09	10.11	12.07	13.99	15.85	17.66
	1.75	62.43	1.60	3.68	5.71	7.68	9.60	11.47	13.29	15.07	16.80
	2.00	51.94	1.51	3.48	5.40	7.27	9.09	10.87	12.60	14.29	15.93
	3.24	0.0	1.08	2.50	3.89	5.25	6.58	7.89	9.17	10.42	11.65
4 YRS.	0.85	100.00	2.42	5.54	8.54	11.44	14.22	16.91	19.49	21.99	24.39
	1.00	91.39	2.33	5.34	8.24	11.03	13.72	16.32	18.82	21.23	23.56
	1.25	76.63	2.18	5.00	7.72	10.34	12.87	15.31	17.67	19.94	22.14
	1.50	61.88	2.03	4.66	7.20	9.65	12.02	14.31	16.52	18.66	20.72
	1.75	47.12	1.88	4.32	6.68	8.96	11.16	13.30	15.37	17.37	19.30
	2.00	32.36	1.73	3.98	6.15	8.26	10.31	12.29	14.21	16.08	17.88
	2.55	0.0	1.40	3.23	5.01	6.75	8.44	10.08	11.69	13.25	14.77
5 YRS.	0.85	100.00	2.87	6.56	10.07	13.43	16.64	19.70	22.63	25.43	28.11
	1.00	88.63	2.74	6.26	9.62	12.83	15.90	18.84	21.65	24.34	26.92
	1.25	69.14	2.52	5.75	8.84	11.83	14.64	17.36	19.97	22.47	24.87
	1.50	49.66	2.29	5.23	8.06	10.78	13.38	15.89	18.29	20.61	22.83
	1.75	30.17	2.06	4.72	7.28	9.75	12.12	14.41	16.61	18.74	20.78
	2.00	10.68	1.84	4.21	6.50	8.72	10.86	12.93	14.93	16.87	18.74
	2.14	0.0	1.71	3.93	6.08	8.16	10.17	12.12	14.01	15.84	17.62
6 YRS.	0.85	100.00	3.28	7.46	11.42	15.17	18.72	22.09	25.29	28.32	31.19
	1.00	85.58	3.10	7.05	10.79	14.35	17.72	20.92	23.97	26.86	29.61
	1.25	60.85	2.78	6.34	9.72	12.94	16.01	18.93	21.71	24.36	26.89
	1.50	36.12	2.47	5.63	8.65	11.53	14.29	16.93	19.45	21.87	24.18
	1.87	0.0	2.01	4.59	7.08	9.48	11.79	14.01	16.16	18.22	20.21
7 YRS.	0.85	100.00	3.65	8.26	12.60	16.68	20.51	24.12	27.53	30.73	33.75
	1.00	82.19	3.41	7.72	11.78	15.62	19.23	22.64	25.85	28.89	31.76
	1.25	51.66	2.99	6.79	10.39	13.80	17.03	20.08	22.98	25.73	28.34
	1.50	21.13	2.58	5.87	9.00	11.98	14.82	17.53	20.12	22.60	24.93
	1.67	0.0	2.29	5.22	8.03	10.72	13.30	15.77	18.13	20.40	22.57
8 YRS.	0.85	100.00	3.98	8.97	13.63	17.99	22.06	25.86	29.42	32.74	35.86
	1.00	78.44	3.67	8.29	12.62	16.67	20.47	24.03	27.38	30.51	33.46
	1.25	41.49	3.15	7.13	10.88	14.42	17.75	20.90	23.87	26.69	29.34
	1.53	0.0	2.56	5.82	8.93	11.89	14.70	17.39	19.95	22.39	24.72
9 YRS.	0.85	100.00	4.27	9.60	14.55	19.13	23.39	27.34	31.02	34.43	37.61
	1.00	74.29	3.90	8.78	13.32	17.55	21.49	25.17	28.60	31.81	34.80
	1.25	30.22	3.25	7.36	11.21	14.84	18.24	21.45	24.46	27.30	29.98
	1.42	0.0	2.81	6.39	9.77	12.97	16.01	18.90	21.62	24.22	26.68
10 YRS.	0.85	100.00	4.54	10.16	15.35	20.13	24.53	28.60	32.37	35.84	39.06
	1.00	69.70	4.09	9.18	13.90	18.27	22.32	26.08	29.58	32.83	35.85
	1.25	17.74	3.32	7.50	11.41	15.08	18.53	21.76	24.80	27.65	30.34
	1.34	0.0	3.66	6.92	10.56	13.99	17.23	20.28	23.16	25.89	28.46
		MONTHS									
UNTIL PAID	1.00	226.36	4.74	10.51	15.75	20.49	24.81	28.74	32.33	35.63	38.65
	1.25	135.20	3.35	7.56	11.50	15.19	18.65	21.89	24.94	27.80	30.49
	1.50	99.08	2.62	5.97	9.15	12.17	15.05	17.79	20.39	22.88	25.24
	1.75	78.73	2.17	4.95	7.62	10.19	12.65	15.01	17.28	19.46	21.56
	2.00	65.49	1.85	4.24	6.54	8.77	10.93	13.00	15.01	16.96	18.83
	2.50	49.15	1.43	3.30	5.12	6.89	8.61	10.28	11.92	13.51	15.06
	3.00	39.40	1.17	2.71	4.21	5.68	7.12	8.52	9.90	11.25	12.57
	4.00	28.24	0.87	2.00	3.12	4.23	5.31	6.38	7.43	8.46	9.48

EXAMPLES *ON PAGES A-382 TO A-397*

MORTGAGE YIELD TABLE
SHOWING DISCOUNT PERCENTAGES AT VARIOUS YIELDS, MONTHLY PAYMENT RATES AND DUE DATES

DUE DATE	20%	21%	22%	23%	24%	25%	26%	27%	28%	29%	30%
1 YR.	8.77	9.62	10.46	11.29	12.12	12.93	13.74	14.54	15.33	16.11	16.88
	8.70	9.54	10.38	11.20	12.02	12.83	13.63	14.42	15.21	15.98	16.75
	8.58	9.41	10.24	11.05	11.86	12.66	13.45	14.23	15.00	15.77	16.52
	8.46	9.28	10.09	10.90	11.69	12.48	13.26	14.03	14.80	15.55	16.30
	8.34	9.15	9.95	10.75	11.53	12.31	13.08	13.84	14.59	15.33	16.07
	8.22	9.02	9.81	10.59	11.37	12.13	12.89	13.64	14.38	15.12	15.85
	4.97	5.46	5.94	6.42	6.90	7.38	7.85	8.32	8.78	9.24	9.70
2 YRS.	15.96	17.43	18.87	20.29	21.67	23.03	24.36	25.67	26.95	28.20	29.44
	15.70	17.15	18.56	19.95	21.32	22.66	23.97	25.25	26.51	27.75	28.97
	15.24	16.65	18.03	19.38	20.71	22.01	23.29	24.54	25.77	26.98	28.16
	14.79	16.16	17.50	18.81	20.10	21.37	22.61	23.83	25.03	26.20	27.35
	14.34	15.66	16.96	18.24	19.49	20.73	21.93	23.12	24.28	25.42	26.54
	13.88	15.17	16.43	17.67	18.89	20.08	21.25	22.41	23.54	24.65	25.74
	9.11	9.97	10.83	11.67	12.50	13.32	14.13	14.93	15.72	16.50	17.26
3 YRS.	21.85	23.78	25.64	27.45	29.21	30.91	32.58	34.19	35.76	37.29	38.77
	21.31	23.18	25.00	26.77	28.49	30.16	31.78	33.36	34.90	36.40	37.85
	20.37	22.16	23.91	25.60	27.26	28.86	30.43	31.95	33.43	34.87	36.27
	19.42	21.14	22.81	24.44	26.02	27.57	29.07	30.53	31.95	33.34	34.69
	18.48	20.12	21.72	23.27	24.79	26.27	27.71	29.11	30.48	31.81	33.11
	17.54	19.10	20.62	22.11	23.56	24.97	26.35	27.70	29.01	30.29	31.53
	12.86	14.04	15.20	16.34	17.46	18.55	19.62	20.67	21.71	22.72	23.71
4 YRS.	26.70	28.93	31.08	33.15	35.15	37.07	38.93	40.72	42.44	44.11	45.71
	25.80	27.96	30.05	32.06	34.00	35.87	37.68	39.42	41.10	42.72	44.29
	24.26	26.31	28.28	30.19	32.04	33.82	35.54	37.20	38.81	40.36	41.86
	22.72	24.65	26.52	28.33	30.07	31.76	33.40	34.98	36.51	37.99	39.43
	21.18	22.99	24.75	26.46	28.11	29.71	31.26	32.76	34.21	35.63	36.99
	19.64	21.34	22.99	24.59	26.14	27.65	29.12	30.54	31.92	33.26	34.56
	16.26	17.71	19.12	20.49	21.84	23.15	24.42	25.67	26.88	28.07	29.23
5 YRS.	30.67	33.11	35.45	37.69	39.83	41.88	43.84	45.71	47.51	49.23	50.87
	29.38	31.74	33.99	36.16	38.23	40.21	42.11	43.93	45.67	47.34	48.95
	27.17	29.38	31.49	33.53	35.47	37.35	39.14	40.87	42.53	44.12	45.65
	24.96	27.02	28.99	30.90	32.72	34.48	36.18	37.81	39.38	40.89	42.35
	22.76	24.66	26.49	28.27	29.97	31.62	33.21	34.75	36.23	37.67	39.05
	20.55	22.30	23.99	25.63	27.22	28.76	30.25	31.69	33.09	34.44	35.75
	19.34	21.01	22.62	24.19	25.72	27.19	28.62	30.01	31.36	32.67	33.95
6 YRS.	33.92	36.51	38.97	41.31	43.52	45.63	47.63	49.54	51.35	53.07	54.71
	32.22	34.70	37.07	39.31	41.45	43.49	45.42	47.27	49.03	50.70	52.30
	29.30	31.61	33.80	35.90	37.90	35.81	41.63	43.38	45.05	46.64	48.17
	26.39	28.51	30.54	32.48	34.34	36.13	37.84	39.49	41.07	42.58	44.04
	22.13	23.98	25.77	27.49	29.15	30.76	32.31	33.80	35.25	36.65	38.00
7 YRS.	36.59	39.27	41.80	44.18	46.44	48.56	50.57	52.47	54.26	55.96	57.56
	34.45	37.32	39.44	41.73	43.90	45.95	47.89	49.73	51.48	53.13	54.70
	30.82	33.17	35.41	37.53	39.55	41.48	43.30	45.04	46.70	48.28	49.79
	27.18	29.32	31.37	33.33	35.21	37.00	38.72	40.36	41.93	43.44	44.88
	24.66	26.66	28.58	30.43	32.20	33.90	35.54	37.11	38.63	40.08	41.49
8 YRS.	38.78	41.51	44.07	46.48	48.73	50.85	52.84	54.71	56.47	58.12	59.68
	36.23	38.83	41.28	43.58	45.75	47.79	49.72	51.54	53.26	54.88	56.41
	31.86	34.23	36.48	38.62	40.64	42.56	44.38	46.11	47.75	49.31	50.80
	26.95	29.07	31.10	33.04	34.90	36.68	38.38	40.01	41.57	43.06	44.49
9 YRS.	40.57	43.33	45.90	48.30	50.54	52.64	54.59	56.43	58.14	59.75	61.26
	37.60	40.22	42.68	44.98	47.14	49.16	51.07	52.86	54.56	56.12	57.62
	32.51	34.90	37.15	39.29	41.30	43.21	45.02	46.74	48.36	49.91	51.37
	29.02	31.25	33.37	35.38	37.30	39.13	40.87	42.54	44.13	45.64	47.09
10 YRS.	42.04	44.81	47.37	49.75	51.97	54.03	55.95	57.74	59.41	60.97	62.43
	38.67	41.29	43.74	46.03	48.17	50.17	52.05	53.81	55.46	57.01	58.47
	32.88	35.27	37.52	39.65	41.66	43.56	45.36	47.06	48.68	50.21	51.67
	30.90	33.21	35.39	37.47	39.43	41.30	43.07	44.76	46.36	47.89	49.34
UNTIL PAID	41.42	43.98	46.35	48.54	50.57	52.45	54.21	55.84	57.37	58.81	60.15
	33.03	35.41	37.67	39.79	41.80	43.69	45.49	47.19	48.80	50.33	51.77
	27.50	29.65	31.71	33.67	35.54	37.34	39.05	40.69	42.26	43.76	45.20
	23.58	25.52	27.38	29.18	30.90	32.57	34.17	35.71	37.20	38.64	40.02
	20.65	22.41	24.10	25.75	27.34	28.88	30.37	31.81	33.21	34.57	35.88
	16.57	18.04	19.47	20.87	22.23	23.56	24.85	26.11	27.34	28.54	29.71
	13.86	15.12	16.35	17.57	18.75	19.91	21.05	22.16	23.25	24.32	25.36
	10.48	11.46	12.43	13.38	14.32	15.25	16.16	17.06	17.94	18.81	19.66

EXAMPLES *ON PAGES A-382 TO A-397*

DUE DATE	PAY'T RATE %	BAL REMAIN %	YIELD PERCENTAGES								
			11%	12%	13%	14%	15%	16%	17%	18%	19%
1 YR.	0.88	100.00	0.47	1.41	2.33	3.25	4.15	5.05	5.94	6.82	7.69
	1.00	98.43	0.47	1.40	2.32	3.23	4.13	5.02	5.90	6.77	7.63
	1.25	95.28	0.46	1.38	2.28	3.18	4.07	4.95	5.82	6.68	7.53
	1.50	92.13	0.46	1.36	2.25	3.14	4.01	4.88	5.74	6.58	7.42
	1.75	88.98	0.45	1.34	2.22	3.09	3.95	4.81	5.65	6.49	7.32
	2.00	85.83	0.44	1.32	2.19	3.05	3.90	4.74	5.57	6.40	7.21
	8.81	0.0	0.26	0.79	1.31	1.82	2.34	2.85	3.35	3.85	4.35
2 YRS.	0.88	100.00	0.89	2.66	4.38	6.07	7.73	9.36	10.96	12.52	14.05
	1.00	96.68	0.88	2.62	4.32	5.99	7.62	9.23	10.80	12.34	13.85
	1.25	90.03	0.85	2.54	4.19	5.80	7.40	8.95	10.48	11.98	13.45
	1.50	83.39	0.83	2.46	4.06	5.63	7.17	8.68	10.17	11.62	13.05
	1.75	76.74	0.80	2.38	3.93	5.45	6.95	8.41	9.85	11.26	12.64
	2.00	70.10	0.78	2.30	3.81	5.28	6.72	8.14	9.53	10.90	12.24
	4.64	0.0	0.50	1.48	2.45	3.41	4.35	5.28	6.20	7.11	8.00
3 YRS.	0.88	100.00	1.27	3.76	6.18	8.53	10.82	13.04	15.19	17.29	19.32
	1.00	94.74	1.24	3.68	6.04	8.34	10.58	12.75	14.86	16.91	18.90
	1.25	84.21	1.19	3.51	5.77	7.96	10.09	12.17	14.19	16.15	18.06
	1.50	73.69	1.13	3.34	5.49	7.58	9.61	11.59	13.52	15.40	17.22
	1.75	63.16	1.07	3.17	5.21	7.20	9.13	11.02	12.85	14.64	16.38
	2.00	52.64	1.01	3.00	4.93	6.81	8.65	10.44	12.18	13.88	15.54
	3.25	0.0	0.72	2.14	3.54	4.90	6.24	7.55	8.84	10.10	11.33
4 YRS.	0.88	100.00	1.61	4.75	7.77	10.67	13.47	16.17	18.77	21.28	23.69
	1.00	92.58	1.56	4.60	7.53	10.35	13.07	15.69	18.22	20.65	23.00
	1.25	77.75	1.46	4.31	7.05	9.70	12.26	14.72	17.10	19.40	21.62
	1.50	62.92	1.36	4.02	6.58	9.05	11.45	13.76	15.99	18.15	20.23
	1.75	48.08	1.26	3.72	6.10	8.41	10.63	12.79	14.88	16.90	18.85
	2.00	33.25	1.16	3.43	5.63	7.76	9.82	11.82	13.76	15.64	17.47
	2.56	0.0	0.94	2.77	4.56	6.31	8.00	9.66	11.27	12.84	14.37
5 YRS.	0.88	100.00	1.92	5.62	9.16	12.53	15.76	18.85	21.80	24.61	27.31
	1.00	90.19	1.84	5.40	8.83	12.05	15.16	18.14	20.98	23.70	26.31
	1.25	70.57	1.69	4.96	8.09	11.09	13.96	16.72	19.36	21.89	24.32
	1.50	50.96	1.54	4.52	7.38	10.13	12.77	15.30	17.73	20.07	22.32
	1.75	31.34	1.39	4.08	6.67	9.16	11.57	13.88	16.11	18.26	20.33
	2.00	11.72	1.23	3.64	5.96	8.20	10.37	12.46	14.49	16.44	18.33
	2.15	0.0	1.14	3.37	5.53	7.63	9.65	11.61	13.51	15.36	17.14
6 YRS.	0.88	100.00	2.19	6.39	10.38	14.15	17.73	21.13	24.35	27.40	30.30
	1.00	87.54	2.08	6.09	9.89	13.50	16.92	20.17	23.26	26.19	28.98
	1.25	62.61	1.87	5.48	8.91	12.18	15.29	18.25	21.07	23.76	26.33
	1.50	37.68	1.66	4.87	7.93	10.86	13.66	16.33	18.89	21.33	23.67
	1.88	0.0	1.34	3.94	6.45	8.87	11.19	13.43	15.59	17.66	19.67
7 YRS.	0.88	100.00	2.43	7.08	11.45	15.56	19.43	23.08	26.51	29.74	32.78
	1.00	84.59	2.29	6.68	10.81	14.71	18.38	21.85	25.12	28.20	31.11
	1.25	53.76	2.02	5.88	9.54	13.00	16.29	19.39	22.34	25.13	27.78
	1.50	22.94	1.74	5.08	8.27	11.30	14.19	16.94	19.56	22.06	24.45
	1.77	0.0	1.53	4.49	7.32	10.09	12.62	15.11	17.49	19.78	21.97
8 YRS.	0.88	100.00	2.65	7.69	12.40	16.79	20.90	24.74	28.33	31.69	34.84
	1.00	81.32	2.48	7.19	11.60	15.73	19.60	23.23	26.63	29.83	32.82
	1.25	43.95	2.12	6.18	10.01	13.61	17.01	20.21	23.24	26.10	28.80
	1.54	0.0	1.71	5.00	8.13	11.12	13.96	16.67	19.25	21.72	24.07
9 YRS.	0.88	100.00	2.85	8.23	13.22	17.86	22.16	26.15	29.87	33.32	36.54
	1.00	77.68	2.63	7.62	12.26	16.58	20.61	24.36	27.86	31.13	34.18
	1.25	33.05	2.20	6.40	10.33	14.03	17.50	20.77	23.84	26.74	29.47
	1.44	0.0	1.88	5.49	8.90	12.14	15.21	18.11	20.87	23.49	25.98
10 YRS.	0.88	100.00	3.02	8.71	13.95	18.78	23.24	27.36	31.17	34.69	37.95
	1.00	73.65	2.77	7.98	12.81	17.29	21.43	25.28	28.85	32.16	35.25
	1.25	20.94	2.25	6.53	10.53	14.29	17.80	21.11	24.21	27.12	29.86
	1.35	0.0	2.04	5.95	9.63	13.09	16.36	19.45	22.36	25.11	27.72
		MONTHS									
UNTIL PAID	1.00	238.69	3.27	9.30	14.74	19.66	24.12	28.18	31.87	35.24	38.33
	1.25	138.20	2.28	6.60	10.64	14.42	17.96	21.28	24.39	27.31	30.06
	1.50	100.49	1.77	5.19	8.43	11.51	14.44	17.22	19.87	22.40	24.80
	1.75	79.56	1.46	4.29	7.00	9.61	12.11	14.50	16.81	19.02	21.14
	2.00	66.04	1.24	3.67	6.00	8.26	10.44	12.54	14.58	16.54	18.44
	2.50	49.45	0.96	2.85	4.68	6.47	8.21	9.90	11.55	13.15	14.72
	3.00	39.58	0.79	2.33	3.85	5.33	6.78	8.20	9.58	10.94	12.27
	4.00	28.34	0.58	1.72	2.85	3.96	5.05	6.12	7.18	8.22	9.24

EXAMPLES *ON PAGES A-382 TO A-397*

MORTGAGE YIELD TABLE
SHOWING DISCOUNT PERCENTAGES AT VARIOUS
YIELDS, MONTHLY PAYMENT RATES AND DUE DATES

DUE DATE	YIELD PERCENTAGES										
	20%	21%	22%	23%	24%	25%	26%	27%	28%	29%	30%
1 YR.	8.55	9.40	10.24	11.07	11.90	12.71	13.52	14.32	15.11	15.89	16.67
	8.49	9.33	10.17	11.00	11.82	12.63	13.43	14.22	15.01	15.79	16.56
	8.37	9.21	10.03	10.85	11.66	12.46	13.25	14.03	14.81	15.57	16.33
	8.25	9.08	9.89	10.70	11.49	12.28	13.06	13.84	14.60	15.36	16.11
	8.14	8.95	9.75	10.55	11.33	12.11	12.88	13.65	14.40	15.15	15.89
	8.02	8.82	9.61	10.40	11.17	11.94	12.70	13.45	14.20	14.93	15.66
	4.84	5.33	5.82	6.30	6.78	7.26	7.73	8.20	8.66	9.12	9.58
2 YRS.	15.55	17.03	18.47	19.89	21.28	22.64	23.98	25.28	26.57	27.83	29.06
	15.33	16.79	18.21	19.61	20.98	22.32	23.64	24.93	26.20	27.44	28.66
	14.89	16.30	17.69	19.05	20.38	21.69	22.97	24.23	25.47	26.68	27.87
	14.45	15.82	17.17	18.49	19.78	21.06	22.30	23.53	24.73	25.91	27.07
	14.00	15.34	16.64	17.93	19.19	20.42	21.64	22.83	24.00	25.14	26.27
	13.56	14.85	16.12	17.37	18.59	15.79	20.97	22.13	23.26	24.38	25.47
	8.88	9.75	10.61	11.45	12.28	13.11	13.92	14.72	15.51	16.29	17.06
3 YRS.	21.30	23.22	25.09	26.91	28.67	30.39	32.06	33.68	35.26	36.79	38.28
	20.84	22.73	24.56	26.34	28.07	29.75	31.39	32.98	34.53	36.03	37.50
	19.92	21.73	23.48	25.10	26.86	28.47	30.05	31.58	33.07	34.52	35.94
	19.00	20.73	22.41	24.05	25.64	27.20	28.71	30.18	31.62	33.01	34.37
	18.08	19.73	21.34	22.90	24.43	25.92	27.37	28.78	30.16	31.50	32.81
	17.15	18.73	20.26	21.76	23.22	24.64	26.03	27.38	28.70	29.99	31.25
	12.54	13.73	14.89	16.04	17.16	18.25	19.33	20.39	21.42	22.44	23.44
4 YRS.	26.02	28.26	30.42	32.50	34.51	36.44	38.31	40.11	41.84	43.52	45.13
	25.26	27.45	29.55	31.58	33.54	35.43	37.25	39.01	40.71	42.35	43.93
	23.76	25.82	27.82	29.74	31.61	33.40	35.14	36.82	38.44	40.00	41.52
	22.25	24.20	26.09	27.91	29.67	31.38	33.03	34.62	36.17	37.66	39.11
	20.74	22.58	24.35	26.07	27.74	29.35	30.91	32.43	33.90	35.32	36.70
	19.24	20.95	22.62	24.23	25.80	27.32	28.80	30.23	31.63	32.98	34.29
	15.86	17.32	18.74	20.12	21.47	22.78	24.06	25.32	26.54	27.73	28.89
5 YRS.	29.88	32.34	34.70	36.95	39.11	41.17	43.14	45.03	46.84	48.57	50.23
	28.80	31.19	33.47	35.66	37.75	39.76	41.68	43.52	45.28	46.97	48.59
	26.64	28.87	31.01	33.07	35.04	36.93	38.75	40.49	42.17	43.78	45.32
	24.48	26.56	28.56	30.48	32.33	34.11	35.82	37.47	39.05	40.58	42.06
	22.32	24.25	26.10	27.89	29.62	31.28	32.89	34.44	35.94	37.39	38.79
	20.16	21.93	23.64	25.30	26.91	28.46	29.96	31.42	32.83	34.19	35.52
	18.87	20.55	22.18	23.75	25.29	26.77	28.21	29.61	30.97	32.29	33.57
6 YRS.	33.05	35.66	38.14	40.50	42.73	44.86	46.88	48.80	50.62	52.36	54.02
	31.62	34.14	36.54	38.81	40.98	43.04	45.00	46.87	48.65	50.35	51.97
	28.77	31.10	33.32	35.45	37.47	39.41	41.26	43.02	44.71	46.33	47.87
	25.91	28.05	30.11	32.08	33.97	35.78	37.51	39.17	40.77	42.30	43.77
	21.60	23.46	25.26	27.00	28.67	30.29	31.85	33.35	34.81	36.22	37.58
7 YRS.	35.65	38.36	40.91	43.32	45.59	47.74	49.77	51.68	53.50	55.21	56.83
	33.87	36.47	38.92	41.25	43.45	45.53	47.50	49.36	51.13	52.81	54.40
	30.39	32.68	34.95	37.11	39.16	41.10	42.96	44.72	46.40	48.00	49.53
	26.73	28.90	30.98	32.97	34.86	36.68	38.42	40.08	41.67	43.20	44.66
	24.07	26.09	28.03	29.89	31.67	33.39	35.04	36.62	38.15	39.62	41.03
8 YRS.	37.78	40.54	43.13	45.56	47.85	49.99	52.00	53.89	55.67	57.35	58.93
	35.64	38.29	40.77	43.12	45.32	47.40	49.35	51.20	52.94	54.59	56.14
	31.35	33.77	36.05	38.22	40.27	42.22	44.06	45.82	47.48	49.06	50.57
	26.31	28.46	30.50	32.46	34.33	36.13	37.84	39.48	41.06	42.56	44.01
9 YRS.	39.53	42.37	44.97	47.35	49.62	51.74	53.73	55.58	57.32	58.95	60.48
	37.03	39.70	42.20	44.54	46.74	48.80	50.73	52.55	54.26	55.87	57.38
	32.04	34.47	36.76	38.92	40.97	42.91	44.74	46.48	48.13	49.69	51.18
	28.34	30.59	32.73	34.76	36.70	38.55	40.31	41.99	43.59	45.12	46.58
10 YRS.	40.96	43.76	46.36	48.78	51.02	53.12	55.06	56.88	58.58	60.16	61.64
	38.12	40.80	43.30	45.63	47.80	49.84	51.75	53.53	55.21	56.78	58.26
	32.44	34.87	37.16	39.32	41.36	43.29	45.11	46.84	48.48	50.03	51.50
	30.18	32.51	34.72	36.81	38.80	40.69	42.48	44.18	45.80	47.34	48.81
UNTIL PAID	41.16	43.77	46.17	48.39	50.44	52.35	54.12	55.77	57.32	58.76	60.11
	32.64	35.07	37.36	39.51	41.55	43.47	45.29	47.01	48.64	50.18	51.65
	27.09	29.28	31.36	33.35	35.25	37.07	38.80	40.46	42.05	43.56	45.02
	23.19	25.15	27.04	28.86	30.60	32.29	33.91	35.47	36.97	38.42	39.81
	20.28	22.06	23.77	25.43	27.04	28.60	30.10	31.56	32.97	34.34	35.66
	16.24	17.72	19.17	20.58	21.95	23.29	24.59	25.87	27.11	28.31	29.49
	13.57	14.84	16.09	17.30	18.50	15.67	20.81	21.93	23.03	24.10	25.15
	10.25	11.24	12.21	13.17	14.11	15.04	15.96	16.86	17.75	18.62	19.48

EXAMPLES *ON PAGES A-382 TO A-397*

MORTGAGE YIELD TABLE
SHOWING DISCOUNT PERCENTAGES AT VARIOUS
YIELDS, MONTHLY PAYMENT RATES AND DUE DATES

DUE DATE	PAY'T RATE %	BAL REMAIN %	11%	12%	13%	14%	15%	16%	17%	18%	19%
						YIELD PERCENTAGES					
1 YR.	0.90	100.00	0.24	1.17	2.10	3.02	3.92	4.82	5.71	6.59	7.46
	1.00	98.69	0.23	1.17	2.09	3.00	3.90	4.79	5.68	6.55	7.42
	1.25	95.53	0.23	1.15	2.06	2.96	3.85	4.73	5.60	6.46	7.32
	1.50	92.38	0.23	1.13	2.03	2.92	3.79	4.66	5.52	6.37	7.21
	1.75	89.23	0.22	1.12	2.00	2.87	3.74	4.60	5.44	6.28	7.11
	2.00	86.08	0.22	1.10	1.97	2.83	3.69	4.53	5.36	6.19	7.01
	8.83	0.0	0.13	0.66	1.18	1.70	2.21	2.72	3.22	3.72	4.22
2 YRS.	0.90	100.00	0.45	2.21	3.94	5.64	7.30	8.94	10.53	12.10	13.64
	1.00	97.22	0.44	2.19	3.90	5.57	7.22	8.83	10.41	11.96	13.48
	1.25	90.56	0.43	2.12	3.78	5.41	7.00	8.57	10.10	11.61	13.08
	1.50	83.90	0.42	2.06	3.66	5.24	6.79	8.31	9.80	11.26	12.69
	1.75	77.24	0.40	1.99	3.55	5.08	6.58	8.05	9.49	10.91	12.30
	2.00	70.58	0.39	1.93	3.43	4.91	6.37	7.79	9.19	10.56	11.91
	4.65	0.0	0.25	1.24	2.21	3.17	4.11	5.05	5.97	6.87	7.77
3 YRS.	0.90	100.00	0.64	3.14	5.56	7.92	10.22	12.44	14.61	16.71	18.76
	1.00	95.60	0.62	3.08	5.46	7.78	10.03	12.21	14.34	16.41	18.41
	1.25	85.03	0.60	2.93	5.21	7.42	9.57	11.66	13.69	15.67	17.60
	1.50	74.47	0.57	2.79	4.96	7.06	9.11	11.11	13.05	14.94	16.78
	1.75	63.90	0.54	2.65	4.71	6.71	8.66	10.56	12.41	14.21	15.96
	2.00	53.34	0.51	2.51	4.45	6.35	8.20	10.00	11.76	13.47	15.14
	3.26	0.0	0.36	1.79	3.19	4.56	5.90	7.21	8.51	9.77	11.01
4 YRS.	0.90	100.00	0.81	3.96	6.99	9.91	12.73	15.44	18.05	20.57	22.99
	1.00	93.79	0.79	3.85	6.81	9.66	12.41	15.05	17.60	20.06	22.43
	1.25	78.88	0.73	3.61	6.38	9.06	11.64	14.13	16.53	18.85	21.09
	1.50	63.96	0.68	3.36	5.95	8.45	10.87	13.20	15.46	17.63	19.74
	1.75	49.05	0.63	3.12	5.52	7.85	10.10	12.28	14.38	16.42	18.39
	2.00	34.14	0.58	2.87	5.09	7.25	9.33	11.35	13.31	15.21	17.05
	2.57	0.0	0.47	2.31	4.11	5.86	7.57	9.23	10.85	12.43	13.97
5 YRS.	0.90	100.00	0.96	4.68	8.24	11.64	14.89	17.99	20.96	23.79	26.50
	1.00	91.77	0.93	4.53	7.97	11.27	14.41	17.42	20.30	23.06	25.69
	1.25	72.02	0.85	4.16	7.33	10.37	13.28	16.06	18.74	21.30	23.75
	1.50	52.28	0.77	3.79	6.69	9.47	12.14	14.70	17.17	19.53	21.81
	1.75	32.53	0.70	3.42	6.05	8.57	11.00	13.34	15.60	17.77	19.86
	2.00	12.78	0.62	3.05	5.40	7.67	9.87	11.98	14.03	16.01	17.92
	2.16	0.0	0.57	2.82	4.99	7.09	9.13	11.10	13.02	14.87	16.66
6 YRS.	0.90	100.00	1.09	5.33	9.34	13.14	16.75	20.17	23.41	26.49	29.41
	1.00	89.53	1.05	5.12	8.97	12.63	16.10	19.40	22.53	25.51	28.33
	1.25	64.40	0.94	4.60	8.09	11.40	14.56	17.56	20.42	23.15	25.75
	1.50	39.27	0.84	4.09	7.20	10.17	13.01	15.72	18.31	20.79	23.16
	1.89	0.0	0.67	3.29	5.82	8.25	10.59	12.84	15.01	17.11	19.12
7 YRS.	0.90	100.00	1.22	5.90	10.31	14.45	18.35	22.03	25.49	28.75	31.82
	1.00	87.03	1.16	5.62	9.83	13.79	17.52	21.04	24.37	27.50	30.46
	1.25	55.91	1.02	4.95	8.67	12.19	15.53	18.69	21.68	24.52	27.21
	1.50	24.79	0.88	4.28	7.52	10.60	13.54	16.33	18.99	21.53	23.96
	1.70	0.0	0.77	3.75	6.60	9.33	11.95	14.45	16.86	19.16	21.37
8 YRS.	0.90	100.00	1.33	6.41	11.16	15.59	19.74	23.61	27.24	30.63	33.81
	1.00	84.25	1.25	6.06	10.55	14.77	18.71	22.41	25.87	29.12	32.17
	1.25	46.46	1.07	5.21	9.11	12.78	16.24	19.51	22.59	25.50	28.24
	1.56	0.0	0.86	4.18	7.34	10.35	13.22	15.95	18.55	21.04	23.41
9 YRS.	0.90	100.00	1.42	6.86	11.90	16.58	20.93	24.96	28.72	32.21	35.46
	1.00	81.16	1.33	6.43	11.17	15.59	19.70	23.53	27.10	30.43	33.54
	1.25	35.95	1.12	5.40	9.42	13.20	16.74	20.07	23.21	26.16	28.93
	1.45	0.0	0.94	4.59	8.03	11.30	14.40	17.33	20.12	22.76	25.27
10 YRS.	0.90	100.00	1.51	7.26	12.56	17.44	21.95	26.12	29.97	33.53	36.83
	1.00	77.72	1.40	6.75	11.70	16.27	20.51	24.44	28.09	31.48	34.63
	1.25	24.25	1.14	5.53	9.63	13.46	17.06	20.43	23.59	26.56	29.36
	1.36	0.0	1.02	4.97	8.69	12.19	15.49	18.61	21.55	24.33	26.96
		MONTHS									
UNTIL PAID	1.00	253.61	1.69	8.02	13.70	18.81	23.43	27.61	31.40	34.86	38.02
	1.25	141.41	1.16	5.61	9.76	13.64	17.26	20.66	23.84	26.82	29.61
	1.50	101.97	0.90	4.38	7.69	10.83	13.81	16.65	19.35	21.91	24.36
	1.75	80.42	0.74	3.61	6.37	9.02	11.55	13.99	16.32	18.56	20.72
	2.00	66.61	0.63	3.08	5.45	7.74	9.95	12.08	14.14	16.12	18.05
	2.50	49.75	0.48	2.39	4.24	6.05	7.80	9.51	11.18	12.80	14.37
	3.00	39.77	0.40	1.96	3.48	4.98	6.44	7.86	9.26	10.63	11.97
	4.00	28.43	0.29	1.44	2.58	3.69	4.79	5.87	6.93	7.97	9.00

EXAMPLES *ON PAGES A-382 TO A-397*

MORTGAGE YIELD TABLE

SHOWING DISCOUNT PERCENTAGES AT VARIOUS
YIELDS, MONTHLY PAYMENT RATES AND DUE DATES

DUE DATE	20%	21%	22%	23%	24%	25%	26%	27%	28%	29%	30%
					YIELD PERCENTAGES						
1 YR.	8.32	9.17	10.02	10.85	11.68	12.49	13.30	14.10	14.90	15.68	16.46
	8.27	9.12	9.96	10.79	11.61	12.42	13.23	14.02	14.81	15.59	16.36
	8.16	9.00	9.82	10.64	11.45	12.25	13.05	13.83	14.61	15.38	16.14
	8.05	8.87	9.69	10.50	11.29	12.09	12.87	13.64	14.41	15.17	15.92
	7.93	8.75	9.55	10.35	11.14	11.92	12.69	13.45	14.21	14.96	15.70
	7.82	8.62	9.41	10.20	10.98	11.75	12.51	13.26	14.01	14.75	15.48
	4.72	5.21	5.69	6.18	6.66	7.13	7.60	8.07	8.54	9.00	9.46
2 YRS.	15.15	16.62	18.07	19.49	20.88	22.25	23.59	24.90	26.19	27.45	28.69
	14.97	16.43	17.86	19.26	20.64	21.99	23.31	24.61	25.89	27.14	28.36
	14.53	15.95	17.35	18.71	20.05	21.37	22.66	23.92	25.16	26.38	27.57
	14.10	15.48	16.83	18.16	19.46	20.74	22.00	23.23	24.44	25.62	26.78
	13.67	15.01	16.32	17.61	18.88	20.12	21.34	22.54	23.71	24.86	26.00
	13.24	14.53	15.81	17.06	18.29	19.50	20.68	21.84	22.99	24.11	25.21
	8.65	9.52	10.38	11.23	12.07	12.89	13.70	14.51	15.30	16.08	16.85
3 YRS.	20.74	22.67	24.55	26.37	28.14	29.87	31.54	33.17	34.75	36.29	37.79
	20.37	22.26	24.11	25.90	27.65	29.34	30.99	32.59	34.15	35.67	37.14
	19.47	21.29	23.06	24.78	26.45	28.08	29.67	31.21	32.71	34.18	35.60
	18.57	20.31	22.00	23.63	25.26	26.83	28.35	29.83	31.28	32.68	34.05
	17.67	19.33	20.95	22.53	24.07	25.57	27.03	28.45	29.84	31.19	32.51
	16.77	18.35	19.90	21.41	22.88	24.31	25.71	27.07	28.40	29.70	30.96
	12.22	13.42	14.58	15.73	16.85	17.96	19.04	20.10	21.14	22.16	23.16
4 YRS.	25.33	27.58	29.76	31.85	33.87	35.81	37.69	39.50	41.25	42.93	44.55
	24.72	26.92	29.05	31.10	33.07	34.98	36.82	38.60	40.31	41.96	43.56
	23.25	25.33	27.35	29.29	31.17	32.98	34.74	36.43	38.07	39.65	41.17
	21.78	23.74	25.65	27.49	29.27	30.99	32.65	34.26	35.82	37.33	38.79
	20.30	22.15	23.95	25.68	27.36	28.99	30.57	32.09	33.58	35.01	36.40
	18.83	20.57	22.25	23.88	25.46	26.99	28.48	29.93	31.33	32.69	34.02
	15.47	16.93	18.35	19.74	21.10	22.42	23.71	24.96	26.19	27.39	28.56
5 YRS.	29.09	31.57	33.94	36.21	38.38	40.46	42.45	44.35	46.17	47.91	49.58
	28.22	30.63	32.94	35.15	37.27	39.30	41.24	43.10	44.89	46.59	48.23
	26.10	28.36	30.53	32.60	34.60	36.51	38.35	40.11	41.80	43.43	44.99
	23.99	26.09	28.11	30.06	31.93	33.72	35.45	37.12	38.72	40.27	41.76
	21.88	23.83	25.70	27.51	29.25	30.94	32.56	34.13	35.64	37.10	38.52
	19.77	21.56	23.29	24.96	26.58	28.15	29.67	31.14	32.56	33.94	35.28
	18.40	20.09	21.73	23.31	24.85	26.35	27.80	29.20	30.57	31.89	33.18
6 YRS.	32.18	34.81	37.31	39.69	41.94	44.08	46.12	48.06	49.90	51.65	53.32
	31.02	33.57	36.00	38.30	40.50	42.59	44.58	46.47	48.27	49.99	51.63
	28.22	30.59	32.84	34.99	37.04	39.00	40.87	42.66	44.37	46.00	47.57
	25.43	27.60	29.69	31.68	33.59	35.42	37.17	38.85	40.47	42.02	43.50
	21.07	22.94	24.75	26.50	28.19	29.81	31.38	32.90	34.37	35.79	37.16
7 YRS.	34.71	37.44	40.02	42.45	44.75	46.92	48.96	50.90	52.73	54.46	56.10
	33.26	35.90	38.39	40.75	42.98	45.09	47.09	48.99	50.78	52.48	54.09
	29.76	32.19	34.49	36.67	38.75	40.72	42.60	44.39	46.09	47.71	49.26
	26.27	28.47	30.58	32.59	34.51	36.35	38.11	39.79	41.40	42.95	44.42
	23.48	25.52	27.47	29.34	31.14	32.87	34.53	36.13	37.67	39.15	40.58
8 YRS.	36.79	39.58	42.20	44.65	46.96	49.13	51.16	53.08	54.88	56.57	58.17
	35.04	37.73	40.26	42.64	44.88	46.99	48.98	50.85	52.62	54.29	55.87
	30.84	33.29	35.61	37.81	39.90	41.87	43.74	45.52	47.20	48.81	50.33
	25.67	27.84	29.90	31.88	33.77	35.57	37.30	38.96	40.55	42.07	43.52
9 YRS.	38.49	41.21	43.95	46.41	48.70	50.85	52.86	54.74	56.50	58.16	59.71
	36.45	39.17	41.71	44.10	46.33	48.42	50.39	52.23	53.97	55.60	57.14
	31.55	34.02	36.35	38.55	40.63	42.59	44.45	46.22	47.89	49.47	50.98
	27.66	29.92	32.08	34.14	36.09	37.96	39.74	41.43	43.05	44.60	46.07
10 YRS.	39.89	42.72	45.36	47.80	50.08	52.20	54.17	56.02	57.74	59.35	60.85
	37.56	40.29	42.83	45.21	47.42	49.50	51.44	53.25	54.95	56.55	58.05
	31.98	34.45	36.78	38.98	41.05	43.01	44.86	46.61	48.27	49.84	51.33
	29.45	31.81	34.04	36.16	38.16	40.07	41.88	43.60	45.24	46.80	48.28
UNTIL PAID	40.91	43.56	46.00	48.25	50.33	52.26	54.05	55.71	57.27	58.72	60.08
	32.24	34.72	37.04	39.23	41.30	43.25	45.09	46.83	48.48	50.04	51.52
	26.68	28.90	31.02	33.03	34.96	36.80	38.55	40.23	41.83	43.37	44.84
	22.79	24.78	26.69	28.53	30.30	32.00	33.64	35.22	36.73	38.20	39.61
	19.90	21.70	23.44	25.11	26.74	28.31	29.83	31.30	32.73	34.11	35.44
	15.91	17.41	18.87	20.29	21.67	23.02	24.34	25.62	26.87	28.09	29.27
	13.28	14.56	15.81	17.04	18.24	19.42	20.57	21.70	22.80	23.89	24.95
	10.01	11.01	11.99	12.95	13.90	14.84	15.76	16.66	17.55	18.43	19.29

EXAMPLES ON PAGES A-382 TO A-397

11%
INTEREST

MORTGAGE YIELD TABLE
SHOWING DISCOUNT PERCENTAGES AT VARIOUS
YIELDS, MONTHLY PAYMENT RATES AND DUE DATES

11%
INTEREST

DUE DATE	PAY'T RATE %	BAL REMAIN %	YIELD PERCENTAGES 12%	13%	14%	15%	16%	17%	18%	19%	20%
1 YR.	0.92	100.00	0.94	1.87	2.78	3.69	4.59	5.48	6.36	7.23	8.10
	1.25	95.79	0.92	1.83	2.73	3.63	4.51	5.38	6.25	7.10	7.95
	1.50	92.64	0.91	1.81	2.69	3.57	4.44	5.31	6.16	7.00	7.84
	1.75	89.48	0.89	1.78	2.66	3.52	4.38	5.23	6.07	6.90	7.73
	2.00	86.32	0.88	1.75	2.62	3.47	4.32	5.16	5.98	6.80	7.62
	2.25	83.17	0.87	1.73	2.58	3.42	4.26	5.08	5.90	6.71	7.51
	2.50	80.01	0.86	1.70	2.54	3.37	4.19	5.01	5.81	6.61	7.40
	8.84	0.0	0.53	1.05	1.57	2.08	2.59	3.10	3.60	4.10	4.59
2 YRS.	0.92	100.00	1.77	3.51	5.21	6.87	8.51	10.11	11.68	13.23	14.74
	1.25	91.10	1.70	3.37	5.00	6.61	8.18	9.72	11.24	12.72	14.17
	1.50	84.42	1.65	3.27	4.85	6.41	7.93	9.43	10.90	12.34	13.75
	1.75	77.74	1.60	3.16	4.70	6.21	7.69	9.14	10.56	11.96	13.33
	2.00	71.07	1.54	3.06	4.55	6.01	7.44	8.85	10.23	11.58	12.91
	2.25	64.39	1.49	2.96	4.39	5.81	7.19	8.55	9.89	11.20	12.49
	2.50	57.71	1.44	2.85	4.24	5.61	6.95	8.26	9.55	10.82	12.07
	4.66	0.0	0.99	1.96	2.93	3.87	4.81	5.73	6.64	7.54	8.42
3 YRS.	0.92	100.00	2.51	4.95	7.31	9.62	11.85	14.02	16.14	18.19	20.18
	1.25	85.86	2.36	4.65	6.88	9.04	11.15	13.20	15.19	17.13	19.01
	1.50	75.25	2.24	4.42	6.55	8.61	10.62	12.58	14.48	16.33	18.13
	1.75	64.65	2.13	4.20	6.22	8.18	10.09	11.96	13.77	15.54	17.26
	2.00	54.04	2.01	3.98	5.89	7.75	9.57	11.34	13.06	14.74	16.38
	2.25	43.44	1.90	3.75	5.56	7.32	9.04	10.71	12.35	13.94	15.50
	2.50	32.83	1.79	3.53	5.23	6.89	8.51	10.09	11.64	13.15	14.62
	3.27	0.0	1.43	2.84	4.21	5.56	6.88	8.17	9.44	10.69	11.91
4 YRS.	0.92	100.00	3.16	6.21	9.15	11.98	14.70	17.33	19.86	22.30	24.65
	1.25	80.01	2.90	5.73	8.40	11.01	13.52	15.95	18.29	20.55	22.73
	1.50	65.03	2.71	5.32	7.84	10.28	12.64	14.92	17.12	19.24	21.30
	1.75	50.04	2.51	4.94	7.29	9.56	11.75	13.88	15.94	17.93	19.86
	2.00	35.05	2.31	4.55	6.73	8.83	10.87	12.85	14.76	16.62	18.42
	2.25	20.06	2.12	4.17	6.17	8.10	9.99	11.81	13.59	15.31	16.99
	2.50	5.07	1.92	3.79	5.61	7.38	9.10	10.78	12.41	14.00	15.55
	2.58	0.0	1.85	3.66	5.42	7.13	8.80	10.43	12.02	13.56	15.07
5 YRS.	0.92	100.00	3.75	7.33	10.74	14.01	17.13	20.12	22.97	25.70	28.31
	1.25	73.49	3.35	6.56	9.63	12.58	15.40	18.10	20.69	23.18	25.56
	1.50	53.61	3.06	5.99	8.80	11.50	14.10	16.59	18.99	21.29	23.50
	1.75	33.73	2.76	5.41	7.97	10.43	12.80	15.08	17.28	19.39	21.43
	2.00	13.86	2.46	4.84	7.14	9.36	11.50	13.57	15.57	17.50	19.37
	2.17	0.0	2.26	4.44	6.56	8.61	10.59	12.51	14.38	16.18	17.93
6 YRS.	0.92	100.00	4.26	8.30	12.13	15.76	19.21	22.48	25.58	28.52	31.31
	1.25	66.22	3.71	7.25	10.61	13.81	16.86	19.76	22.53	25.16	27.67
	1.50	40.88	3.30	6.46	9.47	12.35	15.10	17.72	20.24	22.64	24.94
	1.75	15.55	2.89	5.67	8.33	10.88	13.33	15.69	17.95	20.12	22.21
	1.90	0.0	2.64	5.18	7.63	5.98	12.25	14.44	16.55	18.58	20.54
7 YRS.	0.92	100.00	4.72	9.16	13.34	17.27	20.98	24.47	27.75	30.85	33.77
	1.25	58.10	4.00	7.79	11.37	14.76	17.97	21.01	23.89	26.62	29.22
	1.50	26.68	3.46	6.75	9.89	12.87	15.71	18.42	20.99	23.45	25.80
	1.71	0.0	3.00	5.88	8.63	11.27	13.79	16.21	18.53	20.76	22.89
8 YRS.	0.92	100.00	5.13	9.92	14.39	18.57	22.49	26.15	29.58	32.79	35.79
	1.25	49.05	4.22	8.19	11.94	15.46	18.79	21.92	24.88	27.67	30.31
	1.50	10.83	3.54	6.90	10.10	13.13	16.01	18.75	21.35	23.83	26.20
	1.57	0.0	3.35	6.54	9.57	12.47	15.22	17.85	20.36	22.75	25.03
9 YRS.	0.92	100.00	5.49	10.58	15.31	19.70	23.78	27.57	31.10	34.39	37.45
	1.25	38.94	4.38	8.49	12.34	15.96	19.36	22.55	25.56	28.39	31.05
	1.46	0.0	3.68	7.16	10.46	13.58	16.54	19.36	22.02	24.56	26.97
10 YRS.	0.92	100.00	5.81	11.16	16.10	20.66	24.87	28.77	32.37	35.71	38.81
	1.25	27.67	4.49	8.69	12.62	16.29	19.73	22.96	25.99	28.84	31.51
	1.38	0.0	3.99	7.74	11.28	14.62	17.77	20.74	23.55	26.21	28.72
UNTIL PAID	MONTHS										
	1.25	144.85	4.58	8.84	12.82	16.54	20.01	23.26	26.31	29.16	31.84
	1.50	103.50	3.56	6.93	10.13	13.17	16.06	18.81	21.42	23.90	26.26
	1.75	81.31	2.92	5.73	8.41	10.99	13.46	15.83	18.10	20.29	22.38
	2.00	67.19	2.49	4.89	7.21	9.44	11.60	13.69	15.70	17.64	19.52
	2.50	50.06	1.92	3.80	5.62	7.39	9.12	10.80	12.43	14.03	15.58
	3.00	39.96	1.57	3.11	4.62	6.09	7.53	8.94	10.32	11.66	12.98
	3.50	33.28	1.33	2.64	3.93	5.19	6.42	7.64	8.83	10.00	11.15
	4.00	28.52	1.16	2.30	3.42	4.52	5.61	6.68	7.73	8.76	9.78

EXAMPLES *ON PAGES A-382 TO A-397*

MORTGAGE YIELD TABLE
SHOWING DISCOUNT PERCENTAGES AT VARIOUS
YIELDS, MONTHLY PAYMENT RATES AND DUE DATES

DUE DATE	YIELD PERCENTAGES										
	21%	22%	23%	24%	25%	26%	27%	28%	29%	30%	31%
1 YR.	8.95	9.79	10.63	11.46	12.27	13.08	13.89	14.68	15.46	16.24	17.01
	8.79	9.62	10.44	11.25	12.05	12.85	13.64	14.42	15.19	15.95	16.71
	8.66	9.48	10.29	11.09	11.89	12.67	13.45	14.22	14.98	15.73	16.48
	8.54	9.35	10.15	10.94	11.72	12.50	13.26	14.02	14.77	15.52	16.25
	8.42	9.22	10.00	10.78	11.55	12.32	13.07	13.82	14.56	15.30	16.02
	8.30	9.08	9.86	10.63	11.39	12.14	12.89	13.63	14.36	15.08	15.80
	8.18	8.95	9.71	10.47	11.22	11.97	12.70	13.43	14.15	14.86	15.57
	5.08	5.57	6.05	6.53	7.01	7.48	7.95	8.42	8.88	9.34	9.80
2 YRS.	16.22	17.67	19.09	20.49	21.86	23.20	24.52	25.81	27.08	28.32	29.54
	15.60	17.00	18.37	19.72	21.04	22.34	23.61	24.86	26.08	27.28	28.46
	15.14	16.50	17.83	19.14	20.43	21.69	22.93	24.14	25.33	26.50	27.65
	14.68	16.00	17.29	18.57	19.81	21.04	22.24	23.42	24.58	25.72	26.84
	14.22	15.50	16.75	17.99	19.20	20.39	21.56	22.71	23.83	24.94	26.03
	13.75	14.99	16.21	17.41	18.59	19.74	20.88	21.99	23.09	24.16	25.22
	13.29	14.49	15.67	16.83	17.97	19.09	20.19	21.28	22.34	23.38	24.41
	9.30	10.16	11.01	11.85	12.67	13.49	14.29	15.09	15.87	16.64	17.40
3 YRS.	22.12	24.00	25.83	27.61	29.34	31.02	32.66	34.25	35.79	37.30	38.76
	20.84	22.63	24.36	26.05	27.69	29.29	30.84	32.35	33.83	35.26	36.65
	19.89	21.60	23.26	24.88	26.45	27.99	29.48	30.93	32.35	33.73	35.07
	18.93	20.56	22.15	23.70	25.21	26.68	28.12	29.51	30.87	32.20	33.49
	17.98	19.53	21.05	22.53	23.97	25.38	26.75	28.09	29.40	30.67	31.91
	17.02	18.50	19.95	21.36	22.73	24.08	25.39	26.67	27.92	29.14	30.33
	16.06	17.47	18.84	20.18	21.49	22.78	24.03	25.25	26.45	27.61	28.75
	13.10	14.28	15.43	16.55	17.66	18.74	19.81	20.85	21.88	22.88	23.87
4 YRS.	26.91	29.09	31.22	33.23	35.19	37.07	38.89	40.65	42.34	43.97	45.55
	24.84	26.87	28.83	30.73	32.56	34.33	36.04	37.69	39.28	40.83	42.32
	23.28	25.20	27.06	28.86	30.59	32.27	33.90	35.47	36.99	38.46	39.89
	21.73	23.53	25.29	26.98	28.52	30.21	31.76	33.25	34.70	36.10	37.46
	20.17	21.87	23.51	25.11	26.65	28.16	29.62	31.03	32.41	33.74	35.04
	18.62	20.20	21.74	23.23	24.69	26.10	27.47	28.81	30.11	31.38	32.61
	17.06	18.53	19.96	21.36	22.72	24.04	25.33	26.59	27.82	29.02	30.18
	16.53	17.97	19.36	20.72	22.03	23.31	24.61	25.84	27.05	28.22	29.36
5 YRS.	30.80	33.19	35.47	37.66	39.75	41.75	43.67	45.50	47.26	48.94	50.55
	27.84	30.03	32.13	34.15	36.08	37.94	39.72	41.44	43.08	44.66	46.18
	25.62	27.66	29.63	31.52	33.34	35.08	36.76	38.38	39.93	41.45	42.90
	23.40	25.30	27.12	28.89	30.59	32.23	33.81	35.34	36.82	38.24	39.62
	21.18	22.93	24.62	26.26	27.84	29.37	30.86	32.29	33.69	35.03	36.34
	19.63	21.28	22.87	24.42	25.92	27.38	28.80	30.17	31.50	32.80	34.05
6 YRS.	33.96	36.48	38.88	41.15	43.31	45.37	47.32	49.18	50.95	52.63	54.23
	30.07	32.35	34.53	36.61	38.59	40.49	42.30	44.03	45.68	47.26	48.77
	27.14	29.25	31.27	33.20	35.05	36.83	38.53	40.16	41.73	43.23	44.67
	24.22	26.15	28.01	29.79	31.51	33.17	34.76	36.30	37.78	39.20	40.58
	22.42	24.25	26.00	27.70	29.34	30.92	32.45	33.93	35.35	36.73	38.06
7 YRS.	36.53	39.13	41.58	43.90	46.09	48.16	50.12	51.97	53.72	55.37	56.94
	31.67	34.01	36.23	38.33	40.34	42.24	44.05	45.78	47.42	48.98	50.47
	28.03	30.17	32.21	34.16	36.02	37.80	39.50	41.13	42.69	44.19	45.62
	24.94	26.91	28.80	30.61	32.35	34.03	35.64	37.19	38.68	40.12	41.50
8 YRS.	38.61	41.26	43.74	46.07	48.26	50.32	52.26	54.08	55.80	57.42	58.94
	32.80	35.16	37.40	39.51	41.51	43.41	45.21	46.92	48.55	50.09	51.56
	28.45	30.59	32.64	34.59	36.45	38.23	39.93	41.55	43.11	44.59	46.02
	27.21	29.30	31.27	33.17	35.02	36.76	38.43	40.03	41.57	43.04	44.45
9 YRS.	40.31	42.97	45.46	47.79	49.96	51.99	53.90	55.69	57.36	58.93	60.41
	33.56	35.93	38.16	40.28	42.27	44.16	45.95	47.64	49.25	50.77	52.21
	29.26	31.44	33.51	35.49	37.37	39.16	40.88	42.51	44.07	45.56	46.99
10 YRS.	41.68	44.35	46.83	49.14	51.28	53.29	55.16	56.90	58.53	60.06	61.49
	34.03	36.40	38.63	40.74	42.72	44.60	46.38	48.06	49.65	51.15	52.58
	31.10	33.36	35.49	37.52	39.45	41.28	43.02	44.67	46.25	47.75	49.18
UNTIL PAID	34.36	36.72	38.95	41.05	43.03	44.89	46.66	48.33	49.90	51.40	52.82
	28.52	30.66	32.71	34.66	36.52	38.30	40.00	41.62	43.17	44.66	46.08
	24.40	26.34	28.20	29.99	31.71	33.37	34.96	36.50	37.98	39.40	40.77
	21.34	23.09	24.79	26.43	28.02	29.56	31.04	32.48	33.88	35.22	36.53
	17.09	18.56	19.99	21.39	22.75	24.08	25.37	26.63	27.86	29.05	30.22
	14.27	15.54	16.78	17.99	19.17	20.33	21.47	22.58	23.67	24.73	25.78
	12.27	13.38	14.47	15.54	16.58	17.61	18.62	19.62	20.59	21.55	22.49
	10.78	11.76	12.73	13.69	14.63	15.55	16.46	17.36	18.24	19.11	19.96

EXAMPLES *ON PAGES A-382 TO A-397*

MORTGAGE YIELD TABLE
SHOWING DISCOUNT PERCENTAGES AT VARIOUS YIELDS, MONTHLY PAYMENT RATES AND DUE DATES

DUE DATE	PAY'T RATE %	BAL REMAIN %	12%	13%	14%	15%	16%	17%	18%	19%	20%
						YIELD PERCENTAGES					
1 YR.	0.94	100.00	0.70	1.63	2.55	3.46	4.36	5.25	6.14	7.01	7.87
	1.25	96.05	0.69	1.60	2.51	3.40	4.29	5.16	6.03	6.89	7.74
	1.50	92.89	0.68	1.58	2.47	3.35	4.23	5.09	5.95	6.79	7.63
	1.75	89.73	0.67	1.56	2.44	3.31	4.17	5.02	5.86	6.70	7.52
	2.00	86.57	0.66	1.54	2.40	3.26	4.11	4.95	5.78	6.60	7.41
	2.25	83.41	0.65	1.51	2.37	3.21	4.05	4.87	5.69	6.50	7.31
	2.50	80.25	0.64	1.49	2.33	3.16	3.99	4.80	5.61	6.41	7.20
	8.85	0.0	0.39	0.92	1.44	1.95	2.46	2.97	3.47	3.97	4.47
2 YRS.	0.94	100.00	1.33	3.07	4.77	6.45	8.08	9.69	11.27	12.81	14.33
	1.25	91.63	1.28	2.95	4.60	6.21	7.79	9.34	10.86	12.35	13.81
	1.50	84.94	1.24	2.86	4.46	6.02	7.56	9.06	10.54	11.98	13.40
	1.75	78.25	1.20	2.77	4.32	5.83	7.32	8.78	10.21	11.61	12.99
	2.00	71.55	1.16	2.68	4.18	5.65	7.09	8.50	9.89	11.25	12.58
	2.25	64.86	1.12	2.59	4.04	5.46	6.85	8.22	9.56	10.88	12.17
	2.50	58.16	1.08	2.50	3.90	5.27	6.62	7.94	9.24	10.51	11.76
	4.67	0.0	0.74	1.72	2.68	3.64	4.57	5.50	6.41	7.31	8.20
3 YRS.	0.94	100.00	1.88	4.33	6.71	9.01	11.26	13.44	15.56	17.62	19.62
	1.25	86.69	1.77	4.08	6.33	8.51	10.63	12.69	14.70	16.65	18.55
	1.50	76.05	1.69	3.89	6.02	8.10	10.13	12.10	14.02	15.88	17.70
	1.75	65.40	1.60	3.69	5.72	7.70	9.63	11.50	13.33	15.11	16.84
	2.00	54.75	1.52	3.49	5.42	7.30	9.12	10.91	12.64	14.34	15.99
	2.25	44.11	1.43	3.30	5.12	6.89	8.62	10.31	11.96	13.56	15.13
	2.50	33.46	1.34	3.10	4.81	6.49	8.12	9.71	11.27	12.79	14.28
	3.29	0.0	1.08	2.48	3.86	5.22	6.54	7.84	9.11	10.36	11.59
4 YRS.	0.94	100.00	2.37	5.44	8.39	11.23	13.97	16.61	19.15	21.60	23.96
	1.25	81.17	2.19	5.02	7.74	10.37	12.91	15.36	17.73	20.01	22.21
	1.50	66.10	2.04	4.68	7.23	9.69	12.07	14.37	16.59	18.74	20.81
	1.75	51.03	1.89	4.34	6.72	9.01	11.23	13.38	15.45	17.46	19.41
	2.00	35.96	1.75	4.01	6.20	8.33	10.39	12.38	14.32	16.19	18.01
	2.25	20.90	1.60	3.67	5.69	7.64	9.54	11.39	13.18	14.92	16.61
	2.50	5.83	1.45	3.34	5.17	6.96	8.70	10.39	12.04	13.65	15.21
	2.60	0.0	1.39	3.21	4.97	6.70	8.37	10.01	11.60	13.15	14.67
5 YRS.	0.94	100.00	2.81	6.41	9.85	13.14	16.28	19.28	22.15	24.90	27.52
	1.25	74.98	2.53	5.78	8.89	11.87	14.73	17.46	20.08	22.60	25.01
	1.50	54.97	2.31	5.28	8.13	10.86	13.49	16.01	18.43	20.76	22.99
	1.75	34.96	2.08	4.77	7.36	9.85	12.25	14.55	16.78	18.92	20.98
	2.00	14.95	1.86	4.27	6.59	8.84	11.00	13.10	15.12	17.08	18.97
	2.19	0.0	1.70	3.89	6.02	8.08	10.08	12.01	13.89	15.70	17.46
6 YRS.	0.94	100.00	3.20	7.26	11.12	14.78	18.25	21.54	24.66	27.63	30.44
	1.25	68.07	2.81	6.40	9.81	13.05	16.14	19.09	21.89	24.56	27.11
	1.50	42.53	2.50	5.70	8.76	11.67	14.46	17.13	19.67	22.11	24.44
	1.75	16.98	2.19	5.00	7.70	10.29	12.78	15.17	17.46	19.66	21.77
	1.92	0.0	1.98	4.54	7.00	9.38	11.66	13.86	15.98	18.03	20.00
7 YRS.	0.94	100.00	3.54	8.02	12.23	16.19	19.93	23.45	26.76	29.89	32.84
	1.25	60.34	3.03	6.88	10.52	13.97	17.23	20.32	23.25	26.03	28.66
	1.50	28.61	2.62	5.97	9.16	12.19	15.08	17.82	20.44	22.94	25.31
	1.73	0.0	2.26	5.15	7.93	10.59	13.13	15.57	17.91	20.15	22.30
8 YRS.	0.94	100.00	3.85	8.68	13.19	17.41	21.36	25.06	28.52	31.76	34.80
	1.25	51.69	3.20	7.25	11.07	14.66	18.04	21.23	24.24	27.09	29.77
	1.50	13.04	2.69	6.12	9.37	12.46	15.39	18.17	20.82	23.34	25.74
	1.58	0.0	2.52	5.73	8.80	11.71	14.49	17.14	19.67	22.08	24.39
9 YRS.	0.94	100.00	4.12	9.26	14.03	18.46	22.59	26.42	29.99	33.31	36.41
	1.25	42.02	3.33	7.53	11.47	15.16	18.62	21.88	24.94	27.82	30.53
	1.48	0.0	2.76	6.28	9.61	12.76	15.75	18.59	21.29	23.84	26.28
10 YRS.	0.94	100.00	4.36	9.77	14.76	19.37	23.63	27.57	31.22	34.60	37.73
	1.25	31.20	3.42	7.72	11.74	15.50	19.01	22.31	25.40	28.30	31.03
	1.39	0.0	3.00	6.79	10.37	13.74	16.92	19.92	22.76	25.45	27.99
		MONTHS									
UNTIL PAID	1.25	148.56	3.50	7.89	11.98	15.79	19.35	22.68	25.79	28.70	31.44
	1.50	105.11	2.71	6.15	9.42	12.52	15.46	18.25	20.91	23.44	25.84
	1.75	82.22	2.22	5.07	7.80	10.41	12.92	15.32	17.63	19.85	21.97
	2.00	67.78	1.88	4.32	6.67	8.93	11.12	13.23	15.27	17.24	19.14
	2.50	50.37	1.45	3.35	5.19	6.98	8.72	10.42	12.07	13.68	15.24
	3.00	40.15	1.19	2.74	4.26	5.74	7.19	8.61	10.00	11.36	12.69
	3.50	33.41	1.00	2.32	3.61	4.88	6.13	7.35	8.55	9.73	10.88
	4.00	28.62	0.87	2.02	3.15	4.26	5.35	6.42	7.48	8.52	9.54

EXAMPLES *ON PAGES A-382 TO A-397*

MORTGAGE YIELD TABLE
SHOWING DISCOUNT PERCENTAGES AT VARIOUS YIELDS, MONTHLY PAYMENT RATES AND DUE DATES

DUE DATE	21%	22%	23%	24%	25%	26%	27%	28%	29%	30%	31%
1 YR.	8.73	9.57	10.41	11.24	12.06	12.87	13.67	14.46	15.25	16.03	16.80
	8.58	9.41	10.23	11.05	11.85	12.65	13.44	14.22	14.99	15.76	16.52
	8.46	9.28	10.09	10.89	11.69	12.48	13.25	14.03	14.79	15.54	16.29
	8.34	9.15	9.95	10.74	11.53	12.30	13.07	13.83	14.58	15.33	16.07
	8.22	9.02	9.81	10.59	11.36	12.13	12.89	13.64	14.38	15.11	15.84
	8.10	8.89	9.67	10.44	11.20	11.95	12.70	13.44	14.17	14.90	15.62
	7.98	8.76	9.52	10.28	11.04	11.78	12.52	13.25	13.97	14.68	15.39
	4.96	5.44	5.93	6.41	6.89	7.36	7.83	8.30	8.76	9.22	9.68
2 YRS.	15.81	17.27	18.70	20.10	21.47	22.82	24.14	25.43	26.70	27.95	29.17
	15.25	16.65	18.03	19.39	20.71	22.02	23.29	24.55	25.78	26.98	28.17
	14.80	16.16	17.50	18.82	20.11	21.38	22.62	23.84	25.04	26.21	27.36
	14.35	15.67	16.98	18.25	19.51	20.74	21.95	23.13	24.30	25.44	26.56
	13.89	15.18	16.45	17.69	18.90	20.10	21.27	22.43	23.56	24.67	25.76
	13.44	14.69	15.92	17.12	18.30	19.46	20.60	21.72	22.82	23.90	24.96
	12.99	14.20	15.39	16.55	17.70	18.82	19.93	21.01	22.08	23.13	24.16
	9.07	9.94	10.79	11.63	12.46	13.27	14.08	14.87	15.66	16.43	17.20
3 YRS.	21.57	23.46	25.30	27.08	28.82	30.51	32.15	33.75	35.30	36.81	38.29
	20.40	22.19	23.94	25.64	27.29	28.90	30.47	31.99	33.47	34.92	36.32
	19.46	21.18	22.86	24.49	26.07	27.62	29.12	30.59	32.01	33.40	34.76
	18.53	20.17	21.77	23.33	24.85	26.34	27.78	29.18	30.56	31.89	33.19
	17.59	19.16	20.69	22.18	23.63	25.05	26.43	27.78	29.10	30.38	31.63
	16.66	18.15	19.61	21.03	22.41	23.77	25.09	26.38	27.64	28.87	30.07
	15.73	17.14	18.52	19.87	21.19	22.48	23.74	24.98	26.18	27.35	28.50
	12.79	13.96	15.12	16.25	17.36	18.45	19.52	20.56	21.59	22.60	23.59
4 YRS.	26.24	28.43	30.55	32.59	34.56	36.46	38.29	40.05	41.75	43.40	44.98
	24.34	26.39	28.37	30.28	32.13	33.92	35.64	37.31	38.92	40.47	41.98
	22.82	24.75	26.63	28.44	30.19	31.89	33.55	35.12	36.65	38.14	39.57
	21.29	23.12	24.89	26.60	28.25	29.86	31.41	32.92	34.38	35.80	37.17
	19.77	21.48	23.14	24.75	26.31	27.83	29.30	30.73	32.11	33.46	34.77
	18.25	19.85	21.40	22.91	24.37	25.80	27.19	28.54	29.85	31.12	32.36
	16.73	18.21	19.66	21.06	22.44	23.77	25.07	26.34	27.58	28.79	29.96
	16.14	17.58	18.98	20.35	21.68	22.99	24.26	25.49	26.70	27.88	29.03
5 YRS.	30.03	32.44	34.73	36.93	39.04	41.05	42.98	44.83	46.60	48.29	49.92
	27.32	29.53	31.66	33.69	35.65	37.53	39.33	41.06	42.72	44.32	45.86
	25.14	27.21	29.19	31.10	32.94	34.71	36.41	38.05	39.62	41.14	42.60
	22.97	24.88	26.73	28.51	30.23	31.89	33.49	35.03	36.52	37.96	39.35
	20.79	22.56	24.27	25.92	27.52	29.07	30.57	32.02	33.42	34.79	36.10
	19.17	20.82	22.43	23.99	25.50	26.96	28.39	29.77	31.11	32.41	33.68
6 YRS.	33.11	35.65	38.07	40.36	42.54	44.61	46.58	48.45	50.24	51.94	53.55
	29.53	31.85	34.06	36.16	38.17	40.09	41.92	43.67	45.35	46.95	48.48
	26.67	28.80	30.85	32.80	34.68	36.47	38.20	39.85	41.43	42.95	44.41
	23.81	25.76	27.64	29.45	31.19	32.86	34.47	36.02	37.52	38.96	40.35
	21.90	23.74	25.51	27.21	28.86	30.46	31.99	33.48	34.92	36.30	37.65
7 YRS.	35.62	38.24	40.72	43.06	45.27	47.36	49.33	51.20	52.97	54.65	56.23
	31.15	33.52	35.77	37.91	39.94	41.87	43.71	45.45	47.12	48.70	50.21
	27.58	29.75	31.82	33.79	35.68	37.48	39.20	40.85	42.43	43.94	45.39
	24.36	26.35	28.25	30.08	31.83	33.52	35.15	36.71	38.21	39.66	41.05
8 YRS.	37.65	40.32	42.83	45.19	47.40	49.48	51.44	53.29	55.02	56.66	58.20
	32.30	34.70	36.97	39.12	41.15	43.07	44.90	46.63	48.28	49.84	51.33
	28.03	30.20	32.28	34.26	36.14	37.95	39.67	41.31	42.88	44.37	45.83
	26.59	28.69	30.70	32.62	34.46	36.22	37.90	39.52	41.06	42.55	43.97
9 YRS.	39.30	41.99	44.51	46.87	49.07	51.13	53.06	54.87	56.56	58.16	59.66
	33.09	35.50	37.77	39.91	41.94	43.86	45.67	47.39	49.01	50.55	52.02
	28.59	30.79	32.88	34.87	36.78	38.59	40.32	41.96	43.53	45.05	46.48
10 YRS.	40.64	43.34	45.85	48.19	50.37	52.40	54.29	56.06	57.72	59.27	60.72
	33.59	36.00	38.27	40.41	42.43	44.33	46.13	47.83	49.45	50.97	52.42
	30.39	32.67	34.83	36.88	38.82	40.67	42.43	44.10	45.69	47.21	48.65
UNTIL PAID	34.00	36.40	38.67	40.80	42.80	44.70	46.48	48.17	49.77	51.28	52.71
	28.12	30.30	32.38	34.36	36.24	38.04	39.76	41.41	42.98	44.48	45.91
	24.02	25.98	27.86	29.67	31.42	33.09	34.70	36.26	37.75	39.19	40.58
	20.97	22.75	24.46	26.12	27.73	29.28	30.78	32.23	33.64	35.00	36.32
	16.76	18.25	19.69	21.10	22.48	23.81	25.12	26.39	27.62	28.83	30.01
	13.99	15.26	16.51	17.73	18.92	20.09	21.23	22.35	23.46	24.52	25.57
	12.02	13.13	14.23	15.30	16.35	17.39	18.41	19.41	20.39	21.35	22.30
	10.55	11.54	12.51	13.47	14.42	15.35	16.26	17.16	18.05	18.92	19.78

EXAMPLES *ON PAGES A-382 TO A-397*

DUE DATE	PAY'T RATE %	BAL REMAIN %	12%	13%	14%	15%	16%	17%	18%	19%	20%
						YIELD PERCENTAGES					
1 YR.	0.96	100.00	0.47	1.40	2.32	3.23	4.13	5.03	5.91	6.78	7.65
	1.25	96.31	0.46	1.38	2.28	3.18	4.07	4.94	5.81	6.67	7.52
	1.50	93.15	0.45	1.36	2.25	3.13	4.01	4.88	5.73	6.58	7.42
	1.75	89.98	0.45	1.34	2.22	3.09	3.95	4.81	5.65	6.49	7.32
	2.00	86.82	0.44	1.32	2.19	3.05	3.90	4.74	5.57	6.39	7.21
	2.25	83.66	0.44	1.30	2.15	3.00	3.84	4.67	5.49	6.30	7.11
	2.50	80.49	0.43	1.28	2.12	2.96	3.78	4.60	5.41	6.21	7.00
	8.86	0.0	0.26	0.79	1.31	1.82	2.33	2.84	3.34	3.84	4.34
2 YRS.	0.96	100.00	0.89	2.63	4.34	6.02	7.66	9.27	10.85	12.40	13.92
	1.25	92.17	0.85	2.54	4.19	5.81	7.40	8.96	10.48	11.98	13.45
	1.50	85.46	0.83	2.46	4.06	5.63	7.18	8.69	10.17	11.63	13.05
	1.75	78.75	0.80	2.38	3.94	5.46	6.95	8.42	9.86	11.27	12.65
	2.00	72.04	0.78	2.31	3.81	5.28	6.73	8.15	9.54	10.91	12.25
	2.25	65.33	0.75	2.23	3.68	5.11	6.51	7.88	9.23	10.55	11.85
	2.50	58.62	0.72	2.15	3.55	4.93	6.28	7.61	8.92	10.20	11.46
	4.68	0.0	0.50	1.48	2.44	3.40	4.34	5.26	6.18	7.08	7.97
3 YRS.	0.96	100.00	1.25	3.71	6.10	8.41	10.67	12.86	14.98	17.05	19.06
	1.25	87.53	1.19	3.51	5.77	7.97	10.11	12.19	14.21	16.18	18.09
	1.50	76.84	1.13	3.34	5.50	7.59	9.63	11.62	13.55	15.43	17.26
	1.75	66.16	1.07	3.18	5.22	7.22	9.16	11.05	12.89	14.68	16.42
	2.00	55.47	1.02	3.01	4.95	6.84	8.68	10.47	12.22	13.93	15.59
	2.25	44.78	0.96	2.84	4.67	6.46	8.20	9.90	11.56	13.18	14.76
	2.50	34.10	0.90	2.67	4.40	6.08	7.73	9.33	10.90	12.43	13.92
	3.30	0.0	0.72	2.13	3.52	4.87	6.20	7.51	8.79	10.04	11.27
4 YRS.	0.96	100.00	1.58	4.66	7.62	10.48	13.23	15.88	18.44	20.90	23.28
	1.25	82.33	1.47	4.32	7.08	9.73	12.30	14.77	17.16	19.46	21.68
	1.50	67.18	1.37	4.03	6.61	9.09	11.50	13.82	16.06	18.23	20.32
	1.75	52.04	1.27	3.74	6.14	8.46	10.70	12.86	14.96	16.99	18.96
	2.00	36.89	1.17	3.46	5.67	7.82	9.89	11.91	13.86	15.76	17.59
	2.25	21.74	1.07	3.17	5.20	7.18	9.09	10.96	12.76	14.52	16.23
	2.61	6.60	0.97	2.88	4.73	6.54	8.29	10.00	11.66	13.28	14.86
	2.61	0.0	0.93	2.75	4.53	6.26	7.94	9.59	11.19	12.75	14.27
5 YRS.	0.96	100.00	1.87	5.49	8.95	12.26	15.42	18.44	21.33	24.09	26.74
	1.25	76.50	1.70	4.99	8.14	11.15	14.04	16.81	19.47	22.01	24.45
	1.50	56.35	1.55	4.55	7.44	10.21	12.86	15.42	17.87	20.22	22.48
	1.75	36.20	1.40	4.12	6.74	9.26	11.68	14.02	16.27	18.43	20.52
	2.00	16.06	1.25	3.69	6.04	8.31	10.50	12.62	14.67	16.64	18.55
	2.20	0.0	1.13	3.34	5.48	7.55	9.56	11.51	13.39	15.22	16.99
6 YRS.	0.96	100.00	2.13	6.23	10.11	13.79	17.29	20.60	23.75	26.74	29.57
	1.25	69.96	1.89	5.53	8.99	12.28	15.42	18.40	21.25	23.95	26.53
	1.50	44.20	1.68	4.93	8.03	10.99	13.82	16.52	19.10	21.57	23.93
	1.75	18.45	1.47	4.33	7.07	9.69	12.21	14.63	16.96	19.19	21.33
	1.93	0.0	1.32	3.90	6.38	8.77	11.07	13.28	15.42	17.48	19.46
7 YRS.	0.96	100.00	2.36	6.87	11.12	15.11	18.88	22.43	25.77	28.92	31.90
	1.25	62.62	2.04	5.96	9.66	13.17	16.48	19.62	22.60	25.42	28.09
	1.50	30.58	1.77	5.18	8.41	11.49	14.43	17.22	19.88	22.41	24.82
	1.74	0.0	1.51	4.43	7.22	9.90	12.46	14.92	17.28	19.54	21.70
8 YRS.	0.96	100.00	2.56	7.44	11.99	16.25	20.24	23.97	27.46	30.74	33.81
	1.25	54.40	2.16	6.29	10.18	13.84	17.28	20.53	23.60	26.49	29.21
	1.50	15.31	1.82	5.31	8.62	11.77	14.75	17.59	20.28	22.84	25.28
	1.60	0.0	1.68	4.93	8.01	10.96	13.76	16.43	18.98	21.41	23.74
9 YRS.	0.96	100.00	2.74	7.93	12.75	17.23	21.40	25.27	28.88	32.24	35.37
	1.25	45.18	2.25	6.54	10.56	14.33	17.87	21.19	24.31	27.24	30.00
	1.49	0.0	1.85	5.40	8.76	11.94	14.96	17.82	20.54	23.13	25.58
10 YRS.	0.96	100.00	2.90	8.37	13.42	18.08	22.39	26.37	30.06	33.48	36.65
	1.25	34.84	2.32	6.72	10.83	14.67	18.27	21.64	24.79	27.75	30.53
	1.41	0.0	2.00	5.84	9.45	12.85	16.07	19.10	21.97	24.68	27.25
		MONTHS									
UNTIL PAID	1.25	152.58	2.39	6.91	11.11	15.02	18.67	22.08	25.26	28.24	31.02
	1.50	106.79	1.83	5.35	8.68	11.84	14.84	17.69	20.39	22.96	25.40
	1.75	83.17	1.50	4.39	7.17	9.82	12.37	14.81	17.15	19.40	21.56
	2.00	68.39	1.27	3.74	6.12	8.41	10.63	12.76	14.83	16.82	18.74
	2.50	50.69	0.98	2.89	4.75	6.56	8.32	10.03	11.70	13.32	14.90
	3.00	40.35	0.80	2.36	3.89	5.39	6.85	8.28	9.68	11.05	12.39
	3.50	33.55	0.67	2.00	3.30	4.58	5.83	7.06	8.27	9.45	10.62
	4.00	28.72	0.58	1.74	2.87	3.99	5.09	6.17	7.23	8.27	9.30

EXAMPLES *ON PAGES A-382 TO A-397*

MORTGAGE YIELD TABLE
SHOWING DISCOUNT PERCENTAGES AT VARIOUS YIELDS, MONTHLY PAYMENT RATES AND DUE DATES

DUE DATE	21%	22%	23%	24%	25%	26%	27%	28%	29%	30%	31%
				YIELD	PERCENTAGES						
1 YR.	8.50	9.35	10.19	11.02	11.84	12.65	13.45	14.25	15.03	15.81	16.59
	8.37	9.20	10.03	10.84	11.65	12.45	13.24	14.02	14.80	15.57	16.33
	8.25	9.07	9.89	10.69	11.49	12.28	13.06	13.83	14.60	15.35	16.10
	8.13	8.95	9.75	10.54	11.33	12.11	12.88	13.64	14.39	15.14	15.88
	8.02	8.82	9.61	10.39	11.17	11.94	12.70	13.45	14.19	14.93	15.66
	7.90	8.69	9.47	10.24	11.01	11.76	12.51	13.26	13.99	14.72	15.44
	7.79	8.56	9.33	10.09	10.85	11.59	12.33	13.06	13.79	14.50	15.21
	4.83	5.32	5.81	6.29	6.76	7.24	7.71	8.18	8.64	9.10	9.56
2 YRS.	15.41	16.87	18.30	19.70	21.08	22.43	23.75	25.05	26.32	27.57	28.80
	14.89	16.31	17.69	19.05	20.39	21.69	22.98	24.24	25.47	26.68	27.87
	14.45	15.83	17.17	18.50	19.79	21.07	22.32	23.54	24.74	25.92	27.08
	14.01	15.35	16.65	17.94	19.20	20.44	21.65	22.84	24.01	25.16	26.29
	13.57	14.87	16.14	17.38	18.61	19.81	20.99	22.15	23.28	24.40	25.50
	13.13	14.39	15.62	16.83	18.01	19.18	20.32	21.45	22.55	23.64	24.70
	12.69	13.91	15.10	16.27	17.42	18.55	19.66	20.75	21.82	22.88	23.91
	8.85	9.71	10.56	11.41	12.24	13.06	13.87	14.66	15.45	16.23	16.99
3 YRS.	21.01	22.91	24.76	26.55	28.29	29.99	31.64	33.24	34.80	36.32	37.79
	19.95	21.76	23.52	25.23	26.89	28.51	30.09	31.63	33.12	34.57	35.98
	19.04	20.77	22.45	24.10	25.69	27.25	28.76	30.24	31.68	33.08	34.44
	18.12	19.78	21.39	22.96	24.49	25.98	27.44	28.85	30.23	31.58	32.89
	17.21	18.79	20.33	21.83	23.29	24.72	26.11	27.47	28.79	30.08	31.34
	16.30	17.80	19.27	20.70	22.09	23.46	24.79	26.08	27.35	28.59	29.80
	15.38	16.81	18.20	19.56	20.89	22.19	23.46	24.70	25.91	27.09	28.25
	12.47	13.65	14.81	15.95	17.06	18.15	19.23	20.28	21.31	22.32	23.31
4 YRS.	25.57	27.77	29.90	31.95	33.93	35.84	37.68	39.45	41.16	42.82	44.41
	23.83	25.90	27.90	29.84	31.70	33.50	35.24	36.92	38.55	40.12	41.63
	22.34	24.30	26.19	28.02	29.79	31.50	33.16	34.76	36.31	37.80	39.25
	20.86	22.70	24.48	26.21	27.88	29.50	31.07	32.59	34.06	35.49	36.88
	19.37	21.10	22.77	24.39	25.97	27.50	28.98	30.42	31.82	33.18	34.50
	17.88	19.49	21.06	22.58	24.06	25.50	26.90	28.26	29.58	30.86	32.12
	16.40	17.89	19.35	20.77	22.15	23.50	24.81	26.09	27.33	28.55	29.74
	15.75	17.19	18.60	19.98	21.32	22.62	23.90	25.14	26.36	27.54	28.70
5 YRS.	29.26	31.68	33.99	36.21	38.33	40.36	42.30	44.16	45.94	47.65	49.29
	26.78	29.02	31.17	33.23	35.21	37.11	38.93	40.68	42.36	43.98	45.53
	24.66	26.74	28.75	30.68	32.54	34.33	36.05	37.70	39.30	40.83	42.31
	22.53	24.47	26.33	28.13	29.87	31.55	33.16	34.72	36.23	37.68	39.09
	20.40	22.19	23.91	25.58	27.20	28.76	30.28	31.74	33.16	34.53	35.86
	18.71	20.17	21.99	23.55	25.07	26.55	27.98	29.37	30.71	32.02	33.30
6 YRS.	32.27	34.82	37.26	39.57	41.76	43.85	45.84	47.73	49.53	51.25	52.88
	28.99	31.34	33.57	35.71	37.74	39.69	41.54	43.32	45.01	46.63	48.19
	26.19	28.35	30.42	32.40	34.30	36.12	37.86	39.53	41.13	42.67	44.14
	23.39	25.36	27.26	29.09	30.85	32.55	34.18	35.74	37.26	38.71	40.11
	21.38	23.22	25.00	26.72	28.38	29.99	31.54	33.03	34.48	35.88	37.23
7 YRS.	34.70	37.35	39.85	42.21	44.45	46.56	48.55	50.44	52.23	53.92	55.52
	30.62	33.03	35.31	37.48	39.54	41.49	43.35	45.12	46.81	48.41	49.94
	27.12	29.32	31.42	33.42	35.33	37.15	38.90	40.57	42.17	43.70	45.16
	23.78	25.78	27.70	29.54	31.31	33.01	34.65	36.22	37.74	39.19	40.60
8 YRS.	36.68	39.38	41.92	44.30	46.54	48.65	50.63	52.49	54.25	55.90	57.47
	31.79	34.23	36.53	38.71	40.77	42.73	44.58	46.34	48.01	49.59	51.09
	27.60	29.81	31.91	33.92	35.83	37.66	39.40	41.06	42.65	44.18	45.63
	25.96	28.08	30.10	32.04	33.89	35.67	37.37	39.00	40.56	42.05	43.49
9 YRS.	38.29	41.02	43.57	45.95	48.18	50.26	52.22	54.05	55.77	57.38	58.90
	32.60	35.05	37.36	39.54	41.60	43.54	45.38	47.12	48.77	50.33	51.82
	27.91	30.13	32.25	34.26	36.18	38.01	39.75	41.42	43.01	44.53	45.98
10 YRS.	39.60	42.33	44.88	47.25	49.45	51.51	53.43	55.23	56.91	58.48	59.96
	33.13	35.59	37.90	40.07	42.12	44.05	45.88	47.60	49.24	50.78	52.25
	29.68	31.98	34.16	36.23	38.20	40.07	41.84	43.53	45.14	46.67	48.13
UNTIL PAID	33.63	36.08	38.38	40.55	42.58	44.50	46.31	48.02	49.63	51.16	52.60
	27.73	29.94	32.04	34.05	35.96	37.79	39.53	41.19	42.78	44.29	45.75
	23.63	25.61	27.52	29.36	31.12	32.81	34.45	36.01	37.52	38.98	40.38
	20.60	22.40	24.13	25.81	27.43	29.00	30.52	31.98	33.40	34.78	36.11
	16.44	17.94	19.39	20.81	22.20	23.55	24.86	26.14	27.39	28.61	29.79
	13.70	14.98	16.24	17.46	18.67	19.84	20.99	22.12	23.23	24.31	25.37
	11.76	12.88	13.98	15.06	16.12	17.17	18.19	19.19	20.18	21.15	22.10
	10.32	11.31	12.29	13.26	14.21	15.14	16.06	16.97	17.86	18.74	19.60

EXAMPLES *ON PAGES A-382 TO A-397*

MORTGAGE YIELD TABLE

SHOWING DISCOUNT PERCENTAGES AT VARIOUS
YIELDS, MONTHLY PAYMENT RATES AND DUE DATES

DUE DATE	PAY'T RATE %	BAL REMAIN %	12%	13%	14%	15%	16%	17%	18%	19%	20%
1 YR.	0.98	100.00	0.23	1.17	2.09	3.00	3.90	4.80	5.68	6.56	7.42
	1.25	96.57	0.23	1.15	2.06	2.96	3.85	4.73	5.60	6.46	7.31
	1.50	93.40	0.23	1.13	2.03	2.91	3.79	4.66	5.52	6.37	7.21
	1.75	90.24	0.22	1.12	2.00	2.87	3.74	4.59	5.44	6.28	7.11
	2.00	87.07	0.22	1.10	1.97	2.83	3.68	4.53	5.36	6.19	7.01
	2.25	83.90	0.22	1.08	1.94	2.79	3.63	4.46	5.28	6.10	6.91
	2.50	80.73	0.21	1.07	1.91	2.75	3.58	4.40	5.21	6.01	6.80
	8.87	70.3	0.13	0.66	1.18	1.69	2.20	2.71	3.22	3.72	4.21
2 YRS.	0.98	100.00	0.44	2.19	3.91	5.59	7.23	8.85	10.43	11.99	13.51
	1.25	92.71	0.43	2.12	3.78	5.41	7.00	8.57	10.11	11.61	13.09
	1.50	85.99	0.42	2.06	3.67	5.25	6.79	8.31	9.80	11.27	12.70
	1.75	79.26	0.40	1.99	3.55	5.08	6.58	8.06	9.50	10.92	12.31
	2.00	72.53	0.39	1.93	3.44	4.92	6.37	7.80	9.20	10.57	11.92
	2.25	65.81	0.38	1.86	3.32	4.75	6.16	7.54	8.90	10.23	11.54
	2.50	59.08	0.36	1.80	3.21	4.59	5.95	7.28	8.60	9.88	11.15
	4.70	0.0	0.25	1.23	2.20	3.16	4.10	5.03	5.94	6.85	7.74
3 YRS.	0.98	100.00	0.63	3.09	5.49	7.81	10.07	12.27	14.41	16.48	18.50
	1.25	88.38	0.60	2.94	5.22	7.43	9.58	11.68	13.72	15.70	17.62
	1.50	77.65	0.57	2.80	4.97	7.08	9.13	11.13	13.08	14.97	16.81
	1.75	66.92	0.54	2.66	4.72	6.73	8.68	10.59	12.44	14.24	16.00
	2.00	56.19	0.51	2.52	4.47	6.37	8.23	10.04	11.80	13.52	15.19
	2.25	45.47	0.48	2.37	4.22	6.02	7.78	9.49	11.16	12.79	14.38
	2.50	34.74	0.45	2.23	3.97	5.67	7.33	8.94	10.52	12.07	13.57
	3.31	0.0	0.36	1.78	3.17	4.53	5.87	7.17	8.46	9.71	10.95
4 YRS.	0.98	100.00	0.79	3.88	6.86	9.73	12.50	15.16	17.73	20.21	22.59
	1.25	83.51	0.74	3.62	6.40	9.09	11.67	14.17	16.58	18.91	21.15
	1.50	68.28	0.69	3.38	5.98	8.49	10.92	13.26	15.52	17.71	19.82
	1.75	53.05	0.64	3.14	5.56	7.89	10.16	12.35	14.46	16.51	18.50
	2.00	37.83	0.59	2.90	5.13	7.30	9.40	11.43	13.40	15.31	17.17
	2.25	22.60	0.54	2.66	4.71	6.70	8.64	10.52	12.34	14.12	15.84
	2.50	7.38	0.49	2.41	4.29	6.11	7.88	9.60	11.28	12.92	14.51
	2.62	0.0	0.47	2.30	4.08	5.82	7.51	9.16	10.77	12.34	13.86
5 YRS.	0.98	100.00	0.94	4.58	8.06	11.38	14.56	17.60	20.51	23.29	25.95
	1.25	78.03	0.86	4.19	7.37	10.43	13.35	16.15	18.84	21.41	23.88
	1.50	57.75	0.78	3.82	6.74	9.54	12.23	14.81	17.29	19.68	21.96
	1.75	37.47	0.71	3.46	6.11	8.66	11.11	13.48	15.75	17.94	20.05
	2.00	17.18	0.63	3.10	5.48	7.78	9.99	12.14	14.21	16.20	18.14
	2.21	0.0	0.57	2.79	4.94	7.03	9.05	11.00	12.90	14.73	16.52
6 YRS.	0.98	100.00	1.07	5.19	9.10	12.81	16.33	19.67	22.84	25.84	28.70
	1.25	71.87	0.95	4.65	8.16	11.50	14.68	17.71	20.59	23.34	25.95
	1.50	45.91	0.85	4.14	7.29	10.29	13.16	15.90	18.52	21.02	23.41
	1.75	19.94	0.74	3.64	6.42	9.08	11.64	14.09	16.44	18.70	20.87
	1.94	0.0	0.66	3.26	5.75	8.16	10.47	12.70	14.85	16.92	18.92
7 YRS.	0.98	100.00	1.18	5.73	10.01	14.04	17.83	21.41	24.78	27.96	30.96
	1.25	64.95	1.03	5.02	8.78	12.34	15.72	18.91	21.93	24.79	27.51
	1.50	32.60	0.89	4.36	7.65	10.78	13.76	16.60	19.30	21.87	24.32
	1.75	0.0	0.76	3.70	6.51	9.21	11.80	14.27	16.65	18.92	21.11
8 YRS.	0.98	100.00	1.28	6.20	10.79	15.09	19.11	22.88	26.41	29.71	32.81
	1.25	57.17	1.09	5.31	9.27	13.00	16.51	19.81	22.93	25.87	28.65
	1.50	17.64	0.92	4.48	7.86	11.06	14.10	16.98	19.72	22.33	24.80
	1.61	0.0	0.84	4.11	7.23	10.20	13.02	15.72	18.29	20.74	23.09
9 YRS.	0.98	100.00	1.37	6.61	11.48	16.00	20.21	24.12	27.77	31.16	34.33
	1.25	48.43	1.14	5.53	9.63	13.48	17.09	20.48	23.66	26.65	29.46
	1.50	0.0	0.93	4.51	7.90	11.11	14.16	17.05	19.80	22.40	24.88
10 YRS.	0.98	100.00	1.45	6.98	12.08	16.79	21.14	25.17	28.91	32.37	35.57
	1.25	38.60	1.18	5.69	9.90	13.83	17.50	20.94	24.16	27.18	30.01
	1.42	0.0	1.00	4.88	8.53	11.97	15.21	18.28	21.18	23.92	26.51
		MONTHS									
UNTIL PAID	1.25	156.96	1.22	5.88	10.21	14.23	17.97	21.46	24.72	27.76	30.60
	1.50	108.56	0.93	4.52	7.93	11.15	14.21	17.11	19.86	22.48	24.96
	1.75	84.14	0.76	3.70	6.52	9.22	11.81	14.29	16.67	18.94	21.13
	2.00	69.02	0.64	3.14	5.56	7.88	10.13	12.29	14.38	16.40	18.35
	2.50	51.01	0.49	2.42	4.30	6.13	7.91	9.64	11.32	12.96	14.55
	3.00	40.55	0.40	1.98	3.52	5.03	6.50	7.95	9.36	10.74	12.09
	3.50	33.68	0.34	1.67	2.98	4.27	5.53	6.77	7.99	9.18	10.35
	4.00	28.81	0.29	1.45	2.59	3.72	4.82	5.91	6.98	8.03	9.06

EXAMPLES *ON PAGES A-382 TO A-397*

DUE DATE	YIELD PERCENTAGES										
	21%	22%	23%	24%	25%	26%	27%	28%	29%	30%	31%
1 YR.	8.28	9.13	9.97	10.80	11.62	12.43	13.24	14.03	14.82	15.60	16.37
	8.16	8.99	9.82	10.64	11.45	12.25	13.04	13.83	14.60	15.37	16.13
	8.04	8.87	9.68	10.49	11.29	12.08	12.86	13.64	14.40	15.16	15.91
	7.93	8.74	9.55	10.34	11.13	11.91	12.68	13.45	14.21	14.95	15.70
	7.82	8.62	9.41	10.20	10.97	11.74	12.51	13.26	14.01	14.74	15.48
	7.70	8.49	9.28	10.05	10.82	11.58	12.33	13.07	13.81	14.53	15.26
	7.59	8.37	9.14	9.90	10.66	11.41	12.15	12.88	13.61	14.33	15.04
	4.71	5.20	5.68	6.16	6.64	7.12	7.59	8.06	8.52	8.98	9.44
2 YRS.	15.00	16.46	17.90	19.31	20.69	22.04	23.37	24.67	25.95	27.20	28.43
	14.54	15.96	17.35	18.72	20.06	21.37	22.66	23.93	25.17	26.39	27.58
	14.11	15.49	16.84	18.17	19.47	20.75	22.01	23.24	24.45	25.63	26.80
	13.68	15.02	16.33	17.62	18.89	20.13	21.35	22.55	23.73	24.88	26.01
	13.25	14.55	15.82	17.08	18.31	19.51	20.70	21.86	23.01	24.13	25.23
	12.82	14.08	15.32	16.53	17.72	18.90	20.05	21.18	22.29	23.38	24.45
	12.39	13.61	14.81	15.98	17.14	18.28	19.39	20.49	21.57	22.62	23.66
	8.62	9.49	10.34	11.19	12.02	12.84	13.65	14.45	15.24	16.02	16.79
3 YRS.	20.46	22.37	24.22	26.02	27.77	29.47	31.13	32.74	34.30	35.83	37.31
	19.50	21.32	23.09	24.81	26.49	28.12	29.71	31.26	32.76	34.22	35.65
	18.60	20.35	22.05	23.70	25.31	26.88	28.40	29.89	31.34	32.74	34.12
	17.71	19.38	21.01	22.59	24.13	25.63	27.10	28.52	29.91	31.27	32.59
	16.82	18.41	19.96	21.47	22.95	24.39	25.79	27.15	28.49	29.79	31.05
	15.93	17.44	18.92	20.36	21.77	23.14	24.48	25.79	27.06	28.31	29.52
	15.04	16.48	17.88	19.25	20.59	21.89	23.17	24.42	25.64	26.83	27.99
	12.16	13.34	14.50	15.64	16.76	17.86	18.93	19.99	21.03	22.04	23.04
4 YRS.	24.89	27.11	29.25	31.31	33.30	35.22	37.07	38.85	40.58	42.24	43.84
	23.32	25.41	27.43	29.38	31.26	33.08	34.84	36.54	38.17	39.76	41.29
	21.87	23.84	25.75	27.60	29.38	31.11	32.78	34.39	35.96	37.47	38.93
	20.41	22.27	24.07	25.81	27.50	29.14	30.72	32.25	33.74	35.18	36.58
	18.96	20.70	22.39	24.03	25.62	27.16	28.66	30.11	31.52	32.89	34.22
	17.51	19.14	20.71	22.25	23.74	25.19	26.60	27.97	29.30	30.60	31.86
	16.06	17.57	19.03	20.47	21.86	23.22	24.54	25.83	27.09	28.31	29.51
	15.35	16.81	18.22	19.60	20.95	22.26	23.54	24.79	26.01	27.20	28.36
5 YRS.	28.49	30.93	33.26	35.49	37.62	39.66	41.62	43.49	45.29	47.01	48.65
	26.24	28.51	30.68	32.77	34.77	36.69	38.53	40.30	42.00	43.63	45.20
	24.16	26.27	28.31	30.26	32.14	33.94	35.68	37.35	38.96	40.51	42.00
	22.08	24.04	25.93	27.75	29.50	31.20	32.83	34.41	35.93	37.39	38.81
	20.00	21.81	23.55	25.24	26.87	28.45	29.98	31.46	32.89	34.28	35.62
	18.24	19.92	21.54	23.11	24.64	26.13	27.56	28.96	30.32	31.64	32.91
6 YRS.	31.42	34.00	36.45	38.78	40.99	43.10	45.10	47.01	48.82	50.55	52.20
	28.44	30.82	33.09	35.25	37.31	39.28	41.16	42.95	44.67	46.30	47.87
	25.70	27.89	29.99	31.99	33.91	35.75	37.52	39.21	40.83	42.38	43.87
	22.96	24.96	26.88	28.73	30.51	32.23	33.87	35.46	36.99	38.46	39.88
	20.85	22.71	24.50	26.23	27.90	29.52	31.08	32.58	34.04	35.45	36.81
7 YRS.	33.79	36.46	38.99	41.37	43.62	45.75	47.77	49.67	51.48	53.19	54.81
	30.08	32.52	34.84	37.04	39.12	41.11	42.99	44.79	46.50	48.12	49.67
	26.65	28.88	31.01	33.03	34.97	36.82	38.59	40.28	41.90	43.44	44.92
	23.20	25.21	27.15	29.00	30.79	32.50	34.15	35.73	37.26	38.73	40.14
8 YRS.	35.72	38.45	41.01	43.42	45.68	47.81	49.81	51.70	53.47	55.15	56.73
	31.27	33.74	36.08	38.30	40.39	42.37	44.25	46.03	47.73	49.33	50.85
	27.16	29.40	31.54	33.57	35.51	37.36	39.12	40.81	42.42	43.96	45.43
	25.32	27.46	29.51	31.46	33.33	35.12	36.83	38.48	40.05	41.56	43.01
9 YRS.	37.28	40.04	42.62	45.03	47.28	49.39	51.37	53.23	54.97	56.61	58.15
	32.10	34.59	36.94	39.16	41.25	43.22	45.09	46.85	48.53	50.11	51.61
	27.24	29.48	31.61	33.64	35.58	37.43	39.19	40.87	42.47	44.01	45.47
10 YRS.	38.55	41.32	43.90	46.30	48.54	50.62	52.57	54.39	56.09	57.69	59.19
	32.66	35.16	37.51	39.72	41.80	43.77	45.62	47.37	49.02	50.59	52.07
	28.96	31.29	33.49	35.58	37.57	39.45	41.25	42.95	44.58	46.12	47.60
UNTIL PAID	33.26	35.76	38.10	40.29	42.36	44.30	46.13	47.86	49.49	51.04	52.50
	27.32	29.57	31.70	33.74	35.68	37.53	39.29	40.97	42.58	44.11	45.58
	23.23	25.24	27.18	29.03	30.82	32.53	34.18	35.77	37.30	38.77	40.18
	20.23	22.04	23.80	25.49	27.13	28.72	30.25	31.73	33.16	34.55	35.90
	16.11	17.62	19.09	20.52	21.92	23.28	24.60	25.89	27.15	28.38	29.57
	13.41	14.70	15.96	17.20	18.41	19.60	20.76	21.89	23.00	24.09	25.16
	11.50	12.63	13.74	14.82	15.89	16.94	17.97	18.98	19.97	20.95	21.90
	10.08	11.08	12.07	13.04	13.99	14.93	15.86	16.77	17.66	18.55	19.41

EXAMPLES *ON PAGES A-382 TO A-397*

12% INTEREST

MORTGAGE YIELD TABLE
SHOWING DISCOUNT PERCENTAGES AT VARIOUS YIELDS, MONTHLY PAYMENT RATES AND DUE DATES

12% INTEREST

DUE DATE	PAY'T RATE %	BAL REMAIN %	YIELD PERCENTAGES								
			13%	14%	15%	16%	17%	18%	19%	20%	21%
1 YR.	1.00	100.00	0.93	1.86	2.77	3.67	4.57	5.45	6.35	7.20	8.05
	1.25	96.83	0.92	1.83	2.73	3.62	4.51	5.38	6.24	7.10	7.94
	1.50	93.66	0.91	1.80	2.69	3.57	4.44	5.30	6.16	7.00	7.83
	1.75	90.49	0.89	1.78	2.65	3.52	4.38	5.23	6.07	6.90	7.72
	2.00	87.32	0.88	1.75	2.62	3.47	4.32	5.15	5.98	6.80	7.61
	2.25	84.15	0.87	1.73	2.58	3.42	4.25	5.08	5.90	6.70	7.50
	2.50	80.98	0.86	1.70	2.54	3.37	4.19	5.00	5.81	6.61	7.39
	8.88	0.0	0.52	1.05	1.56	2.07	2.58	3.09	3.59	4.09	4.58
2 YRS.	1.00	100.00	1.75	3.47	5.16	6.81	8.43	10.02	11.57	13.10	14.60
	1.25	93.26	1.70	3.37	5.00	6.61	8.18	9.72	11.24	12.72	14.18
	1.50	86.51	1.65	3.27	4.85	6.41	7.94	9.43	10.90	12.34	13.76
	1.75	79.77	1.60	3.16	4.70	6.21	7.69	9.14	10.57	11.97	13.34
	2.00	73.03	1.55	3.06	4.55	6.01	7.45	8.85	10.24	11.59	12.92
	2.25	66.28	1.49	2.96	4.40	5.81	7.20	8.56	9.90	11.21	12.50
	2.50	59.54	1.44	2.86	4.25	5.61	6.96	8.27	9.57	10.84	12.09
	4.71	0.0	0.99	1.96	2.91	3.86	4.79	5.71	6.62	7.51	8.39
3 YRS.	1.00	100.00	2.47	4.88	7.21	9.48	11.69	13.83	15.91	17.94	19.91
	1.25	89.23	2.36	4.65	6.89	9.06	11.16	13.22	15.21	17.15	19.04
	1.50	78.46	2.25	4.43	6.56	8.63	10.64	12.60	14.51	16.36	18.17
	1.75	67.69	2.13	4.21	6.23	8.20	10.12	11.99	13.81	15.58	17.30
	2.00	56.92	2.02	3.99	5.91	7.78	9.60	11.37	13.10	14.79	16.43
	2.25	46.15	1.91	3.77	5.58	7.35	9.08	10.76	12.40	14.00	15.56
	2.50	35.38	1.79	3.55	5.26	6.93	8.55	10.15	11.70	13.21	14.69
	3.32	0.0	1.42	2.82	4.19	5.53	6.84	8.13	9.39	10.63	11.84
4 YRS.	1.00	100.00	3.11	6.10	8.98	11.76	14.44	17.02	19.51	21.91	24.22
	1.25	84.69	2.91	5.72	8.43	11.05	13.57	16.00	18.35	20.62	22.80
	1.50	69.39	2.72	5.34	7.88	10.33	12.69	14.98	17.19	19.32	21.39
	1.75	54.08	2.52	4.97	7.33	9.61	11.82	13.96	16.03	18.03	19.97
	2.00	38.78	2.33	4.59	6.78	8.90	10.95	12.94	14.87	16.74	18.55
	2.25	23.47	2.14	4.21	6.22	8.18	10.08	11.92	13.71	15.44	17.13
	2.50	8.17	1.94	3.83	5.67	7.46	9.20	10.90	12.55	14.15	15.71
	2.63	0.0	1.84	3.63	5.38	7.08	8.74	10.35	11.93	13.46	14.96
5 YRS.	1.00	100.00	3.66	7.16	10.51	13.71	16.77	19.69	22.49	25.16	27.72
	1.25	79.58	3.37	6.60	9.69	12.65	15.49	18.20	20.81	23.30	25.69
	1.50	59.17	3.08	6.03	8.87	11.59	14.20	16.71	19.12	21.44	23.66
	1.75	38.75	2.79	5.47	8.05	10.53	12.92	15.23	17.44	19.57	21.63
	2.00	18.33	2.50	4.91	7.23	9.48	11.64	13.74	15.76	17.71	19.60
	2.22	0.0	2.24	4.40	6.50	8.53	10.49	12.40	14.25	16.04	17.78
6 YRS.	1.00	100.00	4.15	8.09	11.82	15.37	18.73	21.92	24.95	27.83	30.57
	1.25	73.82	3.75	7.31	10.70	13.93	17.00	19.92	22.71	25.36	27.88
	1.50	47.65	3.34	6.54	9.58	12.49	15.27	17.92	20.46	22.88	25.20
	1.75	21.47	2.94	5.76	8.46	11.05	13.54	15.92	18.21	20.41	22.52
	1.96	0.0	2.61	5.12	7.54	9.87	12.12	14.28	16.37	18.38	20.32
7 YRS.	1.00	100.00	4.58	8.89	12.96	16.78	20.39	23.79	27.00	30.02	32.88
	1.25	67.33	4.05	7.88	11.51	14.93	18.18	21.25	24.16	26.91	29.53
	1.50	34.66	3.52	6.87	10.06	13.09	15.97	18.71	21.32	23.80	26.17
	1.77	0.0	2.96	5.80	8.52	11.12	13.62	16.01	18.30	20.51	22.62
8 YRS.	1.00	100.00	4.96	9.59	13.93	17.99	21.79	25.35	28.69	31.82	34.75
	1.25	60.02	4.29	8.33	12.13	15.71	19.08	22.25	25.24	28.06	30.73
	1.50	20.04	3.63	7.07	10.33	13.43	16.36	19.15	21.80	24.31	26.71
	1.63	0.0	3.30	6.44	9.43	12.28	15.00	17.60	20.07	22.43	24.69
9 YRS.	1.00	100.00	5.29	10.20	14.77	19.02	22.97	26.66	30.09	33.29	36.28
	1.25	51.78	4.48	8.68	12.61	16.29	19.74	22.99	26.03	28.90	31.59
	1.52	0.0	3.61	7.04	10.28	13.36	16.28	19.05	21.68	24.18	26.56
10 YRS.	1.00	100.00	5.58	10.73	15.50	19.90	23.97	27.75	31.25	34.50	37.51
	1.25	42.49	4.62	8.93	12.95	16.71	20.22	23.51	26.59	29.47	32.18
	1.43	0.0	3.91	7.60	11.07	14.35	17.45	20.38	23.14	25.76	28.24
		MONTHS									
UNTIL PAID	1.25	161.75	4.81	9.27	13.41	17.25	20.83	24.16	27.27	30.18	32.89
	1.50	110.41	3.68	7.15	10.45	13.56	16.52	19.32	21.98	24.51	26.91
	1.75	85.15	3.00	5.86	8.61	11.24	13.76	16.17	18.48	20.70	22.83
	2.00	69.66	2.54	4.99	7.34	9.62	11.81	13.93	15.97	17.94	19.84
	2.50	51.34	1.95	3.85	5.70	7.49	9.24	10.94	12.59	14.20	15.77
	3.00	40.75	1.59	3.15	4.67	6.15	7.61	9.03	10.42	11.78	13.11
	3.50	33.82	1.35	2.67	3.96	5.23	6.48	7.70	8.90	10.08	11.24
	4.00	28.91	1.17	2.32	3.44	4.56	5.65	6.72	7.78	8.82	9.85

EXAMPLES *ON PAGES A-382 TO A-397*

DUE DATE	22%	23%	24%	25%	26%	27%	28%	29%	30%	31%	32%
	YIELD PERCENTAGES										
1 YR.	8.90	9.74	10.58	11.40	12.21	13.02	13.82	14.61	15.39	16.16	16.93
	8.78	9.61	10.43	11.24	12.05	12.84	13.63	14.41	15.18	15.94	16.70
	8.66	9.48	10.29	11.09	11.88	12.67	13.44	14.21	14.97	15.73	16.47
	8.54	9.35	10.14	10.93	11.72	12.49	13.26	14.02	14.77	15.51	16.24
	8.42	9.21	10.00	10.78	11.55	12.31	13.07	13.82	14.56	15.29	16.02
	8.30	9.08	9.86	10.62	11.39	12.14	12.88	13.62	14.35	15.08	15.79
	8.17	8.95	9.71	10.47	11.22	11.96	12.70	13.42	14.15	14.86	15.56
	5.07	5.56	6.04	6.52	6.99	7.47	7.93	8.40	8.86	9.32	9.77
2 YRS.	16.06	17.50	18.91	20.30	21.66	22.99	24.29	25.57	26.83	28.06	29.27
	15.60	17.00	18.38	19.72	21.05	22.34	23.61	24.86	26.08	27.28	28.46
	15.15	16.51	17.84	19.15	20.44	21.70	22.94	24.15	25.34	26.51	27.66
	14.69	16.01	17.31	18.58	19.83	21.05	22.26	23.44	24.60	25.74	26.85
	14.23	15.51	16.77	18.01	19.22	20.41	21.58	22.73	23.86	24.96	26.05
	13.77	15.01	16.23	17.43	18.61	19.77	20.90	22.02	23.11	24.19	25.25
	13.31	14.52	15.70	16.86	18.00	19.12	20.22	21.31	22.37	23.41	24.44
	9.26	10.12	10.97	11.80	12.62	13.44	14.24	15.03	15.81	16.58	17.34
3 YRS.	21.82	23.68	25.49	27.25	28.96	30.62	32.23	33.81	35.33	36.82	38.27
	20.87	22.66	24.40	26.09	27.73	29.33	30.88	32.40	33.87	35.31	36.70
	19.93	21.64	23.30	24.92	26.50	28.04	29.54	30.99	32.41	33.79	35.14
	18.98	20.62	22.21	23.76	25.28	26.75	28.19	29.58	30.95	32.28	33.57
	18.03	19.60	21.12	22.60	24.05	25.46	26.84	28.18	29.49	30.76	32.01
	17.09	18.57	20.02	21.44	22.82	24.17	25.49	26.77	28.02	29.25	30.44
	16.14	17.55	18.93	20.28	21.59	22.88	24.14	25.36	26.56	27.74	28.88
	13.03	14.20	15.34	16.46	17.56	18.64	19.70	20.74	21.76	22.76	23.74
4 YRS.	26.45	28.60	30.67	32.67	34.60	36.46	38.26	39.99	41.66	43.27	44.83
	24.91	26.95	28.92	30.82	32.66	34.43	36.14	37.80	39.39	40.94	42.43
	23.38	25.31	27.17	28.97	30.71	32.40	34.03	35.60	37.13	38.61	40.04
	21.84	23.66	25.42	27.12	28.77	30.37	31.91	33.41	34.87	36.27	37.64
	20.31	22.01	23.66	25.27	26.82	28.33	29.80	31.22	32.60	33.94	35.24
	18.77	20.36	21.91	23.42	24.88	26.30	27.68	29.03	30.34	31.61	32.84
	17.24	18.72	20.16	21.57	22.94	24.27	25.57	26.84	28.07	29.27	30.45
	16.42	17.84	19.23	20.58	21.90	23.19	24.44	25.67	26.86	28.03	29.17
5 YRS.	30.17	32.52	34.76	36.91	38.97	40.54	42.82	44.63	46.36	48.02	49.61
	27.99	30.18	32.29	34.32	36.26	38.12	39.91	41.63	43.28	44.86	46.38
	25.80	27.85	29.83	31.72	33.55	35.31	37.00	38.62	40.19	41.70	43.15
	23.61	25.52	27.36	29.13	30.84	32.49	34.08	35.62	37.10	38.53	39.92
	21.42	23.19	24.89	26.54	28.14	29.68	31.17	32.62	34.02	35.37	36.68
	19.46	21.09	22.68	24.21	25.70	27.15	28.56	29.92	31.25	32.53	33.78
6 YRS.	33.17	35.64	37.98	40.22	42.34	44.36	46.29	48.12	49.86	51.52	53.10
	30.29	32.59	34.78	36.87	38.86	40.76	42.58	44.32	45.97	47.56	49.07
	27.42	29.54	31.57	33.52	35.38	37.17	38.88	40.52	42.09	43.60	45.04
	24.55	26.50	28.37	30.17	31.90	33.57	35.17	36.72	38.20	39.63	41.01
	22.19	24.00	25.74	27.42	29.05	30.62	32.13	33.60	35.02	36.38	37.71
7 YRS.	35.57	38.12	40.53	42.80	44.95	46.98	48.91	50.73	52.46	54.10	55.65
	32.00	34.35	36.58	38.70	40.72	42.63	44.45	46.18	47.82	49.39	50.88
	28.43	30.59	32.64	34.61	36.48	38.27	39.98	41.63	43.18	44.68	46.12
	24.64	26.59	28.46	30.26	31.99	33.65	35.24	36.78	38.26	39.69	41.06
8 YRS.	37.91	40.10	42.53	44.82	46.97	48.99	50.90	52.70	54.39	55.99	57.50
	33.25	35.62	37.87	40.00	42.01	43.92	45.72	47.44	49.06	50.61	52.07
	28.98	31.15	33.21	35.18	37.05	38.84	40.55	42.18	43.73	45.22	46.64
	26.85	28.91	30.88	32.76	34.57	36.30	37.95	39.54	41.06	42.52	43.92
9 YRS.	39.07	41.67	44.11	46.39	48.53	50.53	52.41	54.17	55.83	57.39	58.86
	34.12	36.51	38.76	40.89	42.89	44.79	46.58	48.27	49.88	51.40	52.84
	28.82	30.97	33.02	34.98	36.84	38.62	40.31	41.93	43.48	44.96	46.38
10 YRS.	40.32	42.93	45.36	47.62	49.73	51.71	53.55	55.28	56.90	58.42	59.84
	34.72	37.11	39.36	41.47	43.47	45.35	47.12	48.80	50.39	51.89	53.31
	30.59	32.82	34.93	36.93	38.84	40.65	42.37	44.01	45.58	47.07	48.49
UNTIL PAID	35.43	37.81	40.04	42.14	44.11	45.96	47.71	49.36	50.92	52.39	53.79
	29.19	31.36	33.42	35.39	37.26	39.05	40.75	42.38	43.93	45.41	46.83
	24.87	26.83	28.71	30.51	32.25	33.92	35.52	37.06	38.55	39.98	41.35
	21.68	23.46	25.17	26.83	28.43	29.98	31.47	32.92	34.32	35.68	36.99
	17.30	18.78	20.23	21.64	23.01	24.34	25.64	26.91	28.15	29.35	30.53
	14.41	15.69	16.93	18.15	19.35	20.51	21.66	22.78	23.87	24.95	26.00
	12.37	13.49	14.58	15.66	16.71	17.75	18.76	19.76	20.74	21.71	22.65
	10.85	11.84	12.82	13.78	14.72	15.65	16.57	17.47	18.36	19.23	20.09

EXAMPLES *ON PAGES A-382 TO A-397*

12¼% MORTGAGE YIELD TABLE 12¼%

INTEREST — SHOWING DISCOUNT PERCENTAGES AT VARIOUS YIELDS, MONTHLY PAYMENT RATES AND DUE DATES — **INTEREST**

DUE DATE	PAY'T RATE %	BAL REMAIN %	13%	14%	15%	16%	17%	18%	19%	20%	21%
							YIELD PERCENTAGES				
1 YR.	1.02	100.00	0.70	1.62	2.54	3.44	4.34	5.23	6.10	6.97	7.83
	1.25	97.09	0.69	1.60	2.51	3.40	4.29	5.16	6.03	6.88	7.73
	1.50	93.92	0.68	1.58	2.47	3.35	4.23	5.09	5.94	6.79	7.63
	1.75	90.74	0.67	1.56	2.44	3.31	4.17	5.02	5.86	6.69	7.52
	2.00	87.57	0.66	1.54	2.40	3.26	4.11	4.94	5.78	6.60	7.41
	2.25	84.39	0.65	1.51	2.37	3.21	4.05	4.87	5.69	6.50	7.30
	2.50	81.22	0.64	1.49	2.33	3.16	3.99	4.80	5.61	6.41	7.20
	8.90	0.0	0.39	0.91	1.43	1.95	2.45	2.96	3.46	3.96	4.45
2 YRS.	1.02	100.00	1.31	3.04	4.73	6.38	8.01	9.60	11.16	12.69	14.19
	1.25	93.80	1.28	2.96	4.60	6.21	7.79	9.34	10.86	12.35	13.82
	1.50	87.04	1.24	2.87	4.46	6.02	7.56	9.06	10.54	11.99	13.41
	1.75	80.28	1.20	2.78	4.32	5.84	7.33	8.79	10.22	11.62	13.00
	2.00	73.52	1.16	2.69	4.18	5.65	7.09	8.51	9.89	11.26	12.59
	2.25	66.76	1.12	2.60	4.04	5.46	6.86	8.23	9.57	10.89	12.19
	2.50	60.00	1.08	2.51	3.91	5.28	6.63	7.95	9.25	10.53	11.78
	4.72	0.0	0.74	1.71	2.67	3.62	4.55	5.48	6.38	7.28	8.16
3 YRS.	1.02	100.00	1.85	4.27	6.61	8.89	11.10	13.25	15.35	17.38	19.35
	1.25	90.09	1.78	4.09	6.34	8.52	10.65	12.71	14.72	16.68	18.58
	1.50	79.28	1.69	3.89	6.04	8.12	10.15	12.12	14.04	15.91	17.73
	1.75	68.47	1.61	3.70	5.74	7.72	9.65	11.53	13.36	15.15	16.88
	2.00	57.66	1.52	3.51	5.44	7.32	9.16	10.94	12.69	14.38	16.04
	2.25	46.85	1.44	3.31	5.14	6.92	8.66	10.35	12.01	13.62	15.19
	2.50	36.04	1.35	3.12	4.84	6.52	8.16	9.76	11.33	12.85	14.34
	3.33	0.0	1.07	2.47	3.84	5.19	6.50	7.80	9.06	10.31	11.52
4 YRS.	1.02	100.00	2.33	5.34	8.23	11.03	13.72	16.31	18.81	21.22	23.55
	1.25	85.90	2.20	5.03	7.77	10.41	12.96	15.41	17.78	20.07	22.28
	1.50	70.51	2.05	4.70	7.26	9.73	12.12	14.43	16.66	18.82	20.90
	1.75	55.12	1.90	4.37	6.75	9.06	11.29	13.45	15.54	17.56	19.51
	2.00	39.74	1.76	4.04	6.25	8.39	10.46	12.47	14.42	16.30	18.13
	2.25	24.35	1.61	3.71	5.74	7.71	9.63	11.49	13.29	15.05	16.75
	2.50	8.97	1.47	3.38	5.23	7.04	8.80	10.51	12.17	13.79	15.37
	2.65	0.0	1.38	3.18	4.93	6.65	8.31	9.93	11.52	13.06	14.56
5 YRS.	1.02	100.00	2.75	6.27	9.63	12.85	15.93	18.87	21.68	24.38	26.95
	1.25	81.16	2.55	5.81	8.94	11.94	14.81	17.56	20.19	22.72	25.14
	1.50	60.60	2.33	5.32	8.19	10.94	13.59	16.12	18.56	20.90	23.15
	1.75	40.05	2.11	4.82	7.43	9.95	12.36	14.69	16.93	19.09	21.17
	2.00	19.49	1.89	4.33	6.68	8.95	11.14	13.26	15.31	17.28	19.19
	2.24	0.0	1.68	3.86	5.96	8.01	9.99	11.90	13.76	15.56	17.31
6 YRS.	1.02	100.00	3.11	7.08	10.84	14.41	17.79	21.01	24.06	26.96	29.72
	1.25	75.81	2.83	6.45	9.89	13.16	16.28	19.24	22.07	24.75	27.32
	1.50	49.41	2.53	5.77	8.86	11.81	14.63	17.32	19.89	22.35	24.70
	1.75	23.02	2.23	5.09	7.83	10.45	12.97	15.39	17.71	19.94	22.08
	1.97	0.0	1.96	4.49	6.93	9.27	11.53	13.71	15.81	17.84	19.79
7 YRS.	1.02	100.00	3.44	7.78	11.88	15.73	19.37	22.80	26.03	29.08	31.96
	1.25	65.76	3.07	6.97	10.65	14.14	17.43	20.55	23.51	26.31	28.96
	1.50	36.77	2.67	6.08	9.31	12.39	15.32	18.10	20.75	23.28	25.68
	1.78	0.0	2.23	5.09	7.83	10.45	12.96	15.37	17.68	19.90	22.03
8 YRS.	1.02	100.00	3.72	8.39	12.77	16.87	20.70	24.29	27.66	30.82	33.79
	1.25	62.93	3.26	7.38	11.25	14.89	18.32	21.55	24.60	27.47	30.18
	1.50	22.49	2.76	6.27	9.59	12.74	15.73	18.56	21.25	23.81	26.24
	1.64	0.0	2.48	5.65	8.66	11.54	14.28	16.90	19.39	21.78	24.05
9 YRS.	1.02	100.00	3.97	8.93	13.54	17.83	21.83	25.55	29.01	32.25	35.27
	1.25	55.22	3.41	7.69	11.71	15.47	18.99	22.30	25.40	28.32	31.06
	1.53	0.0	2.72	6.17	9.45	12.55	15.50	18.29	20.95	23.47	25.87
10 YRS.	1.02	100.00	4.19	9.39	14.20	18.66	22.78	26.59	30.13	33.42	36.47
	1.25	46.50	3.52	7.93	12.03	15.89	19.48	22.84	25.98	28.92	31.68
	1.45	0.0	2.94	6.66	10.17	13.49	16.62	19.57	22.37	25.01	27.52

		MONTHS									
UNTIL PAID	1.25	167.02	3.69	8.29	12.56	16.51	20.18	23.60	26.78	29.74	32.51
	1.50	112.36	2.80	6.35	9.72	12.90	15.91	18.77	21.48	24.05	26.49
	1.75	86.20	2.27	5.19	7.98	10.65	13.21	15.66	18.01	20.26	22.42
	2.00	70.32	1.92	4.40	6.80	9.10	11.32	13.47	15.54	17.53	19.46
	2.50	51.67	1.47	3.39	5.26	7.07	8.84	10.55	12.22	13.85	15.43
	3.00	40.95	1.20	2.77	4.30	5.80	7.27	8.70	10.10	11.47	12.81
	3.50	33.95	1.01	2.34	3.65	4.93	6.18	7.41	8.62	9.81	10.97
	4.00	29.01	0.88	2.03	3.17	4.29	5.39	6.47	7.53	8.58	9.61

EXAMPLES *ON PAGES A-382 TO A-397*

MORTGAGE YIELD TABLE
SHOWING DISCOUNT PERCENTAGES AT VARIOUS YIELDS, MONTHLY PAYMENT RATES AND DUE DATES

DUE DATE	22%	23%	24%	25%	26%	27%	28%	29%	30%	31%	32%
1 YR.	8.68	9.52	10.36	11.18	11.99	12.80	13.60	14.39	15.17	15.95	16.71
	8.57	9.40	10.23	11.04	11.85	12.64	13.43	14.21	14.99	15.75	16.51
	8.45	9.27	10.08	10.89	11.68	12.47	13.25	14.02	14.78	15.54	16.28
	8.34	9.14	9.94	10.74	11.52	12.30	13.06	13.82	14.58	15.32	16.06
	8.22	9.01	9.80	10.58	11.36	12.12	12.88	13.63	14.37	15.11	15.84
	8.10	8.88	9.66	10.43	11.19	11.95	12.70	13.44	14.17	14.89	15.61
	7.98	8.75	9.52	10.28	11.03	11.78	12.51	13.24	13.96	14.68	15.39
	4.95	5.43	5.92	6.40	6.87	7.34	7.81	8.28	8.74	9.20	9.66
2 YRS.	15.66	17.10	18.52	19.91	21.27	22.60	23.91	25.20	26.45	27.69	28.90
	15.25	16.66	18.04	19.39	20.72	22.02	23.30	24.55	25.78	26.99	28.17
	14.80	16.17	17.51	18.83	20.12	21.39	22.63	23.85	25.05	26.22	27.38
	14.36	15.68	16.99	18.27	19.52	20.75	21.96	23.15	24.31	25.46	26.58
	13.91	15.20	16.46	17.70	18.92	20.12	21.29	22.45	23.58	24.69	25.79
	13.46	14.71	15.94	17.14	18.32	19.49	20.63	21.75	22.85	23.93	24.99
	13.01	14.22	15.41	16.58	17.72	18.85	19.96	21.05	22.11	23.16	24.19
	9.04	9.90	10.74	11.58	12.41	13.22	14.03	14.82	15.60	16.37	17.13
3 YRS.	21.27	23.14	24.96	26.72	28.44	30.11	31.73	33.31	34.84	36.34	37.79
	20.43	22.23	23.97	25.68	27.33	28.94	30.51	32.04	33.52	34.96	36.37
	19.50	21.22	22.90	24.53	26.12	27.67	29.18	30.65	32.07	33.47	34.82
	18.58	20.22	21.83	23.39	24.92	26.40	27.85	29.26	30.63	31.97	33.27
	17.65	19.22	20.76	22.25	23.71	25.13	26.52	27.87	29.18	30.47	31.72
	16.73	18.22	19.68	21.11	22.50	23.86	25.18	26.48	27.74	28.97	30.18
	15.80	17.22	18.61	19.97	21.29	22.59	23.85	25.09	26.29	27.47	28.63
	12.72	13.89	15.04	16.16	17.27	18.35	19.41	20.46	21.48	22.48	23.47
4 YRS.	25.79	27.95	30.03	32.04	33.98	35.85	37.66	39.40	41.08	42.70	44.27
	24.41	26.47	28.46	30.37	32.23	34.02	35.75	37.41	39.03	40.59	42.09
	22.91	24.86	26.74	28.55	30.31	32.01	33.66	35.25	36.79	38.28	39.72
	21.41	23.24	25.01	26.73	28.40	30.01	31.57	33.08	34.55	35.97	37.34
	19.91	21.63	23.29	24.91	26.48	28.00	29.48	30.92	32.31	33.66	34.97
	18.40	20.01	21.57	23.09	24.57	26.00	27.39	28.75	30.07	31.35	32.60
	16.90	18.40	19.85	21.27	22.65	23.99	25.31	26.58	27.83	29.04	30.22
	16.03	17.46	18.85	20.21	21.53	22.83	24.09	25.32	26.52	27.69	28.84
5 YRS.	29.42	31.78	34.06	36.26	38.27	40.25	42.15	43.97	45.72	47.39	48.99
	27.46	29.68	31.81	33.86	35.82	37.71	39.52	41.25	42.92	44.52	46.06
	25.31	27.39	29.39	31.31	33.15	34.93	36.64	38.28	39.86	41.39	42.85
	23.17	25.10	26.96	28.76	30.48	32.15	33.76	35.31	36.81	38.25	39.65
	21.03	22.81	24.54	26.20	27.81	29.37	30.88	32.34	33.75	35.12	36.44
	19.00	20.64	22.24	23.78	25.28	26.74	28.15	29.52	30.85	32.15	33.40
6 YRS.	32.34	34.83	37.19	39.44	41.58	43.62	45.56	47.41	49.17	50.84	52.44
	29.76	32.08	34.30	36.42	38.44	40.36	42.20	43.96	45.64	47.24	48.78
	26.94	29.09	31.15	33.12	35.00	36.81	38.54	40.20	41.79	43.31	44.78
	24.13	26.10	28.00	29.82	31.57	33.26	34.88	36.44	37.94	39.39	40.78
	21.67	23.49	25.25	26.94	28.58	30.15	31.68	33.16	34.58	35.96	37.29
7 YRS.	34.68	37.25	39.68	41.98	44.15	46.20	48.15	49.99	51.73	53.39	54.95
	31.47	33.86	36.12	38.27	40.31	42.25	44.10	45.85	47.52	49.10	50.62
	27.97	30.16	32.24	34.23	36.13	37.95	39.69	41.33	42.92	44.43	45.89
	24.07	26.03	27.92	29.73	31.47	33.14	34.75	36.30	37.79	39.23	40.61
8 YRS.	36.57	39.19	41.64	43.95	46.13	48.18	50.11	51.92	53.64	55.26	56.78
	32.74	35.15	37.44	39.60	41.64	43.57	45.41	47.14	48.79	50.36	51.84
	28.55	30.75	32.85	34.84	36.74	38.55	40.28	41.93	43.50	45.01	46.45
	26.23	28.30	30.29	32.19	34.01	35.76	37.43	39.03	40.56	42.04	43.45
9 YRS.	38.09	40.72	43.19	45.50	47.66	49.69	51.59	53.38	55.06	56.63	58.12
	33.64	36.07	38.36	40.52	42.55	44.48	46.29	48.01	49.64	51.18	52.64
	28.16	30.33	32.40	34.37	36.25	38.05	39.76	41.39	42.96	44.45	45.88
10 YRS.	39.31	41.95	44.41	46.70	48.85	50.85	52.72	54.47	56.11	57.65	59.10
	34.27	36.70	38.99	41.14	43.16	45.07	46.87	48.57	50.18	51.70	53.14
	29.89	32.14	34.27	36.30	38.22	40.05	41.79	43.45	45.03	46.53	47.97
UNTIL PAID	35.10	37.52	39.79	41.92	43.92	45.80	47.57	49.23	50.81	52.30	53.70
	28.81	31.01	33.11	35.10	37.00	38.81	40.53	42.17	43.74	45.24	46.67
	24.48	26.47	28.37	30.20	31.96	33.65	35.27	36.83	38.33	39.78	41.17
	21.32	23.11	24.85	26.52	28.14	29.70	31.22	32.68	34.09	35.46	36.79
	16.97	18.47	19.93	21.35	22.73	24.08	25.39	26.67	27.92	29.13	30.32
	14.13	15.41	16.66	17.89	19.09	20.27	21.42	22.55	23.65	24.73	25.79
	12.12	13.24	14.34	15.42	16.48	17.52	18.55	19.55	20.54	21.51	22.46
	10.62	11.62	12.60	13.56	14.51	15.45	16.37	17.27	18.16	19.04	19.91

EXAMPLES *ON PAGES A-382 TO A-397*

MORTGAGE YIELD TABLE
SHOWING DISCOUNT PERCENTAGES AT VARIOUS
YIELDS, MONTHLY PAYMENT RATES AND DUE DATES

DUE DATE	PAY'T RATE %	BAL REMAIN %	YIELD PERCENTAGES								
			13%	14%	15%	16%	17%	18%	19%	20%	21%
1 YR.	1.04	100.00	0.47	1.39	2.31	3.21	4.11	5.00	5.88	6.75	7.61
	1.25	97.35	0.46	1.38	2.28	3.18	4.06	4.94	5.81	6.67	7.52
	1.50	94.17	0.45	1.36	2.25	3.13	4.01	4.87	5.73	6.58	7.42
	1.75	91.00	0.45	1.34	2.22	3.09	3.95	4.80	5.65	6.48	7.31
	2.00	87.82	0.44	1.32	2.19	3.04	3.89	4.74	5.57	6.39	7.21
	2.25	84.64	0.44	1.30	2.15	3.00	3.84	4.67	5.49	6.30	7.10
	2.50	81.55	0.43	1.28	2.12	2.96	3.78	4.60	5.41	6.21	7.00
	8.91	0.0	0.26	0.78	1.30	1.82	2.33	2.83	3.34	3.83	4.33
2 YRS.	1.04	100.00	0.88	2.60	4.30	5.96	7.58	9.18	10.75	12.28	13.78
	1.25	94.35	0.85	2.54	4.19	5.81	7.40	8.96	10.49	11.98	13.45
	1.50	87.58	0.83	2.46	4.07	5.64	7.18	8.69	10.17	11.63	13.06
	1.75	80.80	0.80	2.39	3.94	5.46	6.96	8.42	9.86	11.28	12.66
	2.00	74.02	0.78	2.31	3.81	5.29	6.74	8.16	9.55	10.92	12.27
	2.25	67.25	0.75	2.23	3.69	5.11	6.51	7.89	9.24	10.57	11.87
	2.50	60.47	0.72	2.16	3.56	4.94	6.29	7.62	8.93	10.21	11.47
	4.73	0.0	0.49	1.47	2.43	3.38	4.32	5.24	6.15	7.05	7.94
3 YRS.	1.04	100.00	1.24	3.66	6.01	8.30	10.52	12.68	14.78	16.82	18.80
	1.25	90.96	1.19	3.52	5.78	7.98	10.12	12.21	14.23	16.20	18.11
	1.50	80.10	1.13	3.35	5.51	7.61	9.65	11.64	13.58	15.46	17.29
	1.75	69.25	1.08	3.18	5.24	7.24	9.18	11.07	12.92	14.72	16.47
	2.00	58.40	1.02	3.02	4.96	6.86	8.71	10.51	12.26	13.97	15.64
	2.25	47.55	0.96	2.85	4.69	6.49	8.24	9.94	11.61	13.23	14.82
	2.50	36.70	0.91	2.68	4.42	6.11	7.76	9.38	10.95	12.49	13.99
	3.35	0.0	0.71	2.12	3.50	4.85	6.17	7.46	8.74	9.98	11.20
4 YRS.	1.04	100.00	1.55	4.57	7.49	10.29	13.00	15.60	18.12	20.54	22.87
	1.25	87.11	1.47	4.34	7.10	9.77	12.34	14.82	17.21	19.52	21.75
	1.50	71.64	1.37	4.05	6.64	9.13	11.55	13.88	16.13	18.30	20.40
	1.75	56.18	1.28	3.77	6.17	8.50	10.76	12.93	15.04	17.08	19.06
	2.00	40.71	1.18	3.48	5.71	7.87	9.97	11.99	13.96	15.86	17.71
	2.25	25.24	1.08	3.20	5.25	7.24	9.17	11.05	12.87	14.64	16.36
	2.50	9.78	0.98	2.91	4.79	6.61	8.38	10.11	11.79	13.42	15.01
	2.66	0.0	0.92	2.73	4.49	6.21	7.88	9.51	11.10	12.65	14.16
5 YRS.	1.04	100.00	1.83	5.37	8.76	11.99	15.09	18.05	20.88	23.59	26.18
	1.25	82.76	1.71	5.02	8.18	11.22	14.12	16.90	19.57	22.12	24.57
	1.50	62.06	1.56	4.59	7.50	10.28	12.96	15.53	17.99	20.36	22.64
	1.75	41.37	1.42	4.16	6.81	9.35	11.80	14.15	16.42	18.60	20.70
	2.00	20.68	1.27	3.74	6.12	8.42	10.64	12.78	14.84	16.84	18.77
	2.25	0.0	1.12	3.31	5.43	7.48	9.47	11.40	13.27	15.08	16.84
6 YRS.	1.04	100.00	2.08	6.07	9.85	13.45	16.86	20.10	23.17	26.09	28.87
	1.25	77.82	1.91	5.58	9.07	12.39	15.55	18.55	21.42	24.14	26.74
	1.50	51.21	1.70	4.99	8.12	11.12	13.97	16.70	19.31	21.80	24.18
	1.75	24.60	1.50	4.40	7.18	9.84	12.40	14.85	17.20	19.46	21.62
	1.98	0.0	1.31	3.86	6.31	8.67	10.95	13.14	15.25	17.29	19.26
7 YRS.	1.04	100.00	2.29	6.67	10.80	14.68	18.35	21.81	25.07	28.15	31.05
	1.25	72.24	2.07	6.03	9.78	13.32	16.67	19.84	22.85	25.69	28.38
	1.50	38.93	1.80	5.26	8.56	11.68	14.66	17.49	20.18	22.74	25.18
	1.79	0.0	1.49	4.37	7.13	9.77	12.30	14.73	17.06	19.30	21.44
8 YRS.	1.04	100.00	2.48	7.20	11.61	15.74	19.61	23.24	26.64	29.83	32.82
	1.25	65.91	2.20	6.40	10.34	14.05	17.55	20.84	23.94	26.86	29.61
	1.50	25.01	1.86	5.44	8.82	12.03	15.07	17.96	20.70	23.29	25.76
	1.65	0.0	1.66	4.85	7.89	10.79	13.56	16.20	18.71	21.12	23.41
9 YRS.	1.04	100.00	2.64	7.65	12.31	16.64	20.68	24.44	27.94	31.21	34.26
	1.25	58.75	2.30	6.68	10.78	14.62	18.22	21.59	24.75	27.73	30.52
	1.55	0.0	1.82	5.30	8.61	11.74	14.71	17.54	20.22	22.76	25.19
10 YRS.	1.04	100.00	2.79	8.05	12.91	17.41	21.58	25.44	29.02	32.34	35.43
	1.25	50.64	2.38	6.90	11.12	15.05	18.71	22.14	25.35	28.35	31.16
	1.46	0.0	1.97	5.73	9.27	12.62	15.78	18.76	21.59	24.26	26.79
		MONTHS									
UNTIL PAID	1.25	172.90	2.52	7.28	11.67	15.74	19.52	23.02	26.27	29.30	32.13
	1.50	114.41	1.96	5.53	8.97	12.22	15.29	18.21	20.96	23.58	26.06
	1.75	87.28	1.54	4.50	7.34	10.06	12.66	15.15	17.53	19.81	22.00
	2.00	71.00	1.29	3.81	6.24	8.57	10.83	13.00	15.09	17.11	19.06
	2.50	52.01	0.99	2.93	4.81	6.65	8.43	10.16	11.85	13.49	15.09
	3.00	41.16	0.80	2.39	3.93	5.44	6.92	8.37	9.78	11.16	12.51
	3.50	34.09	0.68	2.02	3.33	4.62	5.88	7.12	8.34	9.53	10.71
	4.00	29.11	0.59	1.75	2.89	4.02	5.12	6.21	7.28	8.33	9.37

EXAMPLES *ON PAGES A-382 TO A-397*

MORTGAGE YIELD TABLE
SHOWING DISCOUNT PERCENTAGES AT VARIOUS
YIELDS, MONTHLY PAYMENT RATES AND DUE DATES

DUE DATE	YIELD PERCENTAGES										
	22%	23%	24%	25%	26%	27%	28%	29%	30%	31%	32%
1 YR.	8.46	9.30	10.13	10.96	11.78	12.58	13.38	14.18	14.96	15.73	16.50
	8.36	9.20	10.02	10.84	11.64	12.44	13.23	14.02	14.79	15.56	16.32
	8.25	9.07	9.88	10.69	11.48	12.27	13.05	13.83	14.59	15.35	16.10
	8.13	8.94	9.74	10.54	11.32	12.10	12.87	13.63	14.39	15.14	15.87
	8.02	8.81	9.61	10.39	11.16	11.93	12.69	13.44	14.19	14.92	15.65
	7.90	8.69	9.47	10.24	11.00	11.76	12.51	13.25	13.99	14.71	15.43
	7.78	8.56	9.33	10.09	10.84	11.59	12.33	13.06	13.78	14.50	15.21
	4.82	5.31	5.79	6.27	6.75	7.22	7.69	8.16	8.62	9.08	9.54
2 YRS.	15.25	16.71	18.13	19.52	20.88	22.22	23.53	24.82	26.08	27.32	28.54
	14.90	16.31	17.70	19.06	20.39	21.70	22.98	24.24	25.48	26.69	27.88
	14.46	15.83	17.18	18.50	19.80	21.08	22.32	23.55	24.75	25.93	27.09
	14.02	15.36	16.67	17.95	19.21	20.45	21.67	22.86	24.03	25.18	26.31
	13.58	14.88	16.15	17.40	18.62	19.83	21.01	22.17	23.30	24.42	25.52
	13.15	14.40	15.64	16.85	18.03	19.20	20.35	21.47	22.58	23.67	24.73
	12.71	13.93	15.12	16.29	17.45	18.58	19.69	20.78	21.86	22.91	23.95
	8.81	9.67	10.52	11.36	12.19	13.01	13.81	14.61	15.39	16.16	16.93
3 YRS.	20.73	22.60	24.43	26.20	27.92	29.60	31.23	32.81	34.35	35.85	37.31
	19.98	21.79	23.55	25.26	26.93	28.55	30.13	31.67	33.16	34.62	36.03
	19.07	20.81	22.50	24.14	25.74	27.30	28.82	30.30	31.74	33.14	34.50
	18.17	19.83	21.45	23.02	24.55	26.05	27.51	28.92	30.31	31.66	32.97
	17.27	18.85	20.39	21.90	23.37	24.80	26.19	27.55	28.88	30.17	31.44
	16.36	17.87	19.34	20.78	22.18	23.54	24.88	26.18	27.45	28.69	29.90
	15.46	16.89	18.29	19.65	20.99	22.29	23.56	24.81	26.02	27.21	28.37
	12.40	13.58	14.73	15.86	16.97	18.06	19.12	20.17	21.20	22.20	23.19
4 YRS.	25.13	27.30	29.40	31.42	33.37	35.25	37.06	38.81	40.50	42.13	43.71
	23.90	25.98	27.99	29.92	31.79	33.60	35.34	37.03	38.66	40.23	41.75
	22.44	24.40	26.30	28.13	29.91	31.62	33.28	34.89	36.44	37.94	39.40
	20.97	22.82	24.61	26.34	28.02	29.65	31.22	32.75	34.23	35.66	37.05
	19.50	21.24	22.92	24.55	26.13	27.67	29.16	30.61	32.01	33.37	34.70
	18.03	19.65	21.23	22.76	24.25	25.69	27.10	28.47	29.79	31.09	32.34
	16.56	18.07	19.54	20.97	22.36	23.72	25.04	26.32	27.58	28.80	29.99
	15.64	17.07	18.47	19.84	21.17	22.47	23.73	24.97	26.18	27.36	28.51
5 YRS.	28.66	31.04	33.31	35.49	37.57	39.57	41.48	43.32	45.08	46.76	48.37
	26.92	29.17	31.33	33.40	35.38	37.29	39.12	40.87	42.56	44.17	45.73
	24.82	26.92	28.94	30.88	32.75	34.54	36.27	37.93	39.53	41.07	42.55
	22.73	24.68	26.56	28.37	30.12	31.80	33.43	34.99	36.51	37.97	39.38
	20.63	22.44	24.18	25.86	27.49	29.06	30.58	32.06	33.48	34.86	36.20
	18.54	20.19	21.80	23.35	24.86	26.32	27.74	29.12	30.46	31.76	33.03
6 YRS.	31.51	34.02	36.40	38.67	40.83	42.88	44.84	46.70	48.48	50.17	51.78
	29.21	31.57	33.82	35.96	38.01	39.96	41.82	43.60	45.30	46.92	48.47
	26.46	28.63	30.72	32.71	34.62	36.45	38.20	39.88	41.49	43.03	44.51
	23.70	25.70	27.62	29.46	31.23	32.94	34.58	36.15	37.67	39.13	40.54
	21.15	22.98	24.75	26.45	28.10	29.69	31.23	32.71	34.15	35.54	36.88
7 YRS.	33.79	36.39	38.84	41.15	43.35	45.42	47.38	49.24	51.00	52.67	54.26
	30.94	33.36	35.65	37.83	39.90	41.87	43.74	45.52	47.21	48.81	50.34
	27.51	29.72	31.84	33.85	35.78	37.61	39.37	41.04	42.65	44.18	45.65
	23.50	25.47	27.37	29.20	30.95	32.64	34.26	35.82	37.32	38.77	40.16
8 YRS.	35.63	38.27	40.76	43.09	45.29	47.36	49.31	51.15	52.88	54.52	56.07
	32.21	34.67	36.99	39.18	41.26	43.22	45.08	46.84	48.51	50.10	51.60
	28.11	30.34	32.47	34.49	36.42	38.25	40.00	41.67	43.27	44.79	46.25
	25.60	27.70	29.70	31.62	33.46	35.22	36.90	38.51	40.06	41.55	42.97
9 YRS.	37.11	39.78	42.27	44.61	46.79	48.85	50.77	52.58	54.28	55.88	57.39
	33.14	35.61	37.94	40.13	42.20	44.16	46.00	47.74	49.39	50.95	52.43
	27.49	29.68	31.77	33.76	35.66	37.47	39.20	40.85	42.43	43.94	45.38
10 YRS.	38.30	40.97	43.47	45.79	47.96	49.98	51.88	53.66	55.32	56.88	58.35
	33.80	36.28	38.60	40.79	42.85	44.78	46.61	48.34	49.97	51.51	52.96
	29.18	31.46	33.61	35.66	37.60	39.45	41.21	42.88	44.47	45.99	47.44
UNTIL PAID	34.77	37.23	39.54	41.70	43.73	45.63	47.42	49.11	50.70	52.20	53.62
	28.42	30.66	32.78	34.80	36.73	38.56	40.31	41.97	43.56	45.07	46.52
	24.10	26.11	28.04	29.89	31.67	33.38	35.02	36.60	38.11	39.57	40.97
	20.94	22.76	24.51	26.21	27.84	29.43	30.95	32.43	33.86	35.24	36.56
	16.64	18.15	19.63	21.06	22.46	23.81	25.14	26.43	27.68	28.91	30.10
	13.83	15.13	16.39	17.63	18.84	20.03	21.19	22.32	23.42	24.52	25.58
	11.86	12.99	14.09	15.18	16.25	17.30	18.33	19.34	20.33	21.31	22.26
	10.39	11.39	12.38	13.35	14.30	15.24	16.17	17.08	17.97	18.85	19.72

EXAMPLES *ON PAGES A-382 TO A-397*

DUE DATE	PAY'T RATE %	BAL REMAIN %	13%	14%	15%	16%	17%	18%	19%	20%	21%
			YIELD PERCENTAGES								
1 YR.	1.00	100.00	0.23	1.16	2.08	2.99	3.88	4.77	5.65	6.52	7.38
	1.25	97.61	0.23	1.15	2.06	2.95	3.84	4.72	5.59	6.45	7.31
	1.50	94.43	0.23	1.13	2.03	2.91	3.79	4.66	5.52	6.37	7.21
	1.75	91.25	0.22	1.12	2.00	2.87	3.74	4.59	5.44	6.28	7.11
	2.00	88.07	0.22	1.10	1.97	2.83	3.68	4.53	5.36	6.19	7.00
	2.25	84.89	0.22	1.08	1.94	2.79	3.63	4.46	5.28	6.10	6.90
	2.50	81.71	0.21	1.07	1.91	2.75	3.57	4.39	5.20	6.01	6.80
	8.92	0.0	0.13	0.65	1.17	1.69	2.20	2.71	3.21	3.71	4.20
2 YRS.	1.00	100.00	0.44	2.17	3.87	5.53	7.16	8.76	10.33	11.87	13.38
	1.25	94.90	0.43	2.12	3.78	5.41	7.01	8.57	10.11	11.61	13.09
	1.50	88.11	0.42	2.06	3.67	5.25	6.80	8.32	9.81	11.27	12.71
	1.75	81.32	0.40	1.99	3.55	5.09	6.59	8.06	9.51	10.93	12.32
	2.00	74.52	0.39	1.93	3.44	4.92	6.38	7.81	9.21	10.58	11.93
	2.25	67.73	0.38	1.86	3.33	4.76	6.17	7.55	8.91	10.24	11.55
	2.50	60.94	0.36	1.80	3.21	4.60	5.96	7.30	8.61	9.90	11.16
	4.74	0.0	0.25	1.23	2.19	3.14	4.08	5.00	5.92	6.82	7.73
3 YRS.	1.00	100.00	0.62	3.05	5.41	7.70	9.93	12.10	14.21	16.26	18.25
	1.25	91.83	0.60	2.94	5.22	7.44	9.60	11.70	13.73	15.72	17.65
	1.50	80.94	0.57	2.80	4.98	7.09	9.15	11.15	13.10	15.00	16.84
	1.75	70.04	0.54	2.66	4.73	6.74	8.70	10.61	12.47	14.28	16.04
	2.00	59.15	0.51	2.52	4.49	6.40	8.26	10.07	11.84	13.56	15.24
	2.25	48.25	0.48	2.39	4.24	6.05	7.81	9.53	11.21	12.84	14.44
	2.50	37.36	0.45	2.25	3.99	5.70	7.36	8.99	10.58	12.12	13.64
	3.36	0.0	0.36	1.77	3.15	4.50	5.83	7.13	8.41	9.66	10.89
4 YRS.	1.00	100.00	0.78	3.81	6.74	9.56	12.27	14.89	17.42	19.85	22.20
	1.25	88.34	0.74	3.63	6.42	9.12	11.71	14.22	16.63	18.97	21.22
	1.50	72.79	0.69	3.39	6.01	8.53	10.96	13.32	15.59	17.78	19.91
	1.75	57.24	0.64	3.16	5.60	7.94	10.21	12.41	14.54	16.60	18.59
	2.00	41.69	0.59	2.92	5.17	7.35	9.46	11.51	13.50	15.42	17.28
	2.25	26.14	0.54	2.68	4.75	6.76	8.72	10.61	12.45	14.24	15.97
	2.50	10.60	0.50	2.44	4.33	6.18	7.97	9.71	11.40	13.05	14.66
	2.67	0.0	0.46	2.28	4.05	5.78	7.46	9.09	10.69	12.25	13.76
5 YRS.	1.00	100.00	0.92	4.48	7.88	11.14	14.25	17.23	20.08	22.80	25.41
	1.25	84.38	0.86	4.21	7.41	10.48	13.42	16.24	18.94	21.52	24.00
	1.50	63.54	0.79	3.85	6.79	9.61	12.32	14.92	17.42	19.81	22.12
	1.75	42.71	0.71	3.50	6.17	8.74	11.22	13.60	15.90	18.10	20.23
	2.00	21.88	0.64	3.14	5.55	7.87	10.12	12.29	14.38	16.40	18.35
	2.26	0.0	0.56	2.76	4.90	6.96	8.96	10.90	12.78	14.60	16.37
6 YRS.	1.00	100.00	1.04	5.06	8.87	12.49	15.92	19.18	22.28	25.22	28.02
	1.25	79.88	0.96	4.69	8.23	11.60	14.80	17.85	20.75	23.52	26.15
	1.50	53.04	0.86	4.19	7.37	10.41	13.31	16.07	18.72	21.24	23.65
	1.75	26.21	0.76	3.70	6.52	9.22	11.81	14.30	16.68	18.97	21.16
	1.99	0.0	0.66	3.22	5.69	8.05	10.36	12.56	14.69	16.74	18.72
7 YRS.	1.00	100.00	1.15	5.56	9.72	13.64	17.33	20.82	24.10	27.21	30.14
	1.25	74.77	1.04	5.08	8.89	12.49	15.90	19.12	22.17	25.06	27.79
	1.50	43.13	0.91	4.43	7.78	10.96	13.98	16.86	19.59	22.19	24.67
	1.81	0.0	0.75	3.65	6.43	9.09	11.64	14.09	16.44	18.69	20.85
8 YRS.	1.00	100.00	1.24	6.00	10.45	14.62	18.52	22.18	25.61	28.83	31.86
	1.25	68.97	1.11	5.39	9.42	13.20	16.76	20.11	23.26	26.23	29.04
	1.50	27.60	0.94	4.59	8.04	11.31	14.40	17.34	20.12	22.77	25.28
	1.67	0.0	0.83	4.05	7.12	10.04	12.83	15.49	18.03	20.45	22.77
9 YRS.	1.00	100.00	1.32	6.38	11.08	15.45	19.53	23.32	26.86	30.17	33.25
	1.25	62.39	1.17	5.64	9.83	13.75	17.42	20.86	24.09	27.12	29.96
	1.56	0.0	0.91	4.43	7.76	10.93	13.93	16.78	19.48	22.05	24.50
10 YRS.	1.00	100.00	1.40	6.71	11.62	16.17	20.38	24.28	27.90	31.26	34.39
	1.25	54.92	1.21	5.84	10.15	14.17	17.92	21.43	24.70	27.76	30.63
	1.48	0.0	0.99	4.78	8.36	11.74	14.94	17.95	20.80	23.50	26.05
		MONTHS									
UNTIL PAID	1.25	179.50	1.29	6.22	10.75	14.95	18.83	22.42	25.76	28.86	31.74
	1.50	116.58	0.96	4.68	8.20	11.52	14.66	17.63	20.44	23.10	25.63
	1.75	88.40	0.78	3.80	6.69	9.45	12.09	14.62	17.04	19.36	21.57
	2.00	71.69	0.65	3.21	5.67	8.04	10.32	12.52	14.64	16.69	18.66
	2.50	52.36	0.50	2.46	4.36	6.22	8.02	9.77	11.47	13.13	14.74
	3.00	41.37	0.40	2.00	3.56	5.08	6.57	8.03	9.45	10.85	12.21
	3.50	34.23	0.34	1.69	3.01	4.31	5.58	6.83	8.06	9.28	10.44
	4.00	29.21	0.30	1.46	2.61	3.74	4.86	5.95	7.03	8.09	9.13

EXAMPLES *ON PAGES A-382 TO A-397*

MORTGAGE YIELD TABLE

12¾% INTEREST

SHOWING DISCOUNT PERCENTAGES AT VARIOUS
YIELDS, MONTHLY PAYMENT RATES AND DUE DATES

12¾% INTEREST

DUE DATE	22%	23%	24%	25%	26%	27%	28%	29%	30%	31%	32%
1 YR.	8.24	9.08	9.91	10.74	11.56	12.37	13.17	13.96	14.75	15.52	16.29
	8.15	8.99	9.81	10.63	11.44	12.24	13.03	13.82	14.60	15.37	16.13
	8.04	8.86	9.68	10.48	11.28	12.07	12.86	13.63	14.40	15.16	15.91
	7.93	8.74	9.54	10.34	11.13	11.91	12.68	13.44	14.20	14.95	15.69
	7.81	8.61	9.41	10.19	10.97	11.74	12.50	13.25	14.00	14.74	15.47
	7.70	8.49	9.27	10.05	10.81	11.57	12.32	13.07	13.80	14.53	15.25
	7.59	8.37	9.14	9.90	10.66	11.40	12.14	12.88	13.60	14.32	15.03
	4.70	5.18	5.67	6.15	6.63	7.10	7.57	8.04	8.50	8.96	9.42
2 YRS.	14.86	16.31	17.73	19.13	20.50	21.84	23.15	24.44	25.71	26.95	28.17
	14.54	15.96	17.35	18.72	20.06	21.38	22.67	23.93	25.17	26.39	27.59
	14.11	15.49	16.85	18.18	19.48	20.76	22.02	23.25	24.46	25.64	26.81
	13.69	15.03	16.34	17.64	18.90	20.15	21.37	22.57	23.74	24.90	26.03
	13.26	14.56	15.84	17.09	18.32	19.53	20.72	21.88	23.03	24.15	25.25
	12.83	14.10	15.33	16.55	17.74	18.92	20.07	21.20	22.31	23.40	24.48
	12.41	13.63	14.83	16.01	17.17	18.30	19.42	20.52	21.60	22.66	23.70
	8.58	9.45	10.30	11.14	11.97	12.79	13.60	14.40	15.18	15.96	16.72
3 YRS.	20.18	22.07	23.90	25.67	27.41	29.09	30.72	32.31	33.86	35.37	36.83
	19.52	21.35	23.12	24.85	26.53	28.16	29.75	31.30	32.80	34.27	35.69
	18.64	20.39	22.09	23.75	25.36	26.93	28.46	29.94	31.39	32.80	34.18
	17.76	19.43	21.06	22.64	24.19	25.69	27.16	28.59	29.98	31.34	32.66
	16.88	18.47	20.03	21.54	23.02	24.46	25.87	27.24	28.57	29.88	31.15
	16.00	17.51	18.99	20.44	21.85	23.23	24.57	25.88	27.16	28.41	29.63
	15.11	16.56	17.96	19.34	20.68	21.99	23.28	24.53	25.75	26.95	28.11
	12.09	13.27	14.42	15.56	16.67	17.76	18.83	19.88	20.91	21.92	22.92
4 YRS.	24.47	26.65	28.76	30.79	32.75	34.64	36.46	38.22	39.92	41.56	43.15
	23.39	25.49	27.51	29.47	31.35	33.18	34.94	36.64	38.28	39.87	41.40
	21.96	23.94	25.85	27.71	29.50	31.23	32.90	34.52	36.09	37.61	39.07
	20.52	22.39	24.20	25.95	27.64	29.28	30.87	32.41	33.90	35.35	36.75
	19.09	20.84	22.54	24.18	25.78	27.33	28.84	30.29	31.71	33.08	34.42
	17.65	19.29	20.88	22.42	23.92	25.38	26.80	28.18	29.52	30.82	32.09
	16.22	17.74	19.22	20.66	22.07	23.43	24.77	26.06	27.33	28.56	29.76
	15.24	16.09	18.09	19.46	20.80	22.11	23.38	24.62	25.84	27.02	28.17
5 YRS.	27.91	30.30	32.59	34.78	36.88	38.89	40.82	42.66	44.43	46.13	47.75
	26.37	28.65	30.83	32.93	34.93	36.86	38.71	40.48	42.19	43.82	45.39
	24.83	26.45	28.49	30.45	32.34	34.16	35.90	37.58	39.19	40.75	42.25
	23.28	24.25	26.15	27.98	29.75	31.45	33.09	34.68	36.20	37.68	39.10
	20.23	22.05	23.81	25.51	27.16	28.75	30.28	31.77	33.21	34.60	35.95
	18.08	19.74	21.35	22.92	24.43	25.90	27.33	28.72	30.07	31.38	32.65
6 YRS.	30.68	33.21	35.61	37.90	40.07	42.14	44.12	45.99	47.78	49.49	51.11
	28.66	31.05	33.32	35.50	37.57	39.54	41.43	43.23	44.95	46.59	48.16
	25.96	28.17	30.28	32.30	34.23	36.08	37.85	39.55	41.18	42.74	44.23
	23.26	25.29	27.23	29.09	30.89	32.61	34.27	35.86	37.40	38.88	40.30
	20.63	22.47	24.25	25.97	27.62	29.23	30.77	32.27	33.71	35.11	36.46
7 YRS.	32.91	35.52	37.99	40.33	42.54	44.64	46.62	48.50	50.27	51.96	53.56
	30.39	32.84	35.18	37.35	39.49	41.48	43.37	45.18	46.84	48.52	50.07
	27.03	29.28	31.42	33.46	35.41	37.27	39.05	40.75	42.37	43.92	45.39
	22.92	24.91	26.83	28.66	30.43	32.13	33.76	35.34	36.85	38.31	39.71
8 YRS.	34.70	37.36	39.87	42.23	44.45	46.54	48.51	50.37	52.13	53.78	55.35
	31.68	34.18	36.53	38.76	40.87	42.86	44.75	46.53	48.23	49.83	51.36
	27.66	29.93	32.08	34.12	36.09	37.95	39.72	41.41	43.03	44.57	46.04
	24.98	27.09	29.11	31.05	32.90	34.67	36.37	38.00	39.56	41.06	42.49
9 YRS.	36.14	38.83	41.35	43.71	45.93	48.00	49.95	51.78	53.51	55.12	56.65
	32.63	35.15	37.51	39.74	41.84	43.83	45.70	47.47	49.14	50.72	52.22
	26.82	29.04	31.14	33.15	35.07	36.90	38.64	40.31	41.90	43.42	44.87
10 YRS.	37.29	40.00	42.52	44.87	47.07	49.12	51.04	52.84	54.53	56.11	57.60
	33.32	35.84	38.20	40.43	42.52	44.49	46.34	48.09	49.75	51.31	52.78
	28.48	30.77	32.95	35.01	36.98	38.84	40.62	42.31	43.92	45.45	46.92
UNTIL PAID	34.43	36.94	39.29	41.48	43.54	45.47	47.28	48.99	50.59	52.11	53.54
	28.02	30.30	32.45	34.51	36.46	38.31	40.08	41.77	43.37	44.90	46.37
	23.70	25.74	27.70	29.57	31.37	33.10	34.76	36.36	37.89	39.36	40.78
	20.57	22.41	24.18	25.89	27.55	29.15	30.69	32.18	33.62	35.02	36.37
	16.31	17.84	19.32	20.77	22.18	23.55	24.88	26.18	27.45	28.68	29.88
	13.54	14.84	16.12	17.36	18.58	19.78	20.95	22.09	23.21	24.30	25.37
	11.60	12.73	13.85	14.94	16.02	17.07	18.11	19.12	20.12	21.10	22.07
	10.15	11.16	12.15	13.13	14.09	15.03	15.96	16.88	17.78	18.66	19.54

EXAMPLES *ON PAGES A-382 TO A-397*

MORTGAGE YIELD TABLE
SHOWING DISCOUNT PERCENTAGES AT VARIOUS
YIELDS, MONTHLY PAYMENT RATES AND DUE DATES

DUE DATE	PAY'T RATE %	BAL REMAIN %	14%	15%	16%	17%	18%	19%	20%	21%	22%
			YIELD PERCENTAGES								
1 YR.	1.08	100.00	0.93	1.85	2.76	3.65	4.54	5.43	6.30	7.16	8.01
	1.25	97.88	0.92	1.83	2.73	3.62	4.50	5.38	6.24	7.09	7.94
	1.50	94.69	0.91	1.80	2.69	3.57	4.44	5.30	6.15	7.00	7.83
	1.75	91.51	0.89	1.78	2.65	3.52	4.38	5.23	6.07	6.90	7.72
	2.00	88.32	0.88	1.75	2.62	3.47	4.31	5.15	5.98	6.80	7.61
	2.25	85.13	0.87	1.73	2.58	3.42	4.25	5.08	5.89	6.70	7.50
	2.50	81.95	0.86	1.7C	2.54	3.37	4.19	5.00	5.81	6.60	7.39
	8.93	0.0	0.52	1.04	1.56	2.07	2.58	3.08	3.58	4.08	4.57
2 YRS.	1.08	100.00	1.74	3.44	5.11	6.74	8.35	9.92	11.46	12.97	14.46
	1.25	95.46	1.70	3.37	5.01	6.61	8.18	9.73	11.24	12.72	14.18
	1.50	88.65	1.65	3.27	4.86	6.41	7.94	9.44	10.91	12.35	13.76
	1.75	81.84	1.60	3.17	4.71	6.22	7.70	9.15	10.58	11.98	13.35
	2.00	75.03	1.55	3.07	4.56	6.02	7.45	8.86	10.24	11.60	12.93
	2.25	68.22	1.50	2.96	4.41	5.82	7.21	8.57	9.91	11.23	12.52
	2.50	61.41	1.44	2.86	4.26	5.62	6.97	8.29	9.58	10.85	12.10
	4.75	0.0	0.98	1.95	2.90	3.84	4.77	5.69	6.59	7.48	8.36
3 YRS.	1.08	100.00	2.44	4.81	7.11	9.35	11.53	13.64	15.70	17.70	19.64
	1.25	92.71	2.36	4.66	6.90	9.07	11.18	13.23	15.23	17.18	19.07
	1.50	81.77	2.25	4.44	6.57	8.65	10.66	12.63	14.54	16.40	18.20
	1.75	70.84	2.14	4.22	6.25	8.23	10.15	12.02	13.84	15.62	17.34
	2.00	59.90	2.03	4.00	5.93	7.80	9.63	11.41	13.15	14.84	16.48
	2.25	48.97	1.92	3.78	5.61	7.38	9.11	10.80	12.45	14.06	15.62
	2.50	38.03	1.80	3.56	5.28	6.96	8.60	10.20	11.75	13.28	14.76
	3.37	0.0	1.42	2.80	4.16	5.49	6.80	8.08	9.34	10.57	11.77
4 YRS.	1.08	100.00	3.05	5.99	8.82	11.55	14.18	16.72	19.17	21.53	23.80
	1.25	89.58	2.92	5.74	8.46	11.08	13.61	16.05	18.41	20.68	22.87
	1.50	73.95	2.73	5.37	7.91	10.37	12.75	15.04	17.26	19.40	21.47
	1.75	58.32	2.54	4.99	7.37	9.67	11.89	14.04	16.11	18.13	20.07
	2.00	42.69	2.35	4.62	6.82	8.96	11.03	13.03	14.97	16.85	18.67
	2.25	27.06	2.16	4.25	6.28	8.25	10.16	12.02	13.82	15.57	17.27
	2.50	11.43	1.97	3.88	5.74	7.54	9.30	11.01	12.68	14.30	15.87
	2.68	0.0	1.83	3.60	5.34	7.03	8.67	10.28	11.84	13.36	14.85
5 YRS.	1.08	100.00	3.58	7.01	10.28	13.41	16.41	19.27	22.02	24.64	27.16
	1.25	86.02	3.39	6.64	9.74	12.72	15.57	18.30	20.91	23.42	25.82
	1.50	65.04	3.10	6.08	8.94	11.68	14.31	16.83	19.26	21.59	23.82
	1.75	44.07	2.82	5.53	8.13	10.64	13.05	15.37	17.60	19.75	21.82
	2.00	23.10	2.53	4.97	7.32	9.59	11.79	13.90	15.94	17.92	19.82
	2.28	0.0	2.21	4.36	6.44	8.45	10.40	12.29	14.12	15.90	17.62
6 YRS.	1.08	1C0.00	4.04	7.88	11.53	14.98	18.27	21.39	24.35	27.17	29.85
	1.25	81.96	3.78	7.37	10.79	14.04	17.14	20.08	22.88	25.55	28.09
	1.50	54.91	3.38	6.61	9.69	12.63	15.44	18.11	20.67	23.12	25.46
	1.75	27.86	2.99	5.85	8.59	11.22	13.74	16.15	18.47	20.69	22.82
	2.01	0.0	2.58	5.06	7.46	9.76	11.99	14.13	16.19	18.19	20.11
7 YRS.	1.08	100.00	4.45	8.64	12.59	16.31	19.82	23.14	26.27	29.22	32.02
	1.25	77.35	4.10	7.98	11.64	15.10	18.38	21.48	24.41	27.19	29.82
	1.50	43.38	3.58	6.99	10.22	13.29	16.21	18.99	21.63	24.14	26.54
	1.82	0.0	2.92	5.73	8.41	1C.98	13.45	15.81	18.08	20.25	22.34
8 YRS.	1.08	1C0.00	4.80	9.29	13.49	17.43	21.13	24.59	27.84	30.89	33.76
	1.25	72.10	4.36	8.47	12.32	15.95	19.36	22.57	25.59	28.44	31.13
	1.50	36.25	3.72	7.23	10.56	13.72	16.70	19.54	22.22	24.77	27.20
	1.68	0.0	3.25	6.34	9.29	12.10	14.78	17.34	19.79	22.12	24.35
9 YRS.	1.08	100.00	5.10	9.85	14.27	18.38	22.21	25.79	29.13	32.25	35.16
	1.25	66.13	4.58	8.86	12.86	16.60	20.11	23.40	26.49	29.39	32.11
	1.58	0.0	3.55	6.92	10.11	13.14	16.01	18.74	21.34	23.80	26.15
10 YRS.	1.08	100.00	5.37	1C.33	14.92	19.18	23.12	26.78	30.18	33.34	36.29
	1.25	59.33	4.74	9.16	13.27	17.11	20.69	24.03	27.16	30.08	32.82
	1.49	0.0	3.84	7.45	10.87	14.09	17.13	20.01	22.74	25.32	27.76
		MONTHS									
UNTIL PAID	1.25	187.00	5.10	9.80	14.13	18.12	21.82	25.24	28.41	31.36	34.10
	1.50	118.88	3.81	7.40	10.80	14.00	17.03	19.90	22.61	25.18	27.62
	1.75	89.57	3.08	6.02	8.83	11.51	14.08	16.54	18.89	21.14	23.30
	2.00	72.40	2.59	5.09	7.49	9.81	12.04	14.19	16.26	18.26	20.19
	2.50	52.71	1.98	3.91	5.78	7.60	9.37	11.09	12.76	14.39	15.97
	3.00	41.58	1.61	3.18	4.72	6.22	7.69	9.13	10.53	11.90	13.24
	3.50	34.37	1.36	2.69	4.00	5.28	6.53	7.77	8.98	10.17	11.33
	4.00	29.31	1.18	2.33	3.47	4.59	5.69	6.77	7.84	8.88	9.91

EXAMPLES *ON PAGES A-382 TO A-397*

DUE DATE	23%	24%	25%	26%	27%	28%	29%	30%	31%	32%	33%
					YIELD PERCENTAGES						
1 YR.	8.86	9.69	10.52	11.34	12.15	12.95	13.75	14.53	15.31	16.08	16.84
	8.78	9.61	10.43	11.24	12.04	12.84	13.62	14.40	15.17	15.93	16.69
	8.66	9.47	10.28	11.08	11.88	12.66	13.44	14.21	14.97	15.72	16.46
	8.54	9.34	10.14	10.93	11.71	12.49	13.25	14.01	14.76	15.50	16.24
	8.41	9.21	10.00	10.78	11.55	12.31	13.07	13.81	14.55	15.29	16.01
	8.29	9.08	9.85	10.62	11.38	12.13	12.88	13.62	14.35	15.07	15.79
	8.17	8.94	9.71	10.47	11.22	11.96	12.69	13.42	14.14	14.85	15.56
	5.06	5.54	6.03	6.50	6.98	7.45	7.92	8.38	8.84	9.30	9.75
2 YRS.	15.91	17.34	18.74	20.11	21.45	22.77	24.07	25.34	26.58	27.80	29.00
	15.61	17.01	18.38	19.73	21.05	22.35	23.62	24.87	26.09	27.29	28.47
	15.15	16.51	17.85	19.16	20.45	21.71	22.95	24.16	25.35	26.52	27.67
	14.70	16.02	17.32	18.59	19.84	21.07	22.27	23.45	24.61	25.75	26.87
	14.24	15.53	16.79	18.02	19.24	20.43	21.60	22.75	23.88	24.98	26.07
	13.79	15.03	16.25	17.45	18.63	19.79	20.93	22.04	23.14	24.22	25.27
	13.33	14.54	15.72	16.88	18.03	19.15	20.25	21.34	22.40	23.45	24.48
	9.23	10.08	10.92	11.75	12.58	13.38	14.18	14.97	15.75	16.52	17.27
3 YRS.	21.53	23.36	25.15	26.89	28.58	30.22	31.82	33.37	34.88	36.35	37.78
	20.90	22.69	24.43	26.12	27.77	29.37	30.93	32.44	33.92	35.35	36.75
	19.97	21.68	23.35	24.97	26.55	28.09	29.59	31.05	32.47	33.85	35.20
	19.03	20.67	22.27	23.82	25.34	26.81	28.25	29.66	31.02	32.35	33.65
	18.09	19.66	21.18	22.67	24.12	25.54	26.92	28.26	29.57	30.85	32.10
	17.15	18.65	20.10	21.52	22.91	24.26	25.58	26.87	28.13	29.35	30.55
	16.22	17.63	19.02	20.37	21.69	22.98	24.24	25.48	26.68	27.85	29.00
	12.96	14.12	15.26	16.37	17.47	18.54	19.60	20.63	21.64	22.64	23.62
4 YRS.	26.00	28.12	30.16	32.13	34.03	35.87	37.64	39.35	40.99	42.59	44.12
	24.99	27.03	29.01	30.91	32.75	34.53	36.24	37.90	39.50	41.05	42.55
	23.47	25.41	27.28	29.08	30.83	32.52	34.16	35.74	37.27	38.75	40.18
	21.96	23.78	25.55	27.25	28.91	30.51	32.07	33.57	35.03	36.44	37.81
	20.44	22.15	23.82	25.43	26.99	28.51	29.98	31.41	32.79	34.14	35.44
	18.92	20.53	22.08	23.60	25.07	26.50	27.89	29.24	30.55	31.83	33.07
	17.41	18.90	20.35	21.77	23.15	24.49	25.80	27.07	28.32	29.53	30.71
	16.30	17.71	19.09	20.43	21.75	23.02	24.27	25.49	26.68	27.84	28.97
5 YRS.	29.56	31.86	34.07	36.18	38.21	40.15	42.01	43.79	45.50	47.13	48.70
	28.12	30.33	32.45	34.48	36.43	38.30	40.09	41.81	43.47	45.05	46.58
	25.97	28.03	30.02	31.93	33.76	35.52	37.22	38.85	40.42	41.94	43.39
	23.82	25.74	27.59	29.37	31.09	32.75	34.35	35.89	37.38	38.82	40.21
	21.66	23.44	25.16	26.82	28.42	29.98	31.48	32.93	34.34	35.70	37.02
	19.29	20.91	22.48	24.01	25.49	26.92	28.32	29.67	30.99	32.27	33.51
6 YRS.	32.40	34.82	37.12	39.32	41.40	43.39	45.29	47.09	48.81	50.45	52.01
	30.51	32.82	35.02	37.12	39.12	41.03	42.86	44.60	46.26	47.85	49.37
	27.69	29.83	31.87	33.83	35.70	37.50	39.21	40.86	42.44	43.95	45.40
	24.87	26.83	28.72	30.54	32.28	33.96	35.57	37.12	38.62	40.05	41.44
	21.96	23.75	25.48	27.15	28.76	30.31	31.82	33.27	34.68	36.04	37.35
7 YRS.	34.65	37.15	39.51	41.74	43.85	45.85	47.75	49.55	51.25	52.87	54.40
	32.32	34.69	36.93	39.06	41.08	43.00	44.83	46.56	48.21	49.78	51.28
	28.82	30.99	33.06	35.04	36.93	38.73	40.45	42.09	43.66	45.16	46.60
	24.35	26.28	28.13	29.91	31.62	33.27	34.85	36.38	37.84	39.26	40.62
8 YRS.	36.45	38.99	41.37	43.61	45.73	47.72	49.60	51.37	53.05	54.63	56.12
	33.67	36.07	38.33	40.47	42.49	44.40	46.22	47.93	49.56	51.11	52.57
	29.50	31.69	33.77	35.75	37.62	39.43	41.15	42.78	44.34	45.83	47.25
	26.48	28.52	30.47	32.34	34.12	35.84	37.48	39.05	40.56	42.01	43.40
9 YRS.	37.88	40.43	42.82	45.06	47.16	49.13	50.99	52.73	54.37	55.91	57.37
	34.67	37.07	39.34	41.47	43.49	45.39	47.18	48.88	50.48	52.00	53.44
	28.33	30.51	32.54	34.47	36.32	38.08	39.76	41.36	42.90	44.37	45.77
10 YRS.	39.02	41.58	43.96	46.18	48.26	50.21	52.03	53.74	55.34	56.85	58.27
	35.39	37.79	40.06	42.18	44.18	46.07	47.84	49.52	51.10	52.60	54.01
	30.08	32.28	34.37	36.35	38.23	40.03	41.74	43.36	44.91	46.39	47.80
UNTIL PAID	36.66	39.04	41.27	43.36	45.31	47.15	48.87	50.49	52.02	53.47	54.83
	29.93	32.12	34.21	36.18	38.07	39.86	41.56	43.19	44.74	46.21	47.62
	25.37	27.35	29.25	31.07	32.82	34.50	36.12	37.67	39.16	40.59	41.97
	22.05	23.84	25.57	27.25	28.86	30.42	31.93	33.39	34.79	36.16	37.47
	17.51	19.01	20.47	21.89	23.27	24.62	25.93	27.21	28.45	29.66	30.85
	14.56	15.84	17.10	18.33	19.53	20.70	21.86	22.98	24.08	25.16	26.22
	12.48	13.60	14.70	15.78	16.84	17.88	18.91	19.91	20.90	21.87	22.82
	10.93	11.93	12.91	13.87	14.82	15.76	16.68	17.58	18.47	19.35	20.21

EXAMPLES *ON PAGES A-382 TO A-397*

MORTGAGE YIELD TABLE
SHOWING DISCOUNT PERCENTAGES AT VARIOUS
YIELDS, MONTHLY PAYMENT RATES AND DUE DATES

DUE DATE	PAY'T RATE %	BAL REMAIN %	YIELD PERCENTAGES								
			14%	15%	16%	17%	18%	19%	20%	21%	22%
1 YR.	1.10	100.00	0.70	1.62	2.53	3.43	4.32	5.20	6.07	6.94	7.79
	1.25	98.14	0.69	1.60	2.51	3.40	4.28	5.16	6.02	6.88	7.73
	1.50	94.95	0.68	1.58	2.47	3.35	4.22	5.09	5.96	6.81	7.62
	1.75	91.76	0.67	1.56	2.44	3.30	4.16	5.01	5.86	6.69	7.52
	2.00	88.57	0.66	1.54	2.40	3.26	4.10	4.94	5.77	6.59	7.41
	2.25	85.38	0.65	1.51	2.37	3.21	4.04	4.87	5.69	6.50	7.30
	2.50	82.19	0.64	1.49	2.33	3.16	3.98	4.80	5.61	6.40	7.19
	8.94	0.0	0.39	0.91	1.43	1.94	2.45	2.95	3.45	3.95	4.44
2 YRS.	1.10	100.00	1.30	3.01	4.68	6.32	7.93	9.51	11.05	12.57	14.06
	1.25	96.02	1.28	2.96	4.60	6.21	7.79	9.34	10.87	12.36	13.82
	1.50	89.19	1.24	2.87	4.46	6.03	7.56	9.07	10.54	11.99	13.42
	1.75	82.36	1.20	2.78	4.32	5.84	7.33	8.79	10.22	11.63	13.01
	2.00	75.54	1.16	2.69	4.19	5.65	7.10	8.51	9.90	11.27	12.61
	2.25	68.71	1.12	2.60	4.05	5.47	6.87	8.24	9.58	10.90	12.20
	2.50	61.88	1.09	2.51	3.91	5.29	6.64	7.96	9.26	10.54	11.80
	4.77	0.0	0.74	1.71	2.66	3.61	4.54	5.45	6.36	7.25	8.13
3 YRS.	1.10	100.00	1.83	4.21	6.52	8.77	10.95	13.07	15.14	17.14	19.09
	1.25	93.60	1.78	4.09	6.35	8.53	10.66	12.73	14.74	16.70	18.60
	1.50	82.62	1.70	3.90	6.05	8.14	10.17	12.15	14.07	15.94	17.77
	1.75	71.64	1.61	3.71	5.75	7.74	9.68	11.56	13.40	15.19	16.93
	2.00	60.66	1.53	3.52	5.46	7.35	9.19	10.98	12.73	14.43	16.09
	2.25	49.68	1.44	3.33	5.16	6.95	8.69	10.40	12.05	13.67	15.25
	2.50	38.71	1.36	3.13	4.86	6.55	8.20	9.81	11.38	12.92	14.41
	3.38	0.0	1.06	2.45	3.82	5.16	6.47	7.75	9.01	10.25	11.46
4 YRS.	1.10	100.00	2.29	5.24	8.09	10.83	13.48	16.03	18.48	20.86	23.14
	1.25	90.83	2.20	5.05	7.79	10.44	13.00	15.46	17.84	20.13	22.35
	1.50	75.12	2.06	4.72	7.29	9.78	12.18	14.49	16.73	18.89	20.98
	1.75	59.41	1.92	4.40	6.79	9.11	11.35	13.52	15.62	17.65	19.62
	2.00	43.69	1.77	4.07	6.29	8.45	10.53	12.55	14.51	16.41	18.25
	2.25	27.98	1.63	3.74	5.79	7.78	9.71	11.59	13.40	15.17	16.89
	2.50	12.27	1.48	3.41	5.29	7.12	8.89	10.62	12.30	13.93	15.52
	2.70	0.0	1.37	3.16	4.90	6.60	8.25	9.86	11.43	12.96	14.46
5 YRS.	1.10	100.00	2.69	6.13	9.42	12.57	15.59	18.47	21.23	23.87	26.40
	1.25	87.68	2.56	5.85	8.99	12.00	14.89	17.65	20.30	22.83	25.26
	1.50	66.57	2.34	5.36	8.25	11.02	13.68	16.24	18.69	21.05	23.31
	1.75	45.45	2.13	4.87	7.51	10.04	12.48	14.83	17.09	19.26	21.36
	2.00	24.34	1.91	4.38	6.76	9.06	11.28	13.42	15.48	17.48	19.40
	2.29	0.0	1.66	3.82	5.91	7.93	9.89	11.79	13.64	15.42	17.15
6 YRS.	1.10	100.00	3.03	6.90	10.56	14.05	17.36	20.50	23.48	26.32	29.02
	1.25	84.09	2.86	6.51	9.97	13.27	16.41	19.39	22.24	24.94	27.52
	1.50	56.81	2.56	5.84	8.96	11.94	14.79	17.50	20.10	22.57	24.94
	1.75	29.53	2.26	5.17	7.95	10.61	13.16	15.61	17.96	20.21	22.37
	2.02	0.0	1.94	4.44	6.85	9.17	11.41	13.56	15.64	17.65	19.58
7 YRS.	1.10	100.00	3.34	7.56	11.54	15.29	18.83	22.18	25.33	28.31	31.13
	1.25	79.99	3.11	7.05	10.77	14.30	17.63	20.78	23.76	26.58	29.25
	1.50	45.68	2.72	6.18	9.47	12.59	15.55	18.37	21.06	23.61	26.04
	1.83	0.0	2.20	5.02	7.72	10.31	12.80	15.18	17.46	19.66	21.76
8 YRS.	1.10	100.00	3.60	8.13	12.37	16.34	20.07	23.56	26.85	29.93	32.82
	1.25	75.31	3.31	7.49	11.42	15.11	18.59	21.86	24.94	27.84	30.57
	1.50	32.97	2.82	6.41	9.80	13.01	16.05	18.93	21.67	24.26	26.72
	1.65	0.0	2.44	5.56	8.53	11.37	14.07	16.65	19.12	21.47	23.72
9 YRS.	1.10	100.00	3.83	8.62	13.08	17.23	21.10	24.72	28.09	31.24	34.18
	1.25	69.97	3.48	7.85	11.94	15.76	19.34	22.70	25.84	28.80	31.57
	1.59	0.0	2.67	6.07	9.29	12.34	15.24	18.00	20.62	23.11	25.47
10 YRS.	1.10	100.00	4.03	9.04	13.68	17.98	21.97	25.67	29.11	32.30	35.28
	1.25	63.88	3.61	8.14	12.35	16.27	19.93	23.34	26.53	29.51	32.30
	1.51	0.0	2.88	6.54	9.98	13.24	16.31	19.22	21.97	24.58	27.05
		MONTHS									
UNTIL PAID	1.25	195.65	3.93	8.80	13.27	17.39	21.19	24.70	27.96	30.97	33.77
	1.50	121.32	2.91	6.59	10.06	13.33	16.43	19.35	22.12	24.73	27.21
	1.75	90.78	2.34	5.33	8.19	10.92	13.53	16.03	18.42	20.70	22.89
	2.00	73.14	1.96	4.50	6.93	9.28	11.54	13.72	15.82	17.85	19.80
	2.50	53.07	1.50	3.44	5.33	7.17	8.96	10.70	12.39	14.03	15.63
	3.00	41.79	1.21	2.80	4.35	5.86	7.35	8.79	10.21	11.59	12.94
	3.50	34.52	1.02	2.36	3.68	4.97	6.24	7.48	8.70	9.89	11.07
	4.00	29.42	0.89	2.05	3.19	4.32	5.43	6.52	7.59	8.64	9.68

EXAMPLES ON PAGES A-382 TO A-397

DUE DATE	YIELD PERCENTAGES										
	23%	24%	25%	26%	27%	28%	29%	30%	31%	32%	33%
1 YR.	8.64	9.47	10.30	11.12	11.93	12.74	13.53	14.32	15.10	15.87	16.63
	8.57	9.40	10.22	11.03	11.84	12.64	13.42	14.21	14.98	15.74	16.50
	8.45	9.27	10.08	10.88	11.68	12.46	13.24	14.01	14.77	15.53	16.28
	8.33	9.14	9.94	10.73	11.52	12.29	13.06	13.82	14.57	15.32	16.05
	8.21	9.01	9.80	10.58	11.35	12.12	12.88	13.63	14.37	15.10	15.83
	8.10	8.88	9.66	10.43	11.19	11.95	12.69	13.43	14.16	14.89	15.61
	7.98	8.75	9.52	10.28	11.03	11.77	12.51	13.24	13.96	14.68	15.38
	4.93	5.42	5.90	6.38	6.86	7.33	7.80	8.26	8.72	9.18	9.63
2 YRS.	15.51	16.94	18.35	19.72	21.07	22.39	23.69	24.96	26.21	27.44	28.64
	15.25	16.66	18.04	19.40	20.72	22.03	23.30	24.56	25.79	26.99	28.18
	14.81	16.18	17.52	18.84	20.13	21.40	22.64	23.86	25.06	26.23	27.39
	14.36	15.69	17.00	18.28	19.53	20.77	21.98	23.16	24.33	25.47	26.60
	13.92	15.21	16.48	17.72	18.94	20.14	21.31	22.47	23.60	24.72	25.81
	13.48	14.73	15.95	17.16	18.34	19.51	20.65	21.77	22.87	23.96	25.02
	13.03	14.24	15.43	16.60	17.75	18.88	19.99	21.08	22.14	23.20	24.23
	9.00	9.86	10.70	11.54	12.36	13.17	13.97	14.76	15.54	16.31	17.07
3 YRS.	20.99	22.83	24.63	26.37	28.07	29.72	31.32	32.88	34.40	35.87	37.31
	20.46	22.26	24.01	25.71	27.37	28.98	30.55	32.08	33.56	35.01	36.42
	19.54	21.27	22.95	24.58	26.17	27.72	29.23	30.70	32.13	33.53	34.88
	18.62	20.27	21.88	23.45	24.98	26.46	27.91	29.33	30.70	32.04	33.35
	17.71	19.28	20.82	22.32	23.78	25.21	26.59	27.95	29.27	30.56	31.82
	16.79	18.29	19.76	21.19	22.59	23.95	25.28	26.57	27.84	29.08	30.28
	15.88	17.30	18.70	20.06	21.39	22.69	23.96	25.20	26.41	27.59	28.75
	12.65	13.81	14.95	16.07	17.17	18.25	19.31	20.35	21.36	22.36	23.34
4 YRS.	25.35	27.48	29.53	31.51	33.42	35.27	37.05	38.77	40.43	42.03	43.57
	24.48	26.55	28.54	30.46	32.32	34.11	35.85	37.52	39.13	40.70	42.21
	23.00	24.95	26.84	28.66	30.43	32.13	33.78	35.38	36.92	38.41	39.86
	21.52	23.36	25.14	26.87	28.54	30.15	31.72	33.24	34.71	36.13	37.51
	20.04	21.76	23.44	25.07	26.64	28.17	29.66	31.10	32.50	33.85	35.17
	18.55	20.17	21.74	23.27	24.75	26.19	27.60	28.96	30.28	31.57	32.82
	17.07	18.58	20.04	21.47	22.86	24.21	25.53	26.82	28.07	29.29	30.48
	15.91	17.33	18.72	20.07	21.38	22.67	23.92	25.15	26.34	27.51	28.65
5 YRS.	28.82	31.14	33.36	35.49	37.52	39.48	41.35	43.14	44.86	46.51	48.10
	27.59	29.82	31.97	34.02	35.99	37.88	39.69	41.44	43.11	44.71	46.25
	25.48	27.57	29.58	31.51	33.36	35.14	36.86	38.51	40.09	41.62	43.09
	23.37	25.32	27.19	28.99	30.73	32.40	34.02	35.58	37.08	38.53	39.93
	21.26	23.06	24.80	26.48	28.10	29.67	31.18	32.65	34.07	35.45	36.78
	18.83	20.46	22.04	23.58	25.07	26.51	27.91	29.28	30.60	31.89	33.13
6 YRS.	31.59	34.03	36.35	38.56	40.67	42.67	44.58	46.40	48.13	49.78	51.36
	29.97	32.31	34.54	36.67	38.70	40.63	42.48	44.24	45.92	47.53	49.07
	27.21	29.37	31.44	33.42	35.32	37.13	38.87	40.54	42.14	43.67	45.13
	24.44	26.43	28.34	30.18	31.94	33.64	35.27	36.84	38.35	39.80	41.20
	21.45	23.25	24.99	26.67	28.29	29.86	31.37	32.83	34.25	35.62	36.94
7 YRS.	33.79	36.30	38.68	40.94	43.07	45.09	47.00	48.82	50.54	52.17	53.72
	31.79	34.19	36.46	38.62	40.68	42.62	44.47	46.23	47.90	49.50	51.01
	28.35	30.56	32.66	34.66	36.57	38.40	40.14	41.80	43.39	44.91	46.36
	23.78	25.72	27.59	29.38	31.11	32.77	34.36	35.90	37.38	38.80	40.18
8 YRS.	35.54	38.10	40.51	42.77	44.91	46.92	48.82	50.62	52.31	53.91	55.42
	33.15	35.59	37.89	40.06	42.11	44.05	45.89	47.64	49.29	50.85	52.34
	29.06	31.28	33.39	35.40	37.31	39.13	40.87	42.53	44.10	45.61	47.05
	25.87	27.92	29.89	31.77	33.58	35.30	36.96	38.54	40.07	41.53	42.93
9 YRS.	36.94	39.51	41.93	44.20	46.32	48.32	50.19	51.95	53.61	55.18	56.65
	34.17	36.62	38.92	41.10	43.14	45.07	46.89	48.61	50.24	51.78	53.24
	27.73	29.88	31.92	33.87	35.73	37.51	39.21	40.83	42.38	43.86	45.28
10 YRS.	38.05	40.63	43.04	45.29	47.40	49.37	51.22	52.95	54.58	56.10	57.54
	34.92	37.37	39.67	41.84	43.87	45.78	47.58	49.28	50.89	52.40	53.83
	29.39	31.61	33.72	35.72	37.62	39.43	41.16	42.80	44.37	45.86	47.28
UNTIL PAID	36.37	38.80	41.06	43.18	45.16	47.02	48.76	50.40	51.94	53.40	54.77
	29.56	31.79	33.90	35.91	37.82	39.63	41.36	43.00	44.57	46.06	47.48
	24.99	27.00	28.92	30.77	32.54	34.24	35.87	37.44	38.95	40.39	41.79
	21.68	23.50	25.25	26.94	28.57	30.15	31.67	33.14	34.57	35.94	37.27
	17.19	18.70	20.17	21.61	23.00	24.36	25.68	26.97	28.22	29.44	30.63
	14.27	15.56	16.83	18.07	19.28	20.46	21.62	22.75	23.86	24.95	26.01
	12.22	13.35	14.46	15.54	16.61	17.66	18.69	19.70	20.69	21.67	22.62
	10.70	11.70	12.69	13.66	14.61	15.55	16.48	17.39	18.28	19.16	20.03

EXAMPLES *ON PAGES A-382 TO A-397*

DUE DATE	PAY'T RATE %	BAL REMAIN %	YIELD PERCENTAGES								
			14%	15%	16%	17%	18%	19%	20%	21%	22%
1 YR.	1.13	100.00	0.46	1.38	2.30	3.20	4.09	4.97	5.85	6.71	7.57
	1.25	98.40	0.46	1.38	2.28	3.18	4.06	4.94	5.81	6.67	7.52
	1.50	95.21	0.45	1.36	2.25	3.13	4.01	4.87	5.73	6.57	7.41
	1.75	92.02	0.45	1.34	2.22	3.09	3.95	4.80	5.65	6.48	7.31
	2.00	88.83	0.44	1.32	2.18	3.04	3.89	4.73	5.57	6.39	7.21
	2.25	85.63	0.44	1.30	2.15	3.00	3.84	4.66	5.49	6.30	7.10
	2.50	82.44	0.43	1.28	2.12	2.95	3.78	4.60	5.40	6.21	7.C0
	8.96	0.0	0.26	0.78	1.30	1.81	2.32	2.83	3.33	3.83	4.32
2 YRS.	1.13	100.00	0.87	2.58	4.25	5.90	7.51	9.09	10.64	12.16	13.65
	1.25	96.58	0.85	2.54	4.19	5.81	7.40	8.96	10.49	11.99	13.46
	1.50	89.73	0.83	2.46	4.07	5.64	7.18	8.69	10.18	11.64	13.06
	1.75	82.89	0.80	2.39	3.94	5.47	6.96	8.43	9.87	11.28	12.67
	2.00	76.05	0.78	2.31	3.82	5.29	6.74	8.16	9.56	10.93	12.28
	2.25	69.20	0.75	2.23	3.69	5.12	6.52	7.90	9.25	10.58	11.88
	2.50	62.36	0.73	2.16	3.57	4.95	6.30	7.63	8.94	10.23	11.49
	4.78	0.0	0.49	1.46	2.42	3.37	4.30	5.22	6.13	7.02	7.91
3 YRS.	1.13	100.00	1.22	3.61	5.93	8.18	10.37	12.50	14.58	16.59	18.55
	1.25	94.49	1.19	3.52	5.79	8.00	10.14	12.24	14.25	16.22	18.14
	1.50	83.47	1.13	3.36	5.52	7.62	9.67	11.66	13.60	15.49	17.32
	1.75	72.45	1.08	3.19	5.25	7.25	9.20	11.10	12.95	14.75	16.51
	2.00	61.43	1.02	3.03	4.98	6.88	8.74	10.54	12.30	14.02	15.69
	2.25	50.41	0.97	2.86	4.71	6.51	8.27	9.98	11.66	13.29	14.87
	2.50	39.39	0.91	2.70	4.44	6.14	7.80	9.42	11.01	12.55	14.06
	3.39	0.0	0.71	2.11	3.48	4.82	6.13	7.42	8.69	9.93	11.14
4 YRS.	1.13	100.00	1.52	4.49	7.35	10.11	12.77	15.33	17.80	20.18	22.48
	1.25	92.10	1.48	4.35	7.12	9.80	12.38	14.86	17.26	19.58	21.82
	1.50	76.31	1.38	4.07	6.67	9.17	11.60	13.93	16.19	18.38	20.49
	1.75	60.51	1.28	3.79	6.21	8.55	10.81	13.00	15.12	17.17	19.16
	2.00	44.71	1.19	3.51	5.75	7.93	10.03	12.08	14.05	15.97	17.83
	2.25	28.92	1.09	3.23	5.30	7.30	9.25	11.15	12.98	14.76	16.50
	2.50	13.12	1.00	2.94	4.84	6.68	8.47	10.22	11.91	13.56	15.16
	2.71	0.0	0.92	2.71	4.46	6.16	7.83	9.44	11.02	12.56	14.06
5 YRS.	1.13	100.00	1.79	5.25	8.57	11.74	14.77	17.67	20.44	23.10	25.65
	1.25	89.37	1.72	5.04	8.23	11.28	14.20	16.99	19.67	22.24	24.69
	1.50	68.11	1.57	4.62	7.55	10.36	13.05	15.64	18.12	20.50	22.79
	1.75	46.85	1.43	4.20	6.87	9.44	11.91	14.28	16.57	18.77	20.89
	2.00	25.59	1.28	3.78	6.20	8.52	10.76	12.93	15.02	17.03	18.98
	2.30	0.0	1.11	3.28	5.38	7.41	9.39	11.30	13.15	14.95	16.69
6 YRS.	1.13	100.00	2.02	5.91	9.60	13.11	16.44	19.61	22.61	25.47	28.19
	1.25	86.25	1.92	5.62	9.14	12.49	15.67	18.70	21.58	24.32	26.93
	1.50	58.74	1.72	5.05	8.21	11.24	14.12	16.88	19.51	22.02	24.42
	1.75	31.24	1.52	4.47	7.29	9.99	12.58	15.06	17.44	19.72	21.91
	2.03	0.0	1.29	3.81	6.24	8.57	10.82	12.99	15.09	17.11	19.05
7 YRS.	1.13	100.00	2.22	6.48	10.49	14.27	17.84	21.21	24.39	27.40	30.24
	1.25	82.67	2.09	6.10	9.89	13.47	16.86	20.06	23.09	25.95	28.67
	1.50	48.02	1.83	5.35	8.69	11.87	14.88	17.75	20.47	23.06	25.53
	1.85	0.0	1.47	4.31	7.03	9.64	12.15	14.55	16.85	19.06	21.18
8 YRS.	1.13	100.00	2.40	6.97	11.24	15.25	19.01	22.54	25.89	28.96	31.88
	1.25	78.59	2.23	6.50	10.50	14.26	17.80	21.13	24.27	27.22	30.00
	1.50	35.77	1.91	5.56	9.02	12.29	15.38	18.31	21.09	23.73	26.23
	1.71	0.0	1.63	4.78	7.78	10.63	13.36	15.96	18.45	20.82	23.09
9 YRS.	1.13	100.00	2.55	7.39	11.89	16.08	19.99	23.64	27.05	30.23	33.21
	1.25	73.92	2.35	6.82	10.99	14.90	18.55	21.97	25.18	28.19	31.01
	1.60	0.0	1.78	5.21	8.46	11.55	14.47	17.25	19.89	22.41	24.80
10 YRS.	1.13	100.00	2.68	7.75	12.44	16.78	20.81	24.55	28.03	31.26	34.27
	1.25	68.57	2.45	7.08	11.39	15.40	19.14	22.63	25.88	28.93	31.77
	1.52	0.0	1.93	5.62	9.10	12.38	15.49	18.43	21.21	23.84	26.33
		MONTHS									
UNTIL PAID	1.25	205.82	2.70	7.75	12.39	16.84	20.56	24.17	27.50	30.58	33.44
	1.50	123.92	1.97	5.74	9.29	12.64	15.80	18.79	21.61	24.27	26.79
	1.75	92.04	1.58	4.63	7.54	10.32	12.97	15.51	17.94	20.26	22.48
	2.00	73.90	1.32	3.89	6.37	8.75	11.04	13.25	15.38	17.43	19.40
	2.50	53.44	1.01	2.97	4.88	6.74	8.55	10.30	12.01	13.67	15.29
	3.00	42.01	0.81	2.41	3.98	5.50	7.00	8.46	9.89	11.28	12.64
	3.50	34.66	0.69	2.04	3.36	4.66	5.94	7.19	8.41	9.62	10.80
	4.00	29.52	0.59	1.76	2.92	4.05	5.16	6.26	7.35	8.39	9.44

EXAMPLES *ON PAGES A-382 TO A-397*

DUE DATE	23%	24%	25%	26%	27%	28%	29%	30%	31%	32%	33%
1 YR.	8.42	9.25	10.08	10.90	11.72	12.52	13.32	14.10	14.88	15.66	16.42
	8.36	9.19	10.01	10.83	11.64	12.44	13.23	14.01	14.78	15.55	16.31
	8.24	9.06	9.88	10.68	11.48	12.27	13.05	13.82	14.58	15.34	16.09
	8.13	8.94	9.74	10.53	11.32	12.10	12.87	13.63	14.38	15.13	15.87
	8.01	8.81	9.60	10.38	11.16	11.93	12.69	13.44	14.18	14.92	15.65
	7.90	8.68	9.46	10.24	11.00	11.76	12.51	13.25	13.98	14.71	15.43
	7.78	8.56	9.33	10.09	10.84	11.59	12.33	13.06	13.78	14.50	15.21
	4.81	5.30	5.79	6.26	6.73	7.21	7.67	8.14	8.60	9.06	9.51
2 YRS.	15.12	16.55	17.96	19.34	20.69	22.01	23.32	24.59	25.84	27.07	28.28
	14.90	16.31	17.70	19.06	20.40	21.70	22.99	24.25	25.48	26.70	27.89
	14.46	15.84	17.19	18.51	19.81	21.08	22.33	23.56	24.76	25.95	27.10
	14.03	15.37	16.68	17.96	19.23	20.46	21.68	22.87	24.05	25.19	26.32
	13.60	14.89	16.17	17.41	18.64	19.84	21.03	22.19	23.33	24.44	25.54
	13.16	14.42	15.65	16.87	18.06	19.22	20.37	21.50	22.61	23.69	24.76
	12.73	13.95	15.14	16.32	17.47	18.60	19.72	20.81	21.89	22.94	23.98
	8.78	9.63	10.48	11.32	12.14	12.96	13.76	14.55	15.33	16.10	16.86
3 YRS.	20.45	22.30	24.10	25.85	27.56	29.21	30.82	32.39	33.91	35.40	36.84
	20.00	21.82	23.58	25.30	26.97	28.59	30.17	31.71	33.21	34.66	36.08
	19.11	20.85	22.54	24.19	25.79	27.35	28.87	30.35	31.79	33.20	34.56
	18.21	19.88	21.51	23.08	24.61	26.11	27.57	28.99	30.38	31.73	33.04
	17.32	18.91	20.46	21.97	23.44	24.87	26.27	27.63	28.96	30.26	31.53
	16.43	17.94	19.41	20.85	22.26	23.63	24.97	26.28	27.55	28.80	30.01
	15.53	16.97	18.37	19.74	21.08	22.39	23.67	24.92	26.14	27.33	28.49
	12.33	13.50	14.65	15.77	16.88	17.96	19.02	20.06	21.08	22.09	23.07
4 YRS.	24.70	26.84	28.90	30.89	32.82	34.67	36.46	38.19	39.86	41.47	43.02
	23.97	26.06	28.07	30.01	31.88	33.69	35.44	37.13	38.76	40.34	41.86
	22.53	24.50	26.40	28.24	30.02	31.74	33.41	35.02	36.57	38.08	39.54
	21.08	22.93	24.73	26.47	28.16	29.79	31.37	32.90	34.38	35.82	37.21
	19.63	21.37	23.06	24.70	26.29	27.84	29.33	30.79	32.20	33.56	34.89
	18.18	19.81	21.39	22.93	24.43	25.88	27.30	28.67	30.01	31.31	32.57
	16.73	18.25	19.73	21.17	22.57	23.93	25.26	26.56	27.82	29.05	30.24
	15.52	16.95	18.34	19.70	21.02	22.31	23.57	24.80	26.00	27.17	28.32
5 YRS.	28.08	30.42	32.65	34.79	36.84	38.81	40.69	42.50	44.23	45.89	47.49
	27.05	29.31	31.48	33.55	35.55	37.46	39.29	41.05	42.74	44.36	45.92
	24.99	27.10	29.13	31.08	32.93	34.76	36.49	38.16	39.76	41.30	42.79
	22.92	24.89	26.78	28.60	30.36	32.05	33.69	35.26	36.78	38.25	39.66
	20.86	22.68	24.43	26.13	27.77	29.35	30.88	32.37	33.80	35.19	36.53
	18.38	20.02	21.61	23.15	24.65	26.10	27.51	28.88	30.21	31.50	32.76
6 YRS.	30.78	33.24	35.58	37.80	39.93	41.95	43.87	45.71	47.45	49.12	50.71
	29.42	31.79	34.05	36.21	38.26	40.22	42.09	43.87	45.58	47.21	48.76
	26.71	28.91	31.00	33.01	34.93	36.77	38.53	40.21	41.83	43.38	44.86
	24.01	26.02	27.96	29.81	31.60	33.32	34.96	36.55	38.08	39.55	40.96
	20.93	22.74	24.49	26.19	27.82	29.40	30.92	32.39	33.82	35.20	36.53
7 YRS.	32.92	35.46	37.86	40.13	42.29	44.33	46.26	48.09	49.83	51.47	53.04
	31.24	33.68	35.99	38.18	40.26	42.24	44.11	45.89	47.59	49.20	50.73
	27.88	30.11	32.24	34.27	36.21	38.06	39.82	41.50	43.11	44.65	46.12
	23.21	25.17	27.05	28.86	30.59	32.27	33.87	35.42	36.91	38.35	39.73
8 YRS.	34.63	37.21	39.65	41.94	44.09	46.13	48.05	49.86	51.57	53.19	54.72
	32.62	35.10	37.43	39.64	41.72	43.70	45.56	47.33	49.00	50.59	52.10
	28.61	30.86	33.01	35.04	36.98	38.83	40.59	42.26	43.86	45.39	46.84
	25.25	27.33	29.31	31.21	33.02	34.76	36.43	38.03	39.57	41.04	42.46
9 YRS.	35.99	38.60	41.04	43.33	45.48	47.50	49.39	51.18	52.86	54.44	55.94
	33.66	36.16	38.50	40.71	42.78	44.74	46.59	48.34	49.99	51.55	53.03
	27.07	29.24	31.30	33.27	35.15	36.94	38.65	40.29	41.85	43.35	44.78
10 YRS.	37.07	39.69	42.13	44.41	46.54	48.53	50.40	52.16	53.81	55.36	56.81
	34.44	36.94	39.28	41.48	43.54	45.49	47.32	49.04	50.67	52.20	53.65
	28.69	30.94	33.06	35.09	37.01	38.84	40.58	42.24	43.82	45.32	46.76
UNTIL PAID	36.09	38.56	40.86	43.01	45.01	46.89	48.66	50.31	51.87	53.33	54.72
	29.18	31.45	33.59	35.63	37.56	39.40	41.15	42.81	44.40	45.91	47.35
	24.60	26.64	28.59	30.46	32.26	33.98	35.63	37.21	38.74	40.20	41.60
	21.31	23.15	24.92	26.63	28.28	29.88	31.41	32.90	34.34	35.73	37.07
	16.86	18.38	19.87	21.32	22.72	24.09	25.43	26.73	27.99	29.22	30.42
	13.98	15.28	16.55	17.80	19.02	20.21	21.38	22.52	23.64	24.74	25.81
	11.96	13.09	14.21	15.30	16.38	17.43	18.47	19.49	20.49	21.47	22.43
	10.46	11.47	12.46	13.44	14.40	15.34	16.27	17.19	18.09	18.98	19.85

EXAMPLES *ON PAGES A-382 TO A-397*

MORTGAGE YIELD TABLE
SHOWING DISCOUNT PERCENTAGES AT VARIOUS
YIELDS, MONTHLY PAYMENT RATES AND DUE DATES

DUE DATE	PAY'T RATE %	BAL REMAIN %	YIELD PERCENTAGES								
			14%	15%	16%	17%	18%	19%	20%	21%	22%
1 YR.	1.15	100.00	0.23	1.15	2.07	2.97	3.86	4.75	5.62	6.49	7.35
	1.25	98.67	0.23	1.15	2.05	2.95	3.84	4.72	5.59	6.45	7.30
	1.50	95.47	0.23	1.13	2.03	2.91	3.79	4.65	5.51	6.36	7.20
	1.75	92.28	0.22	1.12	2.00	2.87	3.73	4.59	5.44	6.27	7.10
	2.00	89.08	0.22	1.10	1.97	2.83	3.68	4.52	5.36	6.18	7.00
	2.25	85.88	0.22	1.08	1.94	2.79	3.63	4.46	5.28	6.09	6.90
	2.50	82.69	0.21	1.07	1.91	2.75	3.57	4.39	5.20	6.01	6.80
	8.97	0.0	0.13	0.65	1.17	1.68	2.19	2.70	3.20	3.70	4.19
2 YRS.	1.15	100.00	0.43	2.15	3.83	5.48	7.09	8.68	10.23	11.76	13.25
	1.25	97.14	0.43	2.12	3.78	5.41	7.01	8.57	10.11	11.62	13.09
	1.50	90.28	0.42	2.06	3.67	5.25	6.80	8.32	9.81	11.27	12.71
	1.75	83.42	0.40	1.99	3.56	5.09	6.59	8.07	9.51	10.93	12.33
	2.00	76.56	0.39	1.93	3.44	4.93	6.38	7.81	9.22	10.59	11.95
	2.25	69.70	0.38	1.87	3.33	4.77	6.18	7.56	8.92	10.25	11.56
	2.50	62.83	0.36	1.80	3.22	4.61	5.97	7.31	8.62	9.91	11.18
	4.79	0.0	0.25	1.22	2.18	3.13	4.06	4.99	5.90	6.79	7.68
3 YRS.	1.15	100.00	0.61	3.00	5.33	7.60	9.80	11.94	14.01	16.04	18.00
	1.25	95.39	0.60	2.95	5.23	7.45	9.61	11.71	13.75	15.74	17.67
	1.50	84.33	0.57	2.81	4.99	7.11	9.17	11.18	13.13	15.03	16.88
	1.75	73.26	0.54	2.67	4.74	6.76	8.73	10.64	12.50	14.32	16.08
	2.00	62.20	0.51	2.53	4.50	6.42	8.29	10.10	11.88	13.61	15.29
	2.25	51.14	0.49	2.40	4.26	6.07	7.84	9.57	11.25	12.89	14.50
	2.50	40.08	0.46	2.26	4.01	5.73	7.40	9.03	10.63	12.18	13.70
	3.41	0.0	0.35	1.76	3.13	4.48	5.80	7.09	8.36	9.61	10.83
4 YRS.	1.15	100.00	0.76	3.74	6.62	9.39	12.06	14.63	17.12	19.51	21.82
	1.25	93.38	0.74	3.64	6.44	9.14	11.75	14.26	16.69	19.02	21.28
	1.50	77.50	0.69	3.41	6.03	8.56	11.01	13.37	15.65	17.86	19.99
	1.75	61.62	0.65	3.17	5.62	7.98	10.27	12.48	14.62	16.69	18.69
	2.00	45.74	0.60	2.94	5.21	7.40	9.53	11.59	13.59	15.52	17.40
	2.25	29.86	0.55	2.70	4.79	6.82	8.79	10.70	12.55	14.35	16.10
	2.50	13.98	0.50	2.47	4.38	6.24	8.05	9.81	11.52	13.19	14.80
	2.72	0.0	0.46	2.26	4.02	5.73	7.40	9.03	10.61	12.16	13.66
5 YRS.	1.15	100.00	0.90	4.38	7.71	10.90	13.95	16.87	19.66	22.33	24.89
	1.25	91.08	0.87	4.23	7.46	10.54	13.50	16.32	19.03	21.63	24.12
	1.50	69.68	0.79	3.88	6.84	9.68	12.41	15.03	17.54	19.95	22.26
	1.75	48.28	0.72	3.53	6.23	8.83	11.33	13.73	16.04	18.27	20.41
	2.00	26.87	0.65	3.18	5.62	7.97	10.24	12.43	14.54	16.58	18.55
	2.31	0.0	0.56	2.74	4.85	6.90	8.88	10.80	12.66	14.47	16.22
6 YRS.	1.15	100.00	1.01	4.93	8.64	12.17	15.53	18.72	21.74	24.62	27.36
	1.25	88.44	0.97	4.72	8.29	11.69	14.92	17.99	20.91	23.69	26.34
	1.50	60.71	0.87	4.24	7.46	10.52	13.45	16.24	18.91	21.46	23.89
	1.75	32.97	0.77	3.76	6.62	9.36	11.98	14.50	16.91	19.22	21.44
	2.05	0.0	0.65	3.18	5.62	7.97	10.24	12.43	14.53	16.56	18.52
7 YRS.	1.15	100.00	1.11	5.40	9.44	13.25	16.85	20.25	23.45	26.48	29.35
	1.25	85.42	1.06	5.14	8.99	12.63	16.07	19.32	22.40	25.31	28.07
	1.50	50.42	0.93	4.51	7.90	11.13	14.19	17.11	19.87	22.50	25.01
	1.86	0.0	0.74	3.60	6.34	8.97	11.49	13.91	16.23	18.46	20.59
8 YRS.	1.15	100.00	1.20	5.80	10.12	14.16	17.96	21.52	24.86	28.00	30.94
	1.25	81.95	1.13	5.48	9.56	13.39	17.00	20.39	23.58	26.58	29.41
	1.50	38.63	0.96	4.69	8.21	11.54	14.70	17.68	20.51	23.19	25.73
	1.72	0.0	0.82	3.99	7.01	9.89	12.64	15.27	17.77	20.16	22.45
9 YRS.	1.15	100.00	1.28	6.15	10.70	14.93	18.88	22.57	26.01	29.22	32.23
	1.25	77.97	1.19	5.76	10.02	14.01	17.74	21.23	24.50	27.57	30.44
	1.62	0.0	0.89	4.35	7.63	10.74	13.70	16.50	19.17	21.70	24.12
10 YRS.	1.15	100.00	1.34	6.46	11.19	15.58	19.66	23.44	26.95	30.22	33.06
	1.25	73.42	1.24	5.99	10.40	14.50	18.33	21.89	25.22	28.32	31.23
	1.54	0.0	0.97	4.69	8.21	11.53	14.66	17.63	20.43	23.09	25.61
		MONTHS									
UNTIL PAID	1.25	218.10	1.39	6.66	11.47	15.87	19.91	23.62	27.04	30.20	33.11
	1.50	126.69	1.00	4.87	8.51	11.93	15.16	18.21	21.09	23.80	26.37
	1.75	93.35	0.80	3.91	6.87	9.70	12.40	14.98	17.44	19.80	22.06
	2.00	74.67	0.67	3.28	5.79	8.20	10.53	12.77	14.92	17.00	19.00
	2.50	53.81	0.51	2.50	4.43	6.31	8.13	9.91	11.63	13.31	14.94
	3.00	42.23	0.41	2.02	3.60	5.14	6.65	8.12	9.56	10.96	12.34
	3.50	34.81	0.34	1.70	3.04	4.35	5.63	6.89	8.13	9.34	10.53
	4.00	29.62	0.30	1.48	2.63	3.77	4.89	6.00	7.08	8.14	9.19

EXAMPLES *ON PAGES A-382 TO A-397*

DUE DATE	23%	24%	25%	26%	27%	28%	29%	30%	31%	32%	33%
					YIELD PERCENTAGES						
1 YR	8.19	9.03	9.86	10.69	11.50	12.30	13.10	13.89	14.67	15.44	16.21
	8.15	8.98	9.81	10.63	11.43	12.24	13.03	13.81	14.59	15.36	16.12
	8.03	8.86	9.67	10.48	11.28	12.07	12.85	13.62	14.39	15.15	15.90
	7.92	8.73	9.54	10.33	11.12	11.90	12.67	13.44	14.19	14.94	15.68
	7.81	8.61	9.40	10.19	10.97	11.73	12.50	13.25	14.00	14.73	15.46
	7.70	8.49	9.27	10.04	10.81	11.57	12.32	13.06	13.80	14.53	15.25
	7.59	8.36	9.14	9.90	10.65	11.40	12.14	12.87	13.60	14.31	15.03
	4.68	5.17	5.65	6.13	6.61	7.08	7.55	8.02	8.48	8.94	9.40
2 YRS.	14.72	16.16	17.57	18.95	20.30	21.63	22.94	24.22	25.47	26.71	27.91
	14.54	15.96	17.36	18.72	20.07	21.38	22.67	23.94	25.18	26.40	27.59
	14.12	15.50	16.86	18.19	19.49	20.77	22.03	23.26	24.47	25.66	26.82
	13.70	15.04	16.35	17.65	18.92	20.16	21.38	22.58	23.76	24.91	26.05
	13.27	14.57	15.85	17.11	18.34	19.55	20.74	21.90	23.05	24.17	25.28
	12.85	14.11	15.35	16.57	17.77	18.94	20.09	21.23	22.34	23.43	24.50
	12.43	13.65	14.85	16.03	17.19	18.33	19.45	20.55	21.63	22.69	23.73
	8.55	9.41	10.26	11.10	11.93	12.74	13.55	14.34	15.12	15.90	16.66
3 YRS.	19.91	21.77	23.58	25.34	27.05	28.71	30.33	31.90	33.43	34.92	36.37
	19.55	21.38	23.15	24.88	26.56	28.20	29.79	31.34	32.85	34.31	35.74
	18.68	20.43	22.13	23.79	25.41	26.98	28.51	30.00	31.45	32.86	34.24
	17.80	19.48	21.11	22.70	24.25	25.76	27.23	28.66	30.05	31.41	32.74
	16.93	18.53	20.09	21.61	23.09	24.53	25.94	27.32	28.66	29.98	31.24
	16.06	17.58	19.07	20.52	21.93	23.31	24.66	25.98	27.26	28.51	29.73
	15.18	16.63	18.05	19.43	20.77	22.09	23.38	24.63	25.86	27.06	28.23
	12.02	13.19	14.34	15.47	16.58	17.67	18.73	19.78	20.80	21.81	22.79
4 YRS.	24.05	26.20	28.27	30.28	32.21	34.07	35.87	37.61	39.29	40.91	42.47
	23.46	25.56	27.59	29.55	31.44	33.27	35.03	36.74	38.39	39.98	41.51
	22.04	24.03	25.95	27.81	29.61	31.35	33.03	34.65	36.22	37.74	39.21
	20.63	22.50	24.32	26.07	27.77	29.42	31.02	32.56	34.06	35.51	36.91
	19.21	20.97	22.66	24.33	25.94	27.50	29.01	30.47	31.89	33.27	34.61
	17.80	19.44	21.04	22.60	24.11	25.57	27.00	28.38	29.73	31.04	32.31
	16.38	17.91	19.40	20.86	22.27	23.65	24.99	26.29	27.56	28.80	30.01
	15.13	16.57	17.96	19.33	20.66	21.95	23.22	24.45	25.66	26.84	27.98
5 YRS.	27.34	29.69	31.94	34.10	36.16	38.14	40.04	41.86	43.60	45.27	46.88
	26.50	28.79	30.98	33.08	35.10	37.03	38.88	40.66	42.37	44.01	45.59
	24.49	26.62	28.67	30.65	32.54	34.36	36.11	37.80	39.42	40.98	42.48
	22.47	24.45	26.37	28.21	29.99	31.70	33.35	34.94	36.47	37.95	39.38
	20.45	22.29	24.06	25.77	27.43	29.03	30.58	32.08	33.52	34.92	36.28
	17.92	19.57	21.17	22.72	24.22	25.68	27.10	28.48	29.82	31.12	32.38
6 YRS.	29.97	32.44	34.80	37.05	39.19	41.22	43.16	45.01	46.78	48.46	50.06
	28.86	31.27	33.55	35.74	37.82	39.80	41.70	43.50	45.23	46.88	48.45
	26.21	28.43	30.56	32.59	34.53	36.39	38.17	39.88	41.51	43.08	44.58
	23.56	25.60	27.56	29.44	31.25	32.99	34.65	36.26	37.80	39.28	40.71
	20.41	22.24	24.00	25.70	27.35	28.93	30.47	31.95	33.38	34.77	36.11
7 YRS.	32.06	34.62	37.04	39.33	41.50	43.56	45.51	47.36	49.11	50.78	52.36
	30.68	33.16	35.50	37.73	39.84	41.84	43.74	45.55	47.27	48.90	50.45
	27.39	29.66	31.82	33.88	35.84	37.71	39.50	41.20	42.83	44.39	45.88
	22.64	24.61	26.51	28.33	30.08	31.76	33.38	34.94	36.44	37.89	39.28
8 YRS.	33.72	36.33	38.78	41.10	43.28	45.33	47.27	49.11	50.84	52.47	54.02
	32.08	34.59	36.97	39.21	41.33	43.33	45.22	47.01	48.71	50.32	51.85
	28.14	30.43	32.61	34.68	36.64	38.52	40.30	42.00	43.61	45.16	46.63
	24.63	26.72	28.72	30.64	32.47	34.23	35.91	37.52	39.07	40.55	41.98
9 YRS.	35.04	37.68	40.15	42.48	44.64	46.68	48.60	50.40	52.10	53.71	55.22
	33.14	35.68	38.06	40.30	42.42	44.41	46.28	48.06	49.73	51.31	52.81
	26.41	28.60	30.68	32.67	34.56	36.37	38.10	39.75	41.33	42.83	44.28
10 YRS.	36.10	38.74	41.21	43.52	45.68	47.70	49.59	51.37	53.04	54.61	56.08
	33.94	36.49	38.87	41.11	43.21	45.18	47.04	48.79	50.44	52.00	53.47
	27.99	30.26	32.41	34.45	36.39	38.24	40.00	41.67	43.27	44.79	46.24
UNTIL PAID	35.82	38.33	40.67	42.85	44.88	46.78	48.56	50.23	51.80	53.28	54.67
	28.80	31.10	33.28	35.35	37.31	39.17	40.94	42.63	44.23	45.75	47.21
	24.21	26.28	28.26	30.15	31.97	33.68	35.38	36.98	38.52	40.00	41.42
	20.93	22.79	24.59	26.32	27.99	29.60	31.15	32.66	34.11	35.51	36.86
	16.52	18.06	19.56	21.02	22.44	23.82	25.17	26.48	27.75	29.00	30.21
	13.68	14.99	16.28	17.54	18.76	19.97	21.14	22.29	23.42	24.52	25.60
	11.69	12.94	13.96	15.06	16.15	17.21	18.25	19.27	20.28	21.26	22.23
	10.22	11.24	12.24	13.22	14.18	15.13	16.07	16.99	17.90	18.79	19.66

EXAMPLES *ON PAGES A-382 TO A-397*

14%
INTEREST

MORTGAGE YIELD TABLE
SHOWING DISCOUNT PERCENTAGES AT VARIOUS
YIELDS, MONTHLY PAYMENT RATES AND DUE DATES

14%
INTEREST

DUE DATE	PAY'T RATE %	BAL REMAIN %	YIELD PERCENTAGES								
			15%	16%	17%	18%	19%	20%	21%	22%	23%
1 YR.	1.17	100.00	0.92	1.84	2.74	3.64	4.52	5.40	6.26	7.12	7.97
	1.25	98.93	0.92	1.83	2.73	3.62	4.50	5.37	6.24	7.09	7.94
	1.50	95.73	0.91	1.80	2.69	3.57	4.44	5.30	6.15	6.99	7.83
	1.75	92.53	0.89	1.78	2.65	3.52	4.38	5.22	6.06	6.89	7.72
	2.00	89.33	0.88	1.75	2.61	3.47	4.31	5.15	5.98	6.80	7.61
	2.25	86.13	0.87	1.73	2.58	3.42	4.25	5.08	5.89	6.70	7.50
	2.50	82.93	0.85	1.70	2.54	3.37	4.19	5.00	5.81	6.60	7.39
	8.98	0.0	0.52	1.04	1.55	2.06	2.57	3.07	3.57	4.07	4.56
2 YRS.	1.17	100.00	1.72	3.40	5.06	6.68	8.27	9.82	11.35	12.85	14.32
	1.25	97.71	1.70	3.37	5.01	6.61	8.19	9.73	11.24	12.73	14.18
	1.50	90.83	1.65	3.27	4.86	6.42	7.94	9.44	10.91	12.36	13.77
	1.75	83.95	1.60	3.17	4.71	6.22	7.70	9.16	10.58	11.98	13.36
	2.00	77.07	1.55	3.07	4.56	6.02	7.46	8.87	10.25	11.61	12.95
	2.25	70.19	1.50	2.97	4.41	5.83	7.22	8.58	9.92	11.24	12.53
	2.50	63.32	1.45	2.87	4.26	5.63	6.98	8.30	9.60	10.87	12.12
	4.80	0.0	0.98	1.94	2.89	3.83	4.75	5.66	6.56	7.45	8.33
3 YRS.	1.17	100.00	2.40	4.74	7.01	9.22	11.37	13.45	15.48	17.46	19.37
	1.25	96.30	2.37	4.67	6.91	9.08	11.20	13.25	15.25	17.20	19.09
	1.50	85.19	2.26	4.45	6.59	8.66	10.68	12.65	14.57	16.43	18.24
	1.75	74.09	2.15	4.23	6.27	8.25	10.17	12.05	13.88	15.66	17.39
	2.00	62.98	2.03	4.02	5.95	7.83	9.66	11.45	13.19	14.88	16.54
	2.25	51.88	1.92	3.80	5.63	7.41	9.15	10.85	12.50	14.11	15.69
	2.50	40.77	1.81	3.58	5.31	6.99	8.64	10.24	11.81	13.34	14.83
	3.42	0.0	1.41	2.79	4.14	5.46	6.76	8.03	9.28	10.51	11.71
4 YRS.	1.17	100.00	2.99	5.88	8.66	11.35	13.94	16.43	18.84	21.16	23.40
	1.25	94.68	2.93	5.76	8.48	11.11	13.65	16.10	18.46	20.74	22.94
	1.50	78.71	2.74	5.39	7.95	10.42	12.80	15.10	17.33	19.48	21.56
	1.75	62.75	2.55	5.02	7.41	9.72	11.95	14.11	16.20	18.22	20.17
	2.00	46.79	2.37	4.66	6.87	9.02	11.10	13.12	15.07	16.96	18.79
	2.25	30.82	2.18	4.29	6.34	8.32	10.25	12.12	13.94	15.70	17.41
	2.50	14.86	1.99	3.92	5.80	7.62	9.40	11.13	12.81	14.44	16.03
	2.73	0.0	1.81	3.58	5.30	6.97	8.61	10.20	11.75	13.27	14.74
5 YRS.	1.17	100.00	3.50	6.85	10.06	13.13	16.06	18.87	21.56	24.14	26.60
	1.25	92.82	3.41	6.67	9.79	12.78	15.65	18.39	21.02	23.54	25.95
	1.50	71.27	3.13	6.12	9.00	11.76	14.41	16.95	19.39	21.73	23.98
	1.75	45.72	2.84	5.58	8.21	10.73	13.17	15.50	17.76	19.92	22.01
	2.00	28.17	2.56	5.03	7.41	9.71	11.92	14.06	16.12	18.11	20.04
	2.33	0.0	2.19	4.32	6.37	8.37	10.30	12.18	13.99	15.75	17.46
6 YRS.	1.17	100.00	3.94	7.68	11.24	14.61	17.82	20.87	23.77	26.53	29.16
	1.25	90.68	3.81	7.43	10.88	14.15	17.27	20.23	23.05	25.74	28.29
	1.50	62.71	3.42	6.69	9.80	12.77	15.60	18.30	20.88	23.35	25.70
	1.75	34.74	3.03	5.94	8.72	11.38	13.93	16.37	18.71	20.96	23.11
	2.06	0.0	2.55	5.01	7.37	9.65	11.85	13.97	16.02	17.99	19.89
7 YRS.	1.17	100.00	4.32	8.39	12.23	15.86	19.28	22.52	25.57	28.46	31.19
	1.25	88.22	4.15	8.07	11.77	15.27	18.57	21.70	24.66	27.46	30.11
	1.50	52.87	3.64	7.10	10.38	13.49	16.45	19.26	21.93	24.47	26.89
	1.87	0.0	2.89	5.65	8.36	10.84	13.27	15.61	17.85	20.00	
8 YRS.	1.17	100.00	4.64	9.00	13.07	16.90	20.49	23.86	27.03	30.01	32.81
	1.25	85.39	4.43	8.59	12.50	16.17	19.63	22.87	25.93	28.81	31.52
	1.50	41.57	3.80	7.39	10.78	13.99	17.03	19.91	22.63	25.22	27.67
	1.74	0.0	3.20	6.25	9.15	11.92	14.57	17.09	19.51	21.81	24.01
9 YRS.	1.17	100.00	4.92	9.51	13.78	17.77	21.49	24.97	28.21	31.25	34.10
	1.25	82.14	4.67	9.03	13.10	16.90	20.47	23.80	26.93	29.86	32.60
	1.63	0.0	3.49	6.80	9.94	12.92	15.75	18.44	21.00	23.43	25.75
10 YRS.	1.17	100.00	5.17	9.95	14.38	18.50	22.32	25.87	29.18	32.25	35.12
	1.25	78.41	4.86	9.38	13.58	17.49	21.13	24.53	27.70	30.66	33.43
	1.55	0.0	3.76	7.31	10.66	13.83	16.82	19.66	22.34	24.88	27.29
		MONTHS									
UNTIL PAID	1.25	233.47	5.50	10.51	15.07	19.24	23.07	26.58	29.82	32.80	35.56
	1.50	129.67	3.97	7.69	11.20	14.51	17.62	20.55	23.32	25.94	28.41
	1.75	94.72	3.17	6.18	9.06	11.81	14.44	16.94	19.34	21.63	23.82
	2.00	75.48	2.65	5.20	7.65	10.01	12.28	14.46	16.57	18.62	20.55
	2.50	54.19	2.01	3.97	5.86	7.71	9.50	11.24	12.94	14.58	16.18
	3.00	42.46	1.63	3.22	4.77	6.29	7.77	9.22	10.64	12.03	13.38
	3.50	34.96	1.37	2.71	4.03	5.33	6.59	7.84	9.06	10.25	11.43
	4.00	29.73	1.19	2.35	3.50	4.62	5.73	6.82	7.89	8.95	9.99

EXAMPLES *ON PAGES A-382 TO A-397*

MORTGAGE YIELD TABLE
SHOWING DISCOUNT PERCENTAGES AT VARIOUS
YIELDS, MONTHLY PAYMENT RATES AND DUE DATES

DUE DATE	24%	25%	26%	27%	28%	29%	30%	31%	32%	33%	34%
					YIELD PERCENTAGES						
1 YR.	8.81	9.64	10.47	11.28	12.09	12.89	13.68	14.46	15.23	16.00	16.76
	8.77	9.60	10.42	11.23	12.03	12.83	13.62	14.39	15.16	15.93	16.68
	8.65	9.47	10.28	11.08	11.87	12.65	13.43	14.20	14.96	15.71	16.46
	8.53	9.34	10.14	10.92	11.71	12.48	13.25	14.00	14.75	15.50	16.23
	8.41	9.21	9.99	10.77	11.54	12.31	13.06	13.81	14.55	15.28	16.01
	8.29	9.07	9.85	10.62	11.38	12.13	12.88	13.61	14.34	15.07	15.78
	8.17	8.94	9.71	10.46	11.21	11.96	12.69	13.42	14.14	14.85	15.56
	5.05	5.53	6.01	6.49	6.96	7.43	7.90	8.36	8.82	9.28	9.73
2 YRS.	15.76	17.18	18.56	19.92	21.26	22.56	23.85	25.11	26.34	27.55	28.74
	15.61	17.01	18.39	19.73	21.06	22.35	23.62	24.87	26.10	27.30	28.48
	15.16	16.52	17.86	19.17	20.45	21.72	22.96	24.17	25.36	26.53	27.68
	14.71	16.03	17.33	18.60	19.85	21.08	22.29	23.47	24.63	25.77	26.89
	14.25	15.54	16.80	18.04	19.25	20.45	21.62	22.77	23.90	25.01	26.10
	13.80	15.05	16.27	17.47	18.65	19.81	20.95	22.07	23.17	24.24	25.30
	13.35	14.56	15.74	16.91	18.05	19.18	20.28	21.37	22.43	23.48	24.51
	9.19	10.04	10.88	11.71	12.53	13.33	14.13	14.91	15.69	16.45	17.21
3 YRS.	21.24	23.06	24.82	26.54	28.21	29.83	31.41	32.94	34.44	35.89	37.31
	20.93	22.72	24.46	26.16	27.80	29.41	30.97	32.48	33.96	35.40	36.80
	20.00	21.72	23.39	25.02	26.60	28.14	29.64	31.10	32.53	33.91	35.26
	19.08	20.72	22.32	23.88	25.40	26.88	28.32	29.72	31.09	32.43	33.73
	18.15	19.72	21.25	22.74	24.20	25.61	27.00	28.35	29.66	30.94	32.19
	17.22	18.72	20.18	21.60	22.99	24.35	25.67	26.97	28.23	29.46	30.66
	16.29	17.72	19.11	20.46	21.79	23.08	24.35	25.59	26.79	27.97	29.13
	12.89	14.04	15.17	16.28	17.37	18.44	19.49	20.52	21.53	22.52	23.49
4 YRS.	25.56	27.65	29.66	31.60	33.47	35.28	37.03	38.72	40.35	41.92	43.44
	25.06	27.11	29.09	31.00	32.84	34.62	36.34	38.00	39.61	41.16	42.66
	23.56	25.50	27.38	29.19	30.95	32.64	34.28	35.86	37.40	38.88	40.32
	22.07	23.90	25.67	27.39	29.05	30.66	32.22	33.73	35.19	36.60	37.98
	20.57	22.29	23.96	25.58	27.15	28.68	30.15	31.59	32.98	34.33	35.64
	19.07	20.69	22.25	23.78	25.26	26.69	28.09	29.45	30.77	32.05	33.30
	17.57	19.08	20.54	21.97	23.36	24.71	26.03	27.31	28.56	29.77	30.96
	16.18	17.58	18.95	20.29	21.59	22.86	24.11	25.32	26.50	27.65	28.78
5 YRS.	28.97	31.23	33.40	35.48	37.47	39.38	41.21	42.97	44.65	46.27	47.82
	28.26	30.48	32.60	34.64	36.59	38.47	40.27	42.00	43.65	45.24	46.77
	26.14	28.21	30.21	32.12	33.96	35.74	37.44	39.08	40.65	42.17	43.63
	24.01	25.95	27.81	29.61	31.34	33.00	34.61	36.16	37.65	39.10	40.49
	21.89	23.68	25.42	27.09	28.71	30.27	31.78	33.24	34.65	36.02	37.35
	19.12	20.73	22.28	23.80	25.27	26.70	28.08	29.43	30.73	32.00	33.24
6 YRS.	31.65	34.03	36.29	38.45	40.50	42.46	44.32	46.10	47.79	49.41	50.95
	30.73	33.05	35.26	37.37	39.38	41.30	43.13	44.87	46.54	48.13	49.65
	27.95	30.10	32.16	34.13	36.01	37.82	39.54	41.19	42.78	44.30	45.75
	25.18	27.16	29.06	30.89	32.65	34.34	35.96	37.52	39.02	40.46	41.85
	21.73	23.50	25.22	26.87	28.47	30.01	31.51	32.95	34.35	35.70	37.00
7 YRS.	33.77	36.22	38.53	40.72	42.80	44.76	46.63	48.40	50.08	51.68	53.20
	32.63	35.01	37.26	39.41	41.44	43.37	45.20	46.94	48.59	50.17	51.66
	29.19	31.38	33.47	35.46	37.36	39.17	40.90	42.54	44.12	45.63	47.07
	24.06	25.76	27.80	29.56	31.26	32.89	34.46	35.97	37.43	38.83	40.19
8 YRS.	35.44	37.92	40.26	42.46	44.54	46.50	48.35	50.10	51.75	53.32	54.80
	34.08	36.49	38.77	40.92	42.95	44.87	46.69	48.41	50.05	51.59	53.06
	29.99	32.20	34.30	36.30	38.20	40.00	41.72	43.36	44.92	46.41	47.84
	26.12	28.14	30.07	31.91	33.68	35.38	37.01	38.57	40.06	41.50	42.88
9 YRS.	36.76	39.25	41.60	43.79	45.86	47.80	49.63	51.35	52.97	54.50	55.95
	35.19	37.61	39.89	42.04	44.06	45.97	47.77	49.46	51.07	52.59	54.02
	27.95	30.05	32.06	33.97	35.80	37.54	39.20	40.80	42.32	43.78	45.17
10 YRS.	37.80	40.29	42.63	44.81	46.86	48.78	50.58	52.27	53.86	55.36	56.77
	36.02	38.45	40.73	42.86	44.87	46.76	48.53	50.21	51.76	53.27	54.68
	29.58	31.75	33.81	35.77	37.64	39.41	41.10	42.71	44.25	45.72	47.12
UNTIL PAID	38.11	40.49	42.69	44.75	46.67	48.47	50.16	51.74	53.23	54.63	55.95
	30.75	32.97	35.07	37.06	38.94	40.74	42.44	44.06	45.60	47.07	48.47
	25.91	27.92	29.84	31.68	33.44	35.13	36.75	38.31	39.80	41.24	42.62
	22.43	24.25	26.00	27.69	29.32	30.69	32.44	33.87	35.29	36.66	37.98
	17.74	19.25	20.73	22.16	23.55	24.91	26.23	27.52	28.77	29.99	31.18
	14.71	16.00	17.27	18.51	19.72	20.90	22.06	23.19	24.30	25.39	26.45
	12.58	13.71	14.82	15.91	16.98	18.03	19.06	20.07	21.06	22.03	22.99
	11.01	12.01	13.00	13.97	14.92	15.86	16.79	17.70	18.60	19.48	20.34

EXAMPLES *ON PAGES A-382 TO A-397*

DUE DATE	PAY'T RATE %	BAL REMAIN %	15%	16%	17%	18%	19%	20%	21%	22%	23%
1 YR.	1.19	100.00	0.69	1.61	2.51	3.41	4.30	5.17	6.04	6.90	7.75
	1.25	99.20	0.69	1.60	2.50	3.40	4.28	5.15	6.02	6.88	7.72
	1.50	96.00	0.68	1.58	2.47	3.35	4.22	5.08	5.94	6.78	7.62
	1.75	92.79	0.67	1.56	2.43	3.30	4.16	5.01	5.85	6.69	7.51
	2.00	89.59	0.66	1.53	2.40	3.26	4.10	4.94	5.77	6.59	7.41
	2.25	86.38	0.65	1.51	2.36	3.21	4.04	4.87	5.69	6.50	7.30
	2.50	83.18	0.64	1.49	2.33	3.16	3.98	4.80	5.60	6.40	7.19
	8.99	0.0	0.39	0.91	1.43	1.94	2.44	2.95	3.45	3.94	4.43
2 YRS.	1.19	100.00	1.29	2.98	4.64	6.26	7.85	9.41	10.95	12.45	13.92
	1.25	98.28	1.28	2.96	4.60	6.21	7.80	9.35	10.87	12.36	13.82
	1.50	91.38	1.24	2.87	4.46	6.03	7.57	9.07	10.55	12.00	13.42
	1.75	84.49	1.20	2.78	4.33	5.85	7.34	8.80	10.23	11.64	13.02
	2.00	77.59	1.16	2.69	4.19	5.66	7.11	8.52	9.91	11.28	12.62
	2.25	70.69	1.13	2.60	4.05	5.48	6.88	8.25	9.59	10.92	12.22
	2.50	63.80	1.09	2.52	3.92	5.29	6.65	7.97	9.28	10.56	11.81
	4.81	0.0	0.73	1.70	2.65	3.59	4.52	5.43	6.33	7.22	8.10
3 YRS.	1.19	100.00	1.80	4.15	6.43	8.64	10.80	12.89	14.93	16.91	18.84
	1.25	97.21	1.78	4.10	6.35	8.55	10.68	12.75	14.76	16.72	18.63
	1.50	86.06	1.70	3.91	6.06	8.15	10.19	12.17	14.10	15.97	17.80
	1.75	74.92	1.62	3.72	5.77	7.76	9.70	11.59	13.43	15.22	16.97
	2.00	63.77	1.53	3.53	5.47	7.37	9.22	11.01	12.77	14.48	16.14
	2.25	52.62	1.45	3.34	5.18	6.98	8.73	10.44	12.10	13.73	15.31
	2.50	41.47	1.37	3.15	4.89	6.58	8.24	9.86	11.44	12.98	14.48
	3.43	0.0	1.06	2.44	3.80	5.13	6.43	7.71	8.96	10.19	11.39
4 YRS.	1.19	100.00	2.25	5.15	7.94	10.64	13.24	15.75	18.17	20.50	22.75
	1.25	95.99	2.21	5.07	7.82	10.47	13.04	15.51	17.89	20.19	22.41
	1.50	75.94	2.07	4.74	7.32	9.82	12.23	14.55	16.80	18.97	21.06
	1.75	63.89	1.93	4.42	6.83	9.16	11.41	13.59	15.70	17.74	19.72
	2.00	47.84	1.78	4.10	6.34	8.50	10.60	12.64	14.61	16.52	18.37
	2.25	31.79	1.64	3.77	5.84	7.85	9.79	11.68	13.51	15.29	17.02
	2.50	15.74	1.50	3.45	5.35	7.19	8.98	10.73	12.42	14.07	15.67
	2.75	0.0	1.36	3.13	4.86	6.55	8.19	9.79	11.35	12.87	14.35
5 YRS.	1.19	100.00	2.63	6.00	9.22	12.31	15.26	18.09	20.79	23.38	25.87
	1.25	94.58	2.57	5.88	9.04	12.07	14.96	17.74	20.40	22.94	25.38
	1.50	72.88	2.36	5.40	8.31	11.10	13.78	16.35	18.82	21.19	23.46
	1.75	51.18	2.15	4.92	7.58	10.13	12.59	14.96	17.24	19.43	21.54
	2.00	29.49	1.94	4.44	6.85	9.17	11.41	13.57	15.66	17.67	19.61
	2.34	0.0	1.65	3.78	5.85	7.86	9.80	11.69	13.51	15.28	17.00
6 YRS.	1.19	100.00	2.96	6.72	10.30	13.70	16.93	20.00	22.93	25.70	28.35
	1.25	92.95	2.88	6.56	10.05	13.37	16.53	19.54	22.40	25.12	27.71
	1.50	64.75	2.59	5.90	9.06	12.07	14.94	17.68	20.30	22.80	25.18
	1.75	36.55	2.30	5.24	8.06	10.76	13.35	15.82	18.20	20.47	22.65
	2.07	0.0	1.92	4.39	6.77	9.07	11.28	13.41	15.47	17.46	19.37
7 YRS.	1.19	100.00	3.24	7.34	11.21	14.87	18.32	21.58	24.66	27.57	30.32
	1.25	91.08	3.14	7.13	10.89	14.45	17.81	20.99	24.00	26.84	29.53
	1.50	55.38	2.76	6.28	9.61	12.78	15.78	18.64	21.35	23.93	26.38
	1.89	0.0	2.17	4.95	7.62	10.18	12.63	14.99	17.24	19.41	21.49
8 YRS.	1.19	100.00	3.48	7.87	11.98	15.84	19.47	22.87	26.06	29.07	31.90
	1.25	88.92	3.36	7.61	11.59	15.33	18.85	22.15	25.26	28.19	30.95
	1.50	44.58	2.88	6.54	10.00	13.27	16.36	19.29	22.06	24.69	27.18
	1.75	0.0	2.40	5.48	8.41	11.20	13.87	16.41	18.84	21.17	23.39
9 YRS.	1.19	100.00	3.69	8.32	12.64	16.66	20.42	23.93	27.21	30.28	33.15
	1.25	86.43	3.55	8.00	12.16	16.05	19.68	23.08	26.27	29.25	32.05
	1.65	0.0	2.62	5.96	9.13	12.14	14.99	17.71	20.29	22.74	25.08
10 YRS.	1.19	100.00	3.87	8.71	13.19	17.34	21.20	24.79	28.13	31.25	34.15
	1.25	83.56	3.70	8.33	12.63	16.63	20.35	23.82	27.06	30.08	32.90
	1.57	0.0	2.83	6.41	9.80	12.99	16.02	18.88	21.59	24.15	26.59
		MONTHS									
UNTIL PAID	1.25	253.77	4.27	9.50	14.25	18.57	22.52	26.13	29.45	32.50	35.31
	1.50	132.88	3.03	6.86	10.45	13.83	17.01	20.01	22.83	25.50	28.02
	1.75	96.14	2.41	5.48	8.42	11.21	13.88	16.43	18.86	21.19	23.41
	2.00	76.31	2.01	4.60	7.08	9.48	11.78	14.00	16.13	18.18	20.16
	2.50	54.58	1.52	3.54	5.41	7.28	9.09	10.85	12.56	14.22	15.84
	3.00	42.69	1.23	2.83	4.40	5.93	7.43	8.89	10.32	11.72	13.08
	3.50	35.11	1.03	2.39	3.71	5.02	6.29	7.55	8.77	9.98	11.16
	4.00	29.84	0.89	2.07	3.22	4.35	5.47	6.56	7.64	8.70	9.75

EXAMPLES *ON PAGES A-382 TO A-397*

DUE DATE	24%	25%	26%	27%	28%	29%	30%	31%	32%	33%	34%
1 YR.	8.59	9.43	10.25	11.07	11.87	12.67	13.46	14.25	15.02	15.79	16.55
	8.56	9.39	10.21	11.03	11.83	12.63	13.42	14.20	14.97	15.73	16.49
	8.45	9.26	10.08	10.88	11.67	12.46	13.24	14.01	14.77	15.52	16.27
	8.33	9.14	9.94	10.73	11.51	12.29	13.05	13.81	14.57	15.31	16.05
	8.21	9.01	9.80	10.58	11.35	12.11	12.87	13.62	14.36	15.10	15.82
	8.09	8.88	9.66	10.43	11.19	11.94	12.69	13.43	14.16	14.89	15.60
	7.98	8.75	9.52	10.28	11.03	11.77	12.51	13.24	13.96	14.67	15.38
	4.92	5.41	5.89	6.37	6.84	7.31	7.78	8.24	8.70	9.16	9.61
2 YRS.	15.37	16.78	18.17	19.54	20.88	22.19	23.47	24.74	25.97	27.19	28.38
	15.26	16.66	18.05	19.40	20.73	22.03	23.31	24.56	25.79	27.00	28.18
	14.82	16.18	17.53	18.84	20.14	21.41	22.65	23.87	25.07	26.25	27.40
	14.37	15.70	17.01	18.29	19.55	20.78	21.99	23.18	24.35	25.49	26.62
	13.93	15.22	16.49	17.74	18.96	20.16	21.33	22.49	23.62	24.74	25.83
	13.49	14.74	15.97	17.18	18.37	19.53	20.67	21.80	22.90	23.98	25.05
	13.05	14.26	15.45	16.63	17.78	18.90	20.01	21.10	22.18	23.23	24.26
	8.97	9.82	10.66	11.49	12.31	13.12	13.92	14.70	15.48	16.25	17.00
3 YRS.	20.71	22.53	24.30	26.03	27.70	29.33	30.92	32.46	33.96	35.42	36.84
	20.48	22.29	24.04	25.75	27.41	29.02	30.59	32.12	33.61	35.05	36.46
	19.58	21.31	22.99	24.63	26.22	27.77	29.29	30.76	32.19	33.59	34.94
	18.67	20.32	21.94	23.51	25.04	26.53	27.98	29.39	30.77	32.12	33.43
	17.76	19.34	20.89	22.39	23.85	25.28	26.67	28.03	29.36	30.65	31.91
	16.86	18.36	19.83	21.27	22.67	24.03	25.37	26.67	27.94	29.18	30.39
	15.95	17.38	18.78	20.15	21.48	22.79	24.06	25.31	26.52	27.71	28.87
	12.58	13.73	14.87	15.99	17.08	18.15	19.20	20.24	21.25	22.24	23.22
4 YRS.	24.92	27.02	29.04	30.99	32.88	34.70	36.45	38.15	39.79	41.37	42.89
	24.56	26.62	28.62	30.55	32.41	34.21	35.94	37.62	39.24	40.80	42.32
	21.43	23.47	25.26	27.00	28.67	30.30	31.87	33.39	34.87	36.29	37.68
	20.16	21.90	23.59	25.22	26.80	28.34	29.83	31.28	32.68	34.04	35.36
	18.70	20.33	21.91	23.44	24.93	26.38	27.79	29.16	30.49	31.79	33.04
	17.23	18.75	20.23	21.67	23.07	24.43	25.76	27.05	28.31	29.53	30.73
	15.80	17.21	18.58	19.92	21.23	22.51	23.76	24.97	26.16	27.32	28.45
5 YRS.	28.24	30.52	32.70	34.80	36.80	38.72	40.57	42.34	44.03	45.66	47.22
	27.72	29.97	32.12	34.18	36.15	38.05	39.87	41.61	43.29	44.90	46.44
	26.65	27.74	29.76	31.70	33.56	35.35	37.07	38.73	40.32	41.85	43.33
	23.57	25.52	27.41	29.22	30.97	32.65	34.28	35.84	37.35	38.81	40.21
	21.49	23.30	25.05	26.74	28.38	29.95	31.48	32.96	34.38	35.76	37.10
	18.67	20.28	21.85	23.37	24.85	26.29	27.68	29.03	30.35	31.62	32.87
6 YRS.	30.86	33.26	35.54	37.71	39.78	41.75	43.63	45.42	47.13	48.76	50.32
	30.18	32.53	34.77	36.91	38.95	40.89	42.74	44.51	46.20	47.81	49.35
	27.46	29.64	31.73	33.72	35.63	37.45	39.20	40.87	42.47	44.01	45.48
	24.74	26.75	28.68	30.53	32.31	34.01	35.65	37.23	38.75	40.21	41.61
	21.22	23.01	24.73	26.40	28.00	29.56	31.06	32.51	33.92	35.28	36.59
7 YRS.	32.93	35.39	37.73	39.94	42.03	44.02	45.90	47.69	49.39	51.00	52.53
	32.09	34.50	36.79	38.96	41.03	42.98	44.84	46.60	48.28	49.87	51.39
	28.72	30.94	33.06	35.07	37.00	38.83	40.58	42.25	43.85	45.37	46.83
	23.49	25.42	27.26	29.04	30.75	32.39	33.98	35.50	36.97	38.38	39.74
8 YRS.	34.56	37.06	39.42	41.64	43.74	45.72	47.59	49.36	51.03	52.62	54.11
	33.55	36.01	38.32	40.50	42.57	44.52	46.36	48.11	49.76	51.33	52.82
	29.54	31.79	33.92	35.94	37.87	39.70	41.44	43.10	44.68	46.19	47.63
	26.81	27.89	29.49	31.35	33.14	34.05	36.49	38.06	39.37	41.02	42.41
9 YRS.	35.84	38.36	40.73	42.95	45.04	47.00	48.85	50.59	52.24	53.78	55.25
	34.08	37.15	39.47	41.65	43.71	45.64	47.47	49.19	50.82	52.36	53.81
	27.31	29.43	31.45	33.38	35.22	36.98	38.66	40.26	41.80	43.27	44.68
10 YRS.	36.85	39.38	41.74	43.95	46.02	47.97	49.79	51.50	53.11	54.63	56.06
	35.54	38.02	40.33	42.51	44.55	46.46	48.27	49.96	51.57	53.08	54.50
	28.89	31.09	33.17	35.15	37.03	38.82	40.53	42.16	43.71	45.19	46.60
UNTIL PAID	37.91	40.32	42.56	44.64	46.58	48.40	50.09	51.69	53.18	54.59	55.92
	30.40	32.65	34.78	36.80	38.71	40.53	42.26	43.89	45.45	46.94	48.35
	25.54	27.57	29.52	31.38	33.17	34.88	36.52	38.09	39.60	41.05	42.44
	22.07	23.91	25.68	27.38	29.03	30.62	32.16	33.64	35.07	36.45	37.78
	17.41	18.94	20.43	21.87	23.28	24.65	25.98	27.28	28.54	29.77	30.97
	14.42	15.72	17.00	18.24	19.46	20.66	21.82	22.97	24.08	25.18	26.25
	12.32	13.46	14.58	15.67	16.75	17.80	18.84	19.85	20.85	21.83	22.79
	10.77	11.78	12.77	13.75	14.71	15.66	16.59	17.50	18.40	19.29	20.16

EXAMPLES *ON PAGES A-382 TO A-397*

MORTGAGE YIELD TABLE

SHOWING DISCOUNT PERCENTAGES AT VARIOUS
YIELDS, MONTHLY PAYMENT RATES AND DUE DATES

DUE DATE	PAY'T RATE %	BAL REMAIN %	YIELD PERCENTAGES								
			15%	16%	17%	18%	19%	20%	21%	22%	23%
1 YR.	1.21	100.00	0.46	1.38	2.28	3.18	4.07	4.95	5.82	6.68	7.53
	1.25	99.47	0.46	1.37	2.28	3.17	4.06	4.94	5.80	6.66	7.51
	1.50	96.26	0.45	1.36	2.25	3.13	4.00	4.87	5.72	6.57	7.41
	1.75	93.05	0.45	1.34	2.22	3.09	3.95	4.80	5.64	6.48	7.31
	2.00	89.84	0.44	1.32	2.18	3.04	3.89	4.73	5.56	6.39	7.20
	2.25	86.63	0.43	1.30	2.15	3.00	3.83	4.66	5.48	6.30	7.10
	2.50	83.43	0.43	1.28	2.12	2.95	3.78	4.60	5.40	6.20	7.00
	9.00	0.0	0.26	0.78	1.30	1.81	2.32	2.82	3.32	3.82	4.31
2 YRS.	1.21	100.00	0.86	2.55	4.21	5.84	7.44	9.01	10.54	12.05	13.52
	1.25	98.85	0.86	2.54	4.19	5.81	7.40	8.96	10.49	11.99	13.46
	1.50	91.94	0.83	2.46	4.07	5.64	7.18	8.70	10.18	11.64	13.07
	1.75	85.02	0.80	2.39	3.94	5.47	6.97	8.44	9.88	11.29	12.68
	2.00	78.11	0.78	2.31	3.82	5.30	6.75	8.17	9.57	10.94	12.29
	2.25	71.20	0.75	2.24	3.69	5.13	6.53	7.91	9.26	10.59	11.90
	2.50	64.29	0.73	2.16	3.57	4.95	6.31	7.65	8.96	10.24	11.51
	4.82	0.0	0.49	1.46	2.41	3.35	4.28	5.20	6.10	6.99	7.87
3 YRS.	1.21	100.00	1.20	3.56	5.84	8.07	10.23	12.33	14.38	16.37	18.30
	1.25	98.13	1.19	3.53	5.80	8.01	10.15	12.24	14.27	16.24	18.16
	1.50	86.94	1.14	3.36	5.53	7.64	9.69	11.69	13.63	15.52	17.36
	1.75	75.75	1.08	3.20	5.26	7.27	9.23	11.13	12.99	14.79	16.55
	2.00	64.56	1.03	3.04	5.00	6.91	8.77	10.58	12.34	14.06	15.74
	2.25	53.37	0.97	2.87	4.73	6.54	8.30	10.02	11.70	13.34	14.93
	2.50	42.18	0.91	2.71	4.46	6.17	7.84	9.47	11.06	12.61	14.12
	3.44	0.0	0.70	2.09	3.45	4.79	6.10	7.38	8.64	9.87	11.08
4 YRS.	1.21	100.00	1.50	4.41	7.22	9.93	12.54	15.06	17.49	19.84	22.10
	1.25	97.31	1.48	4.36	7.14	9.83	12.41	14.91	17.32	19.64	21.88
	1.50	81.18	1.39	4.09	6.69	9.21	11.64	13.99	16.26	18.45	20.57
	1.75	65.04	1.29	3.81	6.24	8.60	10.87	13.07	15.20	17.26	19.25
	2.00	48.91	1.20	3.53	5.79	7.98	10.10	12.16	14.14	16.07	17.94
	2.25	32.77	1.10	3.25	5.34	7.37	9.33	11.24	13.09	14.88	16.63
	2.50	16.64	1.01	2.98	4.89	6.75	8.56	10.32	12.03	13.69	15.31
	2.76	0.0	0.91	2.69	4.43	6.12	7.77	9.37	10.94	12.47	13.96
5 YRS.	1.21	100.00	1.75	5.14	8.38	11.49	14.46	17.30	20.02	22.63	25.13
	1.25	96.36	1.73	5.07	8.27	11.34	14.27	17.08	19.77	22.34	24.81
	1.50	74.52	1.59	4.66	7.60	10.43	13.14	15.74	18.24	20.64	22.94
	1.75	52.67	1.44	4.24	6.94	9.53	12.02	14.41	16.71	18.93	21.06
	2.00	30.83	1.30	3.83	6.27	8.62	10.89	13.08	15.19	17.22	19.19
	2.35	0.0	1.10	3.25	5.33	7.34	9.30	11.19	13.03	14.81	16.54
6 YRS.	1.21	100.00	1.97	5.76	9.36	12.79	16.04	19.13	22.08	24.87	27.54
	1.25	95.26	1.94	5.67	9.21	12.58	15.79	18.84	21.74	24.50	27.13
	1.50	66.82	1.74	5.10	8.30	11.36	14.27	17.05	19.70	22.24	24.65
	1.75	38.38	1.54	4.53	7.39	10.13	12.75	15.26	17.67	19.97	22.18
	2.09	0.0	1.28	3.77	6.17	8.48	10.70	12.85	14.92	16.92	18.85
7 YRS.	1.21	100.00	2.16	6.29	10.19	13.88	17.35	20.64	23.74	26.68	29.46
	1.25	93.99	2.12	6.17	10.00	13.62	17.03	20.26	23.32	26.21	28.94
	1.50	57.94	1.86	5.44	8.83	12.04	15.10	18.00	20.75	23.37	25.86
	1.90	0.0	1.45	4.25	6.94	9.52	11.99	14.36	16.64	18.82	20.92
8 YRS.	1.21	100.00	2.32	6.75	10.90	14.79	18.44	21.87	25.10	28.13	30.98
	1.25	92.52	2.27	6.59	10.65	14.47	18.05	21.41	24.58	27.56	30.37
	1.50	47.67	1.95	5.68	9.20	12.53	15.68	18.66	21.48	24.15	26.68
	1.77	0.0	1.61	4.70	7.66	10.47	13.16	15.73	18.18	20.52	22.76
9 YRS.	1.21	100.00	2.46	7.13	11.49	15.55	19.35	22.89	26.20	29.30	32.20
	1.25	90.83	2.40	6.95	11.20	15.16	18.87	22.34	25.59	28.63	31.49
	1.66	0.0	1.75	5.12	8.32	11.35	14.23	16.97	19.58	22.05	24.41
10 YRS.	1.21	100.00	2.58	7.46	11.99	16.19	20.09	23.72	27.09	30.24	33.17
	1.25	88.88	2.51	7.24	11.65	15.74	19.55	23.09	26.40	29.48	32.36
	1.58	0.0	1.89	5.51	8.92	12.15	15.21	18.09	20.83	23.42	25.88
		MONTHS									
UNTIL PAID	1.25	283.18	2.97	8.45	13.41	17.90	21.98	25.70	29.10	32.22	35.08
	1.50	136.34	2.06	5.99	9.67	13.13	16.39	19.45	22.34	25.05	27.62
	1.75	97.64	1.63	4.76	7.75	10.60	13.32	15.91	18.38	20.74	23.00
	2.00	77.16	1.35	3.98	6.51	8.94	11.27	13.52	15.68	17.76	19.77
	2.50	54.98	1.02	3.02	4.96	6.84	8.67	10.45	12.18	13.86	15.49
	3.00	42.92	0.82	2.44	4.02	5.57	7.08	8.55	9.99	11.40	12.78
	3.50	35.26	0.69	2.06	3.39	4.70	5.99	7.25	8.49	9.70	10.89
	4.00	29.94	0.60	1.78	2.94	4.08	5.20	6.30	7.39	8.46	9.50

EXAMPLES *ON PAGES A-382 TO A-397*

DUE DATE	YIELD PERCENTAGES										
	24%	25%	26%	27%	28%	29%	30%	31%	32%	33%	34%
1 YR.	8.37	9.21	10.03	10.85	11.66	12.46	13.25	14.03	14.81	15.58	16.34
	8.35	9.19	10.01	10.82	11.63	12.43	13.22	14.00	14.78	15.54	16.30
	8.24	9.06	9.87	10.68	11.47	12.26	13.04	13.81	14.58	15.33	16.08
	8.12	8.93	9.74	10.53	11.31	12.09	12.86	13.62	14.38	15.12	15.86
	8.01	8.81	9.60	10.38	11.16	11.92	12.68	13.43	14.18	14.91	15.64
	7.89	8.68	9.46	10.23	11.00	11.75	12.50	13.24	13.98	14.70	15.42
	7.78	8.56	9.32	10.09	10.84	11.58	12.32	13.05	13.78	14.49	15.20
	4.80	5.28	5.77	6.24	6.72	7.19	7.66	8.12	8.58	9.04	9.49
2 YRS.	14.97	16.39	17.79	19.16	20.50	21.81	23.10	24.37	25.61	26.83	28.02
	14.90	16.32	17.70	19.06	20.40	21.71	22.99	24.25	25.49	26.70	27.89
	14.47	15.85	17.20	18.52	19.82	21.09	22.34	23.57	24.77	25.96	27.12
	14.04	15.38	16.69	17.97	19.24	20.48	21.69	22.89	24.06	25.21	26.34
	13.61	14.91	16.18	17.43	18.66	19.86	21.04	22.21	23.35	24.47	25.56
	13.18	14.44	15.67	16.89	18.08	19.25	20.40	21.52	22.63	23.72	24.79
	12.75	13.97	15.16	16.34	17.50	18.63	19.75	20.84	21.92	22.97	24.01
	8.74	9.60	10.44	11.27	12.10	12.91	13.71	14.50	15.27	16.04	16.80
3 YRS.	20.18	22.01	23.79	25.52	27.20	28.83	30.43	31.98	33.48	34.95	36.38
	20.03	21.85	23.61	25.33	27.00	28.63	30.21	31.75	33.25	34.71	36.13
	19.15	20.89	22.58	24.23	25.84	27.40	28.92	30.41	31.85	33.25	34.62
	18.26	19.93	21.55	23.13	24.67	26.17	27.64	29.06	30.45	31.80	33.12
	17.37	18.97	20.52	22.03	23.51	24.95	26.35	27.71	29.05	30.35	31.62
	16.49	18.01	19.49	20.93	22.34	23.72	25.06	26.37	27.65	28.90	30.11
	15.60	17.05	18.46	19.83	21.18	22.49	23.77	25.02	26.25	27.44	28.61
	12.26	13.43	14.57	15.69	16.78	17.86	18.92	19.95	20.97	21.97	22.95
4 YRS.	24.28	26.39	28.42	30.38	32.28	34.11	35.87	37.58	39.23	40.82	42.35
	24.04	26.13	28.15	30.09	31.97	33.79	35.54	37.23	38.86	40.44	41.97
	22.61	24.59	26.50	28.35	30.13	31.86	33.53	35.14	36.70	38.21	39.67
	21.18	23.05	24.85	26.60	28.29	29.93	31.52	33.05	34.54	35.98	37.38
	19.75	21.50	23.20	24.85	26.45	28.00	29.50	30.96	32.38	33.75	35.08
	18.32	19.96	21.56	23.11	24.61	26.07	27.49	28.87	30.22	31.52	32.79
	16.89	18.42	19.91	21.36	22.77	24.14	25.48	26.78	28.05	29.29	30.49
	15.41	16.83	18.21	19.56	20.87	22.15	23.41	24.63	25.82	26.99	28.12
5 YRS.	27.52	29.81	32.01	34.11	36.13	38.07	39.92	41.70	43.41	45.05	46.62
	27.18	29.45	31.62	33.71	35.71	37.62	39.46	41.23	42.92	44.55	46.11
	25.15	27.27	29.31	31.27	33.15	34.96	36.70	38.37	39.98	41.53	43.02
	23.11	25.09	27.00	28.83	30.60	32.30	33.94	35.52	37.05	38.52	39.94
	21.08	22.91	24.68	26.39	28.04	29.63	31.18	32.67	34.11	35.50	36.85
	18.21	19.84	21.42	22.95	24.43	25.88	27.28	28.64	29.96	31.24	32.49
6 YRS.	30.07	32.48	34.78	36.97	39.05	41.04	42.94	44.74	46.47	48.11	49.68
	29.63	32.01	34.28	36.44	38.51	40.47	42.35	44.14	45.85	47.48	49.04
	26.97	29.17	31.28	33.30	35.23	37.08	38.85	40.54	42.16	43.71	45.20
	24.30	26.34	28.29	30.16	31.96	33.68	35.34	36.94	38.47	39.94	41.36
	20.71	22.51	24.24	25.90	27.54	29.10	30.61	32.08	33.49	34.86	36.18
7 YRS.	32.08	34.57	36.92	39.15	41.27	43.27	45.17	46.98	48.69	50.32	51.87
	31.53	33.99	36.31	38.52	40.61	42.59	44.47	46.26	47.96	49.58	51.11
	28.23	30.49	32.64	34.68	36.63	38.49	40.26	41.95	43.57	45.11	46.58
	22.93	24.87	26.73	28.52	30.24	31.90	33.49	35.02	36.50	37.93	39.30
8 YRS.	33.67	36.20	38.58	40.83	42.95	44.95	46.84	48.63	50.32	51.91	53.43
	33.01	35.51	37.86	40.08	42.17	44.15	46.03	47.80	49.48	51.06	52.57
	29.08	31.36	33.52	35.58	37.53	39.39	41.15	42.83	44.44	45.96	47.42
	24.90	26.95	28.91	30.79	32.59	34.32	35.97	37.56	39.08	40.54	41.94
9 YRS.	34.92	37.47	39.86	42.11	44.22	46.21	48.08	49.84	51.50	53.07	54.55
	34.16	36.67	39.03	41.25	43.34	45.31	47.16	48.91	50.56	52.12	53.60
	26.66	28.80	30.84	32.78	34.64	36.41	38.11	39.73	41.28	42.76	44.19
10 YRS.	35.91	38.46	40.85	43.09	45.19	47.15	49.00	50.73	52.36	53.90	55.35
	35.05	37.57	39.93	42.14	44.21	46.16	47.99	49.72	51.34	52.87	54.32
	28.21	30.42	32.52	34.52	36.42	38.23	39.96	41.60	43.17	44.66	46.09
UNTIL PAID	37.73	40.17	42.44	44.55	46.51	48.34	50.05	51.65	53.15	54.57	55.90
	30.04	32.33	34.49	36.54	38.48	40.32	42.07	43.73	45.31	46.80	48.23
	25.16	27.22	29.19	31.08	32.89	34.62	36.28	37.87	39.40	40.87	42.27
	21.70	23.56	25.35	27.08	28.74	30.35	31.90	33.40	34.84	36.24	37.59
	17.08	18.62	20.12	21.58	23.00	24.38	25.73	27.04	28.31	29.55	30.75
	14.12	15.44	16.72	17.98	19.21	20.41	21.59	22.74	23.86	24.96	26.04
	12.06	13.20	14.33	15.43	16.51	17.57	18.62	19.64	20.64	21.63	22.60
	10.54	11.55	12.55	13.53	14.50	15.45	16.38	17.30	18.21	19.10	19.98

EXAMPLES ON PAGES A-382 TO A-397

MORTGAGE YIELD TABLE
SHOWING DISCOUNT PERCENTAGES AT VARIOUS
YIELDS, MONTHLY PAYMENT RATES AND DUE DATES

DUE DATE	PAY'T RATE %	BAL REMAIN %	15%	16%	17%	18%	19%	20%	21%	22%	23%
						YIELD PERCENTAGES					
1 YR.	1.23	100.00	0.23	1.15	2.06	2.95	3.84	4.72	5.59	6.46	7.31
	1.25	99.73	0.23	1.15	2.05	2.95	3.84	4.72	5.59	6.45	7.30
	1.50	96.52	0.23	1.13	2.02	2.91	3.79	4.65	5.51	6.36	7.20
	1.75	93.31	0.22	1.11	2.00	2.87	3.73	4.59	5.43	6.27	7.10
	2.00	90.10	0.22	1.10	1.97	2.83	3.68	4.52	5.36	6.18	7.00
	2.25	86.89	0.22	1.08	1.94	2.79	3.63	4.46	5.28	6.09	6.90
	2.50	83.68	0.21	1.07	1.91	2.75	3.57	4.39	5.20	6.00	6.80
	9.01	0.0	0.13	0.65	1.17	1.68	2.19	2.69	3.19	3.69	4.18
2 YRS.	1.23	100.00	0.43	2.13	3.79	5.42	7.03	8.60	10.14	11.65	13.13
	1.25	99.42	0.43	2.12	3.78	5.41	7.01	8.58	10.11	11.62	13.10
	1.50	92.49	0.42	2.06	3.67	5.25	6.80	8.32	9.82	11.28	12.72
	1.75	85.56	0.40	2.00	3.56	5.09	6.60	8.07	9.52	10.94	12.34
	2.00	78.63	0.39	1.93	3.45	4.93	6.39	7.82	9.22	10.60	11.96
	2.25	71.70	0.38	1.87	3.33	4.77	6.18	7.57	8.93	10.27	11.58
	2.50	64.77	0.36	1.81	3.22	4.61	5.98	7.32	8.63	9.93	11.20
	4.84	0.0	0.24	1.22	2.17	3.12	4.05	4.97	5.87	6.77	7.65
3 YRS.	1.23	100.00	0.60	2.96	5.26	7.49	9.66	11.77	13.82	15.82	17.76
	1.25	99.06	0.60	2.95	5.24	7.46	9.63	11.73	13.77	15.76	17.69
	1.50	87.83	0.57	2.81	5.00	7.12	9.19	11.20	13.15	15.06	16.91
	1.75	76.59	0.54	2.68	4.76	6.78	8.75	10.67	12.53	14.35	16.12
	2.00	65.36	0.52	2.54	4.52	6.44	8.31	10.14	11.92	13.65	15.34
	2.25	54.12	0.49	2.40	4.27	6.10	7.87	9.61	11.30	12.94	14.55
	2.50	42.89	0.46	2.27	4.03	5.76	7.44	9.08	10.68	12.24	13.76
	3.45	0.0	0.35	1.75	3.11	4.45	5.76	7.05	8.31	9.55	10.76
4 YRS.	1.23	100.00	0.75	3.68	6.50	9.22	11.84	14.38	16.82	19.18	21.45
	1.25	98.65	0.74	3.66	6.46	9.17	11.78	14.30	16.73	19.08	21.34
	1.50	82.43	0.70	3.42	6.06	8.60	11.05	13.42	15.71	17.93	20.06
	1.75	66.21	0.65	3.19	5.65	8.03	10.32	12.55	14.70	16.77	18.78
	2.00	49.99	0.60	2.96	5.24	7.45	9.59	11.67	13.68	15.62	17.51
	2.25	33.77	0.55	2.73	4.84	6.88	8.86	10.79	12.66	14.47	16.23
	2.50	17.55	0.51	2.50	4.43	6.31	8.13	9.91	11.64	13.31	14.95
	4.04	0.0	0.45	2.24	3.99	5.69	7.34	8.96	10.53	12.07	13.56
5 YRS.	1.23	100.00	0.88	4.28	7.54	10.67	13.65	16.51	19.25	21.88	24.39
	1.25	98.17	0.87	4.25	7.49	10.60	13.56	16.41	19.13	21.74	24.24
	1.50	76.17	0.80	3.91	6.89	9.75	12.50	15.13	17.65	20.08	22.41
	1.75	54.18	0.73	3.56	6.29	8.91	11.43	13.85	16.18	18.42	20.58
	2.00	32.19	0.66	3.22	5.69	8.06	10.36	12.57	14.71	16.76	18.75
	2.37	0.0	0.55	2.71	4.80	6.83	8.80	10.70	12.55	14.34	16.07
6 YRS.	1.23	100.00	0.99	4.80	8.43	11.87	15.15	18.27	21.23	24.05	26.73
	1.25	97.61	0.98	4.76	8.36	11.78	15.03	18.12	21.06	23.86	26.53
	1.50	68.93	0.88	4.29	7.54	10.64	13.59	16.41	19.10	21.67	24.12
	1.75	40.26	0.78	3.81	6.71	9.49	12.15	14.69	17.13	19.47	21.71
	2.10	0.0	0.64	3.15	5.56	7.88	10.13	12.29	14.37	16.38	18.32
7 YRS.	1.23	100.00	1.08	5.24	9.18	12.89	16.39	19.70	22.83	25.79	28.59
	1.25	96.97	1.07	5.19	9.09	12.76	16.24	19.52	22.62	25.56	28.34
	1.50	60.55	0.94	4.58	8.02	11.30	14.40	17.35	20.15	22.81	25.33
	1.92	0.0	0.73	3.55	6.26	8.85	11.34	13.73	16.02	18.22	20.34
8 YRS.	1.23	100.00	1.16	5.62	9.81	13.73	17.42	20.88	24.13	27.19	30.07
	1.25	96.22	1.15	5.56	9.70	13.58	17.23	20.66	23.88	26.92	29.77
	1.50	50.84	0.99	4.79	8.38	11.77	14.98	18.01	20.88	23.60	26.17
	1.78	0.0	0.80	3.93	6.91	9.75	12.46	15.04	17.52	19.88	22.13
9 YRS.	1.23	100.00	1.23	5.94	10.34	14.44	18.27	21.85	25.19	28.32	31.25
	1.25	95.35	1.21	5.87	10.21	14.26	18.05	21.59	24.90	28.00	30.90
	1.68	0.0	0.88	4.28	7.50	10.56	13.47	16.23	18.86	21.36	23.74
10 YRS.	1.23	100.00	1.29	6.22	10.79	15.03	18.97	22.64	26.05	29.23	32.19
	1.25	94.35	1.27	6.13	10.63	14.82	18.71	22.34	25.71	28.86	31.80
	1.60	0.0	0.95	4.60	8.05	11.31	14.39	17.31	20.07	22.69	25.17
		MONTHS									
UNTIL PAID	1.25	335.11	1.56	7.36	12.56	17.23	21.46	25.29	28.78	31.97	34.90
	1.50	140.11	1.05	5.09	8.87	12.42	15.75	18.88	21.83	24.60	27.21
	1.75	99.20	0.82	4.02	7.07	9.97	12.74	15.37	17.89	20.29	22.58
	2.00	78.04	0.68	3.35	5.92	8.38	10.75	13.03	15.23	17.34	19.37
	2.50	55.38	0.51	2.54	4.50	6.40	8.25	10.05	11.80	13.49	15.14
	3.00	43.15	0.41	2.05	3.64	5.20	6.72	8.21	9.66	11.08	12.47
	3.50	35.41	0.35	1.72	3.07	4.39	5.68	6.95	8.20	9.42	10.62
	4.00	30.05	0.30	1.49	2.65	3.80	4.93	6.04	7.13	8.21	9.26

EXAMPLES ON PAGES A-382 TO A-397

MORTGAGE YIELD TABLE

SHOWING DISCOUNT PERCENTAGES AT VARIOUS YIELDS, MONTHLY PAYMENT RATES AND DUE DATES

DUE DATE	24%	25%	26%	27%	28%	29%	30%	31%	32%	33%	34%
					YIELD PERCENTAGES						
1 YR.	8.15	8.99	9.81	10.63	11.44	12.24	13.04	13.82	14.60	15.37	16.13
	8.14	8.98	9.80	10.62	11.43	12.23	13.02	13.81	14.58	15.35	16.11
	8.03	8.85	9.67	10.47	11.27	12.06	12.84	13.62	14.38	15.14	15.89
	7.92	8.73	9.53	10.33	11.12	11.90	12.67	13.43	14.19	14.94	15.68
	7.81	8.61	9.40	10.19	10.96	11.73	12.49	13.24	13.99	14.73	15.46
	7.70	8.49	9.27	10.04	10.81	11.56	12.31	13.06	13.79	14.52	15.24
	7.58	8.36	9.13	9.90	10.65	11.40	12.14	12.87	13.60	14.31	15.03
	4.67	5.16	5.64	6.12	6.60	7.07	7.54	8.00	8.46	8.92	9.37
2 YRS.	14.58	16.00	17.40	18.77	20.12	21.44	22.73	24.00	25.24	26.46	27.66
	14.54	15.97	17.36	18.73	20.07	21.38	22.68	23.94	25.18	26.40	27.60
	14.12	15.51	16.86	18.19	19.50	20.78	22.04	23.27	24.48	25.67	26.83
	13.70	15.05	16.36	17.66	18.93	20.17	21.40	22.60	23.77	24.93	26.06
	13.28	14.59	15.87	17.12	18.36	19.57	20.76	21.92	23.07	24.19	25.30
	12.86	14.13	15.37	16.59	17.79	18.96	20.12	21.25	22.36	23.46	24.53
	12.44	13.67	14.87	16.05	17.21	18.36	19.48	20.58	21.66	22.72	23.76
	8.52	9.37	10.22	11.06	11.88	12.69	13.49	14.29	15.07	15.84	16.60
3 YRS.	19.65	21.48	23.27	25.00	26.69	28.34	29.94	31.49	33.00	34.48	35.91
	19.58	21.40	23.18	24.91	26.60	28.24	29.83	31.38	32.89	34.36	35.79
	18.71	20.47	22.17	23.83	25.45	27.03	28.56	30.05	31.51	32.92	34.30
	17.85	19.53	21.16	22.75	24.31	25.82	27.29	28.72	30.12	31.48	32.81
	16.98	18.59	20.15	21.67	23.16	24.61	26.02	27.40	28.74	30.05	31.32
	16.12	17.65	19.14	20.59	22.01	23.40	24.75	26.07	27.36	28.61	29.84
	15.25	16.71	18.13	19.51	20.87	22.19	23.48	24.74	25.97	27.17	28.35
	11.95	13.12	14.27	15.39	16.49	17.57	18.63	19.67	20.69	21.69	22.67
4 YRS.	23.64	25.76	27.80	29.78	31.68	33.52	35.30	37.01	38.66	40.26	41.81
	23.53	25.64	27.67	29.63	31.53	33.36	35.13	36.84	38.49	40.08	41.62
	22.13	24.12	26.05	27.92	29.72	31.46	33.14	34.77	36.35	37.87	39.35
	20.73	22.61	24.44	26.20	27.91	29.56	31.16	32.71	34.21	35.66	37.07
	19.33	21.10	22.82	24.48	26.09	27.66	29.17	30.65	32.07	33.46	34.80
	17.93	19.59	21.20	22.76	24.28	25.76	27.19	28.58	29.93	31.25	32.53
	16.54	18.08	19.58	21.05	22.47	23.86	25.20	26.52	27.80	29.04	30.25
	15.02	16.45	17.83	19.19	20.51	21.80	23.06	24.28	25.48	26.65	27.80
5 YRS.	26.79	29.10	31.31	33.43	35.46	37.41	39.28	41.07	42.79	44.44	46.03
	26.63	28.92	31.12	33.23	35.25	37.19	39.05	40.84	42.55	44.19	45.77
	24.64	26.79	28.85	30.83	32.74	34.56	36.32	38.02	39.64	41.21	42.71
	22.65	24.65	26.58	28.43	30.22	31.94	33.60	35.19	36.73	38.22	39.65
	20.67	22.52	24.31	26.03	27.70	29.31	30.87	32.37	33.83	35.23	36.59
	17.76	19.39	20.98	22.52	24.01	25.46	26.87	28.24	29.57	30.86	32.12
6 YRS.	29.28	31.71	34.02	36.23	38.33	40.33	42.24	44.06	45.80	47.46	49.04
	29.06	31.48	33.78	35.97	38.06	40.05	41.95	43.77	45.50	47.15	48.73
	26.46	28.69	30.83	32.88	34.83	36.70	38.49	40.20	41.84	43.41	44.92
	23.85	25.91	27.89	29.78	31.60	33.35	35.03	36.64	38.19	39.68	41.11
	20.20	22.01	23.75	25.44	27.07	28.64	30.16	31.64	33.06	34.44	35.77
7 YRS.	31.24	33.75	36.12	38.37	40.50	42.53	44.45	46.27	48.00	49.64	51.20
	30.97	33.46	35.82	38.06	40.18	42.19	44.10	45.91	47.63	49.27	50.83
	27.74	30.03	32.20	34.28	36.25	38.14	39.93	41.64	43.28	44.84	46.33
	22.37	24.32	26.19	27.99	29.73	31.40	33.00	34.55	36.04	37.47	38.86
8 YRS.	32.78	35.34	37.74	40.01	42.15	44.17	46.08	47.89	49.60	51.21	52.74
	32.46	35.00	37.39	39.64	41.77	43.78	45.68	47.48	49.18	50.79	52.32
	28.41	30.72	33.12	35.20	37.18	39.07	40.86	42.56	44.18	45.73	47.20
	24.29	26.36	28.34	30.23	32.04	33.78	35.45	37.05	38.59	40.06	41.47
9 YRS.	34.00	36.58	39.00	41.27	43.40	45.41	47.30	49.08	50.76	52.35	53.85
	33.63	36.19	38.59	40.85	42.97	44.97	46.85	48.62	50.30	51.88	53.38
	26.00	28.16	30.22	32.18	34.06	35.85	37.56	39.19	40.76	42.26	43.69
10 YRS.	34.96	37.55	39.96	42.23	44.35	46.34	48.21	49.96	51.61	53.17	54.64
	34.54	37.11	39.51	41.76	43.87	45.85	47.71	49.46	51.11	52.66	54.12
	27.52	29.75	31.88	33.89	35.81	37.64	39.38	41.04	42.62	44.13	45.57
UNTIL PAID	37.58	40.06	42.35	44.48	46.45	48.29	50.01	51.62	53.13	54.55	55.89
	29.68	32.01	34.20	36.28	38.25	40.12	41.89	43.56	45.16	46.67	48.11
	24.77	26.86	28.86	30.78	32.61	34.36	36.04	37.65	39.20	40.68	42.10
	21.32	23.20	25.02	26.77	28.45	30.08	31.65	33.16	34.62	36.03	37.39
	16.74	18.30	19.82	21.29	22.72	24.12	25.47	26.79	28.08	29.32	30.54
	13.82	15.15	16.45	17.71	18.95	20.16	21.35	22.50	23.64	24.75	25.83
	11.79	12.95	14.08	15.19	16.28	17.35	18.40	19.42	20.43	21.43	22.40
	10.30	11.32	12.32	13.31	14.28	15.24	16.18	17.10	18.02	18.91	19.79

EXAMPLES *ON PAGES A-382 TO A-397*

MORTGAGE YIELD TABLE
SHOWING DISCOUNT PERCENTAGES AT VARIOUS YIELDS, MONTHLY PAYMENT RATES AND DUE DATES

DUE DATE	PAY'T RATE %	BAL REMAIN %	16%	17%	18%	19%	20%	21%	22%	23%	24%
1 YR.	1.25	100.00	0.92	1.83	2.73	3.62	4.50	5.37	6.23	7.09	7.93
	1.50	96.78	0.91	1.80	2.69	3.57	4.44	5.30	6.15	6.99	7.82
	1.75	93.57	0.89	1.78	2.65	3.52	4.37	5.22	6.06	6.89	7.71
	2.00	90.35	0.88	1.75	2.61	3.47	4.31	5.15	5.98	6.79	7.61
	2.25	87.14	0.87	1.73	2.58	3.42	4.25	5.07	5.89	6.70	7.50
	2.50	83.92	0.85	1.70	2.54	3.37	4.19	5.00	5.80	6.60	7.39
	2.75	80.71	0.84	1.68	2.50	3.32	4.13	4.93	5.72	6.50	7.28
	9.03	0.0	0.52	1.04	1.55	2.06	2.57	3.07	3.56	4.06	4.55
2 YRS.	1.25	100.00	1.70	3.37	5.01	6.61	8.19	9.73	11.24	12.73	14.19
	1.50	93.05	1.65	3.27	4.86	6.42	7.95	9.45	10.92	12.36	13.78
	1.75	86.11	1.60	3.17	4.71	6.22	7.71	9.16	10.59	11.99	13.37
	2.00	79.16	1.55	3.07	4.56	6.03	7.47	8.88	10.26	11.62	12.96
	2.25	72.21	1.50	2.97	4.42	5.83	7.23	8.59	9.94	11.25	12.55
	2.50	65.26	1.45	2.87	4.27	5.64	6.99	8.31	9.61	10.89	12.14
	2.75	58.32	1.40	2.77	4.12	5.45	6.75	8.03	9.28	10.52	11.73
	4.85	0.0	0.97	1.93	2.88	3.81	4.73	5.64	6.54	7.42	8.29
3 YRS.	1.25	100.00	2.37	4.67	6.92	9.09	11.21	13.27	15.27	17.22	19.12
	1.50	88.72	2.26	4.46	6.60	8.68	10.71	12.68	14.59	16.46	18.27
	1.75	77.44	2.15	4.24	6.28	8.27	10.20	12.08	13.91	15.69	17.43
	2.00	66.16	2.04	4.03	5.97	7.85	9.69	11.48	13.23	14.93	16.59
	2.25	54.88	1.93	3.82	5.65	7.44	9.19	10.89	12.55	14.17	15.74
	2.50	43.61	1.82	3.60	5.34	7.03	8.68	10.29	11.87	13.40	14.90
	2.75	32.33	1.71	3.39	5.02	6.61	8.17	9.70	11.18	12.64	14.06
	3.47	0.0	1.40	2.77	4.11	5.43	6.72	7.99	9.23	10.45	11.64
4 YRS.	1.25	100.00	2.94	5.78	8.51	11.15	13.69	16.15	18.51	20.80	23.00
	1.50	83.69	2.75	5.41	7.98	10.46	12.85	15.16	17.40	19.56	21.64
	1.75	67.39	2.57	5.05	7.45	9.77	12.01	14.18	16.28	18.31	20.27
	2.00	51.08	2.38	4.69	6.92	9.08	11.17	13.20	15.16	17.07	18.91
	2.25	34.77	2.20	4.32	6.39	8.39	10.33	12.22	14.05	15.82	17.54
	2.50	18.46	2.01	3.96	5.86	7.70	9.49	11.24	12.93	14.58	16.18
	2.75	2.16	1.82	3.60	5.33	7.01	8.65	10.25	11.81	13.33	14.81
	2.78	0.0	1.80	3.55	5.26	6.92	8.54	10.12	11.67	13.17	14.63
5 YRS.	1.25	100.00	3.43	6.71	9.85	12.85	15.73	18.48	21.12	23.65	26.07
	1.50	77.86	3.15	6.17	9.06	11.84	14.50	17.06	19.51	21.87	24.13
	1.75	55.71	2.87	5.63	8.28	10.83	13.28	15.64	17.91	20.09	22.19
	2.00	33.57	2.59	5.09	7.50	9.82	12.06	14.22	16.30	18.31	20.25
	2.25	11.43	2.32	4.55	6.72	8.81	10.84	12.80	14.69	16.53	18.31
	2.38	0.0	2.17	4.28	6.31	8.29	10.21	12.06	13.86	15.61	17.30
6 YRS.	1.25	100.00	3.84	7.49	10.96	14.26	17.40	20.38	23.22	25.92	28.49
	1.50	71.08	3.46	6.76	9.90	12.90	15.75	18.48	21.08	23.57	25.94
	1.75	42.16	3.08	6.02	8.84	11.53	14.11	16.59	18.95	21.22	23.40
	2.00	13.24	2.70	5.29	7.78	10.17	12.47	14.69	16.82	18.87	20.85
	2.11	0.0	2.52	4.95	7.29	9.55	11.72	13.82	15.84	17.80	19.68
7 YRS.	1.25	100.00	4.20	8.16	11.89	15.43	18.76	21.92	24.90	27.72	30.39
	1.50	63.22	3.70	7.21	10.53	13.69	16.68	19.52	22.23	24.79	27.23
	1.75	26.44	3.20	6.26	9.17	11.95	14.60	17.13	19.55	21.86	24.07
	1.93	0.0	2.85	5.57	8.19	10.70	13.10	15.41	17.63	19.75	21.80
8 YRS.	1.25	100.00	4.50	8.72	12.68	16.39	19.89	23.17	26.26	29.16	31.90
	1.50	54.09	3.88	7.54	10.99	14.26	17.35	20.27	23.03	25.65	28.12
	1.75	8.18	3.26	6.36	9.31	12.13	14.81	17.36	19.80	22.13	24.35
	1.79	0.0	3.15	6.15	9.01	11.75	14.35	16.85	19.23	21.50	23.68
9 YRS.	1.25	100.00	4.76	9.19	13.33	17.19	20.81	24.18	27.35	30.31	33.08
	1.50	43.49	4.01	7.77	11.32	14.66	17.80	20.77	23.57	26.21	28.71
	1.69	0.0	3.43	6.68	9.77	12.70	15.49	18.14	20.66	23.06	25.35
10 YRS.	1.25	100.00	4.97	9.59	13.87	17.86	21.56	25.01	28.22	31.22	34.02
	1.50	31.20	4.09	7.93	11.53	14.91	18.09	21.08	23.90	26.56	29.07
	1.61	0.0	3.69	7.17	10.46	13.57	16.52	19.30	21.95	24.45	26.83
		MONTHS									
UNTIL PAID	1.50	144.23	4.15	8.04	11.68	15.09	18.30	21.31	24.14	26.80	29.31
	1.75	100.85	3.26	6.37	9.33	12.14	14.83	17.39	19.83	22.15	24.38
	2.00	78.96	2.71	5.32	7.82	10.23	12.54	14.76	16.90	18.96	20.94
	2.25	65.28	2.33	4.58	6.75	8.86	10.89	12.86	14.76	16.60	18.38
	2.50	55.80	2.04	4.03	5.95	7.82	9.64	11.41	13.12	14.79	16.40
	3.00	43.39	1.65	3.26	4.83	6.36	7.86	9.33	10.76	12.16	13.52
	3.50	35.57	1.38	2.74	4.07	5.37	6.65	7.91	9.14	10.34	11.53
	4.00	30.16	1.19	2.37	3.52	4.66	5.78	6.87	7.95	9.02	10.06

EXAMPLES *ON PAGES A-382 TO A-397*

MORTGAGE YIELD TABLE

SHOWING DISCOUNT PERCENTAGES AT VARIOUS
YIELDS, MONTHLY PAYMENT RATES AND DUE DATES

DUE DATE	25%	26%	27%	28%	29%	30%	31%	32%	33%	34%	35%
					YIELD PERCENTAGES						
1 YR.	8.77	9.60	10.41	11.23	12.03	12.82	13.61	14.39	15.16	15.92	16.67
	8.65	9.46	10.27	11.07	11.86	12.65	13.42	14.19	14.95	15.70	16.45
	8.53	9.33	10.13	10.92	11.70	12.47	13.24	14.00	14.75	15.49	16.23
	8.41	9.20	9.99	10.77	11.54	12.30	13.06	13.80	14.54	15.28	16.00
	8.29	9.07	9.85	10.61	11.37	12.13	12.87	13.61	14.34	15.06	15.78
	8.17	8.94	9.70	10.46	11.21	11.95	12.69	13.41	14.13	14.85	15.55
	8.C5	8.81	9.5c	10.31	11.05	11.78	12.50	13.22	13.93	14.63	15.33
	5.C4	5.52	6.00	6.47	6.95	7.42	7.88	8.34	8.8C	9.26	9.71
2 YRS.	15.61	17.01	18.39	19.74	21.06	22.36	23.63	24.88	26.10	27.30	28.48
	15.16	16.53	17.86	19.18	20.46	21.73	22.96	24.18	25.37	26.54	27.69
	14.72	16.04	17.34	18.62	19.87	21.10	22.30	23.48	24.65	25.79	26.91
	14.27	15.55	16.82	18.05	19.27	20.47	21.64	22.79	23.92	25.03	26.12
	13.82	15.07	16.29	17.49	18.67	19.83	20.97	22.09	23.19	24.27	25.33
	13.37	14.58	15.77	16.93	18.08	19.20	20.31	21.40	22.46	23.51	24.54
	12.92	14.09	15.24	16.37	17.48	18.57	19.65	20.70	21.74	22.75	23.76
	9.15	10.00	10.84	11.66	12.48	13.28	14.07	14.86	15.63	16.39	17.14
3 YRS.	20.96	22.75	24.49	26.19	27.84	29.45	31.01	32.53	34.00	35.44	36.84
	20.04	21.76	23.43	25.06	26.65	28.19	29.70	31.16	32.58	33.97	35.32
	19.12	20.77	22.37	23.94	25.46	26.94	28.39	29.79	31.16	32.50	33.80
	18.20	19.78	21.31	22.81	24.27	25.69	27.07	28.43	29.74	31.03	32.28
	17.28	18.79	20.25	21.68	23.07	24.44	25.76	27.06	28.32	29.56	30.76
	16.37	17.79	19.19	20.55	21.88	23.18	24.45	25.69	26.90	28.09	29.24
	15.45	16.80	18.13	19.43	20.69	21.93	23.14	24.33	25.48	26.62	27.72
	12.91	13.96	15.09	16.19	17.28	18.34	19.39	20.41	21.41	22.40	23.37
4 YRS.	25.13	27.19	29.17	31.08	32.93	34.72	36.44	38.10	39.71	41.27	42.77
	23.65	25.60	27.48	29.30	31.06	32.76	34.40	35.99	37.53	39.02	40.45
	22.18	24.01	25.79	27.52	29.18	30.80	32.36	33.88	35.34	36.77	38.14
	20.70	22.43	24.11	25.73	27.31	28.64	30.32	31.76	33.16	34.51	35.83
	19.22	20.84	22.42	23.95	25.44	26.88	28.29	29.65	30.98	32.26	33.52
	17.74	19.25	20.73	22.17	23.56	24.92	26.25	27.54	28.79	30.01	31.20
	16.26	17.67	19.04	20.38	21.69	22.96	24.21	25.42	26.61	27.76	28.89
	16.06	17.46	18.82	20.15	21.44	22.71	23.94	25.14	26.32	27.47	28.59
5 YRS.	28.39	30.62	32.75	34.79	36.75	38.64	40.44	42.17	43.83	45.43	46.96
	26.30	28.39	30.39	32.31	34.16	35.94	37.65	39.30	40.88	42.40	43.86
	24.21	26.15	28.03	29.83	31.57	33.25	34.86	36.42	37.92	39.37	40.76
	22.12	23.92	25.67	27.35	28.98	30.55	32.07	33.54	34.96	36.34	37.67
	20.03	21.69	23.31	24.87	26.39	27.86	29.28	30.67	32.01	33.31	34.57
	18.95	20.54	22.09	23.59	25.05	26.47	27.84	29.18	30.48	31.74	32.97
6 YRS.	30.94	33.27	35.49	37.61	39.63	41.55	43.39	45.14	46.81	48.41	49.93
	28.21	30.37	32.44	34.42	36.32	38.13	39.86	41.52	43.11	44.63	46.09
	25.48	27.48	29.40	31.24	33.01	34.70	36.34	37.90	39.41	40.86	42.25
	22.75	24.59	26.35	28.06	29.70	31.28	32.81	34.28	35.71	37.08	38.41
	21.50	23.26	24.96	26.60	28.18	29.71	31.19	32.63	34.01	35.35	36.65
7 YRS.	32.92	35.32	37.59	39.74	41.78	43.72	45.56	47.30	48.96	50.54	52.04
	29.55	31.75	33.87	35.87	37.78	39.60	41.33	42.99	44.57	46.08	47.52
	26.18	28.21	30.14	32.00	33.77	35.47	37.11	38.67	40.17	41.62	43.00
	23.76	25.65	27.47	29.21	30.89	32.51	34.07	35.57	37.02	38.41	39.75
8 YRS.	34.47	36.90	39.19	41.36	43.40	45.33	47.15	48.88	50.51	52.06	53.53
	30.47	32.70	34.82	36.83	38.74	40.55	42.28	43.92	45.49	46.98	48.40
	26.47	28.50	30.44	32.30	34.08	35.78	37.41	38.97	40.46	41.90	43.28
	25.76	27.75	29.66	31.44	33.24	34.43	36.54	38.08	39.57	41.00	42.37
9 YRS.	35.69	38.13	40.42	42.58	44.61	46.53	48.33	50.03	51.63	53.15	54.58
	31.07	33.31	35.43	37.44	39.34	41.15	42.86	44.49	46.04	47.52	48.93
	27.53	29.60	31.58	33.47	35.28	37.01	38.66	40.23	41.74	43.19	44.57
10 YRS.	36.63	39.08	41.37	43.51	45.53	47.42	49.19	50.87	52.44	53.93	55.33
	31.44	33.07	35.79	37.79	39.69	41.49	43.19	44.81	46.36	47.82	49.21
	29.08	31.22	33.26	35.20	37.04	38.80	40.47	42.07	43.60	45.05	46.44
UNTIL PAID	31.68	33.91	36.03	38.02	39.91	41.70	43.40	45.01	46.54	48.00	49.38
	26.50	28.53	30.47	32.33	34.10	35.80	37.43	38.99	40.49	41.93	43.30
	22.85	24.68	26.45	28.16	29.80	31.39	32.91	34.39	35.81	37.19	38.51
	20.11	21.78	23.40	24.97	26.48	27.96	29.38	30.76	32.11	33.41	34.67
	17.98	19.51	20.99	22.44	23.85	25.21	26.54	27.84	29.10	30.33	31.52
	14.86	16.17	17.44	18.69	19.91	21.10	22.27	23.41	24.53	25.62	26.69
	12.69	13.83	14.94	16.04	17.12	18.17	19.21	20.22	21.22	22.20	23.16
	11.09	12.10	13.09	14.07	15.03	15.97	16.90	17.82	18.72	19.61	20.48

EXAMPLES *ON PAGES A-382 TO A-397*

MORTGAGE YIELD TABLE

SHOWING DISCOUNT PERCENTAGES AT VARIOUS
YIELDS, MONTHLY PAYMENT RATES AND DUE DATES

DUE DATE	PAY'T RATE %	BAL REMAIN %	YIELD PERCENTAGES								
			16%	17%	18%	19%	20%	21%	22%	23%	24%
1 YR.	1.27	100.00	0.69	1.60	2.50	3.39	4.27	5.15	6.01	6.86	7.71
	1.50	97.05	0.68	1.58	2.47	3.35	4.22	5.08	5.93	6.78	7.61
	1.75	93.83	0.67	1.56	2.43	3.30	4.16	5.01	5.85	6.68	7.51
	2.00	90.61	0.66	1.53	2.40	3.25	4.10	4.94	5.77	6.59	7.40
	2.25	87.39	0.65	1.51	2.36	3.21	4.04	4.87	5.69	6.50	7.30
	2.50	84.17	0.64	1.49	2.33	3.16	3.98	4.80	5.60	6.40	7.19
	2.75	80.96	0.63	1.47	2.29	3.11	3.92	4.73	5.52	6.31	7.09
	9.04	0.0	0.39	0.91	1.42	1.93	2.44	2.94	3.44	3.93	4.42
2 YRS.	1.27	100.00	1.28	2.95	4.59	6.20	7.78	9.32	10.84	12.33	13.79
	1.50	93.62	1.24	2.87	4.47	6.03	7.57	9.08	10.55	12.00	13.43
	1.75	86.65	1.20	2.78	4.33	5.85	7.34	8.80	10.24	11.65	13.03
	2.00	79.69	1.17	2.69	4.19	5.67	7.11	8.53	9.92	11.29	12.63
	2.25	72.72	1.13	2.61	4.06	5.48	6.88	8.26	9.61	10.93	12.23
	2.50	65.76	1.09	2.52	3.92	5.30	6.66	7.98	9.29	10.57	11.83
	2.75	58.79	1.05	2.43	3.79	5.12	6.43	7.71	8.97	10.21	11.43
	4.86	0.0	0.73	1.69	2.64	3.58	4.50	5.41	6.31	7.19	8.07
3 YRS.	1.27	100.00	1.78	4.09	6.34	8.53	10.65	12.72	14.73	16.68	18.59
	1.50	89.62	1.70	3.92	6.07	8.17	10.21	12.19	14.12	16.00	17.83
	1.75	78.30	1.62	3.73	5.78	7.78	9.73	11.62	13.47	15.26	17.01
	2.00	66.98	1.54	3.54	5.49	7.39	9.24	11.05	12.81	14.52	16.19
	2.25	55.65	1.46	3.35	5.20	7.00	8.76	10.48	12.15	13.78	15.37
	2.50	44.33	1.37	3.16	4.91	6.62	8.28	9.90	11.49	13.04	14.55
	2.75	33.01	1.29	2.98	4.62	6.23	7.80	9.33	10.83	12.29	13.72
	3.48	0.0	1.05	2.43	3.77	5.10	6.39	7.66	8.91	10.13	11.33
4 YRS.	1.27	100.00	2.21	5.05	7.80	10.45	13.01	15.47	17.85	20.15	22.37
	1.50	84.97	2.08	4.76	7.35	9.86	12.27	14.61	16.86	19.04	21.15
	1.75	68.58	1.94	4.44	6.87	9.21	11.47	13.66	15.78	17.83	19.81
	2.00	52.18	1.80	4.12	6.38	8.56	10.67	12.72	14.70	16.62	18.48
	2.25	35.79	1.66	3.81	5.89	7.91	9.87	11.78	13.62	15.41	17.15
	2.50	19.40	1.52	3.49	5.40	7.26	9.07	10.83	12.54	14.20	15.82
	2.75	3.00	1.38	3.17	4.91	6.62	8.27	9.89	11.46	12.99	14.49
	2.80	0.0	1.35	3.11	4.83	6.50	8.13	9.71	11.26	12.77	14.25
5 YRS.	1.27	100.00	2.57	5.87	9.02	12.05	14.94	17.71	20.37	22.91	25.35
	1.50	79.56	2.38	5.43	8.36	11.18	13.87	16.46	18.94	21.32	23.61
	1.75	57.27	2.17	4.96	7.65	10.23	12.71	15.09	17.38	19.59	21.71
	2.00	34.97	1.96	4.49	6.93	9.27	11.54	13.72	15.83	17.86	19.82
	2.25	12.68	1.75	4.02	6.21	8.32	10.37	12.35	14.27	16.13	17.92
	2.39	0.0	1.63	3.75	5.80	7.78	9.71	11.58	13.39	15.14	16.85
6 YRS.	1.27	100.00	2.88	6.58	10.05	13.37	16.53	19.53	22.39	25.11	27.70
	1.50	73.27	2.62	5.96	9.15	12.19	15.09	17.85	20.49	23.01	25.42
	1.75	44.11	2.33	5.32	8.17	10.91	13.52	16.03	18.43	20.73	22.93
	2.00	14.94	2.04	4.67	7.20	9.62	11.96	14.20	16.36	18.44	20.44
	2.13	0.0	1.89	4.34	6.69	8.96	11.15	13.27	15.30	17.27	19.17
7 YRS.	1.27	100.00	3.15	7.14	10.90	14.46	17.83	21.00	24.01	26.86	29.55
	1.50	65.94	2.80	6.37	9.75	12.96	16.00	18.89	21.63	24.24	26.72
	1.75	28.79	2.43	5.53	8.49	11.32	14.01	16.58	19.04	21.38	23.62
	1.94	0.0	2.14	4.89	7.52	10.05	12.47	14.79	17.03	19.17	21.23
8 YRS.	1.27	100.00	3.37	7.63	11.62	15.37	18.89	22.20	25.32	28.25	31.01
	1.50	57.42	2.94	6.68	10.20	13.52	16.67	19.64	22.45	25.11	27.63
	1.75	10.97	2.48	5.64	8.65	11.51	14.24	16.84	19.31	21.68	23.93
	1.81	0.0	2.37	5.39	8.28	11.03	13.66	16.17	18.57	20.87	23.06
9 YRS.	1.27	100.00	3.57	8.04	12.22	16.12	19.77	23.18	26.37	29.36	32.16
	1.50	47.50	3.05	6.90	10.51	13.92	17.13	20.15	23.01	25.70	28.24
	1.71	0.0	2.58	5.86	8.97	11.93	14.74	17.42	19.96	22.38	24.69
10 YRS.	1.27	100.00	3.73	8.39	12.72	16.74	20.48	23.97	27.21	30.24	33.07
	1.50	35.96	3.12	7.04	10.73	14.19	17.43	20.49	23.37	26.07	28.63
	1.63	0.0	2.77	6.29	9.61	12.75	15.72	18.54	21.20	23.73	26.13
		MONTHS									
UNTIL PAID	1.50	148.78	3.18	7.18	10.91	14.41	17.70	20.77	23.66	26.38	28.94
	1.75	102.57	2.48	5.65	8.67	11.54	14.27	16.87	19.35	21.72	23.98
	2.00	79.90	2.06	4.70	7.25	9.69	12.03	14.29	16.46	18.54	20.55
	2.25	65.88	1.76	4.04	6.25	8.38	10.43	12.43	14.35	16.21	18.02
	2.50	56.22	1.54	3.55	5.50	7.39	9.23	11.01	12.74	14.42	16.06
	3.00	43.63	1.24	2.87	4.45	6.00	7.51	8.99	10.43	11.84	13.22
	3.50	35.72	1.04	2.41	3.75	5.06	6.35	7.61	8.85	10.07	11.26
	4.00	30.27	0.90	2.08	3.24	4.39	5.51	6.61	7.70	8.77	9.82

EXAMPLES *ON PAGES A-382 TO A-397*

MORTGAGE YIELD TABLE
SHOWING DISCOUNT PERCENTAGES AT VARIOUS
YIELDS, MONTHLY PAYMENT RATES AND DUE DATES

DUE DATE	25%	26%	27%	28%	29%	30%	31%	32%	33%	34%	35%
					YIELD PERCENTAGES						
1 YR.	8.55	9.38	10.20	11.01	11.81	12.61	13.40	14.17	14.95	15.71	16.46
	8.44	9.26	10.07	10.87	11.67	12.45	13.23	14.00	14.76	15.52	16.26
	8.32	9.13	9.93	10.72	11.51	12.28	13.05	13.81	14.56	15.30	16.04
	8.21	9.00	9.79	10.57	11.34	12.11	12.87	13.62	14.36	15.09	15.82
	8.09	8.88	9.65	10.42	11.18	11.94	12.69	13.42	14.16	14.88	15.60
	7.97	8.75	9.51	10.27	11.02	11.77	12.50	13.23	13.95	14.67	15.38
	7.86	8.62	9.37	10.12	10.86	11.60	12.32	13.04	13.75	14.46	15.16
	4.91	5.39	5.88	6.35	6.82	7.29	7.76	8.22	8.68	9.14	9.59
2 YRS.	15.22	16.63	18.01	19.36	20.68	21.98	23.26	24.51	25.74	26.94	28.12
	14.82	16.19	17.53	18.85	20.15	21.41	22.66	23.88	25.08	26.26	27.41
	14.38	15.71	17.02	18.30	19.56	20.79	22.01	23.19	24.36	25.51	26.63
	13.95	15.24	16.51	17.75	18.97	20.17	21.35	22.51	23.64	24.76	25.85
	13.51	14.76	15.99	17.20	18.39	19.55	20.70	21.82	22.92	24.01	25.07
	13.07	14.28	15.48	16.65	17.80	18.93	20.04	21.13	22.21	23.26	24.30
	12.63	13.81	14.96	16.10	17.21	18.31	19.39	20.45	21.49	22.51	23.52
	8.93	9.78	10.62	11.45	12.26	13.07	13.86	14.65	15.42	16.19	16.94
3 YRS.	20.44	22.23	23.98	25.69	27.34	28.95	30.52	32.05	33.53	34.98	36.38
	19.61	21.34	23.03	24.67	26.27	27.82	29.34	30.81	32.25	33.64	35.00
	18.71	20.37	21.99	23.56	25.10	26.59	28.04	29.46	30.84	32.19	33.50
	17.82	19.40	20.95	22.45	23.92	25.35	26.75	28.11	29.44	30.73	32.00
	16.92	18.43	19.91	21.35	22.75	24.12	25.46	26.76	28.04	29.28	30.49
	16.02	17.46	18.86	20.24	21.58	22.89	24.16	25.41	26.63	27.82	28.99
	15.12	16.49	17.82	19.13	20.40	21.65	22.87	24.06	25.23	26.37	27.48
	12.50	13.66	14.79	15.90	16.99	18.05	19.10	20.13	21.14	22.13	23.10
4 YRS.	24.50	26.57	28.56	30.49	32.34	34.14	35.87	37.54	39.16	40.72	42.23
	23.18	25.14	27.04	28.88	30.65	32.37	34.03	35.63	37.18	38.68	40.13
	21.73	23.59	25.38	27.12	28.80	30.43	32.01	35.54	35.02	36.45	37.84
	20.29	22.03	23.73	25.37	26.96	28.50	30.00	31.45	32.86	34.23	35.55
	18.84	20.48	22.07	23.61	25.11	26.57	27.99	29.36	30.70	32.00	33.26
	17.39	18.92	20.41	21.86	23.27	24.64	25.97	27.27	28.54	29.77	30.97
	15.95	17.37	18.75	20.10	21.42	22.71	23.96	25.18	26.38	27.54	28.68
	15.68	17.08	18.45	19.78	21.08	22.35	23.59	24.80	25.98	27.14	28.26
5 YRS.	27.68	29.92	32.07	34.12	36.10	37.99	39.81	41.55	43.23	44.83	46.37
	25.81	27.91	29.94	31.89	33.76	35.55	37.28	38.94	40.54	42.08	43.56
	23.76	25.73	27.62	29.44	31.20	32.89	34.53	36.10	37.61	39.08	40.49
	21.71	23.54	25.30	27.00	28.65	30.23	31.77	33.25	34.69	36.07	37.42
	19.66	21.35	22.98	24.56	26.09	27.57	29.01	30.41	31.76	33.07	34.34
	18.50	20.10	21.66	23.17	24.64	26.06	27.45	28.79	30.10	31.36	32.60
6 YRS.	30.16	32.51	34.75	36.88	38.92	40.86	42.71	44.47	46.16	47.77	49.31
	27.71	29.91	32.00	34.01	35.92	37.76	39.51	41.19	42.80	44.34	45.82
	25.10	27.06	29.01	30.87	32.66	34.38	36.03	37.61	39.13	40.60	42.01
	22.	24.22	26.04	27.73	29.39	30.99	32.54	34.03	35.47	36.86	38.20
	21.00	22.77	24.47	26.13	27.72	29.26	30.75	32.19	33.59	34.94	36.24
7 YRS.	32.10	34.52	36.83	38.98	41.03	42.99	44.84	46.61	48.28	49.87	51.39
	29.07	31.31	33.44	35.48	37.41	39.25	41.01	42.69	44.29	45.81	47.27
	25.77	27.82	29.78	31.66	33.46	35.18	36.83	38.41	39.93	41.39	42.79
	23.22	25.11	26.94	28.70	30.39	32.02	33.59	35.10	36.56	37.96	39.31
8 YRS.	33.61	36.06	38.38	40.56	42.62	44.57	46.42	48.16	49.81	51.37	52.86
	30.01	32.28	34.43	36.46	38.40	40.24	41.99	43.66	45.24	46.75	48.19
	26.09	28.19	30.11	31.99	33.79	35.52	37.16	38.74	40.26	41.71	43.10
	25.16	27.17	29.10	30.94	32.71	34.40	36.02	37.58	39.08	40.52	41.90
9 YRS.	34.79	37.26	39.58	41.76	43.82	45.75	47.57	49.29	50.92	52.45	53.90
	30.64	32.92	35.07	37.10	39.04	40.87	42.61	44.26	45.83	47.32	48.75
	26.09	28.90	30.90	32.89	34.71	36.45	38.11	39.71	41.23	42.69	44.09
10 YRS.	35.72	38.19	40.50	42.68	44.71	46.63	48.43	50.12	51.71	53.22	54.64
	31.04	33.31	35.46	37.49	39.42	41.24	42.97	44.61	46.17	47.65	49.06
	28.41	30.57	32.65	34.58	36.44	38.22	39.91	41.52	43.06	44.53	45.93
UNTIL PAID	31.35	33.62	35.77	37.79	39.71	41.52	43.24	44.87	46.42	47.89	49.29
	26.13	28.19	30.16	32.04	33.84	35.56	37.21	38.79	40.30	41.75	43.14
	22.48	24.34	26.13	27.86	29.52	31.12	32.67	34.16	35.60	36.98	38.32
	19.76	21.45	23.09	24.67	26.20	27.69	29.13	30.53	31.88	33.19	34.46
	17.65	19.19	20.69	22.15	23.57	24.95	26.29	27.60	28.87	30.11	31.31
	14.57	15.88	17.17	18.43	19.66	20.86	22.04	23.18	24.31	25.41	26.48
	12.43	13.57	14.70	15.80	16.88	17.95	18.99	20.01	21.02	22.00	22.97
	10.85	11.87	12.87	13.85	14.82	15.77	16.70	17.62	18.53	19.42	20.29

EXAMPLES *ON PAGES A-382 TO A-397*

MORTGAGE YIELD TABLE
SHOWING DISCOUNT PERCENTAGES AT VARIOUS YIELDS, MONTHLY PAYMENT RATES AND DUE DATES

DUE DATE	PAY'T RATE %	BAL REMAIN %	16%	17%	18%	19%	20%	21%	22%	23%	24%
1 YR.	1.29	100.00	0.46	1.37	2.27	3.16	4.05	4.92	5.79	6.64	7.49
	1.50	97.31	0.45	1.35	2.25	3.13	4.00	4.87	5.72	6.57	7.41
	1.75	94.09	0.45	1.34	2.21	3.08	3.95	4.80	5.64	6.48	7.30
	2.00	90.87	0.44	1.32	2.18	3.04	3.89	4.73	5.56	6.38	7.20
	2.25	87.65	0.43	1.30	2.15	3.00	3.83	4.66	5.48	6.29	7.10
	2.50	84.42	0.43	1.28	2.12	2.95	3.78	4.59	5.40	6.20	6.99
	2.75	81.20	0.42	1.26	2.09	2.91	3.72	4.53	5.32	6.11	6.89
	9.05	0.0	0.26	0.78	1.29	1.80	2.31	2.81	3.31	3.81	4.30
2 YRS.	1.29	100.00	0.85	2.53	4.17	5.79	7.37	8.92	10.44	11.93	13.40
	1.50	94.18	0.83	2.47	4.07	5.64	7.19	8.70	10.19	11.64	13.07
	1.75	87.20	0.80	2.39	3.95	5.47	6.97	8.44	9.88	11.30	12.69
	2.00	80.22	0.78	2.32	3.82	5.30	6.75	8.18	9.58	10.95	12.30
	2.25	73.24	0.75	2.24	3.70	5.13	6.54	7.92	9.27	10.60	11.91
	2.50	66.26	0.73	2.16	3.58	4.96	6.32	7.66	8.97	10.26	11.52
	2.75	59.27	0.70	2.09	3.45	4.79	6.10	7.40	8.66	9.91	11.14
	4.87	0.0	0.49	1.45	2.40	3.34	4.27	5.18	6.08	6.97	7.84
3 YRS.	1.29	100.00	1.19	3.51	5.76	7.96	10.09	12.17	14.18	16.15	18.05
	1.50	90.53	1.14	3.37	5.54	7.65	9.71	11.71	13.65	15.55	17.39
	1.75	79.16	1.08	3.21	5.28	7.29	9.25	11.16	13.02	14.83	16.59
	2.00	67.79	1.03	3.05	5.01	6.93	8.79	10.61	12.38	14.11	15.79
	2.25	56.43	0.97	2.89	4.75	6.56	8.34	10.06	11.75	13.39	14.99
	2.50	45.06	0.92	2.72	4.48	6.20	7.88	9.51	11.11	12.67	14.19
	2.75	33.69	0.86	2.56	4.22	5.84	7.42	8.96	10.47	11.95	13.39
	3.49	0.0	0.70	2.08	3.43	4.76	6.06	7.34	8.59	9.81	11.02
4 YRS.	1.29	100.00	1.47	4.33	7.09	9.75	12.32	14.80	17.19	19.50	21.73
	1.50	86.27	1.39	4.10	6.72	9.25	11.69	14.05	16.32	18.52	20.65
	1.75	69.78	1.30	3.83	6.28	8.64	10.93	13.14	15.28	17.35	19.35
	2.00	53.30	1.20	3.56	5.83	8.03	10.17	12.23	14.23	16.17	18.05
	2.25	36.82	1.11	3.28	5.39	7.43	9.41	11.33	13.19	15.00	16.75
	2.50	20.34	1.02	3.01	4.94	6.82	8.65	10.42	12.15	13.82	15.46
	2.75	3.86	0.92	2.73	4.50	6.21	7.89	9.52	11.10	12.65	14.16
	2.81	0.0	0.90	2.67	4.39	6.07	7.71	9.30	10.86	12.38	13.85
5 YRS.	1.29	100.00	1.71	5.03	8.20	11.24	14.15	16.94	19.61	22.17	24.62
	1.50	81.29	1.60	4.69	7.66	10.50	13.23	15.85	18.36	20.77	23.08
	1.75	58.84	1.46	4.28	7.00	9.61	12.12	14.53	16.85	19.09	21.23
	2.00	36.40	1.32	3.88	6.34	8.72	11.01	13.22	15.35	17.40	19.39
	2.25	13.95	1.18	3.47	5.69	7.83	9.90	11.91	13.85	15.72	17.54
	2.41	0.0	1.09	3.22	5.28	7.28	9.21	11.09	12.91	14.68	16.39
6 YRS.	1.29	100.00	1.92	5.62	9.13	12.48	15.66	18.68	21.56	24.30	26.91
	1.50	75.49	1.76	5.15	8.39	11.47	14.41	17.22	19.89	22.44	24.88
	1.75	46.08	1.57	4.60	7.50	10.27	12.92	15.46	17.89	20.22	22.45
	2.00	16.57	1.37	4.04	6.60	9.06	11.43	13.71	15.89	18.00	20.02
	2.14	0.0	1.26	3.72	6.10	8.38	10.58	12.71	14.76	16.74	18.65
7 YRS.	1.29	100.00	2.10	6.12	9.91	13.49	16.89	20.09	23.12	25.99	28.71
	1.50	68.73	1.89	5.52	8.95	12.21	15.31	18.24	21.03	23.67	26.19
	1.75	31.20	1.64	4.80	7.80	10.67	13.41	16.02	18.51	20.89	23.17
	1.96	0.0	1.43	4.20	6.85	9.39	11.83	14.18	16.42	18.58	20.66
8 YRS.	1.29	100.00	2.25	6.54	10.56	14.34	17.90	21.24	24.38	27.34	30.13
	1.50	60.83	1.99	5.79	9.38	12.77	15.97	18.99	21.85	24.56	27.12
	1.75	13.84	1.67	4.89	7.96	10.87	13.65	16.29	18.81	21.22	23.51
	1.82	0.0	1.58	4.63	7.54	10.32	12.97	15.50	17.92	20.23	22.44
9 YRS.	1.29	100.00	2.38	6.89	11.11	15.04	18.73	22.17	25.39	28.41	31.24
	1.50	51.63	2.06	5.99	9.69	13.17	16.44	19.52	22.43	25.17	27.75
	1.72	0.0	1.72	5.03	8.17	11.16	14.00	16.69	19.26	21.70	24.03
10 YRS.	1.29	100.00	2.49	7.19	11.56	15.62	19.40	22.92	26.21	29.27	32.13
	1.50	40.89	2.11	6.13	9.90	13.44	16.76	19.88	22.81	25.57	28.17
	1.64	0.0	1.85	5.40	8.75	11.93	14.93	17.77	20.46	23.01	25.43
		MONTHS									
UNTIL PAID	1.50	153.82	2.17	6.28	10.13	13.72	17.08	20.23	23.18	25.96	28.57
	1.75	104.39	1.68	4.92	7.99	10.91	13.70	16.35	18.87	21.28	23.57
	2.00	80.88	1.39	4.08	6.66	9.14	11.52	13.81	16.01	18.12	20.16
	2.25	66.50	1.19	3.50	5.73	7.89	9.97	11.99	13.94	15.82	17.65
	2.50	56.65	1.04	3.07	5.04	6.95	8.81	10.61	12.36	14.06	15.71
	3.00	43.88	0.83	2.47	4.07	5.63	7.16	8.65	10.10	11.53	12.92
	3.50	35.88	0.70	2.08	3.42	4.75	6.05	7.32	8.56	9.79	10.99
	4.00	30.39	0.60	1.79	2.96	4.11	5.24	6.35	7.44	8.52	9.58

EXAMPLES *ON PAGES A-382 TO A-397*

DUE DATE	YIELD PERCENTAGES										
	25%	26%	27%	28%	29%	30%	31%	32%	33%	34%	35%
1 YR.	8.33	9.16	9.98	10.79	11.60	12.39	13.18	13.96	14.74	15.50	16.26
	8.23	9.05	9.87	10.67	11.47	12.25	13.03	13.81	14.57	15.33	16.07
	8.12	8.93	9.73	10.52	11.31	12.09	12.86	13.62	14.37	15.12	15.86
	8.01	8.80	9.59	10.38	11.15	11.92	12.68	13.43	14.17	14.91	15.64
	7.89	8.68	9.46	10.23	10.99	11.75	12.50	13.24	13.97	14.70	15.42
	7.78	8.55	9.32	10.08	10.84	11.58	12.32	13.05	13.77	14.49	15.20
	7.66	8.43	9.19	9.94	10.68	11.41	12.14	12.86	13.57	14.28	14.98
	4.79	5.27	5.75	6.23	6.70	7.17	7.64	8.10	8.56	9.02	9.47
2 YRS.	14.83	16.24	17.62	18.98	20.31	21.61	22.89	24.15	25.38	26.58	27.77
	14.48	15.85	17.20	18.53	19.83	21.10	22.35	23.58	24.79	25.97	27.13
	14.05	15.39	16.70	17.99	19.25	20.49	21.71	22.90	24.08	25.23	26.36
	13.62	14.92	16.19	17.45	18.67	19.88	21.06	22.23	23.37	24.49	25.59
	13.19	14.45	15.69	16.90	18.10	19.27	20.42	21.55	22.66	23.75	24.82
	12.77	13.99	15.19	16.36	17.52	18.66	19.77	20.87	21.95	23.01	24.05
	12.34	13.52	14.68	15.82	16.94	18.05	19.13	20.19	21.24	22.27	23.28
	8.71	9.56	10.40	11.23	12.05	12.86	13.65	14.44	15.22	15.98	16.73
3 YRS.	19.91	21.72	23.47	25.18	26.85	28.46	30.04	31.57	33.06	34.51	35.92
	19.18	20.92	22.62	24.28	25.88	27.45	28.97	30.46	31.90	33.31	34.68
	18.30	19.97	21.60	23.19	24.73	26.23	27.70	29.13	30.52	31.87	33.19
	17.43	19.02	20.58	22.10	23.58	25.02	26.42	27.79	29.13	30.43	31.70
	16.55	18.07	19.56	21.01	22.42	23.80	25.15	26.46	27.74	28.99	30.22
	15.67	17.12	18.54	19.92	21.27	22.59	23.87	25.13	26.36	27.56	28.73
	14.80	16.17	17.52	18.83	20.11	21.37	22.60	23.80	24.97	26.12	27.24
	12.20	13.35	14.49	15.60	16.69	17.76	18.81	19.85	20.86	21.85	22.83
4 YRS.	23.88	25.95	27.95	29.89	31.76	33.56	35.30	36.98	38.61	40.18	41.70
	22.70	24.68	26.60	28.45	30.24	31.97	33.65	35.26	36.83	38.34	39.81
	21.28	23.16	24.97	26.72	28.42	30.07	31.66	33.20	34.69	36.14	37.54
	19.87	21.63	23.34	25.00	26.60	28.16	29.67	31.14	32.56	33.93	35.27
	18.46	20.11	21.71	23.27	24.79	26.26	27.68	29.07	30.42	31.73	33.00
	17.04	18.59	20.09	21.55	22.97	24.35	25.70	27.01	28.28	29.52	30.73
	15.63	17.06	18.46	19.82	21.15	22.45	23.71	24.94	26.15	27.32	28.47
	15.30	16.70	18.08	19.42	20.72	22.00	23.24	24.46	25.65	26.80	27.93
5 YRS.	26.97	29.22	31.38	33.46	35.44	37.35	39.18	40.93	42.62	44.23	45.79
	25.30	27.44	29.48	31.45	33.34	35.16	36.91	38.59	40.21	41.76	43.25
	23.30	25.29	27.20	29.05	30.82	32.54	34.18	35.77	37.30	38.78	40.21
	21.30	23.14	24.92	26.64	28.31	29.91	31.46	32.96	34.41	35.81	37.16
	19.29	21.00	22.64	24.24	25.79	27.29	28.74	30.15	31.51	32.83	34.12
	18.05	19.66	21.23	22.75	24.22	25.65	27.05	28.40	29.71	30.99	32.23
6 YRS.	29.39	31.76	34.01	36.16	38.21	40.07	42.03	43.81	45.51	47.13	48.68
	27.21	29.43	31.56	33.58	35.53	37.38	39.16	40.86	42.48	44.04	45.53
	24.59	26.64	28.61	30.49	32.30	34.04	35.71	37.31	38.85	40.33	41.76
	21.97	23.85	25.65	27.40	29.08	30.70	32.26	33.77	35.22	36.62	37.98
	20.49	22.27	23.99	25.65	27.26	28.81	30.31	31.76	33.16	34.52	35.83
7 YRS.	31.28	33.71	36.02	38.21	40.29	42.26	44.13	45.91	47.60	49.21	50.73
	28.58	30.85	33.02	35.07	37.04	38.90	40.68	42.38	44.00	45.55	47.03
	25.34	27.42	29.41	31.31	33.13	34.88	36.55	38.15	39.69	41.16	42.57
	22.65	24.57	26.41	28.18	29.89	31.53	33.11	34.63	36.10	37.51	38.87
8 YRS.	32.75	35.23	37.56	39.77	41.85	43.82	45.68	47.44	49.11	50.69	52.19
	29.54	31.84	34.02	36.09	38.06	39.92	41.70	43.38	44.99	46.52	47.98
	25.69	27.78	29.78	31.68	33.50	35.25	36.92	38.52	40.05	41.51	42.92
	24.56	26.59	28.52	30.38	32.16	33.87	35.51	37.08	38.59	40.04	41.43
9 YRS.	33.90	36.40	38.74	40.95	43.02	44.98	46.82	48.56	50.20	51.75	53.22
	30.20	32.51	34.69	36.76	38.72	40.58	42.35	44.02	45.61	47.12	48.56
	26.24	28.36	30.37	32.30	34.14	35.89	37.57	39.18	40.71	42.19	43.60
10 YRS.	34.80	37.30	39.64	41.84	43.90	45.84	47.66	49.37	50.99	52.51	53.95
	30.62	32.93	35.12	37.18	39.14	40.99	42.74	44.40	45.98	47.48	48.91
	27.73	29.91	31.99	33.96	35.84	37.63	39.34	40.97	42.52	44.00	45.42
UNTIL PAID	31.02	33.33	35.51	37.56	39.51	41.34	43.08	44.73	46.29	47.78	49.19
	25.76	27.85	29.84	31.75	33.57	35.32	36.98	38.58	40.11	41.58	42.98
	22.11	24.00	25.81	27.56	29.24	30.86	32.42	33.93	35.38	36.78	38.13
	19.41	21.12	22.77	24.37	25.92	27.42	28.88	30.28	31.65	32.97	34.26
	17.32	18.87	20.39	21.86	23.30	24.69	26.04	27.36	28.64	29.89	31.10
	14.27	15.60	16.90	18.18	19.40	20.61	21.80	22.96	24.09	25.20	26.28
	12.16	13.32	14.45	15.56	16.65	17.72	18.77	19.80	20.81	21.80	22.77
	10.61	11.64	12.64	13.63	14.60	15.56	16.50	17.42	18.33	19.23	20.11

EXAMPLES *ON PAGES A-382 TO A-397*

MORTGAGE YIELD TABLE
SHOWING DISCOUNT PERCENTAGES AT VARIOUS
YIELDS, MONTHLY PAYMENT RATES AND DUE DATES

DUE DATE	PAY'T RATE %	BAL REMAIN %	YIELD PERCENTAGES								
			16%	17%	18%	19%	20%	21%	22%	23%	24%
1 YR.	1.31	100.00	0.23	1.14	2.05	2.94	3.82	4.70	5.56	6.42	7.27
	1.50	97.58	0.23	1.13	2.02	2.91	3.78	4.65	5.51	6.36	7.20
	1.75	94.35	0.22	1.11	2.00	2.87	3.73	4.58	5.43	6.27	7.10
	2.00	91.13	0.22	1.10	1.97	2.83	3.68	4.52	5.35	6.18	7.00
	2.25	87.90	0.22	1.08	1.94	2.79	3.62	4.46	5.28	6.09	6.90
	2.50	84.67	0.21	1.07	1.91	2.75	3.57	4.39	5.20	6.00	6.80
	2.75	81.45	0.21	1.05	1.88	2.70	3.52	4.33	5.12	5.91	6.70
	9.06	0.0	0.13	0.65	1.16	1.68	2.18	2.69	3.19	3.68	4.17
2 YRS.	1.31	100.00	0.43	2.11	3.76	5.37	6.96	8.51	10.04	11.54	13.00
	1.50	94.75	0.42	2.06	3.67	5.25	6.81	8.33	9.82	11.28	12.72
	1.75	87.75	0.40	2.00	3.56	5.09	6.60	8.08	9.53	10.95	12.34
	2.00	80.75	0.39	1.93	3.45	4.94	6.40	7.83	9.23	10.61	11.97
	2.25	73.75	0.38	1.87	3.34	4.78	6.19	7.58	8.94	10.28	11.59
	2.50	66.75	0.37	1.81	3.23	4.62	5.99	7.33	8.65	9.94	11.21
	2.75	59.76	0.35	1.75	3.12	4.46	5.78	7.08	8.35	9.61	10.84
	4.88	0.0	0.24	1.21	2.16	3.10	4.03	4.95	5.85	6.74	7.62
3 YRS.	1.31	100.00	0.59	2.92	5.19	7.39	9.53	11.61	13.64	15.61	17.52
	1.50	91.44	0.57	2.82	5.01	7.13	9.20	11.22	13.18	15.08	16.94
	1.75	80.03	0.54	2.68	4.77	6.80	8.77	10.69	12.57	14.39	16.16
	2.00	68.62	0.52	2.55	4.53	6.46	8.34	10.17	11.95	13.69	15.38
	2.25	57.21	0.49	2.41	4.29	6.12	7.90	9.64	11.34	12.99	14.61
	2.50	45.80	0.46	2.28	4.05	5.78	7.47	9.12	10.73	12.30	13.83
	2.75	34.39	0.43	2.14	3.81	5.44	7.04	8.59	10.11	11.60	13.05
	3.50	0.0	0.35	1.74	3.09	4.43	5.73	7.01	8.27	9.50	10.70
4 YRS.	1.31	100.00	0.74	3.61	6.38	9.06	11.64	14.13	16.53	18.85	21.09
	1.50	87.57	0.70	3.44	6.08	8.63	11.10	13.48	15.78	18.00	20.14
	1.75	71.00	0.65	3.21	5.68	8.07	10.38	12.61	14.77	16.86	18.88
	2.00	54.43	0.61	2.98	5.28	7.50	9.66	11.74	13.76	15.72	17.61
	2.25	37.86	0.56	2.75	4.88	6.94	8.94	10.87	12.76	14.58	16.35
	2.50	21.29	0.51	2.52	4.47	6.37	8.21	10.01	11.75	13.44	15.09
	2.75	4.72	0.46	2.29	4.07	5.81	7.49	9.14	10.74	12.30	13.82
	2.82	0.0	0.45	2.23	3.96	5.64	7.29	8.89	10.45	11.98	13.46
5 YRS.	1.31	100.00	0.86	4.19	7.38	10.44	13.37	16.17	18.86	21.43	23.90
	1.50	83.05	0.80	3.94	6.94	9.82	12.58	15.23	17.77	20.21	22.55
	1.75	60.44	0.73	3.60	6.34	8.99	11.53	13.97	16.32	18.57	20.75
	2.00	37.84	0.66	3.25	5.75	8.16	10.47	12.71	14.86	16.94	18.94
	2.25	15.24	0.59	2.91	5.16	7.33	9.42	11.45	13.41	15.31	17.14
	2.42	0.0	0.55	2.68	4.76	6.77	8.71	10.60	12.43	14.21	15.93
6 YRS.	1.31	100.00	0.96	4.68	8.22	11.59	14.79	17.83	20.73	23.49	26.11
	1.50	77.76	0.89	4.33	7.61	10.74	13.72	16.57	19.28	21.87	24.34
	1.75	48.10	0.79	3.87	6.81	9.62	12.31	14.88	17.35	19.71	21.97
	2.00	18.44	0.69	3.40	6.00	8.49	10.89	13.20	15.42	17.55	19.60
	2.16	0.0	0.63	3.11	5.50	7.80	10.01	12.15	14.22	16.21	18.13
7 YRS.	1.31	100.00	1.05	5.10	8.92	12.53	15.95	19.18	22.23	25.12	27.86
	1.50	71.57	0.95	4.64	8.14	11.45	14.60	17.58	20.41	23.10	25.65
	1.75	33.66	0.83	4.04	7.10	10.02	12.80	15.45	17.98	20.39	22.70
	1.97	0.0	0.72	3.52	6.18	8.74	11.20	13.56	15.82	17.99	20.08
8 YRS.	1.31	100.00	1.12	5.45	9.51	13.32	16.90	20.27	23.44	26.43	29.24
	1.50	64.33	1.01	4.88	8.54	11.99	15.25	18.33	21.24	23.99	26.59
	1.75	16.78	0.85	4.13	7.25	10.22	13.05	15.74	18.30	20.74	23.07
	1.84	0.0	0.79	3.87	6.80	9.60	12.27	14.82	17.26	19.59	21.82
9 YRS.	1.31	100.00	1.19	5.74	10.00	13.97	17.68	21.16	24.42	27.47	30.33
	1.50	55.87	1.04	5.06	8.84	12.39	15.73	18.87	21.83	24.62	27.25
	1.74	0.0	0.86	4.20	7.37	10.38	13.24	15.97	18.55	21.02	23.36
10 YRS.	1.31	100.00	1.24	5.99	10.41	14.51	18.33	21.88	25.20	28.29	31.18
	1.50	45.98	1.07	5.19	9.05	12.67	16.06	19.24	22.23	25.05	27.70
	1.66	0.0	0.93	4.51	7.90	11.10	14.12	16.99	19.71	22.29	24.73
		MONTHS									
UNTIL PAID	1.50	159.47	1.11	5.35	9.31	13.00	16.45	19.67	22.70	25.53	28.19
	1.75	106.31	0.85	4.16	7.29	10.28	13.11	15.81	18.38	20.83	23.16
	2.00	81.89	0.70	3.44	6.06	8.58	11.00	13.32	15.55	17.69	19.76
	2.25	67.14	0.60	2.94	5.20	7.39	9.50	11.54	13.52	15.42	17.27
	2.50	57.09	0.52	2.58	4.57	6.50	8.38	10.20	11.97	13.69	15.36
	3.00	44.12	0.42	2.07	3.69	5.26	6.80	8.30	9.77	11.21	12.61
	3.50	36.04	0.35	1.74	3.10	4.43	5.74	7.02	8.27	9.51	10.71
	4.00	30.50	0.30	1.50	2.68	3.83	4.97	6.09	7.19	8.27	9.33

EXAMPLES *ON PAGES A-382 TO A-397*

DUE DATE	25%	26%	27%	28%	29%	30%	31%	32%	33%	34%	35%
					YIELD PERCENTAGES						
1 YR.	8.11	8.94	9.76	10.58	11.38	12.18	12.97	13.75	14.52	15.29	16.05
	8.03	8.85	9.66	10.47	11.27	12.06	12.84	13.61	14.38	15.14	15.89
	7.92	8.73	9.53	10.33	11.11	11.89	12.66	13.43	14.18	14.93	15.67
	7.80	8.60	9.40	10.18	10.96	11.73	12.49	13.24	13.99	14.72	15.45
	7.69	8.48	9.26	10.04	10.80	11.56	12.31	13.05	13.79	14.52	15.24
	7.58	8.36	9.13	9.89	10.65	11.40	12.13	12.87	13.59	14.31	15.02
	7.47	8.24	9.00	9.75	10.49	11.23	11.96	12.68	13.40	14.10	14.81
	4.66	5.15	5.63	6.11	6.58	7.05	7.52	7.98	8.44	8.90	9.35
2 YRS.	14.44	15.85	17.24	18.60	19.93	21.24	22.52	23.78	25.01	26.22	27.41
	14.13	15.51	16.87	18.20	19.51	20.79	22.04	23.28	24.49	25.68	26.84
	13.71	15.06	16.38	17.67	18.94	20.19	21.41	22.61	23.79	24.94	26.08
	13.30	14.60	15.88	17.14	18.37	19.58	20.77	21.94	23.09	24.21	25.32
	12.88	14.14	15.39	16.61	17.81	18.98	20.14	21.27	22.39	23.48	24.56
	12.46	13.69	14.89	16.08	17.24	18.38	19.50	20.60	21.69	22.75	23.80
	12.04	13.23	14.40	15.55	16.67	17.78	18.87	19.94	20.99	22.02	23.03
	8.43	9.34	10.18	11.01	11.83	12.64	13.44	14.23	15.01	15.78	16.53
3 YRS.	19.39	21.20	22.96	24.68	26.35	27.97	29.55	31.09	32.59	34.04	35.46
	18.75	20.50	22.21	23.88	25.50	27.07	28.61	30.10	31.56	32.98	34.36
	17.89	19.57	21.21	22.81	24.35	25.88	27.35	28.79	30.19	31.55	32.88
	17.03	18.64	20.21	21.74	23.23	24.68	26.09	27.47	28.82	30.13	31.41
	16.18	17.71	19.21	20.67	22.09	23.48	24.84	26.16	27.45	28.71	29.94
	15.32	16.78	18.21	19.60	20.96	22.28	23.58	24.84	26.08	27.29	28.47
	14.47	15.85	17.20	18.53	19.82	21.08	22.32	23.53	24.71	25.86	26.99
	11.89	13.05	14.19	15.30	16.40	17.47	18.53	19.56	20.58	21.58	22.55
4 YRS.	23.25	25.33	27.35	29.29	31.17	32.98	34.73	36.42	38.06	39.64	41.16
	22.21	24.21	26.15	28.02	29.82	31.57	33.26	34.89	36.47	38.00	39.48
	20.83	22.72	24.55	26.32	28.03	29.69	31.30	32.85	34.36	35.82	37.23
	19.45	21.23	22.99	24.62	26.24	27.82	29.34	30.82	32.25	33.64	34.99
	18.07	19.74	21.36	22.93	24.45	25.94	27.38	28.78	30.14	31.46	32.74
	16.69	18.24	19.76	21.23	22.66	24.06	25.42	26.74	28.02	29.27	30.49
	15.31	16.75	18.16	19.53	20.87	22.18	23.45	24.70	25.91	27.09	28.25
	14.91	16.33	17.71	19.05	20.36	21.65	22.90	24.12	25.31	26.47	27.61
5 YRS.	26.26	28.53	30.70	32.79	34.79	36.70	38.54	40.31	42.01	43.64	45.20
	24.79	26.95	29.02	31.01	32.92	34.76	36.53	38.23	39.86	41.43	42.94
	22.84	24.85	26.78	28.65	30.44	32.17	33.84	35.44	36.99	38.48	39.92
	20.88	22.74	24.54	26.28	27.96	29.58	31.15	32.66	34.12	35.54	36.90
	18.92	20.64	22.30	23.92	25.48	26.99	28.46	29.88	31.26	32.59	33.89
	17.60	19.22	20.80	22.32	23.81	25.25	26.64	28.00	29.32	30.61	31.85
6 YRS.	28.62	31.00	33.27	35.44	37.50	39.47	41.35	43.15	44.86	46.50	48.06
	26.70	28.95	31.10	33.15	35.12	37.00	38.80	40.52	42.16	43.74	45.25
	24.14	26.21	28.20	30.11	31.94	33.70	35.39	37.01	38.57	40.06	41.50
	21.57	23.48	25.31	27.07	28.77	30.40	31.98	33.50	34.97	36.39	37.75
	19.98	21.77	23.50	25.18	26.79	28.35	29.86	31.32	32.74	34.10	35.42
7 YRS.	30.45	32.91	35.24	37.45	39.54	41.53	43.42	45.21	46.92	48.54	50.08
	28.08	30.38	32.58	34.66	36.65	38.55	40.35	42.07	43.71	45.28	46.77
	24.91	27.11	29.03	30.96	32.80	34.57	36.26	37.88	39.43	40.92	42.35
	22.09	24.02	25.88	27.66	29.38	31.03	32.62	34.16	35.63	37.06	38.43
8 YRS.	31.89	34.39	36.75	38.97	41.07	43.06	44.94	46.72	48.41	50.00	51.52
	29.06	31.39	33.61	35.71	37.70	39.60	41.39	43.10	44.73	46.28	47.75
	25.29	27.40	29.43	31.36	33.21	34.97	36.66	38.28	39.83	41.31	42.74
	23.96	26.20	27.95	29.03	31.62	33.34	34.99	36.58	38.10	39.56	40.96
9 YRS.	33.01	35.93	37.90	40.13	42.22	44.20	46.06	47.82	49.48	51.05	52.53
	29.74	32.09	34.31	36.41	38.40	40.29	42.07	43.77	45.38	46.92	48.37
	25.60	27.73	29.77	31.71	33.56	35.33	37.03	38.65	40.20	41.68	43.10
10 YRS.	33.88	36.41	38.76	41.00	43.09	45.05	46.89	48.62	50.26	51.80	53.25
	30.19	32.54	34.77	36.86	38.85	40.72	42.50	44.19	45.78	47.30	48.74
	27.05	29.25	31.35	33.34	35.24	37.05	38.77	40.41	41.98	43.48	44.91
UNTIL PAID	30.69	33.04	35.25	37.34	39.31	41.17	42.93	44.60	46.18	47.67	49.10
	25.38	27.50	29.53	31.46	33.30	35.07	36.76	38.38	39.92	41.40	42.82
	21.74	23.65	25.46	27.25	28.95	30.59	32.17	33.69	35.16	36.57	37.94
	19.05	20.78	22.45	24.07	25.63	27.15	28.62	30.04	31.42	32.76	34.05
	16.98	18.55	20.08	21.57	23.02	24.42	25.79	27.12	28.41	29.67	30.89
	13.97	15.31	16.62	17.90	19.14	20.36	21.56	22.72	23.86	24.98	26.07
	11.90	13.06	14.20	15.32	16.41	17.49	18.55	19.58	20.60	21.60	22.57
	10.38	11.40	12.41	13.41	14.38	15.35	16.29	17.22	18.14	19.04	19.92

EXAMPLES *ON PAGES A-382 TO A-397*

MORTGAGE YIELD TABLE
SHOWING DISCOUNT PERCENTAGES AT VARIOUS YIELDS, MONTHLY PAYMENT RATES AND DUE DATES

DUE DATE	PAY'T RATE %	BAL REMAIN %	YIELD PERCENTAGES								
			17%	18%	19%	20%	21%	22%	23%	24%	25%
1 YR.	1.33	100.00	0.91	1.82	2.71	3.60	4.47	5.34	6.20	7.05	7.89
	1.50	97.85	0.91	1.80	2.69	3.57	4.43	5.29	6.14	6.99	7.82
	1.75	94.62	0.89	1.78	2.65	3.52	4.37	5.22	6.06	6.89	7.71
	2.00	91.39	0.88	1.75	2.61	3.47	4.31	5.15	5.97	6.79	7.60
	2.25	88.16	0.87	1.73	2.57	3.42	4.25	5.07	5.89	6.69	7.49
	2.50	84.93	0.85	1.70	2.54	3.37	4.19	5.00	5.80	6.60	7.39
	2.75	81.70	0.84	1.67	2.50	3.32	4.12	4.92	5.72	6.50	7.28
	9.07	0.0	0.52	1.04	1.55	2.06	2.56	3.06	3.56	4.05	4.54
2 YRS.	1.33	100.00	1.69	3.34	4.96	6.55	8.11	9.64	11.14	12.61	14.05
	1.50	95.32	1.65	3.27	4.86	6.42	7.95	9.45	10.92	12.37	13.78
	1.75	88.31	1.60	3.17	4.71	6.23	7.71	9.17	10.60	12.00	13.38
	2.00	81.29	1.55	3.07	4.57	6.03	7.47	8.89	10.27	11.63	12.97
	2.25	74.27	1.50	2.97	4.42	5.84	7.24	8.60	9.95	11.27	12.56
	2.50	67.26	1.45	2.88	4.27	5.65	7.00	8.32	9.62	10.90	12.16
	2.75	60.24	1.40	2.78	4.13	5.46	6.76	8.04	9.30	10.53	11.75
	4.90	0.0	0.97	1.92	2.87	3.80	4.71	5.62	6.51	7.39	8.26
3 YRS.	1.33	100.00	2.34	4.61	6.82	8.97	11.06	13.09	15.07	16.99	18.86
	1.50	92.36	2.27	4.47	6.61	8.70	10.73	12.70	14.62	16.49	18.31
	1.75	80.91	2.16	4.26	6.30	8.29	10.22	12.11	13.94	15.73	17.47
	2.00	69.45	2.05	4.04	5.99	7.88	9.72	11.52	13.27	14.98	16.64
	2.25	58.00	1.94	3.83	5.67	7.47	9.22	10.93	12.59	14.22	15.80
	2.50	46.54	1.83	3.62	5.36	7.06	8.72	10.34	11.92	13.46	14.97
	2.75	35.09	1.72	3.40	5.05	6.65	8.22	9.75	11.24	12.71	14.13
	3.52	0.0	1.39	2.75	4.09	5.40	6.68	7.94	9.18	10.39	11.58
4 YRS.	1.33	100.00	2.89	5.67	8.36	10.95	13.46	15.87	18.20	20.45	22.62
	1.50	88.89	2.77	5.43	8.01	10.50	12.90	15.22	17.46	19.63	21.72
	1.75	72.24	2.58	5.08	7.49	9.82	12.07	14.25	16.36	18.40	20.37
	2.00	55.58	2.40	4.72	6.96	9.14	11.24	13.28	15.26	17.17	19.02
	2.25	38.92	2.21	4.36	6.44	8.45	10.42	12.31	14.16	15.94	17.68
	2.50	22.26	2.03	4.00	5.92	7.78	9.59	11.34	13.05	14.71	16.33
	2.75	5.60	1.85	3.64	5.39	7.10	8.76	10.37	11.95	13.48	14.98
	2.83	0.0	1.78	3.52	5.22	6.87	8.48	10.05	11.58	13.07	14.53
5 YRS.	1.33	100.00	3.35	6.56	9.64	12.58	15.40	18.10	20.69	23.17	25.55
	1.50	84.83	3.17	6.21	9.12	11.92	14.60	17.17	19.64	22.00	24.28
	1.75	62.07	2.90	5.68	8.35	10.92	13.39	15.77	18.05	20.25	22.36
	2.00	39.31	2.62	5.15	7.58	9.93	12.19	14.37	16.47	18.50	20.45
	2.25	16.55	2.35	4.62	6.81	8.94	10.99	12.97	14.89	16.74	18.54
	2.43	0.0	2.14	4.23	6.25	8.21	10.11	11.95	13.74	15.47	17.15
6 YRS.	1.33	100.00	3.75	7.31	10.69	13.92	16.98	19.90	22.68	25.32	27.84
	1.50	80.06	3.50	6.83	10.00	13.02	15.91	18.66	21.28	23.78	26.17
	1.75	50.15	3.12	6.10	8.96	11.68	14.29	16.79	19.19	21.48	23.67
	2.00	20.24	2.75	5.38	7.91	10.35	12.68	14.93	17.09	19.17	21.17
	2.17	0.0	2.49	4.89	7.21	9.44	11.59	13.67	15.67	17.61	19.47
7 YRS.	1.33	100.00	4.08	7.93	11.57	15.01	18.27	21.34	24.26	27.02	29.63
	1.50	74.47	3.75	7.31	10.68	13.87	16.90	19.78	22.51	25.10	27.56
	1.75	36.18	3.27	6.38	9.34	12.17	14.86	17.43	19.88	22.22	24.46
	1.99	0.0	2.81	5.50	8.08	10.56	12.93	15.21	17.40	19.51	21.53
8 YRS.	1.33	100.00	4.36	8.45	12.29	15.91	19.31	22.51	25.52	28.35	31.03
	1.50	67.92	3.95	7.68	11.20	14.52	17.65	20.61	23.41	26.06	28.56
	1.75	19.80	3.35	6.53	9.55	12.43	15.17	17.77	20.25	22.61	24.87
	1.85	0.0	3.10	6.06	8.88	11.57	14.14	16.60	18.95	21.20	23.35
9 YRS.	1.33	100.00	4.59	8.89	12.90	16.64	20.15	23.44	26.52	29.41	32.12
	1.50	60.24	4.11	7.96	11.59	14.99	18.20	21.21	24.06	26.74	29.27
	1.75	0.0	3.37	6.57	9.60	12.49	15.23	17.84	20.33	22.70	24.95
10 YRS.	1.33	100.00	4.79	9.25	13.39	17.25	20.84	24.19	27.32	30.24	32.97
	1.50	51.24	4.22	8.17	11.87	15.33	18.58	21.64	24.51	27.21	29.75
	1.68	0.0	3.62	7.03	10.26	13.32	16.21	18.96	21.56	24.02	26.37
		MONTHS									
UNTIL PAID	1.50	165.89	4.38	8.46	12.26	15.80	19.11	22.20	25.09	27.81	30.35
	1.75	108.35	3.38	6.58	9.62	12.51	15.26	17.88	20.37	22.74	25.00
	2.00	82.94	2.78	5.45	8.01	10.46	12.82	15.08	17.26	19.35	21.36
	2.25	67.79	2.38	4.67	6.88	9.02	11.09	13.09	15.02	16.88	18.69
	2.50	57.54	2.08	4.09	6.05	7.95	9.79	11.58	13.31	15.00	16.64
	3.00	44.38	1.67	3.30	4.89	6.44	7.95	9.43	10.88	12.29	13.67
	3.50	36.21	1.40	2.77	4.11	5.43	6.72	7.98	9.22	10.44	11.63
	4.00	30.61	1.20	2.39	3.55	4.70	5.82	6.93	8.01	9.08	10.13

EXAMPLES *ON PAGES A-382 TO A-397*

MORTGAGE YIELD TABLE
SHOWING DISCOUNT PERCENTAGES AT VARIOUS YIELDS, MONTHLY PAYMENT RATES AND DUE DATES

DUE DATE	YIELD PERCENTAGES										
	26%	27%	28%	29%	30%	31%	32%	33%	34%	35%	36%
1 YR.	8.72	9.55	10.36	11.17	11.97	12.76	13.54	14.31	15.08	15.84	16.59
	8.64	9.46	10.27	11.07	11.86	12.64	13.42	14.19	14.95	15.70	16.44
	8.52	9.33	10.13	10.92	11.70	12.47	13.23	13.99	14.74	15.48	16.22
	8.40	9.20	9.98	10.76	11.53	12.30	13.05	13.80	14.54	15.27	16.00
	8.29	9.07	9.84	10.61	11.37	12.12	12.87	13.60	14.33	15.06	15.77
	8.17	8.94	9.70	10.46	11.21	11.95	12.68	13.41	14.13	14.84	15.55
	8.05	8.81	9.56	10.31	11.05	11.78	12.50	13.22	13.93	14.63	15.33
	5.02	5.51	5.98	6.46	6.93	7.40	7.86	8.32	8.78	9.24	9.69
2 YRS.	15.47	16.86	18.22	19.55	20.87	22.15	23.41	24.65	25.87	27.06	28.23
	15.17	16.53	17.87	19.18	20.47	21.73	22.97	24.19	25.38	26.56	27.70
	14.73	16.05	17.35	18.63	19.88	21.11	22.31	23.50	24.66	25.80	26.92
	14.28	15.57	16.83	18.07	19.29	20.48	21.66	22.81	23.94	25.05	26.14
	13.83	15.08	16.31	17.51	18.70	19.86	21.00	22.12	23.22	24.30	25.36
	13.39	14.60	15.79	16.96	18.10	19.23	20.34	21.43	22.49	23.54	24.58
	12.94	14.12	15.27	16.40	17.51	18.60	19.68	20.73	21.77	22.79	23.79
	9.12	9.96	10.80	11.62	12.43	13.23	14.02	14.80	15.57	16.33	17.08
3 YRS.	20.63	22.45	24.18	25.85	27.48	29.07	30.61	32.12	33.58	35.00	36.39
	20.03	21.80	23.48	25.11	26.70	28.24	29.75	31.21	32.64	34.03	35.38
	19.17	20.82	22.42	23.99	25.52	27.00	28.45	29.86	31.23	32.57	33.88
	18.26	19.84	21.37	22.87	24.34	25.76	27.15	28.51	29.83	31.12	32.37
	17.35	18.85	20.32	21.76	23.16	24.52	25.85	27.15	28.42	29.66	30.87
	16.44	17.87	19.27	20.64	21.98	23.28	24.55	25.80	27.01	28.20	29.36
	15.53	16.89	18.22	19.52	20.80	22.04	23.26	24.45	25.61	26.74	27.86
	12.74	13.88	15.00	16.10	17.18	18.24	19.28	20.30	21.30	22.28	23.24
4 YRS.	24.72	26.74	28.69	30.58	32.40	34.16	35.86	37.51	39.09	40.63	42.11
	23.74	25.69	27.58	29.40	31.17	32.87	34.52	36.11	37.65	39.15	40.59
	22.28	24.13	25.91	27.64	29.32	30.94	32.51	34.03	35.50	36.92	38.30
	20.82	22.56	24.25	25.88	27.47	29.00	30.49	31.94	33.34	34.70	36.02
	19.36	20.99	22.58	24.12	25.61	27.07	28.48	29.85	31.18	32.47	33.73
	17.90	19.43	20.91	22.36	23.76	25.13	26.46	27.76	29.02	30.25	31.45
	16.44	17.86	19.24	20.60	21.91	23.20	24.45	25.67	26.86	28.03	29.16
	15.95	17.33	18.68	20.00	21.29	22.55	23.77	24.97	26.14	27.28	28.39
5 YRS.	27.83	30.02	32.12	34.13	36.06	37.91	39.69	41.40	43.04	44.61	46.13
	26.46	28.55	30.57	32.50	34.36	36.14	37.86	39.51	41.09	42.62	44.09
	24.40	26.36	28.24	30.06	31.80	33.49	35.11	36.67	38.18	39.63	41.03
	22.34	24.16	25.91	27.61	29.25	30.83	32.36	33.84	35.26	36.64	37.98
	20.28	21.96	23.59	25.17	26.69	28.17	29.61	31.00	32.35	33.65	34.92
	18.78	20.36	21.90	23.39	24.84	26.24	27.61	28.94	30.23	31.48	32.70
6 YRS.	30.24	32.53	34.71	36.79	38.78	40.67	42.48	44.21	45.86	47.44	48.94
	28.46	30.63	32.72	34.71	36.61	38.43	40.17	41.84	43.43	44.96	46.42
	25.77	27.79	29.72	31.58	33.35	35.06	36.70	38.28	39.79	41.24	42.64
	23.09	24.94	26.73	28.44	30.10	31.69	33.23	34.72	36.15	37.53	38.86
	21.28	23.02	24.70	26.32	27.90	29.42	30.89	32.31	33.68	35.01	36.30
7 YRS.	32.11	34.46	36.68	38.80	40.80	42.71	44.52	46.24	47.88	49.43	50.92
	29.90	32.13	34.25	36.26	38.18	44.01	41.75	43.41	45.00	46.51	47.96
	26.60	28.64	30.59	32.46	34.25	35.96	37.60	39.18	40.68	42.13	43.52
	23.47	25.34	27.14	28.87	30.54	32.14	33.68	35.17	36.60	37.99	39.32
8 YRS.	33.55	35.93	38.18	40.30	42.31	44.21	46.00	47.71	49.32	50.85	52.30
	30.94	33.19	35.32	37.34	39.26	41.08	42.82	44.47	46.03	47.53	48.95
	27.02	29.07	31.03	32.90	34.69	36.40	38.04	39.61	41.11	42.56	43.92
	25.41	27.38	29.27	31.07	32.81	34.47	36.07	37.61	39.08	40.49	41.85
9 YRS.	34.66	37.06	39.31	41.43	43.42	45.31	47.09	48.76	50.35	51.85	53.27
	31.65	33.91	36.05	38.07	39.98	41.80	43.52	45.15	46.70	48.18	49.58
	27.10	29.15	31.11	32.98	34.77	36.48	38.11	39.68	41.17	42.61	43.98
10 YRS.	35.52	37.92	40.17	42.27	44.26	46.12	47.87	49.53	51.09	52.56	53.96
	32.14	34.40	36.53	38.55	40.45	42.24	43.96	45.58	47.12	48.58	49.96
	28.59	30.71	32.72	34.63	36.46	38.19	39.85	41.44	42.95	44.39	45.77
UNTIL PAID	32.75	35.00	37.12	39.11	41.00	42.78	44.46	46.06	47.57	49.01	50.37
	27.15	29.20	31.16	33.03	34.82	36.53	38.17	39.73	41.23	42.66	44.04
	23.29	25.15	26.94	28.66	30.32	31.92	33.45	34.94	36.37	37.75	39.08
	20.44	22.13	23.76	25.34	26.87	28.36	29.79	31.19	32.54	33.84	35.11
	18.23	19.77	21.27	22.73	24.15	25.53	26.87	28.18	29.44	30.68	31.88
	15.02	16.34	17.63	18.88	20.11	21.31	22.49	23.64	24.76	25.86	26.94
	12.80	13.95	15.07	16.18	17.26	18.32	19.36	20.39	21.39	22.37	23.34
	11.17	12.18	13.18	14.17	15.13	16.09	17.02	17.94	18.85	19.74	20.61

EXAMPLES *ON PAGES A-382 TO A-397*

16¼%
INTEREST

MORTGAGE YIELD TABLE
SHOWING DISCOUNT PERCENTAGES AT VARIOUS
YIELDS, MONTHLY PAYMENT RATES AND DUE DATES

16¼%
INTEREST

DUE DATE	PAY'T RATE %	BAL REMAIN %	17%	18%	19%	20%	21%	22%	23%	24%	25%
1 YR.	1.35	100.00	0.69	1.59	2.49	3.37	4.25	5.12	5.98	6.83	7.67
	1.50	98.11	0.68	1.58	2.47	3.35	4.22	5.08	5.93	6.78	7.61
	1.75	94.88	0.67	1.56	2.43	3.30	4.16	5.01	5.85	6.68	7.51
	2.00	91.65	0.66	1.53	2.40	3.25	4.10	4.94	5.77	6.59	7.40
	2.25	88.41	0.65	1.51	2.36	3.21	4.04	4.87	5.68	6.49	7.29
	2.50	85.18	0.64	1.49	2.33	3.16	3.98	4.80	5.60	6.40	7.19
	2.75	81.94	0.63	1.47	2.29	3.11	3.92	4.72	5.52	6.31	7.08
	9.08	0.0	0.39	0.91	1.42	1.93	2.43	2.93	3.43	3.92	4.41
2 YRS.	1.35	100.00	1.26	2.92	4.55	6.14	7.70	9.24	10.74	12.22	13.66
	1.50	95.90	1.24	2.87	4.47	6.03	7.57	9.08	10.56	12.01	13.43
	1.75	88.86	1.20	2.78	4.33	5.85	7.34	8.81	10.24	11.65	13.04
	2.00	81.83	1.17	2.70	4.20	5.67	7.12	8.54	9.93	11.30	12.64
	2.25	74.79	1.13	2.61	4.06	5.49	6.89	8.27	9.62	10.94	12.24
	2.50	67.76	1.09	2.52	3.93	5.31	6.66	8.00	9.30	10.59	11.85
	2.75	60.73	1.05	2.44	3.79	5.13	6.44	7.73	8.99	10.23	11.45
	4.91	0.0	0.73	1.69	2.63	3.56	4.48	5.39	6.28	7.17	8.04
3 YRS.	1.35	100.00	1.75	4.03	6.25	8.41	10.51	12.55	14.53	16.46	18.34
	1.50	93.29	1.71	3.93	6.08	8.18	10.23	12.22	14.15	16.03	17.86
	1.75	81.79	1.62	3.74	5.80	7.80	9.75	11.65	13.50	15.30	17.05
	2.00	70.29	1.54	3.55	5.51	7.42	9.27	11.08	12.85	14.56	16.24
	2.25	58.79	1.46	3.37	5.22	7.03	8.80	10.52	12.19	13.83	15.42
	2.50	47.29	1.38	3.18	4.93	6.65	8.32	9.95	11.54	13.09	14.61
	2.75	35.79	1.30	2.99	4.65	6.26	7.84	9.38	10.89	12.36	13.80
	3.53	0.0	1.04	2.41	3.75	5.07	6.36	7.62	8.86	10.07	11.27
4 YRS.	1.35	100.00	2.17	4.96	7.66	10.27	12.78	15.21	17.55	19.81	21.99
	1.50	90.23	2.09	4.78	7.38	9.90	12.32	14.66	16.93	19.11	21.22
	1.75	73.48	1.95	4.47	6.90	9.26	11.53	13.73	15.86	17.92	19.91
	2.00	56.73	1.81	4.15	6.42	8.62	10.74	12.80	14.79	16.72	18.59
	2.25	39.98	1.67	3.84	5.94	7.98	9.95	11.87	13.73	15.53	17.28
	2.50	23.24	1.53	3.52	5.46	7.34	9.16	10.93	12.66	14.34	15.96
	2.75	6.49	1.39	3.21	4.97	6.70	8.37	10.00	11.59	13.14	14.65
	2.89	0.0	1.34	3.09	4.79	6.45	8.06	9.64	11.18	12.68	14.14
5 YRS.	1.35	100.00	2.51	5.74	8.83	11.80	14.63	17.35	19.95	22.45	24.84
	1.50	86.63	2.39	5.47	8.42	11.25	13.96	16.56	19.06	21.45	23.75
	1.75	63.72	2.19	5.01	7.71	10.31	12.81	15.22	17.53	19.75	21.89
	2.00	40.80	1.98	4.54	7.00	9.38	11.66	13.87	15.99	18.04	20.02
	2.25	17.89	1.78	4.07	6.29	8.44	10.52	12.52	14.46	16.34	18.15
	2.45	0.0	1.62	3.71	5.74	7.71	9.62	11.47	13.26	15.01	16.70
6 YRS.	1.35	100.00	2.81	6.39	9.80	13.05	16.13	19.07	21.87	24.53	27.07
	1.50	82.40	2.64	6.02	9.24	12.31	15.23	18.02	20.68	23.22	25.64
	1.75	52.24	2.36	5.39	8.28	11.05	13.70	16.23	18.65	20.97	23.20
	2.00	22.08	2.08	4.75	7.32	9.79	12.16	14.43	16.62	18.73	20.75
	2.18	0.0	1.87	4.29	6.62	8.86	11.03	13.12	15.14	17.08	18.96
7 YRS.	1.35	100.00	3.06	6.94	10.61	14.07	17.35	20.45	23.39	26.17	28.81
	1.50	77.44	2.84	6.46	9.89	13.13	16.21	19.13	21.91	24.54	27.04
	1.75	38.75	2.48	5.64	8.65	11.53	14.26	16.87	19.36	21.74	24.01
	2.00	0.0	2.11	4.82	7.42	9.91	12.31	14.60	16.81	18.93	20.97
8 YRS.	1.35	100.00	3.27	7.39	11.27	14.91	18.34	21.57	24.62	27.47	30.16
	1.50	71.60	3.00	6.80	10.38	13.76	16.96	19.97	22.82	25.51	28.06
	1.75	22.91	2.54	5.79	8.85	11.79	14.58	17.23	19.75	22.15	24.44
	1.87	0.0	2.33	5.31	8.13	10.87	13.46	15.94	18.31	20.57	22.74
9 YRS.	1.35	100.00	3.45	7.77	11.82	15.60	19.15	22.46	25.57	28.49	31.22
	1.50	64.74	3.12	7.06	10.76	14.24	17.51	20.58	23.48	26.21	28.78
	1.77	0.0	2.53	5.76	8.92	11.73	14.50	17.13	19.64	22.03	24.30
10 YRS.	1.35	100.00	3.60	8.09	12.28	16.17	19.80	23.18	26.34	29.29	32.05
	1.50	56.67	3.22	7.26	11.04	14.59	17.91	21.02	23.95	26.70	29.29
	1.69	0.0	2.72	6.17	9.43	12.51	15.43	18.20	20.83	23.32	25.68
		MONTHS									
UNTIL PAID	1.50	173.28	3.37	7.58	11.49	15.13	18.53	21.69	24.66	27.43	30.02
	1.75	110.50	2.57	5.85	8.95	11.90	14.70	17.37	19.90	22.31	24.60
	2.00	84.04	2.11	4.82	7.42	9.92	12.31	14.61	16.82	18.94	20.97
	2.25	68.47	1.80	4.12	6.37	8.54	10.63	12.65	14.61	16.50	18.32
	2.50	58.00	1.57	3.61	5.59	7.51	9.37	11.18	12.93	14.64	16.29
	3.00	44.63	1.26	2.90	4.51	6.07	7.60	9.09	10.55	11.98	13.37
	3.50	36.37	1.05	2.43	3.79	5.11	6.41	7.69	8.93	10.16	11.36
	4.00	30.73	0.91	2.10	3.27	4.42	5.55	6.67	7.76	8.84	9.89

EXAMPLES *ON PAGES A-382 TO A-397*

MORTGAGE YIELD TABLE

SHOWING DISCOUNT PERCENTAGES AT VARIOUS
YIELDS, MONTHLY PAYMENT RATES AND DUE DATES

DUE DATE	26%	27%	28%	29%	30%	31%	32%	33%	34%	35%	36%
					YIELD PERCENTAGES						
1 YR.	8.51	9.33	10.15	10.95	11.75	12.55	13.33	14.10	14.87	15.63	16.38
	8.44	9.26	10.07	10.87	11.66	12.45	13.22	13.99	14.75	15.51	16.25
	8.32	9.13	9.93	10.72	11.50	12.28	13.04	13.80	14.55	15.30	16.03
	8.20	9.00	9.79	10.57	11.34	12.11	12.86	13.61	14.35	15.09	15.81
	8.09	8.87	9.65	10.42	11.18	11.93	12.68	13.42	14.15	14.88	15.59
	7.97	8.74	9.51	10.27	11.02	11.76	12.50	13.23	13.95	14.67	15.37
	7.85	8.62	9.37	10.12	10.86	11.59	12.32	13.04	13.75	14.45	15.15
	4.90	5.38	5.86	6.34	6.81	7.28	7.74	8.20	8.66	9.12	9.57
2 YRS.	15.08	16.47	17.84	19.18	20.49	21.78	23.05	24.29	25.51	26.70	27.87
	14.83	16.20	17.54	18.86	20.15	21.42	22.67	23.89	25.09	26.27	27.42
	14.39	15.72	17.03	18.31	19.57	20.81	22.02	23.21	24.38	25.52	26.65
	13.96	15.25	16.52	17.77	18.99	20.19	21.37	22.53	23.66	24.78	25.87
	13.52	14.78	16.01	17.22	18.41	19.57	20.72	21.84	22.95	24.04	25.10
	13.09	14.30	15.50	16.67	17.82	18.96	20.07	21.16	22.24	23.29	24.33
	12.65	13.83	14.99	16.12	17.24	18.34	19.42	20.48	21.52	22.55	23.56
	8.89	9.74	10.58	11.40	12.22	13.02	13.81	14.59	15.36	16.12	16.88
3 YRS.	20.17	21.94	23.67	25.35	26.99	28.58	30.13	31.64	33.11	34.54	35.93
	19.65	21.38	23.07	24.71	26.31	27.87	29.39	30.86	32.30	33.70	35.06
	18.76	20.42	22.04	23.62	25.15	26.65	28.11	29.53	30.91	32.26	33.57
	17.87	19.46	21.01	22.52	23.99	25.43	26.83	28.19	29.52	30.82	32.08
	16.98	18.50	19.98	21.42	22.83	24.20	25.54	26.85	28.13	29.38	30.59
	16.09	17.54	18.95	20.32	21.67	22.98	24.26	25.52	26.74	27.93	29.10
	15.20	16.57	17.92	19.23	20.51	21.76	22.98	24.18	25.35	26.49	27.61
	12.43	13.58	14.71	15.81	16.89	17.95	19.00	20.02	21.02	22.01	22.97
4 YRS.	24.10	26.13	28.09	29.99	31.82	33.59	35.30	36.95	38.55	40.09	41.58
	23.26	25.23	27.14	28.98	30.76	32.48	34.14	35.75	37.31	38.81	40.26
	21.84	23.70	25.50	27.25	28.94	30.57	32.15	33.69	35.17	36.61	38.00
	20.41	22.16	23.86	25.51	27.11	28.66	30.16	31.62	33.04	34.41	35.74
	18.99	20.63	22.23	23.78	25.29	26.75	28.18	29.56	30.90	32.21	33.47
	17.55	19.09	20.59	22.05	23.46	24.84	26.19	27.49	28.77	30.00	31.21
	16.12	17.55	18.95	20.31	21.64	22.94	24.20	25.43	26.63	27.80	28.95
	15.57	16.96	18.32	19.64	20.93	22.20	23.43	24.63	25.80	26.95	28.07
5 YRS.	27.14	29.34	31.45	33.47	35.42	37.28	39.07	40.79	42.44	44.03	45.55
	25.96	28.08	30.11	32.07	33.95	35.75	37.49	39.15	40.76	42.30	43.78
	23.94	25.92	27.83	29.66	31.43	33.13	34.77	36.35	37.87	39.34	40.75
	21.93	23.77	25.54	27.25	28.91	30.51	32.05	33.54	34.98	36.38	37.72
	19.91	21.61	23.25	24.85	26.39	27.89	29.33	30.74	32.10	33.42	34.69
	18.33	19.93	21.47	22.97	24.42	25.84	27.21	28.55	29.84	31.10	32.33
6 YRS.	29.49	31.79	33.99	36.09	38.09	40.00	41.82	43.56	45.22	46.81	48.33
	27.95	30.16	32.27	34.29	36.21	38.06	39.82	41.50	43.12	44.66	46.14
	25.33	27.37	29.32	31.20	33.00	34.73	36.39	37.98	39.51	40.98	42.39
	22.70	24.57	26.38	28.12	29.79	31.40	32.96	34.46	35.90	37.30	38.64
	20.77	22.53	24.22	25.86	27.44	28.97	30.45	31.88	33.26	34.60	35.90
7 YRS.	31.30	33.67	35.92	38.05	40.07	42.00	43.82	45.56	47.21	48.78	50.28
	29.41	31.67	33.82	35.86	37.81	39.66	41.43	43.11	44.72	46.25	47.71
	26.17	28.24	30.22	32.11	33.93	35.66	37.32	38.91	40.44	41.90	43.30
	22.92	24.81	26.62	28.36	30.04	31.65	33.21	34.71	36.15	37.54	38.89
8 YRS.	32.71	35.11	37.38	39.52	41.55	43.47	45.28	47.00	48.63	50.18	51.65
	30.47	32.75	34.92	36.97	38.92	40.77	42.52	44.19	45.78	47.29	48.74
	26.62	28.70	30.69	32.59	34.40	36.13	37.79	39.38	40.89	42.35	43.74
	24.81	26.80	28.70	30.53	32.28	33.95	35.56	37.11	38.59	40.02	41.39
9 YRS.	33.80	36.21	38.49	40.63	42.65	44.55	46.35	48.05	49.65	51.17	52.61
	31.21	33.51	35.68	37.73	39.67	41.51	43.26	44.91	46.48	47.97	49.39
	26.47	28.54	30.52	32.40	34.20	35.93	37.58	39.15	40.66	42.11	43.50
10 YRS.	34.64	37.06	39.33	41.46	43.47	45.35	47.13	48.80	50.38	51.87	53.28
	31.73	34.03	36.19	38.24	40.17	42.00	43.73	45.37	46.93	48.40	49.81
	27.92	30.06	32.09	34.02	35.86	37.62	39.29	40.89	42.41	43.87	45.27
UNTIL PAID	32.46	34.74	36.90	38.92	40.83	42.63	44.34	45.95	47.43	48.92	50.30
	26.79	28.88	30.86	32.76	34.57	36.30	37.96	39.54	41.05	42.50	43.89
	22.93	24.81	26.62	28.37	30.04	31.66	33.21	34.71	36.16	37.55	38.89
	20.09	21.80	23.45	25.05	26.60	28.10	29.55	30.95	32.31	33.63	34.91
	17.90	19.46	20.97	22.45	23.88	25.27	26.62	27.94	29.22	30.46	31.67
	14.73	16.06	17.35	18.62	19.86	21.07	22.25	23.41	24.54	25.65	26.73
	12.54	13.69	14.83	15.94	17.03	18.10	19.14	20.17	21.18	22.17	23.15
	10.93	11.95	12.96	13.95	14.92	15.88	16.82	17.74	18.65	19.55	20.43

EXAMPLES *ON PAGES A-382 TO A-397*

MORTGAGE YIELD TABLE
SHOWING DISCOUNT PERCENTAGES AT VARIOUS
YIELDS, MONTHLY PAYMENT RATES AND DUE DATES

DUE DATE	PAY'T RATE %	BAL REMAIN %	17%	18%	19%	20%	21%	22%	23%	24%	25%
						YIELD PERCENTAGES					
1 YR.	1.38	100.00	0.46	1.36	2.26	3.15	4.03	4.90	5.76	6.61	7.45
	1.50	98.38	0.45	1.35	2.24	3.13	4.00	4.86	5.72	6.56	7.40
	1.75	95.14	0.45	1.33	2.21	3.08	3.94	4.80	5.64	6.47	7.30
	2.00	91.91	0.44	1.32	2.18	3.04	3.89	4.73	5.56	6.38	7.20
	2.25	88.67	0.43	1.30	2.15	3.00	3.83	4.66	5.48	6.29	7.09
	2.50	85.43	0.43	1.28	2.12	2.95	3.78	4.59	5.40	6.20	6.99
	2.75	82.19	0.42	1.26	2.09	2.91	3.72	4.52	5.32	6.11	6.89
	9.10	0.0	0.26	0.78	1.29	1.80	2.30	2.81	3.30	3.60	4.29
2 YRS.	1.38	100.00	0.84	2.50	4.13	5.73	7.30	8.83	10.34	11.82	13.27
	1.50	96.47	0.83	2.47	4.07	5.65	7.19	8.71	10.19	11.65	13.08
	1.75	89.42	0.80	2.39	3.95	5.48	6.98	8.45	9.89	11.30	12.69
	2.00	82.37	0.78	2.32	3.83	5.31	6.76	8.19	9.59	10.96	12.31
	2.25	75.32	0.75	2.24	3.70	5.14	6.55	7.93	9.28	10.62	11.92
	2.50	68.27	0.73	2.17	3.58	4.97	6.33	7.67	8.98	10.27	11.54
	2.75	61.22	0.70	2.09	3.46	4.80	6.12	7.41	8.68	9.93	11.15
	4.92	0.0	0.49	1.45	2.39	3.33	4.25	5.16	6.05	6.94	7.81
3 YRS.	1.38	100.00	1.17	3.46	5.68	7.85	9.95	12.00	13.99	15.93	17.82
	1.50	94.23	1.14	3.38	5.55	7.67	9.73	11.73	13.68	15.57	17.42
	1.75	82.68	1.09	3.22	5.29	7.31	9.27	11.19	13.05	14.86	16.63
	2.00	71.14	1.03	3.06	5.03	6.95	8.82	10.64	12.42	14.15	15.84
	2.25	59.59	0.98	2.90	4.77	6.59	8.37	10.10	11.79	13.44	15.04
	2.50	48.05	0.92	2.74	4.50	6.23	7.91	9.56	11.16	12.72	14.25
	2.75	36.50	0.87	2.58	4.24	5.87	7.46	9.01	10.53	12.01	13.46
	3.54	0.0	0.70	2.07	3.41	4.73	6.03	7.30	8.54	9.76	10.95
4 YRS.	1.38	100.00	1.44	4.26	6.97	9.58	12.11	14.55	16.90	19.17	21.36
	1.50	91.58	1.40	4.12	6.75	9.29	11.73	14.10	16.38	18.59	20.72
	1.75	74.74	1.31	3.85	6.31	8.69	10.98	13.21	15.35	17.43	19.44
	2.00	57.90	1.21	3.58	5.87	8.09	10.23	12.31	14.32	16.27	18.16
	2.25	41.07	1.12	3.31	5.43	7.49	9.48	11.42	13.29	15.11	16.88
	2.50	24.23	1.03	3.04	4.99	6.89	8.73	10.52	12.26	13.95	15.60
	2.75	7.39	0.93	2.77	4.55	6.29	7.98	9.63	11.23	12.79	14.32
	2.86	0.0	0.89	2.65	4.36	6.02	7.65	9.23	10.78	12.28	13.75
5 YRS.	1.38	100.00	1.68	4.92	8.03	11.01	13.86	16.59	19.21	21.73	24.13
	1.50	91.58	1.61	4.72	7.71	10.57	13.32	15.95	18.47	20.90	23.22
	1.75	65.39	1.47	4.32	7.06	9.69	12.22	14.65	16.99	19.24	21.40
	2.00	42.31	1.33	3.92	6.41	8.82	11.13	13.36	15.51	17.58	19.58
	2.25	19.24	1.19	3.52	5.77	7.94	10.04	12.07	14.03	15.92	17.76
	2.46	0.0	1.08	3.19	5.23	7.21	9.13	10.99	12.79	14.54	16.24
6 YRS.	1.38	100.00	1.87	5.48	8.91	12.18	15.28	18.24	21.06	23.74	26.30
	1.50	84.79	1.78	5.21	8.47	11.58	14.55	17.38	20.08	22.65	25.10
	1.75	54.37	1.59	4.66	7.60	10.40	13.09	15.65	18.11	20.46	22.71
	2.00	23.95	1.40	4.11	6.72	9.22	11.62	13.93	16.14	18.28	20.33
	2.20	0.0	1.25	3.68	6.03	8.29	10.47	12.57	14.60	16.56	18.45
7 YRS.	1.38	100.00	2.04	5.95	9.64	13.13	16.44	19.57	22.53	25.33	27.98
	1.50	80.46	1.92	5.59	9.08	12.38	15.51	18.48	21.29	23.96	26.50
	1.75	41.39	1.67	4.89	7.95	10.87	13.65	16.30	18.83	21.24	23.54
	2.01	0.0	1.41	4.14	6.78	9.27	11.68	13.99	16.22	18.35	20.40
8 YRS.	1.38	100.00	2.18	6.34	10.25	13.92	17.38	20.63	23.69	26.58	29.30
	1.50	75.36	2.03	5.90	9.55	12.99	16.24	19.31	22.21	24.95	27.54
	1.75	26.09	1.72	5.02	8.16	11.14	13.98	16.67	19.23	21.67	24.00
	1.88	0.0	1.56	4.56	7.43	16.16	12.78	15.27	17.66	19.94	22.13
9 YRS.	1.38	100.00	2.30	6.66	10.75	14.56	18.14	21.49	24.62	27.57	30.33
	1.50	69.36	2.11	6.14	9.92	13.46	16.80	19.93	22.88	25.66	28.28
	1.78	0.0	1.69	4.94	8.03	10.97	13.76	16.42	18.95	21.36	23.65
10 YRS.	1.38	100.00	2.40	6.94	11.16	15.09	18.76	22.17	25.37	28.35	31.14
	1.50	62.28	2.18	6.32	10.19	13.81	17.21	20.39	23.38	26.18	28.82
	1.71	0.0	1.82	5.30	8.59	11.70	14.65	17.44	20.09	22.60	24.99
		MONTHS									
UNTIL PAID	1.50	181.96	2.31	6.86	10.70	14.45	17.93	21.18	24.21	27.04	29.69
	1.75	112.80	1.74	5.09	8.26	11.27	14.13	16.84	19.42	21.87	24.21
	2.00	85.17	1.42	4.18	6.83	9.36	11.79	14.12	16.36	18.51	20.58
	2.25	69.16	1.21	3.57	5.84	8.04	10.16	12.21	14.19	16.10	17.95
	2.50	58.47	1.06	2.12	5.12	7.06	8.95	10.77	12.55	14.27	15.94
	3.00	44.00	0.84	2.50	4.12	5.70	7.24	8.75	10.22	11.66	13.06
	3.50	36.54	0.71	2.10	3.46	4.79	6.10	7.39	8.64	9.88	11.09
	4.00	30.84	0.61	1.81	2.99	4.14	5.28	6.40	7.50	8.58	9.65

EXAMPLES *ON PAGES A-382 TO A-397*

DUE DATE	26%	27%	28%	29%	30%	31%	32%	33%	34%	35%	36%
					YIELD PERCENTAGES						
1 YR.	8.29	9.11	9.93	10.74	11.54	12.33	13.12	13.89	14.66	15.42	16.18
	8.23	9.05	9.86	10.67	11.46	12.25	13.03	13.80	14.56	15.32	16.07
	8.12	8.93	9.73	10.52	11.30	12.08	12.85	13.61	14.36	15.11	15.85
	8.00	8.80	9.59	10.37	11.15	11.91	12.67	13.42	14.17	14.90	15.63
	7.89	8.68	9.46	10.23	10.99	11.75	12.49	13.24	13.97	14.69	15.41
	7.78	8.55	9.32	10.08	10.83	11.58	12.32	13.05	13.77	14.49	15.20
	7.66	8.43	9.18	9.93	10.68	11.41	12.14	12.86	13.57	14.28	14.98
	4.78	5.26	5.74	6.21	6.69	7.16	7.62	8.08	8.54	9.00	9.45
2 YRS.	14.69	16.09	17.46	18.80	20.12	21.41	22.68	23.93	25.15	26.34	27.52
	14.48	15.86	17.21	18.53	19.83	21.11	22.36	23.59	24.79	25.98	27.14
	14.06	15.40	16.71	18.00	19.26	20.50	21.72	22.92	24.09	25.24	26.37
	13.63	14.93	16.21	17.46	18.69	19.90	21.08	22.24	23.39	24.51	25.61
	13.21	14.47	15.71	16.92	18.12	19.29	20.44	21.57	22.68	23.77	24.84
	12.78	14.01	15.21	16.39	17.54	18.68	19.80	20.90	21.98	23.04	24.08
	12.56	13.54	14.71	15.85	16.97	18.08	19.16	20.23	21.27	22.30	23.31
	8.67	9.52	10.36	11.19	12.00	12.81	13.60	14.38	15.16	15.92	16.67
3 YRS.	19.65	21.43	23.17	24.86	26.50	28.10	29.66	31.17	32.65	34.08	35.48
	19.21	20.96	22.66	24.32	25.93	27.50	29.02	30.51	31.96	33.37	34.74
	18.35	20.02	21.65	23.24	24.79	26.29	27.76	29.19	30.56	31.94	33.27
	17.48	19.08	20.64	22.16	23.64	25.09	26.50	27.87	29.21	30.52	31.79
	16.61	18.14	19.63	21.08	22.50	23.88	25.23	26.55	27.84	29.09	30.32
	15.74	17.20	18.62	20.00	21.36	22.68	23.97	25.23	26.46	27.67	28.84
	14.87	16.25	17.61	18.92	20.21	21.47	22.71	23.91	25.09	26.24	27.37
	12.13	13.28	14.41	15.51	16.60	17.67	18.71	19.74	20.75	21.73	22.70
4 YRS.	23.48	25.52	27.50	29.40	31.24	33.02	34.74	36.40	38.01	39.56	41.06
	22.78	24.77	26.69	28.55	30.35	32.08	33.76	35.38	36.95	38.47	39.94
	21.38	23.27	25.09	26.85	28.55	30.20	31.80	33.34	34.84	36.29	37.70
	19.99	21.76	23.48	25.14	26.75	28.32	29.83	31.30	32.73	34.11	35.45
	18.59	20.25	21.87	23.44	24.96	26.44	27.87	29.26	30.62	31.93	33.21
	17.20	18.75	20.26	21.73	23.16	24.55	25.91	27.22	28.51	29.75	30.97
	15.80	17.24	18.65	20.03	21.37	22.67	23.94	25.18	26.40	27.58	28.73
	15.19	16.58	17.95	19.28	20.58	21.84	23.08	24.29	25.47	26.62	27.74
5 YRS.	26.44	28.66	30.78	32.82	34.77	36.65	38.45	40.18	41.84	43.44	44.97
	25.45	27.60	29.66	31.63	33.53	35.36	37.11	38.79	40.41	41.97	43.47
	23.48	25.48	27.41	29.26	31.05	32.77	34.42	36.02	37.56	39.04	40.47
	21.51	23.37	25.16	26.89	28.57	30.18	31.74	33.25	34.70	36.11	37.47
	19.53	21.25	22.91	24.52	26.08	27.59	29.05	30.47	31.84	33.17	34.46
	17.89	19.49	21.04	22.55	24.01	25.43	26.82	28.16	29.46	30.73	31.96
6 YRS.	28.73	31.05	33.27	35.38	37.40	39.32	41.16	42.91	44.59	46.19	47.72
	27.44	29.60	31.86	33.86	35.81	37.68	39.46	41.17	42.80	44.36	45.86
	24.87	26.94	28.92	30.82	32.64	34.39	36.07	37.68	39.22	40.71	42.14
	22.30	24.20	26.02	27.78	29.47	31.10	32.68	34.19	35.65	37.06	38.42
	20.27	22.04	23.74	25.39	26.98	28.52	30.00	31.44	32.84	34.19	35.49
7 YRS.	30.50	32.89	35.15	37.30	39.35	41.28	43.13	44.88	46.55	48.13	49.64
	28.91	31.21	33.38	35.46	37.43	39.31	41.10	42.80	44.43	45.98	47.46
	25.74	27.84	29.84	31.76	33.60	35.35	37.03	38.64	40.18	41.66	43.08
	22.37	24.27	26.09	27.85	29.54	31.16	32.73	34.24	35.69	37.10	38.45
8 YRS.	31.87	34.30	36.59	38.75	40.80	42.73	44.57	46.30	47.95	49.51	50.99
	29.99	32.31	34.50	36.59	38.56	40.44	42.22	43.91	45.52	47.06	48.51
	26.21	28.33	30.34	32.27	34.10	35.84	37.54	39.14	40.66	42.19	43.55
	24.22	26.22	28.14	29.98	31.74	33.43	35.05	36.61	38.11	39.55	40.93
9 YRS.	32.93	35.37	37.67	39.83	41.87	43.80	45.61	47.33	48.95	50.49	51.94
	30.76	33.09	35.29	37.38	39.35	41.22	42.99	44.66	46.26	47.77	49.20
	25.84	27.92	29.92	31.82	33.64	35.37	37.04	38.63	40.15	41.61	42.01
10 YRS.	33.75	36.20	38.49	40.65	42.68	44.58	46.38	48.07	49.67	51.18	52.61
	31.30	33.64	35.84	37.92	39.88	41.74	43.49	45.16	46.73	48.23	49.65
	27.26	29.41	31.46	33.41	35.27	37.04	38.73	40.34	41.88	43.35	44.76
'UNTIL PAID	32.17	34.50	36.68	38.74	40.67	42.50	44.22	45.85	47.39	48.85	50.23
	26.43	28.54	30.56	32.48	34.32	36.07	37.75	39.35	40.88	42.34	43.75
	22.56	24.47	26.30	28.07	29.77	31.40	32.97	34.49	35.95	37.35	38.71
	19.74	21.46	23.13	24.75	26.32	27.83	29.29	30.71	32.09	33.42	34.71
	17.56	19.14	20.67	22.16	23.60	25.01	26.37	27.70	28.99	30.24	31.46
	14.43	15.77	17.08	18.35	19.60	20.82	22.02	23.18	24.32	25.44	26.53
	12.27	13.44	14.58	15.69	16.79	17.87	18.92	19.96	20.98	21.97	22.95
	10.69	11.72	12.73	13.73	14.71	15.67	16.61	17.54	18.46	19.36	20.25

EXAMPLES *ON PAGES A-382 TO A-397*

DUE DATE	PAY'T RATE %	BAL REMAIN %	17%	18%	19%	20%	21%	22%	23%	24%	25%
						YIELD PERCENTAGES					
1 YR.	1.40	100.00	0.23	1.14	2.03	2.92	3.80	4.67	5.54	6.39	7.23
	1.50	98.65	0.23	1.13	2.02	2.91	3.78	4.65	5.50	6.35	7.19
	1.75	95.41	0.22	1.11	1.99	2.87	3.73	4.58	5.43	6.26	7.09
	2.00	92.17	0.22	1.10	1.97	2.83	3.68	4.52	5.35	6.18	6.99
	2.25	88.93	0.22	1.08	1.94	2.78	3.62	4.45	5.28	6.09	6.89
	2.50	85.68	0.21	1.07	1.91	2.74	3.57	4.39	5.20	6.00	6.79
	2.75	82.44	0.21	1.05	1.88	2.70	3.52	4.32	5.12	5.91	6.69
	9.11	0.0	0.13	0.65	1.16	1.67	2.18	2.68	3.18	3.67	4.16
2 YRS.	1.40	100.00	0.42	2.09	3.72	5.32	6.89	8.43	9.94	11.43	12.88
	1.50	97.05	0.42	2.06	3.67	5.26	6.81	8.33	9.82	11.29	12.73
	1.75	89.99	0.40	2.00	3.56	5.10	6.60	8.08	9.53	10.95	12.35
	2.00	82.92	0.39	1.94	3.45	4.94	6.40	7.83	9.24	10.62	11.98
	2.25	75.85	0.38	1.87	3.34	4.78	6.20	7.59	8.95	10.29	11.60
	2.50	68.78	0.37	1.81	3.23	4.63	5.99	7.34	8.66	9.96	11.23
	2.75	61.71	0.35	1.75	3.12	4.47	5.79	7.09	8.37	9.62	10.85
	4.93	0.0	0.24	1.21	2.16	3.09	4.02	4.93	5.83	6.71	7.59
3 YRS.	1.40	100.00	0.58	2.88	5.12	7.29	9.40	11.46	13.45	15.40	17.29
	1.50	95.17	0.57	2.83	5.02	7.15	9.22	11.24	13.20	15.11	16.97
	1.75	83.58	0.55	2.69	4.78	6.81	8.79	10.72	12.60	14.42	16.20
	2.00	71.99	0.52	2.56	4.54	6.48	8.36	10.20	11.99	13.73	15.43
	2.25	60.40	0.49	2.42	4.31	6.14	7.93	9.68	11.38	13.04	14.66
	2.50	48.81	0.46	2.29	4.07	5.81	7.51	9.16	10.77	12.35	13.89
	2.75	37.22	0.44	2.16	3.84	5.47	7.08	8.64	10.17	11.66	13.12
	3.55	0.0	0.35	1.73	3.08	4.40	5.70	6.97	8.22	9.44	10.64
4 YRS.	1.40	100.00	0.72	3.55	6.27	8.90	11.44	13.89	16.25	18.53	20.73
	1.50	92.95	0.70	3.45	6.11	8.67	11.14	13.53	15.84	18.06	20.21
	1.75	76.02	0.66	3.23	5.71	8.11	10.43	12.67	14.84	16.94	18.97
	2.00	59.09	0.61	3.00	5.31	7.55	9.72	11.82	13.85	15.81	17.72
	2.25	42.16	0.56	2.77	4.92	6.99	9.01	10.96	12.85	14.69	16.47
	2.50	25.23	0.52	2.55	4.52	6.43	8.29	10.10	11.86	13.56	15.22
	2.75	8.30	0.47	2.32	4.12	5.88	7.58	9.24	10.86	12.44	13.98
	2.87	0.0	0.45	2.21	3.93	5.60	7.23	8.82	10.38	11.89	13.36
5 YRS.	1.40	100.00	0.84	4.10	7.23	10.22	13.09	15.84	18.48	21.00	23.42
	1.50	90.32	0.81	3.96	6.98	9.88	12.66	15.32	17.88	20.33	22.68
	1.75	67.08	0.74	3.63	6.40	9.06	11.62	14.08	16.45	18.72	20.91
	2.00	43.85	0.67	3.29	5.82	8.25	10.59	12.84	15.02	17.11	19.13
	2.25	20.62	0.60	2.96	5.23	7.43	9.55	11.60	13.59	15.50	17.36
	2.47	0.0	0.54	2.66	4.71	6.70	8.63	10.50	12.32	14.08	15.78
6 YRS.	1.40	100.00	0.94	4.57	8.02	11.31	14.43	17.41	20.25	22.95	25.52
	1.50	87.22	0.90	4.38	7.69	10.85	13.85	16.72	19.46	22.06	24.55
	1.75	56.54	0.80	3.92	6.90	9.74	12.46	15.07	17.56	19.94	22.22
	2.00	25.86	0.71	3.46	6.10	8.64	11.07	13.41	15.66	17.82	19.89
	2.21	0.0	0.63	3.07	5.43	7.71	9.90	12.02	14.06	16.03	17.93
7 YRS.	1.40	100.00	1.02	4.96	8.68	12.20	15.53	18.68	21.66	24.48	27.16
	1.50	83.55	0.97	4.71	8.25	11.61	14.79	17.80	20.67	23.38	25.96
	1.75	44.08	0.84	4.12	7.23	10.20	13.02	15.71	18.28	20.73	23.06
	2.03	0.0	0.71	3.48	6.09	8.62	11.05	13.38	15.62	17.77	19.83
8 YRS.	1.40	100.00	1.09	5.28	9.22	12.93	16.41	19.69	22.78	25.69	28.44
	1.50	79.23	1.03	4.98	8.70	12.20	15.51	18.64	21.58	24.37	27.00
	1.75	29.37	0.87	4.24	7.44	10.47	13.36	16.10	18.71	21.19	23.55
	1.90	0.0	0.78	3.81	6.70	9.45	12.09	14.60	17.01	19.31	21.51
9 YRS.	1.40	100.00	1.15	5.55	9.67	13.52	17.13	20.51	23.68	26.65	29.44
	1.50	74.11	1.07	5.18	9.04	12.67	16.07	19.26	22.27	25.10	27.77
	1.80	0.0	0.85	4.13	7.24	10.21	13.02	15.70	18.25	20.68	22.99
10 YRS.	1.40	100.00	1.20	5.78	10.04	14.01	17.71	21.17	24.39	27.40	30.22
	1.50	68.00	1.11	5.35	9.31	13.02	16.48	19.73	22.78	25.64	28.33
	1.72	0.0	0.91	4.42	7.74	10.89	13.86	16.68	19.35	21.89	24.30
		MONTHS									
UNTIL PAID	1.50	192.42	1.19	5.70	9.87	13.74	17.33	20.66	23.77	26.66	29.36
	1.75	115.25	0.89	4.31	7.55	10.63	13.54	16.31	18.93	21.43	23.80
	2.00	86.36	0.72	3.53	6.22	8.79	11.26	13.63	15.90	18.09	20.18
	2.25	69.87	0.61	3.00	5.31	7.54	9.68	11.76	13.76	15.70	17.57
	2.50	58.45	0.53	2.62	4.65	6.61	8.51	10.36	12.16	13.90	15.58
	3.00	45.16	0.42	2.10	3.73	5.32	6.88	8.40	9.89	11.33	12.75
	3.50	36.71	0.35	1.76	3.13	4.47	5.79	7.08	8.35	9.59	10.81
	4.00	30.96	0.31	1.51	2.70	3.86	5.01	6.14	7.24	8.33	9.40

EXAMPLES *ON PAGES A-382 TO A-397*

MORTGAGE YIELD TABLE
SHOWING DISCOUNT PERCENTAGES AT VARIOUS YIELDS, MONTHLY PAYMENT RATES AND DUE DATES

DUE DATE	26%	27%	28%	29%	30%	31%	32%	33%	34%	35%	36%
1 YR.	8.07	8.90	9.71	10.52	11.33	12.12	12.91	13.68	14.45	15.21	15.97
	8.02	8.85	9.66	10.46	11.26	12.05	12.83	13.61	14.37	15.13	15.88
	7.91	8.72	9.53	10.32	11.11	11.89	12.66	13.42	14.18	14.92	15.66
	7.80	8.60	9.39	10.18	10.95	11.72	12.48	13.23	13.98	14.72	15.45
	7.69	8.48	9.26	10.03	10.80	11.56	12.31	13.05	13.78	14.51	15.23
	7.58	8.36	9.13	9.89	10.64	11.39	12.13	12.86	13.59	14.31	15.02
	7.47	8.24	8.99	9.75	10.49	11.23	11.96	12.68	13.39	14.10	14.80
	4.65	5.14	5.62	6.09	6.57	7.04	7.50	7.96	8.42	8.88	9.33
2 YRS.	14.31	15.71	17.08	18.43	19.75	21.04	22.32	23.56	24.79	25.99	27.17
	14.14	15.52	16.88	18.21	19.51	20.80	22.05	23.29	24.50	25.69	26.85
	13.72	15.07	16.39	17.68	18.95	20.20	21.42	22.62	23.80	24.96	26.10
	13.31	14.61	15.89	17.15	18.39	19.60	20.79	21.96	23.11	24.23	25.34
	12.89	14.16	15.40	16.63	17.83	19.00	20.16	21.30	22.41	23.51	24.58
	12.48	13.71	14.91	16.10	17.26	18.41	19.53	20.63	21.72	22.78	23.83
	12.00	13.25	14.42	15.57	16.70	17.81	18.90	19.97	21.02	22.05	23.07
	8.45	9.30	10.14	10.97	11.79	12.59	13.39	14.18	14.95	15.72	16.47
3 YRS.	19.13	20.92	22.66	24.38	26.01	27.62	29.18	30.70	32.18	33.62	35.02
	18.78	20.54	22.25	23.92	25.54	27.12	28.66	30.16	31.61	33.03	34.41
	17.93	19.62	21.26	22.86	24.42	25.93	27.53	28.85	30.26	31.62	32.96
	17.08	18.70	20.27	21.80	23.29	24.75	26.17	27.55	28.90	30.21	31.50
	16.24	17.78	19.28	20.74	22.17	23.56	24.92	26.25	27.54	28.80	30.04
	15.39	16.85	18.28	19.68	21.04	22.37	23.67	24.94	26.18	27.40	28.58
	14.93	16.29	17.62	18.92	20.19	21.43	22.64	23.83	24.99	26.12	27.12
	11.82	12.97	14.11	15.22	16.31	17.38	18.43	19.46	20.47	21.46	22.43
4 YRS.	22.86	24.92	26.90	28.82	30.67	32.45	34.18	35.85	37.46	39.02	40.53
	22.29	24.30	26.24	28.12	29.93	31.68	33.37	35.01	36.60	38.13	39.61
	21.22	23.33	24.66	26.04	28.16	29.83	31.44	33.00	34.51	35.97	37.39
	19.57	21.35	23.09	24.76	26.39	27.97	29.50	30.98	32.42	33.81	35.17
	18.20	19.88	21.51	23.09	24.62	26.11	27.56	28.97	30.33	31.66	32.95
	16.84	18.40	19.93	21.41	22.85	24.26	25.62	26.95	28.24	29.50	30.73
	15.47	16.93	18.35	19.74	21.09	22.40	23.69	24.94	26.16	27.35	28.51
	14.80	16.21	17.58	18.91	20.22	21.49	22.74	23.95	25.13	26.29	27.42
5 YRS.	25.75	27.97	30.11	32.18	34.13	36.02	37.83	39.57	41.25	42.85	44.40
	24.94	27.11	29.19	31.19	33.11	34.95	36.73	38.43	40.07	41.64	43.16
	23.01	25.04	26.99	28.86	30.66	32.40	34.07	35.69	37.24	38.74	40.18
	21.08	22.96	24.78	26.53	28.22	29.85	31.42	32.94	34.41	35.83	37.21
	19.15	20.89	22.57	24.20	25.77	27.29	28.77	30.20	31.59	32.93	34.23
	17.44	19.05	20.61	22.13	23.60	25.03	26.42	27.77	29.08	30.35	31.59
6 YRS.	27.98	30.31	32.54	34.67	36.70	38.64	40.49	42.26	43.95	45.56	47.11
	26.93	29.19	31.38	33.42	35.40	37.29	39.09	40.82	42.47	44.06	45.57
	24.41	26.50	28.51	30.43	32.28	34.04	35.74	37.37	38.93	40.44	41.88
	21.89	23.81	25.66	27.44	29.15	30.80	32.39	33.92	35.40	36.82	38.19
	19.77	21.54	23.26	24.92	26.52	28.07	29.56	31.01	32.41	33.77	35.08
7 YRS.	29.70	32.11	34.39	36.56	38.62	40.57	42.43	44.20	45.88	47.48	49.01
	28.40	30.73	32.94	35.04	37.04	38.94	40.76	42.48	44.13	45.70	47.20
	25.29	27.42	29.45	31.40	33.26	35.04	36.74	38.37	39.93	41.42	42.86
	21.82	23.73	25.56	27.33	29.03	30.67	32.25	33.77	35.23	36.65	38.01
8 YRS.	31.03	33.48	35.79	37.97	40.04	42.00	43.85	45.60	47.26	48.84	50.34
	29.49	31.85	34.08	36.20	38.20	40.11	41.91	43.63	45.26	46.81	48.29
	25.80	27.94	29.98	31.94	33.80	35.57	37.27	38.90	40.45	41.94	43.36
	23.62	25.64	27.57	29.42	31.20	32.91	34.54	36.11	37.62	39.07	40.46
9 YRS.	32.06	34.53	36.85	39.04	41.10	43.04	44.88	46.61	48.25	49.81	51.28
	30.29	32.66	34.90	37.02	39.02	40.91	42.71	44.41	46.02	47.55	49.01
	25.20	27.31	29.32	31.23	33.07	34.82	36.50	38.10	39.64	41.11	42.52
10 YRS.	32.86	35.33	37.66	39.84	41.89	43.81	45.63	47.34	48.96	50.49	51.93
	30.86	33.24	35.48	37.59	39.58	41.47	43.25	44.93	46.53	48.04	49.48
	26.59	28.76	30.83	32.80	34.67	36.46	38.16	39.79	41.34	42.83	44.25
UNTIL PAID	31.89	34.25	36.47	38.56	40.52	42.36	44.11	45.75	47.30	48.78	50.17
	26.06	28.21	30.25	32.21	34.07	35.84	37.54	39.16	40.70	42.18	43.60
	22.19	24.12	25.98	27.77	29.48	31.14	32.73	34.28	35.73	37.16	38.53
	19.38	21.13	22.81	24.45	26.03	27.56	29.04	30.47	31.86	33.21	34.51
	17.22	18.82	20.36	21.86	23.32	24.74	26.12	27.46	28.76	30.02	31.26
	14.13	15.48	16.80	18.09	19.34	20.57	21.78	22.95	24.10	25.22	26.32
	12.01	13.18	14.33	15.45	16.56	17.64	18.70	19.74	20.77	21.77	22.75
	10.45	11.49	12.51	13.51	14.49	15.46	16.41	17.34	18.26	19.17	20.06

EXAMPLES *ON PAGES A-382 TO A-397*

MORTGAGE YIELD TABLE
SHOWING DISCOUNT PERCENTAGES AT VARIOUS YIELDS, MONTHLY PAYMENT RATES AND DUE DATES

DUE DATE	PAY'T RATE %	BAL REMAIN %	18%	19%	20%	21%	22%	23%	24%	25%	26%
			YIELD PERCENTAGES								
1 YR.	1.42	100.00	0.91	1.81	2.70	3.58	4.45	5.31	6.17	7.01	7.85
	1.50	98.92	0.90	1.80	2.69	3.56	4.43	5.29	6.14	6.98	7.81
	1.75	95.67	0.89	1.77	2.65	3.51	4.37	5.22	6.06	6.89	7.71
	2.00	92.43	0.88	1.75	2.61	3.46	4.31	5.14	5.97	6.79	7.60
	2.25	89.18	0.87	1.72	2.57	3.41	4.25	5.07	5.89	6.69	7.49
	2.50	85.94	0.85	1.70	2.54	3.36	4.18	5.00	5.80	6.60	7.38
	2.75	82.69	0.84	1.67	2.50	3.32	4.12	4.92	5.72	6.50	7.28
	9.12	0.0	0.52	1.03	1.54	2.05	2.55	3.05	3.55	4.04	4.53
2 YRS.	1.42	100.00	1.67	3.31	4.91	6.49	8.03	9.55	11.03	12.49	13.92
	1.50	97.64	1.65	3.27	4.86	6.42	7.95	9.45	10.93	12.37	13.79
	1.75	90.55	1.60	3.18	4.72	6.23	7.72	9.17	10.60	12.01	13.38
	2.00	83.46	1.55	3.08	4.57	6.04	7.48	8.89	10.28	11.64	12.98
	2.25	76.38	1.50	2.98	4.43	5.85	7.24	8.61	9.96	11.28	12.58
	2.50	69.29	1.45	2.88	4.28	5.66	7.01	8.33	9.64	10.92	12.17
	2.75	62.20	1.40	2.78	4.13	5.46	6.77	8.05	9.31	10.55	11.77
	4.94	0.0	0.97	1.92	2.86	3.78	4.70	5.60	6.49	7.36	8.23
3 YRS.	1.42	100.00	2.31	4.55	6.73	8.85	10.91	12.92	14.87	16.77	18.61
	1.50	96.12	2.27	4.48	6.62	8.71	10.74	12.72	14.65	16.52	18.34
	1.75	84.49	2.16	4.27	6.31	8.31	10.25	12.14	13.98	15.77	17.51
	2.00	72.85	2.05	4.06	6.00	7.90	9.75	11.55	13.31	15.02	16.69
	2.25	61.22	1.95	3.84	5.69	7.50	9.26	10.97	12.64	14.27	15.86
	2.50	49.58	1.84	3.63	5.39	7.09	8.76	10.39	11.97	13.52	15.03
	2.75	37.94	1.73	3.42	5.08	6.69	8.26	9.80	11.30	12.77	14.21
	3.57	0.0	1.38	2.74	4.07	5.37	6.64	7.90	9.13	10.33	11.51
4 YRS.	1.42	100.00	2.84	5.57	8.22	10.76	13.22	15.60	17.89	20.11	22.24
	1.50	94.33	2.78	5.46	8.04	10.54	12.95	15.28	17.53	19.70	21.80
	1.75	77.31	2.59	5.10	7.53	9.87	12.13	14.32	16.44	18.49	20.47
	2.00	60.29	2.41	4.75	7.01	9.20	11.31	13.37	15.35	17.27	19.13
	2.25	43.27	2.23	4.39	6.49	8.52	10.50	12.41	14.26	16.06	17.81
	2.50	26.25	2.05	4.04	5.97	7.85	9.68	11.45	13.17	14.85	16.47
	2.75	9.23	1.87	3.69	5.46	7.18	8.86	10.49	12.08	13.63	15.14
	2.89	0.0	1.77	3.50	5.18	6.82	8.41	9.97	11.49	12.97	14.42
5 YRS.	1.42	100.00	3.28	6.42	9.44	12.32	15.09	17.74	20.28	22.71	25.05
	1.50	92.20	3.19	6.25	9.18	11.99	14.69	17.28	19.76	22.14	24.42
	1.75	68.81	2.92	5.73	8.43	11.02	13.50	15.90	18.20	20.42	22.55
	2.00	45.41	2.65	5.21	7.67	10.04	12.32	14.52	16.64	18.68	20.65
	2.25	22.02	2.38	4.69	6.91	9.06	11.13	13.14	15.08	16.95	18.77
	2.49	0.0	2.13	4.19	6.20	8.13	10.02	11.84	13.61	15.33	16.99
6 YRS.	1.42	100.00	3.65	7.13	10.44	13.59	16.58	19.44	22.16	24.75	27.22
	1.50	89.69	3.53	6.89	10.10	13.15	16.05	18.83	21.47	23.99	26.40
	1.75	58.74	3.16	6.18	9.07	11.83	14.47	17.00	19.41	21.72	23.94
	2.00	27.80	2.79	5.47	8.05	10.51	12.89	15.16	17.35	19.45	21.48
	2.22	0.0	2.46	4.84	7.13	9.33	11.46	13.52	15.50	17.41	19.26
7 YRS.	1.42	100.00	3.96	7.71	11.26	14.61	17.79	20.79	23.64	26.34	28.90
	1.50	86.71	3.81	7.41	10.82	14.05	17.12	20.02	22.78	25.40	27.88
	1.75	46.83	3.33	6.50	9.51	12.38	15.12	17.72	20.21	22.58	24.84
	2.04	0.0	2.77	5.42	7.97	10.42	12.76	15.02	17.18	19.26	21.26
8 YRS.	1.42	100.00	4.23	8.20	11.93	15.45	18.75	21.87	24.81	27.58	30.19
	1.50	83.18	4.03	7.82	11.39	14.76	17.94	20.94	23.78	26.46	28.99
	1.75	32.72	3.44	6.69	9.79	12.72	15.51	18.16	20.68	23.08	25.37
	1.91	0.0	3.05	5.96	8.74	11.40	13.93	16.36	18.68	20.90	23.02
9 YRS.	1.42	100.00	4.44	8.60	12.48	16.12	19.53	22.73	25.73	28.55	31.20
	1.50	79.01	4.20	8.15	11.84	15.32	18.58	21.64	24.53	27.24	29.80
	1.81	0.0	3.31	6.45	9.44	12.28	14.98	17.55	20.00	22.34	24.56
10 YRS.	1.42	100.00	4.62	8.93	12.94	16.67	20.16	23.41	26.46	29.30	31.97
	1.50	74.06	4.34	8.40	12.19	15.74	19.06	22.17	25.09	27.83	30.40
	1.74	0.0	3.54	6.90	10.07	13.07	15.92	18.61	21.17	23.60	25.91
		MONTHS									
UNTIL PAID	1.50	205.47	4.69	9.02	13.01	16.71	20.14	23.32	26.28	29.04	31.62
	1.75	117.88	3.50	6.82	9.96	12.94	15.76	18.44	20.98	23.39	25.69
	2.00	87.59	2.86	5.59	8.21	10.72	13.13	15.44	17.65	19.77	21.81
	2.25	70.61	2.43	4.76	7.02	9.20	11.30	13.33	15.29	17.19	19.01
	2.50	59.45	2.11	4.16	6.15	8.08	9.95	11.76	13.52	15.22	16.88
	3.00	45.43	1.69	3.34	4.95	6.52	8.05	9.55	11.01	12.43	13.83
	3.50	36.88	1.41	2.79	4.15	5.48	6.78	8.06	9.31	10.53	11.74
	4.00	31.08	1.21	2.41	3.58	4.73	5.87	6.98	8.08	9.15	10.21

EXAMPLES *ON PAGES A-382 TO A-397*

MORTGAGE YIELD TABLE

17% INTEREST

SHOWING DISCOUNT PERCENTAGES AT VARIOUS
YIELDS, MONTHLY PAYMENT RATES AND DUE DATES

17% INTEREST

DUE DATE	27%	28%	29%	30%	31%	32%	33%	34%	35%	36%	37%
	YIELD PERCENTAGES										
1 YR.	8.68	9.50	10.31	11.11	11.91	12.69	13.47	14.24	15.01	15.76	16.51
	8.64	9.46	10.26	11.06	11.85	12.64	13.41	14.18	14.94	15.69	16.43
	8.52	9.33	10.12	10.91	11.69	12.46	13.23	13.99	14.75	15.48	16.21
	8.40	9.20	9.98	10.76	11.53	12.29	13.05	13.79	14.53	15.26	15.99
	8.28	9.07	9.84	10.61	11.37	12.12	12.86	13.60	14.33	15.05	15.77
	8.16	8.94	9.70	10.46	11.21	11.95	12.68	13.41	14.13	14.84	15.55
	8.04	8.81	9.56	10.30	11.04	11.77	12.50	13.22	13.92	14.63	15.32
	5.01	5.49	5.97	6.44	6.91	7.38	7.84	8.30	8.76	9.21	9.66
2 YRS.	15.32	16.70	18.05	19.38	20.67	21.95	23.20	24.43	25.63	26.81	27.97
	15.18	16.54	17.88	19.19	20.48	21.74	22.98	24.20	25.39	26.57	27.72
	14.73	16.06	17.36	18.64	19.89	21.12	22.33	23.51	24.68	25.82	26.94
	14.29	15.58	16.84	18.09	19.30	20.50	21.67	22.83	23.96	25.07	26.16
	13.85	15.10	16.33	17.53	18.72	19.88	21.02	22.14	23.24	24.32	25.38
	13.41	14.62	15.81	16.98	18.13	19.26	20.37	21.45	22.52	23.58	24.61
	12.96	14.14	15.29	16.43	17.54	18.63	19.71	20.77	21.81	22.83	23.83
	9.08	9.92	10.75	11.57	12.38	13.18	13.97	14.74	15.51	16.27	17.01
3 YRS.	20.41	22.16	23.88	25.52	27.13	28.70	30.23	31.71	33.16	34.57	35.94
	20.11	21.84	23.52	25.15	26.74	28.29	29.80	31.27	32.69	34.09	35.44
	19.21	20.87	22.48	24.04	25.57	27.06	28.51	29.93	31.30	32.64	33.95
	18.31	19.89	21.44	22.94	24.40	25.83	27.23	28.58	29.91	31.20	32.46
	17.41	18.92	20.40	21.83	23.24	24.60	25.94	27.24	28.52	29.76	30.97
	16.51	17.95	19.35	20.73	22.07	23.38	24.65	25.90	27.12	28.31	29.48
	15.61	16.98	18.31	19.62	20.90	22.15	23.37	24.56	25.73	26.87	27.98
	12.67	13.81	14.92	16.02	17.09	18.14	19.18	20.19	21.19	22.16	23.12
4 YRS.	24.31	26.30	28.23	30.09	31.88	33.62	35.30	36.92	38.49	40.01	41.47
	23.83	25.79	27.68	29.51	31.28	32.98	34.64	36.23	37.78	39.27	40.72
	22.38	24.24	26.03	27.77	29.45	31.07	32.65	34.17	35.65	37.08	38.46
	20.94	22.69	24.38	26.03	27.62	29.16	30.66	32.11	33.51	34.88	36.20
	19.50	21.14	22.74	24.29	25.79	27.25	28.67	30.04	31.38	32.68	33.94
	18.06	19.59	21.09	22.54	23.96	25.34	26.68	27.98	29.25	30.48	31.68
	16.61	18.05	19.44	20.80	22.13	23.42	24.69	25.91	27.11	28.28	29.43
	15.83	17.21	18.55	19.86	21.14	22.39	23.61	24.80	25.96	27.09	28.20
5 YRS.	27.29	29.44	31.50	33.48	35.39	37.21	38.96	40.65	42.27	43.82	45.31
	26.04	28.72	30.74	32.68	34.55	36.34	38.06	39.72	41.31	42.84	44.31
	24.58	26.55	28.45	30.27	32.03	33.72	35.35	36.92	38.43	39.89	41.29
	22.55	24.39	26.15	27.86	29.51	31.10	32.64	34.12	35.56	36.94	38.28
	20.52	22.22	23.86	25.45	26.99	28.48	29.93	31.32	32.68	33.99	35.27
	18.61	20.18	21.70	23.18	24.62	26.02	27.37	28.69	29.97	31.22	32.43
6 YRS.	29.57	31.82	33.96	36.01	37.96	39.83	41.61	43.31	44.94	46.49	47.98
	28.70	30.89	32.98	34.98	36.90	38.72	40.47	42.14	43.74	45.28	46.74
	26.06	28.09	30.04	31.90	33.69	35.41	37.06	38.64	40.16	41.62	43.02
	23.42	25.29	27.09	28.82	30.49	32.10	33.64	35.14	36.57	37.96	39.30
	21.05	22.77	24.44	26.05	27.61	29.12	30.58	31.99	33.35	34.67	35.95
7 YRS.	31.32	33.63	35.81	37.89	39.86	41.74	43.52	45.22	46.83	48.37	49.84
	30.24	32.48	34.62	36.64	38.57	40.41	42.16	43.83	45.42	46.94	48.38
	27.00	29.06	31.03	32.91	34.71	36.44	38.08	39.66	41.18	42.63	44.02
	23.19	25.04	26.82	28.53	30.18	31.77	33.30	34.77	36.20	37.57	38.89
8 YRS.	32.66	34.99	37.20	39.28	41.26	43.13	44.90	46.58	48.17	49.69	51.12
	31.38	33.65	35.80	37.83	39.76	41.60	43.34	44.99	46.56	48.06	49.48
	27.54	29.62	31.60	33.48	35.28	37.01	38.65	40.22	41.73	43.17	44.55
	25.05	27.00	28.87	30.66	32.38	34.03	35.61	37.13	38.59	39.99	41.35
9 YRS.	33.69	36.03	38.24	40.32	42.29	44.14	45.90	47.55	49.12	50.61	52.02
	32.22	34.50	36.65	38.68	40.60	42.42	44.15	45.78	47.34	48.81	50.21
	26.68	28.71	30.65	32.50	34.26	35.95	37.57	39.12	40.61	42.03	43.39
10 YRS.	34.47	36.82	39.02	41.09	43.05	44.88	46.62	48.25	49.80	51.26	52.64
	32.82	35.10	37.25	39.27	41.19	42.99	44.70	46.32	47.85	49.31	50.69
	28.11	30.19	32.18	34.07	35.88	37.60	39.24	40.81	42.30	43.74	45.11
UNTIL PAID	34.02	36.28	38.39	40.38	42.24	44.00	45.66	47.23	48.71	50.12	51.45
	27.87	29.95	31.92	33.81	35.61	37.32	38.96	40.53	42.02	43.46	44.83
	23.77	25.65	27.46	29.20	30.87	32.48	34.03	35.52	36.96	38.34	39.67
	20.78	22.49	24.14	25.74	27.29	28.78	30.23	31.63	32.99	34.30	35.58
	18.49	20.05	21.57	23.04	24.47	25.86	27.21	28.53	29.80	31.04	32.25
	15.19	16.52	17.82	19.08	20.32	21.53	22.72	23.87	25.00	26.11	27.19
	12.92	14.07	15.21	16.32	17.41	18.48	19.53	20.55	21.56	22.55	23.53
	11.25	12.28	13.28	14.27	15.24	16.20	17.14	18.07	18.98	19.87	20.75

EXAMPLES *ON PAGES A-382 TO A-397*

MORTGAGE YIELD TABLE

17¼% INTEREST   **17¼%** INTEREST

SHOWING DISCOUNT PERCENTAGES AT VARIOUS
YIELDS, MONTHLY PAYMENT RATES AND DUE DATES

DUE DATE	PAY'T RATE %	BAL REMAIN %	18%	19%	20%	21%	22%	23%	24%	25%	26%
1 YR.	1.44	100.00	0.68	1.58	2.47	3.36	4.23	5.09	5.95	6.80	7.63
	1.50	99.19	0.68	1.58	2.47	3.34	4.21	5.07	5.93	6.77	7.61
	1.75	95.94	0.67	1.55	2.43	3.30	4.16	5.01	5.85	6.68	7.50
	2.00	92.69	0.66	1.53	2.40	3.25	4.10	4.93	5.76	6.58	7.40
	2.25	89.44	0.65	1.51	2.36	3.20	4.04	4.86	5.68	6.49	7.29
	2.50	86.19	0.64	1.49	2.33	3.16	3.98	4.79	5.60	6.40	7.19
	2.75	82.94	0.63	1.47	2.29	3.11	3.92	4.72	5.52	6.30	7.08
	9.13	0.0	0.39	0.90	1.42	1.92	2.43	2.93	3.42	3.91	4.40
2 YRS.	1.44	100.00	1.25	2.89	4.50	6.08	7.63	9.15	10.64	12.10	13.53
	1.50	98.22	1.24	2.87	4.47	6.04	7.57	9.08	10.56	12.01	13.44
	1.75	91.12	1.21	2.79	4.34	5.86	7.35	8.81	10.25	11.66	13.04
	2.00	84.01	1.17	2.70	4.20	5.68	7.12	8.54	9.94	11.31	12.65
	2.25	76.91	1.13	2.61	4.07	5.50	6.90	8.28	9.63	10.95	12.26
	2.50	69.80	1.09	2.53	3.93	5.32	6.67	8.01	9.32	10.60	11.86
	2.75	62.70	1.06	2.44	3.80	5.14	6.45	7.74	9.00	10.25	11.47
	4.96	0.0	0.72	1.68	2.62	3.55	4.46	5.37	6.26	7.14	8.00
3 YRS.	1.44	100.00	1.73	3.98	6.17	8.29	10.36	12.38	14.34	16.24	18.10
	1.50	97.08	1.71	3.93	6.10	8.20	10.25	12.24	14.18	16.06	17.90
	1.75	85.40	1.63	3.75	5.81	7.82	9.77	11.68	13.53	15.33	17.09
	2.00	73.72	1.55	3.56	5.53	7.44	9.30	11.12	12.88	14.61	16.29
	2.25	62.04	1.47	3.38	5.24	7.06	8.83	10.56	12.24	13.88	15.48
	2.50	50.36	1.39	3.19	4.96	6.68	8.36	9.99	11.59	13.15	14.67
	2.75	38.67	1.30	3.01	4.67	6.30	7.88	9.43	10.95	12.42	13.87
	3.58	0.0	1.04	2.40	3.73	5.04	6.32	7.58	8.81	10.02	11.20
4 YRS.	1.44	100.00	2.13	4.88	7.53	10.09	12.56	14.95	17.25	19.48	21.63
	1.50	95.72	2.09	4.80	7.41	9.93	12.37	14.72	16.99	19.18	21.30
	1.75	78.61	1.96	4.49	6.94	9.30	11.59	13.80	15.94	18.00	20.00
	2.00	61.50	1.82	4.18	6.46	8.67	10.81	12.88	14.88	16.82	18.70
	2.25	44.39	1.68	3.87	5.98	8.04	10.03	11.96	13.83	15.64	17.41
	2.50	27.27	1.55	3.56	5.51	7.41	9.25	11.04	12.77	14.46	16.11
	2.75	10.16	1.41	3.25	5.03	6.77	8.47	10.12	11.72	13.28	14.81
	2.90	0.0	1.33	3.06	4.75	6.40	8.00	9.57	11.09	12.58	14.04
5 YRS.	1.44	100.00	2.46	5.62	8.65	11.55	14.33	17.00	19.55	22.00	24.35
	1.50	94.11	2.41	5.51	8.48	11.32	14.05	16.67	19.18	21.58	23.89
	1.75	70.55	2.21	5.05	7.78	10.40	12.92	15.34	17.67	19.90	22.05
	2.00	46.99	2.00	4.59	7.08	9.48	11.79	14.01	16.15	18.22	20.21
	2.25	23.44	1.80	4.13	6.38	8.55	10.65	12.68	14.64	16.54	18.37
	2.50	0.0	1.60	3.68	5.69	7.64	9.53	11.36	13.14	14.87	16.54
6 YRS.	1.44	100.00	2.74	6.24	9.57	12.74	15.75	18.63	21.37	23.98	26.46
	1.50	92.20	2.67	6.08	9.33	12.43	15.38	18.19	20.87	23.42	25.86
	1.75	60.99	2.39	5.46	8.39	11.19	13.86	16.42	18.87	21.21	23.46
	2.00	29.78	2.12	4.83	7.44	9.95	12.35	14.66	16.87	19.00	21.05
	2.24	0.0	1.85	4.24	6.54	8.76	10.91	12.97	14.97	16.90	18.76
7 YRS.	1.44	100.00	2.97	6.75	10.32	13.70	16.90	19.93	22.80	25.52	28.09
	1.50	89.93	2.88	6.55	10.02	13.30	16.42	19.37	22.17	24.83	27.35
	1.75	49.64	2.52	5.74	8.81	11.73	14.50	17.15	19.67	22.08	24.37
	2.06	0.0	2.08	4.76	7.32	9.78	12.15	14.42	16.60	18.69	20.71
8 YRS.	1.44	100.00	3.17	7.17	10.94	14.48	17.82	20.96	23.92	26.72	29.36
	1.50	87.23	3.06	6.92	10.57	14.00	17.23	20.29	23.17	25.90	28.47
	1.75	36.17	2.61	5.93	9.08	12.07	14.91	17.61	20.17	22.61	24.93
	1.93	0.0	2.29	5.23	8.03	10.70	13.26	15.70	18.04	20.28	22.42
9 YRS.	1.44	100.00	3.33	7.52	11.44	15.11	18.56	21.78	24.81	27.66	30.33
	1.50	84.04	3.20	7.22	11.00	14.54	17.87	21.00	23.94	26.70	29.31
	1.83	0.0	2.49	5.66	8.67	11.53	14.26	16.85	19.32	21.68	23.92
10 YRS.	1.44	100.00	3.47	7.81	11.86	15.63	19.15	22.44	25.51	28.39	31.08
	1.50	80.24	3.31	7.46	11.34	14.97	18.36	21.54	24.51	27.31	29.93
	1.75	0.0	2.66	6.05	9.25	12.28	15.15	17.87	20.45	22.91	25.23
		MONTHS									
UNTIL PAID	1.50	222.67	3.63	8.13	12.27	16.09	19.61	22.88	25.91	28.73	31.35
	1.75	120.70	2.67	6.07	9.28	12.32	15.20	17.93	20.52	22.97	25.31
	2.00	88.88	2.17	4.95	7.62	10.17	12.61	14.96	17.20	19.36	21.43
	2.25	71.37	1.84	4.21	6.50	8.71	10.84	12.89	14.88	16.79	18.65
	2.50	59.95	1.60	3.67	5.68	7.63	9.52	11.36	13.13	14.86	16.53
	3.00	45.70	1.28	2.94	4.56	6.15	7.69	9.20	10.68	12.12	13.52
	3.50	37.05	1.06	2.46	3.82	5.16	6.47	7.76	9.02	10.25	11.46
	4.00	31.20	0.91	2.12	3.30	4.46	5.60	6.72	7.82	8.90	9.97

EXAMPLES *ON PAGES A-382 TO A-397*

MORTGAGE YIELD TABLE
SHOWING DISCOUNT PERCENTAGES AT VARIOUS YIELDS, MONTHLY PAYMENT RATES AND DUE DATES

DUE DATE	27%	28%	29%	30%	31%	32%	33%	34%	35%	36%	37%
					YIELD PERCENTAGES						
1 YR.	8.46	9.28	10.09	10.90	11.69	12.48	13.26	14.03	14.80	15.55	16.30
	8.43	9.25	10.06	10.86	11.65	12.44	13.22	13.99	14.75	15.50	16.25
	8.32	9.12	9.92	10.71	11.50	12.27	13.04	13.80	14.55	15.29	16.03
	8.20	9.00	9.78	10.56	11.34	12.10	12.86	13.61	14.35	15.08	15.81
	8.09	8.87	9.65	10.42	11.18	11.93	12.68	13.42	14.15	14.87	15.59
	7.97	8.74	9.51	10.27	11.02	11.76	12.50	13.23	13.95	14.66	15.37
	7.85	8.62	9.37	10.12	10.86	11.59	12.32	13.04	13.75	14.45	15.15
	4.89	5.37	5.85	6.32	6.79	7.26	7.72	8.19	8.64	9.10	9.55
2 YRS.	14.94	16.32	17.67	19.00	20.31	21.58	22.84	24.07	25.28	26.46	27.62
	14.83	16.20	17.55	18.87	20.16	21.43	22.68	23.90	25.10	26.28	27.43
	14.40	15.73	17.04	18.32	19.58	20.82	22.03	23.22	24.39	25.54	26.66
	13.97	15.26	16.53	17.78	19.00	20.21	21.39	22.55	23.68	24.80	25.90
	13.54	14.79	16.03	17.24	18.43	19.59	20.74	21.87	22.97	24.06	25.13
	13.10	14.32	15.52	16.69	17.85	18.98	20.10	21.19	22.27	23.32	24.36
	12.67	13.85	15.01	16.15	17.27	18.37	19.45	20.51	21.56	22.58	23.59
	8.86	9.70	10.54	11.36	12.17	12.97	13.76	14.54	15.30	16.06	16.81
3 YRS.	19.90	21.66	23.37	25.03	26.65	28.22	29.75	31.25	32.70	34.11	35.49
	19.68	21.42	23.11	24.76	26.36	27.92	29.44	30.92	32.35	33.76	35.12
	18.80	20.47	22.09	23.67	25.21	26.71	28.17	29.59	30.98	32.33	33.64
	17.92	19.31	21.07	22.58	24.06	25.50	26.90	28.27	29.60	30.90	32.17
	17.04	18.56	20.05	21.50	22.91	24.29	25.63	26.94	28.22	29.47	30.69
	16.16	17.61	19.03	20.41	21.76	23.08	24.36	25.62	26.85	28.05	29.22
	15.28	16.66	18.01	19.32	20.61	21.86	23.09	24.29	25.47	26.62	27.74
	12.36	13.51	14.62	15.72	16.80	17.86	18.89	19.91	20.91	21.89	22.85
4 YRS.	23.70	25.70	27.64	29.51	31.32	33.06	34.75	36.38	37.96	39.48	40.95
	23.35	25.32	27.23	29.08	30.87	32.59	34.26	35.87	37.43	38.94	40.39
	21.94	23.81	25.62	27.37	29.06	30.70	32.29	33.83	35.32	36.76	38.16
	20.53	22.29	24.00	25.66	27.26	28.82	30.33	31.79	33.21	34.58	35.92
	19.11	20.77	22.38	23.94	25.46	26.93	28.36	29.75	31.10	32.41	33.68
	17.70	19.25	20.76	22.23	23.66	25.05	26.40	27.71	28.99	30.23	31.44
	16.29	17.74	19.15	20.52	21.86	23.16	24.43	25.67	26.88	28.06	29.21
	15.45	16.84	18.18	19.50	20.79	22.04	23.26	24.46	25.63	26.77	27.88
5 YRS.	26.61	28.77	30.85	32.84	34.75	36.59	38.35	40.05	41.68	43.24	44.75
	26.11	28.24	30.28	32.25	34.13	35.94	37.68	39.36	40.97	42.51	44.00
	24.12	26.11	28.03	29.87	31.65	33.36	35.01	36.59	38.12	39.59	41.01
	22.14	23.99	25.78	27.50	29.17	30.77	32.33	33.82	35.27	36.67	38.02
	20.15	21.86	23.52	25.13	26.68	28.19	29.65	31.06	32.43	33.75	35.04
	18.17	19.75	21.28	22.77	24.21	25.62	26.98	28.31	29.59	30.85	32.06
6 YRS.	28.84	31.10	33.26	35.32	37.28	39.16	40.96	42.67	44.31	45.88	47.38
	28.19	30.41	32.53	34.56	36.49	38.35	40.12	41.81	43.43	44.98	46.46
	25.60	27.66	29.63	31.52	33.33	35.07	36.74	38.34	39.88	41.35	42.77
	23.02	24.91	26.73	28.49	30.17	31.80	33.36	34.87	36.32	37.72	39.08
	20.55	22.29	23.97	25.59	27.16	28.67	30.14	31.56	32.93	34.26	39.55
7 YRS.	30.54	32.86	35.07	37.16	39.15	41.04	42.84	44.55	46.18	47.73	49.21
	29.74	32.02	34.18	36.24	38.20	40.06	41.83	43.52	45.13	46.67	48.13
	26.56	28.65	30.65	32.56	34.38	36.13	37.90	39.40	40.93	42.39	43.80
	22.64	24.50	26.30	28.02	29.68	31.28	32.83	34.31	35.74	37.13	38.46
8 YRS.	31.85	34.20	36.42	38.53	40.52	42.41	44.20	45.89	47.50	49.03	50.49
	30.90	33.21	35.39	37.46	39.41	41.27	43.04	44.71	46.31	47.82	49.26
	27.14	29.24	31.25	33.16	34.90	36.73	38.39	39.99	41.51	42.96	44.36
	24.47	26.43	28.31	30.12	31.85	33.51	35.11	36.64	38.11	39.53	40.89
9 YRS.	32.85	35.21	37.44	39.55	41.53	43.41	45.18	46.85	48.44	49.94	51.37
	31.75	34.08	36.26	38.33	40.28	42.13	43.88	45.54	47.11	48.60	50.02
	26.06	28.10	30.06	31.92	33.70	35.41	37.04	38.60	40.10	41.54	42.91
10 YRS.	33.61	35.98	38.21	40.30	42.28	44.13	45.89	47.54	49.10	50.58	51.98
	32.39	34.71	36.90	38.95	40.90	42.73	44.46	46.10	47.66	49.13	50.53
	27.45	29.56	31.56	33.47	35.29	37.03	38.68	40.27	41.78	43.22	44.61
UNTIL PAID	33.80	36.09	38.24	40.25	42.13	43.91	45.58	47.16	48.66	50.07	51.41
	27.52	29.63	31.64	33.55	35.38	37.11	38.77	40.35	41.87	43.31	44.70
	23.41	25.32	27.15	28.91	30.60	32.23	33.80	35.30	36.76	38.15	39.50
	20.44	22.16	23.83	25.45	27.01	28.52	29.99	31.40	32.77	34.10	35.38
	18.16	19.74	21.27	22.76	24.20	25.60	26.97	28.29	29.58	30.83	32.05
	14.89	16.23	17.54	18.82	20.07	21.29	22.48	23.65	24.79	25.90	26.99
	12.65	13.82	14.96	16.08	17.17	18.25	19.31	20.34	21.36	22.35	23.33
	11.02	12.04	13.06	14.05	15.03	15.99	16.94	17.87	18.78	19.68	20.57

EXAMPLES ON PAGES A-382 TO A-397

MORTGAGE YIELD TABLE
SHOWING DISCOUNT PERCENTAGES AT VARIOUS
YIELDS, MONTHLY PAYMENT RATES AND DUE DATES

DUE DATE	PAY'T RATE %	BAL REMAIN %	18%	19%	20%	21%	22%	23%	24%	25%	26%
1 YR.	1.46	100.00	0.45	1.36	2.25	3.13	4.01	4.87	5.73	6.58	7.41
	1.50	99.46	0.45	1.35	2.24	3.13	4.00	4.86	5.72	6.56	7.40
	1.75	96.21	0.45	1.33	2.21	3.08	3.94	4.79	5.64	6.47	7.30
	2.00	92.95	0.44	1.32	2.18	3.04	3.89	4.73	5.56	6.38	7.19
	2.25	89.70	0.43	1.30	2.15	2.99	3.83	4.66	5.48	6.29	7.09
	2.50	86.45	0.43	1.28	2.12	2.95	3.78	4.59	5.40	6.20	6.99
	2.75	83.19	0.42	1.26	2.09	2.91	3.72	4.52	5.32	6.11	6.89
	9.14	0.0	0.26	0.78	1.29	1.80	2.30	2.80	3.30	3.79	4.28
2 YRS.	1.46	100.00	0.83	2.48	4.09	5.68	7.23	8.75	10.25	11.71	13.15
	1.50	98.81	0.83	2.47	4.07	5.65	7.19	8.71	10.20	11.65	13.08
	1.75	91.69	0.81	2.39	3.95	5.48	6.98	8.45	9.89	11.31	12.70
	2.00	84.57	0.78	2.32	3.83	5.31	6.77	8.19	9.59	10.97	12.32
	2.25	77.45	0.76	2.25	3.71	5.14	6.55	7.94	9.29	10.63	11.94
	2.50	70.32	0.73	2.17	3.59	4.97	6.34	7.68	8.99	10.29	11.55
	2.75	63.20	0.71	2.10	3.46	4.81	6.13	7.42	8.69	9.94	11.17
	4.97	0.0	0.48	1.44	2.38	3.31	4.23	5.14	6.03	6.91	7.78
3 YRS.	1.46	100.00	1.15	3.41	5.61	7.74	9.82	11.84	13.81	15.72	17.58
	1.50	98.05	1.14	3.38	5.56	7.68	9.74	11.75	13.70	15.60	17.45
	1.75	86.32	1.09	3.22	5.30	7.33	9.30	11.21	13.08	14.90	16.67
	2.00	74.59	1.04	3.07	5.04	6.97	8.85	10.67	12.46	14.19	15.88
	2.25	62.87	0.98	2.91	4.78	6.61	8.40	10.14	11.83	13.49	15.10
	2.50	51.14	0.93	2.75	4.53	6.26	7.95	9.60	11.21	12.78	14.31
	2.75	39.41	0.87	2.59	4.27	5.90	7.50	9.06	10.59	12.07	13.53
	3.59	0.0	0.69	2.06	3.39	4.71	5.99	7.25	8.49	9.70	10.89
4 YRS.	1.46	100.00	1.42	4.18	6.85	9.42	11.90	14.30	16.61	18.85	21.01
	1.50	97.13	1.40	4.14	6.77	9.32	11.78	14.15	16.44	18.66	20.80
	1.75	79.93	1.31	3.87	6.34	8.73	11.04	13.27	15.43	17.51	19.53
	2.00	62.72	1.22	3.60	5.91	8.14	10.30	12.39	14.41	16.37	18.27
	2.25	45.52	1.13	3.33	5.47	7.54	9.55	11.50	13.39	15.22	17.00
	2.50	28.31	1.04	3.07	5.04	6.95	8.81	10.62	12.37	14.08	15.73
	2.75	11.11	0.95	2.80	4.60	6.36	8.07	9.73	11.35	12.93	14.47
	2.91	0.0	0.89	2.63	4.32	5.98	7.59	9.16	10.70	12.19	13.65
5 YRS.	1.46	100.00	1.64	4.82	7.86	10.78	13.58	16.26	18.83	21.29	23.66
	1.50	98.05	1.62	4.75	7.76	10.64	13.40	16.05	18.59	21.02	23.36
	1.75	72.32	1.48	4.36	7.12	9.77	12.32	14.77	17.13	19.39	21.56
	2.00	48.60	1.35	3.96	6.48	8.91	11.25	13.50	15.66	17.75	19.77
	2.25	24.88	1.21	3.57	5.85	8.04	10.17	12.22	14.20	16.12	17.98
	2.51	0.0	1.07	3.15	5.18	7.14	9.04	10.88	12.67	14.41	16.09
6 YRS.	1.46	100.00	1.83	5.35	8.70	11.89	14.92	17.82	20.57	23.20	25.71
	1.50	94.75	1.80	5.26	8.55	11.69	14.68	17.54	20.25	22.84	25.32
	1.75	63.28	1.61	4.72	7.69	10.53	13.24	15.84	18.32	20.70	22.97
	2.00	31.80	1.42	4.18	6.83	9.37	11.80	14.14	16.39	18.55	20.62
	2.25	0.0	1.24	3.64	5.96	8.19	10.35	12.43	14.44	16.38	18.25
7 YRS.	1.46	100.00	1.98	5.78	9.38	12.79	16.01	19.06	21.95	24.69	27.29
	1.50	93.22	1.94	5.67	9.20	12.54	15.70	18.70	21.54	24.23	26.81
	1.75	52.52	1.70	4.98	8.09	11.06	13.88	16.57	19.13	21.57	23.90
	2.07	0.0	1.39	4.08	6.67	9.15	11.53	13.81	16.01	18.12	20.15
8 YRS.	1.46	100.00	2.11	6.15	9.94	13.51	16.88	20.05	23.04	25.86	28.52
	1.50	91.39	2.06	6.00	9.72	13.21	16.51	19.62	22.55	25.32	27.94
	1.75	39.71	1.76	5.15	8.36	11.40	14.29	17.03	19.64	22.12	24.48
	1.94	0.0	1.53	4.49	7.31	10.01	12.58	15.05	17.40	19.66	21.81
9 YRS.	1.46	100.00	2.22	6.45	10.40	14.11	17.58	20.84	23.89	26.76	29.46
	1.50	89.21	2.16	6.28	10.13	13.75	17.14	20.33	23.33	26.14	28.80
	1.84	0.0	1.66	4.86	7.90	10.78	13.53	16.15	18.64	21.01	23.28
10 YRS.	1.46	100.00	2.31	6.70	10.78	14.59	18.14	21.46	24.57	27.47	30.20
	1.50	86.62	2.24	6.50	10.46	14.17	17.64	20.88	23.92	26.77	29.44
	1.77	0.0	1.78	5.19	8.42	11.48	14.38	17.12	19.73	22.20	24.56
		MONTHS									
UNTIL PAID	1.50	247.51	2.51	7.20	11.50	15.46	19.09	22.45	25.56	28.44	31.11
	1.75	123.76	1.81	5.29	8.58	11.68	14.62	17.41	20.05	22.55	24.92
	2.00	90.22	1.46	4.30	7.01	9.60	12.09	14.47	16.75	18.94	21.04
	2.25	72.15	1.24	3.64	5.97	8.20	10.36	12.45	14.46	16.40	18.27
	2.50	60.47	1.07	3.17	5.21	7.18	9.09	10.95	12.75	14.49	16.18
	3.00	45.98	0.86	2.54	4.17	5.77	7.33	8.86	10.34	11.79	13.21
	3.50	37.23	0.71	2.12	3.49	4.84	6.16	7.46	8.73	9.97	11.19
	4.00	31.32	0.61	1.82	3.01	4.18	5.33	6.45	7.56	8.65	9.72

EXAMPLES *ON PAGES A-382 TO A-397*

MORTGAGE YIELD TABLE
SHOWING DISCOUNT PERCENTAGES AT VARIOUS YIELDS, MONTHLY PAYMENT RATES AND DUE DATES

DUE DATE	27%	28%	29%	30%	31%	32%	33%	34%	35%	36%	37%
1 YR.	8.25	9.07	9.88	10.69	11.48	12.27	13.05	13.82	14.59	15.35	16.10
	8.23	9.05	9.86	10.66	11.46	12.24	13.02	13.79	14.56	15.31	16.06
	8.11	8.92	9.72	10.51	11.30	12.08	12.84	13.61	14.36	15.10	15.84
	8.00	8.80	9.59	10.37	11.14	11.91	12.67	13.42	14.16	14.90	15.63
	7.89	8.67	9.45	10.22	10.99	11.74	12.49	13.23	13.96	14.69	15.41
	7.77	8.55	9.32	10.08	10.83	11.58	12.31	13.04	13.77	14.48	15.19
	7.66	8.42	9.18	9.93	10.67	11.41	12.14	12.86	13.57	14.28	14.97
	4.76	5.25	5.73	6.20	6.67	7.14	7.60	8.07	8.52	8.98	9.43
2 YRS.	14.56	15.94	17.30	18.63	19.94	21.22	22.48	23.71	24.92	26.11	27.27
	14.49	15.86	17.22	18.54	19.84	21.12	22.37	23.60	24.80	25.99	27.15
	14.07	15.40	16.72	18.01	19.27	20.52	21.73	22.93	24.10	25.26	26.39
	13.64	14.94	16.22	17.47	18.70	19.91	21.10	22.26	23.41	24.53	25.63
	13.22	14.48	15.72	16.94	18.14	19.31	20.46	21.59	22.71	23.80	24.87
	12.80	14.03	15.23	16.41	17.57	18.71	19.83	20.93	22.01	23.07	24.11
	12.38	13.57	14.73	15.87	17.00	18.10	19.19	20.26	21.31	22.34	23.35
	8.64	9.48	10.32	11.14	11.95	12.76	13.55	14.35	15.10	15.86	16.61
3 YRS.	19.39	21.15	22.87	24.54	26.16	27.74	29.28	30.78	32.24	33.66	35.04
	19.25	21.00	22.70	24.36	25.97	27.54	29.07	30.56	32.01	33.42	34.80
	18.39	20.07	21.70	23.29	24.84	26.35	27.82	29.25	30.65	32.01	33.34
	17.53	19.13	20.70	22.22	23.71	25.16	26.57	27.95	29.29	30.60	31.88
	16.67	18.20	19.70	21.15	22.58	23.97	25.32	26.64	27.93	29.19	30.41
	15.81	17.27	18.69	20.09	21.45	22.77	24.07	25.33	26.57	27.77	28.95
	14.95	16.34	17.69	19.02	20.31	21.58	22.82	24.03	25.21	26.36	27.49
	12.06	13.20	14.33	15.43	16.51	17.57	18.61	19.63	20.63	21.62	22.58
4 YRS.	23.09	25.11	27.05	28.93	30.75	32.50	34.20	35.84	37.42	38.95	40.43
	22.86	24.86	26.79	28.65	30.45	32.19	33.87	35.50	37.07	38.59	40.07
	21.48	23.37	25.20	26.97	28.68	30.33	31.93	33.48	34.99	36.44	37.85
	20.10	21.88	23.61	25.28	26.90	28.47	29.99	31.47	32.90	34.29	35.63
	18.72	20.40	22.02	23.60	25.13	26.61	28.05	29.45	30.81	32.13	33.42
	17.34	18.91	20.43	21.91	23.35	24.75	26.11	27.44	28.73	29.98	31.20
	15.97	17.42	18.84	20.23	21.58	22.89	24.17	25.42	26.64	27.83	28.99
	12.96	14.11	15.22	16.31	17.39	18.44	19.48	20.49	21.47	22.44	27.56
5 YRS.	25.93	28.10	30.19	32.20	34.12	35.97	37.75	39.45	41.09	42.67	44.18
	25.60	27.76	29.82	31.81	33.71	35.55	37.30	39.00	40.62	42.18	43.69
	23.66	25.67	27.61	29.47	31.27	32.99	34.66	36.26	37.80	39.29	40.73
	21.71	23.59	25.39	27.14	28.82	30.44	32.01	33.52	34.99	36.40	37.76
	19.77	21.50	23.18	24.80	26.37	27.89	29.36	30.79	32.17	33.51	34.80
	17.73	19.31	20.85	22.35	23.80	25.21	26.59	27.92	29.21	30.47	31.70
6 YRS.	28.10	30.37	32.55	34.63	36.61	38.50	40.31	42.04	43.69	45.27	46.78
	27.67	29.93	32.07	34.13	36.09	37.96	39.75	41.47	43.10	44.67	46.17
	25.14	27.23	29.22	31.14	32.97	34.73	36.41	38.03	39.59	41.08	42.51
	22.61	24.53	26.37	28.15	29.85	31.49	33.08	34.60	36.07	37.48	38.85
	20.06	21.80	23.49	25.12	26.70	28.23	29.70	31.13	32.51	33.85	35.15
7 YRS.	29.76	32.10	34.32	36.43	38.44	40.34	42.16	43.89	45.53	47.10	48.59
	29.24	31.55	33.74	35.83	37.81	39.70	41.49	43.21	44.84	46.39	47.87
	26.12	28.24	30.26	32.20	34.05	35.81	37.50	39.12	40.67	42.15	43.57
	22.10	23.97	25.78	27.51	29.19	30.80	32.35	33.85	35.29	36.68	38.03
8 YRS.	31.03	33.40	35.65	37.77	39.78	41.69	43.50	45.21	46.84	48.38	49.85
	30.41	32.75	34.97	37.07	39.06	40.94	42.73	44.43	46.04	47.58	49.04
	26.72	28.85	30.89	32.83	34.68	36.45	38.13	39.74	41.28	42.76	44.17
	23.88	25.86	27.75	29.57	31.32	32.99	34.60	36.14	37.62	39.05	40.43
9 YRS.	32.00	34.39	36.65	38.77	40.78	42.67	44.46	46.16	47.76	49.28	50.72
	31.29	33.65	35.87	37.97	39.95	41.83	43.60	45.28	46.88	48.39	49.82
	25.43	27.50	29.46	31.34	33.14	34.86	36.51	38.08	39.59	41.04	42.43
10 YRS.	32.75	35.15	37.40	39.51	41.51	43.39	45.16	46.83	48.41	49.91	51.32
	31.95	34.31	36.53	38.62	40.60	42.46	44.22	45.88	47.45	48.94	50.36
	26.79	28.92	30.94	32.87	34.70	36.45	38.13	39.72	41.25	42.71	44.10
UNTIL PAID	33.60	35.93	38.10	40.13	42.04	43.83	45.52	47.11	48.61	50.03	51.38
	27.18	29.32	31.36	33.30	35.14	36.90	38.58	40.18	41.71	43.17	44.57
	23.05	24.98	26.84	28.62	30.33	31.98	33.56	35.09	36.55	37.96	39.32
	20.08	21.83	23.52	25.15	26.73	28.26	29.74	31.17	32.55	33.89	35.19
	17.82	19.42	20.96	22.47	23.93	25.34	26.72	28.05	29.35	30.62	31.84
	14.59	15.95	17.26	18.55	19.81	21.04	22.24	23.42	24.56	25.69	26.78
	12.39	13.56	14.71	15.83	16.94	18.02	19.08	20.13	21.15	22.15	23.14
	10.78	11.81	12.83	13.83	14.81	15.78	16.73	17.67	18.59	19.49	20.38

EXAMPLES *ON PAGES A-382 TO A-397*

MORTGAGE YIELD TABLE
SHOWING DISCOUNT PERCENTAGES AT VARIOUS
YIELDS, MONTHLY PAYMENT RATES AND DUE DATES

DUE DATE	PAY'T RATE %	BAL REMAIN %	YIELD PERCENTAGES								
			18%	19%	20%	21%	22%	23%	24%	25%	26%
1 YR.	1.48	100.00	0.23	1.13	2.02	2.91	3.78	4.65	5.51	6.36	7.20
	1.50	99.73	0.23	1.13	2.02	2.91	3.78	4.65	5.50	6.35	7.19
	1.75	96.47	0.22	1.11	1.99	2.86	3.73	4.58	5.43	6.26	7.09
	2.00	93.22	0.22	1.10	1.97	2.82	3.67	4.52	5.35	6.17	6.99
	2.25	89.96	0.22	1.08	1.94	2.78	3.62	4.45	5.27	6.09	6.89
	2.50	86.70	0.21	1.07	1.91	2.74	3.57	4.39	5.20	6.00	6.79
	2.75	83.45	0.21	1.05	1.88	2.70	3.52	4.32	5.12	5.91	6.69
	9.16	0.0	0.13	0.65	1.16	1.67	2.17	2.67	3.17	3.66	4.15
2 YRS.	1.48	100.00	0.42	2.07	3.68	5.27	6.83	8.35	9.85	11.32	12.76
	1.50	99.40	0.42	2.06	3.67	5.26	6.81	8.33	9.83	11.29	12.73
	1.75	92.26	0.40	2.00	3.57	5.10	6.61	8.09	9.54	10.96	12.36
	2.00	85.12	0.39	1.94	3.46	4.94	6.41	7.84	9.25	10.63	11.99
	2.25	77.98	0.38	1.88	3.35	4.79	6.20	7.59	8.96	10.30	11.62
	2.50	70.84	0.37	1.81	3.24	4.63	6.00	7.35	8.67	9.97	11.24
	2.75	63.70	0.35	1.75	3.13	4.48	5.80	7.10	8.38	9.64	10.87
	4.98	0.0	0.24	1.20	2.15	3.08	4.00	4.91	5.80	6.69	7.56
3 YRS.	1.48	100.00	0.58	2.84	5.05	7.19	9.27	11.30	13.28	15.20	17.06
	1.50	99.02	0.57	2.83	5.03	7.16	9.24	11.26	13.23	15.14	17.00
	1.75	87.25	0.55	2.70	4.79	6.83	8.81	10.74	12.62	14.45	16.24
	2.00	75.47	0.52	2.57	4.56	6.50	8.39	10.23	12.02	13.77	15.47
	2.25	63.70	0.49	2.43	4.32	6.17	7.96	9.72	11.42	13.09	14.71
	2.50	51.93	0.47	2.30	4.09	5.84	7.54	9.20	10.82	12.40	13.95
	2.75	40.16	0.44	2.17	3.86	5.50	7.11	8.69	10.22	11.72	13.18
	3.60	0.0	0.35	1.72	3.06	4.37	5.66	6.93	8.17	9.39	10.58
4 YRS.	1.48	100.00	0.71	3.48	6.16	8.75	11.24	13.65	15.98	18.22	20.39
	1.50	98.56	0.71	3.47	6.13	8.70	11.18	13.58	15.89	18.13	20.29
	1.75	81.26	0.66	3.24	5.74	8.19	10.48	12.73	14.91	17.02	19.06
	2.00	63.96	0.61	3.02	5.35	7.60	9.78	11.89	13.93	15.91	17.82
	2.25	46.67	0.57	2.80	4.95	7.05	9.07	11.04	12.95	14.80	16.59
	2.50	29.37	0.52	2.57	4.56	6.49	8.37	10.19	11.97	13.69	15.36
	2.75	12.07	0.48	2.35	4.17	5.94	7.67	9.35	10.98	12.58	14.13
	2.92	0.0	0.44	2.19	3.90	5.56	7.18	8.76	10.30	11.80	13.27
5 YRS.	1.48	100.00	0.82	4.02	7.08	10.01	12.82	15.52	18.10	20.58	22.96
	1.50	98.01	0.81	3.99	7.03	9.94	12.74	15.42	17.99	20.45	22.82
	1.75	74.12	0.75	3.66	6.45	9.14	11.72	14.20	16.58	18.87	21.07
	2.00	50.24	0.68	3.33	5.88	8.33	10.70	12.97	15.17	17.28	19.32
	2.25	26.35	0.61	3.00	5.30	7.53	9.68	11.75	13.76	15.70	17.57
	2.53	0.0	0.53	2.63	4.67	6.64	8.55	10.40	12.20	13.95	15.64
6 YRS.	1.48	100.00	0.91	4.46	7.83	11.04	14.10	17.01	19.78	22.43	24.95
	1.50	97.35	0.91	4.42	7.76	10.95	13.98	16.87	19.63	22.25	24.76
	1.75	65.61	0.81	3.97	6.98	9.86	12.61	15.25	17.76	20.17	22.47
	2.00	33.86	0.72	3.52	6.20	8.78	11.25	13.62	15.89	18.08	20.18
	2.27	0.0	0.62	3.04	5.37	7.62	9.79	11.88	13.90	15.85	17.74
7 YRS.	1.48	100.00	0.99	4.82	8.44	11.87	15.12	18.19	21.11	23.87	26.49
	1.50	96.57	0.98	4.77	8.36	11.76	14.97	18.02	20.91	23.65	26.25
	1.75	55.45	0.86	4.19	7.36	10.37	13.24	15.97	18.57	21.05	23.41
	2.09	0.0	0.70	3.41	6.01	8.51	10.90	13.21	15.42	17.54	19.58
8 YRS.	1.48	100.00	1.06	5.12	8.95	12.55	15.94	19.14	22.15	24.99	27.68
	1.50	95.64	1.04	5.06	8.85	12.41	15.77	18.93	21.92	24.73	27.40
	1.75	43.34	0.89	4.34	7.61	10.71	13.65	16.45	19.10	21.62	24.01
	1.98	0.0	0.77	3.75	6.59	9.31	11.91	14.39	16.76	19.03	21.21
9 YRS.	1.48	100.00	1.11	5.37	9.36	13.10	16.60	19.89	22.97	25.87	28.60
	1.50	94.53	1.10	5.30	9.24	12.93	16.39	19.65	22.70	25.57	28.27
	1.86	0.0	0.83	4.06	7.12	10.03	12.80	15.44	17.95	20.35	22.63
10 YRS.	1.48	100.00	1.16	5.58	9.70	13.55	17.13	20.49	23.62	26.56	29.31
	1.50	93.21	1.14	5.50	9.56	13.35	16.89	20.21	23.31	26.21	28.94
	1.79	0.0	0.89	4.34	7.59	10.68	13.60	16.38	19.00	21.50	23.87
		MONTHS									
UNTIL PAID	1.50	291.26	1.31	6.24	10.73	14.83	18.59	22.05	25.23	28.18	30.90
	1.75	127.07	0.92	4.49	7.85	11.03	14.03	16.88	19.57	22.11	24.53
	2.00	91.63	0.74	3.63	6.39	9.03	11.55	13.97	16.29	18.51	20.64
	2.25	72.95	0.63	3.07	5.42	7.69	9.88	11.99	14.03	16.00	17.89
	2.50	61.00	0.54	2.67	4.73	6.72	8.66	10.53	12.35	14.11	15.83
	3.00	46.27	0.43	2.13	3.78	5.39	6.97	8.51	10.00	11.47	12.90
	3.50	37.41	0.36	1.77	3.16	4.52	5.85	7.15	8.43	9.69	10.91
	4.00	31.44	0.31	1.52	2.72	3.90	5.05	6.19	7.30	8.40	9.48

EXAMPLES *ON PAGES A-382 TO A-397*

MORTGAGE YIELD TABLE
SHOWING DISCOUNT PERCENTAGES AT VARIOUS YIELDS, MONTHLY PAYMENT RATES AND DUE DATES

DUE DATE	27%	28%	29%	30%	31%	32%	33%	34%	35%	36%	37%
1 YR.	8.03	8.85	9.67	10.47	11.27	12.06	12.84	13.61	14.38	15.14	15.89
	8.02	8.84	9.65	10.46	11.26	12.05	12.83	13.60	14.36	15.12	15.87
	7.91	8.72	9.52	10.32	11.10	11.88	12.65	13.41	14.17	14.92	15.66
	7.80	8.60	9.39	10.17	10.95	11.72	12.48	13.23	13.97	14.71	15.44
	7.69	8.48	9.26	10.03	10.80	11.55	12.30	13.05	13.78	14.51	15.23
	7.58	8.36	9.13	9.89	10.64	11.39	12.13	12.86	13.59	14.30	15.01
	7.47	8.23	8.99	9.74	10.49	11.22	11.95	12.68	13.39	14.10	14.80
	4.84	5.12	5.60	6.08	6.55	7.02	7.48	7.95	8.41	8.86	9.31
2 YRS.	14.17	15.56	16.92	18.26	19.57	20.85	22.11	23.35	24.56	25.76	26.93
	14.14	15.52	16.88	18.21	19.52	20.80	22.06	23.30	24.51	25.70	26.86
	13.73	15.07	16.39	17.69	18.96	20.21	21.43	22.64	23.82	24.97	26.11
	13.32	14.63	15.91	17.17	18.40	19.62	20.81	21.98	23.13	24.25	25.36
	12.91	14.18	15.42	16.64	17.84	19.02	20.18	21.32	22.44	23.53	24.61
	12.50	13.73	14.93	16.12	17.29	18.43	19.55	20.66	21.74	22.81	23.86
	12.03	13.28	14.45	15.60	16.73	17.84	18.93	20.00	21.05	22.09	23.11
	8.42	9.26	10.10	10.93	11.74	12.55	13.34	14.12	14.89	15.66	16.41
3 YRS.	18.88	20.65	22.37	24.05	25.68	27.26	28.81	30.31	31.78	33.20	34.59
	18.81	20.57	22.29	23.96	25.58	27.17	28.71	30.21	31.67	33.09	34.47
	17.97	19.66	21.31	22.91	24.47	25.99	27.47	28.92	30.32	31.69	33.03
	17.13	18.75	20.33	21.86	23.36	24.82	26.24	27.63	28.98	30.29	31.58
	16.29	17.84	19.34	20.81	22.24	23.64	25.00	26.33	27.63	28.90	30.13
	15.45	16.93	18.36	19.76	21.13	22.47	23.77	25.04	26.29	27.50	28.69
	14.62	16.01	17.38	18.71	20.02	21.29	22.54	23.75	24.94	26.11	27.24
	11.75	12.90	14.03	15.13	16.22	17.28	18.33	19.35	20.36	21.34	22.31
4 YRS.	22.48	24.51	26.46	28.35	30.18	31.94	33.65	35.29	36.89	38.43	39.92
	22.37	24.39	26.33	28.21	30.03	31.79	33.49	35.13	36.71	38.25	39.73
	21.03	22.93	24.77	26.56	28.28	29.95	31.57	33.14	34.65	36.12	37.54
	19.68	21.47	23.22	24.90	26.54	28.12	29.66	31.14	32.59	33.99	35.35
	18.33	20.02	21.66	23.25	24.79	26.29	27.74	29.15	30.52	31.86	33.15
	16.98	18.56	20.10	21.59	23.04	24.45	25.83	27.16	28.46	29.73	30.96
	15.64	17.11	18.54	19.93	21.29	22.62	23.91	25.17	26.40	27.60	28.76
	14.70	16.09	17.45	18.78	20.07	21.34	22.58	23.78	24.96	26.11	27.23
5 YRS.	25.24	27.43	29.54	31.55	33.49	35.35	37.14	38.85	40.50	42.09	43.61
	25.09	27.26	29.35	31.36	33.29	35.14	36.92	38.63	40.27	41.85	43.37
	23.18	25.22	27.18	29.06	30.88	32.62	34.30	35.92	37.48	38.99	40.44
	21.28	23.18	25.00	26.76	28.47	30.11	31.69	33.22	34.70	36.12	37.50
	19.38	21.13	22.83	24.47	26.05	27.59	29.07	30.51	31.91	33.26	34.57
	17.28	18.88	20.43	21.93	23.39	24.81	26.19	27.53	28.83	30.10	31.33
6 YRS.	27.36	29.65	31.84	33.93	35.93	37.84	39.66	41.40	43.07	44.66	46.18
	27.15	29.43	31.61	33.69	35.67	37.57	39.38	41.12	42.78	44.36	45.88
	24.67	26.78	28.81	30.74	32.60	34.38	36.08	37.72	39.29	40.80	42.25
	22.20	24.14	26.00	27.80	29.52	31.18	32.78	34.32	35.81	37.24	38.62
	19.56	21.31	23.01	24.66	26.24	27.78	29.26	30.70	32.09	33.44	34.74
7 YRS.	28.97	31.33	33.57	35.70	37.73	39.65	41.48	43.22	44.88	46.46	47.97
	28.72	31.06	33.29	35.40	37.42	39.33	41.15	42.88	44.54	46.11	47.61
	25.67	27.82	29.87	31.83	33.70	35.49	37.21	38.84	40.41	41.91	43.34
	21.55	23.44	25.25	27.00	28.69	30.31	31.88	33.38	34.84	36.24	37.59
8 YRS.	30.21	32.61	34.87	37.02	39.05	40.97	42.79	44.52	46.17	47.73	49.21
	29.91	32.29	34.54	36.67	38.69	40.60	42.42	44.14	45.77	47.33	48.80
	26.29	28.46	30.52	32.49	34.37	36.16	37.86	39.50	41.05	42.54	43.97
	23.29	25.28	27.19	29.03	30.79	32.47	34.09	35.65	37.14	38.58	39.96
9 YRS.	31.16	33.58	35.85	38.00	40.02	41.94	43.74	45.46	47.08	48.61	50.07
	30.81	33.21	35.47	37.60	39.61	41.52	43.32	45.02	46.64	48.17	49.62
	24.81	26.88	28.87	30.77	32.58	34.31	35.97	37.56	39.08	40.54	41.94
10 YRS.	31.89	34.31	36.58	38.72	40.74	42.64	44.43	46.12	47.72	49.23	50.67
	31.50	33.90	36.16	38.28	40.29	42.18	43.96	45.65	47.25	48.76	50.19
	26.13	28.27	30.31	32.26	34.11	35.88	37.57	39.18	40.72	42.19	43.60
UNTIL PAID	33.44	35.79	37.99	40.05	41.97	43.78	45.47	47.07	48.58	50.01	51.36
	26.82	29.00	31.07	33.04	34.91	36.69	38.39	40.01	41.55	43.03	44.44
	22.68	24.64	26.52	28.33	30.06	31.73	33.33	34.87	36.35	37.78	39.15
	19.73	21.49	23.22	24.86	26.45	28.00	29.49	30.93	32.33	33.68	34.99
	17.48	19.09	20.66	22.17	23.65	25.08	26.47	27.82	29.13	30.40	31.64
	14.29	15.66	16.99	18.28	19.55	20.79	22.00	23.19	24.34	25.47	26.58
	12.12	13.30	14.45	15.59	16.70	17.79	18.86	19.91	20.94	21.95	22.94
	10.53	11.58	12.60	13.61	14.60	15.57	16.53	17.47	18.39	19.30	20.20

EXAMPLES *ON PAGES A-382 TO A-397*

MORTGAGE YIELD TABLE
SHOWING DISCOUNT PERCENTAGES AT VARIOUS
YIELDS, MONTHLY PAYMENT RATES AND DUE DATES

DUE DATE	PAY'T RATE %	BAL REMAIN %	YIELD PERCENTAGES								
			19%	20%	21%	22%	23%	24%	25%	26%	27%
1 YR.	1.50	100.00	0.90	1.80	2.68	3.56	4.43	5.29	6.14	6.98	7.81
	1.75	96.74	0.89	1.77	2.65	3.51	4.37	5.21	6.05	6.88	7.70
	2.00	93.48	0.88	1.75	2.61	3.46	4.31	5.14	5.97	6.79	7.60
	2.25	90.22	0.87	1.72	2.57	3.41	4.24	5.07	5.88	6.69	7.49
	2.50	86.96	0.85	1.70	2.54	3.36	4.18	5.00	5.80	6.59	7.38
	2.75	83.70	0.84	1.67	2.50	3.31	4.12	4.92	5.71	6.50	7.27
	3.00	80.44	0.83	1.65	2.46	3.26	4.06	4.85	5.63	6.40	7.17
	3.25	77.18	0.82	1.62	2.42	3.22	4.00	4.78	5.54	6.31	7.06
	9.17	0.0	0.52	1.03	1.54	2.05	2.55	3.05	3.54	4.03	4.52
2 YRS.	1.50	100.00	1.65	3.27	4.87	6.43	7.96	9.46	10.93	12.37	13.79
	1.75	92.84	1.60	3.18	4.72	6.23	7.72	9.18	10.61	12.01	13.39
	2.00	85.68	1.55	3.08	4.58	6.04	7.49	8.90	10.29	11.65	12.99
	2.25	78.52	1.50	2.98	4.43	5.85	7.25	8.62	9.97	11.29	12.59
	2.50	71.37	1.46	2.88	4.29	5.66	7.02	8.35	9.65	10.93	12.19
	2.75	64.21	1.41	2.79	4.14	5.47	6.78	8.07	9.33	10.57	11.79
	3.00	57.05	1.36	2.69	4.00	5.28	6.55	7.79	9.01	10.21	11.39
	3.25	49.89	1.31	2.59	3.85	5.09	6.31	7.51	8.69	9.85	10.99
	4.99	0.0	0.96	1.91	2.84	3.77	4.68	5.57	6.46	7.33	8.19
3 YRS.	1.50	100.00	2.27	4.48	6.64	8.73	10.76	12.74	14.67	16.55	18.37
	1.75	88.18	2.17	4.28	6.33	8.33	10.27	12.17	14.01	15.80	17.55
	2.00	76.36	2.06	4.07	6.02	7.93	9.78	11.59	13.35	15.06	16.73
	2.25	64.54	1.95	3.86	5.72	7.53	9.29	11.01	12.69	14.32	15.92
	2.50	52.72	1.85	3.65	5.41	7.12	8.80	10.43	12.02	13.58	15.10
	2.75	40.91	1.74	3.44	5.10	6.72	8.31	9.85	11.36	12.84	14.28
	3.00	29.09	1.64	3.23	4.80	6.32	7.82	9.27	10.70	12.10	13.46
	3.62	0.0	1.37	2.72	4.04	5.34	6.61	7.85	9.07	10.27	11.45
4 YRS.	1.50	100.00	2.79	5.48	8.07	10.58	13.00	15.34	17.59	19.77	21.88
	1.75	82.61	2.61	5.13	7.56	9.92	12.19	14.39	16.52	18.57	20.56
	2.00	65.22	2.43	4.78	7.05	9.25	11.38	13.44	15.44	17.37	19.25
	2.25	47.83	2.25	4.43	6.54	8.59	10.57	12.50	14.37	16.18	17.93
	2.50	30.43	2.07	4.08	6.03	7.93	9.77	11.55	13.29	14.98	16.62
	2.75	13.04	1.89	3.73	5.52	7.26	8.96	10.61	12.21	13.78	15.30
	2.94	0.0	1.76	3.47	5.14	6.76	8.35	9.90	11.41	12.88	14.31
5 YRS.	1.50	100.00	3.21	6.29	9.24	12.07	14.78	17.38	19.87	22.27	24.56
	1.75	75.95	2.95	5.78	8.49	11.10	13.61	16.02	18.34	20.56	22.70
	2.00	51.89	2.68	5.26	7.75	10.14	12.44	14.66	16.80	18.86	20.85
	2.25	27.84	2.42	4.75	7.00	9.17	11.27	13.30	15.26	17.16	18.99
	2.50	3.79	2.15	4.23	6.25	8.21	10.11	11.94	13.73	15.45	17.13
	2.54	0.0	2.11	4.15	6.14	8.06	9.92	11.73	13.48	15.19	16.84
6 YRS.	1.50	100.00	3.56	6.96	10.19	13.27	16.20	18.99	21.66	24.19	26.62
	1.75	67.98	3.20	6.26	9.18	11.97	14.64	17.19	19.63	21.96	24.20
	2.00	35.96	2.84	5.56	8.17	10.68	13.08	15.39	17.60	19.73	21.78
	2.25	3.94	2.48	4.87	7.17	9.39	11.53	13.59	15.58	17.50	19.35
	2.28	0.0	2.43	4.78	7.04	9.23	11.33	13.37	15.33	17.23	19.06
7 YRS.	1.50	100.00	3.86	7.51	10.96	14.23	17.33	20.29	23.05	25.69	28.19
	1.75	58.46	3.39	6.61	9.67	12.59	15.36	18.00	20.52	22.92	25.20
	2.00	16.91	2.92	5.72	8.39	10.95	13.40	15.74	17.99	20.15	22.21
	2.10	0.0	2.73	5.35	7.87	10.28	12.60	14.82	16.96	19.02	21.00
8 YRS.	1.50	100.00	4.10	7.95	11.58	15.00	18.23	21.26	24.13	26.84	29.40
	1.75	47.07	3.52	6.85	10.01	13.00	15.84	18.54	21.10	23.54	25.85
	1.97	0.0	3.00	5.87	8.61	11.22	13.73	16.12	18.41	20.60	22.70
9 YRS.	1.50	100.00	4.30	8.32	12.09	15.63	18.94	22.05	24.98	27.73	30.32
	1.75	33.46	3.60	7.00	10.22	13.26	16.14	18.87	21.45	23.90	26.23
	1.88	0.0	3.25	6.34	9.28	12.07	14.73	17.26	19.68	21.98	24.18
10 YRS.	1.50	100.00	4.46	8.62	12.50	16.13	19.51	22.68	25.64	28.42	31.03
	1.75	17.18	3.65	7.08	10.33	13.39	16.29	19.03	21.63	24.09	26.42
	1.80	0.0	3.48	6.76	9.88	12.83	15.62	18.28	20.80	23.19	25.46
		MONTHS									
UNTIL PAID	1.75	130.70	3.66	7.10	10.36	13.43	16.33	19.08	21.67	24.13	26.47
	2.00	93.11	2.94	5.75	8.44	11.01	13.47	15.82	18.08	20.24	22.31
	2.25	73.79	2.48	4.87	7.17	9.39	11.53	13.59	15.59	17.51	19.36
	2.50	61.54	2.15	4.24	6.26	8.21	10.11	11.95	13.73	15.46	17.14
	2.75	52.96	1.91	3.76	5.56	7.31	9.02	10.68	12.29	13.87	15.40
	3.00	46.56	1.71	3.38	5.01	6.60	8.15	9.66	11.14	12.58	13.99
	3.50	37.59	1.43	2.82	4.19	5.53	6.85	8.14	9.40	10.63	11.85
	4.00	31.57	1.23	2.43	3.61	4.77	5.92	7.04	8.14	9.23	10.29

EXAMPLES *ON PAGES A-382 TO A-397*

18% INTEREST

MORTGAGE YIELD TABLE

SHOWING DISCOUNT PERCENTAGES AT VARIOUS YIELDS, MONTHLY PAYMENT RATES AND DUE DATES

18% INTEREST

DUE DATE	28%	29%	30%	31%	32%	33%	34%	35%	36%	37%	38%
					YIELD PERCENTAGES						
1 YR.	8.64	9.45	10.26	11.06	11.85	12.63	13.41	14.17	14.93	15.68	16.43
	8.52	9.32	10.12	10.91	11.69	12.46	13.22	13.98	14.73	15.47	16.21
	8.40	9.19	9.98	10.75	11.52	12.29	13.04	13.79	14.53	15.26	15.98
	8.28	9.06	9.84	10.60	11.36	12.12	12.86	13.60	14.33	15.05	15.76
	8.16	8.93	9.70	10.45	11.20	11.94	12.68	13.40	14.12	14.84	15.54
	8.04	8.80	9.56	10.30	11.04	11.77	12.50	13.21	13.92	14.62	15.32
	7.92	8.67	9.42	10.15	10.88	11.60	12.31	13.02	13.72	14.41	15.10
	7.81	8.54	9.28	10.00	10.72	11.43	12.13	12.83	13.52	14.20	14.88
	5.00	5.48	5.96	6.43	6.90	7.36	7.83	8.29	8.74	9.19	9.64
2 YRS.	15.18	16.55	17.88	19.20	20.49	21.75	22.99	24.21	25.40	26.58	27.73
	14.74	16.07	17.37	18.65	19.90	21.13	22.34	23.53	24.69	25.83	26.95
	14.30	15.59	16.86	18.10	19.32	20.52	21.69	22.85	23.98	25.09	26.18
	13.86	15.12	16.34	17.55	18.74	19.90	21.04	22.16	23.27	24.35	25.41
	13.42	14.64	15.83	17.00	18.15	19.28	20.39	21.48	22.55	23.61	24.64
	12.99	14.16	15.32	16.45	17.57	18.66	19.74	20.80	21.84	22.86	23.87
	12.55	13.68	14.80	15.90	16.98	18.05	19.09	20.12	21.13	22.12	23.10
	12.11	13.21	14.29	15.35	16.40	17.43	18.44	19.44	20.42	21.38	22.33
	9.04	9.88	10.71	11.53	12.33	13.13	13.91	14.69	15.45	16.20	16.95
3 YRS.	20.15	21.87	23.56	25.19	26.79	28.34	29.85	31.32	32.75	34.14	35.50
	19.25	20.91	22.53	24.10	25.63	27.12	28.57	29.99	31.37	32.71	34.02
	18.36	19.95	21.50	23.00	24.47	25.90	27.30	28.66	29.99	31.28	32.54
	17.47	18.99	20.47	21.91	23.31	24.69	26.03	27.33	28.61	29.85	31.07
	16.58	18.02	19.43	20.81	22.16	23.47	24.75	26.00	27.23	28.42	29.59
	15.69	17.06	18.40	19.72	21.00	22.25	23.48	24.68	25.85	26.99	28.11
	14.79	16.10	17.37	18.62	19.84	21.04	22.21	23.35	24.47	25.56	26.63
	12.60	13.73	14.84	15.93	16.99	18.04	19.07	20.08	21.07	22.04	23.00
4 YRS.	23.91	25.38	27.77	29.61	31.36	33.09	34.75	36.35	37.90	39.40	40.85
	22.49	24.35	26.15	27.89	29.57	31.20	32.78	34.31	35.79	37.23	38.61
	21.06	22.82	24.52	26.17	27.77	29.31	30.82	32.27	33.68	35.05	36.38
	19.63	21.29	22.89	24.45	25.96	27.43	28.85	30.23	31.58	32.88	34.15
	18.21	19.76	21.26	22.73	24.15	25.54	26.88	28.19	29.47	30.71	31.92
	16.78	18.23	19.64	21.01	22.34	23.65	24.92	26.15	27.36	28.54	29.68
	15.72	17.08	18.42	19.72	20.99	22.23	23.44	24.62	25.78	26.91	28.01
5 YRS.	26.76	28.38	30.91	32.86	34.73	36.53	38.26	39.92	41.51	43.05	44.52
	24.76	26.74	28.65	30.48	32.25	33.95	35.58	37.16	38.68	40.14	41.55
	22.76	24.61	26.39	28.11	29.76	31.36	32.91	34.40	35.84	37.23	38.58
	20.76	22.47	24.13	25.73	27.23	28.78	30.24	31.64	33.00	34.32	35.60
	18.76	20.34	21.87	23.35	24.80	26.20	27.56	28.88	30.17	31.42	32.63
	18.44	20.00	21.51	22.98	24.41	25.79	27.14	28.45	29.72	30.96	32.16
6 YRS.	28.93	31.13	33.24	35.25	37.17	39.01	40.76	42.44	44.05	45.58	47.05
	26.33	28.38	30.34	32.22	34.02	35.75	37.40	38.99	40.52	41.98	43.39
	23.74	25.63	27.44	29.19	30.87	32.49	34.04	35.54	36.99	38.38	39.72
	21.14	22.87	24.54	26.16	27.72	29.23	30.68	32.09	33.44	34.78	36.06
	20.82	22.53	24.19	25.78	27.33	28.82	30.27	31.67	33.02	34.34	35.61
7 YRS.	30.57	32.33	34.97	37.01	38.95	40.80	42.56	44.23	45.83	47.35	48.80
	27.38	29.46	31.45	33.35	35.16	36.89	38.55	40.14	41.66	43.11	44.50
	24.20	26.10	27.93	29.68	31.37	32.99	34.55	36.05	37.49	38.88	40.21
	22.90	24.73	26.49	28.19	29.82	31.40	32.92	34.38	35.79	37.15	38.47
8 YRS.	31.81	34.10	36.26	38.31	40.25	42.09	43.84	45.50	47.07	48.57	49.99
	28.05	30.15	32.14	34.04	35.86	37.59	39.24	40.82	42.33	43.77	45.15
	24.71	26.63	28.48	30.25	31.95	33.50	35.19	36.66	38.11	39.50	40.84
9 YRS.	32.76	35.05	37.22	39.27	41.20	43.03	44.76	46.39	47.95	49.42	50.82
	28.44	30.54	32.54	34.44	36.25	37.98	39.62	41.19	42.69	44.12	45.49
	26.27	28.27	30.18	32.01	33.76	35.44	37.04	38.57	40.05	41.46	42.81
10 YRS.	33.47	35.77	37.93	39.97	41.89	43.70	45.41	47.03	48.56	50.01	51.38
	28.63	30.73	32.73	34.63	36.43	38.16	39.80	41.36	42.85	44.28	45.64
	27.63	29.69	31.65	33.52	35.30	37.00	38.63	40.18	41.67	43.09	44.45
UNTIL PAID	28.68	30.78	32.78	34.67	36.48	38.20	39.84	41.40	42.89	44.32	45.68
	24.29	26.20	28.03	29.78	31.47	33.09	34.65	36.14	37.59	38.97	40.31
	21.15	22.38	24.55	26.17	27.73	29.23	30.69	32.10	33.47	34.79	36.07
	18.77	20.35	21.88	23.37	24.81	26.21	27.57	28.90	30.18	31.43	32.64
	16.89	18.34	19.75	21.13	22.47	23.77	25.04	26.28	27.49	28.67	29.82
	15.36	16.70	18.01	19.29	20.54	21.76	22.95	24.12	25.26	26.37	27.45
	13.03	14.20	15.34	16.46	17.56	18.64	19.69	20.73	21.74	22.74	23.72
	11.34	12.37	13.38	14.38	15.36	16.32	17.26	18.20	19.11	20.01	20.90

EXAMPLES *ON PAGES A-382 TO A-397*

DUE DATE	PAY'T RATE %	BAL REMAIN %	19%	20%	21%	22%	23%	24%	25%	26%	27%
1 YR.	1.52	100.00	0.68	1.57	2.46	3.34	4.21	5.07	5.92	6.76	7.59
	1.75	97.01	0.67	1.55	2.43	3.30	4.15	5.00	5.84	6.68	7.50
	2.00	93.74	0.66	1.53	2.40	3.25	4.10	4.93	5.76	6.58	7.39
	2.25	90.48	0.65	1.51	2.36	3.20	4.04	4.86	5.68	6.49	7.29
	2.50	87.22	0.64	1.49	2.33	3.16	3.98	4.79	5.60	6.40	7.18
	2.75	83.95	0.63	1.47	2.29	3.11	3.92	4.72	5.52	6.30	7.08
	3.00	80.69	0.62	1.44	2.26	3.06	3.86	4.65	5.43	6.21	6.98
	3.25	77.42	0.61	1.42	2.22	3.02	3.80	4.58	5.35	6.12	6.87
	9.18	0.0	0.39	0.90	1.41	1.92	2.42	2.92	3.41	3.91	4.39
2 YRS.	1.52	100.00	1.24	2.87	4.46	6.02	7.56	9.06	10.54	11.99	13.41
	1.75	93.42	1.21	2.79	4.34	5.86	7.35	8.82	10.26	11.67	13.05
	2.00	86.25	1.17	2.70	4.21	5.68	7.13	8.55	9.95	11.32	12.66
	2.25	79.07	1.13	2.62	4.07	5.50	6.91	8.28	9.64	10.97	12.27
	2.50	71.89	1.09	2.53	3.94	5.32	6.68	8.02	9.33	10.62	11.88
	2.75	64.72	1.06	2.44	3.81	5.15	6.46	7.75	9.02	10.27	11.49
	3.00	57.54	1.02	2.36	3.67	4.97	6.24	7.48	8.71	9.92	11.10
	3.25	50.36	0.98	2.27	3.54	4.79	6.01	7.22	8.40	9.57	10.71
	5.00	0.0	0.72	1.67	2.61	3.53	4.45	5.35	6.23	7.11	7.97
3 YRS.	1.52	100.00	1.71	3.92	6.08	8.18	10.23	12.21	14.15	16.03	17.86
	1.75	89.12	1.63	3.76	5.82	7.84	9.80	11.70	13.56	15.37	17.13
	2.00	77.26	1.55	3.57	5.54	7.46	9.33	11.15	12.92	14.65	16.33
	2.25	65.39	1.47	3.39	5.26	7.08	8.86	10.59	12.28	13.93	15.53
	2.50	53.53	1.39	3.21	4.98	6.71	8.39	10.04	11.64	13.21	14.74
	2.75	41.66	1.31	3.03	4.70	6.33	7.93	9.48	11.00	12.49	13.94
	3.00	29.80	1.23	2.84	4.42	5.95	7.46	8.93	10.36	11.77	13.14
	3.63	0.0	1.03	2.38	3.71	5.01	6.28	7.53	8.76	9.96	11.14
4 YRS.	1.52	100.00	2.09	4.79	7.40	9.92	12.35	14.70	16.96	19.15	21.27
	1.75	83.97	1.97	4.51	6.97	9.35	11.64	13.86	16.01	18.09	20.09
	2.00	66.49	1.83	4.20	6.50	8.72	10.87	12.95	14.97	16.92	18.81
	2.25	49.00	1.70	3.90	6.03	8.10	10.10	12.05	13.93	15.76	17.53
	2.50	31.51	1.56	3.59	5.56	7.47	9.33	11.14	12.89	14.59	16.25
	2.75	14.03	1.43	3.28	5.09	6.85	8.56	10.23	11.85	13.43	14.96
	2.95	0.0	1.32	3.04	4.71	6.35	7.94	9.50	11.01	12.49	13.93
5 YRS.	1.52	100.00	2.41	5.50	8.47	11.31	14.04	16.66	19.16	21.57	23.88
	1.75	77.80	2.23	5.09	7.84	10.48	13.02	15.46	17.80	20.05	22.22
	2.00	53.57	2.03	4.64	7.15	9.57	11.90	14.15	16.31	18.40	20.40
	2.25	29.35	1.83	4.19	6.47	8.67	10.79	12.84	14.82	16.74	18.59
	2.50	5.13	1.63	3.74	5.78	7.76	9.67	11.53	13.34	15.08	16.78
	2.55	0.0	1.58	3.64	5.63	7.56	9.44	11.26	13.02	14.73	16.39
6 YRS.	1.52	100.00	2.67	6.09	9.34	12.44	15.39	18.20	20.88	23.44	25.88
	1.75	70.40	2.42	5.53	8.49	11.32	14.02	16.61	19.08	21.45	23.71
	2.00	38.10	2.15	4.91	7.56	10.10	12.54	14.88	17.12	19.27	21.34
	2.25	5.80	1.88	4.30	6.63	8.88	11.05	13.14	15.16	17.10	18.98
	2.29	0.0	1.83	4.19	6.47	8.66	10.78	12.83	14.80	16.71	18.55
7 YRS.	1.52	100.00	2.89	6.57	10.05	13.34	16.46	19.42	22.22	24.88	27.41
	1.75	61.53	2.57	5.85	8.96	11.92	14.74	17.42	19.98	22.41	24.73
	2.00	19.55	2.22	5.06	7.77	10.37	12.86	15.24	17.53	19.71	21.81
	2.12	0.0	2.05	4.69	7.22	9.65	11.99	14.23	16.38	18.45	20.45
8 YRS.	1.52	100.00	3.07	6.96	10.62	14.07	17.31	20.38	23.27	26.00	28.58
	1.75	50.89	2.67	6.07	9.29	12.34	15.23	17.97	20.57	23.05	25.40
	1.99	0.0	2.26	5.15	7.90	10.54	13.06	15.47	17.78	19.99	22.10
9 YRS.	1.52	100.00	3.22	7.28	11.08	14.65	17.99	21.14	24.09	26.86	29.48
	1.75	38.15	2.74	6.22	9.50	12.60	15.54	18.31	20.95	23.44	25.81
	1.89	0.0	2.44	5.56	8.52	11.34	14.02	16.57	19.01	21.33	23.54
10 YRS.	1.52	100.00	3.35	7.55	11.46	15.12	18.54	21.73	24.73	27.53	30.16
	1.75	22.88	2.78	6.30	9.62	12.75	15.71	18.50	21.15	23.65	26.02
	1.82	0.0	2.61	5.93	9.07	12.05	14.87	17.54	20.09	22.50	24.80
		MONTHS									
UNTIL PAID	1.75	134.69	2.80	6.33	9.67	12.81	15.77	18.58	21.23	23.73	26.11
	2.00	94.66	2.23	5.10	7.83	10.45	12.95	15.34	17.63	19.83	21.93
	2.25	74.65	1.88	4.30	6.64	8.89	11.06	13.15	15.17	17.12	18.99
	2.50	62.10	1.63	3.74	5.78	7.77	9.68	11.55	13.35	15.10	16.79
	2.75	53.35	1.44	3.31	5.13	6.91	8.63	10.31	11.94	13.52	15.07
	3.00	46.85	1.29	2.98	4.62	6.23	7.79	9.32	10.81	12.26	13.68
	3.50	37.77	1.08	2.48	3.86	5.21	6.54	7.83	9.11	10.35	11.57
	4.00	31.69	0.92	2.13	3.32	4.49	5.64	6.77	7.88	8.97	10.05

EXAMPLES *ON PAGES A-382 TO A-397*

DUE DATE	YIELD PERCENTAGES										
	28%	29%	30%	31%	32%	33%	34%	35%	36%	37%	38%
1 YR.	8.42	9.24	10.04	10.84	11.64	12.42	13.20	13.96	14.72	15.48	16.22
	8.31	9.12	9.92	10.71	11.49	12.26	13.03	13.79	14.54	15.28	16.02
	8.20	8.99	9.78	10.56	11.33	12.10	12.85	13.60	14.34	15.08	15.80
	8.08	8.87	9.64	10.41	11.17	11.93	12.67	13.41	14.14	14.87	15.58
	7.97	8.74	9.51	10.26	11.01	11.76	12.49	13.22	13.94	14.66	15.36
	7.85	8.61	9.37	10.12	10.86	11.59	12.31	13.03	13.74	14.45	15.15
	7.74	8.49	9.23	9.97	10.70	11.42	12.14	12.84	13.55	14.24	14.93
	7.62	8.36	9.09	9.82	10.54	11.25	11.96	12.65	13.35	14.03	14.71
	4.88	5.36	5.83	6.31	6.78	7.24	7.71	8.17	8.62	9.08	9.53
2 YRS.	14.30	16.17	17.51	18.83	20.12	21.39	22.63	23.85	25.05	26.23	27.38
	14.41	15.74	17.05	18.33	19.59	20.83	22.04	23.24	24.41	25.55	26.68
	13.98	15.28	16.55	17.80	19.02	20.22	21.40	22.56	23.70	24.82	25.92
	13.55	14.81	16.04	17.26	18.45	19.62	20.76	21.89	23.00	24.09	25.15
	13.12	14.34	15.54	16.72	17.87	19.01	20.12	21.22	22.29	23.35	24.39
	12.69	13.88	15.04	16.18	17.30	18.40	19.48	20.55	21.59	22.62	23.63
	12.26	13.41	14.53	15.64	16.72	17.79	18.84	19.87	20.89	21.88	22.87
	11.84	12.94	14.03	15.10	16.15	17.18	18.20	19.20	20.18	21.15	22.10
	8.82	9.67	10.49	11.31	12.12	12.92	13.70	14.48	15.25	16.00	16.75
3 YRS.	19.64	21.38	23.07	24.71	26.31	27.87	29.38	30.86	32.29	33.69	35.06
	18.84	20.51	22.14	23.72	25.26	26.77	28.23	29.65	31.04	32.40	33.71
	17.97	19.57	21.13	22.65	24.12	25.57	26.97	28.34	29.68	30.98	32.25
	17.10	18.63	20.12	21.57	22.99	24.37	25.72	27.03	28.31	29.57	30.79
	16.23	17.68	19.10	20.49	21.85	23.17	24.46	25.72	26.95	28.15	29.33
	15.36	16.74	18.09	19.42	20.71	21.97	23.20	24.41	25.59	26.74	27.87
	14.48	15.80	17.08	18.34	19.57	20.77	21.95	23.10	24.22	25.32	26.40
	12.30	13.43	14.54	15.63	16.71	17.76	18.79	19.80	20.80	21.77	22.73
4 YRS.	23.31	25.20	27.19	29.04	30.82	32.54	34.21	35.82	37.37	38.88	40.34
	22.03	23.91	25.73	27.49	29.19	30.83	32.43	33.97	35.46	36.91	38.31
	20.64	22.41	24.13	25.79	27.41	28.97	30.48	31.95	33.38	34.76	36.10
	19.25	20.91	22.55	24.10	25.63	27.11	28.54	29.94	31.29	32.61	33.89
	17.85	19.42	20.93	22.41	23.85	25.24	26.60	27.92	29.21	30.46	31.67
	16.44	17.92	19.34	20.72	22.07	23.38	24.66	25.91	27.12	28.31	29.46
	15.34	16.71	18.05	19.36	20.64	21.88	23.10	24.29	25.45	26.58	27.69
5 YRS.	26.10	28.22	30.26	32.23	34.11	35.92	37.66	39.33	40.94	42.48	43.97
	24.30	26.30	28.23	30.08	31.87	33.58	35.24	36.83	38.36	39.84	41.27
	22.34	24.21	26.01	27.74	29.42	31.03	32.59	34.10	35.56	36.96	38.32
	20.38	22.11	23.78	25.40	26.97	28.48	29.95	31.37	32.75	34.08	35.39
	18.42	20.02	21.56	23.06	24.52	25.94	27.31	28.64	29.94	31.20	32.42
	18.01	19.57	21.09	22.57	24.00	25.40	26.75	28.07	29.35	30.59	31.80
6 YRS.	28.21	30.43	32.55	34.57	36.51	38.36	40.13	41.82	43.44	44.98	46.47
	25.87	27.95	29.93	31.84	33.66	35.41	37.08	38.69	40.23	41.71	43.13
	23.53	25.24	27.08	28.85	30.55	32.18	33.76	35.27	36.73	38.14	39.50
	20.79	22.54	24.23	25.86	27.44	28.96	30.43	31.86	33.24	34.57	35.86
	20.33	22.05	23.72	25.32	26.88	28.38	29.84	31.25	32.61	33.93	35.21
7 YRS.	29.80	32.08	34.24	36.30	38.26	40.12	41.89	43.58	45.19	46.72	48.19
	26.94	29.05	31.06	32.99	34.82	36.58	38.26	39.86	41.40	42.87	44.28
	23.82	25.75	27.60	29.37	31.08	32.72	34.29	35.81	37.27	38.67	40.02
	22.36	24.21	25.98	27.69	29.33	30.92	32.45	33.92	35.34	36.72	38.05
8 YRS.	31.02	33.32	35.51	37.57	39.53	41.39	43.15	44.83	46.42	47.93	49.37
	27.63	29.76	31.79	33.71	35.55	37.31	38.98	40.58	42.10	43.56	44.96
	24.13	26.07	27.93	29.71	31.43	33.07	34.65	36.17	37.63	39.03	40.38
9 YRS.	31.94	34.26	36.45	38.51	40.46	42.31	44.06	45.71	47.28	48.77	50.18
	28.05	30.19	32.21	34.14	35.98	37.72	39.39	40.98	42.50	43.94	45.33
	25.66	27.67	29.60	31.45	33.21	34.90	36.51	38.06	39.54	40.97	42.33
10 YRS.	32.63	34.76	37.14	39.20	41.14	42.97	44.70	46.34	47.89	49.35	50.74
	28.27	30.41	32.43	34.36	36.19	37.94	39.60	41.18	42.69	44.13	45.51
	26.98	29.06	31.04	32.92	34.72	36.44	38.08	39.65	41.15	42.58	43.95
UNTIL PAID	28.36	30.49	32.52	34.44	36.27	38.01	39.67	41.25	42.76	44.19	45.57
	23.94	25.87	27.73	29.50	31.21	32.85	34.42	35.94	37.39	38.80	40.14
	20.81	22.56	24.25	25.88	27.45	28.98	30.45	31.88	33.26	34.59	35.88
	18.44	20.03	21.58	23.08	24.54	25.95	27.33	28.66	29.96	31.22	32.44
	16.57	18.04	19.46	20.85	22.20	23.52	24.80	26.05	27.27	28.46	29.62
	15.07	16.42	17.74	19.03	20.29	21.52	22.72	23.89	25.04	26.16	27.25
	12.77	13.94	15.09	16.22	17.33	18.41	19.47	20.51	21.54	22.54	23.52
	11.10	12.14	13.16	14.16	15.14	16.11	17.06	18.00	18.92	19.82	20.71

EXAMPLES *ON PAGES A-382 TO A-397*

MORTGAGE YIELD TABLE

SHOWING DISCOUNT PERCENTAGES AT VARIOUS YIELDS, MONTHLY PAYMENT RATES AND DUE DATES

DUE DATE	PAY'T RATE %	BAL REMAIN %	YIELD PERCENTAGES								
			19%	20%	21%	22%	23%	24%	25%	26%	27%
1 YR.	1.54	100.00	0.45	1.35	2.24	3.12	3.99	4.85	5.70	6.54	7.38
	1.75	97.28	0.45	1.33	2.21	3.08	3.94	4.79	5.63	6.47	7.29
	2.00	94.01	0.44	1.31	2.18	3.04	3.88	4.72	5.55	6.38	7.19
	2.25	90.74	0.43	1.30	2.15	2.99	3.83	4.66	5.48	6.29	7.09
	2.50	87.47	0.43	1.28	2.12	2.95	3.77	4.59	5.40	6.20	6.99
	2.75	84.21	0.42	1.26	2.09	2.91	3.72	4.52	5.32	6.11	6.89
	3.00	80.94	0.42	1.24	2.06	2.86	3.66	4.46	5.24	6.02	6.78
	3.25	77.67	0.41	1.22	2.02	2.82	3.61	4.39	5.16	5.93	6.68
	9.19	0.0	0.26	C.77	1.28	1.79	2.29	2.79	3.29	3.78	4.27
2 YRS.	1.54	100.00	0.83	2.46	4.05	5.62	7.16	8.67	10.15	11.60	13.03
	1.75	94.00	0.81	2.39	3.95	5.43	6.98	8.46	9.90	11.32	12.71
	2.00	86.81	0.78	2.32	3.83	5.32	6.77	8.20	9.60	10.98	12.33
	2.25	79.62	0.76	2.25	3.71	5.15	6.56	7.94	9.30	10.64	11.95
	2.50	72.42	0.73	2.17	3.59	4.98	6.35	7.69	9.01	10.30	11.57
	2.75	65.23	0.71	2.10	3.47	4.81	6.14	7.43	8.71	9.96	11.19
	3.00	58.03	0.68	2.03	3.35	4.65	5.92	7.18	8.41	9.62	10.81
	3.25	50.84	0.66	1.95	3.23	4.48	5.71	6.92	8.11	9.28	10.43
	5.02	0.0	0.48	1.43	2.37	3.30	4.21	5.12	6.01	6.88	7.75
3 YRS.	1.54	100.00	1.14	3.36	5.53	7.64	9.69	11.68	13.62	15.51	17.35
	1.75	90.07	1.09	3.23	5.32	7.34	9.32	11.24	13.11	14.93	16.70
	2.00	78.16	1.04	3.08	5.06	6.99	8.87	10.71	12.49	14.23	15.93
	2.25	66.25	0.99	2.92	4.80	6.64	8.43	10.17	11.87	13.53	15.15
	2.50	54.34	0.93	2.76	4.55	6.29	7.98	9.64	11.26	12.83	14.39
	2.75	42.42	0.88	2.60	4.29	5.93	7.54	9.11	10.64	12.14	13.60
	3.00	30.51	0.83	2.45	4.03	5.58	7.10	8.58	10.02	11.44	12.82
	3.64	0.0	0.69	2.04	3.37	4.68	5.96	7.21	8.44	9.65	10.83
4 YRS.	1.54	100.00	1.39	4.11	6.73	9.26	11.70	14.06	16.34	18.54	20.66
	1.75	85.35	1.32	3.89	6.37	8.77	11.09	13.33	15.50	17.59	19.62
	2.00	67.77	1.23	3.62	5.94	8.19	10.36	12.46	14.49	16.46	18.37
	2.25	50.19	1.14	3.36	5.51	7.60	9.62	11.59	13.49	15.33	17.12
	2.50	32.61	1.05	3.10	5.09	7.02	8.89	10.71	12.48	14.20	15.87
	2.75	15.03	0.96	2.83	4.66	6.43	8.16	9.84	11.48	13.07	14.62
	2.90	0.0	0.88	2.61	4.29	5.93	7.53	9.09	10.62	12.10	13.55
5 YRS.	1.54	100.00	1.61	4.72	7.70	10.56	13.30	15.93	18.45	20.87	23.20
	1.75	79.67	1.49	4.39	7.18	9.85	12.42	14.89	17.26	19.53	21.72
	2.00	55.28	1.36	4.01	6.55	9.00	11.36	13.63	15.82	17.92	19.95
	2.25	30.89	1.23	3.62	5.92	8.15	10.30	12.37	14.38	16.31	18.19
	2.50	6.50	1.09	3.23	5.29	7.30	9.24	11.12	12.94	14.70	16.42
	2.57	0.0	1.06	3.12	5.13	7.07	8.95	10.78	12.56	14.28	15.95
6 YRS.	1.54	100.00	1.78	5.22	8.49	11.61	14.58	17.41	20.11	22.68	25.14
	1.75	72.85	1.63	4.78	7.78	10.66	13.40	16.02	18.53	20.92	23.21
	2.00	40.28	1.45	4.25	6.94	9.51	11.98	14.35	16.63	18.81	20.91
	2.25	7.71	1.26	3.72	6.09	8.37	10.57	12.68	14.73	16.70	18.60
	2.31	0.0	1.22	3.60	5.89	8.10	10.23	12.29	14.28	16.20	18.05
7 YRS.	1.54	100.00	1.93	5.63	9.13	12.45	15.59	18.57	21.40	24.08	26.62
	1.75	64.66	1.73	5.06	8.23	11.24	14.10	16.83	19.42	21.89	24.25
	2.00	22.25	1.49	4.38	7.15	9.79	12.31	14.73	17.04	19.27	21.39
	2.13	0.0	1.37	4.03	6.58	9.02	11.37	13.63	15.80	17.89	19.89
8 YRS.	1.54	100.00	2.05	5.97	9.65	13.13	16.40	19.49	22.41	25.16	27.76
	1.75	54.82	1.80	5.27	8.54	11.65	14.59	17.38	20.03	22.55	24.93
	2.00	0.0	1.51	4.42	7.20	9.86	12.40	14.82	17.15	19.37	21.50
9 YRS.	1.54	100.00	2.15	6.24	10.08	13.67	17.05	20.22	23.20	26.00	28.63
	1.75	42.99	1.85	5.40	8.75	11.92	14.91	17.74	20.42	22.96	25.37
	1.91	0.0	1.63	4.77	7.76	10.60	13.30	15.88	18.33	20.67	22.91
10 YRS.	1.54	100.00	2.23	6.47	10.42	14.11	17.56	20.79	23.81	26.64	29.30
	1.75	28.77	1.88	5.49	8.88	12.08	15.10	17.96	20.65	23.20	25.62
	1.83	0.0	1.74	5.09	8.26	11.26	14.11	16.81	19.37	21.81	24.13
		MONTHS									
UNTIL PAID	1.75	139.11	1.90	5.53	8.95	12.17	15.20	18.07	20.77	23.33	25.74
	2.00	98.30	1.51	4.43	7.21	9.88	12.42	14.85	17.18	19.41	21.54
	2.25	75.55	1.27	3.73	6.10	8.38	10.58	12.70	14.75	16.72	18.62
	2.50	62.67	1.10	3.23	5.30	7.31	9.25	11.13	12.96	14.72	16.44
	2.75	53.75	0.97	2.86	4.70	6.49	8.23	9.93	11.57	13.18	14.74
	3.00	47.15	0.87	2.57	4.23	5.85	7.43	8.97	10.47	11.94	13.37
	3.50	37.95	0.72	2.14	3.53	4.89	6.22	7.53	8.81	10.07	11.30
	4.00	31.82	0.62	1.84	3.04	4.21	5.37	6.51	7.62	8.72	9.80

EXAMPLES *ON PAGES A-382 TO A-397*

18½% INTEREST

MORTGAGE YIELD TABLE
SHOWING DISCOUNT PERCENTAGES AT VARIOUS YIELDS, MONTHLY PAYMENT RATES AND DUE DATES

18½% INTEREST

DUE DATE	28%	29%	30%	31%	32%	33%	34%	35%	36%	37%	38%
1 YR.	8.20	9.02	9.83	10.63	11.42	12.21	12.99	13.76	14.52	15.27	16.02
	8.11	8.92	9.72	10.51	11.29	12.07	12.84	13.60	14.35	15.10	15.84
	8.00	8.79	9.58	10.37	11.14	11.90	12.66	13.41	14.16	14.89	15.62
	7.83	8.67	9.45	10.22	10.98	11.74	12.49	13.23	13.96	14.69	15.40
	7.77	8.55	9.31	10.07	10.83	11.57	12.31	13.04	13.76	14.48	15.19
	7.66	8.42	9.18	9.93	10.67	11.41	12.13	12.85	13.57	14.27	14.97
	7.55	8.30	9.05	9.78	10.52	11.24	11.96	12.67	13.37	14.07	14.76
	7.43	8.18	8.91	9.64	10.36	11.07	11.78	12.48	13.17	13.86	14.54
	4.75	5.24	5.71	6.19	6.66	7.12	7.59	8.05	8.50	8.96	9.41
2 YRS.	14.42	15.79	17.14	18.46	19.76	21.03	22.27	23.50	24.70	25.88	27.03
	14.07	15.41	16.73	18.02	19.28	20.53	21.75	22.94	24.12	25.27	26.40
	13.66	14.96	16.23	17.49	18.72	19.93	21.12	22.28	23.42	24.55	25.65
	13.24	14.50	15.74	16.96	18.16	19.33	20.48	21.62	22.73	23.82	24.90
	12.82	14.04	15.25	16.43	17.59	18.73	19.85	20.95	22.03	23.10	24.14
	12.40	13.59	14.75	15.90	17.03	18.13	19.22	20.29	21.34	22.37	23.39
	11.98	13.13	14.26	15.37	16.46	17.53	18.59	19.63	20.65	21.65	22.63
	11.56	12.67	13.77	14.84	15.90	16.94	17.96	18.96	19.95	20.92	21.88
	8.60	9.45	10.28	11.10	11.91	12.71	13.50	14.27	15.04	15.80	16.55
3 YRS.	19.14	20.88	22.57	24.22	25.83	27.39	28.91	30.40	31.84	33.24	34.61
	18.43	20.11	21.75	23.34	24.90	26.41	27.88	29.32	30.72	32.08	33.41
	17.58	19.19	20.76	22.28	23.77	25.23	26.64	28.02	29.37	30.68	31.96
	16.73	18.26	19.76	21.23	22.65	24.04	25.40	26.73	28.02	29.28	30.51
	15.88	17.34	18.77	20.17	21.53	22.86	24.16	25.43	26.67	27.88	29.06
	15.02	16.42	17.78	19.11	20.41	21.68	22.92	24.14	25.32	26.48	27.62
	14.17	15.49	16.79	18.05	19.29	20.50	21.68	22.84	23.98	25.08	26.17
	11.99	13.13	14.25	15.34	16.42	17.47	18.51	19.52	20.52	21.50	22.46
4 YRS.	22.71	24.70	26.62	28.47	30.26	31.99	33.66	35.28	36.85	38.36	39.82
	21.58	23.47	25.31	27.08	28.80	30.46	32.07	33.62	35.13	36.59	38.01
	20.22	22.01	23.74	25.42	27.04	28.62	30.15	31.63	33.07	34.46	35.81
	18.85	20.54	22.17	23.75	25.29	26.78	28.23	29.64	31.00	32.33	33.62
	17.49	19.07	20.60	22.09	23.54	24.95	26.31	27.65	28.94	30.20	31.43
	16.13	17.60	19.03	20.43	21.78	23.11	24.40	25.65	26.88	28.07	29.24
	14.96	16.34	17.69	19.00	20.28	21.54	22.76	23.95	25.12	26.26	27.37
5 YRS.	25.43	27.57	29.62	31.59	33.49	35.31	37.06	38.74	40.36	41.92	43.41
	23.83	25.85	27.80	29.68	31.48	33.21	34.89	36.49	38.04	39.54	40.98
	21.91	23.80	25.62	27.37	29.07	30.70	32.27	33.80	35.27	36.68	38.06
	19.99	21.74	23.43	25.07	26.65	28.18	29.66	31.10	32.49	33.83	35.13
	18.08	19.69	21.25	22.77	24.24	25.67	27.05	28.40	29.71	30.98	32.21
	17.57	19.14	20.67	22.15	23.60	25.00	26.36	27.68	28.97	30.22	31.43
6 YRS.	27.48	29.72	31.86	33.90	35.84	37.71	39.49	41.19	42.82	44.38	45.88
	25.41	27.51	29.52	31.44	33.29	35.06	36.75	38.38	39.94	41.44	42.87
	22.92	24.85	26.71	28.50	30.22	31.87	33.47	35.00	36.47	37.90	39.27
	20.43	22.20	23.91	25.56	27.15	28.69	30.18	31.62	33.01	34.36	35.66
	19.84	21.57	23.24	24.86	26.43	27.94	29.40	30.82	32.19	33.52	34.81
7 YRS.	29.04	31.34	33.52	35.59	37.56	39.44	41.23	42.93	44.55	46.10	47.58
	26.49	28.63	30.67	32.62	34.48	36.26	37.96	39.58	41.14	42.63	44.05
	23.43	25.38	27.26	29.06	30.78	32.44	34.04	35.57	37.04	38.46	39.82
	21.82	23.68	25.46	27.18	28.84	30.44	31.98	33.46	34.89	36.27	37.61
8 YRS.	30.22	32.55	34.75	36.84	38.81	40.69	42.47	44.16	45.76	47.29	48.74
	27.20	29.36	31.42	33.38	35.24	37.02	38.71	40.33	41.87	43.35	44.76
	23.54	25.50	27.38	29.17	30.90	32.56	34.15	35.68	37.15	38.57	39.93
9 YRS.	31.12	33.46	35.67	37.76	39.73	41.59	43.36	45.03	46.61	48.12	49.55
	27.65	29.82	31.88	33.83	35.69	37.47	39.15	40.76	42.30	43.76	45.16
	25.04	27.07	29.02	30.88	32.65	34.35	35.98	37.55	39.04	40.48	41.85
10 YRS.	31.80	34.14	36.35	38.43	40.39	42.24	43.99	45.65	47.21	48.69	50.10
	27.90	30.07	32.13	34.08	35.94	37.71	39.39	40.99	42.52	43.97	45.37
	26.33	28.43	30.42	32.33	34.14	35.88	37.53	39.11	40.62	42.07	43.45
UNTIL PAID	28.03	30.20	32.26	34.21	36.06	37.82	39.50	41.10	42.62	44.07	45.46
	23.58	25.54	27.42	29.22	30.95	32.61	34.20	35.73	37.20	38.62	39.98
	20.45	22.23	23.93	25.59	27.18	28.72	30.21	31.65	33.04	34.39	35.69
	18.10	19.71	21.28	22.79	24.27	25.69	27.08	28.43	29.74	31.01	32.24
	16.26	17.73	19.17	20.57	21.94	23.26	24.56	25.82	27.05	28.25	29.41
	14.77	16.13	17.46	18.76	20.03	21.27	22.48	23.66	24.82	25.95	27.05
	12.50	13.68	14.84	15.98	17.09	18.18	19.25	20.30	21.33	22.34	23.33
	10.86	11.90	12.93	13.93	14.92	15.90	16.86	17.80	18.72	19.63	20.53

EXAMPLES *ON PAGES A-382 TO A-397*

18¾%
INTEREST

MORTGAGE YIELD TABLE
SHOWING DISCOUNT PERCENTAGES AT VARIOUS
YIELDS, MONTHLY PAYMENT RATES AND DUE DATES

18¾%
INTEREST

DUE DATE	PAY'T RATE %	BAL REMAIN %	YIELD PERCENTAGES								
			19%	20%	21%	22%	23%	24%	25%	26%	27%
1 YR.	1.56	100.00	0.23	1.12	2.01	2.89	3.76	4.63	5.48	6.32	7.16
	1.75	97.55	0.22	1.11	1.99	2.86	3.73	4.58	5.42	6.26	7.09
	2.00	94.27	0.22	1.10	1.96	2.82	3.67	4.51	5.35	6.17	6.99
	2.25	91.00	0.22	1.08	1.94	2.78	3.62	4.45	5.27	6.08	6.89
	2.50	87.73	0.21	1.07	1.91	2.74	3.57	4.39	5.20	6.00	6.79
	2.75	84.46	0.21	1.05	1.88	2.70	3.52	4.32	5.12	5.91	6.69
	3.00	81.19	0.21	1.03	1.85	2.66	3.46	4.26	5.04	5.82	6.59
	3.25	77.92	0.20	1.02	1.82	2.62	3.41	4.19	4.97	5.74	6.49
	9.20	0.0	0.13	0.64	1.16	1.66	2.17	2.67	3.16	3.66	4.15
2 YRS.	1.56	100.00	0.41	2.05	3.65	5.22	6.76	8.27	9.76	11.21	12.64
	1.75	94.59	0.40	2.00	3.57	5.10	6.61	8.09	9.54	10.97	12.37
	2.00	87.38	0.39	1.94	3.46	4.95	6.41	7.85	9.26	10.64	12.00
	2.25	80.17	0.38	1.88	3.35	4.79	6.21	7.60	8.97	10.31	11.63
	2.50	72.95	0.37	1.82	3.24	4.64	6.01	7.36	8.68	9.98	11.26
	2.75	65.74	0.35	1.76	3.13	4.48	5.81	7.11	8.40	9.65	10.89
	3.00	58.53	0.34	1.69	3.02	4.33	5.61	6.87	8.11	9.33	10.52
	3.25	51.32	0.33	1.63	2.91	4.17	5.41	6.63	7.82	9.00	10.15
	5.03	0.0	0.24	1.20	2.14	3.07	3.98	4.89	5.78	6.66	7.53
3 YRS.	1.56	100.00	0.57	2.80	4.98	7.09	9.15	11.15	13.10	15.00	16.84
	1.75	91.03	0.55	2.70	4.80	6.85	8.83	10.77	12.65	14.49	16.27
	2.00	79.07	0.52	2.57	4.57	6.52	8.41	10.26	12.06	13.81	15.52
	2.25	67.11	0.49	2.44	4.34	6.19	7.99	9.75	11.46	13.13	14.76
	2.50	55.15	0.47	2.31	4.11	5.86	7.57	9.24	10.87	12.46	14.01
	2.75	43.19	0.44	2.18	3.88	5.53	7.15	8.73	10.27	11.78	13.25
	3.00	31.24	0.41	2.05	3.64	5.21	6.73	8.22	9.68	11.10	12.50
	3.65	0.0	0.34	1.71	3.04	4.35	5.63	6.89	8.12	9.33	10.52
4 YRS.	1.56	100.00	0.70	3.42	6.06	8.60	11.05	13.42	15.71	17.92	20.05
	1.75	86.74	0.66	3.26	5.76	8.19	10.53	12.79	14.98	17.10	19.14
	2.00	69.07	0.62	3.04	5.38	7.64	9.84	11.96	14.01	16.00	17.92
	2.25	51.39	0.57	2.82	4.99	7.10	9.14	11.12	13.04	14.90	16.71
	2.50	33.71	0.53	2.60	4.60	6.55	8.45	10.29	12.07	13.80	15.49
	2.75	16.04	0.48	2.38	4.22	6.01	7.75	9.45	11.10	12.71	14.27
	2.98	0.0	0.44	2.18	3.87	5.52	7.12	8.69	10.22	11.71	13.17
5 YRS.	1.56	100.00	0.80	3.93	6.93	9.81	12.56	15.21	17.74	20.18	22.51
	1.75	81.58	0.75	3.69	6.51	9.21	11.81	14.30	16.70	19.01	21.22
	2.00	57.02	0.69	3.36	5.94	8.42	10.80	13.10	15.31	17.44	19.50
	2.25	32.45	0.62	3.04	5.37	7.62	9.80	11.90	13.92	15.88	17.77
	2.50	7.89	0.55	2.71	4.80	6.83	8.79	10.69	12.53	14.32	16.05
	2.58	0.0	0.53	2.61	4.62	6.57	8.47	10.31	12.09	13.82	15.50
6 YRS.	1.56	100.00	0.89	4.35	7.64	10.78	13.77	16.62	19.34	21.93	24.40
	1.75	75.36	0.82	4.02	7.07	9.98	12.76	15.42	17.96	20.39	22.71
	2.00	42.50	0.73	3.57	6.30	8.91	11.42	13.82	16.12	18.33	20.46
	2.25	9.64	0.64	3.13	5.53	7.84	10.07	12.22	14.29	16.28	18.21
	2.32	0.0	0.61	3.00	5.31	7.53	9.66	11.75	13.75	15.68	17.53
7 YRS.	1.56	100.00	0.96	4.69	8.22	11.56	14.73	17.73	20.58	23.28	25.84
	1.75	67.86	0.87	4.26	7.48	10.54	13.45	16.22	18.85	21.36	23.75
	2.00	25.00	0.76	3.69	6.50	9.19	11.75	14.21	16.56	18.81	20.96
	2.15	0.0	0.69	3.36	5.93	8.39	10.76	13.03	15.22	17.32	19.34
8 YRS.	1.56	100.00	1.02	4.97	8.69	12.19	15.49	18.61	21.55	24.32	26.95
	1.75	58.84	0.91	4.44	7.78	10.95	13.94	16.78	19.48	22.03	24.46
	2.02	0.0	0.75	3.69	6.49	9.17	11.73	14.17	16.52	18.76	20.90
9 YRS.	1.56	100.00	1.07	5.20	9.07	12.70	16.10	19.30	22.30	25.13	27.79
	1.75	47.97	0.94	4.57	7.99	11.22	14.27	17.16	19.89	22.47	24.92
	1.92	0.0	0.82	3.98	7.00	9.86	12.59	15.18	17.66	20.02	22.27
10 YRS.	1.56	100.00	1.12	5.39	9.38	13.10	16.58	19.84	22.89	25.76	28.44
	1.75	34.88	0.96	4.65	8.12	11.39	14.48	17.39	20.14	22.74	25.19
	1.85	0.0	0.87	4.25	7.45	10.48	13.35	16.07	18.66	21.12	23.45
		MONTHS									
UNTIL PAID	1.75	144.06	0.97	4.74	8.21	11.51	14.62	17.55	20.31	22.91	25.38
	2.00	98.03	0.77	3.74	6.58	9.29	11.88	14.35	16.72	18.98	21.15
	2.25	76.47	0.64	3.14	5.55	7.86	10.09	12.24	14.32	16.31	18.24
	2.50	63.26	0.55	2.72	4.81	6.84	8.81	10.71	12.56	14.35	16.08
	2.75	54.16	0.49	2.40	4.26	6.07	7.83	9.54	11.21	12.83	14.40
	3.00	47.45	0.44	2.15	3.83	5.46	7.06	8.61	10.13	11.61	13.05
	3.50	38.14	0.36	1.79	3.19	4.57	5.91	7.23	8.52	9.78	11.02
	4.00	31.95	0.31	1.54	2.74	3.93	5.09	6.24	7.36	8.47	9.55

EXAMPLES *ON PAGES A-382 TO A-397*

MORTGAGE YIELD TABLE
SHOWING DISCOUNT PERCENTAGES AT VARIOUS
YIELDS, MONTHLY PAYMENT RATES AND DUE DATES

DUE DATE	YIELD PERCENTAGES										
	28%	29%	30%	31%	32%	33%	34%	35%	36%	37%	38%
1 YR.	7.99	8.81	9.62	10.42	11.21	12.00	12.78	13.55	14.31	15.06	15.81
	7.91	8.72	9.52	10.31	11.10	11.88	12.65	13.41	14.16	14.91	15.65
	7.80	8.59	9.39	10.17	10.95	11.71	12.47	13.23	13.97	14.71	15.44
	7.69	8.47	9.25	10.03	10.79	11.55	12.30	13.04	13.78	14.50	15.22
	7.58	8.35	9.12	9.88	10.64	11.39	12.13	12.86	13.58	14.30	15.01
	7.47	8.23	8.99	9.74	10.49	11.22	11.95	12.67	13.39	14.10	14.80
	7.36	8.11	8.86	9.60	10.33	11.06	11.78	12.49	13.19	13.89	14.58
	7.25	7.99	8.73	9.46	10.18	10.90	11.60	12.31	13.00	13.69	14.37
	4.63	5.11	5.59	6.06	6.54	7.00	7.47	7.93	8.39	8.84	9.29
2 YRS.	14.04	15.42	16.77	18.09	19.39	20.66	21.91	23.14	24.34	25.53	26.69
	13.74	15.08	16.40	17.70	18.97	20.22	21.45	22.65	23.83	24.99	26.13
	13.33	14.64	15.92	17.18	18.42	19.63	20.82	22.00	23.14	24.27	25.38
	12.92	14.19	15.44	16.66	17.86	19.04	20.20	21.34	22.46	23.56	24.63
	12.51	13.74	14.95	16.14	17.31	18.45	19.58	20.69	21.77	22.84	23.89
	12.10	13.30	14.47	15.62	16.75	17.87	18.96	20.03	21.09	22.12	23.14
	11.70	12.85	13.99	15.10	16.20	17.28	18.34	19.38	20.40	21.41	22.40
	11.29	12.40	13.50	14.58	15.64	16.69	17.71	18.72	19.72	20.69	21.65
	8.38	9.23	10.06	10.88	11.70	12.50	13.29	14.07	14.84	15.60	16.34
3 YRS.	18.64	20.38	22.08	23.74	25.35	26.92	28.45	29.94	31.38	32.79	34.17
	18.01	19.71	21.35	22.96	24.52	26.05	27.53	28.98	30.38	31.76	33.09
	17.18	18.80	20.38	21.92	23.42	24.88	26.31	27.70	29.05	30.37	31.66
	16.35	17.90	19.41	20.88	22.32	23.72	25.09	26.42	27.72	28.99	30.23
	15.52	17.00	18.44	19.84	21.22	22.56	23.86	25.14	26.39	27.61	28.80
	14.69	16.09	17.46	18.80	20.11	21.39	22.64	23.86	25.06	26.23	27.37
	13.86	15.19	16.49	17.76	19.01	20.23	21.42	22.59	23.73	24.84	25.93
	11.69	12.83	13.95	15.05	16.13	17.19	18.23	19.25	20.25	21.23	22.19
4 YRS.	22.12	24.11	26.04	27.90	29.70	31.44	33.12	34.75	36.32	37.84	39.31
	21.12	23.03	24.88	26.67	28.40	30.08	31.70	33.27	34.79	36.26	37.69
	19.79	21.59	23.34	25.04	26.68	28.27	29.81	31.30	32.75	34.16	35.52
	18.46	20.15	21.80	23.40	24.95	26.46	27.92	29.34	30.71	32.05	33.35
	17.13	18.72	20.26	21.76	23.22	24.64	26.03	27.37	28.67	29.95	31.18
	15.79	17.28	18.72	20.13	21.50	22.83	24.13	25.40	26.64	27.84	29.01
	14.59	15.97	17.32	18.64	19.93	21.19	22.42	23.61	24.79	25.93	27.05
5 YRS.	24.76	26.91	28.98	30.96	32.87	34.70	36.46	38.16	39.78	41.35	42.85
	23.35	25.40	27.37	29.26	31.09	32.84	34.53	36.16	37.72	39.23	40.68
	21.48	23.38	25.22	27.00	28.71	30.36	31.95	33.49	34.97	36.40	37.79
	19.60	21.37	23.08	24.73	26.33	27.88	29.37	30.82	32.22	33.58	34.89
	17.73	19.36	20.93	22.47	23.95	25.39	26.79	28.15	29.47	30.75	32.00
	17.13	18.71	20.25	21.74	23.19	24.60	25.96	27.28	28.56	29.85	31.07
6 YRS.	26.76	29.01	31.16	33.22	35.18	37.06	38.85	40.57	42.21	43.78	45.29
	24.93	27.06	29.09	31.04	32.91	34.70	36.42	38.04	39.64	41.15	42.61
	22.50	24.46	26.34	28.15	29.89	31.56	33.17	34.72	36.21	37.65	39.03
	20.06	21.85	23.58	25.25	26.86	28.42	29.92	31.37	32.78	34.14	35.45
	19.35	21.09	22.77	24.40	25.97	27.49	28.97	30.39	31.77	33.11	34.40
7 YRS.	28.28	30.59	32.79	34.88	36.87	38.76	40.56	42.28	43.92	45.48	46.97
	26.03	28.20	30.27	32.24	34.13	35.93	37.65	39.30	40.87	42.38	43.82
	23.03	25.01	26.91	28.73	30.48	32.16	33.77	35.32	36.81	38.24	39.62
	21.28	23.15	24.95	26.68	28.35	29.96	31.51	33.00	34.44	35.83	37.17
8 YRS.	29.43	31.77	34.00	36.10	38.10	39.99	41.78	43.49	45.11	46.65	48.12
	26.77	28.96	31.04	33.03	34.92	36.72	38.44	40.07	41.63	43.12	44.56
	22.96	24.93	26.82	28.63	30.37	32.04	33.65	35.19	36.67	38.10	39.47
9 YRS.	30.30	32.66	34.89	37.00	38.99	40.88	42.66	44.35	45.95	47.47	48.91
	27.24	29.44	31.53	33.52	35.40	37.20	38.91	40.54	42.09	43.57	44.99
	24.42	26.47	28.43	30.30	32.10	33.81	35.45	37.03	38.54	39.98	41.37
10 YRS.	30.96	33.33	35.56	37.66	39.65	41.52	43.28	44.95	46.54	48.03	49.46
	27.52	29.72	31.81	33.80	35.68	37.47	39.18	40.80	42.34	43.82	45.22
	25.68	27.79	29.81	31.73	33.56	35.31	36.98	38.57	40.10	41.56	42.95
UNTIL PAID	27.70	29.91	32.00	33.98	35.86	37.64	39.34	40.95	42.49	43.96	45.36
	23.22	25.21	27.11	28.93	30.68	32.36	33.98	35.52	37.01	38.44	39.82
	20.10	21.89	23.62	25.29	26.90	28.46	29.96	31.42	32.82	34.18	35.50
	17.76	19.39	20.97	22.50	23.99	25.43	26.83	28.19	29.51	30.79	32.04
	15.93	17.43	18.88	20.29	21.67	23.01	24.31	25.58	26.82	28.03	29.21
	14.46	15.84	17.18	18.49	19.77	21.02	22.24	23.43	24.59	25.73	26.84
	12.23	13.42	14.59	15.73	16.85	17.95	19.03	20.08	21.12	22.13	23.13
	10.62	11.67	12.70	13.71	14.71	15.69	16.65	17.59	18.53	19.44	20.34

EXAMPLES *ON PAGES A-382 TO A-397*

19%
INTEREST

MORTGAGE YIELD TABLE
SHOWING DISCOUNT PERCENTAGES AT VARIOUS
YIELDS, MONTHLY PAYMENT RATES AND DUE DATES

19%
INTEREST

DUE DATE	PAY'T RATE %	BAL REMAIN %	YIELD PERCENTAGES								
			20%	21%	22%	23%	24%	25%	26%	27%	28%
1 YR.	1.58	100.00	0.90	1.79	2.67	3.54	4.41	5.26	6.11	6.94	7.77
	1.75	97.82	0.89	1.77	2.65	3.51	4.37	5.21	6.05	6.88	7.70
	2.00	94.54	0.88	1.75	2.61	3.46	4.30	5.14	5.97	6.78	7.59
	2.25	91.27	0.87	1.72	2.57	3.41	4.24	5.07	5.88	6.69	7.49
	2.50	87.99	0.85	1.70	2.53	3.36	4.18	4.99	5.80	6.59	7.38
	2.75	84.71	0.84	1.67	2.50	3.31	4.12	4.92	5.71	6.50	7.27
	3.00	81.44	0.83	1.65	2.46	3.26	4.06	4.85	5.63	6.40	7.17
	3.25	78.16	0.82	1.62	2.42	3.22	4.00	4.78	5.54	6.31	7.06
	9.22	0.0	0.52	1.03	1.54	2.04	2.54	3.04	3.53	4.02	4.51
2 YRS.	1.58	100.00	1.64	3.24	4.82	6.36	7.88	9.37	10.83	12.26	13.66
	1.75	95.18	1.60	3.18	4.72	6.24	7.73	9.18	10.62	12.02	13.40
	2.00	87.95	1.56	3.08	4.58	6.05	7.49	8.91	10.30	11.66	13.00
	2.25	80.72	1.51	2.98	4.44	5.86	7.26	8.63	9.98	11.30	12.60
	2.50	73.49	1.46	2.89	4.29	5.67	7.03	8.36	9.66	10.95	12.21
	2.75	66.26	1.41	2.79	4.15	5.48	6.79	8.08	9.34	10.59	11.81
	3.00	59.03	1.36	2.69	4.01	5.29	6.56	7.80	9.03	10.23	11.41
	3.25	51.80	1.31	2.60	3.86	5.10	6.33	7.53	8.71	9.87	11.01
	5.04	0.0	0.96	1.90	2.83	3.75	4.66	5.55	6.43	7.30	8.16
3 YRS.	1.58	100.00	2.24	4.42	6.55	8.61	10.62	12.58	14.48	16.33	18.13
	1.75	92.00	2.17	4.29	6.34	8.35	10.30	12.19	14.04	15.84	17.59
	2.00	79.99	2.07	4.08	6.04	7.95	9.81	11.62	13.39	15.11	16.78
	2.25	67.98	1.96	3.87	5.74	7.55	9.32	11.05	12.73	14.37	15.97
	2.50	55.98	1.86	3.67	5.43	7.16	8.84	10.48	12.08	13.64	15.16
	2.75	43.97	1.75	3.46	5.13	6.76	8.35	9.90	11.42	12.90	14.35
	3.00	31.97	1.65	3.25	4.83	6.36	7.86	9.33	10.77	12.17	13.54
	3.67	0.0	1.37	2.70	4.02	5.31	6.57	7.81	9.02	10.21	11.38
4 YRS.	1.58	100.00	2.74	5.38	7.93	10.42	12.78	15.08	17.30	19.45	21.52
	1.75	88.15	2.62	5.15	7.60	9.96	12.25	14.46	16.59	18.66	20.65
	2.00	70.38	2.44	4.81	7.09	9.31	11.45	13.52	15.53	17.47	19.35
	2.25	52.61	2.27	4.46	6.59	8.65	10.65	12.59	14.47	16.29	18.05
	2.50	34.83	2.09	4.12	6.09	8.00	9.85	11.65	13.40	15.10	16.76
	2.75	17.06	1.91	3.77	5.58	7.34	9.05	10.72	12.34	13.92	15.46
	2.99	0.0	1.74	3.44	5.10	6.71	8.29	9.82	11.32	12.78	14.21
5 YRS.	1.58	100.00	3.15	6.16	9.05	11.82	14.48	17.04	19.48	21.83	24.09
	1.75	83.51	2.97	5.82	8.56	11.19	13.72	16.14	18.47	20.71	22.87
	2.00	58.78	2.71	5.32	7.83	10.24	12.56	14.80	16.96	19.04	21.04
	2.25	34.04	2.45	4.81	7.09	9.29	11.41	13.46	15.44	17.36	19.21
	2.50	9.31	2.19	4.30	6.35	8.34	10.26	12.12	13.93	15.68	17.37
	2.59	0.0	2.09	4.11	6.08	7.98	9.83	11.62	13.36	15.05	16.69
6 YRS.	1.58	100.00	3.48	6.79	9.95	12.96	15.83	18.56	21.17	23.66	26.04
	1.75	77.91	3.24	6.34	9.29	12.11	14.81	17.38	19.84	22.20	24.45
	2.00	44.75	2.89	5.65	8.30	10.84	13.27	15.61	17.85	20.00	22.06
	2.25	11.62	2.53	4.97	7.31	9.57	11.74	13.84	15.86	17.81	19.69
	2.34	0.0	2.41	4.72	6.96	9.12	11.21	13.22	15.16	17.04	18.85
7 YRS.	1.58	100.00	3.75	7.31	10.67	13.86	16.89	19.75	22.48	25.06	27.51
	1.75	71.14	3.45	6.72	9.83	12.79	15.60	18.28	20.82	23.25	25.56
	2.00	27.85	2.99	5.84	8.57	11.18	13.67	16.06	18.34	20.53	22.62
	2.16	0.0	2.69	5.28	7.76	10.14	12.43	14.63	16.75	18.78	20.74
8 YRS.	1.58	100.00	3.98	7.72	11.25	14.58	17.72	20.68	23.48	26.13	28.63
	1.75	62.97	3.60	7.00	10.22	13.28	16.17	18.91	21.50	23.97	26.31
	2.03	0.0	2.96	5.78	8.48	11.06	13.52	15.88	18.14	20.30	22.37
9 YRS.	1.58	100.00	4.16	8.06	11.72	15.15	18.38	21.41	24.26	26.95	29.48
	1.75	53.10	3.71	7.20	10.50	13.61	16.55	19.33	21.96	24.45	26.81
	1.94	0.0	3.19	6.23	9.12	11.87	14.48	16.98	19.36	21.63	23.79
10 YRS.	1.58	100.00	4.31	8.34	12.09	15.61	18.90	21.98	24.87	27.58	30.12
	1.75	41.19	3.78	7.33	10.68	13.83	16.80	19.61	22.25	24.76	27.12
	1.87	0.0	3.41	6.63	9.69	12.59	15.33	17.94	20.42	22.78	25.02
		MONTHS									
UNTIL PAID	1.75	149.68	3.84	7.45	10.84	14.02	17.02	19.84	22.50	25.00	27.38
	2.00	99.85	3.03	5.93	8.69	11.33	13.84	16.25	18.55	20.75	22.85
	2.25	77.43	2.54	4.98	7.33	9.60	11.78	13.88	15.90	17.85	19.74
	2.50	63.87	2.19	4.32	6.37	8.36	10.29	12.16	13.96	15.72	17.42
	2.75	54.58	1.94	3.82	5.65	7.42	9.15	10.83	12.47	14.06	15.61
	3.00	47.76	1.74	3.43	5.08	6.69	8.25	9.79	11.28	12.73	14.16
	3.50	38.33	1.44	2.85	4.24	5.59	6.92	8.22	9.49	10.74	11.96
	4.00	32.08	1.24	2.45	3.64	4.81	5.97	7.10	8.21	9.30	10.37

EXAMPLES *ON PAGES A-382 TO A-397*

DUE DATE	29%	30%	31%	32%	33%	34%	35%	36%	37%	38%	39%
					YIELD PERCENTAGES						
1 YR.	8.59	9.40	10.21	11.00	11.79	12.57	13.34	14.10	14.86	15.60	16.35
	8.51	9.32	10.11	10.90	11.68	12.45	13.22	13.97	14.72	15.46	16.20
	8.39	9.19	9.97	10.75	11.52	12.28	13.04	13.78	14.52	15.25	15.98
	8.28	9.06	9.83	10.60	11.36	12.11	12.86	13.59	14.32	15.04	15.76
	8.16	8.93	9.69	10.45	11.20	11.94	12.67	13.40	14.12	14.83	15.54
	8.04	8.90	9.55	10.30	11.04	11.77	12.49	13.21	13.92	14.62	15.32
	7.92	8.67	9.41	10.15	10.88	11.60	12.31	13.02	13.72	14.41	15.10
	7.80	8.54	9.28	10.00	10.72	11.43	12.13	12.83	13.52	14.20	14.88
	4.99	5.47	5.94	6.41	6.88	7.35	7.81	8.27	8.72	9.17	9.62
2 YRS.	15.04	16.39	17.72	19.02	20.30	21.55	22.78	23.99	25.18	26.34	27.48
	14.75	16.08	17.38	18.66	19.91	21.15	22.35	23.54	24.71	25.85	26.97
	14.32	15.61	16.87	18.11	19.33	20.53	21.71	22.86	24.00	25.11	26.20
	13.88	15.13	16.36	17.57	18.76	19.92	21.06	22.19	23.29	24.37	25.44
	13.44	14.66	15.85	17.02	18.18	19.31	20.42	21.51	22.58	23.64	24.67
	13.01	14.18	15.34	16.48	17.60	18.69	19.77	20.83	21.87	22.90	23.91
	12.57	13.71	14.83	15.93	17.02	18.08	19.13	20.16	21.17	22.16	23.14
	12.13	13.24	14.32	15.39	16.44	17.47	18.48	19.48	20.46	21.42	22.37
	9.01	9.34	10.67	11.48	12.28	13.08	13.86	14.63	15.39	16.14	16.88
3 YRS.	19.89	21.59	23.26	24.87	26.45	27.98	29.48	30.93	32.34	33.72	35.07
	19.30	20.96	22.57	24.15	25.68	27.18	28.63	30.05	31.43	32.78	34.09
	18.41	20.00	21.55	23.07	24.54	25.97	27.37	28.74	30.07	31.36	32.63
	17.53	19.05	20.53	21.98	23.39	24.77	26.11	27.42	28.70	29.95	31.16
	16.65	18.10	19.51	20.90	22.25	23.56	24.85	26.11	27.33	28.53	29.70
	15.76	17.14	18.49	19.81	21.10	22.36	23.59	24.79	25.96	27.11	28.24
	14.88	16.19	17.47	18.73	19.95	21.15	22.33	23.47	24.60	25.70	26.77
	12.53	13.65	14.76	15.84	16.90	17.94	18.97	19.97	20.96	21.93	22.88
4 YRS.	23.52	25.46	27.33	29.14	30.89	32.58	34.21	35.79	37.32	38.80	40.24
	22.58	24.45	26.26	28.01	29.70	31.33	32.92	34.45	35.93	37.37	38.76
	21.18	22.94	24.65	26.31	27.91	29.47	30.97	32.43	33.85	35.23	36.56
	19.77	21.43	23.04	24.61	26.13	27.60	29.03	30.42	31.77	33.08	34.35
	18.36	19.92	21.43	22.91	24.34	25.73	27.09	28.40	29.68	30.93	32.14
	16.95	18.41	19.83	21.21	22.55	23.87	25.14	26.39	27.60	28.78	29.94
	15.60	16.95	18.28	19.58	20.84	22.07	23.28	24.45	25.60	26.72	27.82
5 YRS.	26.25	28.33	30.33	32.25	34.09	35.87	37.57	39.21	40.78	42.30	43.76
	24.94	26.93	28.84	30.69	32.46	34.17	35.81	37.39	38.92	40.39	41.80
	22.96	24.82	26.62	28.35	30.01	31.62	33.17	34.67	36.12	37.52	38.87
	20.99	22.72	24.39	26.00	27.56	29.08	30.54	31.95	33.32	34.65	35.93
	19.02	20.61	22.16	23.66	25.12	26.53	27.90	29.23	30.52	31.78	33.00
	18.28	19.82	21.32	22.78	24.19	25.57	26.91	28.21	29.47	30.70	31.90
6 YRS.	28.30	30.47	32.54	34.52	36.41	38.22	39.95	41.60	43.18	44.70	46.15
	26.60	28.66	30.64	32.53	34.34	36.08	37.74	39.34	40.87	42.34	43.75
	24.05	25.95	27.79	29.55	31.24	32.87	34.43	35.94	37.39	38.79	40.14
	21.50	23.25	24.93	26.56	28.14	29.66	31.13	32.54	33.92	35.24	36.53
	20.00	22.30	23.93	25.52	27.05	28.53	29.97	31.35	32.70	34.00	35.26
7 YRS.	29.84	32.06	34.17	36.17	38.08	39.90	41.63	43.28	44.85	46.36	47.79
	27.76	29.86	31.86	33.77	35.60	37.34	39.00	40.60	42.12	43.58	44.96
	24.63	26.55	28.40	30.17	31.87	33.50	35.07	36.57	38.02	39.42	40.76
	22.62	24.43	26.17	27.35	29.47	31.03	32.53	33.99	35.39	36.74	38.04
8 YRS.	31.00	33.24	35.36	37.38	39.29	41.10	42.82	44.46	46.01	47.49	48.90
	28.54	30.66	32.67	34.59	36.41	38.15	39.81	41.40	42.91	44.35	45.73
	24.36	26.26	28.09	29.84	31.53	33.14	34.70	36.19	37.63	39.01	40.34
9 YRS.	31.87	34.12	36.25	38.26	40.16	41.96	43.67	45.28	46.82	48.28	49.66
	29.05	31.17	33.19	35.11	36.93	38.66	40.31	41.88	43.38	44.81	46.19
	25.86	27.84	29.73	31.54	33.27	34.92	36.51	38.03	39.49	40.89	42.23
10 YRS.	32.52	34.77	36.90	38.90	40.79	42.57	44.26	45.86	47.38	48.81	50.18
	29.36	31.49	33.50	35.41	37.23	38.96	40.60	42.16	43.65	45.07	46.43
	27.16	29.19	31.13	32.97	34.74	36.42	38.03	39.57	41.04	42.45	43.80
UNTIL PAID	29.62	31.74	33.75	35.65	37.46	39.18	40.81	42.37	43.85	45.26	46.60
	24.87	26.80	28.65	30.42	32.12	33.75	35.31	36.82	38.26	39.65	40.99
	21.55	23.30	24.99	26.62	28.19	29.72	31.18	32.60	33.98	35.30	36.59
	19.06	20.66	22.21	23.71	25.17	26.58	27.95	29.28	30.58	31.83	33.05
	17.11	18.58	20.01	21.39	22.75	24.06	25.35	26.59	27.81	29.00	30.15
	15.54	16.90	18.22	19.51	20.77	22.00	23.20	24.37	25.52	26.64	27.73
	13.16	14.33	15.48	16.61	17.72	18.80	19.86	20.91	21.93	22.93	23.91
	11.43	12.47	13.48	14.49	15.47	16.44	17.39	18.33	19.25	20.15	21.04

EXAMPLES *ON PAGES A-382 TO A-397*

MORTGAGE YIELD TABLE

19¼% INTEREST **19¼% INTEREST**

SHOWING DISCOUNT PERCENTAGES AT VARIOUS YIELDS, MONTHLY PAYMENT RATES AND DUE DATES

DUE DATE	PAY'T RATE %	BAL REMAIN %	YIELD PERCENTAGES								
			20%	21%	22%	23%	24%	25%	26%	27%	28%
1 YR.	1.60	100.00	0.67	1.57	2.45	3.32	4.19	5.04	5.89	6.73	7.56
	1.75	98.09	0.67	1.55	2.43	3.29	4.15	5.00	5.84	6.67	7.49
	2.00	94.81	0.66	1.53	2.39	3.25	4.09	4.93	5.76	6.58	7.39
	2.25	91.53	0.65	1.51	2.36	3.20	4.04	4.86	5.68	6.49	7.29
	2.50	88.25	0.64	1.49	2.33	3.16	3.98	4.79	5.60	6.39	7.18
	2.75	84.97	0.63	1.47	2.29	3.11	3.92	4.72	5.52	6.30	7.08
	3.00	81.69	0.62	1.44	2.26	3.06	3.86	4.65	5.43	6.21	6.97
	3.25	78.41	0.61	1.42	2.22	3.02	3.80	4.58	5.35	6.12	6.87
	9.23	0.0	0.39	0.90	1.41	1.91	2.42	2.91	3.41	3.90	4.38
2 YRS.	1.60	100.00	1.23	2.84	4.42	5.97	7.49	8.98	10.44	11.88	13.28
	1.75	95.77	1.21	2.79	4.34	5.86	7.36	8.82	10.26	11.67	13.06
	2.00	88.52	1.17	2.70	4.21	5.69	7.14	8.56	9.96	11.33	12.67
	2.25	81.27	1.13	2.62	4.08	5.51	6.91	8.29	9.65	10.98	12.28
	2.50	74.03	1.10	2.53	3.94	5.33	6.69	8.03	9.34	10.63	11.90
	2.75	66.78	1.06	2.45	3.81	5.15	6.47	7.76	9.03	10.28	11.51
	3.00	59.53	1.02	2.36	3.68	4.98	6.25	7.50	8.73	9.94	11.12
	3.25	52.28	0.98	2.28	3.55	4.80	6.03	7.23	8.42	9.59	10.73
	5.05	0.0	0.72	1.66	2.60	3.52	4.43	5.32	6.21	7.08	7.94
3 YRS.	1.60	100.00	1.68	3.87	6.00	8.07	10.09	12.05	13.96	15.82	17.63
	1.75	92.97	1.64	3.77	5.84	7.86	9.82	11.73	13.59	15.40	17.17
	2.00	80.92	1.58	3.58	5.56	7.48	9.36	11.18	12.96	14.69	16.38
	2.25	68.86	1.48	3.40	5.28	7.11	8.89	10.63	12.33	13.98	15.59
	2.50	56.81	1.40	3.22	5.00	6.74	8.43	10.08	11.69	13.26	14.80
	2.75	44.75	1.32	3.04	4.72	6.36	7.97	9.53	11.06	12.55	14.01
	3.00	32.70	1.24	2.86	4.44	5.99	7.50	8.98	10.43	11.84	13.22
	3.68	0.0	1.03	2.37	3.69	4.98	6.25	7.49	8.71	9.90	11.08
4 YRS.	1.60	100.00	2.05	4.71	7.27	9.75	12.14	14.45	16.68	18.84	20.92
	1.75	89.58	1.98	4.53	7.00	9.39	11.70	13.93	16.08	18.17	20.18
	2.00	71.71	1.84	4.23	6.54	8.77	10.94	13.03	15.06	17.02	18.92
	2.25	53.84	1.71	3.93	6.08	8.16	10.18	12.13	14.03	15.87	17.65
	2.50	35.97	1.58	3.62	5.61	7.54	9.41	11.23	13.00	14.71	16.38
	2.75	18.10	1.44	3.32	5.15	6.92	8.65	10.33	11.97	13.56	15.11
	3.00	0.0	1.31	3.01	4.68	6.30	7.88	9.42	10.93	12.40	13.83
5 YRS.	1.60	100.00	2.36	5.39	8.36	11.09	13.76	16.33	18.79	21.15	23.42
	1.75	85.47	2.24	5.13	7.90	10.56	13.12	15.57	17.93	20.20	22.38
	2.00	60.56	2.05	4.69	7.22	9.67	12.02	14.28	16.47	18.57	20.59
	2.25	35.65	1.85	4.24	6.55	8.77	10.92	13.00	15.00	16.93	18.80
	2.50	10.74	1.65	3.80	5.87	7.88	9.82	11.71	13.53	15.30	17.01
	2.61	0.0	1.57	3.60	5.58	7.49	9.35	11.15	12.90	14.60	16.24
6 YRS.	1.60	100.00	2.61	5.94	9.12	12.15	15.04	17.79	20.41	22.92	25.31
	1.75	80.50	2.45	5.59	8.59	11.45	14.18	16.79	19.29	21.67	23.96
	2.00	47.07	2.18	4.99	7.68	10.25	12.72	15.09	17.36	19.54	21.63
	2.25	13.64	1.92	4.39	6.76	9.05	11.26	13.38	15.43	17.40	19.30
	2.35	0.0	1.81	4.14	6.39	8.56	10.66	12.69	14.64	16.53	18.35
7 YRS.	1.60	100.00	2.81	6.39	9.78	13.00	16.04	18.93	21.67	24.28	26.75
	1.75	74.48	2.61	5.94	9.10	12.11	14.97	17.68	20.27	22.73	25.07
	2.00	30.74	2.27	5.17	7.94	10.59	13.12	15.55	17.86	20.08	22.21
	2.18	0.0	2.02	4.63	7.13	9.52	11.83	14.04	16.17	18.22	20.19
8 YRS.	1.60	100.00	2.98	6.76	10.31	13.67	16.83	19.82	22.65	25.31	27.84
	1.75	67.20	2.73	6.20	9.48	12.59	15.53	18.32	20.96	23.47	25.85
	2.05	0.0	2.22	5.07	7.78	10.38	12.87	15.24	17.52	19.70	21.79
9 YRS.	1.60	100.00	3.12	7.05	10.74	14.21	17.46	20.52	23.40	26.11	28.66
	1.75	58.39	2.82	6.39	9.76	12.93	15.53	18.76	21.44	23.98	26.38
	1.95	0.0	2.40	5.46	8.37	11.14	13.78	16.30	18.70	20.99	23.17
10 YRS.	1.60	100.00	3.23	7.29	11.09	14.63	17.95	21.06	23.98	26.72	29.29
	1.75	47.72	2.88	6.52	9.94	13.16	16.20	19.06	21.75	24.30	26.71
	1.88	0.0	2.56	5.81	8.90	11.82	14.59	17.22	19.73	22.10	24.36
		MONTHS									
UNTIL PAID	1.75	156.14	2.95	6.66	10.14	13.41	16.47	19.36	22.07	24.63	27.05
	2.00	101.79	2.31	5.26	8.08	10.76	13.32	15.77	18.11	20.34	22.48
	2.25	78.43	1.93	4.41	6.79	9.09	11.30	13.43	15.49	17.46	19.37
	2.50	64.49	1.66	3.81	5.89	7.91	9.86	11.75	13.58	15.35	17.07
	2.75	55.01	1.46	3.37	5.21	7.01	8.76	10.46	12.11	13.72	15.28
	3.00	48.08	1.31	3.02	4.68	6.31	7.89	9.44	10.94	12.41	13.85
	3.50	38.53	1.09	2.51	3.90	5.27	6.60	7.91	9.20	10.45	11.68
	4.00	32.21	0.93	2.15	3.35	4.53	5.69	6.83	7.95	9.05	10.13

EXAMPLES *ON PAGES A-382 TO A-397*

19¼% INTEREST — MORTGAGE YIELD TABLE — 19¼% INTEREST

SHOWING DISCOUNT PERCENTAGES AT VARIOUS
YIELDS, MONTHLY PAYMENT RATES AND DUE DATES

DUE DATE	29%	30%	31%	32%	33%	34%	35%	36%	37%	38%	39%
1 YR.	8.38	9.19	9.99	10.79	11.58	12.36	13.13	13.89	14.65	15.40	16.14
	8.31	9.12	9.91	10.70	11.49	12.26	13.03	13.78	14.53	15.28	16.01
	8.19	8.99	9.78	10.56	11.33	12.09	12.85	13.60	14.34	15.07	15.80
	8.08	8.86	9.64	10.41	11.17	11.92	12.67	13.41	14.14	14.86	15.58
	7.96	8.74	9.50	10.26	11.01	11.75	12.49	13.22	13.94	14.65	15.36
	7.85	8.61	9.37	10.11	10.85	11.59	12.31	13.03	13.74	14.45	15.14
	7.73	8.49	9.23	9.97	10.70	11.42	12.13	12.84	13.54	14.24	14.93
	7.62	8.36	9.09	9.82	10.54	11.25	11.96	12.65	13.35	14.03	14.71
	4.87	5.35	5.82	6.29	6.76	7.23	7.69	8.15	8.60	9.06	9.50
2 YRS.	14.67	16.02	17.35	18.66	19.94	21.20	22.43	23.64	24.83	25.99	27.14
	14.42	15.75	17.06	18.35	19.61	20.85	22.06	23.25	24.42	25.57	26.70
	13.99	15.29	16.56	17.81	19.04	20.24	21.42	22.58	23.72	24.84	25.94
	13.57	14.82	16.06	17.27	18.47	19.64	20.79	21.91	23.02	24.11	25.18
	13.14	14.36	15.56	16.74	17.90	19.03	20.15	21.25	22.32	23.38	24.42
	12.71	13.90	15.06	16.20	17.33	18.43	19.51	20.58	21.62	22.65	23.66
	12.29	13.43	14.56	15.67	16.76	17.82	18.88	19.91	20.93	21.92	22.91
	11.86	12.97	14.06	15.13	16.19	17.22	18.24	19.24	20.23	21.20	22.15
	8.79	9.63	10.45	11.27	12.07	12.87	13.65	14.42	15.19	15.94	16.68
3 YRS.	19.39	21.10	22.77	24.39	25.98	27.52	29.01	30.47	31.90	33.28	34.63
	18.89	20.56	22.19	23.77	25.32	26.82	28.29	29.72	31.11	32.46	33.78
	18.02	19.62	21.16	22.71	24.19	25.63	27.04	28.42	29.76	31.06	32.33
	17.16	18.69	20.18	21.64	23.06	24.45	25.80	27.12	28.40	29.66	30.89
	16.30	17.76	19.18	20.57	21.93	23.26	24.55	25.82	27.05	28.26	29.44
	15.43	16.82	18.18	19.51	20.80	22.07	23.31	24.52	25.70	26.86	27.99
	14.57	15.89	17.18	18.44	19.68	20.88	22.06	23.22	24.35	25.46	26.54
	12.23	13.35	14.46	15.55	16.61	17.66	18.69	19.70	20.68	21.66	22.61
4 YRS.	22.93	24.68	26.76	28.58	30.34	32.04	33.68	35.27	36.81	38.29	39.73
	22.13	24.02	25.84	27.60	29.31	30.96	32.56	34.11	35.60	37.05	38.46
	20.75	22.53	24.26	25.93	27.55	29.12	30.64	32.11	33.54	34.93	36.27
	19.38	21.05	22.68	24.26	25.79	27.28	28.72	30.12	31.48	32.80	34.09
	18.00	19.57	21.10	22.59	24.03	25.44	26.80	28.13	29.42	30.68	31.90
	16.62	18.09	19.52	20.92	22.27	23.59	24.88	26.14	27.36	28.55	29.71
	15.23	16.59	17.92	19.22	20.49	21.73	22.94	24.12	25.27	26.40	27.50
5 YRS.	25.60	27.69	29.70	31.63	33.48	35.27	36.98	38.63	40.22	41.74	43.21
	24.47	26.48	28.42	30.28	32.08	33.80	35.46	37.06	38.60	40.08	41.51
	22.54	24.42	26.23	27.98	29.66	31.29	32.86	34.37	35.83	37.24	38.60
	20.61	22.35	24.04	25.67	27.25	28.77	30.25	31.68	33.06	34.40	35.70
	18.68	20.29	21.85	23.36	24.83	26.26	27.64	28.99	30.29	31.56	32.79
	17.84	19.40	20.90	22.37	23.79	25.18	26.52	27.83	29.10	30.33	31.53
6 YRS.	27.60	29.78	31.86	33.85	35.76	37.58	39.32	40.99	42.58	44.11	45.58
	26.14	28.23	30.22	32.14	33.97	35.73	37.41	39.03	40.58	42.06	43.48
	23.64	25.57	27.42	29.20	30.91	32.56	34.14	35.67	37.13	38.55	39.91
	21.14	22.90	24.61	26.26	27.85	29.39	30.87	32.30	33.69	35.03	36.33
	20.12	21.82	23.47	25.06	26.60	28.09	29.54	30.93	32.29	33.60	34.87
7 YRS.	29.10	31.33	33.45	35.48	37.40	39.23	40.98	42.64	44.23	45.75	47.19
	27.31	29.44	31.47	33.40	35.25	37.02	38.71	40.32	41.86	43.34	44.75
	24.24	26.19	28.06	29.85	31.57	33.22	34.81	36.33	37.80	39.21	40.56
	22.08	23.91	25.66	27.36	28.99	30.56	32.07	33.53	34.96	36.30	37.62
8 YRS.	30.22	32.49	34.63	36.66	38.59	40.41	42.15	43.80	45.37	46.87	48.29
	28.11	30.26	32.30	34.25	36.10	37.86	39.54	41.15	42.68	44.14	45.53
	23.79	25.71	27.55	29.31	31.01	32.64	34.20	35.71	37.15	38.55	39.89
9 YRS.	31.07	33.34	35.49	37.52	39.44	41.26	42.98	44.62	46.17	47.64	49.04
	28.65	30.81	32.85	34.80	36.64	38.40	40.07	41.66	43.18	44.63	46.01
	25.25	27.25	29.15	30.97	32.72	34.39	35.99	37.52	38.99	40.40	41.76
10 YRS.	31.71	33.98	36.13	38.15	40.06	41.86	43.57	45.19	46.72	48.17	49.55
	28.99	31.15	33.20	35.14	36.98	38.73	40.39	41.97	43.48	44.92	46.29
	26.52	28.57	30.52	32.39	34.16	35.86	37.49	39.04	40.52	41.94	43.31
UNTIL PAID	29.33	31.48	33.52	35.45	37.28	39.02	40.67	42.24	43.74	45.16	46.52
	24.52	26.48	28.35	30.15	31.87	33.52	35.10	36.62	38.08	39.49	40.83
	21.21	22.98	24.69	26.34	27.93	29.46	30.95	32.38	33.77	35.11	36.40
	18.73	20.34	21.91	23.43	24.90	26.32	27.71	29.05	30.36	31.63	32.86
	16.60	18.28	19.72	21.12	22.48	23.81	25.10	26.36	27.59	28.79	29.95
	15.25	16.61	17.94	19.24	20.51	21.75	22.96	24.14	25.30	26.43	27.53
	12.89	14.07	15.23	16.37	17.48	18.57	19.64	20.69	21.72	22.73	23.72
	11.19	12.23	13.26	14.27	15.26	16.23	17.19	18.13	19.05	19.96	20.86

EXAMPLES *ON PAGES A-382 TO A-397*

MORTGAGE YIELD TABLE

19½% INTEREST   **19½%** INTEREST

SHOWING DISCOUNT PERCENTAGES AT VARIOUS
YIELDS, MONTHLY PAYMENT RATES AND DUE DATES

DUE DATE	PAY'T RATE %	BAL REMAIN %	20%	21%	22%	23%	24%	25%	26%	27%	28%
						YIELD PERCENTAGES					
1 YR.	1.63	100.00	0.45	1.34	2.23	3.10	3.97	4.82	5.67	6.51	7.34
	1.75	98.36	0.45	1.33	2.21	3.08	3.94	4.79	5.63	6.46	7.29
	2.00	95.08	0.44	1.31	2.18	3.04	3.88	4.72	5.55	6.37	7.19
	2.25	91.79	0.43	1.30	2.15	2.99	3.83	4.66	5.47	6.28	7.09
	2.50	88.51	0.43	1.28	2.12	2.95	3.77	4.59	5.40	6.19	6.99
	2.75	85.23	0.42	1.26	2.09	2.91	3.72	4.52	5.32	6.10	6.88
	3.00	81.94	0.42	1.24	2.06	2.86	3.66	4.45	5.24	6.02	6.78
	3.25	78.66	0.41	1.22	2.02	2.82	3.61	4.39	5.16	5.93	6.68
	9.24	0.0	0.26	0.77	1.28	1.79	2.29	2.79	3.28	3.77	4.26
2 YRS.	1.63	100.00	0.82	2.43	4.02	5.57	7.09	8.59	10.05	11.49	12.90
	1.75	96.37	0.81	2.40	3.96	5.49	6.99	8.46	9.91	11.32	12.72
	2.00	89.10	0.78	2.32	3.84	5.32	6.78	8.21	9.61	10.99	12.34
	2.25	81.83	0.76	2.25	3.72	5.15	6.57	7.95	9.31	10.65	11.96
	2.50	74.57	0.73	2.18	3.60	4.99	6.36	7.70	9.02	10.31	11.59
	2.75	67.30	0.71	2.10	3.48	4.82	6.15	7.45	8.72	9.98	11.21
	3.00	60.03	0.68	2.03	3.36	4.66	5.94	7.19	8.43	9.64	10.83
	3.25	52.76	0.66	1.96	3.24	4.49	5.73	6.94	8.13	9.30	10.46
	5.07	0.0	0.48	1.43	2.36	3.29	4.20	5.10	5.98	6.86	7.72
3 YRS.	1.63	100.00	1.12	3.32	5.46	7.53	9.56	11.53	13.44	15.31	17.12
	1.75	93.95	1.09	3.24	5.33	7.36	9.34	11.26	13.14	14.96	16.74
	2.00	81.85	1.04	3.08	5.07	7.01	8.90	10.74	12.55	14.27	15.97
	2.25	69.75	0.99	2.93	4.82	6.66	8.46	10.21	11.92	13.58	15.20
	2.50	57.65	0.94	2.77	4.57	6.31	8.02	9.68	11.30	12.89	14.43
	2.75	45.55	0.88	2.62	4.31	5.96	7.58	9.15	10.69	12.20	13.66
	3.00	33.44	0.83	2.46	4.06	5.62	7.14	8.63	10.08	11.50	12.89
	3.69	0.0	0.68	2.03	3.35	4.65	5.92	7.17	8.39	9.59	10.77
4 YRS.	1.63	100.00	1.37	4.04	6.61	9.10	11.50	13.82	16.06	18.23	20.32
	1.75	91.02	1.32	3.91	6.40	8.81	11.14	13.39	15.57	17.67	19.71
	2.00	73.05	1.24	3.65	5.98	8.23	10.42	12.53	14.58	16.55	18.47
	2.25	55.08	1.15	3.39	5.55	7.66	9.69	11.67	13.58	15.44	17.24
	2.50	37.12	1.06	3.13	5.13	7.08	8.97	10.81	12.59	14.32	16.00
	2.75	19.15	0.97	2.86	4.71	6.50	8.25	9.94	11.60	13.20	14.77
	3.02	0.0	0.87	2.59	4.26	5.89	7.48	9.03	10.54	12.01	13.45
5 YRS.	1.63	100.00	1.57	4.62	7.54	10.35	13.04	15.62	18.09	20.47	22.75
	1.75	87.46	1.51	4.43	7.23	9.93	12.51	15.00	17.38	19.67	21.88
	2.00	62.37	1.37	4.05	6.62	9.09	11.47	13.76	15.96	18.09	20.13
	2.25	37.29	1.24	3.66	6.00	8.25	10.42	12.52	14.55	16.50	18.39
	2.50	12.21	1.11	3.28	5.38	7.41	9.38	11.28	13.13	14.92	16.65
	2.62	0.0	1.05	3.09	5.08	7.00	8.87	10.68	12.44	14.14	15.80
6 YRS.	1.63	100.00	1.74	5.09	8.29	11.34	14.24	17.01	19.66	22.18	24.59
	1.75	83.14	1.65	4.83	7.87	10.78	13.55	16.19	18.72	21.14	23.45
	2.00	49.42	1.47	4.32	7.04	9.65	12.16	14.55	16.86	19.06	21.18
	2.25	15.70	1.29	3.80	6.21	8.53	10.76	12.92	14.99	16.99	18.91
	2.37	0.0	1.21	3.55	5.82	8.01	10.11	12.15	14.12	16.02	17.85
7 YRS.	1.63	100.00	1.88	5.48	8.89	12.13	15.20	18.11	20.87	23.49	25.98
	1.75	77.90	1.76	5.15	8.36	11.42	14.32	17.08	19.70	22.20	24.58
	2.00	33.70	1.53	4.48	7.30	9.99	12.56	15.02	17.37	19.63	21.78
	2.19	0.0	1.35	3.96	6.49	8.90	11.22	13.45	15.60	17.66	19.64
8 YRS.	1.63	100.00	1.99	5.79	9.38	12.76	15.95	18.96	21.81	24.50	27.04
	1.75	71.54	1.84	5.38	8.73	11.89	14.88	17.72	20.41	22.96	25.38
	2.06	0.0	1.48	4.35	7.09	9.71	12.21	14.60	16.90	19.09	21.20
9 YRS.	1.63	100.00	2.08	6.05	9.77	13.26	16.54	19.63	22.53	25.27	27.84
	1.75	63.83	1.91	5.55	8.99	12.23	15.29	18.18	20.90	23.48	25.93
	1.97	0.0	1.60	4.69	7.62	10.42	13.08	15.62	18.03	20.34	22.54
10 YRS.	1.63	100.00	2.16	6.25	10.08	13.66	17.01	20.15	23.09	25.85	28.45
	1.75	54.47	1.95	5.68	9.18	12.47	15.57	18.49	21.24	23.84	26.29
	1.90	0.0	1.71	4.99	8.10	11.05	13.85	16.50	19.02	21.42	23.70
UNTIL PAID		MONTHS									
	1.75	163.72	2.01	5.84	9.42	12.77	15.92	18.87	21.65	24.26	26.72
	2.00	103.85	1.56	4.57	7.44	10.18	12.79	15.28	17.66	19.93	22.10
	2.25	79.47	1.30	3.82	6.24	8.58	10.82	12.98	15.06	17.06	19.00
	2.50	65.13	1.12	3.30	5.40	7.44	9.42	11.33	13.18	14.97	16.71
	2.75	55.45	0.98	2.91	4.78	6.59	8.36	10.08	11.74	13.37	14.95
	3.00	48.40	0.88	2.60	4.29	5.93	7.52	9.08	10.60	12.09	13.53
	3.50	38.72	0.73	2.16	3.57	4.94	6.29	7.61	8.90	10.17	11.41
	4.00	32.34	0.62	1.85	3.06	4.25	5.42	6.56	7.69	8.79	9.88

EXAMPLES *ON PAGES A-382 TO A-397*

DUE DATE	YIELD PERCENTAGES										
	29%	30%	31%	32%	33%	34%	35%	36%	37%	38%	39%
1 YR.	8.16	8.98	9.78	10.58	11.37	12.15	12.92	13.69	14.44	15.19	15.94
	8.11	8.91	9.71	10.51	11.29	12.07	12.83	13.59	14.35	15.09	15.83
	7.99	8.79	9.58	10.36	11.13	11.90	12.66	13.41	14.15	14.89	15.61
	7.88	8.67	9.45	10.22	10.98	11.73	12.48	13.22	13.96	14.68	15.40
	7.77	8.54	9.31	10.07	10.82	11.57	12.31	13.04	13.76	14.48	15.18
	7.66	8.42	9.18	9.93	10.67	11.40	12.13	12.85	13.56	14.27	14.97
	7.54	8.30	9.04	9.78	10.51	11.24	11.96	12.67	13.37	14.06	14.75
	7.43	8.17	8.91	9.64	10.36	11.07	11.78	12.48	13.17	13.86	14.54
	4.74	5.22	5.70	6.17	6.64	7.11	7.57	8.03	8.49	8.94	9.39
2 YRS.	14.29	15.65	16.98	18.29	19.58	20.84	22.07	23.29	24.48	25.65	26.79
	14.08	15.42	16.74	18.03	19.30	20.54	21.76	22.96	24.13	25.29	26.42
	13.67	14.97	16.25	17.50	18.74	19.94	21.13	22.30	23.44	24.57	25.67
	13.25	14.52	15.76	16.98	18.17	19.35	20.50	21.64	22.75	23.85	24.92
	12.84	14.06	15.27	16.45	17.61	18.76	19.88	20.98	22.06	23.13	24.17
	12.42	13.61	14.78	15.93	17.05	18.16	19.25	20.32	21.37	22.41	23.42
	12.00	13.16	14.29	15.40	16.49	17.57	18.62	19.66	20.68	21.69	22.67
	11.59	12.70	13.80	14.87	15.93	16.97	18.00	19.00	19.99	20.97	21.92
	8.57	9.41	10.24	11.06	11.86	12.66	13.44	14.22	14.98	15.74	16.48
3 YRS.	18.89	20.61	22.29	23.92	25.50	27.05	28.55	30.02	31.45	32.84	34.19
	18.47	20.15	21.79	23.39	24.95	26.46	27.94	29.38	30.78	32.14	33.47
	17.63	19.24	20.81	22.34	23.84	25.29	26.71	28.10	29.44	30.76	32.04
	16.78	18.33	19.83	21.30	22.73	24.12	25.48	26.81	28.11	29.37	30.61
	15.94	17.41	18.85	20.25	21.62	22.95	24.26	25.53	26.77	27.99	29.17
	15.10	16.50	17.86	19.20	20.51	21.78	23.03	24.25	25.44	26.60	27.74
	14.25	15.58	16.88	18.15	19.40	20.61	21.80	22.96	24.10	25.22	26.30
	11.92	13.06	14.17	15.26	16.33	17.38	18.41	19.42	20.41	21.39	22.34
4 YRS.	22.35	24.30	26.19	28.02	29.78	31.49	33.14	34.74	36.29	37.78	39.23
	21.67	23.58	25.42	27.20	28.92	30.58	32.20	33.76	35.27	36.73	38.15
	20.33	22.12	23.87	25.55	27.18	28.77	30.30	31.79	33.23	34.63	35.98
	18.98	20.67	22.31	23.91	25.45	26.95	28.41	29.82	31.19	32.52	33.82
	17.63	19.22	20.76	22.26	23.72	25.14	26.51	27.85	29.15	30.42	31.65
	16.29	17.77	19.21	20.62	21.99	23.32	24.62	25.08	27.11	28.32	29.49
	14.85	16.22	17.56	18.87	20.14	21.38	22.60	23.78	24.94	26.07	27.18
5 YRS.	24.94	27.05	29.07	31.01	32.88	34.67	36.39	38.05	39.65	41.18	42.66
	24.00	26.03	27.99	29.87	31.69	33.43	35.11	36.72	38.28	39.78	41.22
	22.11	24.01	25.84	27.60	29.31	30.95	32.53	34.06	35.54	36.96	38.34
	20.22	21.98	23.68	25.33	26.93	28.47	29.96	31.40	32.80	34.15	35.46
	18.33	19.95	21.53	23.06	24.55	25.99	27.38	28.74	30.06	31.33	32.57
	17.41	18.97	20.48	21.96	23.39	24.78	26.13	27.44	28.72	29.96	31.17
6 YRS.	26.89	29.09	31.18	33.19	35.11	36.94	38.70	40.38	41.99	43.53	45.00
	25.66	27.78	29.80	31.74	33.60	35.38	37.08	38.71	40.28	41.78	43.23
	23.22	25.17	27.04	28.85	30.58	32.24	33.85	35.39	36.87	38.30	39.67
	20.77	22.56	24.28	25.95	27.56	29.11	30.61	32.06	33.46	34.81	36.12
	19.63	21.34	23.00	24.60	26.15	27.65	29.10	30.51	31.87	33.19	34.47
7 YRS.	28.35	30.60	32.74	34.78	36.72	38.57	40.33	42.01	43.61	45.14	46.59
	26.85	29.01	31.07	33.03	34.90	36.69	38.40	40.03	41.59	43.09	44.52
	23.84	25.82	27.71	29.53	31.27	32.94	34.55	36.09	37.57	38.99	40.36
	21.55	23.39	25.15	26.86	28.50	30.08	31.61	33.08	34.50	35.87	37.19
8 YRS.	29.45	31.73	33.89	35.94	37.88	39.73	41.48	43.15	44.73	46.24	47.68
	27.67	29.86	31.93	33.90	35.78	37.57	39.27	40.89	42.44	43.92	45.33
	23.21	25.15	27.00	28.78	30.49	32.13	33.71	35.22	36.68	38.08	39.43
9 YRS.	30.27	32.57	34.74	36.79	38.72	40.56	42.30	43.95	45.52	47.00	48.42
	28.24	30.43	32.51	34.48	36.35	38.13	39.83	41.44	42.98	44.44	45.84
	24.64	26.65	28.57	30.41	32.17	33.85	35.47	37.01	38.50	39.92	41.28
10 YRS.	30.89	33.19	35.36	37.40	39.33	41.15	42.88	44.51	46.06	47.53	48.92
	28.61	30.80	32.88	34.85	36.72	38.49	40.18	41.78	43.30	44.76	46.14
	25.88	27.94	29.92	31.80	33.59	35.30	36.94	38.51	40.00	41.44	42.81
UNTIL PAID	29.04	31.23	33.30	35.26	37.11	38.87	40.54	42.13	43.64	45.07	46.44
	24.17	26.16	28.06	29.88	31.62	33.29	34.89	36.43	37.90	39.32	40.68
	20.86	22.65	24.38	26.05	27.66	29.21	30.71	32.16	33.56	34.91	36.22
	18.39	20.03	21.61	23.14	24.62	26.07	27.46	28.82	30.14	31.42	32.66
	16.48	17.97	19.43	20.84	22.22	23.56	24.86	26.13	27.37	28.57	29.75
	14.94	16.32	17.66	18.98	20.26	21.51	22.73	23.92	25.08	26.22	27.32
	12.62	13.81	14.98	16.12	17.25	18.34	19.42	20.48	21.51	22.53	23.52
	10.95	12.00	13.03	14.04	15.04	16.02	16.98	17.93	18.86	19.77	20.67

MORTGAGE YIELD TABLE
SHOWING DISCOUNT PERCENTAGES AT VARIOUS YIELDS, MONTHLY PAYMENT RATES AND DUE DATES

DUE DATE	PAY'T RATE %	BAL REMAIN %	20%	21%	22%	23%	24%	25%	26%	27%	28%
1 YR.	1.65	100.00	0.22	1.12	2.00	2.88	3.75	4.60	5.45	6.29	7.12
	1.75	98.63	0.22	1.11	1.99	2.86	3.72	4.58	5.42	6.26	7.08
	2.00	95.34	0.22	1.10	1.96	2.82	3.67	4.51	5.35	6.17	6.98
	2.25	92.06	0.22	1.08	1.94	2.78	3.62	4.45	5.27	6.08	6.89
	2.50	88.77	0.21	1.07	1.91	2.74	3.57	4.39	5.19	6.00	6.79
	2.75	85.48	0.21	1.05	1.88	2.70	3.52	4.32	5.12	5.91	6.69
	3.00	82.20	0.21	1.03	1.85	2.66	3.46	4.26	5.04	5.82	6.59
	3.25	78.91	0.20	1.02	1.82	2.62	3.41	4.19	4.97	5.73	6.49
	9.25	0.0	0.13	0.64	1.15	1.66	2.16	2.66	3.16	3.65	4.14
2 YRS.	1.65	100.00	0.41	2.03	3.61	5.17	6.70	8.20	9.67	11.11	12.53
	1.75	96.96	0.40	2.00	3.57	5.11	6.62	8.10	9.55	10.97	12.37
	2.00	89.58	0.39	1.94	3.46	4.95	6.42	7.85	9.26	10.65	12.01
	2.25	82.39	0.38	1.88	3.35	4.80	6.22	7.61	8.98	10.32	11.64
	2.50	75.11	0.37	1.82	3.24	4.64	6.02	7.37	8.69	10.00	11.27
	2.75	67.82	0.35	1.76	3.14	4.49	5.82	7.13	8.41	9.67	10.91
	3.00	60.54	0.34	1.70	3.03	4.34	5.62	6.88	8.12	9.34	10.54
	3.25	53.25	0.33	1.64	2.92	4.18	5.42	6.64	7.84	9.02	10.17
	5.08	0.0	0.24	1.19	2.13	3.05	3.97	4.87	5.76	6.63	7.50
3 YRS.	1.65	100.00	0.56	2.76	4.91	7.00	9.05	11.00	12.93	14.80	16.62
	1.75	94.94	0.55	2.71	4.81	6.86	8.85	10.79	12.68	14.52	16.31
	2.00	82.79	0.52	2.58	4.58	6.54	8.44	10.29	12.09	13.85	15.56
	2.25	70.64	0.50	2.45	4.36	6.21	8.02	9.78	11.50	13.18	14.81
	2.50	58.49	0.47	2.32	4.13	5.89	7.60	9.28	10.91	12.51	14.06
	2.75	46.34	0.44	2.19	3.90	5.56	7.19	8.77	10.32	11.84	13.32
	3.00	34.19	0.42	2.06	3.67	5.24	6.77	8.27	9.74	11.17	12.57
	3.70	0.0	0.34	1.70	3.02	4.32	5.60	6.85	8.08	9.28	10.46
4 YRS.	1.65	100.00	0.68	3.36	5.95	8.45	10.86	13.19	15.45	17.62	19.73
	1.75	92.47	0.67	3.27	5.79	8.23	10.58	12.85	15.05	17.17	19.23
	2.00	74.41	0.62	3.06	5.41	7.69	9.89	12.03	14.09	16.09	18.02
	2.25	56.34	0.58	2.84	5.03	7.15	9.21	11.20	13.13	15.00	16.82
	2.50	38.28	0.53	2.62	4.65	6.61	8.52	10.37	12.17	13.92	15.62
	2.75	20.21	0.49	2.40	4.26	6.07	7.84	9.55	11.22	12.84	14.41
	3.03	0.0	0.44	2.16	3.84	5.47	7.07	8.63	10.14	11.62	13.07
5 YRS.	1.65	100.00	0.79	3.85	6.79	9.61	12.31	14.91	17.40	19.79	22.08
	1.75	89.47	0.76	3.72	6.56	9.28	11.90	14.41	16.83	19.14	21.37
	2.00	64.21	0.69	3.40	6.00	8.50	10.91	13.22	15.46	17.60	19.67
	2.25	38.95	0.63	3.08	5.44	7.72	9.92	12.04	14.09	16.06	17.97
	2.50	13.69	0.56	2.76	4.88	6.93	8.92	10.85	12.72	14.52	16.28
	2.64	0.0	0.52	2.58	4.58	6.51	8.39	10.21	11.98	13.69	15.35
6 YRS.	1.65	100.00	0.87	4.25	7.46	10.53	13.45	16.24	18.90	21.44	23.87
	1.75	85.83	0.83	4.06	7.15	10.09	12.90	15.59	18.15	20.60	22.94
	2.00	51.81	0.74	3.63	6.39	9.04	11.58	14.01	16.34	18.58	20.73
	2.25	17.80	0.65	3.19	5.64	7.99	10.26	12.44	14.54	16.56	18.51
	2.38	0.0	0.60	2.97	5.25	7.44	9.57	11.62	13.59	15.51	17.35
7 YRS.	1.65	100.00	0.94	4.57	8.00	11.26	14.35	17.28	20.07	22.71	25.22
	1.75	81.39	0.89	4.33	7.60	10.71	13.66	16.46	19.13	21.66	24.08
	2.00	36.73	0.77	3.77	6.64	9.38	11.99	14.49	16.87	19.16	21.34
	2.21	0.0	0.68	3.32	5.85	8.28	10.62	12.86	15.02	17.10	19.09
8 YRS.	1.65	100.00	0.99	4.83	8.44	11.85	15.06	18.10	20.97	23.68	26.25
	1.75	75.99	0.93	4.54	7.95	11.17	14.22	17.11	19.84	22.43	24.89
	2.08	0.0	0.74	3.63	6.39	9.03	11.55	13.96	16.27	18.48	20.60
9 YRS.	1.65	100.00	1.04	5.04	8.79	12.31	15.62	18.73	21.66	24.42	27.02
	1.75	69.49	0.97	4.69	8.20	11.51	14.63	17.57	20.35	22.98	25.46
	1.99	0.0	0.80	3.91	6.87	9.69	12.37	14.93	17.37	19.69	21.91
10 YRS.	1.65	100.00	1.08	5.21	9.07	12.68	16.06	19.23	22.20	24.99	27.61
	1.75	61.45	0.99	4.81	8.39	11.76	14.92	17.90	20.71	23.35	25.85
	1.92	0.0	0.86	4.17	7.30	10.28	13.10	15.78	18.32	20.74	23.04
		MONTHS									
UNTIL PAID	1.75	172.83	1.03	4.99	8.68	12.13	15.36	18.38	21.22	23.88	26.39
	2.00	106.05	0.79	3.87	6.30	9.59	12.25	14.78	17.20	19.51	21.71
	2.25	80.54	0.66	3.22	5.68	8.05	10.33	12.52	14.63	16.66	18.62
	2.50	65.79	0.56	2.77	4.91	6.97	8.97	10.91	12.78	14.60	16.35
	2.75	55.90	0.50	2.44	4.33	6.17	7.95	9.69	11.37	13.01	14.61
	3.00	48.73	0.44	2.19	3.88	5.54	7.15	8.73	10.26	11.76	13.22
	3.50	38.92	0.37	1.81	3.23	4.61	5.97	7.30	8.60	9.88	11.13
	4.00	32.47	0.31	1.55	2.77	3.96	5.14	6.29	7.42	8.54	9.63

EXAMPLES *ON PAGES A-382 TO A-397*

MORTGAGE YIELD TABLE
SHOWING DISCOUNT PERCENTAGES AT VARIOUS YIELDS, MONTHLY PAYMENT RATES AND DUE DATES

DUE DATE	29%	30%	31%	32%	33%	34%	35%	36%	37%	38%	39%
1 YR.	7.95	8.76	9.57	10.37	11.16	11.94	12.71	13.48	14.24	14.99	15.73
	7.90	8.71	9.51	10.31	11.09	11.87	12.64	13.40	14.16	14.90	15.64
	7.79	8.59	9.38	10.17	10.94	11.71	12.47	13.22	13.96	14.70	15.43
	7.68	8.47	9.25	10.02	10.79	11.55	12.30	13.04	13.77	14.50	15.22
	7.57	8.35	9.12	9.88	10.64	11.38	12.12	12.85	13.58	14.30	15.01
	7.46	8.23	8.99	9.74	10.48	11.22	11.95	12.67	13.39	14.09	14.79
	7.35	8.11	8.86	9.60	10.33	11.06	11.78	12.49	13.19	13.89	14.58
	7.25	7.99	8.73	9.46	10.18	10.89	11.60	12.30	13.00	13.69	14.37
	4.62	5.10	5.58	6.05	6.52	6.99	7.45	7.91	8.37	8.82	9.27
2 YRS.	13.91	15.28	16.61	17.93	19.21	20.48	21.72	22.93	24.13	25.30	26.45
	13.75	15.09	16.41	17.71	18.98	20.23	21.46	22.66	23.84	25.00	26.14
	13.34	14.65	15.93	17.19	18.43	19.65	20.84	22.01	23.16	24.29	25.40
	12.93	14.21	15.45	16.68	17.88	19.06	20.22	21.36	22.48	23.58	24.66
	12.53	13.76	14.97	16.16	17.33	18.48	19.61	20.71	21.80	22.87	23.92
	12.12	13.32	14.49	15.65	16.78	17.89	18.99	20.06	21.12	22.16	23.18
	11.72	12.98	14.01	15.13	16.23	17.31	18.37	19.41	20.44	21.45	22.44
	11.31	12.43	13.53	14.61	15.68	16.72	17.75	18.76	19.76	20.74	21.70
	8.35	9.19	10.02	10.84	11.65	12.45	13.23	14.01	14.78	15.54	16.28
3 YRS.	18.39	20.12	21.80	23.44	25.03	26.58	28.09	29.56	31.00	32.39	33.75
	18.05	19.75	21.40	23.01	24.58	26.10	27.59	29.04	30.45	31.82	33.16
	17.23	18.85	20.44	21.98	23.48	24.95	26.38	27.77	29.13	30.45	31.74
	16.41	17.96	19.47	20.95	22.39	23.80	25.17	26.50	27.81	29.08	30.32
	15.58	17.06	18.51	19.92	21.30	22.64	23.96	25.24	26.49	27.71	28.91
	14.76	16.17	17.55	18.89	20.21	21.49	22.75	23.97	25.17	26.34	27.49
	13.94	15.27	16.58	17.86	19.11	20.34	21.53	22.71	23.85	24.97	26.07
	11.62	12.76	13.87	14.97	16.04	17.09	18.13	19.14	20.14	21.12	22.08
4 YRS.	21.76	23.72	25.62	27.46	29.23	30.95	32.61	34.22	35.77	37.27	38.73
	21.21	23.13	24.99	26.78	28.52	30.20	31.83	33.40	34.93	36.40	37.83
	20.11	21.71	23.47	25.17	26.82	28.41	29.96	31.46	32.91	34.32	35.69
	18.98	20.29	21.94	23.55	25.11	26.62	28.09	29.51	30.90	32.24	33.55
	17.27	18.87	20.42	21.93	23.40	24.83	26.22	27.57	28.88	30.16	31.40
	15.95	17.45	18.90	20.32	21.70	23.04	24.35	25.62	26.87	28.08	29.26
	14.48	15.35	17.20	18.51	19.79	21.04	22.26	23.45	24.61	25.75	26.86
5 YRS.	24.28	26.40	28.43	30.39	32.27	34.07	35.81	37.48	39.08	40.63	42.12
	23.51	25.57	27.55	29.46	31.29	33.05	34.75	36.38	37.95	39.47	40.93
	21.67	23.99	25.44	27.22	28.94	30.60	32.21	33.75	35.24	36.68	38.07
	19.82	21.60	23.32	24.99	26.60	28.16	29.66	31.12	32.53	33.89	35.21
	17.97	19.62	21.21	22.76	24.25	25.71	27.12	26.49	29.82	31.10	32.36
	16.97	18.54	20.06	21.55	22.98	24.38	25.74	27.06	28.35	29.59	30.81
6 YRS.	26.18	28.39	30.51	32.53	34.46	36.31	38.07	39.77	41.39	42.94	44.42
	25.18	27.33	29.38	31.34	33.22	35.02	36.74	38.39	39.98	41.50	42.96
	22.79	24.76	26.66	28.49	30.24	31.92	33.54	35.10	36.60	38.04	39.43
	20.39	22.20	23.95	25.63	27.26	28.83	30.35	31.81	33.22	34.59	35.91
	19.14	20.86	22.53	24.14	25.70	27.21	28.67	30.09	31.46	32.78	34.07
7 YRS.	27.61	29.87	32.03	34.08	36.04	37.90	39.68	41.37	42.98	44.53	46.00
	26.38	28.57	30.66	32.65	34.55	36.36	38.09	39.74	41.32	42.83	44.28
	23.45	25.44	27.36	29.20	30.96	32.65	34.27	35.83	37.33	38.77	40.15
	22.11	22.86	24.64	26.36	28.01	29.60	31.14	32.62	34.05	35.43	36.76
8 YRS.	28.67	30.97	33.15	35.22	37.18	39.04	40.81	42.50	44.10	45.62	47.07
	27.22	29.44	31.54	33.55	35.45	37.26	38.99	40.63	42.20	43.70	45.13
	22.64	24.50	26.45	28.24	29.97	31.62	33.21	34.73	36.20	37.62	38.98
9 YRS.	29.48	31.79	33.98	36.05	38.01	39.86	41.62	43.28	44.87	46.37	47.80
	27.81	30.04	32.15	34.15	36.05	37.86	39.58	41.21	42.77	44.25	45.66
	24.03	26.06	27.99	29.85	31.62	33.32	34.94	36.50	38.00	39.43	40.81
10 YRS.	30.08	32.40	34.59	36.65	38.60	40.45	42.19	43.84	45.40	46.89	48.30
	28.21	30.44	32.55	34.55	36.45	38.25	39.95	41.58	43.12	44.59	45.99
	25.23	27.32	29.31	31.20	33.01	34.74	36.39	37.97	39.48	40.93	42.32
UNTIL PAID	28.75	30.98	33.08	35.07	36.95	38.73	40.42	42.02	43.54	44.99	46.37
	23.82	25.83	27.76	29.60	31.37	33.06	34.68	36.23	37.73	39.16	40.53
	20.50	22.32	24.07	25.76	27.38	28.96	30.47	31.94	33.35	34.72	36.04
	18.05	19.70	21.30	22.85	24.35	25.81	27.22	28.59	29.92	31.21	32.46
	16.16	17.67	19.13	20.56	21.95	23.30	24.62	25.90	27.14	28.36	29.54
	14.64	16.03	17.38	18.71	20.00	21.26	22.49	23.69	24.86	26.00	27.12
	12.35	13.55	14.73	15.88	17.01	18.11	19.20	20.26	21.30	22.32	23.32
	10.70	11.76	12.80	13.82	14.82	15.80	16.77	17.73	18.66	19.58	20.49

EXAMPLES *ON PAGES A-382 TO A-397*

DUE DATE	PAY'T RATE %	BAL REMAIN %	21%	22%	23%	24%	25%	26%	27%	28%	29%
						YIELD PERCENTAGES					
1 YR.	1.67	100.00	0.89	1.78	2.66	3.53	4.38	5.23	6.08	6.91	7.73
	1.75	98.90	0.89	1.77	2.65	3.51	4.36	5.21	6.05	6.88	7.70
	2.00	95.61	0.88	1.75	2.61	3.46	4.30	5.14	5.96	6.78	7.59
	2.25	92.32	0.87	1.72	2.57	3.41	4.24	5.06	5.88	6.69	7.48
	2.50	89.03	0.85	1.70	2.53	3.36	4.18	4.99	5.80	6.59	7.38
	2.75	85.74	0.84	1.67	2.50	3.31	4.12	4.92	5.71	6.49	7.27
	3.00	82.45	0.83	1.65	2.46	3.26	4.06	4.85	5.63	6.40	7.16
	3.25	79.16	0.82	1.62	2.42	3.21	4.00	4.77	5.54	6.30	7.06
	9.26	0.0	0.51	1.03	1.53	2.04	2.54	3.03	3.52	4.01	4.50
2 YRS.	1.67	100.00	1.62	3.21	4.77	6.30	7.81	9.28	10.73	12.15	13.54
	1.75	97.57	1.61	3.18	4.73	6.24	7.73	9.19	10.62	12.03	13.41
	2.00	90.26	1.56	3.08	4.58	6.05	7.50	8.92	10.31	11.67	13.01
	2.25	82.96	1.51	2.99	4.44	5.87	7.27	8.64	9.99	11.32	12.62
	2.50	75.65	1.46	2.89	4.30	5.68	7.04	8.37	9.68	10.96	12.22
	2.75	68.35	1.41	2.80	4.16	5.49	6.80	8.09	9.36	10.60	11.83
	3.00	61.05	1.36	2.70	4.01	5.30	6.57	7.82	9.04	10.25	11.43
	3.25	53.74	1.31	2.60	3.87	5.12	6.34	7.55	8.73	9.89	11.04
	5.09	0.0	0.95	1.89	2.82	3.74	4.64	5.53	6.41	7.27	8.13
3 YRS.	1.67	100.00	2.21	4.36	6.46	8.50	10.48	12.41	14.29	16.12	17.90
	1.75	95.93	2.18	4.30	6.36	8.37	10.32	12.22	14.07	15.87	17.63
	2.00	83.74	2.07	4.09	6.06	7.97	9.84	11.65	13.42	15.15	16.83
	2.25	71.54	1.97	3.89	5.76	7.58	9.36	11.09	12.77	14.42	16.02
	2.50	59.34	1.86	3.68	5.46	7.19	8.87	10.52	12.13	13.69	15.22
	2.75	47.15	1.76	3.48	5.16	6.79	8.39	9.95	11.48	12.97	14.42
	3.00	34.95	1.66	3.27	4.86	6.40	7.91	9.39	10.83	12.24	13.62
	3.72	0.0	1.36	2.69	3.99	5.27	6.53	7.76	8.97	10.15	11.32
4 YRS.	1.67	100.00	2.69	5.29	7.80	10.22	12.57	14.83	17.02	19.13	21.17
	1.75	93.95	2.63	5.18	7.63	10.01	12.30	14.52	16.67	18.74	20.74
	2.00	75.78	2.46	4.84	7.14	9.36	11.51	13.60	15.62	17.57	19.46
	2.25	57.62	2.28	4.50	6.64	8.71	10.73	12.68	14.57	16.40	18.18
	2.50	39.45	2.11	4.15	6.14	8.07	9.94	11.75	13.52	15.23	16.89
	2.75	21.29	1.93	3.81	5.64	7.42	9.15	10.83	12.47	14.06	15.61
	3.04	0.0	1.73	3.41	5.06	6.66	8.22	9.75	11.24	12.69	14.10
5 YRS.	1.67	100.00	3.08	6.03	8.87	11.59	14.20	16.70	19.10	21.41	23.63
	1.75	91.52	2.99	5.87	8.63	11.27	13.82	16.26	18.61	20.86	23.03
	2.00	66.08	2.74	5.37	7.90	10.34	12.68	14.94	17.11	19.21	21.22
	2.25	40.64	2.48	4.87	7.18	9.40	11.55	13.62	15.62	17.55	19.42
	2.50	15.20	2.22	4.37	6.45	8.46	10.41	12.30	14.13	15.90	17.61
	2.65	0.0	2.07	4.07	6.02	7.90	9.74	11.51	13.24	14.91	16.53
6 YRS.	1.67	100.00	3.40	6.63	9.72	12.66	15.47	18.15	20.70	23.14	25.47
	1.75	88.56	3.28	6.41	9.39	12.24	14.97	17.57	20.05	22.42	24.69
	2.00	54.25	2.93	5.73	8.42	10.99	13.46	15.82	18.09	20.26	22.35
	2.25	19.94	2.58	5.06	7.45	9.74	11.95	14.08	16.13	18.10	20.01
	2.40	0.0	2.38	4.67	6.88	9.02	11.08	13.07	14.99	16.85	18.65
7 YRS.	1.67	100.00	3.65	7.11	10.40	13.51	16.46	19.26	21.93	24.46	26.86
	1.75	84.96	3.50	6.83	9.98	12.98	15.83	18.54	21.11	23.57	25.90
	2.00	39.83	3.05	5.97	8.75	11.40	13.94	16.36	18.68	20.90	23.02
	2.22	0.0	2.66	5.21	7.66	10.01	12.27	14.44	16.53	18.54	20.48
8 YRS.	1.67	100.00	3.86	7.55	10.94	14.18	17.24	20.13	22.86	25.45	27.90
	1.75	80.56	3.68	7.15	10.43	13.54	16.48	19.26	21.89	24.39	26.76
	2.10	0.0	2.91	5.69	8.35	10.89	13.32	15.65	17.87	20.01	22.06
9 YRS.	1.67	100.00	4.03	7.81	11.37	14.70	17.84	20.80	23.58	26.21	28.68
	1.75	75.20	3.81	7.39	10.77	13.95	16.95	19.78	22.46	24.98	27.38
	2.00	0.0	3.14	6.12	8.96	11.66	14.24	16.70	19.04	21.28	23.42
10 YRS.	1.67	100.00	4.17	8.06	11.71	15.12	18.32	21.31	24.13	26.78	29.27
	1.75	68.66	3.91	7.57	11.02	14.25	17.29	20.16	22.85	25.40	27.80
	1.93	0.0	3.34	6.50	9.53	12.35	15.05	17.62	20.06	22.38	24.59
		MONTHS									
UNTIL PAID	1.75	184.19	4.09	7.91	11.46	14.78	17.88	20.79	23.51	26.07	28.48
	2.00	108.40	3.14	6.13	8.98	11.69	14.27	16.73	19.08	21.32	23.46
	2.25	81.67	2.60	5.11	7.51	9.82	12.05	14.19	16.25	18.23	20.14
	2.50	66.46	2.24	4.40	6.50	8.52	10.48	12.38	14.21	15.99	17.71
	2.75	56.36	1.97	3.88	5.74	7.54	9.29	11.00	12.66	14.27	15.83
	3.00	49.06	1.76	3.48	5.15	6.78	8.36	9.91	11.42	12.90	14.33
	3.50	39.12	1.46	2.88	4.28	5.65	6.99	8.30	9.59	10.84	12.08
	4.00	32.61	1.25	2.47	3.67	4.86	6.02	7.16	8.28	9.38	10.46

EXAMPLES *ON PAGES A-382 TO A-397*

MORTGAGE YIELD TABLE
SHOWING DISCOUNT PERCENTAGES AT VARIOUS YIELDS, MONTHLY PAYMENT RATES AND DUE DATES

DUE DATE	30%	31%	32%	33%	34%	35%	36%	37%	38%	39%	40%
					YIELD PERCENTAGES						
1 YR.	8.55	9.36	10.16	10.95	11.73	12.50	13.27	14.03	14.78	15.53	16.26
	8.51	9.31	10.11	10.90	11.68	12.45	13.21	13.97	14.72	15.46	16.19
	8.39	9.18	9.97	10.75	11.52	12.28	13.03	13.78	14.52	15.25	15.97
	8.27	9.06	9.83	10.60	11.36	12.11	12.85	13.59	14.32	15.04	15.75
	8.16	8.93	9.69	10.45	11.20	11.94	12.67	13.40	14.12	14.83	15.53
	8.04	8.80	9.55	10.30	11.04	11.77	12.49	13.21	13.92	14.62	15.31
	7.92	8.67	9.41	10.15	10.88	11.60	12.31	13.02	13.72	14.41	15.09
	7.80	8.54	9.27	10.00	10.72	11.43	12.13	12.83	13.52	14.20	14.88
	4.98	5.46	5.93	6.40	6.87	7.33	7.79	8.25	8.70	9.15	9.60
2 YRS.	14.90	16.24	17.56	18.85	20.12	21.36	22.58	23.78	24.95	26.11	27.24
	14.76	16.09	17.39	18.67	19.93	21.16	22.37	23.55	24.72	25.86	26.98
	14.33	15.62	16.88	18.13	19.35	20.55	21.73	22.88	24.02	25.13	26.22
	13.89	15.13	16.39	17.59	18.77	19.94	21.09	22.21	23.31	24.40	25.46
	13.46	14.68	15.87	17.05	18.20	19.33	20.44	21.54	22.61	23.67	24.70
	13.03	14.21	15.37	16.50	17.62	18.72	19.80	20.86	21.91	22.93	23.94
	12.59	13.74	14.86	15.96	17.05	18.11	19.16	20.19	21.21	22.20	23.18
	12.16	13.27	14.35	15.42	16.47	17.51	18.52	19.52	20.50	21.47	22.42
	8.97	9.81	10.63	11.44	12.24	13.03	13.81	14.57	15.33	16.08	16.82
3 YRS.	19.63	21.32	22.96	24.56	26.12	27.63	29.11	30.55	31.95	33.31	34.64
	19.34	21.00	22.62	24.20	25.74	27.23	28.69	30.11	31.50	32.85	34.16
	18.46	20.06	21.61	23.13	24.60	26.04	27.44	28.81	30.14	31.44	32.71
	17.59	19.11	20.60	22.05	23.47	24.85	26.19	27.51	28.79	30.04	31.26
	16.71	18.17	19.59	20.98	22.33	23.65	24.94	26.20	27.43	28.64	29.81
	15.84	17.23	18.58	19.90	21.20	22.46	23.69	24.90	26.08	27.23	28.36
	14.96	16.28	17.57	18.83	20.06	21.27	22.44	23.60	24.73	25.83	26.91
	12.46	13.58	14.67	15.75	16.81	17.85	18.86	19.86	20.84	21.81	22.75
4 YRS.	23.14	25.05	26.90	28.68	30.41	32.07	33.69	35.25	36.76	38.22	39.64
	22.68	24.55	26.37	28.12	29.82	31.46	33.05	34.59	36.07	37.52	38.91
	21.29	23.06	24.78	26.44	28.05	29.61	31.13	32.59	34.02	35.39	36.73
	19.90	21.57	23.19	24.76	26.29	27.77	29.21	30.60	31.96	33.27	34.55
	18.51	20.08	21.60	23.08	24.52	25.92	27.29	28.61	29.90	31.15	32.37
	17.12	18.58	20.01	21.40	22.76	24.08	25.36	26.62	27.84	29.03	30.18
	15.49	16.83	18.15	19.44	20.69	21.92	23.11	24.28	25.42	26.54	27.63
5 YRS.	25.76	27.80	29.77	31.66	33.47	35.22	36.90	38.52	40.07	41.57	43.01
	25.11	27.11	29.04	30.89	32.67	34.38	36.03	37.62	39.15	40.62	42.04
	23.16	25.04	26.84	28.58	30.25	31.87	33.43	34.94	36.39	37.79	39.15
	21.22	22.96	24.64	26.27	27.84	29.36	30.83	32.25	33.63	34.96	36.26
	19.27	20.88	22.44	23.96	25.43	26.85	28.23	29.57	30.87	32.13	33.36
	18.11	19.64	21.13	22.58	23.98	25.35	26.68	27.97	29.22	30.44	31.63
6 YRS.	27.70	29.83	31.86	33.81	35.67	37.45	39.15	40.79	42.35	43.85	45.28
	26.86	28.94	30.93	32.83	34.65	36.40	38.07	39.67	41.21	42.68	44.10
	24.35	26.27	28.12	29.89	31.60	33.24	34.81	36.33	37.79	39.19	40.54
	21.84	23.61	25.31	26.96	28.54	30.08	31.55	32.98	34.38	35.70	36.99
	20.38	22.06	23.68	25.25	26.77	28.24	29.66	31.04	32.37	33.67	34.93
7 YRS.	29.14	31.32	33.39	35.38	37.24	39.03	40.73	42.36	43.92	45.40	46.82
	28.12	30.24	32.26	34.18	36.02	37.77	39.44	41.04	42.57	44.03	45.43
	25.05	26.99	28.86	30.64	32.35	34.00	35.57	37.09	38.54	39.94	41.28
	22.34	24.13	25.86	27.52	29.12	30.67	32.16	33.60	34.99	36.33	37.62
8 YRS.	30.22	32.42	34.50	36.48	38.36	40.14	41.84	43.46	44.99	46.46	47.85
	29.01	31.15	33.18	35.11	36.95	38.70	40.37	41.95	43.47	44.91	46.29
	24.02	25.90	27.71	29.44	31.11	32.71	34.25	35.73	37.15	38.52	39.84
9 YRS.	31.02	33.23	35.31	37.29	39.16	40.94	42.62	44.22	45.73	47.18	48.55
	29.64	31.78	33.82	35.75	37.58	39.32	40.97	42.55	44.05	45.48	46.84
	25.46	27.41	29.28	31.07	32.78	34.42	35.99	37.49	38.94	40.33	41.66
10 YRS.	31.61	33.82	35.91	37.87	39.74	41.50	43.16	44.74	46.24	47.67	49.02
	30.07	32.22	34.25	36.17	37.99	39.73	41.37	42.93	44.42	45.83	47.18
	26.69	28.70	30.61	32.44	34.18	35.84	37.44	38.96	40.42	41.82	43.16
UNTIL PAID	30.74	32.88	34.89	36.79	38.59	40.30	41.92	43.45	44.91	46.30	47.63
	25.50	27.46	29.33	31.11	32.83	34.47	36.04	37.55	38.99	40.38	41.72
	21.98	23.75	25.46	27.11	28.70	30.23	31.71	33.14	34.52	35.85	37.14
	19.38	20.99	22.55	24.07	25.54	26.97	28.35	29.69	30.99	32.26	33.48
	17.35	18.83	20.28	21.68	23.04	24.37	25.66	26.92	28.14	29.34	30.50
	15.73	17.10	18.43	19.73	21.00	22.24	23.45	24.63	25.79	26.91	28.01
	13.29	14.47	15.63	16.77	17.88	18.97	20.04	21.09	22.12	23.13	24.11
	11.52	12.56	13.59	14.60	15.59	16.56	17.52	18.46	19.39	20.30	21.19

EXAMPLES *ON PAGES A-382 TO A-397*

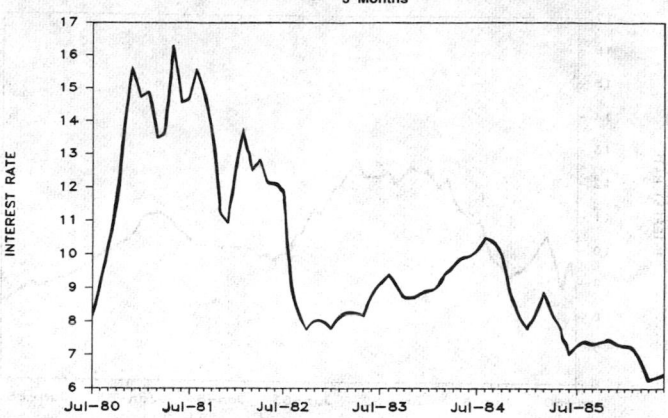

U.S. Treasury Bills Auction Average
3 Months

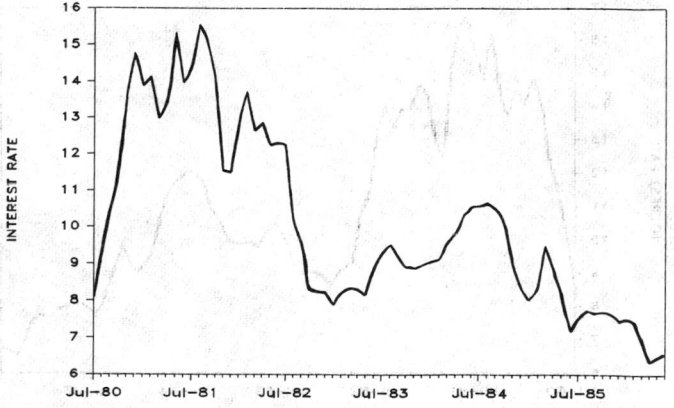

U.S. Treasury Bills Auction Average
6 Months

Eleventh District Monthly Weighted
Cost of Funds

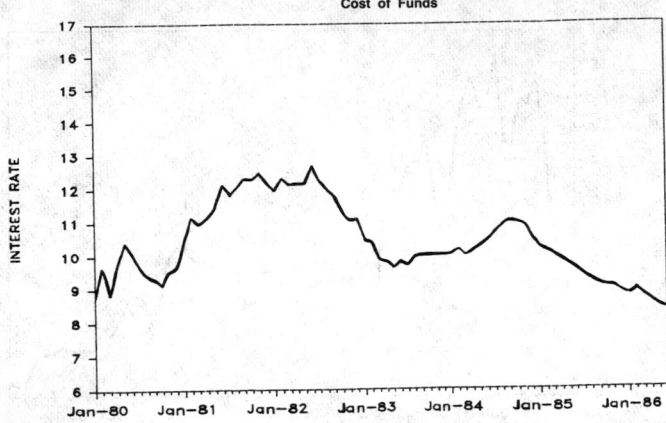

U.S. Treasury Notes and Bonds
1 Year Constant Maturity

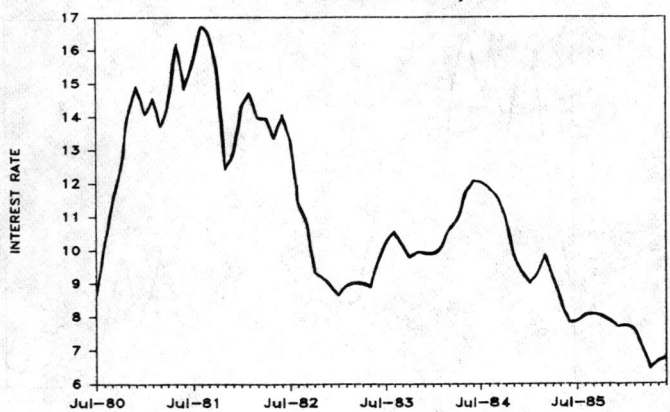

A-301.2

U.S. Treasury Notes and Bonds
3 Year Constant Maturity

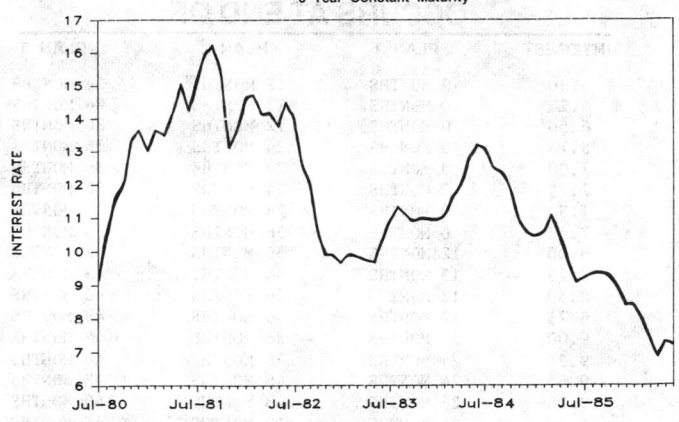

U.S. Treasury Notes and Bonds
5 Year Constant Maturity

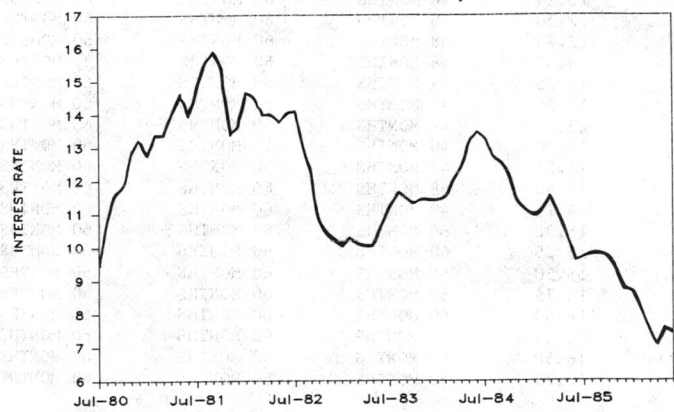

A-301.3

GPM HIGHEST OUTSTANDING BALANCE OCCURS AT END OF:

INTEREST	PLAN 1	PLAN 2	PLAN 3
6.00	0 MONTHS	12 MONTHS	24 MONTHS
6.25	0 MONTHS	12 MONTHS	24 MONTHS
6.50	0 MONTHS	12 MONTHS	36 MONTHS
6.75	0 MONTHS	24 MONTHS	36 MONTHS
7.00	0 MONTHS	24 MONTHS	36 MONTHS
7.25	0 MONTHS	24 MONTHS	36 MONTHS
7.50	0 MONTHS	24 MONTHS	36 MONTHS
7.75	0 MONTHS	36 MONTHS	36 MONTHS
8.00	12 MONTHS	36 MONTHS	48 MONTHS
8.25	12 MONTHS	36 MONTHS	48 MONTHS
8.50	12 MONTHS	36 MONTHS	48 MONTHS
8.75	12 MONTHS	36 MONTHS	48 MONTHS
9.00	24 MONTHS	36 MONTHS	48 MONTHS
9.25	24 MONTHS	36 MONTHS	48 MONTHS
9.50	24 MONTHS	48 MONTHS	48 MONTHS
9.75	24 MONTHS	48 MONTHS	48 MONTHS
10.00	24 MONTHS	48 MONTHS	48 MONTHS
10.25	36 MONTHS	48 MONTHS	48 MONTHS
10.50	36 MONTHS	48 MONTHS	48 MONTHS
10.75	36 MONTHS	48 MONTHS	60 MONTHS
11.00	36 MONTHS	48 MONTHS	60 MONTHS
11.25	36 MONTHS	48 MONTHS	60 MONTHS
11.50	36 MONTHS	48 MONTHS	60 MONTHS
11.75	36 MONTHS	48 MONTHS	60 MONTHS
12.00	48 MONTHS	48 MONTHS	60 MONTHS
12.25	48 MONTHS	60 MONTHS	60 MONTHS
12.50	48 MONTHS	60 MONTHS	60 MONTHS
12.75	48 MONTHS	60 MONTHS	60 MONTHS
13.00	48 MONTHS	60 MONTHS	60 MONTHS
13.25	48 MONTHS	60 MONTHS	60 MONTHS
13.50	48 MONTHS	60 MONTHS	60 MONTHS
13.75	48 MONTHS	60 MONTHS	60 MONTHS
14.00	48 MONTHS	60 MONTHS	60 MONTHS
14.25	48 MONTHS	60 MONTHS	60 MONTHS
14.50	48 MONTHS	60 MONTHS	60 MONTHS
14.75	48 MONTHS	60 MONTHS	60 MONTHS
15.00	60 MONTHS	60 MONTHS	60 MONTHS
15.25	60 MONTHS	60 MONTHS	60 MONTHS
15.50	60 MONTHS	60 MONTHS	60 MONTHS
15.75	60 MONTHS	60 MONTHS	60 MONTHS
16.00	60 MONTHS	60 MONTHS	60 MONTHS
16.25	60 MONTHS	60 MONTHS	60 MONTHS
16.50	60 MONTHS	60 MONTHS	60 MONTHS
16.75	60 MONTHS	60 MONTHS	60 MONTHS

HIGHEST OUTSTANDING BALANCE
FACTORS FOR $1000 GPM

INTEREST	PLAN 1	PLAN 2	PLAN 3
6.00	1.0000000	1.0011164	1.0098941
6.25	1.0000000	1.0019924	1.0118886
6.50	1.0000000	1.0028495	1.0145304
6.75	1.0000000	1.0043290	1.0173401
7.00	1.0000000	1.0059388	1.0200991
7.25	1.0000000	1.0075117	1.0228056
7.50	1.0000000	1.0090487	1.0254642
7.75	1.0000000	1.0107019	1.0280728
8.00	1.0000195	1.0128612	1.0309550
8.25	1.0005895	1.0149700	1.0341945
8.50	1.0011422	1.0170321	1.0373748
8.75	1.0016774	1.0190464	1.0404961
9.00	1.0023085	1.0210154	1.0435617
9.25	1.0033130	1.0229397	1.0465678
9.50	1.0042870	1.0251491	1.0495186
9.75	1.0052329	1.0275358	1.0524197
10.00	1.0061505	1.0298668	1.0552637
10.25	1.0071479	1.0321469	1.0580559
10.50	1.0084361	1.0343732	1.0607998
10.75	1.0096866	1.0365482	1.0635966
11.00	1.0108994	1.0386770	1.0667347
11.25	1.0120765	1.0407556	1.0698110
11.50	1.0132190	1.0427859	1.0728295
11.75	1.0143280	1.0447740	1.0757962
12.00	1.0154746	1.0467166	1.0787075
12.25	1.0168544	1.0486287	1.0815692
12.50	1.0181935	1.0508556	1.0843740
12.75	1.0194922	1.0530313	1.0871336
13.00	1.0207547	1.0551590	1.0898424
13.25	1.0219801	1.0572369	1.0925044
13.50	1.0231699	1.0592689	1.0951202
13.75	1.0243257	1.0612612	1.0976904
14.00	1.0254476	1.0632080	1.1002174
14.25	1.0265382	1.0651109	1.1026993
14.50	1.0275961	1.0669754	1.1051467
14.75	1.0286283	1.0688029	1.1075476
15.00	1.0296759	1.0705897	1.1099107
15.25	1.0308638	1.0723406	1.1122353
15.50	1.0320183	1.0740560	1.1145245
15.75	1.0331387	1.0757364	1.1167789
16.00	1.0342318	1.0773807	1.1189949
16.25	1.0352944	1.0789991	1.1211798
16.50	1.0363243	1.0805804	1.1233313
16.75	1.0373310	1.0821356	1.1254505

FHA GPM PLAN I

RATE	YEAR 1	YEAR 2	YEAR 3	YEAR 4	YEAR 5	REMAIN.
6.000	5.4229	5.5585	5.6974	5.8399	5.9859	6.1355
6.250	5.5720	5.7113	5.8541	6.0005	6.1505	6.3042
6.500	5.7230	5.8661	6.0127	6.1630	6.3171	6.4751
6.750	5.8758	6.0227	6.1732	6.3276	6.4858	6.6479
7.000	6.0303	6.1811	6.3356	6.4940	6.6563	6.8227
7.250	6.1865	6.3412	6.4997	6.6622	6.8288	6.9995
7.500	6.3444	6.5030	6.6656	6.8323	7.0031	7.1781
7.750	6.5039	6.6665	6.8332	7.0040	7.1791	7.3586
8.000	6.6651	6.8317	7.0025	7.1775	7.3570	7.5409
8.250	6.8277	6.9984	7.1733	7.3527	7.5365	7.7249
8.500	6.9918	7.1666	7.3458	7.5294	7.7177	7.9106
8.750	7.1574	7.3364	7.5198	7.7078	7.9005	8.0980
9.000	7.3244	7.5075	7.6952	7.8876	8.0848	8.2869
9.250	7.4928	7.6801	7.8721	8.0689	8.2706	8.4774
9.500	7.6625	7.8541	8.0504	8.2517	8.4580	8.6694
9.750	7.8335	8.0293	8.2300	8.4358	8.6467	8.8629
10.000	8.0057	8.2058	8.4110	8.6213	8.8368	9.0577
10.250	8.1791	8.3836	8.5932	8.8080	9.0282	9.2539
10.500	8.3537	8.5626	8.7767	8.9961	9.2210	9.4515
10.750	8.5295	8.7427	8.9613	9.1853	9.4150	9.6503
11.000	8.7063	8.9240	9.1471	9.3757	9.6101	9.8504
11.250	8.8842	9.1063	9.3340	9.5673	9.8065	10.0516
11.500	9.0631	9.2897	9.5219	9.7600	10.0040	10.2541
11.750	9.2430	9.4740	9.7109	9.9537	10.2025	10.4576
12.000	9.4238	9.6594	9.9009	10.1484	10.4021	10.6622
12.250	9.6056	9.8457	10.0918	10.3441	10.6027	10.8678
12.500	9.7882	10.0329	10.2837	10.5408	10.8043	11.0744
12.750	9.9717	10.2210	10.4765	10.7384	11.0069	11.2820
13.000	10.1560	10.4099	10.6701	10.9369	11.2103	11.4906
13.250	10.3411	10.5996	10.8646	11.1362	11.4146	11.7000
13.500	10.5269	10.7901	11.0599	11.3364	11.6198	11.9103
13.750	10.7135	10.9814	11.2559	11.5373	11.8257	12.1214
14.000	10.9008	11.1734	11.4527	11.7390	12.0325	12.3333
14.250	11.0888	11.3660	11.6502	11.9415	12.2400	12.5460
14.500	11.2775	11.5594	11.8484	12.1446	12.4482	12.7594
14.750	11.4667	11.7534	12.0472	12.3484	12.6571	12.9736
15.000	11.6566	11.9480	12.2467	12.5529	12.8667	13.1884
15.250	11.8471	12.1432	12.4468	12.7580	13.0769	13.4039
15.500	12.0381	12.3390	12.6475	12.9637	13.2878	13.6200
15.750	12.2297	12.5354	12.8488	13.1700	13.4992	13.8367
16.000	12.4217	12.7323	13.0506	13.3768	13.7113	14.0541
16.250	12.6143	12.9297	13.2529	13.5842	13.9238	14.2719
16.500	12.8074	13.1276	13.4558	13.7921	14.1370	14.4904
16.750	13.0009	13.3259	13.6591	14.0006	14.3506	14.7093

FHA GPM PLAN II

RATE	YEAR 1	YEAR 2	YEAR 3	YEAR 4	YEAR 5	REMAIN.
6.000	4.9095	5.1550	5.4127	5.6833	5.9675	6.2659
6.250	5.0470	5.2993	5.5643	5.8425	6.1346	6.4413
6.500	5.1862	5.4455	5.7178	6.0037	6.3039	6.6191
6.750	5.3273	5.5937	5.8733	6.1670	6.4754	6.7991
7.000	5.4701	5.7436	6.0308	6.3323	6.6489	6.9814
7.250	5.6146	5.8953	6.1901	6.4996	6.8246	7.1658
7.500	5.7607	6.0488	6.3512	6.6688	7.0022	7.3523
7.750	5.9085	6.2040	6.5142	6.8399	7.1819	7.5410
8.000	6.0579	6.3608	6.6789	7.0128	7.3634	7.7316
8.250	6.2089	6.5193	6.8453	7.1875	7.5469	7.9243
8.500	6.3613	6.6794	7.0134	7.3640	7.7322	8.1188
8.750	6.5153	6.8410	7.1831	7.5422	7.9193	8.3153
9.000	6.6706	7.0042	7.3544	7.7221	8.1082	8.5136
9.250	6.8274	7.1688	7.5272	7.9036	8.2988	8.7137
9.500	6.9856	7.3349	7.7016	8.0867	8.4910	8.9156
9.750	7.1451	7.5023	7.8775	8.2713	8.6849	9.1191
10.000	7.3059	7.6712	8.0547	8.4575	8.8804	9.3244
10.250	7.4679	7.8413	8.2334	8.6451	9.0773	9.5312
10.500	7.6312	8.0128	8.4134	8.8341	9.2758	9.7396
10.750	7.7957	8.1855	8.5948	9.0245	9.4757	9.9495
11.000	7.9613	8.3594	8.7774	9.2162	9.6771	10.1609
11.250	8.1281	8.5345	8.9612	9.4093	9.8798	10.3737
11.500	8.2960	8.7108	9.1463	9.6036	10.0838	10.5880
11.750	8.4649	8.8881	9.3325	9.7992	10.2891	10.8036
12.000	8.6348	9.0666	9.5199	9.9959	10.4957	11.0205
12.250	8.8058	9.2461	9.7084	10.1938	10.7035	11.2386
12.500	8.9777	9.4266	9.8979	10.3928	10.9124	11.4581
12.750	9.1505	9.6081	10.0885	10.5929	11.1225	11.6787
13.000	9.3243	9.7905	10.2800	10.7940	11.3338	11.9004
13.250	9.4990	9.9739	10.4726	10.9962	11.5460	12.1233
13.500	9.6745	10.1582	10.6661	11.1994	11.7594	12.3473
13.750	9.8508	10.3433	10.8605	11.4035	11.9737	12.5724
14.000	10.0279	10.5293	11.0558	11.6086	12.1890	12.7985
14.250	10.2059	10.7161	11.2520	11.8145	12.4053	13.0255
14.500	10.3845	10.9038	11.4489	12.0214	12.6225	13.2536
14.750	10.5639	11.0921	11.6467	12.2291	12.8405	13.4825
15.000	10.7440	11.2812	11.8453	12.4376	13.0595	13.7124
15.250	10.9248	11.4711	12.0446	12.6469	13.2792	13.9432
15.500	11.1063	11.6616	12.2447	12.8569	13.4998	14.1748
15.750	11.2884	11.8528	12.4455	13.0678	13.7211	14.4072
16.000	11.4712	12.0447	12.6470	13.2793	13.9433	14.6404
16.250	11.6545	12.2372	12.8491	13.4915	14.1661	14.8744
16.500	11.8384	12.4304	13.0519	13.7045	14.3897	15.1092
16.750	12.0229	12.6241	13.2553	13.9180	14.6140	15.3446

FHA GPM PLAN III, VA GPM, 5-YEAR GPARM

RATE	YEAR 1	YEAR 2	YEAR 3	YEAR 4	YEAR 5	REMAIN.
6.000	4.4491	4.7828	5.1415	5.5271	5.9417	6.3873
6.125	4.5122	4.8506	5.2144	5.6055	6.0259	6.4779
6.250	4.5758	4.9189	5.2879	5.6845	6.1108	6.5691
6.375	4.6397	4.9877	5.3618	5.7639	6.1962	6.6610
6.500	4.7042	5.0570	5.4363	5.8440	6.2823	6.7534
6.625	4.7690	5.1267	5.5112	5.9245	6.3689	6.8466
6.750	4.8343	5.1969	5.5867	6.0057	6.4561	6.9403
6.875	4.9000	5.2675	5.6626	6.0873	6.5438	7.0346
7.000	4.9662	5.3386	5.7390	6.1695	6.6322	7.1296
7.125	5.0327	5.4102	5.8160	6.2521	6.7211	7.2251
7.250	5.0997	5.4822	5.8934	6.3354	6.8105	7.3213
7.375	5.1671	5.5546	5.9712	6.4191	6.9005	7.4180
7.500	5.2349	5.6275	6.0496	6.5033	6.9910	7.5154
7.625	5.3031	5.7008	6.1284	6.5880	7.0821	7.6133
7.750	5.3717	5.7746	6.2077	6.6732	7.1737	7.7118
7.875	5.4407	5.8487	6.2874	6.7590	7.2659	7.8108
8.000	5.5101	5.9233	6.3676	6.8452	7.3585	7.9104
8.125	5.5799	5.9983	6.4482	6.9318	7.4517	8.0106
8.250	5.6500	6.0738	6.5293	7.0190	7.5454	8.1113
8.375	5.7206	6.1496	6.6108	7.1066	7.6396	8.2126
8.500	5.7915	6.2258	6.6928	7.1947	7.7343	8.3144
8.625	5.8628	6.3025	6.7752	7.2833	7.8295	8.4168
8.750	5.9344	6.3795	6.8580	7.3723	7.9252	8.5196
8.875	6.0064	6.4569	6.9412	7.4618	8.0214	8.6230
9.000	6.0788	6.5347	7.0248	7.5517	8.1181	8.7269
9.125	6.1516	6.6129	7.1089	7.6421	8.2152	8.8314
9.250	6.2246	6.6915	7.1934	7.7329	8.3128	8.9363
9.375	6.2981	6.7704	7.2782	7.8241	8.4109	9.0417
9.500	6.3719	6.8498	7.3635	7.9158	8.5094	9.1476
9.625	6.4460	6.9294	7.4491	8.0078	8.6084	9.2541
9.750	6.5204	7.0095	7.5352	8.1003	8.7079	9.3609
9.875	6.5952	7.0899	7.6216	8.1932	8.8077	9.4683
10.000	6.6704	7.1706	7.7084	8.2866	8.9081	9.5762
10.125	6.7458	7.2517	7.7956	8.3803	9.0088	9.6845
10.250	6.8216	7.3332	7.8832	8.4744	9.1100	9.7932
10.375	6.8976	7.4150	7.9711	8.5689	9.2116	9.9024
10.500	6.9740	7.4971	8.0594	8.6638	9.3136	10.0121
10.625	7.0507	7.5795	8.1480	8.7591	9.4160	10.1222
10.750	7.1277	7.6623	8.2370	8.8548	9.5189	10.2328
10.875	7.2050	7.7454	8.3263	8.9508	9.6221	10.3438
11.000	7.2826	7.8288	8.4160	9.0472	9.7257	10.4552
11.125	7.3605	7.9126	8.5060	9.1440	9.8298	10.5670
11.250	7.4387	7.9966	8.5964	9.2411	9.9342	10.6793
11.375	7.5172	8.0810	8.6871	9.3386	10.0390	10.7919

FHA GPM PLAN III, VA GPM, 5-YEAR GPARM

RATE	YEAR 1	YEAR 2	YEAR 3	YEAR 4	YEAR 5	REMAIN.
11.500	7.5960	8.1657	8.7781	9.4364	10.1442	10.9050
11.625	7.6750	8.2506	8.8694	9.5346	10.2497	11.0185
11.750	7.7543	8.3359	8.9611	9.6332	10.3556	11.1323
11.875	7.8339	8.4214	9.0530	9.7320	10.4619	11.2466
12.000	7.9138	8.5073	9.1453	9.8312	10.5686	11.3612
12.125	7.9939	8.5934	9.2379	9.9308	10.6756	11.4762
12.250	8.0742	8.6798	9.3308	10.0306	10.7829	11.5916
12.375	8.1549	8.7665	9.4240	10.1308	10.8906	11.7074
12.500	8.2358	8.8535	9.5175	10.2313	10.9986	11.8235
12.625	8.3169	8.9407	9.6112	10.3321	11.1070	11.9400
12.750	8.3983	9.0282	9.7053	10.4332	11.2157	12.0569
12.875	8.4800	9.1160	9.7997	10.5346	11.3247	12.1741
13.000	8.5618	9.2040	9.8943	10.6363	11.4341	12.2916
13.125	8.6440	9.2923	9.9892	10.7384	11.5437	12.4095
13.250	8.7263	9.3808	10.0843	10.8407	11.6537	12.5277
13.375	8.8089	9.4696	10.1798	10.9433	11.7640	12.6463
13.500	8.8917	9.5586	10.2755	11.0461	11.8746	12.7652
13.625	8.9748	9.6479	10.3715	11.1493	11.9855	12.8844
13.750	9.0580	9.7374	10.4677	11.2527	12.0967	13.0040
13.875	9.1415	9.8271	10.5642	11.3565	12.2082	13.1238
14.000	9.2252	9.9171	10.6609	11.4604	12.3200	13.2440
14.125	9.3091	10.0073	10.7579	11.5647	12.4321	13.3645
14.250	9.3933	10.0978	10.8551	11.6692	12.5444	13.4852
14.375	9.4776	10.1884	10.9525	11.7740	12.6570	13.6063
14.500	9.5621	10.2793	11.0502	11.8790	12.7699	13.7277
14.625	9.6469	10.3704	11.1482	11.9843	12.8831	13.8494
14.750	9.7318	10.4617	11.2464	12.0898	12.9966	13.9713
14.875	9.8170	10.5533	11.3448	12.1956	13.1103	14.0936
15.000	9.9023	10.6450	11.4434	12.3016	13.2243	14.2161
15.125	9.9879	10.7370	11.5422	12.4079	13.3385	14.3389
15.250	10.0736	10.8291	11.6413	12.5144	13.4530	14.4619
15.375	10.1595	10.9215	11.7406	12.6211	13.5677	14.5853
15.500	10.2456	11.0140	11.8401	12.7281	13.6827	14.7089
15.625	10.3319	11.1068	11.9398	12.8353	13.7979	14.8328
15.750	10.4183	11.1997	12.0397	12.9427	13.9134	14.9569
15.875	10.5050	11.2929	12.1398	13.0503	14.0291	15.0813
16.000	10.5918	11.3862	12.2402	13.1582	14.1450	15.2059
16.125	10.6788	11.4797	12.3407	13.2662	14.2612	15.3308
16.250	10.7660	11.5734	12.4414	13.3745	14.3776	15.4559
16.375	10.8533	11.6673	12.5423	13.4830	14.4942	15.5813
16.500	10.9408	11.7613	12.6435	13.5917	14.6111	15.7069
16.625	11.0285	11.8556	12.7448	13.7006	14.7282	15.8328
16.750	11.1163	11.9500	12.8463	13.8097	14.8454	15.9589
16.875	11.2043	12.0446	12.9479	13.9190	14.9630	16.0852

1 TO 3 YEAR GPARM

RATE	YEAR 1	YEAR 2	YEAR 3	REMAIN.
6.000	4.9587	5.3306	5.7304	6.1602
6.125	5.0270	5.4041	5.8094	6.2451
6.250	5.0958	5.4780	5.8888	6.3305
6.375	5.1650	5.5523	5.9688	6.4164
6.500	5.2346	5.6272	6.0492	6.5029
6.625	5.3046	5.7024	6.1301	6.5899
6.750	5.3750	5.7782	6.2115	6.6774
6.875	5.4459	5.8543	6.2934	6.7654
7.000	5.5172	5.9310	6.3758	6.8540
7.125	5.5889	6.0080	6.4586	6.9430
7.250	5.6609	6.0855	6.5419	7.0326
7.375	5.7334	6.1634	6.6257	7.1226
7.500	5.8063	6.2417	6.7099	7.2131
7.625	5.8795	6.3205	6.7945	7.3041
7.750	5.9531	6.3996	6.8796	7.3956
7.875	6.0271	6.4792	6.9651	7.4875
8.000	6.1015	6.5591	7.0511	7.5799
8.125	6.1762	6.6395	7.1374	7.6727
8.250	6.2514	6.7202	7.2242	7.7660
8.375	6.3268	6.8013	7.3114	7.8598
8.500	6.4026	6.8828	7.3990	7.9540
8.625	6.4788	6.9647	7.4870	8.0486
8.750	6.5553	7.0469	7.5754	8.1436
8.875	6.6321	7.1295	7.6642	8.2391
9.000	6.7093	7.2125	7.7534	8.3349
9.125	6.7868	7.2958	7.8430	8.4312
9.250	6.8646	7.3795	7.9329	8.5279
9.375	6.9428	7.4635	8.0232	8.6250
9.500	7.0212	7.5478	8.1139	8.7225
9.625	7.1000	7.6325	8.2049	8.8203
9.750	7.1791	7.7175	8.2963	8.9185
9.875	7.2585	7.8028	8.3881	9.0172
10.000	7.3381	7.8885	8.4801	9.1161
10.125	7.4181	7.9745	8.5725	9.2155
10.250	7.4984	8.0607	8.6653	9.3152
10.375	7.5789	8.1473	8.7584	9.4153
10.500	7.6597	8.2342	8.8518	9.5157
10.625	7.7408	8.3214	8.9455	9.6164
10.750	7.8222	8.4089	9.0395	9.7175
10.875	7.9038	8.4966	9.1339	9.8189
11.000	7.9857	8.5847	9.2285	9.9207
11.125	8.0679	8.6730	9.3235	10.0227
11.250	8.1503	8.7616	9.4187	10.1251
11.375	8.2330	8.8505	9.5142	10.2278
11.500	8.3159	8.9396	9.6101	10.3308
11.625	8.3991	9.0290	9.7062	10.4341
11.750	8.4824	9.1186	9.8025	10.5377
11.875	8.5661	9.2085	9.8992	10.6416

1 TO 3 YEAR GPARM

RATE	YEAR 1	YEAR 2	YEAR 3	REMAIN.
12.000	8.6499	9.2987	9.9961	10.7458
12.125	8.7340	9.3891	10.0933	10.8503
12.250	8.8184	9.4797	10.1907	10.9550
12.375	8.9029	9.5706	10.2884	11.0600
12.500	8.9876	9.6617	10.3863	11.1653
12.625	9.0726	9.7531	10.4845	11.2709
12.750	9.1578	9.8446	10.5830	11.3767
12.875	9.2432	9.9364	10.6817	11.4828
13.000	9.3288	10.0284	10.7806	11.5891
13.125	9.4146	10.1207	10.8797	11.6957
13.250	9.5005	10.2131	10.9791	11.8025
13.375	9.5867	10.3057	11.0787	11.9096
13.500	9.6731	10.3986	11.1785	12.0169
13.625	9.7597	10.4916	11.2785	12.1244
13.750	9.8464	10.5849	11.3788	12.2322
13.875	9.9333	10.6783	11.4792	12.3401
14.000	10.0204	10.7720	11.5799	12.4484
14.125	10.1077	10.8658	11.6807	12.5568
14.250	10.1952	10.9598	11.7818	12.6654
14.375	10.2828	11.0540	11.8830	12.7743
14.500	10.3706	11.1484	11.9845	12.8833
14.625	10.4585	11.2429	12.0861	12.9926
14.750	10.5466	11.3376	12.1880	13.1021
14.875	10.6349	11.4325	12.2900	13.2117
15.000	10.7233	11.5276	12.3922	13.3216
15.125	10.8119	11.6228	12.4945	13.4316
15.250	10.9007	11.7182	12.5971	13.5419
15.375	10.9896	11.8138	12.6998	13.6523
15.500	11.0786	11.9095	12.8027	13.7629
15.625	11.1678	12.0053	12.9057	13.8737
15.750	11.2571	12.1014	13.0090	13.9846
15.875	11.3465	12.1975	13.1123	14.0958
16.000	11.4361	12.2938	13.2159	14.2071
16.125	11.5258	12.3903	13.3196	14.3185
16.250	11.6157	12.4869	13.4234	14.4302
16.375	11.7057	12.5836	13.5274	14.5420
16.500	11.7958	12.6805	13.6315	14.6539
16.625	11.8861	12.7775	13.7358	14.7660
16.750	11.9764	12.8747	13.8403	14.8783
16.875	12.0669	12.9720	13.9449	14.9907
17.000	12.1575	13.0694	14.0496	15.1033
17.125	12.2483	13.1669	14.1544	15.2160
17.250	12.3391	13.2646	14.2594	15.3289
17.375	12.4301	13.3624	14.3645	15.4419
17.500	12.5212	13.4603	14.4698	15.5550
17.625	12.6124	13.5583	14.5752	15.6683
17.750	12.7037	13.6564	14.6807	15.7817
17.875	12.7951	13.7547	14.7863	15.8953

2% ANNUAL INCREASE GEM

	YEAR 1	YEAR 2	YEAR 3	YEAR 4	YEAR 5	YEAR 6
6.00	5.995506	6.115416	6.237724	6.362478	6.489728	6.619523
6.25	6.157173	6.280316	6.405922	6.534040	6.664721	6.798015
6.50	6.320681	6.447095	6.576037	6.707558	6.841709	6.978543
6.75	6.485981	6.615701	6.748015	6.882975	7.020635	7.161048
7.00	6.653025	6.786086	6.921808	7.060244	7.201449	7.345478
7.25	6.821763	6.958198	7.097362	7.239309	7.384095	7.531777
7.50	6.992146	7.131989	7.274629	7.420122	7.568524	7.719894
7.75	7.164123	7.307405	7.453553	7.602624	7.754676	7.909770
8.00	7.337646	7.484399	7.634087	7.786769	7.942504	8.101354
8.25	7.512667	7.662920	7.816178	7.972502	8.131952	8.294591
8.50	7.689135	7.842918	7.999776	8.159772	8.322967	8.489426
8.75	7.867005	8.024345	8.184832	8.348529	8.515500	8.685810
9.00	8.046227	8.207152	8.371295	8.538721	8.709495	8.883685
9.25	8.226755	8.391290	8.559116	8.730298	8.904904	9.083002
9.50	8.408543	8.576714	8.748248	8.923213	9.101677	9.283711
9.75	8.591545	8.763376	8.938644	9.117417	9.299765	9.485760
10.00	8.775716	8.951230	9.130255	9.312860	9.499117	9.689099
10.25	8.961013	9.140233	9.323038	9.509499	9.699689	9.893683
10.50	9.147393	9.330341	9.516948	9.707287	9.901433	10.099462
10.75	9.334814	9.521510	9.711940	9.906179	10.104303	10.306389
11.00	9.523234	9.713699	9.907973	10.106132	10.308255	10.514420
11.25	9.712614	9.906866	10.105003	10.307103	10.513245	10.723510
11.50	9.902915	10.100973	10.302992	10.509052	10.719233	10.933618
11.75	10.094098	10.295980	10.501900	10.711938	10.926177	11.144701
12.00	10.286126	10.491849	10.701686	10.915720	11.134034	11.356715
12.25	10.478965	10.688544	10.902315	11.120361	11.342768	11.569623
12.50	10.672578	10.886030	11.103751	11.325826	11.552343	11.783390
12.75	10.866933	11.084272	11.305957	11.532076	11.762718	11.997972
13.00	11.061996	11.283236	11.508901	11.739079	11.973861	12.213338
13.25	11.257736	11.482891	11.712549	11.946800	12.185736	12.429451
13.50	11.454122	11.683204	11.916868	12.155205	12.398309	12.646275
13.75	11.651126	11.884149	12.121832	12.364269	12.611554	12.863785
14.00	11.848718	12.085692	12.327406	12.573954	12.825433	13.081942
14.25	12.046871	12.287808	12.533564	12.784235	13.039920	13.300718
14.50	12.245560	12.490471	12.740280	12.995086	13.254988	13.520088
14.75	12.444758	12.693653	12.947526	13.206477	13.470607	13.740019
15.00	12.644441	12.897330	13.155277	13.418383	13.686751	13.960486
15.25	12.844586	13.101478	13.363508	13.630778	13.903394	14.181462
15.50	13.045170	13.306073	13.572194	13.843638	14.120511	14.402921
15.75	13.246172	13.511095	13.781317	14.056943	14.338082	14.624844
16.00	13.447570	13.716521	13.990851	14.270668	14.556081	14.847203
16.25	13.649347	13.922334	14.200781	14.484797	14.774493	15.069983
16.50	13.851481	14.128511	14.411081	14.699303	14.993289	15.293155
16.75	14.053956	14.335035	14.621736	14.914171	15.212454	15.516703

2% ANNUAL INCREASE GEM

	YEAR 7	YEAR 8	YEAR 9	YEAR 10	REMAIN.	TERM
6.00	6.751913	6.886951	7.024690	7.165184	7.308488	266
6.25	6.933975	7.072655	7.214108	7.358390	7.505558	264
6.50	7.118114	7.260476	7.405686	7.553800	7.704876	262
6.75	7.304269	7.450354	7.599361	7.751348	7.906375	259
7.00	7.492388	7.642236	7.795081	7.950983	8.110003	257
7.25	7.682413	7.836061	7.992782	8.152638	8.315691	255
7.50	7.874292	8.031778	8.192414	8.356262	8.523387	253
7.75	8.067965	8.229324	8.393910	8.561788	8.733024	251
8.00	8.263381	8.428649	8.597222	8.769166	8.944549	249
8.25	8.460483	8.629693	8.802287	8.978333	9.157900	246
8.50	8.659215	8.832399	9.009047	9.189228	9.373013	244
8.75	8.859526	9.036717	9.217451	9.401800	9.589836	242
9.00	9.061359	9.242586	9.427438	9.615987	9.808307	240
9.25	9.264662	9.449955	9.638954	9.831733	10.028368	237
9.50	9.469385	9.658773	9.851948	10.048987	10.249967	235
9.75	9.675475	9.868985	10.066365	10.267692	10.473046	233
10.00	9.882881	10.080539	10.282150	10.487793	10.697549	231
10.25	10.091557	10.293388	10.499256	10.709241	10.923426	229
10.50	10.301451	10.507480	10.717630	10.931983	11.150623	227
10.75	10.512517	10.722767	10.937222	11.155966	11.379085	224
11.00	10.724708	10.939202	11.157986	11.381146	11.608769	222
11.25	10.937980	11.156740	11.379875	11.607473	11.839622	220
11.50	11.152290	11.375336	11.602843	11.834900	12.071598	218
11.75	11.367595	11.594947	11.826846	12.063383	12.304651	216
12.00	11.583849	11.815526	12.051837	12.292874	12.538731	214
12.25	11.801015	12.037035	12.277776	12.523332	12.773799	212
12.50	12.019058	12.259439	12.504628	12.754721	13.009815	210
12.75	12.237931	12.482690	12.732344	12.986991	13.246731	208
13.00	12.457605	12.706757	12.960892	13.220110	13.484512	206
13.25	12.678040	12.931601	13.190233	13.454038	13.723119	204
13.50	12.899201	13.157185	13.420329	13.688736	13.962511	202
13.75	13.121061	13.383482	13.651152	13.924175	14.202659	200
14.00	13.343581	13.610453	13.882662	14.160315	14.443521	198
14.25	13.566732	13.838067	14.114828	14.397125	14.685068	196
14.50	13.790490	14.066300	14.347626	14.634579	14.927271	194
14.75	14.014819	14.295115	14.581017	14.872637	15.170090	193
15.00	14.239696	14.524490	14.814980	15.111280	15.413506	191
15.25	14.465091	14.754393	15.049481	15.350471	15.657480	189
15.50	14.690979	14.984799	15.284495	15.590185	15.901989	187
15.75	14.917341	15.215688	15.520002	15.830402	16.147010	186
16.00	15.144147	15.447030	15.755971	16.071090	16.392512	184
16.25	15.371383	15.678811	15.992387	16.312235	16.633480	182
16.50	15.599018	15.910998	16.229218	16.553802	16.884878	181
16.75	15.827037	16.143578	16.466450	16.795779	17.131695	179

3% ANNUAL INCREASE GEM

	YEAR 1	YEAR 2	YEAR 3	YEAR 4	YEAR 5	YEAR 6
6.00	5.995506	6.175371	6.360632	6.551451	6.747995	6.950435
6.25	6.157173	6.341888	6.532145	6.728109	6.929952	7.137851
6.50	6.320681	6.510301	6.705610	6.906778	7.113981	7.327400
6.75	6.485981	6.680560	6.880977	7.087406	7.300028	7.519029
7.00	6.653025	6.852616	7.058194	7.269940	7.488038	7.712679
7.25	6.821763	7.026416	7.237208	7.454324	7.677954	7.908293
7.50	6.992146	7.201910	7.417967	7.640506	7.869721	8.105813
7.75	7.164123	7.379047	7.600418	7.828431	8.063284	8.305183
8.00	7.337646	7.557775	7.784508	8.018043	8.258584	8.506342
8.25	7.512667	7.738047	7.970188	8.209294	8.455573	8.709240
8.50	7.689135	7.919809	8.157403	8.402125	8.654189	8.913815
8.75	7.867005	8.103015	8.346105	8.596488	8.854383	9.120014
9.00	8.046227	8.287614	8.536242	8.792329	9.056099	9.327782
9.25	8.226755	8.473558	8.727765	8.989598	9.259286	9.537065
9.50	8.408543	8.660799	8.920623	9.188242	9.463889	9.747806
9.75	8.591545	8.849291	9.114770	9.388213	9.669859	9.959955
10.00	8.775716	9.038987	9.310157	9.589462	9.877146	10.173460
10.25	8.961013	9.229843	9.506738	9.791940	10.085698	10.388269
10.50	9.147393	9.421815	9.704469	9.995603	10.295471	10.604335
10.75	9.334814	9.614858	9.903304	10.200403	10.506415	10.821607
11.00	9.523234	9.808931	10.103199	10.406295	10.718484	11.040039
11.25	9.712614	10.003992	10.304112	10.613235	10.931632	11.259581
11.50	9.902915	10.200002	10.506002	10.821182	11.145817	11.480192
11.75	10.094098	10.396921	10.708829	11.030094	11.360997	11.701827
12.00	10.286126	10.594710	10.912551	11.239928	11.577126	11.924440
12.25	10.478965	10.793334	11.117134	11.450648	11.794167	12.147992
12.50	10.672578	10.992755	11.322538	11.662214	12.012080	12.372442
12.75	10.866933	11.192941	11.528729	11.874591	12.230829	12.597754
13.00	11.061996	11.393856	11.735672	12.087742	12.450374	12.823885
13.25	11.257736	11.595468	11.943332	12.301632	12.670681	13.050801
13.50	11.454122	11.797746	12.151678	12.516228	12.891715	13.278456
13.75	11.651126	12.000660	12.360680	12.731500	13.113445	13.506848
14.00	11.848718	12.204180	12.570305	12.947414	13.335836	13.735911
14.25	12.046871	12.408277	12.780525	13.163941	13.558859	13.965625
14.50	12.245560	12.612927	12.991315	13.381054	13.782486	14.195961
14.75	12.444758	12.818101	13.202644	13.598723	14.006685	14.426886
15.00	12.644441	13.023774	13.414487	13.816922	14.231430	14.658373
15.25	12.844586	13.229924	13.626822	14.035627	14.456696	14.890397
15.50	13.045170	13.436525	13.839621	14.254810	14.682454	15.122928
15.75	13.246172	13.643557	14.052864	14.474450	14.908684	15.355945
16.00	13.447570	13.850997	14.266527	14.694523	15.135359	15.589420
16.25	13.649347	14.058827	14.480592	14.915010	15.362460	15.823334
16.50	13.851481	14.267025	14.695036	15.135887	15.589964	16.057663
16.75	14.053956	14.475575	14.909842	15.357137	15.817851	16.292387

3% ANNUAL INCREASE GEM

	YEAR 7	YEAR 8	YEAR 9	YEAR 10	REMAIN.	TERM
6.00	7.158948	7.373716	7.594927	7.822775	8.057458	237
6.25	7.351987	7.572547	7.799723	8.033715	8.274726	235
6.50	7.547222	7.773639	8.006848	8.247053	8.494465	232
6.75	7.744600	7.976938	8.216246	8.462733	8.716615	230
7.00	7.944059	8.182381	8.427852	8.680688	8.941109	228
7.25	8.145542	8.389908	8.641605	8.900853	9.167879	226
7.50	8.348987	8.599457	8.857441	9.123164	9.396859	223
7.75	8.554338	8.810968	9.075297	9.347556	9.627983	221
8.00	8.761532	9.024378	9.295109	9.573962	9.861181	219
8.25	8.970517	9.239633	9.516822	9.802327	10.096397	217
8.50	9.181229	9.456666	9.740366	10.032577	10.333554	215
8.75	9.393614	9.675422	9.965685	10.264656	10.572596	212
9.00	9.607615	9.895843	10.192718	10.498500	10.813455	210
9.25	9.823177	10.117872	10.421408	10.734050	11.056072	208
9.50	10.040240	10.341447	10.651690	10.971241	11.300378	206
9.75	10.258754	10.566517	10.883513	11.210018	11.546319	204
10.00	10.478664	10.793024	11.116815	11.450319	11.793829	202
10.25	10.699917	11.020915	11.351542	11.692088	12.042851	200
10.50	10.922465	11.250139	11.587643	11.935272	12.293330	198
10.75	11.146255	11.480643	11.825062	12.179814	12.545208	196
11.00	11.371240	11.712377	12.063748	12.425660	12.798430	194
11.25	11.597368	11.945289	12.303648	12.672757	13.052940	192
11.50	11.824598	12.179336	12.544716	12.921057	13.308689	190
11.75	12.052882	12.414468	12.786902	13.170509	13.565624	188
12.00	12.282173	12.650638	13.030157	13.421062	13.823694	186
12.25	12.512432	12.887805	13.274439	13.672672	14.082852	185
12.50	12.743615	13.125923	13.519701	13.925292	14.343051	183
12.75	12.975687	13.364958	13.765907	14.178884	14.604251	181
13.00	13.208602	13.604860	14.013006	14.433396	14.866398	179
13.25	13.442325	13.845595	14.260963	14.688792	15.129456	177
13.50	13.676820	14.087125	14.509739	14.945031	15.393382	176
13.75	13.912053	14.329415	14.759297	15.202076	15.658138	174
14.00	14.147988	14.572428	15.009601	15.459889	15.923686	173
14.25	14.384594	14.816132	15.260616	15.718434	16.189987	171
14.50	14.621840	15.060495	15.512310	15.977679	16.457009	169
14.75	14.859693	15.305484	15.764649	16.237588	16.724716	168
15.00	15.098124	15.551068	16.017600	16.498128	16.993072	166
15.25	15.337109	15.797222	16.271139	16.759273	17.262051	165
15.50	15.576616	16.043914	16.525231	17.020988	17.531618	163
15.75	15.816623	16.291122	16.779856	17.283252	17.801750	162
16.00	16.057103	16.538816	17.034980	17.546029	18.072410	160
16.25	16.298034	16.786975	17.290584	17.809302	18.343581	159
16.50	16.539393	17.035575	17.546642	18.073041	18.615232	158
16.75	16.781159	17.284594	17.803132	18.337226	18.887343	156

LOAN TO VALUE RATIOS FOR FHA LOANS

APPROVED NEW CONSTRUCTION – APPROVED EXISTING CONSTRUCTION
LESS THAN ONE YEAR OLD – EXISTING CONSTRUCTION OVER ONE YEAR OLD

Appr. Val. + Cl. Costs	Maximum Loans Regular 203-B	Veteran 203-B	Appr. Val. + Cl. Costs	Maximum Loans Regular 203-B	Veteran 203-B
25000	24250	25000	36000	34700	35450
25200	24440	25190	36200	34890	35640
25400	24630	25380	36400	35080	35830
25600	24820	25570	36600	35270	36020
25800	25010	25760	36800	35460	36210
26000	25200	25950	37000	35650	36400
26200	25390	26140	37200	35840	36590
26400	25580	26330	37400	36030	36780
26600	25770	26520	37600	36220	36970
26800	25960	26710	37800	36410	37160
27000	26150	26900	38000	36600	37350
27200	26340	27090	38200	36790	37540
27400	26530	27280	38400	36980	37730
27600	26720	27470	38600	37170	37920
27800	26910	27660	38800	37360	38110
28000	27100	27850	39000	37550	38300
28200	27290	28040	39200	37740	38490
28400	27480	28230	39400	37930	38680
28600	27670	28420	39600	38120	38870
28800	27860	28610	39800	38310	39060
29000	28050	28800	40000	38500	39250
29200	28240	28990	40200	38690	39440
29400	28430	29180	40400	38880	39630
29600	28620	29370	40600	39070	39820
29800	28810	29560	40800	39260	40010
30000	29000	29750	41000	39450	40200
30200	29190	29940	41200	39640	40390
30400	29380	30130	41400	39830	40580
30600	29570	30320	41600	40020	40770
30800	29760	30510	41800	40210	40960
31000	29950	30700	42000	40400	41150
31200	30140	30890	42200	40590	41340
31400	30330	31080	42400	40780	41530
31600	30520	31270	42600	40970	41720
31800	30710	31460	42800	41160	41910
32000	30900	31650	43000	41350	42100
32200	31090	31840	43200	41540	42290
32400	31280	32030	43400	41730	42480
32600	31470	32220	43600	41920	42670
32800	31660	32410	43800	42110	42860
33000	31850	32600	44000	42300	43050
33200	32040	32790	44200	42490	43240
33400	32230	32980	44400	42680	43430
33600	32420	33170	44600	42870	43620
33800	32610	33360	44800	43060	43810
34000	32800	33550	45000	43250	44000
34200	32990	33740	45200	43440	44190
34400	33180	33930	45400	43630	44380
34600	33370	34120	45600	43820	44570
34800	33560	34310	45800	44010	44760
35000	33750	34500	46000	44200	44950
35200	33940	34690	46200	44390	45140
35400	34130	34880	46400	44580	45330
35600	34320	35070	46600	44770	45520
35800	34510	35260	46800	44960	45710

LOAN TO VALUE RATIOS FOR FHA LOANS

APPROVED NEW CONSTRUCTION – APPROVED EXISTING CONSTRUCTION
LESS THAN ONE YEAR OLD – EXISTING CONSTRUCTION OVER ONE YEAR OLD

Appr. Val. + Cl. Costs	Maximum Loans Regular 203-B	Veteran 203-B	Appr. Val. + Cl. Costs	Maximum Loans Regular 203-B	Veteran 203-B
47000	45150	45900	58000	55600	56350
47200	45340	46090	58200	55790	56540
47400	45530	46280	58400	55980	56730
47600	45720	46470	58600	56170	56920
47800	45910	46660	58800	56360	57110
48000	46100	46850	59000	56550	57300
48200	46290	47040	59200	56740	57490
48400	46480	47230	59400	56930	57680
48600	46670	47420	59600	57120	57870
48800	46860	47610	59800	57310	58060
49000	47050	47800	60000	57500	58250
49200	47240	47990	60200	57690	58440
49400	47430	48180	60400	57880	58630
49600	47620	48370	60600	58070	58820
49800	47810	48560	60800	58260	59010
50000	48000	48750	61000	58450	59200
50200	48190	48940	61200	58640	59390
50400	48380	49130	61400	58830	59580
50600	48570	49320	61600	59020	59770
50800	48760	49510	61800	59210	59960
51000	48950	49700	62000	59400	60150
51200	49140	49890	62200	59590	60340
51400	49330	50080	62400	59780	60530
51600	49520	50270	62600	59970	60720
51800	49710	50460	62800	60160	60910
52000	49900	50650	63000	60350	61100
52200	50090	50840	63200	60540	61290
52400	50280	51030	63400	60730	61480
52600	50470	51220	63600	60920	61670
52800	50660	51410	63800	61110	61860
53000	50850	51600	64000	61300	62050
53200	51040	51790	64200	61490	62240
53400	51230	51980	64400	61680	62430
53600	51420	52170	64600	61870	62620
53800	51610	52360	64800	62060	62810
54000	51800	52550	65000	62250	63000
54200	51990	52740	65200	62440	63190
54400	52180	52930	65400	62630	63380
54600	52370	53120	65600	62820	63570
54800	52560	53310	65800	63010	63760
55000	52750	53500	66000	63200	63950
55200	52940	53690	66200	63390	64140
55400	53130	53880	66400	63580	64330
55600	53320	54070	66600	63770	64520
55800	53510	54260	66800	63960	64710
56000	53700	54450	67000	64150	64900
56200	53890	54640	67200	64340	65090
56400	54080	54830	67400	64530	65280
56600	54270	55020	67600	64720	65470
56800	54460	55210	67800	64910	65660
57000	54650	55400	68000	65100	65850
57200	54840	55590	68200	65290	66040
57400	55030	55780	68400	65480	66230
57600	55220	55970	68600	65670	66420
57800	55410	56160	68800	65860	66610

LOAN TO VALUE RATIOS FOR FHA LOANS

APPROVED NEW CONSTRUCTION – APPROVED EXISTING CONSTRUCTION
LESS THAN ONE YEAR OLD – EXISTING CONSTRUCTION OVER ONE YEAR OLD

Appr. Val. + Cl. Costs	Maximum Loans Regular 203-B	Veteran 203-B	Appr. Val. + Cl. Costs	Maximum Loans Regular 203-B	Veteran 203-B
65000	66050	66800	80000	76500	77250
65200	66240	66590	80200	76690	77440
65400	66430	67180	80400	76880	77630
65600	66620	67370	80600	77070	77820
65800	66810	67560	80800	77260	78010
70000	67000	67750	81000	77450	78200
70200	67190	67940	81200	77640	78390
70400	67380	68130	81400	77830	78580
70600	67570	68320	81600	78020	78770
70800	67760	68510	81800	78210	78960
71000	67950	68700	82000	78400	79150
71200	68140	68890	82200	78590	79340
71400	68330	69080	82400	78780	79530
71600	68520	69270	82600	78970	79720
71800	68710	69460	82800	79160	79910
72000	68900	69650	83000	79350	80100
72200	69090	69840	83200	79540	80290
72400	69280	70030	83400	79730	80480
72600	69470	70220	83600	79920	80670
72800	69660	70410	83800	80110	80860
73000	69850	70600	84000	80300	81050
73200	70040	70790	84200	80490	81240
73400	70230	70980	84400	80680	81430
73600	70420	71170	84600	80870	81620
73800	70610	71360	84800	81060	81810
74000	70800	71550	85000	81250	82000
74200	70990	71740	85200	81440	82190
74400	71180	71930	85400	81630	82380
74600	71370	72120	85600	81820	82570
74800	71560	72310	85800	82010	82760
75000	71750	72500	86000	82200	82950
75200	71940	72690	86200	82390	83140
75400	72130	72880	86400	82580	83330
75600	72320	73070	86600	82770	83520
75800	72510	73260	86800	82960	83710
76000	72700	73450	87000	83150	83900
76200	72890	73640	87200	83340	84090
76400	73080	73830	87400	83530	84280
76600	73270	74020	87600	83720	84470
76800	73460	74210	87800	83910	84660
77000	73650	74400	88000	84100	84850
77200	73840	74590	88200	84290	85040
77400	74030	74780	88400	84480	85230
77600	74220	74970	88600	84670	85420
77800	74410	75160	88800	84860	85610
78000	74600	75350	89000	85050	85800
78200	74790	75540	89200	85240	85990
78400	74980	75730	89400	85430	86180
78600	75170	75920	89600	85620	86370
78800	75360	76110	89800	85810	86560
79000	75550	76300	90000	86000	86750
79200	75740	76490	90200	86190	86940
79400	75930	76680	90400	86380	87130
79600	76120	76870	90600	86570	87320
79800	76310	77060	90800	86760	87510

LOAN TO VALUE RATIOS FOR FHA LOANS
APPROVED NEW CONSTRUCTION – APPROVED EXISTING CONSTRUCTION
LESS THAN ONE YEAR OLD – EXISTING CONSTRUCTION OVER ONE YEAR OLD

Appr. Val. + Cl. Costs	Maximum Loans Regular 203-B	Veteran 203-B	Appr. Val. + Cl. Costs	Maximum Loans Regular 203-B	Veteran 203-B
91000	86950	87700	102000	97400	98150
91200	87140	87890	102200	97590	98340
91400	87330	88080	102400	97780	98530
91600	87520	88270	102600	97970	98720
91800	87710	88460	102800	98160	98910
92000	87900	88650	103000	98350	99100
92200	88090	88840	103200	98540	99290
92400	88280	89030	103400	98730	99480
92600	88470	89220	103600	98920	99670
92800	88660	89410	103800	99110	99860
93000	88850	89600	104000	99300	100050
93200	89040	89790	104200	99490	100240
93400	89230	89980	104400	99680	100430
93600	89420	90170	104600	99870	100620
93800	89610	90360	104800	100060	100810
94000	89800	90550	105000	100250	101000
94200	89990	90740	105200	100440	101190
94400	90180	90930	105400	100630	101380
94600	90370	91120	105600	100820	101570
94800	90560	91310	105800	101010	101760
95000	90750	91500	106000	101200	101950
95200	90940	91690	106200	101390	102140
95400	91130	91880	106400	101580	102330
95600	91320	92070	106600	101770	102520
95800	91510	92260	106800	101960	102710
96000	91700	92450	107000	102150	102900
96200	91890	92640	107200	102340	103090
96400	92080	92830	107400	102530	103280
96600	92270	93020	107600	102720	103470
96800	92460	93210	107800	102910	103660
97000	92650	93400	108000	103100	103850
97200	92840	93590	108200	103290	104040
97400	93030	93780	108400	103480	104230
97600	93220	93970	108600	103670	104420
97800	93410	94160	108800	103860	104610
98000	93600	94350	109000	104050	104800
98200	93790	94540	109200	104240	104990
98400	93980	94730	109400	104430	105180
98600	94170	94920	109600	104620	105370
98800	94360	95110	109800	104810	105560
99000	94550	95300	110000	105000	105750
99200	94740	95490	110200	105190	105940
99400	94930	95680	110400	105380	106130
99600	95120	95870	110600	105570	106320
99800	95310	96060	110800	105760	106510
100000	95500	96250	111000	105950	106700
100200	95690	96440	111200	106140	106890
100400	95880	96630	111400	106330	107080
100600	96070	96820	111600	106520	107270
100800	96260	97010	111800	106710	107460
101000	96450	97200	112000	106900	107650
101200	96640	97390	112200	107090	107840
101400	96830	97580	112400	107280	108030
101600	97020	97770	112600	107470	108220
101800	97210	97960	112800	107660	108410

LOAN TO VALUE RATIOS FOR FHA LOANS

APPROVED NEW CONSTRUCTION – APPROVED EXISTING CONSTRUCTION
LESS THAN ONE YEAR OLD – EXISTING CONSTRUCTION OVER ONE YEAR OLD

Appr. Val. + Cl. Costs	Maximum Loans Regular 203-B	Veteran 203-B	Appr. Val. + Cl. Costs	Maximum Loans Regular 203-B	Veteran 203-B
113000	107850	108600	124000	118300	119050
113200	108040	108790	124200	118490	119240
113400	108230	108980	124400	118680	119430
113600	108420	109170	124600	118870	119620
113800	108610	109360	124800	119060	119810
114000	108800	109550	125000	119250	120000
114200	108990	109740	125200	119440	120190
114400	109180	109930	125400	119630	120380
114600	109370	110120	125600	119820	120570
114800	109560	110310	125800	120010	120760
115000	109750	110500	126000	120200	120950
115200	109940	110690	126200	120390	121140
115400	110130	110880	126400	120580	121330
115600	110320	111070	126600	120770	121520
115800	110510	111260	126800	120960	121710
116000	110700	111450	127000	121150	121900
116200	110890	111640	127200	121340	122090
116400	111080	111830	127400	121530	122280
116600	111270	112020	127600	121720	122470
116800	111460	112210	127800	121910	122660
117000	111650	112400	128000	122100	122850
117200	111840	112590	128200	122290	123040
117400	112030	112780	128400	122480	123230
117600	112220	112970	128600	122670	123420
117800	112410	113160	128800	122860	123610
118000	112600	113350	129000	123050	123800
118200	112790	113540	129200	123240	123990
118400	112980	113730	129400	123430	124180
118600	113170	113920	129600	123620	124370
118800	113360	114110	129800	123810	124560
119000	113550	114300	130000	124000	124750
119200	113740	114490	130200	124190	124940
119400	113930	114680	130400	124380	125130
119600	114120	114870	130600	124570	125320
119800	114310	115060	130800	124760	125510
120000	114500	115250	131000	124950	125700
120200	114690	115440	131200	125140	125890
120400	114880	115630	131400	125330	126080
120600	115070	115820	131600	125520	126270
120800	115260	116010	131800	125710	126460
121000	115450	116200	132000	125900	126650
121200	115640	116390	132200	126090	126840
121400	115830	116580	132400	126280	127030
121600	116020	116770	132600	126470	127220
121800	116210	116960	132800	126660	127410
122000	116400	117150	133000	126850	127600
122200	116590	117340	133200	127040	127790
122400	116780	117530	133400	127230	127980
122600	116970	117720	133600	127420	128170
122800	117160	117910	133800	127610	128360
123000	117350	118100	134000	127800	128550
123200	117540	118290	134200	127990	128740
123400	117730	118480	134400	128180	128930
123600	117920	118670	134600	128370	129120
123800	118110	118860	134800	128560	129310

LOAN TO VALUE RATIOS FOR FHA LOANS

APPROVED NEW CONSTRUCTION – APPROVED EXISTING CONSTRUCTION
LESS THAN ONE YEAR OLD – EXISTING CONSTRUCTION OVER ONE YEAR OLD

Appr. Val. + Cl. Costs	Maximum Loans Regular 203-B	Maximum Loans Veteran 203-B	Appr. Val. + Cl. Costs	Maximum Loans Regular 203-B	Maximum Loans Veteran 203-B
135000	128750	129500	146000	139200	139950
135200	128940	129690	146200	139390	140140
135400	129130	129880	146400	139580	140330
135600	129320	130070	146600	139770	140520
135800	129510	130260	146800	139960	140710
136000	129700	130450	147000	140150	140900
136200	129890	130640	147200	140340	141090
136400	130080	130830	147400	140530	141280
136600	130270	131020	147600	140720	141470
136800	130460	131210	147800	140910	141660
137000	130650	131400	148000	141100	141850
137200	130840	131590	148200	141290	142040
137400	131030	131780	148400	141480	142230
137600	131220	131970	148600	141670	142420
137800	131410	132160	148800	141860	142610
138000	131600	132350	149000	142050	142800
138200	131790	132540	149200	142240	142990
138400	131980	132730	149400	142430	143180
138600	132170	132920	149600	142620	143370
138800	132360	133110	149800	142810	143560
139000	132550	133300	150000	143000	143750
139200	132740	133490	150200	143190	143940
139400	132930	133680	150400	143380	144130
139600	133120	133870	150600	143570	144320
139800	133310	134060	150800	143760	144510
140000	133500	134250	151000	143950	144700
140200	133690	134440	151200	144140	144890
140400	133880	134630	151400	144330	145080
140600	134070	134820	151600	144520	145270
140800	134260	135010	151800	144710	145460
141000	134450	135200	152000	144900	145650
141200	134640	135390	152200	145090	145840
141400	134830	135580	152400	145280	146030
141600	135020	135770	152600	145470	146220
141800	135210	135960	152800	145660	146410
142000	135400	136150	153000	145850	146600
142200	135590	136340	153200	146040	146790
142400	135780	136530	153400	146230	146980
142600	135970	136720	153600	146420	147170
142800	136160	136910	153800	146610	147360
143000	136350	137100	154000	146800	147550
143200	136540	137290	154200	146990	147740
143400	136730	137480	154400	147180	147930
143600	136920	137670	154600	147370	148120
143800	137110	137860	154800	147560	148310
144000	137300	138050	155000	147750	148500
144200	137490	138240	155200	147940	148690
144400	137680	138430	155400	148130	148880
144600	137870	138620	155600	148320	149070
144800	138060	138810	155800	148510	149260
145000	138250	139000	156000	148700	149450
145200	138440	139190	156200	148890	149640
145400	138630	139380	156400	149080	149830
145600	138820	139570	156600	149270	150020
145800	139010	139760	156800	149460	150210

LOAN TO VALUE RATIOS FOR FHA LOANS

APPROVED NEW CONSTRUCTION – APPROVED EXISTING CONSTRUCTION
LESS THAN ONE YEAR OLD – EXISTING CONSTRUCTION OVER ONE YEAR OLD

Appr. Val. + Cl Costs	Maximum Loans Regular 203-B	Veteran 203-B	Appr. Val. + Cl Costs	Maximum Loans Regular 203-B	Veteran 203-B
157000	149650	150400	168000	160100	160850
157200	149840	150590	168200	160290	161040
157400	150030	150780	168400	160480	161230
157600	150220	150970	168600	160670	161420
157800	150410	151160	168800	160860	161610
158000	150600	151350	169000	161050	161800
158200	150790	151540	169200	161240	161990
158400	150980	151730	169400	161430	162180
158600	151170	151920	169600	161620	162370
158800	151360	152110	169800	161810	162560
159000	151550	152300	170000	162000	162750
159200	151740	152490	170200	162190	162940
159400	151930	152680	170400	162380	163130
159600	152120	152870	170600	162570	163320
159800	152310	153060	170800	162760	163510
160000	152500	153250	171000	162950	163700
160200	152690	153440	171200	163140	163890
160400	152880	153630	171400	163330	164080
160600	153070	153820	171600	163520	164270
160800	153260	154010	171800	163710	164460
161000	153450	154200	172000	163900	164650
161200	153640	154390	172200	164090	164840
161400	153830	154580	172400	164280	165030
161600	154020	154770	172600	164470	165220
161800	154210	154960	172800	164660	165410
162000	154400	155150	173000	164850	165600
162200	154590	155340	173200	165040	165790
162400	154780	155530	173400	165230	165980
162600	154970	155720	173600	165420	166170
162800	155160	155910	173800	165610	166360
163000	155350	156100	174000	165800	166550
163200	155540	156290	174200	165990	166740
163400	155730	156480	174400	166180	166930
163600	155920	156670	174600	166370	167120
163800	156110	156860	174800	166560	167310
164000	156300	157050	175000	166750	167500
164200	156490	157240	175200	166940	167690
164400	156680	157430	175400	167130	167880
164600	156870	157620	175600	167320	168070
164800	157060	157810	175800	167510	168260
165000	157250	158000	176000	167700	168450
165200	157440	158190	176200	167890	168640
165400	157630	158380	176400	168080	168830
165600	157820	158570	176600	168270	169020
165800	158010	158760	176800	168460	169210
166000	158200	158950	177000	168650	169400
166200	158390	159140	177200	168840	169590
166400	158580	159330	177400	169030	169780
166600	158770	159520	177600	169220	169970
166800	158960	159710	177800	169410	170160
167000	159150	159900	178000	169600	170350
167200	159340	160090	178200	169790	170540
167400	159530	160280	178400	169980	170730
167600	159720	160470	178600	170170	170920
167800	159910	160660	178800	170360	171110

LOAN TO VALUE RATIOS FOR FHA LOANS

APPROVED NEW CONSTRUCTION – APPROVED EXISTING CONSTRUCTION
LESS THAN ONE YEAR OLD – EXISTING CONSTRUCTION OVER ONE YEAR OLD

Appr. Val. + Cl. Costs	Maximum Loans Regular 203-B	Veteran 203-B	Appr. Val. + Cl. Costs	Maximum Loans Regular 203-B	Veteran 203-B
179000	170550	171300	190000	181000	181750
179200	170740	171490	190200	181190	181940
179400	170930	171680	190400	181380	182130
179600	171120	171870	190600	181570	182320
179800	171310	172060	190800	181760	182510
180000	171500	172250	191000	181950	182700
180200	171690	172440	191200	182140	182890
180400	171880	172630	191400	182330	183080
180600	172070	172820	191600	182520	183270
180800	172260	173010	191800	182710	183460
181000	172450	173200	192000	182900	183650
181200	172640	173390	192200	183090	183840
181400	172830	173580	192400	183280	184030
181600	173020	173770	192600	183470	184220
181800	173210	173960	192800	183660	184410
182000	173400	174150	193000	183850	184600
182200	173590	174340	193200	184040	184790
182400	173780	174530	193400	184230	184980
182600	173970	174720	193600	184420	185170
182800	174160	174910	193800	184610	185360
183000	174350	175100	194000	184800	185550
183200	174540	175290	194200	184990	185740
183400	174730	175480	194400	185180	185930
183600	174920	175670	194600	185370	186120
183800	175110	175860	194800	185560	186310
184000	175300	176050	195000	185750	186500
184200	175490	176240	195200	185940	186690
184400	175680	176430	195400	186130	186880
184600	175870	176620	195600	186320	187070
184800	176060	176810	195800	186510	187260
185000	176250	177000	196000	186700	187450
185200	176440	177190	196200	186890	187640
185400	176630	177380	196400	187080	187830
185600	176820	177570	196600	187270	188020
185800	177010	177760	196800	187460	188210
186000	177200	177950	197000	187650	188400
186200	177390	178140	197200	187840	188590
186400	177580	178330	197400	188030	188780
186600	177770	178520	197600	188220	188970
186800	177960	178710	197800	188410	189160
187000	178150	178900	198000	188600	189350
187200	178340	179090	198200	188790	189540
187400	178530	179280	198400	188980	189730
187600	178720	179470	198600	189170	189920
187800	178910	179660	198800	189360	190110
188000	179100	179850	199000	189550	190300
188200	179290	180040	199200	189740	190490
188400	179480	180230	199400	189930	190680
188600	179670	180420	199600	190120	190870
188800	179860	180610	199800	190310	191060
189000	180050	180800	200000	190500	191250
189200	180240	180990	200200	190690	191440
189400	180430	181180	200400	190880	191630
189600	180620	181370	200600	191070	191820
189800	180810	181560	200800	191260	192010

PAYMENTS FOR $1000 FHA LOAN
INCLUDING PMI
(not applicable to Sections 203(b), 203(i) and 245)

	.5% REGULAR P&I	.5% PLAN 3 GPM P&I
5.00	5.78209	4.37795
5.25	5.93604	4.49745
5.50	6.09201	4.61886
5.75	6.24997	4.74206
6.00	6.40986	4.86705
6.25	6.57163	4.99394
6.50	6.73524	5.12253
6.75	6.90065	5.25281
7.00	7.06778	5.38489
7.25	7.23661	5.51857
7.50	7.40708	5.65394
7.75	7.57914	5.79091
8.00	7.75274	5.92948
8.25	7.92784	6.06954
8.50	8.10439	6.21120
8.75	8.28233	6.35425
9.00	8.46161	6.49881
9.25	8.64221	6.64476
9.50	8.82406	6.79220
9.75	9.00712	6.94085
10.00	9.19134	7.09099
10.25	9.37670	7.24232
10.50	9.56313	7.39486
10.75	9.75060	7.54869
11.00	9.93906	7.70372
11.25	10.12849	7.85995
11.50	10.31883	8.01737
11.75	10.51005	8.17579
12.00	10.70212	8.33541
12.25	10.89499	8.49593
12.50	11.08864	8.65764
12.75	11.28303	8.82025
13.00	11.47812	8.98386
13.25	11.67389	9.14847
13.50	11.87031	9.31398
13.75	12.06734	9.48038
14.00	12.26495	9.64769
14.25	12.46314	9.81589
14.50	12.66184	9.98478
14.75	12.86106	10.15458
15.00	13.06076	10.32517
15.25	13.26093	10.49657
15.50	13.46153	10.66866
15.75	13.66256	10.84145
16.00	13.86396	11.01504
16.25	14.06576	11.18932
16.50	14.26791	11.36421
16.75	14.47040	11.53979
17.00	14.67321	11.71597
17.25	14.87632	11.89286
17.50	15.07973	12.07024
17.75	15.28342	12.24831

INCOME CONVERSION

HOUR	WEEK	MONTH	YEAR	HOUR	WEEK	MONTH	YEAR
4.00	160.00	693.33	8320.00	17.00	680.00	2946.67	35360.00
4.25	170.00	736.67	8840.00	17.25	690.00	2990.00	35880.00
4.50	180.00	780.00	9360.00	17.50	700.00	3033.33	36400.00
4.75	190.00	823.33	9880.00	17.75	710.00	3076.67	36920.00
5.00	200.00	866.67	10400.00	18.00	720.00	3120.00	37440.00
5.25	210.00	910.00	10920.00	18.25	730.00	3163.33	37960.00
5.50	220.00	953.33	11440.00	18.50	740.00	3206.67	38480.00
5.75	230.00	996.67	11960.00	18.75	750.00	3250.00	39000.00
6.00	240.00	1040.00	12480.00	19.00	760.00	3293.33	39520.00
6.25	250.00	1083.33	13000.00	19.25	770.00	3336.67	40040.00
6.50	260.00	1126.67	13520.00	19.50	780.00	3380.00	40560.00
6.75	270.00	1170.00	14040.00	19.75	790.00	3423.33	41080.00
7.00	280.00	1213.33	14560.00	20.00	800.00	3466.67	41600.00
7.25	290.00	1256.67	15080.00	20.25	810.00	3510.00	42120.00
7.50	300.00	1300.00	15600.00	20.50	820.00	3553.33	42640.00
7.75	310.00	1343.33	16120.00	20.75	830.00	3596.67	43160.00
8.00	320.00	1386.67	16640.00	21.00	840.00	3640.00	43680.00
8.25	330.00	1430.00	17160.00	21.25	850.00	3683.33	44200.00
8.50	340.00	1473.33	17680.00	21.50	860.00	3726.67	44720.00
8.75	350.00	1516.67	18200.00	21.75	870.00	3770.00	45240.00
9.00	360.00	1560.00	18720.00	22.00	880.00	3813.33	45760.00
9.25	370.00	1603.33	19240.00	22.25	890.00	3856.67	46280.00
9.50	380.00	1646.67	19760.00	22.50	900.00	3900.00	46800.00
9.75	390.00	1690.00	20280.00	22.75	910.00	3943.33	47320.00
10.00	400.00	1733.33	20800.00	23.00	920.00	3986.67	47840.00
10.25	410.00	1776.67	21320.00	23.25	930.00	4030.00	48360.00
10.50	420.00	1820.00	21840.00	23.50	940.00	4073.33	48880.00
10.75	430.00	1863.33	22360.00	23.75	950.00	4116.67	49400.00
11.00	440.00	1906.67	22880.00	24.00	960.00	4160.00	49920.00
11.25	450.00	1950.00	23400.00	24.25	970.00	4203.33	50440.00
11.50	460.00	1993.33	23920.00	24.50	980.00	4246.67	50960.00
11.75	470.00	2036.67	24440.00	24.75	990.00	4290.00	51480.00
12.00	480.00	2080.00	24960.00	25.00	1000.00	4333.33	52000.00
12.25	490.00	2123.33	25480.00	25.25	1010.00	4376.67	52520.00
12.50	500.00	2166.67	26000.00	25.50	1020.00	4420.00	53040.00
12.75	510.00	2210.00	26520.00	25.75	1030.00	4463.33	53560.00
13.00	520.00	2253.33	27040.00	26.00	1040.00	4506.67	54080.00
13.25	530.00	2296.67	27560.00	26.25	1050.00	4550.00	54600.00
13.50	540.00	2340.00	28080.00	26.50	1060.00	4593.33	55120.00
13.75	550.00	2383.33	28600.00	26.75	1070.00	4636.67	55640.00
14.00	560.00	2426.67	29120.00	27.00	1080.00	4680.00	56160.00
14.25	570.00	2470.00	29640.00	27.25	1090.00	4723.33	56680.00
14.50	580.00	2513.33	30160.00	27.50	1100.00	4766.67	57200.00
14.75	590.00	2556.67	30680.00	27.75	1110.00	4810.00	57720.00
15.00	600.00	2600.00	31200.00	28.00	1120.00	4853.33	58240.00
15.25	610.00	2643.33	31720.00	28.25	1130.00	4896.67	58760.00
15.50	620.00	2686.67	32240.00	28.50	1140.00	4940.00	59280.00
15.75	630.00	2730.00	32760.00	28.75	1150.00	4983.33	59800.00
16.00	640.00	2773.33	33280.00	29.00	1160.00	5026.67	60320.00
16.25	650.00	2816.67	33800.00	29.25	1170.00	5070.00	60840.00
16.50	660.00	2860.00	34320.00	29.50	1180.00	5113.33	61360.00
16.75	670.00	2903.33	34840.00	29.75	1190.00	5156.67	61880.00

ANNUAL COMPOUND INTEREST AND
ANNUAL PRESENT VALUE TABLES

The publisher is indebted to Professor Stephen E. Roulac of Stanford University, for his assistance in programming these tables and for preparing the directions for use of the Present Value and Compound Interest Tables.

If you are familiar with present value techniques, you will find these tables a convenient reference. The constants for single sums and annuities are both listed for each combination of interest rate and number of years. The constants are the values for one dollar, the value for larger sums is the dollar amount times the constant. The present value tables tell what future payments are worth today. The compound interest tables, sometimes called future value tables, tell what a simple sum or annuity contract entered today would be worth at some future time.

If you are unfamiliar with the concept of present and future values, they are merely a way to quantify what most people know intuitively, that there is a time value associated with money. Aside from the risk involved, the promise of $1.00 ten years from now is just not worth $1.00 today. This is because the $1.00 available now could be put in the bank or invested in a business venture at your required rate of return. Some examples will demonstrate the use and power of these tables.

Please refer to Directions for Use of Compound Interest Tables and Present Value Tables

FUTURE VALUE OF $1 COMPOUNDED ANNUALLY

YEAR	SINGLE SUM	ANNUITY	SINGLE SUM	ANNUITY	SINGLE SUM	ANNUITY	SINGLE SUM	ANNUITY
	4%		4½%		5%		5½%	
1	1.0400	1.040	1.0450	1.045	1.0500	1.050	1.0550	1.055
2	1.0816	2.122	1.0920	2.137	1.1025	2.153	1.1130	2.168
3	1.1249	3.246	1.1412	3.278	1.1576	3.310	1.1742	3.342
4	1.1699	4.416	1.1925	4.471	1.2155	4.526	1.2388	4.581
5	1.2167	5.633	1.2462	5.717	1.2763	5.802	1.3070	5.888
6	1.2653	6.898	1.3023	7.019	1.3401	7.142	1.3788	7.267
7	1.3159	8.214	1.3609	8.380	1.4071	8.549	1.4547	8.722
8	1.3686	9.583	1.4221	9.802	1.4775	10.027	1.5347	10.256
9	1.4233	11.006	1.4861	11.288	1.5513	11.578	1.6191	11.875
10	1.4802	12.486	1.5530	12.841	1.6289	13.207	1.7081	13.583
11	1.5395	14.026	1.6229	14.464	1.7103	14.917	1.8021	15.386
12	1.6010	15.627	1.6959	16.160	1.7959	16.713	1.9012	17.287
13	1.6651	17.292	1.7722	17.932	1.8856	18.599	2.0058	19.293
14	1.7317	19.024	1.8519	19.784	1.9799	20.579	2.1161	21.409
15	1.8009	20.825	1.9353	21.719	2.0789	22.657	2.2325	23.641
16	1.8730	22.698	2.0224	23.742	2.1829	24.840	2.3553	25.996
17	1.9479	24.645	2.1134	25.855	2.2920	27.132	2.4848	28.481
18	2.0258	26.671	2.2085	28.064	2.4066	29.539	2.6215	31.103
19	2.1068	28.778	2.3079	30.371	2.5270	32.066	2.7656	33.868
20	2.1911	30.969	2.4117	32.783	2.6533	34.719	2.9178	36.786
21	2.2788	33.248	2.5202	35.303	2.7860	37.505	3.0782	39.864
22	2.3699	35.618	2.6337	37.937	2.9253	40.430	3.2475	43.112
23	2.4647	38.083	2.7522	40.689	3.0715	43.502	3.4262	46.538
24	2.5633	40.646	2.8760	43.565	3.2251	46.727	3.6146	50.153
25	2.6658	43.312	3.0054	46.571	3.3864	50.113	3.8134	53.966
26	2.7725	46.084	3.1407	49.711	3.5557	53.669	4.0231	57.989
27	2.8834	48.968	3.2820	52.993	3.7335	57.403	4.2444	62.234
28	2.9987	51.966	3.4297	56.423	3.9201	61.323	4.4778	66.711
29	3.1187	55.085	3.5840	60.007	4.1161	65.439	4.7241	71.435
30	3.2434	58.328	3.7453	63.752	4.3219	69.761	4.9840	76.419

YEAR	SINGLE SUM	ANNUITY	SINGLE SUM	ANNUITY	SINGLE SUM	ANNUITY	SINGLE SUM	ANNUITY
	6%		6½%		7%		7½%	
1	1.0600	1.060	1.0650	1.065	1.0700	1.070	1.0750	1.075
2	1.1236	2.184	1.1342	2.199	1.1449	2.215	1.1556	2.231
3	1.1910	3.375	1.2079	3.407	1.2250	3.440	1.2423	3.473
4	1.2625	4.637	1.2865	4.694	1.3108	4.751	1.3355	4.808
5	1.3382	5.975	1.3701	6.064	1.4026	6.153	1.4356	6.244
6	1.4185	7.394	1.4591	7.523	1.5007	7.654	1.5433	7.787
7	1.5036	8.897	1.5540	9.077	1.6058	9.260	1.6590	9.446
8	1.5938	10.491	1.6550	10.732	1.7182	10.978	1.7835	11.230
9	1.6895	12.181	1.7626	12.494	1.8385	12.816	1.9172	13.147
10	1.7900	13.972	1.8771	14.372	1.9672	14.784	2.0610	15.208
11	1.8983	15.870	1.9992	16.371	2.1049	16.888	2.2156	17.424
12	2.0122	17.882	2.1291	18.500	2.2522	19.141	2.3818	19.806
13	2.1329	20.015	2.2675	20.767	2.4098	21.550	2.5604	22.366
14	2.2609	22.276	2.4149	23.182	2.5785	24.129	2.7524	25.118
15	2.3966	24.673	2.5718	25.754	2.7590	26.888	2.9589	28.077
16	2.5404	27.213	2.7390	28.493	2.9522	29.840	3.1808	31.258
17	2.6928	29.906	2.9170	31.410	3.1588	32.999	3.4194	34.677
18	2.8543	32.760	3.1067	34.517	3.3799	36.379	3.6758	38.353
19	3.0256	35.786	3.3086	37.825	3.6165	39.995	3.9515	42.305
20	3.2071	38.993	3.5236	41.349	3.8697	43.865	4.2479	46.553
21	3.3996	42.392	3.7527	45.102	4.1406	48.006	4.5664	51.119
22	3.6035	45.996	3.9966	49.098	4.4304	52.436	4.9089	56.028
23	3.8197	49.816	4.2564	53.355	4.7405	57.177	5.2771	61.305
24	4.0489	53.865	4.5331	57.888	5.0724	62.249	5.6729	66.978
25	4.2919	58.156	4.8277	62.715	5.4274	67.676	6.0983	73.076
26	4.5494	62.706	5.1415	67.857	5.8074	73.484	6.5557	79.632
27	4.8223	67.528	5.4757	73.333	6.2139	79.698	7.0474	86.679
28	5.1117	72.640	5.8316	79.164	6.6488	86.347	7.5759	94.255
29	5.4184	78.058	6.2107	85.375	7.1143	93.461	8.1441	102.399
30	5.7435	83.802	6.6144	91.989	7.6123	101.073	8.7550	111.154

FUTURE VALUE OF $1 COMPOUNDED ANNUALLY

YEAR	SINGLE SUM	ANNUITY	SINGLE SUM	ANNUITY	SINGLE SUM	ANNUITY	SINGLE SUM	ANNUITY
	8%		**8½%**		**9%**		**9½%**	
1	1.0800	1.080	1.0850	1.085	1.0900	1.090	1.0950	1.095
2	1.1664	2.246	1.1772	2.262	1.1881	2.278	1.1990	2.294
3	1.2597	3.506	1.2773	3.540	1.2950	3.573	1.3129	3.607
4	1.3605	4.867	1.3859	4.925	1.4116	4.985	1.4377	5.045
5	1.4693	6.336	1.5037	6.429	1.5386	6.523	1.5742	6.619
6	1.5869	7.923	1.6315	8.060	1.6771	8.200	1.7238	8.343
7	1.7138	9.637	1.7701	9.831	1.8280	10.028	1.8876	10.230
8	1.8509	11.488	1.9206	11.751	1.9926	12.021	2.0669	12.297
9	1.9990	13.487	2.0839	13.835	2.1719	14.193	2.2632	14.560
10	2.1589	15.645	2.2610	16.096	2.3674	16.560	2.4782	17.039
11	2.3316	17.977	2.4532	18.549	2.5804	19.141	2.7137	19.752
12	2.5182	20.495	2.6617	21.211	2.8127	21.953	2.9715	22.724
13	2.7196	23.215	2.8879	24.099	3.0658	25.019	3.2537	25.977
14	2.9372	26.152	3.1334	27.232	3.3417	28.361	3.5629	29.540
15	3.1722	29.324	3.3997	30.632	3.6425	32.003	3.9013	33.442
16	3.4259	32.750	3.6887	34.321	3.9703	35.974	4.2719	37.714
17	3.7000	36.450	4.0023	38.323	4.3276	40.301	4.6778	42.391
18	3.9960	40.446	4.3425	42.665	4.7171	45.018	5.1222	47.513
19	4.3157	44.762	4.7116	47.377	5.1417	50.160	5.6088	53.122
20	4.6610	49.423	5.1120	52.489	5.6044	55.765	6.1416	59.264
21	5.0338	54.457	5.5466	58.036	6.1088	61.873	6.7251	65.989
22	5.4365	59.893	6.0180	64.054	6.6586	68.532	7.3639	73.353
23	5.8715	65.765	6.5296	70.583	7.2579	75.790	8.0635	81.416
24	6.3412	72.106	7.0846	77.668	7.9111	83.701	8.8296	90.246
25	6.8485	78.954	7.6868	85.355	8.6231	92.324	9.6684	99.914
26	7.3964	86.351	8.3401	93.695	9.3992	101.723	10.5869	110.501
27	7.9881	94.339	9.0490	102.744	10.2451	111.968	11.5926	122.094
28	8.6271	102.966	9.8182	112.562	11.1671	123.135	12.6939	134.788
29	9.3173	112.283	10.6528	123.215	12.1722	135.308	13.8998	148.688
30	10.0627	122.346	11.5583	134.773	13.2677	148.575	15.2203	163.908
	10%		**10½%**		**11%**		**11½%**	
1	1.1000	1.100	1.1050	1.105	1.1100	1.110	1.1150	1.115
2	1.2100	2.310	1.2210	2.326	1.2321	2.342	1.2432	2.358
3	1.3310	3.641	1.3492	3.675	1.3676	3.710	1.3862	3.744
4	1.4641	5.105	1.4909	5.166	1.5181	5.228	1.5456	5.290
5	1.6105	6.716	1.6474	6.814	1.6851	6.913	1.7234	7.013
6	1.7716	8.487	1.8204	8.634	1.8704	8.783	1.9215	8.935
7	1.9487	10.436	2.0116	10.646	2.0762	10.859	2.1425	11.077
8	2.1436	12.579	2.2228	12.868	2.3045	13.164	2.3889	13.466
9	2.3579	14.937	2.4562	15.325	2.5580	15.722	2.6636	16.130
10	2.5937	17.531	2.7141	18.039	2.8394	18.561	2.9699	19.100
11	2.8531	20.384	2.9991	21.038	3.1518	21.713	3.3115	22.411
12	3.1384	23.523	3.3140	24.352	3.4985	25.212	3.6923	26.104
13	3.4523	26.975	3.6619	28.014	3.8833	29.095	4.1169	30.221
14	3.7975	30.772	4.0464	32.060	4.3104	33.405	4.5904	34.811
15	4.1772	34.950	4.4713	36.531	4.7846	38.190	5.1183	39.929
16	4.5950	39.545	4.9408	41.472	5.3109	43.501	5.7069	45.636
17	5.0545	44.599	5.4596	46.932	5.8951	49.396	6.3632	51.999
18	5.5599	50.159	6.0328	52.965	6.5436	55.939	7.0949	59.094
19	6.1159	56.275	6.6663	59.631	7.2633	63.203	7.9108	67.005
20	6.7275	63.002	7.3662	66.997	8.0623	71.265	8.8206	75.826
21	7.4002	70.403	8.1397	75.137	8.9492	80.214	9.8350	85.661
22	8.1403	78.543	8.9944	84.131	9.9336	90.148	10.9660	96.627
23	8.9543	87.497	9.9388	94.070	11.0263	101.174	12.2271	108.854
24	9.8497	97.347	10.9823	105.052	12.2392	113.413	13.6332	122.487
25	10.8347	108.182	12.1355	117.188	13.5855	126.999	15.2010	137.688
26	11.9182	120.100	13.4097	130.597	15.0799	142.079	16.9491	154.637
27	13.1100	133.210	14.8177	145.415	16.7386	158.817	18.8982	173.535
28	14.4210	147.631	16.3736	161.789	18.5799	177.397	21.0715	194.607
29	15.8631	163.494	18.0928	179.881	20.6237	198.021	23.4948	218.101
30	17.4494	180.943	19.9926	199.874	22.8923	220.913	26.1967	244.298

FUTURE VALUE OF $1 COMPOUNDED ANNUALLY

YEAR	SINGLE SUM	ANNUITY	SINGLE SUM	ANNUITY	SINGLE SUM	ANNUITY	SINGLE SUM	ANNUITY
	12%		12½%		13%		13½%	
1	1.1200	1.120	1.1250	1.125	1.1300	1.130	1.1350	1.135
2	1.2544	2.374	1.2656	2.391	1.2769	2.407	1.2882	2.423
3	1.4049	3.779	1.4238	3.814	1.4429	3.850	1.4621	3.885
4	1.5735	5.353	1.6018	5.416	1.6305	5.480	1.6595	5.545
5	1.7623	7.115	1.8020	7.218	1.8424	7.323	1.8836	7.428
6	1.9738	9.089	2.0273	9.246	2.0820	9.405	2.1378	9.566
7	2.2107	11.300	2.2807	11.526	2.3526	11.757	2.4264	11.993
8	2.4760	13.776	2.5658	14.092	2.6584	14.416	2.7540	14.747
9	2.7731	16.549	2.8865	16.979	3.0040	17.420	3.1258	17.873
10	3.1058	19.655	3.2473	20.226	3.3946	20.814	3.5478	21.420
11	3.4785	23.133	3.6532	23.879	3.8359	24.650	4.0267	25.447
12	3.8960	27.029	4.1099	27.989	4.3345	28.985	4.5704	30.017
13	4.3635	31.393	4.6236	32.613	4.8980	33.883	5.1874	35.205
14	4.8871	36.280	5.2016	37.814	5.5348	39.417	5.8877	41.092
15	5.4736	41.753	5.8518	43.666	6.2543	45.672	6.6825	47.775
16	6.1304	47.884	6.5833	50.249	7.0673	52.739	7.5846	55.360
17	6.8660	54.750	7.4062	57.655	7.9861	60.725	8.6085	63.968
18	7.6900	62.440	8.3319	65.987	9.0243	69.749	9.7707	73.739
19	8.6128	71.052	9.3734	75.361	10.1974	79.947	11.0897	84.829
20	9.6463	80.699	10.5451	85.906	11.5231	91.470	12.5869	97.415
21	10.8038	91.503	11.8632	97.769	13.0211	104.491	14.2861	111.701
22	12.1003	103.603	13.3461	111.115	14.7138	119.205	16.2147	127.916
23	13.5523	117.155	15.0144	126.130	16.6266	135.831	18.4037	146.320
24	15.1786	132.334	16.8912	143.021	18.7881	154.620	20.8882	167.208
25	17.0001	149.334	19.0026	162.023	21.2305	175.850	23.7081	190.916
26	19.0401	168.374	21.3779	183.401	23.9905	199.841	26.9087	217.825
27	21.3249	189.699	24.0502	207.452	27.1093	226.950	30.5414	248.366
28	23.8839	213.583	27.0564	234.508	30.6335	257.583	34.6644	283.031
29	26.7499	240.333	30.4385	264.946	34.6158	292.199	39.3441	322.375
30	29.9599	270.293	34.2433	299.190	39.1159	331.315	44.6556	367.030
	14%		14½%		15%		15½%	
1	1.1400	1.140	1.1450	1.145	1.1500	1.150	1.1550	1.155
2	1.2996	2.440	1.3110	2.456	1.3225	2.473	1.3340	2.489
3	1.4815	3.921	1.5011	3.957	1.5209	3.993	1.5408	4.030
4	1.6890	5.610	1.7188	5.676	1.7490	5.742	1.7796	5.809
5	1.9254	7.536	1.9680	7.644	2.0114	7.754	2.0555	7.865
6	2.1950	9.730	2.2534	9.897	2.3131	10.067	2.3741	10.239
7	2.5023	12.233	2.5801	12.477	2.6600	12.727	2.7420	12.981
8	2.8526	15.085	2.9542	15.432	3.0590	15.786	3.1671	16.148
9	3.2519	18.337	3.3826	18.814	3.5179	19.304	3.6580	19.806
10	3.7072	22.045	3.8731	22.687	4.0456	23.349	4.2249	24.031
11	4.2262	26.271	4.4347	27.122	4.6524	28.002	4.8798	28.911
12	4.8179	31.089	5.0777	32.200	5.3503	33.352	5.6362	34.547
13	5.4924	36.581	5.8140	38.014	6.1520	39.505	6.5098	41.057
14	6.2613	42.842	6.6570	44.671	7.0757	46.580	7.5188	48.575
15	7.1379	49.980	7.6222	52.293	8.1371	54.717	8.6842	57.260
16	8.1372	58.118	8.7275	61.020	9.3576	64.075	10.0302	67.290
17	9.2765	67.394	9.9929	71.013	10.7613	74.836	11.5849	78.875
18	10.5752	77.969	11.4419	82.455	12.3755	87.212	13.3806	92.255
19	12.0557	90.025	13.1010	95.556	14.2318	101.444	15.4546	107.710
20	13.7435	103.768	15.0006	110.557	16.3665	117.810	17.8501	125.560
21	15.6676	119.436	17.1757	127.732	18.8215	136.632	20.6168	146.177
22	17.8610	137.297	19.6662	147.399	21.6447	158.276	23.8124	169.989
23	20.3616	157.659	22.5178	169.917	24.8915	183.168	27.5034	197.493
24	23.2122	180.871	25.7829	195.699	28.6252	211.793	31.7664	229.259
25	26.4619	207.333	29.5214	225.221	32.9190	244.712	36.6902	265.949
26	30.1666	237.499	33.8020	259.023	37.8568	282.569	42.3771	308.326
27	34.3899	271.889	38.7033	297.726	43.5353	326.104	48.9456	357.272
28	39.2045	311.094	44.3153	342.041	50.0656	376.170	56.5322	413.804
29	44.6931	355.787	50.7410	392.782	57.5755	433.745	65.2946	479.099
30	50.9502	406.737	58.0985	450.881	66.2118	499.957	75.4153	554.514

YEAR	SINGLE SUM	ANNUITY	SINGLE SUM	ANNUITY	SINGLE SUM	ANNUITY	SINGLE SUM	ANNUITY
	16%		16½%		17%		17½%	
1	1.1600	1.160	1.1650	1.165	1.1700	1.170	1.1750	1.175
2	1.3456	2.506	1.3572	2.522	1.3689	2.539	1.3806	2.556
3	1.5609	4.066	1.5812	4.103	1.6016	4.141	1.6222	4.178
4	1.8106	5.877	1.8421	5.945	1.8739	6.014	1.9061	6.084
5	2.1003	7.977	2.1460	8.091	2.1924	8.207	2.2397	8.324
6	2.4364	10.414	2.5001	10.592	2.5652	10.772	2.6316	10.955
7	2.8262	13.240	2.9126	13.504	3.0012	13.773	3.0922	14.048
8	3.2784	16.519	3.3932	16.897	3.5115	17.285	3.6333	17.681
9	3.8030	20.321	3.9531	20.850	4.1084	21.393	4.2691	21.950
10	4.4114	24.733	4.6053	25.456	4.8068	26.200	5.0162	26.966
11	5.1173	29.850	5.3652	30.821	5.6240	31.824	5.8941	32.860
12	5.9360	35.786	6.2504	37.071	6.5801	38.404	6.9256	39.786
13	6.8858	42.672	7.2818	44.353	7.6987	46.103	8.1375	47.923
14	7.9875	50.660	8.4833	52.836	9.0075	55.110	9.5616	57.485
15	9.2655	59.925	9.8830	62.719	10.5387	65.649	11.2349	68.720
16	10.7480	70.673	11.5137	74.233	12.3303	77.979	13.2010	81.921
17	12.4677	83.141	13.4135	87.647	14.4265	92.406	15.5111	97.432
18	14.4625	97.603	15.6267	103.273	16.8790	109.285	18.2256	115.658
19	16.7765	114.380	18.2051	121.478	19.7484	129.033	21.4151	137.073
20	19.4608	133.841	21.2089	142.687	23.1056	152.139	25.1627	162.235
21	22.5745	156.415	24.7084	167.396	27.0336	179.172	29.5662	191.801
22	26.1864	182.601	28.7853	196.181	31.6293	210.801	34.7403	226.542
23	30.3762	212.978	33.5348	229.716	37.0062	247.808	40.8198	267.362
24	35.2364	248.214	39.0681	268.784	43.2973	291.105	47.9633	315.325
25	40.8742	289.088	45.5143	314.298	50.6578	341.763	56.3568	371.682
26	47.4141	336.502	53.0242	367.322	59.2697	401.032	66.2193	437.901
27	55.0004	391.503	61.7732	429.096	69.3455	470.378	77.8077	515.709
28	63.8004	455.303	71.9658	501.061	81.1342	551.512	91.4240	607.133
29	74.0085	529.312	83.8401	584.901	94.9271	646.439	107.4232	714.556
30	85.8499	615.162	97.6737	682.575	111.0647	757.504	126.2223	840.778

YEAR	SINGLE SUM	ANNUITY	SINGLE SUM	ANNUITY	SINGLE SUM	ANNUITY	SINGLE SUM	ANNUITY
	18%		18½%		19%		19½%	
1	1.1800	1.180	1.1850	1.185	1.1900	1.190	1.1950	1.195
2	1.3924	2.572	1.4042	2.589	1.4161	2.606	1.4280	2.623
3	1.6430	4.215	1.6640	4.253	1.6852	4.291	1.7065	4.330
4	1.9388	6.154	1.9718	6.225	2.0053	6.297	2.0393	6.369
5	2.2878	8.442	2.3366	8.562	2.3864	8.683	2.4369	8.806
6	2.6996	11.142	2.7689	11.331	2.8398	11.523	2.9121	11.718
7	3.1855	14.327	3.2812	14.612	3.3793	14.902	3.4800	15.198
8	3.7589	18.086	3.8882	18.500	4.0214	18.923	4.1586	19.356
9	4.4355	22.521	4.6075	23.107	4.7854	23.709	4.9695	24.326
10	5.2338	27.755	5.4599	28.567	5.6947	29.404	5.9385	30.264
11	6.1759	33.931	6.4700	35.037	6.7767	36.180	7.0965	37.361
12	7.2876	41.219	7.6669	42.704	8.0642	44.244	8.4804	45.841
13	8.5994	49.818	9.0853	51.790	9.5964	53.841	10.1340	55.975
14	10.1472	59.965	10.7661	62.556	11.4198	65.261	12.1102	68.085
15	11.9737	71.939	12.7578	75.313	13.5895	78.850	14.4717	82.557
16	14.1290	86.068	15.1180	90.431	16.1715	95.022	17.2936	99.851
17	16.6722	102.740	17.9148	108.346	19.2441	114.266	20.6659	120.517
18	19.6733	122.414	21.2290	129.575	22.9005	137.166	24.6958	145.212
19	23.2144	145.628	25.1564	154.732	27.2516	164.418	29.5114	174.724
20	27.3930	173.021	29.8103	184.542	32.4294	196.847	35.2662	209.990
21	32.3238	205.345	35.3253	219.867	38.5910	235.438	42.1431	252.133
22	38.1421	243.487	41.8604	261.728	45.9233	281.362	50.3610	302.494
23	45.0076	288.494	49.6046	311.332	54.6487	336.010	60.1813	362.675
24	53.1090	341.603	58.7815	370.114	65.0320	401.042	71.9167	434.592
25	62.6686	404.272	69.6560	439.770	77.3881	478.431	85.9405	520.533
26	73.9490	478.221	82.5424	522.312	92.0918	570.522	102.6988	623.231
27	87.2598	565.481	97.8127	620.125	109.5893	680.112	122.7251	745.956
28	102.9666	668.447	115.9081	736.033	130.4112	810.523	146.6565	892.613
29	121.5005	789.948	137.3511	873.384	155.1893	965.712	175.2545	1067.868
30	143.3706	933.319	162.7611	1036.145	184.6753	1150.387	209.4292	1277.297

Notes:

FUTURE VALUE OF $1 COMPOUNDED MONTHLY

YEAR	SINGLE SUM	ANNUITY	SINGLE SUM	ANNUITY	SINGLE SUM	ANNUITY	SINGLE SUM	ANNUITY
	4%		4½%		5%		5½%	
1	1.0407	12.222	1.0459	12.251	1.0512	12.279	1.0564	12.307
2	1.0831	24.943	1.0940	25.064	1.1049	25.186	1.1160	25.309
3	1.1273	38.182	1.1442	38.466	1.1615	38.753	1.1789	39.043
4	1.1732	51.960	1.1968	52.484	1.2209	53.015	1.2455	53.553
5	1.2210	66.299	1.2518	67.146	1.2834	68.006	1.3157	68.881
6	1.2707	81.223	1.3093	82.481	1.3490	83.764	1.3899	85.073
7	1.3225	96.754	1.3695	98.521	1.4180	100.329	1.4683	102.179
8	1.3764	112.919	1.4324	115.297	1.4906	117.741	1.5511	120.250
9	1.4325	129.741	1.4982	132.845	1.5668	136.043	1.6386	139.341
10	1.4908	147.250	1.5670	151.198	1.6470	155.282	1.7311	159.508
11	1.5516	165.471	1.6390	170.395	1.7313	175.506	1.8287	180.812
12	1.6148	184.435	1.7143	190.473	1.8198	196.764	1.9319	203.319
13	1.6806	204.172	1.7930	211.474	1.9130	219.109	2.0409	227.095
14	1.7490	224.713	1.8754	233.440	2.0108	242.598	2.1560	252.212
15	1.8203	246.090	1.9616	256.415	2.1137	267.289	2.2776	278.746
16	1.8945	268.339	2.0517	280.445	2.2218	293.243	2.4061	306.776
17	1.9716	291.494	2.1459	305.579	2.3355	320.525	2.5418	336.388
18	2.0520	315.592	2.2445	331.868	2.4550	349.202	2.6852	367.670
19	2.1356	340.673	2.3476	359.365	2.5806	379.347	2.8366	400.717
20	2.2226	366.775	2.4555	388.124	2.7126	411.034	2.9966	435.627
21	2.3131	393.940	2.5683	418.205	2.8514	444.342	3.1657	472.507
22	2.4074	422.212	2.6863	449.668	2.9973	479.354	3.3442	511.468
23	2.5055	451.636	2.8097	482.577	3.1507	516.158	3.5329	552.626
24	2.6075	482.259	2.9387	516.997	3.3118	554.844	3.7321	596.105
25	2.7138	514.130	3.0737	552.998	3.4813	595.510	3.9427	642.037
26	2.8243	547.298	3.2149	590.653	3.6594	638.256	4.1651	690.561
27	2.9394	581.819	3.3626	630.038	3.8466	683.189	4.4000	741.821
28	3.0592	617.745	3.5171	671.233	4.0434	730.421	4.6482	795.972
29	3.1838	655.136	3.6787	714.320	4.2503	780.070	4.9104	853.179
30	3.3135	694.049	3.8477	759.386	4.4677	832.259	5.1874	913.612
	6%		6½%		7%		7½%	
1	1.0617	12.336	1.0670	12.364	1.0723	12.393	1.0776	12.421
2	1.1272	25.432	1.1384	25.556	1.1498	25.681	1.1613	25.807
3	1.1967	39.336	1.2147	39.632	1.2329	39.930	1.2514	40.231
4	1.2705	54.098	1.2960	54.650	1.3221	55.209	1.3486	55.776
5	1.3489	69.770	1.3828	70.674	1.4176	71.593	1.4533	72.527
6	1.4320	86.409	1.4754	87.771	1.5201	89.161	1.5661	90.579
7	1.5204	104.074	1.5742	106.013	1.6300	107.999	1.6877	110.032
8	1.6141	122.829	1.6797	125.477	1.7478	128.199	1.8187	130.995
9	1.7137	142.740	1.7922	146.245	1.8742	149.859	1.9599	153.586
10	1.8194	163.879	1.9122	168.403	2.0097	173.085	2.1121	177.930
11	1.9316	186.323	2.0402	192.045	2.1549	197.990	2.2760	204.165
12	2.0508	210.150	2.1769	217.271	2.3107	224.695	2.4527	232.436
13	2.1772	235.447	2.3227	244.186	2.4778	253.331	2.6431	262.902
14	2.3115	262.305	2.4782	272.904	2.6569	284.037	2.8483	295.733
15	2.4541	290.819	2.6442	303.545	2.8489	316.962	3.0695	331.112
16	2.6055	321.091	2.8213	336.238	3.0549	352.268	3.3077	369.239
17	2.7662	353.231	3.0102	371.120	3.2757	390.126	3.5645	410.325
18	2.9368	387.353	3.2118	408.339	3.5125	430.721	3.8413	454.601
19	3.1179	423.580	3.4269	448.050	3.7665	474.250	4.1395	502.314
20	3.3102	462.041	3.6564	490.421	4.0387	520.927	4.4608	553.731
21	3.5144	502.874	3.9013	535.629	4.3307	570.977	4.8071	609.139
22	3.7311	546.226	4.1626	583.865	4.6438	624.646	5.1803	668.850
23	3.9613	592.251	4.4414	635.332	4.9795	682.194	5.5825	733.196
24	4.2056	641.116	4.7388	690.245	5.5394	743.902	6.0159	802.537
25	4.4650	692.994	5.0562	748.837	5.7254	810.072	6.4829	877.261
26	4.7404	748.072	5.3948	811.352	6.1393	881.024	6.9862	957.786
27	5.0327	806.547	5.7561	878.053	6.5831	957.106	7.5285	1044.563
28	5.3431	868.628	6.1416	949.222	7.0590	1038.688	8.1130	1138.076
29	5.6727	934.539	6.5529	1025.157	7.5693	1126.168	8.7428	1238.849
30	6.0226	1004.515	6.9918	1106.178	8.1165	1219.971	9.4215	1347.445

FUTURE VALUE OF $1 COMPOUNDED MONTHLY

YEAR	SINGLE SUM	ANNUITY	SINGLE SUM	ANNUITY	SINGLE SUM	ANNUITY	SINGLE SUM	ANNUITY
	8%		8½%		9%		9½%	
1	1.0830	12.533	1.0884	12.567	1.0938	12.601	1.0992	12.636
2	1.1729	26.106	1.1846	26.245	1.1964	26.385	1.2083	26.526
3	1.2702	40.806	1.2893	41.132	1.3086	41.461	1.3283	41.794
4	1.3757	56.726	1.4033	57.335	1.4314	57.952	1.4601	58.578
5	1.4898	73.967	1.5273	74.970	1.5657	75.990	1.6050	77.027
6	1.6135	92.639	1.6623	94.163	1.7126	95.720	1.7643	97.308
7	1.7474	112.861	1.8092	115.054	1.8732	117.300	1.9394	119.601
8	1.8925	134.761	1.9692	137.791	2.0489	140.905	2.1319	144.107
9	2.0495	158.479	2.1432	162.537	2.2411	166.724	2.3435	171.045
10	2.2196	184.166	2.3326	189.471	2.4514	194.966	2.5761	200.657
11	2.4039	211.984	2.5388	218.786	2.6813	225.856	2.8317	233.207
12	2.6034	242.112	2.7632	250.691	2.9328	259.644	3.1128	268.988
13	2.8195	274.740	3.0075	285.417	3.2080	296.602	3.4217	308.320
14	3.0535	310.076	3.2733	323.213	3.5089	337.027	3.7613	351.556
15	3.3069	348.345	3.5627	364.349	3.8380	381.244	4.1346	399.083
16	3.5814	389.791	3.8776	409.121	4.1981	429.609	4.5449	451.327
17	3.8786	434.676	4.2203	457.851	4.5919	482.510	4.9960	508.756
18	4.2006	483.287	4.5933	510.888	5.0226	540.374	5.4919	571.885
19	4.5492	535.932	4.9993	568.613	5.4938	603.667	6.0369	641.278
20	4.9268	592.947	5.4412	631.440	6.0092	672.896	6.6361	717.560
21	5.3357	654.694	5.9222	699.821	6.5729	748.620	7.2947	801.411
22	5.7786	721.567	6.4457	774.246	7.1894	831.447	8.0187	893.585
23	6.2582	793.989	7.0154	855.249	7.8638	922.044	8.8145	994.907
24	6.7776	872.423	7.6355	943.413	8.6015	1021.139	9.6893	1106.285
25	7.3402	957.367	8.3104	1039.369	9.4084	1129.530	10.6509	1228.711
26	7.9494	1049.360	9.0450	1143.807	10.2910	1248.089	11.7080	1363.300
27	8.6092	1148.990	9.8445	1257.476	11.2564	1377.770	12.8700	1511.240
28	9.3238	1256.888	10.7146	1381.192	12.3123	1519.616	14.1473	1673.866
29	10.0976	1373.742	11.6617	1515.844	13.4673	1674.768	15.5514	1852.626
30	10.9357	1500.295	12.6925	1662.398	14.7306	1844.474	17.0949	2049.130
	10%		10½%		11%		11½%	
1	1.1047	12.670	1.1102	12.705	1.1157	12.740	1.1213	12.774
2	1.2204	26.667	1.2326	26.810	1.2448	26.953	1.2572	27.098
3	1.3482	42.130	1.3684	42.469	1.3889	42.812	1.4097	43.158
4	1.4894	59.212	1.5192	59.854	1.5496	60.506	1.5806	61.166
5	1.6453	78.082	1.6866	79.156	1.7289	80.247	1.7723	81.357
6	1.8176	98.929	1.8725	100.584	1.9290	102.273	1.9872	103.997
7	2.0079	121.958	2.0788	124.373	2.1522	126.847	2.2281	129.382
8	2.2182	147.399	2.3079	150.784	2.4013	154.265	2.4983	157.845
9	2.4504	175.504	2.5623	180.106	2.6791	184.856	2.8013	189.760
10	2.7070	206.552	2.8446	212.659	2.9891	218.987	3.1409	225.544
11	2.9905	240.851	3.1581	248.800	3.3351	257.068	3.5218	265.668
12	3.3036	278.742	3.5062	288.924	3.7210	299.555	3.9489	310.657
13	3.6496	320.600	3.8925	333.469	4.1516	346.959	4.4277	361.102
14	4.0317	366.841	4.3215	382.923	4.6320	399.848	4.9646	417.663
15	4.4539	417.924	4.7978	437.828	5.1680	458.858	5.5666	481.083
16	4.9203	474.357	5.3265	498.783	5.7660	524.696	6.2416	552.193
17	5.4355	536.698	5.9135	566.455	6.4333	598.152	6.9985	631.926
18	6.0047	605.568	6.5652	641.585	7.1777	680.109	7.8471	721.327
19	6.6335	681.649	7.2887	724.995	8.0083	771.551	8.7986	821.569
20	7.3281	765.697	8.0919	817.597	8.9350	873.573	9.8656	933.967
21	8.0954	858.546	8.9837	920.404	9.9690	987.402	11.0618	1059.993
22	8.9431	961.117	9.9737	1034.540	11.1226	1114.402	12.4032	1201.302
23	9.8796	1074.429	11.0728	1161.255	12.4097	1256.099	13.9072	1359.745
24	10.9141	1199.606	12.2931	1301.934	13.8457	1414.193	15.5936	1537.401
25	12.0569	1337.890	13.6479	1458.117	15.4479	1590.581	17.4844	1736.600
26	13.3195	1490.655	15.1519	1631.511	17.2355	1787.381	19.6046	1959.953
27	14.7142	1659.417	16.8217	1824.014	19.2300	2006.954	21.9818	2210.390
28	16.2550	1845.849	18.6755	2037.732	21.4552	2251.936	24.6473	2491.195
29	17.9571	2051.804	20.7336	2275.002	23.9380	2525.267	27.6361	2806.050
30	19.8374	2279.325	23.0185	2538.419	26.7081	2830.228	30.9872	3159.084

FUTURE VALUE OF $1 COMPOUNDED MONTHLY

YEAR	SINGLE SUM	ANNUITY	SINGLE SUM	ANNUITY	SINGLE SUM	ANNUITY	SINGLE SUM	ANNUITY
		12%		12½%		13%		13½%
1	1.1268	12.809	1.1324	12.844	1.1380	12.879	1.1437	12.915
2	1.2697	27.243	1.2824	27.390	1.2951	27.537	1.3080	27.685
3	1.4308	43.508	1.4522	43.861	1.4739	44.217	1.4959	44.577
4	1.6122	61.835	1.6445	62.513	1.6773	63.200	1.7108	63.897
5	1.8167	82.486	1.8622	83.635	1.9089	84.803	1.9566	85.992
6	2.0471	105.757	2.1088	107.554	2.1723	109.388	2.2378	111.261
7	2.3067	131.979	2.3880	134.640	2.4722	137.367	2.5593	140.161
8	2.5993	161.527	2.7043	165.313	2.8134	169.208	2.9270	173.214
9	2.9289	194.822	3.0623	200.047	3.2018	205.443	3.3475	211.015
10	3.3004	232.339	3.4678	239.381	3.6437	246.681	3.8285	254.247
11	3.7190	274.615	3.9270	283.924	4.1467	293.610	4.3785	303.691
12	4.1906	322.252	4.4471	334.364	4.7191	347.017	5.0076	360.238
13	4.7221	375.931	5.0359	391.484	5.3704	407.796	5.7271	424.910
14	5.3210	436.418	5.7027	456.167	6.1117	476.965	6.5499	498.873
15	5.9958	504.576	6.4579	529.415	6.9554	555.681	7.4909	583.463
16	6.7562	581.378	7.3130	612.362	7.9154	645.263	8.5672	680.207
17	7.6131	667.921	8.2814	706.293	9.0080	747.210	9.7981	790.850
18	8.5786	765.439	9.3780	812.662	10.2514	863.228	11.2058	917.389
19	9.6666	875.325	10.6197	933.116	11.6664	995.261	12.8158	1062.110
20	10.8926	999.148	12.0260	1069.520	13.2768	1145.519	14.6571	1227.622
21	12.2740	1138.674	13.6184	1223.985	15.1094	1316.517	16.7630	1416.915
22	13.8307	1295.896	15.4217	1398.905	17.1950	1511.119	19.1714	1633.400
23	15.5847	1473.057	17.4638	1596.987	19.5685	1732.582	21.9258	1880.997
24	17.5613	1672.687	19.7763	1821.298	22.2696	1984.614	25.0760	2164.163
25	19.7885	1897.635	22.3950	2075.312	25.3435	2271.435	28.6788	2488.013
26	22.2981	2151.112	25.3604	2362.960	28.8417	2597.846	32.7992	2858.392
27	25.1261	2436.736	28.7185	2688.699	32.8228	2969.313	37.5116	3281.984
28	28.3127	2758.585	32.5213	3057.570	37.3534	3392.054	42.9010	3766.436
29	31.9035	3121.252	36.8277	3475.286	42.5094	3873.147	49.0648	4320.492
30	35.9496	3529.914	41.7043	3948.313	48.3771	4420.647	56.1142	4954.151
		14%		14½%		15%		15½%
1	1.1493	12.950	1.1550	12.986	1.1608	13.021	1.1665	13.057
2	1.3210	27.834	1.3341	27.984	1.3474	28.135	1.3607	28.288
3	1.5183	44.941	1.5409	45.308	1.5639	45.679	1.5873	46.054
4	1.7450	64.603	1.7798	65.318	1.8154	66.044	1.8516	66.779
5	2.0056	87.201	2.0558	88.431	2.1072	89.682	2.1598	90.954
6	2.3051	113.174	2.3745	115.126	2.4459	117.120	2.5195	119.155
7	2.6494	143.025	2.7426	145.960	2.8391	148.968	2.9390	152.051
8	3.0450	177.335	3.1678	181.575	3.2955	185.937	3.4283	190.424
9	3.4998	216.769	3.6590	222.711	3.8253	228.840	3.9991	235.187
10	4.0225	262.091	4.2262	270.224	4.4402	278.657	4.6649	287.402
11	4.6232	314.183	4.8814	325.104	5.1540	336.474	5.4417	348.311
12	5.3136	374.054	5.6382	388.492	5.9825	403.585	6.3477	419.362
13	6.1072	442.865	6.5124	461.708	6.9442	481.484	7.4046	502.242
14	7.0192	521.954	7.5220	546.275	8.0606	571.906	8.6374	598.922
15	8.0675	612.854	8.6882	643.952	9.3563	676.863	10.0756	711.699
16	9.2723	717.329	10.0352	756.773	10.8604	798.693	11.7531	843.254
17	10.6571	837.406	11.5910	887.085	12.6063	940.108	13.7100	996.712
18	12.2486	975.416	13.3880	1037.600	14.6328	1104.255	15.9927	1175.721
19	14.0779	1134.037	15.4636	1211.450	16.9851	1294.790	18.6555	1384.535
20	16.1803	1316.346	17.8610	1412.253	19.7155	1515.955	21.7617	1628.116
21	18.5967	1525.882	20.6301	1644.188	22.8848	1772.673	25.3850	1912.254
22	21.3739	1766.711	23.8285	1912.081	26.5637	2070.659	29.6116	2243.700
23	24.5660	2043.505	27.5227	2221.507	30.8339	2416.548	34.5419	2630.332
24	28.2347	2361.636	31.7897	2578.904	35.7906	2818.040	40.2931	3081.338
25	32.4513	2727.278	36.7182	2991.711	41.5441	3284.074	47.0019	3607.437
26	37.2977	3147.525	42.4109	3468.518	48.2225	3825.025	54.8277	4221.131
27	42.8678	3630.533	48.9861	4019.246	55.9745	4452.936	63.9565	4937.004
28	49.2697	4185.674	56.5806	4655.357	64.9727	5181.786	74.6052	5772.070
29	56.6278	4823.721	65.3526	5390.087	75.4173	6027.803	87.0269	6746.175
30	65.0847	5557.056	75.4846	6238.727	87.5410	7009.821	101.5169	7882.467

FUTURE VALUE OF $1 COMPOUNDED MONTHLY

YEAR	SINGLE SUM	ANNUITY	SINGLE SUM	ANNUITY	SINGLE SUM	ANNUITY	SINGLE SUM	ANNUITY
	16%		16½%		17%		17½%	
1	1.1723	13.093	1.1781	13.128	1.1839	13.164	1.1897	13.201
2	1.3742	28.441	1.3878	28.595	1.4016	28.750	1.4155	28.906
3	1.6110	46.433	1.6350	46.815	1.6593	47.201	1.6841	47.591
4	1.8885	67.524	1.9261	68.280	1.9645	69.046	2.0036	69.822
5	2.2138	92.249	2.2691	93.567	2.3257	94.907	2.3838	96.271
6	2.5952	121.234	2.6731	123.356	2.7534	125.524	2.8361	127.738
7	3.0423	155.211	3.1491	158.451	3.2597	161.771	3.3742	165.175
8	3.5663	195.042	3.7099	199.794	3.8592	204.684	4.0144	209.717
9	4.1807	241.735	4.3705	248.500	4.5689	255.488	4.7761	262.709
10	4.9009	296.472	5.1488	305.878	5.4090	315.635	5.6823	325.757
11	5.7452	360.637	6.0656	373.474	6.4037	386.842	6.7605	400.767
12	6.7350	435.857	7.1457	453.106	7.5813	471.144	8.0433	490.010
13	7.8952	524.035	8.4181	546.918	8.9754	570.948	9.5694	596.186
14	9.2553	627.404	9.9171	657.435	10.6260	689.105	11.3851	722.508
15	10.8497	748.580	11.6830	787.632	12.5800	828.990	13.5454	872.798
16	12.7188	890.631	13.7634	941.012	14.8933	994.599	16.1155	1051.605
17	14.9099	1057.153	16.2143	1121.705	17.6321	1190.662	19.1732	1264.339
18	17.4785	1252.363	19.1015	1334.574	20.8745	1422.779	22.8112	1517.437
19	20.4895	1481.201	22.5029	1585.347	24.7131	1697.581	27.1394	1818.559
20	24.0192	1749.461	26.5099	1880.776	29.2577	2022.917	32.2889	2176.816
21	28.1570	2063.934	31.2305	2228.810	34.6379	2408.079	38.4155	2603.049
22	33.0077	2432.583	36.7916	2638.819	41.0075	2864.069	45.7045	3110.157
23	38.6939	2864.738	43.3430	3121.837	48.5485	3403.912	54.3766	3713.484
24	45.3598	3371.342	51.0611	3690.865	57.4761	4043.028	64.6941	4431.287
25	53.1739	3965.218	60.1534	4361.219	68.0455	4799.672	76.9692	5285.288
26	62.3342	4661.402	70.8648	5150.941	80.5586	5695.456	91.5735	6301.328
27	73.0726	5477.518	83.4836	6081.288	95.3726	6755.968	108.9488	7510.153
28	85.6609	6434.227	98.3493	7177.300	112.9108	8011.499	129.6210	8948.343
29	100.4177	7555.748	115.8622	8468.477	133.6742	9497.912	154.2155	10659.418
30	117.7168	8870.476	136.4936	9989.572	158.2558	11257.664	183.4766	12695.155

YEAR	SINGLE SUM	ANNUITY	SINGLE SUM	ANNUITY	SINGLE SUM	ANNUITY	SINGLE SUM	ANNUITY
	18%		18½%		19%		19½%	
1	1.1956	13.237	1.2015	13.273	1.2075	13.310	1.2134	13.346
2	1.4295	29.063	1.4437	29.221	1.4579	29.380	1.4724	29.541
3	1.7091	47.985	1.7346	48.383	1.7604	48.785	1.7866	49.191
4	2.0435	70.609	2.0841	71.406	2.1256	72.215	2.1678	73.035
5	2.4432	97.658	2.5041	99.069	2.5665	100.506	2.6305	101.967
6	2.9212	129.998	3.0088	132.307	3.0990	134.665	3.1918	137.074
7	3.4926	168.665	3.6151	172.243	3.7419	175.911	3.8730	179.673
8	4.1758	214.896	4.3436	220.227	4.5181	225.714	4.6995	231.362
9	4.9927	270.170	5.2189	277.881	5.4554	285.848	5.7024	294.083
10	5.9693	336.258	6.2707	347.152	6.5871	358.457	6.9194	370.189
11	7.1370	415.272	7.5344	430.384	7.9536	446.129	8.3960	462.536
12	8.5332	509.744	9.0527	530.389	9.6036	551.989	10.1878	574.591
13	10.2024	622.696	10.8770	650.547	11.5959	679.809	12.3620	710.559
14	12.1982	757.744	13.0689	794.919	14.0015	834.146	15.0001	875.544
15	14.5844	919.209	15.7026	968.385	16.9061	1020.500	18.2012	1075.738
16	17.4373	1112.260	18.8670	1176.809	20.4133	1245.513	22.0855	1318.655
17	20.8484	1343.075	22.6691	1427.234	24.6480	1517.206	26.7987	1613.412
18	24.9267	1619.041	27.2374	1728.125	29.7613	1845.262	32.5178	1971.072
19	29.8028	1948.992	32.7263	2089.652	35.9353	2241.373	39.4573	2405.060
20	35.6328	2343.487	39.3214	2524.034	43.3901	2719.657	47.8778	2931.665
21	42.6032	2815.153	47.2455	3045.954	52.3914	3297.163	58.0953	3570.650
22	50.9372	3379.085	56.7665	3673.051	63.2600	3994.472	70.4932	4346.000
23	60.9015	4053.332	68.2061	4426.522	76.3834	4836.439	85.5370	5286.816
24	72.8149	4859.474	81.9511	5331.833	92.2292	5853.072	103.7913	6428.409
25	87.0588	5823.312	98.4660	6419.584	111.3622	7080.608	125.9411	7813.626
26	104.0891	6975.695	118.3090	7726.540	134.4644	8562.796	152.8179	9494.459
27	124.4508	8353.504	142.1507	9296.875	162.3592	10352.647	185.4304	11533.995
28	148.7956	10000.838	170.7971	11183.666	196.0408	12513.406	225.0027	14008.783
29	177.9028	11970.421	205.2164	13450.685	236.7096	15122.634	273.0200	17011.710
30	212.7038	14325.289	246.5718	16174.557	285.8153	18273.149	331.2845	20655.484

PRESENT VALUE OF $1 COMPOUNDED ANNUALLY

YEAR	SINGLE SUM	ANNUITY	SINGLE SUM	ANNUITY	SINGLE SUM	ANNUITY	SINGLE SUM	ANNUITY
	4%		4½%		5%		5½%	
1	.961538	.9615	.956938	.9569	.952381	.9524	.947867	.9479
2	.924556	1.8861	.915730	1.8727	.907029	1.8594	.898452	1.8463
3	.888996	2.7751	.876297	2.7490	.863838	2.7232	.851614	2.6979
4	.854804	3.6299	.838561	3.5875	.822702	3.5460	.807217	3.5052
5	.821927	4.4518	.802451	4.3900	.783526	4.3295	.765134	4.2703
6	.790315	5.2421	.767896	5.1579	.746215	5.0757	.725246	4.9955
7	.759918	6.0021	.734828	5.8927	.710681	5.7864	.687437	5.6830
8	.730690	6.7327	.703185	6.5959	.676839	6.4632	.651599	6.3346
9	.702587	7.4353	.672904	7.2688	.644609	7.1078	.617629	6.9522
10	.675564	8.1109	.643928	7.9127	.613913	7.7217	.585431	7.5376
11	.649581	8.7605	.616199	8.5289	.584679	8.3064	.554911	8.0925
12	.624597	9.3851	.589664	9.1186	.556837	8.8633	.525982	8.6185
13	.600574	9.9856	.564272	9.6829	.530321	9.3936	.498561	9.1171
14	.577475	10.5631	.539973	10.2228	.505068	9.8986	.472569	9.5896
15	.555265	11.1184	.516720	10.7395	.481017	10.3797	.447933	10.0376
16	.533908	11.6523	.494469	11.2340	.458112	10.8378	.424581	10.4622
17	.513373	12.1657	.473176	11.7072	.436297	11.2741	.402447	10.8646
18	.493628	12.6593	.452800	12.1600	.415521	11.6896	.381466	11.2461
19	.474642	13.1339	.433302	12.5933	.395734	12.0853	.361579	11.6077
20	.456387	13.5903	.414643	13.0079	.376889	12.4622	.342729	11.9504
21	.438834	14.0292	.396787	13.4047	.358942	12.8212	.324862	12.2752
22	.421955	14.4511	.379701	13.7844	.341850	13.1630	.307926	12.5832
23	.405726	14.8568	.363350	14.1478	.325571	13.4886	.291873	12.8750
24	.390121	15.2470	.347703	14.4955	.310068	13.7986	.276657	13.1517
25	.375117	15.6221	.332731	14.8282	.295303	14.0939	.262234	13.4139
26	.360689	15.9828	.318402	15.1466	.281241	14.3752	.248563	13.6625
27	.346817	16.3296	.304691	15.4513	.267848	14.6430	.235605	13.8981
28	.333477	16.6631	.291571	15.7429	.255094	14.8981	.223322	14.1214
29	.320651	16.9837	.279015	16.0219	.242946	15.1411	.211679	14.3331
30	.308319	17.2920	.267000	16.2889	.231377	15.3725	.200644	14.5337

YEAR	SINGLE SUM	ANNUITY	SINGLE SUM	ANNUITY	SINGLE SUM	ANNUITY	SINGLE SUM	ANNUITY
	6%		6½%		7%		7½%	
1	.943396	.9434	.938967	.9390	.934579	.9346	.930233	.9302
2	.889996	1.8334	.881659	1.8206	.873439	1.8080	.865333	1.7956
3	.839619	2.6730	.827849	2.6485	.816298	2.6243	.804961	2.6005
4	.792094	3.4651	.777323	3.3428	.762895	3.3872	.748801	3.3493
5	.747258	4.2124	.729881	4.1557	.712986	4.1002	.696559	4.0459
6	.704961	4.9173	.685334	4.8410	.666342	4.7665	.647962	4.6938
7	.665057	5.5824	.643506	5.4845	.622750	5.3893	.602755	5.2966
8	.627412	6.2098	.604231	6.0888	.582009	5.9713	.560702	5.8573
9	.591898	6.8017	.567353	6.6561	.543934	6.5152	.521583	6.3789
10	.558395	7.3601	.532726	7.1888	.508349	7.0236	.485194	6.8641
11	.526788	7.8869	.500212	7.6890	.475093	7.4987	.451343	7.3154
12	.496969	8.3838	.469683	8.1587	.444012	7.9427	.419854	7.7353
13	.468839	8.8527	.441017	8.5997	.414964	8.3577	.390562	8.1258
14	.442301	9.2950	.414100	9.0138	.387817	8.7455	.363313	8.4492
15	.417265	9.7122	.388827	9.4027	.362446	9.1079	.337966	8.8271
16	.393646	10.1059	.365095	9.7678	.338735	9.4466	.314387	9.1415
17	.371364	10.4773	.342813	10.1106	.316574	9.7632	.292453	9.4340
18	.350344	10.8276	.321890	10.4325	.295864	10.0591	.272049	9.7060
19	.330513	11.1581	.302244	10.7347	.276508	10.3356	.253069	9.9591
20	.311805	11.4699	.283797	11.0185	.258419	10.5940	.235413	10.1945
21	.294155	11.7641	.266476	11.2850	.241513	10.8355	.218989	10.4135
22	.277505	12.0416	.250212	11.5352	.225713	11.0612	.203711	10.6172
23	.261797	12.3034	.234941	11.7701	.210947	11.2722	.189498	10.8067
24	.246979	12.5504	.220602	11.9907	.197147	11.4693	.176277	10.9830
25	.232999	12.7834	.207138	12.1979	.184249	11.6536	.163979	11.1469
26	.219810	13.0032	.194496	12.3924	.172195	11.8258	.152539	11.2995
27	.207368	13.2105	.182625	12.5750	.160930	11.9867	.141896	11.4414
28	.195630	13.4062	.171479	12.7465	.150402	12.1371	.131997	11.5734
29	.184557	13.5907	.161013	12.9075	.140563	12.2777	.122788	11.6962
30	.174110	13.7648	.151186	13.0587	.131367	12.4090	.114221	11.8104

PRESENT VALUE OF $1 COMPOUNDED ANNUALLY

YEAR	SINGLE SUM	ANNUITY	SINGLE SUM	ANNUITY	SINGLE SUM	ANNUITY	SINGLE SUM	ANNUITY
	8%		8½%		9%		9½%	
1	.925926	.9259	.921659	.9217	.917431	.9174	.913242	.9132
2	.857339	1.7833	.849455	1.7711	.841680	1.7591	.834011	1.7473
3	.793832	2.5771	.782908	2.5540	.772183	2.5313	.761654	2.5089
4	.735030	3.3121	.721574	3.2756	.708425	3.2397	.695574	3.2045
5	.680583	3.9927	.665045	3.9406	.649931	3.8897	.635228	3.8397
6	.630170	4.6229	.612945	4.5536	.596267	4.4859	.580117	4.4198
7	.583490	5.2064	.564926	5.1185	.547034	5.0330	.529787	4.9496
8	.540269	5.7466	.520669	5.6392	.501866	5.5348	.483824	5.4334
9	.500249	6.2469	.479880	6.1191	.460428	5.9952	.441848	5.8753
10	.463193	6.7101	.442285	6.5613	.422411	6.4177	.403514	6.2788
11	.428883	7.1390	.407636	6.9690	.387533	6.8052	.368506	6.6473
12	.397114	7.5361	.375702	7.3447	.355535	7.1607	.336535	6.9838
13	.367698	7.9038	.346269	7.6910	.326179	7.4869	.307338	7.2912
14	.340461	8.2442	.319142	8.0101	.299246	7.7862	.280674	7.5719
15	.315242	8.5595	.294140	8.3042	.274538	8.0607	.256323	7.8282
16	.291890	8.8514	.271097	8.5753	.251870	8.3126	.234085	8.0623
17	.270269	9.1216	.249859	8.8252	.231073	8.5436	.213777	8.2760
18	.250249	9.3719	.230285	9.0555	.211994	8.7556	.195230	8.4713
19	.231712	9.6036	.212244	9.2677	.194490	8.9501	.178292	8.6496
20	.214548	9.8181	.195616	9.4633	.178431	9.1285	.162824	8.8124
21	.198656	10.0168	.180292	9.6436	.163698	9.2922	.148697	8.9611
22	.183941	10.2007	.166167	9.8098	.150182	9.4424	.135797	9.0969
23	.170315	10.3711	.153150	9.9629	.137781	9.5802	.124015	9.2209
24	.157699	10.5288	.141152	10.1041	.126405	9.7066	.113256	9.3341
25	.146018	10.6748	.130094	10.2342	.115968	9.8226	.103430	9.4376
26	.135202	10.8100	.119902	10.3541	.106393	9.9290	.094457	9.5320
27	.125187	10.9352	.110509	10.4646	.097608	10.0266	.086262	9.6183
28	.115914	11.0511	.101851	10.5665	.089548	10.1161	.078778	9.6971
29	.107328	11.1584	.093872	10.6603	.082155	10.1983	.071943	9.7690
30	.099377	11.2578	.086518	10.7468	.075371	10.2737	.065702	9.8347
	10%		10½%		11%		11½%	
1	.909091	.9091	.904977	.9050	.900901	.9009	.896861	.8969
2	.826446	1.7355	.818984	1.7240	.811622	1.7125	.804360	1.7012
3	.751315	2.4869	.741162	2.4651	.731191	2.4437	.721399	2.4226
4	.683013	3.1699	.670735	3.1359	.658731	3.1024	.646994	3.0696
5	.620921	3.7908	.607000	3.7429	.593451	3.6959	.580264	3.6499
6	.564474	4.3553	.549321	4.2922	.534641	4.2305	.520416	4.1703
7	.513158	4.8684	.497123	4.7893	.481658	4.7122	.466741	4.6370
8	.466507	5.3349	.449885	5.2392	.433926	5.1461	.418602	5.0556
9	.424098	5.7590	.407136	5.6463	.390925	5.5370	.375428	5.4311
10	.385543	6.1446	.368449	6.0148	.352184	5.8892	.336706	5.7678
11	.350494	6.4951	.333438	6.3482	.317283	6.2065	.301979	6.0697
12	.318631	6.8137	.301754	6.6500	.285841	6.4924	.270833	6.3406
13	.289664	7.1034	.273080	6.9230	.257514	6.7499	.242900	6.5835
14	.263331	7.3667	.247132	7.1702	.231995	6.9819	.217847	6.8013
15	.239392	7.6061	.223648	7.3938	.209004	7.1909	.195379	6.9967
16	.217629	7.8237	.202397	7.5962	.188292	7.3792	.175227	7.1719
17	.197845	8.0216	.183164	7.7794	.169633	7.5488	.157155	7.3291
18	.179859	8.2014	.165760	7.9451	.152822	7.7016	.140946	7.4700
19	.163508	8.3649	.150000	8.0952	.137678	7.8393	.126409	7.5964
20	.148644	8.5136	.135755	8.2309	.124034	7.9633	.113371	7.7098
21	.135131	8.6487	.122855	8.3538	.111742	8.0751	.101678	7.8115
22	.122846	8.7715	.111181	8.4649	.100669	8.1757	.091191	7.9027
23	.111678	8.8832	.100616	8.5656	.090693	8.2664	.081786	7.9845
24	.101526	8.9847	.091055	8.6566	.081705	8.3481	.073351	8.0578
25	.092296	9.0770	.082403	8.7390	.073608	8.4217	.065785	8.1236
26	.083905	9.1609	.074573	8.8136	.066314	8.4881	.059000	8.1826
27	.076278	9.2372	.067487	8.8811	.059742	8.5478	.052915	8.2355
28	.069343	9.3066	.061074	8.9422	.053822	8.6016	.047457	8.2830
29	.063039	9.3696	.055271	8.9974	.048488	8.6501	.042563	8.3255
30	.057309	9.4269	.050019	9.0474	.043683	8.6938	.038173	8.3637

PRESENT VALUE OF $1 COMPOUNDED ANNUALLY

YEAR	SINGLE SUM	ANNUITY	SINGLE SUM	ANNUITY	SINGLE SUM	ANNUITY	SINGLE SUM	ANNUITY
	12%		12½%		13%		13½%	
1	.892857	.8929	.888889	.8889	.884956	.8850	.881057	.8811
2	.797194	1.6901	.790123	1.6790	.783147	1.6681	.776262	1.6573
3	.711780	2.4018	.702332	2.3813	.693050	2.3612	.683931	2.3413
4	.635518	3.0373	.624295	3.0056	.613319	2.9745	.602583	2.9438
5	.567427	3.6048	.554929	3.5606	.542760	3.5172	.530910	3.4747
6	.506631	4.1114	.493270	4.0538	.480319	3.9975	.467762	3.9425
7	.452349	4.5638	.438462	4.4923	.425061	4.4226	.412125	4.3546
8	.403883	4.9676	.389744	4.8820	.376160	4.7988	.363106	4.7177
9	.360610	5.3282	.346439	5.2285	.332885	5.1317	.319917	5.0377
10	.321973	5.6502	.307946	5.5364	.294588	5.4262	.281865	5.3195
11	.287476	5.9377	.273730	5.8102	.260698	5.6869	.248339	5.5679
12	.256675	6.1944	.243315	6.0535	.230706	5.9176	.218801	5.7867
13	.229174	6.4235	.216280	6.2698	.204165	6.1218	.192776	5.9794
14	.204620	6.6282	.192249	6.4620	.180677	6.3025	.169847	6.1493
15	.182696	6.8109	.170888	6.6329	.159891	6.4624	.149645	6.2989
16	.163122	6.9740	.151901	6.7848	.141496	6.6039	.131846	6.4308
17	.145644	7.1196	.135023	6.9198	.125218	6.7291	.116164	6.5469
18	.130040	7.2497	.120020	7.0398	.110812	6.8399	.102347	6.6493
19	.116107	7.3658	.106685	7.1465	.098064	6.9380	.090173	6.7395
20	.103667	7.4694	.094831	7.2414	.086782	7.0248	.079448	6.8189
21	.092560	7.5620	.084294	7.3256	.076798	7.1016	.069998	6.8889
22	.082643	7.6446	.074928	7.4006	.067963	7.1695	.061672	6.9506
23	.073788	7.7184	.066603	7.4672	.060144	7.2297	.054337	7.0049
24	.065883	7.7843	.059202	7.5264	.053225	7.2829	.047874	7.0528
25	.058823	7.8431	.052624	7.5790	.047102	7.3300	.042180	7.0950
26	.052521	7.8957	.046777	7.6258	.041683	7.3717	.037163	7.1321
27	.046894	7.9426	.041580	7.6674	.036888	7.4086	.032742	7.1649
28	.041869	7.9844	.036960	7.7043	.032644	7.4412	.028848	7.1937
29	.037383	8.0218	.032853	7.7372	.028889	7.4701	.025417	7.2191
30	.033378	8.0552	.029203	7.7664	.025565	7.4957	.022394	7.2415
	14%		14½%		15%		15½%	
1	.877193	.8772	.873362	.8734	.869565	.8696	.865801	.8658
2	.769468	1.6467	.762762	1.6361	.756144	1.6257	.749611	1.6154
3	.674972	2.3216	.666168	2.3023	.657516	2.2832	.649014	2.2644
4	.592080	2.9137	.581806	2.8841	.571753	2.8550	.561917	2.8263
5	.519369	3.4331	.508127	3.3922	.497177	3.3522	.486508	3.3129
6	.455587	3.8887	.443779	3.8360	.432328	3.7845	.421219	3.7341
7	.399637	4.2883	.387580	4.2236	.375937	4.1604	.364692	4.0988
8	.350559	4.6389	.338498	4.5621	.326902	4.4873	.315751	4.4145
9	.307508	4.9464	.295631	4.8577	.284262	4.7716	.273377	4.6879
10	.269744	5.2161	.258193	5.1159	.247185	5.0188	.236690	4.9246
11	.236617	5.4527	.225496	5.3414	.214943	5.2337	.204927	5.1295
12	.207559	5.6603	.196940	5.5383	.186907	5.4206	.177426	5.3069
13	.182069	5.8424	.172000	5.7103	.162528	5.5831	.153615	5.4605
14	.159710	6.0021	.150218	5.8606	.141329	5.7245	.133000	5.5935
15	.140096	6.1422	.131195	5.9918	.122894	5.8474	.115152	5.7087
16	.122892	6.2651	.114581	6.1063	.106865	5.9542	.099698	5.8084
17	.107800	6.3729	.100071	6.2064	.092926	6.0472	.086319	5.8947
18	.094561	6.4674	.087398	6.2938	.080805	6.1280	.074735	5.9695
19	.082948	6.5504	.076330	6.3701	.070265	6.1982	.064706	6.0342
20	.072762	6.6231	.066664	6.4368	.061100	6.2593	.056022	6.0902
21	.063826	6.6870	.058222	6.4950	.053131	6.3125	.048504	6.1387
22	.055988	6.7429	.050849	6.5459	.046201	6.3587	.041995	6.1807
23	.049112	6.7921	.044409	6.5903	.040174	6.3988	.036359	6.2170
24	.043081	6.8351	.038785	6.6291	.034934	6.4338	.031480	6.2485
25	.037790	6.8729	.033874	6.6629	.030378	6.4641	.027255	6.2758
26	.033149	6.9061	.029584	6.6925	.026415	6.4906	.023598	6.2994
27	.029078	6.9352	.025838	6.7184	.022970	6.5135	.020431	6.3198
28	.025507	6.9607	.022566	6.7409	.019974	6.5335	.017689	6.3375
29	.022375	6.9830	.019708	6.7606	.017369	6.5509	.015315	6.3528
30	.019627	7.0027	.017212	6.7778	.015103	6.5660	.013260	6.3661

A-334

PRESENT VALUE OF $1 COMPOUNDED ANNUALLY

YEAR	SINGLE SUM	ANNUITY	SINGLE SUM	ANNUITY	SINGLE SUM	ANNUITY	SINGLE SUM	ANNUITY
	16%		16½%		17%		17½%	
1	.862069	.8621	.858369	.8584	.854701	.8547	.851064	.8511
2	.743163	1.6052	.736798	1.5952	.730514	1.5852	.724310	1.5754
3	.640658	2.2459	.632444	2.2276	.624371	2.2096	.616434	2.1918
4	.552291	2.7982	.542871	2.7705	.533650	2.7432	.524624	2.7164
5	.476113	3.2743	.465983	3.2365	.456111	3.1993	.446489	3.1629
6	.410442	3.6847	.399986	3.6365	.389839	3.5892	.379991	3.5429
7	.353830	4.0386	.343335	3.9798	.333195	3.9224	.323396	3.8663
8	.305025	4.3436	.294708	4.2745	.284782	4.2072	.275231	4.1415
9	.262953	4.6065	.252969	4.5275	.243404	4.4506	.234239	4.3758
10	.226684	4.8332	.217140	4.7446	.208037	4.6586	.199352	4.5751
11	.195417	5.0286	.186387	4.9310	.177810	4.8364	.169662	4.7448
12	.168463	5.1971	.159989	5.0910	.151974	4.9884	.144393	4.8892
13	.145227	5.3423	.137329	5.2283	.129892	5.1183	.122888	5.0121
14	.125195	5.4675	.117879	5.3462	.111019	5.2293	.104585	5.1167
15	.107927	5.5755	.101184	5.4474	.094888	5.3242	.089009	5.2057
16	.093041	5.6685	.086853	5.5342	.081101	5.4053	.075752	5.2814
17	.080207	5.7487	.074552	5.6088	.069317	5.4746	.064470	5.3459
18	.069144	5.8178	.063993	5.6728	.059245	5.5339	.054868	5.4008
19	.059607	5.8775	.054930	5.7277	.050637	5.5845	.046696	5.4475
20	.051385	5.9288	.047150	5.7748	.043280	5.6278	.039741	5.4872
21	.044298	5.9731	.040472	5.8153	.036991	5.6648	.033822	5.5210
22	.038188	6.0113	.034740	5.8501	.031616	5.6964	.028785	5.5498
23	.032920	6.0442	.029820	5.8799	.027022	5.7234	.024498	5.5743
24	.028380	6.0726	.025596	5.9055	.023096	5.7465	.020849	5.5951
25	.024465	6.0971	.021971	5.9274	.019740	5.7662	.017744	5.6129
26	.021091	6.1182	.018859	5.9463	.016872	5.7831	.015101	5.6280
27	.018182	6.1364	.016188	5.9625	.014421	5.7975	.012852	5.6408
28	.015674	6.1520	.013895	5.9764	.012325	5.8099	.010938	5.6518
29	.013512	6.1656	.011927	5.9883	.010534	5.8204	.009309	5.6611
30	.011648	6.1772	.010238	5.9986	.009004	5.8294	.007923	5.6690
	18%		18½%		19%		19½%	
1	.847458	.8475	.843882	.8439	.840336	.8403	.836820	.8368
2	.718184	1.5656	.712137	1.5560	.706165	1.5465	.700268	1.5371
3	.608631	2.1743	.600959	2.1570	.593416	2.1399	.585998	2.1231
4	.515789	2.6901	.507139	2.6641	.498669	2.6386	.490375	2.6135
5	.437109	3.1272	.427965	3.0921	.419049	3.0576	.410356	3.0238
6	.370432	3.4976	.361152	3.4532	.352142	3.4098	.343394	3.3672
7	.313925	3.8115	.304770	3.7580	.295918	3.7057	.287359	3.6546
8	.266038	4.0776	.257189	4.0152	.248671	3.9544	.240468	3.8950
9	.225456	4.3030	.217038	4.2322	.208967	4.1633	.201228	4.0963
10	.191064	4.4941	.183154	4.4154	.175602	4.3389	.168392	4.2647
11	.161919	4.6560	.154560	4.5699	.147565	4.4865	.140914	4.4056
12	.137220	4.7932	.130431	4.7004	.124004	4.6105	.117919	4.5235
13	.116288	4.9095	.110068	4.8104	.104205	4.7147	.098677	4.6222
14	.098549	5.0081	.092884	4.9033	.087567	4.8023	.082575	4.7047
15	.083516	5.0916	.078384	4.9817	.073586	4.8759	.069101	4.7738
16	.070776	5.1624	.066146	5.0479	.061837	4.9377	.057825	4.8317
17	.059980	5.2223	.055820	5.1037	.051964	4.9897	.048389	4.8801
18	.050830	5.2732	.047105	5.1508	.043667	5.0333	.040493	4.9205
19	.043077	5.3162	.039751	5.1905	.036695	5.0700	.033885	4.9544
20	.036506	5.3527	.033545	5.2241	.030836	5.1009	.028356	4.9828
21	.030937	5.3837	.028308	5.2524	.025913	5.1268	.023729	5.0065
22	.026218	5.4099	.023889	5.2763	.021775	5.1486	.019857	5.0264
23	.022218	5.4321	.020159	5.2964	.018299	5.1668	.016616	5.0430
24	.018829	5.4509	.017012	5.3134	.015377	5.1822	.013905	5.0569
25	.015957	5.4669	.014356	5.3278	.012922	5.1951	.011636	5.0685
26	.013523	5.4804	.012115	5.3399	.010859	5.2060	.009737	5.0783
27	.011460	5.4919	.010224	5.3501	.009125	5.2151	.008148	5.0864
28	.009712	5.5016	.008628	5.3588	.007668	5.2228	.006819	5.0932
29	.008230	5.5098	.007281	5.3661	.006444	5.2292	.005706	5.0989
30	.006975	5.5168	.006144	5.3722	.005415	5.2347	.004775	5.1037

$1 COMPOUND INTEREST COMPARISON

8.0%

YR	365 DAY	360 DAY	WEEKLY	MONTHLY	QUARTER	SEMI-AN	ANNUAL
1	1.083278	1.083277	1.083220	1.083000	1.082152	1.081600	1.080000
2	1.173490	1.173490	1.173367	1.172888	1.171054	1.169859	1.166400
3	1.271216	1.271215	1.271015	1.270237	1.267258	1.265319	1.259712
4	1.377079	1.377079	1.376789	1.375666	1.371367	1.368569	1.360489
5	1.491759	1.491758	1.491366	1.489846	1.484027	1.480244	1.469328
6	1.615989	1.615988	1.615478	1.613502	1.605944	1.601032	1.586874
7	1.750565	1.750564	1.749919	1.747422	1.737876	1.731676	1.713824
8	1.896348	1.896346	1.895548	1.892457	1.880646	1.872981	1.850930
9	2.054271	2.054269	2.053297	2.049530	2.035146	2.025817	1.999005
10	2.225346	2.225343	2.224173	2.219640	2.202337	2.191123	2.158925

8.5%

YR	365 DAY	360 DAY	WEEKLY	MONTHLY	QUARTER	SEMI-AN	ANNUAL
1	1.088706	1.088706	1.088642	1.088391	1.087431	1.086806	1.085000
2	1.185281	1.185281	1.185140	1.184595	1.182506	1.181148	1.177225
3	1.290423	1.290423	1.290193	1.289302	1.285894	1.283679	1.277289
4	1.404892	1.404891	1.404558	1.403265	1.398321	1.395110	1.385859
5	1.529515	1.529514	1.529060	1.527301	1.520578	1.516214	1.503657
6	1.665192	1.665191	1.664598	1.662300	1.653524	1.647831	1.631468
7	1.812905	1.812904	1.812150	1.809232	1.798093	1.790873	1.770142
8	1.973721	1.973719	1.972782	1.969152	1.955302	1.946332	1.920604
9	2.148803	2.148800	2.147653	2.143207	2.126257	2.115286	2.083856
10	2.339415	2.339412	2.338024	2.332647	2.312157	2.298906	2.260983

9.0%

YR	365 DAY	360 DAY	WEEKLY	MONTHLY	QUARTER	SEMI-AN	ANNUAL
1	1.094162	1.094162	1.094089	1.093807	1.092727	1.092025	1.090000
2	1.197191	1.197190	1.197031	1.196414	1.194052	1.192519	1.188100
3	1.309921	1.309920	1.309659	1.308645	1.304773	1.302260	1.295029
4	1.433266	1.433265	1.432883	1.431405	1.425761	1.422101	1.411582
5	1.568225	1.568224	1.567702	1.565681	1.557967	1.552969	1.538624
6	1.715893	1.715891	1.715206	1.712553	1.702433	1.695881	1.677100
7	1.877465	1.877463	1.876588	1.873202	1.860295	1.851945	1.828039
8	2.054251	2.054248	2.053155	2.048921	2.032794	2.022370	1.992563
9	2.247684	2.247680	2.246335	2.241124	2.221289	2.208479	2.171893
10	2.459330	2.459326	2.457690	2.451357	2.427262	2.411714	2.367364

9.5%

YR	365 DAY	360 DAY	WEEKLY	MONTHLY	QUARTER	SEMI-AN	ANNUAL
1	1.099645	1.099645	1.099564	1.099248	1.098040	1.097256	1.095000
2	1.209220	1.209219	1.209040	1.208345	1.205692	1.203971	1.199025
3	1.329713	1.329712	1.329416	1.328271	1.323898	1.321065	1.312932
4	1.462212	1.462211	1.461778	1.460098	1.453693	1.449547	1.437661
5	1.607915	1.607913	1.607317	1.605009	1.596214	1.590524	1.574239
6	1.768136	1.768134	1.767348	1.764303	1.752706	1.745213	1.723791
7	1.944322	1.944320	1.943311	1.939406	1.924542	1.914946	1.887552
8	2.138065	2.138062	2.136794	2.131887	2.113224	2.101186	2.066869
9	2.351113	2.351109	2.349541	2.343472	2.320405	2.305540	2.263222
10	2.585390	2.585386	2.583470	2.576055	2.547898	2.529768	2.478228

$1 COMPOUND INTEREST COMPARISON

10.0%

YR	365 DAY	360 DAY	WEEKLY	MONTHLY	QUARTER	SEMI-AN	ANNUAL
1	1.105156	1.105156	1.105065	1.104713	1.103370	1.102500	1.100000
2	1.221369	1.221369	1.221168	1.220391	1.217426	1.215506	1.210000
3	1.349803	1.349803	1.349470	1.348182	1.343272	1.340096	1.331000
4	1.491743	1.491742	1.491252	1.489354	1.482126	1.477455	1.464100
5	1.648608	1.648607	1.647930	1.645309	1.635334	1.628895	1.610510
6	1.821969	1.821967	1.821069	1.817594	1.804380	1.795856	1.771561
7	2.013560	2.013557	2.012399	2.007920	1.990899	1.979932	1.948717
8	2.225297	2.225294	2.223832	2.218176	2.196699	2.182875	2.143589
9	2.459300	2.459296	2.457478	2.450448	2.423773	2.406619	2.357948
10	2.717910	2.717904	2.715673	2.707041	2.674319	2.653298	2.593742

10.5%

YR	365 DAY	360 DAY	WEEKLY	MONTHLY	QUARTER	SEMI-AN	ANNUAL
1	1.110694	1.110694	1.110593	1.110203	1.108718	1.107756	1.105000
2	1.233641	1.233640	1.233417	1.232552	1.229255	1.227124	1.221025
3	1.370197	1.370196	1.369824	1.368383	1.362897	1.359354	1.349233
4	1.521870	1.521868	1.521317	1.519184	1.511069	1.505833	1.490902
5	1.690331	1.690329	1.689564	1.686603	1.675349	1.668096	1.647447
6	1.877440	1.877438	1.876418	1.872472	1.857489	1.847844	1.820429
7	2.085262	2.085259	2.083937	2.078825	2.059431	2.046961	2.011574
8	2.316087	2.316083	2.314406	2.307919	2.283328	2.267533	2.222789
9	2.572464	2.572459	2.570363	2.562260	2.531567	2.511874	2.456182
10	2.857220	2.857214	2.854627	2.844630	2.806794	2.782544	2.714081

11.0%

YR	365 DAY	360 DAY	WEEKLY	MONTHLY	QUARTER	SEMI-AN	ANNUAL
1	1.116260	1.116259	1.116148	1.115719	1.114083	1.113025	1.110000
2	1.246035	1.246035	1.245787	1.244829	1.241180	1.238825	1.232100
3	1.390899	1.390898	1.390483	1.388879	1.382777	1.378843	1.367631
4	1.552604	1.552603	1.551986	1.549598	1.540528	1.534687	1.518070
5	1.733109	1.733107	1.732246	1.728916	1.716276	1.708144	1.685058
6	1.934600	1.934597	1.933444	1.928984	1.912073	1.901207	1.870415
7	2.159516	2.159512	2.158010	2.152204	2.130207	2.116091	2.076160
8	2.410592	2.410576	2.408660	2.401254	2.373227	2.355263	2.304538
9	2.690833	2.690828	2.688422	2.679124	2.643971	2.621466	2.558037
10	3.003668	3.003661	3.000678	2.989150	2.945602	2.917757	2.839421

11.5%

YR	365 DAY	360 DAY	WEEKLY	MONTHLY	QUARTER	SEMI-AN	ANNUAL
1	1.121853	1.121853	1.121731	1.121259	1.119465	1.118306	1.115000
2	1.258554	1.258554	1.258280	1.257222	1.253201	1.250609	1.243225
3	1.411913	1.411912	1.411452	1.409672	1.402914	1.398564	1.386196
4	1.583959	1.583958	1.583270	1.580608	1.570513	1.564023	1.545608
5	1.776970	1.776967	1.776003	1.772272	1.758134	1.749056	1.723353
6	1.993499	1.993496	1.992197	1.987176	1.968169	1.955980	1.921539
7	2.236413	2.236409	2.234709	2.228140	2.203295	2.187385	2.142516
8	2.508927	2.508922	2.506743	2.498323	2.466511	2.446167	2.388905
9	2.814647	2.814641	2.811891	2.801268	2.761172	2.735563	2.663629
10	3.157621	3.157613	3.154185	3.140948	3.091035	3.059198	2.969947

$1 COMPOUND INTEREST COMPARISON

12.0%

YR	365 DAY	360 DAY	WEEKLY	MONTHLY	QUARTER	SEMI-AN	ANNUAL
1	1.127475	1.127474	1.127341	1.126825	1.124864	1.123600	1.120000
2	1.271199	1.271198	1.270898	1.269735	1.265319	1.262477	1.254400
3	1.433245	1.433243	1.432735	1.430769	1.423312	1.418519	1.404928
4	1.615947	1.615945	1.615181	1.612226	1.601032	1.593848	1.573519
5	1.821939	1.821937	1.820860	1.816697	1.800944	1.790848	1.762342
6	2.054190	2.054187	2.052730	2.047099	2.025817	2.012196	1.973823
7	2.316047	2.316043	2.314126	2.306723	2.278768	2.260904	2.210681
8	2.611284	2.611279	2.608810	2.599273	2.563304	2.540352	2.475963
9	2.944157	2.944150	2.941018	2.928926	2.883369	2.854339	2.773079
10	3.319462	3.319453	3.315530	3.300387	3.243398	3.207135	3.105848

12.5%

YR	365 DAY	360 DAY	WEEKLY	MONTHLY	QUARTER	SEMI-AN	ANNUAL
1	1.133124	1.133124	1.132978	1.132416	1.130281	1.128906	1.125000
2	1.283970	1.283970	1.283640	1.282366	1.277534	1.274429	1.265625
3	1.454898	1.454897	1.454337	1.452172	1.443972	1.438711	1.423828
4	1.648580	1.648578	1.647732	1.644463	1.632094	1.624170	1.601807
5	1.868046	1.868043	1.866845	1.862216	1.844724	1.833536	1.802032
6	2.116728	2.116724	2.115096	2.108803	2.085056	2.069890	2.027287
7	2.398516	2.398511	2.396358	2.388043	2.356699	2.336712	2.280697
8	2.717816	2.717810	2.715022	2.704258	2.663731	2.637928	2.565785
9	3.079624	3.079615	3.076061	3.062345	3.010764	2.977974	2.886508
10	3.489596	3.489586	3.485111	3.467849	3.403008	3.361853	3.247321

13.0%

YR	365 DAY	360 DAY	WEEKLY	MONTHLY	QUARTER	SEMI-AN	ANNUAL
1	1.138802	1.138802	1.138644	1.138032	1.135715	1.134225	1.130000
2	1.296870	1.296869	1.296509	1.295118	1.289848	1.286466	1.276900
3	1.476878	1.476877	1.476262	1.473886	1.464899	1.459142	1.442897
4	1.681872	1.681870	1.680937	1.677330	1.663708	1.654996	1.630474
5	1.915319	1.915316	1.913988	1.908857	1.889497	1.877137	1.842435
6	2.181169	2.181165	2.179350	2.172341	2.145930	2.129096	2.081952
7	2.483920	2.483914	2.481503	2.472194	2.437164	2.414874	2.352605
8	2.828693	2.828686	2.825548	2.813437	2.767923	2.739011	2.658444
9	3.221321	3.221312	3.217292	3.201783	3.143571	3.106654	3.004042
10	3.668447	3.668436	3.663349	3.643733	3.570199	3.523645	3.394567

13.5%

YR	365 DAY	360 DAY	WEEKLY	MONTHLY	QUARTER	SEMI-AN	ANNUAL
1	1.144508	1.144508	1.144337	1.143674	1.141166	1.139556	1.135000
2	1.309899	1.309898	1.309506	1.307991	1.302260	1.298588	1.288225
3	1.499190	1.499189	1.498516	1.495916	1.486095	1.479815	1.462135
4	1.715836	1.715833	1.714807	1.710841	1.695881	1.686332	1.659524
5	1.963788	1.963784	1.962316	1.956645	1.935282	1.921670	1.883559
6	2.247571	2.247567	2.245550	2.237765	2.208479	2.189851	2.137840
7	2.572364	2.572358	2.569665	2.559275	2.520241	2.495459	2.426448
8	2.944092	2.944083	2.940561	2.926977	2.876014	2.843715	2.754019
9	3.369537	3.369527	3.364992	3.347509	3.282010	3.240574	3.125811
10	3.856463	3.856450	3.850683	3.828460	3.745318	3.692816	3.547796

$1 COMPOUND INTEREST COMPARIS

14.0%

YR	365 DAY	360 DAY	WEEKLY	MONTHLY	QUARTER	SEMI-AN	ANNUAL
1	1.150243	1.150242	1.150057	1.149342	1.146635	1.144900	1.140000
2	1.323059	1.323058	1.322632	1.320987	1.314772	1.310796	1.299600
3	1.521839	1.521837	1.521103	1.518266	1.507563	1.500730	1.481544
4	1.750485	1.750482	1.749356	1.745007	1.728625	1.718186	1.688960
5	2.013482	2.013479	2.011859	2.005610	1.982102	1.967151	1.925415
6	2.315994	2.315989	2.313754	2.305132	2.272747	2.252192	2.194973
7	2.663956	2.663949	2.660950	2.649385	2.606011	2.578534	2.502269
8	3.064196	3.064187	3.060245	3.045049	2.988143	2.952164	2.852586
9	3.524570	3.524558	3.519458	3.499803	3.426310	3.379932	3.251949
10	4.054112	4.054096	4.047578	4.022471	3.928727	3.869684	3.707221

14.5%

YR	365 DAY	360 DAY	WEEKLY	MONTHLY	QUARTER	SEMI-AN	ANNUAL
1	1.156006	1.156006	1.155806	1.155035	1.152121	1.150256	1.145000
2	1.336351	1.336349	1.335888	1.334107	1.327383	1.323089	1.311025
3	1.544830	1.544828	1.544028	1.540940	1.529307	1.521892	1.501124
4	1.785833	1.785830	1.784597	1.779841	1.761947	1.750566	1.718787
5	2.064434	2.064430	2.062649	2.055779	2.029976	2.013599	1.968011
6	2.386499	2.386493	2.384023	2.374497	2.338779	2.316155	2.253372
7	2.758807	2.758800	2.755468	2.742628	2.694557	2.664172	2.580111
8	3.189199	3.189188	3.184788	3.167833	3.104456	3.064480	2.954227
9	3.686734	3.686720	3.680998	3.658959	3.576709	3.524937	3.382590
10	4.261887	4.261870	4.254521	4.226227	4.120803	4.054581	3.873066

15.0%

YR	365 DAY	360 DAY	WEEKLY	MONTHLY	QUARTER	SEMI-AN	ANNUAL
1	1.161798	1.161798	1.161583	1.160755	1.157625	1.155625	1.150000
2	1.349776	1.349774	1.349276	1.347351	1.340096	1.335469	1.322500
3	1.568167	1.568165	1.567297	1.563944	1.551328	1.543302	1.520875
4	1.821894	1.821891	1.820546	1.815355	1.795856	1.783478	1.749006
5	2.116674	2.116669	2.114716	2.107181	2.078928	2.061032	2.011357
6	2.459148	2.459142	2.456419	2.445920	2.406619	2.381780	2.313061
7	2.857035	2.857026	2.853335	2.839113	2.785963	2.752444	2.660020
8	3.319299	3.319282	3.314387	3.295513	3.225100	3.180793	3.059023
9	3.856356	3.856341	3.849936	3.825282	3.733456	3.675804	3.517876
10	4.480308	4.480289	4.472022	4.440213	4.321942	4.247851	4.045558

15.5%

YR	365 DAY	360 DAY	WEEKLY	MONTHLY	QUARTER	SEMI-AN	ANNUAL
1	1.167620	1.167619	1.167389	1.166500	1.163146	1.161006	1.155000
2	1.363335	1.363334	1.362797	1.360721	1.352909	1.347936	1.334025
3	1.591857	1.591855	1.590913	1.587281	1.573631	1.564962	1.540799
4	1.858683	1.858680	1.857215	1.851563	1.830363	1.816930	1.779623
5	2.170235	2.170230	2.168091	2.159847	2.128980	2.109467	2.055464
6	2.534009	2.534002	2.531006	2.519461	2.476315	2.449105	2.374061
7	2.958758	2.958749	2.954668	2.938950	2.880317	2.843426	2.742041
8	3.454704	3.454691	3.449246	3.428284	3.350230	3.301235	3.167057
9	4.033780	4.033763	4.026611	3.999093	3.896807	3.832755	3.657951
10	4.709920	4.709899	4.700620	4.664940	4.532557	4.449852	4.224933

16.0%

	360 DAY	WEEKLY	MONTHLY	QUARTER	SEMI-AN	ANNUAL
	1.173469	1.173223	1.172271	1.168685	1.166400	1.160000
	1.377030	1.376451	1.374219	1.365825	1.360489	1.345600
	1.615902	1.614884	1.610957	1.596219	1.586874	1.560896
	1.896211	1.894618	1.888477	1.865477	1.850930	1.810639
	2.225145	2.222809	2.213807	2.180155	2.158925	2.100342
6	2.611147	2.611140	2.607850	2.595181	2.547915	2.436396
7	3.064102	3.064092	3.059589	3.042255	2.977710	2.826290
8	3.595631	3.595617	3.589579	3.566347	3.480005	3.278415
9	4.219364	4.219346	4.211375	4.180724	4.067030	3.802961
10	4.951296	4.951272	4.940880	4.900941	4.753077	4.411435

16.5%

YR	365 DAY	360 DAY	WEEKLY	MONTHLY	QUARTER	SEMI-AN	ANNUAL
1	1.179349	1.179349	1.179085	1.178068	1.174241	1.171806	1.165000
2	1.390864	1.390863	1.390242	1.387845	1.378843	1.373130	1.357225
3	1.640315	1.640312	1.639213	1.634975	1.619094	1.609042	1.581167
4	1.934504	1.934500	1.932772	1.926112	1.901207	1.885486	1.842060
5	2.281455	2.281450	2.278902	2.269092	2.232476	2.209424	2.146000
6	2.690632	2.690624	2.687020	2.673145	2.621466	2.589017	2.500089
7	3.173195	3.173184	3.168225	3.149146	3.078234	3.033826	2.912604
8	3.742305	3.742289	3.735606	3.709909	3.614590	3.555056	3.393184
9	4.413484	4.413464	4.404598	4.370526	4.244401	4.165837	3.953059
10	5.205039	5.205012	5.193396	5.148777	4.983951	4.881554	4.605314

17.0%

YR	365 DAY	360 DAY	WEEKLY	MONTHLY	QUARTER	SEMI-AN	ANNUAL
1	1.185258	1.185257	1.184976	1.183892	1.179815	1.177225	1.170000
2	1.404836	1.404835	1.404169	1.401600	1.391964	1.385859	1.368900
3	1.665093	1.665091	1.663907	1.659342	1.642261	1.631468	1.601613
4	1.973565	1.973561	1.971690	1.964482	1.937564	1.920604	1.873887
5	2.339184	2.339177	2.336405	2.325733	2.285968	2.260983	2.192448
6	2.772536	2.772527	2.768585	2.753417	2.697020	2.661686	2.565164
7	3.286171	3.286158	3.280707	3.259747	3.181985	3.133404	3.001242
8	3.894960	3.894943	3.887560	3.859188	3.754155	3.688721	3.511453
9	4.616532	4.616509	4.606666	4.568860	4.429209	4.342455	4.108400
10	5.471781	5.471751	5.458790	5.409036	5.225649	5.112046	4.806828

17.5%

YR	365 DAY	360 DAY	WEEKLY	MONTHLY	QUARTER	SEMI-AN	ANNUAL
1	1.191196	1.191196	1.190896	1.189742	1.185407	1.182656	1.175000
2	1.418949	1.418947	1.418234	1.415485	1.405189	1.398676	1.380625
3	1.690246	1.690243	1.688969	1.684062	1.665721	1.654153	1.622234
4	2.013415	2.013410	2.011387	2.003599	1.974557	1.956294	1.906125
5	2.398372	2.398365	2.395354	2.383765	2.340653	2.313623	2.239697
6	2.856932	2.856922	2.852618	2.836065	2.774627	2.736221	2.631644
7	3.403167	3.403153	3.397172	3.374184	3.289061	3.236009	3.092182
8	4.053840	4.053821	4.045679	4.014408	3.898876	3.827086	3.633314
9	4.828919	4.828893	4.817985	4.776108	4.621754	4.526127	4.269144
10	5.752190	5.752156	5.737720	5.682335	5.478659	5.352853	5.016244

$1 COMPOUND INTEREST COMPARISON

18.0%

YR	365 DAY	360 DAY	WEEKLY	MONTHLY	QUARTER	SEMI-AN	ANNUAL
1	1.197164	1.197164	1.196845	1.195618	1.191016	1.188100	1.180000
2	1.433202	1.433200	1.432439	1.429503	1.418519	1.411582	1.392400
3	1.715778	1.715775	1.714407	1.709140	1.689479	1.677100	1.643032
4	2.054069	2.054064	2.051881	2.043478	2.012196	1.992563	1.938778
5	2.459058	2.459050	2.455784	2.443220	2.396558	2.367364	2.287758
6	2.943896	2.943885	2.939193	2.921158	2.854339	2.812665	2.699554
7	3.524327	3.524312	3.517759	3.492590	3.399564	3.341727	3.185474
8	4.219198	4.219177	4.210214	4.175804	4.048935	3.970306	3.758859
9	5.051073	5.051045	5.038975	4.992667	4.822346	4.717120	4.435454
10	6.046964	6.046927	6.030873	5.969323	5.743491	5.604411	5.233836

18.5%

YR	365 DAY	360 DAY	WEEKLY	MONTHLY	QUARTER	SEMI-AN	ANNUAL
1	1.203162	1.203161	1.202823	1.201521	1.196643	1.193556	1.185000
2	1.447599	1.447597	1.446784	1.443653	1.431954	1.424577	1.404225
3	1.741696	1.741693	1.740226	1.734580	1.713538	1.700312	1.664007
4	2.095543	2.095537	2.093185	2.084135	2.050492	2.029418	1.971848
5	2.521277	2.521269	2.517732	2.504132	2.453707	2.422225	2.336640
6	3.033505	3.033493	3.028387	3.008768	2.936211	2.891062	2.768918
7	3.649798	3.649782	3.642615	3.615099	3.513596	3.450645	3.281168
8	4.391299	4.391276	4.381423	4.343618	4.204519	4.118539	3.888184
9	5.283444	5.283413	5.270078	5.218949	5.031308	4.915707	4.607498
10	6.356840	6.356798	6.338974	6.270678	6.020679	5.867173	5.459885

19.0%

YR	365 DAY	360 DAY	WEEKLY	MONTHLY	QUARTER	SEMI-AN	ANNUAL
1	1.209190	1.209189	1.208831	1.207451	1.202287	1.199025	1.190000
2	1.462140	1.462138	1.461272	1.457938	1.445495	1.437661	1.416100
3	1.768005	1.768001	1.766431	1.760389	1.737900	1.723791	1.685159
4	2.137853	2.137848	2.135317	2.125583	2.089456	2.066869	2.005339
5	2.585071	2.585062	2.581237	2.566537	2.512126	2.478228	2.386354
6	3.125841	3.125828	3.120279	3.098968	3.020297	2.971457	2.839761
7	3.779735	3.779717	3.771890	3.741852	3.631265	3.562851	3.379315
8	4.570417	4.570392	4.559577	4.518103	4.365825	4.271948	4.021385
9	5.526502	5.526468	5.511758	5.455388	5.248976	5.122172	4.785449
10	6.682590	6.682544	6.662783	6.587114	6.310777	6.141612	5.694684

19.5%

YR	365 DAY	360 DAY	WEEKLY	MONTHLY	QUARTER	SEMI-AN	ANNUAL
1	1.215248	1.215247	1.214868	1.213408	1.207950	1.204506	1.195000
2	1.476827	1.476825	1.475904	1.472358	1.459142	1.450835	1.428025
3	1.794711	1.794707	1.793028	1.786570	1.762570	1.747540	1.706490
4	2.181018	2.181012	2.178292	2.167838	2.129096	2.104923	2.039255
5	2.650477	2.650467	2.646337	2.630471	2.571841	2.535393	2.436910
6	3.220986	3.220972	3.214950	3.191833	3.106654	3.053897	2.912108
7	3.914296	3.914276	3.905739	3.872995	3.752682	3.678438	3.479969
8	4.756839	4.756812	4.744957	4.699521	4.533051	4.430701	4.158563
9	5.780738	5.780700	5.764495	5.702435	5.475697	5.336807	4.969482
10	7.025029	7.024978	7.003100	6.919378	6.614366	6.428218	5.938531

FEDERAL DISCOUNT RATE

The following is a list of rates of interest on advances to, and discounts for, member banks and other depository institutions under Sections 13 and 13a of the Federal Reserve Act. Each rate (also referred to as the "discount rate") was in effect until the next date indicated.

	Effective Date		Rate (% per annum)
1979	July	20	10
	August	20	10½
	September	19	11
	October	8	12
1980	February	15	13
	May	29	12
	June	13	11
	July	28	10
	September	26	11
	November	17	12
	December	5	13
1981	May	5	14
	November	2	13
	December	4	12
1982	July	20	11½
	August	2	11
	August	16	10½
	August	27	10
	October	11	9½
	November	22	9
	December	14	8½
1984	April	13	9
	November	21	8½
	December	24	8
1985	May	21	7½
1986	March	7	7
	April	21	6½
	July	11	6
	August	21	5½
1987	September	9	6
1988	August	9	6½

Notes:

YEAR	Annual %	Cum. %	Annual %	Cum. %	Annual %	Cum. %	Annual %	Cum. %
	8% Int.		8¼% Int.		8½% Int.		8¾% Int.	
1	30.714	30.714	30.633	30.633	30.553	30.553	30.473	30.473
2	33.263	63.976	33.258	63.892	33.254	63.807	33.249	63.722
3	36.024	100.000	36.108	100.000	36.193	100.000	36.278	100.000
	9% Int.		9¼% Int.		9½% Int.		9¾% Int.	
1	30.393	30.393	30.313	30.313	30.233	30.233	30.154	30.154
2	33.244	63.637	33.239	63.552	33.234	63.468	33.229	63.383
3	36.363	100.000	36.448	100.000	36.532	100.000	36.617	100.000
	10% Int.		10¼% Int.		10½% Int.		10¾% Int.	
1	30.074	30.074	29.995	29.995	29.915	29.915	29.836	29.836
2	33.223	63.298	33.218	63.213	33.212	63.128	33.206	63.043
3	36.702	100.000	36.787	100.000	36.872	100.000	36.957	100.000
	11% Int.		11¼% Int.		11½% Int.		11¾% Int.	
1	29.757	29.757	29.678	29.678	29.599	29.599	29.520	29.520
2	33.201	62.958	33.194	62.872	33.188	62.787	33.182	62.702
3	37.042	100.000	37.128	100.000	37.213	100.000	37.298	100.000

EXAMPLES *ON PAGES A-382 TO A-397*

3

IN PERCENT OF ORIGINAL LOAN AMOUNT
FOR FIRST 15 YEARS

3

YEAR	Annual %	Cum. %	Annual %	Cum. %	Annual %	Cum. %	Annual %	Cum. %
	12% Int.		12¼% Int.		12½% Int.		12¾% Int.	
1	29.442	29.442	29.363	29.363	29.284	29.284	29.206	29.206
2	33.175	62.617	33.169	62.532	33.162	62.447	33.155	62.361
3	37.383	100.000	37.468	100.000	37.553	100.000	37.639	100.000
	13% Int.		13¼% Int.		13½% Int.		13¾% Int.	
1	29.128	29.128	29.050	29.050	28.972	28.972	28.894	28.894
2	33.148	62.276	33.141	62.191	33.134	62.106	33.127	62.020
3	37.724	100.000	37.809	100.000	37.894	100.000	37.980	100.000
	14% Int.		14¼% Int.		14½% Int.		14¾% Int.	
1	28.816	28.816	28.738	28.738	28.660	28.660	28.583	28.583
2	33.119	61.935	33.111	61.849	33.104	61.764	33.096	61.679
3	38.065	100.000	38.151	100.000	38.236	100.000	38.321	100.000
	15% Int.		15¼% Int.		15½% Int.		15¾% Int.	
1	28.505	28.505	28.428	28.428	28.351	28.351	28.274	28.274
2	33.086	61.593	33.080	61.508	33.071	61.422	33.063	61.337
3	38.407	100.000	38.492	100.000	38.578	100.000	38.663	100.000

EXAMPLES *ON PAGES A-382 TO A-397*

YEAR	Annual %	Cum. %	Annual %	Cum. %	Annual %	Cum. %	Annual %	Cum. %
	8% Int.		8¼% Int.		8½% Int.		8¾% Int.	
1	22.094	22.094	22.006	22.006	21.919	21.919	21.832	21.832
2	23.928	46.022	23.892	45.898	23.856	45.775	23.820	45.652
3	25.914	71.935	25.939	71.838	25.965	71.740	25.990	71.642
4	28.065	100.000	28.162	100.000	28.260	100.000	28.358	100.000

	Annual %	Cum. %	Annual %	Cum. %	Annual %	Cum. %	Annual %	Cum. %
	9% Int.		9¼% Int.		9½% Int.		9¾% Int.	
1	21.744	21.744	21.658	21.658	21.571	21.571	21.484	21.484
2	23.784	45.529	23.748	45.406	23.712	45.283	23.675	45.160
3	26.015	71.544	26.040	71.446	26.065	71.348	26.090	71.250
4	28.456	100.000	28.554	100.000	28.652	100.000	28.750	100.000

	Annual %	Cum. %	Annual %	Cum. %	Annual %	Cum. %	Annual %	Cum. %
	10% Int.		10¼% Int.		10½% Int.		10¾% Int.	
1	21.398	21.398	21.312	21.312	21.226	21.226	21.141	21.141
2	23.639	45.037	23.602	44.914	23.566	44.792	23.529	44.669
3	26.114	71.151	26.138	71.053	26.163	70.954	26.186	70.856
4	28.849	100.000	28.947	100.000	29.046	100.000	29.144	100.000

	Annual %	Cum. %	Annual %	Cum. %	Annual %	Cum. %	Annual %	Cum. %
	11% Int.		11¼% Int.		11½% Int.		11¾% Int.	
1	21.055	21.055	20.970	20.970	20.885	20.885	20.800	20.800
2	23.492	44.547	23.455	44.424	23.417	44.302	23.380	44.180
3	26.210	70.757	26.234	70.658	26.257	70.559	26.280	70.460
4	29.243	100.000	29.342	100.000	29.441	100.000	29.540	100.000

EXAMPLES *ON PAGES A-382 TO A-397*

YEAR	Annual %	Cum. %	Annual %	Cum. %	Annual %	Cum. %	Annual %	Cum. %
	12% Int.		12¼% Int.		12½% Int.		12¾% Int.	
1	20.715	20.715	20.631	20.631	20.547	20.547	20.463	20.463
2	23.343	44.058	23.305	43.936	23.267	43.814	23.230	43.692
3	26.303	70.361	26.326	70.262	26.348	70.163	26.371	70.063
4	29.639	100.000	29.738	100.000	29.837	100.000	29.937	100.000

	13% Int.		13¼% Int.		13½% Int.		13¾% Int.	
1	20.379	20.379	20.295	20.295	20.212	20.212	20.129	20.129
2	23.192	43.571	23.154	43.449	23.116	43.328	23.078	43.206
3	26.393	69.964	26.415	69.864	26.437	69.765	26.459	69.665
4	30.036	100.000	30.136	100.000	30.235	100.000	30.335	100.000

	14% Int.		14¼% Int.		14½% Int.		14¾% Int.	
1	20.046	20.046	19.963	19.963	19.880	19.880	19.798	19.798
2	23.039	43.085	23.001	42.964	22.963	42.843	22.924	42.722
3	26.480	69.565	26.501	69.465	26.523	69.366	26.543	69.266
4	30.435	100.000	30.535	100.000	30.634	100.000	30.734	100.000

	15% Int.		15¼% Int.		15½% Int.		15¾% Int.	
1	19.716	19.716	19.634	19.634	19.552	19.552	19.471	19.471
2	22.885	42.601	22.847	42.481	22.808	42.360	22.769	42.239
3	26.564	69.165	26.585	69.065	26.605	68.965	26.625	68.865
4	30.835	100.000	30.935	100.000	31.035	100.000	31.135	100.000

EXAMPLES *ON PAGES A-382 TO A-397*

YEAR	Annual %	Cum. %	Annual %	Cum. %	Annual %	Cum. %	Annual %	Cum. %
	8% Int.		8¼% Int.		8½% Int.		8¾% Int.	
1	16.944	16.944	16.853	16.853	16.763	16.763	16.673	16.673
2	18.350	35.294	18.298	35.151	18.245	35.008	18.192	34.864
3	19.873	55.168	19.865	55.016	19.857	54.865	19.849	54.713
4	21.523	76.691	21.568	76.584	21.612	76.477	21.657	76.370
5	23.309	100.000	23.416	100.000	23.523	100.000	23.630	100.000

	9% Int.		9¼% Int.		9½% Int.		9¾% Int.	
1	16.583	16.583	16.494	16.494	16.404	16.404	16.315	16.315
2	18.139	34.722	18.086	34.579	18.032	34.437	17.979	34.295
3	19.840	54.562	19.831	54.410	19.822	54.259	19.813	54.107
4	21.701	76.263	21.745	76.156	21.789	76.048	21.833	75.940
5	23.737	100.000	23.844	100.000	23.952	100.000	24.060	100.000

	10% Int.		10¼% Int.		10½% Int.		10¾% Int.	
1	16.227	16.227	16.139	16.139	16.051	16.051	15.963	15.963
2	17.926	34.153	17.873	34.011	17.819	33.870	17.766	33.729
3	19.803	53.956	19.793	53.804	19.783	53.653	19.773	53.502
4	21.877	75.833	21.920	75.724	21.963	75.616	22.006	75.508
5	24.167	100.000	24.276	100.000	24.384	100.000	24.492	100.000

	11% Int.		11¼% Int.		11½% Int.		11¾% Int.	
1	15.875	15.875	15.788	15.788	15.702	15.702	15.615	15.615
2	17.713	33.588	17.659	33.448	17.606	33.307	17.552	33.167
3	19.762	53.350	19.751	53.199	19.740	53.048	19.729	52.896
4	22.049	75.399	22.092	75.291	22.134	75.182	22.176	75.073
5	24.601	100.000	24.709	100.000	24.818	100.000	24.927	100.000

EXAMPLES *ON PAGES A-382 TO A-397*

YEAR	Annual %	Cum. %	Annual %	Cum. %	Annual %	Cum. %	Annual %	Cum. %
	12% Int.		12¼% Int.		12½% Int.		12¾% Int.	
1	15.529	15.529	15.443	15.443	15.358	15.358	15.272	15.272
2	17.498	33.028	17.445	32.888	17.391	32.749	17.338	32.610
3	19.718	52.745	19.706	52.594	19.694	52.443	19.682	52.292
4	22.218	74.964	22.260	74.854	22.302	74.745	22.343	74.635
5	25.036	100.000	25.146	100.000	25.255	100.000	25.365	100.000
	13% Int.		13¼% Int.		13½% Int.		13¾% Int.	
1	15.187	15.187	15.103	15.103	15.019	15.019	14.935	14.935
2	17.284	32.471	17.230	32.333	17.176	32.195	17.123	32.057
3	19.670	52.141	19.657	51.990	19.644	51.839	19.631	51.688
4	22.385	74.526	22.426	74.416	22.467	74.306	22.507	74.195
5	25.474	100.000	25.584	100.000	25.694	100.000	25.805	100.000
	14% Int.		14¼% Int.		14½% Int.		14¾% Int.	
1	14.851	14.851	14.768	14.768	14.684	14.684	14.602	14.602
2	17.069	31.920	17.015	31.782	16.961	31.646	16.907	31.509
3	19.618	51.537	19.604	51.387	19.591	51.236	19.577	51.086
4	22.548	74.085	22.588	73.975	22.628	73.864	22.668	73.753
5	25.915	100.000	26.025	100.000	26.136	100.000	26.247	100.000
	15% Int.		15¼% Int.		15½% Int.		15¾% Int.	
1	14.519	14.519	14.437	14.437	14.355	14.355	14.274	14.274
2	16.853	31.373	16.799	31.237	16.745	31.101	16.692	30.965
3	19.563	50.935	19.548	50.785	19.534	50.634	19.519	50.484
4	22.707	73.642	22.747	73.531	22.786	73.420	22.825	73.309
5	26.358	100.000	26.469	100.000	26.580	100.000	26.691	100.000

EXAMPLES *ON PAGES A-382 TO A-397*

YEAR	Annual %	Cum. %	Annual %	Cum. %	Annual %	Cum. %	Annual %	Cum. %
	8% Int.		8¼% Int.		8½% Int.		8¾% Int.	
1	13.529	13.529	13.437	13.437	13.346	13.346	13.255	13.255
2	14.652	28.180	14.589	28.026	14.526	27.872	14.463	27.718
3	15.868	44.048	15.839	43.865	15.810	43.681	15.780	43.498
4	17.185	61.233	17.196	61.061	17.207	60.889	17.218	60.716
5	18.611	79.844	18.670	79.730	18.728	79.617	18.786	79.502
6	20.156	100.000	20.270	100.000	20.383	100.000	20.498	100.000

	Annual %	Cum. %	Annual %	Cum. %	Annual %	Cum. %	Annual %	Cum. %
	9% Int.		9¼% Int.		9½% Int.		9¾% Int.	
1	13.165	13.165	13.075	13.075	12.985	12.985	12.896	12.896
2	14.400	27.565	14.337	27.412	14.274	27.260	14.211	27.108
3	15.751	43.315	15.721	43.133	15.691	42.950	15.661	42.768
4	17.228	60.544	17.238	60.371	17.248	60.198	17.258	60.026
5	18.844	79.388	18.902	79.273	18.960	79.158	19.017	79.043
6	20.612	100.000	20.727	100.000	20.842	100.000	20.957	100.000

	Annual %	Cum. %	Annual %	Cum. %	Annual %	Cum. %	Annual %	Cum. %
	10% Int.		10¼% Int.		10½% Int.		10¾% Int.	
1	12.807	12.807	12.719	12.719	12.631	12.631	12.544	12.544
2	14.149	26.956	14.086	26.805	14.023	26.654	13.961	26.504
3	15.630	42.586	15.599	42.404	15.569	42.223	15.537	42.042
4	17.267	59.853	17.276	59.680	17.284	59.507	17.293	59.334
5	19.075	78.928	19.132	78.812	19.189	78.696	19.246	78.580
6	21.072	100.000	21.188	100.000	21.304	100.000	21.420	100.000

	Annual %	Cum. %	Annual %	Cum. %	Annual %	Cum. %	Annual %	Cum. %
	11% Int.		11¼% Int.		11½% Int.		11¾% Int.	
1	12.456	12.456	12.370	12.370	12.283	12.283	12.198	12.198
2	13.898	26.354	13.835	26.205	13.773	26.056	13.711	25.908
3	15.506	41.861	15.475	41.680	15.443	41.499	15.411	41.319
4	17.301	59.161	17.308	58.988	17.316	58.815	17.323	58.642
5	19.303	78.464	19.359	78.347	19.415	78.230	19.471	78.113
6	21.536	100.000	21.653	100.000	21.770	100.000	21.887	100.000

EXAMPLES *ON PAGES A-382 TO A-397*

YEAR	Annual %	Cum. %	Annual %	Cum. %	Annual %	Cum. %	Annual %	Cum. %
	12% Int.		12¼% Int.		12½% Int.		12¾% Int.	
1	12.112	12.112	12.027	12.027	11.942	11.942	11.858	11.858
2	13.648	25.760	13.586	25.613	13.524	25.466	13.461	25.319
3	15.379	41.139	15.347	40.960	15.314	40.780	15.282	40.601
4	17.330	58.469	17.336	58.296	17.342	58.122	17.348	57.949
5	19.527	77.996	19.583	77.879	19.639	77.761	19.694	77.643
6	22.004	100.000	22.121	100.000	22.239	100.000	22.357	100.000
	13% Int.		13¼% Int.		13½% Int.		13¾% Int.	
1	11.774	11.774	11.691	11.691	11.608	11.608	11.525	11.525
2	13.399	25.173	13.337	25.028	13.275	24.883	13.213	24.738
3	15.249	40.422	15.216	40.244	15.183	40.065	15.149	39.888
4	17.354	57.776	17.359	57.603	17.364	57.429	17.369	57.256
5	19.749	77.525	19.804	77.407	19.859	77.288	19.913	77.169
6	22.475	100.000	22.593	100.000	22.712	100.000	22.831	100.000
	14% Int.		14¼% Int.		14½% Int.		14¾% Int.	
1	11.443	11.443	11.361	11.361	11.279	11.279	11.198	11.198
2	13.152	24.594	13.090	24.451	13.028	24.308	12.967	24.165
3	15.116	39.710	15.082	39.533	15.048	39.356	15.014	39.179
4	17.373	57.083	17.377	56.910	17.381	56.736	17.384	56.563
5	19.968	77.050	20.022	76.931	20.076	76.812	20.129	76.692
6	22.950	100.000	23.069	100.000	23.188	100.000	23.308	100.000
	15% Int.		15¼% Int.		15½% Int.		15¾% Int.	
1	11.118	11.118	11.038	11.038	10.958	10.958	10.878	10.878
2	12.905	24.023	12.844	23.881	12.782	23.740	12.721	23.599
3	14.980	39.002	14.945	38.826	14.911	38.651	14.876	38.475
4	17.388	56.390	17.391	56.217	17.393	56.044	17.395	55.871
5	20.183	76.573	20.236	76.453	20.289	76.333	20.342	76.213

EXAMPLES *ON PAGES A-382 TO A-397*

YEAR	Annual %	Cum. %	Annual %	Cum. %	Annual %	Cum. %	Annual %	Cum. %
	8% Int.		8¼% Int.		8½% Int.		8¾% Int.	
1	11.105	11.105	11.014	11.014	10.923	10.923	10.833	10.833
2	12.026	23.131	11.957	22.971	11.888	22.811	11.819	22.652
3	13.025	36.156	12.982	35.953	12.939	35.750	12.896	35.548
4	14.106	50.262	14.094	50.047	14.083	49.833	14.071	49.619
5	15.276	65.538	15.302	65.349	15.328	65.161	15.353	64.972
6	16.544	82.082	16.613	81.963	16.682	81.843	16.751	81.723
7	17.918	100.000	18.037	100.000	18.157	100.000	18.277	100.000

	Annual %	Cum. %	Annual %	Cum. %	Annual %	Cum. %	Annual %	Cum. %
	9% Int.		9¼% Int.		9½% Int.		9¾% Int.	
1	10.743	10.743	10.654	10.654	10.565	10.565	10.477	10.477
2	11.751	22.493	11.682	22.336	11.613	22.178	11.545	22.022
3	12.853	35.346	12.810	35.145	12.766	34.945	12.722	34.744
4	14.059	49.405	14.046	49.191	14.033	48.978	14.020	48.764
5	15.377	64.782	15.402	64.593	15.426	64.403	15.450	64.214
6	16.820	81.602	16.888	81.481	16.957	81.360	17.025	81.239
7	18.398	100.000	18.519	100.000	18.640	100.000	18.761	100.000

	Annual %	Cum. %	Annual %	Cum. %	Annual %	Cum. %	Annual %	Cum. %
	10% Int.		10¼% Int.		10½% Int.		10¾% Int.	
1	10.389	10.389	10.302	10.302	10.215	10.215	10.129	10.129
2	11.477	21.866	11.409	21.711	11.341	21.556	11.273	21.402
3	12.679	34.545	12.635	34.345	12.591	34.147	12.546	33.949
4	14.006	48.551	13.992	48.338	13.978	48.125	13.964	47.912
5	15.473	64.024	15.496	63.834	15.519	63.644	15.541	63.453
6	17.093	81.117	17.161	80.995	17.229	80.872	17.296	80.750
7	18.883	100.000	19.005	100.000	19.128	100.000	19.250	100.000

	Annual %	Cum. %	Annual %	Cum. %	Annual %	Cum. %	Annual %	Cum. %
	11% Int.		11¼% Int.		11½% Int.		11¾% Int.	
1	10.043	10.043	9.958	9.958	9.873	9.873	9.789	9.789
2	11.205	21.249	11.138	21.096	11.071	20.944	11.003	20.793
3	12.502	33.751	12.458	33.554	12.413	33.357	12.368	33.161
4	13.949	47.700	13.934	47.487	13.918	47.275	13.903	47.064
5	15.563	63.263	15.585	63.072	15.606	62.881	15.627	62.691
6	17.364	80.627	17.431	80.503	17.498	80.380	17.565	80.256
7	19.373	100.000	19.497	100.000	19.620	100.000	19.744	100.000

EXAMPLES ON PAGES A-382 TO A-397

YEAR	Annual %	Cum. %	Annual %	Cum. %	Annual %	Cum. %	Annual %	Cum. %
	12% Int.		12¼% Int.		12½% Int.		12¾% Int.	
1	9.706	9.706	9.622	9.622	9.540	9.540	9.458	9.458
2	10.938	20.642	10.870	20.492	10.803	20.343	10.736	20.194
3	12.324	32.966	12.279	32.771	12.233	32.576	12.188	32.382
4	13.896	46.852	13.870	46.641	13.853	46.430	13.836	46.219
5	15.648	62.500	15.668	62.309	15.688	62.117	15.707	61.926
6	17.632	80.132	17.699	80.007	17.765	79.883	17.831	79.757
7	19.868	100.000	19.993	100.000	20.117	100.000	20.243	100.000
	13% Int.		13¼% Int.		13½% Int.		13¾% Int.	
1	9.376	9.376	9.295	9.295	9.214	9.214	9.134	9.134
2	10.670	20.046	10.604	19.899	10.538	19.752	10.472	19.606
3	12.143	32.189	12.098	31.996	12.052	31.804	12.006	31.613
4	13.819	46.008	13.802	45.798	13.784	45.588	13.765	45.378
5	15.727	61.735	15.745	61.543	15.764	61.352	15.782	61.160
6	17.897	79.632	17.963	79.507	18.029	79.381	18.094	79.255
7	20.368	100.000	20.493	100.000	20.619	100.000	20.745	100.000
	14% Int.		14¼% Int.		14½% Int.		14¾% Int.	
1	9.054	9.054	8.975	8.975	8.897	8.897	8.819	8.819
2	10.407	19.461	10.341	19.316	10.276	19.173	10.211	19.029
3	11.961	31.422	11.915	31.231	11.869	31.042	11.823	30.852
4	13.747	45.169	13.728	44.960	13.709	44.751	13.690	44.542
5	15.800	60.969	15.817	60.777	15.835	60.585	15.851	60.394
6	18.160	79.128	18.225	79.002	18.290	78.875	18.354	78.748
7	20.872	100.000	20.998	100.000	21.125	100.000	21.252	100.000
	15% Int.		15¼% Int.		15½% Int.		15¾% Int.	
1	8.741	8.741	8.664	8.664	8.587	8.587	8.511	8.511
2	10.146	18.887	10.081	18.745	10.017	18.604	9.953	18.464
3	11.777	30.664	11.731	30.476	11.685	30.289	11.638	30.102
4	13.670	44.334	13.650	44.126	13.630	43.919	13.610	43.712
5	15.868	60.202	15.884	60.010	15.900	59.818	15.915	59.626
6	18.419	78.621	18.483	78.493	18.547	78.365	18.611	78.237
7	21.379	100.000	21.507	100.000	21.635	100.000	21.763	100.000

EXAMPLES *ON PAGES A-382 TO A-397*

YEAR	Annual %	Cum. %	Annual %	Cum. %	Annual %	Cum. %	Annual %	Cum. %
	8% Int.		8¼% Int.		8½% Int.		8¾% Int.	
1	6.805	6.805	6.719	6.719	6.633	6.633	6.548	6.548
2	7.370	14.175	7.294	14.013	7.219	13.852	7.144	13.692
3	7.982	22.157	7.919	21.932	7.857	21.709	7.795	21.487
4	8.644	30.801	8.598	30.530	8.552	30.260	8.505	29.992
5	9.362	40.163	9.335	39.865	9.307	39.568	9.280	39.272
6	10.139	50.302	10.135	50.000	10.130	49.698	10.125	49.397
7	10.980	61.282	11.003	61.003	11.026	60.724	11.047	60.444
8	11.892	73.174	11.946	72.949	12.000	72.724	12.054	72.498
9	12.879	86.052	12.970	85.919	13.061	85.785	13.152	85.650
10	13.948	100.000	14.081	100.000	14.215	100.000	14.350	100.000
	9% Int.		9¼% Int.		9½% Int.		9¾% Int.	
1	6.463	6.463	6.380	6.380	6.297	6.297	6.215	6.215
2	7.070	13.533	6.996	13.376	6.922	13.219	6.849	13.064
3	7.733	21.266	7.671	21.047	7.609	20.829	7.548	20.612
4	8.458	29.724	8.411	29.458	8.364	29.193	8.317	28.929
5	9.252	38.976	9.223	38.681	9.195	38.388	9.165	38.095
6	10.120	49.096	10.114	48.795	10.107	48.495	10.100	48.195
7	11.069	60.165	11.090	59.885	11.110	59.605	11.130	59.325
8	12.107	72.272	12.160	72.045	12.213	71.818	12.265	71.590
9	13.243	85.515	13.334	85.379	13.425	85.243	13.516	85.106
10	14.485	100.000	14.621	100.000	14.757	100.000	14.894	100.000
	10% Int.		10¼% Int.		10½% Int.		10¾% Int.	
1	6.134	6.134	6.054	6.054	5.974	5.974	5.896	5.896
2	6.777	12.911	6.704	12.758	6.633	12.607	6.561	12.457
3	7.486	20.397	7.425	20.183	7.364	19.971	7.303	19.760
4	8.270	28.667	8.223	28.406	8.175	28.146	8.128	27.887
5	9.136	37.803	9.106	37.512	9.076	37.222	9.046	36.933
6	10.093	47.895	10.085	47.596	10.076	47.298	10.067	47.000
7	11.149	59.045	11.168	58.765	11.187	58.485	11.205	58.205
8	12.317	71.362	12.368	71.133	12.419	70.904	12.470	70.675
9	13.607	84.969	13.697	84.831	13.788	84.692	13.879	84.553
10	15.031	100.000	15.169	100.000	15.308	100.000	15.447	100.000
	11% Int.		11¼% Int.		11½% Int.		11¾% Int.	
1	5.818	5.818	5.740	5.740	5.664	5.664	5.588	5.588
2	6.491	12.308	6.420	12.161	6.351	12.014	6.281	11.869
3	7.242	19.550	7.181	19.342	7.121	19.135	7.060	18.930
4	8.080	27.630	8.032	27.374	7.984	27.119	7.936	26.866
5	9.015	36.645	8.984	36.358	8.952	36.071	8.921	35.787
6	10.058	46.703	10.048	46.406	10.038	46.109	10.027	45.814
7	11.222	57.924	11.239	57.644	11.255	57.364	11.271	57.084
8	12.520	70.445	12.570	70.215	12.620	69.984	12.669	69.753
9	13.969	84.414	14.060	84.274	14.150	84.134	14.240	83.993
10	15.586	100.000	15.726	100.000	15.866	100.000	16.007	100.000

EXAMPLES ON PAGES A-382 TO A-397

EQUITY BUILD-UP
IN PERCENT OF ORIGINAL LOAN AMOUNT
FOR FIRST 15 YEARS

YEAR	Annual %	Cum. %	Annual %	Cum. %	Annual %	Cum. %	Annual %	Cum. %
	12% Int.		12¼% Int.		12½% Int.		12¾% Int.	
1	5.513	5.513	5.439	5.439	5.366	5.366	5.293	5.293
2	6.212	11.726	6.144	11.583	6.076	11.442	6.009	11.302
3	7.000	18.726	6.940	18.523	6.881	18.323	6.821	18.123
4	7.888	26.614	7.840	26.364	7.792	26.114	7.744	25.867
5	8.889	35.503	8.856	35.220	8.824	34.938	8.791	34.657
6	10.016	45.518	10.004	45.224	9.992	44.930	9.979	44.637
7	11.286	56.804	11.301	56.525	11.315	56.245	11.329	55.966
8	12.717	69.522	12.766	69.290	12.813	69.058	12.861	68.826
9	14.330	83.852	14.420	83.711	14.510	83.569	14.600	83.426
10	16.148	100.000	16.289	100.000	16.431	100.000	16.574	100.000

YEAR	Annual %	Cum. %	Annual %	Cum. %	Annual %	Cum. %	Annual %	Cum. %
	13% Int.		13¼% Int.		13½% Int.		13¾% Int.	
1	5.221	5.221	5.150	5.150	5.080	5.080	5.010	5.010
2	5.942	11.163	5.875	11.025	5.809	10.889	5.744	10.754
3	6.762	17.925	6.703	17.728	6.644	17.533	6.585	17.339
4	7.695	25.620	7.647	25.375	7.599	25.132	7.550	24.890
5	8.758	34.378	8.724	34.099	8.690	33.822	8.656	33.546
6	9.966	44.344	9.953	44.052	9.939	43.761	9.925	43.471
7	11.342	55.686	11.355	55.407	11.367	55.128	11.379	54.849
8	12.908	68.594	12.954	68.361	13.000	68.128	13.046	67.895
9	14.689	83.283	14.779	83.140	14.868	82.996	14.957	82.852
10	16.717	100.000	16.860	100.000	17.004	100.000	17.148	100.000

YEAR	Annual %	Cum. %	Annual %	Cum. %	Annual %	Cum. %	Annual %	Cum. %
	14% Int.		14¼% Int.		14½% Int.		14¾% Int.	
1	4.941	4.941	4.873	4.873	4.805	4.805	4.739	4.739
2	5.679	10.620	5.614	10.487	5.550	10.356	5.487	10.226
3	6.527	17.147	6.469	16.956	6.411	16.767	6.353	16.579
4	7.502	24.649	7.453	24.410	7.405	24.172	7.356	23.936
5	8.622	33.271	8.588	32.997	8.553	32.725	8.518	32.454
6	9.910	43.181	9.895	42.892	9.879	42.604	9.863	42.317
7	11.390	54.571	11.400	54.292	11.411	54.014	11.420	53.737
8	13.091	67.662	13.135	67.428	13.180	67.194	13.223	66.960
9	15.046	82.707	15.134	82.562	15.223	82.417	15.311	82.271
10	17.293	100.000	17.438	100.000	17.583	100.000	17.729	100.000

YEAR	Annual %	Cum. %	Annual %	Cum. %	Annual %	Cum. %	Annual %	Cum. %
	15% Int.		15¼% Int.		15½% Int.		15¾% Int.	
1	4.673	4.673	4.608	4.608	4.543	4.543	4.479	4.479
2	5.424	10.097	5.361	9.969	5.299	9.842	5.238	9.717
3	6.296	16.393	6.239	16.208	6.182	16.024	6.125	15.842
4	7.308	23.701	7.260	23.467	7.211	23.235	7.163	23.005
5	8.483	32.184	8.447	31.915	8.412	31.647	8.376	31.381
6	9.846	42.030	9.830	41.744	9.812	41.459	9.795	41.175
7	11.429	53.459	11.438	53.182	11.446	52.905	11.454	52.629
8	13.267	66.726	13.309	66.492	13.352	66.257	13.394	66.023
9	15.399	82.125	15.487	81.979	15.575	81.832	15.662	81.685
10	17.875	100.000	18.021	100.000	18.168	100.000	18.315	100.000

EXAMPLES ON PAGES A-382 TO A-397

YEAR	Annual %	Cum. %	Annual %	Cum. %	Annual %	Cum. %	Annual %	Cum. %
	8% Int.		8¼% Int.		8½% Int.		8¾% Int.	
1	3.598	3.598	3.523	3.523	3.449	3.449	3.377	3.377
2	3.896	7.494	3.825	7.348	3.754	7.203	3.684	7.061
3	4.220	11.714	4.153	11.500	4.086	11.289	4.020	11.081
4	4.570	16.284	4.508	16.009	4.447	15.736	4.386	15.467
5	4.949	21.234	4.895	20.903	4.840	20.576	4.786	20.253
6	5.360	26.594	5.314	26.218	5.268	25.844	5.222	25.474
7	5.805	32.399	5.770	31.987	5.734	31.578	5.697	31.171
8	6.287	38.686	6.264	38.251	6.240	37.818	6.216	37.388
9	6.809	45.495	6.801	45.052	6.792	44.610	6.783	44.170
10	7.374	52.869	7.384	52.435	7.392	52.003	7.400	51.571
11	7.986	60.855	8.016	60.452	8.046	60.048	8.075	59.645
12	8.649	69.503	8.703	69.155	8.757	68.805	8.810	68.455
13	9.367	78.870	9.449	78.604	9.531	78.336	9.613	78.068
14	10.144	89.014	10.259	88.862	10.373	88.710	10.488	88.556
15	10.986	100.000	11.138	100.000	11.290	100.000	11.444	100.000

YEAR	Annual %	Cum. %	Annual %	Cum. %	Annual %	Cum. %	Annual %	Cum. %
	9% Int.		9¼% Int.		9½% Int.		9¾% Int.	
1	3.305	3.305	3.235	3.235	3.166	3.166	3.098	3.098
2	3.615	6.921	3.547	6.783	3.480	6.647	3.414	6.513
3	3.955	10.875	3.890	10.673	3.826	10.473	3.763	10.275
4	4.326	15.201	4.265	14.938	4.206	14.678	4.146	14.421
5	4.731	19.932	4.677	19.615	4.623	19.301	4.569	18.991
6	5.175	25.107	5.128	24.743	5.082	24.383	5.035	24.026
7	5.661	30.768	5.624	30.367	5.586	29.969	5.548	29.574
8	6.192	36.959	6.166	36.533	6.141	36.110	6.114	35.688
9	6.772	43.732	6.762	43.295	6.750	42.860	6.738	42.426
10	7.408	51.139	7.414	50.709	7.420	50.279	7.425	49.851
11	8.103	59.242	8.130	58.839	8.156	58.436	8.182	58.033
12	8.863	68.105	8.915	67.753	8.966	67.402	9.016	67.049
13	9.694	77.799	9.775	77.528	9.856	77.257	9.936	76.985
14	10.603	88.402	10.719	88.247	10.834	88.091	10.949	87.934
15	11.598	100.000	11.753	100.000	11.909	100.000	12.066	100.000

YEAR	Annual %	Cum. %	Annual %	Cum. %	Annual %	Cum. %	Annual %	Cum. %
	10% Int.		10¼% Int.		10½% Int.		10¾% Int.	
1	3.032	3.032	2.966	2.966	2.902	2.902	2.839	2.839
2	3.349	6.381	3.285	6.251	3.222	6.123	3.159	5.998
3	3.700	10.081	3.638	9.889	3.577	9.700	3.516	9.514
4	4.087	14.168	4.029	13.918	3.971	13.671	3.913	13.427
5	4.515	18.683	4.462	18.380	4.408	18.079	4.355	17.782
6	4.988	23.671	4.941	23.321	4.894	22.973	4.847	22.629
7	5.510	29.182	5.472	28.793	5.434	28.407	5.395	28.024
8	6.087	35.269	6.060	34.853	6.032	34.439	6.004	34.028
9	6.725	41.994	6.711	41.564	6.697	41.136	6.682	40.710
10	7.429	49.423	7.432	48.997	7.435	48.572	7.437	48.147
11	8.207	57.630	8.231	57.228	8.255	56.826	8.277	56.425
12	9.066	66.697	9.116	66.344	9.164	65.990	9.212	65.637
13	10.016	76.712	10.095	76.439	10.174	76.164	10.253	75.889
14	11.065	87.777	11.180	87.619	11.295	87.460	11.411	87.300
15	12.223	100.000	12.381	100.000	12.540	100.000	12.700	100.000

YEAR	Annual %	Cum. %	Annual %	Cum. %	Annual %	Cum. %	Annual %	Cum. %
	11% Int.		11¼% Int.		11½% Int.		11¾% Int.	
1	2.776	2.776	2.715	2.715	2.655	2.655	2.596	2.596
2	3.098	5.874	3.037	5.752	2.978	5.633	2.919	5.515
3	3.456	9.330	3.397	9.149	3.338	8.971	3.281	8.795
4	3.856	13.186	3.799	12.949	3.743	12.714	3.687	12.483
5	4.302	17.488	4.250	17.198	4.197	16.911	4.145	16.628
6	4.800	22.289	4.753	21.951	4.706	21.617	4.659	21.287
7	5.356	27.644	5.316	27.267	5.277	26.894	5.237	26.524
8	5.975	33.619	5.946	33.214	5.916	32.810	5.886	32.410
9	6.667	40.286	6.651	39.864	6.634	39.444	6.617	39.027
10	7.438	47.724	7.439	47.303	7.438	46.883	7.437	46.464
11	8.299	56.023	8.320	55.623	8.340	55.223	8.360	54.824
12	9.259	65.283	9.306	64.929	9.352	64.575	9.397	64.220
13	10.331	75.614	10.408	75.337	10.486	75.060	10.562	74.783
14	11.526	87.140	11.642	86.979	11.757	86.817	11.872	86.655
15	12.860	100.000	13.021	100.000	13.183	100.000	13.345	100.000

EXAMPLES ON PAGES A-382 TO A-397

EQUITY BUILD-UP

15 YEAR TERM

IN PERCENT OF ORIGINAL LOAN AMOUNT FOR FIRST 15 YEARS

15 YEAR TERM

YEAR	Annual %	Cum. %	Annual %	Cum. %	Annual %	Cum. %	Annual %	Cum. %
	12% Int.		12¼% Int.		12½% Int.		12¾% Int.	
1	2.539	2.539	2.482	2.482	2.426	2.426	2.371	2.371
2	2.861	5.399	2.804	5.285	2.747	5.174	2.692	5.064
3	3.223	8.623	3.167	8.452	3.111	8.285	3.056	8.120
4	3.632	12.255	3.577	12.030	3.523	11.808	3.469	11.589
5	4.093	16.348	4.041	16.071	3.990	15.798	3.939	15.528
6	4.612	20.960	4.565	20.636	4.518	20.316	4.471	19.999
7	5.197	26.156	5.157	25.793	5.116	25.432	5.076	25.075
8	5.856	32.012	5.825	31.618	5.794	31.226	5.762	30.837
9	6.599	38.611	6.580	38.198	6.561	37.787	6.541	37.378
10	7.435	46.046	7.433	45.631	7.430	45.216	7.426	44.804
11	8.378	54.425	8.396	54.027	8.413	53.630	8.430	53.233
12	9.441	63.866	9.485	63.512	9.528	63.157	9.570	62.803
13	10.638	74.504	10.714	74.226	10.789	73.946	10.864	73.667
14	11.988	86.492	12.103	86.328	12.218	86.164	12.333	86.000
15	13.508	100.000	13.672	100.000	13.836	100.000	14.000	100.000
	13% Int.		13¼% Int.		13½% Int.		13¾% Int.	
1	2.318	2.318	2.265	2.265	2.213	2.213	2.163	2.163
2	2.638	4.955	2.584	4.849	2.531	4.745	2.480	4.642
3	3.002	7.957	2.948	7.797	2.895	7.640	2.843	7.485
4	3.416	11.373	3.363	11.161	3.311	10.951	3.259	10.745
5	3.888	15.261	3.837	14.998	3.787	14.738	3.737	14.482
6	4.424	19.685	4.378	19.376	4.331	19.069	4.284	18.766
7	5.035	24.720	4.994	24.370	4.953	24.022	4.912	23.678
8	5.733	30.450	5.698	30.067	5.665	29.687	5.632	29.310
9	6.521	36.971	6.500	36.567	6.479	36.166	6.457	35.767
10	7.421	44.392	7.416	43.983	7.410	43.576	7.403	43.170
11	8.445	52.838	8.460	52.443	8.474	52.050	8.487	51.657
12	9.611	62.449	9.652	62.095	9.692	61.741	9.731	61.388
13	10.938	73.387	11.011	73.106	11.084	72.825	11.156	72.544
14	12.448	85.834	12.562	85.668	12.677	85.502	12.791	85.335
15	14.166	100.000	14.332	100.000	14.498	100.000	14.665	100.000
	14% Int.		14¼% Int.		14½% Int.		14¾% Int.	
1	2.113	2.113	2.064	2.064	2.017	2.017	1.970	1.970
2	2.429	4.542	2.378	4.443	2.329	4.346	2.281	4.250
3	2.791	7.333	2.740	7.183	2.690	7.036	2.641	6.891
4	3.208	10.541	3.158	10.341	3.107	10.143	3.058	9.949
5	3.687	14.229	3.638	13.979	3.589	13.732	3.541	13.489
6	4.238	18.467	4.192	18.171	4.146	17.878	4.100	17.589
7	4.871	23.338	4.830	23.000	4.788	22.666	4.747	22.336
8	5.598	28.936	5.565	28.565	5.531	28.197	5.496	27.832
9	6.434	35.370	6.411	34.976	6.388	34.585	6.364	34.196
10	7.395	42.766	7.387	42.364	7.378	41.963	7.369	41.565
11	8.500	51.266	8.511	50.875	8.522	50.486	8.532	50.098
12	9.769	61.035	9.807	60.682	9.844	60.329	9.880	59.977
13	11.228	72.263	11.299	71.981	11.370	71.699	11.440	71.417
14	12.905	85.168	13.019	85.000	13.132	84.832	13.246	84.663
15	14.832	100.000	15.000	100.000	15.168	100.000	15.337	100.000
	15% Int.		15¼% Int.		15½% Int.		15¾% Int.	
1	1.924	1.924	1.879	1.879	1.835	1.835	1.791	1.791
2	2.233	4.157	2.186	4.065	2.140	3.975	2.095	3.886
3	2.592	6.749	2.544	6.609	2.496	6.471	2.450	6.336
4	3.009	9.757	2.960	9.569	2.912	9.383	2.865	9.200
5	3.492	13.250	3.444	13.013	3.397	12.780	3.350	12.550
6	4.054	17.303	4.008	17.021	3.962	16.742	3.917	16.467
7	4.705	22.009	4.664	21.685	4.622	21.365	4.581	21.048
8	5.462	27.470	5.427	27.112	5.392	26.756	5.356	26.404
9	6.340	33.810	6.315	33.427	6.290	33.046	6.264	32.668
10	7.359	41.169	7.348	40.775	7.337	40.383	7.325	39.992
11	8.542	49.711	8.550	49.325	8.558	48.941	8.565	48.558
12	9.915	59.626	9.949	59.275	9.983	58.924	10.016	58.574
13	11.509	71.135	11.577	70.852	11.645	70.569	11.713	70.287
14	13.359	84.494	13.472	84.324	13.584	84.154	13.697	83.983
15	15.506	100.000	15.676	100.000	15.846	100.000	16.017	100.000

EXAMPLES *ON PAGES A-382 TO A-397*

YEAR	Annual %	Cum. %	Annual %	Cum. %	Annual %	Cum. %	Annual %	Cum. %
	8% Int.		8¼% Int.		8½% Int.		8¾% Int.	
1	2.114	2.114	2.051	2.051	1.990	1.990	1.931	1.931
2	2.289	4.403	2.227	4.278	2.166	4.156	2.107	4.037
3	2.479	6.882	2.418	6.696	2.358	6.514	2.299	6.336
4	2.685	9.567	2.625	9.321	2.566	9.080	2.508	8.844
5	2.908	12.474	2.850	12.171	2.793	11.873	2.736	11.580
6	3.149	15.623	3.094	15.265	3.040	14.912	2.986	14.566
7	3.410	19.034	3.359	18.624	3.308	18.221	3.258	17.823
8	3.693	22.727	3.647	22.271	3.601	21.822	3.554	21.378
9	4.000	26.727	3.960	26.231	3.919	25.741	3.878	25.256
10	4.332	31.059	4.299	30.530	4.265	30.006	4.231	29.487
11	4.692	35.751	4.667	35.198	4.643	34.649	4.617	34.104
12	5.081	40.832	5.067	40.265	5.053	39.702	5.038	39.142
13	5.503	46.335	5.502	45.767	5.499	45.201	5.496	44.638
14	5.959	52.294	5.973	51.740	5.986	51.187	5.997	50.635
15	6.454	58.748	6.485	58.224	6.515	57.701	6.543	57.179
	9% Int.		9¼% Int.		9½% Int.		9¾% Int.	
1	1.873	1.873	1.816	1.866	1.761	1.761	1.707	1.707
2	2.048	3.921	1.991	3.808	1.936	3.697	1.881	3.588
3	2.241	6.162	2.184	5.991	2.128	5.824	2.073	5.661
4	2.451	8.612	2.394	8.386	2.339	8.163	2.284	7.946
5	2.681	11.293	2.626	11.011	2.571	10.735	2.517	10.463
6	2.932	14.225	2.879	13.890	2.826	13.561	2.774	13.238
7	3.207	17.432	3.157	17.047	3.107	16.668	3.057	16.295
8	3.508	20.940	3.462	20.508	3.415	20.083	3.369	19.664
9	3.837	24.777	3.796	24.304	3.754	23.837	3.712	23.376
10	4.197	28.974	4.162	28.466	4.127	27.964	4.091	27.467
11	4.591	33.565	4.564	33.030	4.536	32.500	4.508	31.975
12	5.021	38.586	5.004	38.034	4.986	37.487	4.968	36.943
13	5.492	44.078	5.487	43.522	5.481	42.968	5.474	42.417
14	6.008	50.086	6.017	49.539	6.025	48.993	6.033	48.450
15	6.571	56.657	6.598	56.136	6.623	55.617	6.648	55.098
	10% Int.		10¼% Int.		10½% Int.		10¾% Int.	
1	1.655	1.655	1.604	1.604	1.554	1.554	1.505	1.505
2	1.828	3.483	1.776	3.380	1.725	3.279	1.676	3.181
3	2.019	5.502	1.967	5.347	1.915	5.194	1.865	5.046
4	2.231	7.733	2.178	7.525	2.126	7.321	2.075	7.121
5	2.464	10.198	2.412	9.537	2.361	9.681	2.310	9.431
6	2.723	12.920	2.671	12.608	2.621	12.302	2.571	12.002
7	3.008	15.928	2.959	15.567	2.910	15.212	2.861	14.863
8	3.323	19.250	3.276	18.843	3.230	18.442	3.184	18.048
9	3.671	22.921	3.628	22.472	3.586	22.029	3.544	21.592
10	4.055	26.976	4.018	26.490	3.982	26.010	3.944	25.536
11	4.479	31.455	4.450	30.940	4.420	30.431	4.390	29.926
12	4.949	36.404	4.928	35.869	4.907	35.338	4.886	34.812
13	5.467	41.870	5.458	41.327	5.448	40.786	5.438	40.250
14	6.039	47.909	6.044	47.371	6.049	46.835	6.052	46.302
15	6.671	54.581	6.694	54.065	6.715	53.551	6.736	53.038
	11% Int.		11¼% Int.		11½% Int.		11¾% Int.	
1	1.458	1.458	1.412	1.412	1.368	1.368	1.324	1.324
2	1.627	3.085	1.580	2.992	1.534	2.901	1.489	2.813
3	1.815	4.901	1.767	4.759	1.720	4.621	1.673	4.486
4	2.025	6.926	1.976	6.735	1.928	6.549	1.881	6.367
5	2.260	9.186	2.210	8.946	2.162	8.711	2.114	8.481
6	2.521	11.707	2.472	11.418	2.424	11.135	2.376	10.857
7	2.813	14.520	2.765	14.184	2.718	13.853	2.671	13.528
8	3.139	17.659	3.093	17.277	3.048	16.901	3.002	16.530
9	3.502	21.161	3.459	20.736	3.417	20.318	3.375	19.905
10	3.907	25.068	3.869	24.606	3.831	24.149	3.793	23.698
11	4.359	29.427	4.328	28.933	4.296	28.445	4.264	27.962
12	4.864	34.291	4.841	33.774	4.817	33.262	4.793	32.755
13	5.426	39.717	5.414	39.188	5.401	38.663	5.387	38.142
14	6.054	45.772	6.056	45.244	6.056	44.719	6.055	44.198
15	6.755	52.527	6.773	52.017	6.790	51.510	6.807	51.004

EXAMPLES *ON PAGES A-382 TO A-397*

YEAR	Annual %	Cum. %	Annual %	Cum. %	Annual %	Cum. %	Annual %	Cum. %
	12% Int.		12¼% Int.		12½% Int.		12¾% Int.	
1	1.282	1.282	1.241	1.241	1.201	1.201	1.162	1.162
2	1.445	2.727	1.402	2.643	1.360	2.561	1.319	2.481
3	1.628	4.354	1.583	4.226	1.540	4.101	1.498	3.979
4	1.834	6.189	1.789	6.015	1.744	5.845	1.700	5.679
5	2.067	8.256	2.021	8.035	1.975	7.820	1.930	7.609
6	2.329	10.585	2.282	10.318	2.236	10.056	2.191	9.800
7	2.624	13.209	2.578	12.896	2.533	12.589	2.487	12.287
8	2.957	16.166	2.912	15.809	2.868	15.457	2.824	15.111
9	3.332	19.499	3.290	19.099	3.248	18.704	3.205	18.316
10	3.755	23.254	3.716	22.815	3.678	22.382	3.639	21.955
11	4.231	27.485	4.198	27.013	4.165	26.547	4.131	26.086
12	4.768	32.253	4.742	31.755	4.716	31.263	4.689	30.776
13	5.372	37.625	5.357	37.112	5.341	36.604	5.324	36.099
14	6.054	43.679	6.051	43.164	6.048	42.652	6.043	42.143
15	6.822	50.501	6.836	49.999	6.849	49.500	6.861	49.003
	13% Int.		13¼% Int.		13½% Int.		13¾% Int.	
1	1.124	1.124	1.088	1.088	1.052	1.052	1.017	1.017
2	1.280	2.404	1.241	2.328	1.203	2.255	1.166	2.184
3	1.456	3.860	1.416	3.744	1.376	3.631	1.337	3.521
4	1.657	5.517	1.615	5.359	1.574	5.205	1.533	5.054
5	1.886	7.403	1.842	7.202	1.800	7.005	1.758	6.812
6	2.146	9.549	2.102	9.304	2.058	9.063	2.015	8.828
7	2.442	11.992	2.398	11.702	2.354	11.417	2.311	11.139
8	2.780	14.771	2.736	14.438	2.692	14.110	2.649	13.788
9	3.163	17.935	3.121	17.559	3.079	17.189	3.037	16.825
10	3.600	21.534	3.561	21.119	3.522	20.711	3.482	20.308
11	4.097	25.631	4.062	25.182	4.028	24.739	3.993	24.300
12	4.662	30.293	4.635	29.816	4.606	29.344	4.577	28.878
13	5.306	35.599	5.287	35.104	5.268	34.612	5.248	34.126
14	6.038	41.637	6.032	41.136	6.025	40.637	6.017	40.143
15	6.872	48.509	6.882	48.017	6.891	47.528	6.899	47.041
	14% Int.		14¼% Int.		14½% Int.		14¾% Int.	
1	0.984	0.984	0.951	0.951	0.919	0.919	0.889	0.889
2	1.131	2.115	1.096	2.047	1.062	1.982	1.029	1.918
3	1.300	3.414	1.263	3.310	1.227	3.208	1.192	3.109
4	1.494	4.908	1.455	4.765	1.417	4.625	1.380	4.489
5	1.717	6.624	1.676	6.441	1.637	6.262	1.598	6.087
6	1.973	8.598	1.931	8.372	1.890	8.152	1.850	7.936
7	2.268	10.865	2.225	10.598	2.183	10.335	2.142	10.078
8	2.606	13.472	2.564	13.162	2.522	12.857	2.480	12.558
9	2.996	16.467	2.954	16.116	2.913	15.770	2.872	15.430
10	3.443	19.911	3.404	19.519	3.364	19.134	3.325	18.755
11	3.957	23.868	3.922	23.441	3.886	23.020	3.850	22.605
12	4.548	28.416	4.519	27.960	4.488	27.509	4.458	27.063
13	5.227	33.644	5.206	33.166	5.184	32.693	5.162	32.225
14	6.008	39.652	5.999	39.164	5.988	38.681	5.977	38.201
15	6.905	46.557	6.911	46.076	6.916	45.597	6.920	45.122
	15% Int.		15¼% Int.		15½% Int.		15¾% Int.	
1	0.859	0.859	0.830	0.830	0.802	0.802	0.775	0.775
2	0.997	1.856	0.966	1.796	0.935	1.737	0.906	1.681
3	1.157	3.013	1.124	2.920	1.091	2.829	1.059	2.740
4	1.343	4.357	1.308	4.227	1.273	4.102	1.239	3.979
5	1.559	5.916	1.522	5.749	1.485	5.586	1.449	5.428
6	1.810	7.726	1.771	7.520	1.732	7.319	1.694	7.122
7	2.101	9.827	2.060	9.580	2.020	9.339	1.981	9.103
8	2.439	12.265	2.398	11.978	2.357	11.696	2.317	11.420
9	2.831	15.096	2.790	14.768	2.749	14.445	2.709	14.129
10	3.286	18.382	3.246	18.014	3.207	17.652	3.168	17.297
11	3.814	22.196	3.778	21.792	3.741	21.394	3.704	21.001
12	4.427	26.622	4.396	26.187	4.364	25.757	4.332	25.333
13	5.139	31.761	5.115	31.302	5.091	30.848	5.066	30.399
14	5.965	37.726	5.952	37.254	5.938	36.786	5.924	36.322
15	6.924	44.649	6.926	44.180	6.927	43.713	6.927	43.250

EXAMPLES *ON PAGES A-382 TO A-397*

YEAR	Annual %	Cum. %	Annual %	Cum. %	Annual %	Cum. %	Annual %	Cum. %
	8% Int.		8¼% Int.		8½% Int.		8¾% Int.	
1	1.309	1.309	1.258	1.258	1.209	1.209	1.162	1.162
2	1.418	2.727	1.366	2.624	1.316	2.525	1.267	2.429
3	1.535	4.262	1.483	4.108	1.432	3.957	1.383	3.812
4	1.663	5.925	1.610	5.718	1.559	5.516	1.509	5.321
5	1.801	7.726	1.748	7.466	1.697	7.213	1.646	6.967
6	1.950	9.676	1.898	9.364	1.847	9.060	1.796	8.763
7	2.112	11.789	2.061	11.425	2.010	11.070	1.960	10.723
8	2.288	14.076	2.237	13.662	2.188	13.257	2.138	12.861
9	2.477	16.554	2.429	16.091	2.381	15.638	2.333	15.195
10	2.683	19.237	2.637	18.728	2.591	18.229	2.546	17.740
11	2.906	22.142	2.863	21.591	2.820	21.050	2.778	20.518
12	3.147	25.289	3.108	24.700	3.070	24.120	3.031	23.549
13	3.408	28.697	3.375	28.075	3.341	27.461	3.307	26.855
14	3.691	32.388	3.664	31.739	3.636	31.097	3.608	30.463
15	3.997	36.386	3.978	35.717	3.958	35.055	3.937	34.400
	9% Int.		9¼% Int.		9½% Int.		9¾% Int.	
1	1.116	1.116	1.071	1.071	1.028	1.028	0.987	0.987
2	1.220	2.336	1.175	2.246	1.130	2.159	1.088	2.075
3	1.335	3.671	1.288	3.534	1.243	3.401	1.199	3.273
4	1.460	5.131	1.412	4.946	1.366	4.767	1.321	4.594
5	1.597	6.728	1.549	6.495	1.502	6.269	1.455	6.049
6	1.747	8.474	1.698	8.193	1.651	7.919	1.604	7.653
7	1.911	10.385	1.862	10.055	1.814	9.734	1.767	9.421
8	2.090	12.475	2.042	12.097	1.994	11.728	1.948	11.368
9	2.286	14.761	2.239	14.336	2.192	13.921	2.146	13.515
10	2.500	17.261	2.455	16.791	2.410	16.331	2.365	15.880
11	2.735	19.996	2.692	19.483	2.649	18.980	2.606	18.486
12	2.991	22.987	2.952	22.435	2.912	21.892	2.872	21.358
13	3.272	26.259	3.237	25.671	3.201	25.093	3.165	24.523
14	3.579	29.838	3.549	29.221	3.519	28.612	3.488	28.011
15	3.915	33.752	3.892	33.112	3.868	32.480	3.843	31.855
	10% Int.		10¼% Int.		10½% Int.		10¾% Int.	
1	0.947	0.947	0.908	0.908	0.871	0.871	0.835	0.835
2	1.046	1.993	1.006	1.915	0.967	1.839	0.930	1.765
3	1.156	3.149	1.114	3.029	1.074	2.913	1.035	2.800
4	1.277	4.426	1.234	4.263	1.192	4.105	1.152	3.952
5	1.410	5.836	1.367	5.629	1.324	5.429	1.282	5.234
6	1.558	7.394	1.513	7.143	1.470	6.898	1.427	6.661
7	1.721	9.116	1.676	8.819	1.632	8.530	1.588	8.248
8	1.902	11.017	1.856	10.675	1.811	10.341	1.767	10.016
9	2.101	13.118	2.056	12.730	2.011	12.352	1.967	11.983
10	2.321	15.439	2.276	15.007	2.233	14.585	2.189	14.172
11	2.564	18.002	2.521	17.528	2.479	17.063	2.436	16.608
12	2.832	20.834	2.792	20.320	2.752	19.815	2.711	19.319
13	3.129	23.963	3.092	23.412	3.055	22.870	3.018	22.337
14	3.456	27.419	3.424	26.836	3.392	26.261	3.359	25.696
15	3.818	31.238	3.792	30.628	3.765	30.027	3.738	29.434
	11% Int.		11¼% Int.		11½% Int.		11¾% Int.	
1	0.801	0.801	0.768	0.768	0.736	0.736	0.705	0.705
2	0.894	1.695	0.859	1.626	0.825	1.560	0.792	1.497
3	0.997	2.692	0.960	2.587	0.925	2.485	0.890	2.387
4	1.112	3.804	1.074	3.661	1.037	3.522	1.001	3.388
5	1.241	5.045	1.201	4.862	1.163	4.685	1.125	4.513
6	1.385	6.430	1.344	6.206	1.304	5.989	1.265	5.778
7	1.545	7.975	1.503	7.709	1.462	7.450	1.421	7.199
8	1.724	9.699	1.681	9.390	1.639	9.089	1.598	8.797
9	1.923	11.622	1.880	11.270	1.838	10.927	1.796	10.593
10	2.146	13.768	2.103	13.373	2.061	12.988	2.019	12.611
11	2.394	16.162	2.352	15.725	2.310	15.298	2.269	14.880
12	2.671	18.833	2.631	18.356	2.591	17.889	2.550	17.431
13	2.980	21.813	2.943	21.299	2.905	20.794	2.867	20.297
14	3.325	25.138	3.291	24.590	3.257	24.051	3.222	23.520
15	3.710	28.848	3.681	28.271	3.652	27.703	3.622	27.142

EXAMPLES *ON PAGES A-382 TO A-397*

YEAR	Annual %	Cum. %	Annual %	Cum. %	Annual %	Cum. %	Annual %	Cum. %
	12% Int.		12¼% Int.		12½% Int.		12¾% Int.	
1	0.675	0.675	0.646	0.646	0.619	0.619	0.592	0.592
2	0.761	1.436	0.730	1.377	0.701	1.320	0.673	1.265
3	0.857	2.293	0.825	2.201	0.794	2.113	0.764	2.029
4	0.966	3.259	0.932	3.133	0.899	3.012	0.867	2.895
5	1.088	4.347	1.053	4.186	1.018	4.030	0.984	3.879
6	1.226	5.573	1.189	5.375	1.153	5.183	1.117	4.996
7	1.382	6.955	1.343	6.718	1.305	6.488	1.268	6.264
8	1.557	8.512	1.517	8.235	1.478	7.966	1.440	7.704
9	1.755	10.267	1.714	9.949	1.674	9.639	1.634	9.338
10	1.977	12.244	1.936	11.885	1.895	11.535	1.855	11.193
11	2.228	14.471	2.187	14.072	2.146	13.681	2.106	13.299
12	2.510	16.982	2.470	16.542	2.430	16.112	2.391	15.690
13	2.829	19.811	2.791	19.333	2.752	18.864	2.714	18.404
14	3.187	22.998	3.152	22.485	3.117	21.981	3.081	21.485
15	3.592	26.590	3.561	26.046	3.530	25.510	3.498	24.983
	13% Int.		13¼% Int.		13½% Int.		13¾% Int.	
1	0.567	0.567	0.543	0.543	0.519	0.519	0.497	0.497
2	0.645	1.212	0.619	1.162	0.594	1.113	0.569	1.066
3	0.734	1.947	0.706	1.868	0.679	1.792	0.653	1.718
4	0.836	2.782	0.806	2.673	0.776	2.568	0.748	2.467
5	0.951	3.733	0.919	3.593	0.888	3.456	0.858	3.325
6	1.082	4.816	1.049	4.641	1.016	4.472	0.984	4.308
7	1.232	6.048	1.196	5.837	1.162	5.633	1.128	5.436
8	1.402	7.449	1.365	7.202	1.328	6.962	1.293	6.729
9	1.595	9.045	1.557	8.759	1.519	8.481	1.482	8.211
10	1.815	10.860	1.776	10.535	1.738	10.219	1.699	9.910
11	2.066	12.926	2.026	12.562	1.987	12.206	1.948	11.859
12	2.351	15.277	2.312	14.874	2.273	14.479	2.234	14.093
13	2.676	17.953	2.638	17.511	2.599	17.078	2.561	16.654
14	3.045	20.998	3.009	20.520	2.973	20.051	2.936	19.590
15	3.465	24.464	3.433	23.953	3.400	23.451	3.367	22.957
	14% Int.		14¼% Int.		14½% Int.		14¾% Int.	
1	0.475	0.475	0.454	0.454	0.434	0.434	0.415	0.415
2	0.546	1.021	0.523	0.977	0.501	0.935	0.480	0.895
3	0.627	1.648	0.603	1.580	0.579	1.514	0.556	1.452
4	0.721	2.369	0.694	2.274	0.669	2.183	0.644	2.096
5	0.829	3.197	0.800	3.074	0.773	2.956	0.746	2.841
6	0.952	4.150	0.922	3.996	0.892	3.848	0.864	3.705
7	1.095	5.244	1.062	5.059	1.031	4.879	1.000	4.705
8	1.258	6.502	1.224	6.283	1.190	6.069	1.158	5.862
9	1.446	7.948	1.410	7.693	1.375	7.444	1.341	7.203
10	1.662	9.610	1.625	9.317	1.588	9.032	1.552	8.755
11	1.910	11.520	1.872	11.189	1.834	10.867	1.797	10.552
12	2.195	13.715	2.157	13.346	2.119	12.986	2.081	12.633
13	2.523	16.238	2.485	15.831	2.447	15.433	2.410	15.043
14	2.900	19.138	2.863	18.695	2.827	18.260	2.790	17.833
15	3.333	22.471	3.299	21.994	3.265	21.525	3.231	21.063
	15% Int.		15¼% Int.		15½% Int.		15¾% Int.	
1	0.396	0.396	0.379	0.379	0.362	0.362	0.346	0.346
2	0.460	0.857	0.441	0.820	0.422	0.784	0.404	0.750
3	0.534	1.391	0.513	1.333	0.493	1.277	0.473	1.223
4	0.620	2.011	0.597	1.930	0.575	1.851	0.553	1.776
5	0.720	2.731	0.695	2.624	0.670	2.521	0.646	2.422
6	0.835	3.566	0.808	3.432	0.782	3.303	0.756	3.178
7	0.970	4.536	0.940	4.373	0.912	4.215	0.884	4.062
8	1.126	5.662	1.094	5.467	1.064	5.279	1.034	5.096
9	1.307	6.968	1.273	6.741	1.241	6.520	1.209	6.305
10	1.517	8.485	1.482	8.222	1.447	7.967	1.414	7.718
11	1.761	10.246	1.724	9.947	1.688	9.655	1.653	9.372
12	2.044	12.289	2.006	11.953	1.970	11.625	1.933	11.305
13	2.372	14.661	2.335	14.288	2.297	13.922	2.261	13.565
14	2.753	17.415	2.717	17.004	2.680	16.602	2.643	16.209
15	3.196	20.610	3.161	20.166	3.126	19.729	3.091	19.300

EXAMPLES *ON PAGES A-382 TO A-397*

YEAR	Annual %	Cum. %	Annual %	Cum. %	Annual %	Cum. %	Annual %	Cum. %
	8% Int.		8¼% Int.		8½% Int.		8¾% Int.	
1	0.835	0.835	0.795	0.795	0.756	0.756	0.719	0.719
2	0.905	1.740	0.863	1.658	0.823	1.579	0.784	1.503
3	0.980	2.720	0.937	2.595	0.896	2.474	0.856	2.359
4	1.061	3.781	1.017	3.612	0.975	3.449	0.934	3.292
5	1.149	4.930	1.104	4.716	1.061	4.510	1.019	4.311
6	1.245	6.175	1.199	5.915	1.155	5.664	1.111	5.423
7	1.348	7.523	1.302	7.217	1.257	6.921	1.213	6.635
8	1.460	8.982	1.413	8.630	1.368	8.289	1.323	7.959
9	1.581	10.563	1.534	10.164	1.489	9.777	1.444	9.402
10	1.712	12.275	1.666	11.830	1.620	11.397	1.575	10.978
11	1.854	14.130	1.809	13.639	1.763	13.161	1.719	12.696
12	2.008	16.138	1.964	15.602	1.919	15.080	1.875	14.572
13	2.175	18.312	2.132	17.734	2.089	17.169	2.046	16.618
14	2.355	20.668	2.314	20.048	2.274	19.443	2.233	18.851
15	2.551	23.218	2.513	22.561	2.475	21.917	2.436	21.287
	9% Int.		9¼% Int.		9½% Int.		9¾% Int.	
1	0.683	0.683	0.649	0.649	0.617	0.617	0.586	0.586
2	0.747	1.430	0.712	1.361	0.678	1.294	0.645	1.231
3	0.817	2.248	0.781	2.142	0.745	2.040	0.711	1.942
4	0.894	3.142	0.856	2.997	0.819	2.859	0.784	2.726
5	0.978	4.120	0.938	3.936	0.900	3.759	0.864	3.589
6	1.070	5.190	1.029	4.965	0.990	4.749	0.952	4.541
7	1.170	6.360	1.128	6.093	1.088	5.837	1.049	5.589
8	1.280	7.639	1.237	7.331	1.196	7.033	1.156	6.745
9	1.400	9.039	1.357	8.687	1.315	8.347	1.273	8.018
10	1.531	10.570	1.488	10.175	1.445	9.792	1.403	9.421
11	1.675	12.245	1.631	11.807	1.589	11.381	1.546	10.968
12	1.832	14.077	1.789	13.595	1.746	13.127	1.704	12.672
13	2.004	16.081	1.961	15.557	1.919	15.046	1.878	14.549
14	2.192	18.272	2.151	17.708	2.110	17.156	2.069	16.619
15	2.397	20.670	2.358	20.066	2.319	19.476	2.280	18.899
	10% Int.		10¼% Int.		10½% Int.		10¾% Int.	
1	0.556	0.556	0.528	0.528	0.501	0.501	0.475	0.475
2	0.614	1.170	0.584	1.112	0.556	1.056	0.528	1.003
3	0.678	1.848	0.647	1.759	0.617	1.673	0.588	1.591
4	0.749	2.598	0.717	2.475	0.685	2.358	0.654	2.246
5	0.828	3.426	0.794	3.269	0.760	3.118	0.728	2.974
6	0.915	4.340	0.879	4.148	0.844	3.962	0.811	3.785
7	1.010	5.351	0.973	5.121	0.937	4.900	0.902	4.687
8	1.116	6.467	1.078	6.199	1.040	5.940	1.004	5.691
9	1.233	7.700	1.194	7.392	1.155	7.095	1.118	6.808
10	1.362	9.062	1.322	8.714	1.282	8.378	1.244	8.052
11	1.505	10.567	1.464	10.178	1.424	9.801	1.384	9.436
12	1.662	12.229	1.621	11.799	1.581	11.382	1.541	10.977
13	1.836	14.066	1.795	13.595	1.755	13.137	1.715	12.692
14	2.029	16.094	1.988	15.583	1.948	15.085	1.908	14.600
15	2.241	18.335	2.202	17.785	2.163	17.248	2.124	16.724
	11% Int.		11¼% Int.		11½% Int.		11¾% Int.	
1	0.450	0.450	0.427	0.427	0.404	0.404	0.383	0.383
2	0.502	0.952	0.477	0.904	0.453	0.858	0.431	0.814
3	0.560	1.513	0.534	1.438	0.508	1.366	0.484	1.298
4	0.625	2.138	0.597	2.035	0.570	1.936	0.544	1.842
5	0.698	2.835	0.668	2.703	0.639	2.575	0.612	2.453
6	0.778	3.614	0.747	3.449	0.717	3.292	0.687	3.141
7	0.868	4.482	0.835	4.285	0.804	4.096	0.773	3.914
8	0.969	5.451	0.934	5.219	0.901	4.997	0.869	4.782
9	1.081	6.532	1.045	6.264	1.010	6.007	0.976	5.758
10	1.206	7.737	1.169	7.433	1.133	7.140	1.097	6.856
11	1.345	9.083	1.307	8.741	1.270	8.410	1.234	8.089
12	1.501	10.584	1.462	10.203	1.424	9.834	1.387	9.476
13	1.675	12.259	1.636	11.839	1.597	11.431	1.558	11.034
14	1.869	14.128	1.829	13.668	1.790	13.221	1.752	12.786
15	2.085	16.213	2.046	15.714	2.008	15.229	1.969	14.755

EXAMPLES *ON PAGES A-382 TO A-397*

YEAR	Annual %	Cum. %	Annual %	Cum. %	Annual %	Cum. %	Annual %	Cum. %
	12% Int.		12¼% Int.		12½% Int.		12¾% Int.	
1	0.363	0.363	0.344	0.344	0.325	0.325	0.308	0.308
2	0.409	0.772	0.388	0.732	0.368	0.694	0.350	0.657
3	0.461	1.233	0.438	1.170	0.417	1.111	0.397	1.054
4	0.519	1.752	0.495	1.666	0.472	1.583	0.450	1.505
5	0.585	2.337	0.560	2.225	0.535	2.118	0.511	2.016
6	0.659	2.996	0.632	2.857	0.606	2.724	0.581	2.597
7	0.743	3.739	0.714	3.571	0.686	3.410	0.659	3.256
8	0.837	4.576	0.807	4.378	0.777	4.187	0.748	4.004
9	0.943	5.519	0.911	5.289	0.880	5.067	0.849	4.853
10	1.063	6.582	1.029	6.318	0.996	6.063	0.964	5.817
11	1.198	7.780	1.163	7.480	1.128	7.191	1.094	6.912
12	1.350	9.129	1.313	8.793	1.278	8.469	1.242	8.154
13	1.521	10.650	1.483	10.277	1.447	9.915	1.411	9.565
14	1.714	12.363	1.676	11.953	1.638	11.553	1.601	11.166
15	1.931	14.294	1.893	13.845	1.855	13.409	1.818	12.984
	13% Int.		13¼% Int.		13½% Int.		13¾% Int.	
1	0.291	0.291	0.276	0.276	0.261	0.261	0.247	0.247
2	0.332	0.623	0.314	0.590	0.298	0.559	0.283	0.529
3	0.377	1.000	0.359	0.949	0.341	0.900	0.324	0.853
4	0.429	1.430	0.409	1.358	0.390	1.290	0.371	1.225
5	0.489	1.918	0.467	1.825	0.446	1.736	0.426	1.651
6	0.556	2.474	0.533	2.358	0.510	2.246	0.488	2.139
7	0.633	3.107	0.608	2.965	0.583	2.829	0.560	2.699
8	0.720	3.828	0.693	3.659	0.667	3.496	0.642	3.341
9	0.820	4.647	0.791	4.450	0.763	4.259	0.736	4.077
10	0.933	5.580	0.902	5.352	0.873	5.132	0.844	4.920
11	1.062	6.642	1.029	6.381	0.998	6.130	0.967	5.888
12	1.208	7.850	1.174	7.556	1.141	7.271	1.109	6.997
13	1.375	9.225	1.340	8.896	1.305	8.577	1.272	8.268
14	1.565	10.789	1.529	10.424	1.493	10.070	1.458	9.726
15	1.781	12.570	1.744	12.168	1.707	11.777	1.671	11.397
	14% Int.		14¼% Int.		14½% Int.		14¾% Int.	
1	0.233	0.233	0.220	0.220	0.208	0.208	0.197	0.197
2	0.268	0.501	0.254	0.474	0.240	0.449	0.228	0.424
3	0.308	0.809	0.292	0.766	0.278	0.726	0.264	0.688
4	0.354	1.163	0.337	1.103	0.321	1.047	0.305	0.993
5	0.407	1.569	0.388	1.492	0.370	1.417	0.353	1.347
6	0.467	2.037	0.447	1.939	0.428	1.845	0.409	1.756
7	0.537	2.574	0.515	2.454	0.494	2.340	0.474	2.230
8	0.617	3.191	0.594	3.048	0.571	2.910	0.549	2.779
9	0.710	3.901	0.684	3.732	0.659	3.570	0.635	3.414
10	0.816	4.716	0.788	4.520	0.762	4.331	0.736	4.150
11	0.937	5.654	0.908	5.428	0.880	5.211	0.852	5.002
12	1.077	6.731	1.046	6.475	1.016	6.227	0.986	5.988
13	1.238	7.969	1.206	7.680	1.174	7.401	1.142	7.130
14	1.423	9.393	1.389	9.069	1.356	8.756	1.322	8.453
15	1.636	11.028	1.600	10.670	1.566	10.322	1.531	9.984
	15% Int.		15¼% Int.		15½% Int.		15¾% Int.	
1	0.186	0.186	0.175	0.175	0.166	0.166	0.156	0.156
2	0.216	0.401	0.204	0.380	0.193	0.359	0.183	0.339
3	0.250	0.652	0.238	0.617	0.225	0.584	0.214	0.553
4	0.291	0.942	0.276	0.893	0.263	0.847	0.250	0.803
5	0.337	1.279	0.322	1.215	0.307	1.154	0.292	1.096
6	0.391	1.671	0.374	1.589	0.358	1.512	0.342	1.437
7	0.454	2.125	0.435	2.025	0.417	1.929	0.400	1.837
8	0.527	2.653	0.507	2.532	0.487	2.416	0.468	2.305
9	0.612	3.265	0.590	3.121	0.568	2.984	0.547	2.852
10	0.711	3.975	0.686	3.807	0.662	3.646	0.639	3.491
11	0.825	4.800	0.798	4.606	0.773	4.419	0.748	4.239
12	0.957	5.757	0.929	5.535	0.901	5.320	0.874	5.113
13	1.111	6.869	1.081	6.616	1.051	6.372	1.022	6.136
14	1.290	8.159	1.258	7.874	1.227	7.598	1.196	7.331
15	1.497	9.656	1.464	9.338	1.431	9.029	1.398	8.729

EXAMPLES *ON PAGES A-382 TO A-397*

YEAR	Annual %	Cum. %	Annual %	Cum. %	Annual %	Cum. %	Annual %	Cum. %
	8% Int.		8¼% Int.		8½% Int.		8¾% Int.	
1	0.543	0.543	0.511	0.511	0.481	0.481	0.452	0.452
2	0.588	1.131	0.555	1.066	0.523	1.004	0.493	0.946
3	0.637	1.767	0.602	1.668	0.570	1.574	0.538	1.484
4	0.689	2.457	0.654	2.322	0.620	2.193	0.587	2.071
5	0.747	3.203	0.710	3.032	0.675	2.868	0.641	2.712
6	0.809	4.012	0.771	3.802	0.734	3.602	0.699	3.412
7	0.876	4.887	0.837	4.639	0.799	4.402	0.763	4.175
8	0.948	5.836	0.908	5.548	0.870	5.271	0.832	5.007
9	1.027	6.863	0.986	6.534	0.947	6.218	0.908	5.915
10	1.112	7.975	1.071	7.605	1.030	7.248	0.991	6.906
11	1.205	9.180	1.163	8.767	1.121	8.370	1.081	7.988
12	1.305	10.485	1.262	10.029	1.221	9.591	1.180	9.168
13	1.413	11.898	1.370	11.400	1.328	10.919	1.287	10.455
14	1.530	13.428	1.488	12.888	1.446	12.365	1.405	11.860
15	1.657	15.085	1.615	14.503	1.574	13.939	1.533	13.392
	9% Int.		9¼% Int.		9½% Int.		9¾% Int.	
1	0.425	0.425	0.400	0.400	0.375	0.375	0.353	0.353
2	0.465	0.890	0.438	0.838	0.413	0.788	0.389	0.741
3	0.509	1.399	0.480	1.318	0.454	1.242	0.428	1.169
4	0.556	1.955	0.527	1.845	0.499	1.740	0.472	1.641
5	0.609	2.564	0.578	2.423	0.548	2.288	0.520	2.161
6	0.666	3.230	0.633	3.056	0.603	2.891	0.573	2.734
7	0.728	3.958	0.695	3.751	0.662	3.553	0.631	3.365
8	0.796	4.754	0.762	4.512	0.728	4.281	0.696	4.061
9	0.871	5.625	0.835	5.348	0.800	5.082	0.767	4.827
10	0.953	6.578	0.916	6.263	0.880	5.961	0.845	5.672
11	1.042	7.620	1.004	7.267	0.967	6.929	0.931	6.603
12	1.140	8.760	1.101	8.368	1.063	7.992	1.026	7.629
13	1.247	10.007	1.207	9.576	1.169	9.160	1.131	8.760
14	1.364	11.371	1.324	10.900	1.285	10.445	1.246	10.006
15	1.492	12.863	1.452	12.351	1.412	11.857	1.373	11.379
	10% Int.		10¼% Int.		10½% Int.		10¾% Int.	
1	0.331	0.331	0.311	0.311	0.291	0.291	0.273	0.273
2	0.366	0.697	0.344	0.655	0.323	0.615	0.304	0.577
3	0.404	1.100	0.381	1.035	0.359	0.974	0.338	0.916
4	0.446	1.547	0.422	1.457	0.399	1.373	0.377	1.292
5	0.493	2.040	0.467	1.925	0.443	1.815	0.419	1.712
6	0.545	2.584	0.517	2.442	0.491	2.307	0.467	2.178
7	0.602	3.186	0.573	3.015	0.546	2.852	0.519	2.698
8	0.665	3.850	0.635	3.649	0.606	3.458	0.578	3.276
9	0.734	4.584	0.703	4.352	0.672	4.130	0.643	3.919
10	0.811	5.395	0.778	5.130	0.747	4.877	0.716	4.635
11	0.896	6.291	0.862	5.992	0.829	5.706	0.797	5.431
12	0.990	7.281	0.954	6.947	0.920	6.626	0.887	6.318
13	1.093	8.375	1.057	8.004	1.022	7.648	0.987	7.305
14	1.208	9.582	1.171	9.175	1.134	8.782	1.098	8.404
15	1.334	10.917	1.296	10.471	1.259	10.041	1.222	9.626
	11% Int.		11¼% Int.		11½% Int.		11¾% Int.	
1	0.256	0.256	0.240	0.240	0.225	0.225	0.211	0.211
2	0.286	0.542	0.268	0.509	0.252	0.477	0.237	0.447
3	0.319	0.861	0.300	0.809	0.283	0.760	0.266	0.714
4	0.356	1.217	0.336	1.145	0.317	1.077	0.299	1.013
5	0.397	1.614	0.376	1.520	0.355	1.432	0.336	1.349
6	0.443	2.056	0.420	1.941	0.399	1.831	0.378	1.727
7	0.494	2.550	0.470	2.411	0.447	2.278	0.425	2.152
8	0.551	3.102	0.526	2.936	0.501	2.779	0.478	2.629
9	0.615	3.717	0.588	3.524	0.562	3.341	0.537	3.166
10	0.686	4.403	0.658	4.182	0.630	3.971	0.603	3.769
11	0.766	5.169	0.736	4.917	0.706	4.677	0.678	4.447
12	0.854	6.023	0.823	5.740	0.792	5.469	0.762	5.210
13	0.953	6.976	0.920	6.660	0.888	6.357	0.857	6.067
14	1.063	8.040	1.029	7.690	0.996	7.353	0.963	7.030
15	1.186	9.226	1.151	8.841	1.117	8.470	1.083	8.112

EXAMPLES *ON PAGES A-382 TO A-397*

YEAR	Annual %	Cum. %	Annual %	Cum. %	Annual %	Cum. %	Annual %	Cum. %
	12% Int.		12¼% Int.		12½% Int.		12¾% Int.	
1	0.197	0.197	0.185	0.185	0.173	0.173	0.162	0.162
2	0.222	0.419	0.209	0.393	0.196	0.368	0.183	0.345
3	0.250	0.670	0.236	0.629	0.221	0.590	0.208	0.553
4	0.282	0.952	0.266	0.895	0.251	0.841	0.236	0.790
5	0.318	1.270	0.301	1.195	0.284	1.125	0.268	1.058
6	0.358	1.628	0.340	1.535	0.322	1.446	0.305	1.363
7	0.404	2.032	0.384	1.918	0.364	1.811	0.346	1.708
8	0.455	2.487	0.433	2.352	0.412	2.223	0.393	2.101
9	0.513	2.999	0.489	2.841	0.467	2.690	0.446	2.547
10	0.578	3.577	0.553	3.394	0.529	3.219	0.506	3.053
11	0.651	4.228	0.624	4.018	0.599	3.818	0.574	3.627
12	0.733	4.961	0.705	4.724	0.678	4.496	0.652	4.279
13	0.826	5.788	0.797	5.521	0.768	5.265	0.740	5.019
14	0.931	6.719	0.900	6.421	0.870	6.134	0.840	5.860
15	1.049	7.768	1.017	7.438	0.985	7.119	0.954	6.814
	13% Int.		13¼% Int.		13½% Int.		13¾% Int.	
1	0.151	0.151	0.141	0.141	0.132	0.132	0.123	0.123
2	0.172	0.323	0.161	0.302	0.151	0.283	0.141	0.265
3	0.196	0.519	0.184	0.486	0.173	0.456	0.162	0.427
4	0.223	0.742	0.210	0.696	0.198	0.653	0.186	0.613
5	0.253	0.995	0.239	0.935	0.226	0.879	0.213	0.826
6	0.288	1.283	0.273	1.209	0.258	1.138	0.244	1.071
7	0.328	1.612	0.312	1.520	0.296	1.433	0.280	1.351
8	0.374	1.985	0.355	1.875	0.338	1.771	0.321	1.672
9	0.425	2.410	0.405	2.281	0.387	2.158	0.368	2.041
10	0.484	2.894	0.463	2.743	0.442	2.600	0.422	2.463
11	0.551	3.445	0.528	3.271	0.506	3.105	0.484	2.947
12	0.627	4.071	0.602	3.873	0.578	3.684	0.555	3.503
13	0.713	4.785	0.687	4.560	0.661	4.345	0.637	4.139
14	0.812	5.596	0.784	5.343	0.756	5.101	0.730	4.869
15	0.924	6.520	0.894	6.237	0.865	5.966	0.837	5.706
	14% Int.		14¼% Int.		14½% Int.		14¾% Int.	
1	0.115	0.115	0.108	0.108	0.101	0.101	0.094	0.094
2	0.133	0.248	0.124	0.232	0.116	0.217	0.109	0.203
3	0.152	0.400	0.143	0.375	0.134	0.351	0.126	0.328
4	0.175	0.575	0.165	0.539	0.155	0.506	0.146	0.474
5	0.201	0.776	0.190	0.729	0.179	0.685	0.169	0.643
6	0.231	1.008	0.219	0.948	0.207	0.891	0.195	0.838
7	0.266	1.273	0.252	1.200	0.239	1.130	0.226	1.065
8	0.305	1.579	0.290	1.490	0.276	1.406	0.262	1.326
9	0.351	1.930	0.334	1.825	0.319	1.725	0.303	1.630
10	0.403	2.333	0.385	2.210	0.368	2.093	0.351	1.981
11	0.464	2.797	0.444	2.654	0.425	2.517	0.407	2.388
12	0.533	3.330	0.512	3.165	0.491	3.008	0.471	2.859
13	0.613	3.943	0.589	3.755	0.567	3.575	0.545	3.404
14	0.704	4.647	0.679	4.434	0.655	4.230	0.631	4.035
15	0.809	5.456	0.782	5.216	0.756	4.987	0.731	4.766
	15% Int.		15¼% Int.		15½% Int.		15¾% Int.	
1	0.088	0.088	0.082	0.082	0.076	0.076	0.071	0.071
2	0.102	0.189	0.095	0.177	0.089	0.165	0.083	0.154
3	0.118	0.307	0.111	0.288	0.104	0.269	0.097	0.252
4	0.137	0.444	0.129	0.416	0.121	0.390	0.114	0.365
5	0.159	0.603	0.150	0.566	0.141	0.531	0.133	0.499
6	0.185	0.788	0.174	0.741	0.165	0.696	0.156	0.654
7	0.214	1.002	0.203	0.944	0.192	0.888	0.182	0.836
8	0.249	1.251	0.236	1.180	0.224	1.113	0.213	1.049
9	0.289	1.540	0.275	1.455	0.262	1.374	0.249	1.298
10	0.335	1.875	0.320	1.775	0.305	1.679	0.291	1.589
11	0.389	2.264	0.372	2.147	0.356	2.035	0.340	1.929
12	0.452	2.716	0.433	2.580	0.415	2.450	0.398	2.327
13	0.524	3.240	0.504	3.084	0.484	2.934	0.465	2.792
14	0.608	3.848	0.586	3.670	0.565	3.499	0.544	3.336
15	0.706	4.555	0.682	4.352	0.659	4.158	0.636	3.972

EXAMPLES *ON PAGES A-382 TO A-397*

YEAR	Annual %	Cum. %	Annual %	Cum. %	Annual %	Cum. %	Annual %	Cum. %
	8% Int.		8¼% Int.		8½% Int.		8¾% Int.	
1	0.357	0.357	0.332	0.332	0.309	0.309	0.287	0.287
2	0.386	0.743	0.360	0.693	0.336	0.645	0.314	0.601
3	0.418	1.161	0.391	1.084	0.366	1.011	0.342	0.943
4	0.453	1.614	0.425	1.509	0.398	1.410	0.373	1.316
5	0.491	2.105	0.461	1.970	0.434	1.843	0.407	1.724
6	0.531	2.636	0.501	2.471	0.472	2.315	0.444	2.168
7	0.575	3.211	0.544	3.015	0.514	2.829	0.485	2.653
8	0.623	3.835	0.590	3.605	0.559	3.388	0.529	3.182
9	0.675	4.510	0.641	4.246	0.608	3.996	0.577	3.759
10	0.731	5.240	0.696	4.942	0.662	4.658	0.630	4.389
11	0.792	6.032	0.756	5.698	0.721	5.379	0.687	5.076
12	0.857	6.889	0.820	6.518	0.784	6.164	0.750	5.826
13	0.928	7.818	0.891	7.408	0.854	7.017	0.818	6.644
14	1.006	8.823	0.967	8.375	0.929	7.947	0.893	7.537
15	1.089	9.912	1.050	9.425	1.011	8.958	0.974	8.511
	9% Int.		9¼% Int.		9½% Int.		9¾% Int.	
1	0.267	0.267	0.248	0.248	0.231	0.231	0.214	0.214
2	0.292	0.559	0.272	0.521	0.253	0.484	0.236	0.450
3	0.320	0.879	0.299	0.819	0.279	0.763	0.260	0.710
4	0.350	1.229	0.327	1.146	0.306	1.069	0.287	0.997
5	0.382	1.611	0.359	1.505	0.337	1.406	0.316	1.312
6	0.418	2.029	0.394	1.899	0.370	1.776	0.348	1.660
7	0.458	2.487	0.432	2.330	0.407	2.183	0.383	2.044
8	0.500	2.988	0.473	2.804	0.447	2.630	0.423	2.466
9	0.547	3.535	0.519	3.323	0.492	3.122	0.466	2.932
10	0.599	4.134	0.569	3.892	0.540	3.662	0.513	3.445
11	0.655	4.789	0.624	4.515	0.594	4.256	0.565	4.010
12	0.716	5.505	0.684	5.200	0.653	4.909	0.623	4.633
13	0.784	6.289	0.750	5.950	0.718	5.627	0.687	5.320
14	0.857	7.146	0.823	6.772	0.789	6.416	0.757	6.076
15	0.938	8.083	0.902	7.674	0.867	7.283	0.834	6.910
	10% Int.		10¼% Int.		10½% Int.		10¾% Int.	
1	0.199	0.199	0.184	0.184	0.171	0.171	0.158	0.158
2	0.219	0.418	0.204	0.388	0.190	0.361	0.176	0.335
3	0.242	0.661	0.226	0.615	0.211	0.571	0.196	0.531
4	0.268	0.929	0.250	0.865	0.234	0.805	0.218	0.749
5	0.296	1.224	0.277	1.142	0.260	1.065	0.243	0.992
6	0.327	1.551	0.307	1.449	0.288	1.353	0.271	1.263
7	0.361	1.913	0.340	1.789	0.320	1.673	0.301	1.564
8	0.399	2.311	0.377	2.166	0.355	2.028	0.335	1.899
9	0.441	2.752	0.417	2.583	0.394	2.423	0.373	2.272
10	0.487	3.239	0.462	3.045	0.438	2.861	0.415	2.687
11	0.538	3.777	0.511	3.556	0.486	3.347	0.462	3.149
12	0.594	4.371	0.566	4.123	0.540	3.887	0.514	3.663
13	0.656	5.028	0.627	4.750	0.599	4.486	0.572	4.235
14	0.725	5.753	0.695	5.445	0.665	5.151	0.637	4.872
15	0.801	6.554	0.769	6.214	0.739	5.890	0.709	5.581
	11% Int.		11¼% Int.		11½% Int.		11¾% Int.	
1	0.147	0.147	0.136	0.136	0.126	0.126	0.117	0.117
2	0.164	0.311	0.152	0.288	0.141	0.267	0.131	0.247
3	0.183	0.493	0.170	0.458	0.158	0.425	0.147	0.395
4	0.204	0.697	0.190	0.648	0.177	0.603	0.165	0.560
5	0.227	0.925	0.213	0.861	0.199	0.802	0.186	0.746
6	0.254	1.178	0.238	1.099	0.223	1.025	0.209	0.955
7	0.283	1.462	0.266	1.365	0.250	1.275	0.235	1.190
8	0.316	1.777	0.298	1.663	0.280	1.555	0.264	1.454
9	0.352	2.130	0.333	1.996	0.314	1.870	0.297	1.751
10	0.393	2.523	0.372	2.368	0.353	2.223	0.334	2.085
11	0.439	2.962	0.417	2.785	0.395	2.618	0.375	2.460
12	0.490	3.452	0.466	3.251	0.443	3.061	0.422	2.882
13	0.546	3.998	0.521	3.772	0.497	3.558	0.474	3.356
14	0.609	4.607	0.583	4.355	0.557	4.116	0.533	3.888
15	0.680	5.287	0.652	5.007	0.625	4.741	0.599	4.487

EXAMPLES *ON PAGES A-382 TO A-397*

EQUITY BUILD-UP
IN PERCENT OF ORIGINAL LOAN AMOUNT
FOR FIRST 15 YEARS

YEAR	Annual %	Cum. %	Annual %	Cum. %	Annual %	Cum. %	Annual %	Cum. %
	12% Int.		12¼% Int.		12½% Int.		12¾% Int.	
1	0.108	0.108	0.100	0.100	0.092	0.092	0.085	0.085
2	0.121	0.229	0.113	0.212	0.104	0.197	0.097	0.182
3	0.137	0.366	0.127	0.340	0.118	0.315	0.110	0.292
4	0.154	0.520	0.144	0.483	0.134	0.449	0.125	0.416
5	0.174	0.694	0.162	0.646	0.152	0.600	0.142	0.558
6	0.196	0.890	0.183	0.829	0.172	0.772	0.161	0.719
7	0.221	1.111	0.207	1.036	0.194	0.966	0.182	0.901
8	0.249	1.359	0.234	1.270	0.220	1.187	0.207	1.108
9	0.280	1.640	0.264	1.535	0.249	1.436	0.235	1.343
10	0.316	1.955	0.299	1.833	0.282	1.718	0.267	1.610
11	0.356	2.311	0.337	2.171	0.320	2.038	0.303	1.913
12	0.401	2.712	0.381	2.552	0.362	2.400	0.344	2.257
13	0.452	3.164	0.430	2.982	0.410	2.810	0.390	2.647
14	0.509	3.673	0.486	3.468	0.464	3.274	0.443	3.091
15	0.574	4.246	0.549	4.018	0.526	3.800	0.503	3.594
	13% Int.		13¼% Int.		13½% Int.		13¾% Int.	
1	0.079	0.079	0.073	0.073	0.067	0.067	0.062	0.062
2	0.090	0.168	0.083	0.156	0.077	0.144	0.071	0.133
3	0.102	0.270	0.095	0.250	0.088	0.232	0.082	0.215
4	0.116	0.386	0.108	0.358	0.101	0.332	0.093	0.308
5	0.132	0.519	0.123	0.482	0.115	0.447	0.107	0.415
6	0.150	0.669	0.141	0.622	0.131	0.579	0.123	0.538
7	0.171	0.840	0.160	0.783	0.150	0.729	0.141	0.679
8	0.195	1.035	0.183	0.966	0.172	0.901	0.162	0.841
9	0.222	1.256	0.209	1.174	0.197	1.098	0.185	1.026
10	0.252	1.508	0.238	1.413	0.225	1.323	0.212	1.238
11	0.287	1.795	0.272	1.684	0.257	1.580	0.243	1.482
12	0.327	2.122	0.310	1.994	0.294	1.874	0.279	1.761
13	0.372	2.494	0.354	2.348	0.336	2.211	0.320	2.081
14	0.423	2.916	0.403	2.752	0.385	2.595	0.367	2.448
15	0.481	3.398	0.460	3.212	0.440	3.036	0.421	2.868
	14% Int.		14¼% Int.		14½% Int.		14¾% Int.	
1	0.057	0.057	0.053	0.053	0.049	0.049	0.045	0.045
2	0.066	0.123	0.061	0.114	0.056	0.105	0.052	0.097
3	0.076	0.199	0.070	0.184	0.065	0.170	0.060	0.157
4	0.087	0.286	0.081	0.265	0.075	0.245	0.070	0.227
5	0.100	0.386	0.093	0.358	0.087	0.332	0.081	0.308
6	0.115	0.500	0.107	0.465	0.100	0.432	0.094	0.402
7	0.132	0.632	0.124	0.589	0.116	0.548	0.108	0.510
8	0.152	0.784	0.142	0.731	0.134	0.682	0.125	0.635
9	0.174	0.959	0.164	0.895	0.154	0.836	0.145	0.781
10	0.200	1.159	0.189	1.084	0.178	1.014	0.168	0.949
11	0.230	1.389	0.218	1.302	0.206	1.221	0.195	1.144
12	0.265	1.654	0.251	1.553	0.238	1.458	0.226	1.369
13	0.304	1.958	0.289	1.843	0.275	1.733	0.261	1.630
14	0.350	2.308	0.333	2.176	0.317	2.051	0.302	1.933
15	0.402	2.710	0.384	2.560	0.367	2.418	0.350	2.283
	15% Int.		15¼% Int.		15½% Int.		15¾% Int.	
1	0.041	0.041	0.038	0.038	0.035	0.035	0.032	0.032
2	0.048	0.090	0.044	0.083	0.041	0.076	0.038	0.070
3	0.056	0.145	0.052	0.134	0.048	0.124	0.044	0.115
4	0.065	0.210	0.060	0.195	0.056	0.180	0.052	0.167
5	0.075	0.286	0.070	0.265	0.065	0.245	0.061	0.227
6	0.087	0.373	0.082	0.346	0.076	0.322	0.071	0.298
7	0.101	0.474	0.095	0.441	0.089	0.410	0.083	0.381
8	0.118	0.592	0.110	0.552	0.104	0.514	0.097	0.479
9	0.137	0.729	0.128	0.680	0.121	0.635	0.114	0.592
10	0.159	0.887	0.150	0.830	0.141	0.776	0.133	0.725
11	0.184	1.071	0.174	1.004	0.164	0.940	0.155	0.880
12	0.214	1.285	0.202	1.206	0.192	1.132	0.182	1.062
13	0.248	1.533	0.236	1.442	0.224	1.355	0.212	1.274
14	0.288	1.821	0.274	1.716	0.261	1.616	0.248	1.522
15	0.334	2.155	0.319	2.035	0.304	1.920	0.290	1.812

EXAMPLES *ON PAGES A-382 TO A-397*

MACRS TABLES
For Assets Placed in Service After December 31, 1986

General Depreciation System
Applicable Depreciation Method: 200 or 150 Percent Declining Balance Switching to Straight Line
Applicable Recovery Periods: 3,5,7,10,15,20 years
Applicable Convention: Half-year

If the Recovery Year is:	and the Recovery Period is:					
	3-year	5-year	7-year	10-year	15-year	20-year
	the Depreciation Rate is:					
1	33.33	20.00	14.29	10.00	5.00	3.750
2	44.45	32.00	24.49	18.00	9.50	7.219
3	14.81	19.20	17.49	14.40	8.55	6.677
4	7.41	11.52	12.49	11.52	7.70	6.177
5		11.52	8.93	9.22	6.93	5.713
6		5.76	8.92	7.37	6.23	5.285
7			8.93	6.55	5.90	4.888
8			4.46	6.55	5.90	4.522
9				6.56	5.91	4.462
10				6.55	5.90	4.462
11				3.28	5.91	4.461
12					5.90	4.462
13					5.91	4.461
14					5.90	4.461
15					5.91	4.461
16					2.95	4.462
17						4.461
18						4.461
19						4.462
20						4.461
21						2.231

MACRS TABLES
For Assets Placed in Service After December 31, 1986

General Depreciation System
Applicable Depreciation Method: Straight Line
Applicable Recovery Periods: 27.5 years
Applicable Convention: Mid-month

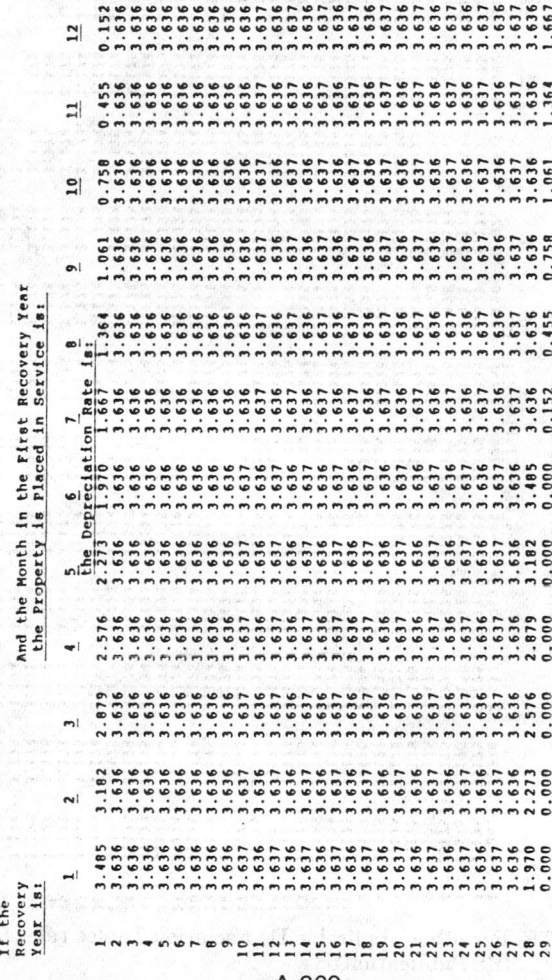

If the Recovery Year is:	And the Month in the First Recovery Year the Property is Placed in Service is:											
	1	2	3	4	5	6	7	8	9	10	11	12
	the Depreciation Rate is:											
1	3.485	3.182	2.879	2.576	2.273	1.970	1.667	1.364	1.061	0.758	0.455	0.152
2	3.636	3.636	3.636	3.636	3.636	3.636	3.636	3.636	3.636	3.636	3.636	3.636
3	3.636	3.636	3.636	3.636	3.636	3.636	3.636	3.636	3.636	3.636	3.636	3.636
4	3.636	3.636	3.636	3.636	3.636	3.636	3.636	3.636	3.636	3.636	3.636	3.636
5	3.636	3.636	3.636	3.636	3.636	3.636	3.636	3.636	3.636	3.636	3.636	3.636
6	3.636	3.636	3.636	3.636	3.636	3.636	3.636	3.636	3.636	3.636	3.636	3.636
7	3.636	3.636	3.636	3.636	3.637	3.636	3.636	3.636	3.636	3.636	3.636	3.636
8	3.636	3.637	3.636	3.636	3.636	3.636	3.636	3.636	3.636	3.636	3.636	3.636
9	3.636	3.636	3.637	3.636	3.636	3.636	3.636	3.636	3.636	3.636	3.636	3.636
10	3.637	3.636	3.636	3.637	3.636	3.636	3.636	3.636	3.637	3.636	3.636	3.636
11	3.636	3.637	3.636	3.636	3.637	3.636	3.636	3.636	3.636	3.637	3.636	3.636
12	3.637	3.636	3.637	3.636	3.636	3.637	3.636	3.636	3.636	3.636	3.637	3.636
13	3.636	3.637	3.636	3.637	3.636	3.636	3.637	3.636	3.636	3.636	3.636	3.637
14	3.637	3.636	3.637	3.636	3.637	3.636	3.636	3.637	3.636	3.636	3.636	3.636
15	3.636	3.637	3.636	3.637	3.636	3.637	3.636	3.636	3.637	3.636	3.636	3.636
16	3.637	3.636	3.637	3.636	3.637	3.636	3.637	3.636	3.636	3.637	3.636	3.636
17	3.636	3.637	3.636	3.637	3.636	3.637	3.636	3.637	3.636	3.636	3.637	3.636
18	3.637	3.636	3.637	3.636	3.637	3.636	3.637	3.636	3.637	3.636	3.636	3.637
19	3.636	3.637	3.636	3.637	3.636	3.637	3.636	3.637	3.636	3.637	3.636	3.636
20	3.637	3.636	3.637	3.636	3.637	3.636	3.637	3.636	3.637	3.636	3.637	3.636
21	3.636	3.637	3.636	3.637	3.636	3.637	3.636	3.637	3.636	3.637	3.636	3.637
22	3.637	3.636	3.637	3.636	3.637	3.636	3.637	3.636	3.637	3.636	3.637	3.636
23	3.636	3.637	3.636	3.637	3.636	3.637	3.636	3.637	3.636	3.637	3.636	3.637
24	3.637	3.636	3.637	3.636	3.637	3.636	3.637	3.636	3.637	3.636	3.637	3.636
25	3.636	3.637	3.636	3.637	3.636	3.637	3.636	3.637	3.636	3.637	3.636	3.637
26	3.637	3.636	3.637	3.636	3.637	3.636	3.637	3.636	3.637	3.636	3.637	3.636
27	3.636	3.637	3.636	3.637	3.636	3.637	3.636	3.637	3.636	3.637	3.636	3.637
28	1.970	2.273	2.576	2.879	3.182	3.485	3.636	3.636	3.636	3.636	3.636	3.636
29	0.000	0.000	0.000	0.000	0.000	0.000	0.152	0.455	0.758	1.061	1.364	1.667

MACRS TABLES
For Assets Placed in Service After December 31, 1986

General Depreciation System
Applicable Depreciation Method: Straight Line
Applicable Recovery Periods: 31.5 years
Applicable Convention: Mid-month

If the Recovery Year is:	And the Month in the First Recovery Year the Property is Placed in Service is:											
	the Depreciation Rate is:											
	1	2	3	4	5	6	7	8	9	10	11	12
1	3.042	2.778	2.513	2.249	1.984	1.720	1.455	1.190	0.926	0.661	0.397	0.132
2	3.175	3.175	3.175	3.175	3.175	3.175	3.175	3.175	3.175	3.175	3.175	3.175
3	3.175	3.175	3.175	3.175	3.175	3.175	3.175	3.175	3.175	3.175	3.175	3.175
4	3.175	3.175	3.175	3.175	3.175	3.175	3.175	3.175	3.175	3.175	3.175	3.175
5	3.175	3.175	3.175	3.175	3.175	3.175	3.175	3.175	3.175	3.175	3.175	3.175
6	3.175	3.175	3.175	3.175	3.175	3.175	3.175	3.175	3.175	3.175	3.175	3.175
7	3.175	3.175	3.175	3.175	3.175	3.175	3.175	3.175	3.175	3.175	3.175	3.175
8	3.175	3.175	3.175	3.175	3.175	3.175	3.175	3.175	3.175	3.175	3.175	3.175
9	3.174	3.174	3.174	3.174	3.174	3.174	3.174	3.174	3.174	3.174	3.174	3.174
10	3.175	3.175	3.175	3.175	3.175	3.175	3.175	3.175	3.175	3.175	3.175	3.175
11	3.174	3.174	3.174	3.174	3.174	3.174	3.174	3.174	3.174	3.174	3.174	3.174
12	3.175	3.175	3.175	3.175	3.175	3.175	3.175	3.175	3.175	3.175	3.175	3.175
13	3.174	3.174	3.174	3.174	3.174	3.174	3.174	3.174	3.174	3.174	3.174	3.174
14	3.175	3.175	3.175	3.175	3.175	3.175	3.175	3.175	3.175	3.175	3.175	3.175
15	3.174	3.174	3.174	3.174	3.174	3.174	3.174	3.174	3.174	3.174	3.174	3.174
16	3.175	3.175	3.175	3.175	3.175	3.175	3.175	3.175	3.175	3.175	3.175	3.175
17	3.174	3.174	3.174	3.174	3.174	3.174	3.174	3.174	3.174	3.174	3.174	3.174
18	3.175	3.175	3.175	3.175	3.175	3.175	3.175	3.175	3.175	3.175	3.175	3.175
19	3.174	3.174	3.174	3.174	3.174	3.174	3.174	3.174	3.174	3.174	3.174	3.174
20	3.175	3.175	3.175	3.175	3.175	3.175	3.175	3.175	3.175	3.175	3.175	3.175
21	3.174	3.174	3.174	3.174	3.174	3.174	3.174	3.174	3.174	3.174	3.174	3.174
22	3.175	3.175	3.175	3.175	3.175	3.175	3.175	3.175	3.175	3.175	3.175	3.175
23	3.174	3.174	3.174	3.174	3.174	3.174	3.174	3.174	3.174	3.174	3.174	3.174
24	3.175	3.175	3.175	3.175	3.175	3.175	3.175	3.175	3.175	3.175	3.175	3.175
25	3.174	3.174	3.174	3.174	3.174	3.174	3.174	3.174	3.174	3.174	3.174	3.174
26	3.175	3.175	3.175	3.175	3.175	3.175	3.175	3.175	3.175	3.175	3.175	3.175
27	3.174	3.174	3.174	3.174	3.174	3.174	3.174	3.174	3.174	3.174	3.174	3.174
28	3.175	3.175	3.175	3.175	3.175	3.175	3.175	3.175	3.175	3.175	3.175	3.175
29	3.174	3.174	3.174	3.174	3.174	3.174	3.174	3.174	3.174	3.174	3.174	3.174
30	3.175	3.175	3.175	3.175	3.175	3.175	3.175	3.175	3.175	3.175	3.175	3.175
31	3.174	3.174	3.174	3.174	3.174	3.174	3.174	3.174	3.174	3.174	3.174	3.174
32	1.720	1.984	2.249	2.513	2.778	3.042	3.175	3.175	3.175	3.175	3.175	3.175
33	0.000	0.000	0.000	0.000	0.000	0.000	0.132	0.397	0.661	0.926	1.190	1.455

NOTE: For other applicable Depreciation Tables refer to IRS Publication 534.

Notes:

FEDERAL INCOME TAX RATES
EFFECTIVE 1987

Married Individuals Filing Joint Returns and Surviving Spouses

TAXABLE INCOME*	PAY
$ 0 – $ 3,000	11%
3,001 – 28,000	330 + 15% ON EXCESS OVER 3,000
28,001 – 45,000	4,080 + 28% ON EXCESS OVER 28,000
45,001 – 90,000	8,840 + 35% ON EXCESS OVER 45,000
Over 90,000	24,590 + 38.5% ON EXCESS OVER 90,000

Standard Deduction – 3,760
Additional Standard – 600 for 65 and over or blind
Personal Exemption – 1,900 for each individual and dependent

Heads of Household

TAXABLE INCOME*	PAY
$ 0 – $ 2,500	11%
2,501 – 23,000	275 + 15% ON EXCESS OVER 2,500
23,001 – 38,000	3,350 + 28% ON EXCESS OVER 23,000
38,001 – 80,000	7,550 + 35% ON EXCESS OVER 38,000
Over 80,000	22,250 + 38.5% ON EXCESS OVER 80,000

Standard Deduction – 2,540
Additional Standard – 750 for 65 and over or blind
Personal Exemption – 1,900 for each individual and dependent

Single Individuals

TAXABLE INCOME*	PAY
$ 0 – $ 1,800	11%
1,801 – 16,800	198 + 15% ON EXCESS OVER 1,800
16,801 – 27,000	2,448 + 28% ON EXCESS OVER 16,800
27,001 – 54,000	5,304 + 35% ON EXCESS OVER 27,000
Over 54,000	14,754 + 38.5% ON EXCESS OVER 54,000

Standard Deduction – 1,880
Additional Standard – 750 for 65 and over or blind
Personal Exemption – 1,900 for each individual and dependent

LONG-TERM CAPITAL GAINS

Taxed as ordinary income with maximum rate of 28% (no 60% exclusion).

*Adjusted gross income less itemized or standard deduction and personal exemptions.

FEDERAL INCOME TAX RATES
EFFECTIVE 1988

Married Individuals Filing Joint Returns and Surviving Spouses

TAXABLE INCOME*	PAY
$ 0 – $29,750	15%
29,751 – 71,900	4,463 + 28% ON EXCESS OVER 29,750
71,901 – 149,250	16,265 + 33% ON EXCESS OVER 71,900
Over 149,250	41,790 + 28% ON EXCESS OVER 149,250

Standard Deduction – 5,000
Additional Standard – 600 for 65 and over or blind
Personal Exemption** – 1,950 for each individual and dependent

Heads of Household

TAXABLE INCOME*	PAY
$ 0 – $23,900	15%
23,901 – 61,650	3,585 + 28% ON EXCESS OVER 23,900
61,650 – 123,790	20,984 + 33% ON EXCESS OVER 61,650
Over 123,790	41,490 + 28% ON EXCESS OVER 123,790

Standard Deduction – 4,400
Additional Standard – 750 for 65 and over or blind
Personal Exemption** – 1,950 for each individual and dependent

Single Individuals

TAXABLE INCOME*	PAY
$ 0 – $17,850	15%
17,851 – 43,150	2,678 + 28% ON EXCESS OVER 17,850
43,131 – 89,650	9,762 + 33% ON EXCESS OVER 43,150
Over 89,650	25,107 + 28% ON EXCESS OVER 89,650

Standard Deduction – 3,000
Additional Standard – 750 for 65 and over or blind
Personal Exemption** – 1,950 for each individual and dependent

*Adjusted gross income less itemized or standard deduction and personal exemptions.

**In 1988, personal exemptions are phased out by increasing the tax rate by 5% after the benefit of the 15% tax rate has been phased out. For example: an additional tax of 5% on income in excess of $149,250 for a married couple filing jointly would be changed until an amount equal to all exemptions had been recovered.

MEASUREMENTS

Computing Square Feet

SQ. FT.	ACRES	SQ. FT.	ACRES	SQ. FT.	ACRES	SQ. FT.	ACRES
1,742,400	40	217,800	5	26,136	0.6	3,049.2	0.07
1,306,800	30	174,240	4	21,780	0.5	2,613.6	0.06
871,200	20	130,680	3	17,424	0.4	2,178	0.05
435,600	10	87,120	2	13,068	0.3	1,742.4	0.04
392,040	9	43,560	1	8,712	0.2	1,306.8	0.03
348,480	8	39,204	0.9	4,356	0.1	871.2	0.02
304,920	7	34,848	0.8	3,920.4	0.09	435.6	0.01
261,360	6	30,492	0.7	3,484.8	0.08		

Number of Various Lots per Acre

For the purpose of subdivision, the number of lots
per acre given below must be adjusted to allow
for streets and other dedications.

LOT SIZE	Approx. No. of Lots per Acre	LOT SIZE	Approx. No. of Lots per Acre	LOT SIZE	Approx. No. of Lots per Acre	LOT SIZE	Approx. No. of Lots per Acre
25 × 100	17.42	30 × 100	14.52	50 × 100	8.71	100 × 100	4.35
25 × 120	14.52	30 × 120	12.1	50 × 120	7.26	100 × 120	3.63

Widths Times Depths Equaling One Acre

1 ACRE EQUALS		1 ACRE EQUALS		1 ACRE EQUALS	
Length	Width	Length	Width	Length	Width
16.5 ft.	2640. ft.	66. ft.	660. ft.	132. ft.	330. ft.
33.	1320.	75.	580.8	150.	290.4
50.	871.2	100.	435.6	208.71	208.71

Price Per Acre Produced by Certain Prices Per Square Foot

CENTS PER SQ. FOOT	$ PER ACRE	CENTS PER SQ. FOOT	$ PER ACRE	CENTS PER SQ. FOOT	$ PER ACRE	CENTS PER SQ. FOOT	$ PER ACRE
1¢	$ 435.60	9¢	$3,920.40	30¢	$13,068	70¢	$30,492
2	871.20	10	4,356.00	35	15,246	75	32,670
3	1,306.80	12	5,227.20	40	17,424	80	34,848
4	1,742.40	14	6,098.40	45	19,602	85	37,026
5	2,178.00	16	6,969.60	50	21,780	90	39,204
6	2,613.60	18	7,840.80	55	23,958	95	41,382
7	3,049.20	20	8,712.00	60	26,136	100	43,560
8	3,484.80	25	10,890.00	65	28,314		

1 Link = 7.92 Inches

1 Rod = 16½ Feet

5½ Yards = 25 Links

1 Chain = 66 Feet = 4 Rods = 100 Links

1 Furlong = 660 Feet = 40 Rods

1 Mile = 8 Furlongs = 320 Rods = 80 Chains = 5280 Feet

1 Square Mile = 1 Section = 640 Acres

1 Township = 36 Sections or square miles

1 Sq. Rod = 272¼ Sq. Feet = 30¼ Sq. Yards

1 Acre = 43560 Square Feet

1 Acre = 160 Square Rods

1 Acre is about 208¾ Feet Square

1 Acre is 8 Rods × 20 Rods (or any two numbers of rods whose product is 160)

ONE SECTION OF LAND CONTAINS ONE SQUARE MILE OR 640 ACRES

DETERMINING SQUARE FOOTAGE

a = area   b = base   h = height

① SQUARES

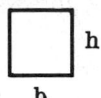

$$a = b \times h$$

② RECTANGLES

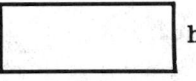

$$a = b \times h$$

③ PARALLELOGRAMS
(4-sided figure with parallel opposite sides)

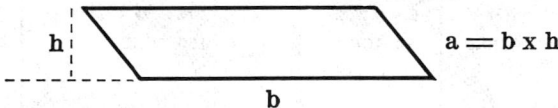

$$a = b \times h$$

④ TRAPEZOID
(4-sided figure with only 2 parallel sides)

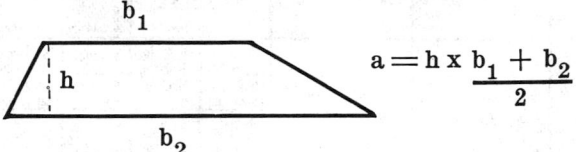

$$a = h \times \frac{b_1 + b_2}{2}$$

⑤ TRIANGLES WITH 90° ANGLE

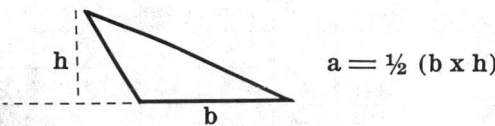

$$a = \frac{1}{2} (b \times h)$$

⑥ TRIANGLES WITHOUT 90° ANGLE

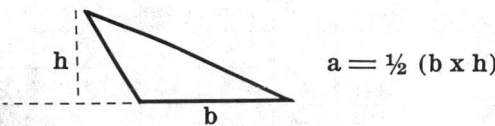

$$a = \frac{1}{2} (b \times h)$$

⑦ CIRCLE
R = radius

$a = R^2 \times 3.1416$

If radius is 14 ft.,

$a = 14 \times 14 \times 3.1416 = 615.75$

⑧ SEGMENT OF CIRCLE

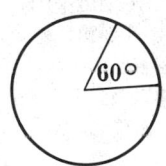

Since there are 360° in a circle, the area of a 60° section is $\frac{60}{360}$, or $\frac{1}{6}$ of the entire circle.

⑨ SEGMENT OF CIRCLE

If the radius and length of an arc are given:

$$a = \text{length of arc} \times \frac{1}{2} \text{ radius}$$

METRIC MEASUREMENTS AND CONVERSIONS

DISTANCE

km = kilometer   cm = centimeter

m = meter   mm = millimeter

dm = decimeter

	km	m	dm	cm	mm	mile	yard	foot	inch
1 km	1	1000	10,000	100,000	1,000,000	0.6214	1,093.64	3280.9	
1 m	$\frac{1}{1000}$	1	10	100	1,000	0.00062	1.0936	3.2809	39.371
1 dm	$\frac{1}{10,000}$	$\frac{1}{10}$	1	10	100		0.1094	0.3281	3.9371
1 cm		$\frac{1}{100}$	$\frac{1}{10}$	1	10		0.0109	0.0328	0.3937
1 mm		$\frac{1}{1000}$	$\frac{1}{100}$	$\frac{1}{10}$	1			0.0033	0.0394
1 mile	1.6093	1609.33				1	1760	5280	63360
1 yard		0.9144	9.1438	91.438	914.38		1	3	36
1 foot		0.3048	3.0479	30.479	304.79		$\frac{1}{3}$	1	12
1 inch		0.0254	0.254	2.54	25.4		0.0277	0.0833	1

VOLUME

1 cu. yd = 0.7646 cu. m   1 cu. m = 1.308 cu. yd

1 cu. ft. = 0.0283 cu. m   1 cu. m = 35.31 cu. ft.

LIQUID VOLUME

10 milliliters = 1 centiliter = 0.338 fluid ounce

10 centiliters = 1 deciliter = 0.845 liquid gill

10 deciliters = 1 liter = 1.0567 liquid quarts

10 liters = 1 dekaliter = 2.6417 liquid gallons

10 dekaliters = 1 hectoliter = 2.8375 U.S. bu.

10 hectoliters = 1 kiloliter = 28.375 U.S. bu.

(or stere)

WEIGHT

kg = kilogram   g = gram

1 kg = 1000 grams

1 kg = 2.205 lbs   1 lb = 0.4536 kg

1 g = 0.0353 ounce   1 oz = 28.35 g

DISTANCE CONVERSIONS

Inches	Centi- meters	Centi- meters	Inches	Feet	Meters	Meters	Feet
1	2.54	1	.3937	1	.3048	1	3.281
2	5.08	2	.7874	2	.6096	2	6.562
3	7.62	3	1.181	3	.9144	3	9.843
4	10.16	4	1.575	4	1.219	4	13.12
5	12.70	5	1.969	5	1.524	5	16.40
6	15.24	6	2.362	6	1.829	6	19.69
7	17.78	7	2.756	7	2.133	7	22.97
8	20.32	8	3.150	8	2.438	8	26.25
9	22.86	9	3.543	9	2.743	9	29.53
10	25.40	10	3.937	10	3.048	10	32.81
20	50.80	20	7.874	20	6.096	20	65.62
30	76.20	30	11.81	30	9.144	30	98.43
40	101.6	40	15.75	40	12.19	40	131.2
50	127.0	50	19.69	50	15.24	50	164.0
60	152.4	60	23.62	60	18.29	60	196.9
70	177.8	70	27.56	70	21.33	70	229.7
80	203.2	80	31.50	80	24.38	80	262.5
90	228.6	90	35.43	90	27.43	90	295.3
100	254.0	100	39.37	100	30.48	100	328.1
200	508.0	200	78.74	200	60.96	200	656.2
300	762.0	300	118.1	300	91.44	300	984.3
400	1016	400	157.5	400	121.9	400	1312
500	1270	500	196.9	500	152.4	500	1640
600	1524	600	236.2	600	182.9	600	1969
700	1778	700	275.6	700	213.3	700	2297
800	2032	800	315.0	800	243.8	800	2625
900	2286	900	354.3	900	274.3	900	2953
1000	2540	1000	393.7	1000	304.8	1000	3281

TEMPERATURE

°F	°C	°F	°C	°C	°F	°C	°F
−10	−23.0	90	32.2	−20	− 4	40	104
0	−17.8	100	37.8	−10	14	50	122
10	−12.2	110	43	0	32	60	140
20	− 6.7	120	49	5	41	80	176
30	− 1.1	130	54	10	50	100	212
40	4.4	150	66	15	59	120	248
50	10	200	93	20	68	150	302
60	15.6	300	149	25	77	180	356
70	21.1	400	204	30	86	200	392
80	26.7	500	260	35	95	250	482

DISTANCE CONVERSIONS

Yards	Meters	Meters	Yards	Miles	Kilo-meters	Kilo-meters	Miles
1	.9144	1	1.094	1	1.609	1	.6214
2	1.829	2	2.188	2	3.218	2	1.243
3	2.743	3	3.282	3	4.828	3	1.864
4	3.658	4	4.376	4	6.437	4	2.486
5	4.572	5	5.470	5	8.047	5	3.107
6	5.486	6	6.564	6	9.656	6	3.728
7	6.401	7	7.658	7	11.27	7	4.350
8	7.315	8	8.752	8	12.87	8	4.971
9	8.230	9	9.846	9	14.48	9	5.592
10	9.144	10	10.94	10	16.09	10	6.214
20	18.29	20	21.88	20	32.18	20	12.43
30	27.43	30	32.82	30	48.28	30	18.64
40	36.58	40	43.76	40	64.37	40	24.86
50	45.72	50	54.70	50	80.47	50	31.07
60	54.86	60	65.64	60	96.56	60	37.28
70	64.01	70	76.58	70	112.7	70	43.50
80	73.15	80	87.52	80	128.7	80	49.71
90	82.30	90	98.46	90	144.8	90	55.92
100	91.44	100	109.4	100	160.9	100	62.14
200	182.9	200	218.8	200	321.8	200	124.3
300	274.3	300	328.2	300	482.8	300	186.4
400	365.8	400	437.6	400	643.7	400	248.6
500	457.2	500	547.0	500	804.7	500	310.7
600	548.6	600	656.4	600	965.6	600	372.8
700	640.1	700	765.8	700	1127	700	435.0
800	731.5	800	875.2	800	1287	800	497.1
900	823.0	900	984.6	900	1448	900	559.2
1000	914.4	1000	1094	1000	1609	1000	621.4

FRACTIONAL EQUIVALENTS

Fractional Inches	Decimal Inches	MM	Fractional Inches	Decimal Inches	MM
1/16	.0625	1.587	9/16	.5625	14.287
1/8	.1250	3.175	5/8	.6250	15.875
3/16	.1875	4.762	11/16	.6875	17.462
1/4	.2500	6.350	3/4	.7500	19.050
5/16	.3125	7.937	13/16	.8125	20.637
3/8	.3750	9.525	7/8	.8750	22.225
7/16	.4375	11.112	15/16	.9375	23.812
1/2	.5000	12.700	1	1	25.400

AREA CONVERSIONS

Sq. In.	Sq. CM	Sq. CM	Sq. In.	Square Yards	Square Meters	Square Meters	Square Yards
1	6.452	1	.1550	1	.8361	1	1.196
2	12.90	2	.3100	2	1.672	2	2.392
3	19.36	3	.4650	3	2.508	3	3.588
4	25.81	4	.6200	4	3.344	4	4.784
5	32.26	5	.7750	5	4.181	5	5.980
6	38.71	6	.9300	6	5.017	6	7.176
7	45.16	7	1.085	7	5.853	7	8.372
8	51.62	8	1.240	8	6.689	8	9.568
9	58.07	9	1.395	9	7.525	9	10.76
10	64.52	10	1.550	10	8.361	10	11.96
20	129.0	20	3.100	20	16.72	20	23.92
30	193.6	30	4.650	30	25.08	30	35.88
40	258.1	40	6.200	40	33.44	40	47.84
50	322.6	50	7.750	50	41.81	50	59.80
60	387.1	60	9.300	60	50.17	60	71.76
70	451.6	70	10.85	70	58.53	70	83.72
80	516.2	80	12.40	80	66.89	80	95.68
90	580.7	90	13.95	90	75.25	90	107.6
100	645.2	100	15.50	100	83.61	100	119.6
200	1290	200	31.00	200	167.2	200	239.2
300	1936	300	46.50	300	250.8	300	358.8
400	2581	400	62.00	400	334.4	400	478.4
500	3226	500	77.50	500	418.1	500	598.0
600	3871	600	93.00	600	501.7	600	717.6
700	4516	700	108.5	700	585.3	700	837.2
800	5162	800	124.0	800	668.9	800	956.8
900	5807	900	139.5	900	752.5	900	1076
1000	6452	1000	155.0	1000	836.1	1000	1196

AREA

1 sq. mile = 2.59 sq. km

1 acre = 4068.8 sq. m

1 sq. yd. = 0.836 sq. m

1 sq. ft. = 0.0929 sq. m = 929 sq. cm

DIRECTIONS FOR USE OF TABLES

CONSTANT ANNUAL PERCENT TABLE (Beginning on page A-129)

The values in this table represent "Annual Constants." An Annual Constant is the sum of 12 monthly payments expressed in percent of a principal loan amount. As an example, it takes $8.78 per month to amortize a $1,000 loan for 30 years at 10% interest. 12 times $8.78 equals $105.36 and $105.36 is 10.53% of $1,000. The Annual Constant is, therefore: 10.53. Expressed in a formula:

$$\text{Annual Constant} = \frac{1200 \times \text{Monthly Payment}}{\text{Loan Amount}}$$

This formula is applied in all of the following examples.

Applications of Constant Annual Percent Table

CASE I – To find the remaining term of a loan

PROBLEM:
Find the remaining term of a loan if you have the following data:
Remaining loan balance: $55,000
Monthly payment: $860
Interest rate: 10%

ANSWER:
Apply the formula:

$$\text{Annual Constant} = \frac{1200 \times \text{Monthly Payment}}{\text{Loan Amount}}$$

$$\text{Annual Constant} = \frac{1200 \times 860}{55,000} = 18.76$$

In the 10% INTEREST column on page A-129 find a spot closest to 18.76 (between 19.01 and 18.21). By following a horizontal line from that spot to the left, the remaining term of the loan can be found in the YEAR column, in this case between 7.5 and 8 years.

The exact term of 7.66 can be interpolated.
At 7.5 years the constant is 19.01
At 8.0 years the constant is 18.21
At X years the constant is 18.76
Solution:
$19.01 - 18.21 = 0.8$ $8.0 - 7.5 = 0.5$
$19.01 - 18.76 = 0.25$
The difference between 7.5 and the number of years corresponding to a constant of 18.76 is:
$0.25 \div 0.8 \times 0.5 = 0.15625$
Therefore, the number of years corresponding to a constant of 18.76 is: $7.5 + 0.15625 = 7.65625$ years.

CASE II — To find the amount which a specified monthly payment will amortize.

PROBLEM:
Find the maximum amount that can be borrowed based on the following data:
Amount available for monthly payments: $850
Interest rate: 14%
Term of loan: 15 years

ANSWER:
Find the Annual Constant for a 15-year loan at 14% interest on page A-131, at the intersection of the 14% INTEREST column and the 15.0 YEAR line: 15.98.

Then apply the formula:

$$\text{A.C.} = \frac{1200 \times \text{Monthly Payment}}{\text{Loan Amount}}$$

$$15.98 = \frac{1200 \times 850}{\text{Loan Amount}}$$

$$\text{Loan Amount} = \frac{1200 \times 850}{15.98} = \underline{\$63,829.79}$$

The maximum amount that can be borrowed is therefore: $63,829.79.

CASE III — To find the interest rate of a loan

PROBLEM:
Find the interest rate if the following data are known:
Loan amount: $50,000
Monthly payments: $498.33
Term of loan: 23 years

ANSWER:
Apply the formula:

$$A.C. = \frac{1200 \times \text{Monthly Payment}}{\text{Loan Amount}}$$

$$A.C. = \frac{1200 \times 498.33}{50,000} = 11.96$$

The interest rate can now be found on page A-129 by following the 23 YEAR line horizontally to the Annual Constant of 11.96 which is located in the 11% INTEREST column.

CASE IV — To find the remaining balance of a loan

The Remaining Balance Tables cannot be used if the original term in years is not known. Therefore the following method may be used if the following data are known:
Original loan amount
Monthly payment
Interest rate
Age of loan

PROBLEM:
Find the remaining loan balance using the following data:
Original loan amount: $47,500
Monthly payment: $430
Interest rate: 9¾%
Age of loan: 8½ years

ANSWER:

Step A: Apply the formula:

$$A.C. = \frac{1200 \times \text{Monthly Payment}}{\text{Loan Amount}}$$

$$A.C. = \frac{1200 \times 430}{47,500} = \underline{10.863157} - [A]$$

Step B: Find the Annual Constant for a 9¾% loan fully amortized in 8½ years, on page A-128, at the intersection of the 9¾% INTEREST column and the 8.5 YEAR line: <u>17.35</u> . . . . [B]

Step C: Find the difference between [B] and [A].
17.35 - 10.863157 = <u>6.486843</u> . [C]

Step D: Find the difference between [B] and the interest rate:
17.35 - 9.75 = <u>7.6</u> . . . . [D]

Step E: Divide [C] by [D]:
6.486843 ÷ 7.6 = <u>0.8535319</u> . [E]

Step F: The remaining balance is [E] multiplied by the original loan amount:
0.8535319 x 47,500 = <u>$40,542.77</u>

CASE IV-A — Negative amortization

PROBLEM: The annual interest rate of an Adjustable Mortgage Loan has been increased to 17%. The loan balance at the time of the increase was $85,000. The monthly payments, however, have not been increased but remain at the old rate of $1,074 including principal and interest. Since 17% interest on $85,000 for one month amounts to $1,204 (17/100 x 85,000 ÷ 12), the payments of $1,074 obviously is not sufficient to cover the interest. The deficit is therefore added to the principal.

QUESTION: What will the loan balance be at the end of three years, at interest compounded monthly?

ANSWER:

Use the same procedure as in CASE IV.

Step A: Apply the formula:

$$A.C. = \frac{1200 \times \text{Monthly Payment}}{\text{Loan Amount}}$$

$$A.C. = \frac{1200 \times 1074}{85,000} = \underline{15.162352} \text{ - [A]}$$

Step B: Find the Annual Constant for a 17% loan fully amortized in 3 years, on page A-132, at the intersection of the 17% INTEREST column and the 3 YEAR line: $\underline{42.79}$ . . . . [B]

Step C: Find the difference between [B] and [A].
42.79 - 15.162352 = $\underline{27.627648}$
. . . . [C]

Step D: Find the difference between [B] and the interest rate:
42.79 - 17 = $\underline{25.79}$ . . . . [D]

Step E: Divide [C] by [D]:
27.627648 ÷ 25.79 = $\underline{1.0712542}$
. . . . [E]

Step F: The loan balance at the end of 3 years is [E] multiplied by the balance at the beginning of the 3-year period:
1.0712542 x 85,000 = $\underline{\$91,056.61}$

REMAINING BALANCE TABLES
(Beginning on page A-150)

Each remaining Balance Table shows the INTEREST rate in bold at the top of the page. Under the heading ORIGINAL TERM IN YEARS, the years 2 thru 20 are shown horizontally across the top of the upper section of the page, continued across the top of the lower section with 21 thru 40. The AGE OF LOAN is indicated in the shaded columns on both sides of the tables. The numbers in the body of the tables express the REMAINING BALANCE of a loan as a percentage of the original loan amount (for example: 91.0 means 91% of the original loan amount). Use of the tables requires the following data:

Original loan amount
Interest rate
Original term of loan
Age of loan

PROBLEM:

Find the remaining balance of the following loan obtained nine years ago:
Original loan amount: $61,000
Interest rate: 9%
Original term of loan: 30 years
Age of loan: 9 years

ANSWER:

Find the 9% Remaining Balance table on page A-158. In the lower section of the page find the intersection of the 30 YEAR ORIGINAL TERM column and the 9 YEAR AGE OF LOAN line: 91.0. The remaining balance is therefore 91% of the original loan amount, or .91 x 61,000 = $55,510.

BALLOON PAYMENT TABLES
(Beginning on page A-200)

A Balloon Payment is a remaining balance due and payable before the loan is amortized. In many junior mortgages the monthly payment is expressed as a percent of the face value of the note, referred to as payment rate, pay-back rate or pay-off rate. For instance, a 1% pay-back rate means that the monthly payment on a $10,000 note is $100. In order to use the Balloon Payment tables it is necessary to know the pay-back rate. If only the dollar amount of the monthly payment is known, the pay-back rate can easily be calculated by dividing the monthly payment by the face value of the note and multiplying the result by 100. For instance, if the monthly payment of a $10,000 loan were $140, the pay-back rate would be $140 \div 10,000 \times 100 = 1.4$.

PROBLEM:
Find the balloon payment of a loan based on the following data:
Face value of the note (original loan amount): $16,000
Monthly payment: $272
Interest rate: 11%
Due date: 5 years

ANSWER:

Step A: Determine the pay-back rate:
$272 \div 16,000 \times 100 = 1.7$

Step B: On page A-203 select the 11% INTEREST section. Find the intersection of the 5 YEAR DUE DATE column (the numbers shown horizontally across the top of the page) and the 1.7 PAY-BACK line: 37.71. This is the balloon payment expressed as a percent of the face value of the note.

Step C: Multiply the face value of the note by 37.71 and divide by 100: 16,000 x 37.71 ÷ 100 = 6,033.60

The balloon payment is therefore $6,033.60.

MORTGAGE YIELD TABLES
(Beginning on page A-212)

Yield: The return to the investor in % of the price he pays for the note. The yield percentages are shown across the top of the tables.

Discount: The difference between the balance due on the note and the amount an investor pays for it. Discount percentages are shown in the body of the yield tables.

Due Date: A specified period at the end of which the entire unpaid balance of a note becomes due and payable in full. Any balance remaining at that time is referred to as "Balloon Payment." Due Dates are shown in the extreme left hand columns of the yield tables.

Monthly Payment Rate (also referred to as PAY-BACK RATE or PAY-OFF RATE): The monthly installment payments expressed in percent of the face value of the note. For instance, a 1% Payment Rate means that the monthly payment on a $10,000 note is $100.

Balance Remaining: The third column from the left shows the balances remaining at the end of the respective Due Dates and at various Monthly Payment Rates.

The FIRST LINE in each DUE DATE section shows a BALANCE REMAINING of 100%, which means the monthly payments are for INTEREST

ONLY. For instance, the 10% Yield Table shows that a Monthly Payment Rate of 0.83% pays INTEREST ONLY, since the balance remains 100%.

The LAST LINE in each DUE DATE section shows a BALANCE REMAINING of ZERO, which means the loan is FULLY AMORTIZED. For instance, the Yield Table for 10% interest shows that a $10,000 loan at 10% interest, with a Payment Rate of 3.23% or $323 per month, is fully amortized at the end of three years.

The other figures in the BALANCE REMAINING column are Balloon Payment rates. For instance, the Yield Table for 10% interest shows the balance remaining at the end of three years on a $10,000 loan at 10% interest, with a Payment Rate of 1.5% or $150 per month, is 72.15% or $7,215.

Applications of Mortgage Yield Table

CASE I — To determine the discount at a Specified Yield.

PROBLEM: Mr. Buyer offers to purchase a property whereby Mr. Seller would be expected to carry back a second mortgage of $10,000, payable at $150 per month (1.5% payment rate), including 10% interest, due and payable in full at the end of 4 years. At what discount must the note be sold to an investor requiring a yield of 15%?

ANSWER: Turn to the YIELD TABLE for 10% INTEREST and locate the point of intersection of the 15% YIELD column and the 1.5% PAYMENT RATE line in the 4 YR. DUE DATE section. The figure at that intersection is 12.58, which is the discount rate at which the note must be sold in order to yield the investor a return of 15%. The discount is, therefore, 12.58% of $10,000, or $1,258.

CASE II — To determine the Monthly Payment Rate needed to fully amortize a mortgage.

PROBLEM: When the buyer in Case I realizes that he will have a balance remaining of 60.85% or $6,085, due and payable in full at the end of 4 years (balloon payment), he prefers to increase his payments to a rate that will fully amortize the loan over the 4-year period. What would his monthly payment have to be?

ANSWER: In the 4 YR. DUE DATE section fine 0.0 in the BALANCE REMAINING column. The figure on that line in the adjoining PAYMENT RATE column is 2.54% or $254, the rate required to retire the note in 4 years.

CASE III — How does the above buyer's decision to increase his monthly payments to $254 affect the seller?

ANSWER: The discount of 12.58% in Case I is reduced to 8.87%, which is the figure found at the intersection of the 15% YIELD column and the 2.54% PAYMENT RATE line in the 4 YR. DUE DATE section. The Seller therefore saves the difference between 12.58% and 8.87% or 3.71% of $10,000, amounting to a cash saving of $371.

CASE IV — To determine the yield at a specified discount.

PROBLEM: A mortgage with a remaining balance of $10,000, payable at $200 per month (2% payment rate) including 10% interest per annum, due and payable in full at the end of 5 years, is offered at a 15% discount. What is the yield of this investment?

ANSWER: Turn to the YIELD TABLE for 10% INTEREST and find the 2% PAYMENT RATE in the 5 YR. DUE DATE section. Follow that line horizontally to the Discount Rate closest to 15% (in this case 15.37%). Follow that column upward, to find the YIELD, in this case 17%. The exact amount may be determined by interpolation.

COMPOUND INTEREST TABLES
(Beginning on page A-322)

PROBLEM: What would $1,000 be worth in 20 years compounded annually at 15% interest?

SOLUTION: On the compound interest table on page A-325 in the Single Sum column of 15% interest on the 20 YEAR line, find the Future Value of one dollar: $16.3665. Therefore, $1,000 will be worth 16.3665 x $1,000 = $16,366.50.

PROBLEM: If you invest $500 at the end of each year at 8% compounded annually, what will your investment be worth at the end of 15 years?

SOLUTION: Use the annuity constants in the compound interest table on page A-324. The 8% 15-year annuity constant is 29.324, so the investment at the end of 15 years would be worth: 29.324 x $500 = $14,662.

PRESENT VALUE TABLES
(Beginning on page A-332)

The publisher is indebted to Professor Stephen E. Roulac of Stanford University, for his assistance in programming these tables and for preparing the directions for use of the Present Value and Compound Interest Tables.

If you are familiar with present value techniques, you will find these tables a convenient reference. The constants for single sums and annuities are both listed for each combination of interest rate and number of years. The constants are the values for one dollar, the value for larger sums is the dollar amount times the constant. The present value tables tell what future tables, sometimes called future value tables, tell what a simple sum or annuity contract entered today would be worth at some future time.

If you are unfamiliar with the concept of present and future values, they are merely a way to quantify what most people know intuitively, that there is a time value associated with money. Aside from the risk involved, the promise of $1.00 ten years from now is just not worth $1.00 today. This is because the $1.00 available now could be put in the bank or invested in a business venture at your required rate of return. Some examples will demonstrate the use and power of these tables.

PROBLEM A: An investor has the opportunity to purchase the right to receive $5,000 at the end of 10 years; other investment alternatives offer yields of 15½% per year on a compounded basis. What is today's value to the investor of the $5,000 to be received at the end of 10 years?

SOLUTION: On page A-334 in the "Single Sum" column under 15½% discount on the 10 YEAR line, you'll find .236690 which is the Present Value of a single sum of $1.00 returned at the end of 10 years, discounted at 15½%. The present value of $5,000 at the end of 10 years is, therefore, 5,000 x .23669 = $1,183.45.

PROBLEM B: What is the Present Value of the following stream of cash flows: $500 in year 1, $1,000 in year 2 and $2,000 in year 3? Use a discount rate of 12%.

SOLUTION: This would be the sum of the present values of the three flows (see page A-334):

$ 500 x .892857 =	$ 446.42
$1,000 x .797194 =	$ 797.19
$2,000 x .711780 =	$1,423.56
Total Present Value =	$2,667.17

PROBLEM C: What is the Present Value of an even stream of $5,000 cash flows over each of 10 years, discounted at 14%?

SOLUTION: This could be calculated as in the last problem but would be tedious. Fortunately the constants for even flows (called annuities) are included in the tables following the Single Sum constant. On page A-334, in the "Annuity" column of 14% Discount, on the 10 YEAR line, find 5.2161, which is the Present Value of a one-dollar, 10-year annuity. The Present Value of a $5,000 10-year annuity is therefore, 5,000 x 5.2161 = $26,080.50.

PROBLEM D: Compare the "Net Present Values" of the following investments A, B and C, using a discount of 16%.

	Investment A	Investment B	Investment C
Initial Investment	100,000	110,000	100,000
After Tax Cash Flow:			
First year	8,000	6,000	7,000
Second year	8,000	7,000	7,000
Third year	5,000	9,000	7,000
Fourth year	8,000	10,000	7,000
Fifth year	10,000	11,000	7,000

SOLUTION: Using the 16% Present Value table on page A-335, discount all future cash flows as follows:

	Constants	Present Values A	Present Values B	Present Values C
1st year	.862069	6896.55	5172.40	6034.48
2nd year	.743163	5945.30	5202.14	5202.14
3rd year	.640658	3202.29	5765.92	4484.61
4th year	.552291	4418.33	5522.91	3866.04
5th year	.476113	4761.13	5237.24	3332.79
Sum Present Values		25,223.60	26,900.61	22,920.06
Initial Investments		100,000	110,000	100,000
Rate of Return		25.22%	24.46%	22.92%

All other things being equal, the investment with the largest Rate of Return should be selected.

Internal Rate of Return

The INTERNAL RATE OF RETURN (IRR) is usually defined as that rate of return which equates the present value of future benefits to the Present Value of the investment outlay. The IRR, therefore, considers not only the amount of return received on a given investment, but also the timing of the receipt of these returns. The IRR enables an investor to compare and rank investments of varying sizes and durations.

The computation of an IRR must be by trial and error. The procedure begins by choosing an arbitrary rate of return which is probably close to the actual IRR. The net cash flows are discounted to their present value using this trial rate. Should the computed Present Value of the future returns equal the amount of the initial investment, then the trial rate is the IRR. If the two are not equal on the first attempt, a new rate of return is chosen and the computation is made again. This process is repeated until the equation between the initial investment and the Present Value of future returns is achieved. The trial rate used for that last computation will be the IRR. While the IRR can be computed using Present Value Tables, as explained above, there are computer programs which calculate Internal Rates of Return.

EQUITY BUILD-UP TABLES
(Beginning on page A-344)

These tables show the amount paid toward principal, expressed as a percent of the original loan amount. The numbers in the YEAR column at the extreme left of each Equity Build-up table indicate the age of the loan (up to 15 years). Two columns are provided for each Interest Rate, one for Annual, the other for Cumulative equity build-up.

PROBLEM: What is the amount paid toward principal since the following loan was made ten years ago?
Original loan amount: $40,000
Interest rate: 9%
Original term of loan: 30 years
Age of loan: 10 years

ANSWER: Find the equity Build-up table for 30-year loan on page A-362. Under the 9% INTEREST heading find the intersection of the CUMULATIVE COLUMN and the 10 YEAR line: 10.570. This is what has been paid toward principal since the loan was made, expressed as a percent of the original loan amount, or:
10.570 ÷ 100 x 40,000 = $4,228

PROBLEM:

What is the amount paid toward principal during the 10th year of the above loan, and the average monthly amount paid toward principal during that year?

ANSWER:

Find the intersection of the ANNUAL column and the 10 YEAR line: 1.531. This is what has been paid toward principal during the 10th year, again expressed in percent of the original loan amount, or: 1.531 ÷ 100 x 40,000 = $612.40.

The average monthly amount paid toward principal during the tenth year is:
612.40 ÷ 12 = $51.03.

NOTES:

The publisher is indebted to
M.B.A., real estate broker and inst
development of the Hewlett-Packard tle,
Business Consultant calculator keysthis
dures and explanations for solving samd
lems which the corresponding tables addre
for his preparation of the section on the deriv
of factors in the select tables. Mr. Little is the
thor of <u>The HP-12C Calculator Course,</u> and <u>T.</u>
<u>HP-17B, HP-18C and HP-19B Business Consul</u>
<u>tant Calculator Course.</u> For information about
these courses, which can be used toward state continuing education license renewal requirements
in many jurisdictions, please contact the publisher at: (415) 472-1964.

₋EM:

₋rmine the monthly payment necessary to
₋ortize a $1,000 loan, bearing interest at 11%
₋r annum, fully amortized over thirty years.

SOLUTION:

THE HEWLETT-PACKARD HP-12C

Keystroke:	Display:	Comments:
f, CLEAR, REG	0.00	Clears Calculator
f, 4	0.0000	Sets Display Format
g, END	0.0000	Sets Payment Mode to End[1]
1,000, PV	1,000.0000	Stores Loan Amount
30, g, n	360.0000	Stores Monthly Term
11, g, i	0.9167	Stores Monthly Interest Rate
PMT	**-9.5232**	Computes Monthly Payment[2]

Notes:
(1) Unless "BEGIN" appears in the display, the calculator is set to "END" mode. Most annuity and compound interest problems use "END" mode.
(2) Hewlett Packard financial calculators utilize a cash flow sign convention of " + " for cash received and " − " for cash paid. Therefore, payments are entered and computed as " − " cash flows.

THE HEWLETT-PACKARD
BUSINESS CONSULTANT
(HP-17B, HP-18C, HP-19B)

Keystroke:	Display:	Comments:
DISP,FIX,4,INPUT		Sets Display Format
FIN, TVM		Displays TVM Menu
GOLD, CLEAR ALL	0.0000	Clears History Stack and TVM Variables
OTHER	0.0000	Displays Secondary TVM Menu
GOLD,CLEAR ALL	0.0000	Sets to 12 Payments/Year, End Mode[1]
EXIT	0.0000	Displays TVM Menu
1,000, PV	PV = 1,000.0000	Stores Loan Amount
30, x, 12, N	N = 360.0000	Stores Monthly Term
11, I%YR	I%YR = 11.0000	Stores Annual Interest Rate
PMT	**PMT = -9.5232**	Computes Monthly Payment[2][3]

Notes:

(1) Before solving problems utilizing the TVM menu, the calculator will display either "BEGIN MODE" or "END MODE". Most annuity and compound interest problems use "END MODE" since these problems customarily provide for payments made (received) in arrears (i.e., at the end of the period).

(2) Hewlett Packard financial calculators utilize a cash flow sign convention of " + " for cash received and " – " for cash paid. Therefore, payments are entered and computed as " – " cash flows.

(3) It is important to note that while the calculator is set to display 4 decimal places, internal calculations are done with 12-digit numbers, except for the values of PV, PMT, and INT used in amortization problems, which are rounded to the display setting.

QUARTERLY PAYMENTS
TO AMORTIZE A $1,000 LOAN
(Beginning on Page A-19)

PROBLEM:

Determine the quarterly payment necessary to amortize a $1,000 loan, bearing interest at 11% per annum, fully amortized over thirty years.

SOLUTION:

THE HEWLETT-PACKARD HP-12C

Keystroke:	Display:	Comments:
f, CLEAR, REG	0.00	Clears Calculator
g, END	0.00	Sets Payment Mode to End[1]
1,000, PV	1,000.00	Stores Loan Amount
30,ENTER,4,x,n	120.00	Stores Quarterly Term
11,ENTER,4, ÷ ,i	2.75	Stores Quarterly Interest Rate
PMT	**-28.60**	Computes Quarterly Payment[2]

Notes:

(1) Unless "BEGIN" appears in the display, the calculator is set to "END" mode. Most annuity and compound interest problems use "END" mode.

(2) Hewlett Packard financial calculators utilize a cash flow sign convention of " + " for cash received and " − " for cash paid. Therefore, payments are entered and computed as " − " cash flows.

THE HEWLETT-PACKARD
BUSINESS CONSULTANT
(HP-17B, HP-18C, HP-19B)

Keystroke:	Display:	Comments:
FIN, TVM		Displays TVM Menu
GOLD, CLEAR ALL	0.00	Clears History Stack and TVM Variables
OTHER	0.00	Displays Secondary TVM Menu
4, #P/Y, END	#PMTS/YR = 4.00	Sets to 4 Payments/Year, End Mode[1]
EXIT	4.00	Displays TVM Menu
x, 30, N	N = 120.00	Stores Quarterly Term
1,000, PV	PV = 1,000.00	Stores Loan Amount
11, I%YR	I%YR = 11.00	Stores Annual Interest Rate
PMT	**PMT = -28.60**	Computes Quarterly Payment[2][3]

Notes:

(1) Before solving problems utilizing the TVM menu, the calculator will display either "BEGIN MODE" or "END MODE." Most annuity and compound interest problems use "END MODE" since these problems customarily provide for payments made (received) in arrears (i.e., at the end of the period).

(2) Hewlett Packard financial calculators utilize a cash flow sign convention of " + " for cash received and " − " for cash paid. Therefore, payments are entered and computed as " − " cash flows.

(3) It is important to note that while the calculator is set to display 2 decimal places in its default setting, internal calculations are done with 12-digit numbers, except for the values of PV, PMT, and INT used in amortization problems, which are rounded to the display setting.

SEMI-ANNUAL PAYMENTS
TO AMORTIZE A $1,000 LOAN
(Beginning on Page A-26)

PROBLEM:

Determine the semi-annual payment necessary to amortize a $1,000 loan, bearing interest at 11% per annum, fully amortized over thirty years.

SOLUTION:

THE HEWLETT-PACKARD HP-12C

Keystroke:	Display:	Comments:
f, CLEAR, REG	0.00	Clears Calculator
g, END	0.00	Sets Payment Mode to End[1]
1,000, PV	1,000.00	Stores Loan Amount
30, ENTER, 2, x, n	60.00	Stores Semi-Annual Term
11, ENTER, 2, ÷, i	5.50	Stores Semi-Annual Interest Rate
PMT	**-57.31**	Computes Semi-Annual Payment[2]

Notes:

(1) Unless "BEGIN" appears in the display, the calculator is set to "END" mode. Most annuity and compound interest problems use "END" mode.

(2) Hewlett Packard financial calculators utilize a cash flow sign convention of "+" for cash received and "−" for cash paid. Therefore, payments are entered and computed as "−" cash flows.

THE HEWLETT-PACKARD BUSINESS CONSULTANT (HP-17B, HP-18C, HP-19B)

Keystroke:	Display:	Comments:
FIN, TVM		Displays TVM Menu
GOLD, CLEAR ALL	0.00	Clears History Stack and TVM Variables
OTHER	0.00	Displays Secondary TVM Menu
2, #P/Y, END	#PMTS/YR = 2.00	Sets to 2 Payments/Year, End Mode[1]
EXIT	2.00	Displays TVM Menu
x, 30, N	N = 60.00	Stores Semi-Annual Term
1,000, PV	PV = 1,000.00	Stores Loan Amount
11, I%YR	I%YR = 11.00	Stores Annual Interest Rate
PMT	**PMT = -57.31**	Computes Semi-Annual Payment[2][3]

Notes:

(1) Before solving problems utilizing the TVM menu, the calculator will display either "BEGIN MODE" or "END MODE." Most annuity and compound interest problems use "END MODE" since these problems customarily provide for payments made (received) in arrears (i.e., at the end of the period).

(2) Hewlett Packard financial calculators utilize a cash flow sign convention of " + " for cash received and " − " for cash paid. Therefore, payments are entered and computed as " − " cash flows.

(3) It is important to note that while the calculator is set to display 2 decimal places in its default setting, internal calculations are done with 12-digit numbers, except for the values of PV, PMT, and INT used in amortization problems, which are rounded to the display setting.

ANNUAL PAYMENTS
TO AMORTIZE A $1,000 LOAN
(Beginning on Page A-33)

PROBLEM:

Determine the annual payment necessary to amortize a $1,000 loan, bearing interest at 11% per annum, fully amortized over thirty years.

SOLUTION:

THE HEWLETT-PACKARD HP-12C

Keystroke:	Display:	Comments:
f, CLEAR, REG	0.00	Clears Calculator
g, END	0.00	Sets Payment Mode to End[1]
1,000, PV	1,000.00	Stores Loan Amount
30, n	30.00	Stores Annual Term
11, i	11.00	Stores Annual Interest Rate
PMT	**-115.02**	Computes Annual Payment[2]

Notes:

(1) Unless "BEGIN" appears in the display, the calculator is set to "END" mode. Most annuity and compound interest problems use "END" mode.

(2) Hewlett Packard financial calculators utilize a cash flow sign convention of " + " for cash received and " − " for cash paid. Therefore, payments are entered and computed as " − " cash flows.

THE HEWLETT-PACKARD BUSINESS CONSULTANT (HP-17B, HP-18C, HP-19B)

Keystroke:	Display:	Comments:
FIN, TVM		Displays TVM Menu
GOLD, CLEAR ALL	0.00	Clears History Stack and TVM Variables
OTHER	0.00	Displays Secondary TVM Menu
1, #P/Y, END	#PMTS/YR = 1.00	Sets to 1 Payment/Year, End Mode[1]
EXIT	1.00	Displays TVM Menu
x, 30, N	N = 30.00	Stores Annual Term
1,000, PV	PV = 1,000.00	Stores Loan Amount
11, I%YR	I%YR = 11.00	Stores Annual Interest Rate
PMT	**PMT = -115.02**	Computes Annual Payment[2][3]

Notes:

(1) Before solving problems utilizing the TVM menu, the calculator will display either "BEGIN MODE" or "END MODE." Most annuity and compound interest problems use "END MODE" since these problems customarily provide for payments made (received) in arrears (i.e., at the end of the period).

(2) Hewlett Packard financial calculators utilize a cash flow sign convention of " + " for cash received and " − " for cash paid. Therefore, payments are entered and computed as " − " cash flows.

(3) It is important to note that while the calculator is set to display 2 decimal places in its default setting, internal calculations are done with 12-digit numbers, except for the values of PV, PMT, and INT used in amortization problems, which are rounded to the display setting.

MONTHLY LOAN
AMORTIZATION PAYMENTS
(Beginning on Page A-40)

PROBLEM:

Determine the monthly payment necessary to amortize an $85,000 loan, bearing interest at 11% per annum, fully amortized over twenty-five years.

SOLUTION:

THE HEWLETT-PACKARD HP-12C

Keystroke:	Display:	Comments:
f, CLEAR, REG	0.00	Clears Calculator
g, END	0.00	Sets Payment Mode to End[1]
85,000, PV	85,000.00	Stores Loan Amount
25, g, n	300.00	Stores Monthly Term
11, g, i	0.92	Stores Monthly Interest Rate
PMT	**-833.10**	Computes Monthly Payment[2]

Notes:

(1) Unless "BEGIN" appears in the display, the calculator is set to "END" mode. Most annuity and compound interest problems use "END" mode.

(2) Hewlett Packard financial calculators utilize a cash flow sign convention of " + " for cash received and " − " for cash paid. Therefore, payments are entered and computed as " − " cash flows.

THE HEWLETT-PACKARD
BUSINESS CONSULTANT
(HP-17B, HP-18C, HP-19B)

Keystroke:	Display:	Comments:
FIN, TVM		Displays TVM Menu
GOLD, CLEAR ALL	0.00	Clears History Stack and TVM Variables
OTHER	0.00	Displays Secondary TVM Menu
GOLD, CLEAR ALL	0.00	Sets to 12 Payments/Year, End Mode[1]
EXIT	0.00	Displays TVM Menu
85,000, PV	PV = 85,000.00	Stores Loan Amount
25, x, 12, N	N = 300.00	Stores Monthly Term
11, I%YR	I%YR = 11.00	Stores Annual Interest Rate
PMT	**PMT = -833.10**	Computes Monthly Payment[2][3]

Notes:

(1) Before solving problems utilizing the TVM menu, the calculator will display either "BEGIN MODE" or "END MODE." Most annuity and compound interest problems use "END MODE" since these problems customarily provide for payments made (received) in arrears (i.e., at the end of the period).

(2) Hewlett Packard financial calculators utilize a cash flow sign convention of " + " for cash received and " − " for cash paid. Therefore, payments are entered and computed as " − " cash flows.

(3) It is important to note that while the calculator is set to display 2 decimal places in its default setting, internal calculations are done with 12-digit numbers, except for the values of PV, PMT, and INT used in amortization problems, which are rounded to the display setting.

FNMA WEEKLY PAYMENT PROGRAM
(Page A-127.4)

PROBLEM:

Determine the weekly payment on an $80,000 loan, bearing interest at 12% per annum, under the FNMA weekly payment program. Then determine the annual term of this loan.

SOLUTION:

THE HEWLETT-PACKARD HP-12C

Keystroke:	Display:	Comments:
f, CLEAR, REG	0.00	Clears Calculator
g, END	0.00	Sets Payment Mode to End
80,000, PV	80,000.00	Stores Loan Amount
30, g, n	360.00	Stores Monthly Term
12, g, i	1.00	Stores Monthly Interest Rate
PMT	-822.89	Computes Monthly Payment
4, ÷, PMT	**-205.72**	Stores Weekly Payment
12,ENTER,52, ÷ ,i	0.23	Stores Weekly Interest Rate
n	988.00	Computes Weekly Term[1]
52, ÷	**19.00**	Computes Term in Years

THE HEWLETT-PACKARD
BUSINESS CONSULTANT
(HP-17B, HP-18C, HP-19B)

Keystroke:	Display:	Comments:
FIN, TVM		Displays TVM Menu
GOLD, CLEAR ALL	0.00	Clears History Stack and TVM Variables
OTHER	0.00	Displays Secondary TVM Menu
GOLD, CLEAR ALL	0.00	Sets to 12 Payments/Year, End Mode
EXIT	0.00	Displays TVM Menu
80,000, PV	PV = 80,000.00	Stores Loan Amount
30, x, 12, N	N = 360.00	Stores Monthly Term
12, I%YR	I%YR = 12.00	Stores Annual Interest Rate
PMT	PMT = -822.89	Computes Monthly Payment
÷, 4, PMT	**PMT = -205.72**	Stores Weekly Payment
OTHER	-205.72	Displays Secondary TVM Menu
52, #P/Y	#PMTS/YR = 52.00	Sets to 52 Payments/Year, End Mode
EXIT	52.00	Displays TVM Menu
N	N = 987.80	Computes Weekly Term[1]
÷, 52, =	**19.00**	Computes Term in Years

Notes:
(1) The computed "n" in the HP-12C example (988.00) is different from the computed "N" in the Business Consultant example (987.80) inasmuch as the HP-12C always rounds "n" to the next higher whole number (i.e., integer).

FNMA BIWEEKLY PAYMENT PROGRAM
(Page A-127.4)

PROBLEM:

Determine the biweekly payment on an $80,000 loan, bearing interest at 12% per annum, under the FNMA biweekly payment program. Then determine the annual term of this loan.

SOLUTION:

THE HEWLETT-PACKARD HP-12C

Keystroke:	Display:	Comments:
f, CLEAR, REG	0.00	Clears Calculator
g, END	0.00	Sets Payment Mode to End
80,000, PV	80,000.00	Stores Loan Amount
30, g, n	360.00	Stores Monthly Term
12, g, i	1.00	Stores Monthly Interest Rate
PMT	-822.89	Computes Monthly Payment
2, ÷, PMT	**-411.45**	Stores Biweekly Payment
12,ENTER,26, ÷ ,i	0.46	Stores Biweekly Interest Rate
n	495.00	Computes Biweekly Term[1]
26, ÷	**19.04**	Computes Term in Years[1]

THE HEWLETT-PACKARD BUSINESS CONSULTANT (HP-17B, HP-18C, HP-19B)

Keystroke:	Display:	Comments:
FIN, TVM		Displays TVM Menu
GOLD, CLEAR ALL	0.00	Clears History Stack and TVM Variables
OTHER	0.00	Displays Secondary TVM menu
GOLD, CLEAR ALL	0.00	Sets to 12 Payments/Year, End Mode
EXIT	0.00	Displays TVM Menu
80,000, PV	PV = 80,000.00	Stores Loan Amount
30, x, 12, N	N = 360.00	Stores Monthly Term
12, I%YR	I%YR = 12.00	Stores Annual Interest Rate
PMT	PMT = -822.89	Computes Monthly Payment
÷, 2, PMT	**PMT = -411.45**	Stores Biweekly Payment
OTHER	-411.45	Displays Secondary TVM menu
26, #P/Y	#PMTS/YR = 26.00	Sets to 26 Payments/Year, End Mode
EXIT	26.00	Displays TVM Menu
N	N = 494.47	Computes Biweekly Term[1]
÷, 26, =	**19.02**	Computes Term in Years[1]

Notes:
(1) The computed "n" in the HP-12C example (495.00) is different from the computed "N" in the Business Consultant example (494.47) inasmuch as the HP-12C always rounds "n" to the next higher whole number (i.e., integer). This accounts for the difference in the term in years of 19.04 for the HP-12C versus 19.02 for the Business Consultant.

REMAINING BALANCE
(Beginning on Page A-150)

PROBLEM:

Determine the remaining balance, after ten years, of an $85,000 loan, fully amortized over thirty years, bearing interest at 10.5% per annum.

SOLUTION:

THE HEWLETT-PACKARD HP-12C

Keystroke:	Display:	Comments:
f, CLEAR, REG	0.00	Clears Calculator
g, END	0.00	Sets Payment Mode to End
85,000, PV	85,000.00	Stores Loan Amount
30, g, n	360.00	Stores Monthly Term
10.5, g, i	0.88	Stores Monthly Interest Rate
PMT	-777.53	Computes Monthly Payment
10, g, n	120.00	Stores Monthly Age of Loan
FV	**-77,879.01**	Computes Remaining Balance[1]

THE HEWLETT-PACKARD
BUSINESS CONSULTANT
(HP-17B, HP-18C, HP-19B)

Keystroke:	Display:	Comments:
FIN, TVM		Displays TVM Menu
GOLD, CLEAR ALL	0.00	Clears History Stack and TVM Variables
OTHER	0.00	Displays Secondary TVM Menu
GOLD, CLEAR ALL	0.00	Sets to 12 Payments/Year, End Mode
EXIT	0.00	Displays TVM Menu
85,000, PV	PV = 85,000.00	Stores Loan Amount
30, x, 12, N	N = 360.00	Stores Monthly Term
10.5, I%YR	I%YR = 10.50	Stores Annual Interest Rate
PMT	PMT = -777.53	Computes Monthly Payment
10, x, 12, N	N = 120.00	Stores Monthly Age of Loan
FV	**FV = -77,879.01**	Computes Remaining Balance[1]

Notes:
(1) The "–" sign indicates that this is an amount due.

BALLOON PAYMENT TABLE
(Beginning on Page A-200)

PROBLEM:

Determine the balloon payment on a $125,000 loan, payable at $1,875 per month, bearing interest at 10.5% per annum, due in seven years.

SOLUTION:

THE HEWLETT-PACKARD HP-12C

Keystroke:	Display:	Comments:
f, CLEAR, REG	0.00	Clears Calculator
g, END	0.00	Sets Payment Mode to End
125,000, PV	125,000.00	Stores Loan Amount
1,875, CHS, PMT	-1,875.00	Stores Monthly Payment
7, g, n	84.00	Stores Monthly Term
10.5, g, i	0.88	Stores Monthly Interest Rate
FV	**-28,676.31**	Computes Balloon Payment[1]

THE HEWLETT-PACKARD
BUSINESS CONSULTANT
(HP-17B, HP-18C, HP-19B)

Keystroke:	Display:	Comments:
FIN, TVM		Displays TVM Menu
GOLD, CLEAR ALL	0.00	Clears History Stack and TVM Variables
OTHER	0.00	Displays Secondary TVM Menu
GOLD, CLEAR ALL	0.00	Sets to 12 Payments/Year, End Mode
EXIT	0.00	Displays TVM Menu
125,000, PV	PV = 125,000.00	Stores Loan Amount
1,875, +/-, PMT	PMT = -1,875.00	Stores Monthly Payment
7, x, 12, N	N = 84.00	Stores Monthly Term
10.5, I%YR	I%YR = 10.50	Stores Annual Interest Rate
FV	**FV = -28,676.31**	Computes Balloon Payment[1]

Notes:
(1) The "−" sign indicates that this is an amount due.

MORTGAGE YIELD TABLE
(Beginning on Page A-212)

PROBLEM:

Determine the value and discount required for a $75,000 mortgage, payable at $937.50 per month, bearing interest at 11% per annum, due in seven years, to yield 17%.

SOLUTION:

THE HEWLETT-PACKARD HP-12C

Keystroke:	Display:	Comments:
f, CLEAR, REG	0.00	Clears Calculator
g, END	0.00	Sets Payment Mode to End
75,000, PV, STO, 0	75,000.00	Stores Loan Amount
937.50, CHS, PMT	-937.50	Stores Monthly Payment
7, g, n	84.00	Stores Monthly Term
11, g, i	0.92	Stores Monthly Interest Rate
FV	-43,576.27	Computes Remaining Balance[1]
17, g, i	1.42	Stores Desired Monthly Yield
PV	**59,243.35**	Computes Value of Mortgage
RCL, 0, -, CHS	**15,756.65**	Computes Discount

THE HEWLETT-PACKARD
BUSINESS CONSULTANT
(HP-17B, HP-18C, HP-19B)

Keystroke:	Display:	Comments:
FIN, TVM		Displays TVM Menu
GOLD, CLEAR ALL	0.00	Clears History Stack and TVM Variables
OTHER	0.00	Displays Secondary TVM Menu
GOLD, CLEAR ALL	0.00	Sets to 12 Payments/Year, End Mode
EXIT	0.00	Displays TVM Menu
75,000, PV, STO, 0	75,000.00	Stores Loan Amount
937.50, +/-, PMT	PMT = -937.50	Stores Monthly Payment
7, x, 12, N	N = 84.00	Stores Monthly Term
11, I%YR	I%YR = 11.00	Stores Annual Interest Rate
FV	FV = -43,576.27	Computes Remaining Balance[1]
17, I%YR	I%YR = 17.00	Stores Desired Annual Yield
PV	**PV = 59,243.35**	Computes Value of Mortgage
-, RCL, 0, =, +/-	**15,756.65**	Computes Discount

Notes:
(1) The "-" sign indicates that this is an amount due.

FUTURE VALUE OF $1
COMPOUNDED ANNUALLY
(Beginning on Page A-323)
Single Sum

PROBLEM:

Determine the value in ten years of a $10,000 investment, which will earn 11% interest per annum, compounded annually.

SOLUTION:

THE HEWLETT-PACKARD HP-12C

Keystroke:	Display:	Comments:
f, CLEAR, REG	0.00	Clears Calculator
g, END	0.00	Sets Payment Mode to End
10,000, CHS, PV	-10,000.00	Stores Present Value
10, n	10.00	Stores Annual Term
11, i	11.00	Stores Annual Interest Rate
FV	**28,394.21**	Computes Future Value

THE HEWLETT-PACKARD
BUSINESS CONSULTANT
(HP-17B, HP-18C, HP-19B)

Keystroke:	Display:	Comments:
FIN, TVM		Displays TVM Menu
GOLD, CLEAR ALL	0.00	Clears History Stack and TVM Variables
OTHER	0.00	Displays Secondary TVM Menu
1, #P/Y, END	#PMTS/YR = 1.00	Sets to 1 Payment/Year, End Mode
EXIT	1.00	Displays TVM Menu
10,000, +/-, PV	PV = -10,000.00	Stores Present Value
10, N	N = 10.00	Stores Annual Term
11, I%YR	I%YR = 11.00	Stores Annual Interest Rate
FV	**FV = 28,394.21**	Computes Future Value

FUTURE VALUE OF $1
COMPOUNDED ANNUALLY
(Beginning on Page A-323)
Annuity

PROBLEM:

Determine the value in ten years of an annual $1,000 investment, commencing today, which will earn 10% interest per annum, compounded annually.

SOLUTION:

THE HEWLETT-PACKARD HP-12C

Keystroke:	Display:	Comments:
f, CLEAR, REG	0.00	Clears Calculator
g, BEG	0.00	Sets Payment Mode to Begin
1,000, CHS, PMT	-1,000.00	Stores Annual Payment
10, n	10.00	Stores Annual Term
10, i	10.00	Stores Annual Interest Rate
FV	**17,531.17**	Computes Future Value

THE HEWLETT-PACKARD BUSINESS CONSULTANT (HP-17B, HP-18C, HP-19B)

Keystroke:	Display:	Comments:
FIN, TVM		Displays TVM Menu
GOLD, CLEAR ALL	0.00	Clears History Stack and TVM Variables
OTHER	0.00	Displays Secondary TVM Menu
1, #P/Y, BEG	#PMTS/YR = 1.00	Sets to 1 Payment/Year, Begin Mode
EXIT	1.00	Displays TVM Menu
1,000, +/-, PMT	PMT = -1,000.00	Stores Annual Payment
10, N	N = 10.00	Stores Annual Term
10, I%YR	I%YR = 10.00	Stores Annual Interest Rate
FV	**FV = 17,531.17**	Computes Future Value

FUTURE VALUE OF $1
COMPOUNDED MONTHLY
(Beginning on Page A-328)
Single Sum

PROBLEM:

Determine the value in ten years of a $10,000 investment, which will earn 11% interest per annum, compounded monthly.

SOLUTION:

THE HEWLETT-PACKARD HP-12C

Keystroke:	Display:	Comments:
Convert Simple (Nominal) Interest to Effective Interest		
f, CLEAR, REG	0.00	Clears Calculator
g, END	0.00	Sets Payment Mode to End
1, g, n	12.00	Stores Monthly Term
11, g, i	0.92	Stores Monthly Interest Rate
100, CHS, ENTER, PV	-100.00	Enters and Stores Present Value
FV	111.57	Computes Future Value
+	**11.57**	Effective Annual Interest Rate
Use Effective Interest to Compute Future Value		
f, CLEAR, FIN	11.57	Clears Financial Registers
i	11.57	Stores Effective Annual Interest Rate
10,000, CHS, PV	-10,000.00	Stores Present Value
10, n	10.00	Stores Annual Term
FV	**29,891.50**	Computes Future Value

THE HEWLETT-PACKARD
BUSINESS CONSULTANT
(HP-17B, HP-18C, HP-19B)

Keystroke:	Display:	Comments:
Convert Simple (Nominal) Interest to Effective Interest		
FIN, ICONV, EFFCT		Displays Interest Rate Conversion Menu
11, NOM%	NOM% = 11.00	Stores Nominal Interest Rate
12, P	P = 12.00	Stores Compounding Periods
EFF%	**EFF% = 11.57**	Computes Effective Interest Rate
STO, 0	EFF% = 11.57	Stores Effective Interest Rate
Use Effective Interest to Compute Future Value		
EXIT, EXIT, TVM	11.57	Displays TVM Menu
GOLD, CLEAR ALL	0.00	Clears History Stack and TVM Variables
OTHER	0.00	Displays Secondary TVM Menu
1, #P/Y, END	#PMTS/YR = 1.00	Sets to 1 Payment/Year, End Mode
EXIT	1.00	Displays TVM Menu
10,000, +/-, PV	PV = -10,000.00	Stores Present Value
10, N	N = 10.00	Stores Annual Term
RCL, 0, I%YR	I%YR = 11.57	Stores Annual Interest Rate
FV	**FV = 29,891.50**	Computes Future Value

FUTURE VALUE OF $1
COMPOUNDED MONTHLY
(Beginning on Page A-328)
Annuity

PROBLEM:

Determine the value in ten years of a monthly $1,000 investment, commencing today, which will earn 10% interest per annum, compounded monthly.

SOLUTION:

THE HEWLETT-PACKARD HP-12C

Keystroke:	Display:	Comments:
f, CLEAR, REG	0.00	Clears Calculator
g, BEG	0.00	Sets Payment Mode to Begin
1,000, CHS, PMT	-1,000.00	Stores Monthly Payment
10, g, n	120.00	Stores Monthly Term
10, g, i	0.83	Stores Monthly Interest Rate
FV	**206,552.02**	Computes Future Value

THE HEWLETT-PACKARD
BUSINESS CONSULTANT
(HP-17B, HP-18C, HP-19B)

Keystroke:	Display:	Comments:
FIN, TVM		Displays TVM Menu
GOLD, CLEAR ALL	0.00	Clears History Stack and TVM Variables
OTHER	0.00	Displays Secondary TVM Menu
GOLD, CLEAR ALL, BEG	0.00	Sets to 12 Payments/Year, Begin Mode
EXIT	0.00	Displays TVM Menu
1,000, +/-, PMT	PMT = -1,000.00	Stores Monthly Payment
10, x, 12, N	N = 120.00	Stores Monthly Term
10, I%YR	I%YR = 10.00	Stores Annual Interest Rate
FV	**FV = 206,552.02**	Computes Future Value

PRESENT VALUE OF $1
COMPOUNDED ANNUALLY
(Beginning on Page A-332)
Single Sum

PROBLEM:

An investor has consistently made returns of 11%, compounded annually, on his investments. How much should the investor pay for an investment which will return $10,000 at the end of ten years?

SOLUTION:

THE HEWLETT-PACKARD HP-12C

Keystroke:	Display:	Comments:
f, CLEAR, REG	0.00	Clears Calculator
g, END	0.00	Sets Payment Mode to End
10,000, CHS, FV	-10,000.00	Stores Future Value
10, n	10.00	Stores Annual Term
11, i	11.00	Stores Annual Interest Rate
PV	**3,521.84**	Computes Present Value

THE HEWLETT-PACKARD BUSINESS CONSULTANT
(HP-17B, HP-18C, HP-19B)

Keystroke:	Display:	Comments:
FIN, TVM		Displays TVM Menu
GOLD, CLEAR ALL	0.00	Clears History Stack and TVM Variables
OTHER	0.00	Displays Secondary TVM Menu
1, #P/Y, END	#PMTS/YR = 1.00	Sets to 1 Payment/Year, End Mode
EXIT	1.00	Displays TVM Menu
10,000, +/-, FV	FV = -10,000.00	Stores Future Value
10, N	N = 10.00	Stores Annual Term
11, I%YR	I%YR = 11.00	Stores Annual Interest Rate
PV	**PV = 3,521.84**	Computes Present Value

PRESENT VALUE OF $1
COMPOUNDED ANNUALLY
(Beginning on Page A-332)
Annuity

PROBLEM:

An investor has consistently made returns of 10%, compounded annually, on his investments. How much should the investor pay for an investment which will return $1,000 per year, commencing in one year, for ten years?

SOLUTION:

THE HEWLETT-PACKARD HP-12C

Keystroke:	Display:	Comments:
f, CLEAR, REG	0.00	Clears Calculator
g, END	0.00	Sets Payment Mode to End
1,000, CHS, PMT	-1,000.00	Stores Annual Payment
10, n	10.00	Stores Annual Term
10, i	10.00	Stores Annual Interest Rate
PV	**6,144.57**	Computes Present Value

THE HEWLETT-PACKARD
BUSINESS CONSULTANT
(HP-17B, HP-18C, HP-19B)

Keystroke:	Display:	Comments:
FIN, TVM		Displays TVM Menu
GOLD, CLEAR ALL	0.00	Clears History Stack and TVM Variables
OTHER	0.00	Displays Secondary TVM Menu
1, #P/Y, END	#PMTS/YR = 1.00	Sets to 1 Payment/Year, End Mode
EXIT	1.00	Displays TVM Menu
1,000, +/-, PMT	PMT = -1,000.00	Stores Annual Payment
10, N	N = 10.00	Stores Annual Term
10, I%YR	I%YR = 10.00	Stores Annual Interest Rate
PV	**PV = 6,144.57**	Computes Present Value

EQUITY BUILD-UP
(Beginning on Page A-344)

PROBLEM:

Determine the amount paid toward principal, after ten years, on an $85,000 loan, fully amortized over thirty years, bearing interest at 10.5% per annum.

SOLUTION:

THE HEWLETT-PACKARD HP-12C

Keystroke:	Display:	Comments:
f, CLEAR, REG	0.00	Clears Calculator
g, END	0.00	Sets Payment Mode to End
85,000, PV	85,000.00	Stores Loan Amount
30, g, n	360.00	Stores Monthly Term
10.5, g, i	0.88	Stores Monthly Interest Rate
PMT	-777.53	Computes Monthly Payment
10, g, n	120.00	Stores Monthly Age of Loan
FV	-77,879.01	Computes Remaining Balance[1]
RCL, PV, +	**7,120.99**	Computes Equity Build-Up

THE HEWLETT-PACKARD
BUSINESS CONSULTANT
(HP-17B, HP-18C, HP-19B)

Keystroke:	Display:	Comments:
FIN, TVM		Displays TVM Menu
GOLD, CLEAR ALL	0.00	Clears History Stack and TVM Variables
OTHER	0.00	Displays Secondary TVM Menu
GOLD, CLEAR ALL	0.00	Sets to 12 Payments/Year, End Mode
EXIT	0.00	Displays TVM Menu
85,000, PV	PV = 85,000.00	Stores Loan Amount
30, x, 12, N	N = 360.00	Stores Monthly Term
10.5, I%YR	I%YR = 10.50	Stores Annual Interest Rate
PMT	PMT = -777.53	Computes Monthly Payment
10, x, 12, N	N = 120.00	Stores Monthly Age of Loan
FV	FV = -77,879.01	Computes Remaining Balance[1]
+, RCL, PV, =	**7,120.99**	Computes Equity Build-Up

Notes:

(1) The "-" sign indicates that this is an amount due.

NOTES: